W9-CBA-811

Range of Writing

10. Write routinely over extended time frames (time for research, reflection, and revision) and shorter time frames (a single sitting or a day or two) for a range of tasks, purposes, and audiences.   Chapters 9, 10, 12

College and Career Readiness Anchor Standards for Speaking and Listening

Comprehension and Collaboration

1. Prepare for and participate effectively in a range of conversations and collaborations with diverse partners, building on others' ideas and expressing their own clearly and persuasively.   Chapters 8, 10

2. Integrate and evaluate information presented in diverse media and formats, including visually, quantitatively, and orally.   Chapters 8, 9

3. Evaluate a speaker's point of view, reasoning, and use of evidence and rhetoric.   Chapters 8, 10

Presentation of Knowledge and Ideas

4. Present information, findings, and supporting evidence such that listeners can follow the line of reasoning and the organization, development, and style are appropriate to task, purpose, and audience.   Chapters 8, 10

5. Make strategic use of digital media and visual displays of data to express information and enhance understanding of presentations.   Chapters 12, 13

College and Career Readiness Anchor Standards for Language

Vocabulary Acquisition and Use

4. Determine or clarify the meaning of unknown and multiple-meaning words and phrases by using context clues, analyzing meaningful word parts, and consulting general and specialized reference materials, as appropriate.   Chapter 6

5. Demonstrate understanding of word relationships and nuances in word meanings.   Chapters 6, 8

6. Acquire and use accurately a range of general academic and domain-specific words and phrases sufficient for reading, writing, speaking, and listening at the college and career readiness level; demonstrate independence in gathering vocabulary knowledge when encountering an unknown term important to comprehension or expression.   Chapters 2, 6

College and Career Readiness: Foundational Skills

Print Concepts

1. Demonstrate understanding of the organization and basic features of print.   Chapter 4

Phonological Awareness

2. Demonstrate understanding of spoken words, syllables, and sounds (phonemes).   Chapters 4, 5

Phonics and Word Recognition

3. Know and apply grade-level phonics and word analysis skills in decoding words.   Chapters 4, 5

Fluency

4. Read with sufficient accuracy and fluency to support comprehension.   Chapter 5

Creating Literacy Instruction for All Students

Creating Literacy Instruction for All Students

EIGHTH EDITION

Thomas G. Gunning

Professor Emeritus
Southern Connecticut State University

Adjunct Professor
Central Connecticut State University

PEARSON

Boston • Columbus • Indianapolis • New York • San Francisco • Upper Saddle River
Amsterdam • Cape Town • Dubai • London • Madrid • Milan • Munich • Paris • Montreal • Toronto
Delhi • Mexico City • São Paulo • Sydney • Hong Kong • Seoul • Singapore • Taipei • Tokyo

Vice President/Editor in Chief: Aurora Martínez Ramos
Editor: Erin Grelak
Editorial Assistant: Michelle Hochberg
Executive Marketing Manager: Krista Clark
Production Editor: Paula Carroll
Editorial Production Service: Jouve North America

Manufacturing Buyer: Megan Cochran
Electronic Composition: Jouve India
Interior Design: Anne Flanagan
Photo Researcher: Annie Fuller
Cover Designer: Jennifer Hart

Previous editions were published under the title *Creating Reading Instruction for All Children Copyright* © 2003, 2000, 1996, 1992. Portions of this work were also published under the title *Creating Literacy for All Students in Grades 4-8, Third Edition.*

Library of Congress Cataloging-in-Publication Data
Gunning, Thomas G.

    Creating literacy instruction for all students / Thomas G.Gunning. — 8th ed.
      p. cm.
    ISBN 978-0-13-268579-5 — ISBN 0-13-268579-5
  1. Reading (Elementary) 2. English language—Composition and exercises—Study
and teaching (Elementary) 3. Response to intervention (Learning disabled children) I. Title.
    LB1573.G93 2013
    372.4—dc23

                                          2011050580

10 9 8 7 6 5 4 3 2 1

www.pearsonhighered.com

ISBN-13: 978-0-13-268579-5
ISBN-10: 0-13-268579-5

To my grandchildren...
Alex and Paige Gunning
Andrew Thomas and Timothy Jay Pizzuto
Ariana Rueda
Michael Daniel and Daniel William Mulhall
Ariana, Michael, and Daniel are new to this edition.

About the Author

THOMAS G. GUNNING has taught courses in methods of teaching reading and writing for more than 20 years and was director of the Reading Clinic at Southern Connecticut State University. Before that, as a secondary English teacher, a reading specialist, and an elementary school reading consultant, he worked extensively with achieving and struggling readers and writers. Dr. Gunning is currently working with teachers to help them implement Response to Intervention and Common Core State Standards, as well as serving as an adjunct professor in the Reading/Language Arts Department at Central Connecticut State University.

Over the years, Dr. Gunning's research has explored reading interests, informal reading inventories, decoding strategies, readability, higher-level literacy skills, and response to intervention. As a result of this research, he has created a number of informal assessments and programs for developing decoding and comprehension skills, including an intervention program for students experiencing difficulty learning decoding skills, *Word Building, A Response to Intervention Program* (Phoenix Learning Resources), and a program designed to develop students' comprehension, *Reading Comprehension Boosters: 100 Lessons for Building Higher-Level Literacy* (Grades 3–5) (Jossey-Bass).

Dr. Gunning's books with Pearson Education include:

- *Assessing and Correcting Reading and Writing Difficulties, Fourth Edition,* ©2010, ISBN: 9780136100829
- *Creating Literacy Instruction for All Students in Grades 4–8, Third Edition,* ©2012, ISBN: 9780132317443
- *Creating Literacy Instruction for All Children in Grades Pre-K to 4, Second Edition,* © 2012
- *Building Literacy in Secondary Content Area Classrooms,* ©2012, ISBN: 9780205580811
- *Developing Higher-Level Literacy in All Students: Building Reading, Reasoning, and Responding,* ©2008, ISBN: 9780205522200
- *Closing the Literacy Gap,* ©2006, ISBN: 9780205456260
- *Building Words: A Resource Manual for Teaching Word Analysis and Spelling Strategies,* ©2001, ISBN: 9780205286256

For more information about any of these books, please visit www.pearson highered.com.

Brief Contents

Contents

2 Teaching All Students 26

3 Assessing for Learning

4 Fostering Emergent/Early Literacy 122

5 Teaching Phonics, High-Frequency Words, and Syllabic Analysis 186

6   Building Vocabulary   260

8 Comprehension: Text Structures and Teaching Procedures   360

12 Writing and Reading 496

13 Creating and Managing a Literacy Program   528

Special Features

LESSONS

REINFORCEMENT ACTIVITIES

STUDENT STRATEGIES

Preface

This book will not tell you how to teach reading and writing. Providing literacy instruction is in large measure a matter of making choices: Should you use basal reader anthologies or children's books, or both? Should you teach children to read whole words or to sound out words letter by letter, or both? Should you have three reading groups or four in your class, or no groups? There are no right answers to these questions. The answers depend on your personal philosophy, your interpretation of the research, the level at which you are teaching, the diversity of the students you are teaching, community preferences, and the nature of your school's or school district's reading program.

What this book will do is help you discover approaches and techniques that fit your teaching style and your teaching situation. Its aim is to present as fairly, completely, and clearly as possible the major approaches and techniques shown by research and practice to be successful. This book also presents the theories behind the methods, so you will be free to choose, adapt, and/or construct approaches and techniques that best fit your style and teaching situation. You will be creating literacy instruction.

Although the text emphasizes approaches and techniques, methods are only part of the equation. Reading is not just a process; it is also very much a content area. What students read does matter, and, therefore, I have provided recommendations for specific children's books and other reading materials. The basic premise of this book is that the best reading programs result through a combination of effective techniques and plenty of worthwhile reading material.

Because children differ greatly in their backgrounds, needs, and interests, the book offers a variety of suggestions about techniques and types of reading materials. The intent is to provide you with sufficient background knowledge of teaching methods and children's books and other reading materials to enable you to create effective instruction for all the children you teach, whether they are rich or poor; bright, average, or struggling; with disabilities or without; urban or suburban; or from any of the diverse cultural and ethnic groups found in today's classrooms.

This book also recognizes that reading is part of a larger language process; therefore, considerable attention is paid to writing and the other language arts, especially as these relate to reading instruction. Whether reading or writing is being addressed, the emphasis is on making the students the center of instruction. For instance, I recommend activities that allow students to choose writing topics and reading materials. Approaches that foster a personal response to reading are also advocated. Just as you are encouraged by this text to create your own reading instruction, students must be encouraged to create their own literacy.

Changes to the Eighth Edition

During the time that has elapsed since the publication of the seventh edition of this book, three key but related movements have come into play. The most basic of these is the initiative to prepare every child to be college and career ready. A companion to this is the widespread adoption of the Common Core State Standards. Related to both is the movement to tie teacher evaluation to student achievement. Because of these key movements, the eighth edition stresses doing whatever it takes to help every student become college and career ready. The eighth edition also incorporates the Common Core State Standards (CCSS), which were designed to prepare students to be college and career ready. (The CCSS are listed on the inside front cover.) The text was revised so as to incorporate Common Core Standards. In Chapter 12, for instance, discussions of writing were expanded to include more information on narrative, informational/explanatory 5, and argumentative writing as recommended by Common Core Standards. In Chapter 5, the phonics scope and sequence chart was revised so as to better reflect Common Core terminology. Insofar as possible, throughout the text, revisions, large and small, were made in order to provide readers with a solid grasp of what the CCSS are and how they might be taught. Throughout the text, the CCSS marginal annotations list a standard and mark the place in the text where that standard is addressed.

The eighth edition is also more research-based. Using landmark research that describes the most effective instructional practices, the text highlights highly effective practices, such as setting goals and monitoring progress, and provides information on the average percentage of gains achieved when these practices are instituted. Many of these practices are part of systems now being used to evaluate teachers. The ultimate purpose of this text is to help you become a highly effective teacher so that your students will become proficient readers and writers and will be well on the road to becoming college and career ready.

To accomplish this goal, each chapter concludes with a feature entitled "Extending and Applying" in which you will be asked to extend your knowledge of effective practices discussed in that chapter and apply them. To further foster professional development, there is a "Professional Reflection" at the end of each chapter in which you will be asked to reflect on your ability to implement key assessment and instructional practices. The Professional Reflection checklists are modeled on highly effective teacher evaluation systems in widespread use, so they will be preparing you for the kinds of assessments you will most likely encounter during your professional career. Fleshing out and adding to these general themes, the eighth edition includes the following additions and revisions:

Chapter 1

- Explanation of importance of tying assessment and instruction to student achievement
- Expanded coverage of scientifically based literacy instruction, including a listing of approaches and techniques and their average gains
- Description of the essentials of an effective lesson

Chapter 2

- Expanded coverage of Response to Intervention
- Expanded discussion of scaffolding for English language learners and instruction in academic language

- Addition of a list of high-frequency academic vocabulary that would be especially appropriate for elementary and middle school students

Chapter 3

- Update of informal reading inventories and curriculum-based measures
- Expanded coverage of mazes
- Description of the oral reading fluency scale
- Expanded explanation of performance assessment and using growth measures to assess progress
- Explanation of Mystery Passages as a group or individual think-aloud
- Explanation of reader and task factors in readability

Chapter 4

- Revision and expansion of information on phonemic awareness
- More information on learning centers
- Explanation of individual interactive writing
- Updated explanation of the positions of professional organizations on early literacy instruction

Chapter 5

- Revised sequence of decoding skills that incorporates the teaching of vowels early
- Additional activities for syllabic analysis
- New Exemplary Teaching: Decoding Long Words
- Revised list of syllable patterns, which are listed by ease of analysis
- Explanation of the sequential spelling technique for decoding long words

Chapter 6

- Description of two programs designed to develop academic vocabulary: Word Generation and ALIAS
- Expanded discussion of English language learner dictionaries
- Discussion of techniques for assessing vocabulary development

Chapter 7

- Description of using think-aloud mysteries to motivate and improve strategy use
- Chart explaining steps in a strategy lesson
- Expanded coverage of repair (fix-up) strategies for fostering comprehension, with a new table of strategies
- Using manipulatives to foster comprehension, a research-based technique that works wonders with the poorest of comprehenders
- Expanded explanation of the importance of prior knowledge

Chapter 8

- Discussion of how to use easy books to build background knowledge
- New Exemplary Teaching: A Steppingstone Approach— proceeding from easy to more challenging texts

Chapter 9

- Discussion of the impact of Common Core State Standards on nonfiction reading
- Discussion of creating key questions and understandings as advocated by Understanding by Design
- Expanded explanation of techniques for differentiating instruction
- Explanation of WIRC (Writing Intensive Reading Comprehension) thinksheets, a research-based technique for scaffolding comprehension
- Discussion of the use of e-books and e-readers in the content areas
- Use of quizzes, judicious review, and practice to bolster students' understanding and retention

Chapter 10

- Updated discussion of envisionments, a literature response approach
- Expanded discussion of techniques for fostering voluntary reading

Chapter 11

- Updated information on basal readers/anthologies
- Added information on adapting commercial programs so as to provide adequate instruction and practice

Chapter 12

- In keeping with Common Core State Standards, explanation of the importance of writing in a variety of genres
- Expanded coverage of narrative, informational/explanatory, and argumentative writing
- Expanded coverage of rubrics

Chapter 13

- Expanded coverage of the new literacies and Web 2.0, including blogs and wikis
- Expanded coverage of technology and electronic materials
- Expanded coverage of intervention programs

Features of the Text

Throughout the eighth edition of *Creating Literacy Instruction for All Students*, special pedagogical features draw the reader's attention to issues of recurring importance in literacy instruction as well as aid with review and understanding of key concepts.

Case Study
An Exemplary Writing Program

In the Teachers College Reading and Writing Project, which has been implemented by thousands of teachers over nearly three decades, the ultimate goal is to have kindergarten children write stories that are five or six pages long (Calkins, 2003). Each page has a picture and one or two sentences. The project features a curriculum calendar, in which there is a focus of

Recording sounds and leaving spaces between words are emphasized. In December, the focus is on writing for readers. Emphasis is on beginning sentences with capital letters, recording sounds, and using end punctuation so that readers will find it easier to read the story. The goal is to have most children using letter–sound correspondences by January. Teachers encourage students teach-word;

Case Studies offer perspectives on teachers at work improving their programs.

IRA POSITION STATEMENT ON KEY ISSUE
High-Stakes Testing

As its name suggests, a high-stakes test is one for which an important decision will be based on the outcome. Because of the role they play in decision making, high-stakes tests have the potential to dictate

because that is the way students will be assessed on the state tests. To combat the misuse of tests, the International Reading Association (1999a) has made the following recommendations:

IRA Position Statements sum up key issues, such as high-stakes testing and family-school partnerships, on which the International Reading Association has published position papers.

LESSON 4.1
Elkonin Phonemic Segmentation Technique

Objective

• Students will segment words into phonemes.

Step 1.

Explain the task, model it, and guide the child through it. Explain to students that this will help them read and spell words.

Model Lessons cover nearly every area of literacy instruction.

STUDENT STRATEGIES
Judging Sources

Once students seem to grasp the concept of judging sources for fairness, help them develop a set of questions that they might use to assess printed sources and Web sites they consult:

Student Strategies outline step-by-step strategies to help students become independent learners.

REINFORCEMENT ACTIVITIES
Alphabet Knowledge

• Have children create their own alphabet books.

• Help children create name cards. Explain that names begin with uppercase letters but that the other letters in a name are lowercase.

• Make a big book of the alphabet song, and point to the letters and words as children sing along.

Reinforcement Activities provide practice and application, particularly in the area of reading and writing for real purposes.

Student Reading Lists arc provided in all instructional chapters as a resource for titles that reinforce the particular literacy skills being discussed.

STUDENT READING LIST

Recommended Books for Read-Alouds

Angelou, M. (1994). *My painted house, my friendly chicken, and me.* New York: Clarkson N. Potter. An eight-year-old Ndebele girl tells about life in her village in South Africa.

Barnes-Murphy, F. (1994). *The fables of Aesop.* New York: Lothrop. This collection of fables retold from Aesop includes "The Hare and the Tortoise" and "The Ant and the Grasshopper."

Exemplary Teaching features help make the descriptions of teaching techniques come alive by offering examples of good teaching practices. All are true-life accounts; many were drawn from the memoirs of gifted teachers, and others were garnered from newspaper reports or my own observations.

Exemplary Teaching

Shared Writing in Kindergarten

Using a series of informal assessment devices, Paige Ferguson determined that only half of her kindergarten students could write their names and only two knew the letters of the alphabet. Given the children's low level of literacy development, she decided to use shared writing with them. As part of their literature unit, she read Paul Galdone's (1975) *The Gingerbread Boy* to the class. The class then took a walking tour of the school to find hidden gingerbread boys. After returning to the classroom, the class began creating a shared story. The story consisted of listing the places where they found the gingerbread boys.

Building on the students' knowledge of the sounds and letters in their names, the teacher introduced other sounds and letters as the class created additional shared stories. To reinforce the children's awareness of separate words, she had one student point to each word in the story while the other children read it. As the year progressed, the children learned to hear the separate sounds in words and represent these sounds with letters. They also learned to write in a variety of formats. They wrote shared letters to pen pals, retold stories, made lists, and summarized scientific observations that they had made.

In addition to writing interactively, the children wrote independently each day. Shared writing provided a foundation for their independent writing. They also reread the shared stories that had been hung up around the room. When assessed in the spring, the students demonstrated dramatic progress. They showed growth in phonemic awareness,

Marginal annotations provide the reader with interesting, practical, and handy guidance for planning and adapting instruction. These notes are titled Adapting Instruction for Struggling Readers and Writers, Adapting Instruction for English Language Learners, Using Technology, Assessing for Learning, Building Language, CCSS (marking places in the text where a Common Cores State Standard is being addressed), and FYI (providing information on a variety of topics).

 Assessing for Learning

When choosing informational books, use children's interests and curiosity as your guide. What kinds of questions do they have? Do they wan̲̲ how where fog comes from they clou

Using Technology

Titlewave provides extensive information about books and other media, including interest level, readability level, book reviews, and awards that books have won. You can search by author, title, topic, grade level, subject area, or curriculum standard.
http://www.flr.follett.com/login

Tre pro on htt cor

 Adapting Instruction for Struggling Readers and Writers

In an urban prekindergarten, Maxie Perry enlisted the services of volunteers and aides to read to individual children. Because some of the volunteers had limited reading skills themselves and lacked confidence, she supplied sensitive guidance and suggestions (Strickland & Taylor, 1989). ■

 FYI

For a time, children's concept of letter-sound relationships may be very specific. At age 4, my granddaughter Paige told me that she had a friend named Paul in scho̲ my Pau her her spec her. repr any (see

 Adapting Instruction for English Language Learners

Discussions can take a number of forms. Students might discuss in pairs or in small groups. These discussions can be ends in themselves or preparation for discussions by the whole class. If ELLs discuss a se the larg &V

 **Building Language**

Although predictable books allow students to think of themselves as readers, they aren't the best texts for developing language (Dickinson & Smith, 1994). Books that have more complex plots and better-developed characters or that delve more deeply into topics offer a richer vocabulary and more opportunities for language development. ■

REFLECTION

When selecting books for read-alouds, how might you balance the goal of providing an enriching experience with the

 **CCSS**

Follow words from left to right, top to bottom, and page by page.
Recognize that spoken words are represented in written language by specific sequences of letters.
Understand that words are separated by spaces in print.

Anticipation Guide

For each of the following statements related to the chapter you are about to read, put a check under "Agree" or "Disagree" to show how you feel. Discuss your responses with classmates before you read the chapter.

	Agree	Disagree
1. The structure of a piece of writing influences its level of difficulty.	____	____
2. Talking about the structure of a story ruins the fun of reading it.	____	____
3. How you ask a question is more important than what you ask.	____	____
4. Struggling learners should be asked a greater proportion of lower-level questions.	____	____
5. Students should play the most important role in class discussions.	____	____
6. Structured reading lessons usually work better than unstructured ones.	____	____
7. Critical (evaluative) reading skills have never been more important or more neglected.	____	____

Various learning aids, including **Anticipation Guides,** a page-by-page glossary, and application suggestions, are included so that readers can review concepts and enhance their understanding.

Extending and Applying

1. Using the procedures described in this chapter, plan a lesson teaching letters or beginning sounds. If possible, teach the lesson and make a video recording of it. On a paper copy of the lesson plan, reflect on the effectiveness of the lesson.
2. Administer to one or more kindergarten students assessments of letter knowledge, beginning sounds, letter sounds, and developmental spelling, using measures described in this chapter or the previous one. Also obtain a writing sample. Based on an analysis of

the assessments, highlight the strengths and needs of the student(s), and plan a program for them.
3. Examine stories written by a kindergarten class. What are some characteristics of children's writing at this age? How do the pieces vary?
4. Search out alphabet books, rhyming tales, song books, and other materials that you might use to enhance alphabet knowledge, rhyming, and perception of beginning sounds. Keep an annotated bibliography of these materials.

Each chapter ends with a brief summary and five activities designed to extend understanding of key concepts: **Extending and Applying,** provides suggestions for practical application. **Professional Reflection** asks readers to reflect on their ability to implement key assessment and instructional practices in the chapter. The **Reflection Question** asks readers to consider practical implications of key chapter concepts. **Building Competencies** suggests additional readings that will further students' ability to meet the chapter's standards. **MyEducationLab** takes students into live classrooms via video clips and also provides activities, artifacts, simulations, and study materials.

Professional Reflection

Do I ...

___ Have an understanding of the ways in which young children develop literacy?
___ Have an understanding of the concept of phonological awareness?
___ Have an understanding of how children's concepts of print develop?
___ Have an understanding of how children's writing develops?
___ Have an understanding of developmentally appropriate practice?

Am I able to ...

___ Assess students to determine their phonological awareness, letter knowledge, and concepts of print?
___ Use a variety of techniques to develop phonological awareness?
___ Use a variety of techniques to develop letter knowledge and concepts of print?
___ Develop language and vocabulary skills and build background?
___ Monitor progress and gear instruction to students' needs and adapt instruction as necessary?
___ Work closely with the home?

Reflection Question

What are the most effective ways to develop young children's literacy but also foster their social and emotional growth?

Building Competencies

To build competencies, consult the following sources for more detailed information:

National Reading Panel. (2000). *National Reading Panel report.* Chapter 2, Part I, "Phonemic awareness instruction," pp. 2-1 to 2-86. Washington, DC: U.S. Department of Education. http://www.nationalreadingpanel.org

Texas Education Agency. (2008). *Welcome to the 2008 Texas prekindergarten guidelines.* Austin, TX: Author. http://ritter.tea.state.tx.us/prek_guide/index.htm#

Venn, E. C., & Jahn, M. D. (2004). *Teaching and learning in the preschool.* Newark, DE: International Reading Association.

Webbing into Literacy http://curry.edschool.virginia.

MyEducationLab

Go to the Topic "Emergent Literacy" in the MyEducationLab (www.myeducationlab.com) for your course, where you can:

- Find learning outcomes for "Emergent Literacy" along with the national standards that connect to these outcomes.
- Complete Assignments and Activities that can help you more deeply understand the chapter content.
- Apply and practice your understanding of the core teaching skills identified in the chapter with the Building Teaching Skills and Dispositions learning units.
- Examine challenging situations and cases presented in

Resources for your text. Here you will be able to take a chapter quiz, receive feedback on your answers, and then access Review, Practice, and Enrichment activities to enhance your understanding of chapter content. (optional)

 A+RISE® Standards2Strategy™ is an innovative and interactive online resource that offers new teachers in grades K–12 just-in-time, research-based instructional strategies that meet the linguistic needs of ELLs as they learn content, differentiate instruction for all grades and abilities, and are aligned to Common Core Elementary Language Arts

Organization of the Text

The text's organization has been designed to reflect the order of the growth of literacy. Chapter 1 stresses the construction of a philosophy of teaching reading and writing. Chapter 2 stresses the need to prepare every child to be college and career ready and explains Response to Intervention, and its basic principle, which is to do whatever it takes to bring every student to full literacy. The second part of the chapter discusses the diversity of students in today's schools and some special challenges in bringing all students to full literacy. Chapter 3 presents techniques for evaluating individuals and programs so that assessment becomes an integral part of instruction. Chapters 4 and 5 discuss emergent literacy and basic decoding strategies, including phonics, syllabic analysis, fluency, and high-frequency words. Chapter 6 presents advanced word-recognition skills and strategies: morphemic analysis, dictionary skills, and techniques for building vocabulary. Chapters 7 through 9 are devoted to comprehension: Chapter 7 emphasizes comprehension strategies that students might use; Chapter 8 focuses on text structures and teaching procedures; Chapter 9 covers application of comprehension skills in the content areas and through studying. Chapter 10 takes a step beyond comprehension by focusing on responding to literature and fostering a love of reading.

Chapters 4 through 10, which emphasize essential reading strategies, constitute the core of the book. Chapters 11 through 13 provide information on creating a well-rounded literacy program. Chapter 11 describes approaches to teaching reading. Chapter 12 explains the process approach to writing and discusses how reading and writing are related. Chapter 13 pulls all the topics together in a discussion of principles for organizing and implementing a literacy program. Also included in this final chapter are a section on intervention programs, a section on technology and its place in a program of literacy instruction and a section on professional development.

This text, designed to be practical, offers detailed explanations and numerous examples of applications for every major technique or strategy. Many suggestions for practice activities and reading materials are also included. I hope that this book will furnish an in-depth knowledge of literacy methods and materials so that the teachers and future teachers who use it will be able to construct lively, effective reading and writing instruction for all the students they teach.

New! CourseSmart eBook and Other eBook Options Available

CourseSmart is an exciting new choice for purchasing this book. As an alternative to purchasing the printed book, you may purchase an electronic version of the same content via CourseSmart for reading on PC, Mac, as well as Android devices, iPad, iPhone, and iPod Touch with CourseSmart Apps. With a CourseSmart eBook, readers can search the text, make notes online, and bookmark important passages for later review. For more information or to purchase access to the CourseSmart eBook, visit http://www.coursesmart.com. Also look for availability of this book on a number of other eBook devices and platforms.

Supplements for Instructors and Students

Many of these supplements can be downloaded from the Instructor Resource Center at www.pearsonhighered.com/irc.

Instructor's Manual with Resource Masters For each chapter, the instructor's manual features a series of Learner Objectives, a Chapter Overview, suggestions for Before, After, and During Reading, a list of suggested Teaching Activities, a Resource Master (a graphic organizer designed to help readers organize information from the chapter), and suggestions for Assessment. Also featured are a series of semi-scripted teaching lessons that readers might use to try out key techniques presented in the text. (Available for downloading from the Instructor Resource Center at www.pearsonhighered.com/irc.)

Test Bank The Test Bank has more than 250 questions and includes multiple choice and essay questions. This supplement, like the Instructor's Manual with Resource Masters, has been written completely by the text author, Tom Gunning. Page references to the main text and, suggested answers, have been added to each question to help instructors create and evaluate student tests. (Available for downloading from the Instructor Resource Center at www.pearsonhighered.com/irc.)

Pearson MyTest The printed Test Bank is also available through our computerized testing system, MyTest, a powerful assessment generation program that helps instructors easily create and print quizzes and exams. Questions and tests are authored online, allowing ultimate flexibility and the ability to efficiently create and print assessments anytime, anywhere! Instructors can access Pearson MyTest and their test bank files by going to www.pearsonmytest.com to log in, register, or request access. Features of Pearson MyTest include:

Premium Assessment Content

- Draw from a rich library of assessments that complement your Pearson textbook and your course's learning objectives.
- Edit questions or tests to fit your specific teaching needs.

Instructor-friendly resources

- Easily create and store your own questions, including images, diagrams, and charts using simple drag-and-drop and Word-like controls.
- Use additional information provided by Pearson, such as the question's difficulty level or learning objective, to help you quickly build your test.
- Time-saving enhancements
- Add headers or footers and easily scramble questions and answer choices—all from one simple toolbar.
- Quickly create multiple versions of your test or answer key, and when ready, simply save to Microsoft-Word or PDF format and print!
- Export your exams for import to Blackboard 6.0, CE (WebCT), or Vista (WebCT)!

PowerPoint™ Presentation Designed for teachers using the text, the PowerPoint™ Presentation consists of a series of slides (ten to twenty per chapter) that can be shown as is or used to make overhead transparencies. The presentation highlights key concepts and major topics for each chapter. (Available for downloading from the Instructor Resource Center at www.pearsonhighered.com/irc.)

MyEducationLab™

Proven to **engage students**, provide **trusted content**, and **improve results**, Pearson MyLabs have helped over 8 million registered students reach true understanding in their courses. **MyEducationLab** engages students with real-life teaching situations through dynamic videos, case studies and student artifacts. Student progress is assessed, and a personalized study plan is created based on the student's unique results. Automatic grading and reporting keeps educators informed to quickly address gaps and improve student performance. All of the activities and exercises in MyEducationLab are built around essential learning outcomes for teachers and are mapped to professional teaching standards.

In *Preparing Teachers for a Changing World*, Linda Darling-Hammond and her colleagues point out that grounding teacher education in real classrooms—among real teachers and students and among actual examples of students' and teachers' work—is an important, and perhaps even an essential, part of training teachers for the complexities of teaching in today's classrooms.

In the MyEducationLab for this course you will find the following features and resources.

Study Plan Specific to Your Text

MyEducationLab gives students the opportunity to test themselves on key concepts and skills, track their own progress through the course, and access personalized Study Plan activities.

The customized Study Plan—with enriching activities—is generated based on students' results of a pretest. Study Plans tag incorrect questions from the pretest to the appropriate textbook learning outcome, helping students focus on the topics they need help with. Personalized Study Plan activities may include eBook reading assignments, and review, practice and enrichment activities.

After students complete the enrichment activities, they take a posttest to see the concepts they've mastered or the areas where they may need extra help.

MyEducationLab then reports the Study Plan results to the instructor. Based on these reports, the instructor can adapt course material to suit the needs of individual students or the entire class.

Connection to National Standards

Now it is easier than ever to see how coursework is connected to national standards. Each topic, activity and exercise on MyEducationLab lists intended learning outcomes connected to the either the Common Core State Standards for Language arts or the IRA Standards for Reading Professionals.

Assignments and Activities

Designed to enhance your understanding of concepts covered in class, these assignable exercises show concepts in action (through videos, cases, and/or student and teacher artifacts). They help you deepen content knowledge and synthesize and apply concepts and strategies you read about in the book. (Correct answers for these assignments are available to the instructor only.)

Building Teaching Skills and Dispositions

These unique learning units help users practice and strengthen skills that are essential to effective teaching. After presenting the steps involved in a core teaching process, you are given an opportunity to practice applying this skill via videos, student and teacher artifacts, and/or case studies of authentic classrooms. Providing multiple opportunities to practice a single teaching concept, each activity encourages a deeper understanding and application of concepts, as well as the use of critical thinking skills. After practice, students take a quiz that is reported to the instructor gradebook.

Lesson Plan Builder

The **Lesson Plan Builder** is an effective and easy-to-use tool that you can use to create, update, and share quality lesson plans. The software also makes it easy to integrate state content standards into any lesson plan.

IRIS Center Resources

The IRIS Center at Vanderbilt University (http://iris.peabody.vanderbilt.edu), funded by the U.S. Department of Education's Office of Special Education Programs (OSEP), develops training enhancement materials for preservice and practicing teachers. The Center works with experts from across the country to create challenge-based interactive modules, case study units, and podcasts that provide research-validated information about working with students in inclusive settings. In your MyEducationLab course we have integrated this content where appropriate.

A+RISE Activities

A+RISE activities provide practice in targeting instruction. A+RISE®, developed by three-time Teacher of the Year and administrator, Evelyn Arroyo, provides quick, research-based strategies that get to the "how" of targeting instruction and making content accessible for all students, including English language learners.

A+RISE® Standards2Strategy™ is an innovative and interactive online resource that offers new teachers in grades K-12 just in time, research-based instructional strategies that:

- Meet the linguistic needs of ELLs as they learn content
- Differentiate instruction for all grades and abilities
- Offer reading and writing techniques, cooperative learning, use of linguistic and nonlinguistic representations, scaffolding, teacher modeling, higher order thinking, and alternative classroom ELL assessment
- Provide support to help teachers be effective through the integration of listening, speaking, reading, and writing along with the content curriculum
- Improve student achievement
- Are aligned to Common Core Elementary Language Arts standards (for the literacy strategies) and to English language proficiency standards in WIDA, Texas, California, and Florida.

Course Resources

The Course Resources section of MyEducationLab is designed to help you put together an effective lesson plan, prepare for and begin your career, navigate your first year of teaching, and understand key educational standards, policies, and laws. It includes the following:

The Grammar Tutorial provides content extracted in part from The Praxis Series™ Online Tutorial for the Pre-Professional Skills Test: Writing. Online quizzes built around specific elements of grammar help users strengthen their understanding and proper usage of the English language in writing. Definitions and examples of grammatical concepts are followed by practice exercises to provide the background information and usage examples needed to refresh understandings of grammar, and then apply that knowledge to make it more permanent.

The Database of Children's Literature offers information on thousands of quality literature titles, and the activities provide experience in choosing appropriate literature and integrating the best titles into language arts instruction.

The Preparing a Portfolio module provides guidelines for creating a high-quality teaching portfolio.

Beginning Your Career offers tips, advice, and other valuable information on:

- **Resume Writing and Interviewing:** Includes expert advice on how to write impressive resumes and prepare for job interviews.
- **Your First Year of Teaching:** Provides practical tips to set up a first classroom, manage student behavior, and more easily organize for instruction and assessment.
- **Law and Public Policies:** Details specific directives and requirements you need to understand under the No Child Left Behind Act and the Individuals with Disabilities Education Improvement Act of 2004.

The Certification and Licensure section is designed to help you pass your licensure exam by giving you access to state test requirements, overviews of what tests cover, and sample test items.

The Certification and Licensure section includes the following:

- **State Certification Test Requirements:** Here, you can click on a state and will then be taken to a list of state certification tests.
- You can click on the **Licensure Exams** you need to take to find:
  - basic information about each test;
  - descriptions of what is covered on each test; and
  - sample test questions with explanations of correct answers.
- **National Evaluation Series™ by Pearson:** Here, students can see the tests in the NES, learn what is covered on each exam, and access sample test items with descriptions and rationales of correct answers. You can also purchase interactive online tutorials developed by Pearson Evaluation Systems and the Pearson Teacher Education and Development group.
- **ETS Online Praxis Tutorials:** Here you can purchase interactive online tutorials developed by ETS and by the Pearson Teacher Education and Development group. Tutorials are available for the Praxis I exams and for select Praxis II exams.

Visit www.myeducationlab.com for a demonstration of this exciting new online teaching resource.

Acknowledgments

I am indebted to Aurora Martínez Ramos, executive editor and vice-president at Pearson Education, who, as in past editions, provided knowledgeable suggestions, continuing encouragement, and rich resources, and to Marilyn Hochman, developmental editor, whose conscientious, perceptive reviews of the revisions and practical suggestions helped me better organize and refine the manuscript. I am also grateful to Paula Carol, who guided the project through the production process; to Erin Grelak, literacy and ELL editor, who provided the overall direction needed to bring this project to completion; and to Michelle Hochberg, editorial assistant at Allyn & Bacon, for her gracious and very helpful assistance. I am also grateful to John Shannon and the staff at Jouve India who patiently and expertly edited the manuscript and prepared it for the printer.

The following reviewers provided many perceptive comments and valuable suggestions. They challenged me to write the best book I could, and for this I am grateful.

For the eighth edition:
Lisa Cheek, Eureka College;
Angela J. Cox, Georgetown College;
Lisa N. Mitchell, University of North Carolina at Pembroke;
Shonta M. Smith, Southeast Missouri State University;
Debra F. Whitaker, Cumberland University.

For the seventh edition: Beth A. Childress, Armstrong Atlantic State University; Deborah A. Farrer, California University of Pennsylvania; Shelley Hong Xu, California State University, Long Beach; Lynn Malok, Moravian College; Lucy Maples, Western Kentucky University; Beth Otto, University of Southern Indiana; Sherrie E. Pardieck, Bradley University.

For the sixth edition: Elaine Byrd, Utah Valley State College; Ward Cockrum, Northern Arizona University; Jo Ann Daly, Marymount University; Anita Iaquinta, Robert Morris University; Laura King, Mary Hogan School, VT (in-service); Margaret Malenka, Michigan State University; Melinda Miller, Sam Houston State University; Sherrie Pardieck, Bradley University; Pamela Petty, Western KY University; Gail Singleton Taylor, Old Dominion University.

For previous editions: Jack Bagford, University of Iowa; Suzanne Barchers, University of Colorado at Denver; John Beach, University of Nevada, Reno; Marian Beckman, Edinboro University of Pennsylvania; Barbara J. Chesler, Longwood University; Sharon Y. Cowan, East Central University; Donna Croll, Valdosta State University; Audrey DíAigneault, Pleasant Valley Elementary School; Lauren Freedman, Western Michigan University; Cynthia Gettys, University of Tennessee at Chattanooga; Shelley Hong Xu, California State University, Long Beach; Maudine Jefferson, Kennesaw State University; H. Jon Jones, Oklahoma State University; Joanna Jones, Grand Canyon University; Betty Lou Land, Winthrop University; Janet W. Lerner, Northeastern Illinois University; Barbara Lyman, Southwest Texas University; Karl Matz, Mankato State University; Lea McGee, Boston College; Jean A. McWilliams, Rosemont College; John M. Ponder, Arkansas State University; Laurence Stewart Rice III, Humboldt State University; Judith Scheu, Kamehama Schools, Honolulu, Hawaii; Patricia Shaw, University of Wisconsin, Whitewater; Gail Silkebakken, East Central Oklahoma University; Shela D. Snyder, Central Missouri State University; Steven Stahl, University of Georgia; Donna Topping, Millersville University; Doris J. Walker-Dalhouse, Moorhead State University; Judith Wenrich, Millersville University; Joyce Feist-Willis, Youngstown State University.

My wife, Joan, offered both helpful comments and continuous encouragement. I deeply appreciate her loving support and understanding, especially when deadlines approached.

T. G.

Creating Literacy Instruction for All Students

1

The Nature of Literacy

Anticipation Guide

Complete the anticipation guide below. It will help to activate your prior knowledge so that you interact more fully with the chapter. It is designed to probe your attitudes and beliefs about important and sometimes controversial topics. There are often no right or wrong answers; the statements will alert you to your attitudes about reading instruction and encourage you to become aware of areas where you might require additional information. After completing the chapter, you might respond to the anticipation guide again to see if your answers have changed in light of what you have read. For each of the following statements, put a check under "Agree" or "Disagree" to show how you feel. Discuss your responses with classmates before you read the chapter.

	Agree	Disagree
1. Before children learn to read, they should know the sounds of most letters.	_____	_____
2. Reading should not be fragmented into a series of subskills.	_____	_____
3. Oral reading should be accurate.	_____	_____
4. Phonics should be taught only when a need arises.	_____	_____
5. Reading short passages and answering questions about them provide excellent practice.	_____	_____
6. Mistakes in oral reading should be ignored unless they change the sense of the passage.	_____	_____

Using What You Know

This chapter provides a general introduction to literacy instruction in preschool and grades K–8. Before reading the chapter, examine your personal knowledge of the topic so that you will be better prepared to interact with the information. Sometimes, you may not realize what you know until you stop and think about it. What do you think reading is? What do you do when you read? What do you think the reader's role is? Is it simply to receive the author's message, or should it include some personal input? How about writing? What processes do you use when you write? How would you go about teaching reading and writing to today's students? What do you think the basic principles of a literacy program should be? What elements have worked especially well in programs with which you are familiar?

The Nature of Reading

"Awake! Awake!" These are the first words I remember reading. But the words were as magical as any that I have read since. Even after all these years, I still have vivid memories of that day long ago in first grade when reading came alive for me, and, indeed, awakened a lifetime of reading and a career as a reading teacher.

Reading is, first and foremost, magical, as those who recall learning to read or who have witnessed their students discover the process will attest. It opens the door to a vast world of information, fulfillment, and enjoyment. After having learned to read, a person is never quite the same.

Although magical, reading is complex. Becoming an effective teacher of reading requires a grounding in the theories behind reading acquisition and instruction. As Pinnell, a noted literacy researcher and practitioner, states:

> Understanding learning is the only true foundation for sound teaching. No matter how good the materials, the program, or the instructional approach, teaching will miss the mark if it is not based on a coherent theory of learning. The word *theory* simply refers to the set of understandings that a teacher holds and believes about how children learn. Everything teachers do in the classroom proceeds from this set of beliefs and understandings, whether they are conscious of it or not. (2006, p. 78)

Major Theories of Literacy Learning and Language Development

The first step, then, in understanding reading requires understanding how children learn and how language develops. There are a number of theories that describe how children learn. They fall into two broad areas: behaviorism and cognitivism.

Behaviorism

Behaviorism stresses observable responses to stimuli. In a behavioral approach, learning consists of the acquisition of new behaviors. Responses that are reinforced increase in frequency. Responses that are not reinforced are extinguished (do not occur again). A response that has been conditioned to a particular stimulus should be elicited if that stimulus is presented. Behaviors are learned or increased when a person receives reinforcers such as praise, privileges, gold stars, or monetary rewards or simply sees that the responses are correct. A basic principle of behaviorism is that we tend to repeat behaviors that are rewarding and avoid those that are not. According to behaviorism, we are passive receivers of knowledge rather than active constructors. Behavioral approaches tend to be teacher-centered.

Scripted programs, such as Reading Mastery, often take a behavioral approach. In Reading Mastery, students first learn individual letter sounds and then learn to blend the sounds to form words. The teacher points to a letter and says, "Here is a new sound." The teacher touches the letter and says the sound for the letter. Students are told to say the sound when the teacher touches the letter. Signals are used so that students respond in unison. Then individuals are called on to say the sound. One objective of this procedure is to obtain as many correct responses from each child as possible. Incorrect responses are quickly corrected so that they will be extinguished.

Cognitivism

Behavioral approaches to learning, with their emphasis on external forces, dominated from about the 1890s until about the 1950s. Rejecting a strictly external view of learning, cognitive psychologists became interested in the inner workings of the mind. **Cognitivism** is based on the proposition that mental processes exist and can be studied. A related proposition is that humans are active participants in their learning rather than passive recipients. Reinforcement is seen as being important in learning, not just because it strengthens responses, but because it is a source of information or feedback (Woolfolk, 2001). Cognitive approaches tend to be student-centered.

Piaget's theories are examples of a cognitive approach to learning. Piaget is also known as a constructivist because of his emphasis on the ways in which children construct an understanding of the world.

■ **Behaviorism** is a philosophy of learning that describes all the activities of an organism in terms of observable actions or behaviors.

■ **Cognitivism** is a philosophy of learning that describes the activities of an organism in terms of observable actions or behaviors and internal or mental states.

Piaget's Theories

Jean Piaget, a Swiss psychologist, stressed stages of cognitive development and the unique nature of children's thinking. As an adherent of **constructivism**, he believed that children construct their own understanding of reality and do not simply reproduce what they see and hear. Children's thinking, according to Piaget, is qualitatively different from adults' thinking, and it evolves through a series of hierarchical stages. He also believed that children's thinking develops through direct experience with their environment. Through *adaptation*, or interaction with the environment, the child constructs psychological structures, or *schemes*, which are ways of making sense of the world. Adaptation includes two complementary processes: **assimilation** and **accommodation**. Through assimilation, the child interprets the world in terms of his or her schemes. Seeing a very small dog, the child calls it "doggie" and assimilates this in his or her dog scheme. Seeing a goat for the first time, the child might relate it to his or her dog scheme and call it "doggie." Later, realizing that there is something different about this creature, the child may accommodate the dog scheme and exclude the goat and all creatures with horns. Thus, the child has refined the dog scheme. To Piaget, direct experience rather than language was the key determiner of cognitive development.

Social Cognitive Views of Learning

According to social cognitive theories, people are an important element in the learning equation. We learn from and with others. L. S. Vygotsky, an adherent of **social constructivism**, stressed the importance of social factors in cognitive development (1962). Although both Piaget and Vygotsky believed that children need to interact with the world around them, Vygotsky thought that learning results from both direct experience and social interaction. If, in examining minerals, a teacher emphasizes the hardness of the minerals, that is what the students will learn. If another teacher emphasizes the value or usefulness of the minerals, that is what the students will learn. Vygotsky is best known for the concept of the **zone of proximal development (ZPD)**. He distinguished between actual and potential development. Actual development is a measure of the level at which a child is functioning. In a sense, it is a measure of what the child has learned up to that point. Potential development is a measure of what the child might be capable of achieving. The difference between the two levels is the zone of proximal development. As explained by Vygotsky (1978), the zone of proximal development is "the distance between the actual developmental level as determined by independent problem solving and the level of potential development as determined through problem solving under adult guidance or in collaboration with more capable peers" (p. 84). In other words, the zone of proximal development is the difference between what a child can do on his or her own and what the child can do with help.

Focusing on the importance of interaction with adults or knowledgeable peers, Vygotsky's theory is that children learn through expert guidance. In time, they internalize the concepts and strategies employed by their mentors and so, ultimately, are able to perform on a higher level. The support and guidance provided by an adult or more capable peer is known as **scaffolding** (Bruner, 1975, 1986). When parents

 FYI

Vygotsky differentiated between learning and development. According to him, learning can often cause qualitative changes in the nature of thought. Certain kinds of knowledge can lead to higher levels of thinking (Bodrova & Leong, 2007). Behaviorists assert that the child simply acquires more knowledge. ■

■ **Constructionism (constructivism)** is a cognitive philosophy of learning that describes learning as an active process in which the learner constructs mental models of reality.

■ **Assimilation** is the process of incorporating new ideas into existing ones.

■ **Accommodation** is the process by which concepts or schemes are modified or new ones created to accommodate new knowledge.

■ **Social constructivism** is a cognitive philosophy of learning that describes learning as an active process in which the learner constructs mental models of reality individually and in interaction with others.

■ The **zone of proximal development (ZPD)** is the difference between independent performance and potential performance as determined through problem solving under the guidance of an adult or more capable peer.

■ **Scaffolding** refers to the support and guidance provided by an adult or more capable peer that helps a student function on a higher level.

FYI

Vygotsky neglected the importance of other ways of learning. Children can and do learn through nonverbal imitation and self-discovery (Berk, 1997). ■

R E F L E C T I O N

How might you apply Vygotskyian principles in your classroom?

converse with a child acquiring language, they respond at a higher level of language use but one that is in the child's zone of proximal development. In their responses, they provide contextual support by restating, repeating key words, and/or focusing on meaning rather than form. Support at the beginning levels of language learning is extensive but is gradually decreased as the child progresses.

Ideally, instruction should be pitched somewhat above a child's current level of functioning. Instruction and collaboration with an adult or more capable peers will enable a child to reach a higher level and ultimately function on that level. Instruction and interaction are key elements. The overall theories of evaluation and instruction presented in this book are grounded in Vygotsky's concepts of actual and potential development and the zone of proximal development.

Implications for classroom instruction based on an integration of the theories of Piaget and Vygotsky are listed below:

- Provide students with hands-on experiences and opportunities to make discoveries.
- Be aware of and plan for individual differences. Because children have different experiences and come from different backgrounds, they develop at different rates.
- Children learn best when activities are developmentally appropriate. Careful observation of the processes a child uses provides insight into the child's level of development. According to Piaget, the child's current level of development determines what she or he will learn. Teaching needs to be adjusted to the child. According to Vygotsky, teaching should be directed to a child's emerging skills. It should be in the zone of proximal development.
- According to Vygotsky, classrooms should be rich in verbal guidance. Interactions with the teacher and peers foster learning. Modeling of strategies for improving comprehension and using context clues are examples of ways teachers foster social cognitive learning.

Cognitive Behavioral Approach

Behavioral and cognitive principles have been combined in an approach known as **cognitive behavioral modification**. Our behavior is affected by the set of rewards and punishments we have experienced in the past and by our beliefs, thoughts, and expectations (Westmont Psychology Department, 2008). Suppose that, based on your past experience of receiving low grades on tests, you believe that you are not very smart and therefore it won't make much difference if you study for a test; so you don't study, and you get a poor grade, thus reinforcing your lack of self-efficacy. A cognitive behavioral approach helps students change their attributions, so they see that effort is required for success. They also learn to see themselves as competent learners. Cognitive behavioral classroom management provides techniques for students to gain control of their learning. Students are taught to set goals, establish and follow a plan for reaching each goal, monitor their progress toward reaching that goal, and evaluate whether they have reached it. Along with learning strategies for improving reading and writing, students are taught self-regulation strategies. A student might set as a goal improving comprehension of text content. The student might then use a checklist or self-talk to prompt herself or himself to set a purpose for reading, survey the text, think about what she or he knows about the topic, make predictions, ask questions while reading, and summarize at the end of each section. The student monitors the use of the strategies to see if they are helping and evaluates whether she or he is reaching the goal of improved comprehension of the text. As Meichenbaum and Biemiller (1998) explain, practice usually involves "both physically performing the skill or skills involved in the task and verbally guiding oneself (thinking out loud—demonstrating self-regulation overtly) while carrying out the task" (p. 126).

■ **Cognitive behavioral modification** is an approach to learning in which self-talk and rewards are used to replace faulty learning habits and beliefs with effective habits and strategies and realistic beliefs.

Top-Down and Bottom-Up Approaches

Another way of looking at theories of literacy learning is to note where those who apply them fall on a continuum. On one end of this continuum are those who espouse a subskills, or bottom-up, approach; on the other end, there are those who advocate a holistic, or top-down, approach. In between are the interactionists.

Bottom-Uppers

In the **bottom-up approach**, children literally start at the bottom and work their way up. First, they learn the names and shapes of the letters of the alphabet. Next, they learn consonant sounds, followed by simple and then more complex vowel correspondences. As Carnine, Silbert, and Kame'enui (1990) explain, "Our position is that many students will not become successful readers unless teachers identify the essential reading skills, find out what skills students lack, and teach those skills directly" (p. 3).

Bottom-up procedures are intended to make learning to read easier by breaking complex tasks into their component skills. Instruction proceeds from the simple to the complex. In essence, there are probably no 100 percent bottom-uppers among reading teachers. Even those who strongly favor phonics recognize the importance of higher-level strategies.

Top-Downers

A **top-down approach**, as its name indicates, starts at the top and works downward. Learning to read is seen as being similar to learning to speak; it is holistic and progresses naturally through immersion. Subskills are not taught because it is felt that they fragment the process and make learning to read more abstract and difficult (Goodman, 1986). One of the most influential models of reading is that proposed by Ken Goodman (1994b). According to Goodman, readers use their background knowledge and knowledge of language to predict and infer the content of print. Readers "use their selection strategies to choose only the most useful information from all that is available" (Goodman, 1994b, p. 1125). When reading the sentence "The moon is full tonight," the reader can use his or her knowledge of the moon, context clues, and perhaps the initial consonants *f* and *t* to reconstruct *full* and *tonight*. According to Goodman's theory, it is not necessary for the reader to process all the letters of *full* and *tonight*. However, in order to make use of background knowledge, context clues, and initial consonant cues, the reader must consider the whole text. If the words *full* and *tonight* were read in isolation, the reader would have to depend more heavily on processing all or most of the letters of each word. As far as comprehension is concerned, the top-down view is that students build their understanding through discussions of high-quality literature or informational texts. There is generally no direct, explicit instruction of comprehension strategies.

 FYI

In Goodman's model, students use three cueing systems: semantic, syntactic, and graphophonic. Semantic cues derive from past experiences, so students construct meaning by bringing their background of knowledge to a story. Syntactic cues derive from knowledge of how the structure of language works. Graphophonic cues refer to the ability to sound out words or recognize them holistically. Based on their use of these cues, students predict the content of the text, confirm or revise their predictions, and reread if necessary. ■

Interactionists

Most practitioners tend to be more pragmatic than either strict top-downers or dyed-in-the-wool bottom-uppers and borrow practices from both ends of the continuum. These **interactionists** teach skills directly and systematically—especially in the beginning—but they avoid overdoing it, as they do not want to fragment the process. They also provide plenty of opportunities for students to experience the holistic nature of reading and writing by having them read whole books and write for real purposes. In his study of highly effective teachers, Pressley (2006) found that most were inter-

---

■ **Bottom-up approach** refers to a kind of processing in which meaning is derived from the accurate, sequential processing of words. The emphasis is on the text rather than the reader's background knowledge or language ability.

■ **Top-down approach** refers to deriving meaning by using one's background knowledge, language ability, and expectations. The emphasis is on the reader rather than the text.

■ **Interactionists** hold the theoretical position that reading involves processing text and using one's background knowledge and language ability.

actionists: "There is a great deal of skills instruction, with as many as 20 skills an hour covered, often in response to the needs of a reader or writer. Skills instruction is strongly balanced with holistic reading and writing, with students reading and experiencing substantial authentic literature and other texts that make sense for them to be reading given their needs" (p. 3). As cognitive psychologist M. H. Ashcroft (1994) notes, "Any significant mental task will involve both data-driven (bottom-up) and conceptually driven (top-down) processing" (p. 75).

In an interactive compensatory model, students use top-down processes to compensate for weakness in bottom-up processes or vice versa. For instance, students who have weak decoding skills make heavy use of context to make sense of a passage. On the other hand, when content is unfamiliar, readers get all they can out of the data. They read every word carefully, may reread it several times, and may even read it out loud. Think about how you read a set of directions for completing a complex, unfamiliar activity or a list of new tax regulations.

Where do you fit on the bottom-up, top-down continuum? Go back to the anticipation guide at the beginning of the chapter. Take a look at how you answered the six statements. If you agreed with only the odd-numbered ones, you are a bottom-up advocate. If you agreed with only the even-numbered statements, you are a top-downer. If your answers were mixed, you are probably an interactionist.

Reader Response Theory

Still another way of looking at reading is from a literary, or reader response, view. Literary theory explores the role of the reader. In the past, the reader's role was defined as being passive, getting the author's meaning. Today, reading requires a more active role—the reader must construct meaning from text. The model of transmission of information in which the reader was merely a recipient has given way to transactional theory, a two-way process involving a reader and a text:

> Every reading act is an event, or a **transaction**, involving a particular reader and a particular pattern of signs, a text, and occurring at a particular time in a particular context. Instead of two fixed entities acting on one another, the reader and the text are two aspects of a total dynamic situation. The "meaning" does not reside ready-made "in" the text or "in" the reader but happens or comes into being during the transaction between reader and text. (Rosenblatt, 1994, p. 1063)

In her study of how students read a poem, Rosenblatt (1978) noted that each reader was active:

> He was not a blank tape registering a ready-made message. He was actively involved in building up a poem for himself out of his responses to text. He had to draw on his past experiences with the verbal symbols. . . . The reader was not only paying attention to what the words pointed to in the external world, to their referents; he was also paying attention to the images, feelings, attitudes, associations, and ideas that the words and their referents evoked in him. (p. 10)

The type of reading, of course, has an effect on the transaction. The reader can take an efferent or an aesthetic **stance**. When reading a set of directions, a science text, or a math problem, the reader takes an **efferent** stance, the focus being on obtaining information that can be carried away (*efferent* is taken from the Latin verb *efferre*, "to carry away"). In the **aesthetic** stance, the reader pays attention to the associations, feelings, attitudes, and ideas that the words evoke.

Does it make any difference whether reading is viewed as being transmissional, transactional, or somewhere in between? Absolutely. If reading is viewed as transmissional, students are expected to stick close to the author's message. If reading is viewed as transactional, students are

■ **Transaction** refers to the relationship between the reader and the text in which meaning is created as the text is conditioned by the reader and the reader is conditioned by the text.

■ **Stance** refers to the position or attitude that the reader takes. The two stances are aesthetic and efferent.

■ **Efferent** refers to a kind of reading in which the focus is on obtaining or carrying away information from the reading.

■ **Aesthetic** refers to a type of reading in which the reader focuses on experiencing the piece: the rhythm of the words, the past experiences the words call up (Rosenblatt, 1978, p. 10).

TABLE 1.1 Theories of Learning and Reading Development

Theory	Features	Implementation
Behaviorism	Observable behavior is stressed. Responses to stimuli are reinforced or extinguished. Drills, guided practice, and acquisition of facts, skills, and concepts are emphasized.	Present and reinforce skills, such as phonics, in systematic fashion. Reinforce appropriate behavior.
Cognitivism	Mental processes are important. Students are active learners as they use strategies to acquire facts, skills, and concepts.	Teach strategies. Ask questions that help reveal students' thinking.
Constructivism	Through active experiences, children construct their understanding of the world.	Arrange for learning experiences and opportunities for problem solving. Gear instruction to students' stage of development. Focus on inquiry and discovery learning.
Social Constructivism	Thoughts and ideas of others are an essential element in constructing knowledge. Students learn through expert guidance from more knowledgeable others. Social interaction, the zone of proximal development, and scaffolding are key elements in learning.	Make sure students are in their zone of proximal development. Co-construct knowledge with students. Scaffold students' learning.
Cognitive Behavioral	Learning is affected by the learning task and situation and the ability, interests, and attitudes of the students. Students use self-regulation to acquire facts, skills, and concepts.	Build self-efficacy. Teach students to set goals and self-regulate. Walk students through the process of setting goals, working to reach goals, and monitoring progress.
Interactionist	Both top-down and bottom-up processes are used. Students are active learners as they employ strategies to acquire facts, skills, and concepts.	Teach students to use phonics skills and context. Encourage students to relate new learning to what they already know. Use compensatory mechanisms.
Reader Response	Reading is a transaction in which the reader affects the text and is affected by it.	Emphasize personal responses and interpretations. Encourage students to make personal connections to what they have read.

Source: Portions of the chart are adapted from Woolfolk (2001), Table 9.8, Four Views of Learning (p. 358).

expected to put their personal selves into their reading, especially when encountering literature. From a transactional perspective, building background becomes especially important because it enriches the transaction between reader and text. Personal response and interpretation are at the center of the reading process. The reader's role is enhanced when a transactional view prevails. See Table 1.1 for a summary of theories of learning and language development.

Importance of Literacy Theories

Why is it important to be aware of different theories of teaching reading? For one thing, it is important that you formulate your own personal beliefs about reading and writing instruction. These beliefs will then be the foundation for your instruction. They will determine the goals you set, the instructional techniques you use, the materials you choose, the organization of your classroom, the reading and writing behaviors you expect students to exhibit, and the criteria you use to evaluate students. For instance, whether you use children's books or a basal anthology, how you teach phonics, and whether you expect flawless oral reading or are satisfied if the student's rendition is faithful to the sense of the selection will depend on your theoretical orientation (DeFord, 1985).

Approach Taken by This Book

This book draws heavily on research in cognitive psychology, combines an interactionist point of view with a holistic orientation, and takes an integrated approach. Both the bottom-up and top-down approaches are step by step (Kamhi & Catts, 1999). In the bottom-up model, the reader progresses from letters to sounds to words. Seeing the word *moon*, the novice readers sounds it out as /m-/oo/-/n/ and then blends the sounds to compose the word *moon*. In the top-down process as Goodman explained above, the reader uses language cues to predict and to confirm the word. Seeing the sentence "The wolf howled at the moon," the reader uses her knowledge of language and wolves

FYI

• To clarify your philosophy of teaching, ask: "What are my instructional practices, and why am I doing what I'm doing?" Examining your practices should help you uncover your beliefs.

• This book takes the position that all sources of information—semantic, syntactic, background knowledge, and letter–sound relationships—are essential when processing text and emphasize the use of both context and phonics. However, the book also agrees with the view that even in mature reading, nearly all words are processed. ■

to predict that the word is *moon* because that makes sense in the sentence. She may decode the initial letter but doesn't have to decode all the sounds in the word to predict that the word is *moon*. However, in an integrated approach, the processes occur in parallel fashion. For instance, when students decode words, four processors are at work: orthographic, phonological, meaning, and context (Adams, 1990, 1994). The orthographic processor is responsible for perceiving the sequences of letters in text. The phonological processor is responsible for mapping the letters into their spoken equivalents. The meaning processor contains one's knowledge of word meanings, and the context processor is in charge of constructing a continuing understanding of the text (Stahl, Osborne, & Lehr, 1990). The processors work simultaneously, and they both receive information and send it to the other processors; however, the orthographic and phonological processors are always essential participants. Context may speed and/or assist the interpretation of orthographic and phonological information but does not take its place (see Figure 1.1). (Context would speed the decoding of *moon*.) When information from one processor is weak, another may be called on to give assistance. With a word such as *lead*, the context processor provides extra help to the meaning and phonological processors in assigning the correct meaning and pronunciation.

In an integrated model, both top-down and bottom-up processes are used. However, depending on circumstances, either bottom-up or top-down processes are emphasized. If one is reading a handwritten note in which some words are illegible, top-down processes are stressed as knowledge of language and knowledge of the world are used to fill in what is missing. If one is reading unfamiliar proper names or words in isolation, bottom-up processes are emphasized.

In an integrated approach, reading is considered an active, constructive process, with the focus on the reader, whose experiences, cultural background, and point of view will play a part in her or his comprehension of a written piece. The focus is on cognitive processes or strategies used to decode words and understand and remember

FIGURE 1.1   Modeling the Reading Systems: Four Processors

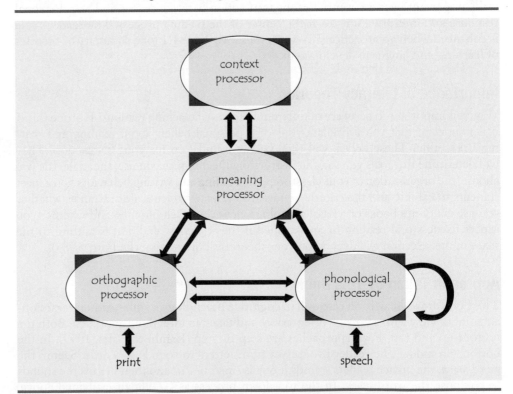

Source: Adams, M. J. (1990). *Beginning to read: Thinking and learning about print: A summary.* Prepared by S. A. Stahl, J. Osborne, & F. Lehr. Urbana-Champaign, IL: Center for the Study of Reading, University of Illinois.

text: using phonics and context to decipher unknown words, activating one's knowledge of a topic, predicting meaning, summarizing, and visualizing.

Stress is also placed on teaching strategies in context and holistically applying them to children's books, periodicals, ads and other real-world materials, and content-area textbooks. The integrated approach is a balanced approach in which systematic instruction and immersion in reading and writing play complementary roles.

The Status of Literacy

According to national testing results, some 67 percent of fourth-graders and 76 percent of eighth-graders can read at least on a basic level (National Center for Educational Statistics, 2011). Some 34 percent of fourth-graders and 34 percent of eighth-graders performed at or above the proficient level. Some 8 percent of fourth-graders and 3 percent of eighth-graders performed at the advanced level. Although there were more fourth- than eight-graders at the advanced level, there were more fourth-graders (33 percent) than eighth-graders (24 percent) at the below-basic level. What do the levels mean? Table 1.2 provides descriptions of the performance at each level. The basic level is a conservative estimate of grade level reading. Students at the below-basic level are reading below grade level. The proficient level is apparently above grade level (Pellegrino, Jones, & Mitchell, 1999). NAEP data provides an overview of the kinds of literacy instruction that students in the elementary grades and middle school will need. Students at the upper end will need to be challenged. Those at the lower end, especially those performing below the basic level, will need extra help and, in some cases, extensive intervention.

Impact of the Elementary and Secondary Act

The Elementary and Secondary Act plays a highly influential role in literacy instruction and assessment. The No Child Left Behind (NCLB) Act of 2001, a version of the Elementary and Secondary Act, had as its goal 100 percent of all students reaching proficiency at their grade level in state math and reading/language arts by the 2013–2014 school year, a provision that was waived in 2011. Although criticized because it led, in many instances, to teaching to the test and a narrowing of the curriculum, and demanded that English language learners be assessed before they have had adequate time to learn English, NCLB succeeded in drawing attention to the neediest students. It conveyed the idea that making provision for all students, including struggling learners, is every teacher's responsibility. The Elementary and Secondary Act (currently

TABLE 1.2   Description of National Assessment of Educational Progress (NAEP) Levels

Grade	Basic	Proficient	Advanced
4	Should be able to locate relevant information, make simple inferences, and use their understanding of the text to identify details that support a given interpretation or conclusion. Students should be able to interpret the meaning of a word as it is used in the text.	Should be able to integrate and interpret texts and apply their understanding of the texts to draw conclusions and make evaluations.	Should be able to make complex inferences and construct and support their inferential understanding of the text and apply their understanding of the texts to make and support a judgment.
8	Should be able to locate information; identify statements of main idea, theme, or author's purpose; and make simple inferences from texts. They should be able to interpret the meaning of a word as it is used in the text. Students performing at this level should also be able to state judgments and give some support about content and presentation of content.	Should be able to provide relevant information and summarize main ideas and themes. They should be able to make and support inferences about a text, connect parts of a text, and analyze text features. Students performing at this level should also be able to fully substantiate judgments about content and presentation of content.	Should be able to make connections with in and across texts and to explain causal relations. They should be able to evaluate and justify the strength of supporting evidence and the quality of an author's presentation. Students performing at this level should also be able to manage the processing demands of analysis and evaluation by stating, explaining, and justifying.

Source: Adapted from National Center for Education Statistics (2011). The Nation's Report Card: Reading 2011 (NCES 2012–458). Institute of Education Sciences, U.S. Department of Education, Washington, DC.

known as No Child Left Behind or NCLB) is up for renewal. Although its basic purpose will remain the same, emphasis will be on improving the effectiveness of teachers, using measures of students' performance as part of teacher evaluation systems, and using measures of growth rather than percentages of students passing a proficiency standard to assess the progress of schools. A key provision will be establishing standards that will prepare students to be college and career ready.

Common Core State Standards

One problem with NCLB was that each state set its own standards and used its own tests to determine proficiency. When individual state standards were translated into NAEP equivalent scores, most states had proficiency levels that were below NAEP's basic level (Bandeira de Mello, 2011). Current emphasis is now on having states adopt a challenging set of standards known as the Common Core State Standards and using an assessment system, now being constructed, that will be aligned with the standards so that every student will be college and career ready. The Common Core State Standards "define the knowledge and skills students should have to succeed in entry-level, credit-bearing, academic college courses and in workforce training programs" (National Governors Association and Council of Chief State School Officers, 2010). There are ten anchor standards for reading, writing, language, and content-area reading and content-area writing. The anchor standards are broad statements of objectives, which are further broken down into more specific grade-specific objectives. The anchor standards are listed on the inside front cover. To find specific standards by grade level, consult the Common Core State Standards at **http://www.corestandards.org/ assets/CCSSI_ELA%20Standards.pdf** for English Language Arts and also Literacy in History/Social Studies, Science, & Technical Subjects.

The Common Core State Standards emphasize teaching for transfer. In other words, for teaching in such a way that the literacy skills presented can be used in other classes and in the world outside school. Emphasis is also placed on helping students see and understand the big ideas and answer essential questions. Higher-level thinking skills and reading informational text are given a more prominent role just as technology is (Kallick, & Troxell, 2011).

In a sense, the primary skill advocated by the Common Core State Standards is the ability to read complex text. ACT researchers (2006) found that "the clearest differentiator in reading between students who are college ready and students who are not is the ability to comprehend complex texts" (pp. 16-17). Since workplace text is equal in complexity to college-level text, the implication is that in order to prepare all students to be college and career ready, it is essential to prepare students to read complex texts. Learning to read complex text is a long-term objective that starts at the earliest levels and develops up through the elementary, middle school, and high school levels, as each level builds on skills and understandings established at earlier levels. Comprehending complex text requires vocabulary and background development, instruction in skills, and the development of higher-level discussion and writing skills. A key feature of the Common Core State Standards is the reading of a greater proportion of informational text. Reading additional informational text should not be interpreted as spending less time reading literary texts (Langer, 2011). It does mean, though, that students should be doing more reading in science and social studies and other content areas.

However, the most drastic change in the Common Core State Standards is the implementation of grade bands. There is an apparent gap between the reading skills possessed by today's students and those required for college and career readiness and also between the difficulty level of materials that students are reading at the end of high school and those that they will be required to read to become college and career ready (National Governors Association and Council of Chief State School Officers, 2010a). To close both gaps, the Common Core State Standards have incorporated a feature known as grade bands. The bands include grades 2–3, 4–5, 6–8, 9–10, and 11–12. The difficulty level at each band has been expanded so that by senior year students will be expected to be able to read at or close to college and career level. In other words, the standards call for students to be able to read more challenging material at every grade level beginning with grade 2. Even though Common Core Standards call for having students read more challenging materials, this does not mean that students should be given material that exceeds their reading ability. Giving students material that is too hard is virtually guaranteed to stunt their literacy growth.

Scientifically Based Literacy Instruction

Because large numbers of students are reading on a basic level or below and because the gap between the reading achievement of poor and middle-class students is substantial, there has been a call in federal regulations for programs that are scientifically based. In federal regulations, scientific evidence is interpreted as meaning studies in which Method A has been compared with Method B and/or a control group and found to be statistically superior. The International Reading Association (2002) uses the term *evidence-based* rather than scientifically based. *Evidence-based* is a broader term and includes qualitative studies as well as the more scientifically based studies that include comparison of experimental and control groups.

The most extensive study of research-based programs was conducted by John Hattie (2009), a New Zealand educator, who analyzed more than 800 meta-analyses. A meta-analysis is a study of studies that use statistical techniques to determine effect size. **Effect size** is the power of the element being tested to improve achievement or some other outcome. The effect size is the degree to which the experimental group did better than a matched group of students. Effect sizes are typically expressed in standard deviations. A **standard deviation** is a measure of the variability of performance and can be translated into percentiles or other units. One standard deviation at the average level is equal to 34 percentile points. For instance, summarizing and note taking have an effect size of 1 (Marzano, Gaddy, & Dean 2000). This is equal to a percentile gain of 34 points. If students were at the fiftieth percentile (an average rank) before the treatment, they would be at the eighty-fourth percentile after the treatment. In other words, instead of doing better than 50 percent of students, they would be doing better than 84 percent.

Average effect size is .4 (13.6 percentile points). An effect size of .2 (6.8 percentile points) is small, and one of .8 (27.2 percentile points) is high (Cohen, 1992). Effect sizes can also be negative. They can detract from progress. Negative effect sizes include summer vacation (–.09), retention (–.16), television (–.18), and mobility (–.34). Throughout the text, effect sizes, if available, will be noted in terms of percentiles so that you can better judge the value of teaching practices and techniques.

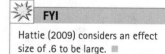

FYI

Hattie (2009) considers an effect size of .6 to be large. ■

Back in the United States, researcher and educator Robert Marzano (2010) identified 41 instructional factors that have a positive impact on learning. In general, the factors he discovered mirror those uncovered by Hattie. Two of Marzano's highest factors are (1) setting goals and (2) tracking student progress and using scoring scales, which are similar to rubrics. These, of course, are key elements in visible teaching and learning. A third meta-analysis was conducted by the National Reading Panel (2000), which restricted its study to literacy. These three main sources and others have been used to help select the research-based strategies presented in this text. Table 1.3 shows the effect sizes of a number of instructional elements.

■ **Effect size** is the power of the element being tested to improve achievement or some other outcome. The effect size is the degree to which the experimental group did better than a matched group of students. Effect sizes are typically expressed in standard deviations. Average effect size is .4. An effect size of .2 is small, and one of .8 is high (Cohen, 1992).

■ **Standard deviation** is a measure of variance or how much dispersion there is from the average. A low standard deviation means there is little variance. Scores cluster around the mean or average. A high standard deviation means that there is a wide variance. Scores are more widely dispersed.

■ **Percentile rank** is the point on a scale of 1 to 99 that shows what percentage of students obtained an equal or lower score. A percentile rank of 75 means that 75 percent of those who took the test received an equal or lower score.

TABLE 1.3 Effect Size of Selected Instructional Elements

Element	Effect Size in Percentiles
Tracking progress	34
Intervention	28
Teacher clarity	27
Feedback	27
Teacher–student relationships	26
Setting goals	25
Professional development	23
Student engagement	21
Not labeling students	21
Teaching strategies	20
Direct instruction	20
Teaching vocabulary	20
Home environment	19
Socioeconomic status	19
Classroom cohesion	18
Peer influences	18
Classroom management	18
Parental involvement	17
Small-group learning	17
Concentration/persistence/engagement	16
Homework	15
Preschool program	15
Expectations	15
Practice	14
Recognition of students' efforts	14

Source: Based on Hattie, J. (2009). *Visible learning.* New York: Routledge; and Marzano, R. J. (2007). *The art and science of teaching.* Alexandria, VA: ASCD.

REFLECTION

What steps might you take to make sure that your teaching is research-based?

Visible Teaching and Learning

Based on his analyses, Hattie (2009) concluded that what is most effective is visible teaching.

> Visible teaching and learning occur when learning is the explicit goal, when it is appropriately challenging, when the teacher and the student both (in their various ways) seek to ascertain whether and to what degree the challenging goal is attained, when there is deliberate practice aimed at attaining mastery of the goal, when there is feedback given and sought, and when there are active, passionate, and engaging people (teacher, student, peers, and so on) participating in the act of learning. It is teachers seeing learning through the eyes of students, and students seeing teaching as the key to their ongoing learning. The remarkable feature of the evidence is that the biggest effects on student learning occur when teachers become learners of their own teaching, and when students become their own teachers. When students become their own teachers, they exhibit the self-regulatory attributes that seem most desirable for learners (self-monitoring, self-evaluation, self-assessment, self-teaching). (p. 22)

The theme of this text will be to make teaching and learning visible. To accomplish that purpose, the text will highlight key effective factors. Each chapter will conclude with a feature entitled "Extending and Applying," in which you will be asked to extend your knowledge of key effective practices and apply them, and also "Professional Reflection," in which you will be asked to reflect on your ability to implement key assessment and instructional practices. The Professional Reflection checklists are modeled on highly effective teacher evaluation systems in widespread use such as those constructed by Robert Marzano (2010), Charlotte Danielson (2010), and those used by charter schools such as Achievement First (2010), and those used by school districts such as the District of Columbia (2010) and also the IRA Standards for Reading

Professionals. The Professional Reflections only cover practices related to literacy instruction. Classroom management and routines are not addressed. The overall intent of this book is to equip you with the knowledge, understanding, and skills to become a highly effective literacy teacher. By focusing on key practices, you can develop the skills and practices needed to become a highly effective teacher.

As a teacher, you should become acquainted with the major findings of literacy research so that you can construct a literacy program that is based on research and so that you can assess whether new techniques or materials that you are thinking about trying are supported by research. You should also assess the research base to see if it is applicable to your students and your situation. A technique that works well on a one-to-one basis may not be effective with small groups. Of course, research doesn't answer all the instructional questions that arise. You need to become a teacher–researcher so that you can test methods and materials and have a better basis for selecting those that are most effective in your situation. You also need to assess all aspects of your program with a view to replacing or improving elements that aren't working and to adding elements that are missing.

As far as possible, the suggestions made in this text are evidence-based. However, in some instances they are based on personal experience or the experience of others. Teaching literacy is an art as well as a science.

Role of Language

As magical as it may be, reading is our second major intellectual accomplishment. Our first, and by far, most important, intellectual accomplishment is our acquisition of language. Without language, of course, there would be no reading. Reading is very much a language activity, and, ultimately, our ability to read is limited by our language skills. We can't read what we can't understand. Even if we can pronounce words we don't understand because of superior phonics skills, we are not reading. **Reading** is a process in which we construct meaning from print. Without meaning, there is no reading.

Components of Language

Language has a number of interacting components: **phonology** (speech sounds known as phonemes), **morphology** (word formation), **syntax** (sentence formation), **semantics** (word and sentence meaning), **prosody** (intonation and rhythm of speech), and **pragmatics** (effective use of language: knowing how to take turns in a conversation, using proper tone, using terms of politeness, etc.) (National Institute on Deafness and Other Communication Disorders, 2003).

Developing Language

Theories of language learning are similar to those of cognitive learning. From the behavioral standpoint, language is learned through reinforcement. As babies make sounds and toddlers say words, they are reinforced by their caregivers. Imitation is also a factor. The nativist viewpoint maintains that children are born with a language acquisition device (LAD) that predisposes them to learn and generate language structures (Chomsky, 1968). According to nativist theorists such as Noam Chomsky, syntax is too complex to be learned by imitation or instruction. The mental structures for syntax are activated by verbal input. Using words that they hear, children are able to understand and generate sentences that follow rules too complex for them to learn simply by imitation or instruction. Interactionists stress the interaction of children's

- **Reading** is a process in which we construct meaning from print.
- **Phonology** is the language component that consists of producing and understanding speech sounds.

- **Morphology** is the component of language that has to do with meaningful word parts, such as roots and affixes.
- **Syntax** is the language component that has to do with the way in which words are arranged in a sentence.

- **Semantics** is the component of language that has to do with word and sentence meaning.
- **Prosody** is the component of language that has to do with the intonation and rhythm of speech: pitch, stress, and juncture.

cognitive abilities and environmental factors, such as input from caregivers and others. Interactionists note that caregivers use a number of strategies, such as speaking slowly, repeating, and filling in missing words, to encourage and scaffold emerging speech. According to social interactionists, humans use these strategies naturally. We have an inborn need and desire to communicate.

Although young children learn many words through imitation, language learning is also a constructive process. If children were mere imitators, they would only be able to repeat what they hear. But they construct sentences such as "Mommy goed work," which is something that adults do not say. Creating a hypothesis about how language works, young children note that *-ed* is used to express past action and then overapply this generalization. With feedback and experience, they revise the hypothesis and ultimately learn that some action words have special past-tense forms.

Learning a Second Language

Large numbers of students learn English as a second or even a third language, so it's important to have some understanding of the acquisition of additional languages. Learning a second language is easier than learning a first language. Students who have a firm foundation in their first language have an easier time learning a second language. Concepts about language and its functions have already been formed. If English is similar to the first language, there may be a transfer of word and syntactical knowledge. Students are best able to learn a second language when their native language is accepted and they feel secure and confident. Input that is comprehensible is another key factor (Krashen, 2003). In reading, **English language learners (ELLs)** will acquire more language and comprehend better if they know 98 percent of the words in the text (Nation, 2001). Input can be enhanced through boldfaced vocabulary words and marginal glosses and illustrations. Speaking slowly, using gestures and visuals, and explaining new words help make oral input comprehensible. Motivation is also a key factor. The desire to make friends can be a powerful motivator (Lessow-Hurley, 2003). Initial success in acquiring language is also a motivator and leads to increased language acquisition.

Growth of Vocabulary

By age 3, children have a speaking vocabulary of about 1,000 words. By the time they enter kindergarten, they may know 5,000 words or more. The major influence on the size of children's vocabularies is the quantity and quality of the kind of talk they are exposed to. According to language expert Todd Risley (2003), the most important thing parents and other caregivers can do for their children is to talk to them. The amount of talk directed toward infants and toddlers is powerfully related to their verbal abilities and their success in school. Hart and Risley (1995) collected data on the quantity and quality of parent talk. They collected enough data on a sufficient number of families that they could reliably estimate the average amount of parent talk. They found that the sheer volume of talk that infants and toddlers hear varies greatly. Some children hear fewer than 500 words in an hour of family life. Others are exposed to 3,000 words in an hour. Some parents express approval or affirmation forty times an hour, whereas others, fewer than four times an hour. These differences add up. By age 4, some children have heard more than 50 million words, while others have heard just 10 million words. By age 4, some children have had 800,000 affirmations, while others have heard just 80,000. But there is more than just a quantitative difference between the most talkative and the least talkative families. The least talkative families use talk primarily to control and guide children. The most talkative families also use talk in this way, but they go beyond giving directions. Much of their extra talk consists of descriptions and explanations and

■ **Pragmatics** is the component of language that has to do with engaging in effective communication.

■ **English language learners (ELLs)** are students who were not born in the United States or whose native language is not English and who cannot participate effectively in the regular curriculum because they have difficulty speaking, understanding, reading, and writing in English-speaking classrooms.

contains a more complex vocabulary and structure and added positive reinforcement. The amount and quality of talk to which children are exposed are correlated with the size of their vocabularies and their later language and cognitive development.

Although studies show that the amount of talk is not strictly related to socioeconomic status, professionals talk the most, and parents on welfare talk the least. However, there is a great variability among the working class. Many of the most talkative parents, along with the quietest, are in the working class. And it is parental talkativeness rather than socioeconomic status that relates to later verbal ability. In other words, it isn't how much money parents have or how much education they have or whether they are members of a minority group that counts; it is how much and how well they talk to their children. As Risley (2003) hypothesized, "The accumulation of language experience is the major determiner of vocabulary growth and verbal intellectual development" (p. 2).

Children learn to read by reading.

In a longitudinal study of children in Bristol, England, Wells (1986) found that children's language was best developed in one-to-one situations in which an adult discussed matters that were of interest and concern to the child or the two talked over a shared activity. It is also essential that the adult adjust his or her language so as to take into consideration and to compensate for the child's limited linguistic ability, something parents seem to do intuitively.

In his extensive study, Wells (1986) found that some parents intuitively provided maximum development for their children's language. Far from being directors of what their children said, these parents were collaborative constructors of meaning. Careful listeners, they made genuine attempts to use both nonverbal and verbal clues to understand what their children were saying. Through careful listening and active involvement in the conversation, parents were able to help the children extend their responses so that both knowledge of the world and linguistic abilities were fostered.

As a teacher, you can't change the quality or quantity of language to which children have been exposed, but you can increase the quantity and quality of talk in your classroom and encourage parents and other caregivers to do the same. This book emphasizes high-quality, language-rich social interactions of the type conducted by the parents who best foster their children's language development.

Importance of the Students' Cultures

Living as we do in a multicultural, pluralistic society, it is important for us to explore and understand the literacy histories of our pupils. We have to ask such questions as these: In students' culture(s), how are reading and writing used? What values are placed on them? What are the ways in which the students have observed and participated in reading and writing? Is literacy in their environment primarily a group or an individual activity? Given this information, instruction should build on the students' experiences and develop and reinforce the skills and values important to their culture(s) as well as those important to the school.

 Using Technology

The Web site of the New Literacies Research Team offers videos and articles exploring the New Literacies.
http://www.newliteracies.uconn.edu/pubs.html ∎

Literacy and Technology: The New Literacies

The New Literacies are the reading, writing, and communication skills that are required for the successful use of information and communications technologies, especially the Internet. The Internet has a number of positive features that can be used to foster higher-level thinking and literacy, and it offers virtually unlimited content that is up-to-date and, in many instances, unavailable elsewhere. Students can work with real-life problems, such as global warming or hunger, and can interact with other students and publish their work on the Internet. However, because of its unlimited and unregulated content, the Internet demands critical thinking, including analysis and evaluation. A key feature of the Internet is the ease with which hyperlinks can be used to go from site to site. Students are able to direct their learning by deciding which links to click on. Again, this means that students must analyze, synthesize, and evaluate as they progress through sites via hyperlinks (Bradshaw, Bishop, Gens, Miller, & Rogers, 2002).

On the minus side, the Internet offers some unique challenges. As Bradshaw and colleagues (2002) warn, "The vast amount of information available can be overwhelming and lead to disorientation, information overload and devaluation of information" (p. 277). Students can suffer from "information fatigue" and simply give up. They might also experience navigational disorientation and have difficulty finding their way around the Internet. Knowledge of the topic and experience with effective search techniques can help overcome these problems. Another problem, and perhaps the most significant, is the danger of falling into shallow thinking patterns. Students might gather a lot of information but not process it. Seeing the amount of information they have collected may give them the false impression of having a greater understanding of the topic than they actually do have. A related issue is the uneven quality of online information. The accuracy, reliability, and depth of information on the Internet can vary dramatically, which calls for careful, critical reading.

"At its best the web offers opportunities that simply cannot be replicated via other media without the learning environment becoming ridiculously clumsy and inefficient. The web offers options and access that can change the way teachers teach and learners learn" (Bradshaw et al., 2002, p. 278). But making the most of the Internet and other technologies requires careful planning and teaching. "Successful searchers used the skills of thinking, acting, integrating, transforming and reaching resolution, but not all searchers are able on their own to use these skills" (p. 279). As researchers note, using the Internet is more complex than traditional inquiry. The New Literacies required for its use include the

> intricacies of rapidly integrating a *physical* process of clicking the mouse, dragging scroll bars, rolling over dynamic images, and navigating pop-up menus that intertwine with a *cognitive* process of planning, predicting, monitoring, and evaluating one's pathway through open Internet text spaces (as opposed to multiple printed texts or closed hypertext systems). In addition, this self-regulated cycle often occurred across much shorter and disparate units of Internet text than the continuous text passages typically included in printed text comprehension tasks. (Coiro & Dobbler, 2007, p. 242)

In addition, as Coiro (2010) notes, "Each online reading activity may require very different skill sets (e.g., informational websites, search engines, email, IM, blogs)." As teachers, we need to determine our students' current level of proficiency in these areas and build on that level.

Adapting Traditional Skills

A key reading skill for the era of the information superhighway is the ability to decide quickly and efficiently whether an article, study, or other document merits reading. With so much information available, it is essential that students not waste time reading texts that are not pertinent or worthwhile. Having more data to work with means that students must be better at organizing information, evaluating it, drawing conclusions from it, and conveying the essence of the information to others. They also need cognitive flexibility in order to utilize the vast amounts of information when proposing diverse solutions to increasingly complex problems. The more complex skills required to make the best use of technology will be addressed in subsequent chapters. Of course, these more complex skills build on traditional comprehension and

Using Technology

Joan Ganz Cooney Center Provides information on using media to advance learning. http://www.joanganzcooneycenter .org ■

Using Technology

The average 5- to 8-year-old spends more than 4 hours each day with recreational media. The average 8- to 10-year-old spends 5 hours and 29 minutes per day with recreational media, but that increases to 8 hours and 40 minutes a day for 11- to 14-year-olds. For 11- to 14-year-olds, much of the media usage occurs on cell phones and other handheld devices (Rideout, Foehr, & Roberts, 2010; Gutnick, Robb, Takeuchi, & Kotler, 2011). ■

study skills. Technology is also changing the way teachers present materials, make assignments, assess students, and manage pupil data. Technology as a teacher tool will be explored in upcoming chapters.

The teacher is the key to effective reading instruction.

A Reading and Writing Program for Today's Students

What kind of program will help meet the literacy needs of today's students? That is a question that the remainder of this book will attempt to answer. However, when all is said and done, the ten principles discussed below, if followed faithfully, should make a difference in determining such a program.

1. *Children learn to read by reading.* Learning to read is a little like learning to drive a car—instruction and guidance are required. In addition to instruction and guidance, novice readers, like novice motorists, require practice. They must read a variety of fiction and nonfiction books, newspapers, and magazines to become truly skilled. In a way, each book or article makes a child a better reader. As Hirsch (1987) pointed out, children must have a broad background in a variety of areas in order to be able to understand much of what is being written and said in today's world. For example, a child who has read the fable "The Boy Who Cried Wolf" will have the background necessary to understand a story that includes the sentence "Frank cried wolf once too often." Reading is not simply a matter of acquiring and perfecting skills; it also requires accumulating vocabulary, concepts, experiences, and background knowledge.

To provide the necessary practice and background, children's books are an essential component of a reading program. Unfortunately, large numbers of students are aliterate: They *can* read, but they *do* not, at least not on a regular basis. Only 56 percent of students ages 6 to 8 are frequent readers, which means they read at least five days a week. That percentage drops to 38 percent for 9- to 11-year-olds and 30 percent for 12- to 14-year-olds (Harrison Group, 2010). Lewis and Samuels (2003) found that additional reading was beneficial for all students. For average students, it added about 17 percentile points, a half-year's gain in reading skills, but it was especially beneficial for ELLs, struggling readers, and students just beginning to learn to read.

The case for including children's books in a reading program is a compelling one. First, as just noted, those who read more, read better. Second, research suggests that students who read widely and are given some choice in what they read have a more favorable attitude toward reading (Harrison Group, 2010). As a practical matter, wide reading builds the skills needed to do well on assessments for the Common Core Standards.

 Using Technology

PARCC
Provides assessment and instructional resources.
http://www.nationalreadingpanel.org ■

> To succeed on the . . . assessments, students need access to a wide range of materials on a variety of topics and genres, both in their classrooms and in their school libraries, to ensure that they have opportunities to independently read widely among texts of their own choosing during and outside of the school day in order to develop their knowledge and joy of reading. (PARCC, 2011, p. 6)

Using children's books in the reading program not only leads to greater enjoyment of reading but also builds skill in reading. In addition, allowing some self-selection should produce students who can and do read. To assist you in choosing or recommending books for your students, lists of appropriate books are presented throughout the text along with a description of several extensive lists of leveled books (see Chapter 3). Chapter 3 also describes a number of devices for leveling or assessing the difficulty level of books.

2. *Reading should be easy—but not too easy.* Think about it this way: If children find reading difficult, they will acquire a distaste for it and will simply stop reading except when they have to. Because of inadequate practice, they will fall further behind, and their distaste for reading will grow. In addition, students will be unable to apply the strategies they have been taught, and learning will be hampered if the text is too difficult (Clay, 1993a). As Fry (1977a) put it years ago, make the match: Give students a book that they can handle with ease. Research by Berliner (1981), and Gambrell, Wilson, and Gantt (1981), and Nation (2001) suggested that students do best with reading materials in which no more than 2 to 5 percent of the words are difficult for them.

3. *Instruction should be functional and contextual.* Do not teach skills or strategies in isolation—teach a word-attack skill because students must have it to decipher words. For example, teach the prefix *pre-* just before the class reads a selection about prehistoric dinosaurs. Students learn better when what they are being taught has immediate value. Suggestions for lessons that are both functional and contextual are presented throughout this book.

4. *Teachers should make connections.* Build a bridge between children's experiences and what they are about to read. Help them see how what they know is related to the story or article. Students in Montana reading about an ice hockey game may have no experience either playing hockey or watching the sport. However, you could help create a bridge of understanding by discussing how hockey is similar to soccer, a sport with which they probably are familiar. You should also help students connect new concepts to old concepts. Relate reading, writing, listening, and speaking—they all build on each other. Reading and talking about humorous stories can expand students' concept of humor and remind them of funny things that have happened to them. They might then write about these events. Also build on what students know. This will make your teaching easier, since you will be starting at the students' level. It will also help students make a connection between what they know and what they are learning.

5. *Teachers should promote independence.* Whenever you teach a skill or strategy, ask yourself: How can I teach this so that students will eventually use it on their own? How will students be called on to use this skill or strategy in school and in the outside world? When you teach students how to summarize, make predictions, or use context, phonics, or another skill or strategy, teach so that there is a gradual release of responsibility (Pearson & Gallagher, 1983). Gradually fade your instruction and guidance so that students are applying the skill or strategy on their own. Do the same with the selection of reading materials. Although you may discuss ways of choosing books with the class, you ultimately want students to reach a point where they select their own books.

6. *Teachers should believe that all children can learn to read and write.* Given the right kind of instruction, virtually all children can learn to read. There is increasing evidence that the vast majority of children can learn to read at least on a basic level. Over the past two decades, research (Reading Recovery Council of North America, 2006) has shown that Reading Recovery, an intensive 12- to 20-week early intervention program, can raise the reading levels of about 76 percent of the lowest achievers to that of average achievers in a class. Reading Recovery uses an inclusive model:

> It has been one of the surprises of Reading Recovery that all kinds of children with all kinds of difficulties can be included, can learn, and can reach average-band performance for their class in both reading and writing achievement. Exceptions are not made for children of lower intelligence, for second-language children, for children with low language skills, for children with poor motor coordination, for children who seem immature, for children who score poorly on readiness measures, or for children who have already been categorized by someone else as learning disabled. (Clay, 1991, p. 60)

A number of intervention programs have succeeded with struggling readers (Hiebert & Taylor, 2000). An important aspect of these efforts is that supplementary assistance is complemented by a strong classroom program. These results demonstrate the power of effective instruction and the belief that all children can learn to read. Actually, a quality program will prevent most problems. A national committee charged with making recommendations to help prevent reading difficulties concluded, "Excellent instruction is the best intervention for children who demonstrate problems learning to read" (Snow, Burns, & Griffin, 1998, p. 33).

7. *The literacy program should be goal-oriented and systematic.* In keeping with the current concern for preparing all students to be college and career ready and the widespread adoption of the Common Core State Standards, this text has incorporated these standards throughout the text. The margin note "CCSS" designates places in the text where suggestions for implementing a particular standard are presented.

8. *Teachers should build students' motivation and sense of competence.* Students perform at their best when they feel competent, view a task as being challenging but doable, understand why they are undertaking a task, are given choices, feel part of the process, and have interesting materials and activities. For many students, working in a group fosters effort and persistence. Students also respond to knowledge of progress. They work harder when they see that they are improving, and they are also energized by praise from teachers, parents, and peers, especially when that praise is honest and specific (Schunk & Zimmerman, 1997; Sweet, 1997; Wigfield, 1997).

9. *Teachers should build students' language proficiency.* Reading and writing are language-based. Students' reading levels are ultimately limited by their language development. Students can't understand what they are reading if they don't know what the words mean or if they get tangled up in the syntax of the piece. One of the best ways to build reading and writing potential is to foster language development. In study after study, knowledge of vocabulary has been found to be the key element in comprehension. Students' listening level has also been found to be closely related to their reading level. The level of material that a student can understand orally is a good gauge of the level at which the student can read with understanding. While fostering language development is important for all students, it is absolutely essential for students who are learning English as a second language.

10. *Teachers need to know how students are progressing so that they can give them extra help or change the program, if necessary.* Assessment need not be formal. Observation can be a powerful assessment tool. However, assessment should be tied to the program's standards and should result in improvement in students' learning. In each chapter in which lessons are presented, suggestions are made for assessing those lessons. Suggestions for assessment can also be found in annotations in the margins and in Chapter 3. In addition, there are several assessment instruments in the Appendix.

Highly Effective Teachers

In the 1960s, the U.S. Department of Education spent millions of dollars in an attempt to find out which method of teaching reading was the best (Bond & Dykstra, 1967; Graves & Dykstra, 1997). More than a dozen approaches were studied. There was no clear winner. No method was superior. Although the research didn't directly prove it, many professionals concluded that the teacher was key. Teachers using the same methods got differing results. Some teachers were simply more effective than others. Hattie's (2009) research found that two of the most powerful factors in student achievement were the clarity of instruction and teacher–student relationships.

What are the characteristics of effective teachers? A number of top researchers have visited the classes of teachers judged to be highly effective. Their students read more books and wrote more stories. Virtually all read on or above grade level. Their writing skills were surprisingly advanced. They also enjoyed school. On many occasions, observers watched in surprise as students skipped recess so that they could continue working on an activity. Their work was more appealing to them than play.

FYI

Differentiated instruction has a powerful impact on achievement. Teachers typically direct most of their questions and reinforcement to the top third of the class. When teachers make successful attempts to direct instruction to all students, including the bottom third of the class, overall achievement improves. ■

Adapting Instruction for Struggling Readers and Writers

Classroom teachers are taking increased responsibility for helping struggling readers and writers. Suggestions for working with struggling readers and writers are made throughout this book. ■

FYI

Fostering student engagement involves proving effective classroom management and routines so that students sense that they are in a safe, productive environment. ■

Caring and High Expectations

Perhaps the most outstanding characteristic of highly effective teachers is that they cared for their students and believed in them (Pressley, Allington, Wharton-McDonald, Block, & Morrow, 2001). They were genuinely convinced that their students could and would learn, and they acted accordingly. In writing, for instance, typical first-grade teachers believed that writing was difficult for young students and expected their students would only be able to produce pieces of writing composed of a sentence or two by year's end (Wharton-McDonald, 2001). Their expectations were discouragingly accurate. By year's end, most students in their classes were producing narratives that consisted of one to three loosely connected sentences with little attention to punctuation or capitalization.

Highly effective teachers had higher expectations. They believed that first-graders were capable of sustained writing. By year's end, they expected a coherent paragraph that consisted of five or even more sentences, each of which started with a capital letter and ended with a period. And that's the kind of writing their students produced. Students have a way of living up to or down to teachers' expectations.

However, the highly effective teachers realized that high expectations are in the same category as good intentions; they need to be acted upon. High expectations were accompanied by the kind of instruction that allowed students to live up to those expectations. Highly effective teachers were also superior motivators. The teachers created a feeling of excitement about the subject matter or skill areas they taught (Ruddell, 1995).

Balanced Instruction

As students evidenced a need for instruction, effective teachers were quick to conduct a mini-lesson. A student attempting to spell *boat*, for instance, would be given an on-the-spot lesson on the *oa* spelling of long *o*. However, essential skills were not relegated to opportunistic teaching. Key skills were taught directly and thoroughly but were related to the reading and writing that students were doing.

Extensive Instruction

Effective teachers used every opportunity to reinforce skills. Wherever possible, connections were made between reading and writing and between reading and writing and content-area concepts. Often, students would develop or apply science and social studies concepts in their writing.

Scaffolding

Exemplary teachers scaffolded students' responses. Instead of simply telling students answers, these teachers used prompts and other devices to help students reason their way to the correct response.

Classroom Management

Highly effective teachers were well organized. Routines were well established and highly effective. The core of their classroom management was building in students a sense of responsibility. Students learned to regulate their own behavior. One of the things that stood out in the rooms of highly effective teachers was the sense of purpose and orderliness. The greatest proportion of time was spent with high-payoff activities. When students composed illustrated booklets, for instance, the bulk of their time was spent researching and composing the booklets. Only a minimum of time was spent illustrating them.

Students learned how to work together. The classroom atmosphere was one of cooperation rather than competition. Effort was emphasized. Praise and reinforcement were used as appropriate. Students were also taught to be competent, independent learners.

They were taught strategies for selecting appropriate-level books, for decoding unfamiliar words, and for understanding difficult text. Their efforts were affirmed so that they would be encouraged to continue using strategies. "Jonathan, I liked the way you previewed that book before selecting it to read. Now you have a better idea of what it is about and whether it is a just-right book for you."

High-Quality Materials

The best teachers used the best materials. Students listened to and read classics as well as outstanding contemporary works from children's literature. There was a decided emphasis on reading. Classrooms were well stocked with materials, and time was set aside for various kinds of reading: shared, partner, and individual.

Matching of Materials and Tasks to Student Competence

Highly effective teachers gave students materials and tasks that were somewhat challenging but not overwhelming. Teachers carefully monitored students and made assignments on the basis of students' performance. If the book students were reading seemed to have too many difficult words and concepts, students were given an easier book. If they mastered writing a brief paragraph, they were encouraged to write a more fully developed piece. However, they were provided with the assistance and instruction needed to cope with more challenging tasks.

REFLECTION

What steps might you take to become a highly effective teacher? What step would you take first? Why?

Becoming a Highly Effective Teacher

Although a great variety of topics will be covered in later chapters, the ten primary principles discussed earlier are emphasized throughout. Teaching suggestions and activities are included for fostering wide reading, keeping reading reasonably easy, keeping reading and writing functional, making connections, setting goals and assessing progress, and, above all, building a sense of competence and promoting independence. This book is based on the premise that virtually all children can learn to read and write.

Essentials for an Effective Lesson

In order to translate the key concepts discussed so far into a practical instructional context, the basic components of an effective lesson are listed below. These components are based on research and incorporate the essential elements contained in widely used teacher evaluation systems, which means that when your lessons are being evaluated, these are the elements that will most likely be considered. A variety of sample lessons are provided in this text. The lessons will incorporate these essential elements.

Objectives: Objectives incorporate key skills or understanding that are based on national, state, or district standards and students' needs. They are clearly stated and shared with students. They might be posted. One way of checking on clarity of objectives would be to ask students to explain what they are learning and why.

Content/Texts/Activities: Content and activities are challenging but engaging. Texts/materials are of high quality and on students' instructional levels. Where appropriate, students are given a choice of activities or texts. Texts might be traditional print, digital, or online.

Instruction: Instruction includes an explanation of what is being taught and why. Skills, strategies, or understandings are presented explicitly through modeling, demonstration, simulation, and/or explanation. Students are provided with guided practice interspersed with additional instruction as needed. The teacher continuously checks for understanding and modifies instruction as necessary. Ultimately, students apply what they have learned. Emphasis is on lots of reading and writing.

Evaluation: Using observation, quizzes, and checks for understanding, and other means, teachers assess students' grasp of the skills, strategies, and understandings presented. Instruction is modified as needed. Teachers document progress and reflect on the effectiveness of the lesson. What went well? What might need improvement?

The following key elements are not specifically described in the sample lessons but are implied:

Differentiation: Students are grouped, as appropriate, and are also provided with additional instruction and practice, as required. Adjustments are made in instruction, activities, and materials to meet the needs of all students.

Classroom Atmosphere: The classroom is set up for maximum efficiency, management routines are established, and students are engaged in learning. Instructional time is maximized. A caring, supportive atmosphere is established, and there is a spirit of mutual cooperation and respect and a we-are-readers-and-writers attitude.

Summary

Reading is an active process in which the reader constructs meaning from text. Key elements in learning to read are cognitive development, language development, and background of experience. Reading development is also affected by one's culture. Approaches to teaching reading can be viewed as being bottom-up, top-down, or interactive. Behavioral theories of learning favor bottom-up approaches, focus on observable phenomena, describe the student as being a passive recipient, tend to be teacher-centered, and emphasize subskills and mastery learning. Cognitive theories tend to be top-down or interactive in their approach, emphasize the active role of the reader as a constructor of meaning, are often student-centered or teacher–student interactive, and stress mental activities. Social cognitive theories stress the social aspects of learning, scaffolding of instruction, and the zone of proximal development.

In their language theories, behaviorists emphasize imitation and reinforcement, nativists stress an inborn propensity for learning language, and interactionists stress the interaction of the learner with opportunities to learn. According to Vygotsky, language is key to the development of thinking.

Learning a second language is easier than learning an original language, but an accepting environment, self-confidence, and motivation foster second-language development.

Current trends in literacy instruction include research-based instruction, Common Core State Standards, educational legislation such as the renewal of the Elementary and Secondary Act, performance on national tests such as the NAEP, and New Literacies. New Literacies build on traditional literacy skills but are more complex.

Widespread reading and functional instruction commensurate with children's abilities are essentials of an effective reading program. Also necessary is instruction that helps students make connections and fosters independence. Believing that virtually every child can learn to read and building students' motivation and sense of competence are important factors in an effective literacy program, as are setting goals; systematic, direct instruction; managing classroom behavior; building language proficiency; building higher-level literacy; and ongoing assessment. These factors can be translated into effective literacy lessons. The ultimate key to a successful program is a highly effective teacher.

Extending and Applying

1. Analyze one or more of your lessons in terms of the Essentials of an Effective Lesson discussed earlier in the chapter. What changes might you need to make to your lessons?

2. Evaluate your literacy program in terms of the major characteristics listed earlier in the chapter. What are

the strengths of your program? What changes might you need to make? How would you go about making those changes?

3. Take another look at the characteristics of Highly Effective Teachers. What are your strengths and weaknesses in this area? What might you do to build on

your strengths and work on your weaknesses?

4. Many school systems require teacher applicants to submit a portfolio. Some require new teachers to complete portfolios as part of the evaluation process. Even if a portfolio is not required in your situation, creating and maintaining one provide you with the opportunity to reflect on your ideas about teaching and your teach-

ing practices. It will help you get to know yourself better as a teacher and so provide a basis for improvement. Set up a professional portfolio. The portfolio should highlight your professional preparation, relevant experience, and mastery of key teaching skills. Also, draw up a statement of your philosophy of teaching reading and writing.

Professional Reflection

Do I

___ Have an understanding of the nature of literacy?
___ Have an understanding of the key components of an effective literacy program and a plan for implementing them in my teaching situation?

___ Have a general understanding of the Common Core State Standards or other standards in the school district where I teach or plan to teach?
___ Have a personal philosophy for teaching literacy?

Reflection Question

In the past, teachers were evaluated on the quality of their presentations. Today, many school districts also evaluate teachers on the basis of how much their students

learn. How might you prepare yourself for an evaluation system that combines quality of presentation with degree of student learning?

Building Competencies

To build competencies, consult the following sources for more detailed information:

Bodrova, E., & Leong, D. J. (2007). *Tools of the mind: The Vygotskian approach to early childhood education* (2nd ed.). Upper Saddle River, NJ: Merrill. Also reread the section on Vygotsky and Piaget in this chapter. Compare and contrast their main beliefs.

Hattie, J. (2009). *Visible learning: A synthesis of over 800 meta-analyses relating to achievement*. New York; Routledge.

The site of the New Literacies Research Team at the University of Connecticut, http://www.newliteracies.uconn.edu, has a wealth of information about the New Literacies.

MyEducationLab™

Go to the Topic "Media/Digital Literacy" in the MyEducationLab (www.myeducationlab.com) for your course, where you can:

- Find learning outcomes for "Media/Digital Literacy" along with the national standards that connect to these outcomes.
- Complete Assignments and Activities that can help you more deeply understand the chapter content.
- Apply and practice your understanding of the core teaching skills identified in the chapter with the Building Teaching Skills and Dispositions learning units.
- Examine challenging situations and cases presented in the IRIS Center Resources.
- Check your comprehension on the content covered in the chapter by going to the Study Plan in the Book

Resources for your text. Here you will be able to take a chapter quiz, receive feedback on your answers, and then access Review, Practice, and Enrichment activities to enhance your understanding of chapter content. (optional)

A+RISE A+RISE® Standards2Strategy™ is an innovative and interactive online resource that offers new teachers in grades K–12 just-in-time, research-based instructional strategies that meet the linguistic needs of ELLs as they learn content, differentiate instruction for all grades and abilities, and are aligned to Common Core Elementary Language Arts standards (for the literacy strategies) and to English language proficiency standards in WIDA, Texas, California, and Florida.

2

Teaching All Students

Anticipation Guide

	Agree	Disagree
1. By and large, techniques used to teach average students also work with those who have special needs.	_____	_____
2. Except for a small percentage of students who have severe disabilities, it is possible to bring virtually all students up to a high level of proficiency.	_____	_____
3. Economically disadvantaged children may have difficulty learning to read because their language is inadequate when they begin school.	_____	_____
4. Of all the special needs students, gifted children require the least help.	_____	_____
5. It is best to teach English language learners to read in their native language.	_____	_____
6. Even students with serious reading or other learning disabilities should be taught in the regular classroom.	_____	_____

Using What You Know

The United States is the most culturally and linguistically diverse nation in the world. Dozens of languages are spoken in U.S. schools, and dozens of cultures are represented. Adding to that diversity is the trend toward inclusion. Increasingly, students who have learning or reading disabilities, visual or hearing impairments, emotional or health problems, or other challenges are being taught in regular classrooms. Because these children have special needs, their programs may have to be adjusted so that they can reach their full potential. Adjustments also need to be made for children who are economically disadvantaged or who are still learning English. The gifted and talented also have special needs and require assistance to reach their full potential. What has been your experience teaching children from other cultures or children who are just learning to speak English? What has been your experience with students who have special needs? Think of some special needs students you have known. What provisions did the school make for these students? Could the school have done more? If so, what? What are some adjustments that you make now or might make in the future for such students?

Teaching All Students

The success of the nation's schools depends increasingly on how we plan for all our children. As a first step, we can put children at the center of the learning process (Crawford, 1993). If, as educators, we focus on all children and use caring and common sense in dealing with their needs, we will have gone a long way toward establishing equity in our schools.

Mandates to prepare every student to be college and career ready (U.S. Department of Education, 2010), the response to intervention (RTI) initiative highlighted in the Individuals with Disabilities Education Improvement Act (IDEIA, 2004), and

FYI

IDEIA is sometimes referred to by its original designation: IDEA. ■

Using Technology

ESEA Reauthorization: A Blueprint for Reform
Provides information about proposals to prepare every child for college or career.

http://www2.ed.gov/policy/elsec/leg/blueprint/index.html ■

FYI

States determine learning disability (LD) eligibility standards but must use multiple measures. To make an LD determination, states may use patterns of strengths and weaknesses, RTI screenings, or discrepancies between ability and achievement. ■

FYI

Levels of prevention are often referred to as tiers of intervention with Tier I being primary; Tier II, secondary; and Tier III, tertiary. ■

Using Technology

The following sites contain extensive information on RTI:

National Center on Response to Intervention
http://www.rti4success.org

Star Legacy Modules on RTI from Vanderbilt University
http://iris.peabody.vanderbilt.edu/resources.html

International Reading Association: Response to Intervention (RTI): Overview
http://www.reading.org/Resources/ResourcesByTopic/ResponseToIntervention/Overview.aspx ■

■ **Response to intervention (RTI)** is an assessment and intervention approach in which students' ability to learn is evaluated by noting how well they respond to instruction of varying degrees of intensity.

Common Core Standards (National Governors Association Center for Best Practices & Council of Chief State School Officers, 2010) have brought into focus the importance of providing for all students. An example of an implementation of the concept of providing every student a high-quality education is California's concept of universal access.

As explained in California's Reading/Language Arts Framework:

> The ultimate goal of language arts programs in California is to ensure access to high-quality curriculum and instruction for all students in order to meet or exceed the state's English language arts content standards. To reach that goal, teachers need assistance in assessing and using the results of that assessment for planning programs, differentiating curriculum and instruction, using grouping strategies effectively, and implementing other strategies for meeting the needs of students with reading difficulties, students with disabilities, advanced learners, English learners, and students with combinations of special instructional needs. Procedures that may be useful in planning for universal access are to:
>
> - Assess each student's understanding at the start of instruction and continue to do so frequently as instruction advances, using the results of assessment for program placement and planning.
> - Diagnose the nature and severity of the student's difficulty and modify curriculum and instruction accordingly when students have trouble with the language arts.
> - Engage in careful organization of resources and instruction and planning to adapt to individual needs. A variety of good teaching strategies that can be used according to the situation should be prepared.
> - Differentiate when necessary as to depth, complexity, novelty, or pacing and focus on the language arts standards and the key concepts within the standards that students must master to move on to the next grade level.
> - Employ flexible grouping strategies according to the students' needs and achievement and the instructional tasks presented.
> - Enlist help from others, such as reading specialists, special education specialists, parents, aides, other teachers, community members, administrators, counselors, and diagnosticians when necessary and explore technology or other instructional devices or instructional materials, such as Braille text, as a way to respond to students' individual needs. (California Department of Education, 2007, p. 263)

Teaching Literacy to All Students: Role of RTI

Response to intervention (RTI) has been designed to raise the achievement of all students but especially those at risk for failure. The reauthorized Individuals with Disabilities Education Improvement Act (IDEIA) of 2004 (PL 108-446) specified a change in the way students are identified as having a learning disability. Previously, students were identified as having a learning disability on the basis of a gap between their ability and their achievement. With IDEIA, they may be identified through a procedure known as response to intervention complemented by other indicators or measures.

RTI is a commonsense approach in which struggling students are offered increasingly intensive instruction. Most students respond favorably when provided with added instruction (Scanlon, 2010; Vellutino et al., 1996). Failure to make adequate progress is an indicator of a possible learning difficulty.

However, RTI is much more than a method for identifying students with learning disabilities. RTI is a whole-school improvement program that enlists all staff members, the community, and parents to ensure that the literacy potential of all students is fully developed. This typically consists of three levels of prevention or intervention: primary, secondary, and tertiary (National Center on Response to Intervention, 2011). The primary level, which is generally referred to as Tier I, is designed to improve the overall instructional program so that everyone benefits. This means that teachers provide enhanced differentiated instruction so that all students have the opportunity to learn. Students in need may be provided with added help within the core program. If the students continue to lag behind despite being provided with differentiated instruction, they are given supplementary secondary level instruction, which is generally referred to as Tier II. This moderately intense intervention is usually provided in a small group for a period of 12 to 20 weeks. If the students still fail to make adequate progress, another secondary intervention might be implemented or the student might be provided tertiary level (Tier III) prevention. Tertiary-level prevention would typically be one-on-one instruction (intervention programs are discussed in Chapter 12). If progress is still inadequate, placement in special education is considered.

Universal Screening

The first step in RTI is to screen all students. The screening measure is designed to identify students who might be at risk, and it is recommended that it be administered three times a year. If given three times a year, students who were doing well in the beginning of the year but have fallen behind can be identified. In addition, screening measures can be used to assess the effectiveness of the classroom program. If large numbers of students are not doing well, this is an indication that the program is not appropriate and/or is not being implemented effectively.

Screening measures are generally assessments of key skills that can be given quickly. At lower levels, alphabet knowledge and ability to read lists of words are frequently used as screening measures. Oral reading is used at the end of grade 1 and higher. Mazes, a comprehension measure focusing on the ability to fill in the blanks in grade-level passages, is used in grade 2 or 3 and higher.

At least 80 percent of students should reach the program's benchmarks. If a number of teachers fail to have at least 80 percent of students meeting the benchmark, this could be an indication that the program is ineffective. If just one or two teachers fail to have at least 80 percent of students meeting the benchmark, this could be an indication that those teachers are not as effective as they should be.

All other things being equal, it is estimated that about 20 percent of public school students will require intervention. Of that 20 percent, 15 percent will need only Tier II (secondary) instruction, but the remaining 5 percent will also need Tier III (tertiary) instruction. On the basis of the screening and other data, instruction is differentiated. Low performers are given extra help from the classroom teacher. Screening at the beginning of the year can over-identify students. The progress of students who do poorly on beginning-of-the-year screenings should be monitored for 4 or 5 weeks. If their performance is still below what is expected, they might then be provided with extra instruction in Tier II.

RTI and English Language Learners

Some teachers might be hesitant to provide or recommend intervention for English language learners (Gersten et al., 2007). For instance, when ELLs experience difficulty learning basic decoding skills, teachers might attribute this to a lack of adequate English and decide to wait until the student acquires more English (Francis, Rivera, Lesaux, Kieffer, & Rivera, 2006). This tactic could delay intervention. Just as a proportion of native English speakers experience difficulty learning decoding skills, so, too, do a proportion of ELLs. However, instruction should be geared to the students' level of language development (see Table 2.2 on page 42). Students should have sufficient command of English so that they are able to benefit from decoding instruction.

Problem-Solving Approach versus Standard Protocol

RTI has two major approaches: problem solving and standard protocol. In a problem-solving approach, the student's strengths and needs are analyzed and a program is created based on that analysis. The program might be assembled by the school's learning

FYI

Up to 15 percent of a school's special education funds can be used to implement RTI. ■

 FYI

Tracking progress results in average gains of 34 percentile points. ■

 FYI

The three-level model is the most popular approach to RTI. However, RTI is a flexible program and may be applied in different ways in different locations. ■

team. The standard protocol is an intervention program that is researched and is delivered in a consistent, standardized fashion (DeRuvo & Barcus, 2008). A number of published programs, such as *Reading Mastery* and *Wilson Language*, are used as standard protocols. Because standardized approaches are consistent, it is easier to assess how well they are working. However, off-the-shelf programs might not meet the specialized needs of all students. Of course, aspects of both approaches can be used.

Monitoring Progress

Continuous monitoring of progress is a key component of RTI. The first steps in progress monitoring are to establish where students are and set goals or benchmarks. Then progress toward reaching those goals or benchmarks can be monitored. Results are used to see if the students are making adequate progress and to plan more intensive instruction, if needed. Results can also be used to assess the effectiveness of the program. The program might require more reinforcement or a slower pace (Johnson, Mellard, Fuchs, & McKnight, 2006).

Progress of English language learners should be monitored and intervention provided as needed. In the primary grades, ELLs often keep up with their classmates on measures of phonological awareness, word reading, and fluency (Gersten et al., 2007). However, as the reading grows more complex, ELLs may experience difficulty because greater demands are being placed on their limited English skills. They will need assessments geared to their language development.

The progress of all students should be monitored at least three times a year. The screening assessments can also be used as monitoring measures. Students judged to be at risk should be monitored more frequently. Depending on the seriousness of their difficulty, they might be monitored monthly, biweekly, or even weekly. Ongoing information about student progress is needed to determine if programs and behavioral supports are working (DeRuvo & Barcus, 2008). Because reading is complex, multiple measures should be used to monitor students' progress. If, for instance, oral reading fluency is the screening and monitoring measure used, this should be complemented with data from measures of comprehension including observations and work samples. See Chapter 3 for more information on screening and monitoring.

Progress monitoring can be implemented as follows:

1. Establish a benchmark for performance and enter it on a chart (e.g., "Read 40 high-frequency words per minute by June" or "Read at Level 18 by June"). The benchmark is an expected level of performance at the end of the school year or other period of time.
2. Record the student's current level of performance (e.g., "50 words per minute").
3. Draw an aimline from the student's current level to the expected benchmark level (as in Figure 5.9 on p. 235). The aimline shows the rate of progress a student needs to make in order to reach the benchmark.
4. Monitor the student's progress frequently if the student is being provided extra help (e.g., every other Friday or at the end of each month). Record scores. (Figure 5.9 on p. 235 shows the progress monitoring of a struggling reader.)
5. Analyze the data on a regular basis. Make adjustments as needed (e.g., "The intervention will be changed after 2 data points are below the aimline").
6. Draw a trendline to see if the student's progress is adequate to meet the goal over time. The trendline is the line that shows the student's progress and projects how the student will do if he or she continues to make progress at the same rate (Lembke, 2008).

Collaboration

RTI requires a high level of collaboration. A schoolwide learning team sets up the framework for RTI and makes decisions about core curriculum and intervention approaches. Students' behavior is also addressed in RTI. The schoolwide team

FYI

Screening measures given three times a year are often used to monitor progress and to see if students are reaching benchmarks. Benchmark measures are generally on grade level. ■

Adapting Instruction for Struggling Readers and Writers

Assessments used to monitor the progress of struggling students must be on their reading level; otherwise, progress cannot be measured. ■

establishes a behavior management system and behavior intervention programs. Grade-level or other teams meet to analyze data and decide whether the core program is effective and to plan ways of increasing its effectiveness. These teams also discuss the progress of pupils, ways to differentiate instruction more efficiently, and other classroom concerns. Another team composed of the school psychologist, reading specialist, special education teacher, and classroom teachers meets to plan interventions for those students who are not making adequate progress in the core program.

Impact of RTI on Your Teaching

As a classroom teacher, you will have primary responsibility for implementing Tier I and, in varying degrees, Tier II interventions. As part of Tier I, you will be working to improve your classroom program and implement it with fidelity to make it as effective as possible. You will be looking for gaps in the program and ways to close up those gaps. You might meet with other teachers in your grade level or department to discuss ways to improve the program. You will be examining data to get a sense of the overall effectiveness of the program and the progress of students, so as to identify those who need more help. You will be differentiating instruction to meet the needs of all students but especially those who struggle. You will be closely monitoring students who struggle to see how they are responding to instruction. Depending on your school's program, you might also be called on to provide some Tier II instruction. Even if another professional provides Tier II instruction, you will need to be knowledgeable about the instruction so that you can coordinate your efforts with those of the Tier II instructor. Best results are obtained when intervention supports the classroom program. In the event that Tier III instruction is required, you will also be coordinating that intervention. Chances are you will also be called on to take part in meetings to discuss the progress of struggling students in your class and to help plan an intervention program. You will be part of a team dedicated to helping all students attain the highest level of literacy of which they are capable.

Providing for the Literacy Needs of All Students

With the recognition that classrooms are becoming increasingly diverse, attempts are being made to provide for the literacy needs of all students. Providing effective instruction requires, first of all, that we get a sense of the diversity of students in today's classrooms. Currently, more than 50 million students are enrolled in public schools (Aud et al., 2010). Forty-three percent of public school students are considered to be part of a racial or ethnic minority group, an increase from 22 percent in 1972. The increase is mainly due to the growth in the number of Hispanic students. Hispanic students currently represent 20 percent of public school enrollment, up from 6 percent in 1972.

Adding to this linguistic, ethnic, and racial diversity in today's classrooms is the inclusion of students with special needs: students who have learning or reading disabilities or physical or emotional difficulties, who are living in poverty, or who need to be challenged because of special gifts or talents they possess. About 6.6 million students or 13 percent of the school population is served under the Individuals with Disabilities Education Act (IDEA). About 57 percent of these students spend most of their day in a regular class. In the typical classroom, as many as one student in three may fit into one or more of these categories and be in need of some sort of differentiation and/or extra attention to reach his or her full literacy potential.

English Language Learners

Some 21 percent of children ages 5–17 (or 10.9 million) speak a language other than English at home, and 5 percent (or 2.7 million) speak English with difficulty (Aud et al., 2010). Seventy-five percent of those who speak English with difficulty speak Spanish.

Using Technology

National Clearinghouse for English
Language Acquisition provides a
wealth of information on bilingual
education and includes excellent
links to useful sites.
http://www.ncela.gwu.edu

Dr. Mora's Web Site is also an
excellent source of information
about bilingual education.
http://edweb.sdsu.edu/people/
jmora ■

FYI

Bilingual programs result in an
average increase of 13 percentile
points (Hattie, 2009). ■

**Adapting Instruction
for English Language
Learners**

English language learners do fairly
well on tests of basic skills up to
fourth grade. In fourth grade and
beyond, as greater demands are
made on language proficiency,
scores begin to decline (Bielenberg &
Fillmore, 2004). ■

Using Technology

Colorín Colorado is an outstanding
source of resources for parents and
teachers of ELLs.
http://www.colorincolorado.org ■

English language learners (ELLs) is the most widely used term for "students who were not born in the United States or whose native language is not English and who cannot participate effectively in the regular curriculum because they have difficulty speaking, understanding, reading, and writing English" (National Clearinghouse, 2008). Children in U.S. schools today come from more than a hundred language communities. Among the languages spoken, in order of number of speakers, are Spanish, Vietnamese, Hmong, Haitian Creole, Korean, Arabic, Chinese (Cantonese), Russian, Tagalog, Navajo, Khmer, Portuguese, Urdu, Chinese (Mandarin), Serbo-Croatian, Lao, and Japanese.

English language learners have diverse backgrounds. Some are new arrivals; others were born in the mainland United States, but grew up in a home where a language other than English was spoken. Some new arrivals have a rich educational background and are literate in their native language. Others have never been to school, or their schooling was interrupted. Some are solidly middle class. However, a large number live in poverty.

The question of how English language learners should be taught to read and write strikes at the core of what reading is—that is, a language activity. Using prior experience and knowledge of language, the reader constructs meaning. Common sense and research (Fillmore & Valdez, 1986) dictate that the best way to teach reading and writing to ELLs is to teach them in their native language. Learning to read and write are complex tasks that involve the total language system—semantic, syntactic, and phonological components. Until children have a basic grasp of the meaning of a language, they will be unable to read it. Even if they are able to sound out the words, they do not understand their meaning.

The prestigious Committee on the Prevention of Reading Difficulties in Young Children recommends teaching ELLs to read in their native language while, at the same time, teaching them to speak English as a second language (Snow, Burns, & Griffin, 1998). Once they have a sufficient grasp of English and of basic reading in their native language, they can then learn to read in English. This type of approach has several advantages. First of all, children build a solid foundation in their native tongue. With language development, thinking skills are enhanced, concepts are clarified and organized, and children learn to use language in an abstract way. Because they are also learning math, science, and social studies in their native language, background experience is being developed.

Thinking skills, background of knowledge, and reading skills learned in students' native language transfer to reading and writing in English. One objection to a bilingual approach is that it delays instruction in reading and writing in English, thereby causing children to lose ground. Research clearly indicates that this is not the case. In several studies, students taught to read in their native language and then later in a second language outperformed those taught to read in the second language (Modiano, 1968). Furthermore, as they progressed through the grades, the difference between the two groups increased (Rosier, 1977). Learning to read in their native language provides ELLs with a solid foundation for learning to read in another language (Constantino, 1999).

The key to a successful bilingual reading program may lie in knowing when to start instruction in the second language. Students should first read relatively proficiently in their native language. Thonis (cited in Fillmore & Valdez, 1986) cautioned that reading in a second language should not be attempted until students have reached a level where they can interpret the text and draw inferences. This indicates that they have developed higher-level comprehension skills, which can then be transferred to reading in the second language. A number of bilingual Spanish–English reading systems include one component in Spanish and one in English. Some also include a transitional component that eases the transfer from Spanish into English.

ESL Only

Not all ELLs have access to a bilingual program. In California and several other states, for instance, most bilingual programs have been terminated, and students are instead being provided with one year of intensive English (Gandara, 2000). If the only program offered is one that teaches the students English as a second language, it is best to delay formal reading instruction until the children have a reasonable command of English (Snow, Burns, & Griffin, 1998). However, students can engage in shared reading, complete language-experience stories, and read predictable books as they learn English. They should also be encouraged to write as best they can. As they gain proficiency in oral English, they can tackle increasingly complex reading and writing tasks. Their oral-language skills will support their reading and writing, and their reading and writing will reinforce and build oral-language skills.

The classroom teacher's role is to support the efforts of bilingual and/or ESL professionals by meeting regularly with them and working with them to plan activities that will enhance students' progress. Even after students have finished the ESL program, they still require special language-development activities. Some adjustments that might be made to adapt classroom instruction to ELLs' needs are described in the following subsections.

Provide a Secure Environment

The first step in helping ELLs build literacy is to provide a safe, secure, and caring environment (Peregoy & Boyle, 2001). As a teacher, you can acquire basic information about the newcomer, seat the student close to you so that you can supply guidance as needed, and assign a buddy. Having a buddy, preferably one who speaks the newcomer's language, will help a newcomer feel welcome and adjust to the school's routines. The buddy can accompany the newcomer during the school day and explain classroom procedures and how to use the cafeteria, line up for the bus, and other routines; such conversation builds language skills. You can also make sure that the newcomer becomes part of the classroom community by introducing him or her, providing information about his or her country of origin, and integrating the newcomer into the classroom's cooperative groups.

> **Building Language**
>
> Monitor the speech you use in your classroom. What you say should be understandable but rich enough that it fosters language growth. Deliberately introduce challenging vocabulary and advanced language structures. ■

Build Language

The greatest need of ELLs is to develop skills in understanding and using English. Students vary in the rate at which they learn a second language. Aptitude for learning language varies. In addition, there are social and psychological factors. More outgoing children will learn a second language more rapidly, as will children who are highly motivated (Tabors, 1997). Children face a double bind when learning a second language. In order to do so, they must be socially accepted by their peers so that they can learn language from them. But to be socially accepted, they need to be able to speak to the other children. Age also has an impact on children's language development. Young children need to learn less language; however, they also have less cognitive capacity than older children, so they may take longer to learn a second language.

When they first enter a school environment in which English is spoken, ELLs may continue to use their native tongue. When they find that this isn't working, many of these students enter a nonverbal period, which may last a few weeks, a few months, or even an entire year. They use gestures and other nonverbal strategies in order to communicate. Gradually, the children use increasingly complex English to communicate. At first, ELLs learn object names: *blocks, water, paint, books*. They might also use commands or comments such as *stop, okay, uh-oh, please, yes, no, hi,* and *bye-bye*. They also pick up a series of useful expressions or routine statements, such as "Good morning. What's happening? How did you do this?" They progress to useful sentence structures, such as "I want _____" or "I like _____," which they complete using a variety of words.

In order to cope with the demands of the school setting, ELLs use any of a number of strategies:

> **Adapting Instruction for English Language Learners**
>
> The social environment of a classroom is important for language learning. Wong (1991, cited in Cummins, 1994) recommends, "Those situations that promote frequent contacts are the best, especially if the contacts last long enough to give learners ample opportunity to observe people using the language for a variety of communication purposes. Those which permit learners to engage in the frequent use of the language with speakers are even better" (p. 54). ■

- Join a group and act as though they know what is going on. This might mean joining a group that is playing with toy cars or building with blocks. ELLs participate by watching the activities of the others.

- Connect what they see with what people are saying. If the teacher holds up a round object and says "ball" several times, they assume that the name of the round object is *ball*.
- Learn some words and expressions, and use them. Even though ELLs know very little English, they become part of a social group by making the most of what they do know and so have the opportunity to expand their language.
- Find and use sources of help. Finding an adult or a friend who will teach them new words or expressions and help resolve confusions fosters language development (Tabors, 1997).
- Use a copying strategy. Not fully understanding directions or the complexity of an assignment, ELLs often imitate their English-speaking classmates. They look to see how they are doing a workbook page or might even copy a sentence composed as part of a writing assignment. This may be viewed by the teacher and classmates as a coping strategy and, thus, tolerated (Weber & Longhi-Chirlin, 2001). When not copying from others, students often copy words that are displayed around the room or words from stories they read. Expression of their own ideas is very limited.

ELLs should be encouraged to ask questions or seek help when they don't understand what they are being taught or what they are supposed to do. These students are often confused by assignments or explanations or don't know what question the teacher is asking because they don't understand enough of the language (Weber & Longhi-Chirlin, 2001). ELLs can do better in small groups because they are in a less intimidating environment and have the opportunity to ask peers for help.

Provide Comprehensible Input

The key to developing language is to provide comprehensible input (Krashen, 2003). To make input more comprehensible, modify the language to make it more accessible. Modification includes speaking more slowly, emphasizing the pronunciation of key words, using shorter sentences, simplifying the syntax, and using a more basic vocabulary. In some instances, you might provide a more elaborate explanation in which each step is more clearly expressed (Díaz-Rico & Weed, 2002). Use the same set of directions for key tasks and routines. Also scaffold language comprehension and development. Use gestures or actions along with words. The request "Line up for lunch" might be accompanied by a gesture for lining up and a gesture for eating (Tabors, 1997). Be repetitious. Repeating statements, key phrases, or words provides ELLs with an added opportunity to catch what is being said (Tabors, 1997). To facilitate understanding of oral language, add illustrative elements to discussions. Use objects, models, and pictures to illustrate vocabulary words that might be difficult. Role-play situations and pantomime activities. When talking about rocks in a geology unit, bring some in and hold them up when mentioning their names. When discussing a story about a tiger, point to a picture of the tiger. When introducing a unit on magnets, hold up a magnet every time you use the word; point to the poles each time you mention them. Supplement oral directions with gestures and demonstrations. Think of yourself as an actor in a silent movie who must use body language to convey meaning.

Find out what words, if any, the student knows in English and build on those. On the other side of the coin, learn a few key expressions in the student's home language and use them: "It is time for lunch." "Line up for lunch." "Line up for recess." "Take out your reading books." Obtain these expressions from online sources, parents, other children who speak the student's language, or the bilingual teacher.

The good news is that ELLs placed in an English-speaking classroom can and do make progress. They develop speaking, listening, reading, and writing skills when their teachers believe that they can learn and present them with meaningful instruction and activities, even though the teachers may not have any training teaching ELLs. Although these students have some success, they would more than likely do even better if teachers were trained or took special steps to assist them (Weber & Longhi-Chirlin, 2001). Some techniques for helping students learn English include modeling, running commentary, expansions, and redirects.

Modeling

Modeling consists of demonstrating some language element that the student is having difficulty with or needs to learn. For instance, to model the use of *this* and *is* and *these* and *are*, you might say, "This is my pencil. These are my pencils. This is my book. These are my books." The student is offered the opportunity to use the constructions but is not required to do so. She or he may need more time to assimilate the structures.

Running Commentary

In a running commentary, you take the role of a sports announcer and describe a process that you are carrying out (Bunce, 1995): "To make a paper bag puppet, first I _____, then I _____, and then I _____." The running commentary helps acquaint students with vocabulary and sentence structure. Since it accompanies an activity, it is concrete. It also provides insight into the teacher's thought processes and problem-solving strategies. Running commentary should be used selectively; if overused, it can be overwhelming to students. It is best used when a process or activity is being demonstrated.

Expansion

In an expansion, you repeat the student's statement but supply a missing part. For example, if a student says, "Car red," you say, "Yes, the car is red." This affirms the student's comment but also gives the student a model of a more advanced form (Bunce, 1995).

Redirect

In a redirect, you encourage a student who has asked you a question or made a request to direct it to another student. If a student says that he wants to play with the blocks, but Martin is playing with them, you direct him to ask Martin. If necessary, you provide a prompt, "Say to Martin, 'May I play with the blocks?' " This prompting fosters both social and language growth.

Increasing the amount of oral language in the classroom enhances English speaking. Structure conversations at the beginning of the school day and at other convenient times to talk about current events, weather, hobbies, sports, or other topics of interest. Encourage students to participate in discussions and provide opportunities for them to use "language for a broad variety of functions, both social and academic" (Allen, 1991, p. 362).

Build Academic Language

Special emphasis should be placed on **academic language**. As students learn English, they first acquire functional structures that allow them to greet others, make conversational statements, and ask questions. This type of everyday communication is heavily contextualized and is augmented by gestures, pointing at objects, and pantomiming. It takes approximately two years for students to become socially proficient in English (Cummins, 2001). However, schooling demands academic language, which is more varied and abstract and relatively decontextualized. This is the language in which math procedures and subject matter concepts are explained. Cummins referred to everyday functional language as Basic Interpersonal Communicative Skills (BICS) and to decontextualized school-type language as Cognitive Academic Language Proficiency (CALP). Proficiency in academic English may take up to five years or more to attain. Even though ELLs may seem proficient in oral English, they may have difficulty with academic language. Mastery of

■ **Academic language** is abstract, decontextualized school-type language that is used to understand and express complex ideas.

conversational English may mask deficiencies in important higher-level language skills (Sutton, 1989). Because of the time required to acquire academic language, ELLs may not demonstrate their true abilities on achievement and cognitive ability tests administered in English.

Learning academic language is more than just learning big words. As Zwiers (2008) explains, it also means learning the smaller words, the grammar, and the thinking skills necessary to put the big words together in an understandable text or utterance. Academic language includes the thinking skills of analyzing, explaining, inferring, and organizing as well as language skills. It requires the ability to think and talk about language as well as use language. And it requires acquisition of background knowledge on a wide range of topics and ideas. "Teachers further the acquisition of CALP by analyzing the conceptual and critical thinking of grade-level curriculum and taking the time to ensure that all students are explicitly taught such requirements" (Díaz-Rico, 2004, p. 305).

Academic vocabulary can be thought of as bricks and mortar (Dutro & Moran, 2003). Bricks are the content-specific technical words such as *cells*, *nucleus*, *hypotenuse*, and *democracy*. Mortar consists of the words used to articulate the concepts represented by the technical words: *require*, *causation*, *temporary*, *determine*. Mortar words can be even more abstract than brick words. Mortar words are also used to describe academic tasks: *analyze*, *contrast*, *synthesize*. Academic language also includes stock phrases, which use figurative language: *when all is said and done*, *what it all boils down to*, *read between the lines*, *see eye to eye* (Zwiers, 2008).

Academic Word List (AWL)

Academic words can be divided into two categories: all-purpose words that appear widely in academic texts but not in everyday texts, and technical words that tend to be discipline-specific (Snow, 2009). Content teachers typically present the technical words necessary to understand key concepts in their disciplines but are less likely to introduce the academic words used to explain the concepts (Snow, 2009). Lack of academic language and especially academic vocabulary has been described as a lexical bar, one that blocks the progress of a large number of students (Corson, 1995). The Academic Word List (AWL) provides a practical starting point for developing the needed academic language skills.

Because it has been drawn from college texts, the AWL has been adapted. Words not typically found in elementary or secondary texts have been eliminated. The 510-word adapted AWL is presented in Table 2.1. In the adapted AWL, words are listed according to three levels of tested difficulty: basic, intermediate, and advanced. Basic words are those known by 40 to 80 percent of students at the end of grade 2. Intermediate words are those known by at least 40 to 80 percent of students in grade 6.

Advanced words are those known by 67 percent or higher of students in grades 8 to 12. Each level is split in two, with the first half being composed of the higher-frequency words and the second half being composed of the lower-frequency words in that level.

Some techniques you can use to foster both general and academic language follow.

Using Cued Elicitation Questions

Cued elicitation questions incorporate a portion of the response: "Gold is called a precious metal because _____." "The main character in this story is similar to the main character in _____." Use these statements and other devices to encourage the students to use more specific or more abstract language (Edwards & Mercer, 1993; Zwiers, 2008).

FYI

Academic language should be emphasized from the beginning of English language learners' schooling. ■

TABLE 2.1 Academic Word List: Basic A1 and A2

Adapted Academic Word List: Basic A1 and A2

A1				
	estimate	remove	convince	plus
	expand	research	cooperate	precise
accurate	expert	respond	detect	predict
achieve	final	reveal	displace	proceed
adult	function	route	display	recover
aid	goal	series	dispose	register
approach	grade	shift	draft	reject
area	grant	similar	drama	relax
assume	image	somewhat	edit	rely
attach	indicate	task	eliminate	resolve
available	individual	team	emerge	restrain
aware	involve	topic	error	restrict
challenge	issue	transfer	export	retain
chapter	label	uniform	foundation	reverse
chart	legal		furthermore	schedule
chemical	link	A2	globe	secure
code	locate		guarantee	structure
communicate	major	adjust	identical	substitute
community	medical	appreciate	index	sufficient
compound	normal	appropriate	initial	sum
contact	obvious	assign	injure	summary
couple	occur	assist	insert	suspend
create	paragraph	author	inspect	target
culture	period	capable	instruct	text
cycle	portion	channel	investigate	tradition
design	positive	clarify	lecture	transmit
device	previous	conduct	likewise	transport
encounter	primary	construct	notion	vehicle
energy	principal	consume	overlap	violate
enormous	publish	contribute	overseas	visible
environment	purchase	convert	participate	vision

Academic Word List: Intermediate B1 and B2

B1					
	category	element	maintain	principle	source
	complex	establish	mental	process	specific
abandon	conclude	expose	method	professional	stable
accompany	conflict	feature	military	project	stress
adapt	considerable	federal	minimum	range	style
alter	consist	file	minor	react	survey
alternative	constant	focus	nevertheless	region	survive
apparent	credit	fundamental	nuclear	release	symbol
approximate	data	generation	obtain	require	tape
aspect	decade	identify	odd	resource	technique
assure	define	illustrate	partner	role	technology
attitude	definite	impact	percent	section	temporary
benefit	demonstrate	item	phase	seek	theory
bond	depress	journal	physical	select	unique
brief	despite	labor	policy	sex	vary
capacity	economy	layer	potential	site	volume

(continued)

TABLE 2.1   (Continued)

B2	derive	generate	network	scheme
	dimension	ignorance	option	sole
access	distribute	imply	outcome	specify
accommodate	document	inevitable	overall	sphere
assemble	domain	insight	parallel	strategy
attain	dominate	institute	perspective	submit
collapse	duration	intense	phenomenon	sustain
commence	ensure	interval	philosophy	tense
comment	equip	liberal	pose	theme
comprise	equivalent	license	preliminary	trace
confer	exceed	manipulate	prime	transit
confirm	exclude	manual	priority	trend
consequent	exhibit	margin	prohibit	undertake
consult	exploit	mechanism	promote	version
contrary	extract	media	publication	visual
converse	fee	medium	random	voluntary
core	flexible	migrate	reside	welfare
correspond	formula	minimize	restore	widespread
debate	fund	monitor	revise	

Academic Word List: Advanced C1 and C2

C1	enable	panel	adjacent	distort
	enforce	perceive	advocate	diverse
accumulate	estate	precede	amend	dynamic
acquire	evaluate	prior	anticipate	enhance
adequate	eventual	proportion	arbitrary	erode
affect	evident	prospect	assess	ethic
ambiguous	evolve	psychology	attribute	ethnic
analyze	explicit	pursue	bias	format
annual	external	radical	cite	hierarchy
authority	factor	ratio	classic	highlight
bulk	finance	regulate	coherent	implement
cease	framework	revenue	colleague	incentive
circumstance	hence	revolution	commit	incline
civil	hypothesis	rigid	commodity	incorporate
clause	impose	sequence	compensate	induce
commission	income	significant	compile	initiate
component	input	statistic	complement	integrate
concentrate	instance	status	comprehensive	integrity
concept	intelligence	subsequent	compute	intermediate
consent	internal	technical	conceive	intervene
constitute	interpret	thereby	confine	model
contemporary	invest	transform	conform	motive
context	isolate	trigger	contradict	nonetheless
contract	justify	ultimate	controversy	offset
contrast	logic	whereas	coordinate	passive
decline	mature		corporate	persist
deny	modify	C2	crucial	practitioner
devote	neutral		currency	predominant
distinct	objective	abstract	denote	quote
domestic	occupy	academy	diminish	rational
emphasis	output	acknowledge	discriminate	refine

Academic Word List: Advanced C1 and C2				
regime	straightforward	terminate	unify	via
reinforce	subordinate	thesis	utilize	whereby
reluctance	successor	undergo	valid	
scope	supplement	underlie		

Source: Adapted from Coxhead, A. (2000) A new academic word list. *TESOL Quarterly 34*, 213–238.

Co-Shaping

In co-shaping, you provide prompts that help the student shape responses that make use of scientific language. Notice how a teacher co-shapes the following interchange:

Student: It happened in some kind of jungle place in olden times.

Teacher: Do you remember where the rain forest was?

Student: South America.

Teacher: Do you recall what part of South America?

Student: It was on the edge.

Teacher: Yes, the setting is the rain forest at the tip of South America. Do you remember when the story took place?

Student: Olden times. About a hundred years ago.

Teacher: Yes, the setting is the rain forest at the tip of South America in the beginning of the 20th century.

Using a Hierarchy of Questions

Match the difficulty level of questions with the students' level of English. At the lowest level, students might nod or shake their heads or answer *yes* or *no.* Either/or questions can be used once students are speaking: "Is this line the latitude or the longitude?" *Wh-* questions come next, with *why* questions being posed last (Díaz-Rico & Weed, 2002).

Collaboration and Negotiation of Meaning

Teacher and student can work together to create meaning, as in the following example in which the student is working in a science lab.

Student: I put it here (points to microscope slide on mounting platform).

Teacher: You mounted the slide.

Student: Yes, it has it—it has plant.

Teacher: You mounted a leaf on the slide?

Student: No, not a leaf. The plant, um, ground (gestures to indicate under the ground).

Teacher: Oh. You mounted a plant root on the slide.

Student: Yes. Root.

Teacher: Can you draw what you see (she makes drawing movements on an imaginary paper)? Make a drawing.

Student: Make a drawing for the root. (Díaz-Rico, 2004, pp. 104–105)

Notice how the teacher collaborates with the student to negotiate meaning. The teacher uses gestures and also rephrasing ("You mounted the slide") to co-construct meaning and to bolster the student's use of academic language. Through the interchange, the teacher helps the student understand what he is to do and also bolsters his language.

Sentence Starters and Word Walls

As you teach new procedures, routines, and concepts, post a list of words needed to carry out those procedures or routines and talk and write about the new concepts. Create a wall of needed words and expressions that students might refer to and that you might review periodically. Also provide sentences that students might use to take part in a discussion: "I think the main character was brave, and here is why I think so. The main character _____." Sentence starters can be used in speaking in much the same way as they are used in writing.

Checking Understanding

Periodically, you should check for understanding. This can be done continually as you look for signs of understanding. Or it can be done by asking the students to give a thumbs up if they understand or a thumbs down if they don't. You might also ask students if they understand, but some students might be reluctant to admit that they don't. Follow up by asking students to show what they are expected to do or explain the concept being discussed or answer a question about it. Students should be taught how to seek help when they don't understand (Díaz-Rico & Weed, 2002). On a practical note, teach students how to ask questions such as "I don't understand. Could you explain that again?" or "I am not sure what to do. Could you show me?" Also explain to students that if they are reluctant to ask for an explanation during class, they might approach the teacher after class.

Empowering Students

Teach students strategies for getting their meaning across: asking for help from listeners if necessary, repeating or using other words if listeners don't seem to understand, showing what they mean, and using gestures. Students might also work with a partner. Older students might keep a dictionary of useful academic terms and expressions.

Recasting

In recasting, you ask students to rephrase what they are saying.

> How could you say that using the new words we learned: *problem, solution, conflict?*
>
> How could you combine those ideas?
>
> What could you add to what you said so that someone who wasn't here would understand it? (Zwiers, 2008)

Correcting Errors

Focus on meaning rather than on correcting errors. Correcting errors during an interchange can be embarrassing and will probably limit a student's willingness to take risks with language. You might provide a rephrase, as long as you believe it will be helpful and not discouraging to the student, or schedule a language session later.

> *Student:* There are too many noises in the room. My ears pain.
>
> *Teacher:* Yes, there is too much noise in the room. No wonder your ears hurt.

Using the Student's Language

Also plan strategic use of the student's native language. Use that level of English that the student is familiar with. However, for developing complex concepts, use the student's native language, if possible, or ask another student who speaks the language to provide a translation. That way the student doesn't have the burden of trying to understand difficult concepts expressed in terms that may be hard to understand.

**Exemplary
Teaching**

Scaffolded Language

Ms. Page uses a scaffolding device known as *semantic contingency* to help English language learners formulate their responses (Manyak, 2008). In semantic contingency, the student recounts an experience or talks about a topic on which she or he is knowledgeable. Because the experience or topic is familiar, the student has an easier time talking about it. The teacher uses spoken prompts and gestures to draw out the student. Aided by the teacher's scaffolding, the student is able to use more English than usual but is also encouraged to use gestures and native language words when English fails him. If unfamiliar with the native language, the teacher has the native words translated. At times, the teacher may be able to use the context and the student's gestures to get the meaning. The teacher's response is phrased in terms of what the student has expressed. The teacher might use many of the same words that the student used. Another strategy that teachers can use is to ask students to translate responses into English.

Fostering Output

Output is also an essential element of second language acquisition (Anthony, 2008). Output has three functions: noticing/triggering, hypothesis testing, and reflecting. When attempting to say or write something, a student might recognize that she doesn't know the required words. She then takes steps to acquire the needed words. Locating the words, the student formulates her message, which leads to the second function of output: hypothesis testing. In hypothesis testing, the student delivers the message and uses feedback to revise the message if necessary. The third function of output is reflecting on what was said and possibly modifying the message. The speaker might realize that what she said didn't sound right and then take steps to correct her statement (Swain, 2005).

Using Technology

Google Translate translates languages and even Web sites. You can type in keywords or phrases and get the equivalent in the students' language. You could also type in summaries of key concepts and have them translated into students' native language. Students could also use these tools to translate difficult English passages into their native language.
http://translate.google.com/ ∎

Assess Students' Academic Language and Background

A first step in fostering academic language is to assess students' academic background and command of academic language. This can be done through informal conversations or interviews and by listening to students as they talk with a reading buddy, in a small group, or on the playground. If students can write, have them write letters in which they introduce themselves, discuss how this school is different from previous schools, explain what their favorite subject is, or tell what they like and dislike about reading and writing. Also read their logs and journals and note their participation in class discussions (Zwiers, 2008). You can obtain from the ESL teacher and the school records data on students' language and academic background. You may find that students have studied English as part of their schooling in their native land. However, they might be better at recognizing English words in print than they are at recognizing them in speech.

Building Academic Language Benefits All Students

Although English learners might be in the most need of academic language, at-risk students, students who speak a dialect other than mainstream English, and native speakers of English who have had limited exposure to school-type language also need academic language.

Gearing Instruction to Stages of Second-Language Acquisition

Although there is some overlap among stages, a second language develops in approximately five stages (see Table 2.2): preproduction, early production, speech emergence, intermediate, and advanced. (Stages are adapted from Díaz-Rico, 2004;

TABLE 2.2   Stages of Second-Language Acquisition

Level of Language	Characteristics of Learner	Teaching Suggestions	Building Literacy
Preproduction	Students know a few English words but primarily use gestures and pointing to communicate. This stage is known as the *silent period*, because students speak only a few words of English or none at all. This stage may last up to six months or a year. Despite not speaking, students may acquire an understanding of up to 500 words.	Use concrete objects, gestures, and pointing; repeat and paraphrase; speak slowly; ask *what, who, where,* and *yes/no* questions.	Students can use books that label illustrations. Encourage drawing and writing of labels and captions.
Early production	Students can understand and use some common words and expressions such as "OK," "That mine," "Can I sharpen pencil?" This stage may last up to six months. Students may acquire a combined listening–speaking vocabulary of 1,000 words.	Use concrete objects, gestures, and pointing; speak slowly; simplify language; build English vocabulary; ask *what, who, where,* and *either/or* questions and questions that elicit a simple list of words.	Students can understand easy predictable text. Encourage writing of brief pieces that use basic sentence patterns. Use repeated sentences from predictable books as models.
Speech emergence	Students can use brief, everyday expressions and have greater receptive than expressive command of English. Students begin to participate in class discussions. This stage may last for up to a year. Most students acquire about 3,000 words by the end of this stage.	Use heavy visual support and gestures; develop English vocabulary; ask *what, who, where,* and *when* questions and questions that can be answered with a phrase or brief sentence.	Students can read more advanced predictable text; they may benefit from interactive writing.
Intermediate	Students have a fairly good grasp of everyday English and begin to grasp and use academic English. They can work in groups. This stage may last for up to a year. Most students acquire about 6,000 words by the end of this stage.	Use visual supports, including graphic organizers, and gestures; use prompts to foster elaboration; ask *what, who, where, when,* and *why* questions and questions that require explanation or elaboration. Some students can benefit from sheltered instruction (see p. 418 of this text).	Students may need easier texts and/or assistance with texts; most benefit from language experience. Scaffold writing by introducing needed vocabulary and forms; use frame paragraphs.
Advanced	Language is comparable to that of a native speaker. Students may take up to 5 years or more to reach this stage.	Continue to provide visual support and build vocabulary.	Students can read grade-level texts. Develop higher-level thinking skills; develop a full array of writing skills.

Adapting Instruction for English Language Learners

Teachers might underestimate the abilities of ELLs. Because they are speaking in broken English, ELLs might not seem as knowledgeable or as intelligent as native English speakers. However, teachers might have unrealistic expectations for ELLs at the intermediate stage. At this stage, students might seem to have more advanced language than they possess (Lalas, Solomon, & Johannessen, 2006). ∎

Guzman-Johannessen, 2006; Northwest Regional Educational Laboratory, 2003). Gear questions and other activities to students' language level (Lalas, Solomon, & Johannessen, 2006). For the lowest levels, for instance, ask *what, who,* and *where* questions. These can be answered with single words. Progress to *when* questions, which might demand a phrase, and then to *how* and *why* questions, which require more elaborate language.

In preparation for teaching ELLs, take note of the students' level of knowledge and language. Plan for the kinds of difficulties they might experience. Ask yourself, "What specifically am I going to do to increase comprehensibility? How will I differentiate for ELLs at different levels?" Develop knowledge of text structures and use graphic organizers. Go through each chapter in any text you plan to use and note features, such as illustrations, that will be of help to ELLs. After each lesson, reflect. Ask yourself, "Have I fostered language development? Was I able to make the text accessible?" (Lalas, Solomon, & Johannessen, 2006).

Use Cooperative Learning and Peer Tutoring Strategies

Working with peers provides excellent opportunities for ELLs to apply language skills. In a small group, they are less reluctant to speak. In addition, they are better able to make themselves understood and better able to understand others. Working

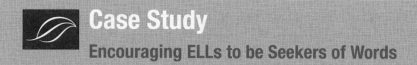

Case Study
Encouraging ELLs to be Seekers of Words

When Josephine Nobisso, a native speaker of Italian, struggled to find a word to express an idea, her parents encouraged her to seek an approximation. This led Josephine to become a seeker of words and a published writer. Based on her experiences as an ELL, she recommends that students pursue a word when they believe that they have heard one that expresses the meaning that they have in mind. She supplies this example:

> *A child asks a teacher, "What's the word for a round thing, like 'circle' but not 'circle'?" Her response, "Do you mean a sphere?" helps the child to enter the word into his lifelong lexicon. (Nobisso, 2002)*

with buddies and in small groups provides context and fosters language learning (Cummins, 1994).

Use Print

Use print to support and expand the oral-language learning of English learners. Label items in the room. Write directions, schedules, and similar information about routines on the chalkboard. As you write them, read them orally (Sutton, 1989). Also encourage students to write:

> Provide experiences in which language is greatly contextualized (as, for example, a field trip, a science experiment, role playing, planning a class party, solving a puzzle). Use print materials with these activities as a natural extension of the oral language generated: write a class language experience report about the field trip; record information on a science chart; write dialogues or captions for a set of pictures; make lists of party items needed; follow written directions to find a hidden treasure. (p. 686)

Also use books to build language. "Children's books can provide a rich input of cohesive language, made comprehensible by patterned language, predictable structure, and strong, supportive illustrations" (Allen, 1994, pp. 117–118). Children's books can be used to stimulate discussion, to show objects that ELLs may not be familiar with, and to build concepts. Books that are well illustrated and whose illustrations support the text are especially helpful. For younger children, a predictable book such as *Cat on the Mat* (Wildsmith, 1982) repeats the simple pattern "The _____ sat on the mat." Eric Carle's *Have You Seen My Cat?* (1973) repeats the question pattern "Have you seen my _____?" For older, more advanced students, First Fact books such as *The Sun* (Winrich, 2005) use primarily simple subject-verb-object sentences. Such books build knowledge of basic syntactical patterns as well as vocabulary. After reading texts of this type, students might use the patterns in their oral language and writing.

Provide Intentional, Systematic Instruction

Instruction in English should be intentional and systematic. A distinguished panel of experts in literacy and language learning recommend the following research-based practices:

> One major theme in our recommendations is the importance of intensive, interactive English language development instruction for all English learners. This instruction needs to focus on developing academic language (the decontextualized language of the schools, the language of academic discourse, of texts, and of formal argument). . . . Ensure that the development of formal or academic English is a key instructional goal for English learners, beginning in the primary grades. . . . Daily academic English instruction should . . . be integrated into the core curriculum. Consider asking teachers to devote a specific block (or blocks) of time each day to building English learners' academic English. . . . Provide

 Using Technology

AR Bookfinder

More than 8,000 books in Spanish, with readability levels provided, can be found at

http://www.arbookfind.com

Click on Advanced Search and Spanish. ∎

R E F L E C T I O N

What specific steps might you take to develop the English language skills of ELL students in your class?

 Adapting Instruction for English Language Learners

In your lesson plans for ELLs, include language objectives that focus on vocabulary, syntax, figurative language, and other elements that might pose problems for your students. In addition to making key concepts more accessible to ELLs, such lessons will build their language skills (Bielenberg & Fillmore, 2004). ∎

high quality vocabulary instruction throughout the day. Teach essential content words in depth. In addition, use instructional time to address the meanings of common words, phrases, and expressions not yet learned. (Gersten et al., p. 2)

Students at Risk

Although widely used, the term **at risk** is avoided by some because it has a negative connotation.

> By focusing primarily on characteristics of the students, their families and their communities, the accompanying responsibility and blame for the at-risk condition is placed on the population themselves.... Instead ... attention should be focused on the educational situation and on the sociocultural factors that have contributed to the at-risk condition. (García, Pearson, & Jiménez, 1994, p. 4)

Moreover, if educators blame the victims or their backgrounds, they may lower their expectations for these students. Slavin (1997–1998) suggests that we start looking at these students as having promise and give them the kinds of high-quality programs that foster success. The Stupiski Foundation uses the term "Our Kids." Our Kids are underserved students living in poverty. Disproportionately, they are African American or Hispanic (Germeroth, Barker, Aren, Wang, 2009).

Hodgkinson (2003) has identified 15 risk factors that include a number of health and economic factors, poor nutrition, and transience and difficulties in parenting. The number one factor is poverty. Some 50 percent of United States children have at least one at-risk factor, with 15 percent having three or more factors (Duncan & Magnson, 2005). The more factors the greater the risk for academic underachievement. Students raised in poverty are most likely to have several at-risk factors.

Economically Disadvantaged Students

The percentage of children living below the poverty level is 20.7 percent (DeNavas-Walt, Proctor, & Smith, 2010). More than 10 million of the nation's school-age children live below the official poverty level. About 800,000 school children are homeless (Kids Count, 2008). Twenty percent of public elementary schools and 9 percent of public secondary schools in the United States are classified as high-poverty schools, which means that at least 75 percent of the students qualify for free or a reduced-price lunch (Aud et al., 2011). High-poverty schools have teachers who are less experienced, are less likely to have advanced degrees, and are more likely to lack certification. Differences in reading achievement between students who attend high-poverty schools and those attending low-poverty schools (25 percent or less qualifying for free or a reduced-cost lunch) are dramatic. In 2009, about 55 percent of fourth-graders from high-poverty schools performed below basic on the NAEP tests, compared with 13 percent of fourth-graders from low-poverty schools. About 47 percent of eighth-graders from high-poverty schools performed below basic, compared with 13 percent of eighth-graders from low-poverty schools. However, when low-income students attended low-poverty schools, their achievement was similar to that of the middle-class students (Kahlenberg, 2009). Some research indicates that low-income students progress at approximately the same rate as middle-income students, especially in the early grades. However, low-income students start out behind and sustain a small loss during summer vacations, whereas middle-class students experience small gains (Barton & Cooley, 2008).

Poverty in and of itself does not mean that children cannot and will not be successful in school. For instance, even in the poorest neighborhoods, about one child out of a hundred enters kindergarten knowing letter–sound relationships and how to read words (West, Denton, & Germino-Hausken, 2000). (The

Using Technology

The following Web site contains resources for helping to educate the homeless:

http://www.ed.gov/programs/ homeless/resources.html ■

FYI

• ELLs and minority students are more likely to live in poverty than white English-speaking students (Aud et al., 2010).
• For suggestions for teaching homeless children, see Noll and Watkins (2003–2004). ■

■ **At risk** refers to students who have been judged likely to have difficulty at school because of poverty, low grades, retention in a grade, excessive absence, or other potentially limiting factors.

proportion is two out of a hundred for middle-class children.) However, because their families and communities generally have fewer resources, low-income students are more reliant on schools.

Principles for Teaching Economically Disadvantaged Children

Build Background   It is important to develop background in reading in all children. For some economically disadvantaged children, this background will have to be extensive. Limited incomes generally mean limited travel and lack of opportunity for vacations, summer camps, and other expensive activities. However, the teacher should not assume that children do not have the necessary background for a particular selection they are about to read. One teacher was somewhat surprised to learn that a group of low-income sixth-graders with whom she was working had a fairly large amount of knowledge about the feudal system (Maria, 1990). Use a technique such as brainstorming or simple questioning to probe students' background to avoid making unwarranted assumptions about knowledge.

Create an Atmosphere of Success   Teachers sometimes emphasize problems, not successes. MacArthur Award recipient L. D. Delpit (1990) said that teachers must maintain visions of success for students who are disadvantaged—to help them get As, not just pass.

Make Instruction Explicit   Middle-class children are more likely to be taught strategies at home that will help them achieve success in school and are more likely to receive help at home if they have difficulty or fail to understand implicit instruction at school. Low-income children need direct, explicit instruction. If such children do not learn skills at school, family members will be less likely to supply or obtain remedial help for them. Disadvantaged students must have better teaching and more of it (Delpit, 1990).

Provide a Balanced Program   Because the economically disadvantaged as a group do less well on skills tests, teachers may overemphasize basic skills (García, 1990). Economically disadvantaged students need higher-level as well as basic skills and strategies. These skills should be taught in context with plenty of opportunity to apply them to high-quality reading materials and real life.

Provide Access to Books and Magazines   One of the most powerful determiners of how well children read is how much they read. Unfortunately, poor children often have few books in their homes. One study found that poor children, on average, had fewer than three books in their homes. What's more, their classrooms, schools, and public libraries had far fewer books than did those in more affluent areas (Krashen, 1997–1998). This is unfortunate, because the number of books a student reads is related to the number of books available and to having a quiet, comfortable place to read (Krashen, 1997–1998).

Counteract the Fourth-Grade Slump   In their study of children of poverty, Chall, Jacobs, and Baldwin (1990) observed a phenomenon known as the *fourth-grade slump*. Students perform well in second and third grades on measures of reading and language, although form lags behind content in writing. However, beginning in fourth grade, many poor students slump in several areas. They have particular difficulty defining abstract, more academically oriented words. In addition to vocabulary, word recognition and spelling scores begin to slip. These are the skills that undergird achievement in reading and writing. They are also the skills for which the schools bear primary responsibility.

From fourth grade on, the school's role in the development of low-income children's literacy capabilities becomes especially important. The school must teach the

FYI

Middle-class children also need instruction to counteract the fourth-grade slump, but economically disadvantaged children must be given extra or more thorough instruction in this area because they are less likely to get help at home. ■

vocabulary and concepts necessary to cope with subject matter texts. Chall, Jacobs, and Baldwin (1990) recommended systematic teaching of word-recognition skills in the primary grades and the use of children's books, both informational and fictional, in all grades. "Exposure to books on a variety of subjects and on a wide range of difficulty levels was particularly effective in the development of vocabulary" (p. 155).

Added opportunity for writing and reading in the content areas was also recommended. The researchers noted that children who wrote more comprehended better, and those who were in classes where the teachers taught content-area reading had higher vocabulary scores. It also helps to "overdetermine success." Overdetermining success "anticipates all the ways children might fail and then plans how each will be prevented or quickly and effectively dealt with" (Slavin, 1997–1998, p. 7). This means making arrangements for tutoring, counseling, and family support.

Students with Learning Disabilities

Using Technology

For more information on learning disabilities, visit these sites:

Learning Disabilities Association of America
http://www.ldanatl.org

The International Dyslexia Association
http://www.interdys.org

Council for Exceptional Children
http://www.cec.sped.org ■

FYI

Intervention programs for students with learning disabilities have an average gain of 28 percentile points (Hattie, 2009). ■

FYI

In general, a learning disability can be caused by a weakness in information processing. Key information-processing skills include visual-perceptual skills, auditory processing and language skills, and attention and motor skills. ■

More than 5 percent of all U.S. students aged 3–21 (about 3 million students) have been determined to have a learning disability (Aud et al., 2010). The term *learning disability* is controversial; experts disagree as to what constitutes a learning disability. The most widely followed definition is that used by the federal government and contained in the Individuals with Disabilities Education Act, or IDEA (PL 108–446):

> Specific **learning disability** means a disorder in one or more of the basic psychological processes involved in understanding or in using language, spoken or written, which disorder may manifest itself in an imperfect ability to listen, think, speak, read, write, spell, or to do mathematical calculations. Such term includes such conditions as perceptual disabilities, brain injury, minimal brain dysfunction, dyslexia, and developmental aphasia. Such term does not include a learning problem that is primarily the result of visual, hearing, or motor disabilities, of mental retardation, of emotional disturbance, or of environmental, cultural, or economic disadvantage. [PL 108–446, section 30(A, B, C)]

In the past, a definition based on some measurable discrepancy between performance and ability was used to identify learning disabilities. However, this definition often delayed services, because a sufficient discrepancy didn't show up until students had been in school for several years. School systems now have the option of using response to instruction as an identification tool. The theory is that if students are offered effective, research-based instruction and they fail to make progress, their lack of progress may indicate a learning disability. However, RTI cannot be the sole determining criterion. States must use multiple measures to determine a learning disability.

Characteristics of Students with Learning Disabilities

R E F L E C T I O N

What impact might RTI have on the number of students diagnosed as having a learning disability? What impact might RTI have on students who have a learning disability?

Because of the broad definition, the learning-disabled group is quite heterogeneous. It includes students who have visual- or auditory-perceptual dysfunction, memory deficits, problems using language to learn, or all of these conditions. Students may have an underlying problem that manifests itself in all school subjects, or the problem may be restricted to a single area, such as reading, writing, or math. The most common reason for referral is a reading problem. About 80 percent of students classified as learning-disabled have a reading difficulty.

Students with Attention Deficit Disorder

About 3 to 5 percent of the school population has **attention deficit disorder** (Children and Adults with Attention-Deficit/Hyperactivity Disorder, 2006). Attention

---

■ **Learning disability** is a general term used to refer to a group of disorders that are evidenced by difficulty learning to read, write, speak, listen, or do math. The speaking and listening difficulties are not caused by articulation disorders or impaired hearing.

■ **Attention deficit disorder** refers to a difficulty focusing and maintaining attention.

deficit disorder (ADD) has as its primary symptom difficulty in focusing and sustaining attention. This may be due to a chemical imbalance and is frequently accompanied by **hyperactivity** or **impulsivity**.

ADD is not classified as a learning or reading disorder. A student can have ADD but demonstrate no difficulty learning. However, there is considerable overlap between the two categories. Many students diagnosed as having a learning disability also have difficulty with attention. ADD students do qualify for special services (U.S. Department of Education, 1991).

Assisting Students with ADD

The nature and extent of ADD are still being debated. However, it is clear that large numbers of students have difficulty learning because of a problem with attention. Literacy educator Constance Weaver (1994), whose son has been diagnosed as having ADHD (the *H* stands for hyperactivity), has a number of humane and practical suggestions for helping these children. Her chief concern is that we not blame the victim. Instead, she suggests that we look at ways in which we can help the student perform better in school and in which the school can adjust to the student's characteristics. For instance, ADHD children, by definition, have difficulty sitting still. Why not allow them stretch breaks or the opportunity to participate in projects that involve movement? Instead of just focusing on trying to change the child, teachers need to work with him or her and modify the program.

Other suggestions include the following, many of which would be beneficial to all students:

- Provide students with tasks that are meaningful and interesting.
- Give students a choice of materials and activities.
- Allow mobility in the classroom; use writing, reading, and other learning centers.
- Allow students to confer with peers or work in cooperative groups.
- Minimize formal tests.
- Make sure students understand directions. Establish eye contact. Give directions one step at a time, writing them on the board as you do so. Make sure that the students have copied the directions accurately and understand them.
- When students have homework assignments, make sure they leave with all the necessary materials and directions.
- Help students keep a schedule for major assignments. Break the assignment down into a series of smaller steps. Check to see that each step is completed.
- Use visual aids, such as pictures, the overhead projector, and videos whenever possible.
- Schedule many brief periods of practice for rote material rather than a few long ones.
- Work closely with parents so that the home supports the school's efforts, and vice versa.
- Minimize distractions. Have ADD students sit near you and put away any books or tools they aren't using.
- Make sure classroom procedures are clear and everyone understands them (Smith, Polloway, Patton, & Dowdy, 1998; Weaver, 1994).
- Highlight important information. In one study, writing the difficult parts of spelling words in red resulted in improved performance for ADD students (Zutell, 1998).
- Use peer tutoring. In several studies, peer tutoring dramatically increased the on-task behavior and performance of both ADD students and non-ADD students (DuPaul & Eckert, 1996).

Using Technology

The Web site of CHADD (Children and Adults with Attention-Deficit/ Hyperactivity Disorder) provides a wealth of information on ADD. http://www.chadd.org ■

Using Technology

National Institute of Mental Health

Provides a wealth of information on ADD. http://www.nimh.nih.gov/health/ publications/attention–deficit– hyperactivity–disorder/complete– index.shtml

Provides information on autism spectrum disorders, depression, and other conditions. http://www.nimh.nih.gov/health/ publications/autism-listing.shtml ■

■ **Hyperactivity** refers to the tendency to be overly active, impulsive, or distractible.

■ **Impulsivity** refers to the tendency to act on the spur of the moment without thinking of the consequences.

- Use computers. Computer programs increased the on-task behavior and academic achievement of ADD students. Programs with games and simulations worked better than programs without such incentives (DuPaul & Eckert, 1996).

Students with Intellectual Disabilities

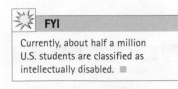

FYI

Currently, about half a million U.S. students are classified as intellectually disabled. ■

Using Technology

The American Association on Intellectual and Developmental Disabilities provides a wealth of information.
http://www.aaidd.org ■

About 1.2 to 1.6 percent of the population is classified as having some degree of intellectual disability, which is sometimes referred to as *cognitive disability* or *mental retardation* (Centers for Disease Control and Prevention, 2011). Intellectual disability is determined by two criteria: low level of intellectual functioning and deficits in adaptive behavior. Low level of intellectual functioning translates into an IQ score below 70, or two standard deviations below the mean.

A primary problem for students with intellectual disabilities is limited reasoning ability. Through modeling and other techniques, the teacher must make explicit the processes of reading and writing that average students often pick up on their own. Book selection and the use of decoding, comprehension, study, and writing skills have to be modeled carefully and continually. The teacher must also model processes that underlie learning: paying attention, staying on task, listening, and determining relevant information.

For most children who have intellectual disabilities, the major obstacles to reading achievement are vocabulary and conceptual development. Because of limited cognitive ability and, perhaps, lack of experiential background, they may have difficulty comprehending what they read. They need to have concepts and background built in functional, concrete ways. They also need appropriate materials. Students need materials that appeal to their age but that are on the appropriate reading level. A language-experience approach, because it is based on students' language, is especially effective.

Some students with intellectual disabilities may never read beyond a second-grade level. Others will never be able to do any sustained reading. Because their literacy development is so limited, it is important that they be taught the literacy skills they need to function in society. These skills include reading traffic and warning signs, labels, simple cooking directions, and common forms. They also have to know how to write their name, address, telephone number, date of birth, names of family members, and other information frequently requested on forms.

Students with intellectual disabilities should also be taught how to read the newspaper and use the Internet, especially for functional items like weather forecasts, movie times, and making purchases. They must know, too, how to use the white, blue, and yellow pages of the telephone book or Internet. Stress should be placed on locating emergency numbers and also making use of assistive devices, such as text-to-speech offered on computers and other digital devices.

Slow Learners

Functioning generally on a higher level than students with intellectual disabilities but on a lower level than average students are a large number of students known as **slow learners**. They make up approximately 14 percent of the school population. Because they have IQ scores between 70 and 85 (approximately), they function on too high a level to be classified as having intellectual disability but are frequently excluded from learning-disabled and remedial reading programs because their IQ scores are too low. Although they have some special needs, slow learners are often denied special services.

Slow learners manifest some of the same characteristics that students with intellectual disabilities display, but to a lesser degree. They tend to be concrete in their thinking, need help with strategies and organization, and are eager for success. They have difficulty with abstract concepts and so need a lot of concrete

■ **Slow learners** have below-average ability but are not intellectually disabled. In general, IQs of slow learners range between 70 and 85.

examples. They also need more practice and more repetition (Cooter & Cooter, 2004). Their executive functioning is on a higher level than that of children with intellectual disabilities. They are better able to decide when and where to use strategies and are better able to classify and group information. They also are more aware of their mental processes and can take more responsibility for their learning.

In terms of instruction, these are "more so" students; they need the same instruction that regular students need, but more so. They must be given more guidance, more practice, and more time to complete learning tasks. One of their greatest needs is to have materials and instruction on their level. (Materials for learning-disabled students can also be used with slow learners.) A slow learner in the fifth grade might be reading on a second- or third-grade level. All too often, slow learners are given a basal that is below grade level but still above their reading level or a content-area textbook that is on grade level and well above their reading level. This is frustrating and leads to lowered self-concept and lowered achievement.

Teaching students with disabilities to read and write may mean adapting techniques and using technology but is mostly a matter of acceptance and caring.

Students with Language and Speech Disorders

Speech impairments do not directly affect reading or writing. The teacher's role consists primarily of being sensitive to the difficulty and helping the child apply skills in the classroom that she or he learned while working with a speech therapist. The teacher should also be supportive and help the child build confidence, providing opportunities for the child to take part in discussions and purposeful oral reading. Consultation with the speech therapist and "promotion of a classroom atmosphere conducive to unpressured verbal interaction" (Cartwright, Cartwright, & Ward, 1989, p. 174) are also recommended.

Although articulation difficulties do not generally impair the acquisition of reading and writing skills, other less noticeable language difficulties may pose significant problems. Some children's language development follows a normal path but is slow. These children may experience a delay acquiring basic reading and writing skills.

Students who suffer from language disorders experience a disruption in the language development process (Hardman, Drew, Egan, & Wolf, 1993). The disruption may be expressive or receptive or a combination of the two. Receptive language disorders affect students' understanding of language. Expressive disorders hinder the ability to communicate. Students with an expressive disorder may possess information but have difficulty communicating it.

Inclusion

Inclusion means teaching students who have disabilities or special needs within the general education classroom. In order to accelerate the trend toward educating special education students within the regular classroom, the concept of inclusion has been widely adopted. Inclusion has come to mean providing support to classroom teachers as they, in turn, provide support for the education of disabled students. Supporting disabled students means creating and maintaining a warm, accepting atmosphere for all students and making whatever accommodations and modifications are required to develop their literacy abilities.

Modifications refers to altering the curriculum, changing the school attendance requirement, or making other changes in school policy designed to aid disabled students. **Accommodations** refers to changes in the way students

 FYI

One expressive language disorder is difficulty finding the words to express what one wants to say. For instance, unable to retrieve the word *bat*, a student might say, "The thing that you hit a ball with." The speech of these students is marked by hesitations, round-about expressions, and "you knows." They may have difficulty using picture and context clues because they cannot retrieve from memory the name of the object shown in the picture or think of the word that might fit the context. These students are helped by graphic organizers. ■

 FYI

Inclusion results in gains of ten percentile points (Hattie, 2009). ■

 Using Technology

The Whole Child

Provides information about inclusion.

http://www.wholechildeducation.org/ ■

■ An **accommodation** is a change in the process of instruction or assessment—allowing a student to listen to rather than read a story or take an exam orally, for example.

Adapting Instruction for Struggling Readers and Writers

If a student will be taking an alternative form of a state test or will be provided with modifications, the IEP must explain why (Office of Special Education and Rehabilitation, 2005). ■

Using Technology

For additional information about giftedness, visit one of the following sites:

The National Research Center on the Gifted and Talented
http://www.gifted.uconn.edu/NRCGT.html

Neag Center for Gifted Education and Talent Development
http://www.gifted.uconn.edu ■

FYI

Enrichment programs have average gains of 10 percentile points (Hattie, 2009). ■

are taught. These could include changes in instruction, assessment, or the assignment of homework (Smith, Polloway, Patton, & Dowdy, 1998). Allowing a test to be taken orally, for instance, would be an accommodation. In making accommodations, it is best if the accommodations benefit all students. Providing a talking software program, such as *Co: Writer* (Don Johnston) or *Doctor Peet's Talk Writer* (Interest-Driven Learning), would be an accommodation that benefits all students.

Gifted and Talented Students

A reading and writing program for **gifted and talented students** should take into account the individual characteristics of the children. About 50 percent of the gifted come to school already reading (Terman, 1954). Provision should be made for them and for those reading above grade level. For example, gifted second-graders reading on a fifth- or sixth-grade level should not be restricted to second-grade material. The materials they read should be on their instructional and interest levels.

Because they master basic reading skills early and may not be sufficiently challenged by the classroom collections of books, gifted students should learn how to select books from the school library. To enable them to investigate areas of special interest, provide early instruction in the use of dictionaries, encyclopedias, the Internet, and other basic references, as well as in the use of research skills. These students may also need help with study skills as they progress through the grades. Some are able to get by in the lower grades because of their ability, but as they reach more advanced grades, they may not have acquired the study habits and skills that will enable them to work up to their abilities.

Reading and writing workshops work quite well for the gifted. Through self-selected reading in reading workshop, gifted students are free to pursue advanced work at an accelerated pace. Through writing workshop, gifted students can also explore a broad range of writing genres. In creating reports on subjects of interest, they can investigate topics in depth and apply a host of practical research skills. Gifted students might also attempt some of the more difficult kinds of writing, such as poetry, drama, and short pieces of fiction.

One program that works exceptionally well with the gifted is Junior Great Books, a program in which students read literary classics and discuss them using a technique known as Shared Inquiry. The group leader, who is trained by the Great Books Foundation, initiates and guides the discussion, but it is up to the group to interpret the reading and validate its interpretation with evidence from the text. In addition to developing skill in the careful reading of complex materials, shared inquiry is designed to develop discussion and thinking skills. As Tierney and Readence (2005) note, "Shared Inquiry offers discussion leaders a systematic approach for preparing for discussions" and "mobilizing student interactions." It also "includes carefully developed guidelines by which group leaders might monitor the success of discussions and initiate strategies to improve them" (p. 401). In an independent study comparing major discussion approaches, Junior Great Books was superior, by far, to all the others in preparing students to obtain higher comprehension scores (Murphy & Edwards, 2005). The program features high-quality selections, excellent discussion

■ **Gifted and talented students** have mental abilities or other talents that are well above average. Approximately the top 2 percent of the population is classified as being gifted or talented.
■ **Inclusion** is the practice of educating within the classroom all students, including those with special needs. In full inclusion, all support services are provided within the classroom setting. In partial inclusion, the student may be pulled out of the classroom for special instruction.
■ **A modification** is a change in the content or structure of instruction—changing the curriculum, for instance.

guides and follow-up materials, and conscientious training of leaders. (Junior Great Books also works well with average and struggling readers.)

Culturally Diverse Students

It is important to value and build on every student's culture. Children from all cultures need to see the connection between their culture and school. First and foremost, it is essential that teachers become acquainted with the children's culture, especially if the teachers' backgrounds are different from those of the children they teach (Strickland, 1998). Reading, discussions with the children, visits to homes, and interaction with those who are knowledgeable about the various cultures represented in the classroom are some informal ways of obtaining information. The teacher should constantly make efforts to become familiar with the literary heritage of the cultures represented in his or her class, and especially with how literacy is used. For example, according to Taylor and Dorsey-Gaines (1988), African American families may read for a wide range of purposes, but the school often fails to reinforce the purposes for reading and writing taught in the home. According to Goldenberg (1994), parents of Hispanic students have high academic aspirations for their children, but the school may not realize this.

Understanding students' cultural background can lead to more effective teaching. Various cultural groups might have socialization practices and expectations that put children at a disadvantage when they attend school. For instance, children of Mexican immigrants are taught to be passive around adults. They are also discouraged from showing off what they know (Valdes, 1996). However, in the typical public school classroom, students are expected to be assertive and demonstrate their knowledge. As a result of a lack of assertiveness and a failure to display what they know, children of Mexican immigrants may be judged to be lacking in skills and background knowledge and placed in lower reading groups.

In working with children and parents from other cultures, you need to be metacognitive: You need to realize that you perceive your students and their parents through your own cultural lens (Maldonado-Colon, 2003) and that the lives of your students are different in some ways from yours. You need to study the culture of your students and find out as much as you can about your students' everyday lives. If you do these things, there is a greater likelihood that your teaching will be more relevant and more effective.

In developing teaching techniques that are appropriate for diverse **learning styles**, you have to be aware of the ways in which students think and process information. Teaching needs to be more collaborative. You have to ask children how they construct meaning so that you can gain insight into their thinking processes. You need to try varied approaches to teaching and organizing classes to learn which ones work best. You also need to give students choices to determine the kinds of activities they prefer. Many suggestions for increasing the achievement of ethnic and linguistic minority children—such as cooperative learning and being sensitive to learning styles—should help all children learn better (Banks, 1994).

Accepting the Student's Language

A student's language is part of who she or he is. Rejecting it is interpreted as a personal rejection. Everyone speaks a dialect, which is determined by place of birth, socioeconomic status, and other factors. Some African American children speak a dialect known as Black English, which is very similar to

> **FYI**
>
> • Although the Junior Great Books shared inquiry program is frequently used with gifted readers, it has been successfully used with below-level readers and could be a part of the classroom routine or an after-school or out-of-class activity. For more information, visit http://www.greatbooks.org/
>
> • Although overrepresented in special needs groups, students still acquiring English, students who are members of a minority group, and students who are poor are underrepresented in programs for the gifted. Special attempts need to be made to identify students from these groups who have special abilities. ∎

> **FYI**
>
> Having a positive view of one's ethnicity results in gains of 10 percentile points (Hattie, 2009). ∎

> **FYI**
>
> As is true of a number of dialects, some African American English pronunciations can cause slight difficulty in phonics. Students might not perceive some final consonant clustering and may confuse word parts, as in *toll* and *told* or *coal* and *cold*. The use of context and added work on auditory discrimination will help take care of this minor interference. ∎

> ∎ The term **learning styles** refers to individual preferences in acquiring, remembering, and applying new information and skills. Learning styles include auditory, visual, or hands-on learning; learning in wholes or pieces; and learning alone or with others.

Today's classrooms are made up of students from diverse ethnic and racial groups.

standard English. The differences between the two dialects are minor and include features such as dropping the suffixes -*ing* and -*ed*, omitting the word *is* ("He busy"), and using some variations in pronunciation such as "pin" for *pen* (Shuy, 1973).

Dialect has no negative effect on reading achievement; it may, however, influence teacher attitude (Goodman & Goodman, 1978). Teachers who form unfavorable opinions on the basis of variant dialects can convey those feelings and associated lowered expectations to students. If they constantly correct language, teachers might also be hindering communication between themselves and their students.

Even when reading orally, a child who uses a variant dialect should not be corrected. In fact, translation of printed symbols into one's dialect is a positive sign (Goodman & Goodman, 1978). It indicates that the student is reading for meaning and not just making sounds.

Teachers should use standard English, thus providing a model for children who speak a variant dialect. Although all dialects are equally acceptable, the use of standard English can be a factor in vocational success. Rather than correcting or eradicating a variant dialect, Brown (1988) recommended that standard English be presented as a second dialect that students may use if they wish. The New Standards Speaking and Listening Committee (2001b) suggests that students who have been in school a few years should be expected to use standard English for academic purposes but not necessarily in social situations. "All students should learn the shared rules of standard English—but not in ways that tread on their heritage" (p. 24).

A Research-Based Approach to Cultural Diversity

Based on an extensive review of the research, Li (2011) recommends the following instructional practices:

1. Acknowledging the importance of students' cultural heritages, individual characteristics, and cultural identities;
2. Recognizing cultural differences between students' home life and school literacy learning and the conflicts these differences may engender;
3. Utilizing a wide array of instructional strategies that emphasize culturally relevant content contexts and interactional structures; and
4. Promoting the development of critical thinking abilities that can help students become better border crossers to tackle the border contextual and societal factors in learning. . . . (pp. 528–529)

Implications of Diversity for Instruction

The diversity present in today's classrooms means that teachers need to be able to differentiate instruction. To do so, teachers should learn about the cognitive, cultural, literacy, and linguistic background of students and use that knowledge to plan instruction. The diversity that students bring to the classroom should be valued and built on. To meet the needs of all students, teachers must apply the principles of RTI by monitoring the progress of each student and modifying and intensifying programs, supplying added help, or getting assistance if students fail to make progress.

Whether all students can be brought to readiness for college or career, only time will tell. However, it is possible to make dramatic improvements in students' literacy achievement. Reading Recovery (What Works Clearinghouse, 2007) and other high-quality programs (Hiebert & Taylor, 2000; Reeves, 2003) have shown that most students will become proficient readers when properly taught. However, achieving this goal will take not just an all-school effort, but the involvement of all of society as evidenced by the success of the Harlem Children's Zone (n.d.), which provides support for low-income children from cradle to college and currently has 500 participants in college and 500 in the pipeline for college. Well-stocked neighborhood and school libraries, adequate health care, parenting programs, contributions from businesses, and the support of all citizens will be needed to foster the high level of literacy achievement being called for. More than ever, parents will need to become partners in their children's education.

Preparing all students to be college and career ready requires taking a long-term view of literacy. As literacy professionals, we need to ask ourselves, "What kind of program will result in literacy proficiency for virtually all students?" The temptation is to drill students on the kinds of items they will be tested on. The drill–skill approach hasn't worked in the past and won't work now. It is too shallow. What is needed is an in-depth approach that builds students' background knowledge and vocabulary, fosters language development, and develops the kinds of skills needed to cope with the literacy demands that students face now and will face in the future so that they are prepared to take their place in postsecondary education and the world of work.

Subsequent chapters will build on the background given in this chapter and will provide specific suggestions for applying the concepts of RTI and differentiating and adapting instruction when working with diverse students. Insofar as possible, the suggestions made in this text are evidence-based. However, in some instances, they are based on personal experience or the experience of others. Teaching literacy is an art as well as a science.

Summary

Mandates to prepare every student to be college and career ready are designed to help the diverse populations found in U.S. schools, especially students at risk, to fully develop literacy skills Growing out of IDEIA 2004 is Response to Intervention (RTI), which uses progress monitoring and intervention to help struggling students. RTI can also be used in the identification of learning disabilities.

Students at risk of failure include English language learners, students raised in poverty, and students who have physical, mental, or cognitive disabilities. Students at risk benefit from instruction that develops language, background, and literacy skills and that respects their native language and culture.

Increasingly, students with a range of learning and physical disabilities are being taught within the regular classroom. Working closely with special education and literacy resource personnel and other specialists, the classroom teacher should make adjustments in the physical environment and/or program so that these students learn to read and write to their full capacities. Gifted and talented students need to be given challenging material and programs.

Extending and Applying

1. Interview the special education, Title 1, or remedial reading specialist at the school where you teach or at a nearby elementary or middle school. Find out what kinds of programs the school offers for special education, Title 1, and remedial students. Also find out whether RTI is being implemented in the school and, if so, how it is structured.

2. Observe a lesson in which English language learners are being taught. Note how the teacher makes adaptations for the students. In particular, what does the

teacher do to make input comprehensible? What is done to encourage output? Does the teacher intentionally present vocabulary or language structures?

3. Observe a classroom in which remedial or special education instruction is offered according to the inclusion model. What arrangements have the specialist and the classroom teacher made for working together? What are the advantages of this type of arrangement? What are some of the disadvantages?

4. Investigate the culture of a minority group that is represented in a class you are now teaching or observing. Find out information about the group's literature, language, and customs. How might you use this information to plan more effective instruction for the class? Plan a lesson using this information. If possible, teach the lesson and evaluate its effectiveness.

 ## Professional Reflection

Do I

___ Have an understanding of the diverse populations served by today's elementary and middle schools?

___ Have an understanding of the principles of RTI?

___ Have an understanding of how I might adapt and differentiate instruction to meet the needs of all learners?

___ Have an understanding of the importance of believing that all students can learn?

Am I able to

___ Differentiate instruction?

___ Build on the culture and background that each student brings to literacy?

 ## Reflection Question

What adaptations might you make for English language learners, even though you don't speak their language?

On what basis would you make these adaptations? What resources might you use?

 ## Building Competencies

To build competencies, consult the following sources for more detailed information:

Start Legacy Modules from Vanderbilt University
http://iris.peabody.vanderbilt.edu/resourcees.html

You can find out more about RTI from this source:

Colorín Colorado
http://www.colorincolorado.org

This site provides information about teaching reading to ELLs.

Information on learning disabilities and ADHD is available at this site:

LD OnLine
http://www.Idonline.org

To find out more about an exemplary approach to developing the literacy abilities of students living in poverty:

Read Harlem Children's Zone (n.d.). *Whatever it takes, A white paper on the Harlem Children's Zone.* http://www.hcz.org/images/stories/HCZ%20White%20Paper.pdf

MyEducationLab™

Go to the Topics "Struggling Readers" and "English Language Learners" in the MyEducationLab (www.myeducationlab.com) for your course, where you can:

• Find learning outcomes for "Struggling Readers" and "English Language Learners" along with the national standards that connect to these outcomes.

• Complete Assignments and Activities that can help you more deeply understand the chapter content.

• Apply and practice your understanding of the core teaching skills identified in the chapter with the Building Teaching Skills and Dispositions learning units.

• Examine challenging situations and cases presented in the IRIS Center Resources.

- Check your comprehension on the content covered in the chapter by going to the Study Plan in the Book Resources for your text. Here you will be able to take a chapter quiz, receive feedback on your answers, and then access Review, Practice, and Enrichment activities to enhance your understanding of chapter content. (optional)

A+RISE® Standards2Strategy™ is an innovative and interactive online resource that offers new teachers in grades K–12 just-in-time, research-based instructional strategies that meet the linguistic needs of ELLs as they learn content, differentiate instruction for all grades and abilities, and are aligned to Common Core Elementary Language Arts standards (for the literacy strategies) and to English language proficiency standards in WIDA, Texas, California, and Florida.

3 Assessing for Learning

Anticipation Guide

For each of the following statements related to the chapter you are about to read, put a check under "Agree" or "Disagree" to show how you feel. Discuss your responses with classmates before you read the chapter.

	Agree	Disagree
1. Nationwide achievement tests are essential for the assessment of literacy.	___	___
2. Setting high standards and assessing student achievement on those standards is a good way to improve the quality of reading and writing instruction.	___	___
3. Most writing assessments are too subjective.	___	___
4. Today's students take too many tests.	___	___
5. Teachers should be evaluated on the basis of how much their students learn.	___	___
6. Observation yields more information about a student's progress in reading and writing than a standardized test does.	___	___

Using What You Know

Evaluation is an essential part of literacy learning. It is a judgment by teachers, children, parents, administrators, and the wider community as to whether instructional goals have been met. Evaluation also helps teachers determine what is and what is not working so that they can plan better programs. Self-evaluation gives students more control over their own learning. Taking all of this into consideration, what kinds of experiences have you had with evaluation? How has your schoolwork been assessed? Do you agree with the assessments, or do you think they were off the mark? Keeping in mind the current emphasis on preparing every student to be college and career ready, what might be some appropriate ways to evaluate the literacy development of today's students?

The Nature of Evaluation

In evaluation, we ask, "How am I doing?" so that we can do better. **Evaluation** is a value judgment. We can also ask, "How is the education program doing?" and base our evaluation on tests, quizzes, records, work samples, observations, anecdotal records, portfolios, and similar information. The evaluation could be made by a student while reviewing her or his writing folder or by parents as they look over a report card. The evaluator could be a teacher, who, after examining a portfolio or collection of a student's work and thinking over recent observations of that student, concludes that the student has done well but could do better.

Evaluation should result in some kind of action. The evaluator must determine what that action should be, based on his or her judgment. The student may decide that he or she has been writing the same type of pieces and needs to branch out, the parents might decide that their child must study more, and the teacher might choose to add more silent reading time to the program.

The Starting Point

Evaluation starts with a set of goals or standards. You cannot tell if you have reached your destination if you do not know where you were headed. For example, a teacher may decide that one of her goals will be to instill in children a love of reading. This is a worthy goal, one that is lacking in many programs. How will the teacher decide whether the goal has been reached, and what will the teacher use as evidence? The goal has to be stated in terms of a specific objective that includes, if possible, observable behavior—for example, students will voluntarily read at least 20 minutes a day or at least one book a month. The objective then becomes measurable, and the teacher can collect information that will provide evidence as to whether it has been met.

Broad goals should be stated for the school year so that you have a map of where you are going. These goals might be stated in the school district's framework. Goals are then broken down into unit objectives and finally lesson objectives. Objectives are sometimes confused with activities. Activities are what students do to achieve a goal. They are the means rather than the end. For example, the statement "Read a story that contains short-*a* words" is an activity. "Be able to read short-*a* words" or "Be able to use short-*a* words to read a story" are objectives. Objectives are what you expect students to know or be able to do as a result of instruction. Learning expert Robert Marzano recommends using the following frames to state objectives:

Students will be able to _____ .

or

Students will understand _____ . (Marzano, 2007, p. 18)

The first objective represents the acquisition of a skill or strategy. In the parlance of cognitive psychology, it is "procedural knowledge"; the second represents "declarative knowledge." You might want to add to the frames a statement that tells how you will know that students have attained the objective or are on track for attaining it. If it's a skill, you might observe how well students use it in their everyday reading and writing, or you might note their performance on a quiz or worksheet. If it's a knowledge objective, you might see how well they do in a discussion or oral or written retelling of the new knowledge.

The Standards Movement

The centerpiece of the standards movement is the statement of goals or objectives. The standards movement grew out of concern for the quality of education in the United States. The basic idea behind standards is that establishing challenging, world-class standards and measuring whether those standards have been reached will lead to instruction geared to the standards and higher achievement. Standards "define our expectations for what's important for children to learn, serve as guideposts for curriculum and instruction, and should be the basis of all assessment" (American Federation of Teachers, 2008, p. 2).

The Common Core State Standards

Because standards vary from state to state, the National Governors Association (NGA) and Council of Chief State School Officers (CCSSO, 2010) have created a set of Common Core State Standards in English language arts and math. The standards are designed to prepare students to be college and career ready. Anchor Standards for Reading are listed on the inside front cover. Anchor standards are broad statements of standards. There are also anchor

■ **Evaluation** is the process of using the results of tests, observations, work samples, and other devices to judge the effectiveness of a program. A program is evaluated in terms of its objectives. The ultimate purpose of evaluation is to improve the program.

standards for writing, language, and speaking and listening. The anchor standards are broken down into more specific grade level standards, which are available at the Common Core State Standards Web site at http://www.corestandards.org.

The Standards' authors recommend holding English language learners (ELLs) to the same standards set for native speakers but more time, instruction, and support should be provided. Similarly, it is also recommended that instruction and assessment of students with disabilities be guided by the standards, the philosophy being that "[t]he common core state standards provide a historic opportunity to improve access to academic content standards for students with disabilities" (National Governors Association and Council of Chief State School Officers, 2010). As the report points out, adjustments, including supports and accommodations, need to be made based on the nature and severity of the disability.

The Key Standard

What is the key ability that predicts success in college? According to studies conducted by ACT (2006), "The clearest differentiator in reading between students who are college ready and students who are not is the ability to comprehend complex texts" (pp. 16–17). The ability to read complex text is a better predictor than gender, race, or socioeconomic status. Of course, what ACT is describing is the outcome goal. This is the kind of reading that students should be able to perform when they are high school juniors or seniors, but obviously, reaching that goal means working toward it in every grade. However, there is a gap between the reading skills of many high school seniors and the reading demands of college and the workplace (National Governors Association and Council of Chief State School Officers, 2010a). There is also a gap between the materials generally read in high school and those read in college and the workplace. To close both gaps, the Common Core Standards have incorporated a feature known as grade bands. The bands include grades 2–3, 4–5, 6–8, 9–10, and 11–12. As stated in the Standards, "Students in the first year(s) of a given band are expected by the end of the year to read and comprehend proficiently within the band, with scaffolding as needed at the high end of the range. Students in the last year of a band are expected by the end of the year to read and comprehend independently and proficiently within the band" (p. 10). However, because of the gaps between what students can read at the end of high school and the demands of college and career and the gap between the difficulty level of high school materials and college and workplace materials, beginning at grade 2 and at every grade level after that, the upper range of that band represents an increase in difficulty. For instance, end-of-third-grade materials will be somewhat more challenging than what has typically been end-of-third-grade material. The difficulty level at every band has been expanded so that by senior year students will be expected to be able to read at or close to college and career level. In other words, the standards call for students to be able to read more challenging material at every grade level beginning with grade 2.

Common Core assessments will be demanding. The ability to read both literary and informational texts will be assessed, and both basic and higher level skills will be evaluated. Students will be expected to demonstrate a "close reading of text." Particular emphasis will be placed on citing evidence to support a position or conclusion along with the ability to analyze that evidence. For some items, students will be expected to draw from two or more sources rather than just one. Vocabulary will be assessed through items that will be embedded in the context of the test selections. The ability to write about texts will be stressed.

FYI

Grade bands represent the most significant change called for in the Common Core State Standards and the most difficult standard to achieve. Beginning in grades 2–3, the bands call for an increase in the overall literacy growth of students and an increase in the difficulty level of materials that they will be expected to read. ▪

FYI

Even though Common Core Standards call for having students read more challenging materials, this does not mean that students should be given material that exceeds their reading ability. Giving students material that is too hard, unless they are adequately prepared for it, is virtually guaranteed to stunt their literacy growth. ▪

Using Technology

Center for K–12 Assessment & Performance Management at ETS Provides information on the development of assessments for Common Core State Standards.
http://www.k12center.org/ ▪

▪ **Standards** are statements of what students should know and be able to do.
▪ **A high-stakes test** is one whose results are used to make an important decision such as passing students, graduating students, or rating a school.

▪ **Assessment** is the process of gathering data about an area of learning through tests, observations, work samples, and other means.

▪ **Authentic assessment** involves using tasks that are typical of the kinds of reading or writing that students perform in school and out.

Common Core assessments will provide information that can be used for planning instruction. Formative, benchmark/interim, and summative assessment will be available. Curriculum frameworks, learning progressions based on the Common Core standards, and other resources will also be available.

Assessing for Learning: Summative and Formative Assessments

Assessment can be characterized as being summative or formative. **Summative assessment** summarizes students' progress at the end of a unit or a semester or at some other point in time. Summative assessment occurs after learning has taken place. Norm-referenced and high-stakes tests are generally summative. **Formative assessment** is ongoing and is used to inform instruction. Formative assessment takes place during learning. "Teachers need to know about their pupils' progress and difficulties with learning so that they can adapt their own work to meet pupils' needs—needs that are often unpredictable and that vary from one pupil to another" (Black & Wiliam, 1998). As Chappuis, Chappuis, and Stiggins (2009) explain, it is not the assessment that is formative. It is the way the information derived from the assessment is used. It is formative if it used to adjust instruction.

Combining characteristics of summative and formative tests is a type of test known as an "interim" test. Interim tests, which are sometimes labeled as through-course, benchmark, or short cycle tests, are often used to determine whether students are on track to reach key instructional goals or benchmarks or to predict how students will perform on the end-of-year state test or other high-stakes tests. They are given periodically: every quarter or month, for instance. Because they are given at intervals during the school year, they can be used to plan future instruction (Hamilton, Halverson, Jackson, Mandinach, Supovitz, & Wayman, 2009).

Assessing for Learning: Using Summative and Interim Assessments

One problem with summative assessments, especially state-mandated tests, is that by the time results are sent to the schools, it is too late to use them. To make summative assessments more useful, they need to occur more frequently so that changes can be made in the program or additional help can be given to students who are not meeting the standards. Many school systems give interim tests that are similar to the state high-stakes tests or are released copies of those tests. Students who do poorly on interim tests are generally provided with added instruction. Areas on which all or most students have difficulty are scheduled for instruction (Stiggins & Chappuis, 2005). Hence, summative assessments are used in formative ways. In another attempt to use summative assessment in a formative way, schools collect and analyze the test data more efficiently so that instructional decisions can be based on that data.

Assessing for Learning: Using Formative Assessments

The basic idea behind assessing for learning is to obtain enough information about students so that you can give them the help they need. Assessing for learning begins with a clear explanation of the standards that students are expected to meet. This means that the classroom teacher may need to break down the state standards into a curriculum map or series of steps that, if followed, will lead to meeting the standard. The standard is expressed in terms that the students can understand. For a writing standard, for example, students are shown writing samples that meet and don't meet the standard so that they have a clear idea of what is expected. As part of instruction, students are

■ **Summative assessment** occurs after learning has taken place and summarizes students' progress at the end of a unit or a semester or at some other point in time.

■ **Formative assessment** takes place during learning and is used to plan or modify instruction.

IRA POSITION STATEMENT ON KEY ISSUE
High-Stakes Testing

As its name suggests, a high-stakes test is one for which an important decision will be based on the outcome. Because of the role they play in decision making, high-stakes tests have the potential to dictate curriculum. Instead of teaching what their community has judged to be important, educators might teach what is tested. This has the effect of narrowing the curriculum. Knowing, for instance, that students will be tested on narrative writing in the fourth grade, teachers in the early grades overemphasize story writing and neglect expository writing. A great deal of time is also spent writing to a prompt because that is the way students will be assessed on the state tests. To combat the misuse of tests, the International Reading Association (1999a) has made the following recommendations:

Teachers should

- construct rigorous classroom assessments to help outside observers gain confidence in teacher techniques.

- educate parents, community members, and policymakers about classroom-based assessment.

- teach students how tests are structured, but not teach to the test.

---

assessed to see where they are in relation to the standard and also what they need to do to achieve the standard. Progress is monitored, and students are informed of their progress along the way. Results of the monitoring are used to inform instruction.

Clear feedback is an essential part of assessing for learning. Feedback should be expressed so that students fully understand what they need to do to improve. Self-assessment is also a key component of formative assessment or assessing for learning. For students to carry out self-assessment, they need to understand what it is they are supposed to know or be able to do (the objective), how they are progressing (status), and what they need to do to reach the goal (corrective action). Students can't work toward a goal if they don't know what it is, don't know what their current capabilities are, or don't know how to take corrective action. As Stiggins (2004) recommends, "We must build classroom environments in which students use assessments to understand what success looks like and how to do better the next time. In effect, we must help students use ongoing classroom assessment to take responsibility for their own academic success" (pp. 25–26).

Formative assessment emphasizes process rather than product. Process assessment seeks to find out how the student learns. Process measures include observing students to see what strategies they use to arrive at a particular answer, to compose a piece of writing, or to study for a test. Having this kind of insight, the teacher is able to redirect errant thought processes, correct poorly applied strategies, or teach needed strategies. Actually, both product and process measures provide useful information. Knowing where a child is and how he or she got there, the teacher is better prepared to map out a successful path toward improvement.

Checking for Understanding

Literacy experts, researchers, and former classroom teachers Douglas Fisher and Nancy Frey (2007) confess to having asked students the question, "Does everybody understand?" and when a lone voice answered "Yes," proceeding with the lesson, only to find out through a quiz or discussion that understanding was not universal. It is vitally important to find out whether students are following along or are lost—or are somewhere in between. However, most students typically don't respond to the "Does everybody understand?" question. To elicit that kind of information, there are a number of

 Using Technology

The Assessment Training Institute site features a number of articles and other resources for assessing for learning.
http://www.assessmentinst.com ■

 Assessing for Learning

Assessment measures should also be fair to all who take them. There should be no biased items; content should be such that all students have had an equal opportunity to learn it. ■

R E F L E C T I O N

What is formative assessment and what is its role in instruction? What are some types of formative assessment you might use in your current or projected teaching situation?

 FYI

Checking for understanding is a key element in an effective lesson and is part of widely used teacher evaluation systems. ■

steps you might take. You might call on a number of students, including those who don't usually raise their hands, or probe incorrect or incomplete responses to determine the nature of the misunderstanding and figure out ways to correct it. You might ask for thumbs up to indicate understanding or thumbs down to signal a lack of understanding. You might use every-pupil response cards. Younger students might hold up letters that represent the sounds that the teacher says. Or students might write their responses on a white board and hold them up. A teacher displaying various examples of energy via a PowerPoint presentation had students hold up cards labeled "kinetic energy" or "potential energy" to indicate their responses. This action, along with having students explain their choices when there was disagreement, allowed him to see how well students were grasping the concept and to remedy confusions immediately (Fisher & Frey, 2007). Listening in on student discussions, using a quick write, and observing students as they write or complete a lab assignment are also helpful checks to gauge students' understanding. An electronic interactive response system used in conjunction with an interactive whiteboard enables teachers to administer quizzes via the whiteboard at any point during the lesson. Students use remotes known as "clickers" to respond to multiple-choice or true-false questions. Students can also respond with very brief responses of about 20 letters or fewer. The response can also be used to take a poll: How many ate breakfast this morning? Responses are checked and compiled immediately: 80 percent had breakfast. Quizzes or questions can be prepared by the teacher or can be purchased or obtained free from a learning community. Some measure of how well teachers check for understanding is a key characteristic assessed on a number of widely used evaluations of teacher effectiveness (iObservation, 2010).

Self-Evaluation

The ultimate evaluation is, of course, self-evaluation. Students should be involved in all phases of the evaluation process and, insofar as possible, take responsibility for assessing their own work. Questionnaires and self-report checklists are especially useful for this. Figure 3.11 shows a self-report checklist with which students in grade 3 and beyond can assess their use of strategies in learning from text.

Self-assessment should begin early. Ahlmann (1992) noted that by October, her first-graders are already evaluating their own work and that of authors they read. To self-assess, students reflect on their learning, assemble portfolios of their work, list their achievements, and, with the guidance of the teacher, put together a plan for what they hope to achieve.

In some classes, students complete exit slips on which they write about what they have learned that day or raise questions that they did not have time to raise in class or were reluctant to raise. Learning logs and journals might perform a similar function. As an alternative, the teacher and the class might design a form on which students write what they learned in a certain class and list questions that they still have. In reading and writing conferences, part of the discussion should center on skills mastered and goals for the future, and how those goals might be met. These conferences, of course, should be genuinely collaborative efforts so that students' input is shown to be valued.

As students engage in a literacy task, they should assess their performance. After reading a selection, they might ask themselves: "How well did I understand this selection? Do I need to reread or take other steps to improve my comprehension?" After completing a piece of writing, they should also evaluate their performance. If a rubric has been constructed for the piece of writing, they should assess their work in terms of the rubric.

Logs and Journals for Self-Evaluation   Reading logs and response journals can also be a part of students' self-evaluation, as well as a source of information for the teacher. Reading logs contain a list of books read and, perhaps, a brief summary or assessment. Response journals provide students with opportunities to record personal reactions to their reading. Both reading logs and response journals offer unique insights into students' growing ability to handle increasingly difficult books, their changing interests, and personal involvement with reading.

 Judging Assessment Measures

Reliability

To be useful, tests and other assessment instruments must be both reliable and valid. **Reliability** is a measure of consistency, which means that if the same test were given to the same students a number of times, the results would be approximately the same. Reliability is usually reported as a coefficient of correlation and ranges from .00 to 1 or −.01 to −1. The higher the positive correlation, the more reliable the test. For tests on which individual decisions are being based, reliability should be in the .90s.

Reliability can also be thought of as generalizability. For observations and other informal approaches to assessment, it means that similar findings have been found by different judges and at different times (Johnston & Rogers, 2001). One way of increasing reliability is by training observers. Another is to have several observations.

A test that is not reliable is of no value. It is the equivalent of an elastic yardstick—the results of measurement would be different each time.

Validity

In general, **validity** means that a test measures what it says it measures: vocabulary knowledge or speed of reading, for instance. Ultimately, it is consequential and means that a particular test will provide the information needed to make a decision, such as placing a student with an appropriate level book or indicating specific strengths and weaknesses in comprehension (Farr & Carey, 1986). Johnston and Rogers (2001) contend that unless an assessment practice helps to improve students' learning, it should not occur. Reading tests need content validity, meaning that the skills and strategies tested must be the same as those taught. To check for **content validity**, list the objectives of the program and note how closely a particular test's objectives match them. The test selections should be examined, too, to see whether they reflect the type of material that the students read. Also, determine how reading is tested. If a test assesses skills or strategies that you do not cover or assesses them in a way that is not suitable, the test is not valid for your class.

Concurrent validity means that an assessment measure correlates with a similar test or other form of assessment occurring at about the same time. *Predictive validity* means that there is a correlation between the assessment measure and some future behavior. This could be a correlation between phonological awareness in kindergarten and reading comprehension in the third grade.

However, a number of assessment measures that have high statistical (concurrent and predictive) validity may be lacking in content validity. For instance, phonics tests that use nonsense words might correlate well with measures of current and future performance but distort the reading process and so have limited content validity and thus limited usefulness for teachers. If an assessment measure doesn't assess what you teach or assesses a skill in a way that differs from the way that students actually apply it, then the measure is lacking in content validity.

 FYI

• Whether assessment is formal or informal, done through observation or paper-and-pencil testing, reliability is essential. As Farr (1991) observes, "If a test or other means of assessment is not reliable, it's no good. . . . If you stand on the bathroom scale and it registers 132 lbs. one morning, but it's 147 the next morning, and 85 the morning after that, you conclude it's time for a new set of bathroom scales" (p. 4).

• One danger in evaluation is the temptation to gather too much information. Be economical. Do not waste time gathering information you are not going to use. ■

R E F L E C T I O N

What is content validity? What is consequential validity? What is the importance of content and consequential validity? Why should they be considered along with concurrent and predictive validity?

■ **Reliability** is the degree to which a test yields consistent results. In other words, if students took a reliable test again, their scores would be approximately the same.

■ **Validity** is the degree to which a test measures what it is supposed to measure, or the extent to which a test will provide information needed to make a decision. Validity should be considered in terms of the consequences of the test results and the use to which the results will be put.

■ **Content validity** means that the tasks of an assessment device are representative of the subject or area being assessed.

■ **Concurrent validity** means that an assessment measure correlates with a similar assessment occurring at about the same time.

■ **Predictive validity** means that there is a correlation between the assessment and some future behavior.

Closely tied to validity are the consequences or uses to which the assessment will be put. A useful assessment answers the following questions: What decision is to be made? By whom? What information will help them? At the classroom level, teachers and students need to know the answer to this question: What do students need to learn next on their way to achieving the standard? At the program support level, which might be the grade-level team or the school learning team, a key question is this: Who needs additional support? At the school and district level, administrators and the public want answers to these questions: How many students are meeting standards or demonstrating adequate growth? Are a sufficient number of students meeting standards? Is growth adequate?

At the classroom level, teachers need to go beyond identifying students who are or are not meeting standards and determine what needs to be learned so that standards are met. This entails obtaining information about foundational skills that might be needed to meet a standard. Summative assessment tools indicate which standards are being met but don't provide information about the steps needed to meet the standards. Observation, quizzes, discussions, and examination of students' work are needed to reveal why the standard isn't being met or growth is not adequate. The students might have difficulty understanding basic details, seeing how details are related, drawing a conclusion based on details, or formulating a response.

General Questions for Evaluation

Essentially, evaluation is the process of asking a series of questions. Specific questions depend on a program's particular goals and objectives. However, some general questions that should be asked about every literacy program include the following:

- Where are students in their literacy development? What might be done to enhance development?
- At what level are they reading?
- Are they reading up to their ability level? If not, what will help them do better?
- Are they making adequate, ongoing progress? If not, what can be done to accelerate progress?
- How well do they comprehend what they read? What will help them improve comprehension?
- How well do they read complex text?
- How adequate are students' reading vocabularies? What can be done to foster vocabulary growth?
- What comprehension and word-analysis strategies do students use? How can the use of such strategies be improved?
- What is the level of students' language development? What can be done to enhance language development?
- What are students' attitudes toward reading? How might their attitudes be improved?
- Do students enjoy a variety of genres? If not, what might be done to entice them to read in a greater number of genres?
- Do students read on their own? What will encourage them to read more?
- How well do students write? What will enable them to improve their writing?
- What kinds of writing tasks have students attempted?
- How well prepared are students for the writing tasks on which they will be assessed? How well do they do when asked to provide constructed responses?
- Which students seem to have special needs in reading and writing?
- Are these special needs being met? If not, what steps might be taken so that all needs are met?
- Are students on track to becoming career and college ready?

Answers to these essential questions help teachers plan, revise, and improve their reading and writing programs. The rest of this chapter explores a number of techniques for gathering the assessment information necessary to answer them. Both traditional and alternative means will be discussed.

Placement Information

The first question the classroom teacher of reading has to answer is "Where are the students in their literacy development?" If they are reading, assessment begins with determining the levels at which they are reading. One of the best placement devices is an informal reading inventory (IRI). In fact, if properly given, it will provide just about everything a teacher needs to know about a student's reading. It will also supply useful information about language development, work habits, interests, and personal development.

Informal Reading Inventory

An **informal reading inventory (IRI)** is a series of graded selections beginning at the very easiest level—pre-primer—and extending up to eighth grade or beyond. Each level has two selections; one is silent and the other oral. Starting at an easy level, the student continues to read until it is obvious that the material has become too difficult.

An IRI yields information about four reading levels: independent, instructional, frustration, and listening capacity. The **independent level**, or the free-reading level, is the point at which students can read on their own without teacher assistance. The **instructional level** refers to the point at which students need assistance because the material contains too many unknown words or concepts, or their background of experience is insufficient. This is also the level of materials used for teaching. Material at the **frustration level** is so difficult that students cannot read it even with teacher assistance. The fourth level is listening capacity, the highest level at which students can understand what has been read to them. **Listening capacity** is an informal measure of ability to comprehend spoken language. Theoretically, it is the level at which students should be able to read if they had all the necessary decoding skills. In practice, a small percentage of students have listening deficiencies, so a listening test might underestimate their true capacity. Younger students also tend to read below capacity because they are still acquiring basic reading skills. As students progress through the grades, listening and reading levels grow closer together (Sticht & James, 1984).

The first IRIs were constructed by teachers and were created using passages from basal readers. This was a good idea because it meant that there was an exact match between the material the student was tested on and the material the student would be reading. Because constructing IRIs is time-consuming, most teachers now use commercially produced ones. (See Table 3.1.) Unfortunately, most inventories are out of sync with the beginning levels of today's reading programs. Up until recently, the major reading programs used a high-frequency approach to teaching beginning reading. This meant that the words of the easiest selections consisted mainly of frequently occurring words. However, all of today's major programs use a decodable text approach. Beginning reading materials are made up primarily of words that incorporate the phonics patterns that students have been taught plus some high-frequency

FYI

Placing students at the appropriate level is more important than ever. Concern with preparing students to be college and career ready may lead to placing students in texts that are too difficult, which will stifle their growth. A key condition for accelerating progress is to make sure students are properly placed. ■

FYI

If students are not yet reading, they can be given an emergent literacy assessment, as explained in Chapter 4. ■

■ An **informal reading inventory (IRI)** is an assessment device in which a student reads a series of selections that gradually increase in difficulty. The teacher records oral reading errors and assesses comprehension in order to determine levels of materials that a student can read.
■ The **independent level** is the level at which a student can read without any assistance.

Comprehension is 90 percent or higher, and word recognition is 99 percent or higher.
■ The **instructional level** is the level at which a student needs a teacher's help. Comprehension is 75 percent or higher, and word recognition is 95 percent or higher.
■ The **frustration level** is the level at which reading material is so difficult that the

student can't read it even with help. Frustration is reached when either word recognition is 90 percent or lower, or comprehension is 50 percent or lower.
■ **Listening capacity** is the highest level of reading material that students can understand with 75 percent comprehension when it is read to them.

TABLE 3.1   Commercial Reading Inventories

Name	Publisher	Grades	Added Skill Areas
Analytical Reading Inventory	Merrill	1–9	
Bader Reading and Language Inventory	Merrill	1–12	phonics, language, emergent literacy
Basic Reading Inventory	Kendall/Hunt	1–8	emergent literacy
Burns and Roe Informal Inventory	Houghton Mifflin	1–12	
Classroom Reading Inventory	McGraw-Hill	1–8	spelling
Comprehensive Reading Inventory	Merrill	K–12	emergent literacy, phonics, reading attitude (Spanish version on CD)
Critical Reading Inventory: Assessing Students' Reading and Thinking	Prentice Hall	1–12	critical thinking
Ekwall/Shanker Reading Inventory	Allyn & Bacon	1–12	emergent literacy, word analysis
English-Español Reading Inventory for the Classroom	Prentice Hall	1–12	emergent literacy (has an English-only version)
Flynt-Cooter Reading Inventory for the Classroom	Merrill	1–12	emergent literacy
Informal Reading Thinking Inventory	Harcourt	1–11	
Phonological Awareness Literacy Screening (PALS)	University of Virginia	K–3	emergent literacy, spelling
Qualitative Reading Inventory 5	Allyn & Bacon	1–12	emergent literacy
Stieglitz Informal Reading Inventory	Allyn & Bacon	1–8	emergent literacy, phonics
Texas Primary Reading Inventory	Texas Education Agency	K–3	(has a Spanish version)

FYI

• The listening portion of the inventory provides only an approximate indication of students' capacity. It tends to be inaccurate with youngsters who have difficulty paying attention, who lack good listening skills, or who are still learning English.

• Standards for determining levels, marking symbols, types of misreadings that are counted as errors, and administration procedures vary, depending on the source consulted. The standards used in this book are taken from Johnson, Kress, and Pikulski (1987) and seem to be the most widely used. ■

words (Gunning, 2008a). However, most commercial reading inventories still take a high-frequency approach and fail to incorporate phonics patterns. At the pre-primer and primer levels, students are not being assessed on what they have been taught. If you are assessing students on the beginning reading levels, obtain passages that are representative of those levels. At the easiest levels, the ninth and tenth editions of the Basic Reading Inventory and the fifth edition of the Qualitative Reading Inventory have passages containing decodable and high-frequency words. Most basal reading programs have IRIs that would be aligned with their instruction.

IRIs can also be based on children's books. If, for instance, your program emphasizes the reading of children's books, you might designate certain titles as benchmark books and construct questions or retelling activities based on these books. Benchmark books can be used to place students and check their progress. Sets of benchmark books and accompanying questions are also available from basal reader publishers, or you can construct your own. This chapter lists benchmark books that can be used to judge the difficulty level of children's books at the beginning levels. You might use these books as the beginning basis for an informal reading inventory.

Determining Placement Levels   Placement levels are determined by having students read two selections, one orally and one silently, at appropriate grade levels. The percentages of oral-reading errors and comprehension questions answered correctly at each level are calculated. This information is then used to determine placement levels. Quantitative criteria for determining levels are presented in Table 3.2.

To be at the independent level, a reader must have, at minimum, both 99 percent word recognition and 90 percent comprehension. At the instructional level, the reader must have at least 95 percent word recognition and at least 75 percent comprehension. The frustration level is reached when word recognition drops to 90 percent or below, or comprehension falls to 50 percent or below. Even with 80 percent comprehension and 90 percent word recognition, readers are at the frustration level because they are encountering too many words that they cannot decode. Listening capacity is the level at which students can understand 75 percent of the material that is read to them.

Level	Word Recognition in Context (%)	Average Comprehension (%)
Independent	99–100	90–100
Instructional	95–98	75–89
Frustration	≤90	≤50
Listening capacity		75

TABLE 3.2 Quantitative Criteria for IRI Placement Levels

Running records and some other placement devices use lower standards for the instructional level, such as 90 to 95 percent word recognition. It is strongly advised that you stick to the 95 to 98 percent word-recognition standard. Research indicates that students do best when they can read at least 95 to 98 percent of the words (Berliner, 1981; Biemiller, 1994; Gambrell, Wilson, & Gantt, 1981; Nation, 2001). It is also important that the examiner adhere to strict standards when marking word reading errors. Enz (1989) found that relaxing IRI standards resulted in a drop in both achievement and attitude. Students placed according to higher standards spent a greater proportion of time on task, had a higher success rate, and had a more positive attitude toward reading.

REFLECTION

What are the most effective procedures for placing students? Some sources say that 90 to 95 percent word recognition is the instructional level. Others say 95 to 98 percent. Which standard do you intend to use? Why?

Administering the Word-List Test   Rather than guessing the grade level at which to begin the IRI, a teacher can administer a word-list test to locate an approximate starting point. This test consists of a series of ten to twenty words at each grade level. Students read the words in isolation, starting with the easiest and continuing until they reach a level where they get half or more of the words wrong. In a simplified administration of the test, students read the words from their copy of the list, and the teacher marks each response as being right or wrong on her or his copy.

In a diagnostic administration, the teacher uses three-by-five cards to flash the words for one second each. When students respond correctly, the teacher moves on to the next word. If the answer is incorrect or if students fail to respond, the teacher stops and lets them look at the word for as long as they wish (within reason). While students examine the missed word, the teacher writes down their response or marks a symbol in the flash (timed) column. If students make a second erroneous response, it is written in the second, or untimed, column. Symbols used to mark word-list tests are presented in Table 3.3. A corrected word-list test is shown in Figure 3.1.

Besides indicating the starting level for the IRI, a word-list test can yield valuable information about students' reading, especially if a diagnostic administration has been used. By comparing flash and untimed scores, teachers can assess the adequacy of students' sight vocabulary (their ability to recognize words immediately) and their proficiency with decoding. Teachers can note which decoding skills students are able to use and which must be taught. Looking at the performance depicted in Figure 3.1, it is clear that the student has a very limited sight vocabulary. The flash column shows that the student recognized few of the words immediately; the untimed column gives an overall picture of the student's ability to apply decoding skills. The student was able to use initial and final consonants and short vowels to decode words; for example, the student was able to read *wet*, *king*, *let*, and *bit* when given time to decode them. However,

Word	Teacher Mark	Meaning
the	✓	Correct
was	✓	Incorrect response or repeated error
have	O	No response
dog	boy	Mispronunciation
are	Dk	Don't know

TABLE 3.3 Word-List Marking Symbols

FIGURE 3.1 A Corrected Word-List Test

		Flash	Untimed
1.	their	*the*	✓
2.	wet	*o*	✓
3.	king	*o*	✓
4.	off	*o*	*dk*
5.	alone	*uh*	*along*
6.	hurt	✓	
7.	near	✓	
8.	tiger	*tie*	✓
9.	stick	*sick*	✓
10.	move	*moo*	*more*
11.	let	*o*	✓
12.	men	✓	
13.	shoe	*o*	✓
14.	wish	✓	
15.	apple	*o*	*dk*
16.	on	*o*	✓
17.	sign	*o*	*o*
18.	bit	*o*	✓
19.	smell	*sell*	✓
20.	floor	*for*	✓
	Percent correct	20%	60%

the student had difficulty with initial clusters; note how the student read *sick* for *stick*, *sell* for *smell*, and *for* for *floor*.

Rechecking Responses When students misread words, the logical assumption is that they are lacking in decoding or word-recognition skills. However, this is not always so. In their analysis of errors made by struggling readers, Cohn and D'Alessandro (1978) found that students were able to correct half their errors when the examiner requested, "Please look at it carefully and try it again" (p. 342). If the student still got the word wrong, the examiner tried a series of prompts to direct the student's attention to the misread word. Through prompting, another 28 percent of errors were corrected. Results of assessments need to be carefully analyzed to make sure that misread words actually indicate difficulty with decoding or word-recognition skills. This is especially true with older struggling readers, who are more likely to be able to correct errors than struggling readers in the first or second grade. To make sure you are getting an accurate picture of students' word reading ability, recheck erroneous responses to any word-list test that you administer. Note if students are able to read the word correctly after you prompt them to look at it carefully and try again. If they still get the word wrong, you might use the sounding out and/or pronounceable word prompts described on pages 226-227. Note how the students do when provided with prompts. This information could help you plan instruction.

Administering the Inventory The IRI is started at the level below the student's last perfect performance on the flash portion of the word-list test. For example, if that perfect performance was at the fourth-grade level, the inventory is started at the third-grade level.

An IRI is like a guided reading lesson, except that its main purpose is to assess a student's reading. To administer an IRI, first explain to the student that she or he will be reading some stories and answering some questions so that you can get some information about her or his reading. Before each selection is read, have the student read its title and predict what it will be about (Johns, 1997). Doing this will help the student set a purpose for reading, and it will give you a sense of the student's prediction ability and background of experience.

The student reads the first selection orally. This is one of the few times at which reading orally without having first read the selection silently is valid. As the student reads, use the symbols shown in Table 3.4 to record her or his performance. Although many different kinds of misreadings are noted, only the following are counted as errors or **miscues**: mispronunciations, omissions, insertions, and words supplied by the examiner because the student asked the examiner to read them or apparently could not read them on her or his own. Self-corrected errors are not counted. Hesitations, repetitions, and other qualitative misreadings are noted but not counted as errors. A corrected inventory selection is shown in Figure 3.2.

After the student finishes reading aloud, ask the series of comprehension questions that accompany the selection or ask for an oral retelling (see pp. 93-94 for information on retelling). Then

■ A **miscue** is an oral reading response that differs from the expected (correct) response. The term *miscue* is used because miscue theory holds that errors are not random but are the attempts of the reader to make sense of the text.

TABLE 3.4 Oral-Reading Symbols

Item	Marking	Meaning
Quantitative errors	the bi͡g dog ^bad^	Mispronounced
	the bi͡g dog	Omitted word
	the (ferocious) dog	Asked for word
	the big͜͜ dog ^bad^	Inserted word
Self-correction	the big͜ dog ^bad✓^	Self-corrected
Qualitative errors	I hit the ball⌄ and George ran.	Omitted punctuation
	The ‖‖ ferocious dog	Hesitation
	the ferocious dog	Repetition
	Good morning!↑	Rising inflection
	Are you reading?↓	Falling inflection
	W × W	Word-by-word reading
	HM	Head movement
	FP	Finger pointing
	PC	Use of picture clue

FIGURE 3.2 Corrected Inventory Selection

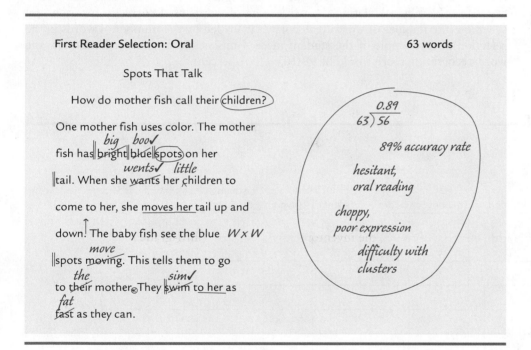

First Reader Selection: Oral   63 words

Spots That Talk

How do mother fish call their (children?)

One mother fish uses color. The mother
fish has ‖bright ‖blue ‖spots on her   *big boo✓*
tail. When she wa͜nts her children to   *wents✓ little*

come to her, she <u>moves her</u> tail up and

down↑ The baby fish see the blue *W × W*

spots mo͜ving. This tells them to go *move*

to their mother⊙ They ‖swim t<u>o her</u> as *the   sim✓*

fast as they can. *fat*

0.89
63) 56

89% accuracy rate

*hesitant,
oral reading*

*choppy,
poor expression*

*difficulty with
clusters*

introduce a silent selection on the same level. Just as with the oral selection, allow a very brief preparation phase and have the student make a prediction. During the silent reading, note finger pointing, head movement, lip movement, and subvocalizing. Symbols for these behaviors are given in Table 3.5. Ask comprehension questions when the student finishes reading. Proceeding level by level, continue to test until the student reaches a frustration level—that is, misreads 10 percent or more of the words or misses at least half the comprehension questions. Comprehension is calculated by averaging comprehension scores for the oral and silent selections at each level. Using the numbers on the summary sheet, determine the placement levels. Refer to the criteria in Table 3.2.

When the frustration level has been reached, read to the student the oral and silent selections at each level beyond the frustration level until the student reaches the highest level at which she or he can answer 75 percent of the comprehension questions.

FYI

Some inventories recommend counting all miscues as errors. Others suggest counting only those that disrupt the meaning or flow of the passage. It is easier and quicker to count all misreadings but make note of whether they fit the sense of the passage. Deciding whether a miscue is significant is subjective. If standards are too lenient, the student being assessed may end up being paired with a text that is too difficult. ∎

TABLE 3.5 Silent-Reading Symbols

Symbol	Meaning
HM	Head movement
FP	Finger pointing
LM	Lip movement
SV	Subvocalizing

This is the student's listening capacity, and it indicates how well the student would be able to read if she or he had the necessary word-recognition skills and related print-processing skills. For children who have limited language skills, limited background of experience, or deficient listening skills, you may have to backtrack and read selections at the frustration level and below. Because students will already have been exposed to the lower-level selections, you will have to use alternative selections to test listening comprehension.

Assessing Fluency To assess reading rate, which is a key element in fluency, time the student's oral and silent reading for each passage. For oral reading, you can note how many words the student reads in the first minute of reading or time how long the student took to read the whole selection and divide that into the number of words read correctly. Silent reading rate is also assessed by dividing the number of words read by the time spent reading. Use timings from the instructional level, not the frustration level. If the student reads more than one passage at the instructional level, average the reading rates.

Tallying up Results After administering the inventory, enter the scores from each level on the inventory's summary sheet (see Figure 3.3). Word-recognition scores are determined by calculating the percentage of words read correctly for each oral selection (the number of words read correctly divided by the number of words in the selection). For example, if the student made 5 miscues in a 103-word selection, the word-recognition score would be 98/103 = 95.1 percent.

FIGURE 3.3 IRI Summary Sheet

Word-List Scores			Inventory Scores						
			Word recognition	Comprehension			Listening	Reading rate	
Level	Flash	Untimed	(in context)	(oral)	(silent)	(avg.)	capacity	(oral)	(silent)
PP	80	95	100	100	90	95		20	15
P	70	80	96	100	80	90		20	20
1	30	55	89	60	60	60		15	20
2							90		
3							80		
4							50		
5									
6									
7									
8									

Levels
Independent _PP_
Instructional _P_
Frustration _1_
Listening capacity _3_

Strengths and weaknesses
Strong language development
Difficulty with high-frequency words and clusters

Interpreting the Inventory   After determining the student's levels, examine her or his performance on the inventory to determine word-recognition and comprehension strengths and weaknesses. What kinds of phonics skills can the student use? Is the student able to decode multisyllabic words? Could the student read words that have prefixes or suffixes? Did the student use context? Did the student integrate the use of decoding skills with context? How did the student's word recognition compare with her or his comprehension? How did the student handle literal and inferential questions? How did comprehension on oral passages compare with comprehension on silent passages? You can also note the quality of the student's responses as she or he answered questions and the way the student approached the tasks. What level of language did the student use to answer questions? What was the student's level of confidence and effort as she or he undertook each task? Through careful observation, you can gain insight into the student's reading processes. For example, you may observe the student decoding unfamiliar words sound by sound or using a combination of context and phonics to handle difficult words. Strengths and weaknesses as well as immediate needs can be noted on the IRI summary sheet.

Probing Comprehension Problems   Most students have difficulty comprehending because there are too many words in a selection that they don't know. However, occasionally there are students who are good decoders but poor comprehenders (see the Case Study). They sail through the word lists and read the oral passages flawlessly and with good expression. But they have difficulty answering the comprehension questions. To assess comprehension difficulties, probe responses so that you can gain some insight into the causes, which often have to do with the students' thinking processes. Some possible causes of poor comprehension are listed below, along with questions that might be asked to determine causes of difficulties (Dewitz & Dewitz, 2003).

- *Inadequate background knowledge.*   Ask questions about items that you believe the students might not know: "What can you tell me about planets? What is an asteroid? Have you ever seen a telescope?"
- *Difficulty with vocabulary.*   Go back to the passage, point to a key word that you believe may be unfamiliar to the student, and ask, "What does this word mean?"
- *Difficulty with syntax.*   Go back to the target sentence, and ask questions about it.
- *Overuse of background knowledge.*   Ask, "What makes you think that the sun is closer to Earth in the summertime? How did you know that? Is that in the article?"
- *Failure to recall or comprehend directly stated information.*   Ask, "Can you find the answer to that in the article?"
- *Failure to link ideas in a passage.*   Ask, "What happened because it rained? What else could have made Lee sad? Who else caused the team to lose?"
- *Failure to make inferences.*   Ask, "Why do you think the family decided to head west? What do you think the long, dry summer will cause to happen?"

Miscue Analysis of IRIS   Students use three cueing systems to decode printed words: syntactic, semantic, and phonic (graphophonic). In other words, they use their sense of how language sounds (syntax), the meaning of the sentence or passage (semantics), and phonics to read. To determine how they are using these systems, analyze their word-recognition errors, or miscues, with a modified **miscue analysis**. On a sheet similar to the one in Figure 3.4, list a student's miscues. Try to list at least ten miscues, but do not analyze any that are at or beyond the frustration level. Miscues can be chosen from the independent and instructional levels and from the buffer zone between the instructional and frustration levels (91 to 94 percent word recognition). Also list the correct version of each error. Put a check in the syntactic column if the miscue is syntactically correct—that is, if it is the same part of speech as the

Building Language

When students are responding orally to IRI questions, note the level and quality of their language and use your observations to plan a program of language development. ■

Adapting Instruction for English Language Learners

ELLs may have particular difficulty with both vocabulary and syntax. Note difficulties and plan instruction, with the ESL teacher if possible, to help them overcome these difficulties. ■

FYI

Through analysis and probing, you can discover ways in which to foster students' thinking. ■

■ **Miscue analysis** is the process of analyzing miscues in order to determine which cueing systems or combination of cueing systems the student is using: semantic, syntactic, and/or phonic (graphophonic).

Case Study

Good Decoding, Poor Comprehending

Although he has excellent decoding skills and reads orally with fluency and expression, Mark has problems understanding what he reads. He also has difficulty answering questions about selections that have been read to him. On a reading inventory known as the QRI-3, Mark was able to read the sixth-grade word list with no difficulty. He was also able to read the words on the sixth-grade oral passage with no errors. However, his comprehension was below 50 percent on the sixth-grade passage and also on the fourth- and fifth-grade passages. Puzzled by Mark's performance, the reading consultant analyzed Mark's responses (Dewitz & Dewitz, 2003). The consultant wanted to get some insight into Mark's thinking processes. The correct responses didn't reveal much about Mark's thinking. They simply restated what was in the text. When erroneous responses were analyzed, patterns appeared. Mark could answer questions that required comprehending only a single sentence. However,

he had difficulty with questions that required linking ideas across sentences or passages. Putting ideas together posed problems for him. Mark could pick up information from one segment but couldn't integrate that with information from another segment.

Mark also overrelied on background knowledge. He made up answers. This happened when he was unable to recall a fact or put pieces of information together. Mark also had some minor difficulty with complex syntactical structures and vocabulary.

Based on an analysis of Mark's responses, the consultant created a program for Mark and other students who had similar difficulties. After instruction, Mark was able to comprehend sixth-grade material. He was no longer overrelying on background knowledge, and he was connecting and integrating ideas.

 FYI

Generally, IRIs are given at the beginning of the school year to obtain placement information, when a new student enters the class, or whenever a student's placement is in doubt. They may also be given as pretests and posttests and are often more sensitive indicators of progress than norm-referenced tests. ■

word in the text or could be used in that context. Put a check in the semantic column if the miscue makes sense in the sentence. In the graphic column, use a check to show whether the miscue is graphically and/or phonically similar to the text word. It is similar if it contains at least half the sounds in the text word. Also use a check to show whether the beginning, middle, and end of the miscue are similar to the text word. Put a check in the nonword column if the miscue is not a real word. Also indicate corrected miscues with a check in the self-correction column.

Tally each column (as shown in Figure 3.4), and convert tallies to percentages. After tallying the columns, examine the numbers to see whether the student is reading for meaning. Miscues that make sense in the context of the selection, self-corrections, and absence of nonwords are positive signs. They show that the student is reading for meaning. Conversely, the presence of nonwords is a negative sign, as are miscues that do not fit the sense of the passage or the syntax.

Also compare the tallies to see whether the cueing systems are being used in a balanced fashion or whether one is being overused or underused. The student could be overusing phonics and underusing semantic context, or vice versa. Draw tentative conclusions about the strategies that the student uses in his or her word recognition. Double-check those conclusions as you observe the student read in the classroom.

As you can see from Figure 3.4, fewer than half of this student's miscues fit the context either syntactically or semantically. Moreover, three of them

An informal inventory or running record yields a wealth of information.

FIGURE 3.4 Miscue Analysis

Name: _____ Date: _____

Miscue	Text	Syntactic similarity	Semantic similarity	Graphic similarity	Beginning	Middle	End	Nonword	Self-correction
gots	gets	✓	✓	✓	✓	—	✓		
will	with	—	—	✓	✓	✓	—		
ran ✓	runs	✓	✓	✓	✓	—	✓		✓
balt	ball	—	—	✓	✓	✓	—	✓	
tricks	kicks	✓	—	✓	—	✓	✓		
my	me	—	✓	✓	✓		—		
trick	trust	✓	—	—	✓	—	—		
bell	ball	✓	—	✓	✓	—	✓		
frain	five	—	—	—	✓	—	—	✓	
grain	gray	—	—	✓	✓	✓			
there	that	—	—	—	✓	—	—		
eak	each	—	—	✓	✓		—	✓	
Totals		5	3	9	11	4	4	3	1
Numbers of miscues analyzed		12	12	12				12	12
Percentage		42	25	75				25	8

are nonwords, and the student had only one self-correction. All indications are that the student is failing to use context clues and is not reading for meaning. The student makes heavy use of phonics, especially at the beginning of words, but must better integrate the use of phonics with syntactic and semantic cues. The student also needs to improve the use of phonics skills with middle and ending elements.

IRIs require training and practice to administer and interpret. In the past, they were generally administered by the school's reading specialist. However, increasingly, classroom teachers are administering IRIs. To make the best possible use of time, classroom teachers might use a streamlined version of an IRI in which they give the full word-list test but administer only the oral passages of the inventory, without the listening portion. It will also save time if the inventory contains brief passages. Giving a shortened inventory reduces its reliability, so results should be regarded as tentative and should be verified by observation of the student's performance when reading books at the estimated instructional level.

Even if you, as a classroom teacher, never formally administer an IRI, it is still essential that you be familiar with the concept. Knowing the IRI standards for instructional and other levels, you have a basis for evaluating your students' reading performance. If students have difficulty orally reading more than five words out of a hundred, or if their oral and written comprehension seem closer to 50 percent than 75 percent, you may have to check the material they are reading to see whether it is too difficult. On the other hand, if both word recognition and comprehension in everyday reading tasks are close to perfect, you may want to try more challenging materials.

FYI

• To simplify the administration of running records, use IRI marking symbols, and record miscues on photocopies of the selection.

• Running records provide indirect evidence of comprehension. "Observation of how a child reads a text—including phrasing, expression, and use of a variety of clues, checking to be sure all sources of information fit to determine when attempts don't make sense—provide evidence of comprehension" (Fountas, 1999, p. 11). ■

As children struggle with difficult words, you may also want to conduct a mental miscue analysis. By closely observing miscues, you can sense whether students might need added instruction in using context or phonics or in integrating the two.

Selecting an IRI   Although they share a common purpose, IRIs vary in length, types of passages included, ways in which comprehension is assessed, presence of supplementary assessments, and technical adequacy. In selecting an IRI, match the inventory with your needs. The Basic Inventory (Johns, 2008) or QRI-5 might be a good choice if you are assessing young children, since they have passages geared to materials being used at the easiest levels. Because none of its passages is more than 100 words long, the Basic Inventory can be administered fairly rapidly. For in-depth analysis of comprehension at higher levels, the QRI-5 might be a good choice since it includes lengthy content area passages and think-alouds. If you are working with Spanish-speaking students, you might want to consider the Comprehensive Reading Inventory, which contains assessments in Spanish. For a comparison of IRIs, see Nilsson (2008).

Running Records

Similar to the IRI and based on K. S. Goodman's (1974) theory of analyzing students' miscues to determine what strategies they are using to decode words, the **running record** has become a popular device for assessing students' progress. Like the IRI, the running record is administered individually. However, only an oral-reading sample is obtained. The running record has two major purposes: to determine whether students' reading materials are on the proper level and to obtain information about the word-recognition processes students are using. To get a fuller assessment of comprehension, some teachers supplement the administration of a running record by having students retell the selection. Teachers often take running records during guided reading, while other students are reading silently.

Although running records may be obtained from older readers, they are most often used to assess the performance of novice readers and are administered daily to Reading Recovery students. As used in Reading Recovery and recommended in *An Observation Survey of Early Literacy Achievement*, 2nd edition (Clay, 2005), running records are administered according to a standardized format in which students' errors and corrections are recorded on a separate sheet. As adapted for use by classroom teachers, running records may be recorded (as long as the fair-use provision of the copyright laws is adhered to or permission is obtained from the publisher) on a photocopy of the text that the student is using (Learning Media, 1991). To assess whether materials are on a suitable level of difficulty and to determine how well the child makes use of previously presented strategies, take a running record on a text that the student has recently read. To assess the student's ability to handle challenging materials and apply strategies independently, take a running record on material that the student has not previously read. If the book or article is very brief, take a running record of the whole piece. If the text is lengthy, select a sample of 100 to 200 words. As the student reads orally, record his or her performance with symbols such as those presented in Table 3.6. However, you may use the IRI symbols if you are more familiar with them. After taking a running record, record the number of words in the selection, number of errors made, error rate, number of self-corrections made, and the accuracy rate.

Clay (1993a) accepts 90 percent as an adequate accuracy rate; however, 95 percent seems more realistic. Word recognition is emphasized in a running record, so comprehension is

Quizzes and unit tests can be used as part of formative assessment.

■ The **running record is** an assessment device in which a student's oral reading errors are noted and classified in order to determine whether the material is on the appropriate level of difficulty and to see which reading strategies the student is using.

TABLE 3.6   Running Record Symbols

Symbol	Text	Example
Words read correctly are marked with a check.	Janice kicked the ball.	✓ ✓ ✓ ✓
Substitutions are written above the line.	A barn owl hooted.	✓ *big* ✓ ✓ *barn*
Self-corrections are marked *SC*.	A barn owl hooted.	✓ *big\Sc* ✓ ✓ *barn*
A dash is used to indicate no response.	I saw her yesterday.	✓ ✓ ✓ — *yesterday*
A dash is used to indicate the insertion of a word. The dash is placed beneath the inserted word.	We saw a big dog.	✓ ✓ ✓ ✓ *bad* ✓
A *T* is used to indicate that a child has been told a word.	Her cat ran away yesterday.	✓ ✓ ✓ ✓ *T* *yesterday*
The letter *A* indicates that the child has asked for help.	A large moose appeared.	✓✓✓ *A* *appeared*
At times, the student becomes so confused by a misreading that it is suggested that she or he "try that again" (coded *TTA*). Brackets are put around the section that has been misread, the whole misreading is counted as one error, and the student reads it again for a new score.	The deer leaped over the fence.	[✓ ✓ *landed* ✓ ✓ *field*] *TTA* *leaped* *fence*
A repetition is indicated with an *R*. Although not counted as errors, repetitions are often part of an attempt to puzzle out a difficult item. The point to which the student returns in the repetition is indicated with an arrow.	The deer leaped over the fence.	✓ ✓ *landed\Sc* ✓ ✓ *field\Sc* *R* *leaped* *fence*

not directly checked. However, you may ask the child to retell the story if you wish to obtain information about comprehension.

It is essential that you analyze a student's miscues in order to determine what strategies she or he is using. As you examine the student's miscues, ask the following questions:

- Is the student reading for meaning? Do the student's miscues make sense?
- Is the student self-correcting miscues, especially those that do not fit the meaning of the sentence? Is the student using meaning cues?
- Is the student using visual or sound-symbol cues (phonics)? Are the student's miscues similar in appearance and sound to the target word?
- Is the student using picture cues?
- Is the student integrating cues? Is the student balancing the use of meaning and sound-symbol cues?
- Based on the student's performance, what strategies does she or he need to work on?

For younger readers in the very early stages, note whether they read from left to right or top to bottom and whether there is a voice-print match (the word the child says matches the one she or he is looking at). For detailed information on analyzing and interpreting running records, see Clay (1993a, 2000, 2005) or Johnston (2000).

Commercial Running Records   The Developmental Reading Assessment (DRA, 2nd edition) functions as an informal reading inventory or running record for students in grades K–3. It also assesses fluency and decoding skills. At its upper levels, students respond in writing to comprehension questions. DRA2 (2nd edition) is designed for grades 4–8. At the upper levels, note taking is assessed. The Fountas and Pinnell Benchmark Assessment System 1 (2nd edition), which is designed for grades K–2, has a format similar to that of DRA2. A word-list test is used to estimate students' reading level, and they read from a series of increasingly difficult booklets until their levels are established. Booklets are leveled according to the Fountas-Pinnell guided reading system. Accuracy, rate, fluency, and comprehension are assessed. A feature called Comprehension Conversation provides information about a reader's thinking. The Fountas and Pinnell Benchmark Assessment System 2 (2nd edition) is designed for grades 3–8. As an option, written responses to reading and note taking are assessed.

Group Inventories

Because of the time involved, it may be impractical to administer individual IRIs. However, you may choose to administer a group reading inventory. QRI-5 incorporates provisions for group administration at levels 3 and above. Students read a passage that is at their grade level. Those who have 70 to 75 percent comprehension or higher are tested with the next higher-level passage. Those who fail to meet the criteria are tested with passages at lower levels until they meet the criteria or they may be assessed with an individual administration of an IRI. Information about constructing and administering group reading inventories can be found in *Informal Reading Inventories* (2nd edition) by Johnson, Kress, and Pikulski (1987). Some reading series contain group reading inventories. There are also three tests that function as group inventories: Degrees of Reading Power, the Scholastic Reading Inventory, and STAR.

Degrees of Reading Power (DRP)   Composed of a series of passages that gradually increase in difficulty, Degrees of Reading Power (DRP) assesses overall reading ability by having students choose from among five options the one that best completes a portion of the passage from which words have been omitted (modified cloze). Each passage has nine deletions.

As in a traditional IRI, the passages gradually increase in difficulty and encompass a wide range of difficulty so that slow, average, and superior readers' ability may be appropriately assessed. Instead of yielding a grade-level score, the assessment provides a DRP score, which indicates what level of material the student should be able to read. A complementary readability formula is used to indicate the difficulty level of books in DRP units. Approximate grade equivalents of DRP units are presented in Table 3.7. The main purpose of DRP is to match students with books that are on their levels.

The Scholastic Reading Inventory   The Scholastic Reading Inventory, which also uses a modified cloze procedure and can be administered and scored manually or by

TABLE 3.7   Comparison of Readability Levels

Grade Equivalent	DRP	Lexile	Guided Reading	DRA	Reading Recovery
Emergent/Picture			A	A, 1	1–2
Frame/Caption (Early PP)			B	2	3
High Frequency PP–1			C	3	4
Pre-primer 2			D	4	5–6
Pre-primer 3			E	6, 8	7–8
Primer		200–300	F	10	9–10
First Reader		300–400	G–I	12, 16	11–17
Grade 2a	24–28	400–500	J–K	18, 20	18–20
Grade 2b	29–33	400–500	L–M	24, 28	
Grade 3	34–42	500–700	N–P	30, 34, 38	
Grade 4	43–49	700–800	Q–S	40	
Grade 5	50–55	800–900	T–V	50	
Grade 6	56–59	900–1000	W–X	60	
Grade 7	60–63	1000–1100	Y	70	
Grade 8	64–66	1000–1100	Z	80	

computer, yields lexile scores. Lexile scores range from about 70 to 1700+. A score of 70 to 200 indicates a reading level of about mid-first grade. A score of 1700 represents the level at which difficult scientific journals are written. Approximate grade equivalents of lexile scores are presented in Table 3.7.

Star   STAR (Advantage Learning Systems), which is administered and scored by computer and so doesn't require valuable teacher time, has a branching component: If students give correct answers, they are given higher-level passages, but if they respond incorrectly, they are given lower-level passages. STAR uses a modified cloze procedure and also assesses vocabulary. Students need a reading vocabulary of one hundred words in order to be able to take STAR. Testing time is 10 minutes or less.

Word-List Tests

To save time, teachers sometimes administer word-list tests instead of IRIs. Because they require only the ability to pronounce words, these tests neglect comprehension and may yield misleading levels for students who are superior decoders but poor comprehenders, or vice versa. One of the most popular word-list tests is the Slosson Oral Reading Test (SORT). SORT presents twenty words at each grade level from pre-primer through grade 12. The student is only required to pronounce the words and does not have to know their meanings.

Screening, Benchmark, and Progress-Monitoring Assessments

Screening measures range from those that assess alphabet knowledge and beginning sounds to those that assess comprehension. Younger readers need assessments that tap into phonological awareness, basic phonics skills, or ability to read high-frequency words. Older students need assessments that tap into comprehension or fluency or both. Screening tests are designed to identify students who are at risk or who are falling behind. Screening assessments are also frequently used to monitor progress and provide an overview of the effectiveness of instruction. If whole groups of students are not making expected progress, this is an indicator that the program might need to be adjusted. If some classes are not doing as well as others, this could be a sign that the teachers in those classes need assistance.

The screening tests that you select should assess the key skills that students need to be successful. In first grade, this might be phonics. In third grade, this might be word recognition, fluency, and/or comprehension. The most useful reading instruments are those that assess actual reading. An oral reading test can be used to assess word recognition, level of reading, fluency, decoding skills, and comprehension. Often the screening instrument is also used for benchmarking. **Benchmark** assessments are measures of expected level of performance *and* are typically based on grade-level performance standards. A benchmark might state that students should be able to read a grade-level passage with 75 percent accuracy or read grade-level material at a rate of 100 words a minute.

Informal reading inventories and running records have been widely used to place and screen students and can be used to monitor progress. Informal reading inventories can be created for children's books. Representative books can be designated as being benchmark books; questions or retelling activities based on these books are then used to assess students' comprehension. Benchmark books can be used to place students and track their progress. In Reading Recovery and a number of other intervention systems, students read books that gradually increase in difficulty. Students' progress from level

■ **Screening measures** are designed to indicate possible difficulties or problems.

■ A **benchmark** is an expected level of performance on a task. Benchmarks have also been defined as scores that can be used to predict later success.

to level is monitored by charting their progress in reading the texts. Failure to move to a higher level is a sign that the students aren't making adequate progress. Many programs also set achievement levels or benchmarks; in a 16-level program, for example, it is expected that students will be at level 4 by November, in level 8 by mid-year, level 12 by spring, and level 16 by year's end.

Curriculum-Based Measures

Curriculum-based measures (CBMs) are frequently recommended for screening and progress monitoring. These measures are actually curriculum-independent and not tied to a particular curriculum or program. CBMs have been described as general outcome assessments. They measure overall indicators of proficiency rather than mastery of specific skills. Thus, the ability to read lists of words or passages orally and to complete maze (fill-in-the-blank) passages are indicators of overall achievement in reading. CBMs are **standardized** and are quick, easy-to-administer probes of students' overall proficiency. They are designed in such a way that multiple but equivalent versions can be created, allowing progress to be monitored frequently, in some cases as often as once a week (Hosp, Hosp, & Howell, 2007). CBMs are most effective when used to measure lower-level skills. They don't do a very good job of measuring comprehension. As Fletcher, Lyon, Fuchs, and Barnes (2006) comment, CBMs

> . . . are best developed for word recognition, reading fluency, math, and spelling. It is possible to assess comprehension with CBM measures using cloze or maze tests, but the format provides a limited assessment of reading comprehension, which in itself is difficult to assess because it reflects so many underlying processes. (p. 67)

Emergent and Early Reading CBMS   Emergent and early literacy are typically assessed by measuring students' ability to name letters of the alphabet, give the sounds represented by letters of the alphabet, identify the first sound of a spoken word, segment spoken words, read nonwords, and read high-frequency (sight) words as in the following assessments.

Letter Name Fluency   Students name as many letters as they can within 1 minute. By timing the naming of the letters, the automaticity of the students' responses is being assessed. Students are asked to point to the letter as they say its name.

First Sound Fluency (DIBELS Next)   The assessor says a word, and the student is asked to say the first sound for the word: "What sound does *man* begin with?"

Phoneme Segmentation Fluency (DIBELS)   Given a spoken word, students are asked to say all the sounds in the word. The tester pronounces the word *stop*, and the student is expected to say "/s/, /t/, /o/, /p/."

Letter Sound Fluency   Letter Sound Fluency (Fuchs & Fuchs, n.d.) assesses students' ability to provide the sounds typically represented by letters shown in isolation. The letters *q* and *x* are not included. Except when used in proper names, *q* always appears with *u*. The letter *x* represents a blend or cluster of sounds or, in a few words, the sound /z/. The consonant digraphs *ch* and *sh* are included. For vowel letters, students are only given credit for giving the short sound of the letter. Limiting students to 1 minute indicates their automaticity, or fluency, and also their speed of processing. In a tryout with 1,500 kindergarten students and 1,500 first-graders, Fuchs and Fuchs judged students to be at risk if they could correctly sound

Adapting Instruction for English Language Learners

For additional information about screening and monitoring ELL, see *RTI for English Language Learners: Appropriately Using Screening and Progress Monitoring Tools to Improve Instructional Outcomes* (Brown & Sanford, 2011). http://www.rti4success.org/pdf/rtiforells.pdf ■

FYI

• Curriculum-based measures are not tied to a particular curriculum or program. Thus, the results are said to be more generalizable. Tasks deemed to be of universal importance are included in these measures.
• Many CBMs provide unofficial norms by supplying tables that indicate students' performance at a range of percentile levels. However, the cut scores or benchmarks can be regarded as criterion-referenced scores. ■

FYI

Multiple copies of the Letter Sound Fluency and the Word Identification Fluency Test are available from Lynn Fuchs, Vanderbilt University, Peabody #328, 230 Appleton Place, Nashville, TN 37203-5721. ■

■ A **curriculum-based measure** (CBM) is a brief, standardized assessment of a general outcome in reading, math, or some other content area.
■ **Standardized** means that a standard format is followed: standard set of directions, standard test items, and standard testing conditions. *Standardized* is often confused with *norm-referenced*. Not all standardized tests provide comparisons with a normative group.

fewer than 12 letters at the end of kindergarten and fewer than 19 at the beginning of first grade.

The results included a number of **false positives** and **false negatives**, so students' progress on this measure should be monitored closely.

Nonsense Word Fluency   Reading nonsense words short-circuits the process of decoding words. When decoding words, students note whether the word they have decoded is a real word. If it is not a real word, then they are apt to try decoding again. When faced with reading nonsense words, many students try to make real words out of them (Moustafa, 1995). Reading nonsense words is a more difficult task than reading real words and so underestimates the reading ability of students (Cunningham et al., 1999; Walmsley, 1978–1979).

Word Reading Fluency   Students are given a list of from 50 to 100 high-frequency words and are asked to read as many as they can in 1 minute. Reading real words proved to be a more valid predictor of reading achievement than reading nonsense words (Fuchs, Fuchs, & Compton, 2004).

Fluency and Comprehension CBMs

Oral Reading Fluency   The most widely used CBM is oral reading fluency, which measures how many words a student can accurately read in 1 minute. Many tests of oral reading fluency only measure the rate of reading. Oral reading fluency should also include accuracy, expression, and comprehension (Valencia, Smith, Reece, Li, Wixson, & Newman, 2010). A rubric for assessing fluency of expression is presented in Table 3.8. Oral reading fluency is a general outcome measure and is a rough indicator of a student's proficiency with lower-level reading skills. It has been compared to a thermometer in that it is an indicator of general reading health. However, in one study, 15 percent of students who had good oral reading fluency had poor comprehension. These students also tended to have low vocabulary scores (Riedel, 2007). Measures of oral reading fluency need to be complemented with measures of comprehension.

Screening and monitoring first-graders' oral reading fluency with passages are somewhat problematic. Because they

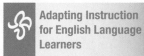

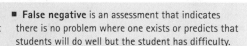

■ **False positive** is an assessment that indicates a problem where none exists or predicts that a student will have difficulty, but the student does well.

■ **False negative** is an assessment that indicates there is no problem where one exists or predicts that students will do well but the student has difficulty.

Fluency Level	Description
4	Reads primarily in larger, meaningful phrase groups. Although some regressions, repetitions, and deviations from text may be present, these do not appear to detract from the overall structure of the story. Preservation of the author's syntax is consistent. Some or most of the story is read with expressive interpretation. Reads with at least 98 percent accuracy.
3	Reads primarily in three- or four-word phrase groups. Some small groupings may be present. However, the majority of phrasing seems appropriate and preserves the syntax of the author. Little or no expressive interpretation is present. Reads with at least 95 percent accuracy.
2	Reads primarily in two-word phrases with some three- or four-word groupings. Some word-by-word reading may be present. Word groupings may seem awkward and unrelated to larger context of sentence or passage. Reads with at least 90 percent accuracy.
1	Reads primarily word-by-word. Occasional two-word or three-word phrases may occur—but these are infrequent and/or they do not preserve meaningful syntax. Accuracy is below 90 percent.

TABLE 3.8   Adapted National Assessment of Educational Progress (NAEP) Oral Reading Fluency Scale

Note: Levels 4 and 3 are adequate. Levels 1 and 2 are not. The scale has been adapted to include reading accuracy, which was not included in the original.

Source: U.S. Department of Education, Institute of Education Sciences, National Center for Education Statistics, National Assessment of Educational Progress (NAEP), 2002 Oral Reading Study.

are still in the beginning stages of learning to read, first-graders aren't given passages to read until the winter of first grade. However, at that point the skills of many first-graders might still be too limited. For instance, the winter first-grade passage of the widely used DIBELS assessment contains words with long vowels, *r* vowels, and other vowels. However, in the winter of the school year, many first-graders would not have been taught these more complex vowel patterns.

The winter test passage would be more appropriate for spring administration. The passage would be overwhelming for struggling readers. A better assessment would be a word-list test.

Maze Passages   In grade 3 and beyond, **maze passages** are preferred to oral reading passages because they provide a measure of basic comprehension, can be administered to groups, and take very little time. Maze passages are 150 to 400 words in length. Every seventh word is deleted but no words are deleted from the first or last sentences. Answer options include the word from the selection, an option that is not the same part of speech and does not make sense in the selection, and another option that may or may not be the right part of speech but doesn't fit the sense of the selection. The two distracters are usually chosen from other parts of the selection (see the sample maze passage in Figure 3.5). Students read for 2.5 or 3 minutes.

Because they are group tests, mazes provide a quick and efficient way to screen a whole class. Students who score poorly on the mazes might be given individual tests, such as an IRI or oral reading test.

One problem with maze passages is that they are not very sensitive to growth. On average, students' scores increase by only half a word per month. AIMSweb has maze passages for grades 1–8. DIBELS Daze has passages for grades 3-6, which can be downloaded free of charge.

Mazes can also function as a group reading inventory. Students who have low scores might be given a maze assessment on a lower level; those with higher scores might be assessed on higher levels in order to obtain approximate reading levels. Assess until an instructional level is obtained. The highest level at which a student achieves a score of 70 to 80 percent is the estimated instructional level. These approximate levels might then be verified by observing students' performance or by administering additional assessments, such as an IRI or oral reading test.

When used for benchmarking or screening, maze and other tests are typically given on grade level. The idea is to see if the student has reached the benchmark. When used

REFLECTION

Take a close look at the sample maze passage. What kind of information might it provide that could be used for planning instruction? What role might mazes play in an assessment program?

FIGURE 3.5 Sample Maze Passage: Kangaroos

Sample Maze Passage
Kangaroos

If you want to see one kind of kangaroo, you have to look up. One kind of kangaroo lives in (foods, trees, even). The tree kangaroo is small, but (it, that, from) has an extra-long tail. It (and, also, in) has long curved claws. The long (tail, fruit, move) and sharp claws help it to (climb, eat, to) trees. The tree kangaroo is a good (person, jumper, up). It can leap 30 feet from (good, one, is) tree branch to another or (even, faster, and) from one tree to another. It (look, can, small) also jump as much as 60 (claws, as, feet) to the ground. But on the (kind, another, ground) the tree kangaroo hops slowly. It (only, quickly, long) hops about as fast as a (person, bird, main) walks. Trees are good places for (see, which, the) tree kangaroo. They can move much (faster, smaller, it) in trees. Besides, their main food (is, want, also) tree leaves. But they also eat (branch, fruit, sharp) and sometimes will even eat small (places, birds, to). In addition, being in a tree helps (keep, jump, but) tree kangaroos safe from enemies.

Source: Gunning, T. (2011). *Success for All Readers: Using Formative Assessment Guide Instruction and Intervention.* San Francisco: Jossey-Bass.

for progress monitoring, tests are given on the students' reading level. The idea is to find out on what level the student is operating so that growth can be measured.

IRIs and Running Records.   Running records and informal reading inventories (IRIs) have been criticized for use as progress-monitoring devices because they focus on specific skills, whereas curriculum-based measures are indicators of overall reading proficiency. Actually, both inventories and oral reading fluency tests assess oral reading. Although some examiners skip this step, it is recommended that inventories be timed so that a rate of reading is obtained. In addition, through retelling and/or questioning, comprehension is assessed. Comprehension is the ultimate aim of reading, so IRIs and running records are better indicators of performance when retelling and/or questioning are included. IRIs and running records are time-consuming, but administration time can be reduced by assessing only oral reading and using brief passages. In addition, if students are tested several times a year, the examiner has a good idea of the level the student is on and so can arrange for the student to read passages on that level.

Using Technology

The University of Southern Maine Assessment Center has maze passages from books selected from the American Library Association's list of recommended books for students in grades 4–6. http://www.usm.maine.edu/cehd/assessment-center/CBM.htm ■

Setting Benchmarks

Many progress-monitoring measures have benchmarks, or expected levels of performance. Some benchmarks have been set because they are desired levels of performance. Others have been set by noting the relationship between students' performance on a benchmark and later performance on an outcome measure. For instance, according to the DIBELS, the benchmark for oral reading rate at the beginning of third grade is 70 words per minute (wpm). Students reading below that level scored below the 40th percentile on the GRADE, a standardized and norm-referenced reading test (Dynamic Measurement Group, 2010). Beginning third-graders reading below 70 wpm would be candidates for additional assessment or intervention. The benchmarks are less than perfect predictors, but they do provide helpful indicators. They need to be complemented with professional judgment and additional assessments.

Table 3.9 shows rates of letter naming and phonological awareness. Table 3.10 presents oral and silent reading rates of students at various percentiles. Note the variation of

REFLECTION

Why is progress monitoring such an essential element? Which progress-monitoring assessments do you think would provide the best information and be efficient in terms of the time needed to administer them?

Grade	Fall	Winter	Spring
K			
Letter Name Fluency	(1) 2–8 (8+)	(1–14) 15–26 (27+)	(1–28) 29–39 (40+)
Initial Sound Fluency	(1–3) 4–7 (8)	(1–9) 10–24 (25+)	NT
Phoneme Segmentation Fluency	NT	(1–6) 7–17 (18+)	(1–9) 10–34 (35+)
Letter Sound Fluency	5 (0)	17	27 (12)
Nonsense Word Fluency	NT	(1–4) 5–12 (13)	(1–14) 15–24 (25+)
Grade 1			
Letter Name Fluency	(1–24) 25–36 (37)		
Phoneme Segmentation Fluency	(1–9) 10–34 (35+)	(1–9) 10–34 (35+)	(1–9) 10–34 (35+)
Letter Sound Fluency	28 (19)	33	47
Nonsense Word Fluency	(1–12) 13–23 (24+)	(1–29) 30–49 (50+)	(1–29) 30–49 (50+)
Word Reading Fluency	6–10	20–25	40–45

TABLE 3.9   Rates of Letter Naming and Phonological Awareness

Scores are based on number of correct responses in 1 minute. Except for Letter Sound Fluency, the range of scores in the middle of the column indicates some risk. The range (or score) in parentheses to the left of the middle indicates at risk. The score in parentheses to the right of the middle indicates low risk. For Letter Sound Fluency, the score without parentheses indicates an average score; the score in parentheses indicates at risk. Scores for Word Reading Fluency are estimates of average performance. Adapted from Fuchs & Fuchs (n.d.), Good & Kaminski (2003), and AIMSweb (2006, as cited in Hosp, Hosp, & Howell, 2007).

TABLE 3.10   Rates of Oral and Silent Reading

Grade	Fall	Winter	Spring	Silent Reading
1		12 (23) 47	28 (53) 82	
2	(25) 51 (79)	(42) 72 (100)	(61) 89 (117)	121
3	(44) 71 (99)	(62) 100 (120)	(78) 107 (137)	135
4	(68) 94 (119)	(87) 112 (139)	(98) 123 (152)	149
5	(85) 110 (139)	(99) 127 (156)	(109) 139 (168)	163
6	(98) 127 (153)	(111) 140 (167)	(122) 150 (177)	177
7	128 (101) 156	136 (109) 165	(123) 150 (177)	191
8	(106) 133 (161)	146 (115) 173	(124) 151 (177)	205

Scores are based on number of words read in 1 minute. The score in the middle of the Fall, Winter, and Spring columns shows oral reading rate at the 50th percentile. The score in parentheses to the left of the middle shows oral reading rate at the 25th percentile. The score in parentheses to the right of the middle shows oral reading rate at the 75th percentile. The scores for oral reading are drawn from Tindal, Hasbrouck, & Jones (2005). The scores for silent reading are drawn from Carver (1990).

reading rate at each grade level. The table can be used to set benchmarks for students and cut points for determining which students are at risk. **Cut points** might be set at the 25th percentile or lower. Table 3.11 shows replacement rates for maze passages. Table 3.12 shows average growth rates for students on a variety of CBMs. In grade 1, students gain about 1.5 words a week and are able to read 1 additional word on a 50-word phonics inventory. In oral fluency, they gain about 1 word per week in grades 2 and 3, but only .5 word a week in grades 7 and 8. Using the tables, you can estimate whether students are making average progress.

The number and nature of monitoring assessments depend on the needs of the students. In Florida, for instance, Broad Screen/Progress Monitoring assessments are administered to all students (Florida Center for Reading Research, 2010). Those judged to be at risk are administered Broad Diagnostic Inventory assessments. If there is still a need for additional information, assessments from the Targeted Diagnostic Inventory are administered. Students judged to be at risk are given ongoing progress-monitoring assessments: Letter Name Knowledge (K), Letter Sound Knowledge (K), Phonemic Awareness (K & 1), Word Building (K & 1); (assembling letters to make words), Oral Reading Fluency (1 & 2), and Word Lists.

A key issue in screening and monitoring is the use of Curriculum-Based Measures versus Mastery Measures. **Mastery measures** assess what is being taught and so can be used to plan instruction. However, they may lack technical adequacy and might measure acquisition of skill rather than growth. Benchmark and screening instruments are often composed of grade-level material. However, monitoring instruments should be provided that are on the student's reading level. Otherwise, they may not be sensitive to growth (Deno, Fuchs, Marston, & Shin, 2001).

Creating Your Own Monitoring System

Because of the overemphasis on speed of responding and a possible lack of correspondence between what current progress-monitoring systems assess and what you teach, you might choose to construct your own system. First, decide what your key objectives are. Determine what it is that students should know and be able to do at the end of the year. These objectives should, of course, include school and district standards but might also include additional goals that you have set for your students. Translate these standards into language that students can

> **FYI**
>
> More frequent monitoring helps you to note which students aren't making adequate progress and so to intervene earlier with more intensive instruction or different materials. DIBELS provides materials for benchmark monitoring, designed to be administered three times a year, and also materials for progress monitoring, which may be given more frequently. ■

■ **Cut points** are the scores that are used to classify performance on a test, such as passing or failing. A cut score of 70 means that anyone who scores below 70 does not meet the benchmark.

■ A **mastery measure** assesses specific content or skills that have been taught to see whether students have learned the skills or content adequately: getting 100 percent on a list of spelling words or 8 percent on a comprehension test.

TABLE 3.11 Rates of Completion for Mazes

Grade	Fall	Winter	Spring
1	(0) 2 (6)	(2) 5 (10)	(3) 7 (13)
2	(2) 4 (8)	(6) 10 (15)	(9) 13 (18)
3	(8) 12 (17)	(10) 15 (19)	(10) 15 (21)
4	(9) 13 (17)	(13) 18 (25)	(14) 19 (25)
5	(12) 17 (22)	(15) 21 (27)	(18) 24 (30)
6	(10) 15 (22)	(13) 20 (28)	(14) 19 (27)
7	(13) 17 (22)	(13) 18 (24)	(15) 21 (28)
8	(14) 18 (23)	(14) 17 (22)	(17) 21 (28)

The score in the middle of each column shows the completion rate at the 50th percentile. The score in parentheses to the left of the middle shows the completion rate at the 25th percentile. The score in parentheses to the right of the middle shows the completion rate at the 75th percentile. Adapted from AIMSweb.

TABLE 3.12 Average Growth Rates per Week on Various CBMs

Grade CBM	K	1	2	3	4	5	6	7	8
Letter Name Fluency	1								
Letter Sound Fluency	1	1.2							
Word Reading Fluency		1.5							
Phonics Inventory	1								
Oral Reading Fluency			1	1	.75	.75	.75	.5	.5
Mazes					.25	.25	.25	.25	.25

Adapted from Good & Kaminski (2003); Gunning (2008); Hosp, Hosp, & Howell (2007); Fuchs & Fuchs (undated).

understand so that they have a clear idea of what is expected of them. You might also list the steps needed to meet the standards. Then create or adapt measures that assess those objectives. For instance, for phonics, you might use the Letter Sound Fluency test if students are at an early level of learning phonics or the Phonics Inventory, explained in Chapter 5, if students are working with vowel patterns. For recognition of words in isolation, you might use the Word Reading Fluency test or word lists from an IRI. For reading rate, you could use the DIBELS oral fluency passages. For comprehension, you might use the maze passages from AIMSweb, DIBELS DAZE, IRI passages, or DIBELS Oral Reading Fluency passages with retellings or questions added.

The phonics and word-recognition tests can be administered rapidly since they only involve reading lists of words. The oral reading rate can also be assessed quickly since it entails reading a passage for just 1 minute. These measures could be given frequently. However, if given individually, comprehension passages are more time-consuming to administer. Because growth in comprehension is generally slower than growth in skills such as phonics and reading lists of words, comprehension tests might be given just three or four times a year. Other measures might be given monthly or even weekly.

Graph performances so that you can see whether students are on track. Mark where you believe students should be by the end of the year. Then mark where students are now. Draw an aimline from where students are to where it is expected they will be at year's end. The slope of the line gives you a sense of the rate of progress necessary for students to reach the end mark. Monitor students' progress at least three times a year and mark their progress. Monitor more frequently if students are struggling. If students fall below the aimline, provide added instruction and arrange for intervention, if necessary. If students are consistently scoring above the aimline, adjust the program

 Using Technology

Curriculum-Based Measurement Warehouse has a wealth of information on curriculum-based measurement.
http://www.interventioncentral.org/cbm_warehouse ∎

to make it more challenging. Monitoring progress is one of the most effective steps you can take to help all students reach their full literacy potential. Figure 3.6 shows a first-grader's progress on the Word Reading Fluency indicator. Note how the student's progress accelerated when he was provided intervention in November but was still below the aimline. The goal for the student was 40 words by the end of the year, which the student missed by 5 words. Summer sessions could help Roberto catch up.

Monitoring Progress and Assessing for Learning

Assessing for learning requires monitoring of progress. However, some CBMs don't do much more than provide a general indication of where students are. For instance, if a student has a low oral reading fluency, you need to determine why so that you can provide an effective intervention. If you analyze the student's miscues, you might find that the student is reading slowly because he or she is having difficulty with high-frequency words or with words containing complex vowels and so needs instruction in basic word recognition. Assessing for learning requires information that might not be provided by progress-monitoring assessments. Information from observations, discussions, work samples, and other sources is also required.

Norm-Referenced versus Criterion-Referenced Tests

Norm-Referenced Tests

Many traditional tests provide some sort of comparison. In a **norm-referenced test**, students are compared with a representative sample of others who are the same age or in the same grade. The scores indicate whether students did as well as the average, better than the average, or below the average. The norm group typically includes students from all sections of the country, from urban and nonurban areas, and from a variety of racial or ethnic and socioeconomic groups. The group is chosen to be representative of the nation's total school population. However, norm-referenced tests can result in unfair comparisons. Urban schools, for example, should only be compared with other urban schools.

Because norm-referenced tests yield comparative results that are generally used by school boards, school administrators, and the general public, they provide one source of information to assess the effectiveness of the school program. Classroom teachers can also make use of the data to complement information from quizzes, informal tests, and observations. Reading scores indicate an approximate level of achievement. If a measure of academic aptitude has been administered, results can be examined to see whether students are reading up to their expected or anticipated level of achievement. If they are not, the teacher can explore the problem.

The tests can also be used as a screening device. Very high-scoring students may be candidates for a gifted or enriched reading program. Low-scoring students may benefit from input from the reading or learning disabilities specialist, especially if there is a marked difference between capacity and performance. Subtest scores of individuals can also be analyzed for patterns of strengths and weaknesses. A high-vocabulary, low-comprehension score, for example, is often a sign that a student needs extra instruction in the use of comprehension strategies. A low-vocabulary, high-comprehension score might indicate the need for language development. Occasionally, norm-referenced tests yield surprises. Sometimes children, because of shyness or other factors, hide their talents. Norm-referenced tests occasionally spotlight a student whose abilities have gone unnoticed.

Some school districts have as a goal that all students will be reading on grade level according to the results of a norm-referenced test. This is the same thing as saying that everyone will be at least average. However, norm-referenced tests are created in such a way that half the students in

FYI

Norm-referenced tests are not a very good source of information in terms of planning classroom instruction. However, in most instances, the decision to give norm-referenced tests is made by the administration. Since the tests are being given anyway, teachers might as well make use of the information they provide. ■

FYI

• Norm-referenced tests provide information desired by school boards, policymakers, and the public. Ease and efficiency of administration and objectivity are key factors.
• To get a better sense of the assessment component of your program, try to experience the assessment instruments. Take the tests that students are required to take; write the stories or essays that they are required to compose for assessment. Imagine that you are one of your students as you take the tests. Getting a feel for the assessment will help you better understand the results. ■

■ **Norm-referenced tests** are those in which students' performance is compared with a norm group, which is a representative sampling of students.

FIGURE 3.6 Progress-Monitoring Chart

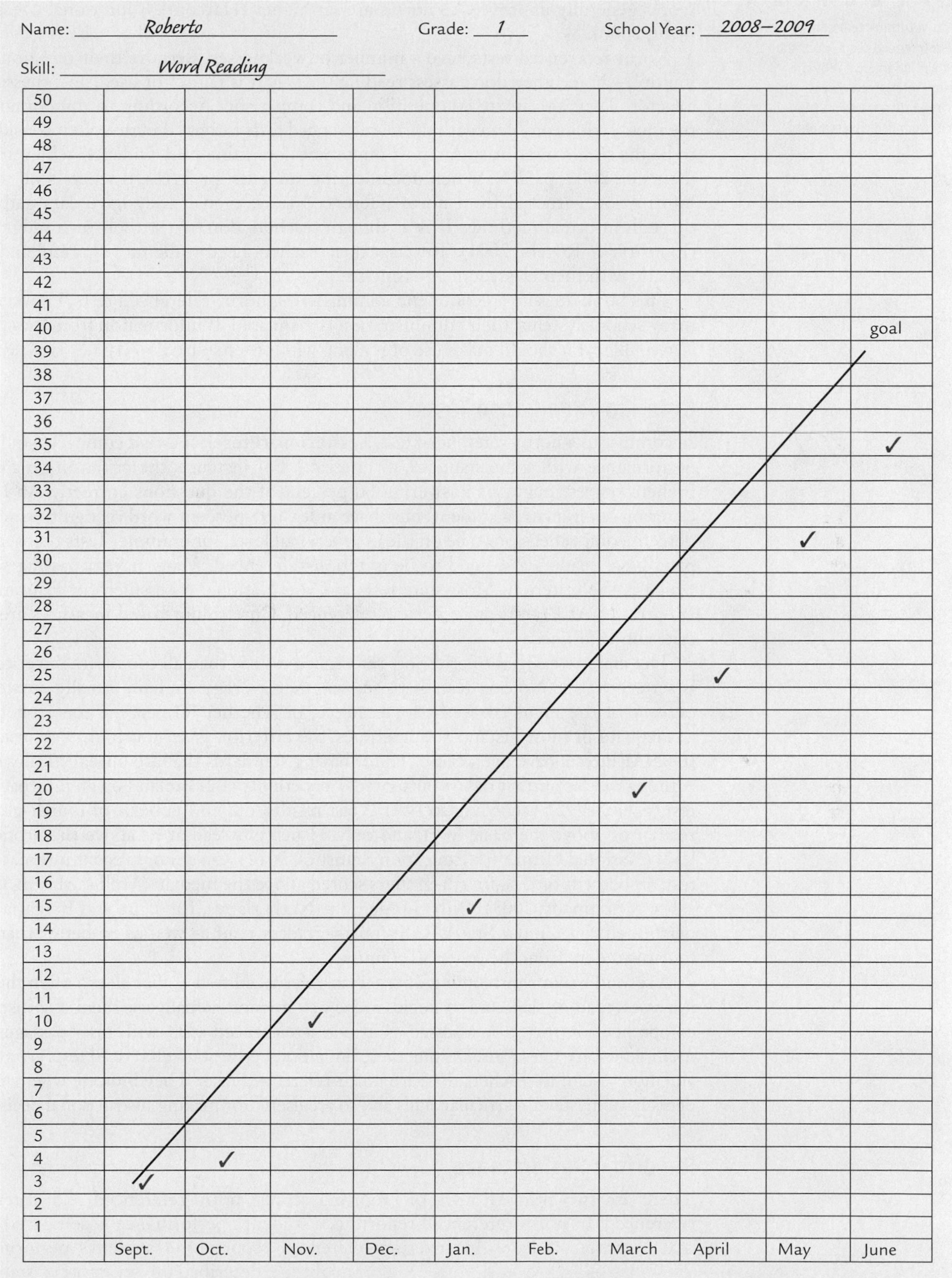

Name: _____Roberto_____   Grade: __1__   School Year: __2008–2009__

Skill: _____Word Reading_____

a typical group will score below average. Even if students' scores improve, this won't make the goal achievable. Test publishers periodically renorm their tests so that if scores generally improve, the norms are set higher (Harcourt Educational Measurement, 2000).

Norm-referenced tests have a number of weaknesses. Because their questions are multiple-choice, they don't assess reading the way it is taught or used, and guessing is a factor. They also invite competition and comparison. According to some theorists, the most serious problem with norm-referenced tests is that "they are often considered to be the single or at least the most important determinant of students' achievement" (Salinger, 2001, p. 394). When documenting students' progress, teachers tend to use information garnered from norm-referenced tests, even if they have data gathered through informal methods. It is as though teachers don't trust their own judgments (Johnston & Rogers, 2001). To offset this, teachers need to be more careful and systematic with their classroom assessments.

This book does not recommend administering norm-referenced tests. However, in many school systems, their administration is mandated. If information from these tests is available, you should make use of it along with other sources of data.

Criterion-Referenced Tests

In contrast to a norm-referenced test, a **criterion-referenced test** compares students' performance with some standard, or criterion. For instance, the criterion on a comprehension test might be answering 80 percent of the questions correctly. An IRI is criterion-referenced; a student must have at least 95 percent word recognition and 75 percent comprehension to be on the instructional level, for example. Tests that accompany basal readers also tend to be criterion-referenced. Many have a passing score, which is the criterion. Most state tests and the National Assessment of Educational Progress (NAEP) tests are criterion-referenced. Curriculum-based measures are also criterion-referenced.

The major weakness of criterion-referenced tests is that, all too often, the criterion is set arbitrarily. No one tests it to see whether average students usually answer 80 percent of the items correctly, for example, or whether 80 percent comprehension is adequate in most instances. Sometimes, the criterion is set too high. For instance, the NAEP tests have been criticized for having standards that are unrealistically high. Although U.S. fourth-graders outscored every country but Finland on an international test (Elley, 1992), according to NAEP test results, only 67 percent of fourth-graders read at or above the basic level, and only 33 percent read at or above the proficient level (National Center for Education Statistics, 2011). On a more recent international test, 68 percent of U.S. fourth-graders scored above the median (Mullis, Martin, Gonzalez, & Kennedy, 2003). Only Sweden, the Netherlands, England, and Bulgaria outperformed the United States. U.S. fourth-graders read as well as or better than the fourth-graders from the other 30 countries.

A second major shortcoming of criterion-referenced tests is that all too often they do not assess reading skills and strategies in the way students actually use them. For instance, comprehension might be assessed as in norm-referenced tests, with brief passages and multiple-choice questions. Despite these limitations, criterion-referenced tests are generally more useful to teachers than are norm-referenced tests. They indicate whether students have mastered particular skills and so are useful for making instructional decisions.

Reporting Performance

There are two primary ways of reporting scores: norm-referenced and criterion-referenced. In norm-referenced reporting, a student's performance is compared with that of other students. In criterion-referenced reporting, a student's performance might be described in terms of a standard or expected performance or in terms of the student's goals.

Norm-Referenced Reporting Tests and other assessment measures yield a number of possible scores. To interpret results correctly, it is important to know the significance of each score. Here are commonly used types of scores:

- A **raw score** represents the total number of correct answers. It has no meaning until it is changed into a percentile rank or other score.

- A **percentile rank** tells where a student's raw score falls on a scale of 1 to 99. A score at the first percentile means that the student did better than 1 percent of those who took the test. A score at the 50th percentile indicates that the student did better than half of those who took the test. A top score is the 99th percentile. Most norm-referenced test results are reported in percentiles; however, the ranks are not equal units and should not be added, subtracted, divided, or used for subtest comparison.

- The **grade-equivalent score** characterizes a student's performance as being equivalent to that of other students in a particular grade. A grade-equivalent score of 5.2 indicates that the student correctly answered the same number of items as the average fifth-grader in the second month of that grade. Note that the grade-equivalent score does not tell on what level the student is operating; that is, a score of 5.2 does not mean that a student is reading on a fifth-grade level. Grade-equivalent scores are more meaningful when the test students have taken is at the right level and when the score that the students achieve is not more than a year above or a year below the average for that grade. Because grade-equivalent scores are misleading and easily misunderstood, they should be used with great care or not at all.

- **Normal curve equivalents** (NCEs) rank scores on a scale of 1 through 99. The main difference between NCEs and percentile ranks is that NCEs represent equal units and so can be added and subtracted and used for comparing performance on subtests. NCEs can be used, for instance, to compare performance on vocabulary and comprehension subtests.

- **Stanine** is a combination of the words *standard* and *nine*. The stanines 4, 5, and 6 are average points, with 1, 2, and 3 being below average, and 7, 8, and 9 above average. Stanines are useful when making comparisons among the subtests of a norm-referenced test.

- **Scaled scores** are a continuous ranking of scores from the lowest levels of a series of norm-referenced tests—first grade, for example—through the highest levels—high school. They start at 000 and end at 999. They are useful for tracking long-term reading development through the grades. Lexiles, DRP units, and grade equivalents are examples of scaled scores.

Grade equivalents and other scaled scores rise over time. However, percentiles, stanines, and normal curve equivalents may stay the same from year to year. If they do, this means that the student is making average progress in comparison with others. For instance, if a student is at the 35th percentile in third grade and then tests again at the 35th percentile in fourth grade, that means that his or her relative standing is the same; the student continues to do better than 35 percent of the students who took the test. However, if the student moves to a higher percentile, this means that he or she outperformed students who started off with similar scores. If the student scores at the 40th percentile in fourth grade, it means that he or she is moving up in the relative standings. Now the student is doing better than 40 percent of those who took the test.

Criterion-Referenced Reporting Criterion-referenced results are reported in terms of a standard, or criterion. For example, the student answered 80 percent of the

FYI

Percentile ranks are not equal because test scores cluster in the middle so that scores in the middle of the range are closer together than are scores at the end of the range. It is easier to move from the 49th to the 59th percentile than it is to move from the 89th to the 99th. ■

FYI

Grade-equivalent scores, which have been opposed by the International Reading Association, are relatively valid when pupils are tested on their instructional level and when extrapolations are limited to a year or two beyond the target grade level. ■

FYI

- For additional information about tests, see the *Eighteenth Mental Measurements Yearbook*, (Spies, Carlson, & (Geisinger, 2010), or *Tests in Print VII* (Murphy, Spies, & Plake, 2006), which lists more than 4,000 tests. You might also consult the Buros Center for Testing, which specializes in test information: http://www.unl.edu/buros
  Another source of information is the ERIC site for assessment: http://ericae.net ■

- A **raw score** is the number of correct answers or points earned on a test.
- The **percentile rank** is the point on a scale of 1 to 99 that shows what percentage of students obtained an equal or lower score. A percentile rank of 75 means that 75 percent of those who took the test received an equal or lower score.

- A **grade-equivalent score** indicates the score that the average student at that grade level achieved.
- A **normal curve equivalent** is the ranking of a score on a scale of 1 through 99.
- A **stanine** is a point on a 9-point scale, with 5 being average.

- A **scaled score** is a continuous ranking from 000 to 999 of scores from a series of norm-referenced tests, from the lowest- to the highest-level test. The first-grade test might have the lowest scores; the twelfth-grade test would have the highest.

comprehension questions correctly. Two types of standards now being used in authentic assessment are the benchmark, which is discussed on pp. 77 and 81, and the rubric, which is a descriptive form of criterion-referenced reporting.

Rubrics   A **rubric** is a written description of what is expected from students in order for them to meet a certain level of performance. It is usually accompanied by samples of several levels of performance. For example, for assessing a piece of writing, the characteristics of four to six levels of performance might be listed. Although rubrics are typically used in the assessment of writing tasks, they can also be used to assess combined reading and writing tasks, portfolios, and creation of Web sites, presentations, and projects. A writing rubric is presented in Table 3.13. A rubric for oral reading fluency was presented in Table 3.8.

In addition to their use as scoring guides, rubrics can be powerful teaching tools (Popham, 2000). Carefully constructed rubrics describe the key tasks that students must complete or the main elements that must be included in order to produce an excellent piece of work. This helps both the teacher and

■ A **rubric** is a written description of the traits or characteristics of standards used to judge a process or product.

TABLE 3.13   Levels of Informational Writing in Primary Grades

	Expanding	Organizing	Elaborating	Expressing	Emerging
Content	Uses a variety of details and examples to develop a topic.	Expands on details by explaining how or why. May address a number of subtopics.	Begins to expand on details by explaining how or why.	Expresses several details related to topic.	Limited topic development. Topic might simply be stated and might be a label that identifies a person, place, or thing, but provides no information beyond a label.
Organization	Uses title, headings, connectives such as *and, also, for example, because,* and, *however* and sequencing to organize information. Has a beginning, middle, and end, but writing may be formulaic. Composes a conclusion that flows from the information provided.	Begins to organize details. Uses repetition of key ideas and connectives, such as *and* and *also* to show relationships among ideas. May use headings and subheadings. Provides a concluding sentence.	Information lacks overall organization. There are no headings or subheadings. Little or no use of connecting words or transitions.	Details follow a list-like structure and are not explained or elaborated upon.	Labels pictures with single words, phrases or sentences.
Writing/ Spelling	Spelling is accurate. May have one or two misspelled words.	Most words are spelled correctly.	Spelling is mostly conventional.	Uses invented and conventional spelling.	May draw, scribble, use random letters, or partial invented spelling.
Language	Uses technical vocabulary, more formal language, and may use some complex sentences.	Begins to use varied sentence patterns. Combines some ideas into compound sentences, but may string clauses together her with a series of *ands.*	Uses simple words and simple sentence patterns.	Uses simple words and brief sentences.	Uses simple words and brief phrases.
Mechanics	Few errors in mechanics. Makes some use of commas and quotation marks.	May have a few errors in capitalization and end punctuation. May use commas and quotation marks.	Increased use of capitalization and end punctuation.	Some use of capitalization and end punctuation.	Limited or lack of correct use of capitalization & punctuation.

Source: Adapted from Donovan, C.A., & Smolkin, L.B. (2011). Supporting informational writing in the elementary grades. *The Reading Teacher, 64,* 406–416. Georgia Department of Education (2000). *Developmental Stages/Scoring Guidelines for Writing.* Atlanta: Author. Resnick, L. B., & Hampton, S. (2009) *Reading and Writing Grade by Grade.* Newark, DE: International Reading Association & Washington, DC: National Center on Education and the Economy. Salahu-Din, D., Persky, H., and Miller, J. (2008). *The Nation's Report Card: Writing 2007*
(NCES 2008–468). National Center for Education Statistics, Institute of Education Sciences, U.S. Department of Education, Washington, D.C.

the student focus on key skills. To be effective, rubrics should contain only three to six evaluative criteria so that students and teachers do not get sidetracked by minor details. More important, each evaluative criterion must encompass a teachable skill. For instance, evaluative criteria for writing a story might call for an exciting plot, believable characters, an interesting setting, and the use of vivid language.

Creating a Rubric   To develop a rubric, first identify the key characteristics or traits of the performance or piece of work to be assessed. For example, for a rubric for a friendly letter, the key traits might include interesting content, chatty style, correct letter format, and correct mechanics. If available, examine finished products to see what their major traits are. Write a definition of each trait. What exactly is meant by "interesting content," "chatty style," "correct letter format," and "correct mechanics"? Develop a scale for the characteristics. It is usually easiest to start with the top performance. If you have examples of students' work, sort them into piles: best, worst, and middle. Look over the best pieces and decide what makes them the best. Look at the poorest and decide where they are deficient. Write a description of the best and poorest performances. Then fill in the middle levels. For the middle levels, divide the remaining papers into two or more piles from best to worst, depending on how many levels you wish to have. However, the more levels you create, the more difficult it becomes to discriminate between adjoining levels. You may find that four suffice. Evaluate your rubric, using the following checklist:

- Does the rubric measure the key traits in the student performance?
- Are differences in the levels clearly specified?
- Does the rubric clearly specify what students are required to do?
- Can the rubric be used as a learning guide by students?
- Can the rubric be used as an instructional guide by the teacher? (Chicago Public Schools, 2000)

Discuss the rubric with students, and invite feedback. Through helping with the creation of the rubric, students form a better idea of what is expected in the task being assessed and also feel more willing to use the rubric because they had a hand in its construction. When fourth-graders used cooperatively created rubrics to assess their writing (Boyle, 1996), their persuasive pieces showed a significant improvement.

Try out the rubric, revise it, and then use it. As you use the rubric with actual pieces of students' work, continue to revise it.

Teachers can align their rubrics with key state, local, or Common Core standards. To ease her students into using rubrics, Ferrell (Skillings & Ferrell, 2000) modeled the process. She also had students create rubrics for everyday activities such as picking the best restaurant. After students caught on to the idea of creating rubrics, she involved them in creating rubrics for basic writing tasks. To keep the rubrics simple, the class had just three levels: best, okay, not so good. Later, the class created rubrics for more complex tasks. Sample rubrics can be found at the following Web sites:

Discovery School Kathy Schrock's Guide for Educators lists sources for sample rubrics and information about rubrics.
http://school.discovery.com/schrockguide/assess.html

Rubistar has a library of rubrics and tools for creating rubrics.
http://rubistar.4teachers.org/

Rubrics for Constructed Responses   Along with rubrics for assessing stories and essays, create rubrics for assessing responses to open-ended questions of the type that your students will be asked to answer, if these are not already available (see Figure 3.7). These could be tests that you make up, tests from the reading program you are using, or state tests. Provide students with practice using the rubrics so that they understand what they are being asked to do. NAEP tests and some state tests supply rubrics and sample (or anchor) answers. Distribute sample answers and rubrics, and have students mark them. Begin with correct answers so that students have some guidance, and then have them assess answers that receive no credit or partial credit.

FYI

Students should participate in the creation of rubrics. Through helping with the creation of rubrics, students form a clearer idea of what is expected in their writing. In one study, students used a rubric they helped create to assess their own writing. They also took part in peer evaluation sessions in which the rubric was used to judge their writing. As a result of creating and using the rubric, students' writing of persuasive pieces showed a significant improvement (Boyle, 1996). ■

FIGURE 3.7   Sample
Scoring Rubric

Score	3	2	1	0
Criterion	Names an important lesson. Gives evidence from the story to support answers.	Names an important lesson. Fails to give evidence from the story to support answer.	Names an unimportant lesson.	Does not state a lesson that could be learned from the story. No response.

As a shared whole-group activity, compose responses to open-ended questions, and then assess the responses with a rubric. Once students have some sense of how to respond to open-ended questions, have them compose individual responses and check them.

Instructionally Supportive Assessment   Most high-stakes tests assess so many items that they fail to provide information that the teacher can use to plan instruction (Popham, 2004). What is more helpful is classroom assessment that tests a limited number of objectives—about six over the course of a year—and that can be used to plan instruction. To make assessment data instructionally useful, select or create a rubric that will help you and your students note the specific requirements for each objective.

Besides being used to support instruction, monitor students' progress, and identify students who need intervention, assessment data can be used in other essential ways. They can indicate what skills are needed and what skills have been mastered. At one urban public school where I worked as a literacy consultant, periodic assessment revealed the need for a strong program covering syllabic analysis, vocabulary instruction, and higher-level literacy skills—areas that were being neglected. However, it also revealed what didn't need to be taught. Most students had mastered phonological awareness and basic phonics, although teachers continued to teach these skills. The assessment data showed that instructional time could be more profitably spent in other areas.

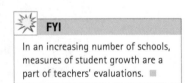

FYI

In an increasing number of schools, measures of student growth are a part of teachers' evaluations. ■

Measuring Growth

In the past, most states reported performance in terms of what percentage of students met the state's proficiency level. This is a threshold or status measures. Threshold testing might mask growth. Results tell what percentage of students have met a certain standard, but not how much students' scores have changed. For instance, students' scores might be increasing, bringing them closer to meeting the standard, but this is not indicated in the results. Unless growth is measured, schools that have large numbers of struggling students might be misjudged. Many urban schools have below-level achievement and might be classified as low-performing or in need of improvement. However, their students might be making better-than-average gains, but not enough to take them over the threshold. Measures of growth can be used to identify students who aren't making adequate progress and teachers whose classes are not making at least average progress.

Measuring growth also means that you need to make a comparison between where students were at the point of initial assessment and where they are at the end of assessment. You need to compare the same students at the beginning and end of the instructional period, not this year's students with last year's students, as most states do. The problem with this common comparison is that there might be significant differences between this year's students and last year's students.

A growth model fits in with the concept of meeting each student where he or she is and moving him or her upward. In addition to recognizing that there are certain key skills that are necessary for students to become college and career ready, such as being able to read and write effectively, it is also necessary to be aware of students' level of achievement. Additional efforts might be required so that all students, even those who are lagging behind, meet these standards (Tanner, 2010). Schools should be judged not just on the percentage of students who meet the standard, but on how much students improve.

Functional-Level Assessment

Measuring growth requires functional-level assessment. The typical elementary or middle school class will exhibit a wide range of reading ability. Just as students need appropriate levels of materials for instruction, they should have appropriate levels of materials for testing. Most literacy tests cover a limited range. For instance, a general reading test designed for fourth-graders will mostly have selections on a fourth-grade level, a selection or two on a third-grade level, and a few selections beyond the fourth-grade level. A fourth-grader reading on a second-grade level should not be given a fourth-grade reading test. It would be frustrating to the student and would yield misleading results. The student should take a test that includes material on her or his level of reading ability. This might mean giving the student a test designed for the third grade but that includes second-grade material. Similarly, a second-grade-level test would probably not be appropriate for a second-grader reading on a fifth-grade level. It would probably lack a high-enough ceiling and so would underestimate the student's true reading ability. With **functional-level testing**, students are tested at their functional level, which is not necessarily their grade level. Students reading significantly above or below grade level should be given out-of-level tests unless the tests they are taking cover a wide range of levels. As a rule of thumb, if a student answers more than 90 percent of the items on a test correctly, the student should be tested at a more difficult level (Touchstone Applied Science Associates, 2006). If a student answers less than 10 percent of the items correctly, she or he should be tested at an easier level. Giving students a test at the wrong level results in erroneous, invalid information. This is true whether a norm-referenced, criterion-referenced, or other type of assessment is being used. If teachers are being assessed on the basis of the progress that their students make, it is absolutely essential that accurate beginning and ending points be established. This requires functional-level assessment. For its assessments, Scholastic makes the following comments and suggestion:

> Traditional standardized grade-level reading tests are designed to measure grade-level standards. The scores' accuracy of these tests is not equal across all levels of ability. The further away from grade-level the student performs, the greater the degree of inaccuracy in the student's score. As a result, test scores of low- and high-ability students might not be accurate enough to be used instructionally or to monitor instructional growth from one year to the next. . . . In the case of Scholastic Reading Inventory (SRI), the accuracy of the test score can be substantially increased if the test is targeted by prior reading ability and grade level instead of by grade level only. (Scholastic Overview, n.d.)

To get a quick estimate of students' reading levels, you can use either your professional judgment or a test such as the GRADE Reading-Level Indicator and Spanish Companion (Pearson Assessments), a brief assessment designed to estimate the reading levels of students in grades 4 through 12. Although designed for students in grade 4 and above, the GRADE Locator Test has items on beginning reading levels as well as advanced reading levels. The test also has a Spanish component that provides an estimate of students' ability to read Spanish. Directions are provided in Spanish but

REFLECTION

How would you go about implementing functional-level testing? Why do you think most assessments incorporate a grade level rather than a functional-level approach? For which students would functional-level testing be especially effective?

■ **Functional-level testing** is the practice of assigning students to a test level on the basis of their reading ability rather than their grade level.

may also be pantomimed. Florida, Massachusetts, and Oregon have locator tests for ELL. The Oregon Department of Education (2008) comments, "Using the locator items improves both the test experience for each student and the precision of the assessment" (p. B1). As the Florida Department of Education (2008) advises,

Administration of the Reading and Writing test at the appropriate functional level is important because it:

- Provides reliable results for all ELLs.
- Avoids student frustration during testing since administering the most appropriate level of Reading and Writing ensures that each student is given only test items that reflect his or her skill level (p. 10).

These benefits should be available to all students. Florida, Oregon, and Massachusetts have valuable suggestions for function level testing, suggestions that could be adapted to most tests.

Universal Design of Assessments   The idea behind universal design of assessments is to design assessments to make them accessible to as many students as possible and "to ensure that each student has a comparable opportunity to demonstrate achievement on the standards being tested" (Abedi, Leon, Kao, Bayley, Ewers, Herman, & Mundhenk, 2010, p. 2). Steps can be taken to make tests more accessible without changing the difficulty level of the test passages. These include making directions more explicit, breaking lengthy passages into shorter portions, allowing students to choose from passages of equivalent difficulty (Thurlow, Laitusis, Dillon, Cook, Moen, Abedi, & O'Brien., 2009) and changing the format of the test such as using a larger font size and putting fewer words on a page (Abedi et al., 2010). For instance, in a math test the directions might be changed from "A certain reference file contains approximately . . ." to, "Mack's company sold . . ." (Abedi, 2009). The simplified version is easier to read and understand but does not change the skill being assessed (Wolf, Herman, Dietel, 2010). Although these steps have the potential to increase the accessibility of assessment, they do not adequately address the needs of students reading significantly below grade level. Although the questions might be more understandable and the format more reader friendly, the grade level test passage would still have a high proportion of words that below-level readers would be unable to decode and/or whose meanings would be unfamiliar. One solution, would be to include some below-level passages in the assessment so that students reading below grade level would have the opportunity to demonstrate their reading skill or to use functional level or adaptive testing.

Adaptive Tests

Adaptive tests are usually taken on a computer. Based on the student's responses, the computer adapts to the student's level. If a student is getting all the questions correct, the computer presents higher-level questions. If the student is getting all or most of the items wrong, the computer switches to lower-level questions. Currently, there are two widely used adaptive tests: Measures of Academic Progress (MAP) and STAR. MAP tests consist of sentences or brief paragraphs and have a multiple-choice format. They can be given in grades 2 through 10 and four times a year to monitor progress. MAP tests, which are used as Idaho's high-stakes tests, can also be used to indicate students' reading level. STAR uses multiple choice and modified cloze.

A key step in assessing students is deciding on the level of material that will be used. Screening or benchmark tests are typically administered on grade level. If possible, select screening instruments that have items that are below level as well as on level so that all students will be able to respond. Progress-monitoring assessments should be on the students' reading levels. Struggling readers, by definition, are typically reading below grade level. If text that is too difficult is used, the assessment will probably not do a very good job of measuring growth or the effectiveness of the intervention. "As selections of text are made, however, one must be aware that using grade-appropriate text is not a simple solution to the question. Such text is certain to be very difficult for students with learning disabilities and that text might not be particularly sensitive to growth and intervention effects" (Deno, Fuchs, Marston, & Shin, 2001, p. 520).

Other Methods of Assessment

Performance Assessment

Performance assessment is just what its name suggests. Instead of showing what they know by answering multiple-choice questions or writing a brief response, students demonstrate knowledge through their performance (Popham, 2000). Students, after consulting several sources on a controversial topic, might write a persuasive essay or letter to the editor or they might compose an informational booklet for younger students. As Darling-Hammond and Pecheone (2010) point out, performance assessments provide opportunities for students to demonstrate "the ability to plan an inquiry and organize their time, develop self-discipline and perseverance as well as intellectual discipline, define problems and determine strategies for how to pursue answers, organize and display data, evaluate findings, draw conclusions, and express and defend their ideas according to standards of evidence" (p. 32).

Performance tasks potentially assess knowledge and skills in a more realistic way at the application level. Students who will be assessed on a performance measure need to be more active learners and must be able to apply knowledge, not merely recite facts. Despite its obvious value, performance assessment does have some limitations. Performance assessment can be more expensive and more time-consuming. However, performance assessments are expected to become part of the Common Core State Standards assessment.

Retelling

Retelling has the potential to supply more information about a student's comprehension than simply asking questions does. In a **retelling**, a student is asked to do what the name suggests: The student may retell a selection that has been read to her or him or one that the student has read independently. The student may do this orally or in writing. In addition to showing what the reader comprehended, retelling shows what she or he added to and inferred from the text (Irwin & Mitchell, 1983). Free from the influence of probes or questions, retelling demonstrates the student's construction of text and provides insight into her or his language and thought processes. It shows how the student organizes and shapes a response. The teacher can also assess the quality of language used by the student in the retelling. However, since retelling requires remembering the whole text, it places greater demands on memory and also communication skills (Caldwell & Leslie, 2010). There may also be cultural variation. Different cultural groups might emphasize different elements of a story. A cultural group might, for instance, emphasize setting and omit the actions in a story. As Leslie and Caldwell (2011), explain "Students who encounter a story structure different from what is familiar to them may retell the story according to their cultural format" (p. 9).

In addition, students typically do better with narrative retellings than they do with expository retellings. On the QRI 5 average narrative retellings ranged from 17 to 41 percent whereas average retellings for expository text ranged from 13 to 31 percent. The low scores on retellings indicate that the average student's ability to retell a story is limited. Correlations between

■ **Retelling** is the process of summarizing or describing a story that one has read. The purpose of retelling is to assess comprehension.

FYI

• Being less time-consuming, informal retellings are more practical for the classroom teacher. Of course, shy children may not perform up to their ability.

• Because the person assessing them obviously knows the story, students might provide a contextualized retelling. They may not give the characters' names, referring to them as *he* or *she* because they assume that the examiner is familiar with the characters. Knowing that the examiner is familiar with the story, they might omit or abbreviate crucial details (Benson & Cummins, 2000). When using a retelling as an assessment, stress that the students should pretend that they are telling the story to someone who has not read it or heard it. ∎

Assessing for Learning

Students score higher on narrative (17 to 41 percent) passages than on expository passages (13 to 33 percent; Leslie & Calwell, 2011). ∎

FIGURE 3.8 Evaluation of an Oral Retelling

retellings and question answering was relatively low (Leslie & Caldwell, 2011). This suggests that if retellings are used to assess comprehension, they need to be accompanied by questions. Otherwise, students' comprehension ability might be greatly underestimated.

To administer a retelling, explain to the student what she or he is supposed to do: Read a selection orally or silently or listen to one read aloud. It may be a narrative or expository piece. Tell the student that she or he will be asked to retell the story in her or his own words. Use neutral phrasing, such as "Tell me about the story that you read." For a young child, say, "Pretend I haven't read the story. Tell it to me in your own words." A shy younger child can use props—such as a puppet—to facilitate the retelling. If a student stops before retelling the whole selection, encourage her or him to continue or elaborate. When the student is finished, ask questions about any key elements that were not included in the retelling.

Evaluating Retellings As the student retells the selection, record it and/or jot down brief notes on the major events or ideas in the order in which the child relates them. Note any recalls that were not spontaneous but were elicited by your questions. Tape recording provides a full and accurate rendition of the retelling but is time-consuming.

Retellings can be scored numerically by giving students credit for each major unit that they retell. However, this is a laborious process. Far less time-consuming, but still useful, is noting the major units in the retelling in one column, comments about it in a second column, and a summary and recommendations in a third. Because the main purpose of the retelling is to gain insight into students' reading processes, you should draw inferences about students' overall understanding of the selection and their ability to use strategies to construct the meaning of the piece. A sample evaluation of a retelling is presented in Figure 3.8.

Name of student: _Jamie S._

	Retelling	Comments	Summary and recommendations
Elves and the shoemaker	Shoemaker said had only one piece of leather left. Elves made shoes.	Drew inference. Started with story problem.	Good grasp of story.
	Man in hat came in. Woman came in. Many people bought shoes.	Told story in sequence.	Used structure of story to retell it.
	Shoemaker and wife waited up to see elves.		Didn't go beyond story to suggest why elves started or stopped helping.
	Elves had ragged clothes. Wife made new clothes.	Used picture to get information about elves. Misinterpreted passage.	
	Elves thought new clothes looked funny. Elves said would no longer be cobras. Never came back.	Missed <u>cobblers</u>.	Failed to use context to help with <u>cobblers</u>. Good average performance. Work on context and drawing conclusions.

Written Retellings Written retellings allow the teacher to assess the class as a group. Using holistic scoring, the teacher can also assess the quality of the responses. It is important to keep in mind that, whether oral or written, the mode of expression will affect the information students convey. Students may have good knowledge of a selection but find it difficult to express their ideas orally and/or in writing. To obtain a better picture of that knowledge, the teacher might have a class discussion after students have completed their written retellings and compare impressions garnered from the discussion with those from the written versions.

Structured Written Retellings In a structured written retelling, the teacher might ask students to read a whole selection and write answers to a series of broad questions. The questions are constructed to assess students' ability to understand major aspects of the text, such as characters, plot, and setting. The questions can also be framed to provide some insight into the strategies students are using. They are scored and analyzed by the teacher.

Think-Aloud Protocols

Think-alouds are used to show the thought processes students use as they attempt to construct meaning. During a think-aloud, the reader explains his or her thought processes while reading a text. These explanations might come after each sentence, at the end of each paragraph, or at the end of the whole selection. Students' thoughts might be expressed as "news bulletins or play-by-play accounts" of what students do mentally as they read (Brown & Lytle, 1988, p. 96).

Informal Think-Alouds Whereas formal think-aloud procedures might be too time-consuming, informal think-alouds can be incorporated into individual and small-group reading conferences and classroom activities. For example, the teacher might simply ask students to share their thoughts on a difficult passage or question, or to tell what strategies they used. Think-aloud questions can include the following:

- Tell me how you figured out that hard word.
- Tell me how you got the answer to that question.
- What were you thinking about when you read that selection?
- Pretend that you are an announcer at a sports game. Tell me play by play what was going on in your mind as you read that sentence (or paragraph) (Brown & Lytle, 1988).
- What do you think will happen next in the selection? What makes you think that?
- How did you feel when you read that passage? What thoughts or pictures were going through your mind?

Think-alouds may also be expressed in writing. In their learning logs, students can note the difficulties they encountered in hard passages and describe the processes they used to comprehend the selections. In follow-up class discussions, they can compare their thought processes and strategies with those of other students (Brown & Lytle, 1988). A simple way for students to keep track of perplexing passages is to record comprehension problems on sticky notes and place them next to the passages.

Mystery Passages

Mystery Passages can be administered as an individual or group think-aloud. Mystery Passages are brief informational selections that have been inverted so that the main idea or topic is not revealed until the last segment has been read. Students read the Mystery Passages in segments and after each segment make a prediction as to what the paragraph is about. A Mystery Passage should be

■ **Think-alouds** are procedures in which students are asked to describe the processes they are using as they engage in reading or another cognitive activity.

on the student's instructional level and should be about a familiar topic. Otherwise, the student will not have the background knowledge needed to make predictions. For example, if a student has no knowledge of polar bears, a polar bear passage would not be appropriate.

Administering a Mystery Passage as a Diagnostic Instrument

In preparation for reading a Mystery Passage, students are told that they will be reading an article in parts and that after each part is read, they are to try to guess what the mystery animal is. After each part is read, the student is asked: "What do you think the mystery animal is?" The student is then asked to explain the reasoning for his or her response: "What makes you think that?" After the student has completed reading all the separate segments, the student is asked to reread the passage and then retell the entire selection. The student's responses are analyzed in light of the following questions:

- How well was the reader able to hypothesize the identity of the animal?
- How well did the reader support her or his hypotheses with reasons, inferences, or predictions?
- At what point did the reader guess the identity of the animal?
- What information from the text did the reader use?
- Did the reader integrate information from the current passage with information from previously read passages? Were clues used in additive fashion?
- Were the reader's inferences and predictions logical?
- How did the reader use her or his background knowledge?
- How well was the reader able to identify key information in the passage?
- What strategies did the reader use?
- How did the reader handle unfamiliar words or puzzling portions of the text? (Wade, 1990; Gunning, 2010)

Note in particular how much background knowledge students have and how well they make use of it. Note also how well students integrate information from succeeding segments and how logical their reasoning processes are.

Mystery Passages can be administered individually. Students' responses are recorded and then analyzed. Mystery Passages can also be administered to a group. In a group administration, ask the students to record their responses. After students have completed recording their responses, discuss them. This gives students the opportunity to expand on their responses. Give students one clue segment at a time. Otherwise, they may read down the page and locate the identity of the mystery animal.

Mystery Animal

- It is a very large animal. When fully grown, it might weigh up to 1,500 pounds or even more.
  My prediction: _____
  Reason(s) for my prediction:

  _____

  _____

- It is a powerful swimmer. It can swim for 10 hours or more.
  My prediction: _____
  Reason(s) for my prediction:

  _____

  _____

- It is a fast swimmer. It can swim 6 miles in an hour's time.
  My prediction: _____
  Reason(s) for my prediction:

  _____

  _____

- It doesn't mind the cold. It swims in icy water and sometimes floats on large sheets of ice.
  My prediction: _____
  Reason(s) for my prediction:

  _____

  _____

- It has a built-in life jacket. It has two coats of hair. The inner coat is made of fine white hair and keeps it warm. The outer coat is made up of longer hairs. These hairs are hollow. The hollow hairs are like tiny life jackets or tubes.
  My prediction: _____
  Reason(s) for my prediction:

  _____

  _____

- The two coats of hair help keep the polar bear floating on top of the water.
  What were the main things that you learned about the mystery animal?

  _____

  _____

  _____

  _____

Analyzing Students' Performance on Mystery Passages   Students to whom the think-aloud Mystery Passage was administered fell into five main categories.

Good Comprehenders: Use information from text and background knowledge to generate and support their hypotheses. They are flexible and change their hypotheses when this is called for by new information in the text.

Non-Risk-Takers: Stick closely to the text and are reluctant to offer a hypothesis. They fail to make adequate use of background knowledge. Nearly one in five students was a non-risk-taker. Most were younger readers or struggling readers.

Nonintegrators: Fail to put together information from various segments of the text. They might pose a new hypothesis based on the current segment of text without regard to previously read segments.

Schema Imposers: Hold onto their first hypothesis. The information in succeeding passages is changed to fit the readers' schema. About one in 10 students is a schema imposer. Schema imposers might overrely on background knowledge because of the difficulty they have processing the text.

Storytellers: Rely heavily on background knowledge to create a plausible scenario that might have little to do with the text. As with schema imposers, they may have difficulty processing the text and find it easier to create their own meaning rather than to construct meaning from the text. About one student in 12 is a storyteller (Wade, 1990; Gunning, 2010).

 Using Technology

Handheld computers can be used to record observational and other assessment data and generate reports. ∎

FYI

• Teachers may resist keeping anecdotal records because they believe they will remember the important things that the student does. Memories are fallible. Teachers may remember only the good things or not so good things that a student does, and thus fail to obtain a balanced view. For additional suggestions for taking and using anecdotal records, see the article by Boyd-Batstone (2004) and extensive coverage provided by Tierney & Readence (2005). ■

Observation

Teachers learn about children "by watching how they learn" (Goodman, 1985, p. 9). As "kidwatchers," teachers are better able to supply the necessary support or ask the kinds of questions that help students build on their evolving knowledge.

Opportunities for Observations   Observations can be made any time students are involved in reading and writing. Some especially fruitful opportunities for observation include shared reading (What emergent literacy behaviors are students evidencing?), reading and writing conferences (What are the students' strengths and weaknesses in these areas? What is their level of development? How might their progress in these areas be characterized?), and sustained silent reading (Do students enjoy reading? Are they able to select appropriate materials? What kinds of materials do they like to read?). Other valuable observation opportunities include author's circle, literature circle, and sharing periods in general (Australian Ministry of Education, 1990).

Teachers using a program known as Bookshop (Mondo) structure their observations. First, the teachers list from one to three focus areas for a lesson. Then they note whether students in the reading group master the focus area(s) or require added instruction. Each student in the group is listed, as shown in Figure 3.9.

Anecdotal Records

An **anecdotal record** is a field note or description of a significant bit of student behavior. It is an observational technique long used by both anthropologists and teachers. Almost any observation that can shed light on a student's literacy endeavors is a suitable entry for an anecdotal record, including notes on strategies, miscues, interests, interactions with others, and work habits (Rhodes, 1990). The anecdotal record should be "recordings of what the child said or did—not interpretations" (Bush & Huebner, 1979, p. 355). Interpretation comes later and is based on several records and other sources of information. It is important to keep in mind that when recording observations of strategy use, the way in which strategies are used may vary according to the nature of

■ An **anecdotal record** is the recording of the description of a significant incident of student behavior; interpretation of the observation comes later.

FIGURE 3.9 Group Observation Sheet

Focuses	Alison	Matt	Stacey	Jesse	Emma
Uses headings to hypothesize main idea					
Locates supporting details					
Summarizes main idea and key details					

Key: S—satisfactory; N—needs additional instruction

Notes for future instruction: _____

_____

_____

the task—the type of story being read, its relative difficulty, and the purpose for reading it. Therefore, it would be helpful to record several observations before coming to a conclusion (Tierney and Readence, and Dishner, 2005). In going over anecdotal records, the teacher should ask what this information reveals about the student and how it can be used to plan her or his instructional program.

To keep track of observations and anecdotal records, you might keep a notebook that has a separate section for each student. Or you might use a handheld computer to record observations, which can then be downloaded into a database, classroom management system, or assessment management software, such as Learner Profile (Sunburst), which allows you to record and organize observations and other data in terms of standards or objectives. Sum up the anecdotal records periodically, and decide on the steps needed to assist each student (Boyd-Batstone, 2004). Observe five or six students a day. Have one sheet for each student.

By examining anecdotal records and other sources of information teachers can plan instruction that matches students' needs.

Ratings

A structured and efficient way to collect data is through the use of **ratings**. Ratings generally indicate the "degree to which the child possesses a given trait or skill" (Bush & Huebner, 1979, p. 353). The three kinds of ratings are checklists, questionnaires, and interviews.

Checklists   Checklists can use a present-absent scale (a student either has the trait or does not have it) or one that shows degrees of involvement. The present-absent scale might be used for traits for which there is no degree of possession, such as knowing one's home address and telephone number. The degree scale is appropriate for traits that vary in the extent to which they are manifested, such as joining in class discussions. Figure 3.10 shows a sample observation checklist designed to assess voluntary reading

FYI

The Metacognitive Awareness of Reading Strategies (MARS) (Mokhtari & Reichard, 2002) can be used to assess reading strategy awareness. The MARS or a similar instrument can also be used to build students' awareness of strategies (Klingner, Vaughn, & Boardman, 2007). ■

■ **Ratings** are an estimation of the degree to which a student possesses a given skill or trait.

FIGURE 3.10   Observation Checklist for Voluntary Reading

	Never	Seldom	Occasionally	Frequently
Name of student: _____ Date: _____				
Reads during free time	_____	_____	_____	_____
Visits the library	_____	_____	_____	_____
Reads books on a variety of topics	_____	_____	_____	_____
Recommends books to others in the class	_____	_____	_____	_____
Talks with others about books	_____	_____	_____	_____
Checks out books from the library	_____	_____	_____	_____

Exemplary Teaching

Ongoing Assessment

To make her instruction as fruitful as possible, Pat Loden, a first-grade teacher, bases it on ongoing assessment of students (Morrow & Asbury, 2001). Each day, she focuses on two students to assess. During the day, she carefully observes these students and records her observations. She keeps running records of their reading, assesses their story retellings, and notes their use of reading strategies. She also has a conference with them and goes over their reading logs. In their reading logs, they record titles and authors of books read and their reading goals for the week. During whole-class activities, Loden makes sure to direct questions to them and notes their responses. She also observes the two students as they work independently. She keeps a file on each student and uses the files when planning instruction, when making decisions about placing students in guided reading groups, and before holding conferences with students. Loden also keeps records of conferences she holds during writing workshop. During the conferences, she asks questions that help reveal students' thought processes as they write and the strategies they use. Emphasis throughout the assessment is on obtaining a deeper understanding of where students are and what processes and strategies they are using so that individual and group instructional activities can be planned to further foster their development.

Questionnaires

Questionnaires can provide information about reading interests, study habits, strategy use, and other areas in reading and writing. They can be forced-choice like ERAS or open-ended and requiring a written response. Questionnaires assessing study habits and skills might cover such topics as how students go about studying for a test, where they study, and how much time they spend doing homework each night.

A good example of a reading attitude questionnaire is the Elementary Reading Attitude Survey (ERAS; McKenna & Kerr, 1990). It includes twenty items designed to measure how students feel about recreational and school reading. ERAS can be read to younger, less-skilled readers; older, more-skilled students can read it themselves. The questionnaire addresses such areas as how children feel when they read a book on a rainy Saturday and how they feel about reading in school. Students respond by circling one of four illustrations of the cartoon cat Garfield, which range from very happy to very sad. Another questionnaire that might be used is the Reading Survey section of the Motivation to Read Profile (MRP), which can be found in the March 1996 issue of *The Reading Teacher*. The survey probes two aspects of reading motivation: self-concept as a reader and value of reading. For older students, administer the Adolescent Motivation to Reading Profile (Pitcher et al., 2007). The Adolescent MRP includes two parts. The first is a written questionnaire, which can be administered to groups. The second is a follow-up interview that is given individually. The questionnaire portion is designed to reveal students' attitudes about reading and common classroom literacy practices. The conversational interview probes the kinds of books the student likes to read, how reading material is chosen, and the kinds of literacy activities in which the student engages, and the kinds of activities that might motivate the student to read.

Interviews   **Interviews** are simply oral questionnaires. Their advantage is that the teacher can probe a student's replies, rephrase questions, and encourage extended answers, thereby obtaining a wide range of information. An interview can focus on such topics as a student's likes and dislikes about a reading

FYI

ERAS has not been copyrighted and was presented, ready to duplicate, in the May 1990 issue of *The Reading Teacher*. ■

■ A **questionnaire** is an instrument in which a subject is asked to respond to a series of questions on some topic.

■ An **interview** is the process of asking a subject a series of questions on a topic.

group, preferences with respect to reading materials, and reasons for these attitudes. A good example of an interview is the Conversational Interview section of the Motivation to Read Profile (Gambrell, Codling, & Palmer, 1996). The Conversational Interview, which complements the Reading Survey, consists of a series of questions about a student's reading interests and habits and possible influences on those habits.

One kind of interview, the process interview, provides insight about the strategies students are using and also helps students become aware of their processes (Jett-Simpson, 1990). The process interview is best conducted informally on a one-to-one basis, but if time is limited, you might ask for written responses to your questions or hold sessions with small groups. Possible process interview questions include the following ones, which are adapted from Jett-Simpson (1990). Only one or two of these questions should be asked at one sitting.

1. If a young child asked you how to read, what would you tell him or her to do?
2. When you come to a word you don't know, what do you do?
3. How do you choose something to read?
4. How do you get ready for reading?
5. Where do you read or study at home?
6. When a paragraph is confusing, what do you do?
7. How do you check your reading?
8. What do you do to help you remember what you've read?

Conferences

Like interviews, conferences can be an excellent source of assessment information. During writing conferences, you might ask such questions as these: "What do you like best about writing? What kind of writing do you like to do? What is easy for you when you are writing? What is hard for you? What are some things that you might do to become an even better writer than you are now? What do you like best about reading? Do you have any favorite authors? Who are they? What is easy for you in reading? What is hard for you? What might you do to become a better reader?"

Checklists, questionnaires, interviews, and conferences have a common weakness. Their usefulness depends on students' ability and willingness to supply accurate information. Students may give answers that they think the teacher wants to hear. Information gathered from these sources, therefore, should be verified with other data.

In this era of mandated high-stakes assessment, informal measures are more important than ever. High-stakes tests tend to narrow the curriculum and lead to teaching to the test. What's more, they generally fail to yield information that is useful to teachers. Using observation, think-alouds, samples of students' work, and other informal measures can broaden the curriculum and yield useful information for teachers.

Using Technology

The National Center for Research on Evaluation, Standards, and Student Testing provides information on assessment:
http://www.cse.ucla.edu
The National Center on Educational Outcomes provides information on assessing students who have disabilities:
http://education.umn.edu/nceo ∎

Basal Reader/Anthology Assessment Devices

Today's basal readers and literature anthologies offer a variety of assessment devices. One especially valuable assessment device is the theme-level test or unit test. These tests assess the strategies and skills taught in a theme or unit. Presenting open-ended as well as multiple-choice items, theme-level or unit tests provide an excellent opportunity to assess students' ability to cope with high-stakes tests. In a sense, there is a bit of a disconnection between daily and unit assessment. Students demonstrate a skill taught during a unit or theme primarily through discussion with the whole class or in small groups. However, the skill is assessed through open-ended questions. Students might do well when answering such questions orally, but have difficulty getting their thoughts down on paper. In discussion, you can provide prompts and ask additional questions to draw out students' responses. However, on written assessments, students are not given these aids. As with any other skill, students need to be taught how to deal with open-ended questions, especially if they have not previously been exposed to such questions.

FIGURE 3.11   Student's Self-Report Checklist on Strategies for Learning from Text

	Usually	Often	Sometimes	Never
Before reading, do I				
1. Read the title, introductory paragraph, headings, and summary?	_____	_____	_____	_____
2. Look at photos, maps, charts, and graphs?	_____	_____	_____	_____
3. Think about what I know about the topic?	_____	_____	_____	_____
4. Predict what the text will be about or make up questions that the text might answer?	_____	_____	_____	_____
During reading, do I				
5. Read to answer questions that the teacher or I have made up?	_____	_____	_____	_____
6. Stop after each section and try to answer my questions?	_____	_____	_____	_____
7. Use headings, maps, charts, and graphs to help me understand the text?	_____	_____	_____	_____
8. Try to make pictures in my mind as I read?	_____	_____	_____	_____
9. Reread a sentence or get help if I don't understand what I am reading?	_____	_____	_____	_____
10. Use context or the glossary if I don't understand what I am reading?	_____	_____	_____	_____
After reading, do I				
11. Review the section to make sure that I know the most important information?	_____	_____	_____	_____
12. Try to organize the information in the text by creating a map, chart, time line, or summary?	_____	_____	_____	_____

Evaluating Writing

Students' writing can be evaluated by holistic scoring, analytic scoring, or a combination of the two.

Holistic Scoring

What captures the essence of a piece of writing—its style, its theme, its development, its adherence to conventions, its originality? The answer is all of these elements and more. Because of the way the parts of the piece work together, it must be viewed as a whole. In **holistic scoring**, instead of noting specific strengths and weaknesses, a teacher evaluates a composition in terms of a limited number of general criteria. The criteria are used "only as a general guide . . . in reaching a holistic judgment" (Cooper & Odell, 1977, p. 4). The teacher does not stop to check the piece to see whether it meets each of the criteria but simply forms a general impression. The teacher can score a piece according to the presence or absence of key elements. There may be a scoring guide, which can be a checklist or a rubric. (A holistic scoring guide in the form of a rubric is shown in Table 3.14). The teacher should also use anchor pieces along with the rubric to assess compositions. Anchor pieces, which may be drawn from the work of past classes or from the compositions that are currently being assessed, are writing samples that provide examples

FYI

When reviewing students' papers, teachers tend to note all errors. However, students do their best when comments are positive and when there is emphasis on one or two areas, such as providing more detail or using more vivid language. This is especially effective when instruction is geared to the areas highlighted and students revise targeted areas in their compositions (Dahl & Farnan, 1998). ■

■ **Holistic scoring** is a process for sorting or ranking students' written pieces on the basis of an overall impression of each piece. Sample pieces (anchors) or a description of standards (rubric) for rating the pieces might be used as guides.

TABLE 3.14   Rubric for Writing to Convey Experience, Real or Imagined

	Skillful	Sufficient	Developing	Needs Support
Re-creation of Experience	Effectively conveys experience. Uses well chosen examples, sensory details, and narrative techniques.	Conveys experience. Uses examples, sensory details, and narrative techniques, but some need more development.	Conveys elements of experience. Examples, sensory details, and narrative techniques are not sufficiently developed.	Details or examples are brief and undeveloped, or not relevant. Little or no use of narrative techniques.
Organization	Ideas are clearly focused on the topic. Logical progression of ideas. Transitions convey relationships.	Ideas are usually focused on the topic. Has an organizational structure. Elements are logically grouped.	Most ideas are focused on the topic. Uses a simple organizational structure.	Shows attempt to organize thoughts by grouping ideas, but groupings are illogical. Some ideas may not be focused on topic.
Sentence Structure	Sentence structure is well controlled and varied.	Sentence structure is adequately controlled and somewhat varied.	Sentence structure is usually correct but shows little variety.	Sentence structure is often incorrect. Little, if any, sentence variety.
Word Choice	Word choice is specific and precise.	Word choice is specific and adequate.	Word choice is not always clear or adequate.	Word choice is not adequate and rarely specific.
Mechanics	May be a few minor errors in mechanics.	Some distracting errors, but meaning is clear.	Some errors that may impede understanding.	Frequent errors that often impede understanding.

Source: Adapted from National Assessment Governing Board. (2010). *Writing Framework for the 2011 National Assessment of Educational Progress.* Washington, DC: Author and National Governors Association Center for Best Practices and Council of Chief State School Officers (2010). *Writing standards K–5, Common Core State Standards for English Language Arts & Literacy in History, Social Studies, Science, and Technical Subjects.*

of deficient, fair, good, and superior pieces. The teacher decides which of the anchor pieces a student's composition most closely resembles.

Before scoring the pieces, the teacher should quickly read them all to get a sense of how well the class did overall. This prevents setting criteria that are too high or too low. After sorting the papers into four groups—beginning, developing, proficient, and advanced—the teacher rereads each work more carefully before confirming its placement. If possible, a second teacher should also evaluate the papers. This is especially important if the works are to be graded.

Analytic Scoring

Analytic scoring involves analyzing pieces and noting specific strengths and weaknesses. It requires the teacher to create a set of specific scoring criteria. (An analytic scoring guide for a friendly letter is presented in Figure 3.12.) Instead of overwhelming students with corrections, it is best to decide on a limited number of key features, such as those that have been emphasized for a particular writing activity. Spandel and Stiggins (1997) suggest the following six characteristics: ideas, organization, voice, word choice, sentence fluency, and conventions. Although more time-consuming than holistic scoring, analytic scoring allows the teacher to make constructive suggestions about students' writing.

Using a Combination of Techniques

In some cases, a combination of holistic and analytic scoring works best. Holistic scoring guards against the teacher's becoming overly caught up in mechanics or stylistics and neglecting the substance of the piece. Analytic scoring provides students with necessary direction for improving their work and becoming more proficient writers. Whichever approach is used,

> **Assessing for Learning**
>
> When students know why they are being assessed and when you share results with them and use results to plan reachable goals, they become more engaged in the learning process. Portfolio conferences are particularly effective for engaging students, especially when they can compare current with past work samples and see progress (Simmons, 1990). ■

> ■ **Analytic scoring** is a process for scoring that uses a description of major features to be considered when assessing a written piece.

FIGURE 3.12 Analytic Scoring Guide for a Friendly Letter

	Beginning	Developing	Proficient	Advanced
Name of student: _____		Date: _____		
Content				
Has a natural but interesting beginning.	_____	_____	_____	_____
Includes several topics of interest.	_____	_____	_____	_____
Develops each topic in sufficient detail.	_____	_____	_____	_____
Shows an interest in what's happening to the reader.	_____	_____	_____	_____
Has a friendly way of ending the letter.	_____	_____	_____	_____
Style				
Has a friendly, natural tone.	_____	_____	_____	_____
Form				
Follows friendly letter form.	_____	_____	_____	_____
Indents paragraphs.	_____	_____	_____	_____
Is neat and legible.	_____	_____	_____	_____
Mechanics				
Begins each sentence with a capital.	_____	_____	_____	_____
Uses correct end punctuation.	_____	_____	_____	_____
Spells words correctly.	_____	_____	_____	_____

it is important that criteria for assessment be clearly understood. As Dahl and Farnan (1998) note, "When writers lack specific standards and intentions, their ability to reflect on and evaluate their writing is severely compromised. It is not surprising that if writers do not know what they want to accomplish with a particular writing, it will be difficult for them to judge whether they have created an effective composition" (p. 121).

Portfolios

Artists, photographers, designers, and others assemble their work in **portfolios** for assessment. Portfolios are now being used in a somewhat modified fashion to assess the literacy growth of elementary and middle school students. Portfolios have a number of advantages. First, they facilitate the assessment of growth over time. Because they provide the teacher with an opportunity to take a broad look at a student's literacy development, they are an appropriate method for assessing holistic approaches. Portfolio assessment can also lead to changes in the curriculum and teaching practices. In Au's (1994) study, for instance, teachers began emphasizing the revision phase of writing when portfolio assessment helped them see that they were neglecting that area. Teachers in Kentucky reported that portfolios were the key element in a program designed to improve writing (Stecher, Barron, Kaganoff, & Goodwin, 1998).

Types of Portfolios

There are five kinds of portfolios, each performing different functions and containing different kinds of materials: showcase, evaluation,

■ A **portfolio** is a collection of work samples, test results, checklists, and other data used to assess a student's performance.

documentation, process, and composite (Valencia & Place, 1994). Like the traditional portfolio used by artists to display their best works, the showcase portfolio is composed of works that students have selected as being their best. The focus in the evaluation portfolio is on collecting representative works from key areas. The samples included might be standardized—that is, based on a common text or a common topic—so that results are comparable across students. A documentation portfolio is designed to provide evidence of students' growth and so might contain the greatest number and variety of work samples. The process portfolio is designed to show how students work, so it includes samples from various stages of a project along with students' comments about how the project is progressing. A composite portfolio contains elements from two or more types of portfolios. For instance, a portfolio designed for district evaluation might contain showcase and process items.

Writing Samples

Collecting representative pieces from several types of writing assignments gives the teacher a broad view of a student's development. Including pieces written at different times of the year allows the teacher to trace the student's growth. Rough drafts as well as final copies illustrate the student's writing progress and indicate how well the student handles the various processes. Each student might include in her or his portfolio lists of pieces written, major writing skills learned, and current goals. Both student and teacher should have access to the portfolio and should agree on which pieces should be included. Teacher and student should also agree on how to choose what goes into the portfolio.

To help students reflect on their learning and make wise choices about the pieces they include, you might have them explain their choices by completing a self-evaluative statement. The statement can be a brief explanation with the heading "Why I Chose This Piece." Initially, reasons for inclusion and comments tend to be vague (Tierney, Carter, & Desai, 1991). However, through classroom discussions and conferences, you can help students explore criteria for including certain pieces rather than others—it tells a good story, it has a beginning that grabs the reader, it has many interesting examples, it seems to flow, and so on.

A portfolio can demonstrate the power of a reader and a writer. Unknown to the teacher, a student may read dozens or hundreds of books or be a budding author. A reading log or sampling of written pieces should reveal this (Tierney, Carter, & Desai, 1991). However, you might invite students to include in their portfolios pieces they have written on their own as nonschool literacy endeavors.

Reading Samples

Some teachers use portfolios primarily to assess writing. If you wish to use portfolios to assess reading, include samples of reading. Samples to be included depend on the goals of the program. Valencia (1990) cautioned, "If the goals of instruction are not specified, portfolios have the potential to become reinforced holding files for odds and ends" (p. 339). If a goal of reading instruction is to teach students to visualize, drawings of reading selections might be included. If you have been working on summaries, you may want to see sample summaries. A list of books read might be appropriate for a goal of wide reading. Running records or informal reading inventories might be included to demonstrate fluency, word recognition in context, comprehension, or overall reading development.

At certain points, reading and writing will converge—written summaries of selections and research reports using several sources might count toward both reading and writing goals. Other items that might be placed in the portfolio are checklists, quizzes, standardized and informal test results, learning logs, written reactions to selections, and graphic organizers.

Assessing for Learning

• Portfolios are most useful when goals are clearly stated and specific criteria are listed for their assessment. It is essential, that goals and criteria be understood by students (Snider, Lima, & DeVito, 1994).

• In Kentucky, teachers reported that the portfolio system was the most influential factor in determining their instructional practice (Stecher, Barron, Kaganoff, & Goodwin, 1998). They also credited the portfolio system with helping them become better teachers. ■

Reviewing Portfolios

To check on students' progress, periodically review their portfolios. Farr and Farr (1990) suggested that this be done a minimum of four times a year. In order to make the best use of your time and to help students organize their work, you might have them prepare a list of the items included in the portfolio. The portfolio should also contain a list of students' learning objectives. Students might write a cover letter or fill out a form summarizing work they have done, explaining which goals they feel they have met, which areas might need improvement, and what their plans for the future are. A sample portfolio evaluation form is presented in Figure 3.13.

Before you start to review a portfolio, decide what you want to focus on. It could be number of books read, changes in writing, or effort put into revisions. Your evaluation should, of course, consider the student's stated goals; it is also important to emphasize the student's strengths. As you assess the portfolio, consider a variety of pieces and look at the work in terms of its changes over time. Ask yourself: "What does the student's work show about her or his progress over the time span covered? What might she or he do to make continued progress?"

To save time and help you organize your assessment of the portfolio, you may want to use a checklist or rubric that is supplemented with personal comments. A sample portfolio review checklist is presented in Figure 3.14. Because the objective of evaluation is to

FIGURE 3.13 Portfolio Evaluation by Student

Name: _____   Date: _____

Portfolio Evaluation

What were my goals in reading for this period?

What progress toward meeting these goals does my portfolio show?

What are my strengths?

What are my weaknesses?

What are my goals for improving as a reader?

How do I plan to meet those goals?

What were my goals in writing for this period?

What progress toward meeting these goals does my portfolio show?

What are my strengths as a writer?

What are my weaknesses?

What are my goals for improving as a writer?

How do I plan to meet these goals?

What questions do I have about my writing or my reading?

Name of student: _____   Date: _____

Voluntary Reading
   Number of books read   _____
   Variety of books read   _____
   Strengths   _____
   Needs   _____

Reading Comprehension
   Construction of meaning   _____
   Extension of meaning   _____
   Use of strategies   _____
   Quality of responses   _____
   Strengths   _____
   Needs   _____

Writing
   Amount of writing   _____
   Variety of writing   _____
   Planning   _____
   Revising   _____
   Self-editing   _____
   Content   _____
   Organization   _____
   Style   _____
   Mechanics   _____
   Strengths   _____
   Needs   _____

Comments: _____
_____
_____

FIGURE 3.14 Portfolio Review Checklist

improve instruction, students should be active partners in the process. "It follows that . . . assessment activities in which students are engaged in evaluating their own learning help them reflect on and understand their own strengths and needs, and it instills responsibility for their own learning" (Tierney, Carter, & Desai, 1991, p. 7).

Alignment of Assessment and Data Analysis

A critical feature of assessment measures is alignment. Alignment means that the curriculum and instruction are based on agreed upon objectives and the tests are assessing what is being taught (Webb, 1999). This is especially important in view of the demands of making adequate yearly progress. Classroom and other assessments should be aligned with standards (objectives) and instruction. Alignment needs to be flexible. Based on a study of fourth-graders' performance on the comprehension section of a state proficiency test, Riddle, Buly, and Valencia (2002) warn:

> Alignment is certainly a centerpiece of standards-based reform and, most of the time, it makes good sense. However, sometimes it can be oversimplified and inadvertently lead to inappropriate instruction. More specifically, aligning instruction with state assessments

REFLECTION

What is the value of portfolios? What might be done to get the most out of portfolios? In what situation might portfolios be especially effective?

 FYI

Tests, observations, work samples, and other assessment devices can be used to verify and complement each other. A student's performance in phonics, for instance, might be assessed through a written quiz, an observation of oral reading, and an examination of his or her spelling. This triangulation of data might reveal that the student can read simple, short-vowel words (*top, pet*) but has difficulty with clusters (*stop, step*). ∎

Adapting Instruction for English Language Learners

Obtaining a valid assessment of the ability and performance of English language learners is a problem. ELLs can obtain conversational proficiency in two years or less.

However, it may take five years or more for ELLs to learn enough academic English so that they can do as well on tests of academic proficiency as native speakers of English do (Cummins, 2001). ■

may help teachers focus on what is tested. . . . It will not address the skills and strategies that underlie such competence. . . . A focus on comprehension would miss those who have difficulty in word identification or fluency, or those with specific second language issues. Similarly, requiring teachers to align their instruction with grade level content standards may also fall short. Assuring, for example, that 4th-grade teachers are teaching the 4th-grade content standards does not assure they are providing appropriate instruction for all students. To be sure, some students would benefit from instruction and practice reading material that is at a lower grade level and some would benefit from more advanced curriculum. It is not that grade level standards or expectations are unimportant or that aligning instruction, assessment, and standards is wrong. However, for many struggling students, grade level standards are goals rather than immediate needs. The teacher's challenge is to bring the students to the point where those grade level goals are within reach. (p. 234)

If you are using a commercial program, chances are that it is aligned. However, examine it closely to see if any revisions are needed. In addition, you might need to make some adjustment to ensure that the program aligns with state, district, and other outside assessments. If you are using a program that you or your school has created, you will need to construct or adopt an assessment system that aligns with your objectives and instruction.

Data Analysis

Along with aligning assessment and instruction, it is essential that you analyze the data so that it can actually be used to plan instruction. Keep a record of students' performance on any assessments that are administered to them. Use that data to make instructional decisions. After an assessment has been administered, organize the results. Note especially students who did not perform adequately. What are some possible reasons for their poor performance? What might be done to assist them? If you have scores from the same or comparable assessments, note whether there has been an improvement and whether the improvement is such that the students are on track to reach the target benchmark by the end of the school year. Also analyze items that students responded to. On a phonics test, for instance, note the items that students got correct. Perhaps the students got most of the short-vowel items correct but had difficulty with clusters (blends). This is the kind of information that you can use to plan instruction. Consider other sources of data. You might have information from an IRI, running record, or personal observation that sheds additional light on students' skill levels and cognitive processes.

Adapting Instruction for English Language Learners

Students whose language is non-alphabetic or doesn't use the Roman alphabet will have a greater adjustment than those whose written language is more similar to English. ■

Adapting Instruction for English Language Learners

ELLs should not be given assessments that are so far beyond their English language capacity that they are overwhelmed. ■

Assessing English Language Learners

Under the No Child Left Behind Act of 2001, the academic progress of every child in grades 3 through 8, including those learning English who have been enrolled in a U.S. school for at least a year, is tested in reading and math. English language learners (ELLs) are tested annually to measure how well they are learning English.

Apart from state and federal regulations, it is essential that you have information about ELLs' proficiency in literacy in their first language. Students who can read in another language will have learned basic concepts of reading. They will have developed phonological awareness, alphabetical knowledge, and knowledge of phonics, if their home language is an alphabetic one. You can build on this knowledge. It is also essential that you have information about the students' proficiency in oral and written English. If students are weak in understanding English, you can plan a literacy program that develops oral language.

Key questions include:

- What is the student's proficiency in speaking her or his first language?
- What is the student's proficiency in speaking English?
- What is the student's proficiency in reading in the first language?
- What is the student's proficiency in reading in English?
- What is the educational background of the student?

The ESL or bilingual specialist should be able to provide information about the students' proficiency in literacy in their first language and also their knowledge of English. If this information is not available, use informal techniques to assess the students' proficiency in reading and writing their first language. Ask students to bring in books in their first language and read them to you and then retell the selection in English. Also ask them to bring in a piece of writing that they have done in their first language and read it to you and then retell it in English. Based on the ease with which they read, you can judge whether they are literate in their first language, even if you don't know the language. You might also obtain or construct a list of common words in their language and ask students to read them. Figure 3.15 contains a list of twenty common Spanish words, phonetically respelled and with their English translations. You might use a list such as this one to get a very rough idea of the students' reading proficiency. (Spanish has a number of dialects. Pronunciations might vary somewhat from those provided.) If students can read all or most of these words, they can read at least at a basic level in Spanish. If you are fluent in Spanish, you might administer the Spanish Reading Inventory (Kendall/Hunt) or the English-Español Reading Inventory for the Classroom (Merrill).

A distinguished panel of experts on English language learners recommended administering measures of phonological awareness, letter knowledge, and word and text reading in English and using the results to identify ELLs who require additional instructional support:

> Research shows that early reading measures, administered in English, can be used to screen English learners for reading problems. This finding is important because until recently it was widely believed that an absence of oral proficiency in English prevented English learners from learning to read in English, thus limiting the utility of early screening measures. The common practice was to wait until English learners reached a reasonable level of oral English proficiency before assessing them on measures of beginning reading. (Gersten, Baker, Shanahan, Linan-Thompson, Collins, & Scarcella, 2007, p. 5)

The panel also recommended using the same early reading standards for ELLs as are used with native speakers of English:

> Schools with performance benchmarks in reading in the early grades can use the same standards for English learners and for native English speakers to make adjustments in instruction when progress is not sufficient. It is the opinion of the panel that schools should not consider below-grade-level performance in reading as "normal" or something that will resolve itself when oral language proficiency in English improves. (Gersten et al., 2007, p. 3)

This recommendation, which applies only to early reading, is somewhat controversial. While it is true that on-grade English reading tests administered to English learners will show whether they have reached a set benchmark or standard, it is easy to picture situations where the students' English is so limited that they are only able to respond to a few items or none at all. This seems to be a needlessly disheartening process. Teacher judgment needs to be exercised so that students are not overwhelmed with assessments that are far beyond their language capabilities. One solution would be to administer screening measures that include items on the lower end of the scale as well as on-grade items so that even students with limited English ability will be able to respond to some items and their performance will provide useful information for instructional planning. The CELLA (Comprehensive English Language Learning Assessment), for instance, is functionally based rather than grade-level based in reading and writing. Level A, which is designed for students in grades 1–2, ranges from

FIGURE 3.15 Spanish Word List

Spanish Word	Pronunciation	Meaning
no	no	no
mi	me	my
uno	OO-no	one
esta	ES-tah	this
ella	AY-yah	she
señor	sen-YOR	mister
leer	lay-AIR	read
libro	LEE-bro	book
amigo	ah-ME-go	friend
pelota	peh-LOH-tah	ball
vaca	BAH-kah	cow
musica	MYEW-see-kah	music
sorpressa	sor-PRES-ah	surprise
leopardo	lay-oh-PAR-doh	leopard
abuela	ah-BWEH-lah	grandmother
bicicleta	bee-see-KLAY-tah	bicycle
mañana	mon-YAH-nah	tomorrow
primavera	pre-mah-BEAR-ah	spring
zapatos	sah-PAH-toes	shoes
elefante	eh-leh-FAHN-teh	elephant
vaca	BAH-kah/VAH-kah	cow

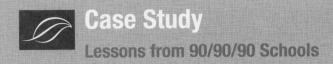

Case Study

Lessons from 90/90/90 Schools

Assessment works best when it is connected to instruction and the attitude that all students can learn if given adequate instruction and whatever assistance they need. Assessment becomes a blueprint for instruction rather than a judgment. In 90/90/90 schools, there was frequent assessment of student progress with multiple opportunities for improvement. A 90/90/90 school was one in which 90 percent of the students were members of minority groups and lived in poverty but attained the proficient level on high-stakes tests. In many instances, assessments in these schools were weekly and were constructed by classroom teachers. Since many of the students in these schools were struggling readers and writers, they often did poorly on assessments. However, the consequence of a poor performance was not a low grade or a sense of failure but additional instruction and practice.

Another characteristic of assessment in 90/90/90 schools was an emphasis on students' written responses in performance assessments. Because the responses were written rather than oral, students were better able to elaborate on their thinking, and teachers were better able to judge the quality of the students' responses. Being better able to examine and analyze students'

responses, teachers had the information they needed to plan effective instructional activities. "By assessing student writing, teachers can discern whether the challenges faced by a student are the result of vocabulary issues, misunderstood directions, reasoning errors, or a host of other causes that are rarely revealed by typical tests" (Reeves, 2003, p. 5).

In 90/90/90 schools, teachers used a common rubric so that there were clear standards for writing and clear standards for assessing (Reeves, 2003). In addition, in many instances teachers would meet to assess papers or to exchange papers, so assessment was the result of applying the rubric rather than simply using highly subjective judgment. Disagreements about scoring generally arise when teachers use implicit criteria rather than stated criteria or when the criteria are not specific enough. For instance, a teacher might judge a paper partly on neatness, which isn't one of the stated criteria. Or a criterion such as "fully develops ideas," which lacks specificity, is interpreted in different ways by different teachers. By talking over standards and disagreements, teachers can clarify the criteria and refrain from adding criteria that are not stated.

---

identifying letters of the alphabet and reading high frequency words to reading brief passages. For grade 3 and beyond, a brief locator test is used to estimate the appropriate assessment level: Level A, B, C, or D. Another solution would be to gear assessment to the students' level of language development.

A second factor in the assessment of ELL is the use of cognitive resources, especially at higher levels. As compared to native speakers of English, ELL must draw on added cognitive resources to process English text (Francis, Rivera, Lesaux, Kieffer, & Rivera, 2006). This means that they may not be able to allocate a full measure of cognitive resources to process complex text, or it may take them longer. Providing them with accessible text and/or more time are possible accommodations. Even so, complex standardized tests may underestimate the abilities of ELL.

Assessing Language

To assess students' ability to understand language, request that they point to various objects: "Point to the book. Point to the red dot. Point to the square. Point to your knee, your foot, your ear" (Law & Eckes, 2002). Start with common objects, and progress to less common ones: "Point to the magnet. Point to the picture of the jet." Real objects work better, but you might also use magazine or other photos to assess students' receptive vocabulary. Also request that students follow a series of commands: "Stand. Sit. Open the book. Raise your hand. Write your name." To assess expressive vocabulary, have the students identify objects that you point to and ask, "What is this? What are those?" Also ask students a series of questions, and note how they respond: "What is your name? How old are you? Where do you live? Count to ten. Name the colors that I point to. Name the letters that I point to." For a copy of informal language tests for English language learners and additional suggestions for assessment, refer to the text by Law and Eckes (2002), which is listed in the References section.

REFLECTION

What are the main obstacles to obtaining valid and reliable information about the literacy development of English language learners? How might these obstacles be overcome?

Creating a Literacy Profile

Jiménez (2004) recommends that a literacy profile be created for English language learners. The profile provides information about the language the students speak at home. It is also important to determine whether there have been gaps in ELLs' schooling. Their schooling may have been fragmented, or they may have been moved from a regular class to an ESL class or to a special education class.

When looking at scores from an ELL student, compare them to the scores of other ELLs. Also consider such factors as when the student began learning English and how many years of exposure to English the student has had. Also find out if the student can read in his or her native language. If so, skills can be transferred. Get information, too, on the students' literacy activities. Some students act as translators for their parents, an activity known as *language brokering* (Lalas, Solomon, & Johannessen, 2006). Language brokering apparently strengthens students' academic achievement. These students might be translating medical forms, advertisements, and even income tax forms. Affirm students' native language, and help them see that their native language can be a source of help in understanding English.

 ## Assessing Materials

Just about the most important instructional decision you will make is selecting the appropriate level of materials for your students. Choose a level that is too easy and students will be bored and unchallenged. Select material that is too difficult and they will be discouraged, have their academic self-concepts demolished, and fail to make progress. Perhaps, worst of all, they will learn to hate reading (Juel, 1994). As noted earlier, students should know at least 95 percent of the words in the materials they are asked to read and should have about 75 percent comprehension.

A three-part approach to estimating the readability of a text is recommended: quantitative measures of text difficulty, qualitative measures of text difficulty, and professional judgment in matching texts to reader and task (National Governors Association Center for Best Practices and Council of Chief State School Officers, 2010b). Quantitative measures consist of the use of formulas. Qualitative measures include leveling systems and checklists. Professional judgment involves considering reader factors in terms of the material to be read and the task to be performed.

Publishers of school materials generally provide reading levels for their texts. Using a formula or subjective leveling scale, they estimate that the material is at, for example, a second-, third-, or fourth-grade level, which means that the average second-, third-, or fourth-grader should be able to read it. Or they may use letters or numbers to indicate a level rather than a grade. Some publishers of children's books also supply **readability levels**. If no readability level is indicated for a book that you wish to use, you can can consult one of the following sources.

ATOS (Advantage-TASA Open Standard)

ATOS is a computerized formula that uses number of words per sentence, characters per word, and average grade level of words and analyzes the entire text to estimate the readability of a book and provide a grade-level equivalent. ATOS scores for more than 50,000 trade books are available from Renaissance Learning, the creators of Accelerated Reading, at http://www.arbookfind.com. Enter the title of the book for which you would like to have an ATOS score. ATOS scores appear in bold type after the abbreviation "BL" (for book level) and are expressed in grade equivalents. First grade is subdivided into a series of levels that are equated with Reading Recovery levels. If the text

 Using Technology

Google Search
By using an advanced Google search, users can determine whether the readability of articles is estimated to be basic, intermediate, or advanced. Basic is about a middle school level. The user can also select to have articles listed by reading level.
http://www.google.com/ support/websearch/bin/answer. py?hl=en&answer=1095407 ■

 Using Technology

Titlewave® provides ATOS, lexile, and its own estimated readability levels.
http://www.flr.follett.com/intro/ titleservices.html ■

■ **Readability level** indicates the difficulty of a selection. A formula may be used to estimate readability by measuring quantitative factors such as sentence length and number of difficult words in the selection. A leveling system may use a number of qualitative factors to estimate the difficulty of the text. Best results are obtained by assessing both qualitative and quantitative factors.

FYI

Lexiles are the most widely used readability estimate. ∎

FYI

Common Core Standards allow lexiles, DRP units, and grade scores to be used to measure text difficulty. ∎

Using Technology

Titlewave provides extensive information about books and other media, including interest level, readability level, book reviews, and awards that books have won. You can search by author, title, topic, grade level, subject area, or curriculum standard.

http://www.flr.follett.com/login ∎

for which you want a readability estimate is not listed, contact Renaissance Learning. They may have the ATOS score. If not, if you provide sample passages from the book, the company will provide an ATOS score for you.

Lexile Scale

The lexile scale is a two-factor computerized formula that consists of a measurement of sentence length and word frequency. Table 3.7 on page 76 provides approximate grade equivalents for lexile scores. A software program for obtaining readability estimates, the *Lexile Analyzer*, is available from MetaMetrics and can be used to calculate your own lexile scores. However, lexile scores for about 40,000 books are available online at http://www.lexile.com. ATOS and DRP seem to provide a more accurate estimate than does the lexile scale (Renaissance Learning, 2006, 2009). However, the lexile scale is more widely used.

Degrees of Reading Power

The Degrees of Reading Power test measures sentence length, number of words not on the Dale List of words known by fourth-graders, and average number of letters per word (Touchstone Applied Science Associates, 1994). Compilations of readability levels expressed in DRP units for some content-area textbooks can be found on the following Web site: http://www.questarai.com/readability.htm. DRP readabilities for trade books are available on easy-to-use software called *BookLink*. DRP units range from 15 for the easiest materials to 85 for the most difficult reading material. Table 3.7 provides approximate grade equivalents for DRP scores.

Other Readability Formulas

If you are unable to get a readability level from one of these sources, or if you prefer to assess the readability of the text yourself, there are a number of formulas you can apply. One of the easiest to use is the Fry Readability Graph, which bases its estimate on two factors: sentence length and number of syllables in a word. Number of syllables in a word is a measure of vocabulary difficulty. In general, the more syllables a word has, the harder it tends to be. The Fry Readability Graph (Fry, 1977b) is presented in Figure 3.16. A formula that counts the number of hard words but is relatively easy to use is the Primary Readability Formula (Gunning, 2002); it can be used to assess the difficulty level of materials in grades 1 to 4. The New Dale-Chall Readability Formula (Chall & Dale, 1995), which also counts the number of difficult words, is recommended for grade 3 and up.

One problem with readability formulas is that they are mechanical and so do not consider subjective factors, such as the density of concepts, use of illustrations, or background required to construct meaning from the text. Readability formulas should be complemented by the use of the subjective factors incorporated in a leveling system (Gunning, 2000b). A leveling system uses subjective or qualitative factors to estimate the difficulty level of materials.

FYI

The Primary Readability Formula, which is designed for grades 1–4, is available in the Instructor's Manual. ∎

Qualitative Factors

In addition to failing to consider qualitative factors, traditional formulas do not work well at the very beginning levels. Formulas don't consider such factors as usefulness of illustrations and number of lines per page, which are major determinants of the difficulty level of beginning materials. Formulas do indicate with reasonable accuracy that materials are on a first-grade level. However, first-grade reading encompasses a wide range of material that includes counting or colorword books that have just one or two easy words per page as well as books, such as the Little Bear series, that contain brief chapters and may contain several hundred words. To make fine discriminations among the range of first-grade books, it is necessary to use a leveling system.

FIGURE 3.16 Fry's Graph
for Estimating Readability

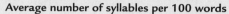

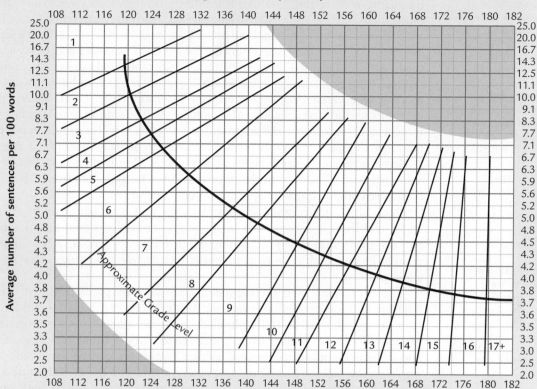

Expanded Directions for Working Readability Graph

1. Randomly select three (3) sample passages and count out exactly 100 words each, beginning with the beginning of a sentence. Do not count proper nouns, initializations, and numerals.

2. Count the number of sentences in the 100 words, estimating length of the fraction of the last sentence to the nearest one-tenth.

3. Count the total number of syllables in the 100-word passage. If you don't have a hand counter available, an easy way is to simply put a mark above every syllable over one in each word, then when you get to the end of the passage, count the number of marks and add 100. Small calculators can also be used by pushing numeral 1, then the + sign for each word or syllable when counting.

4. Enter graph with *average* sentence length and *average* number of syllables; plot dot where the two lines intersect. Area where dot is plotted will give you the approximate grade level.

5. If a great deal of variability is found in syllable count or sentence count, putting more samples into the average is desirable.

6. A word is defined as a group of symbols with space on either side; thus, *Joe, IRA, 1945,* and *&* are each one word.

7. A syllable is defined as a phonetic syllable. Generally, there are as many syllables as vowel sounds. For example, *stopped* is one syllable and *wanted* is two syllables. When counting syllables for numerals and initializations, count one syllable for each symbol. For example, *1945* is four syllables, *IRA* is three syllables, and *&* is one syllable.

Leveling Systems

Although materials for beginning readers may look similar—large print and lots of illustrations—they incorporate different theories of teaching reading and have different uses (Hiebert, 1999). Early reading materials can be classified as being predictable, high-frequency, or decodable. Predictable texts are written in such a way that students can use illustrations or their knowledge of language to "read" the text. A predictable book might have the sentences "I can run. I can jump. I can sing. I can read," each on a separate page accompanied by an illustration showing the action. The reader gets heavy support from the illustrations and the repeated pattern. Predictable books are excellent for reinforcing concepts of print and giving students the feel of reading, and they can also help English language learners learn the patterns of English. Predictable books do a good job of introducing students to reading. Most students will pick up an initial reading vocabulary by repeatedly meeting words in print. However, some will continue to use picture and language clues, and the use of predictable text may actually hinder their progress.

Some texts emphasize high-frequency words. Words such as *of*, *and*, *the*, *was*, and *where* occur so often in print that they are said to be high-frequency. Most predictable books are composed primarily of high-frequency words.

Decodable texts contain phonics elements that have been taught. A story about a *bug* who lived in a *rug* would be decodable to students who have learned the *-ug* pattern. No text is totally decodable. High-frequency words such as *is*, *are*, and *the* need to be included, as do content words such as *bear* and *hungry* if the story is about a hungry bear.

The most widely used leveling system is based on the predictability of text. Adapting a system that was originally devised for Reading Recovery, Fountas and Pinnell (2009) have compiled a list of 18,000 leveled books for students in kindergarten through grade 8. Books are leveled from A through Z, with A being very beginning reading and Z being eighth-grade reading. Table 3.7 provides approximate grade equivalents. Books on the Graded Listing of Outstanding Children's Books at the author's Web site (http://www.wordbuilding.org) have been leveled according to both predictability and decodability, based on quantitative as well as qualitative factors.

However, you may wish to use books that have not been leveled, or you may not have access to a listing of leveled books. In that case, you need to be able to level books on your own. To level books, consider key subjective factors and compare passages from the book you are leveling to passages from benchmark books. *The Qualitative Assessment of Text Difficulty* (Chall, Bissex, Conard, & Harris-Sharples, 1996) provides benchmark passages and directions for leveling both fictional and informational books. For beginning books, use the Basic Leveling Index, which is explained below.

 ## The Basic Leveling Index

Using the Basic Leveling System with Beginning Reading Books

Beginning reading books are more difficult to level than are upper-grade books because they encompass a very wide range of difficulty. The Basic Leveling System has seven beginning-reader through first-grade levels: picture, caption or frame (early pre-primer), pre-primer one, pre-primer two, pre-primer three, primer, and first. To determine the difficulty of an early reading text, compare the text being assessed with a benchmark book or benchmark passage. Ask: Which benchmark book or passage is this text most like? Also consider qualitative factors. Note especially the difficulty level of the words. Would your students be able to read them? Remember that they should be able to read about 95 percent of the words. At this level, most of the words will be in the students' listening vocabulary. Their major task is to pronounce or recognize the printed words. Words such as *the* and *are* appear with high frequency and so are easier to read. Some words such as *cat* and *hat* will be easy to decode. Consider, too, how helpful the illustrations are. Some of the words may be depicted by illustrations, which might also provide an overview of the text or portray significant portions of

Number of hard words depicted by illustrations:

        None _____   Some _____   Most _____   All _____

Number of words that would be easy to decode:

        None _____   Some _____   Most _____   All _____

Difficulty of vocabulary and concepts

_____ Familiar vocabulary and concepts

_____ One or two unfamiliar words or concepts

_____ Several unfamiliar words or concepts

Familiarity of topic or story line

        High _____   Medium _____   Low _____

When compared with benchmark passages or books, what level(s) do the sample passages from the text seem to be most like?

Passage 1 _____

Passage 2 _____

Passage 3 _____

Average   _____

FIGURE 3.17 Worksheet for Estimating Difficulty of First-Grade Materials

it. Be attentive to the overall interest of the selection, familiarity of the topic and language, repetition of elements, use of rhyme, and such format factors as number of lines per page. Also consider the length of the text; short pieces are easier to read than longer ones. Above all, note whether the average beginning reader would have the background information necessary to read the text. A book about the Vietnam War, no matter how simply written, would be beyond most beginning readers. Watch out, too, for the use of figurative language and allusions that are beyond beginning readers. When estimating difficulty level, be conservative. If you are undecided whether a book is on a primer or first level, place it at the higher level. It's better to give a student a book that is on the easy side rather than one that is too difficult.

Consider both objective and subjective information to decide on a difficulty level. Use the worksheet in Figure 3.17 to note quantitative and qualitative factors. As you become familiar with leveling books, your estimates will become more accurate and there will be less need to rely on objective measures. However, objective measures provide a helpful check.

The next few pages provide a description of each level and a sample benchmark passage. Words that are judged to be difficult are boldfaced.

Picture Level In books at the picture level, a single word or phrase is depicted with an illustration (see Figure 3.18). The word *lion*, for instance, is accompanied by a drawing of a lion; the word *three* is accompanied by the numeral 3 and three dots. The text is so fully and clearly depicted that no reading is required. In some books, the student might need to use the initial consonant to help identify the picture. For instance, the student might not know whether a wolf or a dog is being depicted. Seeing that the label for the picture starts with a *w*, the student uses knowledge of initial consonants to reason that a wolf is being depicted.

FIGURE 3.18

I see a lion.   I see a tiger.

FIGURE 3.19

Benchmark books:

Colors by John Burningham

Numbers by Guy Smalley

Caption or Frame Level   The text of caption-level books is illustrated so that the reader can use pictures to identify most but not all of the words (see Figure 3.19). These books feature frame sentences, which are easy sentences, such as: "I can _____," "I am _____," or "_____can swim," that are repeated throughout the text. The name of the object, animal, person, or action that completes the frame is depicted. The student would need to know initial consonants and the few high-frequency words that make up the frame.

Benchmark books:

Have You Seen My Cat? by Eric Carle

My Barn by Craig Brown

Cat on the Mat by Brian Wildsmith

Benchmark passage: *I see _____.*

Pre-primer 1 (Easy, High-Frequency Words)   Pre-primer 1 books are similar to caption-level books but there are a greater number of different words used and more reading is required. Illustrations usually depict some or much of the text. A pre-primer 1 book requires increased knowledge of high-frequency words and some beginning familiarity with short-vowel patterns, such as *-at* and *-am.*

Benchmark books:

Brown Bear, Brown Bear, What Do You See? by Bill Martin, Jr.

Bugs by Patricia and Fredrick McKissack

Benchmark passage: *"The Bad Cat"*

Matt is sad.

Matt had a hat.

Now **Pat** has **Matt's** hat.

Pat is a cat.

Matt ran after Pat.

But Pat ran away.

Pat ran away with Matt's hat.

Pat is a bad cat.

Pre-primer 2   Pre-primer 2 books are similar to pre-primer 1 books, but there are a greater number of different words used and more reading is required. Illustrations usually depict some of the text. This level requires increased knowledge of high-frequency words and some familiarity with most of the short-vowel patterns, such as *-at, -op,* and *-et.*

Benchmark books:

Cat Traps by Molly Coxe

The Carrot Seed by Ruth Krauss

Benchmark passage: *"The Red Kangaroo"*

Hop! Hop! Hop!

Kangaroos like to hop.

The red kangaroo can **hop** the best.

The red kangaroo can hop over you.

The red kangaroo can hop over the top of a **van**.

The red kangaroo is big.

The red kangaroo has big back legs.

Its back legs are very **strong**.

And it has a long **tail**.

The red kangaroo is bigger than a man.

The red kangaroo is the biggest kangaroo of all.

Pre-primer 3   The pre-primer 3 level is similar to pre-primer 2 but requires increased knowledge of high-frequency words and increased familiarity with short-vowel patterns that make use of consonant combinations such as *tr*, *st*, and *sch*.

Benchmark books:

The Foot Book by Dr. Seuss

Sleepy Dog by Harriet Ziefert

Benchmark passage: "Best Pet"

"I have the best pet," said Ted.

"My dog **barks** and **wags** his **tail** when I come home from school."

"No, I have the best pet," said **Robin**. "I have a cat. My cat **wakes** me up so that I can go to school."

"I have the best pet," said Will. "I have a pet pig.

My pig can do many **tricks**."

Then Ted said, "We all have the best pet.

I have the pet that is best for me.

Robin has the pet that is best for her.

And Will has the pet that is best for him."

Primer   At the primer level, vocabulary becomes more diverse, and illustrations are less helpful. Students need to know high-frequency words and short-vowel and long-vowel patterns (*-ake*, *-ike*, *-ope*). A primer-level book might also require some knowledge of *r*-vowel (*-ar*, *-er*) and other-vowel (*-our*, *-ought*) patterns.

Benchmark books:

And I Mean It Stanley by Crosby Bonsall

Jason's Bus Ride by Harriet Ziefert

Benchmark passage: The Little Red Hen

A little red hen lived on a farm with her **chickens**. One day she found a **grain** of **wheat** in the **barnyard**.

"Who will plant this wheat?" she said.

"Not I," said the Cat.

"Not I," said the Duck.

"I will do it **myself**," said the little Red Hen. And she planted the grain of wheat.

When the wheat was ripe she said, "Who will take this wheat to the **mill**?"

"Not I," said the Cat.

REFLECTION

What procedures might be used to assess the difficulty level of materials? Which formula would you use? Why? Why is it important to verify the difficulty level of a text by noting how well students can read the text?

Using Technology

Coh-Metrix Easability is a free text analysis system that uses five key language factors to assess text: word concreteness, narrativity, local cohesion, deep cohesion, and syntactic simplicity. Results can be used to plan instruction. See the Easibility site for more information.

"Not I," said the Duck.

"I will, then," said the little Red Hen, and she took the wheat to the mill.

When she **brought** the **flour** home, she said, "Who will bake some bread with this flour?"

First Grade   At the first-grade level, selections are becoming longer and more complex. Books may be divided into very brief chapters. Students need to know short-vowel, long-vowel, and some of the easier other-vowel (*-ow, -oy, -oo, -aw*), and *r*-vowel (*-ear, -or*) patterns. There may also be some easy two-syllable words. Illustrations support text and may depict a hard word or two.

Benchmark books:

The Cat in the Hat by Dr. Seuss

Little Bear's Visit by Else Minark

Benchmark passage: Johnny Appleseed

John Chapman wore a **tin pan** for a hat. And he was **dressed** in **rags**. But **people** liked John. He was kind to others, and he was kind to animals.

John loved **apples**. He left his home and headed **west** about 200 years ago. He wanted everyone to have apples. On his back he carried a **pack** of apple seeds. Walking from place to place, John planted his apple seeds. As the years **passed** the seeds **grew** into trees. After planting **hundreds** and hundreds of apple trees, John Chapman came to be called "**Johnny Appleseed.**"

Easability

Readability formulas measure surface factors such as word difficulty and sentence length. Using computer analysis, Coh-Metrix Easability attempts to go beyond the text base to the situation and mental model (McNamara, Graesser, Cai, & Kulikowich, 2011). Easability indices include narrativity, syntactic simplicity, word concreteness, referential cohesion, and deep cohesion and measure the degree to which segments in a text are tied together. The proportion of cohesive ties indicates the ease with which readers can go beyond understanding words and individual sentences and integrate ideas in the text and relate these to background knowledge and so form a situation or mental model. Using the Easability indices can shed light on the challenges posed by a text. Texts with the same overall readability level may have significant differences in their makeup. One might be more syntactically complex or less cohesive, or contain a smaller proportion of concrete words. Knowing the challenges posed by the text, it then becomes possible to plan lessons that will help students better understand the text. If referential and deep cohesion are low, you might pose questions that help students tie together ideas. Perhaps they will complete a graphic organizer. If syntactic simplicity is low, you might demonstrate a strategy for translating dense text into understandable English or provide instruction and practice in reading complex constructions. A low score on narrativity or word concreteness suggests the need to work both on vocabulary and background knowledge.

Reader and Task Factors

In addition to assessing the difficulty of the text, it is important to consider reader factors, such as motivation, interest, and background knowledge, and the knowledge of the reading task (National Governors Association and Council of Chief State School Officers, 2010a). The following question assesses the knowledge of the reading task: "Is the text being skimmed to get an overview or is it being read closely in order to learn how to carry out a complex procedure?" Reader factors are listed in

	Low			High	
Reader Factors	1	2	3	4	5
Background knowledge					
Vocabulary					
Overall reading ability					
Interest					
Motivation					

TABLE 3.15   Reader Factors

Source: Adapted from Gunning, T. (2010), *Assessing and Correcting Reading and Writing Difficulties* (3rd ed.). Boston: Allyn & Bacon

	Narrative	Expository	Poetry
Purpose for Reading			
_____Following directions			
_____Learning a new procedure			
_____Reading for pleasure			
_____Evaluating a text			
_____Learning a new concept			
Complexity of Questions			
_____Locate & recall			
_____Integrate & interpret			

TABLE 3.16   Task Difficulty

Table 3.15. Task factors are presented in Table 3.16. Ultimately, the true measure of the difficulty level of a book is the proficiency with which students can read it. Note how well students are able to read books that have been leveled. Based on your observation of students' performance, be prepared to change the estimated difficulty level.

Summary

Evaluation entails making a subjective judgment about the effectiveness of instruction; it is based on data from tests, work samples, and observations. An evaluation is made in terms of standards or objectives and should result in the improvement of instruction.

The standards movement is an attempt to improve the quality of education by setting high, but clear, standards for all. A set of Common Core State Standards is now being emphasized. The purpose of these standards is to prepare all students to be college and career ready.

Assessment is categorized as being summative, formative, or interim. Summative assessment occurs after instruction and is used for grading or to evaluate students' progress or the effectiveness of a program. Formative assessment is administered during instruction and is used to plan and guide instruction. Interim assessment predicts performance on end-of-year summative measures and is used to plan instruction and schedule intervention. Assess-

ing for learning makes use of formative and interim assessment and involves students in the assessment process. This approach builds students' competence and confidence by clarifying standards and helping students see specifically what they need to do to meet standards.

Placement information is necessary to indicate where students are on the road to literacy. Continuous progress monitoring is used to track students' progress. Norm-referenced tests and criterion-referenced tests, as well as a variety of informal measures, are used to assess students' progress. Norm-referenced tests compare students with a norm group. Criterion-referenced assessments indicate whether students have reached a standard or objective. Benchmarks and rubrics are criterion-referenced assessment devices that offer ways of holistically indicating performance. Holistic evaluation of writing, observations, anecdotal records, checklists, and portfolios provide authentic information that complements data yielded by more formal measures. Formative assessment makes use of a variety of measures in order to improve instruction.

Students should be given tests designed for the level on which they are reading. Tests that are too easy or too hard are invalid and yield erroneous information.

A number of objective readability formulas and several subjective leveling systems and a computerized easability system can be used to assess the difficulty level of materials. Difficulty level is best assessed by using quantitative and qualitative measures and professional judgment.

Extending and Applying

1. Select a benchmark or progress-monitoring instrument described in this chapter. In terms of your theory of literacy instruction and/or research in the field, explain why you chose this particular instrument. Analyze the assessment instrument and make a judgment about its content validity. Obtain information on its concurrent and predictive validity and reliability. Make a judgment as to the usefulness and quality of the instrument. If possible, use the instrument with a student or group of students. Analyze the results, and explain what implications they have for instruction.

2. Administer an IRI, running record, or other placement device to one or more students. From the results of the assessment, estimate each student's independent, instructional, and frustration reading levels. Also list any strengths or needs that you noted. Discuss the results with the student and the student's teacher.

3. Create a portfolio system for literacy assessment for a class you are or might be teaching. Decide what kinds of items might be included in the portfolio. Also devise a checklist or summary sheet that can be used to keep track of and summarize the items and a rubric for assessing the portfolio.

4. In your professional portfolio, place any checklists, rubrics, or other assessment devices that you have devised and/or used. Reflect on the effectiveness and usefulness of these devices. If you used the devices, describe how you used the information they yielded to guide instruction.

5. Find out what the standards are for your state, how they are assessed, and how test results are used. Find out also if your state has recommendations for assessments that can be used to screen and monitor progress. Find out if your state has adopted the Common Core State Standards and, if so, how they are being implemented.

Professional Reflection

Do I
___ Have an understanding of the process of evaluation?
___ Have an understanding of test validity, reliability, and fairness?
___ Set realistic goals for instruction and communicate the goals to students?

___ Monitor progress and check for understanding?
___ Place students in the appropriate level of materials?
___ Evaluate progress and make changes as necessary?

Reflection Question

Data from summative tests indicate that Mr. Angelo's class has a general weakness in comprehension. He is in the process of planning an assessment program that he can use to monitor progress and provide information that will help

him plan an effective program. What assessment instruments might Mr. Angelo use that would take a minimum of time but that would provide the information he needs?

🖋 Building Competencies

To build competencies, consult the following sources for more detailed information:

- Assessment Training Institute
  http://www.assessmentinst.com
  The institute advocates the kind of assessment that fosters students' competence and learning.

- National Center on Student Progress Monitoring
  http://www.studentprogress.org
  This site provides good coverage of CBMs but neglects other, more authentic ways of monitoring progress.

- The Lexile Framework® for Reading
  http://www.lexile.com
  The Lexile Framework is becoming the dominant system for estimating the difficulty level of books. This site offers a detailed explanation of the system and a number of resources.

- Colorín Colorado
  http://www.colorincolorado.org
  This site has a broad range of resources in both English and Spanish for teachers and parents of ELLs.

- Gersten, R., Baker, S. K., Shanahan, T., Linan-Thompson, S., Collins, P., & Scarcella, R. (2007). *Effective literacy and English language instruction for English learners in the elementary grades: IES practice guide* (NCEE 2007-4011). Washington, DC: National Center for Education Evaluation and Regional Assistance, Institute of Education Sciences, U.S. Department of Education.
  http://www.ies.ed.gov/ncee/wwc/pdf/practiceguides/20074011.pdf

- This document makes research-based suggestions for assessing and instructing ELLs but includes some recommendations that are controversial.

- LD OnLine
  http://www.ldonline.org
  Excellent source of information and teaching resources regarding learning disabilities and ADHD.

- Brown, J. E., & Sanford, A. (2011). *RTI for English language learners: Appropriately using screening and progress-monitoring tools to improve instructional outcomes.* National Center on Response to Intervention.
  http://www.rti4success.org/pdf/rtiforells.pdf

- National Governors Association Center for Best Practices and the Council of Chief State School Officers (2010). *Common core state standards for English language arts & literacy in history/social studies, science, and technical subjects. Appendix A: Research supporting key elements of the standards. Glossary of key terms.*
  http://www.corestandards.org/assests/Appendix_A.pdf

MyEducationLab™

Go to the Topics "Assessment" and "Fluency" in the MyEducationLab (www.myeducationlab.com) for your course, where you can:

- Find learning outcomes for "Assessment" and "Fluency" along with the national standards that connect to these outcomes.
- Complete Assignments and Activities that can help you more deeply understand the chapter content.
- Apply and practice your understanding of the core teaching skills identified in the chapter with the Building Teaching Skills and Dispositions learning units.
- Examine challenging situations and cases presented in the IRIS Center Resources.
- Check your comprehension on the content covered in the chapter by going to the Study Plan in the Book

Resources for your text. Here you will be able to take a chapter quiz, receive feedback on your answers, and then access Review, Practice, and Enrichment activities to enhance your understanding of chapter content. (optional)

 A+RISE® Standards2Strategy™ is an innovative and interactive online resource that offers new teachers in grades K–12 just-in-time, research-based instructional strategies that meet the linguistic needs of ELLs as they learn content, differentiate instruction for all grades and abilities, and are aligned to Common Core Elementary Language Arts standards (for the literacy strategies) and to English language proficiency standards in WIDA, Texas, California, and Florida.

4 Fostering Emergent/ Early Literacy

Anticipation Guide

For each of the following statements, put a check under "Agree" or "Disagree" to show how you feel. Discuss your responses with classmates before you read the chapter.

	Agree	Disagree
1. An informal, unstructured program works best in kindergarten.	_____	_____
2. Reading books to young children is a better use of instructional time than working on skills.	_____	_____
3. Allowing children to spell any way they can is harmful.	_____	_____
4. Children at risk should have their literacy development accelerated so that they can catch up.	_____	_____
5. The best way for young children to learn reading is through writing.	_____	_____
6. Kindergartners should be taught a full program of beginning phonics.	_____	_____

Using What You Know

This chapter on emergent, or early, literacy is based on the ten principles for teaching reading discussed in Chapter 1. The word *literacy* encompasses both writing and reading; *emergent* indicates that the child has been engaged in reading and writing activities long before coming to school. Putting the two concepts together, Sulzby (1989b) defined emergent literacy as "the reading and writing behaviors that precede and develop into conventional literacy" (p. 84). Reflect on your personal knowledge of emergent literacy. Have you observed young children as they explored reading and writing? How did they do this? What did their writing look like? What did they learn about reading and writing from their homes and the larger environment? How would you go about fostering emergent literacy?

Understanding Emergent Literacy

Children begin developing literacy long before they enter school. Unless they are disabled, all school-age children have acquired a fairly extensive oral language vocabulary and a sophisticated syntactic system. They have seen traffic signs and billboard advertising, printed messages on television, and printing on cereal boxes. They can tell the McDonald's logo from that of Burger King and distinguish a box of Fruit Loops from one of Captain Crunch. They have seen their parents read books, magazines, newspapers, letters, and bills and have observed them writing notes or letters, filling out forms, and making lists. They may also have imitated some of these activities. Their parents may have read books to them and provided them with crayons, pencils, and other tools of literacy. All children, no matter how impoverished their environment may be, have begun the journey along the path that begins with language acquisition and ends in formal literacy. The teacher must find out where each child is on the path and lead him or her on the way. "The issue," explains Purcell-Gates (1997), "is not getting children ready to learn, but rather creating literacy environments within which

FYI

• The term *early literacy* is sometimes used instead of *emergent literacy*. Early literacy suggests that the child already has some knowledge of reading and writing, whereas emergent literacy might suggest that the child is on the verge of acquiring this knowledge.

• Different cultures might value different literacy activities. Therefore, it is important for the teacher to know what kinds of writing and reading activities are stressed in children's homes and communities so that these can be built on in the classroom. ■

FYI

For a time, children's concept of letter-sound relationships may be very specific. At age 4, my granddaughter Paige told me that she had a friend named Paul in school, and commented, "He has my letter." She had noticed that Paul's name began with a *P*, as did hers. She regarded the letters of her name as being personal and specific. The *P* in Paige identified her. She did not realize that *P* represents /p/ and can be used in any word containing a /p/ sound (see Ferreiro, 1986). ■

the learning they already do on an ongoing basis includes the different emergent literacy concepts needed for school success" (p. 427).

The concept of **emergent literacy** is rooted in research conducted a number of years ago. Read (1971) reported on a study of early spellers who had learned to spell in an informal manner. The early spellers were preschoolers who were given help in spelling when they asked for it but were otherwise allowed to spell however they wanted. What surprised Read was that these young children, who had no contact with each other, created spelling systems that were remarkably similar and that, although not correct, made sense phonetically. For instance, *er* at the end of a word such as *tiger* was typically spelled with just an *r*, as in TIGR. In this instance, *r* is syllabic; it functions as a vowel and so does not need to be preceded by an *e*. For long vowels, children generally used the letter name, as in SOP for *soap*, where the name of the letter *o* contains the sound of the vowel. Commenting on his findings, Read stated, "We can no longer assume that children must approach reading with no discernible prior conception of its structure" (p. 34). Landmark studies by researchers in several countries echoed and amplified Read's findings in both reading and writing (Clay, 1972; Ferreiro & Teberosky, 1982; Teale & Sulzby, 1986).

These revelations about children's literacy abilities have a number of implications. First and foremost, we must build on what children already know. In their five or six years before coming to school, they have acquired a great deal of insight into the reading and writing processes. Instead of asking whether they are ready, we have to find out where they are and take it from there. We must value and make use of their knowledge.

As children observe parents and peers reading and writing and as they themselves experiment with reading and writing, they construct theories about how these processes work. For instance, based on their experience with picture books, children may believe that pictures rather than words are read. Initially, children may believe that letters operate as pictures. They may believe that letters represent objects in much the same way that pictures represent objects. Using this hypothesis, they may reason that *snake* would be a long word because a snake is a long animal. *Mouse* would be a short word because a mouse is a short animal. As children notice long words for little creatures (*hummingbird, mosquito*) and short words for large creatures (*whale, tiger*), they assimilate this and make an accommodation by giving up their hypothesis of a physical relationship between size of words and size of objects or creatures represented. They may then theorize that although letters do not represent physical characteristics, letters do somehow identify the person or thing named. They may theorize that the first letters of their names belong uniquely to them (Ferreiro, 1986). Children need to see that other people's names may start with the same letters as theirs but that some or all of the other letters are different. When Paige comments that Paul has her letter, Paige might be told that yes, she and Paul have the same letter at the beginning of their names and even the same second letter, but the other letters are different. She might also be told that both their names begin with a *P* because they both begin with the same sound /p/.

Before children discover the alphabet principle, they may refine their theories of the purpose of letters and conclude that it is the arrangement of letters that matters. Through exposure to print, they will have noticed that words form patterns, and they begin to string letters together in what seem to be reasonable patterns. Usually, the words are between three and seven characters long and only repeat the same letter twice (Schickedanz, 1999). Known as *mock words*, these creations look like real words. After creating mock words, children frequently ask adults what the words say. The adults may attempt sounding out the words and realize that they don't say anything and inform the child of that fact. Realizing that they can't simply string a series of letters together, children may begin asking adults how to spell words or copy words from signs or books. As adults write multisyllabic words for

■ **Emergent literacy** consists of the reading and writing behaviors that evolve from children's earliest experiences with reading and writing and that gradually grow into conventional literacy.

children, they might sound them out as they write each syllable and also say the letters: "An-dy . . . A-N-D-Y spells Andy." Hearing words sounded out, children catch on to the idea that letters represent speech sounds. Since the words they hear have been spoken in syllables while being written, the children may use one letter to represent each syllable and one letter for the final sound and produce spellings such as JRF for *giraffe*.

If you have some insight into students' current scheme for the writing system, you can provide the kind of explanation that will help them to move to a higher level of understanding. For children who are moving from a visual or physical hypothesis about how the alphabetical system operates to a phonological one, sounding out words as you spell them provides helpful information. Providing many opportunities to write also helps students to explore the writing system.

Essential Skills and Understandings for Emergent Literacy

Understanding how print works and the many roles it plays in people's lives is known as seeing the "big picture" (Purcell-Gates, 1997). The big picture is the foundation on which all other information about reading and writing is built. Children also need to become more familiar with the types of language used in books and to acquire a deeper sense of how stories develop. On a more formal level, they need to construct basic **concepts of print**, if they have not already learned them. These concepts of print include the following:

- What we say and what others say can be written down and read.
- Words, not pictures, are read.
- Sentences are made up of words, and words are made up of letters.
- In English, reading goes from left to right and from top to bottom.
- A book is read from front to back in English.
- What we say is divided into words. (Some young students may believe that "How are you?" is a single word, for example.) Students must also grasp the concept of what a word is. Of course, they use words in their oral language, but understanding what a word is occurs on a higher level of abstraction, involving a metalinguistic or metacognitive awareness. This means that they must be able to think about language as well as use it.
- Space separates written words. Students must be able to match words being read orally with their written counterparts. Hearing the sentence "The little dog ran," the student must focus on *the*, *little*, *dog*, and *ran* as each word is read.
- Sentences begin with capital letters.
- Sentences end with periods, question marks, or exclamation marks.
- A book has a title, an author, and sometimes an illustrator.
- Students must also develop phonological awareness and arrive at an understanding of the alphabetic principle. Phonological awareness involves being able to detect separate words in a sentence, to separate syllables in a word, to segment words into their separate sounds, and to perceive beginning, ending, and medial sounds. Understanding the alphabetic principle means grasping the concept that letters represent sounds.

The rate of children's literacy development varies, as does the richness of home environments. A few children will be able to read words or even whole sentences when they enter kindergarten. However, most will still be developing emergent literacy in kindergarten and a few in first grade. The activities and procedures explored in this chapter apply to any students who might benefit from them, whether they are in kindergarten, first grade, or beyond. Very basic activities and procedures, such as developing phonological awareness and learning the names of the letters of the alphabet and the sounds of beginning consonants, may be

C.C.S.S

Demonstrate understanding of the organization and basic features of print.

■ **Concepts of print** are understandings about how print works—that printed words represent spoken words, have boundaries, are read from left to right in English, and so on.

Adapting Instruction for English Language Learners

Make generous use of illustrations and realia. Also post signs and labels in both English and the English learners' first language. ∎

Using Technology

Between the Lions is an award-winning PBS series for children aged 4–7, designed to foster a love of reading and literacy skills. The television programs are complemented by a Web site that features a host of supplementary activities, including reading stories and playing games. A number of the activities are designed for parents to engage in with their children. A teaching guide for kindergarten teachers is available.
http://pbskids.org/lions ∎

FYI

Writing and reading materials should be available in every center. Students might want to write about what they see or do in the science center or building blocks center. ∎

used with preschool children. Literacy instruction has moved downward, but it should always be developmentally appropriate. However, as Strickland (2008) explained, DAP (Developmentally Appropriate Practice) has met the gap (the difference in achievement among groups of children). There has been increased attention on helping students who have not done well in the past. One area of focus has been to help children get off to a better start.

Fostering Emergent Literacy

Regardless of where children are in terms of literacy, an essential step in further development is to create an environment that promotes active reading, writing, listening, and speaking. Getting children to engage in literacy activities is partly a matter of providing an appealing environment. One means of encouragement is to have readily available writing instruments, paper of various kinds, and books and periodicals. In a classroom environment that fosters literacy, print is everywhere. Bulletin boards include words as well as pictures. There is a calendar of students' birthdays and other important upcoming events. Aquariums and terrariums are labeled with the names of their inhabitants. Most important of all, students' stories and booklets are displayed prominently. The classroom might have a student-run post office so that children can correspond with each other. If computer equipment is available, students might even make use of e-mail. Label mailboxes with children's names but also include their pictures so that students who cannot read can find the mailboxes they are looking for. Be sure to include a mailbox for yourself and anyone who regularly visits the class. To encourage the use of the mailboxes and to model the process of writing a letter, let students observe you as you write notes to parents, to the principal, and to the students. Also, encourage adults to write to your class. Read and post their letters (Jurek, 1995).

Although a classroom can be arranged in many ways to induce children to take part in literacy activities, Morrow (1997) recommended that a variety of centers be set up, including areas for writing, math, social studies, science, music, blocks and other manipulatives, **dramatic play**, and a library. A listening/viewing center and a computing center are also possibilities. If the classroom is small, some of these centers could be combined. Centers that are clearly set off from each other by bookcases or racks, shelves, or panels foster quieter, more purposeful behavior (Vukelich, Christie, & Enz, 2012).

The writing center should contain the upper- and lowercase alphabets in manuscript form. Letters, stories, lists, and other models of writing can also be displayed. The materials should be posted at students' eye level for ease of use. A selection of writing instruments and paper should be available. Paper should come in various colors and should be unlined so that students are not unduly concerned with spacing. Small memo pads of paper are also recommended. Writing instruments should include crayons and magic markers, the latter being the choice of most children (Bauman, 1990). If pencils are provided, students should be instructed in using them safely. Other useful items for the writing center are chalkboards, magnetic letters, letter templates, whiteboards and markers, clipboards, blank books, printing sets, and computers with easy-to-use word-processing programs. Paste, glue sticks, tape, safety scissors, and staplers are also useful. Reference materials are important. For kindergarten children, such materials could consist primarily of picture dictionaries, both commercially produced and constructed by students. The center should also invite the sharing of writing by providing a table and two or more chairs so that students can share what they have written and also seek help from classmates: "I don't know what winter starts with. Do you?" (Vukelich et al., 2012)

The library or book corner should feature a wide selection of reading materials attractively displayed, including both commercial and

■ **Dramatic play** refers to a type of activity in which students play at being someone else: a doctor, a teacher, a firefighter.

student-written books. Extra copies of a book currently being read by the teacher or other books by the same author or on the same theme should be given a place of prominence. Rockers, cushions, bean-bag chairs, and pieces of rug will give students comfortable places to read. The listening/viewing center should have a wide variety of audio books and, if available, video versions that display favorite stories so that students can follow the text as the story is being read. Multiple copies of audio recordings of favorite books will allow small groups of students to listen to a book together. The dramatic play and housekeeping centers should be stocked with order blanks, note pads, signs, bills, menus, calendars, and other realia of literacy. Environmental print conveys the message that reading and writing are essential elements in everyday living. A technology center might include software, such as *Dr. Seuss Kindergarten* (Learning Company), *Reader Rabbit Kindergarten* (Learning Company), or *Learn about ABCs and Letter Sounds* (Sunburst), and apps that reinforce key themes or skills. In a classroom that fosters literacy, the tools and products of writing and reading abound.

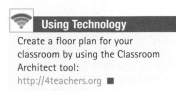

Using Technology

Create a floor plan for your classroom by using the Classroom Architect tool:
http://4teachers.org ∎

An environment that fosters literacy is both physical and attitudinal. Attitudinally, the teacher believes that literacy is a broad-based, naturally occurring process that takes place over a long period of time. Although it can and should be taught, literacy can also be fostered by "setting the scene" and through subtle encouragement. The teacher should lose no opportunity to reinforce literacy concepts. For example, after the class's pet gerbil has been named *George*, a label displaying the name is attached to the cage. While preparing the label, the teacher explains what is being done and shows the class that the letters *G-e-o-r-g-e* spell "George." When students are running software on the computer, the teacher points to the RETURN key and explains what the printing on it means. After turning a page on the calendar, the teacher points to the name of the new month and asks the class to guess what the word is. When a notice is being sent home, the teacher reads it aloud to the class first. If students see any familiar words in the notice, they are encouraged to read them.

Procedures for handling transitions are put into place. Time is spent showing children how to work in each center. Classroom routines are established and placed on charts. For instance, procedures for using the computer, turning on the CD player, and signing out books are posted. Simple words and illustrations that help convey the meaning of the procedures are used (Jurek, 1995).

Labels and signs should be used generously. Cubbies and coat hooks should be labeled with children's names. Places where supplies are stored should be labeled: paper, paints, crayons. Signs should be used to designate learning centers and key locations in the classroom. Signs should also direct students to wash hands, to put away paints when finished, to walk rather than run, and so forth. The room might also have an attendance chart and a helper chart. Students can show that they are present by putting their names in the pockets of the attendance chart. Calendar charts and schedule charts also provide opportunities for discussing print as you talk over the fact that *Monday* and *May* both begin with the same letter, which has an /m/ sound. Special days such as birthdays and holidays can be marked. On the weather chart, students can place in a pocket the cards containing the words *sunny*, *cloudy*, *rainy*, or *snowy*; *cold*, *warm*, or *hot*; *windy* or *calm*. Cards might be illustrated with pictures of the sun, clouds, rain, and snow to help students identify them. Lists, recipes, and schedules for centers also provide opportunities for reading and writing.

The key is to make use of whatever opportunities are available to foster reading and writing concepts and skills. At snack time, point out the writing on the milk cartons and note that *m-i-l-k* spells "milk." On subsequent days, you might read the name of the dairy that produced the milk or have students tell you which word says "milk," what letter *milk* begins with, or what letters *milk* has. Talk about the letters and the words on the packaging of apple juice and crackers or whatever snack foods children are eating.

Students are also encouraged to write or draw, and the emphasis is on expression and exploration rather than on conventional spelling or handwriting. There is plenty of time for conventions later. The class library is an active place. Students read books in school and are allowed to take them home. The inevitable torn pages and jelly-stained covers and the occasional lost books are a small price to pay for the development of literacy skills.

Making Reading and Writing a Part of Classroom Activities

Fostering literacy growth among young children is partly a matter of making reading and writing a natural part of their classroom activities. One way to increase early literacy experiences is to stock centers with the tools of writing and reading that might naturally appear there. In dramatic play centers, children can make use of these as they take on the roles of adults whom they see in their everyday lives. They also are more likely to role-play literacy tasks if the appropriate materials are available. Christie (1990) recommended that dramatic play centers be supplied with pens, pencils, note pads, diaries, cookbooks, telephone books, picture books, magazines, catalogs, and newspapers—in other words, the kinds of materials that might be found in the typical home. Opportunities for dramatic play that can stimulate reading and writing include the following:

1. Grocery store—creating signs, writing checks or food lists
2. Bank—writing deposit and withdrawal slips and checks
3. Doctor's office—writing prescriptions, making appointments, making bills
4. Restaurant—writing and reading menus, taking food orders, creating signs (Christie, 1990)
5. Post office—writing letters, addressing letters, mailing packages, selling stamps, delivering mail

In planning dramatic play centers, find out what kinds of experiences the children have had and how they have seen literacy function in their environments. For instance, if they are more familiar with fast-food eating places than with restaurants that have servers and individual menus, create wall-type menus characteristic of fast-food establishments.

To make dramatic play as valuable as possible, provide an introduction. Discuss the activity, or read students a book about it. Show props and talk about some of the ways they might be used (Bunce, 1995). Provide prompts or model interchanges in the initial stages or when students seem to be floundering.

For dramatic play involving a railroad station, the best preparation would be to actually visit a station and take a short trip on a train. Other possibilities include having a conductor visit the class and talk about the things that a conductor does. Viewing videos and listening to informational books about trains would also extend students' knowledge of the topic. You might model some of the oral language that the children would be using: "Where are you going? A ticket to _____ will cost $100. How will you pay for that? Will you pay in cash? Or will you use a credit card? Train Number 5 to Washington will be leaving from track 5. Train Number 5 will be leaving in 10 minutes" (Bunce, 1995).

Not all play is equal. Mature, or advanced, play provides the most benefit. In mature play, children use pretend objects and prompts. They can pretend that a refrigerator box is an airplane, for instance. They use language to set the stage or advance the action: "Let's pretend that this is an airplane, and it will take us to the ocean." Their play incorporates multiple themes. They might pretend that the dog is sick and they need to go to the vet, but on the way they get lost, thus combining sick-dog-to-the-vet and getting-lost themes. In advanced play, children adopt multiple roles. The vet might be a dad or a mom. Mature play is also extended. It is sustained over a period of time and even continued the next day (Bodrova & Leong, 2007; Ven & Jahn, 2004). Mature play has the following characteristics:

1. Symbolic representations and actions
2. Language used to create a pretend scenario

FYI

When working with difficult students who seemed to be doing everything wrong, one kindergarten teacher discovered that it was better to accept what students could do and shape their behavior rather than criticize everything they did wrong (Edwards, 2000). ■

FYI

Play programs result in average percentile gains of 17 points (Hattie, 2009). ■

FYI

Whenever possible, use naturally occurring activities to develop literacy. By involving students in an activity in which they explore literacy naturally, such as experimenting with a word-processing program in which the letters of the alphabet say their names and sounds when keys are pressed, you know that you have their attention and their interest. ■

3. Complex interwoven themes

4. Rich multifaceted roles

5. Extended time frame (often over several days) (Bodrova & Leong, 2007, p. 142)

There are a number of ways that play can be enriched. Children need long blocks of time so that themes and scenarios can be developed. Initially, play time might be 20 minutes but should be gradually extended to 40 to 60 minutes. Help the children identify a variety of roles and props that might be used. Discuss how these roles might be acted out and how the props might be used. Also monitor children's play. Most important of all, help children plan their play. You might talk over the themes, the roles, and the props. Planning play can be a literacy activity. Students can draw their play plans and then write what they intend to do or dictate their play plans.

Mature play is encouraged when dramatic play centers are carefully planned. Change the play centers frequently. Possible settings for dramatic play activities include airport, bus terminal, train station, dock, grocery store, clothing store, toy store, doctor's office, dentist's office, vet's office, firehouse, police station, recycling station, zoo, circus, movie theater, car wash, campground, beach, fast-food restaurant, pizza parlor, delivery truck, warehouse, beauty parlor, barber shop, hospital, post office, office, hotel, library, or aquarium. Possibilities are many and varied. Select the ones that interest and benefit your students the most.

Playing with print is an important part of literacy development through which children can explore the uses of the medium. After scrawling letterlike figures on a piece of paper, one child pretended he was reading a weather report (McLane & McNamee, 1990). Others have been police officers writing tickets, restaurant owners creating menus, store owners writing receipts, parents writing shopping lists, and authors writing books. Children have also pretended to read books to dolls, teddy bears, friends, and younger siblings. "Through play, children may come to feel that they are writers and readers before they actually have the necessary skills to write and read" (McLane & McNamee, 1990, p. 19).

As children learn about literacy skills through playing and observing how members of their families and communities use these skills, they become motivated to learn more about reading and writing so that they can make fuller use of these skills. In learning literacy, function fosters form. Students learn the what and the why of reading and writing as a prelude to learning the details of how to read and write.

Reading to Students

What are your favorite memories of literacy instruction and activities when you were in elementary or middle school? All these years later, I still recall Sister Irene reading *Mr. Popper's Penguins* (Atwater & Atwater, 1938) to my first-grade class. I was absolutely enchanted with the tale and, to this day, am fascinated by penguins. Surveys of teachers reveal that I am not alone in citing being read to as a favorite school activity (Fisher, Flood, Lapp, & Frey, 2004).

Why is being read to so important? Being read to develops children's vocabulary, expands their experiential background, makes them aware of the language of books, introduces them to basic concepts of print and how books are read, and provides them with many pleasant associations with books. Perhaps most important is the power of books to help children create worlds based on words and story structures (Wells, 1986).

In conversation, the child can use context to help construct the meaning of a situation. For instance, if someone is pointing to a ball and making a throwing motion while saying, "Throw me the ball," then the context for the statement—the pointing, the ball, and the throwing motion—aids understanding. However, in a story, there is no context except for, possibly, illustrations. The child must therefore use language to construct meaning. As parents read storybooks to their children, they provide a bridge between conversation with all its support and the more abstract, noninteractive

 FYI

• At least 20 minutes a day should be set aside for reading aloud, and this period should be held at a regularly scheduled time.

• Reading to students helps them comprehend literary language, which is different from conversation. Conversation is concrete, immediate, and contextual. In storybook reading, there is no physical context or clarifying interchange between author and listener. ■

After hearing a book read aloud, students might listen to a recorded version.

FYI

• Reading both narrative and informational texts is important. Narratives build a sense of story. Informational texts build background and arouse curiosity.

• However you choose to introduce a read-aloud, the introduction should be brief and should provide needed background, motivate students to want to hear the selection, and provide a purpose for listening. ■

REFLECTION

When selecting books for read-alouds, how might you balance the goal of providing an enriching experience with the need to present books that children can grasp and relate to? What provision would you make for ELLs or students who have limited experience being read to?

FYI

If families lack sufficient literacy to read to their children, encourage them to tell stories orally or to talk with their children about the pictures in books. ■

experience of hearing a story read. Intuitively, parents use the illustrations as well as explanations, gestures, and discussion to help children understand the storybook.

Initial readings are highly interactive. Over time, as the child becomes a more sophisticated listener and assimilates the format of storybook reading into her or his own schema or conceptual background, less support is offered by the reader. In the process, however, the child learns invaluable lessons about the language and structure of written text. As they read to their children, parents explain new words and expressions that crop up in storybooks. They also discuss unfamiliar concepts, intuitively relating new concepts to the child's background. Parents do not deliberately set out to teach their children new concepts and words; this happens as a natural part of reading to children. As a result of these interactions, children who are read to the most have the most highly developed language skills. They have larger vocabularies and are better able to narrate an event, describe a scene, and understand the teacher (Strickland & Taylor, 1989).

What kinds of books should be read to children? Books such as *The Very Hungry Caterpillar* (Carle, 1969), *Waiting for Wings* (Ehlert, 2001), and *My Farm Friends* (Minor, 2011) that have a richness of content are excellent choices. They build background. Nursery rhymes and books with repetitive patterns, such as *Are You My Mother?* (Eastman, 1960) and *I Am the Dog* (Pinkewater, 2010), are also excellent choices. Be sure to include informational books as read-alouds. Reading informational text sparks intriguing discussions and raises interesting questions that help foster curiosity and background building. If possible, select books that relate to themes or topics that the class is studying. However, choose books that are on students' level of comprehension and background. A book on ancient Egypt, for instance, would be well beyond the comprehension and background level of most kindergarten or first-grade students. If students seem bored or restless while you are reading a book, make sure that the book is of interest to them, is on the proper level, and is not too long and complex. If students have little experience being read to, you may want to start out with brief, easy-to-understand texts and gradually move into longer, more complex books.

Before reading a selection aloud, preview it. Make sure that it is appropriate for your class and that your students will enjoy it. Note places where you might like to stop for a brief discussion. Also practice reading it aloud so that you get the flow of it.

Schedule read-alouds regularly. Don't withhold read-alouds as a punishment. They are too important a part of the curriculum (Campbell, 2001). Set the mood for read-aloud time. To signal the start of a read-aloud, you might play a little tune, ring a bell, or initiate a chant. Or have a puppet make the announcement.

Also establish a routine for the read-aloud itself. For most read-alouds, students are seated on large rugs. They should be seated far enough apart so that they aren't pushing against each other but can turn and talk to each other when you want them to discuss some aspect of the story with their partners (Fountas & Pinnell, 2006). Research indicates that students who are seated closest to you will gain the most. Change seating places periodically so that those on the far edge are now seated close to you. Those who have been moved to the far edge will continue to make good gains because they have formed the habit of listening and responding (Teale, 2008).

Before starting to read aloud, set the stage. You might set the stage in a number of ways, such as by asking students questions that enable them to make connections between their personal backgrounds and the story. For instance, before reading *What Pet Will I Get?* (Oelschlager, 2008), which is a humorous tale about a boy who has a difficult time selecting a pet, ask students to tell about their pets and what they like about them or, if they don't have pets, what kind of pet they might like to have and why. You might also use your own experiences to introduce a read-aloud selection. In preparation for reading Eric Carle's (1973) *Have You Seen My Cat?*, you could tell about an experience you have had with a lost pet. You also might begin with a general discussion of the topic of the book or with a description that relates the book to one that you read to the class previously. Such discussions build essential concepts and background.

Hold up the book that is to be read. Point to and discuss the title. If the book's title lends itself to it, use the title as a predictive device. Have students think about the title and guess what the story might be about. For example, before reading *Ducks Disappearing* (Naylor, 1997), ask them to tell why ducks might disappear.

As you read a book, stop periodically to review what has happened, and encourage children to discuss the book with you and to make some predictions. Younger children will need more frequent stops, and their story conversations may be less focused. After you have finished reading, talk over whether their predictions came true. For example, when reading *What Pet Will I Get?*, you might ask, "What pet do you think the boy will get? What pet do you think is in the bag? What do you think the boy will do now that he has a pet that he does not like?" Encourage students to modify predictions, if necessary, and make new ones.

Hold the book so that students can see the illustrations as you read the selection. Discuss and ask questions about them. Looking at the picture in *What Pet Will I Get?*, you might ask, "What makes you think that the boy is dreaming? What is he dreaming about?" Point to pictures as you read a book in order to illustrate words and concepts that might be unfamiliar to students. By pointing to the illustration of an unfamiliar word rather than stopping and defining it, you maintain the flow of the story. Another way of handling difficult words is to simply supply a brief meaning. When reading the book *The Relatives Came* (Rylant, 1985), you might explain that relatives are people in the family: mother, father, sisters, brothers, uncles, aunts, cousins, and grandparents. Dramatizing and highlighting onomatopoeia can also help provide meanings for words. For instance, when reading *The Cat in the Hat* (Geisel, 1957), emphasize the sounds of *bump* and *thump* as you read these words. You might even make bumping and thumping sounds (Schickedanz, 1999).

Developing Story Structure   Reading to children develops a sense of story as they become familiar with plot development and the interaction of plot, characters, and setting. This familiarity bolsters comprehension, the ability to discuss stories, and the ability to compose stories.

To develop a sense of story structure, discuss with the class literary language, or words and phrases that are frequently used in stories: "once upon a time," "lived happily ever after," "many years ago," and so on. Point out that most stories have a main character, who may be an older person, a young person, or even an animal that talks and acts like a human. Have students identify the main characters in stories they know. Discuss how setting, too, may be an important element.

After students have grasped the concepts of story language and characters, point out that the main characters usually have problems to solve. Give examples from familiar stories. Discuss how Marylou's problem with having too many books in *Too Many Books* (Bauer, 1984) and the old man's problem in Wanda Gág's (1928) *Millions of Cats* are similar. Discuss the fact that problems are usually solved in some way. Talk over how that occurred for Marylou and the old man. These kinds of questions not only build comprehension, discussion, and composing skills, they also develop and lay the groundwork for an understanding of literary techniques.

Building Comprehension   In your discussions about books, ask students a variety of questions, including those that involve important details, sequence, and drawing conclusions or making inferences and that provide a foundation for reading comprehension (Feitelson, Kita, & Goldstein, 1986). Do not use the questions primarily as a

Assessing for Learning

When choosing informational books, use children's interests and curiosity as your guide. What kinds of questions do they have? Do they want to know where fog comes from or where dinosaurs lived? Are they curious about rainbows or clouds or cows? ■

FYI

Books with subtle character development may be difficult for children who have not had much experience being read to. They may do better with tales in which action is emphasized. ■

Building Language

Although predictable books allow students to think of themselves as readers, they aren't the best texts for developing language (Dickinson & Smith, 1994). Books that have more complex plots and better-developed characters or that delve more deeply into topics offer a richer vocabulary and more opportunities for language development. ■

Adapting Instruction for Struggling Readers and Writers

Dramatizing a story after reading it helps students internalize the story's sequence (Edwards, 2000). ■

Using Technology

Reading Rockets
Repeated Interactive Read-Alouds in Preschool and Kindergarten
Lea M. McGee and Judith Schickedanz
Provides an explanation and examples of interactive reading.
http://www.readingrockets.org/article/1628 ■

technique for gauging depth of understanding but as a means for drawing attention to important details or relating details so that a conclusion can be reached or a main idea constructed. For example, after you have read *The Snowy Day* (Keats, 1962), ask students how Peter felt about the snow. Then ask them how they know that Peter liked the snow. Go back over the story if children have difficulty supplying details that back up the conclusion. Think of your discussions as a way of sharing so that books can be more fully understood and enjoyed.

Making Personal Connections   Students will not fully appreciate reading unless the stories touch their lives. Ask questions that involve personal reactions, such as how a story made them feel, what they liked best, whether they have ever met anyone like the main character, or whether they would like to hear a similar book. After reading *Whistle for Willie*, by Ezra Jack Keats (1964), have students describe how Willie felt at the end, and ask them about a time when they have felt proud.

After discussing a story, you may want to provide follow-up or extension activities. The book could become the focus of learning center activities. Students might listen to a taped version or pretend to read the story to a partner. Pretend reading provides them with the opportunity to use book language. Follow-up activities also include illustrating a portion of the story; watching a videotape or DVD; visiting the author's Web site; or carrying out some activity suggested by the book. After reading *The Gingerbread Boy* (Galdone, 1975), students might have a hunt for a gingerbread man; reading *The Carrot Seed* (Krauss, 1945) might lead to the planting of seeds. Another excellent follow-up is reading another book by the same author.

Planning an Interactive Read Aloud.   Books may be read aloud for a number of different purposes. You might read a book simply to provide an enjoyable experience for children. Or you may want to build students' language and background knowledge along with providing an enjoyable experience. Listening to read-alouds should always be an enjoyable experience. However, if you wish to build language and background, include activities that will help achieve these aims. Interactive read-alouds can help you achieve both aims (McGee & Schickedanz, 2007). In an interactive reading, students become involved in the reading process by responding to the reader's prompts and probes. The reader might also model making predictions or drawing inferences. The following general plan for reading narrative books aloud interactively has been adapted from Mason, Peterman, and Kerr (1988, Fig. 1) and McGee and Schickedanz, 2007.

Before reading the narrative book

Show the cover of the book to the children. Read the title. Encourage discussion about the book's content. Children might predict what is going to happen. Introduce children to the story's main characters. You might also provide a brief overview of the story problem. This story is about a boy and a dog who change places. "Set a purpose for the children to listen to the story, usually to find out what happens to the main character: "Let's find out what happens when the boy and dog change places." Or children might make predictions, which they can verify or modify during the reading: "What do you think will happen to the boy?"

During the reading of the narrative book

Encourage children to react to and comment on the story. Elaborate on the text, when appropriate, in order to help children understand the written language used in the story and the story's components, such as the main character's problem, attempts to resolve the problem, and its resolution. Ask occasional questions to monitor children's comprehension of the story. During the initial reading, you might ask, who, what, where, and when questions to foster a basic understanding of the story. As students demonstrate a basic understanding of the text, ask why and other higher-level questions. Rephrase the text when it is apparent that children are having difficulty with the words or phrases. Briefly define or explain key words: "*reluctant* means 'not wanting to do something.' I was reluctant to eat the strange food." If building vocabulary is a key aim, select five or so key words that you will briefly introduce. At appropriate points in the story, ask children to predict what will happen next or to make inferences about characters. If students have difficulty making inferences, model how you go about the process. "The story says that the boy is running around and smiling. That makes me think he is happy to be a dog."

After reading the narrative book

Discuss students' predictions or the purpose for listening that was established earlier. Review the vocabulary words if one of your aims is building vocabulary. Help children make connections between the events in the story and similar events in their own lives. "Have you ever dreamed of changing places with your pet? If you could be an animal, what kind of animal would you choose to be? Why?" Engage children in some kind of follow-up activity. This could include rereading the selection and building a deeper understanding of the selection or reading another book about the same topic.

For reading informational books aloud, the following general plan has been adapted from Mason, Peterman, and Kerr (1988, Fig. 2).

Before reading the informational book

Read the title of the book, and have students predict what the author will tell them in the book. Determine children's level of understanding of the topic of the book. Do this by discussing the pictures in the text and having the children describe their experiences with the topic. You might also bring in relevant artifacts, such as model trucks when reading a book about trucks. Build background as necessary.

Provide demonstrations and in-context explanations of difficult concepts.

Set a purpose for listening. This often involves finding the answers to questions the children raised in their discussion of the topic. Or students might make predictions and read to see if their predictions are correct or need to be modified.

Provide a link between their experiences with the topic and what they will be learning from the book.

During the reading of the informational book

Ask questions periodically to check children's understanding of the text. Questions that actually appear in the text might provide excellent opportunities for discussion and elucidation of the topic. Through comments about the pictures and through carefully selected questions, help children identify pictures that represent unfamiliar concepts. Briefly define or explain key words.

After reading the informational book

Discuss children's predictions, questions they raised, or questions you posed. Encourage children to ask further questions about the text. Review key vocabulary words. Help them see how informational books can be used to learn more about their own world. Reread the book but set purposes and ask questions that foster a deeper or fuller understanding of the topic or read other books on the same topic. Provide suggestions about activities the children might engage in later to further explore the topic. Students might visit a Web site or view a video clip that extends the topic. After hearing an informational book about bald eagles, students might view the Web cam at http://www.baldeagleinfo.com/eagle/eagle13.html to view a bald eagle nest. Offer activities that will tie the book's concepts to children's experiences.

Reading aloud is particularly effective for developing language when the books are carefully chosen and when there is interaction before, during, and after each book has been read. This is especially true when the reader uses cognitively challenging talk. *Cognitively challenging talk* includes analyzing characters and events, predicting upcoming events, making connections between the text and real-life experiences, discussing or explaining vocabulary words, summarizing portions of the text, and eliciting evaluative responses about the text by asking students to tell whether they liked the story or who the favorite character was and why (Dickinson & Smith, 1994). Although discussions are important, they shouldn't interrupt the flow of the story. Delay extended

Adapting Instruction for English Language Learners

ELLs benefit when read to in small groups. Books and activities can be geared to their level of English (Hickman & Pollard-Durodoa, 2009). ■

FYI

How much children benefit from being read to depends on the quality of the book and the way it is read (Zevenbergen & Whitehurst, 2003). Children show greater gains when the reading is interactive—when they are asked questions or are involved in discussing the story. ■

discussions until after the story has been read. Otherwise, children are likely to lose interest and become restless.

Developing Language and Thinking Skills   Being read to and discussing books also build thinking skills. The questions teachers ask about books they read aloud produce only brief responses, often just a single word (Beck & McKeown, 2001). To encourage students to provide elaborated responses, ask open-ended questions. Open-ended questions for *Harry the Dirty Dog* (Zion, 1956) might include these: "What do we know about Harry? How does what Harry did fit in with what we know about him? Why did the family call Harry a strange dog when they saw him in their backyard?" Since students often have a difficult time providing elaborated responses, the teacher might follow up these queries with prompts. Some of the prompts are general: "What does that mean? What is that all about? Can you tell me more about that? Would you explain what you mean?" Others are specific: "What else do we know about Harry? What else did Harry do?" Repeating what students said also helps. When students are unable to respond, rereading the portion of the story being queried helps them formulate a response. The key to developing language and thinking skills is to pose questions that elicit more elaborated responses and to provide support through prompts or reading that help students formulate a response. By evaluating children's responses, you can help build their language (Zevenbergen & Whitehurst, 2003). For instance, you might help a child use more precise vocabulary or expand a response. If a child identifies a moose as a deer, you might say, "That animal looks like a deer, but we call it a moose." If the child says, "Bad dog!" you might prompt an elaborated response: "Why is that dog bad? Can you tell me what the dog does that is bad?"

To make read-alouds more concrete and to develop language, try creating prop boxes (Wasik, Bond, & Hindman, 2006). Prop boxes contain books to be read and concrete objects that depict vocabulary words to be covered. A prop box for gardens might contain *The Carrot Seed* (Krauss, 1945) and *Jack's Garden* (Cole, 1995). The box might also contain the following props: seeds, a shovel, a rake, a small version of a garden hose, a watering can, plastic insects, plastic flowers, a stalk of corn, and a carrot. The props can be used to create interest and also to develop vocabulary. To develop vocabulary, decide which words you plan to present. Use the props as an aid. Also read the books twice. Discuss or point out vocabulary words as you encounter them. Use the target vocabulary throughout the day.

Selecting Read-Aloud Books   To make your read-alouds as valuable as possible, plan the texts that you intend to read to your students. Most important of all, choose books that students will enjoy and will be able to understand and relate to. If possible, the books should feature a theme currently being explored, reinforce skills that you are working on, and develop students' language. Most published programs offer lengthy lists of suggested read-alouds. By planning ahead for read-alouds, you can build on past read-alouds while reinforcing your curriculum. You might want to form a study group with other teachers and decide which books to read aloud at each grade level so that students in later grades aren't listening to books that were read to them in earlier grades. You can also share suggestions for good read-alouds and discuss how read-alouds can strengthen the school's literacy program (Fountas & Pinnell, 2006). Enlist the help of your school media specialist, and consult Titlewave and/or Trelease-on-Reading. See the Student Reading List for a number of books that are recommended for reading aloud.

Literally thousands of books make enjoyable, worthwhile read-alouds. An excellent source of both titles and techniques for reading aloud is Trelease's (2006) *The New Read-Aloud Handbook*, 6th edition. Other sources of read-aloud titles include the following:

Anderson, N. (2007). *What should I read aloud? A guide to 200 best-selling picture books*. Newark, DE: International Reading Association.

Children's Book Committee at the Bank Street College of Education. (2003). *Books to read aloud*. New York: Author.

FYI

Students who have been read to will pick up many concepts of print through observing and interacting with the person reading. Children may notice how print functions, ask questions about words and letters, or try to match print with the words being read. ■

Using Technology

Titlewave provides extensive information about books and other media, including interest level, readability level, book reviews, and awards that books have won. You can search by author, title, topic, grade level, subject area, or curriculum standard.
http://www.flr.follett.com/login

Trelease-on-Reading.com provides extensive information on read-alouds:
http://www.trelease-on-reading.com ■

STUDENT READING LIST
Recommended Books for Read-Alouds

Angelou, M. (1994). *My painted house, my friendly chicken, and me.* New York: Clarkson N. Potter. An eight-year-old Ndebele girl tells about life in her village in South Africa.

Barnes-Murphy, F. (1994). *The fables of Aesop.* New York: Lothrop. This collection of fables retold from Aesop includes "The Hare and the Tortoise" and "The Ant and the Grasshopper."

Canon, J. (1993). *Stellaluna.* San Diego, CA: Harcourt. After she falls headfirst into a bird's nest, a baby bat is raised like a bird until she is reunited with her mother.

Cowley, J. (2005). *Chameleon, chameleon.* New York: Scholastic. Full-color photos show the chameleon as it tracks down and eats a caterpillar.

Dorros, A. (1991). *Abuela.* New York: Dutton. While riding on a bus with her grandmother, a little girl imagines that they are carried up into the sky and fly over the sights of New York City.

Eastman, P. D. (1960). *Are you my mother?* New York: Random House. After falling out of its nest, a small bird searches for its mother.

Gershator, D., & Gershator, P. (1995). *Bread is for eating.* New York: Holt. When her son leaves bread on his plate, his mother explains why bread is for eating. And she sings him a song in Spanish.

Greenfield, E. *Honey, I love.* (1978, 1995). New York: HarperCollins. A young girl tells about the many things in her life that she loves.

Jango-Cohen, J. (2004). *The bald eagle.* Minneapolis MN: Lerner. Well-illustrated text provides basic information about bald eagles.

Keats, E. J. (1962). *The snowy day.* New York: Viking. A small boy has fun in the snow.

Maitland, B. (2000). *Moo in the morning.* New York: Farrar Straus Giroux. A boy and his mother visit an uncle in the country because the city is noisy, but they find that the country has its own noises.

Martin, B., Jr. (1983). *Brown Bear, Brown Bear, what do you see?* New York: Holt. A brown bear, a blue horse, a purple cat, and other creatures are asked to tell what they see.

McCloskey, R. (1941). *Make way for ducklings.* New York: Viking. With the assistance of a kindly police officer, a mother duck and her brood waddle from the Charles River to the pond in Boston's Public Garden.

Parr, T. (2005). *Otto goes to school.* New York: Little, Brown. Otto, the dog, goes to school for the first time.

Reiser, L. (2006). *Hardworking puppies.* Orlando, FL: Harcourt. Ten puppies find jobs.

Schreiber, A. (2010) *Pandas.* Washington, DC: National Geographic. Well-illustrated book explains where and how pandas live.

Stead, P. C. (2010). *A sick day for Amos McGee.* New York: Roaring Brook Press. When zoo-keeper Amos McGee stays home because he is sick, the animals come to see him.

FYI

Wells (1986) found book reading to be one of the most productive situations for developing language. ■

Children's Book Committee at the Bank Street College of Education. (2010). *The best children's books of the year.* New York: Author. This special anniversary edition has a list of the best books of the last 100 years.

Freeman, J. (2006). *Books kids will sit still for 3: A read-aloud guide.* New Providence, NJ: Libraries Unlimited.

Hansen-Krening, N., Aoki, E. M., & Mizokawa, D. T. (Eds.). (2003). *Kaleidoscope: A multicultural booklist for grades K–8* (4th ed.). Urbana, IL: NCTE.

Indiana Library Federation. (2010). *Read-aloud books too good to miss.* Available at http://www.ilfonline.org/programs-awards/read-aloud-books.

Read Aloud America. http://www.readaloudamerica.org/booklist.htm. Features read-alouds selected by librarians, authors, and teachers.

If students have not been read to on a regular basis, schedule extra read-aloud sessions. When read to systematically on a one-to-one basis, economically disadvantaged

Adapting Instruction for Struggling Readers and Writers

In an urban prekindergarten, Maxie Perry enlisted the services of volunteers and aides to read to individual children. Because some of the volunteers had limited reading skills themselves and lacked confidence, she supplied sensitive guidance and suggestions (Strickland & Taylor, 1989). ■

preschoolers demonstrate a greater involvement with stories and increase the number and complexity of their questions and comments. Together with fostering a sense of story, the sessions apparently develop oral language and social skills (Morrow, 1988). Working with groups of five, Klesius and Griffith (1996) implemented interactive storybook reading with kindergarten children whose language development was below that of the other students in the class and who were not responsive to whole-class read-aloud sessions. In addition to developing overall literacy skills, the children "discovered that books are a source of enchantment and wonder" (p. 560).

A Theme Approach

Instruction is most beneficial when connections are made. Creating units helps to build connections and build background. A unit topic might be transportation, and the theme might be: "We travel in different ways." Activities revolve around the theme. In dramatic play, students manage bus stations, airports, docks, railroad stations, and a taxi company. Read-alouds include books about the various kinds of transportation: *Cars, Boats, Planes* (Emberley, 1987); *School Bus* (Crews, 1984); *The Adventures of Taxi Dog* (Barracca, 1990); *Cars, Trucks and Planes* (Rosa-Mendoza, 2011); *Trucks* (Nixon, 2011); *Boats! Boats! Boats!* (Cleland, 2009); *Trains on the Move* (Sullivan, 2011); *Freight Trains* (Ryan, 2011); or the *See How They Go* series by Dorling Kindersley. Students also sing songs and recite rhymes related to the unit theme: "Row, Row, Row Your Boat," "Wheels on the Bus."

Instruction is also most beneficial when you have specific objectives. If you want to foster language and literacy skills, you need to specify these. You might note vocabulary words and structures that you would like students to learn. Vocabulary words might include *transportation, highway, airport, luggage, tickets, boarding pass, passengers, fuel, pilot, cabin attendants, driver, captain, port, dock, railroad, train station, engineer, conductor, platform, reservation, track,* and *coach*. Also note literacy objectives and activities. Objectives might be to have students read environmental print such as signs and logos, become aware of the uses of print, and engage in writing. Activities such as reading signs at the railroad station, advertisements for recognizable products, an illustrated menu in a food car, or illustrated schedules and writing tickets and credit card slips would help achieve these objectives.

Emergent Storybook Reading

On one visit with my 4-year-old granddaughter Paige, she took me aside and whispered, "I can read." Sitting on the sofa, she "read" *Are You My Mother?* (Eastman, 1960) as she leafed through the pages. Although she was not actually reading the words on the pages—her retelling was guided by the pictures—her voice had the tone and expression of one who is reading aloud rather than of one who is telling a story. Paige was engaged in **emergent storybook reading**, a widespread phenomenon in homes and classrooms where children are read to frequently.

Children who have been read to imitate the process and engage in readinglike behaviors. As a result of being read to, children play with books, often for long periods of time, and gradually learn to reconstruct the stories conveyed in the books that have been read to them. For their pretend reading, or emergent storybook reading, children typically select a favorite storybook, one that has been read to them many times. Children's storybook reading can be placed in any of five broad categories beginning with talking about the illustrations in a storybook (but not creating a story) to actually reading a storybook in conventional fashion. The five categories are presented in Table 4.1.

Encourage students to "read" to themselves, to you, and to each

■ **Emergent storybook reading** is the evolving ability of a child to read storybooks, which progresses from simply telling a story suggested by the book's illustrations or having heard the book read aloud to reading the book conventionally.

Category	Description
Attends to pictures but does not create a story.	The child simply talks about the illustrations and does not attempt to make connections among the pictures so as to tell a story.
Uses pictures to create an oral story.	Using the storybook's illustrations, the child creates a story. However, the child's expression and intonation are those of telling rather than reading a story.
Uses pictures to create a combined oral/reading story.	Using the storybook's illustrations, the child retells a story. Portions of the retelling sound like oral storybook reading; however, other portions sound like an oral retelling of the story or are conversational.
Uses pictures to create a literary retelling.	Using the storybook's illustrations, the child creates a literary rendition of a story. In wording, expression, and intonation, it sounds like the reading of a storybook. The reading may be verbatim but is not just memorized. The verbatim rendition is conceptual. The child uses knowledge of the specific events in the story to help recall the wording of the story (Sulzby, 1985).
Uses print to read.	Ironically, the first subcategory here may be a refusal to read. As a child attempts to use print rather than pictures, the child may realize that she or he cannot decipher the print and therefore might say, "I don't know the words." In the second subcategory, the child pays attention to known aspects of print, such as a few known words or a repeated phrase.

TABLE 4.1 Emergent Reading of Storybooks

Based on Classification Scheme for Children's Emergent Reading of Favorite Storybooks (simplified version) (pp. 137–138) by E. Sulzby (1992). In J. W. Irwin & M. A. Doyle (Eds.), *Reading/Writing Connections: Learning from Research*. Newark, DE: International Reading Association.

other, even though that reading may be a simple retelling of the story. By providing them with opportunities to interact with books in this way, you will be setting the scene for their construction of more advanced understandings about the reading process. You might provide 10 minutes a day for reading time. Schedule it to follow your read-aloud segment so that students can choose to read or retell a book that you have just read. Students can read alone, to you, or to a classmate. Explain to them that they do not have to read like grownups; they can read in their own way (Sulzby & Barnhart, 1992). You might also provide a read-aloud center where students can read to a doll or stuffed animal or read along with a recorded version of a story.

Observe children as they read to themselves (young children's "silent" reading is generally audible), to a stuffed animal, to a friend, or to you. Observing children's storybook reading will provide insight into their understanding of the reading process, which has implications for instruction. If children do not use storybook intonation, for example, they may not have a grasp of the language of books and so may need to be read to more often (Sulzby & Barnhart, 1992). Until they have a sense of literary language, children may have difficulty grasping the concept that the printed words on a page convey the story and can be read aloud.

Using Shared Book Experiences

An excellent way to help students construct concepts of print (words are made up of letters, sentences are made up of words, reading goes from left to right and top to bottom, etc.) and other essential understandings is the **shared book experience**, also known as *shared reading*. Shared book experience is modeled on the bedtime story situation in which a parent or grandparent or other guardian reads to a child, and, through observation and interaction, the child discovers the purpose of and satisfaction provided by books and begins to construct basic concepts of print (Holdaway, 1979). In order to make the print visible to a group, enlarged text or multiple copies are used. There are several ways of providing enlarged text. Holdaway (1979) suggested using a **big book**, an oversized book,

FYI

When young children play at reading, they rehearse the special things a reader does, such as turning the pages, inspecting the pictures, and pausing to savor or to return to particular moments (Learning Media, 1991). ■

Adapting Instruction for Struggling Readers and Writers

Share-read books that are shorter and easier so that students will be better able to follow along. After a shared reading (as compared to a traditional oral reading of a storybook), students, in general, had richer retellings and were more enthusiastic; however, the average and below-average youngsters benefited most (Combs, 1987). ■

■ **Shared book experience,** which is also known as *shared reading*, is the practice of reading repetitive stories, chants, poems, or songs, often in enlarged text, while the class follows along or joins in.

■ A **big book** is a book large enough so that all the words can be seen by all the members of the group or class. A typical size is 15 by 19 inches.

FYI

• The amount of support students are given when reading continually decreases: First comes oral reading to students; then shared reading, in which students follow along; paired reading, in which the teacher or a tutor and students take turns reading; guided reading, in which students receive instructional preparation; buddy reading, in which students take turns reading to each other; and finally independent reading, in which students read on their own.

• Predictable books invite children to chime in as the adult is reading (Schickedanz, 1999). Knowing letters and beginning sounds helps a child point to words. If the text is a memorized one, the child can recite a line of print, but while reciting a word, she or he thinks of the beginning sound of the word and the letter that represents that sound. This enables the child to point to words as she or he reads. ■

CCSS

Follow words from left to right, top to bottom, and page by page.

Recognize that spoken words are represented in written language by specific sequences of letters.

Understand that words are separated by spaces in print.

measuring approximately 15 by 19 inches, in which the text is large enough so that students can follow the print as the teacher reads. Alternatives to a big book include using a document projector, interactive white board, or an overhead projector and transparencies or carefully printing parts of the text on story paper or the board.

Before reading a big book, introduce the selection by discussing the title and cover illustration. Invite students to predict what the story might be about, build background and interest, and set a purpose for reading it. If it is a story that has already been shared with the class, the purpose can grow out of the original reading and discussion. Perhaps some details were not clear, and so children need to listen carefully to those parts. Or they may simply enjoy hearing a certain tale over and over again. The purpose also could lead to deeper involvement with the characters. Say, for example, that you have made a big book out of *Good as New* (Douglas, 1982), the story of a badly damaged teddy bear that was refurbished by its owner's grandfather. Students might imagine being the child who owns the bear. Have them read along with you and describe how they feel when K.C. cries for the bear. As the story progresses, ask them what they think when K.C. plays with the bear and treats it very roughly. What do they feel when the bear is just about ruined?

As you read, point to the words so that students have a sense of going from left to right and also begin to realize that printed words have spoken equivalents, and that sentences are composed of words. Also discuss key happenings, clarify confusing elements, and have students revise or make new predictions. However, do not interrupt the flow of the reading. The focus should be on having students enjoy the experience. After you have shared a book, discuss it with the class, just as you would after reading a book orally to them.

Successive Readings   One goal of shared reading is to involve the students more deeply in the reading. If the book you have shared with students is one they would like to read again, conduct a second shared reading. During this second reading, encourage students to join in by reading refrains, or repeated phrases, sentences, or words that are readily predictable from context or illustrations. They can do this chorally as a group or as individual volunteers. In these subsequent shared readings, continue to point to each word as you read it so that students can see that you are reading individual words. During a second reading of the book *Are You My Mother?* (Eastman, 1960), read the repeated sentence "Are you my mother?" pointing to each word as you read it. Have volunteers read the sentence. Again, point to each word as the sentence is being read. Then read the story once more. Tell students that you are going to read the story, but they are going to help. As you come to "Are you my mother?" pause and have the class read the sentence in unison as you point to each word. Schedule the book for additional readings with choral reading of the repeated sentence. From time to time, have individual volunteers read the line.

Children have a difficult time following along in a shared reading until they learn to identify initial consonants.

During follow-up reading of *Rosie's Walk* (Hutchins, 1987), one teacher began introducing students to concepts of words and letters. Pointing to the first page, she asked the students what the page said. Because the story had been read to them previously, they were able to say that it told that Rosie the hen went for a walk. The teacher asked them to find the word *hen* and point to it with a pointer and to tell what letters were in *hen* (Campbell, 2001). Students might also talk about names of classmates that begin with *h* or about other *h* words in the story.

Concept of word is a key skill in shared reading. Concept of word means that a student can point to separate words in a sentence when that sentence is being read either by the student or by someone else. Concept of word is facilitated by awareness of beginning sounds. Using beginning sounds, students can mark the first sound of a word and use that as an anchor point. Once students have a concept of word, they are better able to build their knowledge of letter–sound relationships. Because they are able to follow along during shared reading, they begin to match sounds with letters and to learn whole words and additional letter–sound relationships, such as ending consonant correspondences. This process is aided if the teacher points to words as a big book is read and if the big book contains just one line on a page so that students can match spoken and printed words (Morris, Bloodgood, Lomax, & Perney, 2003). You can also start a word wall that contains words that have been introduced to the class. On the word wall, place words that have been repeated in the shared reading. Review these words and encourage students to use them in their writing.

Once a big book has been shared, have students engage in follow-up activities. Some may choose to listen to a recorded version while reading a regular-size edition of the book. A small group may want to read the big book once more, with one of their members assuming the role of teacher. Some students may want to read to partners, while still others may want to listen to a new story in the listening center or draw an illustration related to the big book. Students who have listened to *Are You My Mother?* may want to look at Komori's (1983) *Animal Mothers*, which uses realistic paintings to show how animal mothers get their babies to travel with them. Viewing a filmstrip, videotape, CD-ROM, or Web site on animal mothers and their young may be another option. Later, the class as a group might compose a story based on observations of how the class's mother gerbil cares for her young. Some students may want to dictate an individual story telling how their cats or dogs cared for their young. Some students may want to compose their own stories, using drawings and **invented spelling**. Invented spellings, such as "I KN RT" for "I can write," reflect the evolving concept of how letter–sound relationships should be represented.

To help students get started on follow-up stories, you might put three or four key words from the book that was read aloud on the classroom word wall or bulletin board. After sharing *Rosie's Walk* (Hutchins, 1987), one class took a walk around the school grounds to see what they could see. Students then wrote a story about their walk (Campbell, 2001). Words from this story that might be put on a word wall include *walk*, *saw*, and *for*. The students' individual stories were collected in a book. Each student was given two pages. The student's version was pasted on the right-hand page and a correctly spelled rewritten version appeared on the left-hand page, so that other students could read the book.

Periodically, introduce other repetitive selections. They need not be stories— poems, rhymes, songs, easy recipes, craft directions, and even jump-rope chants are suitable. Some of these selections may be in big books; others can be written on the board, interactive white board, or chart paper or displayed with a document camera. As students' understanding of print develops, introduce additional concepts: Point out that words are composed of letters, talk about the sounds in words, discuss words that begin with the same sound, and help students see that some words begin with the same letter and the same sound. Also discuss **print conventions**, such as punctuation marks, capital letters, and quotation marks. And, whenever introducing a new selection, point out the title and author's name.

FYI

Until children know beginning sounds and letters, following along with a shared reading may be difficult and unprofitable. Reading aloud to these children might be a more appropriate activity. ■

■ **Invented spelling** is the intuitive spelling that novices create before learning or while learning the conventional writing system. Invented spelling is also known as temporary, developmental, constructive, phonics-based, or transitional spelling (Strickland, 2011). These terms indicate that this spelling marks a passing stage in the child's development.

■ **Print conventions** refer to generally accepted ways of putting words on a page, such as arranging words from left to right and using capital letters and end punctuation.

Adapting Instruction for English Language Learners

For individual stories, write the story just as the student says it, even if the grammar is not correct or the student uses both English and his native language. For group stories, use correct grammar or students may become confused. ∎

Dialogic Reading   *Dialogic reading* is a form of interactive shared book reading in which the questioning and prompts are used with a small group to develop deeper understanding (Doyle & Bramwell, 2006). Questions are asked on three levels as in interactive reading explained earlier: literal questions, open-ended questions, and connection questions in which the children relate events in the story to another story or an experience in their lives. Vocabulary is also developed through discussion of key ideas in a selection. For instance, a classroom discussion in one dialogic reading session became an extended discussion of why the character in the story was feeling frustrated (a new vocabulary word), about times in which the children had felt frustrated, and about some things they might do when they feel frustrated. Through this and similar discussions, dialogic reading is used to develop social and emotional skills as students read about and discuss challenging situations. Here is an example of dialogic reading used with a storybook about a fish.

Before reading the book, the teacher asks children to point to the title and make predictions about what might happen. This helps children anticipate what's to come and establish a personal incentive to see what happens—to see if their predictions come to pass.

During book reading, the teacher gives explanations, prompts comments, and poses questions to gauge how well students are following and understanding the story. The teacher might ask, "What could Fish do to make friends?" As students share their ideas, the teacher could turn their attention back to the story to show how Fish tries to solve the problem. As she does, the teacher can also build print awareness by tracking with her finger to show that text is read from top to bottom and left to right.

After reading the book, the teacher will discuss it with the children, often drawing connections between events in the story and their everyday lives. For example, she might ask, "How did Fish feel about losing his scales? Have you lost something you loved? How did you feel?" This final level of reflection helps children see reading as a gateway to understanding their own world, helping them establish a personal connection to literacy (Doing What Works, 2007).

Using Language-Experience Stories

Language-experience stories can also be used to introduce the visual aspects of reading. They may be used instead of or in conjunction with big books and may be created by students working in groups or by individuals. As the name suggests, a language-experience story is based on a real-life experience. For instance, the story in Figure 4.1 began with a class trip to a nearby apple orchard. When they returned to school, the students discussed the orchard and drew pictures to illustrate their trip. Pictures often result in more focused, coherent stories because they encapsulate the child's experience (Platt, 1978). The teacher (or an aide) discusses each child's picture, after which the child dictates a story about it. As the teacher writes the child's dictated story, the teacher tells the student what he or she is doing. Then the teacher reads the story back and asks if that is what the child wanted to say. The teacher invites the child to add to the story or make other changes. Once any requested changes have been made, the teacher again reads the story. Then the teacher and the child read the story together. After this shared reading, the child is invited to read his or her story to the teacher. Aided by the drawing and the familiarity of the experience, children usually are able to read their stories.

Individual stories are gathered into books, which children are encouraged to take home and read to their families. During the school year, students may create anywhere from one to a dozen books, depending on their interest in the activity and their emerging skills.

∎ **Language-experience stories** can foster emergent literacy. One student or a group of students dictates a story, which is then used as a basis for reading and writing instruction.

FIGURE 4.1   Language-Experience Story

The Apple Orchard

We went to the apple orchard.
I saw apples on the trees.
I saw a big red apple on the ground.

Miguel

Shared (Interactive) Writing

In **shared (interactive) writing**, which is modeled on experience stories and shared reading, both teacher and student compose a story (Martin, 1995). Just as in traditional language-experience stories, the class writes about experiences they have had or books that have been read to them. Often, a shared reading of a favorite book sets the stage for the class's writing. After share-reading Sarah Albee's *I Can Do It* (1997), in which the Muppets tell about some of the things they can do, one class composed a story about things they can do. In addition to suggesting content, students also participated in the actual writing. The teacher encouraged students to spell or write initial consonants, parts of words, or even whole words. These novice writers were encouraged to use their knowledge of the spellings of their names. For instance, Carl was able to supply the first letter of *can* because *can* begins like *Carl*, and Roberto was able to supply the first letter of *ride*.

In shared writing, the teacher emphasizes reading for meaning and basic concepts of print. For instance, after adding a word to a story, the teacher goes back and reads the portion of the sentence that has been written so far. Focused on the details of the writing of a word, students may have lost the sense of the sentence. Going back over what has been written helps the students keep the story in mind and also helps them make a one-to-one match between written and spoken words. After, for example, adding "ride" to "Roberto can," the teacher rereads all that has been written of the sentence: "Roberto can ride." As part of scaffolding, the teacher also asks such questions as the following:

Where do we begin writing?

How many words are there in our sentence?

Say the word slowly. What sounds do you hear?

Can you write the letter that stands for that sound?

Here is sample dialogue to show how shared writing might be implemented:

Teacher: What are some things that you can do?

Maria: I can ride a bike.

Teacher: How shall we write that in our story?

Felicia: Maria can ride a bike.

Teacher: How many words are in that sentence?

Reginald: Five.

Teacher: What is the first word?

Jason: Maria.

Teacher: (pointing to spot on chalkboard) Maria, will you write your name here?

Teacher: (pointing to and reading *Maria*) What goes next?

Thomas: Can.

Teacher: How many sounds does *can* (teacher stretches out word) have?

James: Three.

Teacher: How does *can* (emphasizes first sound) begin? Who has a name that begins like *can*?

Carl: I do.

Teacher: How does your name begin?

Carl: With a *c*.

Teacher: Would you write a *c* here? (Judging that the students would not be able to spell the short *a* sound, the teacher adds an *a* and says,) "What should we add to /ca/ to make *can*?"

Assessing for Learning

As students participate in shared writing, note what they can do. Can they supply initial or final consonants? Do they seem to know most of the consonant correspondences? Or do they just know the consonants that their names begin with? Can they read some words? What do your observations suggest about the type of instruction they might need? ■

 FYI

• For additional examples of shared (interactive) writing, see the chapters on interactive writing in *Voices in Word Matters*, edited by I. C. Fountas and G. S. Pinnell (Portsmouth, NH: Heinemann, 1999).

• Students are asked to point to the words they read to make sure that they are processing individual words and not just reciting a portion of the text that they have memorized. ■

■ In **shared (interactive) writing**, students may tell the teacher what letters to write or may actually write them in the piece.

Exemplary Teaching
Shared Writing in Kindergarten

Using a series of informal assessment devices, Paige Ferguson determined that only half of her kindergarten students could write their names and only two knew the letters of the alphabet. Given the children's low level of literacy development, she decided to use shared writing with them. As part of their literature unit, she read Paul Galdone's (1975) *The Gingerbread Boy* to the class. The class then took a walking tour of the school to find hidden gingerbread boys. After returning to the classroom, the class began creating a shared story. The story consisted of listing the places where they found the gingerbread boys.

Building on the students' knowledge of the sounds and letters in their names, the teacher introduced other sounds and letters as the class created additional shared stories. To reinforce the children's awareness of separate words, she had one student point to each word in the story while the other children read it. As the year progressed, the children learned to hear the separate sounds in words and represent these sounds with letters. They also learned to write in a variety of formats. They wrote shared letters to pen pals, retold stories, made lists, and summarized scientific observations that they had made.

In addition to writing interactively, the children wrote independently each day. Shared writing provided a foundation for their independent writing. They also reread the shared stories that had been hung up around the room. When assessed in the spring, the students demonstrated dramatic progress. They showed growth in phonemic awareness, knowledge of letter–sound relationships, alphabet knowledge, concepts of print, and writing. Most could also read some beginning first-grade-level books (Button, Johnson, & Ferguson, 1996).

Class: N.

Teacher: Whose name has an *n*?

Nan: Mine does.

Teacher: (After the *n* has been added, she says, pointing to each word) Maria can. What can Maria do?

Class: Ride a bike.

Teacher: How many sounds does *ride* (teacher emphasizes sounds in word) have?

Cynthia: Three.

Teacher: How does *ride* (emphasizes first sound) begin? Whose name begins like *ride*?

Roberto: My name. Roberto begins like *ride*.

Teacher: What other sounds do you hear in *ride*? What comes after *r*? (Teacher stretches the *r* sound.)

Carl: I–duh.

Teacher: What letter spells /ī/?

Carl: That's easy. *I* spells /ī/.

Teacher: What letter spells /d/?

Carl: D.

Teacher: Can you write *i-d* for us?

Carl: I can write *i*, but I forget how *d* goes.

Teacher: Can you find *d* on the alphabet chart?

Teacher: (After adding an *e* to the *d* on the end of the word, she asks) Who will point to and read what we have written so far?

The teacher continues until the story is completed.

Finished pieces are placed on the walls. The teacher share-reads the pieces. As students become familiar with the pieces, they are encouraged to read them. Lists of colors, numbers, and other common words and students' names are also placed on the wall in alphabetical order. If possible, provide illustrations for words so that students can identify the words. For instance, you might accompany children's names with their photos (Bradley & Jones, 2007). Students are encouraged to use the lists and the stories placed on the wall to help them with pieces that they write independently. Because shared writing is a group project, stories are written in standard spelling. When students write independently, they use invented spelling but are encouraged to use words from the wall. Their writing typically contains conventional spellings drawn from lists and stories on the walls.

Individual Interactive Writing

In addition to utilizing share the pen with groups or whole classes, shared interactive writing can be conducted with individual students (Roser, 2011). Using it with individual students helps teachers get a fuller picture of each child's literacy development. The lessons are also especially effective because they build on the child's abilities and focus on the child's specific needs. Using a technique adapted from Ashton-Warner's (1963) organic approach, teachers invite students to dictate stories that are based on a particular word. Whereas Ashton-Warner asked students what word they would like to learn, in this approach the teacher asks, "What word is in your mind?" After saying what their word is, the student is asked to tell about the word. A student who says "dog" is then asked to tell about the word and might say, "I have a dog." Sharing the pen, the student might write "I" and, when prompted, write the *h* in *have*. The teacher finishes the writing of *have*, prompts the writing of *a* and initial *d*, and then writes *og* to complete the word *dog*.

Other prompts to initiate shared interactive writing might include: "What do you want to write about today? What do you want to say?" As the teacher, you might demonstrate how you decide what you want to write about and how you go about writing. This demonstration helps students get their thoughts down on paper. It is more effective than simply inviting them to write.

A New Concept of Writing

Traditionally, writing was not taught until after students started reading. Often, it was equated with handwriting, copying, and spelling instruction. However, writing is not simply a matter of forming letters (Holdaway, 1979); it is a way of representing the world, progressing from apparently random scribbles to meaningful marks to increasingly more conventional letters and spellings. From their first day in school, children should be encouraged to write as best they can, in whatever way they can, whether by drawings, letterlike forms, or invented spellings.

Teachers should encourage students to write and draw, should accept and support their efforts, and should resist correcting "errors." Teachers should model the process, allowing students to see them writing on the chalkboard, chart paper, word processor, notepaper, and so on. Attempts at writing lead to discoveries about the alphabetic system that help students gain essential insights into both writing and reading.

Formation of Speech Sounds

Knowing how speech sounds are formed will help you to do a better job teaching phonological awareness, phonics, and spelling. It will help you to understand why *train* is frequently spelled CHRAN and why *girl* is often spelled GRIL and why clusters such as the *st* in *stop* and the *sp* in *spot* are often misread.

FYI

Until recently, writing was viewed as being more difficult and advanced than reading, so children were taught to write after they learned to read. However, reading and writing are now seen as developing simultaneously and as being interrelated. ■

FYI

Take a bit of time to become acquainted with the speech sounds. Say the labials in the first column of Table 4.2. Notice how /b/ and /p/ are formed with the lips. Note the vibration in your larynx when you say /b/ but not /p/. What happens when you hold your nose while you say /m/? Go through the other consonant sounds in the same way. Notice how and where they are formed. ■

TABLE 4.2   Consonants: Place and Manner of Articulation

	Lips (Labials)	Lips and Teeth (Labio-dentals)	Tongue between Teeth (Dentals)	Tongue behind Teeth (Aveolars)	Roof of Mouth (Palatal-velars)	Back of Mouth (Velars)	Throat (Glottal)
Stops							
Voiced	b (barn)			d (deer)		g (gate)	
Voiceless	p (pot)			t (time)		k (kite)	
Nasals	m (me)			n (now)		ng (sing)	
Fricatives			th (this)	z (zipper)	zh (azure)		h (horse)
Voiced		v (van)	th (thin)	s (sight)	sh (ship)		
Voiceless		f (fan)					
Affricatives							
Voiced					j (jug)		
Voiceless					ch (chip)		
Semivowels	w (we)				y (yacht)		
(glides)	hw (whale)						
Liquids		r (ride)			l (lion)		

Consonant Formation   Consonants are formed by obstructing or interfering in some way with the flow of breath. In English, there are twenty-five consonant sounds (see Table 4.2). Consonants can be distinguished by place and manner of articulation and voice. Say the consonant sounds in Table 4.2. As you do so, focus on the formation of each one. Notice that you are using your tongue, lips, and teeth and that the consonants are formed in various parts of your mouth, nose, and throat. In addition, consonants are either voiced or voiceless. A voiced consonant is one that is accompanied by a vibration of the vocal cords. For example, /b/ is voiced, but /p/ is voiceless. If you say /b/ and /p/, you will notice that both have the same manner and place of articulation. The only difference between them is that one is voiced and the other is not.

Vowel Formation   Vowels are articulated with tongue, lips, and teeth. Vowels are classified according to where they are articulated. Say each of the vowel sounds in Table 4.3. What do you notice about their articulation? What happens to your tongue as you say the various vowels? Notice that your tongue moves from the very front of your mouth to the back. Your tongue also moves lower in your mouth as you say /ē/, /i/, /ā/, /e/, /a/, /ī/, /o/ and then begins to move up. Starting with /ē/, your lips are parted as though you were smiling. Gradually, your lips become rounded. The sounds /oy/ and /ow/ include two sounds.

Effect of Environment on Speech Sounds   Except for words like *I* and *oh*, most speech sounds don't appear in isolation; they have other speech sounds coming before or after them. Often, speech sounds are altered by the sounds surrounding them (Moats, 2000, 2004).

TABLE 4.3   American English Vowels

	Front	Central	Back
High	ē (beat)		o͞o (boot)
	i (bit)		oo (book)
Mid	ā (bait)	u (but)	ō (boat)
	e (bet)	schwa	
Low	a (bat)	o (bottle)	aw (bought)
	ī (bite)	oy ow (combinations of vowel sounds)	

Nasalization   Nasal consonant sounds such as /m/, /n/, and /ŋ/ are partially absorbed by the preceding vowel and sometimes by the following consonant, so a word like *ant* may sound like /at/, and *sand* may sound like /sad/. Because of nasalization, it is difficult to segment the sounds in *ant*, *sand*, and similar words. There is also an increased possibility that *ant* and *sand* will be spelled without the nasal consonant— that is, spelled as AT and SAD. Patterns that end in the nasal consonants /n/ and /m/ may need special handling. Contrast the sound of /a/ in *at* and *an*. When introducing *an* and *am* patterns, present them as a unit. Do not ask students to say the sound of *a* and then the sound of *n* and blend them together, and do not use words with such patterns for segmentation exercises.

Syllabic Consonants   The sound /l/, /r/, /m/, or /n/ at the end of a word can represent a syllable. Therefore, it is logical for novice writers to spell *letter* and *little* as LETR and LITL. *Him* and *Dan* might be spelled HM and DN.

Affrication   The phonemes /ch/ and /j/ are known as affricatives. In an affricative, a stop of breath is followed by a fricative. A fricative is a consonant sound that is produced through friction as in /v/ or /f/. The phonemes /t/ and /d/ are affricated when they appear before the sound /r/, so that /t/ sounds like /ch/ and /d/ sounds like /j/ as in *train* and *drum*. In the process of articulating /r/, the mouth naturally forms a /ch/ or a /j/. Because of affrication, *train* is often spelled CHRAN and *drum* JRM or JM by children who are focusing on the sounds they hear.

Aspiration   Holding a piece of paper a few inches from your mouth, say *pit* out loud. Now say *tip*. When you said *pit*, the paper moved but not when you said *tip*. The pronunciation of *pit* was accompanied by aspiration. Aspiration is a puff of air as when you articulate /h/. The voiceless stop consonants /p/, /t/, and /k/ are usually aspirated when they come at the beginning of a word or syllable. Voiceless stops are not aspirated when they come at the end of a word or syllable or as the second sound in a cluster as in *spot*, *stop*, or *scare*. Being unaspirated, they are harder to detect, so children have more difficulty identifying final sounds and the second sound in a cluster. Students might have a more difficult time segmenting the sounds in words that have unaspirated stops. Because the unaspirated forms may sound like their voiced counterparts, /p/ is often spelled as *b*, /t/ as *d*, and /k/ as *g* as in PIG for *pick*, CUB for *cup*, SGAR for *scare*, and SBOT for *spot* (Moats, 2000).

Vowel Blending   Some vowels are difficult to detect because they blend in with the consonant that follows them. This is especially true of /l/ and /r/, as in *will* and *girl*. Children may spell *bird* as BRID, not because they are confusing the sequence of sounds but because the /i/ and /r/ are blended and the /r/ sound dominates. This also explains the GRIL spelling of *girl*, where the /l/ sound dominates. Segmenting the sounds in these words can be difficult. When students have difficulty spelling these words, encouraging them to sound them out may be counterproductive. If they spell what they hear, chances are they will misspell the words (Moats, 2000). This is also true of words like *train*, *drum*, and *dress*. These elements need to be taught as onset-rime patterns. When taught such a rime as a unit, students aren't asked to separate the sounds in a word like *third* or *fort*.

Development of Spelling   When does writing start? At the age of 18 months, average toddlers will make marks on paper (Gibson & Levin, 1974). By age 3, scribbling is no longer random or unorganized (Harste, Woodward, & Burke, 1984). Because it proceeds in a straight line across the page and may be composed of up-and-down or curved marks, it resembles genuine writing. In time, children may create letterlike figures, use a combination of numbers and letters, and eventually use only letters. Along the way, they discover the concept of sign (Clay, 1972)—that is, they arbitrarily

Assessing for Learning

Examine children's writing and their attempts to spell. Try to figure out the reasoning behind their misspellings. Note examples of nasalization, affrication, aspiration, and vowel blending. Think how you might apply this knowledge to the teaching of spelling and phonics. ∎

FYI

Speech sounds have allophones. Allophones are variant pronunciations of a phoneme. In the word *egg*, the vowel sound is more like /ā/ than /e/ (Moats, 2004). This means that *egg* is not a good candidate for a model word for the short *e*. ∎

FYI

As Elbow (2004) explains, "Even younger children who don't know the alphabet can write if they have seen other people write: They just scribble, scribble, scribble—but with meaning, and they can 'read' their writing back to you. All that's needed is to invite them to use invented spelling or kid spelling, whatever letters come easily. Once this door is opened, teachers find that it helps teach reading" (p. 10). ∎

use a graphic element to represent an idea or a word, a syllable, or a sound. For example, the child may use the letter *b* or *x* or a self-created letterlike form to represent the word *ball*.

The earliest spelling stage is the **prealphabetic (prephonemic) stage**. At this stage, children realize that letters are used to create words but have not caught on to the alphabetic principle—that is, that letters represent sounds. At age 4, Paul Bissex used strings of letters to cheer his mother up. The letters were a random selection and were designed to convey the message "Welcome home" in one instance and "Cheer up" in another (Bissex, 1980).

The next stage of spelling is the **alphabetic (letter name) stage**. In the early part of this stage, children start putting the alphabetic principle to work. Single letters may at first represent whole words but later may stand for syllables and then represent single sounds (Ferreiro, 1986). For instance, the letter *k* may be used to represent the word *car*. In later phases of this stage, a child may add the final consonant, spelling *car* as KR. Some consonant combination spellings may at first seem to have no connection to their sounds: *tr* is frequently spelled CH, and *dr* may be spelled JR. Try saying "train." Listen very carefully to the initial sound. The beginning sound is actually /ch/. Likewise, the *d* in *dr* combinations has a /j/ sound. The child is spelling what she or he hears (Read, 1971).

As the alphabetic (letter name) stage proceeds, children begin representing vowel sounds. Students continue to employ a strategy in which a letter is used to represent the sound heard in the letter's name, so *late* is spelled LAT and *feet* is spelled FET. This works for most consonants and long vowels but not for short ones, as the names of short vowels do not contain their pronunciations. To spell short vowels, children employ the "close to" tactic, in which they use the long-vowel name that is closest to the point in the mouth where the short vowel to be spelled is articulated. For instance, short *e* is formed very close to the point where long *a* is articulated, so the child spells short *e* with an *A*, as in BAD for *bed*. Based on the "close to" tactic, short *i* is spelled with an *e* (SET for *sit*), short *o* with an *i* (HIP for *hop*), and short *u* with an *o* (BOT for *but*; (Read, 1971).

As they are exposed to standard spellings in books and environmental print, children begin to notice that spelling incorporates certain conventions—that final *e* is used to mark long vowels, for instance. They enter the **consolidated alphabetic stage** (also known as the *within word pattern* or *orthographic stage*), in which they begin to consolidate visual or orthographic elements along with sound elements in their spelling (Henderson, 1990). Their spelling is no longer strictly guided by sound. Although their spelling may not always be accurate, they begin to use final *e* markers and double vowel letters to spell long vowel sounds. They may spell *mean* as MEEN or MENE. However, they begin to spell short vowels accurately. As children progress through this stage, their spelling becomes conventional, and ultimately they move into the stages of syllable juncture and derivational constancy, which are advanced stages of conventional spelling involving multisyllabic words (Henderson, 1990). See Table 4.4 for examples of the major stages of spelling.

As can be seen from the description of the stages of spelling, spelling is not merely a matter of memorizing words. Spelling is conceptual and involves three levels of understanding: alphabetic, pattern, and meaning. At the alphabetic level, students understand that letters represent sounds. At the pattern level, they realize that letters often form patterns, as in the spelling of *load* and *rope*, where long *o* is spelled with *oa* and *o-e*. At the meaning level, students conclude that meaning may govern a word's spelling; that is, words that have a similar meaning have a similar spelling even though their pronunciations may differ: *sign/signature* (Bear & Templeton, 1998).

- In the **prealphabetic (or prephonemic) stage,** students use letters but don't realize that the letters represent sounds.
- The **alphabetic stage** is also known as the letter name stage because students use the names of the letters to figure out the sounds they represent. The name of *b*, for instance, contains its sound.
- The **consolidated alphabetic stage** is sometimes known as the within word pattern or orthographic stage because students are beginning to see patterns such as final *e* and double vowels.

Age	Stage	Example
18 months	Random scribbling	
3 years	Wordlike scribbling	
4–5 years	Prealphabetic (prephonemic) writing	LWIↃ
4–6+ years	Early alphabetic (early letter name)	WL
5–7+ years	Alphabetic (letter name)	WAL
6–7+ years	Consolidated alphabetic (within word pattern)	whale
8–10+ years	Syllable juncture	whaling
10–20+ years	Derivational constancy	aquatic

TABLE 4.4 Stages of Spelling

As they have more experience with writing, children develop a deeper understanding of the spelling system. They begin to use visual and meaning features to spell words instead of just relying on sound characteristics. Instruction is most effective when it matches the student's stage of development. For instance, a student in the early letter name (early alphabetic) stage has difficulty with final *e* words. She or he might be able to memorize the spelling of *note* but would not understand the principle of final *e* and so would not apply it to other words.

To determine students' spelling stage, analyze samples of their writing. You might also use the Elementary Spelling Inventory (Bear & Barone, 1989), presented in Table 4.5. The inventory presents twenty-five words that increase in difficulty and embody key elements of the stages. Start with the first word and continue testing until the words become too difficult. Ask students to spell as best they can because even partially spelled words reveal important information about spelling stages. Before administering the inventory, explain to students that you want to see how they spell words. Tell them that some of the words may be hard, but they should do the best they can. Say each word, use it in a sentence, and say the word once more.

Using the error guide, carefully analyze the students' performance. Most novice readers will be in the early alphabetic (early letter name) stage. However, a few might be in a more advanced stage, and some may be in the prealphabetic (prephonemic)

 FYI

Be sure to explain the nature of invented spelling to parents. Let them know that invented spelling is transitional and does not lead to poor spelling. Explain what you will be doing to teach conventional spelling. ■

Assessing for Learning

Invented spelling provides insight into the child's knowledge of letter–sound relationships. By analyzing the child's spelling and noting what the child seems to understand about letter–sound relationships, you can gear your instruction to the child's level of understanding. ■

TABLE 4.5 The Elementary Spelling Inventory (with error guide)

Stages	Early Letter Name	Letter Name	Within Word Pattern
1. bed	b bd	bad	bed
2. ship	s sp shp	sep shep	sip ship
3. drive	jrv drv	griv driv	drieve draive drive
4. bump	h bp bmp	bop bomp bup	bump
5. when	w yn wn	wan whan	wen when
6. train	j t trn	jran chran tan tran	teran traen trane train
7. closet	k cs kt clst	clast clost clozt	clozit closit
8. chase	j jass cs	tas cas chas chass	case chais chase
9. float	f vt ft flt	fot flot flott	flowt floaut flote float
10. beaches	b bs bcs	bechs becis behis	bechise beches beeches beaches
11. preparing			preparng preypering
12. popping			popin poping
13. cattle			catl cadol
14. caught			cot cote cout cought caught
15. inspection			inspshn inspechin

(continued)

TABLE 4.5   The Elementary Spelling Inventory (*Continued*)

Stages	Early Letter Name	Letter Name	Within Word Pattern
16. puncture			pucshr pungchr puncker
17. cellar			salr selr celr seler
18. pleasure			plasr plager plejer pleser plesher
19. squirrel			scrl skwel skwerl
20. fortunate			forhnat frehnit foohinit
21. confident			
22. civilize			
23. flexible			
24. opposition			opasiun opasishan opozcison opishien opasitian
25. emphasize			

Syllable Juncture (Syllabic)			Derivational Constancy (Morphemic)
11. preparing prepairing preparing			
12. popping			
13. catel catle cattel cattle			
15. inspecshum inspecsion inspection			
16. punksher punture puncture			
17. seller sellar celler cellar			
18. plesour plesure			pleasure
19. scqoril sqrarel squirle squirrel			
20. forchenut fochininte fortunet			fortunate
21. confadent confedint confedent confadent conphident confiadent confedent confendent confodent confident			
22. sivils sevelies sivilicse cifillazas sivelize sivalize civalise civilise civilize			
23. flecksibl flexobil fleckuble flecible flexeble flexibel flaxable flexibal flexable			flexible
24. opasition oppasishion oppisition			oposision oposition opposition
25. infaside infacize emfesize emfisize imfasize ephacise empasize emphasise			emphisize emphasize

Note: The Preliterate Stage is not presented here.

Adapted from Bear, D., & Barone, D. (1989). The Elementary Spelling Inventory (with Error Guide). Adapted from *Reading Psychology 10*(3), 1989, pp. 275–292. Reproduced with permission. All rights reserved.

stage. Often, students move back and forth between adjacent stages. Figure 4.2 shows examples of a child's use of invented spelling in kindergarten and in first grade.

Forms of Emergent Writing   Children's writing develops through seven forms, beginning with drawing and ending with conventional spelling. These forms include the spelling stages depicted in Table 4.4 but go beyond spelling to include the writer's intentions. The major forms of emergent writing described in Table 4.6 are based on research completed with kindergarten students (Sulzby, Barnhart, & Hieshima, 1989).

In the beginning stages, children might not distinguish between drawing and writing (Luria, 1983). Students' first attempts at writing might actually be drawings. Young students can use drawing in the same way that writing is used by older students. They can use drawing to record a field trip or retell a story. Drawing aids memory in much

(a) Kindergarten

(b) First Grade

From stories written by Anne Lincoln. Used by permission.

FYI

The kindergarten paper says, "I am playing with my kite." ■

Assessing for Learning

Through observation and discreet probing, find out where children are in their writing development. Some may be drawing or scribbling. Others may have advanced to invented or even conventional spelling. Also note how children approach the task of writing. Do they jump right in, or are they hesitant and unsure? ■

FYI

As Dierking (2006) notes, writing can be used to foster reading, and vice versa, even at the earliest stages. Writing slows down the processing of letters and sounds and so highlights individual sounds. ■

the same way as writing does. After completing a drawing, students might be encouraged to write about the drawing.

At the beginning of the kindergarten year, some children may be "writing" on a scribbling level. Some continue to use that form for a portion of the year. However, even though some students cling to a scribble form of writing, the scribbles in October or November of the year are more advanced than those created at the beginning of the year. How can one scribbled story be more advanced than another? Although, on the surface, two scribbled stories may seem very similar, they may have very different meanings for their creators. In children's writing, there may be more on the page than meets the eye. Sulzby (1989a) cautions, "One can only judge the quality of the form of writing by comparing it with the rereading a child uses with it" (p. 51).

TABLE 4.6   Forms of Emergent Writing

Form	Description
Drawing	The drawing is not an illustration for a story but is the story itself. The child reads the drawing as though it were text.
Scribbling	The scribbling resembles a line of writing. It may have the appearance of a series of waves or, in a more advanced representation, may resemble a series of letterlike forms.
Letterlike forms	Letterlike forms resemble manuscript or cursive letters and are generally written as separate forms rather than the continuous forms seen in scribbling. They are not real letters, and care needs to be taken that poorly formed real letters are not placed in this category.
Prephonemic spelling	The child writes with real letters, but the letters are a random collection or a meaningless pattern, such as repeating the same letter. Although the letters are real, they do not represent sounds.
Copying	The child copies from print found in his or her environment: signs, labels, etc. One child copied from a crayon box but, when asked to read his piece, told a story that had nothing to do with crayons (Sulzby, 1989a).
Invented spelling	Students make use of the alphabetic principle. The letters they write represent sounds. Initially, one letter may represent a whole word. Over time, there is a gradual movement to conventional spelling. See Table 4.4 for a chart of spelling stages, including the several stages of invented spelling.
Conventional spelling	Student's spelling is conventional.

Based on Appendix 2.1, Forms of Writing and Rereading from Writing, Example List (pp. 51–63) by E. Sulzby (1989). In J. M. Mason (Ed.), *Reading and Writing Connections*. Boston: Allyn & Bacon.

Assessing for Learning

Children use different forms of writing for different tasks. When writing brief pieces, kindergarten children tend to use conventional spelling. When writing a long story, they may scribble. ■

FYI

Modeling is an important part of children's early writing attempts. In writing letters and notes, they imitate what they have seen parents, teachers, and older siblings do. ■

R E F L E C T I O N

How might you help students who hesitate to take risks with writing words that they can't spell? How might you help those who continue to use invented spelling with words whose spellings they have been taught.

After students write stories in whatever form or forms they choose, they are asked to read them. Just as in emergent storybook readings, described in Table 4.1, students read their written pieces on a variety of levels of sophistication. A child asked to read a scribbled story may simply retell a story that apparently has no connection with the scribbles. Another child may read the scribbles as though he or she is reading conventional writing. The child's voice may incorporate the intonation of a story, and he or she may even point to the scribbles as they are read as though pointing to a line of words. When the child comes to the end of the scribbles, his or her reading ceases. When asked to reread the scribbles, the child may use exactly the same words to retell the tale. In a sense, the child is reading the scribbles. Categories of reading from emergent writing are presented in Table 4.7.

Encouraging Children to Write   Whether they are drawing, scribbling, copying, creating invented spellings, or entering into a transitional phase, children should be encouraged to write. This writing program should be informal but functional. The first prerequisite is that each student should realize that she or he has something to say. Whatever a student produces should be accepted and valued.

The teacher's role should be an active one, modeling the writing process at every opportunity. When the teacher is writing a note to parents explaining a field trip, the children should be shown what the teacher is doing. They should see the teacher create signs for the room, draw up a list of supplies, complete a book order, and write messages on the board. Seeing real writing done for real purposes is especially important for students who may not have seen their parents do much writing.

Invitations to write should be extended to the children. The teacher might ask them to write about things they like to do. The teacher should model the process by writing a piece that tells what he or she likes to do. In the beginning, students should then be encouraged to write as best they can or in any way they can. If they wish, they can draw pictures showing what they like to do, or they may both draw and write. The teacher should show samples of the various ways children can write—including scribbling, random letter strings, drawings, and invented spellings—and explain that each student

Category	Description
Null	The child refuses to read the story he or she has written, says that he or she cannot read it, or comments that nothing was written or the story does not say anything.
Labeling/describing	The child supplies labels or a description instead of reading. The child says, "Cat" or "This is a cat." A one-word response is a label; a sentence response is a description if it gives information beyond the label.
Dialogue	The child only responds if you ask questions, so the interchange takes on a question–answer format. The question–answer interchange may be initiated by the child.
Oral monologue	The child tells a story in the style of an oral retelling. It does not have the characteristics of the reading of a piece of writing.
Written monologue	The reading sounds as though the child is reading from a written piece. It has the sound and flow of oral reading of written text, but the child is not actually reading from the written piece.
Naming letters	The child names the letters that have been written.
Aspectual/strategic reading	The child is beginning to attend to the writing and may attempt to sound out some words and phrases while skipping others. The child may read the written piece while looking at the written words, but the written words may not completely match up with what the child is reading.
Conventional	The child uses the written words to read. The rendition may sound like written monologue, but the main difference is that the child is deciphering the written words while reading.

TABLE 4.7   Reading from Emergent Writing

Based on Appendix 2.1, Forms of Writing and Rereading from Writing, Example List (pp. 51–63) by E. Sulzby (1989). In J. M. Mason (Ed.), *Reading and Writing Connections*. Boston: Allyn & Bacon.

is to write in her or his own way. However, in time, and as appropriate, students should be provided with the kinds of scaffolding that will move their writing forward (see Chapter 9 for specific suggestions).

During the year, the students should engage in several writing projects, such as letters or invitations to family members and friends, stories, accounts of personal experiences, and lists. After writing a piece, a child should read it to an adult, who might want to transcribe it on another sheet of paper if the original is not readable. Transcriptions should be kept with the written pieces in a writing folder, which becomes a file of the child's writing development. As Sulzby and Barnhart (1992) commented,

> Many people are still shocked at the ease with which children at kindergarten age (or younger) write, when we invite them and if we accept the forms of writing they prefer. From working with and observing hundreds of classrooms, we can say confidently that all kindergartners reared in a literate culture like our own can and will write. (pp. 125–126)

Using Graphics to Prepare Students for Writing   One way to prepare students for writing is to use graphics. Creating graphics provides a foundation for forming letters. By practicing the following marks and shapes (listed in order of increasing difficulty), children can develop the fine motor and visual-motor skills needed to write letters: dots, lines, circles, squares, and triangles (Bodrova et al., 2001). The ways these shapes and marks are made (also listed in order of increasing difficulty) are not touching, touching, big, little, mixture of big and little. To practice these graphics, children can be asked to draw objects that incorporate their features. To make circles with dots that don't touch, children might draw cookies and add chocolate chips or draw pizzas and add mushrooms. For circles and lines that don't touch, children can draw the sun, the moon, or a ball, and rain or grass. To make lines and circles that do touch, children can draw balloons or spiders. For circles, lines, and dots that touch, students can draw stick figures, flowers, or apples on a tree. For circles and triangles, students can make jack-o-lanterns and ice cream cones. As students develop their fine motor and

Adapting Instruction for Struggling Readers and Writers

Kindergarten teacher Linda Edwards (2000) divides her class into five groups for writing so that she is teaching students who are on similar levels and share common needs. She doesn't set up guided writing groups until children can remember what they wrote the day before. ■

Emphasis in a writing program for young children is on writing for a variety of purposes.

FYI

For additional suggestions for using children's names to teach phonics, see *Month-by-Month Phonics for First Grade* (2nd ed.), by P. M. Cunningham and D. P. Hall (Greensboro, NC: Carson-Dellosa, 2008). ■

FYI

As students are learning to compose morning messages, you might supply frame sentences until they catch on to the idea and are able to write their reports on their own. Frame sentences might include "Today is _____. Today the class is going to _____. My news is _____." (Morrow & Asbury, 2001). ■

Adapting Instruction for Struggling Readers and Writers

Encouraging students to spell a word the way it sounds helps them to make discoveries about the spelling system. If they don't know how to begin, help them go through a word sound by sound and talk about the letters that spell those sounds. For words like *train*, *drum*, *girl*, and *bird*, which are not spelled the way they sound, explain to children that these are "tricky" spellings. ■

drawing skills, they can also develop their writing skills. Children might start by labeling their pictures (Venn & Jahn, 2004). As noted earlier, one way of helping children get the most out of dramatic play sessions is to encourage them to plan their play. As children move beyond the ability to label pictures, they can draw and/or write their plans, with the teacher providing needed scaffolding (Bodrova & Leong, 2007).

Real Writing for Real Purposes   Emphasis in a writing program for young children is on writing a variety of pieces for a variety of reasons. Young children adopt different strategies for different tasks. They might use invented spelling when compiling a list but use scribbling for a lengthy tale (Martinez & Teale, 1987). Real-life activities have the effect of motivating them to use more sophisticated techniques. When writing invitations for the class's Thanksgiving feast, many kindergarten children in an experimental writing program, who until that time had used scribble writing, chose to use random strings of letters or even to attempt to spell words (Martinez & Teale, 1987).

Making Lists   One writing activity on which young children thrive is making lists. Clay (1975) called the motivation for this activity the inventory principle. Novice writers enjoy creating an inventory of letters or words that they can write. Suggested assignments include making lists of friends, family members, favorite foods, places visited, favorite toys, and so on.

Writing Names   One of the first words that a child learns to spell is his or her name. Special attention should be given to this task, because once children learn their names, they frequently use the letters to spell other words. Thus, each name becomes a source of known letters that can be used in various sequences and combinations (Temple, Nathan, Temple, & Burris, 1993).

Take full advantage of children's interest in their names. Put name tags on their cubbyholes, coat hooks, and/or shelf spaces. Ask the children to sign all their written work. When scheduling individuals for activities or assignments, write their names on the chalkboard so that they become used to seeing and reading their own names, as well as those of the other children.

Using Routines   Whenever possible, use routines to demonstrate literacy lessons. Written by the teacher, the morning message gives the date and important information about the day's activities. Messages in the beginning of the year are relatively simple, but they become increasingly complex to match the growth in children's skills. A November message might be "Today is Monday, November 12. We will go to the firehouse this morning." The teacher reads it aloud and encourages the students to read along with her. At this juncture, the teacher wants the children to see that writing is functional (it conveys important information), that one reads writing from left to right and top to bottom, and that written messages are made up of individual words and letters. Later, longer messages are written, and more sophisticated skills—such as the concepts that words are made up of sounds and that certain sounds are represented by certain letters—are stressed. As students learn letter–sound relationships, the writing can be more interactive. Students can be asked to tell what letter each word begins with or even spell out high-frequency words they may have learned.

Students can also be encouraged to add to the morning message. This assures them that what they have to say is important. These additions also help students and the teacher get to know each other better, as the students' contributions might include

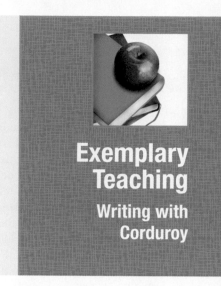

Taking Corduroy home served as a motivation for kindergartners to write journal entries. After teacher Marilyn Cook (2006) read *Corduroy* to her students, she explained that she was taking Corduroy (a stuffed version) home with her. They would have an adventure, and she would write about it. The next day, she brought Corduroy back and shared with her students what she had written. She then invited them to take turns taking Corduroy home and telling about their experiences in their journals. She prompted responses with such questions as "What would you like to do if you were Corduroy?" Students drew an illustration of their experience and composed a journal entry themselves or dictated it to someone.

Corduroy's hosts shared their adventures with the rest of the class, reporting that Corduroy played games, watched TV, and even went swimming. Each day, Cook used the journal entries to prompt a writing skill, such as beginning each sentence with a capital letter or allowing spaces between words. The teacher also modeled such writing skills as adding details and composing dialogue. Students composed a rubric for their journal entries: "I drew a picture of Corduroy's adventure at my house. I wrote two or more sentences about what Corduroy did at my house."

Exemplary Teaching
Writing with Corduroy

---

major family events such as the birth of siblings or the death of grandparents and other news of personal importance.

Help with Spelling   Children should be encouraged to use their knowledge of letter–sound relationships to create spellings, even if the spellings are not accurate. You can foster this process by showing students how to elongate sounds as they spell them. One question that arises in a program emphasizing invented spelling is what to do when children ask how to spell a word. The advice offered most often is to encourage them to spell it as best they can or to say the word very slowly—to stretch it out—and work out the spelling. You might ask, "With what sound does the word start? What letter makes that sound? What sound comes next? What letter spells that sound?" The idea is to have students develop their own sense of the spelling system. If you spell words for students, they will begin to rely on your help instead of constructing their own spellings. Keep in mind that students' invented spellings reflect their understanding of the spelling system. Words that they create belong to them in a way that words that are spelled for them do not (Wilde, 1995) (For words that aren't spelled the way they sound, you might simply spell the word. For instance, if you suggest to a student that she sound out the word *drum*, she might spell it *jrum*, since that is how it sounds).

Providing access to standard spelling could take the form of having picture dictionaries available; placing some frequently requested words on the board; posting word lists of animals, families, colors, foods, or other related items; labeling items; or creating a word wall (see Chapter 5). It could also mean providing assistance when students are unable to work out the spelling of a word and you believe that providing help will further their development. Occasionally, you might have students attempt to spell the word as best they can and then write the conventional spelling above their attempt, saying, "Here's how we usually spell _____. Look how close you came" (Ruddell & Ruddell, 1995, p. 103). Any help that you supply should take into account the student's understanding of the spelling system. If, for instance, the child spells *truck* with CH, you should say, "Truck sounds like it begins with a *ch* as in *Charles*, but it begins with a *t* as in *Tim* and an *r* as in *Raymond*" (Wilde, 1995).

Although students are encouraged to explore the writing system through invented spellings, they should be held accountable for any letter relationships they have been taught. If students have been taught initial *m* or *s*, they should be held accountable for spelling these sounds, although you might provide some prompting such as modeling the process of sounding out the first sound so as to be better able to perceive it (Invernizzi, Meier, Swank, & Juel, 2001).

 Using Technology

Read • Write • Think offers a complete description of Marilyn Cook's lesson "A Journal for Corduroy: Responding to Literature," as well as other high-quality literacy lessons.
http://www.readwritethink.org/lessons/lesson_view.asp?id=30 ■

R E F L E C T I O N

What is the role of invented spelling in assessment and instruction?

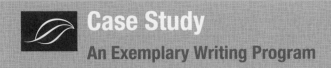

Case Study
An Exemplary Writing Program

In the Teachers College Reading and Writing Project, which has been implemented by thousands of teachers over nearly three decades, the ultimate goal is to have kindergarten children write stories that are five or six pages long (Calkins, 2003). Each page has a picture and one or two sentences. The project features a curriculum calendar, in which there is a focus of instruction for each month. Kindergartners start off by drawing pictures and then writing about the pictures, if they can. After three or four weeks, when the children have learned some or all of the letters of the alphabet, the children who at first only drew pictures begin labeling their drawings. The goal is that by the end of September, each kindergartner will be writing his or her name and labeling a drawing. As they label their drawings, children are encouraged to stretch out the words and write the letters for the sounds they hear. At this point, some of the more advanced children will be writing sentences. The goal is that by the end of October or November, most kindergartners will be writing sentences.

Units of study are blocked out for each month. In November, the focus is on writing about small moments, instead of writing stories that begin with waking up and end with going to bed.

Recording sounds and leaving spaces between words are emphasized. In December, the focus is on writing for readers. Emphasis is on beginning sentences with capital letters, recording sounds, and using end punctuation so that readers will find it easier to read the story. The goal is to have most children using letter–sound correspondences by January. Teachers encourage students to spell as best they can. If students are having difficulty, teachers provide support by having them say the sounds in a word; if students cannot think of the letters that spell the sounds, the teachers supply them. In subsequent units, children write information pieces. They write a procedural text by using pictures and words to explain a process: feeding a dog, kicking a soccer ball, shooting a basket in basketball. Students also write an "All About" book, in which they write about T-ball, taking care of a puppy, or another topic with which they have personal experience.

The program is carefully managed. Students keep their work in writing folders and work at assigned tables. The folders have colored dots that correspond to the table color. A table monitor brings materials to the table. There is a toolbox for each table that contains pencils, markers, paper, staplers, glue sticks, and any other supplies that might be needed.

FYI

- Students need lots of practice with sounding out. When using sounding out, first-graders failed to represent all the sounds in half the words. Second-graders failed to represent all the sounds in one-third of the words (Rittle-Johnson & Siegler, 1999).
- Encourage invented spelling in the beginning stages of literacy development. As you introduce phonological elements and high-frequency words in reading and spelling, begin holding students responsible for the correct spelling of words incorporating those items (Wharton-McDonald, 2001). ■

Whatever you do, have a clear policy—one based on your beliefs about invented spelling. Be sure to explain your policy to both students and their parents. Parents should understand that one reason for encouraging children to write before they can spell conventionally is that it gives them a reason to learn the real system, the "code."

Dictation in the Writing Program

Dictation   In **dictation**, a child recounts an experience or a story and someone else writes it down. Dictation can be used when children have a special message to convey. Although students should be encouraged to write as best they can, they may choose to dictate on occasion, such as when they are expressing heartfelt feelings or recounting events that touch them deeply. The content may be so intense that they cannot handle both it and the form. For example, one young student, who usually wrote on her own, chose to dictate when she told the story of how her mother had been involved in a serious auto accident. Both teacher-initiated and child-initiated writing and dictation are vital elements of a literacy program, as "they provide process as well as content for beginning reading" (Fields, Spangler, & Lee, 1991, p. 52).

Dictation helps children see the relationship between speaking and writing. They can see that if they speak too fast, the scribe has a difficult time keeping up. Over time, they learn to pace their dictation so that it matches the scribe's ability to record it. Of course, the scribe can also point out letters, words, and sentences while writing so that the child is better able to see the relationship between written and spoken language. One thing that should be made clear is the role of dictation.

■ **Dictation** is the process of recounting an experience or a story orally and having someone else write down the words.

The teacher does not want to create the impression that he or she is writing because the student cannot. The teacher should explain that dictating is another way of writing. In addition to being used to capture emotional stories that individuals have to tell, dictated writing can also be used to record a group experience (Sulzby, Teale, & Kamberelis, 1989).

Scaffolded Writing   Students who are hesitant to write might benefit from a form of dictation known as scaffolded writing. Scaffolded writing helps children develop a concept of word. Until children know where a word begins and ends, they will be hindered in learning and applying phonics skills and learning high-frequency words. Young children are assisted in their writing by using scaffolded writing. Initially, the child dictates her or his message. To help convey the concept of word, the teacher draws a line for each word the child says. The child repeats the message and points to a line while saying the word that goes with it. Then the child writes the words, or as much of each word as possible, on the lines. As the child develops a concept of word, she or he draws the lines and then writes the words on the lines. Saying the words while drawing lines provides practice in delineating separate words. Because the line reminds the child of the word, the child is able to repeat the word over and over again, which helps the child focus on representing the sounds of the word. Once the child has internalized the concept of word, she or he can compose sentences without first using lines. In setting the scene for children to draw up their play plans, Bodrova and Leong (2007) suggest using scaffolded writing.

Planned Instruction of Essential Understandings

Setting the stage for developing reading and writing is important, and arranging for many opportunities to read and write is vital, but explicit instruction should also be a key element in the literacy program. This is especially true when students are struggling.

Direct instruction should take place within the context of the kinds of reading and writing activities that are being explored in this chapter. Two areas in which students are most likely to need direct instruction are **phonological awareness** (ability to detect beginning sounds and to hear separate sounds in words) and the alphabetic principle (the system by which speech sounds are represented by letters). In fact, the major cause of difficulty in learning to read is a deficiency in these areas (Adams, 1990).

Children vary greatly in knowledge of the alphabet and phonological awareness. In the fall of 1998, trained assessors conducted standardized, one-on-one assessments with a representative sample of about 22,000 kindergartners (West, Denton, & Germino-Hausken, 2000). A majority of entering kindergartners (66 percent) could recognize letters of the alphabet by name, whether they were upper- or lowercase. However, most kindergartners could not point to letters representing sounds at the beginning or end of simple words, read basic words in isolation, or read more complex words in the context of a sentence. Only about two children out of a hundred could read high-frequency words. And only about one in a hundred could read sentences (see Table 4.8). However, children raised in poverty were less proficient. Only 41 percent of children whose caregivers were receiving welfare benefits could identify the letters of the alphabet.

Learning the Letters of the Alphabet   Although it seems logical that students would learn letters by memorizing their shapes, that is not the way it happens. They learn to tell one letter from another and to identify particular letters by noting distinctive features such as whether lines are curved or slanted, open or closed (Gibson, Gibson, Pick, & Osser, 1962). To perceive distinctive features, students must be given many experiences comparing and contrasting

■ **Phonological awareness** is the consciousness of the sounds in words. It is a broad term and includes the ability to perceive syllables and rhymes, as well as individual speech sounds (phonemes).

TABLE 4.8   Percentage of Kindergartners Passing Each Reading Proficiency Level

Letter Recognition	Beginning Sounds	Ending Sounds	High-Frequency Words	Words in Context
66%	29%	17%	2%	1%

FYI

• Children generally know more uppercase letters than lowercase ones. Uppercase letters are easier to learn, and adults generally write in uppercase when writing for children.

• When should the alphabet be introduced? "As soon as the child is encouraged to write his name, his attention is being directed to letters. Often, the first two or three letters that occur in his name become distinctive because of these efforts" (Clay, 1991, pp. 266–267). ∎

Using Technology

For suggestions on teaching handwriting, see "How to Teach Letter Recognition" at http://www.auburn.edu/rdggenie

The Literacy Center features imaginative, interactive activities for building letter recognition and other emergent literacy skills. http://www.literacycenter.net

Super Why! offers other activities that reinforce alphabet knowledge, phonological awareness, and word and sentence reading. http://pbskids.org/superwhy ∎

letters. When introducing letters, teachers should present at least two at a time so that students can contrast them. It is also a good idea to present letters that have dissimilar appearances—*s* and *b*, for instance. Presenting similar letters such as *b* and *d* together can cause confusion. It is recommended, too, that upper- and lowercase forms of the letters be introduced at the same time, because students will see both in their reading.

Using names is a good way to introduce the alphabet. Discuss the fact that names are made up of letters. Write your name on the board, and talk about the letters in it. Explain that your first and last names begin with capital letters and that the other letters are lowercase. Write the names of some students, perhaps those that begin with the first three or four letters of the alphabet, and then move to other letters on succeeding days.

To emphasize a letter, ask students to raise their hands if their name has that letter—*m*, for example. Ask them to spell out their names; give assistance if they need it. Write the names on the board—*Manuel*, *Marcella*, and *Tom*, for example—and have students tell where the *m* is in each name.

Create signs for the class: "Writing Center," "In," "Out," and so on. Let students see you make the signs, and talk about the letters you used. Bring in familiar objects, such as cereal boxes, signs, and posters, and discuss the words printed on them and the letters that make up the words.

Have students use keyboards. Keyboards invite exploration of the alphabet. If you are using *Dr. Peet's Talk/Writer* (Interest-Driven Learning), which has speech capability, the name of the letter will be pronounced when the child presses the key. Whole words are spoken when the space bar is pressed. *Dr. Peet's Talk/Writer* also has an ABC Discovery module that introduces the alphabet. In one activity, students are prompted to find the letter *P*. When they press the *P* key, they are shown the letter *P* in upper- and lowercase and a picture of two polar bears, and they hear a song that says, "*P* is for polar bear." Stamp printing sets, magnetic letters, and felt letters also encourage working with the alphabet.

Use games such as *Alphabet Walk* to teach the names of the letters of the alphabet. Place large alphabet cards on the floor. Begin playing music. As the music plays, students walk. When the music stops, they stop. Hold up an alphabet card. Ask the student who was standing on that card to identify it. If students are working on letter sounds, ask the student to tell what sound the letter makes and to name some word that begins with that sound (Invernizzi, Meier, Swank, & Juel, 2001).

As with all learning activities, proceed from the concrete to the abstract. Letters by their very nature are abstract; when they are in the contexts of names, signs, and labels, they are more concrete than letters in isolation.

Display a model alphabet so that students can see how letters are formed. Provide each child with his or her own alphabet to refer to as needed. Also teach students how to form the letters of the alphabet. Writing the letters helps students to remember the names of the letters. Demonstrate the formation of the letters and use simplified directions to talk students through the formation of the letters. For lowercase *b*, you might say: "Straight down, back up, and around." However, do not overemphasize letter formation. Students who are overly conscious of forming their letters perfectly will have a difficult time moving beyond that task to writing.

One popular practice activity is to have students say the names of the letters as you point to them. If the letters are covered in order, the middle letters get neglected. The reason? We remember best things that occur first and last, so the middle letters don't stand out the way the beginning and ending letters do. From time to time, don't follow alphabetical order when practicing letter names (Reutzel, 2008). Also, according to research by Reutzel, it's better to present a new letter each day (contrasted with a previously presented letter) rather than devote a whole week to a letter, which is a common practice. The reason? There is not enough time for review. In a letter-a-day program, the letters can be reviewed every 26 days. Students who were taught a letter a day outperformed letter-a-week students by a wide margin.

Read to the class some of the many alphabet books that are available. *A to Zoo: Subject Access to Children's Picture Books*, 8th edition (Lima & Thomas, 2010), lists more than 300 alphabet books. Some of these are included in the following Student Reading List. Look for books that present the letters clearly. Overly ornate letters may be aesthetically pleasing, but they can be distracting and confusing. Many of these books show words containing the beginning sound that a particular letter frequently represents. Do not emphasize these letter–sound relationships, as they require advanced skill. Focus instead on the appearance of each letter and how it differs from a similarly formed letter—for example, how *y* is different from *t*. Point out that letters have two forms—capital and lowercase. Avoid the words *little* and *big* so that children do not use size to determine whether a letter is upper- or lowercase. When possible, choose alphabet books that present both forms. According to Bear and colleagues (2008), children are ready to begin learning letter sounds when they know nine letters.

Building Phonological Awareness   For children, the sounds in a word blend so that the word seems like the continuation of a single sound. In their natural environment,

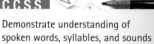

STUDENT READING LIST
Alphabet Books

Aylesworth, J. (1991). *Old black fly.* New York: Holt. Rhyming text follows a mischievous black fly through the alphabet as he has a very busy day.

Ehlert, L. (1989). *Eating the alphabet.* New York: Harcourt. Drawings of foods beginning with the letter being presented are labeled with their names in both upper- and lowercase letters.

Hoban, T. (1982). *A, B, see!* New York: Greenwillow. Uppercase letters are accompanied by objects in silhouette that begin with the letter shown.

Jocelyn, M. (2006). *ABC × 3.* Plattsburgh, NY: Tundra Books. Presents letters and illustrative words in English, Spanish, and French. The letter *p* is accompanied by *pear, pera,* and *poire.* Some words and illustrations will need explaining.

Martin, D. (2010). *David Martin's ABC: Z is for zebra.* North Vancouver, BC, Canada: DJC Kids Media. Clever drawings reinforce the shapes of letters. Each letter is accompanied by a humorous illustration, such as an ant crawling over the letter *A.*

Musgrove, M. (1976). *Ashanti to Zulu.* New York: Dial. This Caldecott winner gives information about African tribes as it presents the alphabet.

Onyefulu, I. (1993). *A is for Africa.* New York: Dutton. Color photos and a brief paragraph using the target letter show everyday life in Africa.

Scarry, R. (1973). *Richard Scarry's find your ABC.* New York: Random House. Each letter is illustrated with numerous objects and creatures whose names contain the letter.

Smith, R. M. (2008). *An A to Z walk in the park.* Alexandria, VA: Clarence Henry Books. Letters are illustrated with more than 200 animals.

Wood, A. (2003). *Alphabet mystery.* New York: Blue Sky Press. When the letter *x* is missing, the other 25 letters search for him.

Wood, J. (1993). *Animal parade.* New York: Bradbury. A parade starts with an aardvark, an antelope, and other animals whose names begin with *A* and proceeds through the rest of the letters of the alphabet.

Ziefert, H. (2006). *Me! Me! ABC.* Maplewood, NJ: Blue Apple Books. Dolls make a series of requests.

REINFORCEMENT ACTIVITIES
Alphabet Knowledge

- Have children create their own alphabet books.

- Help children create name cards. Explain that names begin with uppercase letters but that the other letters in a name are lowercase.

- Make a big book of the alphabet song, and point to the letters and words as children sing along.

- If children are using classroom computers, teach the letters of the alphabet as you teach them keyboarding skills.

- Encourage students to write as best they can. This will foster learning of the alphabet as they move from using pictures and letterlike forms to actual letters to express themselves.

- As you write messages, announcements, or stories on the board, spell out the words so that students will hear the names of the letters in a very natural way.

- Sing songs, such as "Bingo," that spell out words or use letters as part of their lyrics.

- Read books such as *Chicka Chicka Boom Boom* (Martin & Archambault, 1989), in which letters play a prominent role.

- Most important, provide an environment in which children are surrounded by print. Encourage students to engage in reading and writing activities. These might include "reading" a wordless picture book, using a combination of drawings and letterlike figures to compose a story, creating some sort of list, using invented spelling to write a letter to a friend, exploring a computer keyboard, or listening to a taped account of a story. Interaction with print leads to knowledge of print. The ability to form letters improves without direct instruction (Hildreth, 1936). However, systematic instruction should complement the provision of opportunities to learn. Learning the alphabet is too important to be left to chance. ■

FYI

Phonemic awareness is not the same as speech discrimination. Speech discrimination is the ability to discriminate the sounds of language, such as being able to tell the difference between *bat* and *hat*. Students having adequate speech discrimination may have difficulty with phonemic awareness. Speech discrimination does not require abstracting sounds, whereas phonemic awareness does (Snow, Burns, & Griffin, 1998). ■

children do not have to deal with individual sounds; however, the ability to detect speech sounds in words is absolutely crucial for literacy development. Without the ability to abstract separate sounds, they will not be able to understand, for example, that the letter *b* stands for the sound /b/ heard at the beginning of *ball*. They will not even be able to consider a beginning sound because they will not be able to abstract it from the word itself. They may be able to write a few letters, but their writing will not evolve beyond the early alphabetic stage because they will be unable to isolate the sounds of words.

What makes detecting sounds in words difficult? Two factors: metalinguistic awareness and coarticulation. Metalinguistic awareness requires students to reflect on language on an abstract level, to treat language as an object of thought. **Coarticulation** is a feature of language that makes listening and speaking easy but makes reading difficult. For instance, when saying the word *cat*, you do not say /k/, /a/, /t/; you coarticulate the phonemes: As you form the /k/, you also form the /a/, and as the /a/ is being formed, you coarticulate the final sound /t/. Because of coarticulation, *cat* is a blend of sounds, rather than three separate sounds. Coarticulation makes it easier to form and perceive words. However, because the sounds in the words are coarticulated, they seem to be one continuous sound and so are difficult for young children to pry apart (Liberman & Shankweiler, 1991).

Language is the foundation for phonological awareness. The larger children's vocabularies are and the better their articulation of speech sounds, the easier it is for them to acquire phonological awareness. Initially, children learn words as wholes. The ability to segment individual sounds

■ A **phoneme** is the smallest unit of sound that distinguishes one word from another. *Pit* is different from *pat* because of the difference in the phonemes /i/ and /a/.
■ **Phonemic awareness** is the consciousness of individual sounds in words. It is the realization that a spoken word is composed of a sequence of speech sounds.
■ **Coarticulation** is the process of articulating a sound while still articulating the previous sound—for instance, saying /oy/ while still articulating /t/ in *toy*.

in words apparently develops as children's vocabularies grow and they acquire larger numbers of words that have similar pronunciations, such as *cat, can, cap,* and *cab* (Metsala, 1999). For children to be able to distinguish among such words and represent them in memory, they must be able to mentally segment the words into smaller units of pronunciation. It is theorized that children segment words into syllables and segment syllables by onset and rime and, later, sound by sound. Children with larger vocabularies have segmented more words in this way (Metsala, 1999). Because they have elements that occur more frequently, some words are easier to segment than others. Children are better at segmenting *at* words into onset and rime than at segmenting *ud* words. In other words, they are more likely to be able to detect the *at* in *cat* and *rat* than the *ud* in *bud* and *mud*. There are more *at* words than *ud* words, so children know more *at* words and thus have had more experience noting differences among them. Words that children learn early and word elements such as *at* that have a large number of examples are easier to learn (Metsala, 1999). For novice readers, begin instruction in phonemic awareness with patterns that appear in very basic words that students have learned early and patterns that encompass many words. These are more likely to have segmented representations in children's memory (Goswami, 2001).

Word Play   One of the best ways to develop phonological awareness is to have fun with words. As students play and experiment with language, they become aware of it on a more abstract level. They begin to think of words as words and become aware of the sounds of language on an abstract level. In addition to playing games with words in the classroom, read aloud books that have fun with words, especially those that call attention to the parts of words.

An excellent book for developing phonological awareness is *Jamberry* (Degen, 1983), in which both real and nonsense words are formed by adding *berry* to a variety of words. After reading the tale to students, have them create *berry* words. *Don't Forget the Bacon!* (Hutchins, 1976) is another good choice for developing phonological awareness. Afraid that he will forget an item on his shopping list (six farm eggs, a cake for tea, and a pound of pears), the child rehearses the list as he heads for the store. Unfortunately, as he rehearses it, he makes substitutions in some of the words so that "a cake for tea" becomes "a cake for me" and later "a rake for leaves." Read the story to students, and discuss how the boy kept changing the sounds. This will build their awareness of sounds in words. Also have them role-play the rehearsing of the shopping list so that they can see firsthand how the sounds in the words are changed (Griffith & Olson, 1992). In *The Hungry Thing Goes to a Restaurant* (Slepian & Seidler, 1992), initial sounds are substituted. The staff at the restaurant can't understand what the Hungry Thing wants when he orders things such as bapple moose and spoonadish. As you read the story, have students guess what the Hungry Thing was ordering (apple juice and tuna fish). Other books that play with sounds include most of the Dr. Seuss books and the sheep series by Shaw (including *Sheep in a Jeep, Sheep on a Ship,* and *Sheep in a Shop*).

Key Phonological Skills   The main skills developed in phonological awareness are rhyming, blending, and segmenting. Blending involves putting word parts together, combining /h/ +/ /a/ +/t/ to form *hat,* and is easier than segmenting, which involves segmenting *hat* into the phonemes /h-/a/-/t/ and identifying initial sounds in words.

Rhyming   Rhyming is an important concept in its own right. Rhyming has traditionally played a large role in phonological awareness programs. It was believed that rhyming was the easiest of the phonological awareness tasks. However, some experts now believe that rhyming is one of the more difficult of such tasks (Lonigan, Schatschneider, & Westberg, 2007). Gough, Larson, and Yopp (2001) found that some students were better able to identify words that began with the same sound than to supply rhyming words. In addition, research is indicating that blending and segmenting sounds and identifying initial sounds are more effective tasks for building the kind of phonological awareness essential for reading than is rhyming.

FYI

• Phonemic awareness demands that the child ignore meaning and attend to the word's form. This requires a new perspective, a change in the way the child "looks at" a word (Gough, Larson, & Yopp, 2001).
• Students should be taught phonological awareness as long as they need it. Instruction in phonological awareness should be a continuing feature of instruction in phonics. There is a reciprocal relationship between phonemic awareness and reading. Being able to detect phonemes helps the child learn to read. The act of reading fosters growth in phonemic awareness. ■

Adapting Instruction for English Language Learners

ELLs may find detecting beginning sounds easier than detecting rhymes. ■

CCSS

Recognize and produce rhyming words.

Using Technology

Nicky's Nursery Rhymes has an extensive collection of nursery rhymes and songs. Many of the songs are accompanied by music, and many of the rhymes are recited by Nicky, so students can follow along. http://www.nurseryrhymes4u.com ■

FYI

Parents can help their children develop phonological awareness by playing word games with them, reading rhyming stories to them, reciting traditional nursery rhymes, and singing songs. ■

Using Technology

Illustrations for rhyming words and suggestions for teaching rhyming can be found at Webbing into Literacy:
http://curry.edschool.virginia.edu/go/wil/home.html ■

FYI

Stories build sensitivity to and awareness of the sounds of language, since many children's books are told in rhymes or feature alliteration (Schickedanz, 1999). ■

FYI

Engagement is fostered when emergent literacy activities are taught and reinforced within a playful context, such as reciting tongue twisters or nursery rhymes or playing alphabet games. ■

FYI

Being able to detect beginning sounds is a more important skill than being able to detect rhymes. Students are ready for instruction in phonics when they can detect beginning sounds; they are not yet ready when they can detect rhyme but not beginning sounds. Focus instruction on beginning sounds. ■

To develop rhyme, read nursery rhymes and other rhyming tales to the students to help them develop the ability to detect rhyme. At first, just read the nursery rhymes and rhyming tales so that the children enjoy the stories and the sounds. They may memorize some of the rhymes if they wish (see the Student Reading List, Rhyming Books). Discuss any rhyming stories that you read to the children, thereby building a background of literacy. In time, discuss the concept of rhyme itself. Lead students to see that the last word in one line has the same ending sound as the last word in another line. Reread some of the nursery rhymes aloud, emphasizing the rhyming words. Explain what rhyming words are, using examples such as *rake/cake, bell/well, ice/mice,* and so on. Also build rhymes with students. Using the element *an,* here is how a rhyme might be built: Say "an." Have students say "an." Explain to students that you are going to make words that have *an* in them. Say "c-*an,*" emphasizing the *an* portion of the word. Ask students if they can hear the *an* in *c-an.* Holding up a picture of a can, have them say "can" and listen to the *an* in *c-an.* (By using pictures, you are reducing the burden on students' memories.) Hold up a picture of a pan. Have students tell what it is. Tell students that *p-an* has *an* in it. Ask them if they can hear the *an* in *f-an* as you hold up a picture of a fan. Introduce *man* and *van* in the same way. Ask students if they can tell what sound is the same in *can, pan, fan, man,* and *van.* Stress the *an* in each of these words. Explain that *can, pan, fan, man,* and *van* rhyme because they all have *an* at the end. Invite students to suggest other words that rhyme with *can: tan, Dan, Jan, plan, ran* (Gunning, 2000c). Build other rhymes in similar fashion.

Blending Blending prepares students for segmenting and noting the beginning sounds in words. In general, the larger the word part, the easier it is to blend. Blending

STUDENT READING LIST

Rhyming Books

Barrett, J. (2000). *I knew two who said moo.* New York: Atheneum. Humorous sentences contain words that rhyme with the number words *one* to *twenty.*

Cameron, P. (1961). *"I can't," said the ant.* New York: Coward. With the help of an army of ants and some spiders, an ant helps repair a broken teapot amid the encouragement of the kitchen's inhabitants.

dePaola, T. (1985). *Tomie dePaola's Mother Goose.* New York: Putnam. Traditional verses are accompanied by dePaola's lighthearted illustrations.

Fisher, J. (2000). *Pass the celery, Ellery.* New York: Stewart, Tabori & Chang. People pass a food that rhymes with their names: "Pass the egg, Meg."

Franton, D. (2002). *My beastie book of ABC rhymes and woodcuts.* New York: HarperCollins. Humorous animal rhymes.

Hague, M. (1993). *Teddy Bear Teddy Bear.* New York: Morrow. In this action rhyme, Teddy Bear is asked to do such things as turn around, touch the ground, and show his shoes.

Hale, G. (Ed.) (2003). *An illustrated treasury of read-aloud poems for young people: More than 100 of the world's best-loved poems for parent and child to share.* New York: Black Dog & Leventhal. This collection of new and classic poems was selected for young people.

Harwayne, S. (1995). *Jewels: Children's play rhymes.* Greenvale, NY: Mondo. Twenty play rhymes from around the world include brief poems, as well as action, game, jump rope, and song rhymes.

Lobel, A. (1986). *The Random House book of Mother Goose.* New York: Random House. More than 300 nursery rhymes are presented.

Marzollo, J. (1990). *Pretend you're a cat.* New York: Dial. Rhyming verses ask the reader to purr like a cat, scratch like a dog, leap like a squirrel, and so on.

Raffi. (1987). *Down by the bay.* New York: Crown. This song celebrates silly rhymes: "Did you ever see a whale with a polka-dot tail, down by the bay?"

Samuells, J. (2003). *A nose like a hose.* New York: Scholastic. A little elephant has a very long nose.

Tafuri, N. (2006). *Five little chicks.* New York: Simon & Schuster. A mother hen helps her chicks find food.

Thomas, J. (2009). *Rhyming dust bunnies.* New York: Atheneum. Three of the dust bunnies rhyme: Ed, Ned, and Ted, but Bob does not and that sets up a series of humorous encounters.

Wong, E. Y. (1992). *Eek! There's a mouse in the house.* Boston: Houghton Mifflin. After the discovery of a mouse in the house, larger and larger animals are sent in, one after another, with increasingly chaotic results.

 FYI

Send home a letter to each student's family. Mention that you are teaching the concept of rhyme and explain why. List things the family might do to help: read rhyming books, recite rhymes, talk about rhyming words. Send materials that the parents might use. Your letter might contain a series of nursery rhymes (Ericson & Juliebo, 1998). ■

 REINFORCEMENT ACTIVITIES

The Concept of Rhyme

- Have students supply the final rhyming word of a couplet:

  There was an old lady who lived in a shoe. She had so many children she didn't know what to _____.

- I like to run. It's so much _____.

- Students can compose a rhyming pictionary in which they paste on each page illustrations of words that rhyme. A typical page might include pictures of a man, a can, a fan, and a pan. Pictures might come from old magazines, workbooks, or computer clip art, or they can be drawn.

- Read a rhyming story or verse to students. Pause before the rhyming word and have them predict what the word might be.

- Have students sort cards containing illustrations of objects whose names rhyme. Begin by providing a model card (cat) and having students arrange rhyming cards under it (bat, rat, hat). Provide students with cards that do not rhyme with *cat*, as well as those that do. Later, have students sort two or three rhyming patterns at the same time. Discuss students' sorting.

- Play the game *I Spy* using rhyming clues. "I spy something that rhymes with walk and talk" (chalk; Ericson & Juliebo, 1998).

- Sing traditional songs that have a strong rhyming element. After singing a song once, have students listen to a second singing to detect rhyming words. Also sing all of two rhyming lines except the last word, and let students say or sing the missing word.

syllables and **onsets** and **rimes** is easier than blending phonemes. However, blending syllables and onset and rimes has limited payoff. You might want to go directly to blending individual sounds in words. If you decide to blend syllables, explain to students what you are doing. Using a hand puppet, tell students that the puppet says its words in syllables or parts. Instead of saying *basket* the way we do, it says *bas-ket*. Explain that we have to help the puppet by putting the parts of the word together: *bas-ket, basket*. Have the puppet say the following words in parts. Have students repeat the word parts, holding up a finger for each part, and then blend the parts to form words: *monkey, turtle, camel, robin, turkey, penguin, eagle*. You might also have students clap for each syllable in a word.

Onsets and rimes may be blended in this same way. Again using a hand puppet, tell students that the puppet says its words in parts. Instead of saying *moon* the way we do, it says *m-oon*;

 CCSS

Blend and segment onsets and rimes of single-syllable spoken words.

■ The **onset** is the initial part of a word, the part that precedes the first vowel. The onset could be a single consonant (*c* + *at*), a digraph (*sh* + *eep*), or a cluster (*tr* + *ip*). A word that begins with a vowel, such as *owl* or *and*, does not have an onset.

■ The **rime** is the part of a word that rhymes, such as *-ook* in *look* or *-ow* in *cow*.

so we have to help the puppet by putting the parts of the word together. Have students help put the following words together: *m-an, s-and, h-at, r-at, r-an.* To introduce the blending of phonemes, follow the same process but have students blend all the word's individual sounds. Using the hand puppet, tell students that the puppet says its words in separate sounds Instead of saying *cat* the way we do, it says /k/-/a/-/t/, so we have to help the puppet by putting the sounds of the word together. We have to put /k/-/a/-/t/ together and say *cat.* (Hold up a finger for each sound so as to dramatize and mark the separate sounds.) In the activities below in which students blend phonemes, present the words in groups of four. In order to actively involve all students, provide each student with a set of pictures showing the four words. When you say the sounds of the word to be blended, students say the sounds, holding up a finger for each sound as it is spoken. They then say the word and choose the picture that shows the word and hold it up. By observing students, you can tell who is catching on and who is struggling. Discuss the names of the pictures before beginning the activity so that students know them:

pie, tie, bee, key

cat, hat, bat, rat

cap, map, nap, fish

lock, rock, sock, goat

hop, mop, pop, bed

bus, duck, pig, cup

After students have held up the picture for the word being blended, have them say the word. Affirm students' efforts but correct wrong responses. For a correct response, you might say, "Hat. That is correct. When you put /h/ -/a/ - /t/ together, you get *hat.*" For an incorrect response, you might say, "That was a good try. But when I put /h// -/a/ - /t/ together, I get *hat.* You say it: /h/ -/a/- /t/. " After students have completed a group, go through it again. Encourage them to put the words together faster. If students have difficulty with the activity, provide assistance or present words that have just two sounds, as in the first row above.

Segmenting   **Segmentation** typically begins with larger elements and works down to smaller elements until students are segmenting words into their separate sounds, or phonemes. Thus, students are presented with exercises that segment sentences into words, compound words into their component words, words into syllables, syllables into onset and rime, and, finally, words into phonemes.

Segmentation can be introduced as you lead the class in reading a big book, an experience story, or the morning message. Point out separate words as you read enlarged text or as you write stories, announcements, or messages for all to see. Have students count how many words are in a sentence that you say.

To introduce segmenting words into syllables, explain that words are made up of parts. Point out the separate syllables in compound words and other two-syllable words. You might have students clap out the syllables or word parts they hear in *baseball, backpack, sunup, bobcat, outside, puppet, window, pencil, baby, puppy.* Also have students clap out the syllables they hear in each other's names: *Jac-ob, Mi-chelle, Ma-ri-a, Is-a-bell-a.*

More difficult, but providing better preparation for leaning letter–sound relationships is the ability to segment words into phonemes. Choose two-phoneme words whose sounds are easily discriminated, and then elongate the words and discuss their sounds. For instance, after reading "Goldilocks and the Three Bears," stretch out the words *he, me, see,* and *she,* and help students abstract the separate sounds. Because students will be learning short-vowel patterns initially, have them segment two-sound short-vowel words: *at, Ed, it, is, up, us.* Avoid segmenting words that

∎ **Segmentation** is the division of sentences into words, compound words into component words, words into syllables, syllables into onset and rime, and finally, words into phonemes.

contain nasals, such as *an* and *am*, because nasals tend to combine with the preceding vowel. After students can segment two-phoneme words, move on to words that have three phonemes. Focus on words that have **continuants**, such as /s/ or /m/, because these are easier to say and detect than **stops**. Continuants can be stretched out: *ssss*. Stops cannot. The stops /b/, /d/, /k/, /g/, /p/, /t, /j/, and /ch/ should be emphasized but not stretched out. Actually, they should be said fast so as to minimize distortion. Stops spoken in isolation tend to be followed by an "uh" sound so that /b/ might sound like "buh." Also focus on the sounds that students will need to know to read and spell words. If the first words they are going to learn are *sat* and *hat*, present words containing /s/ and /h/.

Attempts at spelling foster phonemic awareness. As students try their hand at spelling, encourage them to stretch out words so that they can hear the sounds. As you write on the board, say the separate sounds that correspond to the letters so that students can hear them. As you write *Sam has a new pet*, say, "S-a-m h-a-z uh n-oo p-e-t." After students have begun to catch on to the concept of sounds, say words slowly and ask students to tell how many sounds are in them.

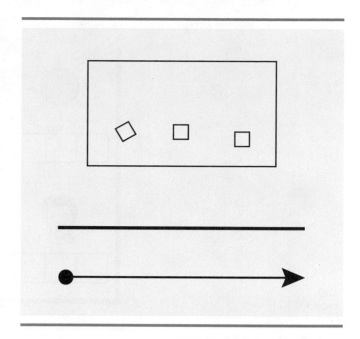

FIGURE 4.3   Say It and Move It

If students experience difficulty learning to segment words, you might try a technique designed by Blachman and colleagues (1994, 2000) known as Say It and Move It. As students say a sound in a word, they move a blank tile from a circle or square at the top of the page down the page past a thick black line to a line that has a dot on the left and an arrow point on the right, as in Figure 4.3. Hearing the word *man*, the students would say /m/ while moving the first tile, /a/ while moving a second tile, and /n/ while moving a third tile. Students then move a finger along the arrow but under the tiles and blend the sounds to form the word *man*. After students learn the sounds for the letters *a, m, t, i, s, r, b,* and *f* they use tiles that have letters to show the spelling of each sound.

Students can also use a procedure suggested by Elkonin (1973) and widely used in intervention programs. Elkonin attempted to make the abstract skill of segmenting more concrete by using drawings and markers. The student is given a drawing of a short word, below which are blocks that correspond to the number of sounds in the word. Below a drawing of the word *sun*, for instance, there are three blocks, as in Figure 4.4. Markers are placed in the blocks to represent the three sounds in *sun*. To introduce the technique, carry out the steps outlined in Lesson 4.1. As students learn letter–sound relationships, they might fill in the blocks with the letters that represent the sounds.

Another technique for helping students grasp the concept of segmenting is to cut a picture of a common word into the number of sounds contained in the word and have students say the elements as they reassemble the picture. The compound word *football* might be represented by pictures of a foot and a ball. A picture of a cat might be cut into three pieces, one for each sound (Lonigan et al., 2007).

 FYI

• In order of difficulty, students detect syllables, rimes and onsets, and then individual sounds. Detection is easier than segmentation. Blending is also easier than segmentation. Segmentation is easier than manipulation.
• Phonemic awareness is a continuously developing skill. When students are learning initial consonants, it is only necessary that they be able to perceive initial sounds. As they learn ending consonants and vowel correspondences, they need to be able to segment all the sounds in a word. ■

FYI

Stretching out sounds works best with continuants. Stops should be repeated: *-b-b-b* rather than stretched. ■

Phonological Awareness and ELLs   Phonemic awareness is a general skill that is not language specific. Phonemic awareness developed in another language will transfer to English (Yopp & Stapleton, 2008). "ELLs, even in the very beginning stages of English language development, benefit from phonological awareness instruction and activities. Those ELLs who demonstrate difficulty developing these abilities, even as early as kindergarten, require extra instruction to support this development. Improved proficiency in English is not

■ **Continuants** are consonant sounds that are articulated with a continuous stream of breath: /s/, /f/, /h/, /w/, /m/, /n/, /r/, /l/, /sh/, /th/, /th/, /y/, /v/, /z/, /zh/, and /ng/.

■ **Stops** are consonant sounds that are articulated by partially obstructing the flow of breath: /b/, /d/, /k/, /g/, /p/, /t, /j/, and /ch/.

FIGURE 4.4   Elkonin Boxes

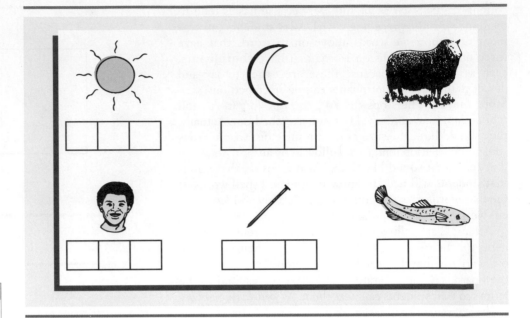

Source: Word Building: Beginnings by T. Gunning, 1994. New York: Phoenix Learning Resources. Reprinted by permission of Galvin Publications.

FYI

The ability to segment words into phonemes emerges as children attempt to write (Venn & Jahn, 2004). ■

Adapting Instruction for Struggling Readers and Writers

Elkonin blocks can be used informally. If a student is struggling with the spelling of a word, draw one box for each sound so that the student can see how many sounds the word has. Encourage the student to spell any sounds that he or she can, and give help with the rest. ■

FYI

According to Elkonin (1973), 5- and 6-year-olds who used his technique were able to learn to segment words. ■

Adapting Instruction for English Language Learners

When working with ELLs, focus on speech sounds that are common to both languages. Avoid sounds that might be unfamiliar to students until they have had a chance to learn them. Spanish has no short *a*, *i*, or *u*, but does have the long vowels. Start phonemic awareness with words containing long vowels. ■

LESSON 4.1
Elkonin Phonemic Segmentation Technique

Objective

• Students will segment words into phonemes.

Step 1.

Explain the task, model it, and guide the child through it. Explain to students that this will help them read and spell words.

Step 2.

Give the child a drawing of the sun. Remind the child to say the word that names the picture and to stretch the word out so that she or he can hear the separate sounds. If the child has difficulty noting the sounds, very carefully and deliberately pronounce the word. Emphasize each sound, but do not distort the word.

Step 3.

Have the child put a marker in each block while saying each sound. The number of blocks tells the child how many separate sounds there are in a word. The child says /s/ and puts a marker in the first block, then says /u/ and puts a marker in the second block, and finally puts a marker in the third block while saying /n/.

Step 4.

As the child becomes more proficient, eliminate the blocks and markers, and have her or him simply tell how many sounds are in a word.

Step 5.

Evaluate the students' ability to segment words. Note how many sounds students are representing in their invented spelling. Provide additional instruction and practice as necessary.

likely to remediate difficulties in understanding the sound structure of the language" (Rivera, Lesaux, Kieffer, & Rivera, 2006, p. 18.).

Perceiving Beginning Consonant Sounds

The ultimate aim of phonemic awareness instruction in general and segmentation in particular is to enable students to learn letter–sound correspondences. Initially, their major task is to learn beginning consonant correspondences such as s/s/ and m/m/. However, students will have difficulty learning phonics if they are unable to perceive the sounds of beginning consonants. For example, when a child who confuses the sound /p/ with the sound /d/ is taught the letter that represents /p/, the child may actually associate it with the sound /d/, or vice versa.

To introduce the concept of beginning sounds, read and discuss *The Story of Z* (Modesitt, 1990), if possible. Tired of being last, Z leaves the alphabet, and so children say things such as "Can we go to the *oo* and see the *ebras*?" Have students supply the missing beginning sound and tell what the sound is. Using the same technique employed in *The Story of Z*, hold up objects or pictures of objects or creatures and ask such questions as "Is this an *ee*? (while holding up a picture of a *bee*). What is it? What sound did I leave off?" While holding up a pen, ask, "Is this an *en*?" Do the same with other objects and pictures. Another easy way to convey the concept of beginning sound is to ask questions such as "Do you hear /s/ in *sock* or *rock*?" (Murray, 2006b). (It's helpful if you are holding a sock and a rock.) Build on the student's response. Say, if the answer is correct, "Yes, you are right: *sssock* begins with a /s/ sound." If the answer is incorrect, say, "That's a good try. But *sock* begins with a /s/ sound."

Also, or as an alternative introduction, read aloud alliterative stories or alphabet books such as *Emma's Elephant & Other Favorite Animal Friends* (Ellwand, 1996), which

FYI

If children cannot abstract the separate sounds in *hat* or the beginning sound of *ball*, they may learn to read a few words by sheer rote memory but will not be able to sound out words. ∎

Adapting Instruction for Struggling Readers and Writers

Read, Write & Type! (Talking Fingers) is a research-based program that reinforces phonological awareness, decoding, writing, and comprehension. Because it uses a talking keyboard that says the sound of the letter being typed, this program is especially effective at building phonemic awareness and beginning consonant correspondences. ∎

Using Technology

Tongue twisters tested with students can be found at Wallach and Wallach's Tongue Twisters: http://www.auburn.edu/~murraba/twisters.html ∎

FYI

• Difficulty with high-frequency sounds, such as /s/ or /f/, or substitution of voiced for voiceless sounds (/b/ for /p/, /v/ for /f/) could be an indication that a student has high-frequency hearing loss. Confer with the school nurse.
• Classrooms should be both print-rich, with many opportunities to explore print, and sound-rich, with many opportunities to explore the sounds of the language (Lonigan et al., 2007). ∎

STUDENT READING LIST

Alliterative Books for Reinforcing Beginning Consonants

Bandes, H. (1993). *Sleepy river.* New York: Philomel. During a canoe ride at nightfall, a Native American mother and child glimpse ducks, fireflies, bats, and other wonders of nature.

Base, G. (1987). *Animalia.* New York: Harry N. Abrams. Each letter is illustrated and accompanied by an alliterative phrase, such as "Lazy lions lounging in the local library."

Bayer, J. (1984). *A, my name is Alice.* New York: Dial. The well-known jump rope rhyme that is built on letters of the alphabet is illustrated with animals from all over the world.

Cole, J., & Calmenson, S. (1993). *Six sick sheep.* New York: Morrow. This is a collection of all kinds of tongue twisters.

Geisel, T. S. (1973). *Dr. Seuss's ABC.* New York: Random House. Letters of the alphabet are accompanied by an alliterative story and humorous illustrations.

Hobby, H. (2000). *Toot and Puddle: Puddle's ABC.* Boston: Little, Brown. Puddle uses alliterative phrases to teach Otto the alphabet.

Kellogg, S. (1987). *Aster Aardvark's alphabet adventures.* New York: Morrow. A highly alliterative story accompanies each letter.

Knutson, K. (1993). *Ska-tat.* New York: Macmillan. Children describe playing in the colorful, crunchy autumn leaves as the leaves fall to the ground.

Schwartz, A. (1972). *Busy buzzing bumblebees and other tongue twisters.* New York: HarperCollins. This is another fun collection of tongue twisters.

Steig, J. (1992). *Alpha beta chowder.* New York: HarperCollins. An alliterative, humorous verse for each letter of the alphabet is presented.

Stevenson, J. (1983). *Grandpa's great city tour.* New York: Greenwillow. Letters in upper- and lowercase are accompanied by numerous unlabeled objects whose names begin with the sound commonly associated with the letter being presented.

features alliterative captions, or *Flatfoot Fox and the Case of the Bashful Beaver* (Clifford, 1995), which has a character who speaks in alliterative sentences. Some other alliterative books that might be used to reinforce the idea of beginning consonant sounds are listed in the Student Reading List. At first, simply read such a book as you would any other picture book, showing pictures and discussing content. Then, lead students to see that many of the words begin with the same sound, and let them read some selections along with you. For instance, read the following from *Nedobeck's Alphabet Book* (Nedobeck, 1981):

> Little Leonard Lion climbs a
> Ladder to mail a Love Letter to Lori.

Also read the *L* page from Judith Gwyn Brown's (1976) *Alphabet Dreams*:

> My name is Lucy,
> And my husband's name is Lee.
> We live in a log,
> And we sell lamps.

Forming Sounds   Being aware of articulation fosters phonological awareness. Skjelfjord (1976) found that students did better when they were trained to prolong continuant sounds such as /s/ and /f/ and to stress stops such as /p/, /b/, and /t/. In segmentation tests, students often said the word silently before responding. The harder a word was to segment, the more they repeated the word.

The easiest sounds to perceive are continuants because they are articulated with a continuous stream of breath: /f/, /h/, /l/, /m/, /n/, /w/, /r/, /s/, /sh/, /th/, /th/, /v/, /z/,

REINFORCEMENT ACTIVITIES
The Concept of Beginning Sounds

- Recite traditional alliterative pieces such as "Peter Piper picked a peck of pickled peppers," and have students attempt to repeat them. See *The Little Book of Big Tongue Twisters* by Foley Curtis (1977) or *Six Sick Sheep: 101 Tongue Twisters* by Cole and Calmenson (1993) for examples of alliterative pieces to accompany nearly every beginning sound. After reading each piece, give students examples of what is meant by "begin with the same sound," and then have them tell which words begin with the same sound.

- Say a word, and have students supply other words that begin with the same sound. Discuss students' names that begin with the same sound, such as *Benjamin*, *Barbara*, and *Billy*.

- Play the game *I Spy* with students. Tell them that you spy something whose name begins like the word *boat*. Encourage them to say the names of objects in the classroom that begin like *boat*. If necessary, give added clues: "It has covers. It can be read."

- Using a troll doll or puppet, have it say that only people whose names begin like the name *Sandy* (or whatever name you choose) may cross the bridge. Supply names, and have students tell which persons are allowed to cross (Stahl, 1990).

- Have students sort cards containing illustrations of objects whose names begin with the same sound (*ball, boy, banana*; *sun, sock*). Sorts can be closed or open. In a closed sort, you provide a model (illustrations of a ball and the sun). In an open sort, you provide the items (illustrations of /b/ words and /s/ words), and children decide how to sort them. Be sure to model sorting.

- Encourage students to stretch out or emphasize the sounds of words as they write them, saying *soap* as "sss-ooo-ppp." This helps build awareness of separate sounds in words as well as perception of beginning sounds. It also helps students determine how to spell words.

Using Technology

DaisyQuest and *Daisy's Castle* (GreatWave Software) are software programs that reinforce a variety of phonological skills. ■

and /zh/. Other consonant sounds cannot be continued: /b/, /d/, /p/, /ch/, /j/, /k/, /t/. To emphasize continuants such as /s/ or /m/, students can simply elongate the sound as in "ssssun" and "mmman." For sounds that cannot be elongated, students may use a process known as iteration, in which they repeat the sound as in "g-g-g-goat."

Sounds differ according to where they are formed, how they are formed, and whether they are voiced or unvoiced (see Tables 4.2 and 4.3). Demonstrating how and where sounds are formed helps students become aware of separate sounds (see Table 4.9). For instance, for the sounds /b/ and /p/, have them note how their lips make a popping sound. For /t/ or /d/, have them notice how they use their tongues to make the sound. For /f/ or /v/, they might note the use of teeth and lips. For /th/, they might note the use of teeth and tongue. For /n/, they might note the use of tongue and nose. For /m/, they might note how their lips come and stay together to make the sound and how the nose is used. Students could see what happens when they hold their noses and try to articulate one of the nasals: /m/, /n/, or /ŋ/. They might note, too, that some sounds—the stops, /b/, /d/, /k/, /g/, /p/, and /t/—pop out, but the continuants are articulated with a continuous stream of breath. Students might note that /p/ and /b/ are both produced in the same way and in the same part of the mouth. However, /b/ is voiced—the larynx vibrates when it is articulated—and /p/ is not. Most consonants occur in pairs of voiced and unvoiced sounds (the first sound in each pair here is the voiced one): /d/–/t/, /g/–/k/, /z/–/s/, /v/–/f/, /zh/ (*pleasure*)–/sh/, /j/–/ch/, /th/ (*that*)–/th/ (*think*). The sound /h/ is formed by forcing air through an opening in the larynx, the glottis (Gunning, 2000c).

FYI

Phonetics: The Sounds of American English

Demonstrates and explains how speech sounds are formed.

TABLE 4.9 Articulation of Consonants

Sound	Articulation	Directions for Students
Stops		
b	Lips popping—voiced.	Lips are pressed together and opened quickly to make a popping /b/ sound as in *ball*. Vocal cords vibrate.
p	Lips popping—voiceless.	Lips are pressed together and opened quickly to make a voiceless popping /p/ sound as in *pen*.
d	Tongue behind ridge—voiced.	Front and sides of the tongue touch the ridge behind the teeth. Tongue is lowered and makes a voiced burst of sound as in *dog*.
t	Tongue behind ridge—voiceless.	Front and sides of the tongue touch the ridge behind the teeth. Tongue is lowered and makes a voiceless burst of sound as in *ten*.
g	Tongue at back of mouth—voiced.	Tongue touches middle of roof of mouth. Tongue is lowered and makes a voiced burst of sound as in *goat*.
k	Tongue at back of mouth—voiceless.	Tongue touches middle of roof of mouth. Tongue is lowered and makes a voiceless burst of sound as in *king*.
Nasals	Lips pressed together. Sound partially absorbed by preceding vowel.	Lips are pressed together. Air is pushed through the nose.
m	Lips are pressed together. Sound partially absorbed by preceding vowel.	Lips are pressed together. Air is pushed through the nose as in *man*.
n	Tongue behind teeth. Sound partially absorbed by preceding vowel.	The front and sides of the tongue touch the ridge. Air is pushed out through the nose as in *nail*.
/ŋ/	Tongue at back of mouth. Sound partially absorbed by preceding vowel.	Tongue touches the roof of the mouth. Air is pushed out through the nose as in the last sound in *ring*.
Fricatives		
v	Teeth touching lower lip. Vocal cords vibrate.	Lower lip presses against upper teeth and pushes air out as in *vase*. Vocal cords vibrate.

(continued)

TABLE 4.9 Articulation of Consonants (*Continued*)

Sound	Articulation	Directions for Students
f	Teeth touching lower lip. Vocal cords do not vibrate.	Lower lip presses against upper teeth and pushes air out as in *fish*. Vocal cords do not vibrate.
th	Tongue behind or just below teeth. Vocal cords vibrate.	Tip of tongue presses against or just below upper teeth and pushes out air to make /th/ as in *this*. Vocal cords vibrate.
th	Tongue behind or just below teeth.	Tip of tongue presses against or just below upper teeth and pushes out air to make /th/ as in *thumb*. Vocal cords do not vibrate.
z	Tongue touching roof of mouth.	The tip of the tongue touches the middle of the roof of your mouth. The sides of your tongue touch your teeth. Air is pushed over your tongue and makes a *zzz* sound: *zzz* as in *zebra*. Vocal cords vibrate.
s	Tongue behind teeth touching roof of mouth. Sides of tongue touch teeth. Students might not articulate this sound until they have their front teeth.	The tip of the tongue touches the middle of the roof of your mouth. The sides of your tongue touch your teeth. Air is pushed over your tongue and makes a snake sound: *sssss* as in *sun*. Vocal cords do not vibrate.
zh	Tongue touching roof of mouth and teeth.	Tongue touches roof of mouth. Sides of tongue touch teeth and push out air to make a /zh/ sound as in the last sound in *garage*. Vocal cords vibrate.
sh	Tongue touching roof of mouth.	Tongue touches roof of mouth. Sides of tongue touch teeth and push out air to make a be quiet /sh/ sound as in *shoe*. Vocal cords do not vibrate.
h	Pushing air through throat.	Air is pushed up through the throat to make a /h/ sound as in *hat*. Vocal cords do not vibrate.
Afficatives		
j	Tongue touching ridge of mouth.	Tongue touches ridge of mouth. Tongue is lowered and sound is pushed out as in *jar*. Vocal cords vibrate.
ch	Tongue touching ridge of mouth.	Tongue touches ridge of mouth. Tongue is lowered and sound is pushed out as in *chair*. Vocal cords do not vibrate.
Glides		
w	Lips are rounded.	Lips are rounded but shape changes to form the vowel that follows as in *wagon*. Vocal cords vibrate.
y	Tongue touching roof of mouth.	Tongue touches roof of mouth but moves to form vowel that follows as in *yo-yo*. Vocal cords vibrate.
Liquids		
r	Tongue touching roof of mouth.	Tongue is pushed up to roof of mouth and pushes out sound as in *ring*.
l	Tip of tongue touches ridge.	Tip of tongue touches ridge on roof of mouth and pushes out sound as in *lion*.

In the LIPS (Lindamood Phoneme Sequencing) Program (Lindamood & Lindamood, 1998), students are taught to become aware of the speech articulation movements involved in creating sounds by analyzing the way in which they form sounds. For instance, students can tell that there are three phonemes in the word *meat* because three movements are needed to articulate the word: lips closing for /m/, lips opening in a smile for /ee/, and tongue tapping the roof of the mouth for the final /t/. Sounds are given names based on the way they are formed. Sounds such as /p/ and /b/, for instance, are known as lip poppers. In the New Phonics program (Birnbaum, 1999), which is designed for kindergartners, students are shown photos of faces of children articulating speech sounds. Each photograph has a descriptive label, such as the "itchy nose card" for the short-*i* sound, and a description of facial characteristics involved in the production of that phoneme. Helping children become aware of how sounds are formed may help them better perceive and then separate sounds in words, especially if they are struggling with this concept. However, this instruction can be informal and need not involve intensive study of how sounds are formed. Learning how sounds are articulated is a means to an end and not an end in itself.

Phonemic awareness may be learned through interaction with print, through specific training in segmenting and other skills, or through some combination of the two. Watson (1984) concluded that the development of phonemic awareness may require an underlying cognitive factor that is above and beyond what is required to develop listening and speaking skills. Thus, students who are skilled users of language may not acquire phonemic awareness, even when working with print, without some sort of intervention.

Integrating Phonological Awareness and Phonics   Although phonological awareness is an essential skill, it should be taught in a functional fashion. Because it is so important, there is a tendency in some programs to teach phonological awareness in isolation and to teach it more than is necessary. Phonological awareness is most effective when students learn to segment and identify phonemes as part of learning to read and write rather than as an isolated skill (Bus & van Ijzendoorn, 1999; Vandervelden & Siegel, 1997). Because the letters in a word represent the word's sounds, working with letters is a way of marking sounds. "Learning to attend to letters in words and relating these to how words sound appeared to make explicit the underlying phonemic structure" (Vandervelden & Siegel, 1997, p. 78). In a series of studies, students taught by an integrated approach outperformed those who were taught either phonemic awareness or phonics in isolation. "Letters may draw the child's attention to the sounds in spoken words, and a distinct visual symbol for each phoneme may anchor the phonemes perceptually" (Bus & van IJzendoorn, 1999, p. 412).

Instruction should also be geared to the students' level of understanding and need to know. Apparently, students do not need a high level of phonemic awareness before being able to tackle phonics. Being able to perceive and segment beginning sounds should be enough to get them started on learning initial consonant correspondences (Stahl, 1998). As they study initial consonant correspondences, they can do so in such a way that their phonemic awareness is enhanced. Stretching out sounds as they spell words ("mmmaaannn"), making new words by changing the initial consonant (making *hat* from *cat* by substituting *h* for *c*), and similar activities build phonemic awareness.

If students are about to be instructed in final consonants, that is the time to teach them to segment or isolate final sounds. If they are about to learn vowel sounds, they need to be able to segment all the sounds in a word (Stahl & McKenna, 2002). Some skills, such as deleting a sound from a word ("Say *sting* without the /t/"), may be beyond what is necessary. On the other hand, phonological awareness should be an integral part of phonics and spelling lessons. Students can't learn to decode or spell sounds if they cannot detect them. Apparently, each phoneme needs to be understood individually. It is possible for a child to be able to abstract initial /s/ from a word but not initial /m/.

When teaching a new phonics element such as *m* = /m/, be sure to teach students how to detect the sound /m/ at the beginning of *m* words (Stahl & McKenna, 2002). One reason students struggle with consonant clusters such as *st* or *bl* is that they may have difficulty segmenting the separate sounds in the clusters. Part of teaching students how to decode clusters is teaching them how to segment the sounds in a cluster. Students also do better when only key skills are emphasized and when they are

FYI

Having phonemic awareness means that the student must be able to abstract the sound from a real word and use it to read that word. Seeing the letter *m*, one struggling student could say /m/, but he could not say and blend /m/ and /ē/ when he saw the word *me*. Though he could say /m/ for the letter *m*, he could not apply this to a real word. He was unable to manipulate phonemes and so lacked genuine phonemic awareness. ∎

R E F L E C T I O N

How might phonological awareness be presented in a developmentally appropriate way?

Using Technology

Alphafriends

Each consonant is introduced with an alliterative song.
http://teacher.ocps.net/janet.cahill/page7.html ∎

FYI

Most major basal series introduce initial consonant correspondences and short-vowel patterns at the kindergarten level. ∎

FYI

Phonics instruction results in an average gain of 14 percentile points (National Reading Panel, 2000). ∎

FYI

- How much phonemic awareness is needed before students are able to grasp phonics? Stahl (1998) asserts that the ability to segment or perceive initial consonants is sufficient.
- Integrating phonemic awareness and instruction in phonics and spelling is the most effective way to foster early literacy. After learning to identify and/or segment initial sounds, students should use this knowledge to read and spell words that begin with the sound taught. ∎

FYI

- According to Bear and colleagues (2008), children are ready to begin learning letter sounds when they know nine letters.
- At-risk students who took part in speech-to-print recognition activities of this type improved in phonemic awareness, letter–sound recognition, and the ability to learn new words (Vandervelden & Siegel, 1997). ∎

Adapting Instruction for Struggling Readers and Writers

Another integrated program is *Road to the Code* (Brookes Publishing). A variety of activities integrate phonemic awareness and phonics by having students learn the short vowels *a* and *i* and the consonants *m, t, s, r, b,* and *f* and then build a series of words using them. This program should be especially helpful to struggling learners. ∎

CCSS

Demonstrate basic knowledge of one-to-one letter–sound correspondences by producing the primary or most frequent sound for each consonant.

taught in small groups (Ehri et al., 2001). Placing students in small groups means that they can be taught according to their needs and they get more individualized attention.

Using Names   Names are a good place to start instruction in learning the names of the letters of the alphabet and beginning sounds. Names are familiar and have a special significance to their owners. In the beginning, children's names can be attached to their photos so that the photo is a clue to the name. As they learn the letters that make up their names, they can recognize the name without the help of the photo. They can match names that begin with the same letter. Shown a letter, they can find names that begin with that letter. As they begin to learn letter sounds, they can find names that begin with the same sound, or they can say the sound of a letter they are shown and find names that begin with that sound (Strickland, 2008).

Letter names also provide clues to the sounds associated with the letters. Except for *h, w,* and *y,* letter names incorporate their sounds. The letters *b, c* (soft sound), *d, g* (soft sound), *j, k, p, q, t,* and *v* incorporate their sounds at the beginning of their names. The letters *f, l, m, n, r,* and *s* incorporate their sounds at the end of their names. The names of the vowel letters incorporate their long sounds (Bradley & Jones, 2007). If students forget the sound that a letter represents, the letter's name may help them remember it. When students learn letter names, they are also learning letter sounds (Bradley & Jones, 2007).

Speech-to-Print Phonics   One highly successful integrated program used speech-to-print recognition. Students were required only to recognize the printed form of a word spoken by the teacher. This is a relatively easy task and is highly recommended for use with students who are struggling with other approaches. The teacher presents a letter-sound correspondence, such as *m* = /m/, and shows students two cards—one of which contains a word that incorporates the correspondence. The teacher then asks students to point to the word that contains that correspondence. After two correspondences have been presented, the students are shown two words, one of which contains the correspondence just taught and one of which contains a correspondence previously taught. For instance, having taught the correspondences *s* = /s/ and *m* = /m/, the teacher presents the words *man* and *sun* and asks students to point to the word that says *man.* After a third correspondence has been taught, students choose from all three. However, as additional correspondences are introduced, one is dropped so that students are not required to choose from more than three correspondences. Choose correspondences whose letter names are known by students. An adapted lesson is presented in Lesson 4.2.

LESSON 4.2
Sample Lesson: Speech-to-Print—Introducing the Correspondence *m* = /m/

Objectives
- Students will understand that *m* stands for /m/.
- Students will be able to say the sound that *m* represents and spell /m/.

Step 1. Phonemic awareness

Teach the correspondence *m* = /m/. You might do this with a storybook such as *Moo in the Morning* (Maitland, 2000). Read the book aloud, and discuss it. Talk about the words *moo* and *morning* and how they begin with the same sound. Emphasize the sound of /m/ as you say *moo* and *morning.* Stress the way that the lips are pressed together to form the sound /m/. Show pictures of a man, moon, mouse, monkey, mirror, and mop. Have students say the name of each item. Repeat the names of the items, emphasizing the beginning sound as you do so. Ask students to tell what is the same about *man, moon, mouse, monkey, mirror,* and *mop.* Help students to see that they all begin with the same sound. Explain that *man, moon, mouse, monkey, mirror,* and *mop* begin with /m/. Have students say the words.

Step 2. Letter–sound integration

Write the words *man* and *moon* on the board. Stress the sounds as you write the letters that represent them. Explain that the letter *m* stands for the sound /m/ heard at the beginning of "mmman" and "mmmoon." If any of your students' names begin with /m/, also write their names—*Maria, Martin, Marisol*—on the board, again emphasizing the beginning sound as you do so.

Step 3. Guided practice

Assuming that the correspondences *s* = /s/ and h = /h/ have been introduced, present a group of three word cards containing the words *man, hat,* and *sun.* Ask: "Which word says *man?*"

After each correct response, ask questions similar to the following: "How do you know this word says *man?*" If the student says, "Because it begins with the letter *m,*" ask, "What sound does *m* stand for?" If the student says he or she chose the word because it begins with an /m/ sound, ask what letter stands for /m/. In that way, students will make connections between the letters and the sounds they represent. If a student has given an incorrect response, read the word that was mistakenly pointed to and then point to the correct word and read it: "No, this word is *sun.* It begins with the letter *s. S* makes a /s/ sound. This is the word *man.* It begins with the letter *m. M* makes the /m/ sound that you hear at the beginning of *man.*" Proceed to additional word groups similar to the following:

Which word says *sun?* man sun hat
Which word says *hat?* man sun hat
Which word says *me?* me see he
Which word says *he?* me see he
Which word says *see?* me see he
Which word says *mat?* mat sat hat
Which word says *had?* mad sad had
Which word says *sat?* mat sat hat
Which word says *had?* mad sad had
Which word says *mad?* mad sad had
Which word says *sad?* mad sad had

Go through the words in groups of three several times or until students seem to have some fluency with the words. To make the activity more concrete, you might have the students place a plastic letter on the word they have identified—placing an *m* on *man,* for example. An informal way to use speech-to-print phonics is to say a sound and have students choose from three letters the one that represents that sound.

Step 4. Guided spelling

In guided spelling, the teacher carefully articulates the word, and the student spells it with a set of plastic letters. Initially, the student might simply select from three plastic letters the one that spells the beginning sound. Later, the student might be asked to spell two- or three-letter words and be given the letters in mixed-up order.

To help students make the transition from recognizing that *m* represents /m/ to retrieving the sound of *m* when they see it, present the letter *m* and have students tell what sound it makes. If necessary, tell them the sound and provide additional practice. Also have students spell the sound. You say the sound for *m* and they spell it. Once students have a solid grasp of m /m/, have them read and write stories that contain m /m/ and other phonic elements that have been taught.

Step 5: Evaluation and review

Note students' ability to provide the sound for *m* and the spelling of /m/. Provide added instruction and practice as needed.

 FYI
- Encourage students to attempt to spell words. As students attempt to spell words, they focus on the sounds of words and make discoveries about the spelling system (Clarke, 1988).
- For additional lessons, see Building Literacy:
  http://www.wordbuilding.org ■

 FYI
In a study of more than 22,000 kindergartners, it was found that by the end of kindergarten, nearly all the children knew their letters (Denton, West, & Walston, 2003). About 70 percent knew beginning letter sounds. About one in four could read some high-frequency words. About one in ten could read brief stories. ■

 FYI
See Chapter 5 for a suggested scope and sequence for introducing consonant and vowel correspondences. ■

Adapting Instruction for Struggling Readers and Writers

Struggling students may lack confidence. They may need more support or just a vote of confidence. They may need one more explanation or another walk-through. Or they may need to work with a partner (Edwards, 2000). ■

Assessing for Learning

To assess students' language development, observe the range of their vocabularies and the complexity of their sentence structures. Observe children in informal situations as well as formal ones. Children who say little in class might be talkative when playing. Based on your assessment, plan a program of vocabulary development. ■

Introducing Other Consonant Correspondences   After students have mastered the first set of consonants /s/, /h/, and /m/, gradually introduce additional correspondences. After students have learned five or six initial consonants, they are introduced to final consonants and make matches based on both the initial and final consonants. For instance, presenting students with the word cards cat, can, and cap, the teacher says, "Which word spells *can*? Which word spells *cat*? Which word spells *cap*?"

Vowel correspondences are introduced so that students can start forming words. After vowels have been introduced, choices are made on the basis of vowels. Given the word cards bit, bet, and but, the students are asked, "Which word spells *but*? Which word spells *bet*? Which word spells *bit*?"

Using Systematic Instruction to Help Underachieving Students

High-readiness kindergartners make dramatically more progress than those with low readiness. In one study, the high-readiness group was able to spell beginning and ending consonants by the middle of kindergarten (Morris, Bloodgood, Lomax, & Perney, 2003). The low-readiness group did not acquire this ability until the second month of first grade. As a result, in first grade, the high-readiness group was able to read more than twice as many words as the low-readiness group. For the most part, students were taught with a holistic program in which the teacher conducted shared reading lessons and children were encouraged to write using invented spelling. However, except for being instructed in the alphabet and beginning consonant sounds, they were not provided with systematic instruction in letter–sound relationships. The high-readiness children picked up these skills through shared reading. The low-readiness students needed a more systematic program. The message is clear. If students are not responding to a holistic, informal approach, they may do better with one that is more systematic and explicit.

Fostering Language Development

Although alphabet knowledge, phonological awareness, phonics, and concepts of print are essential literacy skills, it is language development that predicts students' ultimate literacy development. As students move up through the grades, language skills play a more prominent role in the development of literacy skills. Language development should be an essential goal in any literacy program (Paratore, Cassano, & Schickedanz, 2011).

Although both home and school play key roles in developing a child's language and literacy skills, they do so in somewhat different ways. The school is by necessity more formal and structured than the home; however, there should be continuity between home and school. The school should build on the language and literacy skills and understandings that children have learned at home. It should make use of the learning strategies that children are accustomed to using. As Wells (1986) states,

> As far as learning is concerned, therefore, entry into school should not be thought of as a beginning, but as a transition to a more broadly based community and to a wider range of opportunities for meaning making and mastery. Every child has competencies, and these provide a positive base from which to start. The teacher's responsibility is to discover what they are and to help each child extend and develop them. (pp. 68–69)

To ease the transition from home to school and to make full use of the knowledge and skills that children bring to school, it is important that the school resemble a rich, warm, home environment, using techniques employed by the parents in such homes. In his comparison of home and school conversations, Wells (1986) concluded that home conversations were far richer. At school, the teacher dominates conversations, saying approximately three times as much as the children do. Teachers ask more questions—often of a quizlike nature—make more requests, initiate conversations more often, and choose the topic to be talked about more frequently. Because the teacher dominates conversations and discussions, both the amount and the complexity of students' contributions are drastically reduced. Syntax is less complex, vocabulary is more restricted, and utterances are briefer. Busy answering the teacher's many questions and requests, the students have limited opportunities to make a genuine contribution. Teachers are also only half as likely as parents to help children extend their statements (Wells, 1986).

To foster children's language development, try the following (Wells, 1986):

- Listen very carefully to what the student has to say. Try to see the world from the child's point of view. Do not run away with the topic. For instance, if a child mentions a trip to the zoo, find out what it was about the trip that intrigued her or him. Do not launch into a detailed description of your last trip to the zoo.
- Be open to what children want to talk about. Do not follow a preconceived plan for the direction you want the discussion to take. When discussing a story that you have read to the children, let them tell you what they liked best about it. Do not tell them what they should like best, and, of course, give them the freedom not to like it at all.
- Help students extend their responses by making encouraging comments. If a child says, "I have a new puppy," ask the child to tell you more about the puppy—how old the puppy is, what it looks like, what it eats, where it sleeps, and so forth.
- Provide students with opportunities to initiate conversations and ask questions.
- Arrange for small-group and one-on-one discussions as often as possible. Although whole-class discussions are valuable, they do not allow for much interaction.
- Use language that is on or slightly above their level when you respond to students.
- Use students' comments and questions to help them construct meaning. Students are active learners who are using what they know to try to make sense of their world.
- Give the children something to talk about. Take trips to zoos and museums. Plant seeds, and raise fish or hamsters. Have lots of experiences so that children have lots to talk about. But don't make the mistake of having the experience and not talking about it. It is through talk that students form concepts about what makes plants grow or why hippos at the zoo spend just about all their time in the water. Children develop language and concepts when they talk about what they have experienced.
- Foster conversations among children. One way children learn that talking is satisfying is by having enjoyable interchanges with other children. Fostering conversations can build language as well as social skills. Sometimes, teachers see themselves as the molders or builders of language. While this is so, teachers should also see themselves as the facilitators of language and encourage conversations and discussions among children whenever possible.
- Build on children's talk. Whenever possible, have one-on-one conversations with children. Make certain that children have equal access. Often, the quiet children, those who need one-on-one conversation the most, are given the least. In conversations, ask questions that require extended answers. Also ask real questions, ones you don't already know the answers to. When replying to young children's statements or questions, elaborate. In answer to the statement, "The dog is barking," you might reply, "Yes, the dog is barking. Perhaps it is hungry or maybe it is lonely. It wants its owner to come home and play with it" (Bunce, 1995).
- By listening carefully to children, teach them how to listen to you and to converse with and listen to each other. Also establish routines, such as taking turns and raising hands.
- Model the use of expanded language. Instead of simply saying "Good story!" explain why the story a child has written is good: "I like the way you used what you know about letters and sounds to write your story." Instead of saying "Put the crayons away," say, "Put the crayons on the shelf next to the red box of magic markers."

Adapting Instruction for English Language Learners

Understanding a new language is easier than speaking it. To help ELLs bridge the gap between understanding words and speaking them, use prompts to help them formulate what they would like to say. Also focus on the meaning of what they say and not the form. ■

Assessing for Learning

Using the Teacher Rating of Oral Language and Literacy (TROLL) (*Reading Teacher*, March 2003), teachers can help prevent future failures. Teachers can also use TROLL to challenge high-achieving children. TROLL is an easy-to-use instrument for assessing the language and literacy of 3- to 5-year-olds. TROLL assesses students' oral language and emerging reading and writing behaviors and can be administered in just 5 to 10 minutes. Teachers of ELLs can enlist the help of parents in filling out the scale. ■

Adapting Instruction for Struggling Readers and Writers

In one study, teachers used many of the techniques listed here to expand children's language. When the study began, children were 14 months below average. At the study's end, they were just 6 months behind. Teachers did more defining, recasting, demonstrating, pointing, and using of props (Wasik, Bond, & Hindman, 2006). ■

- Use informational talk, or talk that makes use of vocabulary that students are learning or reinforces concepts: "Make the pirate's hat in the shape of a triangle, so that it has three sides. Make the treasure chest in the shape of a rectangle. Two of its sides will be longer than the other two sides" (Wasik, Bond, & Hindman, 2006). (Adapt these suggestions to fit the needs of ELL students. See pp. 31–44 for more on helping ELLs.)

Core Activities for Building Emergent Literacy

This chapter has presented a number of techniques for building emergent literacy. Listed below are activities that are so highly effective that they should form the core of a literacy program for kindergarten children or other students on an emergent level. These core activities can be supplemented with other activities chosen by the teacher.

- Reading to children
- Shared reading
- Reading by children (could consist of reading along with a taped book or CD-ROM, reading a wordless or highly predictable book, pretend reading, or reading with a partner)
- Language experience/shared writing
- Independent writing
- Other language/literacy building activities

Once students have a sense of story, understand the purpose and the basic concepts of print, can identify most of the letters of the alphabet, and can detect beginning sounds in words, they are prepared for a higher level of instruction. Upcoming chapters contain suggestions for a more intensive and structured approach to reading that fosters children's growth in literacy areas such as phonics, knowledge of high-frequency words, and other word analysis skills. The next sections are devoted to reading in preschool, working with parents, and monitoring emergent literacy.

Reading in Preschool

A joint committee of the International Reading Association (IRA) and the National Association for the Education of Young Children (NAEYC) recommended that preschool children build the foundations for learning to read and write: "Failing to give children literacy experiences until they are school-age can severely limit the reading and writing levels they ultimately obtain" (1998, p. 197). In a more recent position statement, the groups made the following recommendations:

- Children do not become literate automatically; careful planning and instruction are essential. Adults— parents and teachers—must give young children the experiences they need, including exposure to books; rich conversations; experiences in drawing, pretend play, and other symbolic activities; and instruction in recognizing letters and making connections between letters and sounds. At all times, experiences should be challenging yet achievable, creating interest, engagement, and responsiveness.
- As children move from preschool into kindergarten and the primary grades, instruction focused on phonemic awareness, letter recognition, segmenting words into sounds, and decoding printed text will support later reading competence. Many factors influence whether a child becomes a competent reader, but research underscores the importance of alphabet knowledge and an understanding of connections between letters and sounds. The developmental continuum identified by research suggests that children at different ages and developmental levels need different kinds of literacy instruction, with more explicit emphasis on phonics and word analysis as they get older, but still with emphasis on obtaining meaning and enjoyment from books. (2009)

The groups commented that "programs can incorporate a focus on reading and writing into play as well as structured activities, including but not limited to direct teaching of key literacy skills" (NAEYC, 2009).

The concept of readiness to read has been replaced by the concept of preparing to read (Texas Instruments Foundation, Head Start of Greater Dallas, Southern Methodist University, 1996). A prudent course would be to avoid formal instruction in literacy. Reading aloud regularly, doing shared reading, setting up areas for dramatic play and reading and writing and a classroom library, developing oral language skills, modeling reading and writing, and providing opportunities for children to write, draw, and explore language will naturally develop emergent literacy (Campbell, 1998).

Preschool programs have grown in popularity. Although most state-funded preschool programs are designed for poor children, a number of states have universal programs, open to all 4-year-olds. With universal programs, parents choose whether to send their children. In a well-planned preschool program, students make gains of six to eight months in essential prereading skills (Gormley, Gayer, Phillips, & Dawson, 2005).

The National Early Reading Panel (Strickland & Shanahan, 2004) recommended activities to foster development in the following areas: language, alphabetical and phonological knowledge, and print knowledge.

Language

- Listening to and discussing stories, rhymes, and songs
- Engaging in small-group and one-on-one conversations with adults, especially conversations that elicit elaborated talk
- Retelling stories and events
- Listening in order to follow directions and gain information

Alphabetical and Phonological Knowledge

- Engaging in drawing and writing
- Listening to rhymes and tongue twisters and playing word games
- Exploring alphabet books
- Exploring letter names and sounds

Print Knowledge

- Exploring environmental signs
- Observing as adults read and write
- Dictating stories for adults to write down
- Exploring picture books

Effective Preschool Programs

Although there is much agreement on the curriculum for students in K–12, ideas for preschool education range from programs that are play-based and child-centered to those that embody direct instruction. The current trend is toward adding academics to early childhood education. For instance, the Framework for Head Start includes Book Appreciation and Knowledge, Phonological Awareness, Alphabet Knowledge, Print Concepts and Conventions, and Early Writing (National Center on Quality Teaching and Learning, 2011). Language, cognitive, and social skills and emotional development are also emphasized.

Neuman and Roskos (2005) caution that building background knowledge, vocabulary, and thinking skills should be the focus of preschool. These are the areas that will have the biggest payoff in the long term.

> The press for academic success has recently overwhelmed voices that call for the interplay of development and learning. Early childhood curriculum packages, adorned with the trappings of puppets and other playthings, provide hours of activities, all targeted

 FYI

Children's acquisition of emergent literacy is determined in part by their social skills and work habits (Ritchey, 2004). Students who were rated higher on following directions and completing tasks did better on measures of emergent literacy at the end of kindergarten than students who were rated lower on these items. ■

 Using Technology

To get an idea of what a pre-K curriculum might look like, examine the Prekindergarten Curriculum Guidelines from the Texas Education Agency. Emphasis is on cognitive development and language development through meaningful activities.
http://ritter.tea.state.tx.us/prek_guide/index.htm# ■

 Using Technology

Texas Pre-K Guidelines

View the clips of a preschool program in action. Note how the teachers reinforce literacy skills.
http://ritter.tea.state.tx.us/prek_guide/index.htm ■#

 FYI

The highest-scoring 25 percent of Head Start students perform at about the same level as the average kindergarten student. The lowest 25 percent perform like the lowest 2 percent of the larger kindergarten population. However, by the end of kindergarten, Head Start graduates have made substantial gains (Zill et al., 2006). ■

FYI

Early childhood instruction should combine social development with academic competence. Without a nurturing, playful, responsive environment, an academic focus may diminish children's engagement and motivation. But a child-centered environment that lacks intellectual challenge also falls short of what curious young learners deserve (Hyson, Marion, & Hyson, 2003). ■

FYI

• A key element in effective early childhood instruction is intentionality, which is "directed, designed interactions between children and teachers in which teachers purposefully challenged, scaffolded, and extended the children's skills" (Pianta & La Paro, 2003).
• Some parents and teachers favor direct teaching of handwriting and reading and writing skills at the preschool level, but early childhood educators and emergent literacy researchers have recommended exploratory activities in which children are provided with opportunities to try reading and writing for functional purposes (Rowe, 2005). ■

REFLECTION

How might a preschool literacy program differ from a kindergarten or first-grade program?

to basic sounds and letter skills. Described as compensatory, these preschool programs presumably play catch-up, helping children who are considered less fortunate to develop the skills that other children in more privileged circumstances are learning at home where parents read and talk with them regularly and expose them to interesting places, ideas, and concepts. . . . There is a tragic fallacy to this logic. Reading achievement in the earliest years may look like it's just about letters and sounds. But it's not. Reading achievement, as it becomes inevitably clear by grades 3 and 4, is—once again—about meaning (Snow, Burns, & Griffin, 1998). Successful reading ultimately consists of knowing a relatively small tool kit of unconscious procedural skills, accompanied by a massive and slowly built-up store of conscious content knowledge (Neuman, in press). It is the higher-order thinking skills, knowledge, and dispositional capabilities, encouraging children to question, discover, evaluate, and invent new ideas, that enable them to become successful readers.

This doesn't mean that letters and sounds have no place in the preschool. Rather, they should be presented in the context of meaningful activities. As Neuman and Roskos (2005) explain:

> Letter games and sound activities have a place in content-rich literacy instruction. Children learn about the alphabet and sing and play with rhythm and rhymes. In an environment full of vivid displays of developmental writing and functional print, children engage in learning how to write their names and perfecting the sounds of language. But letters and sounds do not take center stage. Rather, these skills serve a supporting role, strategically placed to help children in their content explorations. Driven by their curiosity and interest in communicating and interacting with others, children learn about the uses of literacy in ways that have personal meaning and value for them.

Low-income 4-year-olds showed encouraging gains when stories were read to them on a regular basis and the teacher engaged them in discussions in which they made predictions, reflected on the story, and talked about words (Dickinson & Smith, 1994). When book reading and literacy interactions were enhanced in child care centers for 3- and 4-year-olds by training the teachers and adding a library of children's books, the children outperformed a comparison group on vocabulary, concepts of print, concepts of writing, letter names, and phonemic awareness when assessed in kindergarten (Neuman, 1997). Other effective programs include the following.

Para Los Niños   In Para Los Niños, a child care center in a part of Los Angeles known as Skid Row, a morning language and literacy program was instituted for approximately fifty 4-year-old Spanish-speaking preschool children. The program included big-book shared reading, writing and reading centers, and a take-home library for parents. Workshops for parents were held on book-handling and home reading and writing activities. Students demonstrated encouraging gains in concepts of print, letter knowledge, and recognition of some phonics elements. Many of the families also established read-aloud routines at home (Yaden et al., 2001).

The outcomes of this program included successful transfer of early language awareness in Spanish to English. Although they were taught literacy skills in Spanish, these skills transferred to English. In fact, the students outscored native speakers of English who had participated in other preschool programs, despite the fact that the emergent literacy tests were administered in English.

Harlem Children's Zone   Harlem Children's Zone offers cradle to college services. Its preschool program is Harlem Gems, a Head Start program. Harlem Gems is an all-day pre-kindergarten program that gets children ready to enter kindergarten. Teachers work with parents as well as with students. Classes have a 4:1 child-to-adult ratio and run from 8 a.m. to 6 p.m. Children are assessed when they enter the program so that an individualized program is planned for them. The curriculum is based on the High Scope, Creative Curriculum, and Life Skills Learning Approach. Students learn their numbers, days of the week, and other basic vocabulary words in English, Spanish, and French. Of the 190 four-year-olds who entered the Harlem Gems in the 2009–2010 school year, 16.5 percent had a school readiness classification of delayed or very delayed. By the end of the year, there were no students classified as "very delayed" and the percentage of "advanced" had gone from 21.3 percent to 41.6 percent, with another 6.8 percent at "very advanced," up from 2.1 percent. About 99.5 percent of students attained a school readiness classification of average or above.

Many of the students who take part in Harlem Gems are the children of graduates of Baby College. The Baby College offers a nine-week parenting workshop to expectant parents and those raising a child up to 3 years old. Topics discussed include health, brain development, and discipline. Brain development includes discussion of the importance of reading to children, talking to children, playing with them, and using verbal discipline rather than corporal punishment (Harlem Children's Zone, 2011).

Working with Parents

Because today's emergent literacy practices are different from those parents experienced when they attended school and there was a readiness orientation, it is important that the emergent literacy program be explained to them. Trace the roots of reading and writing, and explain to parents the essential role that they have played and continue to play. Be sensitive to different styles of parenting. Some parents, not having been read to themselves, may not realize the value of reading aloud to their children or, because of limited skills, may not feel able to do it well.

Affirm what parents have done and encourage them to support their children's efforts as best they can. Also, explain each element of the program. Pay special attention to invented spelling and process writing, as these are areas that lend themselves to misunderstanding. Trace the development of children's writing from drawing and scribbling through invented spelling to conventional writing. Show examples of students' writing. Stress the benefits of early writing and assure parents that invented spelling is transitory and will not harm their children's acquisition of conventional spelling. Just as you seek to help parents use effective techniques to help their children, seek from parents an understanding that helps you to more effectively help their children. As Rodriguez-Brown (2011) notes, the home–school connection is a two-way street:

> It is necessary to support culturally diverse families in learning about different ways to support their children's learning at home, but is also important for schools to learn, understand, and recognize the contributions of culturally and linguistically different families to their children's learning in order to find functions and applications of this knowledge in their curricula and methodologies. In a diverse society and in the era of globalization, the application of this knowledge in educational settings will make schooling more relevant to the needs of all children. (pp. 748–749)

The joint position statement of the International Reading Association and the National Association for the Education of Young Children (1998) suggests that parents can help emergent readers in the following ways:

- Read and reread narrative and informational stories to children daily.
- Encourage children's attempts at reading and writing.
- Allow children to participate in activities that involve writing and reading (for example, making grocery lists).
- Play games that involve specific directions (such as Simon Says).
- Have conversations with children during mealtimes and throughout the day.

 Using Technolgy

Literacy Express

Read the report on Literacy Express, which obtained medium to large effects for oral language, print knowledge, and phonological processing according to the What Works Clearinghouse.
http://ies.ed.gov/ncee/wwc/reports/early_ed/lit_express ∎

 Using Technology

Teaching Our Youngest: A Guide for Preschool Teachers and Child Care and Family Providers contains helpful information for preschool instruction.
http://www.ed.gov/teachers/how/early/teachingouryoungest/index.html

The International Reading Association notes that preschools make a difference in children's lives; therefore, every 3- and 4-year-old child should have access to free, high-quality public preschool.
http://www.reading.org/Libraries/Position_Statements_and_Resolutions/ps1066_preschool.sflb.ashx ∎

 FYI

Parents' ways of interacting with their children are determined by cultural factors. Some parents may read in an authoritative style and fail to interact with the child (Leseman & deJong, 1998). Sessions or video recordings that demonstrate effective read-aloud techniques can be helpful to these parents. ∎

R E F L E C T I O N

What role should parents play in the development of their children's early reading skills? What provision might be made for parents who feel that they are unable to help their children?

Adapting Instruction for English Language Learners

Parents of ELLs should be encouraged to use the language that they feel most comfortable with. Advising them to speak only English may hinder communication between them and their children. ■

FYI

Children who are read to at least three times a week are twice as likely to be in the top 25th percentile of readers at the end of first grade (Denton & West, 2002). Parents need specific suggestions for helping their children. Provide a list of possible books and tips for reading aloud. ■

 Assessing for Learning

Based on your observations of a student's reading, plan instruction. For instance, if a student is using initial consonants but not vowels, probe further to see if the student knows common vowels. If not, introduce them. If the student does know common vowels, show him or her how to use vowels to help read words. Present a sentence such as *The (cap, cat) ran*, where the student must use the vowel as well as the final consonant to choose the right word. ■

 Assessing for Learning

Assessment tasks that ask students to produce rhyming words or words that begin with the same sound may be misleading (Anthony & Lonigan, 2004). Students may be able to detect words that rhyme or begin with the same sound without being able to produce them. In some studies, children have cried or refused to participate when asked to produce rhymes or alliterative words. ■

Family Literacy Programs

One highly effective way of assisting children, especially those at risk, to fully develop literacy is to help their parents overcome their own literacy difficulties so that they can then help their children. A **family literacy program** can take several forms. Parents and children may attend sessions held after school or during the summer. The parents and children may be given separate sessions, or the program may be coordinated in such a way that the parents spend some of the time working directly with their children. In another form, just the parents attend sessions, where they are taught reading and writing skills, which they pass on to the children. Parents are then prepared to read storybooks to their children or to assist with homework. In a third version, parents are taught ways to enhance their children's reading and writing skills by reading to them, talking with them, or supervising homework. As they learn ways to help their children, parents' literacy skills improve. Parents may also meet in discussion groups to talk over difficulties they are having and ways in which they might help their children.

Parents may need ongoing, specific guidance in the use of techniques to build their children's literacy. Paratore (1995) found that it wasn't enough to provide parents with storybooks and demonstrations on how to read to children. The parents needed many opportunities to observe read-aloud sessions as well as opportunities to practice reading aloud. Discussing their read-aloud sessions and obtaining practical feedback also helped.

Monitoring Emergent Literacy

Emergent literacy can best be monitored through careful observation. As students read and write, try to get beyond the product to the process. As a student is reading, try to determine what he or she is reading. Is the student reading the pictures? Has the student simply memorized the text? Is it some sort of combination? What is the child attending to? Possibilities include pictures, overall memory of the selection, memorized words or phrases, context, beginning letters, beginning letters and ending letters, all the letters in the word, or a combination of elements. Knowing where the student is, you can build on his or her knowledge and, through scaffolding, lift the student to a higher level. For instance, if the student is simply using picture clues, you can help him or her use highly predictable text along with pictures. A checklist for evaluating a child's use of early reading strategies is presented in Table 4.10.

Note the level of the student's writing. Does the student have a sense of what writing is? Is the student attempting to convey a message? Is the student using invented spelling? Use the observation guide in Figure 4.5 to monitor writing, stages of storybook reading, oral language, concepts about reading, interest in reading and writing, and work habits. The observation guide is generic; use only those parts that fit in with your program.

Observation should be broad-based. Dahl (1992) suggests observing strategies that children use in reading and writing, the routines that students engage in every day, and the products of their efforts and the comments that they make about them.

- *Strategies.* Note what strategies students use as they attempt to read or write a word. Do they elongate the sounds? Ask a teacher?
- *Routines.* How do students choose books? What do they do when they write? Do they typically use a book as a model? Do they use a drawing as a story starter?
- *Products.* What do the illustrations children have made of their reading look like? What do their written pieces look like? Are they scribbling or using a combination of scribbles and invented spelling? How are the products changing over time?

■ A **family literacy program** has as its overall goal the sharing of reading and writing by family members. Although concerned with helping children become proficient readers and writers, another goal is the transmission of the family's culture. In one such program, parents wrote stories about their experiences that they then shared with their children (Akroyd, 1995).

TABLE 4.10 Checklist for Evaluating Early Reading Strategies

Strategy	Never	Seldom	Often
Uses pictures exclusively to retell story.	_____	_____	_____
Uses pictures and text to retell story.	_____	_____	_____
Uses pictures to help with difficult words.	_____	_____	_____
Uses memory of entire piece to read story.	_____	_____	_____
Uses memory of repeated phrases.	_____	_____	_____
Uses context to decipher words.	_____	_____	_____
Uses initial consonants and context to decipher words.	_____	_____	_____
Uses initial and final consonants and context to decipher words.	_____	_____	_____
Uses consonants and vowels to decode words.	_____	_____	_____

Based on Appendix 2.1, Forms of Writing and Rereading, Example List (pp. 51–63) by E. Sulzby (1989). In J. M. Mason (Ed.), *Reading and Writing Connections*. Boston: Allyn & Bacon.

- *Comments.* What are children saying about their work? For instance, when Maurice tossed his piece of scribble writing into the wastebasket, his teacher asked him about it. Maurice replied, "My writing doesn't say anything." Maurice realized that he needed another form of writing in order to express meaning. His rejection of his scribble writing was a sign of development (Dahl, 1992). This is the kind of incident of which perceptive anecdotal records are made.

Observations should focus on what the child can do. For instance, the focus of the observation made about Maurice was his new understanding of what is required to represent spoken words in writing.

Notes taken after a discussion has been completed or a reading or writing conference has been held can also offer valuable insights. If the notes are put on gummed labels or sticky notes, they can be entered into a handheld computer or pasted into a looseleaf notebook that contains separate pages for each child.

Because young children's literacy behavior changes rapidly, observations should be ongoing. However, progress should be checked on a more formal basis approximately once a month. In addition to filling out checklists, keep anecdotal records. Note the emergence of significant behaviors, such as the appearance of finger pointing, word-by-word reading, and the use of invented spelling. Briefly describe the behavior and note the date. See Chapter 3 for more information on using observations and anecdotal records.

Using Technology

PALS

If your program requires a more formal assessment, consider a tool such as PALS Pre-K or K.

http://pals.virginia.edu/tools-prek. html ■

Informal Assessment Measures

Emergent literacy measures need not be purchased. Teachers can put together a measure that is geared to their own concept of literacy and that meshes with their literacy program. Although it can be a paper-and-pencil test to allow for group administration, an informal type of one-to-one assessment often works better. A sample informal assessment, which is administered individually, follows:

- *Letter Knowledge.* Print or type the twenty-six letters of the alphabet on cards. Make a set for uppercase letters and a set for lowercase ones. (Assess knowledge of uppercase letters first.)
- *Writing Sample.* Ask the child to write his or her name as best he or she can. If the child can write his or her name, ask the child to write any other words that he or she knows. Ask the child to write a story as best he or she can. In the story, the child might tell about himself or herself and his or her family. This may be done with letterlike

Assessing for Learning

The copyright-free Yopp-Singer Test of Phoneme Segmentation can be found in *The Reading Teacher 49* (1995), pp. 20–29. The Test of Invented Spelling, which notes how many sounds students are able to represent, can be found in the *Merrill-Palmer Quarterly 33* (1987), pp. 365–389. ■

FIGURE 4.5   Emergent
Literacy Observation Guide

Student's name: _____   Age: _____

Date: _____

Oral language	Below average	Average	Advanced
Uses a vocabulary appropriate for age level	1	2 3 4	5
Uses a sentence structure appropriate for age level	1	2 3 4	5
Can make himself/herself understood	1	2 3 4	5
Listens attentively to directions and stories	1	2 3 4	5
Can retell a story in own words	1	2 3 4	5
Understands oral directions	1	2 3 4	5
Asks questions when doesn't understand something	1	2 3 4	5

Concepts about reading	Below average	Average	Advanced
Knows the parts of a book	1	2 3 4	5
Understands that the print is read	1	2 3 4	5
Can follow a line of print as it is being read	1	2 3 4	5
Can point to words as each is being read	1	2 3 4	5
Can name letters of the alphabet	1	2 3 4	5
Can perceive beginning sounds	1	2 3 4	5
Can detect rhyming words	1	2 3 4	5
Can tell how many sounds are in a word	1	2 3 4	5
Can discriminate between words that have a similar appearance	1	2 3 4	5
Recognizes environmental print signs and labels	1	2 3 4	5
Can read own name	1	2 3 4	5

Interest in reading and writing	Below average	Average	Advanced
Enjoys being read to	1	2 3 4	5
Browses among books in class	1	2 3 4	5
"Reads" picture books	1	2 3 4	5
Asks questions about words, sentences, or other elements in books	1	2 3 4	5

Writing	Below average	Average	Advanced
Shows interest in writing	1	2 3 4	5
Writes or draws stories or letters	1	2 3 4	5
Understands the purpose of writing	1	2 3 4	5
Writes to communicate with others	1	2 3 4	5

For the most part his/her writing is best described as being at the following level:

Unorganized scribbles	_____	(The scribbles have no perceptible pattern.)
Drawings	_____	(Drawing is the child's primary mode of written expression.)
Organized scribbles	_____	(The scribbles show a pattern. They may be linear.)
Letterlike figures	_____	(The characters aren't real letters, but have some of the features of letters.)
Prephonemic spelling	_____	(The child uses real letters, but the letters have no apparent relationship to the sounds of the words he or she is writing.)
Early alphabetic spelling	_____	(Consonant sounds are spelled; *kitten* may be spelled *KTN*.)
Alphabetic spelling	_____	(Vowels are spelled with letter names; *RAN* for *rain*.)
Consolidated alphabetic spelling	_____	(Vowel markers are used; *RANE* for *rain*.)
Standard spelling	_____	

Work habits	Below average	Average	Advanced
Is able to work on own	1	2 3 4	5
Works at task until it is finished	1	2 3 4	5
Works well with others	1	2 3 4	5
Is able to share materials	1	2 3 4	5
Is able to take turns	1	2 3 4	5

forms or drawings or real letters. Note the level of the child's writing and the number of words that he or she can write, if any.

- ***Print Familiarity.*** Give *Have You Seen My Cat?* (Carle, 1973) or a similar book to the child. Discuss the book informally to find out how familiar the child is with print conventions. You might ask, "Have you ever seen this book? What do you think this book is about? How can you tell what the book is about? What do you do with a book?" Open to the first page of the story and say, "I'm going to read this page to you. Show me where I should start reading." (Note whether the child points to the illustration or the first word.) Ask the child if he or she can read any words on the page. Then tell the child that you are going to read the first sentence. Ask him or her to point to each word as you read it. (Note whether the child can do this.) Read the sentence again. Then ask the child to read it. Ask him or her to point to each word as he or she reads it. (Pointing to each word shows whether the child has a concept of separate words.) Point to a line of print and ask, "How many words are in this line?" Point to a word and ask, "How many letters are in this word?"

Other Measures of Emergent Literacy

One of the best-known measures of print concepts is CAP, or Concepts about Print (Clay, 2000). CAP has twenty-four items and takes only 5–10 minutes to administer. Clay (2006) also assembled a battery of reading and writing measures known as the

 Using Technology

Phonological awareness can be measured through the DIBELS Next subtests First Sounds Fluency and Phoneme Segmentation Fluency. Alphabet knowledge is assessed through Letter Name Fluency. All three subtests are 1-minute speed tests that have many versions so that students can be retested many times. This enables teachers to track progress continuously. After administering the timed tests, a teacher can give students untimed versions to see how well they do when speed is not a factor.
http://dibels.org/next.html ■

Exemplary Teaching

Using Assessment to Reduce Potential Reading Problems

The purpose of the Early Intervention Reading Initiative in Virginia is to reduce the number of students in grades kindergarten through 3 with reading problems by using early diagnosis and acceleration of early reading skills. The initiative provides teachers with a screening tool that helps them determine which students would benefit from additional instruction. Schools are also given incentive funds to obtain additional instruction for students in need.

Students are administered the Phonological Awareness Literacy Screening (PALS) instrument. PALS-K (kindergarten) includes measures of rhyme, beginning sounds, alphabet recognition, letter sounds, spelling, concept of word, and word recognition. According to PALS scores, approximately 25 percent of students need additional instruction.

The PALS project makes heavy use of the Internet. When teachers report their scores, they get an immediate summary report. Principals can also get reports for their schools. The site contains instructional suggestions and a listing of materials. Instruction provided to students must be in addition to their regular classroom instruction. When retested in the spring, approximately 80 percent of kindergartners identified as needing added help were making satisfactory progress. Retention is not considered a means of providing additional assistance and is not the purpose of the Early Intervention Reading Initiative.

After screening ninety-two children with PALS, the four kindergarten teachers at the McGuffey School in Virginia found that twenty-three children needed an intervention program. The students worked with a PALS tutor for 30 minutes a day. The focus was on developing phonemic awareness, alphabet skills, and beginning consonants. The lessons also included shared reading of nursery rhymes and simple pattern books. This approach was designed to develop awareness of sounds, letter recognition, concept of word, and writing skills. Although all of the students had low overall scores on emergent literacy skills, some were especially weak in phonological awareness. Others had difficulty with letter recognition or matching beginning sounds. Students were placed in groups of four according to common needs so that instruction would be focused. Skills were introduced in integrated fashion. If the lesson's focus was on beginning sounds, the teacher read aloud a selection that contained the target sounds and discussed them. Students also sorted objects and pictures that shared the target sounds and then attempted to write the name of each object or picture. The lesson ended with a rhyme that contained the target sounds (Invernizzi, Meier, Swank, & Juel, 2001). For more information, go to http://www.pen.k12.va.us/VDOE/Instruction/Reading/readinginitiative.html.

FYI

Tests of phonological awareness may not work well with children younger than 5 (Muter and Snowling, 1998). When given at age 5, such tests were relatively good predictors of later reading achievement, but when given at age 4, the tests failed to provide adequate predictions. ■

Observation Survey, which can be used to assess emergent reading and early reading behaviors (Denton, Ciancio, & Fletcher, 2006). The Bader Reading and Language Inventory (Bader & Pearce, 2009) also includes a number of assessment devices for emergent literacy: Concepts about Print, Blending, Segmentation, Letter Knowledge, Hearing Letter Names in Words, and Syntax Matching (being able to match printed with spoken words).

CAP, the Observation Survey, and the Bader Inventory are individually administered. The Phonological Awareness Literacy Screening (PALS) is a group or individual test that includes measures of rhyme, beginning sounds, alphabet recognition, letter sounds, spelling, concept of word, and word recognition (Invernizzi, Meier, Swank, & Juel, 2001). PALS Pre-K assesses name writing, letter knowledge, beginning sound awareness, print and word awareness, and nursery rhyme awareness. For letter knowledge, children who know 16 or more uppercase letters also take the lowercase alphabet recognition task. Children who know 9 or more lowercase letters are also asked to produce the sounds associated with the letters. As noted in

Chapter 3, there are a number of curriculum-based measures (CBMs) that assess emergent literacy. Measures of emergent literacy are also included with basal reading series, in the teacher's manual or as a separate item. One advantage of basal tests is that they are geared to the program for which they have been constructed. They are also generally accompanied by suggestions for working with students who do poorly on them.

Using the Assessment Results

The results of an emergent literacy assessment should help you plan instruction. Generally, an acceptable standard for phonological awareness is 80 percent. Students falling below that level require additional help. Ultimately, students are required to know all the letters of the alphabet. At the end of preschool or the beginning of kindergarten, knowing ten letters is a reasonable expectation. Children who are lacking in print familiarity need more experience with concepts with which they had difficulty. Writing samples are also indicators of emergent literacy concepts. Based on the samples, note where children are on the path to literacy and, according to their level of development, what experiences will be most beneficial.

As indicated earlier, not every ability important to reading can be measured formally or informally. Learning to read requires hard work, perseverance, and a certain degree of maturity. It also demands reasonably good health, sufficient social skills to allow one to work with others, and adequate language skills so that the teacher's instructions and the material to be read can be understood.

Measures of emergent literacy should be interpreted with care. The pre-K child who seems to be at risk because he or she knows just a few letter sounds might catch on to the system in kindergarten and do quite well. Because children develop at different rates and experience spurts in development, there are a lot of false positives when assessing young children. However, children who seem to be lagging should be closely monitored. Often young children who seem to be at risk do quite well once they get acclimated to school, but some do not. There is no sure way to tell which child will make accelerated progress and which will lag behind and need extensive support.

REFLECTION

Of all the early reading assessments, which ones would you use to assess the early literacy skills of Pre-K or K students? How would you obtain the information you need without overtesting? What are some of the pitfalls of assessing young children? How would you cope with these?

FYI

Intervention programs result in average percentile gains of 28 points (Hattie, 2009). ■

FYI

Each of the phonological assessment tasks has its own cognitive requirements. To blend a string of isolated phonemes, the child must first perceive those phonemes, then hold them in memory while trying to connect them into a word. To detect a rhyme, the child must identify both of the words' rimes, keep them in memory, and then decide if both words end with the same rime. ■

Summary

Emergent literacy instruction attempts to capitalize on the literacy skills that the child brings to school. To foster literacy, the teacher immerses the class in reading and writing activities. By reading to children, the teacher builds knowledge of story structure and story language, vocabulary, and background of experience. To build language, the school should use techniques to make the child an active partner in conversations and discussions. Through shared reading and language-experience stories, including shared writing, dictation, and scaffolded writing, basic literacy concepts and skills are built.

Once primarily a matter of copying and learning letter formation, writing in preschool and kindergarten is now seen as a valid means of expression. Children are invited to write and spell as best they can.

Progress in literacy is closely tied to knowledge of the alphabet, phonological awareness, and students' persistence. Increasingly, preschool and kindergarten programs are including instruction in literacy and preliteracy skills. Several preschool programs have been shown to be highly beneficial to at-risk learners. Parent involvement is an essential ingredient in fostering emergent literacy. A number of formal and informal measures can be used to assess emergent literacy.

Extending and Applying

1. Using the procedures described in this chapter, plan a lesson teaching letters or beginning sounds. If possible, teach the lesson and make a video recording of it. On a paper copy of the lesson plan, reflect on the effectiveness of the lesson.
2. Administer to one or more kindergarten students assessments of letter knowledge, beginning sounds, letter sounds, and developmental spelling, using measures described in this chapter or the previous one. Also obtain a writing sample. Based on an analysis of the assessments, highlight the strengths and needs of the student(s), and plan a program for them.
3. Examine stories written by a kindergarten class. What are some characteristics of children's writing at this age? How do the pieces vary?
4. Search out alphabet books, rhyming tales, song books, and other materials that you might use to enhance alphabet knowledge, rhyming, and perception of beginning sounds. Keep an annotated bibliography of these materials.

Professional Reflection

Do I …
___ Have an understanding of the ways in which young children develop literacy?
___ Have an understanding of the concept of phonological awareness?
___ Have an understanding of how children's concepts of print develop?
___ Have an understanding of how children's writing develops?
___ Have an understanding of developmentally appropriate practice?

Am I able to …
___ Assess students to determine their phonological awareness, letter knowledge, and concepts of print?
___ Use a variety of techniques to develop phonological awareness?
___ Use a variety of techniques to develop letter knowledge and concepts of print?
___ Develop language and vocabulary skills and build background?
___ Monitor progress and gear instruction to students' needs and adapt instruction as necessary?
___ Work closely with the home?

Reflection Question

What are the most effective ways to develop young children's literacy but also foster their social and emotional growth?

Building Competencies

To build competencies, consult the following sources for more detailed information:

National Reading Panel. (2000). *National Reading Panel report*. Chapter 2, Part I, "Phonemic awareness instruction," pp. 2-1 to 2-86. Washington, DC: U.S. Department of Education. http://www.nationalreadingpanel.org

Strickland, D. S., & Schickedanz, J. A. (2004). *Learning about print in preschool: Working with letters, words, and beginning links*. Newark, DE: International Reading Association.

Texas Education Agency. (2008). *Welcome to the 2008 Texas prekindergarten guidelines*. Austin, TX: Author. http://ritter.tea.state.tx.us/prek_guide/index.htm#

Venn, E. C., & Jahn, M. D. (2004). *Teaching and learning in the preschool*. Newark, DE: International Reading Association.

Webbing into Literacy http://curry.edschool.virginia.edu/go/wil/home.html

MyEducationLab™

Go to the Topic "Emergent Literacy" in the MyEducation-Lab (www.myeducationlab.com) for your course, where you can:

- Find learning outcomes for "Emergent Literacy" along with the national standards that connect to these outcomes.
- Complete Assignments and Activities that can help you more deeply understand the chapter content.
- Apply and practice your understanding of the core teaching skills identified in the chapter with the Building Teaching Skills and Dispositions learning units.
- Examine challenging situations and cases presented in the IRIS Center Resources.
- Check your comprehension on the content covered in the chapter by going to the Study Plan in the Book

Resources for your text. Here you will be able to take a chapter quiz, receive feedback on your answers, and then access Review, Practice, and Enrichment activities to enhance your understanding of chapter content. (optional)

A+RISE® Standards2Strategy™ is an innovative and interactive online resource that offers new teachers in grades K–12 just-in-time, research-based instructional strategies that meet the linguistic needs of ELLs as they learn content, differentiate instruction for all grades and abilities, and are aligned to Common Core Elementary Language Arts standards (for the literacy strategies) and to English language proficiency standards in WIDA, Texas, California, and Florida.

5

Teaching Phonics, High-Frequency Words, and Syllabic Analysis

Anticipation Guide

For each of the following statements, put a check under "Agree" or "Disagree" to show how you feel. Discuss your responses with classmates before you read the chapter.

	Agree	Disagree
1. Before they start to read, students should be taught most of the consonant letters and their sounds.	_____	_____
2. Phonics rules have so many exceptions that they are not worth teaching.	_____	_____
3. Phonics is difficult to learn because English is so irregular.	_____	_____
4. The natural way to decode a word is sound by sound or letter by letter.	_____	_____
5. Memorizing is an inefficient way to learn new words.	_____	_____
6. Syllabication is not a very useful skill because you have to know how to decode a word before you can put it into syllables.	_____	_____

Using What You Know

The writing system for the English language is alphabetic. Because a series of twenty-six letters has been created to represent the speech sounds of the language, our thoughts and ideas can be written down. To become literate, we must learn the relationship between letters and speech sounds. Chapter 4 presented techniques for teaching the nature and purpose of writing and reading, concepts of print, the alphabet, and awareness of speech sounds and for presenting initial consonants. These techniques form a foundation for learning phonics, which is the relationship between spelling and speech sounds as applied to reading. This chapter covers high-frequency words, some of which may not lend themselves to phonic analysis. In addition, the chapter explores syllabic analysis, which is the application of phonics to multi-syllabic words, and fluency, which is freedom from word identification problems. This chapter will be more meaningful if you first reflect on what you already know about phonics, syllabic analysis, and fluency. Think about how you use phonics and syllabic analysis to sound out strange names and other unfamiliar words. Think about how you might teach phonics, and ask yourself what role phonics should play in a reading program.

Rationale and Approaches for Phonics Instruction

As you read the following sentence out loud, think about the processes you are using:

> In *Palampam Day*, by David and Phyllis Gershator (1997), Papa Tata Wanga offers sage advice to Turn, who refuses to eat because on this day, the food talks back, as do the animals.

In addition to thinking about what the sentence is saying, did you find that you had to use **phonics** and syllabication skills to read *Palampam*, *Gershator*, and *Tata Wanga*? Phonics skills are absolutely essential for all readers. Most of the words we read are sight words. We've encountered them so many times that we don't need to take time to sound them out. They are in our mental storehouse of words that we recognize automatically. However, we need phonics for names of people or places or events that we have never met in print. Without phonics, we would not be able to read new words.

As adept readers, we use phonics occasionally. Because of our extensive experience in reading, we have met virtually all of the word patterns in the language. Although you may have never seen the word *Palampam* before, you have seen the word patterns *pal* and *am*. Chances are you used these patterns to decode *Palampam*. You probably decoded the word so rapidly that you may not even be conscious of having applied your skills. For novice readers, phonics is a key skill. For a period in their development, novice readers may be using phonics in a conscious, deliberate fashion to decode many of the words that they read. In time, after they've had sufficient experience with a word, that word becomes part of their instant recognition vocabulary.

How Words Are Read

Words are read in one of five, often overlapping, ways. They are predicted, sounded out, chunked, read by analogy, or recognized immediately. Predicting means using context by itself or context and some decoding to read a word. Seeing the letter *w* and using the context "Sam was pulling a red w_____," the student predicts that the missing word is *wagon*. Sounding out entails pronouncing words letter by letter or sound by sound (/h/ + /a/ + /t/) and then blending them into a word. As readers become more advanced, they group or chunk sounds into pronounceable units (/h/ + /at/). Readers may also decode a word because it is analogous to a known word. They can read the new word *net* because it is like the known word *pet*. In the fifth process, the words are recognized with virtually no mental effort. Adept readers have met some words so often that they recognize them just about as soon as they see them. These are called *sight words* because they are apparently recognized at sight (Ehri & McCormick, 1998).

How High-Frequency Words Are Learned

According to Ehri (1998), learning words at sight entails forging links that connect the written form of the word and its pronunciation and meaning. Looking at the spelling of a word, the experienced reader retrieves its pronunciation and meaning from her or his mental dictionary or storehouse of words instantaneously. Beginners might look at a word, analyze it into its component sounds, blend the sounds, and say the word. At the same time, they note how the word's letters symbolize single or groups of sounds. Over time, the connections that the reader makes between letters and sounds enable the reader to retrieve the spoken form and meaning of the word just about instantaneously. The reader makes adjustments for irregular words so that certain letters are flagged as being silent or having an unusual pronunciation. "Knowledge of letter-sound relations provides a powerful mnemonic system that bonds the written forms of specific words to their pronunciations in memory" (Ehri & McCormick, 1998, p. 140).

Stages in Reading Words

Prealphabetic Stage

Students go through stages or phases in their use of word analysis skills. Young children surprise their elders by reading McDonald's signs, soda can and milk carton labels, and the names of cereals. However, for the most part, these children are not translating letters into sounds as more mature readers would do; instead, they are associating "nonphonemic visual characteristics" with spoken words (Ehri, 1994). For instance, a child remembers the word

McDonald's by associating it with the golden arches and the word *Pepsi* by associating it with its logo. At times, teachers take advantage of the nonphonemic characteristics of words. They tell students that the word *tall* might be remembered because it has three tall letters and that *camel* is easy to recall because the *m* in the middle of the word has two humps.

In the prealphabetic (prephonemic) stage, students learn a word by selective association, by selecting some nonphonemic feature that distinguishes it from other words (Gough, Juel, & Griffith, 1992). For the word *elephant*, it could be the length of the word; for the word *look*, it could be the two *o*'s that are like eyes. The problem with selective association is that students run out of distinctive clues, and the clues that they use do not help them decode new words. Students can learn only about forty words using nonphonemic clues (Gough & Hillinger, 1980). In addition, students don't begin to advance in their understanding of the alphabetic nature of the language until they begin to use letter-sound relationships to read words.

Students' invented or spontaneous spelling provides clues to the stage they are in. They may use random letters to represent a word. Or they may even be able to spell their names because they have memorized the letters. As students become aware of individual sounds in words and the fact that letters represent sounds, they move into the second stage of reading, the partial alphabetic stage (Byrne, 1992). It should be kept in mind that stages are fluid and students might be in more than one stage at the same time.

FYI

Most children in preschool and early kindergarten are in the prealphabetic stage. ■

FYI

Spelling and reading experts have chosen different terms to refer to similar stages. The alphabetic stage is the same as the letter name stage. The consolidated alphabetic stage is the same as the within-word pattern stage. ■

Partial Alphabetic Stage

In the alphabetic (letter name) stage, learners use letter-sound relationships to read words. In the partial alphabetic stage, they may use just a letter or two. They may use only the first letter of a word and combine the sound of that letter with context. For instance, in the sentence "The cat meowed," students may process only the initial *m* and then use context and their experience with cats to guess that the word is *meowed*. Or they may use the first and last letter to decode the word *cat* in "I lost my cat," so they read the word *cat* as opposed to *cap* or *car*. Students at this stage cannot use full decoding because they haven't yet learned vowel correspondences. Because they are using partial cues, these students store incomplete representations of words and so confuse words like *where*, *when*, and *were* (Pikulski, 2006).

In their spontaneous spelling, students at this stage may represent a word by using just the first letter, such as K for *car*, or by using the letters that represent the most distinctive sounds, as in KR for *car*. At the end of this stage, they begin using vowels but may not spell the words correctly.

Full Alphabetic Stage

In the full alphabetic stage, students begin to process all the letters in words. As they learn to apply their growing knowledge of letter-sound relationships, their reading may be slow and effortful. Focusing on using their newly learned decoding skills, students cautiously read word by word. Students are "glued to print" (Chall, 1996). The danger at this stage is that too much emphasis will be put on accuracy and sounding out. This could impede students' development. "Too analytical an approach . . . may hold up silent reading comprehension" (Chall, 1996, p. 47). With students glued to print, this is a bottom-up stage. As students build their store of known words, they are better able to see commonalities in words. They note that both *cat* and *hat* have *at*. Encountering the word *mat*, which they have never seen in print, they can decode it by noting the pronounceable part *at* and blending it with *m*. Or they may use an analogy strategy. Seeing that *mat* is similar to *cat* enables them to read the word.

Students spell vowel sounds in this stage but may not spell them correctly. Because they may not perceive patterns until the end of this stage, they may fail to use final e (*hope*) and double vowel letters (*coat*) to represent long vowel sounds.

FYI

Because they begin to notice patterns and don't have to process a word letter by letter, students' reading speed and oral fluency begin to improve at the consolidated alphabetic stage. ■

Consolidated Alphabetic Stage

In the consolidated alphabetic (within-word pattern) stage, students consolidate and process longer and more sophisticated units. For instance, instead of processing *hen* as *h-e-n*, they may divide it into two units: *h + en*. They process *light* as *l + ight* and make use of such elements as a final *e* (as in *cape*) to help them determine the pronunciation of a word. In spelling, they begin using final *e* or use two vowel letters to show that a vowel is long.

As students process the same words over and over again, connections are made, and they do not have to read *cat* as /k/ /a/ /t/, or even /k/ /at/. Rather, the printed representation of the word as a whole elicits its spoken equivalent. The printed representation becomes bonded with the spoken equivalent (Perfetti, 1992). As Ehri (1998) explains, "Sight word learning is at root an alphabetic process in which spellings of specific words are secured to their pronunciations in memory" (p. 105). Gough, Juel, and Griffith (1992) explain the process somewhat differently. They believe that just about all the letters in a word are analyzed. Through practice, access speed increases so that even though words are analyzed element by element, this is done so rapidly as to be almost instantaneous. Perfetti (1985) suggests that even when words are recognized immediately, the decoding processes are still at work but on a subconscious level. This underlying processing verifies our word recognition so that we are alerted when we misread a word. This system also enables us to read very rapidly words we have never seen before.

Regardless of how the process is explained, the end result is the same. In time, nearly all the words expert readers encounter in print are read as sight words. They are recognized virtually instantaneously. What makes the instantaneous recognition possible are the connections that have been created between each word's spelling or phonics elements and its pronunciation and meaning. To create this bond between a word's written appearance and its pronunciation and meaning, students must have many opportunities to encounter the word in print. It is also important that students process the whole word rather than simply look at the initial consonant and guess what the rest of the word is. By processing the whole word, students are creating a stronger, clearer bond between the word and its pronunciation. However, the rate at which individuals create these bonds may vary. Research suggests that there is a processing ability that determines the rate at which these associations are formed (Torgeson, Wagner, Rashotte, Burgess, & Hecht, 1997). This means that some students will need more practice than others, and, in some instances, special help.

Having a firmer command of basic phonics skills, students at this stage begin to incorporate top-down strategies. They begin to rely more on "knowledge of language, of ideas, and of facts to anticipate meanings as well as new words" (Chall, 1996, p. 47). Students begin using an integrated approach. Their decoding also becomes fluent and virtually automatic so that they can devote full attention to comprehension.

In the beginning of this stage, students begin using final *e* and double letters to represent long-vowel sounds but may do so incorrectly. By the end of this stage, their spelling has become conventional.

Implications of Stage Theory

This theory of the stages of reading has two very important implications for the teaching of reading. First, it suggests that nearly all the words we acquire are learned through phonics. Therefore, words to be learned (except for a few highly irregular ones, such as *of* and *one*, and perhaps a few learned in the very beginning) should be taught through a phonics approach rather than through an approach based on visual memory. Most words that have been classified as having irregular spellings are at least partly predictable. For instance, the first and last letters of *was* are regular, as are the first and last letters of *been*. In fact, except for *of*, it is hard to find any word that does not have some degree of spelling-sound predictability. In teaching words, take advantage of that

Building Language

As you develop students' phonics skills, be sure to continue to foster language development through discussions and read-alouds. It doesn't do students much good to sound out words whose meanings they don't know. ■

Assessing for Learning

To determine what stages students are in, note what phonics cues they use to read words and also their spelling. If they are using picture clues primarily, they may be in a prealphabetic stage. If they are using initial consonants primarily, they may be in an early alphabetic stage. Gear instruction to their stage of reading. ■

regularity. It will make the words easier to learn and to recognize. And establishing links between letters and sounds helps fix words in memory so that they are eventually recognized instantaneously, or at sight.

The stage theory also implies that instruction should be geared to the stage that a student is in. Students lacking in phonemic awareness may have difficulty with letter-sound instruction unless it incorporates practice with phonemic awareness. Whereas using picture clues and memorizing predictable stories are appropriate for building emergent literacy, students in the alphabetic stage should be focusing on letters and sounds. This helps foster their decoding ability. Moreover, a student in the partial alphabetic stage is not ready for the final-*e* pattern, as in *pipe* and *late*.

Basic Principles of Phonics Instruction

Phonics instruction is of no value unless it fulfills some specific conditions. First, it must teach skills necessary for decoding words. Being able to read the short *a* in *hat* is an important skill, but knowing whether the *a* is long or short is not important; students can guess that the *a* is short without being able to read the word. Noting so-called silent letters is another useless skill. Knowing that the *k* in *knight* is silent does not ensure that a student can read the word.

Second, the skill should be one that students do not already know. One second-grader who was reading a fourth-grade book was put through a second-grade phonics workbook to make sure she had the necessary skills. If students can read material on a third-grade level or above, they obviously have just about all the phonics skills they will ever need.

Finally, the skills being taught should be related to reading tasks in which students are currently engaged or will soon be engaged. For instance, the time to teach that *ee* = /ē/ in words such as *jeep* and *sheep* is when students are about to read a book like *Sheep in a Jeep* (Shaw, 1986). All too often, they are taught skills far in advance of the time they will use them, or well after the relevant selection has been read, with no opportunity to apply the skills within a reasonable amount of time. This is ineffective instruction. Research indicates that children do not use or internalize information unless the skills they have been taught are applicable in their day-to-day reading (Adams, 1990).

Phonics instruction must be functional, useful, and contextual to be of value. It also should be planned, systematic, and explicit (Fielding-Barnsley, 1997; Foorman, Fletcher, Francis, Schatschneider, & Mehta, 1998). It must also be differentiated.

Differentiation of Phonics Instruction

Often, teachers doing intervention note that students are weak in phonics and decide to begin from the beginning. This is a poor practice. It fails to give students credit for what they know and undermines them by giving them material that is too easy. Phonics instruction should be developmental (Gunning, 2006). Assess students to find out where they are, and begin instruction there, making adjustments as necessary.

Similarly, whole-class instruction in phonics is a poor practice. In virtually all classes, there is a range of phonics knowledge. Students have different levels of understanding of the alphabetic principle. Some are just beginning to grasp that letters represent sounds. Others have a concept that each sound in a word is represented by a letter—as with /h/, /a/, /t/ for *hat*—and are learning short-vowel patterns that, for the most part, show a one-to-one correspondence between letters and sounds. More advanced students realize that not all words can be processed sound by sound. They have come to the understanding that some words have a final-*e* marker that indicates that the preceding vowel is long, as in *hate*, or a vowel digraph that performs a similar function, as in *wait*. Instruction should be geared to students' developmental level. Students who are just beginning to grasp that each sound in a word is represented by a letter and have not mastered short vowel patterns are not ready for instruction in final-*e* or digraph

Using Technology

For a discussion of the research on phonics, see the National Reading Panel's report: http://www.nationalreadingpanel.org ∎

C.C.S.S
Know and apply grade-level phonics and word analysis skills in decoding words.

Adapting Instruction for Struggling Readers and Writers

A study of the oral reading of a large sample of fourth graders suggests a need for word analysis instruction in grades 4 and perhaps beyond for a number of students (Daane et al., 2005). Some 25 percent of the students made more than ten errors on a relatively easy fourth-grade passage and 35 percent read at a rate that was below 105 words per minute. ∎

FYI

When students miss a word here or there, teachers may get the impression that they do not know their phonics and so may review phonics from the beginning. Students become bored when taught skills they already know. Observe students as they read or give them a test, such as the Phonics Inventory presented in the appendix to this book, and see what they know and where they might need help. ∎

patterns. Research clearly indicates that students make the most progress when they are grouped according to their developmental level (Juel & Minden-Cupp, 2000). Some reading programs recommend whole-class instruction in phonics. However, the research clearly favors small-group, targeted instruction (National Reading Panel, 2000).

In her study of the first-grade level of five basal anthology programs, Maslin (2003) noted that most of the programs recommended whole-class instruction and moving all students through phonics lessons at the same pace. Even though the programs recommended differentiating instruction on the basis of assessment, none of them suggested placing students at a lower-grade level if they were significantly behind in reading skills. As Invernizzi and Hayes (2004) comment, classes in which grouping is used to differentiate phonics instruction "seem to be slim to nil" (p. 223). They add, "Because of the ease of implementation, many teachers will want their students to continue through their grade-level program regardless of their instructional level. . . . Contrary to what commercial programs would have us believe, systematic, explicit instruction is not synonymous with everyone [being] on the same page at the same time in the same workbook" (pp. 224, 226).

Dialect Variation

Note whether the words in each row have the same pronunciation or different pronunciations:

balm	bomb	
merry	Mary	marry
pin	pen	
root	route	

In some dialects, each word in a row has the same pronunciation. In other dialects, each word is pronounced differently. American English encompasses a variety of regional dialects. No one dialect is superior to another. However, if you teach a pronunciation that is different from that spoken by your students, it can be confusing. When teaching phonics, use the dialect that your students use. You might also give a brief lesson in dialects. If your dialect differs from that of your students, you might explain why this is so—because you came from a different part of the country, for instance. When you come to an element that you pronounce differently, explain that to students and let them pronounce the word in their own dialect. Some of the major dialect variations include the following:

/aw/ and /o/. Words such as *dog, frog,* and *hog* have an *aw* or short *o* pronunciation.

/ōo/ and /ŏo/. Words such as *room* and *roof* have either a long double-*o* pronunciation or a short double-*o* pronunciation.

/i/ and /e/. In some dialects, short *e* is pronounced as a short *i*, so *pen* and *pin* and *tin* and *ten* are homophones.

/e/ and /ā/. In some dialects, words such as *egg* and *beg* are pronounced with a long *a* instead of the more typical short *e*.

/ōo/ and /ow/. In some dialects, *route* rhymes with *boot*; in others, it rhymes with *bout*.

Phonics and Spelling

Although related, phonics and spelling are not identical. Children who are encouraged to write early and are allowed to spell as best they can develop insights that carry over into their ability to read words (Burns & Richgels, 1989). Although invented spellings and spelling instruction can help children gain insights into the alphabetic principle, a systematic program of teaching phonics is still necessary. Neither invented spelling nor regular spelling instruction provides all the skills necessary to decode printed words. Spelling is best seen as a useful adjunct to phonics instruction, especially in the beginning stages of reading, rather than as a major method of teaching students to crack the code.

Using an Integrated Approach

Although phonics, context clues, and vocabulary are treated as separate topics in this book, students make use of all three when they face an unknown word. In fact, they make use of their total language system. As noted earlier, when students decode words, four processors are at work: orthographic, phonological, meaning, and context (Adams, 1990, 1994). The processors work simultaneously, and each receives information and sends it to the other processors. Therefore, phonics instruction must be viewed as being part of a larger language process. Phonics is easier to apply when context clues are used, and, in turn, it makes those clues easier to use. Students who are adept decoders will be able to recognize more words and so will have more context to use. Moreover, greater knowledge of the world, larger vocabularies, and better command of language increase students' ability to use phonics. If a student has a rich vocabulary, there is a better chance that the word he or she is decoding will be recognized by his or her meaning processor. Even if the word is not known, the student will have a better chance of deriving its meaning from context if most of the other words in the passage are known and if his or her background knowledge of the concepts in the passage is adequate.

To be most effective, therefore, phonics instruction should be presented in context and practiced and applied through extensive reading, which enables students to connect phonics functionally to the total language system. Extensive reading also provides practice for phonics skills so that students' decoding becomes so effortless and automatic that they can devote full attention to comprehension, which is what reading is all about.

Phonics Elements

Before considering how to teach phonics, you need to know the content of phonics. Knowing the content, you are in a better position to decide how to teach phonics elements and in what order these elements might be taught.

The content of phonics is fairly substantial. Depending on the dialect, English has forty or more sounds; however, many of them, especially vowels, may be spelled in more than one way. As a result, children have to learn more than a hundred spellings. The number would be even greater if relatively infrequent spellings were included, such as the *eigh* spelling of /ā/ in *neighbor* or the *o* spelling of /i/ in *women*.

Consonants

There are twenty-five consonant sounds in English (see Table 5.1). Some of the sounds are spelled with two letters (*ch*urch and *sh*ip); two letters that represent just one sound are known as **digraphs**. The most frequently occurring digraphs are *sh* (*sh*op), *ch* (*ch*ild), *ng* (si*ng*), *wh* (*wh*ip), *th* (*th*umb), and *th* (*th*at). Common digraphs are listed in Table 5.2. Doubles are digraphs that are a combination of the same letter to spell one sound: the *ll* in spill. Three-letter spellings of sounds are trigraphs as in the *dge* spelling of /j/ in the word bridge.

Some groups of consonants represent two or even three sounds (*st*op, *str*ike). These are known as **clusters**, or *blends*, and are listed in Table 5.3. Most clusters are composed of *l*, *r*, or *s* and another consonant or two. Because they are composed of two or more sounds, clusters pose special problems for

■ **Digraphs** (di, "two"; *graphs*, "written symbols") are two letters used to spell a single sound. If you look at the consonant chart in Table 5.1, you will notice that some of the sounds are spelled with two letters. The sound /f/ is usually spelled with *f* as in *fox* but may also be spelled with *ph* or *gh*, as in *photograph* or *tough*.

■ A **cluster** is composed of two or more letters that represent two or more sounds, such as the *br* in *broom*. Clusters are sometimes called blends. Because it is difficult to hear the separate sounds in a cluster, this element poses special difficulty for many students.

TABLE 5.1 Consonant Spellings

Sound	Initial	Final	Model Word
/b/	barn	cab, robe	ball
/d/	deer	bad	dog
/f/	fun, photo	laugh	fish
/g/	gate, ghost, guide	rag	goat
/h/	house, who		hat
/hw/	whale		whale
/j/	jug, gym, soldier	age, judge	jar
/k/	can, kite, quick, chaos	back, ache	cat, key
/l/	lion	mail	leaf
/m/	me	him, comb, autumn	man
/n/	now, know, gnu, pneumonia	pan	nail
/p/	pot	top	pen
/r/	ride, write		ring
/s/	sight, city	bus, miss, face	sun
/t/	time	rat, jumped	table
/v/	vase	love	vest
/w/	we, wheel		wagon
/y/	yacht, onion		yo-yo
/z/	zipper	has, buzz	zebra
/ch/	chip, cello, question	match	chair
/sh/	ship, sure, chef, action	push, special, mission	sheep
/th/	thin	breath	thumb
/th/	this	breathe	the
/zh/	azure, version	beige, garage	garage
/ŋ/		sing	ring

TABLE 5.2 Common Consonant Digraphs

Correspondence	Examples	Correspondence	Examples
ch = /ch/	chair, church	sh = /sh/	shoe, shop
ck = /k/	tack, pick	(s)si = /sh/	mission
gh = /f/	rough, tough	th = /th/	there, them
kn = /n/	knot, knob	th = /th/	thumb, thunder
ng = /ŋ/	thing, sing	ti = /sh/	station, action
ph = /f/	phone, photograph	wh = /w/	wheel, where
sc = /s/	scissors, scientist	wr = /r/	wrench, wrestle

TABLE 5.3 Common Consonant Clusters

Initial Clusters							
With l	Example Words	With r	Example Words	With s	Example Words	Other	Example Words
bl	blanket, black	br	broom, bread	sc	score, scale	tw	twelve, twin
cl	clock, clothes	cr	crow, crash	sch	school, schedule	qu	queen, quick
fl	flag, fly	dr	dress, drink	scr	scream, scrub		
gl	glove, glue	fr	frog, from	sk	sky, skin		
pl	plum, place	gr	green, ground	sl	sled, sleep		
sl	slide, slow	pr	prince, prepare	sm	smoke, smile		
				sn	snake, sneakers		

(continued)

TABLE 5.3 Common Consonant Clusters (*Continued*)

Initial Clusters							
With *l*	Example Words	With *r*	Example Words	With *s*	Example Words	Other	Example Words
				sp	spider, spot		
				st	star, stop		
				sw	sweater, swim		

Final Clusters					
With *l*	Example Words	With *n*	Example Words	Other	Example Words
ld	field, old	nce	prince, chance	ct	fact, effect
lf	wolf, self	nch	lunch, bunch	mp	jump, camp
lk	milk, silk	nd	hand, wind	sp	wasp, grasp
lm	film	nk	tank, wink	st	nest, best
lp	help	nt	tent, sent		
lt	salt, belt				
lve	twelve, solve				

students. Novice readers have a difficult time discriminating separate sounds in a cluster and often decode just the first sound, the /s/ in *st*, for example.

Vowels

English has about sixteen vowel sounds. (The number varies somewhat because some dialects have more than others.) Each vowel sound has a variety of spellings. For example, /ā/, which is commonly referred to as long *a*, is usually spelled *a_e*, as in *late*; *a* at the end of a syllable, as in *favor*; or *ai* or *ay*, as in *train* and *tray*. So, the vowel sound /ā/ has four main spellings, two of which are closely related: *ay* appears in the final position, and *ai* is found in initial and medial positions.

All the other vowel sounds are similar to /ā/ in having two to four major spellings. Considering correspondences in this way makes vowel spellings seem fairly regular. It is true that /ā/ and other vowel sounds can each be spelled in a dozen or more ways, but many of these spellings are oddities. Lexicographers Flexner and Hauck (1994) list nineteen spellings of /ā/ in the words *ate*, *Gael*, *champagne*, *rain*, *arraign*, *gaol*, *gauge*, *ray*, *exposé*, *suede*, *steak*, *matinee*, *eh*, *veil*, *feign*, *Marseilles*, *demesne*, *beret*, and *obey*. Many of these are in words borrowed from other languages.

A chart of vowels and their major spellings is presented in Table 5.4. Note that the chart lists twenty-two vowel sounds and includes *r* vowels, which are combinations of *r* and a vowel and so, technically, are not distinct vowels.

Onsets and Rimes

The **onset** is the consonant or consonant cluster preceding the rime: *b-*, *st-*, *scr-*. The **rime** is a vowel or vowels and any consonants that follow: *-at*, *-op*, *-een*. Rimes, which are also known as phonograms and word families, are highly predictable. When considered by itself, *a* can represent several sounds. However, when followed by a consonant, it is almost always short (*-at*, *-an*, *-am*).

- The **onset** is the initial part of a word, the part that precedes the first vowel. The onset could be a single consonant (*c* + *at*), a digraph (*sh* + *eep*), or a cluster (*tr* + *ip*). A word that begins with a vowel, such as *owl* or *and*, does not have an onset.

- The **rime** is the part of a word that rhymes, such as *-ook* in *look* or *-ow* in *cow*.

 FYI

- Go back to Table 4.3 on page 144 to review the formation of vowel sounds.
- Short vowels are the vowel sounds heard in *cat*, *pet*, *sit*, *hot*, and *cut*. Long vowels are the vowel sounds heard in *cake*, *sleep*, *pie*, *boat*, and *use*. ■

 FYI

Although onsets and rimes seem to be natural units of language, some students may have to process individual sounds before being able to group them into rimes. They may need to learn *a* = /a/ and *t* = /t/ before learning the rime *-at*. ■

R E F L E C T I O N

Why do you think that phonics has been a controversial issue for as long as students have been learning how to read? What role do you think phonics should play in early reading instruction?

TABLE 5.4   Vowel Spellings

	Vowel Sound	Major Spellings	Model Word
Short Vowels	/a/	rag, happen, have	cat
	/e/	get, letter, thread	bed
	/i/	wig, middle, event	fish
	/o/	fox, problem, father	mop
	/u/	bus	cup
Long Vowels	/ā/	name, favor, say, sail	rake
	/ē/	he, even, eat, seed, bean, key, these, either, funny, serious	wheel
	/ī/	hide, tiny, high, lie, sky	nine
	/ō/	vote, open, coat, bowl, old, though	nose
	/ū/	use, human	cube
Other Vowels	/aw/	daughter, law, walk, off, bought	saw
	/oi/	noise, toy	boy
	/ŏŏ/	wood, should, push	foot
	/oo/	soon, new, prove, group, two, fruit, truth	school
	/ow/	tower, south	cow
	/ə/	above, operation, similar, opinion, suppose	banana
r Vowels	/ar/	far, large, heart	car
	/air/	hair, care, where, stair, bear	chair
	/i(e)r/	dear, steer, here	deer
	/er/	her, sir, fur, earth	bird
	/iēr/	fire, wire	tire
	/or/	horse, door, tour, more	four

Approaches to Teaching Phonics

There are two main approaches to teaching phonics: analytic and synthetic. In the **analytic approach**, consonants are generally not isolated but are taught within the context of a whole word. For example, the sound /b/ would be referred to as the one heard in the beginning of *ball* and *boy*. The sound /b/ is not pronounced in isolation because that would distort it to "buh." Although somewhat roundabout, the analytic approach does not distort the sound /b/.

In the **synthetic approach**, words are decoded sound by sound, and both consonant and vowel sounds are pronounced in isolation. A child decoding *cat* would say, "Kuh-ah-tuh." This approach is very direct, but it distorts consonant sounds, which cannot be pronounced accurately without a vowel. However, Ehri (1991) maintained that artificial procedures, such as saying the sound represented by each letter in a word, may be necessary to help beginning readers decipher words.

Most literacy programs use a systematic, synthetic approach to phonics, in which students are taught to say individual sounds and blend them. However, this book recommends a combination of the analytic and synthetic approaches. Novice readers need to have the target sound highlighted by hearing it in isolation, which is what the synthetic approach does. And they need to hear it in the context of a real word, which is what the analytic approach does.

Phonics instruction can also be part to whole or whole to part. In a whole-to-part approach, students listen to or share-read a selection. From the selection, the teacher draws the element to be presented. After share-reading "Star Light, Star Bright," the teacher might lead students to see that *bright*, *might*, and *light* contain the *ight* pattern. After discussing the pattern, students then read a selection such as *Sleepy Dog* (Ziefert, 1984)

■ **The analytic approach** involves studying sounds within the context of the whole word; for example, /w/ is referred to as the sound heard at the beginning of *wagon*.

■ **The synthetic approach** involves decoding words sound by sound and then synthesizing the sounds into words.

that contains the element. In a part-to-whole approach, the teacher presents the *ight* pattern in preparation for reading *Sleepy Dog*. Both approaches prepare students for an upcoming selection. However, the whole-to-part approach also helps students to relate the element to a familiar selection and words that they have seen in print (Moustafa & Maldonado-Colon, 1999).

Phonics instruction can be embedded or systematic. In systematic instruction, students are taught all the key elements in a logical sequence. With embedded instruction, students are taught phonics as a need arises and in the context of reading a selection in which the target element occurs. For instance, after share-reading the nursery rhyme "Little Boy Blue," students discuss the fact that *horn* and *corn* rhyme and are spelled with the rime *-orn*. Later, they discover that in the weather rhyme "Red sky at night, Sailor's delight; Red sky in the morning, Sailor's warning," the /orn/ sound is spelled *arn* in *warning*. Noting that the word *war* has an /or/ sound, they come to the conclusion that *w* sometimes has an effect on the vowel that follows it. There is a need for both embedded and systematic phonics instruction. While making discoveries is a highly effective way to learn, students may not make all the discoveries they need to make about phonics.

Teaching Initial Consonants

Phonics instruction typically begins with initial consonants. Being the first sound in a word makes an initial consonant easier to hear. Initial consonants are typically the first element to appear in children's invented spelling. Students may pick up some knowledge of initial consonants through shared reading and through writing activities, but letter-sound relationships should also be taught explicitly to make sure that students have learned these important elements, to clarify any misconceptions that may have arisen, and to provide additional reinforcement. A phonics lesson starts with phonemic awareness to make sure students can perceive the sound of the element and then proceeds to the visual level, where the children integrate sound and letter knowledge. A six-step lesson for teaching initial consonants is detailed in Lesson 5.1. It assumes that the students can segment a word into its separate sounds, have a concept of beginning sounds, and realize that sounds are represented by letters; these skills were explained in Chapter 4. The lesson is synthetic and analytic: The consonant sound is presented both in isolation and in the context of a whole word. If possible, relate your instruction to a story, song, or rhyme or to a language experience story that you have share-read. This whole-to-part approach helps students relate the phonics they are learning to real reading (Moustafa & Maldonado-Colon, 1999).

C C S S

Demonstrate basic knowledge of letter-sound correspondences by producing the primary or most frequent sound for each consonant.

 FYI

Although consonant sounds spoken in isolation are distorted, some youngsters do better when the target sound is presented explicitly. Continuants like /m/, /f/, and /s/ are less distorted because they are articulated with a continuous stream of breath. ■

Assessing for Learning

Observe students as they work with beginning sounds. If students are having difficulty perceiving initial *m*, ask questions that help them focus on the beginning sound. Pointing to a picture of the moon, ask, "Is this an 'oon'? No? What is it? What sound did I leave off?" Use this same procedure with other *m* words: *monkey, man, milk.* ■

 FYI

• If students struggle with this approach to teaching initial consonants, try the speech-to-print approach on pages 170–171. ■

LESSON 5.1

Analytic-Synthetic Introduction of Initial Consonant Correspondence

Objectives

• Students will understand that the letter *m* stands for the sound /m/.
• Students will use their understanding of /m/ to sound out and spell initial *m*.

Step 1. Phonemic awareness

Explain to students that they will be learning about a letter and its sound and that this will help them to read and write. Teach the letter-sound relationship in the initial position of words. In teaching the correspondence (letter-sound relationship) m = /m/, read a story such as *Papa, Please Get the Moon for Me* (Carle, 1987) that contains a number of *m* words. Call students' attention to the *m* words from the book: *moon, me, man.* Explain how the lips are pressed together to form /m/. Stressing the initial sound as you say each word, ask students to tell what is the same about the words: "mmmoon," "mmme," and "mmman." Lead students to see that all the words begin in the same way. Ask them to supply other words that begin like *moon*, *me*, and *man*. Give hints, if necessary—an animal that can climb trees (*monkey*), something that we drink (*milk*).

Step 2. Letter–sound integration

Write the *m* words on the board and ask what is the same about the way *moon*, *me*, and *man* are written. Lead students to see that the words all begin with the letter *m* and that the letter *m* stands for the sound /m/ heard at the beginning of *moon*. At this point, *moon* becomes a model word. This is a simple word that can be depicted and that contains the target letter and sound. When referring to the sound represented by *m*, say that it is /m/, the sound heard at the beginning of *moon*, so that students can hear the sound both in isolation and in the context of a word. You might ask if there is anyone in the class whose name begins like /m/ in *moon*. List the names of students whose names begin like /m/ in *moon*. Explain to students why you are using a capital letter for the names.

Step 3. Guided practice

Provide immediate practice. Help students read food labels that contain /m/ words: *milk*, *mayonnaise*, *margarine*, *mustard*, *marshmallows*. Read a story together about monkeys or masks, or sing a song or read a rhyme that has a generous share of /m/ words. Try to choose some items in which students integrate knowledge of the correspondence with context. Compose sentences such as "I will drink a glass of milk" and "At the zoo, we saw a monkey," and write them on the chalkboard. Read each sentence, stopping at the word beginning with /m/. Have students use context and their knowledge of the correspondence *m* = /m/ to predict the word.

Step 4. Application

As share-reading or on their own, have students read selections that contain /m/ words. Students might read the *M* pages in alphabet books.

Step 5. Writing and spelling

If necessary, review the formation of the letter *m*. Dictate some easy *m* words (*me*, *man*), and have students spell them as best they can. Encourage students to use the letter *m* in their writing.

Step 6. Evaluation and reteaching

Note whether students are able to read at least the initial consonant of *m* words and are using *m* in their writing. Review and reteach as necessary. Throughout the day, call attention to initial consonants that have been recently taught. As you prepare to write the word *Monday*, for instance, ask students to tell what sound *Monday* begins with and what letter makes that sound. Also label items in your class that begin with the letter *m*: *mirror*, *magnets*.

FYI

- Using context to verify decoding is known as cross-checking. The student checks to see whether the decoded word makes sense in the selection.
- When using alphabet books, be on the lookout for confusing presentations. In one book, the words *tiger*, *thin*, and *the* are used to demonstrate the sound usually represented by the letter *t*. However, *th* in *thin* represents a different sound than that heard at the beginning of *tiger*, and *th* in *the* represents the voiced counterpart of *th* in *thin*. ■

Using Children's Books to Reinforce Initial Consonants   A good children's book can be a powerful medium for presenting or providing practice with phonics. A book such as *Easy as Pie* (Folsom & Folsom, 1986) is excellent for integrating knowledge of initial consonants and context (see Figure 5.1). Common similes, except for the last word, are shown on the right-hand page, as is the letter of the missing word. The answer appears when the child turns the page. For instance, the *S* page contains the letter *S* and the words "Deep as the." Read the first part of the simile aloud, and tell the students that the next word begins with the letter *s*. Ask students to guess what they think the word is. Remind them that the word must begin with /s/, the sound heard at the beginning of *sun*. Write their responses on the board. If any word supplied does not begin with /s/, discuss why this could not be the right answer. Turn the page to uncover the word that completes the riddle, and let students read the answer. Discuss why the answer is correct. Emphasize that it makes sense in the phrase and begins with /s/, the same sound heard at the beginning of *sun*.

Deep as the

Sea

FIGURE 5.1 *S* Pages from *Easy as Pie*

STUDENT READING LIST
Books for Reinforcing Initial Consonants

Calmenson, S. (1993). *It begins with an A.* New York: Hyperion. Rhyming riddles challenge the reader to guess objects whose names begin with letters *A* to *Z*.

Cronin, D. (2005). *Click, clack, quackity-quack: An alphabetical adventure.* New York: Simon & Schuster. A summer adventure is told in alliterative phrases.

Ellwand, D. (1996). *Emma's elephant & other favorite animal friends.* New York: Dutton. Black-and-white photos and brief alliterative captions depict children with animals.

Hindley, J. *Crazy ABC.* (1994). Cambridge, MA: Candlewick. Target letters are reinforced with zany alliterative sentences.

Hofbauer, M. (1993). *All the letters.* Bridgeport, CT: Greene Barke Press. Each letter is accompanied by an alliterative story.

Inches, A. (2003). *An ABC adventure.* New York: Simon & Schuster. By lifting flaps, readers find objects that begin with the target letter.

Jocelyn, M (2005). *ABC X 3.* Plattsburgh, NY: Tundra Books. Labels for illustrations are provided in English, Spanish, and French. Only objects whose names in the three languages begin with the same letter were chosen: *pear, pera, poire.*

Joyce, S. (1999). *ABC animal riddles.* Columbus, NC: Peel Productions. Readers are asked to guess the identity of animals based on verbal and picture clues.

Laidlaw, K. (1996). *The amazing I spy ABC.* New York: Dial. Readers spy objects whose names begin with the target letter.

Metropolitan Museum of Art (2002). *Museum ABC.* Boston: Little, Brown. Each letter is illustrated with four paintings. Would be a good choice for use with older students working on initial consonants

Moxley, S. (2001). *ABCD: An alphabet book of cats and dogs.* Boston: Little, Brown. An alliterative tale accompanies each letter.

Wallace, N. E. (2005). *Alphabet house.* New York: Marshall Cavendish. Readers identify objects that begin with the letter sound featured on each page.

Adapting Instruction for English Language Learners

Before teaching elements that are not present in Spanish—*sh*, for instance—make sure that these elements have been introduced in the ESL class. For easily confused auditory items—*sh* and *ch*, for example—provide added auditory-discrimination exercises in which students tell whether pairs of easily confused words such as *choose-shoes* or *cheap-sheep* are the same or different. Also, use the words in sentence context, or use real objects or pictures to illustrate them. When discussing *sheep*, for example, hold up a picture of sheep. ■

 Using Technology

The speech component of Kidspiration and similar software is especially useful for students whose backgrounds are limited and who might not be familiar with some items. It is also helpful to ELLs who might be familiar with the items shown but might not know their English names. ■

Adapting Instruction for English Language Learners

For this and all other activities that use illustrations or objects, make sure that all students know the names of the items. ∎

Using Technology

Word Family Sort

Enables students to sort short-vowel patterns electronically. http://www.readwritethink.org/files/resources/interactives/wordfamily/

DrBarnes1 Word Sort Videos

This is one of numerous videos by one of the pioneers of word sorting. http://www.youtube.com/watch?v=1_wiTAsMnqs ∎

Another book that combines context and knowledge of beginning consonant correspondences is *The Alphabet Tale*, by Jan Garten (1964). Shown on the *S* page is a large red *S*, a seal's tail, and a riddle:

His home is the Arctic

Raw fish is his meal.

This is the tale of a whiskered . . .

The next page shows the rest of the seal and the word *Seal*. The Student Reading List identifies more titles that may be used to reinforce initial consonants.

One problem with using alphabet books is that children might not be familiar with the objects being presented or may call the objects by different names. Children might mistake a wolf for a dog. A cap might be identified as a hat. A piece of software that avoids these difficulties but presents excellent reinforcement is *Kidspiration* (Inspiration). *Kidspiration* has a library of 1,200 illustrations and a speech component that can be used to create excellent phonics reinforcement activities. When working with initial consonant correspondences, students can search through illustrations and select those that begin with a target letter. Figure 5.2 shows a finished exercise in which items whose names begin with *b* have been selected. Because *Kidspiration* has speech capability, children using it can have the name of the item spoken and also spelled out. This is especially helpful for ELL.

After an alphabet or other book has been discussed, place it in the class library so that students may "read" it. Encourage children to check out books for home use.

Be sure to make use of students' emerging knowledge of letter-sound relationships when reading big books. After reading Paul Galdone's (1975) *The Gingerbread Boy*, for instance, turn to the page on which the gingerbread boy meets the cow. Read the words *cow*, *can*, and *catch*. Discuss how the words sound alike and begin with the letter *c*.

Encourage the use of context. Reread the story, stopping when you come to a word that begins with *c*. Encourage students to read the word. Using *cow* as a key word, remind students that the word should begin with /k/ as in *cow*. Also remind them of the context of the sentence to help them learn to integrate letter-sound relationships with context. To further reinforce the *c* = /k/ correspondence, have students draw a picture of something they *can* do and write a short piece about it. Individual stories could be the basis for a group story or booklet that tells about the talents and abilities of all class members.

FIGURE 5.2 Exercise Created with *Kidspiration*

Sorting   One activity that is especially useful in deepening students' understanding about phonics elements is sorting (Bear, 1995). Sorting forces children to analyze the elements in a word or picture and select critical features as they place the words or pictures in piles. Through sorting, students classify words and pictures on the basis of sound and spelling and construct an understanding of the spelling system. They also enjoy this active, hands-on, nonthreatening activity.

Students should sort only elements and words that they know. This allows them to construct basic understandings of the spelling system. Although they may be able to read *cat*, *hat*, and *bat*, they may not realize that the words all rhyme and follow a CVC (consonant-vowel-consonant) pattern. Sorting helps students come to these understandings.

Students' sorting activities are determined by their stage of spelling development. Students in the early alphabetic stage may sort pictures and, later, words according to their beginning sounds. In the consolidated alphabetic stage, students sort words according to whether they have long or short vowels, have an e marker, or have a double-vowel pattern, and then according to the specific long-vowel or other vowel pattern they illustrate. Words can also be sorted according to initial digraphs or consonant clusters or any other element that students need to study.

Lesson 5.2 shows how students in the early alphabetic stage might be taught to sort initial consonant sounds. The lesson is adapted from Bear (1995).

Students might conduct sorts in pairs or small groups. A simple way to sort is to place a target word or illustration in the center of a table and then distribute cards, some of which contain the target element. Have students read or name the target element, and then have them take turns placing cards containing the target element. As students place cards, they should read the words or name the illustrations on them (Temple, Nathan, Temple, & Burris, 1993). For illustrations that can be used for sorting, go to the Webbing into Literacy Web site (**http://curry.edschool.virginia.edu/go /wil/home.html**). Although this site was designed for preschool students, the illustrations and word cards can be used with students of any age.

Sorts can be open or closed. In a closed sort, the teacher provides the basis for sorting the cards, as in Lesson 5.2. In an open sort, students decide the basis for sorting the cards.

Adapting Instruction for English Language Learners

Native speakers of Spanish may have difficulty perceiving /b/, /v/, /k/, /j/, /z/, /sh/, /th/, and /ch/. You may need to spend additional time on auditory discrimination. ■

FYI

Some consonant letters pose special problems. One of these letters is *x*, which is a reverse digraph, except when it represents /z/, as in *xylophone*. It may represent either /ks/, as in *tax*, or /gz/, as in *example*. ■

LESSON 5.2

Sorting by Beginning Consonant Sounds

Objective

Students will distinguish between words that begin with /s/ and /r/.

Step 1. Set up the sort

Set up two columns. At the top of each column, place an illustration of the sound to be sorted. If you plan to have students sort /s/ and /r/ words, use an illustration of the sun and an illustration of a ring. A pocket chart works well for this activity.

Step 2. Explain sorting

Tell students that you will be giving them cards that have pictures on them. Explain that they will be placing the cards under the picture of the sun if the words begin with /s/, the sound heard at the beginning of *sun*, or under the picture of the ring if the words begin with /r/, the sound heard at the beginning of *ring*. Explain that sorting will help them learn their letter sounds.

Step 3. Model the sorting procedure

Shuffle the cards. Tell the students, "Say the name of the picture. Listen carefully to see whether the name of the picture begins like /s/ as in *sun* or /r/ as in *ring*." Model the process with two or three cards: "This is a picture of a saw. *Saw* has an /s/ sound and begins like *sun*, so I will put it under *sun*. *Sun* and *saw* both begin with /s/." Also make sure that students can identify all the objects being pictured.

Step 4. Children sort the cards

Distribute the cards. Have the students take turns placing a card in the /s/ or /r/ column. When students place their cards, have them say the picture's name and the sound it begins with. Correct errors quickly and simply. For instance, if a student puts a picture of a rat in the /s/ column, say, "*Rat* begins with /r/ and goes under *ring*," or ask why *rat* was put under *sun* and discuss its correct placement. A sample sort can be found in Figure 5.3. Have students sort cards a second and third time to solidify their perception of beginning sounds.

Step 5. Application

Have students find objects or pictures of objects whose names begin with /s/ or /r/. Proceed to other initial consonants, or sort known words that begin with /s/ or /r/.

Step 6: Evaluation and Review

Note students' ability to sort accurately and with increasing speed. Provide added instruction and practice as necessary.

FYI

Activities such as making words and sorting require students to be more actively engaged, more individually accountable, and more thoughtful (Mesmer & Griffith, 2005). Because it involves students in seeing similarities and differences and making generalizations, sorting is an excellent activity for building higher-level thinking. ■

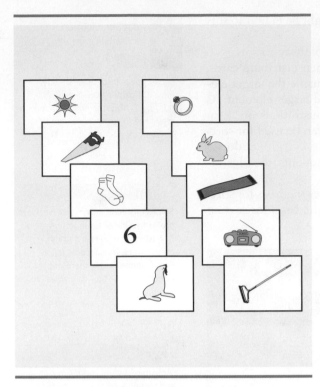

FIGURE 5.3 A Sample Sort

Sometimes, students sort words visually. For example, after one *-at* word has been sorted, they simply put all the other *-at* words under it without actually thinking about the sound that the words have in common. To overcome this practice, use a blind sort. Draw a word from the pile to be sorted, and say it without showing it to the students. Then have them tell in which column it should be placed. After putting the word in the correct column, have a volunteer read it. For instance, picking up the word *rat*, you read it without showing it to students and they tell you whether it goes in the *cat*, *ran*, or *dad* column. After *rat* has been placed in the column, a volunteer reads *rat* and the other words in that column (Johnston, 1999).

Teaching Final Consonants

Final consonants are handled in much the same way as initial consonants. Relate them to their initial counterparts. And do not neglect them. According to a classic research study by Gibson, Osser, and Pick (1963), final consonants are a significant aid in the decoding of printed words. You might teach final consonants as you teach the word patterns that use them. For instance, teach final /t/ before or as you are teaching the *-at* pattern and final /d/ before or as you are teaching the *-ad* pattern. Be sure to develop phonemic awareness of final consonants. Use activities suggested in the lesson for initial consonants.

FYI

The first word that most children learn is their name. To take advantage of this natural learning, create a chart of children's first names. When studying words that begin with a certain sound, refer to names on the chart that also begin with that sound. Attach photos of the students to the chart so that students may learn to associate printed names and faces. ■

Assessing for Learning

Some students need only a few repetitions in order to learn a correspondence. Others need numerous opportunities to practice skills. Note the degree of practice students need and be prepared to move on or to provide added reinforcement, depending on students' performance. ■

REINFORCEMENT ACTIVITIES
Consonant Letter-Sound Relationships

- Have students encounter initial consonants they know in books.
- Creating a language experience story also affords students the opportunity to meet phonics elements in print. While reading the story with an individual or group, the teacher can call attention to any consonants that have already been introduced. The teacher might pause before a word that begins with a known consonant and have a student attempt to read it.
- Play the game *Going to Paris* (Brewster, 1952). Players recite this:
    I'm going to Paris.
    I'm going to pack my bag with _____.
    The first player says an object whose name begins with the first letter of the alphabet. Subsequent players then say the names of all the objects mentioned by previous players and identify an object whose name begins with the next letter of the alphabet.
- Play the game *Alphabet It*. In this counting-out game, one child recites the letters of the alphabet. As the child says each letter, she or he points to the other members of the class whose names begin with the letter being recited. Each child pointed to removes herself or himself from the game. The alphabet is recited until just one child is left. That child is "it" for the next round or next game.
- Use software that helps students discover letter-sound relationships, such as *Dr. Peet's Talk/Writer* (Interest-Driven Learning) or *Write Out Loud* (Don Johnston). These programs will say words that have been typed in. *Dr. Peet's Talk/Writer* also has an ABC Discovery module that introduces the alphabet. *Dr. Peet's WritingBuddy* is a talking word processor available as an app at the APP Store.

- Use software such as *Letter Sounds* (Sunburst). The student matches, sorts, and manipulates consonants and composes tongue twisters and songs based on initial sounds. *Curious George's ABC Adventure* (Sunburst) reinforces letter names and letter sounds. As a review of initial consonant spelling-sound relationships, read the following jump-rope chant with students. Help students extend the chant through all the letters of the alphabet. Adapt the chant for boys by substituting *wife's* for *husband's*.

  A—my name is Alice,

  My husband's name is Andy,

  We live in Alabama,

  And we sell apples.

- Traditional rhymes can also be used to reinforce initial consonant sounds. Do a shared reading of the rhyme first. Stress the target consonant letter-sound correspondence as you read the selection. During subsequent shared readings of the selection, encourage the class to read the words beginning with the target letter.
- Deedle, deedle, dumpling, my son John,

  Went to bed with his stockings on;

  One shoe off, and one shoe on,

  Deedle, deedle, dumpling, my son John.

FYI

- Have students create their own alphabet books. After a letter-sound relationship has been presented, direct students to create a page showing the upper- and lowercase forms of the letter along with a key word and an illustration of the word. As students learn to read words beginning with the letter and sound, they may add them to the page.
- A good source of jump-rope chants and other rhymes is *Favorite Rhymes from a Rocket in My Pocket* (Withers, 1988), which is still available in paperback. ∎

Teaching Consonant Clusters

Although consonants, consonant clusters, and vowel patterns are presented separately, their introduction should be integrated. As discussed earlier, clusters, which are sometimes known as blends, are combinations of consonants, as in *spot* or *straw*, that represent two (/s/ and /p/) or three (/s/ and /t/ and /r/) sounds clustered together. Many children have a great deal of difficulty learning the combination of sounds heard in clusters, such as *st* in *stop* and *fl* in *flag*. The problem is probably rooted in phonemic awareness. Children have difficulty separating the second sound in the cluster from the first. This is especially true of *l* and *r* clusters because they tend to merge with the preceding consonant. When teaching clusters, it is best to start with *s* clusters because they are more distinctive. When presenting a cluster, stress the separate sounds and also emphasize the second sound. To develop students' phonemic awareness, slowly say a word containing the cluster and have students count out the sounds, holding up a finger for each sound. For example, as you say "stick," hold up a finger as you say /s/, a second finger as you say /t/, a third as you say /i/, a fourth as you say /k/. Build on what students already know. In presenting the spelling of the cluster *st*, relate it to known words that begin with *s*. Place the word *sick* on the board, and have students read it. Carefully stretch out and count each sound: /s/, /i/, /k/. Ask them what needs to be added to *sick* to make the word *stick*. As you say "stick," emphasize the /t/. Present *sack–stack*, *sand–stand*, *sill–still*, and *sink–stink*. If students have had long-vowel words, you might also present *say–stay*, *sore–store*, and *seal–steal*. Once students have caught on to the *st* cluster, present other *st* words: *stop, stamp, step*.

Using Technology

For additional sources for rhymes, see Building Literacy:
http://www.wordbuilding.org ∎

Using Technology

The Video App, *Talking Words Factory* (LeapFrog), provides activities in which students build clusters by adding letters.

Jump Rope Rhmes
http://www.gameskidsplay.net/jump_rope_ryhmes/ ∎

FYI

When students misread a cluster—reading "fog" for *frog*, for instance—you might ask questions that lead them to see that they need to process two initial sounds rather than just one: "What letter does the word *fog* begin with? What two letters does the word in the sentence begin with? What sound does *f* stand for? What sound does *r* stand for? What sounds do *f* and *r* make when said together? How would you say the word in the story?" ∎

Troublesome Correspondences   The most difficult consonant letters are *c* and *g*. Both regularly represent two sounds: The letter *c* stands for /k/ and /s/, as in *cake* and *city*; the letter *g* represents /g/ and /j/, as in *go* and *giant*. The letter c represents /k/ far more often than it stands for /s/ (Gunning, 1975), and this is the sound students usually attach to it (Venezky, 1965); the letter *g* more often represents /g/. In teaching the consonant letters *c* and *g*, the more frequent sounds (*c* = /k/, *g* = /g/) should be presented first. The other sound represented by each letter (*c* = /s/, *g* = /j/) should

REINFORCEMENT ACTIVITIES
Consonant Clusters

To help students distinguish between single consonants and clusters, have them sort stacks of word or picture cards representing single consonants and clusters containing that consonant. For instance, have students sort *s* and *st* words. Because students might have difficulty discriminating between the sound of /s/ and the sound of /st/, begin with picture sorts so that students can focus on sounds. Students might sort cards with the following pictures: sun, saw, sandwich, socks, six, seal, star, stick, step, and store. (Make sure students know names of pictures). Pointing to the stack of cards portraying objects whose names begin with /s/ or /st/, tell students, "We're going to sort these picture cards. If the name of the picture begins with /s/ as in *sun*, we're going to put it in the sun column. If the name of the picture begins with /st/ as in *star*, we'll put it in the star column." Holding up a stamp, ask, "What is this? What sounds does it begin with? What column should we put it in?" Affirm or correct students' responses: "Yes, *stamp* begins with the sound /st/ that we hear in the beginning of *ssstttar*, so we'll put it in the star column." Go through the rest of the cards in this fashion. Once all the cards have been categorized, have volunteers say the names of all the cards in a column and note that they all begin with /s/ or /st/. Encourage students to suggest other words that might fit in the columns. Also have students sort the picture cards on their own to promote speed of response. You might then have them sort /s/ and /sp/ pictures (or words) and then /s/, /sp/, and /st/ pictures (or words).

Also try a spelling sort. For a spelling sort, set up two or three columns, and write the target element at the head of each column. For example, when presenting *s* and *st* words, write *s* above one column and *st* above the second, and dictate *s* and *st* words.

You can also use the following reinforcement activities:

- Use real-world materials to reinforce clusters. When introducing *sp*, for example, have students read food labels for spaghetti and spinach and brand names such as Spam and Spaghetti-Os.
- Have students create words by adding newly learned clusters to previously presented word patterns. After being introduced to *st*, for instance, students might add it to short-vowel patterns that they have been taught: *-and*, *-ill*, *-ick*, and *-ing*.
- The best reinforcement is to have students meet clusters in their reading. Clusters occur naturally in most books, so it's simply a matter of looking over texts and deciding which clusters you wish to emphasize. The following books have a high proportion of clusters:

Cronin, D. (2005). *Click, clack, quackity-quack: An alphabetical adventure*. New York: Simon & Schuster. Has a number of alliterative clusters in addition to those contained in the title: *blue blankets*, *flippity flip*, and single cluster words.

Ehlert, L. (1990). *Fish eyes: A book you can count on*. San Diego, CA: Harcourt. The text reinforces several major clusters.

Emberley, Ed. (1992). *Go away, Big Green Monster*. Boston: Little, Brown. This book reinforces *s* clusters.

O'Brien, J. (1995). *Sam and Spot: A silly story*. Boca Raton, FL: Cool Kids. A good alliterative read-aloud that emphasizes *s* clusters.

Rohman, C. (1996). *Stories*. CA: Outside the Box. Part of a series, this book reinforces the *st* cluster. Also available from Zaner-Bloser. See Ray's *Reader: Digraphs and blends*.

Smee, N. (2006). *Clipclop*. New York: Sterling. Good book for introducing *l* clusters.

Spence, R., & Spence, A. (1999). *Clickety clack*. New York: Viking. Repeats *clickety clack* and a number of other cluster words that contain the rime *–ack*.

be taught sometime later. At that point, it would also be helpful to teach the following generalizations:

- The letter *c* usually stands for /k/ when it is followed by *a*, *o*, or *u*, as in *cab*, *cob*, or *cub*.
- The letter *c* usually stands for /s/ when followed by *e*, *i*, or *y*, as in *cereal*, *circle*, or *cycle*.

- The letter *g* usually stands for /g/ when followed by *a, o,* or *u,* as in *gave, go,* or *gum.*
- The letter *g* usually stands for /j/ when followed by *e, i,* or *y,* as in *gem, giant,* or *gym.* (There are a number of exceptions: *geese, get, girl, give.*)

When teaching the *c* and *g* generalizations, do so inductively. For instance, list examples of the *c* spelling of /k/ in one column and the *c* spelling of /s/ in another. Have students read each word in the first column and note the sound that *c* represents and the vowel letter that follows *c.* Do the same with the second column. Then help students draw generalizations based on their observations. Better yet, have students sort *c* = /k/ and *c* = /s/ words and discover the generalizations for themselves.

Variability (Try Another Sound) Strategy   An alternative to presenting the *c* and *g* generalizations is to teach students to be prepared to deal with the variability of the spelling of certain sounds. Students need to learn that, in English, letters can often stand for more than one sound. After learning the two sounds for *c* and *g,* students should be taught to use the following **variability strategy** when they are unsure how to read a word that begins with *c* or *g.*

FYI

- The *g* generalizations help explain the *gu* spelling of /g/, as in *guide* and *guilt.* Without the *u* following the *g,* there would be a tendency to pronounce those words with the /j/ sound (Venezky, 1965). Determining the sound of *c* and *g* at the end of a word is relatively easy. If a word ends in *e, c* represents /s/ and *g* stands for /j/: *lace, page.* The letter *e* serves as a marker to indicate that *c* and *g* have their soft sounds.
- Students need to see that the aim of phonics is to help them construct meaning from print. If they use phonics to decipher a word but end up with a nonword, they should try again. Even when they construct a real word, they should cross-check it by seeing if it makes sense in the sentence they are reading. ◼

STUDENT STRATEGIES

Applying the Variability (Try Another Sound) Strategy to Consonant Correspondences

1. Try the main pronunciation—the one the letter usually stands for.
2. If the main pronunciation gives a word that is not a real one or does not make sense in the sentence, try another sound. Try the other pronunciation that the letter usually stands for.
3. If you still get a word that is not a real word or does not make sense in the sentence, ask for help.

Just as you post a chart to remind students of correct letter formation, display a chart showing all the major consonant correspondences and a key word for each. Students experiencing difficulty sounding out a word can refer to the chart. A child feeling puzzled when pronouncing *cider* as "kider" can look at the chart and note that *c* has two pronunciations: /k/ as in *cat* and /s/ as in *circle.* Since the /k/ pronunciation did not produce a word that made sense, the child tries the /s/ pronunciation. Table 5.1 could be used as a basis for constructing a consonant chart; a sample of such a chart is shown in Figure 5.4. Drawings, photos, or pictures may be used to illustrate each of the sounds. As new correspondences are learned, they can be added to the chart. The chart can also be used as a spelling aid.

FYI

Vowels can be taught in isolation or as part of patterns. In Lesson 5.3, they are taught in isolation. Teaching vowels in isolation is helpful for students who are still learning to detect individual sounds in words.

Teaching Vowel Correspondences

Vowels are taught in the same way as consonants. The main difference is that vowels can be spoken in isolation without distortion, so teaching vowels synthetically should not be confusing to students. Lesson 5.3 outlines how short *a* might be taught.

Teaching the Word-Building Approach

One convenient, economical way of introducing vowels is in rimes or patterns: for example, *-at* in *hat, pat,* and *cat,* or *-et* in *bet, wet,* and *set.* Patterns can be presented in a number of ways. A word-building approach helps children note the onset and the rime in each word (Gunning, 1995). Students are presented with a

◼ The **variability strategy** is a simpler procedure than the application of rules. Rather than trying to remember a rule, all the student has to do is try the major pronunciation, and, if that pronunciation does not work out, try another.

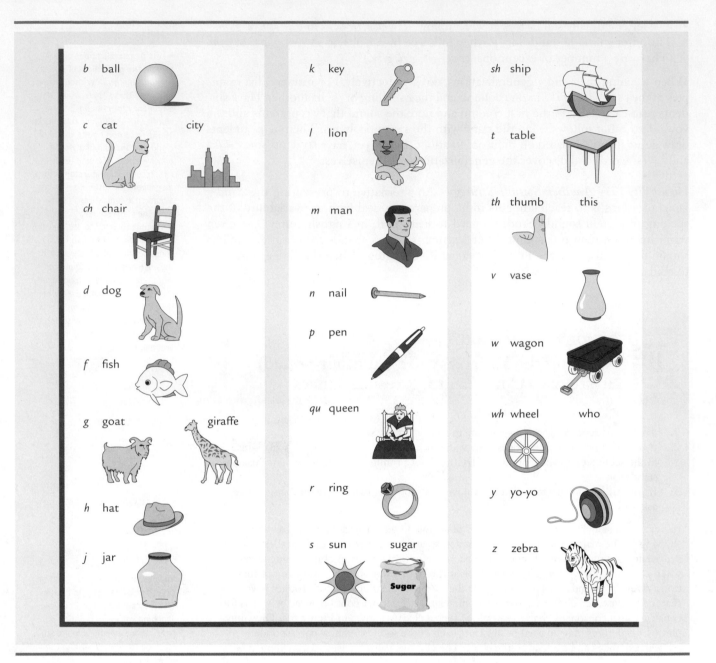

FIGURE 5.4   Beginning
Consonant Chart

rime and then add onsets to create words. Next, students are provided with onsets and add rimes. Because some students have difficulty with rimes (Bruck, 1992; Juel & Minden-Cupp, 2000), rimes are broken down into their individual sounds after being presented as wholes. For example, after introducing the rime -et as a whole, the teacher would highlight its individual sounds: /e/ and /t/. This fosters phonemic awareness. In a study involving high-risk students in four first grades, only the two groups of students taught with an onset–rime approach were reading close to grade level by year's end (Juel & Minden-Cupp, 2000). The students who did the best were those whose teachers broke the rimes into their individual sounds. In their study of disabled readers, Ehri, Satlow, and Gaskins (2009) also found that students taught to fully analyze the sounds of words outperformed students taught only by an onset-rime approach.

LESSON 5.3
Vowel Correspondence

Objectives

- Students will understand that the letter *a* sometimes stands for /a/.
- Students will use their understanding of *a*/a/ to sound out and spell short-*a* words.

Step 1. Phonemic awareness

Phonemic Awareness of the Beginnings of Words

Explain to students that they will be learning a sound and the letter that stands for that sound. Before presenting short *a*, short *e*, or another short vowel either as part of a pattern or as an individual vowel correspondence, introduce the vowel as it occurs at the beginning of words, since it is easier to perceive in that position. In preparation for introducing short *a*, say the words *apple*, *astronaut*, and *add*. Have students say them and note that they all begin with the same sound, which is /a/. Write the words on the board, read them, and lead the class to see that the words all begin with the letter *a* and that the letter *a* makes the sound /a/ as in *apple*. Tell students that the word *apple* will be the model word for the /a/ sound of *a*. On the board, write and say *a apple* /a/. Explain to students that if they come across a word that has an *a* in it and they forget the sound of *a*, they can use the model word routine to help them: They can say "a, apple" and then think of the sound that *apple* begins with and say /a/. Explain that there will also be a hand signal for *a apple* /a/. Demonstrate by pretending to eat an apple and explain that this signals *apple* and the sound at the beginning of *apple*: /a/. Elongate the sound of *a* at the beginning of *apple*: /a/. Have students practice saying *a apple* /a/. Encourage them to use this mnemonic if they need it. Create a vowel chart as in Figure 5.5, and place *a apple* /a/ on it, along with a drawing of an apple. Use this same procedure for introducing the other short vowels. For short *e*, introduce the words *echo*, *Ed*, and *effort*. The hand signal for echo is cupping your hands around your mouth and pretending to call out. Explain what an echo is if students don't know. For short *i*, introduce the words *itch*, *igloo*, and *iguana*. The hand signal is pretending to scratch an itch on your arm. For short *o*, introduce the words *octopus*, *October*, and *ostrich*. The hand signal is locking your thumbs and wiggling your eight fingers so they appear to be an octopus. For short *u*, introduce the words *up*, *us*, and *usher*. The hand signal is pointing up with your index finger.

Phonemic Awareness of the Middles of Words

Read a selection, such as *Cat Traps* (Coxe, 1996) or *The Cat Sat on the Mat* (Cameron, 1994), in which there are a number of short-*a* words. Call students' attention to *a* words from the book: *cat*, *trap*, *sat*. Stressing the vowel sound as you say each word, ask students to tell what is the same about the words: "caaat," "traaap," and "saaat." Lead students to see that they all have an /a/ sound in the middle.

Step 2. Letter–sound integration

Write the words *cat*, *trap*, and *sat* on the board, saying each word as you do so. Ask students whether they can see what is the same about the words. Show them that all three words have an *a*, which stands for the sound /a/, as pronounced in *cat*. Have students read the words. Discuss other words, such as *map*, *bag*, and *dad*, that have the sound /a/. Have students read the words chorally and individually.

Step 3. Guided practice

Share-read a story that contains a number of short-*a* words. Pause before the short-*a* words, and invite students to read them. Also share-read songs, rhymes, announcements, and signs that contain short-*a* words.

Step 4. Application

Have students read selections or create language experience stories that contain short-*a* words.

Adapting Instruction for Struggling Readers and Writers

Struggling readers may have been taught a variety of decoding strategies, some of which may conflict with each other (Stahl, 1998). Focus on the teaching of a few strategies and meet with other professionals in the school to discuss and implement the use of a consistent set of strategies. ■

Adapting Instruction for Struggling Readers and Writers

Struggling readers often fail to process all the letters in a word and so misread it. To help students match all the sounds and letters in a word, say a word such as *snack*, stretching out or emphasizing its sounds as you do so: "sssnnnaaakkk." Have students repeat the word and *explain* how many sounds they hear. Show a card that has the word written on it. Match up the sounds and their spellings. Put the word in Elkonin boxes (see Figure 4.4 on p. 164). Have students tell why there are five letters but only four sounds (Gaskins, 2005). ■

> **Step 5. Evaluation and reteaching**
> Note students' ability to read and write short-*a* words. Review and extend the pattern.

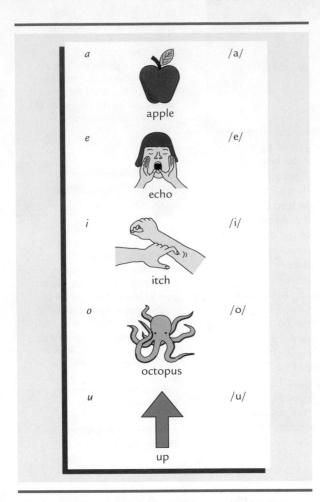

FIGURE 5.5 Short-Vowel Chart
Source: Gunning, T. (2008). *Teacher's guide for word building book B* (2nd ed.). Honesdale, PA: Phoenix Learning Resources.

CCSS

Associate the long and short sounds with the common spellings (graphemes) for the five major vowels.

Students also did their best when given differentiated instruction in word analysis that met their needs. The more time the at-risk students spent working at their level, the better their progress. This suggests that lessons provided to small groups of students who have approximately the same level of development in phonics are more effective than phonics instruction provided to the whole class. Small-group instruction benefits achieving readers as well, because they will not have to be subjected to instruction in skills that they have already mastered. Lesson 5.4 describes how the rime -*et* might be presented.

Teaching Vowels Early

It isn't necessary or even desirable to teach all the major consonant correspondences before introducing vowels. After students have learned five or six consonant correspondences, have them combine the consonants they have learned with a short vowel to form words. For instance after *m*/m/, *s* /s/, *h* /h/, *c*/k/, and *t*/t/ have been taught, introduce a/a/. After students have learned a/a/, they will be able to form, with your help, the words *at*, *sat*, *hat*, *cat*, *mat*, and *rat*. You will need to teach final /t/ as well as initial t/t/ and how to blend sounds to make words. Using a word-building approach, first demonstrate how you add *t* to *a* to make the word *at*. Writing *a* on the board, have students say its sound. Writing *t* on the board, have students say its sound. Moving your hand under the *a* and the *t*, explain that you are blending the sounds /a/ and /t/ to form the word *at*. Have students read the word *at*. Then ask students to tell what you would add to *at* to make the words *mat*, *hat*, *sat*, and *cat*. Stress each sound in the words so that phonemic awareness is fostered.

Teaching Patterns

Most vowels occur in one of four patterns:

- Consonant-vowel-consonant, or closed syllable (*cat*, *hot*, *pattern*). The syllable is closed because it ends with a consonant. The vowel is usually short.
- Consonant-vowel, or open syllable (*he*, *go*, *open*). The syllable is open because it ends with a vowel. The vowel is usually long.
- Final *e* (*wave*, *pine*). The vowel is usually long.
- Vowel digraph (*sheep*, *wait*). The vowel is usually long.

The easiest pattern is the consonant-vowel-consonant (CVC) pattern. In short-vowel words, each letter represents a sound. Such words may be processed in linear fashion: *h-a-t*. Final-*e* words are a major stumbling block for many learners. They represent a higher level of cognitive processing (Bear, personal communication, December 2003). Final-*e* words require the reader to note the final *e* as the word is being processed and use it as a sign that the vowel is probably long. Students need to use orthographic awareness as well as phonics skills when they decode final-*e* words. In addition, when working at the short-vowel level, students generally encountered vowels with a short sound. After long vowels have been introduced, the vowels they see might have a long or a short sound. Decoding becomes a whole lot more difficult.

LESSON 5.4
Word-Building Pattern: -et

Objectives
- Students will understand how the -et pattern is formed.
- Students will be able to use the -et pattern to read and spell words.

Step 1. Introducing the pattern's vowel

Explain to students that they will be learning how to read a group of words. As explained in Lesson 5.3, before presenting short-e or another vowel pattern, introduce the vowel in that pattern by presenting words in which the vowel appears first: *echo*, *Ed*, and *effort*. Discuss the words, the model word for /e/, and the mnemonic: *echo*.

Step 2. Building words by adding onsets

To introduce the -et pattern, share-read a story or rhyme that contains -et words. Then write *et* on the board, and ask the class what letter would have to be added to *et* to make the word *pet*, as in the story that you just read. (This reviews initial consonants and helps students see how words are formed.) As you add *p* to *et*, carefully enunciate the /p/ and the /et/ and then the whole word. Have several volunteers read the word. Then write *et* underneath *pet*, and ask the class what letter should be added to *et* to make the word *wet*. As you add *w* to *et*, carefully enunciate /w/ and /et/ and then the whole word. Have the word *wet* read by volunteers. The word *pet* is then read, and the two words are contrasted. Ask students how the two are different. Other high-frequency -et words are formed in the same way: *get*, *let*, *jet*, and *net*. After the words have been formed, have students tell what is the same about all the words. Have students note that all the words end in the letters *e* and *t*, which make the sounds heard in *et*. Then have them tell which letter makes the /e/ sound and which makes the /t/, or ending, sound in *et*. Calling attention to the individual sounds in *et* will help students discriminate between -et and other short-e patterns. It should also help students improve the perception of individual sounds in words and so help improve their reading and spelling.

In a sense, word building takes a spelling approach. The teacher says a sound, and students supply the letter that would spell that sound. By slightly altering the directions, you can change to a reading approach when building words: Add the target letter, and then have students read the word. For instance, adding *p* to *et*, ask, "If I add *p* to *et*, what word do I make?" If students don't respond to a spelling approach, using a reading approach to building words provides another way of considering the elements in words.

Step 3. Building words by adding rimes to onsets

To make sure that students have a thorough grasp of both key parts of the word—the onset and the rime—present the onset, and have students supply the rime. Write *p* on the board, and have students tell what sound it stands for. Then ask them to tell what should be added to *p* to make the word *pet*. After adding *et* to *p*, say the word in parts—/p/ /e/ /t/—and then as a whole. Pointing to *p*, say the sound /p/. Pointing to *e* and then *t*, say /e/ and then /t/. Running your hand under the whole word, say, "pet." Show *wet*, *get*, *let*, *jet*, and *net* being formed in the same way. After all words have been formed, have students read them.

Step 4. Providing mixed practice

Realizing that they are learning words that all end in the same way, students may focus on the initial letter and fail to take careful note of the rest of the word, the rime. After presenting a pattern, mix in words from previously presented patterns and have students read these. For example, after presenting the -et pattern, you might have students read the following words: *wet*, *when*, *pet*, *pen*, *net*, and *Ned* (assuming that -en and -ed have been previously taught). This gives students practice in processing all the letters in the words and also reviews patterns that have already been introduced.

 Using Technology

Between the Lions features a number of brief film clips of songs and stories that reinforce vowel patterns. The clips are fairly sophisticated, so they can be used with older as well as younger students.
http://pbskids.org/lions

The exercises in *Words and Pictures* have a distinctive British flavor but provide imaginative reinforcement.
http://www.bbc.co.uk/schools/wordsandpictures/index.shtml

Simon Sounds It Out (Don Johnston), pronounces and helps students build words by combining initial consonants (onsets) and patterns (rimes). Featuring an electronic tutor, it provides effective practice for word building. Because it pronounces and shows parts of words, it also helps develop phonemic awareness. ∎

 FYI

- A book that may be used to introduce the concept of building words is dePaola's (1973) *Andy: That's My Name*, in which his name is used to construct words: *and*, *sand*, *handy*, *sandy*, and so on.
- Students who are unable to conserve or pay attention to two aspects of an object or a situation at the same time may have difficulty dealing with word patterns (Moustafa, 1995). Although they may know the words *hat* and *sat*, they may be unable to use their knowledge of these two words to read *bat* or *mat* because they fail to see the -at pattern. These children may still be processing words sound by sound. As their cognitive skills mature, they should be able to grasp patterns. ∎

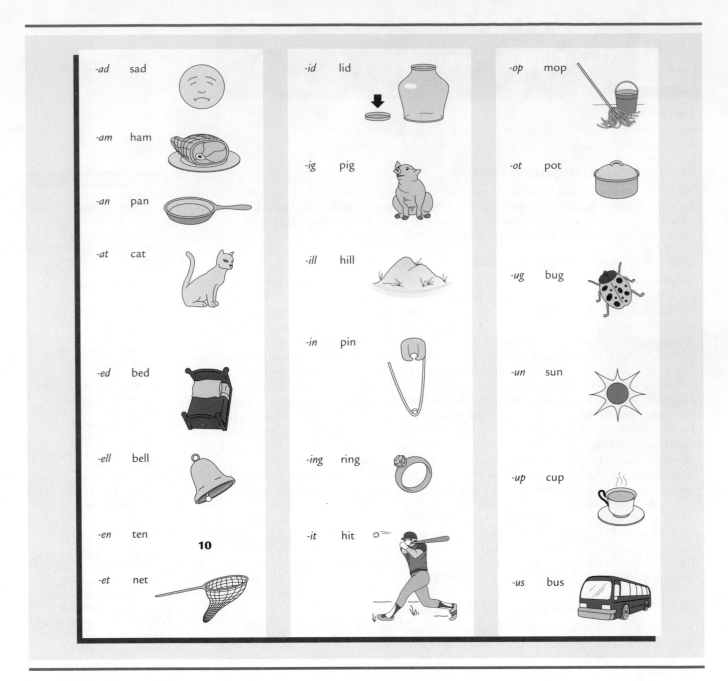

FIGURE 5.6   Model Words
From *Word Building, Book A*, 2nd ed., by T. Gunning (2008). Honesdale, PA: Phoenix Learning Resources.

Step 5. Creating a model word

Create a model word. This should be a word that is easy and can be depicted. Construct a chart on which model words are printed and depicted with a photo or illustration. (A sample chart of model words for short-vowel patterns is presented in Figure 5.6) For the *-et* pattern, the word *net* might be used. Students can use the chart to help them decipher difficult words that incorporate patterns that have already been taught. Place the chart where all can see it. Explain to students that if they come across a word that ends in *-et* and forget how to say it, they can use the chart of model words to help them figure it out. Explain that the model word *net* has a picture that shows the word. In case they forget how to say the model word, the picture will help them.

Step 6. Guided practice

Under the teacher's direction, the class might read sentences or rhymes about a pet that got wet and was caught in a net, or they might create group or individual experience stories about pets they have or wish they had.

Step 7. Application

Students read stories and/or create pieces using -et words. Two very easy books that might be used to reinforce the -et pattern are *Let's Get a Pet* (Greydanus, 1988) and *A Pet for Pat* (Snow, 1984). Also have students read words such as *vet* and *yet*, which incorporate the pattern but which were not presented. As students encounter words such as *letter*, *better*, and *settle*, encourage them to use the known *et* element in each word to help them decode the whole word.

Step 8. Writing and spelling

If necessary, review the formation of the letters *e* and *t*. Dictate some easy but useful -et words (*get, let, wet*), and have students spell them. When dictating the words, stretch out their pronunciations (/g/–/e/–/t/) and encourage students to do the same so that they can better perceive the individual sounds. After students have attempted to spell the words, have them check their attempts against correct spellings placed on the board or overhead. Students should correct any misspellings. Encourage students to use -et words in their writing.

Step 9. Extension

Students learn other short-*e* patterns: *-en*, *-ep*, *-ell*, and so on.

Step 10. Evaluation and review

Note whether students are able to read words containing -et. Note, in particular, whether they are able to decode -et words that have not been taught. Note, too, whether students are spelling -et words in their writing. Provide additional instruction and practice as necessary.

To introduce final-*e* words (CVE pattern), dramatize the impact of a final *e* on a word. When presenting the *a_e* pattern, you might do the following: Holding up a can, tell students that you are going to change the can into a cane (hold up a cane). Ask students to guess how you might do that. Explain that you are not actually going to change the can but are going to change the word *can*. Write *can* on the board. Adding *e*, explain that the word is now *cane*. Write the following words on the board and then add *e* so that they become long-vowel words: *cap, tap, mad, hat, plan, man*. Lead students to see that short *a* is spelled with an *a* in the middle or beginning of a word, as in *cap* or *at*, while long *a* has an *e* at the end of the word as a marker, as in *cape* and *ate*. Explain that long *a* is spelled *a _ e*, with the blank being the space for a consonant letter (Gunning, 2008).

Have students complete exercises similar to the following in which they choose between CVC and CVE words. When discussing the completed exercise, make sure they know the meanings of all the words.

1. The (man, mane) sees a lion.
2. The lion has a (man, mane).
3. The (man, mane) is the hair around the lion's face and on its neck.
4. Lions like to rest in the (shad, shade) of a tree.
5. Lions (can, cane) hunt for food.

Vowel digraphs, which are typically presented after the final-*e* pattern, also pose problems. Present vowel digraphs as another way of spelling long vowels. Write the words *tale* and *tail* on the board. Explain that both are pronounced the same way. Point out that *e* at the end of a word is often used to mark the vowel as being long. Explain that another way of marking a vowel as being long is its placement right before another vowel, as in *tail*. Discuss the different meanings of the two words *tale* and *tail*.

Place the following homophone pairs on the board and discuss them with students: *male–mail*, *pale–pail*, *sale–sail*. Have students sort long-*a* words spelled with final *e* and long-*a* words spelled with a digraph.

 Application Through Reading

As students begin to learn decoding strategies that combine context and knowledge of letter-sound correspondences, it is important that they have opportunities to apply these strategies to whole selections. If they read materials that contain elements they have been taught, they will learn the elements better and also be better at applying them to new words (Juel & Roper-Schneider, 1985). For instance, students who have been introduced to short-*u* correspondences might read *Bugs* (McKissack & McKissack, 1988) and *Joshua James Likes Trucks* (Petrie, 1983), both of which are very easy to read; a somewhat more challenging text is *Buzz Said the Bee* (Lewison, 1992).

Books that might be used to reinforce vowel letter-sound relationships are listed in the following Student Reading List.

 Using Technology

Reading A–Z offers numerous decodable and leveled book and lesson plans for a small subscription fee.

http://www.readinga-z.com ∎

 FYI

• *Mouse's Hide-and-Seek Words* (Heling & Hembrook, 2003) can be used to reinforce finding pronounceable word parts. The book shows readers how to find little words in a big word. (Asking students to find a part they can say works better than finding little words in big words. Not all big words have little words.)

• Display real-world materials that contain the phonics element you are working on. If working on *ch*, for example, bring in a box of Cheerios, chocolate chip cookies, and a menu that features cheeseburgers or chicken. Help students read the items, and encourage them to bring in some of their own. ∎

 Adapting Instruction for Struggling Readers

Books listed in the Student Reading List have varying levels of maturity. When working with older struggling readers, select materials that are on their interest level. ∎

STUDENT READING LIST
Books That Reinforce Vowel Patterns

Short-Vowel Patterns

Level 1

Short a

Antee, N. (1985). *The good bad cat.* Grand Haven, MI: School Zone.
Cameron, A. (1994). *The cat sat on the mat.* Boston: Houghton Mifflin.
Carle, E. (1987). *Have you seen my cat?* New York: Scholastic.
Coxe, M. (1996). *Cat traps.* New York: Random House.
Flanagan, A. K. (2000). *Cats: The sound of short a.* Elgin, IL: Child's World.
Maccarone, G. (1995). *"What is THAT?" said the cat.* New York: Scholastic.
Wildsmith, B. (1982). *Cat on the mat.* New York: Oxford.

Short i

Coxe, M. (1997). *Big egg.* New York: Random.
Greydanus, R. (1988). *Let's get a pet.* New York: Troll.
Meister, C. (1999). *When Tiny was tiny.* New York: Puffin.
Moncure, J. B. (2002). *Play with "i" and "g."* Elgin, IL: Child's World.
Ziefert, H. (2005). *Can you play?* New York: Sterling.

Level 2

Short o

Flanagan, A. K. (2000). *Hot pot: The sound of short o.* Elgin, IL: Child's World.
McKissack, P. C. (1983). *Who is who?* Chicago: Children's Press.
Moncure, J. B. (1981). *No! no! Word Bird.* Elgin, IL: Child's World.
Smee, N. (2006). *Clip-clop.* New York: Sterling.
Weston, M. (2002). *Jack and Jill and big dog Bill.* New York: Random House.
Worth, B. (2003). *Cooking with the cat.* New York: Random House.

Short e

Ada, A. F. (2003). *Daniel's pet.* San Diego, CA: Harcourt.
Flanagan, A. K. (2000). *Ben's pens: The sound of short e.* Elgin, IL: Child's World.
Gregorich, B. (1984). *Nine men chase a hen.* Grand Haven, MI: School Zone.
Snow, P. (1984). *A pet for Pat.* Chicago: Children's Press.

Short u
Capucilli, A. S. (1996). *Biscuit.* New York: HarperCollins.
Gaydos, N. (2008). *The bus stop.* Norwalk, CT: Innovative Kids.
Gaydos, N. (2009). *Frog legs.* Norwalk, CT: Innovative Kids
Gaydos, N. (2009). *The trip.* Norwalk, CT: Innovative Kids.
McKissack, P., & McKissack, F. (1988). *Bugs.* Chicago: Children's Press.
Petrie, C. (1983). *Joshua James likes trucks.* Chicago: Children's Press.
Rylant, C. (2002). *Puppy Mudge takes a bath.* New York: Simon & Schuster.

Levels 3 and 4
Review of Short Vowels
Boegehold, B. D. (1990). *You are much too small.* New York: Bantam.
Kraus, R. (1971). *Leo, the late bloomer.* New York: Simon & Schuster.
Lewison, W. C. (1992). *Buzz said the bee.* New York: Scholastic.

Long-Vowel Patterns
Level 5
Long a
Cohen, C. L. (1998). *How many fish?* New York: HarperCollins.
Flanagan, A. K. (2000). *Play day: The sound of long a.* Elgin, IL: Child's World.
Oppenheim, J. (1990). *Wake up, baby!* New York: Bantam.
Raffi. (1987). *Shake my sillies out.* New York: Crown.
Robart, R. (1986). *The cake that Mack ate.* Toronto: Kids Can Press.
Stadler, J. (1984). *Hooray for Snail!* New York: HarperTrophy.

Long i
Gelman, R. G. (1977). *More spaghetti I say.* New York: Scholastic.
Hoff, S. (1988). *Mrs. Brice's mice.* New York: HarperTrophy.
Kenah, K. (2004). *Animals day and night.* Columbus, OH: Children's Specialty.
Ziefert, H. (1984). *Sleepy dog.* New York: Random House.
Ziefert, H. (1987). *Jason's bus ride.* New York: Random House.
Ziefert, H. (2005). *No more TV, sleepy cat.* New York: Sterling.

Level 6
Long o
Armstrong, J. (1996). *The snowball.* New York: Random House.
Buller, J., & Schade, S. A. (1998). *Pig at play.* New York: Troll.
Cobb, A. (1996). *Wheels.* New York: Random House.
Hamsa, B. (1985). *Animal babies.* Chicago: Children's Press.
Kueffner, S. (1999). *Lucky duck.* Pleasantville, NY: Reader's Digest Children's Books.
McDermott, G. (1999). *Fox and the stork.* San Diego, CA: Harcourt.
Oppenheim, J. (1992). *The show-and-tell frog.* New York: Bantam.
Rader, L. (2005). *Silly pig.* New York: Sterling.
Schade, S. (1992). *Toad on the road.* New York: Random House.

Long e
Bonsall, C. (1974). *And I mean it, Stanley.* New York: Harper.
Milgrim, D. (2003). *See Pip point.* New York: Atheneum.
Shaw, N. (1986). *Sheep in a jeep.* Boston: Houghton Mifflin.
Ziefert, H. (1988). *Dark night, sleepy night.* New York: Puffin.
Ziefert, H. (1995). *The little red hen.* New York: Puffin.

Review of Long Vowels
Heling, K., & Hembrook, D. (2003). *Mouse's hide-and-seek words.* New York: Random House.
Matthias, C. (1983). *I love cats.* Chicago: Children's Press.
Parish, P. (1974). *Dinosaur time.* New York: Harper.
Phillips, J. (1986). *My new boy.* New York: Random House.
Ziefert, H. (1985). *A dozen dogs.* New York: Random House.

Level 7

r Vowels

Arnold, M. (1996). *Quick, quack, quick!* New York: Random House.

Clarke, G. (2001). *Sharks!* New York: Grosset & Dunlap.

Hooks, W. H. (1992). *Feed me!* New York: Bantam.

Penner, R. (1991). *Dinosaur babies.* New York: Random House.

Wynne, P. (1986). *Hungry, hungry sharks.* New York: Random House.

Ziefert, H. (1997). *The magic porridge pot.* New York: Puffin.

Level 8

/oo/ Vowels

Blocksma, M. (1992). *Yoo hoo, Moon!* New York: Bantam.

Marzollo, J. (2004). *I spy a scary monster.* New York: Scholastic.

Phillips, M. (2000). *And the cow said "moo."* New York: Greenwillow.

Silverman, M. (1991). *My tooth is loose.* New York: Viking.

Wiseman, B. (1959). *Morris the moose.* New York: Harper.

Ziefert, H. (1997). *The ugly duckling.* New York: Puffin.

/o̅o̅/ Vowels

Arengo, S. (2000). *The magic cooking pot.* New York: Oxford.

Brenner, B. (1989). *Lion and lamb.* New York: Bantam.

Platt, K. (1965). *Big Max.* New York: Harper.

Level 9

/ow/ Vowels

Arengo, S. (2001). *The fisherman and his wife.* New York: Oxford.

Black, S. W. (1999). *Plenty of penguins,* New York: Scholastic.

Holub, J. (2001). *Scat, cats!* New York: Puffin.

Lobel, A. (1975). *Owl at home.* New York: Harper.

Oppenheim, J. (1989). *"Not now!" said the cow.* New York: Bantam.

Siracusa, C. (1991). *Bingo, the best dog in the world.* New York: HarperCollins.

Level 10

/aw/ Vowels

Crowley, N, (2006). *Ugh! A bug.* Minneapolis, MN: Millbrook Press.

Gaydos, N. (2008). *Where is my home?* Norwalk, CT: Innovative Kids.

Mann, P. Z. (1999). *Meet my monster.* Pleasantville, NY: Reader's Digest Children's Books.

Oppenheim, J. (1991). *The donkey's tale.* New York: Bantam.

Oppenheim, J. (1993). *"Uh-oh!" said the crow.* New York: Bantam.

Rylant, C. (1989). *Henry and Mudge get the cold shivers.* New York: Bradbury.

Wallace, K. (2001). *Diving dolphin.* New York: DK Publishing.

/oy/ Vowels

Marshall, J. (1990). *Fox be nimble.* New York: Puffin.

Witty, B. (1991). *Noises in the night.* Grand Haven, MI: School Zone.

Review of r Vowels and Other Vowel Patterns

Brenner, B. (1989). *Annie's pet.* New York: Bantam.

Hays, A. J. (2003). *The pup speaks up.* New York: Random House.

Hopkins, L. B. (1986). *Surprises.* New York: Harper.

Marshall, E. (1985). *Fox on wheels.* New York: Dutton.

Milton, J. (1985). *Dinosaur days.* New York: Random House.

Rylant, C. (1987). *Henry and Mudge: The first book.* New York: Bradbury.

Stambler, J. (1988). *Cat at bat.* New York: Dutton.

Rhymes

Have students read nursery rhymes that contain the target pattern. Most nursery rhymes contain some unfamiliar words along with the target words. Share-read these rhymes with students until they are able to read them on their own. This builds fluency, automaticity, and confidence.

Word Wall

An excellent device to use for reinforcing both patterns and high-frequency words is a word wall. Words are placed on the wall in alphabetic order. About five new words are added each week (Cunningham & Allington, 1999). They are drawn from basals, trade books, experience stories, and real-world materials that students are reading. You might encourage students to suggest words for the wall from stories they have read or words that they would like to learn.

Kindergarten teachers might start their word wall by placing children's first names on it in alphabetical order. Placing the names in alphabetical order helps reinforce the alphabet (Campbell, 2001).

Before adding a word to the wall, discuss it with the children. Emphasize its spelling, pronunciation, and any distinguishing characteristics. Also talk over how it might relate to other words—for instance, it begins with the same sound, it rhymes, or it is an action word. To reinforce beginning consonants, highlight the first letter of the words containing the consonant you wish to spotlight, for example, the *p* in *pumpkin* and *pull*. To reinforce rimes, highlight the rime you are reinforcing, such as *-at* in *hat* and *cat*.

Because the words are on the wall, they can be used as a kind of dictionary. If students want to know how to spell *there* or *ball*, they can find it on the wall. Being on the wall, the words are readily available for quick review. Troublesome words can be reviewed on a daily basis.

After a pattern has been introduced, place the new pattern words on a separate part of the wall, and arrange model words alphabetically by pattern. The *-ab* pattern would be placed first, followed by the *-ack* and *-ad* patterns, and so on. The model word should be placed first and accompanied by an illustration so that students can refer to the illustration if they forget how to read the model word. When students have difficulty with a pattern word and are unable to use a pronounceable word part to unlock the word's pronunciation, refer them to the word wall. Help them read the model word, and then use an analogy strategy to help them read the word they had difficulty with.

Review the words on the wall periodically, using the following or similar activities:

- Find as many animal names, color names, and number names as you can.
- Pantomime an action (sit, run) or use gestures to indicate an object or other

Adapting Instruction for Struggling Readers and Writers

Struggling youngsters are often given too much phonics. What they need is lots of opportunities to practice their skills by reading easy books. Instruction in phonics should be balanced with application. ∎

 Using Technology

A number of illustrated rhymes can be found at the Web site for Webbing into Literacy:
http://curry.edschool.virginia.edu/go/wil/home.html
For other sources of rhymes, see the Building Literacy Web site:
http://www.wordbuilding.org ∎

 FYI

In the morning message, use words that contain the phonics elements taught recently. Integrate phonics with other subject areas. After c = /k/ has been introduced, you might read about cows or corn, or the class might follow a printed recipe for a custard cake. ∎

Words on the wall will help students with their reading and spelling.

item (pan, hat, cat, pen), and have students write the appropriate pattern word and then hold it up so that you can quickly check everyone's response. Have a volunteer read the word and point to it on the word wall. Before pantomiming the word, tell students what the model word of the pattern is—for example, *cat* or *pan*.

- Have students sort words by pattern. Students might sort a series of short-*a* words into *-at*, *-am*, and *-an* patterns or sort long-*a* words according to their spellings: *a_e*, *-ay*, *-ai*.

Secret Messages

Have students create secret messages by substituting onsets in familiar words and then putting the newly formed words together to create a secret message (QuanSing, 1995). Besides being motivational, secret messages help students focus on the onsets and rimes of words and also foster sentence comprehension. Once students become familiar with the procedure, invite them to create secret messages. Here is a sample secret message.

> Take *H* from *He* and put in *W*. *We*
> Take *l* from *lot* and put in *g*. *got*
> Take *p* from *pen* and put in *t*. *ten*
> Take *st* from *stew* and put in *n*. *new*
> Take *l* from *looks* and put in *b*. *books*
> Secret message: *We got ten new books.*

Secret Word

Try "The Secret Word" (Cunningham & Allington, 1999). Select a word from a pattern, and jot it down on a sheet of paper, but do not reveal its identity. Have students number their papers from 1 to 5. Give a series of five clues as to the identity of the word. After each clue, students should write down their guess. The object of the activity is to guess the word on the basis of the fewest clues. The clues might be as follows:

1. The secret word is in the *-at* pattern.
2. It has three letters.
3. It is an animal.
4. It can fly.
5. The _____ flew into the cave.

Phonics instruction should be differentiated to meet students' needs.

After supplying the five clues, show the secret word (*bat*), and discuss students' responses. See who guessed the secret word first.

Making Words

Students put letters together to create words. Students assemble up to a dozen words, beginning with two-letter words and extending to five-letter or even longer ones (Cunningham & Cunningham, 1992). The last word that the students assemble contains all the letters they were given. For example, students are given the letters *a*, *d*, *n*, *s*, and *t* and are asked to do the following:

- Use two letters to make *at*.
- Add a letter to make *sat*.
- Take away a letter to make *at*.
- Change a letter to make *an*.
- Add a letter to make *Dan*.
- Change a letter to make *tan*.
- Take away a letter to make *an*.
- Add a letter to make *and*.
- Add a letter to make *sand*.
- Now break up your word, and see what word you can make with all the letters (*stand*).

LESSON 5.5
A Making Words Lesson

Objectives
- Students will be able to form words by adding or substituting letters.

Step 1.
Distribute the letters. Explain to students that they will use these letters to make words and that this will help them to become better spellers and readers. You may have one child distribute an *a* to each student, a second child distribute a *t*, and so on. Lowercase letters are written on one side of the card and uppercase on the other. The uppercase letters are used for the spelling of names.

Step 2.
Give the directions for each word: "Use two letters to make *at*." Students form the word.

Step 3.
Have a volunteer assemble the correct response, the word *at*, on the chalkboard ledge (or pocket chart or letter holder). Have the volunteer read the word. Students should check and correct their responses.

Step 4.
Give the directions for the next word. Use the word in a sentence so that students hear it in context. If you have students who are struggling with phonological awareness and letter-sound relationships, slowly articulate each of the target words and encourage them to stretch out the sounds as they spell them with their letters. If a target word is a proper name, make note of that.

Step 5.
On the chalkboard ledge, line up in order enlarged versions of the words the students were asked to make. Have volunteers read each of the words. Also have volunteers help sort the words according to patterns or beginning or ending sounds. For instance, holding up the word *at*, the teacher might ask a student to come up to the ledge and find the words that rhyme with *at*.

Step 5. Evaluation
Note students' ability to make words. Provide added instruction and practice for those who show a need.

FYI

For additional Making Words exercises, go to http://wordbuilding.org. ■

Using Technology

Wordmaker (Don Johnston) is a computer program that students can use to make words. The program provides letters, says the word to be made, and allows students to check their responses. ■

FYI

Scrabble letter holders can be used to hold students' letters, or letter holders can be constructed from cut-up file folders. ■

Assessing for Learning

One first-grader was doing well with phonics exercises until he had to choose among three words to name an illustration. He was picking *bug* for the picture of the bat and *bat* for the picture of the bug. He was only using initial consonants to decode words, which is what he had been taught in kindergarten. Therefore, vowel patterns were reviewed, and he was taught how to use all the letters to decode words. ■

FYI

• Children learn what they are taught. If they are taught to use initial consonants rather than to process the whole word, they will have difficulty with a sentence like "Pam has a pet duck." It could be read as "Pat had a pet dog." ∎

• One way to keep phonics functional is to analyze a text that students are about to read and note which phonics elements students need to know in order to read the text. For instance, if the selection is about trains, you might present or review the *-ain* pattern.

R E F L E C T I O N

What are the characteristics of effective reinforcement for phonics? Which of the reinforcement activities are most effective? Why? How would you rank them in order of importance?

Using Technology

The Electric Company has a variety of video clips for reinforcing phonics elements.
http://pbskids.org/electriccompany

Starfall
Features activities, stories, and short movies designed to introduce single-syllable patterns.
http://www.starfall.com ∎

FYI

Incorporate dialect differences in your planning. Although *egg* is often used as an example of a short *e* word, many people pronounce it as though it begins with a long *a* sound. If that's the way your students pronounce it, don't use it as an example of a short *e* word. ∎

FYI

Based on his experience with instruction in phonics, Engelmann (1999) found that summer forgetting was minimal if students had been taught to mastery. He recommended a week of review, consisting of going over the last ten lessons from the previous school year, when students returned at the end of summer. ∎

To plan a making words lesson, decide which patterns you wish to reinforce and how many letters you wish students to assemble. The letters chosen must form the word, so you may want to select the final word right after you have chosen the pattern. As students grow more adept, they can be given more challenging patterns and asked to make longer words using a greater variety of patterns. You might also include two or more vowels so that students become involved in vowel substitution.

Scope and Sequence

A well-planned program of phonics instruction features a flexible but carefully planned scope and sequence. Although vowels could be introduced first in a reading program, it is recommended that consonants be presented initially, as their sounds have fewer spelling options. The consonant sound /b/, for example, is spelled *b* most of the time. In addition, initial letters, which are usually consonants, yield better clues to the pronunciation of a word than do medial or final letters.

When teaching initial consonants, present consonants that are easiest to say and that appear with the highest frequency first. The sounds /s/ and /m/ are recommended for early presentation because they are easy to distinguish, are among the most frequently occurring sounds in the English language, and can be used to form easy words early on. After students have learned five or six high-frequency consonant correspondences, have them combine the consonants they have learned with a short vowel to form words. Usually, short *a* is introduced first. Short *i*, which is the most frequently occurring vowel, is generally introduced next, followed by short *o*, *e*, and *u*. Long vowels, *r* vowels, and other vowels are presented next.

Phonics instruction begins in preschool with the exploration of beginning consonants. In kindergarten, beginning and ending consonants and short-vowel patterns are introduced. These are reviewed in first grade, and all the major single-syllable vowel patterns and consonant clusters and digraphs are presented. Some programs also introduce syllabic analysis in first grade. In second grade, major patterns and clusters are reviewed, and some advanced patterns and syllabic analysis are presented. In third grade, emphasis is often on syllabic analysis, although this skill tends to be neglected. Table 5.5 is a phonics scope-and-sequence chart that shows the approximate grade levels where key skills are taught in today's reading programs. Correspondences within each level are listed in order of approximate frequency of occurrence. The levels are rough approximations and must be adjusted to suit the needs and abilities of your students and the structure of your specific program. Some advanced kindergartners might be taught correspondences at the grade 1 level and even some at the grade 2 level. On the other hand, a fourth-grader with a reading disability may have difficulty with short vowels and would need to work at the grade 1 level.

Skills taught in one grade are often retaught or reviewed in the next grade. For example, first-grade basal programs typically start off with a review of consonants and short-vowel patterns. The review moves quickly and is usually finished within three weeks. This isn't enough time for students to learn elements that they have forgotten or didn't learn, and much of the review is unnecessary for students who did learn the basic elements. A better plan would be to use kindergarten records to estimate where students are and to assess them to determine what elements they have learned and which need to be taught. This would be especially beneficial for struggling students who need more than a quick review.

Based on records and your assessment, start instruction where students show needs. Don't reteach skills that students have mastered; it's a waste of time teaching them what they already know. Some programs recommend reviewing basic phonics patterns, such as the *ai* or *ay* spelling of long *a* and the *ee* or *ea* spelling of long *e*, in grades 2 and 3. Being able to read second- or third-grade material is usually proof enough that students know these patterns. Use your own judgment and your knowledge of students' abilities when deciding what to teach.

TABLE 5.5 Scope-and-Sequence Chart for Phonics

Level	Categories	Correspondence	Model Word	Correspondence	Model Word
K–1	Letter names, phonemic awareness, rhyming, segmentation, perception of initial consonants				
K–1	High-frequency initial consonants	s = /s/	sea	r = /r/	rug
		f = /f/	fish	l = /l/	lamp
		m = /m/	men	g = /g/	game
		t = /t/	toy	n = /n/	nine
		d = /d/	dog	h = /h/	hit
K–1	Lower-frequency initial consonants and x	c = /k/	can	c = /s/	city
		b = /b/	boy	g = /j/	gym
		v = /v/	vase	y = /y/	yo-yo
		j = /j/	jacket	z = /z/	zebra
		p = /p/	pot	x = /ks/	box
		w = /w/	wagon	x = /gs/	example
		k = /k/	kite		
1	High-frequency initial consonant digraphs	ch = /ch/	church	th = /th/	thumb
		sh = /sh/	ship	wh = /wh/	wheel
		th = /th/	this		
K–1	Short vowels	a = /a/	hat	e = /e/	net
		i = /i/	fish	u = /u/	pup
		o = /o/	pot		
1–2	Initial consonant clusters	st = /st/	stop	fr = /fr/	free
		pl = /pl/	play	fl = /fl/	flood
		pr = /pr/	print	str = /str/	street
		gr = /gr/	green	cr = /kr/	cry
		tr = /tr/	tree	sm = /sm/	small
		cl = /kl/	clean	sp = /sp/	speak
		br = /br/	bring	bl = /bl/	blur
		dr = /dr/	drive		
1–2	Final consonant clusters	ld = /ld/	cold	mp = /mp/	lamp
		lf = /lf/	shelf	nd = /nd/	hand
		sk = /sk/	mask	nt = /nt/	ant
		st = /st/	best	nk = /ŋk/	think
2	Less frequent digraphs and other consonant elements	ck = /k/	lock		
		dge = /j/	bridge		
1–2	Long vowels: final e marker	a-e = /ā/	save	e-e = /ē/	these
		i-e = /ī/	five	u-e = /ū/	use
		o-e = /ō/	hope		
1–2	Long vowels: digraphs	ee = /ē/	green	ow = /ō/	show
		ai/ay = /ā/	aim, play	igh = /ī/	light
		oa = /ō/	boat		
		ea = /ē/	bean		
1–2	r vowels	ar = /ar/	car	are = /air/	care
		er = /er/	her	air = /air/	hair
		ir = /er/	sir	ear = /i(e)r/	fear
		ur = /er/	burn	eer = /i(e)r/	steer
		or = /or/	for		
1–2	Other vowels	ou/ow = /ow/	out, owl	oo = /ŏŏ/	book
		au/aw = /aw/	author, paw	oo = /oo/	tool
		al = /aw/	ball		
		oi/oy = /oi/	oil, toy		
2–3	Consonants/Consonant digraphs	ti = /sh/	action		
		ssi = /sh/	mission		
		t, ti = /ch/	future, question		
		ch = /k/	choir	kn = /n/	knee
		ch = /sh/	chef	wr = /r/	wrap
		gh = /g/	ghost	ph = /f/	photo

(continued)

TABLE 5.5   Scope-and-Sequence Chart for Phonics (*Continued*)

Level	Categories	Correspondence	Model Word	Correspondence	Model Word
2–3	Vowels	$y = /\bar{e}/$	city	$o = /aw/$	off
		$y = /\bar{\imath}/$	why	$ew = /\bar{u}/$	few
		$y = /i/$	gym	$a = /\partial/$	alike
		$a = /o/$	father		
		$e = /i/$	remain		

Major Word Patterns

If you use word building or another pattern approach, you can think of scope and sequence in terms of word patterns. A listing of major word patterns is presented in Table 5.6. The sequence of presentation is similar to the order in which the elements are listed: short-vowel patterns, followed by long-vowel patterns, followed by *r*-vowel patterns and other vowel patterns. However, within each grouping, patterns are presented in alphabetical order. Do not present the patterns in alphabetical order. Start with the easiest and most useful patterns. When teaching short *a* patterns, begin with the *-at* pattern, for instance. When introducing patterns, do not present every word that fits the pattern. Present only words that students know or that they will be likely to meet

TABLE 5.6   Major Word Patterns

Short Vowels									
-ab	**-ack**	**-ad**	**-ag**	**-am**	**-amp**	**-an**	**-and**	**-ang**	**-ank**
cab	back	bad	bag	*ham	camp	an	and	bang	*bank
tab	jack	dad	rag	jam	damp	can	band	gang	sank
*crab	pack	had	tag	slam	*lamp	fan	*hand	hang	tank
	sack	mad	wag	swam	stamp	man	land	*rang	blank
	*tack	*sad	drag			*pan	sand	sang	thank
	black	glad	*flag			tan	stand		
	crack					plan			
	stack					than			
-ap	**-at**		**-ed**	**-ell**	**-en**	**-end**	**-ent**	**-ess**	**-est**
cap	at		*bed	*bell	den	end	bent	guess	best
lap	bat		fed	fell	hen	bend	dent	less	nest
*map	*cat		led	tell	men	lend	rent	mess	pest
tap	fat		red	well	pen	mend	sent	bless	rest
clap	hat		shed	yell	*ten	*send	*tent	*dress	test
slap	pat		sled	shell	then	tend	went	press	*vest
snap	rat			smell	when	spend	spent		west
trap	sat			spell					chest
wrap	that								guest
-et	**-ead**	**-ick**	**-id**	**-ig**	**-ill**	**-im**	**-in**	**-ing**	
bet	dead	kick	did	big	bill	dim	in	king	
get	head	lick	hid	dig	fill	him	fin	*ring	
jet	lead	pick	kid	*pig	*hill	skim	*pin	sing	
let	read	sick	*lid	wig	kill	slim	sin	wing	
met	*bread	click	rid	twig	pill	*swim	tin	bring	
*net	spread	*stick	skid		will		win	sting	
pet	thread	thick	slid		chill		chin	thing	
set		trick			skill		grin		
wet		quick			spill		skin		

(continued)

TABLE 5.6 Major Word Patterns (*Continued*)

				Short Vowels					
						spin thin twin			

-ink	*-ip*	*-it*	*-ob*	*-ock*	*-op*	*-ot*			
link	dip	it	job	dock	cop	dot			
pink	lip	bit	mob	*lock	hop	got			
*sink	rip	fit	rob	rock	*mop	hot			
clink	chip	sit		clock	chop	*pot			
drink	flip	knit		flock	drop	shot			
stink	*ship	quit		knock	shop	spot			
think	skip	split			stop				
	trip								
	whip								

-ub	*-uck*	*-ug*	*-um*	*-ump*	*-un*	*-unk*	*-us(s)*	*-ust*	*-ut*
cub	*duck	bug	bum	bump	bun	bunk	*bus	bust	but
rub	luck	dug	hum	dump	fun	hunk	plus	dust	cut
sub	cluck	hug	yum	hump	gun	junk	us	just	hut
tub	stuck	mug	*drum	*jump	run	sunk	fuss	*must	*nut
*club	struck	*rug	plum	lump	*sun	shrunk	muss	rust	shut
scrub	truck	tug		pump	spun	*skunk		trust	
		chug		thump		stunk			
				stump					

				Long Vowels					

-ace	*-ade*	*-age*	*-ake*	*-ale*	*-ame*	*-ape*	*-ate*	*-ave*	*-ail*
*face	fade	age	bake	pale	came	ape	ate	*cave	fail
race	made	*cage	*cake	sale	game	*cape	date	gave	jail
place	grade	page	lake	tale	*name	tape	*gate	save	mail
space	*shade	rage	make	*scale	same	scrape	hate	wave	*nail
	trade	stage	rake		tame	grape	late	brave	pail
			take		blame	shape	mate		sail
			wake		shame		plate		tail
			flake				skate		snail
			shake				state		trail
			snake						

-ain	*-ay*		*-ea*	*-each*	*-eak*	*-eal*	*-eam*	*-ean*	*-eat*
main	bay		pea	each	*beak	deal	team	*bean	eat
pain	day		sea	beach	leak	heal	*dream	lean	beat
rain	*hay		*tea	*peach	peak	meal	scream	mean	neat
brain	lay		flea	reach	weak	real	stream	clean	*seat
chain	may			teach	creak	*seal			cheat
grain	pay			bleach	sneak	squeal			treat
*train	say				speak	steal			wheat
	way				squeak				
	gray								
	play								

-ee	*-eed*	*-eel*	*-eep*	*-eet*		*-ice*	*-ide*	*-ile*	*-ime*
*bee	deed	feel	beep	*feet		*mice	hide	mile	*dime
see	feed	heel	deep	meet		nice	ride	pile	lime
free	*seed	kneel	*jeep	sheet		rice	side	*smile	time
knee	weed	steel	keep	sleet		slice	wide	while	chime
tree	bleed	*wheel	peep	sweet		twice	*bride		
	freed		weep				slide		

(*continued*)

TABLE 5.6 Major Word Patterns (*Continued*)

Long Vowels

	speed		creep						
			sleep						
			steep						
			sweep						

-ine	-ite	-ive	-ie	-ind	-y		-o, -oe	-oke	-ole
fine	bite	dive	die	find	by		go	joke	hole
line	*kite	*five	lie	kind	guy		*no	poke	mole
mine	quite	hive	pie	*mind	my		so	woke	*pole
*nine	white	live	*tie	blind	dry		doe	broke	stole
pine		drive			fly		hoe	*smoke	whole
					*sky		toe	spoke	
					try				
					why				

-one	-ope	-ose	-ote	-oad	-oat	-ow	-old		u-e
bone	hope	hose	*note	load	boat	bow	old		use
cone	nope	*nose	vote	*road	coat	low	cold		fuse
*phone	*rope	rose	quote	toad	*goat	tow	fold		*mule
shone	slope	chose	wrote		float	blow	hold		huge
		close				glow	*gold		
		those				grow	sold		
						slow	told		
						*snow			

r Vowels

-air	-are	-ear, ere	-ar	-ard	-ark, *shark		-art	-ear
fair	care	*bear	*car	*card	bark		art	*ear
*hair	hare	pear	far	guard	dark		part	dear
pair	share	there	jar	hard	mark		*chart	fear
chair	scare	where	star		park		smart	hear
		spare			spark			year
		*square						clear

-eer		-or	-ore	-orn	-ort
*deer		*or	more	born	*fort
cheer		for	*sore	*corn	port
steer		nor	tore	torn	sort
			wore	worn	short
					sport

Other Vowels

-all	-aw	-au	-ong	-oss	-ost	-ought	-oil	-oy
*ball	caw	fault	bong	boss	cost	ought	*boil	*boy
call	jaw	*caught	gong	loss	*lost	*bought	soil	joy
fall	paw	taught	long	toss	frost	fought		toy
hall	*saw		song	*cross		brought		
wall	claw		strong					
small	draw		wrong					
	straw							

-oud	-our	-out	-ound	-ow	-own	-ood	-ook	-ould
loud	our	out	bound	ow	down	good	*book	*could
*cloud	*hour	*shout	found	bow	gown	hood	cook	would

(continued)

TABLE 5.6   Major Word Patterns (*Continued*)

Other Vowels								
proud	sour	scout	hound	*cow	town	*wood	hook	should
flour	spout		mound	how	brown	stood	look	
			pound	now	clown		took	
			*round	plow	*crown		shook	
			sound					
			wound					
			ground					

*May be used as model words.

From *Assessing and Correcting Reading and Writing Difficulties* (2nd ed.) by T. Gunning, 2002. Boston: Allyn & Bacon. Reprinted by permission of Allyn & Bacon.

in the near future. It's better for them to attain a good grasp of a few high-frequency pattern words than to have an uncertain knowledge of a large number of pattern words. It also saves time to introduce just the important words. It is not necessary to teach every pattern. For instance, after five or six short-*a* patterns have been introduced, help students to generalize that all the patterns contain a short *a* sound and to apply this to short-*a* words from patterns that have not been introduced. Words from low-frequency patterns such as -*ab*, -*ag*, -*aft*, and -*ax* might be presented in this way.

Teaching Vowel Generalizations

"When two vowels go walking, the first one does the talking." Recited by millions of students, this generalization is one of the best known of the vowel rules. It refers to the tendency for the first letter in a digraph to represent the long sound typically associated with that letter: For example, *ea* in *team* represents long *e*, and *ai* in *paid* represents long *a*. Although this generalization is heavily criticized because, as expressed, it applies only about 50 percent of the time, it can be helpful (Gunning, 1975; Johnston, 2001).

About one word out of every five has a digraph; however, the generalization does not apply equally to each situation. For some spellings—*ee*, for example—it applies nearly 100 percent of the time. The letters *ea*, however, represent at least four different sounds (as in *bean*, *bread*, *earth*, and *steak*). Moreover, the generalization does not apply to such vowel-letter combinations as *au*, *aw*, *oi*, *oy*, and *ou*.

This generalization about digraphs should not be taught as a blanket rule because it has too many exceptions. Instead, it should be broken down into a series of minigeneralizations in which the most useful and most consistent correspondences are emphasized. These minigeneralizations include the following:

Instances where digraphs usually represent a long sound

- The letters *ai* and *ay* usually represent long *a*, as in *way* and *wait*.
- The letters *ee* usually represent long *e*, as in *see* and *feet*.
- The letters *ey* usually represent long *e*, as in *key*.
- The letters *oa* usually represent long *o*, as in *boat* and *toad*.

Instances where digraphs regularly represent a long sound or another sound

- Except when followed by *r*, the letters *ea* usually stand for long *e* (*bean*) or short *e* (*bread*).
- The letters *ie* usually stand for long *e* (*piece*) or long *i* (*tie*).
- The letters *ow* usually stand for a long *o* sound (*snow*) or an /ow/ sound (*cow*).

The minigeneralizations could also be taught as patterns, such as *seat*, *heat*, *neat*, and *beat* or *boat*, *goat*, and *float*. Whichever way they are taught, the emphasis should be on providing ample opportunities to meet the double vowels in print. Providing exposure is the

FYI

- Familiar words are easier to decode. A student who has been taught the -*at* pattern may have little difficulty with the high-frequency words *cat*, *that*, and *sat* but may falter when encountering *chat*, *drat*, and *mat*. ■

Adapting Instruction for English Language Learners

Both Chinese- and Spanish-speaking youngsters have difficulty with long *e*. ■

Adapting Instruction for Struggling Readers and Writers

Some students may need more phonics than others. If students don't seem to do well with systematic phonics, try a more holistic approach. Teach a limited amount of phonics, but provide lots of reading practice. Have them read recorded stories that incorporate the element you wish to teach (Carbo, 1997) or try language-experience stories or phonics games. ■

FYI

- A number of vowel combinations are not used to spell long vowels: *au* or *aw* = /aw/ *fault*, *saw*
oi or *oy* = /oy/ *toil*, *toy*
oo = /oo̅/ *moon*
oo = /oŏ/ *book*
ou or *ow* = /ow/ *pout*, *power* ■

FYI

One of the few generalizations that students make use of in their reading is the final *e* generalization. When they reach the consolidated alphabetic stage of reading, students make use of final *e* as part of a larger pattern: *-age, -ate, -ive.* ∎

FYI

• The best way to "learn" generalizations is to have plenty of practice reading open and closed syllable words, final *e* words, and other words covered by generalizations.
• Because there is no way to predict on the basis of spelling whether *ow* will represent /ow/ (*cow*) or /ō/ (*snow*) or *oo* will represent a short vowel sound (*book*) or long one (*boot*), you need to teach students to check whether the sounds they construct create a real word. If not, have them try the other major pronunciation of *ow* or *oo*. Model this process for your students. ∎

key to learning phonics. Generalizations and patterns draw attention to regularities in English spelling, but actually meeting the elements in print is the way students' decoding skills become automatic; they can then direct fuller attention to comprehension.

Most vowel rules are not worth teaching because they have limited utility, have too many exceptions, or are too difficult to apply. However, the following generalizations are relatively useful (Gunning, 1975):

- *Closed syllable generalization.*   A vowel is short when followed by a consonant: *wet, but–ter*. This is known as the closed syllable rule because it applies when a consonant "closes," or ends, a word or syllable.
- *Open syllable generalization.*   A vowel is usually long when it is found at the end of a word or syllable: *so, mo–ment*. This generalization is known as the open syllable rule because the word or syllable ends with a vowel and so is not closed by a consonant.
- *Final-e generalization.*   A vowel is usually long when it is followed by a consonant and a final *e*: *pine, note*.

Vowel generalizations should be taught inductively. After experiencing many words that end in *e* preceded by a consonant, for example, students should conclude that words ending in a consonant and *e* often have long vowels. Students might also discover this by sorting words that end in *e* and words that don't.

The real payoff from learning generalizations comes when students group elements within a word in such a way that they automatically map out the correct pronunciation most of the time. For example, when processing the words *vocal, token,* and *hotel* so that the first syllable is noted as being open (*vo–cal, to–ken, ho–tel*) and the vowel is noted as being long, students are able to decode the words quickly and accurately. This is a result of many hours of actual reading. However, it is also a process that can be taught (Glass, 1976).

Because none of the vowel generalizations applies 100 percent of the time, students should be introduced to the variability principle. They need to learn that digraphs and single vowels can represent a variety of sounds. If they try one pronunciation and it is not a real word or does not make sense in context, then they must try another. A child who read "heevy" for *heavy* would have to try another pronunciation, because *heevy* is not a real word. A child who read "deed" for *dead* would need to check to see whether that pronunciation fit the context of the sentence in which the word was used. Although *deed* is a real word, it does not make sense in the sentence "Jill's cat was dead"; so, the student needs to try another pronunciation. This strategy needs to be taught explicitly, and students must have plenty of opportunity for practice. To sound out a word, they should be taught the general steps outlined in the following Student Strategy.

STUDENT STRATEGIES
Applying the Variability (Try Another Sound) Strategy to Vowel Correspondences

1. Sound out the word as best you can.
2. After sounding out the word, ask yourself, "Is this a real word?" If not, try another sound. (Applying the variability principle to a word containing *ow*, a student might try the long-vowel /ō/ pronunciation first. If that did not work out, he or she would try the /ow/, as in *cow*, pronunciation. If there is a chart of spellings available, students can use it as a source of possible pronunciations.)
3. Read the word in the sentence. Ask yourself, "Does *this* word make sense in the sentence?" If not, try another sound.
4. If you still cannot sound out a word so that it makes sense in the sentence, try context, skip it, or get help.

Introducing Syllabic Analysis Early

Long words pose problems for students. Although students might know the words *car*, *pen*, and *her*, they have difficulty reading the word *carpenter*. Most multisyllabic words are composed of known word parts or patterns. After teaching several short-vowel patterns, present two-syllable words composed of those patterns. For instance, after students have studied the short *a* and short *i* patterns, present words such as *rabbit*, *napkin*, *distant*, and *instant*. When students encounter multisyllabic words, prompt them to use their knowledge of word parts to figure out the words. Also build words. After students have learned a word such as *swim*, have them make words that contain *swim*, including *swims*, *swimming*, and *swimmer* so that they are used with reading words that contain suffixes.

 Strategy Instruction

The ultimate value of phonics instruction is that it provides students with the keys for unlocking the pronunciations of unknown words encountered in print. For instance, a child who has studied both the -*at* and the -*et* patterns but has difficulty with the words *flat* and *yet* needs strategies for decoding those words. There are three powerful decoding strategies that the student might use: pronounceable word part, analogy, and context (Gunning, 1995).

To apply the pronounceable word part strategy, a student who is having difficulty with a word seeks out familiar parts of the word. You might prompt the student by pointing to a word such as *yet* and asking, "Is there any part of the word that you can say?" If the student fails to see a pronounceable word part, cover up all but that part of the word (*et*), and ask the student if she or he can read it. Once the student reads the pronounceable part, she or he adds the onset (*y*) and says the word *yet*. (This assumes that the student knows the *y* = /y/ correspondence.) In most instances, the student will be able to say the pronounceable word part and use it to decode the whole word. (Use the prompt "Is there any part of the word that you can say?" rather than asking students if they can read any chunk of the word. Some students might have difficulty reading chunks but will be able to sound out individual letters.)

If a student is unable to use the pronounceable word part strategy, try the analogy strategy. With the analogy strategy, the student compares an unknown word to a known one. For instance, the student might compare the unknown word *yet* to the known word *net*. The teacher prompts the strategy by asking, "Is the word like any word that you know?" If the student is unable to respond, the teacher writes the model word *net*, has the student read it, and then compares *yet* to *net*. Or the teacher might refer the child to a model words chart.

When students reconstruct a word using the pronounceable word part or analogy strategy, they must always make sure that the word they have constructed is a real word. They must also make sure that it fits the context of the sentence. The pronounceable word part strategy should be tried before the analogy strategy because it is easier to apply and is more direct. Although students may have to be prompted to use these strategies, they should ultimately apply them on their own.

The pronounceable word part and analogy strategies need to be integrated with the use of context clues. There are some situations in which neither of the first two strategies will work. For instance, the first two strategies will not work with *have* in the following sentence, but context clues probably will: "I have three pets." However, context probably will not be of much help in decoding the word trains in the sentence "I like trains," but the pronounceable word part or analogy strategy is likely to work if the student knows the -*ain* pattern or the word *rain*. Based on their own studies and others, New Zealand researchers Chapman, Tunmer, and Prochnow (2001) concluded that in most instances, students will be more successful if they use the pronounceable word part strategy first: "Children . . . should be encouraged to look for familiar spelling

REFLECTION

Which phonics elements are most difficult to learn? Why do you think long vowels are more difficult than short vowels? What are some techniques that might be used to help students who are struggling to learn difficult elements?

 FYI

• The pronounceable word part strategy takes advantage of students' natural tendency to group sounds into pronounceable parts. ■

 FYI

• Do not ask students to "look for the little word in the big word." This may work sometimes but would result in a misleading pronunciation in a word like *mother*. Besides, there are many words that don't have "little words" in them. ■

  **CCSS**

Use context to confirm or self-correct word recognition and understanding, rereading as necessary

FYI

The prompt "Is there any word part that you can say?" allows students to select the word element they can best handle, which might be a single sound, a cluster, or a rime. For the word *blurt*, the student might recognize *b*, *bl*, *ur*, or *urt*. ■

FYI

• Prompting for clues should be closely related to the text (White, 2005). Asking a student to recall and apply a phonics generalization is getting away from the immediate text. Routine prompts, such as "Sound it out," aren't helpful either. The prompt should also match the nature of the word. Don't ask a student to sound out a word such as *were*.
• To provide practice in applying strategies, give students a slip of paper, and have them record on the paper a word they have figured out in the text they are reading. During discussion of the text, have them tell what their word is and how they figured it out (White, 2005). ■

patterns first and use context to confirm what unfamiliar words might be" (pp. 171–172). As McKenna and Picard (2006) explain:

> Our best conceptualization of the reading process suggests that context is used *after* a word is located in memory. It helps us determine which meaning is the one intended by the author. . . . Teachers should view meaningful miscues (like substituting *pony* for *horse*) as evidence of inadequate decoding skills, and not as an end result to be fostered. Because beginning readers will attempt to compensate for weak decoding by reliance on context, teachers should instruct them in how to use the graphophonic, semantic, and syntactic cueing systems to support early reading. . . . When a child struggles to read a word, the teacher responds with prompts such as "What's the first sound?," "Is there a part of the word you know?," "You said _____. Does that make sense?" We have placed the context prompt last for a reason—it should be the child's last resort, not the first. "A major failing" of instruction that places the three cueing systems on equal footing is that it ignores the fact that one of the systems "is more central and important" than the others (Rayner & Pollatsek, 1989, p. 351). (p. 379)

As students encounter difficult words, use a pause-prompt-praise routine (Tunmer & Chapman, 1999). Pause for about 5 seconds to see if students can work out the word on their own. If they cannot, prompt them to use a pronounceable word part or analogy strategy. Listed below is a series of steps that students might take when confronting a word that is unfamiliar in print.

Step 1.   See if there is any part of the word that I can say. (If I can't say any part of the word, go to step 4.)

Step 2.   Say the part of the word I know. Then say the rest of the word. (If I can't say the rest of the word, go to step 4.)

Step 3.   Ask: "Is the word I said a real word? Does it make sense in the story?" (If not, try again or go to step 4.)

Step 4.   Is the word like any word I know? Is it like one of the model words? (If not, go to step 6.)

Step 5.   Say the word. Is it a real word? Does it make sense in the story? (If not, try again, or go to step 6.)

Step 6.   Say "blank" for the word. Read to the end of the sentence. Ask myself: "What word would make sense here?"

Post a simplified list of steps that students might take to decode challenging words and check the results of their efforts.

1. Try to figure out the word.

   • Can I say any part of this word?
     or
   • Is this word like any word I know? Is it like one of the model words?
     or
   • What word would make sense here?

2. After I say the word, check it.
   • Is the word I made a real word?
   • Does the word make sense in its sentence?

As students' understanding of the alphabetic system develops, they begin to use more advanced strategies. Initially, they might use sounding out because that is the simplest strategy. They pronounce the words sound by sound: /h/-/a/-/t/. However, as they begin to see patterns in words, they use pronounceable word parts or chunks (Sharp, Sinatra, & Reynolds, 2008): /h/-/at/. Since some students may not be able to chunk words and may need to decode sound by sound, prompt them to say words sound by sound and then put the sounds together. If the student is encountering a short-vowel word such as *mat* but forgets the short-vowel sound, prompt the use of the model word routine; for example, for the short vowel *a*, the student would say "*a apple* /a/" and then say /m/-/a/-/t/. Use a monitoring prompt if the student produces a nonword or a word that doesn't make sense in the selection: "Is that a real word? Does that make sense?" As students encounter exceptions to the final-*e* generalization (*give, have*) and learn vowel digraphs, such as *ea* and *ow*, which have more than one pronunciation (*beak, bread, low, cow*), they will need to try more than one pronunciation. Model and provide practice in using the try-another-sound strategy (variability strategy). In using the try-another-sound strategy, in most cases, students will try the long-vowel pronunciation and then, if that doesn't work, try the short-vowel or other pronunciation. The strategy can also be used with the consonant letters *c* and *g*. The following are the steps for the try-another-sound strategy:

Step 1. When decoding a word, if the word isn't a real word or doesn't make sense in the sentence, try another pronunciation.

Step 2. Try the long-vowel pronunciation first. If that doesn't work, try the short-vowel pronunciation or another pronunciation. For the word *bow*, the student might try the long *o* pronunciation and then the *ow* as in *cow* pronunciation For the consonant letters *c* and *g*, try the hard pronunciation first and then the soft pronunciation.

Step 3. Check to see if the word is a real word and makes sense in the sentence: After singing her song, Maria took a bow.

Affirm students' use of a strategy. This encourages students to use that strategy again: "I like the way you used a word part that you knew in order to read the whole word." As students grow in skills, instead of affirming students' responses, you might have them affirm their own responses by cross-checking to verify that their response is correct: How do you know that *bow* (as in *cow*) is the correct pronunciation? (Gelzheiser, 2010). At times, none of your prompts will work. In that case, give students a choice between the correct word and an alternative: "Is that word *barked* or *howled*? How do you know?"

Giving students a choice saves face and also involves them in using phonics and/or semantics to respond. Give students as much guidance as they need, but gradually lead them to the point where they can decode independently. See Table 5.7 for a list of strategies students can use.

 FYI

- Stopping occasionally to decode a difficult word or because something does not sound right to the reader does not mean that the reader lacks fluency. It means that the reader is monitoring for meaning, which is something good readers do.
- A coverup can be a prompt. Cover the word with your finger, and then slowly uncover the letters to help the reader sound out and blend. With children just beginning to decode, uncover single letters or digraphs (e.g., *s-a-ck*). With more advanced beginners, uncover syllable chunks (e.g., *news-pa-per*)" (Murray, 2006a). ∎

 Assessing for Learning

As students read, watch their eyes. A glance upward at an illustration generally signals that they have encountered a difficult word and are attempting to use picture clues. ∎

TABLE 5.7 Strategy Prompts for Word Decoding

Strategy	When Used	Prompt
Pronounceable word part	The word contains a pronounceable word part: *an* or *ran* in *ranch*.	"Is there any part of this word that you can say?" (You might need to cover up all of the word except the pronounceable part.)
Analogy	The pronounceable word part strategy doesn't work. The word is like one the student knows: *vain* is like *train*.	"Is this word like any word that you know? Is this word like any of the model words?" (You might need to write or show the known word so that the student can compare the two.)
Context	The word is irregular, or other strategies don't work.	"What word would make sense here?"
Sound by sound	Student doesn't see chunks or parts in words. Needs to decode the word sound by sound.	"What is the first sound? What is the next sound? The last sound? What word do you get when you put the sounds together?"
Try another sound	The vowel or consonant spelling has more than one pronunciation.	"What other sound can that letter (or letters) make?" (Student can refer to a model words chart.) The student also checks that the word is a real one and fits the context.
Sound correction/model word routine	Student says the wrong sound for an element (says "pet" for *pit*) or can't recall the sound. The student is prompted to use model word routine and says the letter, model word from short-vowel chart, and sound of letter. For a long-vowel error (student says "cap" for *cape*), call attention to a final e or digraph.	"What is the vowel? What is the model word for *i*? What sound does *i* make? What would this word be if you put the *i* sound in it?" (Direct student to refer to the model words chart, if you have one.)"What is the vowel? What does the final e tell you about the vowel? What would this word be if you put the long-*a* sound in it?"

(continued)

TABLE 5.7   Strategy Prompts for Word Decoding (*Continued*)

Strategy	When Used	Prompt
Monitoring/cross check	Student produces a nonword or a word that doesn't fit. Student uses context to check the use of a phonological strategy or uses phonics to check the use of a contextual strategy.	Context: "Is that a real word? Does that fit the sense of the sentence?" Phonological: "With what letter does the word in the story begin? What sound does that letter make? What sound does your word begin with?" (Check other letters and sounds as needed.)
Writing	Student fails to process all the letters in a word, even though he knows all the correspondences in the word.	Write the word. As you write the letters, say the sounds that the letters stand for.
Choice	Student is unable to decode a word using any strategy. Provide a choice of two words. Have student select the correct one.	"Is the word *wolf* or *dog*? How do you know?"
Affirmation	Praise student for working out a word. Name the strategy used. This lets the student know what strategy she or he used and encourages the student to continue to use strategies.	"I like the way you used the pronounceable word part to help you read that word."
Diagnostic	To see what strategies a student is using, use a diagnostic prompt after the student has decoded a difficult word.	"How did you figure out that word?"

Source: Teacher's guide for word building book B (2nd ed.), by T. Gunning. Honesdale, PA: Phoenix Learning Resources, 2008.

To help students who rush through their oral reading and produce a host of "careless" errors, stress meaning. Have them focus on accurately reading short segments of text. For a while, they might read one sentence at a time. Initial reading should be silent so that they have time to work out difficult words. Encourage students to request help as needed. After their silent reading, have them read the sentences orally. Prompt the use of integrated clues. Students pay more attention to meaning and make fewer errors because they have spent more time carefully reading the segments. Where they request help, they are provided with prompts that lead them to use effective strategies (Buettner, 2002). Gradually, they incorporate these strategies and become meaning-based readers.

Exemplary Teaching
Lightbulb Reading

When Jake reads "shinny penny" for "shiny penny," his teacher, Patty Nagano, waits to see if Jake notices his miscue and corrects it. Jake continues to read. Patty places her hand on the table palm up and then palm down. "Switch it?" Jake asks. Patty nods her head yes. Jake then reads the phrase correctly (Vogt & Nagano, 2003).

Realizing that reading is a struggle for underachieving readers, reading specialist Patty Nagano uses an external motivator dubbed Lightbulb Reading. Wanting to help as many struggling readers as possible, Nagano schedules brief, high-intensity sessions that focus on providing students with highly effective word recognition and comprehension strategies. Strategies are placed on personalized cards. When a student uses one of the strategies, which have been modeled and practiced, he or she is given a certificate showing a lightbulb. The certificate states, "I earned this lightbulb because I am using some of the reading strategies from my card." Other certificates reward improved use of strategies by noting that the student is using many of the strategies or using most of the strategies. The lightbulb on the certificate for using most of the strategies is colored yellow, and the certificate states, "My lightbulb is shining brightly."

Emphasis in the program is on helping students understand key generalizations, such as the construction of short versus long vowels. Because the terms *short, long, open,* and *closed* are somewhat abstract, students are provided with a card that illustrates with words and pictures the short and long vowels. When a student misreads a short vowel for a long vowel or vice versa, Nagano signals the student to switch sounds. The student can refer to the vowel card and note the spelling of the vowel and its sound. Cards for sound switching are also used for *c* and *s*, *g* and *j*, and other commonly confused consonant pairs.

Sometimes, students fail to process all the letters in a word, even though they know all the correspondences in the word. They might glance at beginning and ending letters and guess at what the word might be. To help students process all the word's elements, have the student write the word, saying each sound as he or she writes the letter or letter group that represents that sound. For instance, after reading the word *problem* as *probably*, the student would write and read the word as: *p-r-o-b-l-e-m-* problem (Dorn, 2010).

If a student is reading orally in a group situation, do not allow another student to correct her or him. This robs the student of her or his academic self-concept and also of the opportunity to apply strategies. If a student misreads a word and does not notice the error, do not immediately supply a correction or even stop the reading. Let the student continue to the end of the sentence or paragraph; there is a good chance that she or he will notice the misreading and correct it.

Miscue Correction

Students, especially those who struggle, may experience a loss of confidence and a feeling of helplessness due to the many errors they have made. Through preparation and careful planning, eliminate sources of their errors. For instance, preteach needed skills and words likely to pose problems. However, even with the best of instruction, miscues or errors will occur. Use the prompts in Table 5.7 and the following procedure to provide corrections. The aim is not just to correct the specific error, but to teach or review the underlying skill so that the student can apply it in the future. Note where the error occurred and plan the correction accordingly. Ask yourself, "What is the nature of the miscue? Is it decodable? Does it have a pronounceable word part? Is it like a word the student knows? Does it lend itself to contextual analysis? What prompts can I use to foster a correction?" If, for instance, the student said "cap" for *cape*, you might ask the student, "What is the vowel? What does the *e* on the end of the word tell you about the vowel?"

Note particular difficulties that a student has. Talk over the difficulties and work on those (Wilson, 1999): "I see you have difficulty with words that begin with *wh*. These words are tough. They have strange spellings. But if you read through the word, if you look at all the letters, especially the ending letters, that will help you. I'll give you some practice exercises that I think will help." Leading students to become aware of their difficult areas and providing strategies for overcoming those difficulties gives them a sense of self-efficacy, and, of course, it also makes them better readers (Gunning, 2008).

Decodable Texts

Ardith Cole (1998) noticed that some of her first-graders who had apparently done well in the first half of the grade began to struggle in the second half. In fact, their progress came to a grinding halt. Heidi Mesmer (1999) observed a similar phenomenon. Both discovered a mismatch between their students and the materials they were reading. Their students did well with texts in which most of the words could be predicted by using illustrations as cues or with the help of repeated, highly predictable language. As students encountered more complex text, they floundered. Cole and Mesmer came to a similar conclusion: Choose texts that provide support to students.

Decodable texts are selections that contain only phonics elements that have been taught. Figure 5.7 shows a page from a well-written decodable text. Note that except for the familiar "Once upon a time" and a few high-frequency words, all of the words can be decoded by the application of short-vowel patterns.

No text is totally decodable. High-frequency words such as *is*, *are*, and *the* need to be included, as do content words such as *angry* and *animal* if the story is about an

FYI

Parents have different styles when helping children with their miscues (Mansell, Evans, & Hamilton-Hulak, 2005). Some supply the words; others encourage sounding out. Provide parents with guidance that fits your program. The safest approach is to have parents pause briefly and then supply the word. This prevents struggles between child and parent. ■

REFLECTION

What are the key strategies that students should learn in order to become independent decoders? What steps might you take to help students who are not making much progress in implementing the strategies?

FYI

When words become too difficult, both high achievers and low achievers experience difficulty using strategies (Sharp, Sinatra, & Reynolds, 2008). ■

REFLECTION

Why do you think decodable texts might be somewhat controversial?

FYI

Setting a high arbitrary level of decodability can result in tongue-twisting language. Texts need to be written in such a way that they are decodable but the language is natural. Books listed on pages 212–214 are decodable but have a natural flow. ■

FIGURE 5.7 Decodable Text

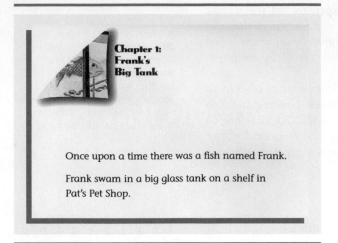

Chapter 1:
Frank's
Big Tank

Once upon a time there was a fish named Frank.

Frank swam in a big glass tank on a shelf in Pat's Pet Shop.

Source: From *Frank the Fish Gets His Wish* by Laura Appleton-Smith, 1998. Lyme, NH: Flyleaf Publishing. Copyright © Laura Appleton-Smith. Reprinted by permission of Laura Appleton-Smith.

Using Technology

Refer to Texas Reading Initiative's *Guidelines for Examining Phonics & Word Recognition Programs* for an excellent explanation of phonics instruction and useful checklist for assessing programs. http://www.tea.state.tx.us/reading/products/products/redbk3.pdf ■

FYI

If beginning readers spend excessive amounts of time reading texts that contain no new words or ideas, they lose an opportunity to develop vocabulary and background. If possible, select texts that foster vocabulary and build background. Richer texts also give students something to talk about and so promote language development. ■

Assessing for Learning

If something isn't working, figure out why and try another approach. Note how Heidi Mesmer (see Case Study) reassessed her instructional program when she saw that Cametera wasn't making adequate progress. She analyzed the program and changed it so that it became effective. ■

angry animal. Two factors have to be considered in order to determine the decodability of a text: the skills the student has learned and the skills demanded by the text.

Some materials emphasize high-frequency words. Most predictable books are composed primarily of high-frequency words. However, as these books become more complex, they become less predictable. If students have not learned basic decoding skills, they will have difficulty coping with them.

Decodable texts are transitional. As students progress in phonics, there is less need for the support of decodable texts. The texts they use can be written in a more natural fashion and include easy children's books such as the *Little Bear* or the *Frog and Toad* series.

As explained in Chapter 1, there are four processors at work when students read: orthographic, phonological, meaning, and context. The processors operate simultaneously. Rich context facilitates the use of phonics. For most students, a word in context is easier to read than a word in a list. In their attempt to provide students with decodable text, authors have sometimes included words that incorporate the phonic element that has been taught but the words are difficult or unusual and the language lacks a natural flow. Because one processor has been over-emphasized and the others neglected, the reading is made more difficult. For instance, in their attempt to include as many decodable words as possible, authors might include unfamiliar words such as *vat* and *drat* while reinforcing the *-at* pattern. Because of the way students process written language, familiar *-at* pattern words are easier to decode than unfamiliar ones.

Because the inclusion of high-frequency words makes for more natural sounding text, because text that is partly predictable is easier to read, and because students should have the opportunity to apply decoding skills, the best texts are those that have a balanced mix of decodable elements, high-frequency words, and predictability. The focus should match students' stage of development. For students in the prealphabetic and early alphabetic stage, highly predictable texts work best. As students move into the alphabetic stage, they need decodable texts that will allow them to apply what they have learned. Over time, an increasing number of high-frequency words should be introduced so that texts have a more natural sound and more complex topics can be covered. Most of the texts contained in the Student Reading List on pages 212–214 in-corporate a balanced blend of decodability and predictability.

Balancing Decodable Texts with Predictable Books

A general principle of teaching phonics is that the books students read should reinforce the words or patterns they have been taught. In general, this means that students should be given decodable rather than predictable books. However, predictable books, with their picture support, are easy to read and so give students a sense of the fun of reading and also build confidence. They are especially important when working with struggling readers who have to work hard to apply their newly learned skills. I realized this when working with short-vowel patterns with a struggling first-grader. After working hard to read a brief, decodable text, she told me that she wasn't a very good reader. After that, I made sure that she spent some of her time with predictable text so that she could see that reading wasn't always a struggle.

Taking a Flexible Approach

As an elementary school reading consultant, I quickly discovered that no method of instruction works for all children. Working with struggling readers, I was having encouraging success with a systematic, structured reading program. Then, unexpectedly, it totally failed with one of the brightest of these struggling readers. He responded to a more holistic approach that included phonics, but that emphasized meaning and context clues. Research by Connor, Morrison, and Katch (2004) confirmed my observations. They found that first-graders who had limited phonics knowledge did better when provided with systematic instruction, but students with solid phonics knowledge did better with a more holistic approach. Juel and Minden-Cupp (2000) reached a similar conclusion. Commenting on the success of the Benchmark School, which was established to instruct struggling readers, Pressley, Gaskins, and Fingeret (2006) stated, "A centerpiece of Benchmark School's instruction is that the teachers are always monitoring whether what they are trying is working, and if it is not, they try something else" (p. 48).

Adapting Instruction for Struggling Readers and Writers

As Pressley (2006) advises, "Excellent primary teachers adjust instruction to the needs of individual children, balancing skills instruction and holistic experiences within their classrooms so that some children receive a greater dose of skills and others are more completely immersed in holistic reading and writing" (p. 12). ■

Teaching Phonics to English Language Learners

In teaching English language learners to read, determine the extent of their literacy in their first language and build on that. Also, be aware of the similarities and differences between the two languages so that you can provide explanations or extra help where it is needed. There are some differences between Spanish and English that require some adjustments in an English phonics program for speakers whose first language is Spanish.

Spanish has a simpler phonology and orthography than English. For one thing it has fewer speech sounds. In addition, there is a near one-to-one correspondence between Spanish sounds and the letters that represent them. However, Spanish has more multisyllabic words than English does.

Adapting Instruction for English Language Learners

Some prompts, such as "Does that sound right?" and "What would make sense here?" would be difficult for ELLs since they have not developed an ear for English (Slavin & Cheung, 2005). ■

Case Study
Adjusting Instruction to Meet the Needs of a Struggling Reader

Despite having been given extra help, second-grader Cametera was in the beginning stages of reading. Based on an analysis of her miscues, Heidi Mesmer, who was instructing her, found that Cametera was making heavy use of context clues but was using phonic clues only 15 percent of the time (Mesmer, 1999). Careful observations revealed that Cametera was making heavy use of picture clues present in the highly predictable books that she was reading. Her miscues made sense but didn't make use of the alphabetic principle. For *pig*, she read *hog*. For *only*, she read *just*. For *plant*, she read *leaf*. Mesmer began teaching Cametera basic phonics skills, including consonant sounds and word patterns. Sorting was a key activity. Provision was also made for including newly introduced elements in Cametera's writing. Mesmer continued to use the predictable books that Cametera had been reading. This turned out to be a mistake. Cametera did well with the phonics activities but did not apply these skills to her reading. Instead of using her newly learned skills to sound out unfamiliar words, Cametera continued to rely too much on picture and other context clues.

Taking a step back, Mesmer analyzed her instruction and her materials. She realized that there was a mismatch between materials and instruction. The books included a variety of patterns, including many that had not yet been introduced. In addition,

there was a lack of continuity. The next book in the series didn't reinforce patterns found in the previous book. Besides not providing sufficient practice with newly learned patterns, the books presented too many new words. Mesmer realized that Cametera needed materials in which patterns were introduced in some sort of controlled fashion. However, she didn't want to use books that were so highly controlled that they made little sense and sounded like tongue twisters. After some searching, Mesmer discovered a series known as the Ready Readers (Modern Curriculum Press) that provided a reasonable balance between controlled introduction of patterns and use of high-frequency words. The books were decodable but not so much so that they sounded unnatural. Texts that are approximately 70 percent decodable would seem to be adequate for helping novice readers learn to apply phonics skills (Beck & Juel, 1995). As a result of careful instruction and matching of materials to instruction, Cametera made encouraging progress. Miscue analysis showed that she made heavier use of phonics skills and also made a greater number of self-corrections. Once Cametera had a firm grasp of basic decoding skills, Mesmer planned to provide her with high-quality children's books. As she explained, "Decodable text is like a set of training wheels on a bicycle; it offers temporary support and is designed to facilitate future independence" (p. 140).

TABLE 5.8 Comparison of English and Spanish Consonants and Their Spellings

Phoneme	English	Spanish
b	b: *ball*	b, v: *bebé, vaca*
d	d: *dog*	d: *dentista*
f	f: *fish*	f: *familia*
g	g: *goat*	g: *gallina*
h	h: *hat*	j: *jardín*
j	j: *jar*	does not occur in Spanish
k	c, k: *cat, key*	c, k, qu: *caimán, kilo, qué*
l	l: *lion*	l: *lobo*
m	m: *man*	m: *mucho*
n	n: *nail*	n: *no*
ñ	like ni in *onion*	ñ: *niña*
p	p: *pen*	p: *papá*
r	r: *ring*	r: *rojo*
rr	does not occur in English	rr: *perro*
s	s: *sun*	s, z: *seis, zapatos*
t	t: *table*	t: *taxi*
v	v: *vest*	in most dialects pronounced as /b/ at beginning of word or after /m or /n/
w	w, qu: *wagon, quiz*	u, hu: *cuarto, huerta*
y	y: *yo-yo*	y, i: *yo, fiambre*
z	z: *zebra*	does not occur in Spanish
ch	ch: *chair*	ch: *chapeo*
sh	sh: *shoe*	does not occur in Spanish
th	th: *thin*	does not occur in some Spanish dialects
th	th: *that*	does not occur in some Spanish dialects
/ŋ/	ng: *ring*	does not occur in Spanish
zh	age: *garage*	does not occur in Spanish

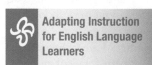

Adapting Instruction for English Language Learners

• In Spanish, the natural word unit is the syllable rather than the onset or the rime (Moustafa & Maldonado-Colon, 1999). When teaching students who can read in Spanish how to read in English, capitalize on their ability to recognize syllables in words by using word building and stressing pronounceable syllables. However, also spend time helping them recognize onsets and rimes.

• Because Spanish has a regular orthography, students learning to read in Spanish can read longer, more complex materials earlier in their reading development (Vaughn et al., 2006). ∎

There are significant differences between consonant sounds in English and Spanish (see Table 5.8). The following consonant sounds are not present in Spanish: /j/, /v/, /sh/, and /ŋ/. In addition, some consonant sounds that are the same in an initial position in English and Spanish do not occur in a final position in Spanish: final /b/ (*cab*), /f/ (*if*), /g/ (*bag*), and /ch/ (*match*). Just as in English, many Spanish words have clusters: There are *l* clusters (*blusa, playa*) and *r* clusters (*frijoles, gratia*) but no *s* clusters in Spanish (*stop, spot*).

Most English reading programs start with short vowels. However, Spanish has no short *a* (*hat*), short *i* (*bit*), short *u* (*cut*), short *oo* (*book*), or schwa (*banana*) vowels (see Table 5.9). Most *r* vowels will also be unfamiliar to Spanish speakers. The sound /r/ has a different pronunciation in Spanish. However, *ar* (*cart, carne*) and *or* (*horn, horno*) have similar pronunciations in Spanish and English. The *r* sounds in *sir, fear, hair,* and *were* will be unfamiliar to Spanish speakers. Both English and Spanish have the /oy/ (*boy, soy*) and /ow/ (*cow*) sounds, but /ow/ is spelled *au* in Spanish (*causa*).

Because of differences in the sound systems of the two languages, Spanish speakers may experience confusion with the following:

final /b/ pronounced as /p/: *cab* becomes *cap*
/j/ pronounced as /y/: *jet* becomes *yet*
/ŋ/ pronounced as /n/: *thing* becomes *thin*
/ch/ pronounced as /sh/: *chin* becomes *shin*
/v/ pronounced as /b/: *vote* becomes *boat*
/y/ pronounced as /j/: *yes* becomes *jes*
s clusters pronounced with an *e*: *speak* becomes *espeak*
/a/ pronounced as /e/: *bat* becomes *bet*

Phoneme	English	Spanish
a	a: *cat*	does not occur in Spanish
e	e: *bed*	e: *es*
i	i: *fish*	does not occur in Spanish
o	o: *mop*	a: *gato*
u	u: *cup*	does not occur in Spanish
ā	a-e, ai, ay: *rake*	ei, ey: *rey, seis*
ē	ee, e, ea, e-e: *wheel*	i, y: *misa, y*
ī	i-e, igh, ie, -y: *nine*	ai, ay: *baile, hay*
ō	o-e, o, ow, oa: *nose*	o: *oso*
ū	u-e, -u: *cube*	yu: *ayuda*
oo	oo, ew, ou, ui: *school*	u: *uno*
oŏ	oo, ou, u: *book*	does not occur in Spanish
aw	aw, au: *saw*	does not occur in Spanish
ow	ow, ou: *cow*	au: *causa*
oy	oi, oy: *boy*	oi, oy: *estoi, soy*
schwa	a, e, i, o, u: *banana*	does not occur in Spanish
ar	ar: *car*	ar: *carpa*
or	or, oor, our: *four*	or: *hora*
air	air, are, ere: *chair*	does not occur in Spanish
eer	ear, eer: *deer*	does not occur in Spanish
ier	ire: *fire*	does not occur in Spanish

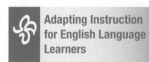

TABLE 5.9 Comparison of English and Spanish Vowels and Their Spellings

/i/ pronounced as /e/: *hit* becomes *heat*
/ē/ pronounced as /i/: *heal* becomes *hill*
/u/ pronounced as /o/: *hut* becomes *hot*
/oŏ/ pronounced as /oo/: *look* becomes *Luke*

When learning English phonics, Spanish-speaking students need exercises that help them to perceive sounds not present in Spanish. When presenting a new phonics element that might be confusing, spend extra time introducing the sound of the element. Have students complete oral exercises such as the following, in which they discriminate between easily confused elements. Students tell which word correctly completes the spoken sentence:

Maria is wearing her new (choose, shoes).
The explorers sailed away on a large (chip, ship).
Little Bo Peep lost her (cheap, sheep).
Which book did you (choose, shoes) to read?
You may not (chew, shoe) gum in class.

You might enlist the help of the ESL or bilingual specialist to help students perceive unfamiliar speech sounds. However, focus on the purpose of phonics instruction. The purpose of instruction in phonics is to provide students with a tool for decoding difficult words. It isn't necessary that they be able to pronounce the words without any trace of an accent. Avoid turning phonics lessons into speech lessons.

Teaching Students Who Are Literate in Spanish

When teaching students who are literate in Spanish to read in English, explain to them that they already know much of the phonics that they will meet in English (Thonis, 1983). You might create a chart showing them skills in Spanish that will transfer to English.

Unfortunately, some of the sounds that are the same in both languages have different spellings. For instance, long *e* is spelled with an *i* in Spanish as in *si*, and long *a* is typically spelled with an *ei* or *ey* as in *rey, seis*. (See Table 5.10 for a listing of divergent

Adapting Instruction for English Language Learners

For more information on teaching Spanish speakers, see: Helman, L. (2004). Building on the sound system of Spanish: Insights from the alphabetic spellings of English-language learners. *The Reading Teacher, 57,* 452–460. ∎

FYI

Long *o* is a good starting point for teaching phonics to Spanish-speaking students because it is spelled the same in both languages. ∎

TABLE 5.10 Phonics Elements with the Same Sounds in Spanish and English but Different Spellings

Phoneme	English	Spanish
ē	e: *me* (i: *spaghetti*)	i: *mi*
o	o: *top* (a: *father*)	a: *gato*
ā	a-e, ai, ay: *rake, rain, ray* (ei, ey: *reign, they*)	ei, ey: *rey, seis*
ī	i-e, igh, ie: *nine, high, tie*	ai, ay: *baile, haya*
ow	ou, ow: *out, owl*	au: *causa*

R E F L E C T I O N

How would you go about planning a phonics program that provides differentiated instruction? What provisions might you make for students whose progress is lagging?

FYI

Monitoring students' progress results in average percentile gains of 34 points (Manzo, 2001)? ■

Adapting Instruction for Struggling Readers and Writers

The student's intervention program included word building, sorting, making words, and reassembling cut-up sentences. He read poems, songs, selections from the lower levels of the classroom basal anthology, and many of the books listed on pages 212–214. Above all, he had a caring, well-prepared tutor. ■

spellings.) In addition, Spanish does not have a final silent *e* that marks vowels as being long. Spanish readers seeing the word *came* might read it as *cahmay*. Such miscues tell you that the student is applying Spanish phonics to English spelling and needs instruction in English phonics. When introducing elements in which there are possible confusions, explain the potentially confusing part.

Phonics Progress Monitoring

Students' progress in phonics should be monitored on a continuing basis to ensure that they are mastering the elements that are being taught. Phonics skills build on each other. Students shouldn't progress to the next level until they have mastered the current level. They need not achieve perfection before moving on, but they should be able to get 80 percent or more of the items correct. If students are struggling, it is essential that they be monitored frequently so that the program can be intensified or changed to produce adequate progress.

The Phonics Inventory, which is presented in the Appendix, can be used to monitor students' progress. It can also be used to determine students' knowledge of single-syllable phonics and to place the students in the appropriate level of instruction. The first ten words of the fifty-word set assess short-vowel patterns; the next ten words assess short-vowel patterns with clusters; the next ten assess long-vowel patterns; the fourth group assesses *r*-vowel patterns; and the last group of ten tests other vowel patterns. Students who get at least eight out of ten of the first ten words but have difficulty with the second group should be instructed in short-vowel patterns that contain clusters.

The Progress Monitoring Chart (Figure 5.8) shows the actual performance of a struggling first-grader on the Phonics Inventory from October through May. The assessment is constructed so that phonics instruction is divided into ten units, with each unit being represented by five words. The goal for first-graders is that they will be able to read forty to forty-five of the fifty words by year's end, meaning that they will have mastered basic single-syllable phonics. It is expected that students will be able to read an additional four or five words each month. Because he was making slow progress in his regular program, the student featured in Figure 5.8, who was in an RTI program, was given Tier II intervention, which provided more intensive instruction and more instructional time, beginning at the end of January. Because he had completed five months of school, his expected performance was between twenty and twenty-five (four to five words a month). However, his score was thirteen. The goal for him was to be able to read forty to forty-five words by the end of the year. By the end of February, even with intervention, he was able to read only two additional test words. But then his progress accelerated. Notice the considerable jump he made from February to March, when he first hit the aimline, and his substantial progress through May. Progress monitoring is a valuable tool for spurring changes in a program when students aren't advancing adequately.

Readability Based on Phonics Elements

As noted in Chapter 3, matching students with an appropriate-level text is absolutely essential. If you are using a program that presents phonics in systematic fashion, it's a good idea to level your books according to the skills needed to read them. In most

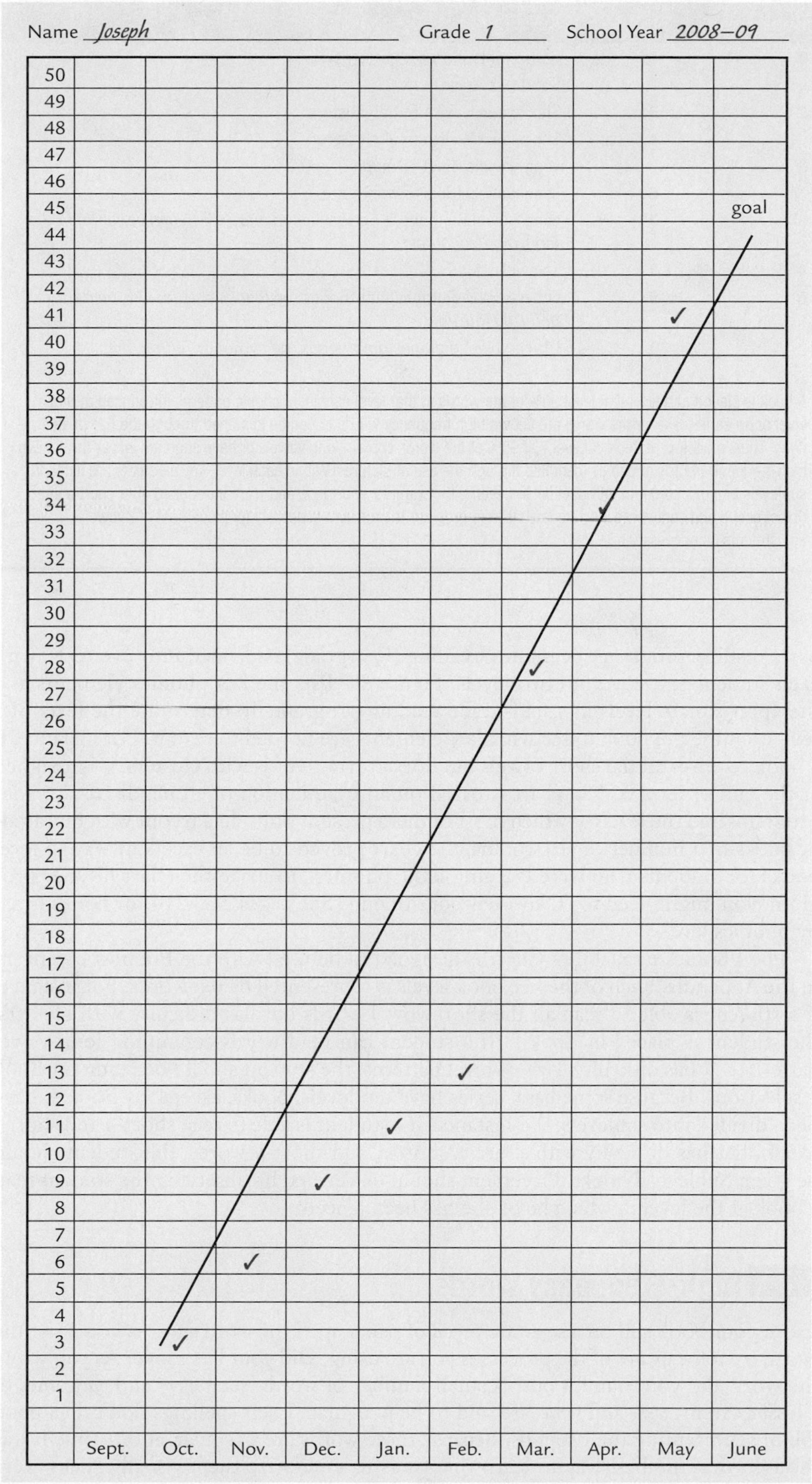

FIGURE 5.8 Progress
Monitoring Chart for Phonics
Inventory

Name _Joseph_ _____   Grade _1_____   School Year _2008–09_ ____

	Sept.	Oct.	Nov.	Dec.	Jan.	Feb.	Mar.	Apr.	May	June
50										
49										
48										
47										
46										
45										goal
44										
43										
42										
41									✓	
40										
39										
38										
37										
36										
35										
34								✓		
33										
32										
31										
30										
29										
28						✓				
27										
26										
25										
24										
23										
22										
21										
20										
19										
18										
17										
16										
15										
14										
13					✓					
12										
11				✓						
10										
9			✓							
8										
7										
6		✓								
5										
4										
3	✓									
2										
1										

FIGURE 5.9　Phonics Readability Chart for First-Grade Reading Programs

Book Level	Sublevel	Key Elements
1	1	ConsonantsShort *a, i* patterns
	2	Short *o, e, u* patterns
2	3	Short vowels with initial clusters
	4	Short vowels with final clusters
3	5	Long vowels (final -*e* marker): *a & i*
	6	Long vowels (final-*e marker*): *o, e, u*
	7	Long-vowel digraphs & open syllable: *ai/ay, e/ee/ea/ei, ie/igh/ind/ild/y (cry), o/oa/ow/oll/old*
4	8	*r*-vowels
5	9	Other-vowel digraphs/diphthongs: *oo (book), ould (could), oo (too)/ew/ ue/ui, ou (out)/ow*
	10	Other-vowel digraphs/diphthongs: *oi/ oy, au/ aw/all/alk/ong*

A book is placed at a level if at least 90% of the words at that level consist of phonic patterns introduced at that level or an earlier level or the words are known high frequency words or can be identified through the use of illustrations. Thus, a book is at Book 3, Level 7, if 90% of the words contain long vowels or have short vowels or are known high-frequency words or can be identified through the use of pictures. Within each level, key elements are listed in sublevels in typical order of introduction. In Level 1, for example, short *o, e,* and *u* are introduced after short *a* and *i*. (Exact scope and sequences vary somewhat from program to program, especially for placement of *r* vowels. Make adjustments as necessary.)

FYI

• A number of phonics tests use nonsense words to assess decoding. The rationale is that students wouldn't have seen these items before and wouldn't be responding to them as words that they had memorized. However, decoding involves using four processors: orthographic (letter), phonological (sound), meaning, and context. When students decode a word, there is a feedback step in which they note whether the item they have decoded is a real word. If the item being decoded is a nonword, then the semantic process cannot be brought into play. Because of this missing feedback step, decoding nonsense words is apparently more difficult than decoding real words (Cunningham, Yoder, & McKenna, 1999). As Invernizzi and Hayes (2004) note, a student's performance on a nonsense word task doesn't give teachers clear guidance in terms of what elements the student has mastered and what elements need to be taught or reviewed. ◼

basal reading programs, beginning reading (first grade) is divided into five texts, with each student text covering two levels. Figure 5.9 lists the key phonics elements and the approximate levels in a first-grade reading program. To determine the level of a text, examine the book to see what key elements are needed to read it. For instance, if a book requires all the short vowels but doesn't have words with clusters, it is assigned at the end of level 2. The chart is based on an examination of all major basal reader programs and the levels at which most of them present skills. In a tryout with hundreds of books in a number of classrooms, the chart proved to be an excellent way to level books for students who were learning basic phonics. To make the chart fit your program, you might need to make a few adjustments. See pages 212–214 for books listed by phonics level.

The Phonics Readability Chart is designed to be used with the Phonics Inventory in the Appendix. Each of the five book levels is represented by ten words. For instance, if a student is able to read all the short-vowel words but has difficulty with clusters, the student is placed in Book 2. If a student can read words containing long-vowel patterns but has difficulty with *r*-vowel patterns, the student should be ready for Book 4 selections. Because some basal series have ten levels, books, except for Book 4, have been divided into sublevels. For instance, if a student is able to read short-*a* and short-*i* words, but has difficulty with short-*o*, short-*e*, and short-*u* words, the student should be given Sublevel 2 books. Placement should be verified by observing the student read a book at the level in which he or she has been placed.

High-Frequency Words

Close your book and on a separate piece of paper spell the word *once*. As you write the word, try to be aware of the processes you are using. Did your lips move? As you wrote the word, did you sound it out? A small number of words, such as *of* and *once*, and, to a lesser extent, *were* and *some*, are said to be irregular. Their spellings don't do a good job of representing their sounds. Because these words are irregular, at one time it was thought that the best way to learn them was to memorize them visually. They were put on cards and studied. Because it is believed that they were memorized visually,

TABLE 5.11   High-Frequency Words

1. the	30. had	59. would	88. find	117. same	146. different	175. am
2. of	31. but	60. other	89. use	118. right	147. number	176. us
3. and	32. what	61. into	90. water	119. look	148. away	177. left
4. a	33. all	62. has	91. little	120. think	149. again	178. end
5. to	34. were	63. more	92. long	121. also	150. off	179. along
6. in	35. when	64. two	93. very	122. around	151. went	180. while
7. is	36. we	65. her	94. after	123. another	152. tell	181. sound
8. you	37. there	66. like	95. word	124. came	153. men	182. house
9. that	38. can	67. him	96. called	125. three	154. say	183. might
10. it	39. an	68. time	97. just	126. high	155. small	184. next
11. he	40. your	69. see	98. new	127. come	156. every	185. below
12. for	41. which	70. no	99. where	128. work	157. found	186. saw
13. was	42. their	71. could	100. most	129. must	158. still	187. something
14. on	43. said	72. make	101. know	130. part	159. big	188. thought
15. are	44. if	73. than	102. get	131. because	160. between	189. both
16. as	45. will	74. first	103. through	132. does	161. name	190. few
17. with	46. do	75. been	104. back	133. even	162. should	191. those
18. his	47. each	76. its	105. much	134. place	163. home	192. school
19. they	48. about	77. who	106. good	135. old	164. give	193. show
20. at	49. how	78. now	107. before	136. well	165. air	194. always
21. be	50. up	79. people	108. go	137. such	166. line	195. until
22. this	51. out	80. my	109. man	138. here	167. mother	196. large
23. from	52. then	81. made	110. our	139. take	168. set	197. often
24. I	53. them	82. over	111. want	140. why	169. world	198. together
25. have	54. she	83. did	112. sat	141. things	170. own	199. ask
26. not	55. many	84. down	113. me	142. great	171. under	200. write
27. or	56. some	85. way	114. day	143. help	172. last	
28. by	57. so	86. only	115. too	144. put	173. read	
29. one	58. these	87. may	116. any	145. years	174. never	

Adapted from *The Educator's Word Frequency Guide* by S. M. Zeno, S. H. Ivens, R. T. Millard, & R. Duvvuri, 1995. Brewster, NY: Touchstone Applied Science Associates.

they became known as **sight words**. However, more recent research indicates that even irregular words are learned phonologically. That's why when you wrote the word *once*, chances are you said the word, at least subvocally, and then said the sounds of the word as you spelled each sound. There is also an element of visual memory involved. Otherwise, you may have spelled *once* as *wuns*.

A list of **high-frequency words** is presented in Table 5.11. Note that these are all common words. Ironically, the words that appear most frequently tend to have the most irregular spellings, mainly because they are some of the oldest words in the language. Over the years, English evolved so that, in many instances, spellings no longer do a very good job of representing pronunciations.

Table 5.11 gives 200 high-frequency words in order of their frequency of appearance. The list is drawn from a compilation of words that appear in books and other materials read by school children (Zeno, Ivens, Millard, & Duvvuri, 1995). These 200 words make up about 60 percent of the words in continuous text. For example, the most frequently occurring word, *the*, comprises about 2 percent of text.

Many students pick up a number of high-frequency words through reading signs and other print to which they are exposed in class

 FYI

- Introducing high-frequency words makes it possible to provide students with more natural-sounding text.
- Knowing how to spell and/or sound out a word partially or fully helps students learn and remember new words (Ehri, 1991), but time spent discussing known definitions may be wasted (Kibby, 1989). However, hearing and seeing function words such as *the* and *are* are helpful. ■

■ A **sight word** is one that is recognized immediately. Many sight words occur with high frequency, and some are learned through visual memorization. However, the vast majority of words are learned through phonics.

■ **High-frequency words** are words such as *the*, *of*, and *them* that appear in printed material with a high rate of occurrence.

and through shared reading of big books and other materials. However, direct teaching is also necessary. When teaching high-frequency words, limit the number being taught to three or four. Choose words that students will soon be meeting in print. If they are about to read Dr. Seuss's *The Cat in the Hat Comes Back* (Geisel, 1961), you might present *this*, *off*, *done*, and *know*, irregular words that figure prominently in the story. Select words that are different in appearance. Presenting *put* and *but* or *where*, *when*, and *were* together is inviting confusion, as students are almost sure to mix them up.

When teaching high-frequency words, take full advantage of phonic regularities, such as initial and final consonant correspondences. "Contrary to past beliefs, sight-word learning does not depend on rote association. Children learn sight words in just a few quality encounters. Quality encounters connect letters in a spelling to phonemes in the pronunciation, usually by sounding out and blending. In other words, we typically learn sight words through careful decoding. Though decoding demands great attention in young readers, it sets up reliable access routes to retrieve the word" (Murray, 2006c).

Also, seek out commonalities of words. For instance, when teaching *at* as a high-frequency word, also teach *that* and show how the two are related; have students note that *that* contains the pronounceable word part *at*. When presenting *all*, relate it to *ball*, *call*, *small*, and *almost*. Other patterns include the following:

Long-*e* words: *he, me, she, we, see*

ou/ow words: *how, now, down, out*

or words: *or, for*

er words: *after, over, other*

Long *oo* words: *do, to, two, too*

ere words: *there, where*

Odd vowels: *what, want, from, come, have, pull, put*

Note that for the words with the odd-vowels pattern, only the vowel spellings are irregular. The rest of each word is highly decodable (Gunning, 2008).

Except for dramatically irregular words like *of* and *one*, help students match up spellings and sounds. For *were*, help students see that *w* represents /w/ and *ere* represents /er/ as in *her*. For the word *some*, match *s* with /s/, note that *o* is a very unusual way of spelling /u/, and match *m* with /m/. Encourage students to spell out the words and provide opportunities for them to meet the words in many contexts so that they form visual images of the words in addition to making phonological connections. As students are learning exception words such as *know* or *sure*, they also need to be taught specific distinguishing features of these words.

Because high-frequency words are such a prominent part of just about everything that students read, it is important that they learn to recognize them rapidly. The idea behind rapid recognition of words is that the human mind has only so much mental-processing ability and time. If students get caught up trying to sound out words, they lose the memory of what they are attempting to read. They need *automaticity*, the ability to process words effortlessly and automatically (Laberge & Samuels, 1974). Students who are able to recognize words rapidly have ample attention and mental energy left to comprehend what they are reading. Ultimately, because of lots of practice, most of the words that skilled readers meet in print, although learned through phonics, are processed as rapid-recognition words. Only when skilled readers meet strange names or unfamiliar words do they resort to decoding.

CCSS

Recognize and read grade-appropriate irregularly spelled words.

Teaching High-Frequency Words

When presenting high-frequency words, emphasize activities that reflect this purpose. Use phonics to help students accurately decode words—accuracy must come first. As

Samuels (1994) notes, accuracy precedes automaticity, or rapid recognition. Use of knowledge of patterns and correspondences facilitates accurate recognition. Once accuracy has been achieved, stress rapid recognition.

As you gradually introduce added phonics skills, include high-frequency words as part of your instruction. For instance, when teaching the consonant cluster *bl*, use the high-frequency words *black* and *blue* as examples. When students are studying short *a*, present the high-frequency words *am*, *an*, and *at*. Being able to relate the printed versions of these words with their sounds gives students another way to process them, which aids memory and speed of processing. Use the steps listed in Lesson 5.6 as a framework for presenting high-frequency words.

CCSS

- When teaching high-frequency words, point out both regularities and irregularities. As Pikulski (2006) explains, "While the word *have* does not follow the generalization about the effect of a final *e* on a preceding vowel sound, the *h*, *v*, and *e* all behave as they should, and the *a* does represent a sound that it often represents." Point out the regular elements of irregular words to help children use these as clues to learning the words.

- Two factors are involved in rapid recognition of words: accuracy and automaticity (Samuels, 1994). To reach an effective level of accuracy, students must process virtually every letter. Students need varying amounts of time to reach a high level of accuracy. However, after achieving accuracy, they seem to gain automaticity at similar rates (Samuels, 1994). Children who seem to take longer to become fluent readers may not have achieved accuracy.

LESSON 5.6
High-Frequency Words

Objectives

- Students will read high-frequency words.
- Students will use known word parts to help them read high-frequency words.

Step 1. Develop understanding of the words

This step is only necessary if students do not have an adequate understanding of the words being presented. Since high-frequency words are among the most common in the language, they will be in the listening vocabularies of the majority of students. However, some high-frequency words may be unknown to English language learners.

Step 2. Present printed words in isolation

Explain to students that they will be learning some small but very important words. Write each word to be learned on the chalkboard, or present each one on a large card. Although students may not be able to read the words, they may know parts of them. Build on any part they know. This will make the task of learning the word easier, as students will be faced with learning only a portion of the word rather than the whole word; it also helps them connect new knowledge with old knowledge. If students know only initial consonant correspondences, build on that knowledge: Emphasize the *y* = /y/ in *you* and the *f* = /f/ in *for*. If they know initial and final consonants, talk about the *c* = /k/ and *n* = /n/ in *can*. If they know word patterns, make use of those: Help them use their knowledge of *-an* to read *man* and their knowledge of *-op* to read *stop*. Present these elements as ways of perceiving and remembering sight words, but do not turn the sight-word lesson into a phonics lesson. For words that are highly irregular, such as *of*, *one*, and *once*, stress the spellings. But note that the *n* in *one* represents /n/ and *nce* in *once* represents /ns/.

After all the words have been introduced, have students read them chorally and individually. Distribute cards containing the words so that each student has a set. The reverse side of each card might contain the word used in a sentence.

Step 3. Present printed words in context

On the board, interactive white board, story paper, document camera, or overhead transparency, present the high-frequency words in context. Underline the target words so that they stand out. Take care to use each word in the same sense in which students will most likely see it. For instance, if the high-frequency word *water* is going to be a verb in an upcoming story, show it as a verb. In composing sample sentences, except for the target high-frequency words, use words already taught so that students can concentrate their efforts on the new ones. Actually, using high-frequency words that have already been taught is a good way to review them. Read the sentences to the students, and then have them read in unison as you sweep your hand under the words. Later, individual volunteers can read the sentences.

FYI

There is some disagreement about how expert readers recognize words. Ehri (1994) theorizes that they are recognized holistically because each word's letters and pronunciation have become bonded through repeated encounters, thus providing an access route that leads instantaneously from the word's graphic representation to the word's pronunciation. Gough and Hillinger (1980) believe that readers process words phonologically, but the processing is so rapid that recognition appears to be instantaneous. ■

Using Technology

E-books that highlight and speak the words that are being read are a good way to build up students' rapid recognition of high-frequency words, especially if the student reads the story several times. It is crucial that students read along as the words are being highlighted. To test themselves, students might turn down the sound and see if they can read the words as they are being highlighted. ■

Step 4. Practice

Provide ample practice for high-frequency words. Practice could be in the form of maze worksheets on which students choose from three words the one that correctly completes the sentence:

            take
   I am new years old.
            five

Practice might also use a brief story, a game, or a piece of computer software such as *Richard Scarry's Busytown* (Paramount Interactive), or an app from the Learning to Read collection at Apple's App Store or from Android sight word listings at Appolicious, or another source. Select programs that have carefully chosen words to be presented, which provide experience seeing the words in context, or involve building the words.

Step 5. Apply

Have students create experience stories or read easy stories that contain target high-frequency words. Experience stories naturally contain a high proportion of sight words. Easy books also provide an opportunity for students to meet sight words in context. In one study, students who read easy books learned more sight words than those who used a basal series (Bridge, Winograd, & Haley, 1983). They also expressed more positive feelings about reading, and, because their books were written about a variety of topics, they had an opportunity to learn more about their world.

Step 6. Evaluate and review

Observe students as they read to see how well they do when they encounter high-frequency words. Provide added instruction and practice as needed.

Using Children's Books to Build a High-Frequency Vocabulary

Several types of children's books, including predictable books, caption books, and label books, can be used to build high-frequency vocabulary. Predictable books are those that follow a set pattern, making it easy for the child to predict what the sentences are going to say. Caption books feature a single sentence per page that describes or relates to the illustration in much the same way that a caption relates to a photo. Label books, as their name suggests, depict a number of objects, actions, or people and provide printed labels for them. All of these kinds of books may be read over and over again.

There are literally thousands of children's books that can be used to foster instant recognition of words. However, it is important that the books be on the right level. Students should know most of the words, so that their focus is on moving just-introduced or barely known words to the category of words that are well known and rapidly recognized. Although it is helpful for students to build fluency by rereading the same book or story, it is also important that they read many different books to see the same words in a variety of contexts. Series of books designed to reinforce high-frequency words include:

Reading Corners.   San Diego, CA: Dominie Press. This series reinforces a number of basic patterns: I like _____; I have _____; I do _____. Consisting of just eight to twelve pages of text, these books are very easy to read.

Read More Books.   San Diego, CA: Dominie Press. This series presents a number of basic sentence patterns. The text is brief and explicitly illustrated with color photos and so is very easy to read.

Seedlings.   Elizabethtown, PA: Continental Press. This series includes texts at levels from beginning reading to second grade.

Wilbooks.   This series has an extensive collection of inexpensive books in English and Spanish, many of which reinforce high-frequency words.

Adapting Instruction for Struggling Readers and Writers

Poor readers may require extra practice to learn high-frequency words. Good readers apparently learn four times as many new words as poor readers (Adams & Higgins, 1985). ■

FYI

Benchmark, Lerner, Rigby, Scholastic, Sundance, and other publishers make available extensive collections of books that provide practice with high-frequency words. Increasingly, texts are being placed on hand-held or computer e-readers that contain text-to-speech capability so that unfamiliar words can be pronounced. ■

Using Word Banks

A *word bank* is a collection of known words and consists primarily of high-frequency words. As students learn new words, these are added to their word banks. Students might also include words that they are working on or want to learn. A good source of words would be the high-frequency words in the books

they are reading. For example, after reading *Cat on the Mat* (Wildsmith, 1982), students might add *cat*, *on*, *the*, and *sat* to their word banks. Word banks should be limited to about a hundred words. Beyond that limit, the bank becomes too extensive to handle, and students' decoding skills should have developed to a point where word banks have lost their usefulness (Graves, Juel, & Graves, 2001).

So that the words in the banks are recognized automatically, students might work with them for brief periods each day. Working in pairs, students can quiz each other on words from their word banks. Using word-bank cards, they might make a list of things they can do. They can sort words by placing color words in one pile, action words in another, and animal words in a third. They can search out opposites or write stories about individual words. For concrete nouns or some action words, students might draw an illustration of the word on the reverse side of the paper or card. They might then quiz themselves by attempting to read the word, turning the card or paper over to see if they got it right. Creating sentences with words from their banks is another possible activity.

Using items from word banks is also one way of introducing or reinforcing phonics elements. After learning *see*, *so*, and *say*, students might be taught that *s* represents /s/. After learning *cat*, *hat*, and *sat*, they might be introduced to the -*at* pattern.

After students have accumulated a number of words in their word banks, they can keep them in alphabetical order by first letter. This will reinforce the use of the alphabet and also help them locate words. In time, the word bank becomes a kind of dictionary as well as a source of motivation: Word banks that are growing signal to the children that they are learning.

Building Fluency

In the beginning stages of learning to read, students may read in slow, halting fashion. This is understandable since students are still learning the code. However, if it persists, comprehension will suffer. Students will expend so much effort decoding that they won't be able to devote mental energy to understanding what they read. Students need to become fluent as well as accurate readers. As Rasinski and Hamman (2010) explain, "Reading fluency is the essential link from word recognition to comprehension" (p. 26). Although often equated with rate of reading or smoothness of oral reading, **fluency** has been defined as "freedom from word identification problems that might hinder comprehension in silent reading or the expression of ideas in oral reading" (Harris & Hodges, 1995, p. 85).

 Adapting Instruction for Struggling Readers and Writers

Word analysis skills are interdependent. For instance, sight words are easier to learn if students know basic phonics. Analogies can only be used on a limited basis if there are few comparison words in the student's store of known words. Therefore, struggling readers often have difficulty in several areas of word analysis and so need broadbased instruction (Ehri & McCormick, 1998). ■

Adapting Instruction for English Language Learners

Drawing illustrations for new words can be especially helpful to ELLs. ■

 FYI

Parents or grandparents can provide struggling readers and writers with the additional practice they need. One grandfather, following the advice of his grandson's teacher, taught his grandson 100 high-frequency words. Although the child was still far behind, the grandfather stopped helping his grandson because he didn't know what else he could do. A little time spent showing the grandfather what he might do would have had an invaluable payoff. ■

■ **Fluency** is freedom from word identification problems that might hinder comprehension in silent reading or the expression of ideas in oral reading. Fluency has levels of complexity. *Surface fluency* refers to rate of reading and reading with expression. *Deep fluency* means that the reader controls rate of reading and reading with expression to maximize comprehension (Topping, 2006). "The critical test of fluency is the ability to decode a text and understand it simultaneously" (Samuels, 2006, p. 41).

■ **Accuracy** means being able to pronounce or sound out a word and also knowing the word's meaning.

■ **Automaticity** refers to tasks that can be performed without attention or conscious effort.

CCSS

Read with sufficient accuracy and fluency to support comprehension. Read grade-level text orally with accuracy, appropriate rate, and expression.

Fluency has two components: **accuracy** and **automaticity**. Students are accurate readers if they can recognize the words. They have automaticity if they recognize the words rapidly. Students can be accurate but slow decoders. As Samuels (2006) explains, fluency is based on automaticity, which is

> . . . the ability to perform two difficult tasks at the same time as the result of extended practice, whereas prior to practice only one task could be performed at a time. If two complex tasks can be performed simultaneously, then at least one of them is automatic. For example, at the beginning stage of reading, only one skill could be done at a time; first decoding, followed by comprehension. However, at the skilled stage, both decoding and comprehension can be performed together. Thus, the critical test of fluency is the ability to decode a text and understand it simultaneously. (pp. 39–41)

Note Samuels' inclusion of understanding in his explanation of fluency. Because DIBELS and other widely used assessments measure rate of reading, reading speed has been overemphasized to the detriment of comprehension. As Rasinski and Hamman (2010) explain, "Reading instruction must be focused on the making of meaning. . . . The importance of speed should be minimized in the fluency debate. Reading requires a level of active awareness and thought about language which diminishes when reading speed is emphasized. Reading at an appropriate rate in meaningful phrases, with prosody and comprehension, should be the fluency goal for all readers" (p. 26).

One way of judging fluency is by noting students' rate of silent reading and their comprehension. If they can read at a reasonable pace, then they probably are able to recognize the words rapidly. If they can answer questions about what they read, their word recognition is probably accurate. Another way of assessing fluency is by having students read a selection orally. If they misread a number of words, this indicates that accuracy is a problem. It also may be an indication that the material is beyond their instructional level. If they read word by word and seem to need to sound out an excessive number of words, then automaticity is an issue.

Comprehension is also an element in fluency. Students' phrasing and expressiveness should be noted. Does their reading indicate an understanding of what they are reading? Understanding what one reads is important for proper expression. Of course, it is essential that students be given material that is on the appropriate level. Given material that is too difficult, even the best readers become dysfluent.

Accuracy and speed of reading have to be balanced. An overemphasis on accuracy will lead to a decrease in reading speed. Do not insist on 100 percent accuracy (Samuels, 1994). An overemphasis on oral reading will decrease reading speed. Students will also get the wrong idea about reading. They will begin to see reading as an oral performance activity in which they are expected to pronounce each word correctly. This could carry over into students' silent reading and so hinder comprehension. When students read orally, their purpose should be to convey the meaning of the passage rather than to render accurate pronunciation of each word.

The foundation for fluency is to build solid word analysis skills (Wolf & Katzir-Cohen, 2001) and to monitor for meaning. Beginning readers need to check themselves as they read by asking: "Do the words that I am reading match the letters? Do the words make sense?" Older readers also need to have well-developed decoding skills. While assessing the fluency of two classes of third-graders, I noticed that slowness in decoding multisyllabic words hampered the reading speed of about one student in ten. Stumbling over multisyllabic words or taking time to put a word into syllables slowed the students' reading and interfered with comprehension. The best way to boost the fluency of these students would have been to provide instruction in decoding multisyllabic words and also lots of practice and opportunities to read texts containing multisyllabic words so that their skills would have become more automatic.

In addition to prompting students to monitor for meaning, activities that foster rapid recognition of high-frequency words will foster fluency, as will wide reading of books at the students' independent level. This reading need not be oral. In fact, silent reading provides more realistic practice. At all levels, silent reading is recommended

Adapting Instruction for Struggling Readers and Writers

If students focus on one word at a time, move a note card over the text to keep them moving (Clay, 1993). ■

Adapting Instruction for English Language Learners

Reading along with a recorded version of a story is especially helpful for students whose reading speed is extremely slow and for students who are still learning English (Blum et al., 1995; Dowhower, 1987). ■

FYI

- Except when working with very beginning readers, the initial reading of a selection should almost always be silent. While discussing a selection read silently, students might read a favorite part orally, dramatize dialogue, or read a passage out loud to provide support for a point they are making.
- Students with faster decoding speeds are more likely to read with expression (Schwanenflugel, Hamilton, Kuhn, Wisenbaker, & Stahl, 2004). Readers who are still slow at decoding read with many pauses that make their reading seem hesitant and expressionless. One theory is that decoding requires so much mental energy that there is none left to devote to reading with expression. ■

for building fluency. As they read books in which nearly all the words are known, students' ability to recognize the words faster should increase. Like any other complex behavior, reading requires substantial practice before it becomes automatic and seemingly effortless. If students persist in reading in a labored, halting fashion, the material is probably too difficult. Try material that is easy, and gradually move up to more difficult selections. Students, especially if they are younger, might also be encouraged to read the same selections a second, a third, or even a fourth time.

The ability to read orally with expression is, in part, a public speaking skill. Its goal is to convey meaning to others rather than to construct meaning. Oral reading should be preceded by silent reading. Readers need to construct a good understanding of the text so that they can then read it orally in such a way as to convey their interpretation. If you wish to promote oral reading skills, use drama and poetry to provide practice. Students don't mind reading a script over and over again if they are going to dramatize it. Students are also motivated to read accurately and expressively if they are reading to others. Having older children read to young children—first-graders reading to kindergartners, fourth-graders reading to second-graders—provides students with a reason to read a selection over and over again.

Choral Reading

Choral reading of selections also fosters fluency (McMaster, 1998). Choral reading involves two or more people but can take many forms. In unison reading, the whole group reads together. In refrain reading, the leader reads most of the text and the group reads the refrain. In antiphonal reading, two or more groups alternate. The boys may read one portion, the girls another. Or one side of the room might read a portion, and the other side reads the other portion. Or one child or group reads a couplet or line, and another reads the next line or couplet (Bromley, 1998). One group might read designated lines in a loud voice; a second group, in a soft voice. Variations are endless.

Choral reading can be a whole-class or small-group activity. Choral reading is an excellent way to foster fluency and expression in reading. In a choral reading lesson, you might emphasize any of a number of oral reading skills: reading with expression, interpreting punctuation, phrasing of words, varying speed of reading. Poems, speeches, and tales with repeated parts lend themselves to choral reading. Choral reading lends itself to repeated reading as the class rereads in order to improve timing or expression or smoothness. It is a nonthreatening way for English language learners and struggling readers to practice their skills.

Because oral reading is used to measure fluency, there is a tendency to overemphasize oral reading as a way of fostering fluency. However, silent reading and oral reading are different tasks. Oral reading focuses the reader's attention on pronouncing words correctly. Silent reading stresses constructing meaning, which is the essence of reading. Silent reading also provides students the opportunity to work out troublesome words on their own without feeling rushed or embarrassed because people are listening to them struggle.

Silent reading is faster and more efficient. Readers can skip unnecessary words or sections. Beyond second grade, silent reading speed should exceed oral reading speed (see Table 5.12). If students are reading at a very slow pace, try to determine why and take corrective action. If the material is too difficult—if they miss more than five words out of one hundred—obtain materials on the appropriate level. If they are having difficulty decoding words, work on decoding skills. If they have mastered decoding skills but are reading in a slow or labored fashion, work on fluency. They may also be very anxious readers who feel they have to read each word carefully.

Modeled Techniques for Building Fluency

A first step in building fluency is to model the process. As you read orally, you are modeling the process of smooth, expressive reading. As you read orally to students, explain the techniques that you use: how you read in phrases, how you use your voice to express the author's meaning, how you read at a pace that listeners can keep up with but that isn't too fast.

FYI

• When students are asked to read orally, they should have a chance to read silently first and should be asked to read in such a way as to convey what the author meant. Students will then have to think about and emphasize the meaning of what they read. Model the process frequently.

• Unrehearsed oral reading in which students take turns reading (round robin) can be painful for struggling readers, who are embarrassed by their mistakes, and for good readers, who are bored by slow, choppy reading. ■

Using Technology

Lerner Digital

Digital books such as those published by Lerner, which read individual words or running text and have one speed for slow reading and another for fluent reading, can be used to foster fluency.
http://www.lernerbooks.com ■

FYI

Less fluent readers comprehend less. In a study of oral fluency among fourth-graders, the more fluent readers had better comprehension (Pinnell et al., 1995; Daane, Campbell, Grigg, Goodman, & Oranje, 2005). ■

Adapting Instruction for Struggling Readers and Writers

Some struggling readers may process written language differently than achieving readers do (Shaywitz, 2003). Because of a disruption in the visual word form area, which fosters rapid recognition of words, these students compensate by using frontal portions of the brain to pronounce letter sounds. Their reading is likely to be more labored as they use phonological processes to compensate for a weakness in visual processes. These students need intensive phonics and many opportunities to practice. ■

TABLE 5.12 End-of-Year Reading Rate in Words per Minute

Instructional Reading Level	Oral reading	Silent reading
Grade 1	55	55
Grade 2	85	85
Grade 3	115	130
Grade 4	135	155
Grade 5	145	185
Grade 6	150	205
Grades 7–8	150	225

Adapted from Powell (1980), cited in Lipson and Wixson (1997) and Harris and Sipay (1990).

Using Technology

The following sites have numerous songs that can be used for choral reading and singing:
NIEHS Sing-Along Songs Index!
http://www.niehs.nih.gov/kids/music.htm#index

Songs for Teaching
http://www.songsforteaching.com/Reading.html ■

FYI

• Pausing for 4 seconds before supplying a word that a student is having difficulty with gives the student the chance to self-correct. Tutors have a tendency to provide a correction too quickly (Topping, 2006).
• For beginning, middle, and end-of-year oral reading norms at various levels, see Hasbrouck, J., & Tindal, G. A. (2006). Oral reading fluency norms: A valuable assessment tool for reading teachers. *The Reading Teacher, 59*, 636–644. ■

Using Technology

TRW Resources provides a wealth of resources for paired reading.
http://www.dundee.ac.uk/fedsoc/research/projects/trwresources/reading ■

Reading along with a recorded version of a selection can build oral fluency. Paired reading, which is also known as Duolog Reading (Topping, 1998), can be effective in building oral fluency. For example, the teacher, a parent, or a child who is a more proficient reader teams up with a student. The less proficient student chooses the book to be read. The book selected is one that would be a little too difficult for the student to read on her or his own. After a brief discussion of the title and cover illustration, the helper and student simultaneously read the book out loud. During this dual reading, the helper adjusts her or his reading rate so that it matches that of the student. When the student feels that she or he can read a portion of the text on her or his own again, the student signals the helper by raising her or his left hand. When the student wants the helper to resume reading with her or him, the student raises her or his right hand. The helper automatically provides assistance when the student stumbles over a word or is unable to read the word within 4 seconds (Topping, 1987, 1989). As an alternative to paired reading, the teacher, parent, or tutor may take turns reading the selection. At first, the teacher might do most of the reading. The student would read any words she or he could. As the student becomes more proficient, she or he can read larger segments. All of these techniques provide a model of phrasing and expression that students might then incorporate into their silent reading.

Repeated Reading

A popular technique for fostering fluency is repeated reading (Samuels, 1979). Repeated reading helps students achieve accuracy and rapid recognition of high-frequency words. In one study, slow-reading second-graders doubled their reading speed after just seven weeks of repeated reading training (Dowhower, 1987). In another study, students enjoyed the fluency exercises so much that after the experiments were concluded, they asked for additional repeated reading sessions (Rashotte & Torgesen, 1985).

Rereadings are effective because students meet high-frequency words over and over, and these become part of their automatic recognition vocabulary (Dowhower, 1987). However, this means that the chosen selections should be on the same approximate level and should be on the students' instructional level. Lesson 5.7 lists suggested steps for a repeated reading lesson.

Variations on Repeated Reading Instead of working with a teacher, students may work in pairs. However, explain and model the procedure first. One student reads while the other charts his or her progress. Then they switch roles. Show students how to time the reading and count errors. To make the charting easier, have students check 100-word samples only. Students might read a selection that contains more than 100 words but only 100 words are used for charting reading rate. Students may hurry through a selection to obtain a fast time. Explain to students that they should read at a normal rate. On occasion, have students read a song or a poem instead of the usual reading selections. Because of their rhythm, narrative poems and songs lend themselves to a rapid reading.

LESSON 5.7
Repeated Reading

Objective

- Students will read with increased speed and fluency.

Step 1. Introducing repeated reading

Explain the reasons behind repeated reading. Discuss how we get better when we practice. Explain to students that they will be practicing by reading the same story over and over. Tell students that this will help them read faster and better.

Step 2. Selecting a passage

Select or have the students choose a short, interesting selection of approximately 100 words. They or you might choose books, such as *The Cat in the Hat* (Geisel, 1957) or *Are You My Mother?* (Eastman, 1960), that are rhythmic and fun to read. Make sure that books are on the students' instructional level.

Step 3. Obtaining an initial timing

Obtain a baseline reading and accuracy rate. Have students read a selection orally. Time the reading, and record the number of words read correctly. If students take more than 2 minutes to read the selection and make more than five errors out of 100 words (not counting missed endings), the selection is too difficult. If students make only one or two errors and read the selection at 85 words per minute or faster, the selection is too easy. If students can read 100 words a minute or close to it, repeated reading is probably a waste of instructional time (Dowhower, 1987). They would be better off with self-selected reading.

Step 4. Rereading

Go over the students' miscues with them. Help them read these words correctly. Also help them with phrasing problems or any other difficulties they may have had. Then direct them to reread the selection until they feel they can read it faster and more smoothly. Practice can take one of three forms: (1) reading the selection to oneself; (2) listening to an audiotape or viewing the selection on a CD-ROM while reading the selection silently, and then reading the selection without the aid of the tape or CD; (3) reading the selection to a partner. If students' reading speed is very slow, below 50 words per minute, they will do better reading along with a person or recorded or CD version (Dowhower, 1987). After they reach speeds of 60 words per minute, they can practice without the tape or CD. Initially, students with very low reading rates will need lots of practice to reach 80 words per minute. But as their reading rate increases, they won't need as many practice readings. Once they get accustomed to the procedure, four or five rereadings should provide optimal returns for time spent. Additional rereadings would provide diminishing returns.

Step 5. Evaluating the reading

Students read the selection to you or to a partner. The number of word recognition errors and reading speed are recorded. Students are informed of their progress. A chart might be constructed to show the degree of improvement. The goal is to have students in grade 3 and beyond read at least 80 to 100 words per minute. Students should practice until they reach that standard. Errors in word recognition should also decrease. However, do not insist on perfect word recognition. Setting a standard of 100 percent accuracy leads students to conclude that reading is a word-pronouncing rather than a meaning-constructing activity. It also slows the reading rate. Afraid of making a mistake, students will read at a slow-but-sure pace (Samuels, 1988b). To reduce anxiety, make sure that students are provided with materials on the appropriate level and are given needed instruction and practice with unfamiliar words. Also downplay miscues, especially those that are insignificant.

Adapting Instruction for Struggling Readers and Writers

In an adaptation of paired reading, children are given high-interest books that they would not be able to read on their own but that explore topics that develop background knowledge and vocabulary. Words that fit patterns that students have been taught are highlighted. The parent or volunteer reads the selection but pauses before highlighted words, which the student then reads. ■

FYI

Results of a study of the oral reading accuracy of a large sample of fourth graders indicate that there is strong relationship among reading rate, accuracy, and a holistic measure of fluency. All three also have a strong relationship with comprehension (Daane et al., 2005). ■

FYI

- Because students read the scripts aloud, *Tales and Plays* (Rigby) and *Primary Reader's Theatre* (Curriculum Associates) provide opportunities for oral reading that have genuine purpose.
- Students in the early stages of learning phonics will not benefit from fluency instruction. They are too busy applying word analysis skills. Fluency instruction may be initiated once students have learned basic single-syllable patterns. Kuhn and Stahl (2003) recommend that fluency instruction not be implemented until students have reached the late pre-primer stage. For students making average progress, this falls during the second half of first grade. Once students are able to read about 100 words a minute, fluency instruction no longer has much power. For most students, this occurs toward the end of second grade. ■

Adapting Instruction for Struggling Readers and Writers

Repeated reading can be used to help struggling readers experience what it is like to read smoothly and with few or no mistakes (Allington, 2006). ■

FYI

Repeated reading results in average percentile gains of 23 points. ■

Recorded-Book Method

To build students' ability to recognize words automatically and to improve their phrasing, have them read along as a selection is read. You or an aide can read selections to students, or you can have them read along with recorded stories. Because recorded stories are read at the pace of normal speech, this may be too rapid for the listener to match printed and spoken words. When a student reads along with a tape, the pace should be at about the same rate as the student can read orally or slightly faster. If the pace is too rapid, the student may not be able to keep up and may become frustrated (Carbo, 1997). In deciding which books to record, select those that are interesting and that students will be able to understand when they hear them read aloud. When recording selections, read with expression but read slowly enough so that students can follow along. Pace your reading at about 80 to 100 words per minute. Also obtain a tape recorder that has a speed regulator. Have students set the speed at a comfortable pace (Shany & Biemiller, 1995). As you encounter words or expressions that might be unfamiliar to students, pause before and after reading them so that students will have time to process them (Carbo, Dunn, & Dunn, 1986).

Recordings should be brief. Record from 5 to 10 minutes of text on each side of a tape or on one track of a CD. Obtain short stories and brief articles that lend themselves to being recorded. Begin the recording by announcing title and author. Provide an overview of the selection to give students an orientation. Also provide a purpose for listening. Signal when it is time to turn a page and announce when the reading has been completed (Carbo, Dunn, & Dunn, 1986).

Encourage students to read along with the recorded selection several times, until they judge that they can read it on their own. When they feel ready to read on their own, students should try reading the selection without the recorded version and note difficult parts. They should then listen to the recorded selection once more and reread the text to practice the parts that proved to be difficult. Students can work alone or with partners. Partners can read to each other after practicing with the recorded selection.

Fluency Read-Alongs   Many reading software programs, such as *Reading Blasters* (Knowledge Adventure), have a feature that allows students to read stories out loud and then hear the read-aloud. INSIGHTS Reading Fluency (Charlesbridge) uses sophisticated speech recognition software to measure and assist students' oral reading. The software tracks a student as she or he reads, corrects errors, and keeps a record of the student's performance. One of the best features of the program is that it presents high-quality selections.

Alternate Reading

In alternate reading, the teacher (or parent or tutor) and the student take turns reading the selection. Initially, the teacher reads most of the selection. The student reads any words or phrases that he or she can. For some students, this might be a few high-frequency and short-vowel words or a repeated sentence. As the student improves, he or she reads larger portions. The teacher reads the first page, and the student reads the second page. Or the teacher might read the difficult parts, and the pupil reads the easy parts. The teacher also provides whatever help the student needs. If the student encounters a difficult word, the teacher tells the student the word or provides prompts that help the student figure out the word.

Increasing the Amount of Reading

Fluency is most effectively fostered by increasing the amount of reading that students do. For example, in one study, second-graders engaged in partner and echo reading of the basal text and silent reading of self-selected books in school and at home. Although the program was only a year long, students gained nearly two years (Stahl, Heubach, & Crammond,

1997). The students who gained the most were reading at least on a late pre-primer level. Apparently, students need some foundational reading skill before they can profit from fluency instruction (Kuhn & Stahl, 2000).

Phrasing of Text

Fluency is more than just accuracy and speed in reading; it also includes proper phrasing. Word-by-word reading is frequently caused by giving students material that is too difficult so that they literally have to figure out just about every word. It also can be caused by a lack of automaticity. Students have to stop and decode a large proportion of words because they don't recognize them immediately. Word-by-word reading should fade as students improve their decoding skills and as their skills become automatic. If word-by-word reading persists even though word recognition is adequate and automatic, model reading orally in logical phrases, and have students read selections in which phrases are marked so that they have practice reading in meaningful chunks.

Why Fluency Instruction Works

Why does fluency instruction work? It seems to work because it increases the amount of reading that students do. Repeated reading and assisted reading may "enable children to read more difficult material than they might otherwise be able to read or may provide a manageable structure to enable increased amounts of reading" (Kuhn & Stahl, 2003, p. 17). In a study comparing repeated reading of a selected number of texts and wider reading of a variety of texts, Van Bon, Bokesbeld, Font Freide, and Van den Hurk (1991) found that reading a variety of texts worked just as well as reading one text over and over.

Putting Fluency in Perspective

The ultimate goal of fluency instruction is constructing meaning. This means that fluency instruction needs to be integrated with reading for meaning. When text is difficult or confusing, readers compensate by pausing and trying to figure out a hard word, rereading, reading more slowly, or pausing to think about what they have read. All of these compensations can improve comprehension but slow down the rate of reading (Walczyk & Griffith-Ross, 2007). Fluency instruction should teach readers to read at different rates for different purposes, and meaning should be emphasized. Overemphasis on reading speed may harm comprehension.

 FYI

- "If students are making adequate progress with fluency, wide reading rather than repeated readings may lead to greater improvements in vocabulary and comprehension. However, for less able readers experiencing particular difficulties with fluency, repeated readings remain an important approach to building fluency" (Mathes & Fuchs, 1993, p. 517).
- Using recorded books, students can read more challenging and more interesting materials. Since the books are recorded, students can decide how many times to read along with a particular book. ■

 Assessing for Learning

Tests that measure only reading rate might give a false impression. Samuels (2006) found that a number of English learners had good decoding skills and a good reading rate, but their comprehension was poor because of their difficulty in understanding the language. ■

 Syllabic Analysis

Fortunately, many of the most frequently used words in English have just one syllable. By the middle first-grade (primer) level, however, 15 percent are polysyllabic (Harris & Jacobson, 1984). Students have to know early on how to deal with

 **Syllabication** is the division of words into syllables. In reading, words are broken down into syllables phonemically, according to their sound (*gen e rous, butt er*), rather than orthographically, according to the rules governing end-of-line word division (*gen er ous, but ter*).

multisyllabic words. **Syllabication,** or structural analysis as it is sometimes called, should be introduced informally in the middle of first grade or after students have learned most of the short-vowel patterns. In Lesson 5.8, students are taught how to read multisyllabic words composed of short-vowel patterns.

Syllabic analysis is deceptively difficult. Surprisingly, in one study of thirty-seven second-graders who were proficient readers and could easily read *let* and *her*, several students read *letter* as *later*, *weeding* as *wedding*, *cabbage* as *cab bag*, and *ribbon* as *rib bahn*, the last two errors being nonwords (Gunning, 2001). For 20 percent of the multisyllabic words, students omitted at least one syllable. An analysis of students' errors has a number of implications for instruction, including the following:

• Students should be taught and prompted to process all the syllables in a word.
• Students need to be taught to see patterns in words. Students who can read *let* and *her* but read *letter* as *later* are not seeing the familiar *-et* pattern.
• Students need to be flexible in their decoding of words. If one pronunciation doesn't work out, they should be prepared to try another. This ties in with reading for meaning. Pronouncing *even* as *ev-en*, the student should note that this is not a word and so should try a long-*e* pronunciation: *e-ven*.
• Students should integrate context and syllabic analysis. A number of students read *wedding* for *weeding* in the sentence: "Amy was weeding her garden," which indicates failure to use context. A number of other students read the sentence as "Amy was watering her garden," which suggests that although they used context, they failed to process the whole word.
• Students need to be reminded to use the orthographic aspects of phonics. Many students had difficulty with words containing final-*e* markers and digraphs. Students did not make use of the final-*e* marker that indicates a soft *g* in *cabbage* or the digraph *ai* in *contain* that indicates a long *a*. When presenting syllable patterns, you may find it helpful to review the single-syllable elements that make up those patterns.
• Students should also be taught that sometimes an element in a multisyllabic word is not read in the same way as when it appears in a single-syllable word. For instance, many students read the *car* in *carrots* as though it were the word *car*. Students also need to know that often the pronunciation of an element changes when it is in a multisyllabic word. Because of reduced stress, the *on* in ribbon has a schwa rather than a short-*o* pronunciation. Many students pronounced it as though it had a short-*o* pronunciation and ended up with the nonword *ribbahn*. Students need to be flexible in their pronunciation of the syllables in multisyllabic words and should also be using context as an aid.
• Elements such as *tion* and *ture* as in *mention* and *future*, which occur only in multisyllabic words, need a careful introduction, frequent review, and a great deal of practice.

Generalization Approach to Teaching Syllabic Analysis

Sort the following words. You can have a question mark category for words that don't seem to fit a pattern.

spider	super	magnet	clever
secret	flavor	bitter	custom
rabbit	hotel	tiger	over
supper	music	fever	elbow
pepper	pupil	wagon	future

How did you sort the words? One way of sorting them is by sound: All the words with long vowels are in one column; all the words with short vowels are in a second column. You can also sort them by sound and spelling. Notice that the vowels in syllables that end in a consonant tend to be short and vowels in syllables that end in a vowel seem to be long. You might also note that the long vowels are followed by one consonant and short vowels are followed by two consonants. However, there are two exception words: *wagon* and *clever*. Sorting is a way of helping students make discoveries about words.

Through sorts of this type, students discover two of the most sweeping generalizations in phonics: The open syllable generalization states that syllables that end in a vowel are generally long, and the closed syllable generalization states that syllables that end in a consonant are generally short.

The two approaches to teaching syllabication are generalization and pattern. The generalization approach is more widespread but probably less effective. It can be combined with a pattern approach.

In the generalization approach, students learn general rules for dividing words into syllables. The generalizations listed below seem to be particularly useful (Gunning, 1975). These should be presented in the following order, which reflects both frequency of occurrence and approximate order of difficulty:

1. *Easy affixes: -ing, -er, -ly.*   Most prefixes and suffixes form separate syllables: *un-safe, re-build, help-ful, quick-ly*. Except for *s* as a plural marker, affixes generally are composed of a vowel and consonant(s). Thus, they are syllables in themselves: *playing, re-play*.
2. *Compound words.*   The words that make up a compound word usually form separate syllables: *sun-set, night-fall*.
3. *Two consonants between two vowels.*   When two consonants appear between two vowels, the word generally divides between them: *win-ter, con-cept*. The place of division is often an indication of the pronunciation of the vowel. The *i* in *winter*, the *o* in the first syllable of *concept*, and the *e* in the second syllable of *concept* are short. Note that all three vowels are in closed syllables—that is, syllables that end in consonants: *win, con, cept*. Closed syllables often contain a short vowel. (The *e* in winter is not short because it is followed by *r*.) Note, too, that digraphs are not split: *broth-er, with-er*.
4. *One consonant between two vowels.*   When one consonant appears between two vowels, it often becomes a part of the syllable on the right: *ma-jor, e-vil*. When the single consonant moves to the right, the syllable to the left is said to be open because it ends in a vowel. If a syllable ends in a vowel, the vowel is generally long. In a number of exception words, however, the consonant becomes a part of the syllable on the left: *sev-en, wag-on*.
5. *The ending le.*   The letters *le* at the end of a word are usually combined with a preceding consonant to create a separate syllable: *cra-dle, ma-ple*.
6. *Two vowels together.*   A limited number of words split between two vowels: *i-de-a, di-al*.

It is important to keep in mind that syllabication is designed to help students decode an unfamiliar word by separating it into its syllabic parts and then recombining the parts into a whole. It is not necessary for students to divide the word exactly right, which is a highly technical process. All that matters is whether students are able to arrive at the approximate pronunciation.

Pattern Approach to Teaching Syllabic Analysis

Knowing syllabic generalizations is one thing; applying them is quite another. Research (Gunning, 1975) and experience suggest that many students apparently do not apply syllabic generalizations. When faced with unfamiliar, multisyllabic words, they attempt to search out pronounceable elements or simply skip the words. These students might fare better with an approach that presents syllables in patterns (Cunningham, 1978).

In a pattern approach, students examine a number of words that contain a syllable that has a high frequency. For example, dozens of words that begin with a consonant and are followed by a long *o* could be presented in pattern form. The advantage of this approach is that students learn to recognize pronounceable units in multisyllabic words and also to apply the open syllable generalization in a specific situation. The pattern could be introduced with a one-syllable word contrasted with multisyllabic words to make it easier for students to grasp the idea. (The following example assumes that the syllables -*da*, -*el*, and -*al* are known.)

FYI

The term *structural analysis* is sometimes used to refer to syllabic analysis and morphemic analysis (study of affixes and roots). ■

Assessing for Learning

To assess and monitor students' ability to read multisyllabic words, administer the Syllable Survey (see the Appendix). ■

FYI

Coping with multisyllabic words is a major obstacle for many students, but is badly neglected in many literacy programs. You may need to provide supplementary instruction in syllabic analysis. If so, you might use the common syllable patterns in Table 5.13 as a framework. ■

Adapting Instruction for Struggling Readers and Writers

Shefelbine and Newman (2000) found that average and poor decoders were two to four times more likely than good decoders to omit syllables when reading multisyllabic words. The researchers suggested a great deal of reading at the independent level. Direct instruction in using multisyllabic words should also be implemented. ■

FYI

Students often confuse open and closed syllables. They tend to read open syllables such as those occurring in even and noticed as closed syllables: *ev-en* (for *e-ven*), *not-iced* (for *no-ticed*). ■

FYI

Although students formulate a generalization, the emphasis is on using patterns or known word parts rather than generalizations to read multisyllabic words. ■

so
soda
total
local
vocal
motel
hotel
notice

The steps to follow in teaching a syllabication lesson using the pattern approach are presented in Lesson 5.8.

FYI

Putting words into syllables can be a challenging task because it's sometimes difficult to tell where one syllable ends and another begins. Even the experts disagree. If you look up the word *vocational*, for instance, you will see that Merriam-Webster dictionaries divide it into syllables in one way and Thorndike-Barnhart dictionaries syllabicate it in another way. ■

Adapting Instruction for Struggling Readers and Writers

When working with struggling readers, especially those who have been unsuccessful with a particular program or approach, try using a new approach and also new materials. Struggling readers don't want to work with a program or text that they associate with failure (Stahl, 1998). ■

FYI

• Why might students who can read elements in single-syllable words have difficulty with those same elements in multisyllabic words? The students may have difficulty locating the known element in a longer word. For instance, *par* is a single-syllable word that appears as an element in *partial*, *parcel*, and *particle* but has a different identity in *parade* and *paradise*. As Shefelbine (1990) notes, "Identifying patterns of syllables requires more developed and complex knowledge of letter and spelling patterns than the knowledge needed for reading single syllable words" (p. 225). ■

LESSON 5.8

Syllabication Using the Pattern Approach

Objectives
• Students will recognize the word pattern *it* in multisyllabic words.
• Students will use the word part *it* to decodable multisyllabic words

Step 1. Introducing the syllabic pattern(s)

To introduce a syllabic pattern, explain the importance of syllabic analysis, and then introduce the pattern with single-syllable words. This helps students to spot familiar parts in what might appear to be unfamiliar polysyllabic words.

Step 2. Presenting the –*it* pattern(s) and selecting a model word

Write the word *kit* on the board, and have students read it. (Remind students that a *kit* is a baby fox.) Then write *kitten* under it, and have students read it. Contrast *kit* and *kitten* by pointing to the sound that each syllable makes. To help students perceive the separate syllables in *kitten*, write them in contrasting colors or underline them. Then have students read *kitten*. Present the words *kitchen, mitten, written* and *rabbit*, in the same way. Then have students read all the words. Tell students that *kit* is the model word for this pattern. If they forget the pattern or have difficulty with a word containing the syllable *it*, they can use the model word to help them. If you have a model words chart, add *kit* to it. If you do not have such a chart, you may wish to start one.

Step 3. Formulating a generalization

Lead students to see that *i* often has the short *i* sound when it is followed by two or more consonants or appears in a closed syllable, as in *kit* and *kitten*.

Step 4. Guided practice

For guided practice, have students search out multisyllabic -*it* words in a reading selection so that they can see this pattern in context. Have students complete exercises similar to the following one or the Additional Practice Activities listed below.

Make a word by putting together two of the three syllables in each row. Write the word on the lines.

mitt	it	en	_____
chen	us	kit	_____
id	mit	ad	_____
it	rabb	on	_____
en	it	happ	_____

Underline the word that better fits the sense of each sentence.

1. Did you give the (kitchen, kitten) some milk?
2. The pitcher of milk is in the (kitchen, kitten).
   3. Sam has (wrapped, written) a story about his kitten.

4. Sam is (fitting, sitting) in the kitchen
5. Sam ate a (batting, biscuit).

Step 5. Application

Have students read selections—stories, informational pieces, and/or real-world materials—that incorporate multisyllabic words containing *it*.

Step 6. Evaluation and review

Note students' ability to read multisyllabic words that follow the patterns introduced. Also note what they do when they encounter multisyllabic words. Are they able to use strategies to decode the words? Are they able to find the *it* in a word such as *admit* and use that to decode the word. Review and reteach as necessary.

Step 7. Extension

Present other short-*i* patterns. After presenting a number of short-vowel patterns, review them. The sample lesson was designed to be taught after students learned short-vowel patterns but before they were introduced to long-vowel patterns. Therefore, only words containing short-vowel patterns were used. As students learn long-vowel and other advanced patterns, words containing these patterns can be used to provide practice.

Adapting Instruction for Struggling Readers and Writers

Students might use an e-dictionary to see how a word they are struggling with is divided into syllables and to see how it is pronounced. ■

Additional Practice Activities for Multisyllabic Words

- Have students read or sing song lyrics in which the separate syllables of multisyllabic words are indicated.
- Have students sort multisyllabic words. This enables them to discover generalizations and patterns. Words to be sorted should be words they can read.
- Make available books in which difficult words are put into syllables and phonetically respelled.
- Have students read words by syllables (Shefelbine & Newman, 2000). Write a syllable on the board and have students read it. Then write another syllable on the board and have students read it. Then have them read the word formed by putting the two syllables together. For example, students read *ab* and then *sent* and then *absent*. Emphasize the need to adjust the pronunciation of a syllable so as to say a real word. When occurring in unaccented syllables, vowels have a reduced pronunciation; for example, the second syllable in *velvet* is pronounced *vit* instead of *vet*.
- Have students use syllabic analysis skills to read whole words. In the Reading Words by Syllables activity, students are provided with practice in recognizing individual syllables and combining them to form words. Reading Whole Words by Syllables is a more advanced activity. Students must note the word's syllables on their own and then reconstruct the word. (Students might use the pronounceable word part, analogy, or Spot and Dot strategy explained below). When reading whole words, students frequently have to adjust the pronunciation so that they are reading a real word rather than just sounding out syllables (Gunning, 2011).
- Encourage students to bring in multisyllabic words that they have noticed in their reading and that they were able to pronounce. They might write their words on the board and have the other students read them.
- When introducing new words that have more than one syllable, write the words on the board and encourage students to read them. Provide help as needed.
- Use software, such as *Tenth Planet: Word Parts* (Sunburst), that challenges students to build words by combining syllables and to use multisyllabic words to compose poems, riddles, and stories.
- To help students differentiate between open and closed syllables, have them read contrasting word pairs (*super, supper; biter, bitter*) or complete sentences by selecting one of two contrasting words: Although the dog looked mean, it was not a (*biter, bitter*). We had chicken and mashed potatoes for (*super, supper*).

FYI

When students decode multisyllabic words, do not insist on exact syllable division. Expect the student to break such a word into smaller units so that she or he can pronounce each one and then put the units back together again to form a whole word. ■

Exemplary Teaching
Decoding Long Words

For students who have difficulty decoding long words, McCabe (2010), a former teacher, created the sequential spelling technique, which happens to be an excellent application of the pronounceable word part strategy. For a student who couldn't read the word *advice*, McCabe would have him or her write the "chunk" *ice* and then keep changing *ice* to words such as *rice, lice, slice, vice,* and finally the word *advice*. For a student who had difficulty with the word *startle*, McCabe would lead him or her through a series of *-ar* words: *car, far, bar, jar, tar, star, starring, starred, startle*. Other *-ar* words could also be presented: *stark, stardom, starfish, starch, starve, starvation, harbor, bargain, sparkle, target, jargon*. Much of McCabe's instruction focused on advanced patterns, such as *ci* = /sh/, that have a high frequency but are not often taught. McCabe's approach is especially appropriate for older struggling readers because it teaches them what they need to know and builds on what they already know. Building step by step on what students know, this technique is practically failure-free.

Multisyllabic Patterns

In approximate order of difficulty, the major multisyllabic patterns are as follows:

Easy affixes: *play-ing, quick-ly*

Compound words: *base-ball, any-one*

Closed-syllable words: *rab-bit, let-ter*

Open-syllable words: *ba-by, ti-ny*

Final-*e* markers: *es-cape, do-nate*

Vowel digraphs: *a-gree, sea-son*

Other patterns: *cir-cle, sir-loin*

Major syllable patterns and example words for the patterns are presented in Table 5.13. The patterns are in approximate order of difficulty. Easy suffixes, such as *–ing*, can be taught when words containing *-ing* inflected endings begin appearing in the texts that students are reading. Compound words are taught when compound words begin appearing in the students' reading. Closed-syllable patterns can be taught as soon as students have learned the single-syllable patterns that make up the closed syllables. For instance, the multisyllabic words *rabbit* and *napkin* can be analyzed after students have learned short-*a* and short-*i* patterns. However, you might want to wait until most of the basic short-vowel patterns have been introduced before presenting closed syllable patterns, but do not wait until all the major single-syllable patterns have been taught before introducing syllabic analysis. Multisyllabic words appear with increasing frequency even in first-grade materials, so students need to be taught how to read them. In Table 5.13, sample words are presented that are restricted to elements previously introduced. For instance, the first group of short-vowel patterns contains only words composed of short-*a* and short-*i* words but are gradually expanded to include short-*o*, short-*e*, and short-*u* words; then they move into long-vowel words.

TABLE 5.13   Common Syllable Patterns

Compound-Word Pattern			
some	day	out	sun
someone	daylight	outside	sunup
sometime	daytime	outdoor	sundown
something	daybreak	outline	sunfish
somehow	daydream	outgrow	sunlight
somewhere		outfield	sunbeam

Short-Vowel Patterns

rabbit	accept
admit	invent
attic	comment
plastic	contest
traffic	suggest
instant	discuss
basket	hundred
magnet	puppet
happen	trumpet
splendid	
absent	
eldest	
expense	

Open Long-Vowel Pattern

vacant	solo
raven	open
evil	hotel
secret	motel
decent	woken
react	vocal
recent	human
minus	menu
tripod	emu
ripen	humid
silent	
robot	
focus	
nomad	

Final-*e* Vowel Pattern

locate	invite
escape	reptile
mistake	recycle
donate	bicycle
vibrate	expose
female	suppose
invade	excuse
inhale	
divide	
advice	
entire	

Vowel Digraphs Pattern

exclaim	approach
obtain	below
remain	shadow
display	
succeed	
peanut	
repeat	

(*continued*)

r Vowel Pattern

artist	confirm
carpet	explore
harvest	fortunate
margin	important
market	restore
participate	support
batter	purpose
enter	surface
concern	murmur
corner	disturb
lumber	absurd
member	confirm
perfect	concern
certain	

le Pattern

saddle	juggle
paddle	jungle
rattle	knuckle
candle	able
example	table
pebble	beetle
dribble	people
pickle	circle
tickle	turtle
riddle	couple
simple	double
puddle	

Long *oo* Pattern

igloo	roofer
kangaroo	noodles
scooter	typhoon
shampoo	
rooster	

ove Spelling of Long *oo* Pattern

prove	approve
proven	remove
improve	movements

u Spelling of Long *oo* Pattern

Sue	studio
super	truly
student	tuna

Short *oo* Pattern

cookie	woolen
rookie	looking
wooden	

(continued)

al Pattern

also	altogether
always	although
already	walrus

au Pattern

because	caution
saucer	faucet
author	sausage
August	daughter
autumn	auditorium
audience	

aw Pattern

draw	strawberry
drawing	awful
crawling	awesome

oi Pattern

point	rejoice
poison	noisy
disappoint	avoid
disappointment	

oy Pattern

joy	annoy
enjoy	royal
destroy	loyal
employ	voyage

ou Pattern

round	fountain
mountain	surround
	compound
	thousand

ow Pattern

power	allow
tower	allowance
flower	

Schwa *a* Pattern

ago	around	about
away	along	announce
alone	alive	amount
awake	apart	
among	across	
asleep	about	

(*continued*)

Adjacent Vowels Pattern

quiet	create
trio	poem
piano	poet
radio	fluid
period	ruin
area	studio

-*ture* Pattern

capture	picture
fracture	nature
pasture	creature
gesture	future
mixture	sculpture

-*tion* Pattern

fraction	decoration
section	demonstration
fiction	exaggeration
nation	exclamation
station	expectation
motion	explanation
portion	investigation
description	illustration
destruction	information
direction	introduction
election	invitation
emotion	multiplication
abbreviation	population
conversation	

-*sion* Pattern

conclusion	explosion
confusion	persuasion
occasion	

y as long *i* Pattern

try	deny
reply	magnify
supply	

Source: Adapted from Gunning, T. (2011). *Teacher's Guide for Word Building Book D* (2nd ed.). Unionville, CT: Galvin; Honesdale, PA: Phoenix Learning Resources.

Combining the Generalization and Pattern Approaches

Although the pattern approach is highly effective and builds on what students know, students sometimes are unable to see patterns in words. In these instances, they should try applying generalizations. In his research, Shefelbine (1990) found that instruction in open (*mo-*, *ta-*, *fi-*) and closed (*-at*, *-em*, *-in*) syllables and affixes (*un-*, *pre-*, *-less*, *-ful*) was especially helpful. After teaching a number of open-syllable patterns, you might have students construct a generalization about the pattern, such as "Syllables that end in a vowel are often long (*ta ble*)." After teaching a number of closed-syllable patterns, you might have students construct a generalization about the pattern, such as "Syllables that end in a consonant are often short (*hap py*)."

To apply generalizations in words that don't have affixes, students should identify the first syllable by locating the first vowel and note whether the syllable is open (ending in a vowel) or closed (ending in a consonant). Students should say the first syllable and then proceed in this same way, syllable by syllable. After they have pronounced all the syllables, they should attempt to say the word, making any adjustments necessary. Prompt students as needed. If students misread an open syllable as a closed one—for instance, reading *notice* as *not-ice*—ask them to tell where the first vowel is so they can see that the vowel should be ending the syllable and should be long. Often, vowel sounds are reduced when they appear in multisyllabic words, as in *educate*, where the *u* has a schwa pronunciation. Explain to students that they should not just pronounce syllables but should change pronunciations if they have to so that they can "read the real word" (Shefelbine & Newman, 2000).

Whether you teach using generalizations, patterns, or, as this book recommends, a combination of approaches, students must have a plan of attack or strategy when facing an unfamiliar multisyllabic word. Students can use the steps in the following Student Strategy on their own.

Using Technology

The Resource Room contains lists of words that can be used for practice with phonics elements and multisyllabic words. http://www.resourceroom.net/readspell/index.asp ■

FYI

Parents might want to know what to do if their children ask for help with a word. Having them simply tell their children unknown words is the safest, least frustrating approach (Topping, 1989). But in some situations, you may want to have them encourage their children to use specific strategies. ■

STUDENT STRATEGIES
Attacking Multisyllabic Words

1. See whether the word has any prefixes or suffixes. If so, pronounce the prefix, then the suffix, and then the remaining part(s) of the word. If the word has no prefix or suffix, start with the beginning of the word and divide it into syllables. Say each syllable.
2. Put the syllables together. If the word does not sound like a real word, try other pronunciations until you get a real word.
3. See if the word makes sense in the sentence in which it appears. If it does not, try other pronunciations.
4. If nothing works, use a dictionary or ask the teacher.

To help students apply this strategy, you might show them how to use *Spot and Dot*. When using *Spot and Dot* (Fast Track Reading, 2002), students spot the vowel and then place a dot over where the syllable ends. If a vowel is followed by one consonant (*bi ter*), the consonant most often goes with the second syllable and the vowel is long. If the vowel is followed by two consonants (*bit ter*), the consonants are usually split; the first syllable ends with a consonant (is closed) and usually has a short vowel. There are exceptions, so students need to be flexible.

Using the Pronounceable Word Part and Analogy Strategies

The pronounceable word part and analogy strategies recommended for decoding single-syllable words may also be used to decode multisyllabic words. For instance, if students are having difficulty with the word *silver*, they might look for a pronounceable word part such as *il* and add /s/ to make *sil*. They would then say *er*, add /v/ to make *ver*, and reconstruct the whole word. In many instances, saying a part of the word—the *sil* in *silver*, for example—is enough of a clue to enable students to say the whole word. If the pronounceable word part strategy does not work, students may use an analogy strategy, in which they employ common words to help them sound out the syllables in a multisyllabic word that is in their listening but not their reading vocabulary. For instance, faced with the word *thunder*, the student works it out by making a series of comparisons. The first syllable is *thun*, which is similar to the known word *sun*, and the second syllable is *der*, which is similar to the known word *her*. Putting them together, the student synthesizes the word *thunder*.

As students read increasingly complex materials and meet a higher proportion of polysyllabic words, their ability to perceive the visual forms of syllables should develop naturally. As with phonics skills, the best way to practice dealing with polysyllabic words is through a combination of instruction and wide reading.

Summary

The ultimate goal of phonics, syllabic analysis, and other word recognition skills is to enable students to become independent readers. Functional practice and extensive reading are recommended to help them reach that goal. Instruction should be developmental and differentiated so that it matches students' understanding of the writing system. Progress should be monitored, and added instruction should be provided as needed. Students should be taught how to use two powerful word identification strategies: pronounceable word part and analogy. Because high-frequency words occur so often, students should be given extra practice with them in order to recognize them rapidly. Although virtually all words are learned by creating a bond between sounds and spellings, most words are ultimately recognized just about instantaneously. Fluency is fostered by providing a solid foundation in word analysis and rapid recognition of high-frequency words. Numerous opportunities to read materials on the appropriate level of challenge also build fluency.

Extending and Applying

1. Using the Phonics Inventory or another decoding assessment tool, assess the phonics skills of one or more novice readers. Check results by giving the student(s) another try at items missed. Analyze the results, and plan a program based on your analysis.
2. Using the word-building (pattern) approach described in this chapter, plan a lesson in which a phonic or syllabic element is introduced. You might teach the lesson to the student or students assessed in item 1. State your objectives, and describe each of the steps of the lesson. List the titles of children's books or other materials that might be used to reinforce or apply the element taught. If possible, teach the lesson and evaluate its effectiveness.
3. Working with a small group of students, note which strategies they use when they encounter difficult words. Providing the necessary instruction and prompts, encourage them to use the pronounceable word part, analogy, and context strategies.
4. Examine the word analysis component of a basal/anthology or other literacy series that contains a phonics program. What is its approach to teaching phonics and syllabic analysis? Are the lessons and activities functional and contextual? Is adequate practice provided? What is your overall evaluation of the word analysis component of this series?
5. Read over the pronunciation key of a dictionary. Notice the spellings given for the consonant sounds and the vowel sounds. Check each of the sounds. Are there any that are not in your dialect? The following words have at least two pronunciations: *dog* ("dawg" or "dog"), *roof* ("rōof" or "roŏf"), *route* ("root" or "rowt"). How do you pronounce them?

Professional Reflection

Do I ...

___ Have an understanding of the stages of learning to read words?

___ Have an understanding of basic principles of teaching phonics and syllabic analysis?

___ Have an understanding of how high-frequency words should be taught?

___ Have an understanding of key strategies that students might use to decode unfamiliar words?

___ Have an understanding of fluency?

Am I able to. . .

___ Teach effective word analysis lessons?

___ Develop fluency?

___ Monitor progress and gear instruction to student needs and adapt instruction as necessary?

___ Provide varied practice?

Reflection Question

What are the instructional implications if a student reads *interior* as *inturur*, but *interior* is in the student's listening vocabulary?

Building Competencies

To build competencies, consult the following sources for more detailed information:

Bear, D. R., Invernizzi, M., Templeton, S., & Johnston, F. (2008). *Words their way: Word study for phonics, vocabulary, and spelling instruction* (4th ed.). Upper Saddle River, NJ: Prentice Hall.

Ganske, K. (2000). *Word journeys.* New York: Guilford.

Gunning, T. (2000). *Building words: A resource manual for teaching word analysis and spelling strategies.* Boston: Allyn & Bacon.

Gunning, T. (2000). *Phonological awareness and primary phonics.* Boston: Allyn & Bacon.

National Reading Panel. (2000). *National Reading Panel report,* Chapter 3, "Fluency," pp. 3-2–3-43. Washington, DC: U.S. Department of Education. http://www.nationalreadingpanel.org

National Reading Panel. (2000). National Reading Panel report, Chapter 2, Part II, "Phonics instruction," pp. 2-89–2-176. Washington, DC: U.S. Department of Education. http://www.nationalreadingpanel.org

View and reflect on the videos noted in this chapter.

MyEducationLab™

Go to the Topics "Phonemic Awareness/Phonics" and "Fluency" in the MyEducationLab (www.myeducationlab.com) for your course, where you can:

- Find learning outcomes for "Phonemic Awareness/Phonics" and "Fluency" along with the national standards that connect to these outcomes.
- Complete Assignments and Activities that can help you more deeply understand the chapter content.
- Apply and practice your understanding of the core teaching skills identified in the chapter with the Building Teaching Skills and Dispositions learning units.
- Examine challenging situations and cases presented in the IRIS Center Resources.
- Check your comprehension on the content covered in the chapter by going to the Study Plan in the Book

Resources for your text. Here you will be able to take a chapter quiz, receive feedback on your answers, and then access Review, Practice, and Enrichment activities to enhance your understanding of chapter content. (optional)

A+RISE A+RISE® Standards2Strategy™ is an innovative and interactive online resource that offers new teachers in grades K–12 just-in-time, research-based instructional strategies that meet the linguistic needs of ELLs as they learn content, differentiate instruction for all grades and abilities, and are aligned to Common Core Elementary Language Arts standards (for the literacy strategies) and to English language proficiency standards in WIDA, Texas, California, and Florida.

6

Building Vocabulary

Anticipation Guide

For each of the following statements, put a check under "Agree" or "Disagree" to show how you feel. Discuss your responses with classmates before you read the chapter.

	Agree	Disagree
1. Vocabulary words should be taught only when students have a need to learn them.	_____	_____
2. All or most of the difficult words in a selection should be taught before the selection is read.	_____	_____
3. Building vocabulary leads to improved comprehension.	_____	_____
4. The best way to build vocabulary is to study a set number of words each week.	_____	_____
5. Using context is the easiest way to get the meaning of an unfamiliar word.	_____	_____
6. The best way to learn about roots, prefixes, and suffixes is to have a lot of experience with these word parts.	_____	_____
7. Using the dictionary as a strategy to get the meanings of unfamiliar words is inefficient.	_____	_____

Using What You Know

Chapter 5 explained techniques for teaching children how to decode words that were in their listening vocabularies but might not be recognizable to them in print. This chapter is also concerned with reading words. However, the focus in this chapter is on dealing with words whose meanings are unknown. In preparation for reading this chapter, explore your knowledge of this topic: How many words would you estimate are in your vocabulary? Where and how did you learn them? Have you ever read a book or taken a course designed to increase your vocabulary? If so, how well did the book or the course work? What strategies do you use when you encounter an unknown word? How would you go about teaching vocabulary to an elementary or middle school class?

The Need for Vocabulary Instruction

Read the following paragraph, which is excerpted from Beverly Cleary's *Ramona Quimby, Age 8* (1981), a book typically read in grade 3. What challenges does the passage present for the typical third-grader?

> Rainy Sunday afternoons in November were always dismal, but Ramona felt this Sunday was the most dismal of all. She pressed her nose against the living-room window, watching the ceaseless rain pelting down as bare black branches clawed at the electric wires in front of the house. Even lunch, leftovers Mrs. Quimby had wanted to clear out of the refrigerator, had been dreary, with her parents, who seemed tired or discouraged or both, having little to say and Beezus mysteriously moody. Ramona longed for sunshine, sidewalks dry enough for roller skating, a smiling happy family. (p. 33)

Although meant for third-graders, the passage has surprisingly advanced vocabulary. Students might have difficulty with *dismal*, *ceaseless*, *pelting*, and *longed*. In the initial stages of reading, virtually all the words are known by readers. They are in the readers' listening vocabularies. But as students advance into higher-level texts, vocabulary becomes more challenging. To be proficient readers and writers, students must build their vocabularies and learn strategies for coping with difficult words. As students progress through the grades, a key element in their growth as readers and writers is vocabulary development.

Word Knowledge Tasks

Knowing a word's meaning is not an either/or proposition. Graves (1987) posited six tasks that lead to word knowledge:

Task 1: Learning to read known words. Learning to read known words involves sounding out words that students understand but do not recognize in print. It includes learning a sight vocabulary and using phonics and syllabication to sound out words.

Task 2: Learning new meanings for known words. Even a cursory examination of a dictionary reveals that most words have more than one meaning. A large part of expanding a student's vocabulary is adding new shades of meaning to known words.

Task 3: Learning new words that represent known concepts. Because the concept is already known, this really is little more than learning a new label.

Task 4: Learning new words that represent new concepts. As Graves (1987) observed, "Learning new words that represent new concepts is the most difficult word-learning task students face" (p. 169).

Task 5: Clarifying and enriching the meanings of known words. Although this task is accomplished when students meet known words in diverse contexts, Graves (1987) felt that more systematic, more direct involvement is called for. Teachers have to help students forge connections among known words and provide a variety of enrichment exercises to ensure greater depth of understanding.

Task 6: Moving words from receptive to expressive vocabulary. It is necessary to teach words in such a way that they appear in students' speaking and writing vocabularies. The ultimate test is whether students actually use newly learned words correctly. As Nagy and Scott (2000) comment, "Knowing a word means being able to do things with it. . . . Knowing a word is more like being able to use a tool than it is like being able to state a fact" (p. 273).

As can be seen from the six tasks just described, word knowledge is often a question of degree. The person who has made a systematic attempt to reduce his or her *carbon footprint* has a better knowledge of the words *carbon footprint* than does one who has simply heard the words mentioned. Instruction needs to be devoted to refining as well as to introducing vocabulary and concepts.

Selecting Words for Instruction

With thousands and thousands of words to be learned, how can teachers select words for instruction? Beck and colleagues (2008) have divided words into three groups: Tier One, Tier Two, and Tier Three. Tier One words are "everyday, basic familiar words" (*look*, *see*) that are learned through speaking and listening. Tier Two are "high-utility words that generally appear primarily in print rather than in conversation" (*gaze*, *glance*, *peer*). Tier Three words are "technical words drawn from specific content areas" (*refraction*, *astigmatism*). Tier One words are learned through conversation and interaction with others. Tier Two words are learned mostly through reading or classroom discussions. Tier Three words are learned primarily through studying or exploring a specific content area. Beck and her colleagues recommend providing instruction in Tier Two words. These words are often simply literate labels for common words: *gaze* for *look*, *amble* for *walk*, *gorgeous* for *pretty*, and so are relatively easy to teach. Tier Two words represent a lexical glass ceiling or lexical bar (Corson, 1985, 1995). Without a grasp of Tier Two words, students' opportunity to advance educationally is limited. However, not all Tier Two words are equal. Some will occur more often and be more useful than others, or as Beck and colleagues (2008) put it, they will have more mileage.

Words for Reading

When comprehension of a reading selection is the goal, select words that students probably don't know and whose meaning is crucial to their understanding of the selection. It isn't necessary to preteach each word that is likely to be unfamiliar to students. Restrict your choices to unknown words essential to an understanding of the selection. The presentation can be relatively brief. You need to balance the goal of having students learn new words with the goal of having them understand the selection. Don't make the presentation of words so extensive that you distract students from the goal of reading the selection with understanding. If the words are ones that you judge should be added to students' vocabulary, spend additional time with the words after the selection has been read. After discussing the selection, you might select additional Tier Two words for further study if you believe your students will encounter those words again and again.

Beck and colleagues (2008) recommend that words needed for clarification of comprehension be presented at point of use. If the teacher is reading aloud, a difficult word can be clarified—that is, briefly explained—when it is encountered. For silent reading, words might be presented near the point of use. This works best if students are reading a work section by section. For instance, if students are reading about a boy who is mocked by his classmates because he is a poor reader, the teacher might explain, "In this section you will read about a boy who is mocked by his classmates. *Mocked* means 'being made fun of.'" Because you are providing clarification of the word, you would not go into a discussion about a time when you were mocked or when a character in another selection was mocked. However, if you want students to add the word to their vocabulary, you can go into this kind of discussion after the selection has been read. Beck and colleagues recommend brief vocabulary instruction before reading, parenthetical clarification during reading, and robust study of words after reading.

Although the focus of vocabulary instruction is on Tier Two words, since these are the kind of words learned by reading and in academic settings, Tier One words can also be part of the vocabulary program. However, Tier One words are not taught in the same way that Tier Two words are. Since Tier One words are learned primarily through conversation and interaction, one way to foster learning of such words is to have more conversation in the classroom. Beck and colleagues (2008) recommend that teachers be more loquacious: "Say things in more elaborated ways, play with language" (p. 29). Create a classroom in which there is a lot of talk. With Tier One words, you are less concerned with definitions and more concerned with students becoming aware of the uses of the words. Take advantage of the numerous opportunities during the day for enriching students' language, especially that of ELLs. When lining students up, use the words *front, forward, rear,* and *march* and the expressions *single file, head of the line,* and *end of the line.* Bond and Wasik (as cited by Beck, Kucan, & McKeown, 2008) suggest setting up conversation stations, which are specific areas of the classroom where students can go at designated times to talk with the teacher or another student.

Living in the moment as they do, students may bring up a topic at an inopportune time. Bond and Wasik recommend that you tell the child that he or she will be listened to at another time: "Diego, I want to hear about your new puppy. Would you tell me about your puppy at lunch time?" Bond and Wasik also recommend that teachers reflect on the following questions:

- Do I actively promote children's listening to and responding to what is being said in a conversation? Do I model it myself? Do I give children time to finish their thoughts?

FYI

Brief introduction works for Tier Two words; however, as mentioned earlier in this chapter, the introduction needs to be more thorough for words that represent new concepts. ■

FYI

Vocabulary instruction results in an average percentile gain of 20 points (Haystead & Marzano, 2009; Hattie, 2009). ■

- Do I show respect for children's unique interests when they go off topic during a conversation? Do I gently steer them back to the topic? Do I make note of their interest and address it at another time of day? (Bond & Wasik, as cited by Beck, Kucan, & McKeown, 2008, p. 31).

Seven Principles of Developing Vocabulary

FYI

Vocabulary instruction should be geared to the students' stage of cognitive development. As students' cognitive ability develops, they learn to use words in hierarchical fashion: *large, larger, largest.* Their understanding moves from the concrete to the abstract and from personal meanings to meanings that are broader in scope and socially shared (Hulit & Howard, 2002). ■

Developing vocabulary is not simply a matter of listing ten or twenty words and their definitions on the board each Monday morning and administering a vocabulary quiz every Friday. In a sense, it is a part of living. Children learn their initial 5,000 to 6,000 words by interacting with parents and peers, gradually learning labels for the people, objects, and ideas in their environment. As children grow and have additional experiences, their vocabularies continue to develop. They learn *pitcher, batter, shortstop,* and *home run* by playing or watching softball or baseball. They learn *gear shift, brake cable, kick stand,* and *reflector* when they begin riding a bicycle.

Depending on the nature of the words to be learned and the students' background knowledge, vocabulary development represents two related but somewhat different cognitive tasks: establishing associations and developing conceptual knowledge (Baumann, Kame'enui, & Ash, 2003). To learn an association between a known concept and a new label for that concept, students don't have to do much more than hear and/or use the label several times or use mnemonic devices to help them remember the word. Intensive instruction is not required.

However, depending on its complexity, a concept might require considerable instruction. Conceptual learning is a far more demanding cognitive task. Such words as *democracy, photosynthesis, personality, state, government, emigration, fossils,* and *poverty* require experience and/or extensive explanation and discussion before understanding is achieved. The new word becomes a label for the concept. Of course, having the label does not guarantee understanding the concept behind the label. Students can tell what state they live in without knowing what a state is.

Concepts are organized into networks. For instance, if I say "cake," chances are you will say something like "ice cream" or "chocolate" or "party." These don't define what a cake is but present associations or experiences that you have with cake. Of course, the more experiences you have with cake, the more associations you can construct. Because our concepts are stored in networks, conceptual words are best presented in frameworks that show how they are related to other concepts and also how they are related to students' background of knowledge. Unfamiliar concepts are best learned when they are presented within the context of known concepts or words. That way they become part of a network. That's one reason why simply presenting words in unrelated lists is the least effective way to present new vocabulary.

Building Experiential Background

The first and most effective step that a teacher can take to build vocabulary is to provide students with a variety of rich experiences. These experiences might involve taking children to an apple orchard, supermarket, zoo, museum, or office. Working on projects, conducting experiments, handling artifacts, and other hands-on activities also build a background of experience.

Not all activities can be direct. Viewing computer simulations and demonstrations, film clips, and special TV shows helps build experience, as do discussing, listening, and reading. The key is to make the activity as concrete as possible.

Talking Over Experiences   Although experiences form the foundation of vocabulary, they are not enough; labels or series of labels must be attached to them. A presurvey and postsurvey of visitors to a large zoo found that people did not know much more about the animals after leaving the park than they did before they arrived. Apparently, simply looking at the animals was not enough; visitors needed words to define their experiences. This is especially true for young children.

Learning Concepts Versus Learning Labels   For maximum benefit, it is important that experiences be discussed. It is also important to distinguish between learning **labels** and building concepts. For example, the words *petrol* and *lorry* would probably be unfamiliar to American students preparing to read a story set in England. The students would readily understand them if the teacher explained that to the British *petrol* means "gasoline" and *lorry* means "truck." Since the concepts of gasoline and truck are already known, it would simply be a matter of learning two new labels. If the word *fossil* appeared in the selection, however, and the students had no idea what a fossil was, the concept would have to be developed. To provide a concrete experience, the teacher might borrow a fossil from the science department and show it to the class while explaining what it is and relating it to the children's experiences. Building the **concept** of fossil would take quite a bit more teaching than would learning the labels *petrol* and *lorry*.

Relating Vocabulary to Background

The second principle of vocabulary development is relating vocabulary to students' background. It is essential to relate new words to experiences that students may have had. To teach the word *compliment*, the teacher might mention some nice things that were said that were complimentary. Working in pairs, students might compose compliments for each other.

Gipe (1980) devised a background-relating technique in which students are asked to respond to new words that require some sort of personal judgment or observation. For example, after studying the word *beacon*, students might be asked, "Where have you seen a beacon that is a warning sign?" (p. 400). In a similar vein, Beck and McKeown (1983) asked students to "tell about someone you might want to eavesdrop on," or "describe the most melodious sound you can think of" (p. 624). Carr (1983) required students to note a personal clue for each new word. It could be an experience, object, or person. One student associated a local creek with *murky*; another related *numbed* to how one's hands feel when shoveling snow.

Building Relationships

The third principle of developing vocabulary is showing how new words are related to each other. For example, students may be about to read a selection on autobiographies and biographies that includes the unfamiliar words *accomplishment*, *obstacles*, and *nonfiction*, as well as *autobiography* and *biography*. Instead of simply presenting these words separately, demonstrate how they are related to each other. Discuss how autobiography and biography are two similar types of nonfiction, and they often describe the subject's accomplishments and some of the obstacles that he or she had to overcome.

Other techniques for establishing relationships include noting synonyms and antonyms, classifying words, and completing graphic organizers. (These devices are covered later in this chapter.)

Developing Depth of Meaning

The fourth vocabulary-building principle is developing depth of meaning. The most frequent method of teaching new words is to define them. Definitions, however, may provide only a superficial level of knowledge (Nagy, 1988). They may be adequate when new labels are being learned for familiar concepts, but they are not sufficient for new concepts. Definitions also may fail to indicate how a word should be used. The following sentences were created by students who had only definitional knowledge. Obviously, they had some understanding of the words, but it was inadequate.

FYI

Younger students learn words more easily when they are provided with perceptual clues. Real experiences and illustrations are especially helpful. In time, students' understanding of words becomes more conceptual. Instead of defining words in functional fashion, they begin to put words into categories (Owens, 1992). When asked to tell what a carrot is, a young child might say that he likes carrots or carrots are something to eat. As understanding becomes more conceptual, the child defines a carrot as being a vegetable. ■

■ A **label** is simply a name for a concept. Students may use labels without really understanding the meanings behind them.

■ A **concept** is a general idea, an abstraction derived from particular experiences with a phenomenon. In the rush to cover content, teachers may not take the time necessary to develop concepts thoroughly; thus, students may simply learn empty labels for complex concepts such as *democracy* or *gravity*.

FYI

• When concerned about comprehension, choose a few key terms for intensive teaching. The words should be taught so well that students don't have to pause when they encounter them.

• Although students may derive only a vague idea of a word's meaning after a single exposure, additional incidental exposures help clarify the meaning. Over a period of time, many words are acquired in this way.

• Vocabulary knowledge is the most important predictor of reading comprehension (Davis, 1968; Thorndike, 1973). ◾

The *vague* windshield needed cleaning.

At noon we *receded* to camp for lunch.

As Beck and colleagues (2008) comment, "The problem is that asking students to write a novel sentence about words they've looked up in the dictionary may be requiring them to generate new information before they know enough about a word to be able to do so" (p. 28). Research by Nichols (2007) confirms the difficulty that students have composing sentences based on dictionary definitions.

It takes time to learn a word well enough to use it appropriately in a sentence. Instead of having students write sentences using newly learned words, have them complete sentence stems, which prompt them to use the word appropriately and show that they know the meaning of the word: The farmers had to irrigate their fields because _____. In order to complete the sentence, students will have to know what *irrigate* means and why farmers might have to irrigate their fields (Beck, McKeown, & Kucan, 2002).

Words may have subtle shades of meanings that dictionary definitions may not quite capture. Most students have difficulty composing sentences using new words when their knowledge of the words is based solely on definitions (McKeown, 1993). Placing words in context (Gipe, 1980) seems to work better, as it illustrates use of the words and thereby helps to define them. However, in order for vocabulary development to aid in the comprehension of a selection, both the definition and the context should reflect the way the word is used in the selection the students are about to read.

Obviously, word knowledge is a necessary part of comprehension. Ideas couched in unfamiliar terms will not be understood. However, preteaching difficult vocabulary has not always resulted in improved comprehension. In their review of the research on teaching vocabulary, Stahl and Fairbanks (1986) found that methods that provided only definitional information about each word to be learned did not produce a significant effect on comprehension; nor did methods that gave only one or two exposures to meaningful information about each word. For vocabulary instruction to have an impact on comprehension, students must acquire knowledge of new words that is both accurate and enriched (Beck, McKeown, & Omanson, 1987). Experiencing a newly learned word in several contexts broadens and deepens understanding of it. For instance, the contexts *persistent detective*, *persistent salesperson*, *persistent pain*, and *persistent rain* provide a more expanded sense of the word *persistent* than might be conveyed by a dictionary or glossary definition.

Presenting Several Exposures

Frequency of exposure is the fifth principle of vocabulary building. Beck, McKeown, and Omanson (1987) suggested that students meet new words at least ten times; however, Stahl and Fairbanks (1986) found that as few as two exposures were effective. It also helps if words appear in different contexts so that students experience their shades of meaning. Frequent exposure to or repetition of vocabulary is essential to comprehension because of limitations of attention and memory. Third-graders reading a selection about the brain that uses the new words *lobe* and *hemisphere* may not recall the words if the teacher has discussed them only once. Although the students may have understood the meanings of the words at the time of the original discussion, when they meet the words in print, they are vague about their definitions and must try to recall what they mean. Because they give so much attention to trying to remember the meanings of the new words, they lose the gist of the fairly complex passage. Preteaching the vocabulary did not improve their comprehension because their reading was interrupted when they failed to recall the words' meanings immediately or because their knowledge of the words was too vague.

FYI

Word Wizard motivates students to notice newly learned words and to share their discoveries. ◾

FYI

A useful resource for word play activities is *Wordworks: Exploring Language Play* by Bonnie von Hoff Johnson. Golden, CO: Fulcrum. ◾

Creating an Interest in Words

Generating interest in words can have a significant impact on vocabulary development. In their experimental program, Beck and McKeown (1983) awarded the title "Word Wizard" to any student who noted an example of a taught word outside of class and reported it to the group. Children virtually swamped their teachers with instances of seeing, hearing, or using the words as they worked toward gaining points on the Word Wizard Chart. On some days, every child in the class came in with a Word Wizard contribution. Teachers also reported that the children would occasionally cause a minor disruption—for example, at an assembly when a speaker used one of the taught words, "the entire class buzzed with recognition" (p. 625).

Teaching Students How to Learn New Words

The seventh and last principle of vocabulary development is promoting independent word-learning skills. Teaching vocabulary thoroughly enough to make a difference takes time. If carefully taught, only about 400 words a year can be introduced (Beck, McKeown, & Omanson, 1987). However, students have to learn thousands of words, so teachers also have to show them how to use such tools of vocabulary acquisition as context clues, morphemic analysis, and dictionary skills. Vocabulary instruction must move beyond the teaching of words directly as a primary activity. Because students derive the meanings of many words incidentally, without instruction, another possible role of instruction is to enhance the strategies readers use when they do learn words incidentally. Directly teaching such strategies holds the promise of helping children become better independent word learners (Kame'enui, Dixon, & Carnine, 1987).

Techniques for Teaching Words

Dozens of techniques are available for introducing and reinforcing new vocabulary. Those discussed here follow all or some of the seven principles just presented.

Graphic Organizers

Graphic organizers are semantic maps, pictorial maps, webs, and other devices that allow students to view and construct relationships among words. Because they are visual displays, they allow students to picture and remember word relationships. Students who listed synonyms and antonyms and created graphic organizers for vocabulary words learned 40 percent more words than students who wrote the vocabulary words and used them in sentences. Processing the words at a deeper level led to increased retention (Boulware-Gooden, Carreker, Thornhill, & Joshi, 2007).

Semantic Maps   Suppose that your students are about to read an informational piece on snakes that introduces a number of new concepts and words. For example, it states that snakes are reptiles, a concept that you believe will be new to the class. You have scheduled an article about alligators and crocodiles for future reading. Wouldn't it be efficient if you could clarify students' concept of snakes and also prepare them to relate it to the upcoming article? There is a device for getting a sense of what your students know about snakes, helping them organize their knowledge, and preparing them for related concepts: semantic mapping, or, simply, mapping.

A **semantic map** is a device for organizing information graphically according to categories. It can be used for concepts, vocabulary, topics, and background. It may also be used as a study device to track the plot and character development of a story or as a prewriting exercise. Mapping may be presented in a variety of ways but is generally introduced through the following steps (Heimlich & Pittelman, 1986; Johnson & Pearson, 1984):

1. **Introduce the concept, term, or topic to be mapped.** Write the key word for it on the board, overhead transparency, interactive white board, or chart paper.

■ A **graphic organizer** is a diagram used to show the interrelationships among words or ideas.

■ A **semantic map** is a graphic organizer that uses lines and circles to organize information according to categories.

2. **Brainstorm.** Ask students to tell what other words come to mind when they think of the key word. Encourage them to volunteer as many words as they can. This may be done orally, or students may write their lists and share them. If the new words that you plan to teach are not suggested, present them and discuss them.
3. **Group the words by category, discussing why certain words go together.** Encourage students to supply category names.
4. **Create the class map, putting it on a large sheet of paper so that the class can refer to it and add to it.**
5. **Discuss the finished map.** Encourage students to add items to already established categories or to suggest new categories.
6. **Extend the map.** As students discover, through further reading, additional new words related to the topic or key word, add these to the map.

Lesson 6.1 shows, in abbreviated form, how a map on *snakes* was produced by a class of third-graders.

 LESSON 6.1
Semantic Mapping

Objective

• Students use a graphic organizer to show relationships among words.

Step 1.

The teacher explains to students that they will be learning a technique that will help them learn words. The teacher writes the word *snakes* on the board and asks the class to tell what words come to mind when they think of snakes.

Step 2.

Students suggest the following words, which are written on the chalkboard: *poisonous, rattlesnakes, nonpoisonous, garter snakes, sneaky, king snakes, dangerous, frightening, deserts, rocky places,* and *forests*. No one mentions *reptiles*, which is a key word in the article students are about to read. The teacher says that he would like to add that word and asks students if they know what a reptile is. One student says reptiles are cold-blooded. This word is also added to the list.

Step 3.

Words are grouped, and category names are elicited. Students have difficulty with the task, so the teacher helps. He points to the words *forests* and *deserts* and asks what these tell about snakes. The class decides that they tell where snakes live. The teacher then asks the class to find another word that tells where snakes live. Other words are categorized in this same way, and category labels are composed.

Step 4.

The map, shown in Figure 6.1, is created.

Step 5.

Students discuss the map. Two of them think of other kinds of snakes—water moccasins and boa constrictors—which are added. During the discussion, the teacher clarifies concepts that seem fuzzy and clears up misconceptions. One student, for instance, thinks that all snakes are poisonous.

Step 6.

Students read to find out more information about snakes. They refer to the map, which is displayed in the front of the room, to help them with vocabulary and concepts. After reading and discussing the selection, students are invited to add words or concepts they learned. The following are added: *dry, smooth skin; scales; vertebrae;* and *flexible jaws.* A few weeks later, the class reads a selection about helpful snakes. The map is reviewed before reading the story and then expanded to include new concepts and vocabulary.

   Maps are created for other topics. Students complete partially finished maps and work in small groups to construct maps. Students are gradually led to compose their own individual maps independently.

Step 7.

Evaluation and review. Note students' ability to see relationships among words and to display those relationships.

After students have grasped the idea of mapping, they can take a greater share of responsibility for creating maps. The sequence listed below gradually gives children ownership of the technique (Johnson & Pearson, 1984).

1. Students cooperatively create a map under the teacher's direction.
2. Students begin assuming some responsibility for creating maps. After a series of items has been grouped, they might suggest a category name.
3. Students are given partially completed maps and asked to finish them. They can work in groups or individually.
4. The teacher supplies the class with a list of vocabulary words. Working in groups, students use the list to create maps.
5. Working in groups or individually, students create their own maps.

FIGURE 6.1   Semantic Map on Snakes

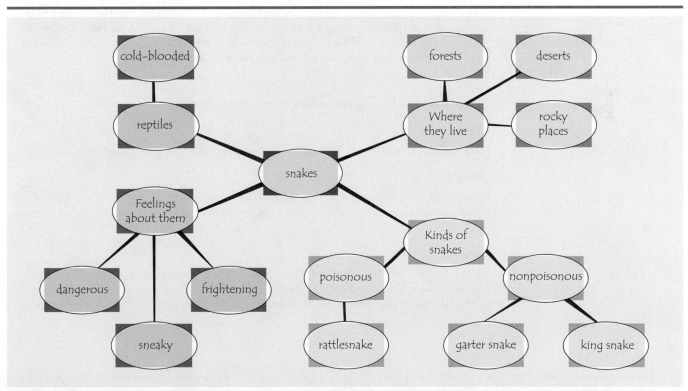

FIGURE 6.2   Web for Mars

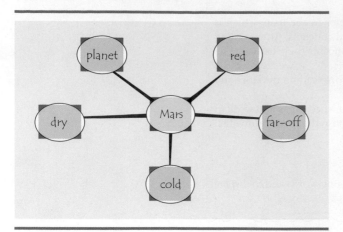

Pictorial Maps and Webs   Pictorial and mixed pictorial–verbal maps work as well as, and sometimes better than, purely verbal maps. A **pictorial map** uses pictures along with words. For some words or concepts, teachers may want to use a more directed approach to constructing semantic maps. After introducing the topic of the planet Mars, the teacher might discuss the characteristics in a **web**, which is a simplified semantic map (see Figure 6.2). A web does not have a hierarchical organization, and it is especially useful for displaying concrete concepts (Marzano & Marzano, 1988).

Semantic Feature Analysis   Semantic feature analysis uses a grid to compare words that fall in a single category. For example, it could be used to compare different mammals, means of transportation, tools, sports, and so on. In constructing a semantic feature analysis, complete the steps outlined in Lesson 6.2, which are adapted from Johnson and Pearson (1984).

LESSON 6.2
Semantic Feature Analysis

Objective

- Students use a graphic organizer to show relationships among words.

Step 1.

The teacher reviews semantic maps and explains to students that they will be learning to create another graphic organizer, a semantic feature analysis, that will help them learn words. The teacher announces the topic and asks students to give examples. In preparation for reading a story about boats, ask students to name different kinds of boats.

Step 2.

List the types of boats in the grid's left-hand column.

Step 3.

Ask students to suggest characteristics that boats have. List these in a row above the grid.

Step 4.

Look over the grid to see if it is complete. Have students add other types of boats and their characteristics. At this point, you might suggest additional kinds of boats or other features of boats.

Step 5.

Complete the grid with the class. A completed grid is shown in Figure 6.3. Put a plus or minus in each square to indicate whether a particular kind of boat usually has the specific characteristic being considered. If unsure, put a question mark in the square. Encourage

---

■ A **pictorial map** uses drawings, with or without labels, to show interrelationships among words or concepts.

■ A **web** is another name for a semantic map, especially a simplified one.

■ A **semantic feature analysis** is a graphic organizer that uses a grid to compare a series of words or other items on a number of characteristics.

students to discuss items about which they may have a question—for example, whether hydrofoils sail above or through the water. As students become proficient with grids, they may complete them independently.

Step 6.

Discuss the grid. Help students get an overview of how boats are alike as well as how specific types differ.

Step 7.

Extend the grid. As students acquire more information, they may want to add other kinds of boats and characteristics.

Students discuss the value of grids. Grids are created for other topics. Students complete partially finished grids and work in small groups to construct grids. Students are gradually led to compose their own individual grids independently. Students also discuss when semantic feature analysis might be used most effectively and when semantic maps or another organizer might be the better choice.

Step 8.

Evaluation and review. Note students' ability to see relationships among words and to display those relationships in grids.

Eventually, students should compose their own grids. Through actively creating categories of qualities and comparing items on the basis of a number of features, students sharpen their sense of the meaning of each word and establish relationships among them.

Venn Diagram   Somewhat similar in intent to the semantic feature analysis grid is the **Venn diagram** (Nagy, 1988), in which two or three concepts or subjects are compared. The main characteristics of each are placed in overlapping circles. Those traits that are shared are entered in the overlapping area, and individual traits are entered in the portions that do not overlap. In discussing crocodiles and alligators, the teacher might encourage students to list the major characteristics of each, noting which belong only to the alligator and which belong only to the crocodile. A Venn diagram like that in Figure 6.4 could then be

FYI

Although Venn diagrams are popular, compare/contrast frames (frame matrixes) work better when a number of elements are being compared or a number of categories are being considered (see Table 9.2, p. 412). ■

■ A **Venn diagram** is a graphic organizer that uses overlapping circles to show relationships between words or other items.

FIGURE 6.3   Semantic Feature Analysis

BOATS	On water	Under water	Above water	Paddles, oars	Sails	Engines
Canoe	+	−	−	+	−	−
Rowboat	+	−	−	+	−	−
Motorboat	+	−	−	?	−	+
Sailboat	+	−	−	?	+	?
Submarine	−	+	−	−	−	+
Hydrofoil	−	−	+	−	−	+
Hovercraft	−	−	+	−	−	+

FIGURE 6.4   A Venn Diagram

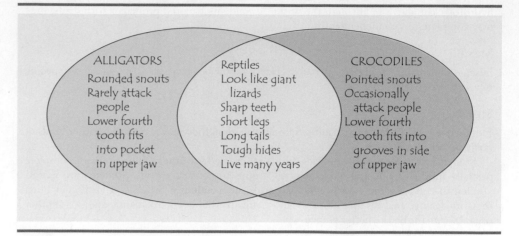

constructed. After they grasp the technique, students should be encouraged to construct their own diagrams. Because this activity requires active comparing and contrasting, it aids both understanding and memory.

Dramatizing

Although direct experience is the best teacher of vocabulary, it is not possible to provide it for all the words that have to be learned. Dramatization can be a reasonable substitute. Putting words in the context of simple skits adds interest and reality.

Dramatizations can be excerpted from a book or created by teachers or students. They need not be elaborate; a simple skit will work in most instances. Here is one dramatizing the word *irate*.

Student 1: Hey, Brian, what's wrong? You seem really mad.

Student 2: Someone's eaten my lunch. They must have known my dad packed my favorite sandwich, peanut butter and banana with raisins. I'm boiling inside. I'm really irate.

Student 1: I'd be irate, too, if someone took my lunch. But before you blow your lid, calm down. Maybe you misplaced it. Say, isn't that your dad coming down the hall? And what's that in his hand? It looks like a lunch bag.

Another way of dramatizing words is to use a hinting strategy (Jiganti & Tindall, 1986). After a series of new words has been introduced and discussed, the teacher distributes cards to individuals or pairs of students; on each card is one of the new words. Each student or pair creates a series of sentences that contain hints to the identity of the target word. Hints for *exaggerate* can be found in the following paragraph:

> I like being around Fred, but he tends to stretch the truth a little. The other day, he caught a fairly large fish. But to hear him tell it, it sounded like a whale. When Fred catches five fish, he pretends that he really caught twenty. And when it's a little chilly, Fred says it's the coldest day of the year. I like Fred, but I wish he'd stick a little closer to the facts.

The new words are written on the chalkboard. Students read their hints, and the class then tries to figure out which of the new words they describe.

Creating Memorable Events

Create events that lead to the introduction of a new word and provide contextual clues to its meaning. To introduce the word *lethargic*, drag yourself around the class and complain that everything takes so much effort. Tell the class that you are feeling lethargic and ask what they think *lethargic* means. To introduce the word *incoherent*, you might try this example provided by Alber and Foil (2003), which is sure to engage students. When the students enter the classroom, you might say something like, "Okay, it's time to get to work. I want you to take out your dog food and write a rocket ship about the computer floating over that tree" (p. 23). If students express puzzlement, say, "Aren't you listening? I want you to go to the ceiling and make up a can opener about a zebra" (p. 23). Then explain that you were being incoherent. Ask students to tell what they think *incoherent* means. Also be sure to introduce *coherent*. This kind of introduction to new words is especially helpful to struggling learners and ELLs.

Determining Shades of Meaning

Semantic gradients, or differentials, can be used to help students note differences in shades of meaning (Greenwood & Flanigan, 2007). Students place words along a continuum based on the words' meanings. They might be given words such as *huge*, *massive*, *mammoth*, and *large* to place on a continuum based on the words' strength or intensity, or they might create a continuum that links opposites, such as *freezing* and *scalding*. The task is more challenging when students have to generate words. Meeting in small groups, students must decide on placement of the words and convince their peers that their placement is accurate. Discussions often involve using dictionaries and thesauruses. Through discussion, students learn to use the tools of vocabulary acquisition and also deepen their knowledge of the words being discussed.

 Using Technology

Read•Write•Think features a sample lesson showing how to use semantic gradients, Solving Word Meanings: Engaging Strategies for Vocabulary Development.
http://www.readwritethink.org/lessons/lesson_view.asp?id=1089 ∎

Exploring Word Histories

Knowing the histories of words helps students in three ways: It sheds light on their meanings and helps students remember them better and longer; it "can function as a memory device by providing additional context" (Dale & O'Rourke, 1971, p. 70); and it can spark an interest in words.

Large numbers of words and expressions are drawn from Greek and Roman mythology. Read Greek and Roman myths to students, or, if they are able, have them read some on their own. As a follow-up, discuss words that have been derived from them. After reading about one of Hercules' adventures, discuss what a herculean task might be. After reading about Mars, the god of war, ask what martial music is. Discuss, too, expressions that are drawn from Greek and Roman mythology: Achilles heel, Midas touch, Gordian knot, Pandora's box, and laconic reply. The books in the following Student Reading List provide word histories.

 FYI

Find the origins of *boycott*, *pasteurized*, and *iridescent*. How would knowing the origins help your students understand the words? ∎

Enjoying Words

In school, words are used to instruct, correct, and direct. They should also be used to have fun, as one of the functions of language is to create enjoyment. Recite appropriate puns, limericks, and jokes to the children, and encourage them to share their favorites. Include word-play collections, such as those listed in the Student Reading List, in the classroom library.

 Using Technology

Funbrain.com features a variety of intriguing activities, including several word games.
http://www.funbrain.com/vocab/index.html ∎

STUDENT READING LIST

Word Histories

Baker, R. F. (2003). *In a word: 750 words and their fascinating stories and origins.* Peterborough, NH: Cobblestone.

Houghton Mifflin. (2004). *Word histories and mysteries: From abracadabra to Zeus.* Boston: Author.

Houghton Mifflin. (2006). *More word histories and mysteries: From aardvark to zombie.* Boston: Author.

Metcalf, A. A. (1999). *The world in so many words: A country-by-country tour of words that have shaped our language.* Boston: Houghton Mifflin.

Umstatter, J. (2002). *Where words come from.* New York: Franklin Watts.

STUDENT READING LIST
Word Play

Cerf, B. (1960). *Bennett Cerf's book of riddles.* New York: Random House. This collection features a variety of easy-to-read riddles.

Christopher, M. (1996). *Baseball jokes and riddles.* Boston: Little, Brown. This book presents more than fifty jokes and riddles.

Clark, E. C. (1991). *I never saw a purple cow and other nonsense rhymes.* Boston: Little, Brown. The collector has illustrated her collection of more than 120 nonsense rhymes about animals.

Hall, K., & Eisenberg, L. (1998). *Puppy riddles.* New York: Dial. Presents a series of forty-two easy-to-read riddles about puppies.

Joyce, S. (1999). *ABC animal riddles.* Gilsum, NH: Peel Productions. Readers use the alphabet to help guess the answers to riddles.

Kitchen, B. (1990). *Gorilla/chinchilla and other animal rhymes.* New York: Dial. Rhymed text describes a variety of animals whose names rhyme but who have very different habits and appearances.

Lederer, R. (1996). *Pun and games: Jokes, riddles, daffynitions, tairy fales, rhymes, and more word play for kids.* Chicago: Chicago Review Press. This book features a variety of word-play activities for older students.

Mathews, J., & Robinson, F. (1993). *Oh, how waffle! Riddles you can eat.* Morton Grove, IL: Whitman, 1993. This book features riddles related to food.

Meddaugh, S. (1992). *Martha speaks.* Boston: Houghton Mifflin. Problems arise when Martha, the family dog, learns to speak after eating alphabet soup.

Rattigan, J. (1994). *Truman's aunt farm.* Boston: Houghton Mifflin. When Truman sends in the coupon for an ant farm, a birthday present from his Aunt Fran, he gets more than he bargains for when aunts instead of ants show up.

Rosen, M. (1995). *Walking the bridge of your nose: Wordplay poems and rhymes.* London: Kingfisher. This collection features a variety of poems and rhymes that play with words.

Terban, M. (1992). *Funny you should ask: How to make up jokes and riddles with wordplay.* Boston: Houghton Mifflin.

Terban, M. (2007). *Eight ate: A feast of homonym riddles.* Boston: Houghton Mifflin. This collection features clever riddles based on homonyms.

Crossword Puzzles   Crossword puzzles are excellent for reinforcing students' vocabulary. When creating them, also use previously introduced words. Puzzles are more valuable if they revolve around a theme—such as farm implements, the parts of the eye, or words that describe moods. For younger readers, start out with limited puzzles that have only five to ten words and expand puzzles as students gain in proficiency.

A dictionary is a valuable word-learning tool.

Riddles   Riddles are inherently interesting to youngsters, and they provide an enjoyable context for developing vocabulary. They can be used to expand knowledge of homonyms, multiple meanings, figurative versus literal language, and intonation as a determiner of word meaning (Tyson & Mountain, 1982). Homonyms can be presented through riddles such as the following:

> Why is Sunday the strongest day?
>
> Because the other days are weak days. (p. 171)

Multiple meanings might be reinforced through riddles of the following type:

> Why couldn't anyone play cards on the boat?
>
> Because the captain was standing on the deck. (p. 171)

Riddles containing figurative language can be used to provide practice with common figures of speech:

> Why were the mice afraid to be out in the storm?
>
> Because it was raining cats and dogs. (p. 172)

Some of the riddle books listed in the Student Reading List might be used to implement these suggestions. Also, plan activities in which riddles and puzzles are not tied to a lesson, so that students can experience them just for the fun of it.

Discovering Sesquipedalian Words

Students enjoy the challenge of sesquipedalian words (Dale & O'Rourke, 1971). Composed of the Latin form *sesqui* ("one and one-half") and *ped* ("foot"), *sesquipedalian* means "foot and a half," or very long words. Long or obviously difficult words tend to be easier to learn than short ones because they are distinctive. Given the prestige and pride involved in learning them, students are also willing to put in more effort. Set up a sesquipedalian bulletin board. Encourage students to contribute to it. They can write the words, including the sentence context in which the words were used, on three-by-five cards, which can then be placed on the bulletin board. Other students should be encouraged to read each word and see whether they can use context to determine its meaning. Then they can use the dictionary to check whether their guess is correct and learn how to pronounce the word. The ultimate aim is to have students become lifetime collectors of long and interesting words.

Word of the Day

A good way to begin the day is with a new word. The word might tie in with the day, the time of year, or some special local or national event. Or choose a word related to a topic the students are studying. Select interesting, useful words. Write the word on the board, or put it on a special bulletin board. Read or write the context in which the word is used. Have students try to guess the meaning of the word. Provide a history of the word, and discuss why it's an important word. Encourage students to collect examples of the word's use. Working alone or in pairs, older students might present their own words of the day.

Labeling

Labeling provides greater depth of meaning to words by offering at least second-hand experience and, in some instances, helps illustrate relationships. The parts of plants, of the human body, of an airplane, or of many other items lend themselves to labeling. For instance, when students are about to read a true-life adventure about a pilot whose life was endangered when the flaps and ailerons froze, present a labeled diagram showing these and other airplane parts, such as fuselage, landing gear, stabilator, fin, rudder, and trim tab. A sample of such a labeled drawing is presented in Figure 6.5. Discuss each part and its function. Relate the parts to each other and show how they work together to make the plane fly. Ask students to picture the parts in operation during

FYI

- Talking about words is important. Many new words are acquired through explanation by others, including explanation in texts (Boote, 2006).
- Place words on the wall, and ask questions about them: Which word means "sad"? What does _____ mean? Which word tells what a quarterback might need? (Richek, 2005). ■

Building Language

Students enjoy the challenge of learning long words. Actually, long words are easier to learn because their length makes them more distinctive. ■

Using Technology

Word Central presents a new word each day, defines it, uses it in a sentence, and helps readers find its root.
http://www.wordcentral.com/buzzword/buzzword.php ■

Adapting Instruction for English Language Learners

Labeling helps students visualize words. Information may be coded in words or images (Sadowski & Paivio, 1994), and if it can be coded into both, memory is enhanced. The *Longman Dictionary of American English* (Pearson, 2008) has an inserted Picture Dictionary that provides labels for a range of illustrations. ■

FIGURE 6.5   Labeled Drawing of an Airplane

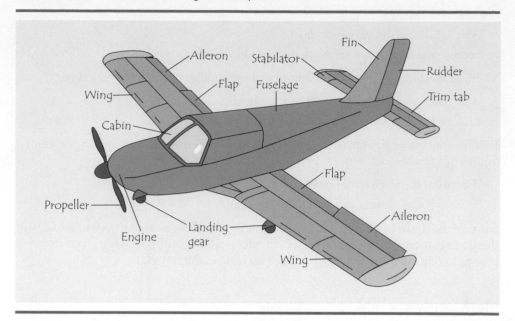

takeoff, level flight, turns, and landing. After the story has been read, give them drawings of a plane. Have them label the parts. Better yet, let them label their own drawings of a plane.

Feature Comparison

Through questions that contain two newly learned words, students can compare major meanings (Beck & McKeown, 1983). For example, ask such questions as "Could a virtuoso be a rival?" and "Could a philanthropist be a miser?" (p. 624). Answering correctly is not the crucial point of this kind of activity. What is important is that students have the opportunity to discuss their responses so as to clarify their reasoning processes and their grasp of the meanings of the words.

Using Word-Building Reference Books

Dictionaries give definitions, illustrative sentences, and sometimes drawings of words. However, this is often not enough, especially for words that apply to concepts that are unknown or vague. For example, a dictionary definition of *laser* is not sufficient for a student who is reading a selection that assumes knowledge of both the operation and the uses of lasers. In contrast, an encyclopedia entry on lasers explains how they work, what their major uses are, and how they were invented. Encourage the use of the encyclopedia so that students eventually refer to it or other suitable references to clarify difficult words on their own.

Predicting Vocabulary Words

The main purpose of studying vocabulary words before reading a selection is to improve comprehension. Two techniques that relate new vocabulary to the selection to be read are the predict-o-gram, which works only with fictional pieces, and possible sentences, which works best with informational text.

Predict-O-Gram   In a predict-o-gram, students organize vocabulary in terms of the story grammar of a selection (Blachowicz, 1977). Students predict which words would be used to describe the setting, the characters, the story problem, the plot, or

Using Technology

The Way Things Work (Dorling Kindersley), a CD-ROM program, uses explanations, labeled illustrations, and animations to show how dozens of technical devices work. Excellent for building background and vocabulary. ■

the resolution. Here's how the technique works: First, the teacher selects key words from the story. The words are written on the board and discussed to make sure students have some grasp of the meanings of the words. Students are then asked to predict which words the author would use to tell about the main parts of a story: the setting, the characters, the story problem, the plot, the resolution. The teacher asks the class to predict which words might fit in each part of the story grammar: "Which words tell about the setting? Which tell about the characters?" and so on. Once all the words have been placed, students might predict what the story is about. A completed predict-o-gram based on *Make Way for Ducklings* (McCloskey, 1941) is presented in Figure 6.6.

The predict-o-gram forces students to think about new vocabulary words in terms of a story that is to be read. It also helps students relate the words to each other. After the story has been read, students should discuss their predictions in terms of the actual content and structure of the story. They should also revise their predict-o-grams, which provides them with additional experience with the new words.

Possible Sentences   Possible sentences is a technique by which students use new vocabulary words to predict sentences that might appear in the selection to be read. Possible sentences has five steps (Moore & Moore, 1986):

1. **List key vocabulary.**   The teacher analyzes the selection to be read and selects two or three concepts that are the most important. Vocabulary words from the selection that are essential to understanding those concepts are chosen. These words are listed on the board, pronounced by the teacher, and briefly discussed with the class.
2. **Elicit sentences.**   Students use the words listed to compose sentences. They must use at least two words in each sentence and create sentences they feel might occur in the selection. It is suggested that the teacher model the creation of a sample sentence and the thinking processes involved. Students' sentences are written on the board even if not correct. Words may be used more than once. This step ends when all the words have been used in sentences or after a specified time.
3. **Read to verify sentences.**   Students read the text to verify the accuracy of their possible sentences.
4. **Evaluate sentences.**   After reading the selection, students evaluate their sentences. They discuss each sentence in terms of whether or not it could appear in the selection. Sentences are modified as needed.
5. **Create new sentences.**   Students use the words to create new sentences. These sentences are also discussed and checked for accuracy of usage.

The value of the possible sentences technique is that, in addition to being motivational, it helps students use informational text to refine their knowledge of new words. Because students write the words, it also helps them put new words into their active vocabularies. Putting new words in sentences is difficult, so the teacher should provide whatever guidance is necessary.

FIGURE 6.6 Predict-o-Gram for *Make Way for Ducklings*

Setting	Characters	Story Problem	Plot	Resolution
Boston	Mr. and Mrs. Mallard	nest	hatched	Michael
Public Garden	Michael	pond	responsibility	police
Charles River		island		
		ducklings		
		eggs		

Story Impressions

Story impressions is an activity that uses vocabulary from a story to activate students' story schema and build word knowledge. Students use vocabulary from a selection to reconstruct the story. Although students are encouraged to create a story that is as close as possible to the original one, faithfulness to the original is not as important as the ability to use the clues to create a logical, coherent story. To present story impressions, adapt the steps described in Lesson 6.3.

LESSON 6.3
Story Impressions

Objective
- Students use key words and knowledge of story structure to predict the development of a story.
- Students use key words and story structure to create a narrative.

Step 1. Developing a set of story impression clues

Read the story to get an overview. Then go back over the story and select words that highlight characters, setting, and key elements of the plot. Use single words or two- or three-word phrases. Select ten to fifteen words or phrases, and list them vertically on the board, interactive white board, or overhead in chronological order under the title of the story. Select words that are easy as well as some that might be challenging to students. Use arrows to show that one word or phrase leads to another. See Figure 6.7, which presents a list of story impression clues based on Gary Soto's (1998) *Big, Bushy Mustache*.

Step 2. Explaining story impressions

Explain the purpose of story impressions and how it works. Point out the title and the list of words and phrases. Explain to students that they will use the words and phrases to create a story and then will read the actual story to compare it with theirs. Explain that the words and phrases are listed in the order in which they appear in the selection.

Step 3. Reading the story's words and phrases

Read the words and phrases with students. Discuss any words that may be unfamiliar. Encourage students to think about the kind of story that might be created, based on the words listed.

Step 4. Creating a story impression

After discussing the words and phrases, you and the class create a story impression based on the clues. All listed words must be used. Students may add words and phrases not presented, may add endings to words, and may use the words more than once. Focus on creating a story that is interesting and logical. Provide help as needed so that a sensible story is formulated. After the story has been written on the board, discuss it, and encourage students to evaluate it and make revisions, if needed.

Step 5. Reading of the author's story

Invite students to read the author's story and then compare their version with it.

Step 6. Discussing the story

Discuss the author's story. Compare the author's and the class's versions. As students grow in proficiency, they might create and discuss story impressions in small cooperative learning groups. Story impressions can also be used as part of the writing program (McGinley & Denner, 1987; Richek, 2005). This activity provides excellent practice in constructing narrative pieces.

Step 7. Evaluation and review

Note students' ability to use key words and story structure to make logical predictions and to create a plausible narrative. Provide additional instruction and practice as necessary.

FIGURE 6.7 Story Impression Clues for *Big, Bushy Mustache*

school
↓
Ricky
↓
play
↓
big, bushy mustache
↓
costume
↓
pocket
↓
grown-up
↓
home
↓
lost
↓
retrace steps
↓
father
↓
told
↓
solve problem
↓
gracias
↓
gift

Word Experts

This activity works well when there are many words to be learned (Richek, 2005). The teacher compiles a list of words from materials that will soon be read. Page numbers on which the words appear are included. After words have been selected, the list is distributed to students. Students are directed to begin constructing their expert cards. Each student is assigned two words and writes each on a three-by-five card. The students locate the words in the reading selection and copy the sentences in which they were used. Students then obtain dictionary definitions for the words. The process of locating appropriate definitions is reviewed. Next, students write the definitions, which must be approved by the teacher, on the cards; they can also include a personal connection to the word and an illustration, if appropriate. The illustration need not be a drawing but can be an image from the Web or a magazine. Students can also dramatize their words.

After completing the expert cards, students pair up and teach their words to a partner. The student shows the first word to the partner and asks the partner if he or she knows what the word means. If not, the first student begins to give clues. The student has the partner read the sentence to see if he or she can figure out the meaning from context. The student then shows the illustration. If that doesn't work, the student may dramatize the word. Finally, the student reveals the dictionary definition and gives any other information about the word that might make it more memorable: its history or etymology, its part of speech, and any other uses that it has. Once a student has taught both words, the other student teaches his or her words. The process is repeated on successive days until all the words have been learned. When taught in this way, 92 to 97 percent of the listed words were learned (Richek, 2005).

Word Sorts

Word sorts is a useful activity when dealing with groups of related words. Sorting forces students to think about each word and to see similarities and differences among words. (Words can also be sorted according to their origins or roots.) Students might sort the following words: *melancholy, weary, tired, sorrowful, exhausted, glad, contented, cheerful, delighted, unhappy, gloomy, overworked, dejected.* The sort could be open, which means that students would decide on categories, or it could be closed. In a closed sort, the teacher decides the categories: happy, sad, tired. After sorting the words, students would discuss why they sorted them the way they did.

Vocabulary Self-Collection Strategy (VSS)

When given the opportunity to personalize their learning, students become more involved (Blachowicz & Fisher, 2000). A device that helps students personalize their learning is the vocabulary self-collection strategy (VSS) (Ruddell, 1992). In VSS, after reading a new selection, each student chooses one word to learn. The word selected should be one that the student believes is important enough for the whole class to learn. VSS is initiated after the text has been read because being familiar with the text helps students select words that are important. The teacher also selects a word. Students record the printed sentence in which they discovered the word. Students also tell what they think the word means in the context in which it was found and explain why they think the class should learn the word.

Words are discussed, and dictionaries and glossaries may be checked to make sure that the correct pronunciation and definition have been obtained. As the words and their possible meanings are discussed, the teacher might model the use of context clues and the dictionary. The teacher adds his or her word, and the class list is reviewed. Words selected are recorded in vocabulary notebooks or study sheets. Realizing that they are responsible for selecting a word for the whole class to study, students suddenly become word-conscious and begin noticing words as possible candidates for selection. As students become more conscious of words, they begin acquiring

FYI

Being involved in selecting words for study can be highly motivating to all students, but especially struggling readers. To limit the number of words chosen for class study, you might have students meet in small groups to discuss their words and select one for class study. Each group then presents its word to the class. ■

R E F L E C T I O N

How can you make vocabulary learning interesting but effective?

Adapting Instruction for Struggling Readers and Writers

- Many students who would benefit the most from wide reading seldom read for pleasure. Reading less, they fall farther behind their peers. One way for at-risk students to catch up is to read on their own.
- The *Early Bird Nature Books* (Lerner) explore a variety of science topics in easy-to-read fashion and develop key vocabulary through previewing, context, and a glossary. ■

new vocabulary words at an increased rate (Shearer, 1999). VSS can be extended by encouraging students to bring in new words they hear in oral contexts—television, radio, or conversations.

Wide Reading

The most productive method for building vocabulary—wide reading—requires no special planning or extra effort (Nagy & Herman, 1987). Research (Herman, Anderson, Pearson, & Nagy, 1987) indicates that average students have between a 1 in 20 and a 1 in 5 chance of learning an unfamiliar word they meet in context. Those who read for twenty-five minutes a day at the rate of 200 words per minute for 200 days of the year will encounter a million words (Nagy & Herman, 1987). About 15,000 to 30,000 of these words will be unfamiliar. Assuming a 1 in 20 chance of learning an unfamiliar word from context, students should pick up between 750 and 1,500 new words. Of course, if they read more, they have even greater opportunity for vocabulary growth. If they read 2 million rather than 1 million words a year, they theoretically would double the number of new words they learn.

Many of today's informational books for young people contain glossaries or phonetic spellings of difficult words and provide definitions in context. Some also contain labeled diagrams of technical terms. Note how the following excerpt from a reader-friendly informational book entitled *Fish That Play Tricks* (Souza, 1998) provides both phonetic respelling and contextual definitions:

> The grouper is only one of more than 20,000 different species (SPEE-sheez), or kinds, of fish that live in waters around the world. All fish are cold-blooded, meaning they cannot make themselves much warmer than the temperature around them. Like you, fish are vertebrates (VUHR-tuh-brits), or animals with skeletons inside their bodies. The skeletons of some fish, such as sharks and rays, are made of cartilage, a flexible tissue. (p. 4)

In addition to encouraging wide reading of varied materials, teachers can also provide students with strategies for using context clues, morphemic analysis, and the dictionary to decipher unknown words. Sternberg (1987) found that average adults trained to use context clues were able to decipher seven times as many words as those who spent the same amount of time memorizing words and definitions. If elementary school students are taught to use such clues with greater efficiency, it should boost their vocabulary development as well. For instance, students reading the book *Fish That Play Tricks*, from which the excerpt above was taken, would benefit if they were helped to discover that many of the terms in the book are explained in context, and the explanatory context often begins with the word *or*. Modeling the use of context clues and guided practice should also prove to be helpful.

Some books are designed to build vocabulary. Jane O'Connor's Fancy Nancy, the main character in a series of books for girls in the primary grades, likes fancy clothes and fancy words. Included in the series is *Fancy Nancy's Favorite Fancy Words* (Harper-Collins), which provides fancy synonyms for plain words. Young boys (and girls) may enjoy the picture books *The Boy Who Loved Words* (Schotter, 2006) and *Max's Words* (Banks, 2006). For older students, there are the Lemony Snickett books in which a number of useful but higher level words are explained. Some other books that are especially effective for building vocabulary are listed below.

FYI

High-quality books that are reasonably challenging are best for building vocabulary. ■

Reading to Students

Read-aloud books are better sources of new words for students in the early grades than are the books they read silently. Up until about grade 3 or 4, the books that students read are composed primarily of known words. At these levels, teachers frequently read books to students that would be too difficult for them to read on their own. Therefore, carefully chosen read-alouds can be effective for building word knowledge. Whereas it is best to introduce words beforehand when students are reading on their own, it is

Agroup of primary grade teachers were surprised that their students did not know many common words such as *circle*, *athlete*, and *umbrella* (Blachowicz & Obrochta, 2005). The teachers decided that students' background and vocabulary needed building. Although field trips are ideal for building background, the teachers decided that they couldn't take enough real-life field trips to build the necessary background. Instead, they decided to take virtual field trips through read-alouds. Using standards in science and social studies to choose suitable curriculum-related topics, the teachers planned virtual field trips, each of which consisted of reading five books on one of the selected topics: the human skeleton, weather and climate, animal habitats, or recycling. Words to be emphasized for each topic were then chosen by the teachers. For the topic of the human skeleton, words included *bone*, *skull*, *leg*, *arm*, *wrist*, *ankle*, *foot*, *ribs*, *brain*, *spine*, *backbone*, and *protect*. The topic was announced to students and they were encouraged to write down any words related to *skeleton* that they knew. These lists functioned as a preassessment, allowing the teachers to get a sense of what topic-related words students already knew and which should be introduced.

A poster of a skeleton was then displayed and students were asked to tell what they saw. Stick-on notes were used to label known parts. Words were discussed and acted on: "Point to your skull. Hold your wrist." The read-alouds were then initiated. Selections were read and discussed with particular emphasis on target words. New words were added to the chart. Students stuck their thumbs up whenever they heard one of the target words in a read-aloud. At the end of each session, students wrote about something they learned or something that interested them. After being read aloud, the books were placed in the reading center and students were encouraged to read them. As one teacher explained:

> These books circulate four or five times more than they did last year. The read-alouds help my kids get interested in the topic and also make the other books accessible to them because they know some of the ideas and the vocabulary. It really works! (Blachowicz & Obrochta, 2005, p. 266)

Students continued to add words to the skeleton. They even added words from their own reading. Parents reported that children asked to be taken to the library to get books on the topic being explored. Not surprisingly, post-assessment showed a gain in words learned, especially among students who initially recorded the fewest words.

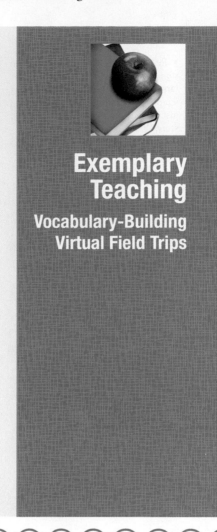

Exemplary Teaching
Vocabulary-Building Virtual Field Trips

STUDENT READING LIST
Building Vocabulary

Frasier, D. (2000). *Miss Alaineus: A vocabulary disaster.* San Diego, CA: Harcourt Brace.
Gibbons, G. (1990). *Weather words and what they mean.* New York: Holiday House.
Hansen, A. S. (2010). *Solar energy: Running on sunshine.* New York: Rosen.
Juster, N. (1961). *The phantom toll booth.* New York: Random House.
Newman, L. (2004). *The boy who cried fabulous.* Berkeley, CA: Tricycle Press.
O'Connor, J. (2008). *Fancy Nancy's favorite fancy words: From accessories to zany.* New York: HarperCollins.
Ravishankar, A. (2007). *Elephants never forget.* Boston: Houghton Mifflin.
Simons, W. (2011). *Exploring countries: Pakistan.* Minneapolis, MN: Bellwhether Media.
Tarsky, S. (1997). *The busy building book.* New York: Putnam.

 Using Technology

Digital books often have features for developing vocabulary. For example, in *The New Kid on the Block* (Broderbund), viewers hear the poems read aloud as text is displayed on the screen with accompanying animation. When words or phrases are clicked on, they are dramatized. ■

 FYI

Reading to students results in average effect sizes of 21 percentile points in oral language and 14 percentile pointsin reading (Hattie, 2009). ■

better to discuss vocabulary words after a selection has been read aloud to students. If words are needed for an understanding of a selection, then they can be explained briefly as the selection is being read. That way, students can immediately use their knowledge of the new words to comprehend the selection.

Beck and McKeown (2001) devised an approach in which a portion of the read-aloud was devoted to developing vocabulary. From each book, two to four words were selected. Words were selected that were probably unknown to students but that labeled concepts or experiences that would be familiar. These included words such as *reluctant*, *immense*, *miserable*, and *searched*. The words were presented in the context of the story, discussed, and later used by students. After reading *A Pocket for Corduroy* (Freeman, 1978) to students, the teacher stated, "In the story, Lisa was reluctant to leave the laundromat without Corduroy. *Reluctant* means you are not sure you want to do something. Say the word for me" (Beck, McKeown, & Kucan, 2002, p. 51). Students say the word so that they gain a phonological representation of it. The teacher then gives examples involving *reluctant*, such as foods that they might be reluctant to eat or amusement park rides that they might be reluctant to go on. Students are then asked to tell about some things that they might be reluctant to do. "Tell about something that you might be reluctant to do. Try to use *reluctant* when you tell about it. You could start by saying something like 'I would be reluctant to _____.'" (p. 51).

Notice how the teacher provided a prompt to help students formulate a sentence using *reluctant*. This would be especially helpful to English language learners. Note, too, the steps in the presentation:

1. Presenting the word in story context.
2. Providing an understandable definition of the word.
3. Providing examples of the use of the word in other contexts, so that the word generalizes. Otherwise, students might form the impression that *reluctant* means "to leave something behind that you don't want to leave behind" as in "leaving the laundromat without Corduroy."
4. Having children relate the word to their own lives. They did this by talking about things that they were reluctant to do. They might also make a list of things that they are reluctant to do or write about a time when they felt reluctant.
5. Reviewing the word. The word is related to other words that are being introduced and to other words that students have learned. For instance, students might discuss how *reluctant* and *eager* are opposites. As occasions arise, the teacher uses newly taught words. She or he might talk about being reluctant to go outside because it is cold and rainy or reluctant to take down the Thanksgiving decorations because they look so nice. She or he might also read aloud *The Reluctant Dragon* (Grahame, 1966).
6. Encouraging students to use the word in their speaking and writing and also to note examples of hearing or seeing the word. As Dale and O'Rourke (1971) explain, learning a new word is serendipitous. Newly learned words have a way of cropping up in our reading and listening.

Some books are better than others for developing vocabulary. The frequency with which a new word appears in the text, whether the word is illustrated, and the helpfulness of the context in which the word appears are factors that promote the learning of a new word (Elley, 1989). Having students retell a story in which a new word appears also seems to foster vocabulary growth. Words are used with more precision and in more elaborated fashion during students' second and third retellings (Leung, 1992).

To be more effective at building vocabulary, the story being read to students should be within their listening comprehension. If the words are too abstract for the students' level, gains may be minimal. In one study in which a fairly difficult text was read to students aged 8 to 10, only the best readers made significant gains (Nicholson & Whyte, 1992). An inspection of the target words in the text suggested that they may have been too far above the level of the average and below-average readers. The study also suggested that while bright students might pick up words from a single reading, average and below-average students may require multiple encounters with the words.

Speaking and Writing

The ultimate aim of vocabulary development is to have students use new words in their speaking and writing. In-depth study of words and multiple exposures will help students attain sufficient understanding of words and how they are used so that they will be able to employ them in their speech and writing. All students, but especially English learners, should be encouraged to use new words in the classroom so that they become comfortable with them and thus feel confident in using them in other situations. Students should also be encouraged to use new words in their written reports and presentations. As part of preparing students for a writing assignment, teachers might highlight words that lend themselves to inclusion in the written pieces.

Using a Thesaurus

Students tend to use familiar, everyday words to express their thoughts. A thesaurus is an excellent tool to help them use a greater range of vocabulary by seeking out and using synonyms. In addition to helping students use a more varied vocabulary, a thesaurus can help students become aware of the shades of meanings of words and can acquaint them with new words for old meanings. By providing synonyms, a thesaurus can also clarify the meaning of the word being looked up. Many thesauruses also provide antonyms. Being provided with a word's opposites also clarifies the meaning of the word. Because most word-processing programs have a thesaurus, using a thesaurus is convenient and easy.

 Using Technology

Thesauruses are available in print and online as well as in apps. ■

To introduce a thesaurus, you may have students brainstorm synonyms for an overused word such as *said*. After listing the synonyms, show students how they can use a thesaurus to accomplish the same purpose. A good practice activity would be to provide students with a paragraph in which overused words are underlined and have them select synonyms for them. Stress the importance of finding the appropriate synonym. The synonym must match the meaning of the word according to the way it is being used. Initially, underline only those words that are relatively easy to find synonyms for. Once students have a basic grasp of how to use a thesaurus, show how it can be used to improve the wording of a written piece. Encourage them to use a thesaurus to provide a more varied vocabulary in their writing.

A thesaurus can be a highly effective tool for building vocabulary, especially for English learners. *The Longman Dictionary of American English* (4th ed.) (Pearson Education, 2008), which is designed for English learners but may be used by all older students, provides thesaurus entries to accompany many of the words being defined. For the word *jubilant*, the thesaurus entry lists *happy, glad, delighted, thrilled, overjoyed, ecstatic, elated*. Users are introduced to a number of words having a similar meaning. This clarifies the meaning of the word being looked up but also has the potential of adding new words to the user's vocabulary.

Introducing New Words

At a minimum, the introduction of new words should include a definition of the word, the use of the word in a sentence or story context, an activity that relates the word to other words being introduced, and an activity that relates the word to the students' background. In the sixth-grade level of one basal series (Flood et al., 2001), the words *participate, ordeals, grimaced, spat, encounter*, and *victorious* are introduced with definitions in preparation for reading the selection *Ta-Na-E-Ka* (Whitebird, 2001). The words are also used in context and discussed. To help students relate the words to their backgrounds of experience, the following types of questions are asked:

- What school activities do you like to participate in?
- Have you ever had to go through something that you consider an ordeal?
- In what contest would you most like to be victorious? (p. 140D)

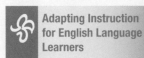

Adapting Instruction for English Language Learners

A key task for ELLs is learning the English labels for concepts that they possess in their native language. ■

FYI

Although cognates are derived from the same word, some words and their cognates may have acquired slightly different meanings over the years. ■

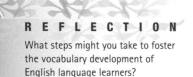

R E F L E C T I O N

What steps might you take to foster the vocabulary development of English language learners?

Developing the Vocabulary of English Language Learners

English language learners know fewer English words than their native speaking peers, and they also possess fewer meanings for these words (Verhallen & Schoonen, 1993). Ironically, when reading, ELLs rely more on their vocabulary knowledge than do native speakers of English. Intensive instruction in vocabulary can make a difference. After two years of systematic instruction, ELLs closed the gap in vocabulary and comprehension that existed between their performance and that of native speakers by about 50 percent (McLaughlin et al., 2000). Taking part in a similar program that lasted for four years, language minority elementary school students in Holland made gains of one or two years beyond that made by a control group (Appel & Vermeer, 1996, as cited in McLaughlin et al., 2000). There were also encouraging gains in reading comprehension. The researchers concluded that language minority students can catch up to native speakers in vocabulary knowledge if they receive targeted vocabulary instruction for about four hours a week throughout the school year and if the instruction is carried out for all eight grades of elementary and middle school.

Knowing how words are stored in bilingual students' minds will help you plan ways to develop their vocabularies. Unfortunately, there is no agreement on how words are stored. Some experts believe that the words are stored separately. Words learned in Spanish are not stored in the same place as words learned in English, so *amigo* and *friend* would not share a storage location. Others believe that there is a single store, so *amigo* and *friend* are stored in the same location. A third possibility is that the English words are linked to the Spanish words. When the student hears *friend*, he or she thinks first of the equivalent in his or her language: *amigo*. The fourth theory is that there are overlapping stores: Some words are linked; some are not. The most reasonable theory seems to be that there is overlap between the two stores (Cook, 2001). With some words, students might have to access the meaning in their native language first. With other words, they can access the meaning without going through a translation process. It is easier for young students to learn a word through translation than it is through an explanation, definition, or even illustration. A young Spanish-speaking student will learn the word *cat* faster if you say it means "el gato" than if you show her or him a picture of a cat or point to a cat (Durgunoglu & Oney, 2000).

To promote full understanding, provide translations of new vocabulary words. If you are unable to translate the words, enlist the services of an older student, a parent, or a bilingual teacher. You might post key vocabulary words in both languages in a prominent spot. Also explore **cognates**. Some cognates have identical spellings, such as *color* (koh-LOR) and *chocolate* (choh-koh-LAH-teh) but, as you can see, do not have the same pronunciations. Others have similar spellings: *calendario, excelente, lista*. Still others have spellings that are similar but might not be similar enough to be recognized: *carro* (*car*), *crema* (*cream*), *difícil* (*difficult*).

Spanish-speaking students may know some advanced English words without realizing it. For instance, the word *luna* (*moon*) would be known by very young Spanish-speaking children. However, *lunar*, as in *lunar landing*, is an advanced word for native speakers of English. Spanish developed from Latin; *luna*, for instance, is a Latin word. Although English has thousands of words borrowed from Latin, English developed primarily from Anglo-Saxon. Its most basic words are derived from Anglo-Saxon. Words derived from Latin tend to be a more advanced way of expressing common concepts encapsulated by the most basic English words. Although Spanish-speaking students have to learn most common English words from scratch, they have a running start on learning many of the more advanced words because a large proportion of these words are derived from Latin. Explain to Spanish-speaking students that they know some of the harder words in English; you might use *lunar* as an example. This will affirm the value of the students' first language but will also provide them with a most valuable tool for learning English. Make use of this

■ **Cognates** are words that are similar in both languages, have a common derivation, and share a common meaning, although the pronunciation may differ.

principle when introducing new vocabulary. For instance, when introducing *annual*, ask Spanish-speaking students to tell you the Spanish word for *year* (*año*). Help them to see that the word *annual* is related to *año*. Follow a similar approach for words like *arbor* (*árbol–tree*), *grand* (*grande–big*), *primary* (*primero–first*), *rapidly* (*rapidamente–quickly*), and *tardy* (*tarde–late*).

Not having had the same opportunity to learn English as native speakers have, ELLs understandably have a more limited store of English words. Experts agree that this is their main stumbling block on the road to literacy in English. They need a long-term, well-planned program of vocabulary development, which builds on their growing knowledge of English and their command of another language. In many instances, vocabulary development for them will simply consist of learning the English label for a familiar concept. In other instances, they might be able to use cognates to help them develop their English vocabulary.

Beyond the Core Program Vocabulary instruction for ELLs has to be more extensive than that provided in the core program (Gersten et al., 2007). Draw up a list of essential vocabulary words. These can be drawn from the core program and from content areas. English learners may not know common words such as *sink*, *bank*, and *can*, which will be known by native speakers. These words can be taught quickly (Gersten et al., 2007). Along with developing the meanings of the words, the instruction should help ELLs understand how to use the words.

Teach Academic Vocabulary Explicitly teach ELLs academic vocabulary in the content areas. For example, in math, you can teach your students the terms for subtraction: *subtract*, *take away*, and *decreased by*. In science, you can teach terms that connect the parts of an experiment: *therefore*, *as a result*, and *for instance*. For social studies, you can teach key words and also the background knowledge that ELLs will

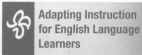

Adapting Instruction for English Language Learners

Television, radio, lessons, lectures, discussions, and conversations are rich sources of new words. Set aside a few minutes each day to discuss new words that your pupils have heard. This could be especially helpful to students still learning English. They may have questions about pronunciation and shades of meaning. ■

Case Study

Teaching Vocabulary to English Language Learners

Edguardo, a sixth-grader, is a conscientious, highly motivated student. Having attended a dual-language school since kindergarten, he is reading on grade level in Spanish and is fluent in English. Although his decoding skills in English reading are on grade level, Edguardo has difficulty with comprehension. He feels overwhelmed when he encounters a number of words that he doesn't know. As might be expected of an ELL, Edguardo's English vocabulary is somewhat below grade level. Because he has had less opportunity to develop English vocabulary, Edguardo could benefit from a program of intensive vocabulary instruction. A general program of vocabulary development would be helpful. But even more effective would be a program designed to teach Edguardo, or any other student in similar circumstances, the words that he is most likely to meet in texts.

For Edguardo and other ELLs, much of their word learning will involve learning the English equivalent of words already known in their first language. When Edguardo learns the word *moon*, he need only associate it with the known Spanish word for moon, *luna*. In addition, there are thousands of cognates, words such as *artista*, *autor*, *contento*. See Table 6.1 for a listing of high-frequency cognates.

TABLE 6.1 Frequently Used Spanish Cognates

artista	famoso	música
autor	foto	necesita
bebé	favorito	nota
biografía	fruta	número
carácter	gigante	oficina
carro	gorila	página
causa	grado	papá
contento	hipopótamo	perfecta
describir	importante	rápido
diferente	insecto	teléfono
difícil	jirafa	tigre
elefante	mamá	tomate
enciclopedia	mágico	uniforme
eléctrica	mayo	vegetales
familia	minuto	zoológico

Science is an excellent source of new words.

need. For example, when you mention Thanksgiving, an English-speaking student is likely to know about the holiday's origins among the early European settlers on the east coast during the seventeenth and eighteenth centuries. But for ELLs, the word *Thanksgiving* may not mean much by itself. In English language arts, you can use basic graphic organizers for word development to visually represent knowledge. ELLs can write a word and then explore its connections and relationships (Colorín Colorado, 2008).

Assessing Vocabulary

An essential ingredient in developing students' literacy so that they are college and career ready is to build their vocabulary. Therefore, it is important to have information about students' vocabulary knowledge, especially students who are struggling or who are not native speakers of English. Most norm-referenced reading tests contain a reading vocabulary subtest. Or, individual students may have been given the Peabody Picture Vocabulary Test or another test of vocabulary. You can also get a general idea of students' listening and speaking vocabularies by noting the kinds of words that they use. An easy-to-administer group measure of students' vocabulary knowledge, The Vocabulary Levels Test, is available at the School of Linguistics and Applied Language (University of Wellington); go to http://www.victoria.ac.nz/lals/resources/vocrefs/default.aspx. The Vocabulary Levels Test assesses students' knowledge of the 10,000 most frequently occurring words and the Academic Word List. Although designed for ELLs, the Vocabulary Levels Test can be used with native speakers of English. Vocabulary knowledge can also be assessed informally. One of the easiest and most flexible vocabulary assessments is a self-reporting scale. In a self-reporting scale, students are given a list of words and asked to check one of four responses.

1. I never saw it before.
2. I have heard of it, but I don't know what it means.
3. I recognize it in context—it has something to do with. . . .
4. I know it. (Dale & O'Rourke, 1971, p. 3)

A Planned Program

Although young people apparently learn an amazing number of words incidentally, a **planned program** of vocabulary development is highly advisable. Research from as far back as the 1930s (Gray & Holmes, 1938, cited in Curtis, 1987) suggested that direct teaching is more effective than a program that relies solely on incidental learning. A more recent review of a number of research studies confirmed these results (Petty, Herold, & Stoll, 1968).

Based on their extensive investigations, Beck, McKeown, and Omanson (1987) opted for a program that includes both direct teaching and incidental learning of words and also differentiates among words. Words especially important to the curriculum are given "rich instruction." These words are chosen from basals, content-area texts, or trade books that are to be read by students, and they are selected on the basis of their importance in understanding the text, frequency of appearance in students' reading, and general usefulness. Rich instruction goes beyond simple definition to include discussion, application, and further activities. Words selected for rich instruction might be presented five to ten times or more. Less important words are simply

■ A **planned program** is one in which a certain amount of time is set aside each week for vocabulary instruction. Vocabulary may be preselected from materials students are about to read or from words they may need to understand content-area concepts.

defined and used in context. This process introduces words that become more familiar as students meet them in new contexts. Any remaining new words are left to incidental learning. Perhaps the most important feature of this program is that words are taught within the context of reading, as opposed to being presented in isolated lists.

Another important component of a planned vocabulary program is motivation. Students will try harder and presumably do better if they encounter intriguing words in interesting stories and if they can relate learning vocabulary to their personal lives. As Sternberg (1987) commented, "In most of one's life, one learns because one wants to or because one truly has to, or both" (p. 96).

Word Generation and Alias

Word generation is an interdisciplinary program designed to develop academic vocabulary. Words are drawn from the Academic Word List (AWL), which is a listing of words frequently used in academic settings, and are embedded in content materials created for the program. The articles in which the words were embedded discuss high-interest but controversial topics, such as cyberbullying or paying students to do well in school. Each content-area teacher spends 15 minutes a week developing the words within his or her content area. On Monday, the English teacher introduces the words. On the next day, the math teacher presents the words in a word problem. On Wednesday, the science teacher presents the words in a science article. On Thursday, the student's social studies teacher has the students debate an article that contains the words. On Friday, the English teacher leads the students to develop a persuasive essay using the words. The persuasive essay is based on the controversial issue that was introduced on Monday. In addition to improving their academic vocabulary, students learn to discuss and write about controversial issues (Strategic Education Research Partnership, 2009).

Academic Language Instruction for All Students (ALIAS) is a vocabulary-building approach similar to Word Generation, except that it is designed to be implemented by language arts teachers. It was effective in building both academic vocabulary and, to a lesser extent, comprehension (Lesaux, Kieffer, Faller, & Kelley, 2010). Academic vocabulary was presented in 45-minute segments to sixth-graders four days a week in eight-day units. Each unit was based on an interesting article from *Time for Kids*, a periodical published for students in grades 4 to 6. Words were introduced in the context of the selection. On day one, students read and discussed the article, and the eight or nine target words were introduced. On day two, use of context clues was discussed. Possible word meanings were brainstormed and the class, under the teacher's direction, created an accurate definition. Class definitions were recorded. Students were encouraged to compose a personal definition by writing the class definition in their own words. On subsequent days, students, working in pairs, responded to questions about the text. The questions contained target words. In other activities, students drew representations of the words and completed similar reinforcement activities. Students then engaged in a morphological analysis of the target words and created a chart in which various forms of the target words were displayed: inflected forms, derived forms, and related words. For the word *suspicious*, the words *suspicion, suspiciously, suspiciousness*, and *suspect* were listed (Word Generation, 2010). Ultimately, words were used in speaking and writing. Discussions or mock interviews were held in which the target words were purposely used. Students then used the target words in written pieces. The writing activities were set up so that they lent themselves to the use of the words. For instance, they responded to the prompt: "What *crucial* invention from the past one hundred years has most *affected* your daily life?" (Lesaux et al., 2010, p. 206). The italicized words are target words.

Teachers liked the program. They were especially pleased with the use of high-interest materials. The use of intriguing topics set the stage for lively debates. Discussions were enlivened because students really wanted to talk about the topics. The ability to present challenging material to all students and the ability to receive effective professional development were also key factors. Teachers had at first feared that the

Using Technology

Word Generation

Provides a wealth of information about Word Generation.
http://wordgeneration.org ■

activities were too difficult, but were happily surprised to see that their students met the challenge.

A Balanced Blend

Vocabulary instruction should be a balanced blend of the planned and the incidental. The **incidental approach** capitalizes on students' immediate need to know words. It gives the program spontaneity and vitality. A planned approach ensures that vocabulary instruction is given the attention it deserves. Important words and techniques for learning words are taught systematically and in depth. Combining these two types of approaches should provide the best possible program and should help close the vocabulary gap.

Closing the Vocabulary Gap

The greatest disparity between educational achievers and nonachievers in U.S. schools lies in vocabulary and background, which means that the single greatest need for underachieving schools and underachieving students is building vocabulary and background. Unlike most reform movements, no money is required, no professional development or outside consultants are needed, no new materials need to be purchased, no schedules need to be adjusted, and no complex procedures need to be put in place. To build vocabulary, all you need to do is make a few adjustments to things you do anyway. Talk in a way that builds vocabulary, read stories aloud using Text Talk or a form of it, make vocabulary development a part of students' reading, make students word-conscious, and have fun with words. Not all vocabulary instruction has to be robust. Briefly introducing words before a story is read builds vocabulary, as does parenthetically mentioning words while reading aloud or having a class discussion in which unfamiliar words might pop up. If you have ELLs or struggling learners in your room, make it a point to briefly explain, illustrate, or demonstrate words that they might have difficulty with. When in doubt, ask students to signal thumbs up if they know a word and thumbs down if they don't.

Teaching Special Features of Words

Many words have special characteristics that have to be learned if the words are to be understood fully. Among such important features are homophones, homographs, figurative language, multiple meanings, connotation, and denotation.

Homophones

Homophones are words that are pronounced the same but differ in spelling and meaning and often have different origins as well: for example, *cheap* and *cheep* or *knew*, *gnu*, and *new*. In reality, homophones are more of a problem for spelling than for reading because context usually clarifies their meaning. In some instances, however, it is important to note spelling to interpret the meaning of a sentence correctly—for example:

He complements his wife.

The shed is dun.

To avoid being tackled, you must feint.

REFLECTION

What steps might be taken to close the vocabulary gap that exists between underachieving and achieving students?

FYI

To convey the concept of homophones, you might have students translate sentences that have been written in homophones, like these: *Aye gnu Gym wood bee hear. Dew ewe no hymn?* ■

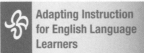

Adapting Instruction for English Language Learners

The Web page ESL: Quizzes: Self-Study offers a variety of self-checking quizzes on common words, idioms, homonyms, and slang expressions. It also includes games and crossword puzzles. Although designed for ESL students, it could be used with native speakers of English.
http://iteslj.org/links/ESL/Quizzes/Self_Study ■

■ The **incidental approach** to vocabulary instruction involves the study of vocabulary words as they occur in the natural course of reading and writing. A balanced vocabulary program is a blend of the incidental and planned approaches.

■ The combining form *phon* means "sound," so **homophones** are words that have the same sound but differ in meaning and often have different origins. They usually do not have the same spelling: *be*, *bee*; *him*, *hymn*.

To build awareness of homophones, discuss riddles. Write a riddle on the chalkboard, and have students identify the word that has a homophone—for example, "What is black and white and read all over?"

(the newspaper). Additional riddles may be found in the books presented in the Student Reading List for Word Play (pp. 273–274). Students might enjoy reading Fred Gwynne's books on homophones, such as *The King Who Rained* (1987), *A Chocolate Moose for Dinner* (1988a), and *A Little Pigeon Toad* (1988b), or one of Peggy Parrish's *Amelia Bedelia* books.

Homographs

Homographs are words that have the same spelling but different meanings and possibly different pronunciations—for example, *palm* (part of the hand or a tree) and *bat* (a club or a mammal). They make spelling easier but reading more difficult. For instance, on seeing the word *page*, the reader must use context to decide whether the word means "a piece of paper" or "someone who attends a knight or runs errands for lawmakers." Homographs may share a single pronunciation or have different pronunciations. Homographs such as the following, which have two distinct pronunciations, can be particularly troublesome for students: *bass, bow, desert, dove, lead, minute, sewer,* and *sow*.

As students learn that a word may have two, three, or even more entirely separate meanings, stress the importance of matching meaning with context. Students may also need to learn an entirely new meaning, and perhaps a pronunciation, for a word that looks familiar. Reading the sentence "The neighbors had a terrible row," students will see that neither of the familiar meanings "paddle a boat" or "in a line" fits this sense of *row*. They must learn from context, a dictionary, or another source that the word's third meaning is "a noisy fight or quarrel." They will also need to learn that *row* in this context is pronounced /rau/.

Figurative Language

Young students tend to interpret language literally and may have difficulty with figurative language. This is especially true for children who have a profound hearing loss and those whose native language is not English. It is important to make young children aware that language is not always to be taken literally. As they grow in their ability to handle figurative expressions, they should be led to appreciate phrases that are especially apt and colorful. The *Amelia Bedelia* books, in which Amelia takes language very literally, can serve as a good introduction. Children might also keep a dictionary of figurative and **idiomatic expressions**. Some books of idioms are included in the following Student Reading List.

Multiple Meanings

One study found that 72 percent of the words that appear frequently in elementary school materials have more than one meaning (Johnson, Moe, & Baumann, 1983). When teaching new meanings for old words, stress the fact that words may have a number of different meanings and that the context is the final determinant of meaning. Some words with apparently multiple meanings are actually homographs. For instance, *bark* means "a noise made by a dog," "the covering of a tree," and "a type of sailing ship." These are really three different words and have separate dictionary entries. Other examples where diverse meanings are associated with one word are

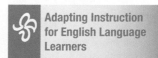

Adapting Instruction for English Language Learners

Figurative language and words with multiple meanings pose special problems for ELLs, who tend to focus on the literal meanings of words. English learners might need additional prompts and explanations when responding to riddles. ■

FYI

• Students may not realize that figures of speech can be found in the dictionary, usually under the key word in the phrase. For instance, the expressions "big heart," "take to heart," and "with all one's heart" can be found under *heart*.

• When learning words that have multiple meanings, students learn concrete and functional meanings first ("The dog barked at me"), followed by more abstract meanings ("The coach barked out instructions for the team") (Asch & Nerlove, 1967). ■

CCSS

Determine or clarify the meaning of unknown and multiple-meaning words and phrases based on grade-level reading and content, choosing flexibly from a range of strategies.

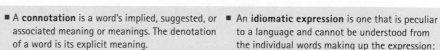

■ *Graph* is a combining form meaning "written element," so **homographs** are two or more words that have the same spelling but different meanings and different word origins. Homographs may have the same or different pronunciations: *bark* (dog), *bark* (tree); *bow* (ribbon), *bow* (front of a boat).

■ A **connotation** is a word's implied, suggested, or associated meaning or meanings. The denotation of a word is its explicit meaning.

■ An **idiomatic expression** is one that is peculiar to a language and cannot be understood from the individual words making up the expression: for example, *call up* a friend.

CCSS

Distinguish among the connotations (associations) of words with similar denotations (definitions) (e.g., *stingy, scrimping, economical, unwasteful, thrifty*).

FYI

- Based on their research, White, Power, and White (1989) estimated that average fourth-graders double their ability to use morphemic analysis after just ten hours of instruction.
- About 50 to 60 percent of the unfamiliar words that students in grades 4 and beyond encounter lend themselves to morphemic analysis because they are orthographically transparent; they contain easily detected prefixes or suffixes or are compounds. In addition, a large percentage of words are semi-transparent (Carlisle & Stone, 2005; Nagy & Anderson, 1984). ■

Adapting Instruction for Struggling Readers and Writers

Students with learning disabilities have especially poor knowledge of morphemic elements. However, given systematic instruction, they make encouraging gains (Henry, 1990). ■

CCSS

Language: Vocabulary Acquisition and Use. Use common, grade-appropriate Greek and Latin affixes and roots as clues to the meaning of a word (e.g., telegraph, photograph, autograph).

STUDENT READING LIST

Figurative Language

Arnold, T. (2001). *More parts.* New York: Dial.
Christopher, M. (1996). *Baseball jokes and riddles.* Boston: Little, Brown.
Leedy, L. (2003). *There's a frog in my throat. 440 animal sayings a little bird told me.* New York: Holiday House.
Rosen, M. (1995). *Walking the bridge of your nose: Wordplay poems and rhymes.* London: Kingfisher.
Terban, M. (1990). *Punching the clock: Funny action idioms.* Boston: Clarion.
Terban, M. (1993). *It figures! Fun figures of speech.* New York: Scholastic.
Terban, M. (2006). *Scholastic dictionary of idioms* (revised). New York: Scholastic.
Terban, M. (2007). *Mad as a wet hen and other funny idioms.* New York: Scholastic

elevator ("platform that moves people up and down," "place for storing grain," "part of airplane") and *magazine* ("periodical" and "building where arms and/or ammunition are stored"). Provide exercises that highlight the new meaning of an old word by asking questions specific to a definition: "What does a plane's elevator do? Why would a fort have a magazine?"

Connotations

It is important to introduce the concept of connotations and denotations of words. Comparing words and noting connotations help students to detect subtle shades of meaning (Dale & O'Rourke, 1971). For example, in comparing the synonyms *slender*, *skinny*, *lanky*, and *scrawny*, students find that, although all refer to being thin, they are not interchangeable. *Scrawny* and *skinny* convey less favorable meanings than do *slender* and *lanky*. Provide students with opportunities to discriminate between synonyms by determining which word in a pair sounds better (for example, *chuckle/guffaw*; *gossip/chat*; *request/demand*) or which word in a pair sounds worse (for example, *scribbled/wrote*; *sip/slurp*; *muttered/said*). Encourage students to find words in their reading that have favorable and unfavorable connotations and discuss them.

Learning How to Learn Words

A key objective for a vocabulary-building program is to teach students how to learn words on their own. Three major skills for learning the meanings of unknown words are morphemic analysis, contextual clues, and dictionary usage.

Morphemic Analysis

One of the most powerful word-attack skills is **morphemic analysis**, determining a word's meaning through examination of its prefix, root, and/or suffix. A **morpheme** is the smallest unit of meaning. It may be a word, a prefix, a suffix, or a root. The word *believe* has a single morpheme; however, *unbelievable* has three: *un-believ(e)-able*. *Telegraph* has two morphemes: *telegraph*. Whereas syllabic analysis involves chunks of sounds, morphemic analysis is concerned with chunks of meaning.

Instruction must be generative and conceptual rather than mechanical and isolated. For example, students can use their knowledge of the familiar word *microscope* to figure out

■ **Morphemic analysis** is the examination of a word in order to locate and derive the meanings of the morphemes.

■ A **morpheme** is the smallest unit of meaning. The word *nervously* has three morphemes: *nerv(e)-ous-ly*.

what *micro* means and to apply that knowledge to *microsecond, microwave, micrometer,* and *microbe*. By considering known words, they can generate a concept of *micro* and apply it to unknown words, which, in turn, enriches that concept (Dale & O'Rourke, 1971). The key to teaching morphemic analysis is to help students note prefixes, suffixes, and roots and discover their meanings. It is also essential that elements having a high transfer value be taught and that students be trained in transferring knowledge (Dale & O'Rourke, 1971).

Frequency of occurrence, number of words in the word family, and transparency also determine whether morphemic units are utilized to learn meaning. There are two kinds of transparency: phonological and orthographical. To be phonologically transparent, the base of a derived word must retain its original pronunciation. Hence, *growth* is phonologically transparent, but *health* is not (Carlisle & Stone, 2005). *Grow* keeps its pronunciation in *growth,* but *heal* changes its pronunciation in *health.* A word is orthographically transparent when the spelling of the base stays the same with the addition of affixes. Both *growth* and *health* are orthographically transparent, but *opportune* (*op* + *port* = "carry toward") is not. If words are not phonologically transparent, orthographical transparency can be helpful, especially to older readers.

Prefixes   In general, **prefixes** are easier to learn than suffixes (Dale & O'Rourke, 1964, cited in O'Rourke, 1974). According to Graves and Hammond (1980), there are relatively few prefixes, and they tend to have constant, concrete meanings and relatively consistent spellings. When learning prefixes and other morphemic elements, students should have the opportunity to observe each one in a number of words so that they have a solid basis for constructing an understanding of the element. Lesson 6.4 describes how the prefix *pre-* might be taught.

FYI

• Prefixes are easier to learn than suffixes and are more useful in decoding words. When applying morphemic analysis, readers remove the prefix and the suffix and then note if there is a root. However, in many instances they might not need to remove the suffix to identify the root word (White, Power, & White, 1989).

• The most frequently occurring prefixes are *un-, re-, in-, im-, ir-, il-, dis-, en-, em-, non-, in-, im-* (meaning "into"), *over-, mis-, sub-, pre-, inter-, fore-, de-, trans-, super-, semi-, anti-, mid-,* and *under-* (White, Sowell, & Yanagihara, 1989).

• Prefixes are most useful when they contribute to the meaning of a word and can be added to other words. The prefix *un-* is both productive and easy to detect (*unafraid, unable, unhappy*), but the prefix *con-* in *condition* is unproductive and difficult to detect (McArthur, 1992).

• Readers who have a good grounding in morphemics can infer the meanings of as many as 60 percent of multisyllabic words they encounter by analyzing roots and affixes (Nagy & Scott, 2000). ■

LESSON 6.4
Prefixes

Objectives
• . Students will understand the meaning of the prefix *pre-*.
• . Students will use the prefix *pre-* to help them derive the meanings of unfamiliar words.

Step 1. Constructing the meaning of the prefix

Place the following words on the board, overhead, or interactive whiteboard:

pregame prepay preview pretest predawn

Discuss the meanings of these words and the places where students may have seen them. Note, in particular, how *pre-* changes the meaning of the word it precedes. Encourage students to construct a definition of *pre-*. Lead students to see that *pre-* is a prefix. Discuss, too, the purpose and value of knowing prefixes. Explain to students how knowing the meanings of prefixes will help them figure out unknown words. Show them how you would syllabicate words that contain prefixes and how you would use knowledge of prefixes to sound out the words and determine their meanings.

Step 2. Guided practice

Have students complete practice exercises similar to the following. Fill in the blanks with these words containing prefixes: *preview, pregame, prepay, predawn, pretest.*

To make sure they had enough money to buy the food, the party's planners asked everyone to _____.
The _____ show starts thirty minutes before the kickoff.
The _____ of the movie made it seem more exciting than it really was.
Everyone got low marks on the spelling _____ because they had not been taught the words yet.

■ A **prefix** is an affix placed at the beginning of a word or root in order to form a new word: for example, *prepay.*

FYI

The most frequently occurring derivational suffixes are -er, -tion (-ion), -ible (-able), -al (-ial), -y, -ness, -ity (-ty), -ment, -ic, -ous (-ious), -en, -ive, -ful, and -less (White, Sowell, & Yanagihara, 1989). ■

FYI

About 80 percent of affixed words are analyzable (White, Power, & White, 1989). Having knowledge of high-frequency affixes should help fourth-graders learn an additional 125 words a year. That figure probably doubles for fifth-graders since they encounter more affixed words. By eighth grade, knowledge of affixes might enable students to learn 500 or more words. ■

In the _____ quiet, only the far-off barking of a dog could be heard.

Step 3. Application

Have students read selections that contain the prefix *pre-* and note its use in real-world materials.

Step 4. Extension

Present the prefix *post-* and contrast it with *pre-*. Since *post-* is an opposite, this will help clarify the meaning of *pre-*.

Step 5. Evaluation and reteaching

Through observation, note whether students are able to use their knowledge of **affixes** to help them pronounce and figure out the meanings of unfamiliar words. Review common affixes from time to time. Discuss affixes that appear in selections that students are reading.

Scope-and-Sequence Chart   Since some prefixes appear in reading materials as early as second grade, this seems to be the appropriate level at which to initiate instruction. A scope-and-sequence chart based on an analysis of current reading programs is presented in table 6.2. At each level, elements from earlier grades should be reviewed. Additional prefixes that students encounter in their reading should also be introduced.

Suffixes   The two kinds of **suffixes** are derivational and inflectional. **Derivational suffixes** change the part of speech of a word or change the function of a word in some way. Common derivational suffixes are presented in Table 6.3. **Inflectional suffixes** mark grammatical items and are learned early. In fact, *-s*, *-ed*, and *-ing* occur in the easiest materials and are taught in first grade; *-er*, *-est*, *-ly* are introduced in most basals by second grade.

TABLE 6.2   Scope-and-Sequence Chart for Common Prefixes

Grade	Prefix	Meaning	Example	Grade	Prefix	Meaning	Example
2–3	*un-*	not	unhappy	5–6	*ex-*	out, out of	exhaust
	un-	opposite	undo		*ex-*	former	explayer
	under	under	underground		*inter-*	between	international
3–4	*dis-*	not	dishonest		*mis-*	not	misunderstanding
	dis-	opposite	disappear		*mis-*	bad	misfortune
	re-	again	reappear	6–7	*en-*	forms verb	enrage
	re-	back	replace		*ir-*	not	irresponsible
4–5	*im-*	not	impossible		*trans-*	across	transatlantic
	in-	not	invisible	8	*anti-*	against	antiwar
	pre-	before	pregame		*pro-*	in favor of	prowar
					sub-	under	submarine
					super-	above	supersonic

■ An **affix** is a morphemic element added to the beginning or ending of a word or root in order to add to the meaning of the word or change its function. Prefixes and suffixes are affixes: for example, *prepayment*.

■ A **suffix** is an affix added to the end of a word or a root in order to form a new word: for example, *helpless*.

■ A **derivational suffix** produces a new word by changing a word's part of speech or meaning: *happy, happiness*.

■ An **inflectional suffix** changes the inflected ending of a word by adding an ending such as *-s* or *-ed* that shows number or tense: *girls, helped*.

TABLE 6.3   Scope-and-Sequence Chart for Common Derivational Suffixes

Grade	Suffix	Meaning	Example	Grade	Suffix	Meaning	Example
1–2	-en	made of	wooden	4–5	-ian	one who	guardian
	-er	one who	painter				
	-or	one who	actor		-ic	of; having the form of	gigantic
2–3	-able	is; can be	comfortable		-ish	having the quality of	foolish
	-ible	is; can be	visible		-ive	being	creative
	-ful	full of; having	joyful	5–6	-ian	one who is in a certain field	musician
	-ness	having	sadness		-ist	a person who	scientist
	-(t)ion	act of	construction		-ity	state of	reality
	-y	being; having	dirty		-ize	forms verbs	apologize
3–4	-al	having	magical	6–7	-ar	forms adjectives	muscular
	-ance	state of	allowance		-age	forms nouns	postage
	-ence	state of; quality of	patience		-ess	female	hostess
	-ify	make	magnify	7–8	-ary	forms adjectives	budgetary
	-less	without	fearless		-ette	small	dinette
	-ment	state of	advertisement		-some	forms adjectives	troublesome
	-ous	having	curious				

Suffixes are taught in the same way as prefixes. As can be seen from Tables 6.2 and 6.3, the definitions of prefixes and suffixes are sometimes vague. Although only one or two definitions are given in the tables, in reality, some affixes have four or five. To give students a sense of the meaning of each affix, provide experience with several examples. Experience is a better teacher than mere definition.

Root Words   As students move through the grades, knowledge of morphemic elements becomes more important for handling increasingly complex reading material. As the reading becomes more abstract and therefore more difficult in every subject area, the number of words made up of **roots** and affixes becomes greater. Science, for instance, often uses Greek and Latin words and compounds (O'Rourke, 1974). As with prefixes and suffixes, roots that should be taught are those that appear with high frequency, transfer to other words, and are on the appropriate level of difficulty. For example, the root *cil (council)*, meaning "call," should probably not be taught because it is difficult to distinguish in a word. Roots such as *graph (autograph)* and *phon (telephone)* are easy to spot and appear in words likely to be read by elementary and middle school students. Table 6.4 shows roots that are good candidates for inclusion in a literacy program. The sequence is based on O'Rourke's research (1974) and an analysis of the roots found in current reading programs.

Teaching Root Words   Teach root words inductively, and take advantage of every opportunity to develop students' knowledge of them. For example, if students wonder what a thermal wind is, discuss known words such as *thermos, thermostat,* and *thermometer.* Lead them to see that in all three words, *therm* has to do with heat; thus, thermal winds are warm winds. Choose elements to be taught from students' reading. If students read about dinosaurs, use the opportunity to introduce *tri, saurus, pod,*

Using Technology

Dictionary of Greek and Latin Roots presents a list of common roots. http://english.glendale.cc.ca.us/roots.dict.html ■

FYI

Included among the list of roots are combining forms. A combining form is a base designed to combine with another combining form (*tri* + *pod*) or a word (*tri* + *angle*). Combining forms differ from affixes because two combining forms can be put together to make a word but two affixes cannot. Although combining forms are not roots, they are included with the roots because that is where they are presented in most texts (McArthur, 1992). ■

■ The **root** of a word is the part of the word that is left after all the affixes have been removed. A root is also defined as the source of present-day words. The Latin verb *decidere* is the root of the English verb *decide* (McArthur, 1992). The words *base, combining form, root,* and *stem* are sometimes used interchangeably but actually have different meanings. To keep matters simple, this text uses the word *root.*

TABLE 6.4   Scope-and-Sequence Chart for Common Roots

Grade	Root	Meaning	Example	Grade	Root	Meaning	Example
3	*graph*	writing	autograph	7	*mid*	middle	midday
	tele	distance	telescope		*ped*	foot	pedestrian
4	*port*	carry	import		*chrono*	time	chronometer
	saur	lizard	dinosaur		*dict*	say	dictate
	phon	sound	telephone		*hemi*	half	hemisphere
	vid, vis	see	visible		*manu*	hand	manuscript
5	*astro*	star	astronaut	8	*bio*	life	biology
	cred	believe	incredible		*geo*	earth	geology
	duct	lead	conductor		*micro*	small	microscope
	tri	three	triangle		*mono*	one	monotone
6	*aud*	hearing	auditorium		*semi*	half, part	semisweet
	auto	self	autobiography		*some*	group	foursome
	bi	two	bicycle				
	ology	study of	geology				
	scrib, script	writing	inscription				
	therm	heat	thermometer				

ornitho, and other roots. This often helps students use the name to identify the distinguishing characteristics of the creature. For example, *triceratops* uses three word parts to describe a dinosaur that has three horns, two of which are over the eyes: *tri*, "three"; *cerat*, "horn"; and *ops*, "eyes." Two of the parts also transfer to a number of other words: *tri* to *triangle*, *tripod*, etc., and *op* to *optical*, *optician*, *optometrist*, etc.

Scope-and-sequence charts for affixes and roots have been provided to give you a sense of when certain ones are usually presented. The real determinants, however, are the needs of the students and the demands of their reading tasks.

Applying Morphemic Analysis to Unfamiliar Words   When students encounter a word that is in their listening vocabulary but not in their reading vocabulary, they should look for a part of the word they know or try to think of a familiar word that is like the unknown word. They might see if the word has a familiar prefix, familiar root, and/or a familiar suffix. Encountering the unfamiliar word *miscalculation*, a student might recognize that *mis* means "wrong," *calculate* means "to figure with numbers," and *tion* means "act of" and conclude that *miscalculation* means "the act of not figuring up correctly." Of course, the student would need to know the meaning of each of the word parts.

Morphemic Analysis for English Language Learners   Just as in English, Spanish has roots, prefixes, and suffixes. In fact, Spanish has more affixes than English does because Spanish nouns and adjectives have endings that show agreement in gender and number. However, there are many similarities between Spanish and English. A number of elements are identical in both languages or altered slightly. For instance, the prefixes *re-* and *sub-* are the same in both languages; so are the suffixes *-able* and *-ion*. The suffix *-tion* is slightly different in Spanish: It is often spelled *-cion* but may also be spelled *-sion* or *-xion*. If students know prefixes, suffixes, and roots in Spanish, they can transfer some of this knowledge to English.

Contextual Analysis

Imagine that you are a fourth-grader who has never seen or heard the word *salutations*. What does the following passage indicate about its meaning?

CCSS

Use common, grade-appropriate Greek and Latin affixes and roots as clues to the meaning of a word (e.g., *telegraph*, *photograph*, *autograph*).

REINFORCEMENT ACTIVITIES

Morphemic Analysis

- Provide students with several long words composed of a number of morphemic units, for example:

unbelievable	improperly	unimaginable
prehistoric	photographer	disagreeable
irregularly	unfavorable	uncomfortable
unreturnable	misjudgment	oceanographer

  Have them determine the morphemic boundaries and try to figure out what the words mean based on analysis of the units. Good sources of other words to analyze are the texts that students are encountering in class.

- Ask students to create webs of roots and affixes in which the element is displayed in several words (Tompkins & Yaden, 1986). A web for the root *loc* might look like Figure 6.8.

- Students can incorporate roots and affixes into their everyday lives by constructing personal experiences. Have them tell or write about times when they were helpful or helpless, careful or careless.

- Using root words, prefixes, and suffixes, let students create words that label a new creature, invention, or discovery. For example, a *quintocycle* would be a cycle with five wheels. A *monovideopod* would be a single walking eye.

- Ask students to bring in examples of roots and affixes from periodicals, children's books, textbooks, signs, and labels or from spoken language. For example, a child who has recently been on an airplane may have noted the word *preboard*. Let the class determine the word's root and/or affix and discuss the word's meaning.

"Salutations!" repeated the voice.

"What are they, and where are you?" screamed Wilbur. "Please, please, tell me where you are. And what are salutations?"

"Salutations are greetings," said the voice. "When I say 'salutations' it's just my fancy way of saying hello or good morning." (White, 1952, p. 35)

FIGURE 6.8   Web for the Root *Loc*

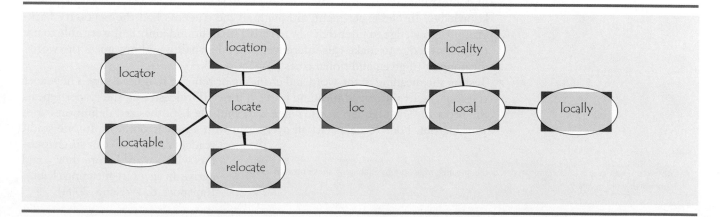

FYI

Even when contextual clues are as rich as they are in this excerpt from *Charlotte's Web*, some students still may not pick up the meaning of *salutations*. After the story has been read, write *salutations* and other words that had rich contextual clues on the board and ask the class what the words mean. This will give you a rough idea of how well students were using context in their reading. ■

FYI

Teaching students to derive the meanings of unfamiliar words requires them to use a number of higher-level thinking skills. Model the reasoning you use as you attempt to figure out new words. ■

FYI

When students are using context to derive word meaning, guide their efforts with prompts. Because students may not be using their understanding of the text as a context clue, ask them to tell what the section containing the target word is about. Often, the general sense of the passage will provide a clue to the meaning of the target word (Beck, McKeown, & Kucan, 2002) ■

Not only does E. B. White define the word *salutations* in context in *Charlotte's Web*, but he also implies that its use is somewhat pompous. Of course, not all difficult words are explained with such care; in fact, in many instances, **contextual analysis** is not at all helpful (Schatz & Baldwin, 1986). Context determines the particular meaning of a word, but it may not reveal it (Deighton, 1959).

However, it is estimated that the average reader is able to use context successfully only between 5 and 20 percent of the time (Jenkins, Matlock, & Slocum, 1989; Nagy, Anderson, & Herman, 1987). Even when context clues are fairly obvious, students may fail to take advantage of them. Fortunately, children do become more proficient at using context clues as they progress through the grades. They also do significantly better with practice. Simply directing students to use context to get the meaning of an unfamiliar word is not effective. The directive has to be accompanied by practice and feedback to let them know whether their contextual guesses are correct (Carnine, Kame'enui, & Coyle, 1984).

Deriving the Meaning of a Word From Context   Deriving the meaning of an unfamiliar word generally involves the following steps (Gunning, 2006):

- Recognizing that the word is unknown (Nation, 2001).
- Deciding to use context to derive the meaning of the unknown word. Many readers simply skip unknown words. Even if they do not, most of their use of context is incidental (Rapaport, 2004). The typical reader doesn't make deliberate use of context until she or he notes a disruption in meaning and makes the decision to use context (Kibby, Rapaport, & Wieland, 2004).
- Applying experience to the word. The reader notes whether she or he has ever seen or heard this word before.
- Noting morphemic units. The student notes prefixes, suffixes, and roots that might provide helpful clues to the word's meaning.
- Selecting clues to the word's meaning. From the passage as a whole, the reader seeks information that might shed light on the word's meaning. These clues constrain the meaning of the word but might not fully reveal it (Kibby, Rapaport, & Wieland, 2004). For instance, they might indicate that the target word is a noun or verb or suggest a negative rather than a positive meaning.
- Using context clues, background, and reasoning to compose a general meaning of the word. The reader uses clues from the text, her or his background of experience, and reasoning to create a hypothesis about the word's meaning. Although the text is used to provide context clues, the reader's background knowledge is often a more important factor. Context leads the reader to use her or his background of experience to make inferences. The reader revises her or his hypothesis based on subsequent encounters with the word (Rapaport, 2004). Subsequent encounters may provide additional clues to the word's meaning. In a sense, context is in the reader's head rather than on the page. One way to increase the effectiveness of students' use of context clues is to show students how to make inferences based on background knowledge. In one experiment, although all the students had the necessary background knowledge to infer that a brachet is a small hound, only half were able to use their knowledge to make this inference. The other half could not guess the word's meaning until given additional clues (Rapaport, 2004).
- Testing the meaning of the word and changing or refining it, if necessary. The reader tries out the hypothesized meaning to see if it fits. If it doesn't fit, the reader repeats the process. Good readers revise when they find the hypothesized definition is not working out. Poor readers start all over again with a new hypothesis. In one study, readers required five or six encounters with a word before they could derive an accurate meaning (Kibby, Rapaport, & Wieland, 2004).

■ **Contextual analysis** is an attempt to derive the meaning of a word by examining the context in which the unknown word appears.

Encourage students to follow these key steps for using context:

1. **Reread and gather clues.**   Reread the sentence and see how the target word is used. Look for clues to the meaning of the word. If there are no clues or the clues don't help, read the sentence before and after the target sentence.
2. **Identify part of speech.**   Determine the word's part of speech.
3. **Summarize.**   In your mind, summarize what the text has said so far. Combine that with all the clues that the text has offered.
4. **Use background knowledge.**   Use what you know, the sense of the passage, and the clues you have gathered. Make a careful guess (hypothesis) as to the word's meaning.
5. **Check your careful guess.**   See if your guess fits the context.
6. **Revise.**   If your careful guess doesn't fit, try again. If the word is used in other places in the selection, get clues from those uses.

Instruction in the use of context clues should make explicit the thinking processes involved. Here is how the key steps would be put to use to figure out the meaning of *dismal* in this passage from Cleary's (1981) *Ramona Quimby, Age 8*:

> Rainy Sunday afternoons in November were always dismal, but Ramona felt this Sunday was the most dismal of all. She pressed her nose against the living-room window, watching the ceaseless rain pelting down as bare black branches clawed at the electric wires in front of the house. Even lunch, leftovers Mrs. Quimby had wanted to clear out of the refrigerator, had been dreary, with her parents, who seemed tired or discouraged or both, having little to say and Beezus mysteriously moody. Ramona longed for sunshine, sidewalks dry enough for roller skating, a smiling happy family. (p. 33)

1. **Reread and gather clues.**   What information in the sentence containing the unknown word will help me figure out what this word means? Is there any information in earlier sentences that will help? Is there any information in later sentences that will help?
   Helpful clues include the rain, Ramona's obvious boredom, the moods of the other family members, and Ramona's longing for sunshine, sidewalks dry enough for roller skating, and a smiling happy family.
2. **Identify part of speech.**   How is the word being used?
   Dismal is identified as being an adjective. The readers infer that *dismal* is being used to describe.
3. **Summarize.**   When I think about all the information given about this unknown word, what does the word seem to mean?
   When readers put all the clues together, they can see that the scene that is being described is a gloomy or unhappy one.
4. **Use background knowledge.**   What do I know that will help me figure out the meaning of this word?
   Using past experience, students can think about days on which it was raining and they couldn't go out and everyone seemed crabby. This will help them decide that *dismal* means "gloomy" or "unhappy."
5. **Check your careful guess.**   Does my meaning seem to fit the context?
   Once readers have used context to construct a tentative meaning for the unknown word, they should try substituting the tentative meaning into the text.
6. **Revise.**   What do I need to do to make a better guess?
   If the meaning does not fit the sense of the text's sentence, students should revise their guess, use the dictionary, or get help.

Types of Context Clues   Listed below, in approximate order of difficulty, are seven main types of context clues. They have been drawn from a variety of materials that elementary or middle school students might read.

FYI

Challenge students to make use of context clues just as a detective or crime scene investigator might do. You might also have them work in teams so that they can share clues and reasoning (Kibby, Rapaport, Wieland, & Dechert, 2006). ■

FYI

• Context clues complement phonics strategies and help students predict the pronunciations of words that are in their listening vocabularies but not in their reading vocabularies. However, context clues in this section are designed to help students derive the meanings of words that are not in their listening or reading vocabularies.
• Oral context is probably more helpful than written context. A "written context lacks many of the features of oral language that support learning new words, such as intonation, body language, and shared physical surroundings" Beck, McKeown, & Kucan, 2002, p. 3). ■

1. **Explicit explanation or definition.**   The easiest clue to use is a definition in context. For instance, the following passage from *The Wright Brothers at Kitty Hawk* (Sobol, 1961) gives a detailed, conceptual explanation of warping:

"Why the wings are twisting!" exclaimed Bill Tate.

"We call it warping," said Orville. "See the wings on the side? Their ends are turned upward and forward."

"And the wings on the left side are pulled downwards and rearward," said Bill Tate.

Orville let go of the rope. "Now, in front—"

"Hold on," said Bill Tate. "I'm not sure I understand what I saw."

"The warping is our idea for keeping the glider level," said Orville. Carefully he explained how it changed the way the wind pushed against the wings. (p. 24)

Explicit definitions are usually more concise, as in this excerpt from *César Chávez: A Hero for Everyone* (Soto, 2003): "The cotton pickers were paid by piecework. This meant they didn't get paid by the hour but by how much they picked" (p. 2).

2. **Appositives.**   Definitions are sometimes supplied in the form of appositives immediately after the difficult word: "On a clear summer morning, a pod, or group, of close to fifty dusky dolphins moves toward deeper water" (Souza, 1998, p. 27).

3. **Synonyms.**   Finding a synonym sometimes takes some searching. It often appears in a sentence after the one that used the target word. In the following passage from *Little House on the Prairie* (Wilder, 1941), the synonym for *ague* is given in a preceding sentence: "Next day he had a little chill and a little fever. Ma blamed the watermelon. But next she had a chill and a little fever. So they did not know what could have caused their fever 'n' ague" (p. 198).

4. **Function indicators.**   Sometimes, context provides clues to meaning because it gives the purpose or function of the difficult word (Sternberg, 1987). In the following sentence, the reader gets an excellent clue to the meaning of *derrick* as the sentence indicates what a derrick does: "The derrick lifted the glider into the sky" (Sobol, 1961, p. 27).

5. **Examples.**   The example—lions—in the following passage gives the reader a sense of the meaning of *predators*: "Only 5 percent of cheetah cubs live to become adults. The remainder die from disease, starvation, or attacks from other predators, such as lions" (Thompson, 1998, p. 7).

6. **Comparison–contrast.**   By contrasting the unknown word *foreigners* with the known word *nationals* in the following passage, readers can gain an understanding of the unknown word: "Halmoni walked Yunni over to the long line that said 'Foreigners.' The line moved slowly as the officer checked each passport. Halmoni got to stand in the fast-moving line that said 'Nationals.' Yunni looked like all the Koreans in the nationals line, but she had to stand in the foreigners line" (Choi, 2001, p. 146). Students must be able to reason that the word *foreigners* is the opposite of *nationals*, however. Being able to use *nationals* as a context clue also requires that students know the meaning of *nationals*.

7. **Experience.**   A main clue to the meaning of an unfamiliar word is students' background of experience. In the following passage, readers can use their own experience of being cut or injured to help them to make an informed guess as to what the unfamiliar word *excruciating* means: "Suddenly, the hedge clippers caught a branch, and my left middle finger was pulled into the blades. I felt an excruciating pain. The tip of my finger was hanging by a thread" (Rolfer, 1990, p. 25).

Presenting Context Clues   Use of context should permeate the reading program from its very beginning. When emerging readers use phonics skills to try to decode words that are in their listening but not in their reading vocabulary, they should use context as well, both as an aid to sounding out and as a check to make sure they have decoded the words correctly. Context clues presented in this chapter are designed to help readers derive the meanings of unknown words—words that are not in the students' listening vocabularies. Although the use of context clues ideally becomes automatic over the years, it should be taught explicitly. Using a direct teaching model, the teacher should explain what the clues are, why it is important to use context, and how they can be applied. Modeling the use of clues, guided practice, and application are important elements in the process. Lesson 6.5 describes how context clues might be presented.

LESSON 6.5
Context Clues

Objective
- Students use context clues to derive the meanings of unfamiliar words.

Step 1. Explain context

Explain the usefulness of context clues. Select five or six difficult words from a book the class is reading, and show how context could be used to derive their meanings.

Step 2. Demonstrate the process of using context

Ask the following questions:

What information in the selection will help me figure out what the unknown word means?
How is the unknown word being used? (What is its part of speech?)
From all the information given about the unknown word, what does it seem to mean?
What do I know from my own experience that will help me figure out the meaning of the word?

Step 3. Try out the tentative meaning of the unknown word

Show students how to try out the tentative meaning of the unknown word by substituting the meaning for the word and reading the sentence to see whether the substitution fits. Explain that if the tentative meaning does not fit the sense of the sentence, they should revise it.

Step 4. Model the process

Model the process of using context with a variety of words. Explain the thinking processes that you go through as you attempt to figure out their meanings and then try out these tentative meanings. Show, for example, how you might interpret examples, use a comparison, search out synonyms, look for appositives, use your background of experience, or try a combination of strategies. Show, too, how you would use context and experience to construct a tentative meaning for the unknown word and then try out the meaning by substituting it in the sentence.

Step 5. Guided practice

Have students use context clues to figure out unfamiliar words in selected passages that provide substantial clues. Do one or two cooperatively; then have students try the process on their own. Discuss the meanings of the unfamiliar words and the types of clues they used.

Step 6. Application

Encourage students to try using context clues for an unknown word in a reading selection. After the reading, talk over the meanings that they derived and the strategies they used.

FYI

As Nagy and Anderson (1984) noted, "For every word a child learns we estimate that there are an average of one to three additional words that should be understandable to the child, the exact number depending on how well the child is able to utilize context and morphology to induce meaning" (p. 304). ■

Using Technology

Vocabulary Drill for Kids presents words in context. Students select from three options the one they think is the correct response.
http://www.edu4kids.com/index.php ■

Ask how they went about determining what the unknown word meant, what clues they used, and how they decided on their definition of the unknown word.

Step 7. Assessment and review

Note how often and how well students apply context clues on their own. From time to time, check on their use of context. Provide additional instruction as needed.

R E F L E C T I O N

What might be done to increase student use of word analysis strategies?

FYI

• Review the use of context clues periodically. Whenever a selection is discussed, talk over passages that contain especially effective context clues so as to remind students to use context clues and also to refine students' usage of them.

• Students can help each other learn new words. If they get stuck on a word while reading and neither context clues nor morphemic analysis or other strategies work, students can place a stick-on note next to the challenging word (Lubliner & Smetana, 2005). Later, working in small groups or during discussion of the selection, they can seek help from their fellow students. ∎

FYI

Dictionaries have been criticized because their definitions are sometimes hard to understand (McKeown, 1993). However, a recent study found that students were able to answer open-ended questions about words about two-thirds of the time after reading the dictionary definitions (Nichols, 2007). ∎

Subsequent Lessons in the Use of Context Clues   In a series of lessons, present other major context clues, emphasizing the thinking processes involved in using each one. After introducing all the types of clues appropriate for students' level, review them. However, instruction should be focused on using context clues effectively rather than on identification of types of clues. Draw sample sentences from children's periodicals, trade books, content-area texts, and the Internet, so that students can see that the skills have relevance and that context clues will help them analyze words. Most important, encourage students to get in the habit of using context to figure out the meanings of unfamiliar words. Instead of merely suggesting that they use clues, model the process from time to time to remind them about it. Also, encourage students to use the dictionary as a means of checking definitions derived by using context clues.

Also integrate the use of context with morphemic and syllabic analysis. Note how morphemic analysis and context clues might be used to derive the meanings of *microbats* and *megabats*.

> Bats are the masters of the ultrasonic world. They are divided into two groups, the microbats and the megabats. Most microbats are insect eaters. All microbats rely on ultrasound to guide them when they fly and to help them find food and communicate with each other. The large, fruit-eating megabats can make ultrasounds, too, but they do not use them when flying or searching for food. (Arnold, 2001)

Dictionary Usage   Context, especially when combined with phonics and morphemic and syllabic analysis, is a powerful word-attack strategy, but some words defy even these four strategies. When all else fails, it is time for the student to consult the world's greatest expert on words, the dictionary. Dictionaries have been criticized because their definitions are sometimes hard to understand or may not provide sufficient information for the user to obtain an understandable meaning (McKeown, 1993). However, in a recent study, fourth- and fifth-graders were able to answer open-ended questions about a word approximately two-thirds of the time, based on a reading of the dictionary definition (Nichols, 2007). Had they been given instruction in obtaining adequate definitions, the students might have done even better.

Although students might not use a real dictionary in first and second grades, preparation begins early. In first grade and, in some cases, kindergarten, students compile word books and picture dictionaries. They also learn alphabetical order (a prerequisite skill for locating words) and phonics (which is necessary for using the pronunciation key).

Using Predictionaries   Most students are not able to use dictionaries until the third grade. However, predictionaries, which can be used by first- and second-graders, have been compiled by several publishers. *Predictionaries* are books in which limited numbers of words are defined through illustrations. A more advanced predictionary, which is usually called the first dictionary, uses sentences and pictures to define words but does not supply syllabications or pronunciation. Predictionaries are available on CD-ROM; the advantage of this format is that the selected words are pronounced orally and their definitions spoken. A **predictionary** is a useful tool but must be used with care. Because it includes only a limited number of words, students may find that many words they want to look up are not there. Locating entry words may also be fairly time-consuming, unless an electronic version is used.

Using Glossaries   Glossaries are included in the anthologies of major reading programs and content-area texts. In some programs, glossaries can be found as early as first grade. Easier to use than dictionaries because they have only a limited number of words and definitions, glossaries are helpful and prepare students for the dictionary.

Using Dictionaries   By third grade, students with average reading achievement are ready to use real dictionaries. They should, of course, use beginning dictionaries that are simplified so that the definitions are readable. For reading, students must have three major skills: locating the target word, finding the proper definition, and learning the pronunciation. For writing, determining correct spelling and usage is also important.

Locating the Words to Be Looked Up   The first thing that students must realize is that words are arranged in alphabetical order—*a* to *z*—by first letter and then by second letter, and, if necessary, by third letter, and so on. From the beginning, train students to use guide words so that they do not adopt the time-wasting habit of simply thumbing through the *s*'s or the *w*'s page by page until they find the appropriate location. Even after they have mastered alphabetical order, students may be confused as they search for some entry words. Entry words often exclude inflected forms. A student looking up *rallies* or *exporter*, for example, will have to look under *rally* or *export*.

Locating and Understanding Meanings   Many words have more than one definition. Students must be taught how to use context to select the meaning that best fits the way a word is used. This skill is best taught through modeling and think-alouds. Students tend to select the first definition when there are several. Even when there is just one definition provided for a word, students may use only part of the information, not the entire definition. For instance, for *altercation*, which is defined as "a heated argument," students might focus on "heated" and neglect the argument part of the definition (Nichols, 2007). Students need lots of instruction and guided practice in selecting a definition that fits and absorbing the whole definition. Dictionary definitions are more useful when you have some sense of the meaning of the word and are looking up the word for confirmation and/or clarification. In your modeling and think-alouds, show how you use context to get a sense of a word's meaning and then use the dictionary to confirm or adjust your guess.

Definitions are not the only way words are explained. Many dictionaries also include synonyms, illustrations, and phrases or sentences in which the word is used. Some give a word history for selected words and explain how words that are synonyms differ in meaning. For instance, *Webster's New World Dictionary* supplies a definition for *kiosk*, gives a history of the term, and includes a photo of a kiosk. For the word *model*, it presents a brief explanatory paragraph that contrasts *model* and *pattern*.

Demonstrate the various ways a dictionary explains words. Start with words that have one concrete meaning. Later, direct students to look up words that are accompanied by illustrations. Discuss the definition, illustration, synonym, and example, if given, for each one. Words likely to have illustrations include the following (this will vary from dictionary to dictionary): *manatee, lattice, isobar, ibex, hoe, heart,* and *funnel*. Choose examples that are at the appropriate level for your students and that would be helpful for them to know.

Once students have a good grasp of how to locate words and how to use the several kinds of defining and

 FYI

• Model the use of a dictionary by letting students see how you use the dictionary to look up an unfamiliar word, check the spelling or pronunciation of a word, or use its style guide section to get information on a question of style.

• Do not make dictionary use so tiresome that students grow to dislike this tool. Looking up all of a set of vocabulary words is just the type of assignment that gives the dictionary a bad name. Make sure that tasks that students are required to do are not too complex. Asking students to use new words in sentences after looking them up is difficult. It often takes a number of experiences with a word before a student acquires enough feeling for it to use it in a sentence. ■

■ A **predictionary** is an easy dictionary that has fewer entries than a regular dictionary, simplifies definitions, but does not contain a pronunciation key.

Adapting Instruction for English Language Learners

For ELLs, a translation dictionary that contains English and their first language could be an invaluable aid. Students might use one of the many language translators found on the Web, such as Web-a-dex Language Translator:

http://www.web-a-dex.com/translate.htm ■

FYI

• Build your pupils' skill in using dictionary phonetic respellings to get the correct pronunciations along with the meanings of unknown words. Just as it's easier to remember a person's name if you can pronounce it, so, too, it's easier to remember a new word if you can say it correctly.

• Merriam-Webster presents a number of vocabulary-building exercises. The site also provides pronunciations for words.

http://www.m-w.com ■

REFLECTION

How can you foster effective and appropriate use of the dictionary?

explanatory information, have them look up words. Choose words that students have a genuine need to know, such as hard words from a content-area text or children's book that they are reading. In the beginning, stress words that have just one or two meanings, like *edifice*, *egret*, or *cellist*.

As students grow in skill in using the dictionary, tell them that some words may have many meanings. Have them look up the following words and count the number of meanings given: *ace*, *bit*, *bowl*, *comb*, and *free*. Emphasize that context can help them choose the correct meaning for a word that has several definitions. Have them practice finding the correct meaning for each of several words that have just two or three distinct meanings:

Because I moved the camera, the photo was a bit *fuzzy*.

The blanket was warm and *fuzzy*.

The explorers packed up their *gear* and left.

Use second *gear* when going up a steep hill.

Homographs   Have students note how homographs are handled in their dictionaries. Usually, they are listed as separate entries and numbered, as in Figure 6.9. For practice, students can use context to help them determine which definition is correct in sentences such as the following:

The doctor gave me medicine for my *sty*.

The king signed the paper and put his *seal* on it.

We landed on a small sandy *key*.

Constructing the Correct Pronunciation   After students have acquired some skill in locating words and choosing appropriate meanings, introduce the concept of phonetic respellings. Display and discuss the pronunciation key contained in the dictionary your class is using. To avoid confusion, have all students use the same dictionary series, if possible, because different publishers use different keys. Help students discover what they already know about the key. Almost all the phonetic respellings of consonants will be familiar, except for, perhaps, *ng* in words like *sung*, which is signified by /ŋ/ in some systems. Short vowels, indicated by *a*, *e*, *i*, *o* (sometimes symbolized as /ä/), and *u*, will also be familiar. Inform the students that long vowels are indicated by a symbol known as a macron, as in /gōt/. Explain that the macron is a diacritical mark and that such marks are used to show pronunciation. Show how diacritical marks are used to indicate the pronunciation of *r* vowels, short

FIGURE 6.9   Homographs in a Dictionary

bay¹ (bā), a part of a sea or lake extending into the land. A bay is usually smaller than a gulf and larger than a cove. *noun.*
bay² (bā), **1** a long, deep barking, especially by a large dog: *We heard the distant bay of the hounds.* **2** to bark with long, deep sounds: *Dogs sometimes bay at the moon.* 1 *noun,* 2 *verb.*
bay³ (bā), **1** reddish-brown. **2** a reddish-brown horse with black mane and tail. 1 *adjective,* 2 *noun.*

Scott, Foresman Beginning Dictionary (p. 51) by E. L. Thorndike & C. L. Barnhart, 1988, Glenview, IL: Scott, Foresman and Company. Copyright © 1988 by Scott, Foresman & Company. Reprinted by permission of Scott, Foresman and Company.

and long double *o*, schwa, the vowel sounds heard in *paw*, *toy*, and *out*, and short *o*. Also have students look up words such as *frog* and *route* and note that they have two pronunciations. Remind students that everyone speaks in a dialect and no one dialect is superior to another (see pp. 51–52 for a discussion).

After providing an overview of the pronunciation key, concentrate on its segments so that students acquire a working knowledge of the system. In order of difficulty, these segments might include consonants and short vowels, long vowels, *r* vowels, short and long double *o*, other vowels, and schwa. After introducing each segment, have students read words using the elements discussed. Encourage the active use of the pronunciation key.

Once students have mastered phonetic respelling, introduce the concept of accent. One way to do this would be to say a series of words whose meaning changes according to whether the first or second syllable is accented: *record, present, desert, minute, object*. As you say the words, stress the accented syllable. Have students listen to hear which syllable is said with more stress. After the class decides which syllable is stressed, write the words on the board and put in the accent marks while explaining what they mean. Discuss how the change in stress changes the pronunciation, meaning, or use of each word. To provide guided practice, select unknown words from materials students are about to read and have students construct their pronunciations. Discuss these constructions, and provide ample opportunity for independent application. Later, introduce the concept of secondary stress.

Electronic Dictionaries   Electronic dictionaries are far easier to use than book versions. Words are easier to look up. All the student has to do is to type in the target word. Some electronic dictionaries accept misspelled words, so students looking up the spelling of a word can find it even if they can't spell it accurately. Speaking dictionaries also pronounce the word being looked up and read the definition, so students don't have to be able to use the pronunciation key before they can use the dictionary. Electronic dictionaries are also motivational: They're more fun to use than a traditional dictionary. Electronic dictionaries come in CD-ROM and handheld versions and are available on the Web and with some computer programs and as apps. Handheld versions have the advantage of being small and portable. And some of the simpler models are not much more expensive than book versions.

The Dictionary as a Tool   Many school dictionaries include generous instructions for use, along with practice exercises. Use these selectively. Avoid isolated drill on dictionary skills. Concentrate on building dictionary skills through functional use—that is, show students how to use the dictionary, and encourage them to incorporate it as a tool for understanding language. For instance, when they have questions about word meaning, pronunciation, spelling, or usage, encourage them to seek help in the dictionary.

One word of caution is in order: For word recognition, the dictionary should generally be used as a last resort. Looking up a word while reading a story interrupts the flow of the story and disturbs comprehension. Students should try context, phonics, and morphemic or syllabic analysis before going to the dictionary. Moreover, unless the word is crucial to understanding the story, they should wait until they have read the selection to look up the word. The dictionary is also a good check on definitions derived from context clues. After reading a story in which they used context clues, students should check their educated guesses against the dictionary's definitions.

English Learner Dictionaries   English learner dictionaries, such as *The Longman Dictionary of American English* (Pearson Education), simplify definitions and provide more examples so that ELLs can see how words are used. They also provide added help with pronunciation and highlight high-frequency words, use more illustrations,

Using Technology

KidsClick provides a list of online dictionaries that range from regular to rhyming.
http://www.kidsclick.org
Many electronic devices contain dictionaries. The advantages of an electronic dictionary are that it locates the word faster and is motivational. An electronic dictionary may also read the word and its definition. This is a help for students whose reading skills are limited.
Handheld electronic dictionaries are available from Franklin Learning Resources, One Franklin Plaza, Burlington, NJ, 08016-4907, 800-266-5626.
My First Incredible Amazing Dictionary (Dorling Kindersley) is an excellent example of a talking predictionary. ∎

and group words by category to foster vocabulary building. And they contain common expressions in English. Both bilingual and English learner dictionaries should be made available to ELLs. Consulting a bilingual dictionary is especially helpful for getting the meaning of a word. Because they are reader-friendly, English learner dictionaries might be made available to native speakers of English as well as to ELLs. Note the difference in the definitions of the word *reluctant* provided by a regular online dictionary and an online English learner dictionary.

> *Word Central Online:* showing doubt or unwillingness <*reluctant* to answer>
>
> *Longman Dictionary of Contemporary English Online:* slow and unwilling: *She gave a reluctant smile.*
>
> reluctant to do something: *Maddox was reluctant to talk about it.*

Supplying Corrective Feedback

A student is reading and is suddenly stopped cold by an unknown word. What should the teacher do? If the student does not self-correct and the error is not substantive—the student says *this* for *that*—you may choose to do nothing. Sometimes, an error is substantive and disturbs the sense of the sentence, but it is obvious that the student will not be able to work out the word using phonics, syllabication, context, or morphemic analysis. In such a case, you might supply the word as one of two options so that the student is involved in the process: "Would *chat* or *champ* fit here?" If there is a chance that the student can use strategies to decode the word, pause briefly—about five seconds or so—to provide an opportunity for the student to work out the word (Harris & Sipay, 1990).

Using Prompts

If the student is struggling with a word but you think he can work it out and the word is in the student's listening vocabulary, try one of the word analysis prompts described in Table 5.7 on pages 227–228. If the word is not in the student's listening vocabulary, try one of the following prompts:

FYI

The probing prompt encourages students to reflect on their knowledge of strategies and to select the most appropriate one. ◼

- *Morphemic analysis.* Are there any parts of the word that you know? If so, put the meanings of those parts together.
- *Dictionary or glossary usage.* Would the dictionary or glossary help?
- *Affirmation.* I like the way you used context (or another strategy) to help you figure out that word.
- *Probing.* What could you do to help you figure out that word?

Using Think-Alouds

To assess students' use of word analysis skills and to provide guidance in their use, conduct a **think-aloud** (Harmon, 1998). In a think-aloud, students stop when they come to a difficult word and then give a description of what is going on in their minds as they try to figure out the word. Instead of providing direct instruction, the teacher offers neutral prompts that encourage students to explain their thinking: "Can you tell me what you are thinking? Can you tell me more?" Once you know what strategies students are using, you can then use the think-aloud as an instructional tool. You might use prompts like these: "Can you find clues to the word's meaning in other sentences or other parts of the article? What might help you to get the word's meaning? Would the glossary help?"

Guidance provided in a think-aloud is designed to help students apply and integrate strategies. It also

◼ **Think-alouds** are procedures in which students are asked to describe the processes they are using as they engage in reading or another cognitive activity.

helps build students' confidence in their word analysis skills and their sense of competence. If individual think-alouds are too time-consuming, group think-alouds might be used instead. That way students learn from each other.

Help for Struggling Readers and Writers

Struggling readers often have poor concepts of themselves as learners. To build their self-concepts and vocabulary, plan a program of vocabulary development that introduces challenging words to them. They will appreciate learning "big" words. Also provide instruction in morphemic analysis, context clues, and dictionary skills to help them become independent word learners. A handheld speaking electronic dictionary or an e-book reader with a built-in dictionary can be a big help for struggling readers and writers. It allows them to obtain the pronunciations of known words that are in in their listening but not their reading vocabularies as well as the meanings of unknown words that are not in their listening or reading vocabularies. It also helps them with their spelling.

Summary

Average first-graders know between 5,000 and 6,000 words and learn about 3,000 new words each year. Having rich experiences and talking about them are important factors in learning new words. Also important are relating vocabulary to background knowledge, building relationships, developing depth of meaning, presenting numerous exposures, creating an interest in words, and promoting transfer. A variety of activities, such as using graphic organizers and playing word games, can be used to develop word knowledge. The most powerful word learning activity is wide reading.

A balanced program of vocabulary development that includes planned and incidental instruction is advisable. Words chosen for intensive instruction should be key words that will be encountered again and again. A balanced program of vocabulary development should include provisions for teaching students how to learn words on their own through the use of morphemic analysis, contextual analysis, and the dictionary.

Extending and Applying

1. Plan a program of vocabulary development. Include a description of the class, your objectives, the source of words, your rationale for choosing words, the activities you will use to reinforce words, and the techniques you will use. Also tell what provision you will make for ELLs and struggling readers and explain how you will evaluate the program.

2. Choose four to six words from a chapter in a children's book. Then, using the steps described in this chapter, create a vocabulary lesson. Teach the lesson to a group of students and critique it. What worked well? What might be changed?

3. Using procedures explained in this chapter, create a semantic map with a class. Evaluate the map's

effectiveness. In what ways did it help students? Did the activity engage their attention?

4. Plan a lesson on morphemic analysis. Select elements that appear in students' texts and have a high degree of utility. If possible, teach the lesson and then reflect on its effectiveness.

5. Try using graphic devices, such as semantic feature analysis, a Venn diagram, or a semantic map, to organize words that you are studying or in which you are interested. Which of these devices works best for you? Why?

6. Investigate one of the vocabulary-building Web sites mentioned in this chapter or one you have discovered. How might you use this site in a class?

Professional Reflection

Do I have an understanding of …

____ The variability of students' vocabulary?

____ Word analysis components?

____ How new words are learned?

____ The special challenges faced by ELLs?

Am I able to …

____ Use a variety of approaches and techniques to develop students' vocabulary?

____ Teach students how to use morphemic and contextual analysis and dictionary skills?

____ Provide varied practice in the use of word analysis skills?

____ Assess and monitor students' vocabulary development and use of word analysis skills?

Reflection Question

Why is it important that every teacher be a teacher of vocabulary development?

Building Competencies

To build competencies, consult the following sources for more detailed information:

Bear, D. R., Invernizzi, M., Templeton, S., & Johnston, F. (2008). *Words their way: Word study for phonics, vocabulary, and spelling instruction* (4th ed.). Upper Saddle River, NJ: Prentice Hall.

Beck, I. L., Kucan, L., & McKeown, G. (2008). *Creating robust vocabulary: Frequently asked questions and extended examples*. New York: Guilford.

Ganske, K. (2000). *Word journeys: Assessment-guided phonics, spelling, and vocabulary instruction*. New York: Guilford.

Ganske, K. (2008). *Mindful of words: Spelling and vocabulary explorations 4–8*. New York: Guilford.

Moats, L. C. (2000). *Speech to print: Language essentials for teachers*, Chapter 4. Baltimore: Brookes.

National Reading Panel. (2000). National Reading Panel report, Chapter 4, Part I, *"Vocabulary instruction,"* pp. 4-15–4-35. Washington, DC: U.S. Department of Education. http://www.nationalreadingpanel.org

This report can be read online or downloaded, or a free copy may be ordered.

MyEducationLab™

Go to the Topics "Phonemic Awareness/Phonics" and "Fluency" (www.myeducationlab.com) for your course, where you can:

- Find learning outcomes for "Phonemic Awareness/ Phonics" and "Fluency" along with the national standards that connect to these outcomes.
- Complete Assignments and Activities that can help you more deeply understand the chapter content.
- Apply and practice your understanding of the core teaching skills identified in the chapter with the Building Teaching Skills and Dispositions learning units.
- Examine challenging situations and cases presented in the IRIS Center Resources.
- Check your comprehension on the content covered in the chapter by going to the Study Plan in the Book

Resources for your text. Here you will be able to take a chapter quiz, receive feedback on your answers, and then access Review, Practice, and Enrichment activities to enhance your understanding of chapter content. (optional)

A+RISE A+RISE® Standards2Strategy™ is an innovative and interactive online resource that offers new teachers in grades K–12 just-in-time, research-based instructional strategies that meet the linguistic needs of ELLs as they learn content, differentiate instruction for all grades and abilities, and are aligned to Common Core Elementary Language Arts standards (for the literacy strategies) and to English language proficiency standards in WIDA, Texas, California, and Florida.

Comprehension
Theory and Strategies

Anticipation Guide

For each of the following statements related to the chapter you are about to read, put a check under "Agree" or "Disagree" to show how you feel. Discuss your responses with classmates before you read the chapter.

	Agree	Disagree
1. Reading comprehension is understanding the author's meaning.	_____	_____
2. The less one knows about a topic, the more one will learn by reading about it.	_____	_____
3. Comprehension is a social activity.	_____	_____
4. Knowledge of words is the most important ingredient in comprehension.	_____	_____
5. As students read, they should be aware of whether they are comprehending what they're reading.	_____	_____
6. Before learning to draw inferences, the reader must master comprehension of literal details.	_____	_____
7. In comprehension instruction, the teacher should focus on the processes students use rather than on whether they obtain the right answers.	_____	_____

Using What You Know

In a sense, all the previous chapters have provided a foundation for this one, which is about comprehension. This chapter begins with a discussion of the nature of comprehension and goes on to describe and suggest how to teach strategies for obtaining meaning from reading. Comprehension is very much a matter of bringing your knowledge to the task. What do you know about comprehension? What strategies do you use as you try to understand what you read? What do you do when you fail to comprehend something you read? What tips for comprehension might you share with a younger reader?

The Process of Comprehending

Comprehension is a constructive, interactive process involving three factors—the reader, the text, and the context in which the text is read. For comprehension to improve, the interaction among all three factors must be taken into consideration. Readers vary in the amount and type of prior knowledge they possess, the strategies they use, their attitudes toward reading, and their work habits. Texts vary in genre, theme or topic, style, difficulty level, and appeal. The context includes when, where, and why a text is being read. Is it being read at home in preparation for a test the next day? Is it an antidote description printed on a can of pesticide, being read by a frantic parent whose child has sprayed her- or himself with the substance? Or is it a novel being read for pleasure in an easy chair on a lazy weekend? Although the bulk of this chapter will discuss comprehension strategies, the use of these strategies will be affected by reader, text, and context.

FYI

Because comprehension is dependent on schemata, building background knowledge lays the foundation for higher-level comprehension. Students who read more, and so have more background knowledge, actually boost their IQ scores. "Those who read a lot will enhance their verbal intelligence; that is, reading will make them smarter" (Cunningham & Stanovich, 1998, p. 7). ■

FYI

Because comprehension is dependent on what we know, one way to foster comprehension is to build background. ■

FYI

• Based on a situation model, you could take at least three steps to improve comprehension: build background, give students material on the appropriate level, and teach strategies, such as generating questions as they read, that will help them make connections.
• Following written directions is an example of the use of a situation model of reading. It requires that students go beyond merely remembering information. They must also put the information to use. ■

Schema Theory

To gain some insight into the process of comprehension, read the following paragraph, which has been divided into a series of sentences. Stop after reading each sentence and ask yourself, "What did the sentence say? How did I go about comprehending it? What does this paragraph seem to be about?"

A hoatzin has a clever way of escaping from its enemies.

It generally builds its home in a branch that extends over a swamp or stream.

If an enemy approaches, the hoatzin plunges into the water below.

Once the coast is clear, it uses its fingerlike claws to climb back up the tree.

Hoatzin are born with claws on their wings but lose the claws as they get older.

To make sense of the selection, you have to rely heavily on the knowledge you bring to the text. One definition of comprehension is that it is the process of building a connection between what we know and what we do not know, or the new and the old (Searfoss & Readence, 1994). Our knowledge is packaged into units known as schemata. A **schema** is the organized knowledge that one has about people, places, things, or events (Rumelhart, 1984). A schema may be very broad and general (for example, a schema for animals) or it may be fairly narrow (for example, a schema for Siamese cats).

In constructing the meaning of the selection on the hoatzin, you used various processes to activate the appropriate schema. In reading the first sentence, assuming that you did not know what a hoatzin is, you may have made a reasoned prediction that it was some kind of animal. The information in the first sentence was probably enough to activate your animal-survival-from-enemies schema. Integrating or summarizing the first three sentences made it possible for you to place "plunges into the water" into the ability-to-flee schema. The fourth sentence, which describes the use of claws to climb, probably activiated your schema for small mammals. However, when you read about the wings in the last sentence, you probably inferred that the hoatzin is a bird, even though it dives into the water. Thus, you were able to fill in the type-of-animal schema. You probably also inferred that the hoatzin's enemies could not reach it in the water. You may have inferred, too, that the creature is not fierce, since it seems to prefer fleeing to fighting. As you can probably see, comprehending the selection about the hoatzin was not so much a question of getting meaning from the text as it was of bringing meaning to it or constructing meaning by transacting with the text.

Not only do readers have schemata for ideas and events, they also have schemata for text structures, which help them organize information. For instance, a selection might be organized in terms of a main idea and details. A reader who realizes this can use the structure of the text to organize the information in his or her memory.

As they transact with text, proficient, active readers are constantly relating what they are reading to other experiences they have had, other information in the text they have read, and texts previously read. Their interest in the text plays a powerful role in the web of linkages that they construct (Hartman, 1994). A student captivated by the idea that a bird has claws on its wings might relate this text to passages that he or she has read or a TV show about unusual animals.

Situation Model Theory

Comprehension can also be thought of as the construction of a mental or **situation model**. According to a mental models theory, comprehension consists of multiple levels

---

■ A **schema** is a unit of organized knowledge. (The plural of *schema* is *schemata*.)
■ A **situation model,** also known as a mental model, views comprehension as a "process of building and maintaining a model of situations and events described in text" (McNamara, Miller, & Bransford, 1991, p. 491). Schema theory describes how familiar situations are understood; situation model theory describes how new situations are comprehended.
■ The **textbase** includes the statements or ideas conveyed by the surface structure.
■ **Propositions** are statements of information.

of understanding and includes surface code, propositional textbase, and the situation or mental model (Kintsch, 1994; Graesser, 2007). The surface code is composed of the exact words and syntax of the written piece. The textbase contains the explicit propositions or ideas conveyed by the surface structure. Propositions are statements of information. The textbase retains the meaning of the text but not the form. The mental model consists of the representation of the situation constructed by the reader.

Constructing a textbase, which is the basis for building a mental model, requires four key processing abilities: understanding essential details at a literal level; integrating text across sentences and paragraphs; making low-level, text-based inferences; and monitoring for meaning. As students read, they link the smaller units of text, the words, phrases, clauses, and sentences and build **local coherence** (Hampton & Resnick, 2009). They transform the words, phrases, and sentences structures into propositions. Using connecting words, the repetition of key words, and other cohesive devices, readers combine and integrate propositions to form **global coherence**, which is a running summary of the text. Constructing a coherent textbase makes it possible to build a mental model as the reader also relates background knowledge to the text and makes higher-level inferences about the text.

Readers construct a mental model when they integrate their prior knowledge or schema, goal for reading, and other reader factors with the textbase. Students reading the same passage would construct a similar textbase, but their mental models would vary because their backgrounds, goals for reading, and perspectives vary. "Whereas the textbase is verbal—it consists of word meanings combined into propositions— the mental model can include imagery and even an emotional component" (Gunning, 2010, p. 4). As Hampton and Resnick (2009) explain, "Readers move back and forth between the textbase and mental model. As they read, strong readers continually check their mental model against the textbase to make certain that the mental model accurately reflects what the text says and is consistent with their knowledge base" (p. 223). However, the text is the "foundation of the mental model" (p. 26) as readers build a representation of the text in their minds by combining schema and information from the text. For instance, in reading about heart disease, a student may find out that blood turns purple when it cannot get rid of carbon dioxide through the lungs. But a student who lacks background knowledge about the circulatory system will not be able to infer why this is so and will therefore be unable to construct a situation model. The student will be able to recite the information that he or she has read but will not be able to explain it because he or she really doesn't understand it (Kintsch, 1994). A student who has knowledge of the circulatory system can create a mental or situation model by combining information from the text with background information to infer why the blood turns purple. Of course, had the text reviewed the operation of the circulatory system, the reader might then have had sufficient background knowledge to infer why the blood turns purple. Or, the teacher could have built the necessary background. Comprehension is a combination of reader, text, and context, so a well-written, very explicit text, the building of necessary background, and instruction in the use of strategies can compensate for weak initial background.

Role of Reasoning

Reasoning is a key component in comprehension. Students may be called on to infer character traits, judge a solution, analyze a situation, compare settings, draw conclusions, form concepts, apply a principle, or evaluate the credibility of information. Reasoning and background knowledge interact. Comprehension relies heavily on the reader's ability to use background knowledge to make inferences. Students who have a richer background and can make more connections between what they know and what they are reading have better comprehension and retention.

■ **Local cohesion** is the use of linguistic devices to signal relationships within and among sentences.

■ **Global cohesion** is the use of linguistic devices to signal relationships among large or major parts of a text.

Role of Attention

Attention is also a factor in comprehension. Constructing meaning is hindered if the student is not reading actively and purposely: "Successful comprehension depends in part on readers' ability to allocate their limited attention efficiently and effectively to the most relevant pieces of information within the text and within memory" (van den Broek & Kremer, 2000, p. 7).

As McKeown (2006) explains, "The core of comprehension is a reader building a coherent representation of a text. Within this process, readers move through text—attending to information, making decisions about which information is important, connecting information to related text information or to what they already know, and eventually putting it all together to develop meaning. In shorthand we might think of the process of comprehension as focused attention, connection, and integration, and the outcome of comprehension as a coherent mental representation of the ideas in a text" (p. 1).

Role of Surface Features

Compare the following two excerpts (Touchstone Applied Science Associates, 2006, p. 2):

> Ford saw all this. But he didn't like it. The workers had to keep going back and forth to get parts. Again and again. Too many minutes and even hours were wasted. Ford was concerned. Such a great waste of _____ was disturbing. "There must be a better way," he thought. (DRP = 43)
>
> Henry Ford was the trailblazer of mass production in the automotive industry. When Ford began manufacturing, automobiles were usually assembled like houses, with the chassis fabricated at stationary locations where mechanics gathered around, attaching various parts. Assistants were constantly required to fetch materials, a practice that consumed numerous man-hours. Ford studied these production methods and was concerned. Such a great waste of _____ was disturbing. (DRP = 73)

Although both excerpts cover the same content, the second is written in a more complex style. In the second excerpt, vocabulary is more advanced, and sentences are longer and more complex. As might be expected, when presented with the full version of the more complex text, students' scores fell. Students were able to fill in 70 percent of the missing words in the less complex version but only 48 percent in the more complex one. As the sample passages suggest, surface features can impede comprehension (Touchstone Applied Science Associates, 2006). Although background knowledge is an essential element in comprehension, decoding and related skills are also important. Students who lack adequate vocabulary or have difficulty with syntax will experience difficulty understanding the more complex passage. The performance on the sample passages underscores the importance of automaticity in decoding and of adequate language skills, including vocabulary. The research also dramatizes the importance of providing students with materials that are on their level.

Developmental Nature of Comprehension

As children's background knowledge increases and their reasoning ability matures, their ability to comprehend improves. Until they reach Piaget's stage of concrete operations, children might have difficulty comprehending tales in which things are not what they seem. They take their reading very literally. For instance, one second-grader had a great deal of difficulty with a trickster tale in which a fox disguised itself as a tree to make a meal of the hens. Despite the fact that the story described the tree's feet and teeth, she was unable to move beyond the textbase and believed that it was still a tree. Between the ages of 5 and 7, children tend to think in one dimension (Donovan & Smolkin, 2001). By about age 8, children are able to think in more than one dimension and so can learn comprehension strategies more readily. Young children also experience difficulty with metacognitive tasks. They have difficulty both explaining their cognitive processes and planning cognitive strategies. Comprehension instruction for young children should be explicit and concrete and in keeping with where they are developmentally. This does not mean that they should not be taught comprehension skills; what it does mean is that they need to be taught skills that coincide with their level of understanding. In discussions, it is important to probe to see how students are understanding what they read and to build on their understanding. Open-ended questions work best at revealing children's thinking: "What is happening here? What is the author telling us? Is there anything that is puzzling you?" Also ask questions that guide children's thinking as they read: "What is different about this tree? Do you know any trees that have feet and teeth? Why do you think this tree has feet and teeth?"

FYI

Students from impoverished backgrounds may do well in the early grades but lose momentum as they advance in the grades (Pearson, 2003). To close this gap, it is recommended that more attention be paid to developing comprehension and high-level thinking skills, applying skills in the content areas, making connections, and integrating instruction (Pearson, 2003). ■

Approaches to Teaching Comprehension

There are two main approaches to teaching comprehension: strategy and content analysis. As McKeown, Beck, and Blake (2009) explain, "A major distinction between the two approaches is that strategy instruction encourages students to think about their mental processes and, on that basis, to execute specific strategies with which to interact with text. In contrast, content instruction attempts to engage students in the process of attending to text ideas and building a mental representation of the ideas, with no direction to consider specific mental processes" (p. 219). Of course, the approaches can be combined so that the reader attends to both strategies and content. In this chapter, strategy, content, and combined approaches are explored. This chapter also takes a look at approaches that are collaborative but that focus on content. That is, they focus on analyzing ideas rather than the strategies used to comprehend those ideas.

Cognitive strategies have a cost. They do require a certain amount of mental input, especially when students are learning to use strategies. However, as students become more proficient, the strategies become more automatic and take little or no extra effort (Graesser, 2007).

Comprehension Strategies

Before you began reading this chapter, what did you do? Did you read the title? Did you ask yourself what you know about comprehension? As you read, did you question what the text was saying? Did you try to relate information in the text to your experience? Did you reread sections because you didn't quite understand what was being said or were momentarily distracted? If you did any of these things, you were using reading strategies.

To help you understand strategies, think about the processes you use as you read. Because you are an experienced reader, your strategies have become relatively automatic. Stop your reading from time to time and think about the processes you are using to comprehend what you are reading. Do this especially when you are reading difficult material. Strategies tend to become more conscious when the material is difficult because we have to take deliberate steps to comprehend it. One group of highly effective staff developers and classroom teachers tried out each strategy on their own reading before teaching it. They discovered that their comprehension as well as their understanding of strategies and ability to teach them to students improved.

> We tested the strategies on our reading. We became more conscious of our own thinking processes as readers. We realized that we could concentrate simultaneously on the text and our ways of thinking about it. What seems most extraordinary, however, was that by thinking about our own thinking—by being metacognitive (literally, to think about one's

thinking)—we could actually deepen and enhance our comprehension of the text. (Keene & Zimmermann, 1997, p. 21)

According to the schema and situation model theories of comprehension, the reader plays a very active role in constructing meaning for and understanding of a text. One way the active reader constructs meaning is by using strategies. **Strategies** are deliberate, planned procedures designed to help the reader reach a goal (Afflerbach, Pearson, & Paris, 2008). Previewing, predicting, summarizing, and questioning are strategies. In contrast to strategies, skills are automatic processes that are usually performed without conscious control. When strategies are applied automatically, they become skills.

Strategies are important at all levels. Research indicates that even sophisticated readers are poor at judging how well they comprehend (Graesser, 2007). Many readers are also satisfied with a shallow level of comprehension. They are satisfied if they recognize the words and can read the sentences. However, effective reading requires being able to organize and integrate information, draw conclusions, and evaluate the information (Graesser, 2007). Added to that, even the best readers struggle with text that is introducing new concepts. The widely adopted Common Core State Standards call for deeper comprehension of challenging text, especially informational text. Such challenges require more proficient use of strategies. As Graesser reminds us, "Cognitive strategies are particularly important when there is a breakdown at any level of comprehension. A successful reader implements deliberate, conscious, effortful, time-consuming strategies to repair or circumvent a reading component that is not intact" (p. 4).

Comprehension strategies can be categorized as preparational, organizational, elaboration, rehearsal, and monitoring. There are also affective strategies (Weinstein & Mayer, 1986), in which motivation and interest play a role in the construction of meaning.

Preparational strategies are processes that readers use to prepare themselves to construct meaning, such as surveying a text and predicting what it will be about. Using organizational strategies, readers construct relationships among ideas in the text, specifically between the main idea and supporting details. Paraphrasing, summarizing, clustering related words, noting and using the structure of a text, and creating semantic maps are also ways of organizing.

Elaborating involves building associations between information being read and prior knowledge or integrating information by manipulating or transforming it. Elaboration strategies include drawing inferences, creating analogies, visualizing, and evaluating, or reading critically. (Evaluating is discussed in Chapter 8.)

Rehearsing involves taking basic steps to remember material. Outlining, taking notes, underlining, testing oneself, and rereading are rehearsal strategies. Organizing, elaborating, and rehearsing are often used in combination to learn complex material.

FYI

• When second-through sixth-graders were surveyed to determine what teachers could do to help them comprehend, the students wanted teachers to (1) describe what they did to understand the "things that occurred in books," (2) show how they knew which meanings went with which words, and (3) explain "just about everything that they did in their minds to comprehend" (Block & Israel, 2004).
• For a discussion of strategies and skills, see Afflerbach, Pearson, and Paris (2008). ■

FYI

In this text, strategies are presented according to the cognitive or affective processes involved. ■

■ A **strategy** is a deliberate, planned procedure designed to achieve a certain goal.

■ **Rehearsing** is studying or repeating something so as to remember it.

TABLE 7.1 Major Comprehension Strategies

Preparational Strategies	Organizational Strategies	Elaboration Strategies	Metacognitive Strategies
Previewing	Comprehending the main idea	Making inferences	Regulating
Activating prior knowledge	Determining important details	Imaging	Checking
Setting purpose and goals	Organizing details	Generating questions	Repairing
Predicting	Sequencing	Evaluating (critical reading)	
	Following directions		
	Summarizing		

Monitoring consists of being aware of one's comprehension and regulating it. Monitoring strategies include setting goals for reading, adjusting reading speed to difficulty of material, checking comprehension, and taking corrective steps when comprehension fails. (Some preparational strategies are actually a special set of monitoring strategies that are employed prior to reading.) See Table 7.1 for a listing of comprehension strategies.

FYI

As you teach strategies, keep in mind that the goal is improved comprehension. Strategy instruction is a means to an end and not an end in itself (Mehigan, 2005). ▪

Strategy Instruction

Whatever the strategy (whether inferring, summarizing, or predicting), strategy instruction has six key steps: introducing the strategy, demonstrating and modeling the strategy, guided practice, independent practice and application, assessment and reteaching, and ongoing reinforcement and implementation. See Table 7.2 for an overview of the main steps in strategy instruction.

FYI

Teaching students to use strategies results in average percentile gains of 20 points (Hattie, 2009). ▪

1. *Introducing the strategy.* Explain what the strategy is, why it is being taught, how it will benefit students, and when and where it might be used.

2. *Demonstrating and modeling the strategy.* Show how the strategy is put to use. Model the process, and do a think-aloud as you demonstrate activation of the strategy. If possible, select a text that genuinely puzzled you so that the think-aloud seems real to the students. Have students note the difficulty you are having and the steps you are taking to resolve the difficulty. Provide examples of situations in which you or others have used the strategy effectively. Sum up by providing students with clear, specific directions for applying the strategy. If possible, incorporate a mnemonic into the steps. Post a list of the steps in the classroom.

3. *Guided practice.* Guidance might be tightly structured initially. Gradually turn over more responsibility to students. Initially, the teacher does most of the talking, but students help out. For a time the guided practice is collaborative as students and teachers work closely together. Later, students do most of the work, but the teacher provides assistance. It is essential that adequate guidance be provided so that students achieve a solid grasp of the strategy. There is a tendency for programs to provide independent practice activities before students are ready for them (Dewitz et al., 2009). Although strategies might be taught to the whole class, Boyles (2004) recommends that guided practice be completed in small groups of from four to six in the earlier grades and up to eight in the upper grades. With this arrangement, students can be grouped according to reading ability, and instruction can be geared to their level of development. As part of guided practice, have students work in pairs in which one student implements the strategy and the other student checks the implementation, and then they switch roles. (They might use a checklist of the steps involved in applying a strategy, as in the explanation of applying the details strategy in Lesson 7.2, under "How do we use this strategy?" on p. 327.) In the initial stages of guided practice, it is a good idea to use materials that are brief and relatively easy. That way, students can focus their full mental energies on applying the strategy.

4. *Independent practice and application.* Strategy learning is contextual. Its application tends to be limited to the context or subject in which it was learned. To promote transfer, have the students apply the strategy to a variety of materials and to other content areas.

5. *Assessment and reteaching.* Observe students to see if they apply the strategy and apply it effectively. Also conduct a written assessment. Reteach and review as necessary.

6. *Ongoing reinforcement and implementation.* After a month or so of practice and application, students should have an initial grasp of

REFLECTION

Students learn at different rates. How will you provide for students who are slower at catching on to a strategy that you are teaching? How will you differentiate instruction so as to provide for all students?

▪ **Monitoring** is being aware of or checking one's cognitive processes. In reading comprehension, the reader monitors his or her understanding of the text.

the strategy. They can add it to their repertoire and move on to the next strategy. However, continue to review the strategy from time to time and also remind students to use it, perhaps by using cues. Cues differ from scaffolds because they provide brief reminders but do not "tell us all that we are to do or say" (Beyer, 2001, p. 421). To cue students, simply mention the name of a strategy to be used, or you might provide a brief description of it; you might also ask students to tell what strategy they plan to use in a particular situation, point out a chart containing the strategy, or refer to a mnemonic that reminds students of the main steps of a strategy. (For example, a mnemonic for one summarizing strategy is WITS: Write the main idea. Include only the key details. Take out unimportant details and unnecessary words. Smooth out the summary. (Students might be told to keep their WITS about them when writing a summary.) Mnemonics or other cues might be placed on charts or bookmarks.

Boyles (2004, p. 15) explains the changing roles of teacher (I) and students (you) as students take on more responsibility for strategy application:

Explain/model	I do; you watch.
Initial guided practice	I do; you help.
Later guided practice	You do; I help.
Independence	You do; I watch.

Assessing for Learning

Observing students as they apply strategies and asking questions about their use of strategies will provide feedback that will allow you to give them the guidance they need. ■

To reinforce strategy use in your post-reading discussion of a selection, talk over the strategies that were used. You might ask, "What strategies did you use?" If there is no response, use more specific questions: "Did you ask questions as you read? Did pictures pop into your mind as you were reading?" Ask students to support their responses by reading portions of the text. "What part of the text caused that picture to pop into your mind? Could you read it for us? What part of the text led you to ask questions?" Also discuss how the strategies helped students understand the text: "How did using that strategy help you to understand what you were reading?"

TABLE 7.2   Steps in a Strategy Lesson

Task	Classroom Usage Example
Introducing the strategy	"Predicting is making guesses about what will come next in the text you are reading. Make predictions often when you read by stopping and thinking about what might come next."
Demonstrating and modeling the strategy	"I am going to predict using the cover of this book. I see a picture of an owl wearing pajamas and carrying a candle. I predict that this story is going to be about this owl, and that it is going to take place at night."
Guided practice (collaborative use)	"I want you to make predictions with me. Each of us should stop and think about what might happen next.... Okay, now, let's hear what you think and why."
Guided practice	"I have given you a list of pages in the book you are reading. After you read a page on the list, make a prediction and write it down. After you read the next page on the list, check off whether your prediction happened, will not happen, or still might happen." Some items are done cooperatively. Teacher provides assistance as needed. Students might work in pairs.
Independent use	"For now you should stop every two pages, evaluate the predictions you have made, and then make some new ones for the next two pages." Students are also reminded to use the strategy with texts that they are reading on their own.
Assessment and reteaching	"In your learning logs, you were asked to describe the strategies you used as you read the selection. How many of you used predictions? What predictions did you make? How did you go about making predictions? How did your predictions work out? What effect did making predictions have on your reading?"
Ongoing reinforcement and implementation	"We've been making predictions for nearly a month, Let's review what we have learned. Why do we make predictions? When do we make predictions? How do we go about making predictions? What have you learned about making predictions? How has making predictions helped you? What would you do to make predictions even more effectively? We've been using predictions with fiction. Now we are going to try using them with nonfiction. We are going to predict what the author is going to tell us. In the selection 'The Power of the Wind,' what do you think the author might tell us?"

Source: Shanahan, T., Callison, K., Carriere, C., Duke, N. K., Pearson, P. D., Schatschneider, C., & Torgesen, J. (2010). *Improving reading comprehension in kindergarten through 3rd grade: A practice guide (NCEE 2010-4038).* Washington, DC: National Center for Education Evaluation and Regional Assistance, Institute of Education Sciences, U.S. Department of Education. Retrieved from whatworks.ed.gov/publications

Teaching Preparational Strategies

Preparational strategies include previewing, activating prior knowledge about a topic before reading, and predicting what a piece is about or what will happen in a story. Setting purposes and setting goals are also preparational strategies.

Activating Prior Knowledge   Because comprehension involves relating the unknown to the known, it is important that students become aware of what they know about a subject. The teacher should model the process. In preparation for reading an article, the teacher should show the class how she or he previews, asks what she or he already knows about the subject, and then decides what she or he would like to find out.

Before students read a selection, the teacher activates students' **prior knowledge** through questioning. This works best when both subject knowledge (school-type knowledge) and personal knowledge are activated. For instance, before reading a story about poisonous snakes, the teacher asks students to tell what they know about poisonous snakes and also relate any personal knowledge they have about snakes. In one study, students who activated both subject knowledge and personal knowledge prior to reading were better able to apply their knowledge and also had a more positive attitude (Spires & Donley, 1998). In time, students should be led to activate both subject and personal knowledge on their own, because much of their reading will be done without the benefit of preparatory discussion or teacher assistance.

Setting Purpose and Goals   Although the teacher often sets the **purpose** for reading a piece by giving students a question to answer, students must be able to set their own purpose. This could fit in with activating prior knowledge. For example, as readers activate knowledge about computers, they may wonder how the machines work, which could be a purpose for reading. Readers also have to decide on their overall **goal** for reading—for pleasure, to gain information, or to study for a test—as each goal requires a different style of reading. Again, these are processes that the teacher should model and discuss. However, students should gradually take responsibility for setting purposes and goals.

Previewing   A strategy that helps readers set a purpose for reading is **previewing**. In previewing, also known as surveying, students read a selection's title, headings, introduction, and summary and look at illustrations to get an overview of the selection. This preview orients them to the piece so that they have some sense of what it will be about. A preview can function as a kind of blueprint for constructing a mental model of the text and also activates readers' schemata. As readers preview, they ask themselves what they know about the subject. Previewing is often used with predicting: Information gathered from previewing can be used to make predictions.

Predicting   Powerful, but relatively easy to use, predicting activates readers' schemata because predictions are made on the basis of prior knowledge. Predicting also gives readers a purpose for reading and turns reading into an active search to see whether a prediction is correct. However, one danger of predicting is that students' predictions run the risk of simply being guesses, with little thought backing them up. To improve predictions, stress the importance of having a solid basis for them. To encourage students to base their predictions on experience and textual clues, ask two questions: one that asks what the prediction is ("What do you think will happen in the

Adapting Instruction for Struggling Readers and Writers

Stress that the goal of reading is to construct meaning. Poor readers may be more concerned with pronouncing words correctly than with making meaning. If students realize that the goal of reading is comprehension, they are more likely to be "actively involved in achieving this goal by monitoring their effectiveness toward it" (Westby, 1999, p. 154). ■

Using Technology

Technology can foster active reading. In *Alex's Scribbles*, Max the koala has a series of adventures. To continue each story, the reader must point and click in response to a question. This site also lends itself to writing. Alex, the coauthor, and Max invite readers to e-mail them. http://www.scribbles.com.au/max/bookmain.html ■

- **Prior knowledge** is the background information that a reader brings to the text.
- The **purpose** for reading is the question that the reader wants to answer or the information the reader is seeking.

- The **goal** of reading is the outcome the reader is seeking: to gain information, to prepare for a test, to learn how to put a toy together, to relax, etc.

- **Previewing** can also be applied during reading. A reader may complete a section and then activate prior knowledge and make predictions for the upcoming section.

story?" or "How do you think the main character will resolve her problem?") and one that asks for support of the prediction ("What makes you predict that?" or "What have you experienced and what clues from the story lead you to make that prediction?") (Nessel, 1987). For nonfiction, have students predict what they might learn about the topic.

If students look at both the title of a selection and the cover illustration, they are likely to rely primarily on the illustration, and this might limit their predictions (Benson-Castagna, 2005). Write the title of a selection that students are about to read on the chalkboard. Have them use just the title to make predictions, if it lends itself to it. Model the process of making predictions. For a story such as *A Bad, Bad Day* (Hall, 1995), explain what you think a bad day would be and how you use your background knowledge to predict what might happen in the story. After making a prediction based on the title, explain how the cover illustration helps you to add to your prediction. You can predict some of the things that might happen because the illustration shows the boy missing the school bus. Also, discuss how the illustration relates to the title.

For nonfiction, students also preview the title and cover illustration, but in addition, they look at headings, additional illustrations, and the table of contents, if there is one. Before students read informational text, it is especially important to activate their prior knowledge. Oczkus (2005) prompts students to activate prior knowledge by first discussing the title and having students tell what they already know about pets, ants, rockets, germs, or whatever the topic happens to be. Once they have discussed what they know about the topic, students are in a better position to make predictions. For informational text, they predict what the author will tell them about the topic or what they will learn about the topic.

As with fiction, model the process of making predictions about informational text. In previewing the title of a selection entitled "Robots at Work," start by telling what you know about robots: "I know that robots help put cars together, but I don't know how they do that. Maybe the article will explain how they assemble cars. A friend of mine has a robot that vacuums his home. I wonder if there are robots that scrub floors. I predict that the article will tell what kinds of jobs robots do besides putting cars together and vacuuming floors. I predict that the author will also explain how robots are able to do certain jobs."

Some students have difficulty making predictions. Possible reasons include limited background of experience, failure to activate prior knowledge, difficulty inferring, or reluctance to take a risk. To get students accustomed to making predictions, have them make predictions about everyday events: "What do you predict will be on the lunch menu today? What do you predict tomorrow's weather will be?" To build confidence and skill in making predictions, provide students with brief fictional selections that lend themselves to making predictions. Do lots of modeling and coaching. For younger children, lift-the-tab books, such as *Where's Spot?* (Hill, 1980), are especially good for making predictions. Another book for young readers that lends itself to making predictions is *Where's the Bear?* (Pomerantz, 1984). For older students, detective stories, such as the *Sebastian Super Sleuth* series, provide continuous opportunities for making predictions. You might also have students make predictions based on illustrations. They can describe what is happening in an illustration and predict what might happen next.

Some students are so reluctant to take a risk and make predictions that they read ahead so that their predictions aren't predictions at all. Emphasize that predictions are just careful guesses; the important thing is that predictions will help them think about their reading. Explain that the key element is the thinking that goes along with the prediction rather than the accuracy of the prediction. Emphasize the importance of well-thought-out predictions. Deemphasize the rightness or wrongness of predictions. Stress plausibility and flexibility. The focus is on building thinking skills. When students are practicing predicting, have them cover up the portions of the text that

FYI

Emphasize the plausibility and flexibility of predictions rather than their accuracy. Explain to students that as they read, they will get more information and can change their predictions to fit with the new information. ■

they haven't read yet. That way, they aren't tempted to read ahead and find out what happens so that their predictions can be "accurate." The prediction chart in Figure 7.1 helps students make reasoned predictions.

To help students build flexibility into their predictions, provide an exercise similar to the following in which they make a prediction after each sentence:

- Sam walked slowly on the way to school.
- She was worried about her test today.
- She wondered how she could help her students. (Scanlon, 2010)

Emphasize that predictions may vary. The whole class or group doesn't have to have the same prediction. Also, stress that predictions are careful guesses, so readers need to be flexible. Based on information obtained as they read, students might wish to change their predictions.

Gradually, students can create their own predictions as they read. Predicting becomes an excellent device for enhancing comprehension when students read independently—ideally, it will become automatic. Predicting should also be a lifelong strategy. As they move into higher grades, students should use predicting as a study technique as well as for other sustained reading.

Part of being an effective user of comprehension strategies is knowing when and where to use a particular strategy. Making predictions requires prior knowledge. Students who are beginning to read about a topic on which they have little background information will have difficulty making reasonable predictions and so should use another strategy.

Teaching Organizational Strategies

Organizational strategies are at the heart of constructing meaning. In contrast to preparational strategies, they are employed during reading as well as after reading. As students read, they form a situation model. Organizational strategies involve selecting important details and building relationships among them. For reading, this entails identifying or constructing the main idea (or gist) of a passage and its supporting details and summarizing.

Comprehending the Main Idea Deriving the main idea is at the core of constructing meaning from text, as the main idea provides a framework for organizing, understanding, and remembering the essential details. Without it, students wander aimlessly among details. Being able to identify or compose main ideas is essential for summarizing, note taking, and outlining. (Although suggestions for teaching comprehension of main ideas and important details are presented separately in this chapter for the sake of clarity, these should be taught together.)

FYI

Students might practice making predictions by looking at an illustration and predicting what the caption will say about it. They then check their predictions by reading the caption. Oczkus (2005) has students examine captionless illustrations and then respond to the statement "I wonder what is going on in this illustration." ■

CCSS

Determine the central ideas or themes of a text and analyze their development; summarize the key supporting details and ideas.

FIGURE 7.1 Prediction Chart

Prediction	Clues What led me to make this prediction?	Changes in Predictions As I read the text, what changes did I have to make in my predictions?

Although it has been defined in a variety of ways (Cunningham & Moore, 1986), in this book, the **main idea** is a summary statement that includes the other details in a paragraph or longer piece; it is what all the sentences are about. It is not the most important idea; rather, it is the gist of the paragraph or piece, a one-sentence summary. It fits in with the strategies of determining importance and summarizing. Although main ideas are key to comprehension, little is known about how elementary and middle school students generate them.

Adept readers tend to use either a whole-to-part strategy, in which they draft or hypothesize the whole and confirm it by reading the parts, or a part-to-whole strategy, in which they note important parts, construct relationships among them, and compose a main idea statement (Afflerbach, 1990; Afflerbach & Johnston, 1986). The whole-to-part strategy fits best with a schema theory of comprehension; the part-to-whole strategy exemplifies the construction of a situation model.

Because of its complexity and importance, main idea comprehension has to be taught step by step. Instruction should include presenting underlying processes, one of which is classifying.

Classifying   Determining the main idea is partly a classification skill. The main idea statement is a category label for all or most of the details in the piece. The best way to convey the concept of a main idea and to provide instruction in its underlying cognitive process is to have students classify a series of objects or words (Baumann, 1986; Johnson & Kress, 1965; Williams, 1986b).

To demonstrate classifying to younger students, bring in a variety of objects and indicate how they might be sorted. For example, display an apple, orange, pear, banana, and book, and ask students to tell which go together. Discuss why the book does not belong. Put the objects in a box. Tell students you want to label the box so that you know what is in it and ask them what word you might use. Students can name other objects that might be put in the box, with a discussion of why they belong there. Follow a similar procedure with tools, toys, and other objects.

Once students have grasped the idea of classifying objects, have them classify words. First, give them lists of words that include labels. Model how you would go about choosing the category label. Tell students that you are looking for a word that tells about all the others. Read a series of related words that have been written on the board, overhead, or interactive white board: *cats, fish, pets, dogs*. Model how you would choose *pets* as the label because it includes the other three words. After working through several sample series of words, have students complete exercises similar to the following, one that contains words that are easy enough for first-graders. For older students, select more challenging items.

ball	toys	blocks	doll
oak	trees	maple	pine
fruit	apple	peach	banana

To vary the activity, include an item in the series that does not belong (*train, bus, car, ball*) and have students identify it. Also, list a series of related items (*three, nine, four, two*) and let students supply a category label.

After students are able to categorize words with ease, have them categorize groups of sentences by identifying the one that tells about all the others. Call this the main idea sentence. To construct exercises of this type, locate brief paragraphs that have an explicitly stated main idea. Write the sentences in list form, and have students point out which sentence tells about all the others. Groups of sentences similar to the following can be used:

The car door locks were frozen.

Small children refused to venture from their warm homes.

It was the coldest day that anyone could remember.

The temperature was twenty below zero.

The lake was frozen solid.

Model the process of choosing the most inclusive sentence, thinking aloud as you choose it. Let students see that the process involves checking each sentence to determine which one includes all the others and then examining the other sentences to make sure that each one can be included under the main sentence. In your explanation, you might use the analogy of a roof. Explain that the main idea sentence is like a roof. The other sentences contain details that hold up the roof. They are like the walls that support a roof. As part of the process, explain how pointing out the inclusive sentence will help them find main ideas in their reading. After students have acquired a concept of an inclusive sentence, have students complete a series of similar exercises under your guidance.

Recognizing Topic Sentences   Once students have a sense of what a main idea is, begin working with brief paragraphs that contain an explicitly stated main idea, a sentence that tells about all the others. Explain that the main idea sentence is called a topic sentence because it contains the topic of the paragraph. It is often the first sentence of a paragraph, but may be last or in the middle. Move the topic sentence in a sample paragraph around to show students how it could make sense in a number of positions. Also point out how the details in the paragraph support the main idea.

Provide students with guided practice in locating topic sentences and supporting details in paragraphs. Locating supporting details is like proving a problem in math: If the details do not support the sentence chosen as the topic sentence, the student has probably not located the real topic sentence. Take practice paragraphs from children's periodicals, books, and textbooks. At first, select paragraphs in which the main idea sentence comes first, as this is the easiest organizational pattern to understand. Students have more difficulty with paragraphs in which the topic sentence occurs last (Kimmel & MacGinitie, 1984). Make sure to choose paragraphs that are interesting and well written and on the students' level. Students will then enjoy the activity more and will pick up incidental information. Using real books and periodicals also demonstrates that recognizing topic sentences is a practical activity, one students can use in their everyday reading. It also makes the practice more realistic because students will be working with the kinds of material they actually read rather than with paragraphs contrived for teaching the main idea. The following is an example of a paragraph that might be used:

> The largest members of the cat family are truly large. They range in size from about 6 feet to 12 feet long, measured from the tips of their noses to the tips of their tails. They weigh from 50 to 500 pounds, and are 22 to 44 inches tall at the shoulder. (Thompson, 1998, p. 26)

Presenting paragraphs that contain topic sentences makes sense in the beginning stages of instruction, as it simplifies identifying the main idea, but you must emphasize that not all paragraphs contain topic sentences. In fact, most do not. Baumann and Serra (1984) found that only 44 percent of the paragraphs in elementary social studies textbooks had explicitly stated main ideas, and only 27 percent of the main ideas occurred in the opening sentence.

Even when the main idea is explicitly stated and is in the opening sentence, readers must still infer that the first sentence tells what the rest of the paragraph is about. Young readers and poor readers tend to select the first sentence as the topic sentence almost automatically (Gold & Fleisher, 1986). To prevent this, ask them to check by specifying the supporting details in this paragraph and to see whether all the other sentences support the first one (Duffelmeyer, 1985). If that is the case, the first sentence is the topic sentence. If not, the students should search for a sentence that does serve that function.

FYI

Young students find it easier to select titles than to identify main idea statements. Titles are more familiar and more concrete. Students' ability to identify main ideas improves with age (van den Broek et al., 2003). ■

FYI

• Although well-formed paragraphs might be used for initial instruction in main ideas, students should apply their strategies to informational trade books and texts. Authors do not begin each paragraph with a main idea. Often, the main idea is implied, and some paragraphs simply provide an introduction or additional information and lack a clear-cut main idea.

• In addition to modeling strategy use and providing practice, develop with students a series of steps to be followed in order to carry out the strategy, such as those listed for determining the main idea. ■

Selecting or Constructing the Main Idea   Most passages do not have an explicitly stated main idea, so it must be constructed. Students might use the following steps (which should be posted in the classroom, as given here or in adapted form) to select a stated main idea or construct a main idea if it is not stated:

1. Use the heading, title, or first sentence to make a hypothesis (careful guess) as to what the main idea is.
2. Read each sentence and see whether it supports the hypothesis. If not, revise the hypothesis.
3. If you can't make a hypothesis about what the main idea is, see what all or most of the sentences have in common or are talking about.
4. Select a sentence or make a sentence that tells what all the sentences are about.

One problem that students have in recognizing or generating main ideas is a tendency to focus on a narrow statement of a single detail instead of on a broad statement that includes all the essential information in a paragraph (Williams, 1986a). As students work with paragraphs, you might use a series of prompts to help them identify what the paragraph is about. Start off by asking them what the general topic of the paragraph is, and then ask them to identify the specific topic and check whether all the details support it. For instance, using the following simple paragraph about robots, you might ask, "What is the general topic of the paragraph? What is the specific topic? What does the paragraph tell us about robots?"

> Robots help us in many ways. Robots work in factories. They help put cars and TVs together. In some offices, robots deliver the mail. And in some hospitals, robots bring food to sick people. A new kind of robot can mow lawns. And some day there may even be robots that can take out the trash and take the dog for a walk.

If students provide the correct specific topic, ask them to verify their response. The class should go over each sentence to determine whether it tells how robots help out. If, on the other hand, students supply a supporting detail rather than a statement of the specific topic, have the class examine the detail to see if it encompassed all the other details in the paragraph. Lesson 7.1 presents suggestions for teaching how to determine the main idea.

FYI

• Noting main ideas in longer sections is the ultimate payoff. This helps pupils better understand and remember information. Today's content-area texts make plentiful use of heads and subheads, which announce main ideas or can be used to construct them.

• If students fail to construct a main idea during their first pass through a text, show them how to skim through the passage and note related words, ideas, or concepts. Have them create a main idea statement that tells what all the sentences are about. As an alternative, show students how to use the draft-and-revise strategy. That is, they use their initial reading to construct a main idea statement and then check the validity of their statement by rereading the passage. ■

LESSON 7.1

Determining the Main Idea and Its Supporting Details

Objectives

• Students will recognize directly stated main ideas.
• Students will infer implied main ideas.
• Students will relate supporting details to main idea.

Step 1. Introducing the strategy

Explain what main ideas and supporting details are and why it is important to locate and understand them in reading. Give a clear definition of what a main idea is—it tells what the paragraph or section is all about. Provide examples of main ideas.

Step 2. Modeling the process

Show how you would go about determining a main idea and its supporting details. Starting off with well-constructed paragraphs, demonstrate the hypothesis strategy, because this is the strategy most frequently used by adept readers. Show students how you would use

FYI

To help them comprehend, students want teachers to describe what they did to understand the "things that occurred in books" and explain "just about everything that they did in their minds to comprehend" (Block & Israel, 2004). ■

a title, heading, graphic clues, and the apparent topic sentence to predict the main idea. Then confirm or revise your hypothesis as you read and see whether the details support your hypothesized main idea. (Even if the main idea is directly stated, it is still necessary to use a hypothesis or other strategy, because readers cannot be sure that the sentence is indeed a topic sentence until they read the rest of the paragraph.)

In subsequent lessons that tackle paragraphs with implied main ideas and no titles or headings that could be clues to the main idea, you may have to use a part-to-whole strategy. Note the details in such a paragraph and then construct a main idea statement after seeing how the details are related or what they have in common. A part-to-whole strategy is best taught after students have a firm grasp of the hypothesis-confirmation strategy. Model the process with a variety of paragraphs.

Step 3. Guided practice

Have students derive main ideas from brief, well-constructed paragraphs. If possible, choose paragraphs that cover familiar topics, as it is easier to construct main ideas when the content and vocabulary are known. Although shorter paragraphs should be used in the beginning stages, have students gradually apply this skill to longer pieces, such as selections from content-area textbooks.

Step 4. Independent practice and application

Have students derive main ideas and supporting details in children's books, textbooks, periodicals, and other materials that they read on their own. From well-written, well-organized science or social studies textbooks or children's books, choose sections that convey an overall main idea or theme and develop it in several paragraphs. At first, choose pieces that have an explicitly stated main idea. Show students how you would use a hypothesis strategy to derive the main idea. Using a selection similar to that illustrated in Figure 7.2, demonstrate how you would use the heading ("The Pilgrim's Voyage to America") and the subheading of each section to guess what the main idea of each section is. Lead students to see that the main idea seems to be stated in the heading and that the main idea of each section is found in the subhead and first sentence of the section.

Step 5. Assessment and reteaching

Observe students as they obtain main ideas from a variety of passages in texts and trade books. Note how well they can do the following:

Identify the main idea and supporting details in a brief, well-constructed paragraph in which the main idea is directly stated in the first sentence.

Identify the main idea and supporting details in a brief, well-constructed paragraph in which the main idea is directly stated in the middle or end of the paragraph.

Infer the main idea in a well-constructed paragraph in which the main idea is not directly stated.

Identify or infer the main idea in general reading.

Based on the results of your assessment, review and reteach.

STUDENT STRATEGIES
Determining the Main Idea

In a discussion with students, create a series of steps that they might use to locate or construct the main idea. Make a chart containing the steps, and put it in a prominent place so that students can refer to it while reading. (Use the steps listed on p. 322 or an adaptation of them.)

REFLECTION

What steps might you take to help students who are having difficulty identifying or constructing main ideas?

FYI

Comprehension instruction requires scaffolding. Teachers provide examples, modeling, explicit instruction, prompts, and discussions in helping students learn strategies (Dole, Duffy, Roehler, & Pearson, 1991). In time, the scaffolding is reduced, and students apply the strategies independently. ■

Extending the Ability to Construct the Main Idea Take advantage of discussions of selections that students have read and other naturally occurring opportunities to apply and extend the skill of constructing main ideas. Note how important details are related to the main idea of a selection. Also apply the concept to writing. Have students create and develop topic sentences on nonfiction subjects of their own choosing.

Graphic displays can help students identify the topic sentence and its supporting details. Use a simplified semantic map, which is sometimes called a *spider web* when the supporting details are of equal importance, as shown in Figure 7.3. Use a linear display like that in Figure 7.4 when the piece has a sequential order, that is, when the ideas are listed in order of occurrence.

Main idea instruction is more appropriate for nonfiction than for fiction. Fiction has a theme rather than a main idea. Identifying a theme can be subtler and more complex than noting a main idea. Most children's fiction also has a central problem that gives coherence to the story (Moldofsky, 1983).

Reviewing the Strategy Learning a strategy may take a month or more. In subsequent lessons, review and extend the strategy. To review the strategy, ask the following kinds of questions:

- What strategy are we learning to use? (main idea)
- How does this strategy help us? (helps us understand and remember what we read; helps us organize important details)
- When do we use this strategy? (with nonfiction)
- How do we use this strategy? (Review the steps presented on p. 322.) Also ask students to tell about instances when they used the strategy on their own. (T. Scott, 1998)

REINFORCEMENT ACTIVITIES

Main Idea Construction

- Cut out newspaper headlines and titles of articles and have students match them with the articles.
- Have students classify lists of items.
- When discussing selections that students have read, include questions that require them to identify and/or construct a main idea.

Semantic maps and other graphic organizers can help students organize information.

Determining the Relative Importance of Information   The ability to determine what is important in a selection is a key factor in comprehension, as it keeps readers from drowning in a sea of details or having to cull out trivial information. Identifying main ideas and determining the relative importance of information should be taught together. Determination of what is important in a selection is often dependent on the derivation of the main idea. Once they know the main idea, readers are in a better position to identify the relative importance of information and to construct a situation model of the text. For instance, once readers know that the main idea of an article is how to use a video camera, they can assume that the steps in the process will be the important details. Readers have to ask themselves which details support or explain a selection's main idea or, if the article is especially rich in details, which are the most important. If an article cites twenty capabilities of lasers, readers might decide which five are most essential or group similar capabilities.

Adept readers will use textual clues to help determine which details are most important. A carefully written text might state which details are essential. Or, the reader might note those details that are discussed first and given the most print. Minor details might be signaled by words such as *also*, as in the sentence "Laser readers are also used to check out books in many libraries and to check times in many competitive sports."

Expert readers also use text structure, relational terms, and repetition of words or concepts to determine importance. Relational terms and expressions such as "most important of all" and "three main causes" help readers determine important ideas. A repeated word or concept is an especially useful clue. The structure of the piece also gives clues as to which details are most essential (Afflerbach & Johnston, 1986). With a problem–solution organization, an adept reader will seek out the problem and solution and ignore extraneous descriptions or examples.

CCSS

Read closely to determine what the text says explicitly and to make logical inferences from it; cite specific textual evidence when writing or speaking to support conclusions drawn from the text

FIGURE 7.2   Main Ideas in a History Text

The Pilgrims' Voyage to America

On September 6, 1620, 102 men, women, and children set sail from England for America. Many of the passengers were Pilgrims. Pilgrims are people who travel to distant places in search of a better life.

A Difficult Journey

The trip across the sea was long and hard. The Pilgrims were traveling on a small ship called the Mayflower. The Mayflower was only built to carry 60 people. The Pilgrims were crowded into an area below the main deck. Their living quarters were stuffy and smelly. There was no place to wash clothes. People wore the same clothes day after day, week after week.

The Pilgrims also ate the same food day after day: cheese, dried meat, fish, and hard chunks of bread known as "hardtack." Some of the food had worms crawling in it. There were no fresh vegetables or fresh fruit.

But the smelly living quarters and wormy food weren't the worst parts of the trip. In the middle of the sea, storms belted the little ship. Giant waves tossed the Mayflower about like it was a play boat. And heavy rains pounded her decks.

A Long Voyage

Besides being difficult and dangerous, the voyage to America was a long one. The weeks passed. Two months had gone by. The Pilgrims wondered if they would ever get to America. At last, the ship's lookout gave the cry everyone had been waiting for. "Land ho!" he sang out. After 67 days at sea, the Pilgrims had reached America and a new life.

FIGURE 7.3 Spider Web for Main Idea and Equally Important Supporting Details

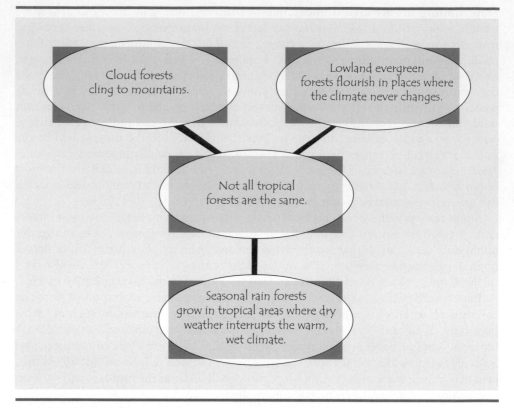

Source: Text from *Weather Words*, by G. Gibbons, 1990, New York: Holiday House.

In addition to using textual clues, readers can use their schemata or background knowledge to determine what is important. A student who raises tropical fish would seek out certain kinds of information when reading about a new species, such as a description of the species, its habits, and where it is found. The purpose for reading is also a factor. A student who is contemplating buying a new tropical fish will realize that details on cost and care are significant.

Expert readers also use their beliefs about the author's intention to determine which details are essential and which are not (Afflerbach & Johnston, 1986). Expert readers are able to step back from the text and consider the author's purpose. If, for instance, the author is trying to establish that a certain point is true, the reader will seek out the details or examples the author provides as proof of the contention. Lesson 7.2 includes some steps that might be used to help students determine important information.

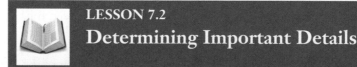

LESSON 7.2
Determining Important Details

Objectives
- Students will differentiate essential from nonessential details.
- Students will understand and recall essential details.

Step 1. Introduction of strategy

Explain what is meant by "important details" and why being able to identify them is an essential skill. Display and discuss several short selections that contain both important and unimportant information, and help students discriminate between the two.

Step 2. Model the process

Determine important information in a sample paragraph. Show how you would use contextual clues: topic sentences, placement of ideas, and graphic aids. In another session, demonstrate how you might use knowledge of the topic or your purpose for reading.

Step 3. Guided practice

Provide guidance as students determine important information in a selection. Start with well-structured texts that supply plenty of clues and gradually work up to selections from their basal readers, content-area textbooks, library books, or periodicals. Ask students to justify their choice of important details, because this skill is somewhat subjective.

Step 4. Application

Have students note important ideas in materials that they read independently. The more experience students have with varied reading materials and the broader and deeper their knowledge base, the better prepared they will be to determine the relative importance of information. Set purposes that lead students to grasp essential information. Ask questions that focus on important information. By asking such questions, you will be modeling the kinds of questions that students should be asking themselves before they read and as they read.

Step 5. Assessment and reteaching

During discussions of selections that have been read, ask questions that require selecting important details. Take note of students' performance. Ask the kinds of questions that provide insight into students' reasoning processes. Supply on-the-spot help if students need it. Also, plan reteaching lessons if needed.

Reviewing the Strategy   In subsequent lessons, review and extend the strategy. To review the strategy, ask the following kinds of questions:

- What strategy are we learning to use? (determining important ideas)
- How does this strategy help us? (helps us understand and remember important details; keeps us from getting lost in too many details)
- When do we use this strategy? (with nonfiction)
- How do we use this strategy? (The following steps should be posted in the classroom.)

1. Use the title, heading, and first sentence to make a hypothesis (careful guess) about what the main idea will be.
2. Read the selection to see whether you have chosen the right main idea. If not, change it.
3. Choose the most important details. These will be details that support the main idea. The author might signal the most important details by using phrases such as "most important of all." (T. Scott, 1998)

Building Language

Having students talk about strategies they are using, especially when they describe specific instances of strategy use, develops academic language. ■

REINFORCEMENT ACTIVITIES
Determining Importance of Information

- Have students predict the important ideas in a selection they are about to read.
- After they have read a selection, ask students to tell which ideas are most important.
- Encourage students to write newspaper stories. In most newspaper stories, the important information is provided in the first paragraph.

FYI

To provide practice with the sequence of steps in a process, you might encourage students to read such books as *Howling Hurricanes* (Richards, 2002) or *Recycle! A Handbook for Kids* (Gibbons, 1992). ■

FIGURE 7.4　Main Idea and Details in Sequential Display

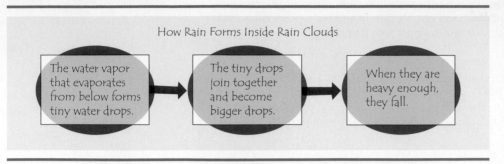

How Rain Forms Inside Rain Clouds

The water vapor that evaporates from below forms tiny water drops. → The tiny drops join together and become bigger drops. → When they are heavy enough, they fall.

Sequencing Because some details have to be comprehended and then remembered in a certain order, readers must organize them sequentially. These include historical or biographical events, steps in a process, and directions. Because the extra step of noting the sequence is involved, organizing sequential details often poses special problems, especially for younger readers. To introduce sequence, have students tell about some simple sequential activities in which they engage, such as washing dishes, playing a favorite game, or assembling a puzzle. Discuss the order of the activities, and place them on the chalkboard, overhead, or interactive white board using cue words such as *first*, *second*, *next*, *then*, *before*, *last*, and *after*.

Place lists of other events on the chalkboard, and ask students to put them in order. Start with a series of three or four events for younger students and work up to six or seven items for more advanced readers. Encourage students to use their sense of the situation or the process to put the events in order. Show how cue words help indicate sequence.

After students have become adept at this activity, let them apply their skill to stories and articles. To help them become aware of the sequence of a story, have them map out the main events, showing how the story progresses to its climax and the resolution of a problem. Help students create causal links between events in a story, as this aids retention (McNamara, Miller, & Bransford, 1991).

For biographies and historical accounts, show students how to use dates to keep events in order. Show students books like *The Ancient Greeks* (Shuter, 1997) or the e-book *Harriet Tubman* (McGowan, 2011), in which the authors use time lines or chronologies to help readers keep track of key events. When time lines have not been included in a selection, encourage students to create them to help keep a sequence of events in order. As students read about the steps in a process (e.g., a caterpillar becoming a butterfly), have them note the sequence and visualize it if possible. Show them how they might use a graphic organizer to display a process or chain of events. Figure 7.4 presents a chain map showing how radar works.

Following Directions　Following directions is a natural outgrowth of sequencing. As students read directions, remind them to make use of cue words such as *first*, *next*, and *last*. Also introduce words such as *list*, *match*, and *underline*, which are frequently found in directions and with which young children often have difficulty (Boehm, 1971). Students can create mental models of directions by visually depicting the process, using an accompanying diagram or other illustration, or by describing the steps. If possible, have students carry out the procedures outlined in the directions.

Using Technology

HyperHistory Online presents a variety of time lines for famous people and key events. http://www.hyperhistory.com/online_n2/History_n2/a.html ■

FYI

• Being able to comprehend and follow directions is more important than ever. Many items that we purchase come unassembled. And many appliances have to be programmed. Downloading a file from the Internet or using a new program requires being able to follow sophisticated directions.

• Use writing to support reading. Encourage students to write a series of directions for a favorite game or other activity. Have students work in pairs. The partners can check the clarity of each other's directions by trying them out and seeing whether they can follow them. ■

Adapting Instruction for Struggling Readers and Writers

Have students practice following directions by reading and responding to books such as those published by Klutz Press that involve making and doing things. ■

STUDENT STRATEGIES
Following Directions

Students can use these steps (which should be posted for them to refer to) to follow directions:

• Read the directions to get an overview.
• Look at any pictures or diagrams that go along with the directions.

- Make sure all parts have been included.
- Get all necessary tools, materials, or ingredients.
- Read and follow each step. Use any pictures or diagrams as an aid.

Other activities that provide natural practice in following directions are planting seeds, caring for classroom animals or plants, using a computer program, finding a site on the Web, and following recipes. The best thing about real-life exercises is that they are self-checking. A computer program that is not used correctly will flash an error message, recipes incorrectly followed result in inedible food, and devices improperly constructed do not work.

Summarizing What is the most effective comprehension strategy of all? When five experts in learning examined the research on comprehension in order to discover which strategies seemed to have the greatest payoff and were the most solidly grounded in research, they listed summarization first (Pressley, Johnson, Symons, McGoldrick, & Kurita, 1989). Summarization, which builds on the organizational strategy of determining main ideas and supporting details, improves comprehension and increases retention. It is also a metacognitive means of monitoring, through which students can evaluate their understanding of a passage that they have just read. If a student has not comprehended a selection, she or he is almost certain to have difficulty summarizing it. Summarizing also helps students understand the structure of text. In writing a summary, students are brought face to face with the organization of a piece of writing. This should help them detect the underlying structure of the text, which is key to understanding text and writing effective summaries (Touchstone Applied Science Associates, 1997).

Summarizing is a complex skill that takes years to develop. Even college students may have difficulty summarizing. Young children realize that a summary is a retelling of material; however, they have difficulty determining what points should be included in a summary. The view of young students seems to be egocentric: They choose details that are personally interesting rather than selecting details that seem important from the author's point of view. Young students also have difficulty with the procedures necessary to summarize (Hidi & Anderson, 1986). They delete information but do not combine or condense details; they also tend to use a copy strategy, recording details word for word in their summaries. Once they learn to put information into their own words, they begin combining and condensing.

Introducing Summarizing Summaries need not be written. All of us make oral summaries of movie and book plots, events, conversations, and so on. Because writing summaries can be difficult (Brown & Day, 1983; Hare & Borchardt, 1984), teachers should first develop students' ability to summarize orally.

Retelling is a natural way to lead into summarizing. Young children tend to recount every incident in a story and give every detail about a topic. Help them structure their retellings so as to emphasize major events and main ideas. Ask questions like these: "What were the two most important things that the main character did? What were the three main things that happened in the story? What are the main things you learned about robots? What are the main ways in which robots are used?" (See Chapter 8 for a fuller discussion of retelling.)

From kindergarten on, teachers can model the process of summarizing by providing summaries of selections read, especially nonfiction, and of discussions and directions. As students get into content-area material, they can be directed to pay special attention to chapter summaries. Although they may not be capable of writing well-formed summaries until the upper elementary or middle school grades, they can begin learning the skill in developmentally appropriate ways from their very first years of school. With younger and less able students, emphasize inclusion of the most important information in a summary. As students become proficient in extracting the most essential information, teach techniques for condensing information.

Building Language

Demonstrate how you would explain a series of directions. Emphasize the use of signal words such as *first, second, last,* and phrases such as "gather all materials" and "next step" that occur frequently in directions. Have students give directions orally and in writing. ■

CCSS

Determine central ideas or themes of a text and analyze their development; summarize the key supporting details and ideas.

FYI

Summarizing results in average percentile gains of 19 points (Haystead & Marzano, 2009). ■

FYI

Organizational strategies are effective. Whether it be creating main ideas, making semantic maps, or summarizing, just about any attempt to organize information results in better understanding and recall. ■

FYI

- Although a complex skill, summarizing begins early. Children summarize when they describe a real event or retell a story.
- Present summarizing as a tool that students can use to share information and better comprehend and remember what they read (Touchstone Applied Science Associates, 1997). When teaching and applying summarization, use students' content-area texts so they can see how summarizing can be a learning aid. ■

Using Technology

Summary Street® software (available from Pearson Education) can be used to guide and check summaries. ■

REFLECTION

What steps might you take to build your students' summarizing skill?

CCSS

Read closely to determine what the text says explicitly and to make logical inferences from it; cite specific textual evidence when writing or speaking to support conclusions drawn from the text.

Certain activities can build summarizing or its underlying skills. Encourage students to use titles, illustrations, topic sentences, headings, and other textual clues. In Taylor's (1986) study, many students failed to use the title and topic sentence when composing their summaries, although both contained the main idea of the selection. Teach students how to read expository text. Ineffectual summarizers read such works as though they are fiction and so fail to note textual cues that could help them create better summaries (Taylor, 1986). Have students compose oral summaries of stories, articles, and class discussions. Also compose group summaries.

To create a group summary, read an informational article aloud and ask students what the most important points are. After listing the points on the board, have the class summarize them. Group summaries provide preparation for the creation of independent summaries (Moore, Moore, Cunningham, & Cunningham, 1986). You might also try the 3-2-1 approach (Serafini, 2006). In the 3-2-1 approach, students are helped through instruction and guided practice to write a three-sentence summary. After discussion, they compose a two-sentence summary and then a one-sentence summary. Through further discussion, students see that writing a briefer summary isn't just a matter of omitting details. The writer has to take a broader view of the piece being summarized and compose a more general or more inclusive summarizing statement.

Summarizing can be an excellent device for checking comprehension. Encourage students to stop after reading key sections of expository text and mentally summarize the materials. Once they have some ability to identify relevant details, make use of structural cues, and identify and construct main ideas, they are ready for a more formal type of instruction in summarizing.

Presenting Summarizing Skills   When teaching summarizing, begin with shorter, easier text. Texts that are shorter and easier to comprehend are easier to summarize. Also, start with narrative text, which is easier than expository text to summarize (Hidi & Anderson, 1986). Focus on the content rather than the form of the summaries. After students become accustomed to summarizing essential details, stress the need for well-formed, polished summaries. Because many students have great difficulty determining which details are important, have them list important details. Discuss these lists before they compose their summaries. Also have students create semantic maps before writing summaries. In addition to helping students select important information, such maps may help them detect important relationships among key ideas. One study found that students who constructed maps before summarizing used a greater number of cohesive ties than those who did not (Ruddell & Boyle, 1989).

Teaching Elaboration Strategies

Elaboration is a generative activity in which the reader constructs connections between information from text and prior knowledge. Like organizational strategies, elaboration strategies are employed both during reading and after reading. The reader generates inferences, images, questions, judgments, and other elaborations. Use of elaboration strategies increased comprehension by 50 percent in a number of studies (Linden & Wittrock, 1981).

Making Inferences   Although children have the cognitive ability to draw inferences, some do not do so spontaneously. A probable cause of this deficiency is a lack of background information about the topic or the failure to process information in the text that would foster drawing inferences. Or, students may not realize that inferences are necessary. They might believe that only literal comprehension is called for (Westby, 1999). Two approaches enhance the ability to make inferences: building background and teaching specific strategies for making

■ **Elaboration** refers to additional processing of text by a reader, which may result in improved comprehension and recall. Elaboration involves building connections between one's background knowledge and the text or integrating new information through manipulating or transforming it.

inferences. However, sustained instruction is required. When students were taught processes for making inferences, no significant change was noted until after four weeks of teaching. The effects were long-lasting, and, as a side benefit, literal comprehension improved (Dewitz, Carr, & Patberg, 1987).

There are two kinds of inferences: schema-based and text-based (Winne, Graham, & Prock, 1993). Schema-based inferences depend on prior knowledge. For instance, inferring from the sentence "They rode into the sunset" that it was late in the day and the riders were heading west is schema-based. The reader uses her or his schema for the position of the sun to infer approximate time and direction. Schema-based inferences allow the reader to elaborate on the text by adding information that has been implied by the author. A text-based inference is one that requires putting together two or more pieces of information from the text. Reading that peanuts have more food energy than sugar and that a pound of peanut butter has more protein than thirty-two eggs but more fat than ice cream, the reader might put all this information together to infer that peanuts are nutritious but fattening.

Making inferences is the most important elaboration strategy. Much of the information in a piece, especially fiction, is implied. Authors show and dramatize rather than tell. Instead of directly stating that a main character is a liar, the author dramatizes situations in which the character lies. This is true even in the simplest of stories. For instance, in the third paragraph of *The Tale of Peter Rabbit*, Beatrix Potter (1908) wrote:

> "Now, my dears," said old Mrs. Rabbit one morning, "you may go into the field or down the lane, but don't go into Mr. McGregor's garden. Your Father had an accident there. He was put in a pie by Mrs. McGregor."

The reader must infer that Father was killed by Mr. McGregor and that Mr. McGregor will harm any rabbits that he catches in his garden. The reader might also infer that the reason Mr. McGregor does not like rabbits is that they eat the vegetables in his garden. None of this is stated, so the reader must use her or his schema for rabbits and gardens, together with her or his comprehension of the story, to produce a series of inferences. In a sense, the author erects the story's framework, and the reader must construct the full meaning by filling in the missing parts.

Activating prior knowledge helps students make inferences. For instance, if the teacher discusses the fact that rabbits anger gardeners by nibbling their vegetables before students read *The Tale of Peter Rabbit*, they will be much more likely to draw appropriate inferences from the passage previously cited. Asking questions that require students to make inferences also helps. It increases both their ability and their inclination to make inferences (Hansen, 1981).

Although above-average students make more inferences than average ones (Carr, 1983), below-average readers can be taught the skill. Hansen and Pearson (1982) combined activation of prior knowledge, direct instruction in an inference-making strategy, posing of inferential questions, and predicting to create a series of lessons in which poor readers improved to such an extent that their inferential comprehension became equal to that of good readers. Here is how Hansen and Pearson's prior knowledge–prediction strategy works:

1. The teacher reads the story and analyzes it for two or three important ideas.
2. For each important idea, the teacher creates a previous-experience question that elicits from students any similar experiences that they may have had. This is a have-you-ever question (Pearson, 1985).
3. For each previous-experience question, an accompanying prediction question is created. This is a what-do-you-think-will-happen question.
4. Students read the selection to check their predictions.
5. Students discuss their predictions. Inferential questions, especially those related to the key ideas, are discussed.

FYI

To make inferences, students must have access to the information necessary to make the inference. If students can't recall the information or can't recall enough of it, they won't be able to make an inference. Adequate literal comprehension is a second prerequisite for inferential comprehension. Also important is being able to implement inference-making procedures such as combining several pieces of text information or combining text information and prior knowledge (Winne, Graham, & Prock, 1993). ■

FYI

Students should only be given text that they can decode with at least 95 percent accuracy and at a reasonable speed. Otherwise, they might expend so much energy decoding text that they have little cognitive energy left for comprehension because they have expended all their cognitive resources on lower-level processes (Sinatra, Brown, & Reynolds, 2002). ■

The following important ideas, previous-experience questions, and prediction questions were used in the study (Pearson, 1985, Appendix B):

Important idea number 1: Even adults can be afraid of things.

Previous-experience question: Tell something an adult you know is afraid of.

Prediction question: In the story, Cousin Alma is afraid of something even though she is an adult. What do you think it is?

Important idea number 2: People sometimes act more bravely than they feel.

Previous-experience question: Tell about how you acted some time when you were afraid and tried not to show it.

Prediction question: How do you think that Fats, the boy in the story, will act when he is afraid and tries not to show it?

Important idea number 3: Our experience sometimes convinces us that we are capable of doing things we thought we couldn't do.

Previous-experience question: Tell about a time when you were able to do something you thought you couldn't do.

Prediction question: In the story, what do you think Cousin Alma is able to do that she thought she couldn't do?

An important element of the technique is the discussion, with students' responses acting as a catalyst. One student's answer reminds others of similar experiences that they have had but do not think apply. For example, a girl mentioning that her uncle is afraid of snakes might trigger in another student the memory that his grandfather is afraid of dogs, even small ones. The teacher also emphasizes that students should compare their real-life experiences with events in the story.

In addition to having background activated and being asked inferential questions, students should be taught a strategy for making inferences. Gordon (1985) mapped out a five-step process, which is outlined in Lesson 7.3.

Adapting Instruction for Struggling Readers and Writers

As Hansen and Pearson (1982) noted, poor readers are typically asked literal questions, so their inferential skills are underdeveloped. If carefully taught, lower-achieving readers can make inferences. ■

LESSON 7.3
Making Inferences

Objectives
- Students will make inferences based on text information and background knowledge.
- Students will support inferences with details from the text and from background knowledge.

Step 1. Explaining the skill

The teacher explains what the skill is, why it is important, and when and how it is used. This explanation might be illustrated with examples.

Step 2. Modeling the process

While modeling how inferences are made with a brief piece of text written on the chalkboard, the overhead, or interactive white board, the teacher reveals her or his thinking processes: "It says here that Jim thought Fred would make a great center when he first saw him walk into the classroom. The center is usually the tallest person on a basketball team, so I inferred that Fred is tall." The teacher also models the process with several other selections, so students see that inferences can be drawn from a variety of materials.

Step 3. Sharing the task

Students are asked to take part in making inferences. The teacher asks an inferential question about a brief sample paragraph or excerpt and then answers it. The students supply supporting evidence for the inference from the selection itself and from their background knowledge.

The reasoning processes involved in making the inference are discussed. The teacher stresses the need to substantiate inferences with details from the story.

Step 4. Reversing the process

The teacher asks an inferential question and the students supply the inference. The teacher provides the evidence. As an alternative, the teacher might supply the evidence and have the students draw an inference based on it. Either way, a discussion of reasoning processes follows.

Step 5. Integrating the process

The teacher just asks the inferential question. The students both make the inference and supply the evidence. As a final step, students might create their own inferential questions and then supply the answers and evidence. Basically, the procedure turns responsibility for the strategy over to students.

Step 6. Application

The students apply the process to texts and trade books.

Step 7. Assessment

Observe students as they make inferences while reading texts and trade books. Note how well they can do the following:

> Make an inference based on two or more pieces of information in the text.
> Make an inference based on information in the text and their own background knowledge.
> Find support for an inference.
> Make increasingly sophisticated inferences.

Reviewing the Strategy In subsequent lessons, review and extend the strategy. To review the strategy, ask the following kinds of questions:

- What strategy are we learning to use? (making inferences)
- How does this strategy help us? (fill in or think of details that the author has hinted at but has not directly stated; helps us to read between the lines)
- When do we use this strategy? (when we have to put together two or more pieces of information in a story or when the author has hinted at but not directly stated information)
- How do we use this strategy? (post these steps for students to refer to)

1. As you read, think, "What is the author suggesting here?"
2. Put together pieces of information from the story, or put together information from the story with what you know.
3. Make an inference or come to a conclusion.

Using QAR Some students are text-bound and may not realize that answers to some questions require putting together several pieces of information from the reading or using their background of experience plus that information to draw inferences. These students have difficulty constructing meaning from prior knowledge and textual content (Carr, Dewitz, & Patberg, 1989). Based on an analysis of thousands of student responses to higher-level questions, Applegate, Quinn, and Applegate (2006) found that a large number of students had difficulty with any questions whose answers could

FYI

Although making inferences is more difficult than understanding the literal content of a text, it isn't necessary for students to master literal comprehension before they are instructed in making inferences. Both can and should be taught simultaneously. ■

Students learn to locate evidence for inferences they have made.

Using Technology

eThemes is an extensive database of reading and writing and other educational resources organized around themes. It lists a number of excellent sites for building comprehension.

http://www.emints.org/ethemes ■

not be found in the text and a number of other students did not use the text to answer questions but relied on their background of experience. Both of these groups of readers may benefit from using QAR (question–answer relationship), in which questions are described as having the following four levels, based on where the answers are found (International Reading Association, 1988):

1. **Right there.** The answer is found within a single sentence in the text.
2. **Put together.** The answer is found in several sentences in the text.
3. **On my own.** The answer is in the student's background of knowledge.
4. **Writer and me.** A combination of information from the text and the reader's background is required to answer the question.

In a series of studies, Raphael (1984) observed that students' comprehension improved when they were introduced to the concept of QAR and given extensive training in locating the source of the answer. Initially, they worked with sentences and very short paragraphs, but they progressed to 400-word selections. Raphael (1986) recommended starting with two categories of answers: "in the book" and "in my head." This would be especially helpful when working with elementary students. "In the book" includes answers that are "right there" or require "putting together." "In my head" items are "on my own" and "writer and me" answers. Based on Raphael's (1986) suggestions, QAR might be presented in the manner described in Lesson 7.4.

LESSON 7.4

Presenting QAR

Objectives
- Students will use the text, text plus background, and personal knowledge to construct meaning from text.
- Students will use knowledge of different sources of textual and personal information to answer questions.

Step 1. Introducing the concept of QAR

Introduce the concept by writing on the board a paragraph similar to the following:

Andy let the first pitch go by. It was too low. The second pitch was too high. But the third toss was letter high. Andy lined it over the left fielder's outstretched glove.

Ask a series of literal questions: "Which pitch did Andy hit? Where did the ball go? Why didn't Andy swing at the first pitch? The second pitch?" Lead students to see that the answers to these questions are "in the book."

Next, ask a series of questions that depend on the readers' background: "What game was Andy playing? What do you think Andy did after he hit the ball? Do you think he scored a run? Why or why not?" Show students that the answers to these questions depend on their knowledge of baseball. Discuss the fact that these answers are "in my head."

Step 2. Extending the concept of QAR

After students have mastered the concept of "in the book" and "in my head," extend the in-the-book category to include both "right there" and "put together." Once students have a solid working knowledge of these, expand the in-my-head category to include both "on my own" and "writer and me." The major difference between these two is whether the student has to read the text for the question to make sense. For instance, the question "Do you think Andy's hit was a home run?" requires knowledge of baseball and information from the story. The question "How do you feel when you get a hit?" involves only experience in hitting a baseball.

Step 3. Providing practice and application

Provide ample opportunity for guided and independent practice. Also refine and extend students' awareness of sources for answers and methods for constructing responses.

Step 4. Evaluating and reviewing

Note students' ability to use different sources of information to understand a text. Provide instruction and practice in needed areas. Review QAR periodically.

FYI

Making inferences about consequences is more difficult than inferring causes because it entails predicting future events, (Graesser & Bertus, 1998). ■

Difficulties in Making Inferences   Some students' responses to inference questions are too specific. In addition to knowing that they can use both text and background knowledge as sources of information, students need to learn to gather all the information that is pertinent (McCormick, 1992). They need to base their inferences on several pieces of textual or background information. Some students choose the wrong information on which to base their inferences, and others do not use the text at all. They overrely on prior knowledge or do not recall or use sufficient pertinent text to make valid inferences (McCormick, 1992). This is especially true of poor readers.

Applying the Skill   Comprehension relies heavily on the reader's ability to use background knowledge to make inferences. Inferencing is a cognitive skill that can be used in all areas of learning. Have students apply it in class discussions and when reading in the content areas. Emphasize the need to go beyond facts and details in order to make inferences.

Making Inferences with It Says–I Say–And So   It Says–I Say–And So is a series of prompts that guide students as they make inferences about a story (Beers, 2003). Students fill in four columns of a chart like the one in Figure 7.6. In the *Question* column, students record the question they are answering. Under *It Says*, they answer the question with information from the text. Under *I Say*, students use their background knowledge to write what they know about the text information recorded in the *It Says* column. In the *And So* column, they use both text and their background knowledge to make an inference.

FYI

Although poor decoding skills are the main cause of poor comprehension, a number of struggling readers are good decoders but poor comprehenders (Shankweiler et al., 1999). As many as 20 percent of struggling readers are good decoders but poor comprehenders (Duke, 2003). See the Case Study that follows.

Students who are good decoders but poor comprehenders have problems with all kinds of comprehension, but they have the most difficulty making inferences (Oakhill & Yuill, 1996). ■

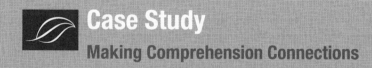

Case Study

Making Comprehension Connections

Mark had difficulty integrating information from different parts of an article and had problems connecting ideas. He often used his background knowledge to answer questions rather than referring to the text. Mark had to learn how to use the text to construct meaning. Mark also had difficulty making inferences. As a starting point, Mark's teacher introduced QAR. QAR might help Mark understand where the answers to questions could be found and highlight the importance of the text and also the importance of combining information from text with background knowledge. His teacher hoped that QAR would help Mark see that "comprehension involves the search for and construction of meaning" (Dewitz & Dewitz, 2003, p. 432). Direct instruction in making text-based inferences was accompanied by modeling and think-alouds. The teacher chose texts that required the kinds of strategies and thinking processes that were being taught. Content-area texts were chosen because they embody the kinds of reading that Mark would be required to do. When planning a lesson, the teacher read each text twice, once to get an overview of the text and once to determine the kinds of strategies and cognitive processes that would be required to comprehend the text. The teacher read the text as though he were Mark.

To help Mark with the difficulty he had making connections, the teacher physically marked where he made connections as he modeled reading the text. The teacher also noted what kinds of connections he was making: connections to other sentences or paragraphs, connections to background knowledge, connections to other texts, and so on. As Mark read, he used sticky notes to indicate connections that he was making. After reading passages, Mark discussed the kinds of connections that he made as he read. As Mark grew proficient at making connections, marking them with sticky notes was phased out. Through discussions and probes, the teacher continued to gain insight into Mark's reasoning process. By year's end, Mark was making text-based responses and was able to comprehend both narrative and expository text at a high level.

FIG☼RE 7.5   A Chain Map

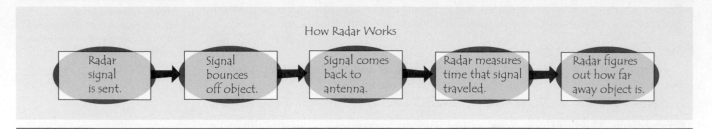

Macro-Cloze   In macro-cloze, students use their background of experience and inferential reasoning to supply a missing sentence (Yuill and Oakhill, 1991).

The team had hoped to play a game of baseball.

_____

They played basketball instead.

Jeff thought he would finish his chores in less than an hour.

_____

He didn't finish until three hours later.

Tanya thought she had scored 100 on the spelling test.

_____

She made up her mind to study harder for the next spelling test.

Explain to students that the macro-cloze activities can be completed in a number of ways. The key element is that the sentences make sense together after the missing sentence is inserted. Help students see that the inferences we make are based on our backgrounds and that each of us sees life in a unique way (Paul & Elder, 2001). Challenge students to create their own macro-cloze activities and share them with classmates.

Difficulty Drawing Conclusions   Working with students who were having difficulty drawing conclusions, McMackin and Witherell (2005) observed that the students failed to consider information provided in the text. Students were urged to think about the passage they had just read, to note what they knew for sure because it was contained in the passage, and then to stop and think about this information so that they could draw a conclusion: "I must combine what I know for sure from the text with what I think about it and then determine what else I can figure out from the information provided." Students were asked, "What were you able to figure out from the passage you read?" They were also asked to cite support for their conclusions. McMackin and Witherell also used graphic organizers to scaffold students' efforts. They differentiated instruction by providing different levels of organizers.

Mystery Passages

Presented in Chapter 3 as a think-aloud assessment, Mystery Passages also function as a highly motivating instructional technique that is particularly effective at developing students' ability to predict, make inferences, draw conclusions, and integrate information from several sentences or passages (see Figure 7.7 for a sample lesson). To construct a mystery passage, adapt articles so that the identity of the object or creature being described is not revealed until the end. The identity is suggested through a series of riddlelike clues. Animals, people, and events make especially good subjects for Mystery Passages (Gunning, 2010).

Here is how the Mystery Passages activity works. Students read a brief segment, of text, write down what they predict the mystery animal is, and then briefly explain what makes them think that. After each segment, their predictions and reasons are discussed. After completing all the segments, they reread the entire passage and tell

R E F L E C T I O N

Which of the techniques designed to teach iinferencing might you use with your students? What adaptations might you make so the techniques fit the needs of your students?

what they learned about the mystery animal, person, or object. When using the activity, distribute the clues one by one, so that students don't read ahead. Encourage students to use their background knowledge and thinking skills. Prompts might be used that lead them to make more carefully considered predictions or to integrate details from the passage. You might also model how you would go about making predictions.

FIGURE 7.6   It Says–I Say-And So Chart

Question Read the question.	It Says Find information from the text that will help you answer the question.	I Say Think about what you know about the information from the text.	And So Put together what the text says and what you know.
How did Jason feel as the lunch period approached?	Jason's stomach was growling. He had skipped breakfast. He didn't want to be late for his first day at the new school. Even so, he wasn't looking forward to lunch. He wondered where he would sit and if anyone would talk to him.	I remember my first day at a new school after we moved. The worst part of the day was lunchtime. Even though I was hungry, I wished they would just skip lunch.	And so that's why I think Jason was nervous and maybe a little bit afraid. He didn't know if anyone would invite him to sit with them or if he would have to sit all by himself or maybe someone would make fun of him.

FIGURE 7.7   Mystery Animals

Use the clues to solve the mystery. After each clue, write down what you think the mystery animal is.

The Most Dangerous Animal

• What is the most dangerous animal in all of Africa?
  My prediction: _____
  Reason(s) for my prediction: _____

  _____

• The most dangerous animal in all of Africa is a huge beast. It can weigh more than 8,000 pounds. Even though it is huge and has short legs, it can run very fast. It can run faster than any human and most animals.
  My prediction: _____
  Reason(s) for my prediction: _____

  _____

• Its mouth is gigantic and it has teeth huge. It has chomped alligators and small boats in half.
  My prediction: _____
  Reason(s) for my prediction: _____

  _____

• Many animal scientists believe that the hippo is the most dangerous creature in Africa. Hippos have killed more people than any other wild animal.
  What are the main things you learned about the mystery animal?

  _____
  _____
  _____
  _____

Source: Gunning, T. (2010).

Exemplary Teaching

Motivating Strategy Use

Strategy use can be fostered through high-interest activities such as Think-Aloud Mysteries. Think-Aloud Mysteries is an activity in which a student or small group of students work together to identify what a passage is about as they read it one sentence at a time (Smith, 2006). The teacher uses questions that incorporate key strategies to guide students through their reading. Sentences are presented separately on strips of paper. The first sentences of the passage provide only a few clues. Succeeding sentences provide more specific information. As they read, students build a hypothesis and gather evidence. Students are urged to use background knowledge and the text to make predictions and inferences. The teacher asks questions, such as "What makes you think it was _____?" The teacher then affirms students' responses: "You made good use of background knowledge. You did a god job of putting the key details together."

Here is an excerpt from a session in which a fifth-grade teacher is helping a struggling reader, using Think-Aloud Mysteries.

Sentence 1. Suddenly I could hear it making noise pounding on the roof of the house.

Teacher: What do you know from your experience that does that?
Student: A storm.
Teacher: Good.

Sentence 2. I could see something bouncing onto the sidewalk and gathering into little white piles.

Student: Still thundering and raining. . . .
Teacher: Well, what are those white piles?
Student: Huh? [rereads] Hah. Snow!
Teacher: Really? What does it say besides "white piles"? Is there another clue?
Student: Gathering . . . bouncing? Let's see what the next sentence says.
Teacher: Good thinking! Keep your mind thinking while you read more. This next one might really throw you.

Sentence 3. It was summertime, but cold bits were falling from the sky.

Student: Oooh, so it was raining?
Teacher: What makes you think so? Does that fit with what you read right before?
Student: Uh huh.
Teacher: But you said "snow" right before.
Student: Oh, man, snow.
Teacher: Okay, let's review what we've read so far. So you have a storm. What else do you have?
Student: Ice. [laughs delightedly and reads next sentence]

Sentence 4. I've heard that sometimes it could get the size of golf balls or break car windshields.

Student: Oh, I know it . . . but I can't get the word out for it!
Teacher: What's it like?
Student: Hail!
Teacher: You think? All right, let's see. (Smith, 2006, p. 769)

After reading additional sentences and discussing them and doing some rereading, the student verified that the passage was about hail. The teacher affirmed the student's efforts by noting that when her predictions and inferences weren't making sense, she went back and reread and reviewed the information in the story until she was able to put all the details together and come to the right conclusion.

The Guess Who series (Benchmark Marshall Cavendish) has a format similar to a Mystery Passage selection. In the book *Who Swims* (Rau, 2009), for instance, students use information about a penguin's behaviors, physical characteristics, and habitat to guess its identity.

Imaging Although readers rely heavily on verbal abilities to comprehend text, they also use imaging. According to a **dual coding** theory of cognitive processing, information can be coded verbally or nonverbally. The word *robot*, for instance, can be encoded verbally. It can also be encoded visually as a mental picture of a robot. Because it can be encoded as a word or mental picture, it can be retrieved from memory either verbally or visually, so it is twice as memorable. In one research study, participants who encoded words visually remembered twice as many words as those who encoded the words just verbally (Schnorr & Atkinson, 1969).

Imaging is relatively easy to teach. In one study, students' comprehension increased after just thirty minutes of instruction (Gambrell & Bales, 1986). The increase was not large, but it was significant. When teaching students to create images, start with single sentences and then move on to short paragraphs and, later, longer pieces. Have students read the sentence or paragraph first, and then ask them to form a picture of it.

Creating images serves three functions: fostering understanding, retaining information, and monitoring for meaning. If students are unable to form an image, or if their image is incomplete or inaccurate, encourage them to reread the section and then add to the picture in their minds or create a new one. As a comprehension strategy, imaging can help students who are having difficulty understanding a high-imagery passage such as the following visual description:

> A comet is like a dirty snowcone. A comet has three parts: a head, coma, and tail. The head is made of ice, gases, and particles of rocks. The heads of most comets are only a few kilometers wide. As a comet nears the sun, gases escape from the head. A large, fuzzy, ball-shaped cloud is formed. This ball-shaped cloud is the coma. The tail is present only when the coma is heated by the sun. The tail is made of fine dust and gas. A comet's tail always points away from the sun. The tail can be millions of kilometers long. (Hackett, Moyer, & Adams, 1989, p. 108)

Imaging can also be used as a pictorial summary. After reading a paragraph similar to the one about comets, students can review what they have read by trying to picture a comet and all its parts. A next step might be to draw a comet based on their visual summary. They might then compare their drawing with an illustration in the text or an encyclopedia and also with the text itself to make sure that they have included all the major components.

Like other elaboration strategies, imaging should be taught directly. The teacher should explain and model the strategy; discuss when, where, and under what conditions it might be used; and provide guided practice and application. From time to time, the teacher should review the strategy and encourage students to apply it.

Questions that ask students to create visual images should become a natural part of postreading discussions. Auditory and kinesthetic or tactile imaging should also be fostered. Students might be asked to tell how the hurricane in a story sounded or what the velvet seats in the limousine they read about felt like. In discussing images that children have formed, remind them that each of us makes our own individual picture in our mind. Ask a variety of students to tell what pictures they formed.

Whether used with fiction or nonfiction, imaging should follow these guidelines (Fredericks, 1986):

- Students create images based on their backgrounds. Images will differ.
- Teachers should not alter students' images but might suggest that students reread a selection and then decide whether they want to change their images.
- Students should be given sufficient time to form images.

FYI

- One way of enhancing imaging is to read high-imagery selections to children and ask them to try to picture the main character, a setting, or a scene. Possibilities include Burton's (1942) *The Little House*, Williams's (1926) *The Velveteen Rabbit*, and Byars's (1970) *Summer of the Swans*.
- Make sure that strategy instruction complements the text. When teaching imaging, for instance, ensure that the text is one that offers many opportunities for imaging. ■

FYI

Use of nonlinguistic representations such as imaging results in average percentile gains of 17 percentile points (Marzano, 2001). ■

Adapting Instruction for English Language Learners

Have students draw pictures of concepts or topics rather than use words to describe or talk about them. This works especially well with students who are still learning English or other students who might have difficulty expressing their ideas through words alone. ■

FYI

- Some teachers encourage students to make clay figures as a way of representing visualizations (Onofrey & Theurer, 2007).
- Younger students might need demonstrations of how to create mental images, whereas older readers might just need timely reminders and encouragement. However, even older readers may need instruction to transfer imaging from one subject to another. ■

■ **Dual coding** is the concept that text can be processed verbally and nonverbally. Nonverbal coding focuses on imaging.

■ **Imaging** refers to creating sensory representations of items in text.

Exemplary Teaching
Using Imaging

Creating images is a powerful strategy for enhancing both comprehension and memory of text. Maria (1990) encouraged fourth-graders to construct images to foster their understanding of a social studies passage that described an Iroquois village. Maria started the lesson by having students study a detailed drawing of an Iroquois village. After shutting their eyes and visualizing the scene, students discussed what they had seen. Their images varied.

Students were then directed to close their eyes as Maria described a scene laden with sensory images and asked image-evoking questions:

You are at an Iroquois village in New York State about the year 1650. It is winter. Feel how cold you are. Feel the snow crunch under your feet. The wind is blowing. You can hear it and feel it right through your clothes. See yourself walk through the gate into the village. See the tall fence all around the village. . . .(p. 198)

After discussing what they saw, heard, and felt, the students read a passage in their social studies textbook about life in an Iroquois longhouse. After each paragraph, they stopped and created images of what they had read and discussed the images. In the discussion, Maria asked questions that focused on the important details so that when students later created images on their own, they, too, would focus on these elements. The images that students created demonstrated that their comprehension was indeed enriched. Best of all, many of the students who responded were those who usually had little to say in class discussions.

FYI

- Dramatizing fosters the creation of images. When called on to act out a scene, readers can be asked to picture the scene and speaker, and try to imagine how the words were spoken. To build imaging ability, students might act the part of a character in a selection the class has read and invite the other class members to guess who the character is (McMaster, 1998).
- The aim of strategy instruction is to have use of the strategy become automatic. As students become more proficient in the application of a strategy, make them responsible for its use (Sinatra, Brown, & Reynolds, 2002). ■

REFLECTION

How might you adapt indexing and imaging to fit the needs of your students? With what students and in what situations might these techniques be most appropriate?

- Teachers should encourage students to elaborate on or expand their images through careful questioning: "What did the truck look like? Was it old or new? What model was it? What color? Did it have any special features?"

Beyond Imaging: Using Manipulatives According to Glenberg and associates, "meaning is tied to action" (Glenberg Jaworski, & Rischal, 2007, p. 223). Thus, students can be led to understand a passage by performing the actions specified by the text. If a passage said, "The enraged rhino charged at the jeep, and smashed its grill," the reader would use toys to show the rhino charging at the jeep and smashing into its grill. In experiments, students who manipulated objects after reading sentences outperformed students who simply read the sentences twice by a 1.39 (47 percentile points) and 0.81 (27 percentile points) effect size for recall and question answering. Even students who simply viewed the manipulations had improved comprehension. The researchers concluded that "meaning arises from simulating the content of sentences. This simulation requires indexing words to the objects and actions those words represent" (Glenberg et al., 2004, p. 435).

In the following paragraph, figures of animals and trees were used to simulate the actions or ideas expressed in the sentences preceded by an asterisk. This and similar paragraph were used to instruct and provide reinforcement for a third-grader whose decoding skills were above grade level but whose comprehension was nearly nonexistent.

Giraffes

Giraffes are tall animals. *A giraffe is taller than an elephant. *A giraffe is so tall that it can eat the leaves on the tops of trees. Giraffes have many enemies. *Lions, hyenas, and Nile crocodiles hunt giraffes. Because they stand tall and have excellent eyesight, giraffes can see far away. *A giraffe can see a lion or hyena that is a mile away. (Gunning, 2010d)

The activity was easy to set up. A plastic elephant, giraffe, lion, and hyena and plastic tress were assembled. After reading that a giraffe is taller than an elephant, the student placed the giraffe next to the elephant. After reading that a giraffe is so tall that it can eat the leaves from the tops of trees, the student showed the giraffe eating the leaves. After reading, "Lions, hyenas, and Nile crocodiles hunt giraffes," the student assembled the animals and showed them approaching the giraffe. After reading, "A giraffe can see a lion or hyena that is a mile away," the student showed the giraffe spotting a lion that was far away. Actively involved and motivated by the task, the third-grader's comprehension was perfect. Over time, more complex tasks were arranged and the third-grader was eventually led to manipulate in his mind by visualizing rather than performing the actions.

Of course, obtaining appropriate manipulatives can be time-consuming and expensive. However, toys can be obtained from parents whose children have outgrown them. Illustrations downloaded from free clip art sites can also be used. Older students might use maps, diagrams, replicas of sports fields, or other manipulatives. Colleagues have used manipulatives with autistic children, developmentally delayed students, poor comprehenders, students with attention deficit disorder, as well as with achieving students. All have praised the power of the technique. Over time, students are taught to use imaging in place of manipulatives.

Question Generation   Accustomed to answering questions posed by teachers and texts, students enjoy composing questions of their own. In addition to being a novel and interesting activity, **question generation** is also an effective strategy for fostering comprehension. It transforms the reader from passive observer to active participant. It also encourages the reader to set purposes for reading and to note important segments of text so that questions can be asked about them and possible answers considered. Creating questions also fosters active awareness of the comprehension process. Students who create questions are likely to be more aware of whether they are understanding the text and are more likely to take corrective action if their comprehension is inadequate (Andre & Anderson, 1978–1979).

ReQuest   One of the simplest and most effective devices for getting children to create questions is **ReQuest**, or reciprocal questioning (Manzo, 1969; Manzo & Manzo, 1993; Manzo, Manzo, & Albee, 2004). Although originally designed for one-on-one instruction of remedial pupils, ReQuest has been adapted for use with groups of students and whole classes. In ReQuest, the teacher and students take turns asking questions. ReQuest can be implemented by following the steps outlined in Lesson 7.5.

FYI

ReQuest can be combined with QAR to guide students to ask questions whose answers involve "putting together" and "writer and me," as well as being "right there." ■

■ **Question generation** is a powerful elaboration strategy. Through creating questions, students' comprehension jumped from the 50th percentile to the 66th percentile and in some instances to the 86th percentile (Rosenshine, Meister, & Chapman, 1996).

■ **ReQuest** is a procedure in which the teacher and student(s) take turns asking and answering questions.

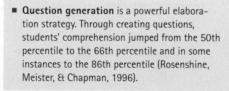

LESSON 7.5
ReQuest Procedure

Objectives
- Students will improve their understanding of text by composing and answering questions.
- Students will compose higher-level questions as well as lower-level ones.

Step 1.

Choose a text that is on the students' level but is fairly dense so that it is possible to ask a number of questions about it.

Step 2.

Explain the ReQuest procedure to students. Tell them that they will be using a technique that will help them better understand what they read. Explain that in ReQuest, they get a chance to be the teacher because they and you take turns asking questions.

Step 3.

Survey the text. Read the title, examine any illustrations that are part of the introduction, and discuss what the selection might be about.

Step 4.

Direct students to read the first significant segment of text. This could be the first sentence or the first paragraph but should not be any longer than a paragraph. Explain that as they read, they are to think up questions to ask you. Students can make up as many questions as they wish. Tell them to ask the kinds of questions that a teacher might ask (Manzo & Manzo, 1993). Model how they might go about composing questions. Read the segment with the students.

Step 5.

Students ask their questions. Your book is placed face down. However, students may refer to their texts. If necessary, questions are restated or clarified. Answers can be checked by referring back to the text.

Step 6.

After students have asked questions, ask your questions. Pupils' books are face down. You might model higher-level questioning by asking for responses that require integrating several details in the text. If difficult concepts or vocabulary words are encountered, they should be discussed.

Step 7.

Go to the next sentence or paragraph. The questioning proceeds until enough information has been gathered to set a purpose for reading the remainder of the text. This could be in the form of a prediction: "What do you think the rest of the article will be about?" Manzo and Manzo (1993) recommended that the questioning be concluded as soon as a logical purpose can be set but no longer than ten minutes after beginning.

Step 8.

After students have read the rest of the selection silently, the purpose question and any related questions are discussed. The discussion might start off with the question "Did we read for the right purpose?" (Manzo, Manzo, & Albee, 2004, p. 303).

Step 9. Evaluation and Review

Note students' ability to ask appropriate questions and answer questions. Pay attention to changes in nature and level of questions the students compose.

Students enjoy reversing roles and asking questions. Initially, they may ask lower-level questions, but with coaching and modeling will soon ask higher-level ones. ReQuest is especially effective with lower-achieving readers.

Other elaboration strategies include applying information that has been obtained from reading, creating analogies to explain it, and evaluating text (covered in Chapter 8). A general principle underlying elaboration is that the more readers do with or to text, the better they will understand and retain it.

Teaching Monitoring (Metacognitive) Strategies

As you were reading this chapter, did you reread a section because you didn't quite understand it? Did you go back and reread any sentences? Were you aware of whether the text was making sense? Did you decide to use a particular strategy such as summarizing or questioning or imaging? If so, you were engaged in metacognition.

Realizing that the norm-referenced tests weren't providing the kind of information that was needed to plan instruction, administrators in the school district where Kelly Krueger teaches fourth grade decided to emphasize classroom-based assessment and require that teachers use a rubric twice a year to analyze students' responses to one narrative and one expository selection (Fiene & McMahon, 2007). The work samples are analyzed to assess students' ability to demonstrate comprehension proficiencies and use key strategies, such as summarizing, generating questions, and visualizing.

Krueger's students used stick-on notes to respond to their reading. The students were also asked to elaborate on their notes in their journals, and responses were discussed in class. Krueger analyzed both the stick-on notes and the journal entries. The stick-on notes, journal entries, and discussions provided insight into students' comprehension and supplied a foundation for planning instruction.

Krueger found a pattern in the responses she analyzed. After reading fourth-grader Justin's notes, which were based on several selections about heroes, she could see that he had listed only three facts. And all of these were literal details. She saw a similar pattern in the work of several other students, revealing a need to teach the students how to see relationships among ideas. She introduced graphic organizers to help students compare, contrast, and evaluate information. She also worked with individual students. Noting that Melissa's responses were vague and lacking in elaboration, Krueger made plans for helping Melissa make more inferences from text so as to be able to provide fuller responses. She also planned to work with Melissa on writing so that the student's responses would better reflect her thinking. According to test data, Melissa was reading on grade level. However, information gathered from stick-on notes, journal entries, and conversations helped Krueger devise plans for refining Melissa's skills. Had she limited her assessment to standardized test results, Krueger would not have realized the specific help that Melissa needed.

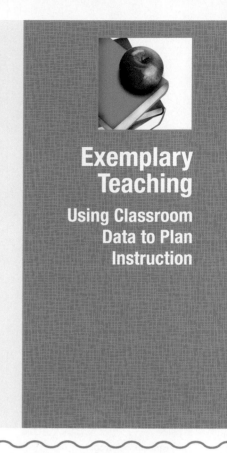

Exemplary Teaching

Using Classroom Data to Plan Instruction

Summarizing, inferring, creating images, predicting, and other strategies are valuable tools for enhancing comprehension. Knowing how to use them is not enough, however; it is also essential to know when and where to use them. For example, visualizing works best with materials that are concrete and lend themselves to being pictured in the imagination (Prawat, 1989). Predictions work best when the reader has a good background of knowledge about the topic. Knowing when and where to use these and other strategies is part of monitoring, which is also known as **metacognition**, or metacognitive awareness.

Monitoring also means recognizing what one does and does not know, which is a valuable asset in reading. If a reader mouths the words of a passage without comprehending their meaning and does not recognize his or her lack of comprehension, the reader will not reread the passage or take other steps to understand it; the reader is not even aware that there is a problem. "Metacognitive awareness is the ability to reflect on one's own cognitive processes, to be aware of one's own activities while reading, solving problems, and so on" (Baker & Brown, 1984, p. 353). A key feature of metacognitive awareness is knowing what one is expected to be able to do as a result of reading a selection. All of the other activities are examined in light of the desired outcome. Students will read a book one way if they are reading it as part of voluntary reading, another way if they are to evaluate it, and still another way if they are taking a test on it. Their criteria for success will depend on their specific goal for reading the text. A critical factor is the level of comprehension that students demand. Proficient readers generally demand a higher level of comprehension than do struggling readers.

The four major aspects of metacognition in reading are knowing oneself as a learner, regulating, checking, and repairing (Baker & Brown, 1984; McNeil, 1987).

■ **Metacognition**, or metacognitive awareness, means being conscious of one's mental processes.

Knowing Oneself as a Learner　The student is aware of what he or she knows, his or her reading abilities, what is easy and what is hard, what he or she likes and dislikes. The student is able to activate his or her prior knowledge in preparation for reading a selection:

> I know that Theodore Roosevelt was a president a long time ago. Was it during the late 1800s or early 1900s? I'm not sure. I remember reading a story about how he was weak as a child and had bad eyesight. I'll read about him in the encyclopedia. I'll try *World Book* instead of *Encyclopedia Britannica*. *Encyclopedia Britannica* is too hard, but I can handle *World Book*.

Regulating　In **regulating**, the student knows what to read and how to read it and is able to put that knowledge to use. The student is aware of the structure of the text and how this might be used to aid comprehension. The student also understands the task he or she will be expected to do as a result of reading this selection: retelling, writing a story, taking a test. He or she surveys the material, gets a sense of organization, sets a purpose, and then chooses and implements an effective strategy:

> Wow! This is a long article about Roosevelt. But I don't have to read all of it. I just need information about his boyhood. These headings will tell me which section I should read. Here's one that says "Early Life." I'll read it to find out what his childhood was like. After I read it, I'll make notes on the important points.

Checking　The student is able to evaluate his or her performance. He or she is aware when comprehension suffers because an unknown term is interfering with meaning or an idea is confusing. Checking also involves noting whether one is focusing on important, relevant information and engaging in self-questioning to determine whether goals are being achieved (Baker & Brown, 1984):

> The part about Roosevelt's great-grandparents isn't important. I'll skim over it. I wonder what *puny* and *asthma* mean. I've heard of asthma, but I don't know what it is. This is confusing, too. It says, "He studied under tutors." What does that mean? Let's see if I have all this straight. Roosevelt's family was wealthy. He was sickly, but then he worked out in the gym until he became strong. He liked studying nature and he was determined. I don't know about his early schooling, though, and I ought to know what *asthma* and *puny* mean.

Repairing　In **repairing**, the student takes corrective action when comprehension falters. Not only is the student aware that there is a problem in understanding the text, he or she also does something about it:

> I'll look up *asthma*, *puny*, and *tutor* in the dictionary. Okay, I see that *tutor* means "a private teacher." Oh, yeah, it's like when my brother Bill had trouble with math and Mom got a college student to help him. Did Roosevelt have trouble in school? Is that why he had tutors? I'm still confused about his early schooling. I think I'll ask the teacher about it.

Failure to comprehend might be caused by a problem at any level of reading (Collins & Smith, 1980):

- Words may be unknown or may be known but used in an unfamiliar way.
- Concepts are unknown.
- Punctuation is misread.
- Words or phrases are given the wrong emphasis.
- Paragraph organization is difficult to follow.
- Pronouns and antecedent relationships are confused. Relationships among ideas are unclear.
- Relationships among paragraphs and sections are not established.
- The reader becomes lost in details. Key ideas are misinterpreted.
- The reader has inadequate prior knowledge, or a conflict exists between that knowledge and the text.

Repair strategies, which are also known as compensations, include slowing reading rate, pausing,

FYI

Repair strategies can also be thought of as revision strategies. You reread a challenging piece and revise your understanding of it as you make new connections, check the meanings of unfamiliar words, and reconsider complex thoughts (Keene & Zimmerman, 2007). ■

■ **Regulating** is a metacognitive process in which the reader guides his or her reading processes.

■ **Repairing** refers to taking steps to correct faulty comprehension.

reading aloud, jumping over (skipping portions of a text), looking back, rereading, paraphrasing, using graphic aids or references, and taking other actions when text is confusing (see Table 7.3). Pausing gives the reader time to try to figure out a word or expression or to think about what the author is saying. Or, a pause might give the reader time to try to figure out why the reading has gone wrong and what can be done to set it right (Walczyk & Griffith-Ross, 2007). The text may be difficult or may require closer reading, so the student may have to slow down, adjusting his or her rate of reading. Reading aloud can help the reader concentrate and overcome distractions by providing auditory feedback. Reading aloud can foster monitoring of comprehension. Jumping over is helpful when a word or detail is not understood but doesn't seem crucial to an understanding of the selection. Experienced readers know that spending too much time on unknown words or confusing details can interfere with comprehension (Walczyk & Griffith-Ross, 2007). Sometimes simply reading to the end of the paragraph or section will provide needed clarification. Looking back enables readers to obtain information that was lost from working memory or overlooked on the first pass through text (e.g., whom the pronoun *he* refers to). If a student cannot remember specific details, she or he should skim back through the text to find them. Rereading is a reprocessing of some or all of a text. Having failed to grasp the gist of a section, the student might reread the preceding section. Rereading is fairly disruptive, so experienced readers use it only when easier-to-apply repair strategies have failed. Rereading can be used to compensate for poor reading skills or poorly written text (Pressley & Afflerbach, 1995). Rereading a sentence or paragraph may clear up a confusing point or provide context for a difficult word.

A second group of repair strategies involves the use of illustrations, maps, charts, graphs, or other graphic materials to provide clarification. A third group of repair strategies involves the use of a reference tool, such as a glossary, dictionary, or encyclopedia, to clarify a confusing concept or obtain needed background information. Some sophisticated readers admit to reading a children's book or children's encyclopedia to get basic information about an unfamiliar concept before tackling a more advanced book on the subject.

REFLECTION
Which of the repair strategies do you find most effective? How might you develop metacognition and greater use of repair strategies in your students?

TABLE 7.3 Repair Strategies

Strategy	Description	When Used
Slowing reading rate	Reads at a pace that allows deeper concentration.	With difficult, complex, and/or confusing text.
Pausing	Stops momentarily and thinks.	To figure out a word or expression or to figure out what might be done to resolve confusion.
Reading aloud	Deliberately reads aloud (or in a whisper) to self.	To achieve greater focus or overcome distraction.
Jumping over	Deliberately skips a word or phrase.	Decides a word or phrase is unimportant or hopes that further reading will clarify meaning.
Looking back	Checks back to locate a forgotten or misunderstood piece of information.	To obtain information lost from working memory or information overlooked on the first pass through text.
Rereading	Reprocesses a portion of text.	To obtain meaning not absorbed on first pass through text or to clarify meaning.
Paraphrasing	Puts text in own words.	To translate a difficult passage into easier-to-understand language.
Using text aids	Looks at illustrations, maps, charts, graphs, and other nontext elements.	To resolve confusion or obtain added input.
Using references	Consults a glossary, dictionary, encyclopedia, or other reference work.	To check an unknown word or concept or obtain needed information to resolve confusion.
Reading an easier version	Uses an easier-to-read or less complex version.	With target text that is too complex or confusing.

Readers can and should be taught repair strategies. Students need to know what the strategies are, what they look like in operation, and how and when they should be used. Repair strategies should be modeled, and students should be given lots of opportunities to apply them under teacher guidance and independently. Proficient readers might pick up these strategies on their own, but struggling readers need explicit instruction and lots of guided and independent practice. To practice, students might apply stick-on notes to portions of text where they used strategies and then discuss in small groups and with the whole class which strategies they used and how the strategies helped. Discussion of strategy use has a secondary benefit. "Knowing that they are not the only students who have difficulties can improve students' self-esteem, which, in turn, can motivate them to work harder to understand text (Winstead, 2004)" (Walczyk & Griffith-Ross, 2007, p. 566).

Figure 7.8 shows a series of questions that students might ask themselves if they encounter difficulties as they read. The questions provide prompts for the major repair strategies and should be posted in a prominent spot in the classroom.

Lookback   One of the most valuable repair strategies is looking back, but it is typically underused. Students may not realize that they can look back at a text when they cannot recall a specific bit of information or do not understand a passage (Garner, Hare, Alexander, Haynes, & Winograd, 1984). If students' overall comprehension of a passage is faulty, they need to reread the entire passage. If, however, they have simply forgotten or misunderstood a detail, they may use **lookback**, a strategy that involves skimming back over the text and locating the portion that contains the information they need.

To present this strategy, the teacher should explain that it is not possible to remember everything (Garner, MacCready, & Wagoner, 1984). Therefore, it is often necessary to go back over a story. The teacher should then model the strategy by showing what he or she does when unable to respond to a question. The teacher should demonstrate how to skim through an article to find pertinent information and then use that information to answer a difficult question. Guided practice and application opportunities should be provided. When students are unable to respond to questions during class discussions or on study sheets or similar projects, they can be reminded to use lookbacks. As they learn how to use lookbacks, students should discover when to use them. Lookbacks are useful only when the information needed to answer the question is present in the text.

Instruction in Metacognitive Strategies   For most students, metacognitive awareness develops automatically over time; however, instruction is also helpful (Anthony, Pearson, & Raphael, 1989). In fact, it should be a part of every reading strategy lesson. During each part of the lesson, the teacher should make explicit the cognitive processes involved. For instance, the teacher might model how he or she recalls prior knowledge, sets a purpose, decides on a reading strategy, executes the strategy, monitors for meaning, organizes information, takes corrective action when necessary, and applies knowledge gained from reading. The teacher should also discuss these processes with students, asking them what they know about a topic, how they plan to read a selection, and what they might do if they do not understand what they are reading. The ultimate aim is to have metacognitive processes become automatic. In the past, teachers have not made their thinking processes explicit. The teaching of reading now follows the novice–expert or master craftsperson–apprentice model. The student learns from the teacher's modeling and guidance as the student progresses from novice reader to expert.

One way of reminding students of metacognitive strategies is to

FYI

Although teachers agree that monitoring strategies are important, they may not spend enough time teaching them. In one study, the teachers assessed and provided opportunities for students to practice using these strategies but spent little time teaching students how to use them (Pressley, Wharton-McDonald, Mistretta-Hampston, & Echevarria, 1998). ■

FIGURE 7.8   Using Repair Strategies

What to Do When I Don't Understand

What is keeping me from understanding?

Should I read the sentence or paragraph again?

Will looking at maps, charts, photos, or drawings help?

Should I look up key words?

Should I keep on reading and see whether my problem is cleared up?

Should I slow down?

Should I ask for help?

■ **Lookback** is the strategy of skimming back over a selection that has already been read in order to locate missed, forgotten, or misunderstood information.

make a list of those that have been introduced and place it in a prominent spot in the classroom. A sample list of metacognitive strategies appears in Figure 7.9. You may want to adapt the list so that it fits the needs of your class. You may also want to have two lists: one for fiction and one for nonfiction.

To reinforce the use of metacognition, ask process, as well as product, questions. Product questions get at the content of a story: You might ask who the main character is, what problem he or she had in the story, and how he or she felt. A process question attempts to uncover how a student arrived at an answer. After a student responds that the main character was angry, ask, "How do you know that?" Other process questions are "How did you figure out that word? How did you find the answer? What did you do when you realized that you had forgotten some main facts?"

Metacognitive awareness has to be built into virtually all reading instruction; "any attempt to comprehend must involve comprehension monitoring" (Baker & Brown, 1984, p. 385). This monitoring need not be on a conscious level. The skilled reader operates on automatic pilot until some sort of triggering event signals that comprehension is not taking place. At that point, the reader slows down, focuses on the problem, and decides how to deal with it (Baker & Brown, 1984).

Click and Clunk To reinforce monitoring for meaning, use the click-and-clunk analogy, in which reading is compared to driving a car: When everything is going smoothly, the car is clicking along. When the car hits a pothole, there is a clunk. Clicks are portions of the text that are easy to understand. Clunks are problem portions. When students hit clunks, which are generally hard words or confusing sentences, they attempt to clarify them. Strategies for dealing with clunks might be listed on a chart or a bookmark. If students are unable to resolve a clunk, they can place a sticky note next to the confusing element and get help later (Vaughn, Klinger, & Schumm, n.d.).

In addition to scheduling lessons devoted to teaching monitoring and repair strategies, be alert for opportunities to do on-the-spot teaching or reinforcement. When a student is reading orally and makes an error, do not immediately correct her or him. Give the student the opportunity to monitor her or his own reading and correct any errors. In fact, if the miscue makes sense in the sentence, you might ignore it. If it changes the meaning of the sentence and the student does not correct it, ask questions like these: "Did that sentence make sense? What might you do to read the sentence correctly?" If the student cannot make the correction after a reasonable effort, supply the correct word and an alternative: "Would [unknown word] or [incorrect alternative] fit here? Why?" However, it is important that students be given a chance to correct their errors. To develop monitoring and repair strategies, students need ample opportunity to apply them. They also need an environment in which they are not afraid to make mistakes.

To promote the use of monitoring and repair strategies during silent reading, review these strategies from time to time. At times when it is not possible for students to get help with comprehension difficulties, have them make a note of problems they encounter. For example, a student might put a sticky note by the word or passage that poses a problem. As part of every postreading discussion, talk over any difficulties that students may have had while reading the text. Also make sure that the text is not too difficult for students. They will have difficulty monitoring for meaning if they are unable to construct a coherent situation model of the text (Paris, Wasik, & Turner, 1991).

FYI

Click and clunk is a useful way to motivate students to become involved in monitoring for meaning. ■

Adapting Instruction for Struggling Readers and Writers

Good readers have good monitoring skills, and poor readers don't. Poor readers are less likely to detect lapses in comprehension and, when they do detect them, are less able to repair them. However, when instructed, poor readers can and do learn to become effective monitors (Palincsar, Winn, David, Snyder, & Stevens, 1993). ■

FIGURE 7.9 Metacognitive Strategies

Thinking and Reading

Before reading

What does this selection seem to be about?
What do I already know about this subject?
What do I want to learn or find out?
Why am I reading this?

While reading

What am I learning or finding out?
Is the selection making sense?
If I'm having trouble understanding the selection, what can I do?

After reading

What have I learned or found out?
How does what I read fit in with what I know?
What questions do I still have?

FYI

Strategy instruction works best when students evidence a need for a strategy, when the strategy taught is applied to a reading selection, when the teacher repeatedly models and explains the strategy, when the students have many opportunities to use the strategy, and when assessment is based on comprehension of the text and the use of the strategy (Duffy, 2002). The key element is the teacher's ability to adapt instruction to students' understanding and to provide sufficient instruction. ■

To understand metacognition and to become aware of the strategies that you use when reading becomes difficult and comprehension breaks down, reflect on the repair strategies that you use.

Using Process Questions and Think-Alouds to Assess Comprehension

In Chapter 5, use of a think-aloud for assessing word analysis was described. Think-alouds can also be used to assess comprehension. In a think-aloud, readers tell what is going on in their minds as they read. Process questions can also be used in assessing comprehension. As you discuss a selection with a student, you can ask process questions such as the following:

- What happened in the story? (fiction)
- What were the main things the author told you? (nonfiction)
- What were you thinking about as you read the selection?
- Were there any confusing parts?
- What did you do when you came to a confusing part?
- What did you do to help yourself understand the selection?
- Did you make any pictures in your mind while you were reading?
- Did you ask yourself any questions as you read? If so, what did you ask yourself?

To get additional information about students' comprehension processes, you might use a more systematic think-aloud. In a systematic think-aloud, students read a text section by section and report on their thinking. Sample texts are usually about 200 words long with four or five stopping places marked. When students get to a stopping point, they are asked to tell what they were thinking as they were reading or what was going on in their minds. Systematic think-alouds for students at the sixth-grade, middle school, and high school levels can be found in the Qualitative Reading Inventory-5 (Leslie & Caldwell, 2011).

It is important to explain the think-aloud process and model it, and then analyze responses. To get the most valid insights into students' comprehension processes, ask process questions and do think-alouds with a number of different kinds of passages. The kinds of comprehension processes students use will be determined in part by the nature of the selection they read (Lipson & Wixson, 2008). Younger readers have difficulty describing their thinking. Process questions are more likely to elicit responses from them.

Scheduling Strategy Instruction

Some schools teach all of the comprehension strategies in all the grades at the same time each year. This makes it easier for content-area and special teachers to rein-force the strategies. Some schools focus on three or four strategies a year. Keene and Zimmermann (2007) recommend teaching one strategy at a time and building on the known strategies. For some kinds of texts, one or two strategies might be most effective.

To create independent learners, a model called Gradual Release of Responsibility is used (Pearson & Gallagher, 1983). To make sure that the responsibility is released to students on a timely basis, Keene and Zimmermann recommend a sequence of four phases: planning, early, middle, and late. In the planning phase, teachers try out the strategy on their own, plan how to introduce the strategy, gather materials, and possibly reassess students. In the early phase, the teacher introduces the strategy and students begin to apply it. In the middle phase, the strategy is applied to longer texts and a variety of genres. In the late phase, the strategy is integrated with other strategies.

Putting Strategies in Perspective   You need to guard against making strategy instruction too intrusive or too burdensome. Students need time to read just for pleasure or for their own purposes (Keene & Zimmermann, 2007). Keene recalls her daughter stating that she hated strategies. The girl's overzealous teacher was having students mark five things that they thought were important on every page (Keene & Zimmermann, 2007). It's important to keep in mind that strategies are a means to an end and not an end in them. As Scanlon and colleagues warn, "When too much emphasis is placed on strategies and too little on the materials being read, children may come to believe that it is the application of strategies that is valued and important rather than comprehension of the text" (p. 286).

Special Comprehension Strategies for Bilingual Readers

Bilingual students find reading and comprehending in their weaker or nondominant language more difficult. One of the major obstacles is vocabulary. If bilingual students have recently learned to speak English, chances are they will encounter a greater number of unknown words than will their same-age English-speaking counterparts. Fortunately, successful bilingual readers do use a repertoire of strategies to aid themselves. For one thing, they seem to be more metacognitively aware. Apparently, the process of learning a second language has provided them with insights into language on an abstract level, as an object of study. They are more likely to notice problems in word recognition or comprehension. While using the same kinds of strategies (predicting, inferencing, monitoring, etc.) as their monolingual counterparts, they also use additional strategies: translating from one language to another and transferring information learned in one language to another.

Achieving bilingual readers see similarities between their native language and their new language. They use their native language as a source of help by activating prior knowledge in both languages and by translating when encountering a difficult passage, especially when they are in the earlier stages of learning English. Transferring, translating, and reflecting on text in their native or stronger language have the potential for improving comprehension (Jiménez, 1997).

Importance of Prior Knowledge

Prior knowledge has been shown to make a greater contribution to text comprehension than decoding or reported use of strategies (Samuelstuen & Bråten, 2005). Building background knowledge is especially effective if facts are tied together into generalizations or concepts so that they represent a depth of understanding. As Romance and Vitale (2006) explain, the main component of effective reading comprehension is well-organized, accessible knowledge that is cumulatively acquired and organized so that it is available for future use.

As Cassidy and colleagues (2010) caution, "The depth and complexity of reading comprehension in middle and high school requires much more than direct, explicit comprehension instruction (Ehren, 2009). The literacy demands at this level suggest students should have a knowledge base of the various content areas they are studying as well as 'facility with the specific discourse used to convey that knowledge'" (Ehren, 2009, p. 192) (p. 451).

Making Connections

Students who have a richer background and can make more connections between what they know and what they are reading have better comprehension and retention. For instance, students reading about germs might relate what they read to a time when they had strep throat and took medicine to get rid of the germs. Comprehension can be thought of as a network of ideas connected largely by causal–logical relationships. Good readers use higher-level thought processes to establish relationships and store information in network form so that the concept of germs, for example, has a number of connections in their schemata.

FYI

Because metacognition depends on developmental level, young students are less adept at it than older readers. However, developmentally appropriate instruction in metacognitive processes is effective. ■

FYI

In addition to being taught how to use metacognitive strategies, students should learn why, where, and when to use them so as to acquire cognitive command of them. ■

Adapting Instruction for English Language Learners

• A bonus for using prompts with ELLS is that the students often follow the teacher's lead and use prompts in their discussion groups.
• When introducing selections to bilingual students, extra time needs to be spent building background and vocabulary. Providing students with high-interest, readable, culturally relevant materials also boosts their motivation and comprehension (Jiménez, 1997).
• Because comprehension improves when ELLs read texts with culturally familiar content, teachers should provide these students with such texts whenever possible (Manyak, 2007b). ■

One way of helping students, especially below-level readers, improve their comprehension is to use causal questioning. In causal questioning, students are asked why and how questions help them to make inferences. These questions can be asked during discussions or can be added to the text at locations where comprehension is likely to falter. This might be at points where important cause–effect relationships are being established (van den Broek & Kremer, 2000).

Social-Constructivist Nature of Comprehension

According to Vygotsky (1978), learning is a social process. Directions and explanations provided by a more knowledgeable other are internalized by the learner and become part of his or her thinking. When a teacher and students or a group of students discuss a reading selection, they help each other construct meaning. Comprehension is still an individual task. Participants discuss their personal understandings of the text, but as they engage in an interchange of ideas, they may modify their understandings as they perceive the selection from other perspectives. This is especially true in reading literature, where understandings are enriched and broadened by discussion with others. However, even when reading informational texts, understandings are deepened and clarified through discussion. When students explain how they comprehended a particular passage or what they did when a passage was confusing, understanding of reading processes is enhanced (Kucan & Beck, 1996).

The degree to which comprehension is fostered depends on the quality of the thinking and the ideas exchanged. The talk must be accountable (New Standards Primary Literacy Committee, 1999). It must go beyond mere opinion. Students must be prepared to back up a judgment about a literary piece by using passages from the text, for instance. Or, if they draw a conclusion from a passage in a social studies text, they must cite supporting details. In this way, students learn to draw evidence from text, check facts, and reason with information. Teachers play a key role in modeling accountable talk and in shaping discussions so that student talk becomes accountable.

Reciprocal Teaching

Reciprocal teaching is a form of social–constructivist learning and cognitive apprenticeship in which students gradually learn key comprehension strategies by imitating and working along with the teacher. Reciprocal teaching introduces group discussion techniques created to improve understanding and retention of the main points of a selection. Reciprocal teaching also has built-in monitoring devices that enable students to check their understanding of what they are reading and to take steps to improve their comprehension if necessary.

In a reciprocal teaching situation, the group reads a story and then discusses it. Members of the group take turns leading the discussion. They use four tried-and-true techniques for building comprehension and for monitoring for meaning—predicting, question generating, clarifying, and summarizing (Palincsar & Brown, 1986):

1. *Predicting.* Students predict what information a section of text will present based on what they have read in a prior section. If they are just starting a selection, their prediction is based on illustrations, headings, or an introductory paragraph. They must activate their background knowledge to guess what the author is going to say next. Predicting makes them active readers and gives them a purpose for reading.

2. *Question generating.* Students must seek out the kinds of information in a text that provides a basis for well-formed questions. Not being able to formulate a question may be a sign that they have failed to understand the significant points in the text and so must reread or take other corrective action.

■ **Reciprocal teaching** is a form of cooperative learning in which students learn to use four key reading strategies in order to achieve improved comprehension: predicting, question generating, clarifying, and summarizing.

3. *Clarifying.* Students note words, concepts, expressions, or other items that hinder comprehension, and they ask for explanations during discussion.

4. *Summarizing.* The discussion leader, with or without the help of the group, retells the selection, highlighting the main points. This retelling reviews and integrates the information and is also a monitoring device. Inability to paraphrase is a sign that comprehension is poor and rereading is in order (Brown, 1985). Summarizing also becomes a springboard for making predictions about the content of the next section.

Using direct instruction, the teacher introduces reciprocal teaching over approximately a week's time but may take longer if necessary. Lesson 7.6 outlines the teacher's role in reciprocal teaching.

LESSON 7.6
Reciprocal Teaching

Objectives

- Students will construct meaning from text by making predictions, summarizing, creating and answering questions, and monitoring.

Step 1. Introduce reciprocal teaching

Ask students whether they have ever wanted to switch places with the teacher. Tell them that they will be using a new method to help them read with better understanding and that each student will have a chance to lead a discussion of a story that the class has read. Outline for the students the four parts of the method: predicting what will happen; making up questions; clarifying, or clearing up details that are hard to understand; and summarizing.

Step 2. Explain the four basic parts

a. Explain that predicting helps readers think what a story might be about and that it gives them a purpose for reading. Students will want to see how their predictions work out, so they will read with greater interest and understanding. Model the process and give students a chance to try it out.

b. Explain to students that asking questions will help them read with better understanding. Model the process by reading a selection and constructing questions. Emphasize the need to ask questions about the important parts of the selection and provide guided practice in constructing some questions.

c. Explain what clarifying is. Tell students that it is important to notice words or ideas that make it hard to understand a selection. Explain that clarifying hard parts of a selection will help them get more meaning out of what they are reading. Have them locate which words, sentences, or ideas in a sample selection need clarifying. Explain that what is clear to one person may not be clear to another.

d. Explain why summarizing is an important skill. Tell students that summarizing a paragraph helps them concentrate on important points while reading. Demonstrate creating a summary for a model paragraph. Explain that if students summarize, they will better understand what they read and remember it longer.

Depending on students' age, ability, and previous experience with the strategies, the teacher might introduce the strategies all at once, one a day, or even one a week. The teacher should not expect students to become proficient in using the strategies or even to fully understand them at this point. That will come when the strategies are applied in a reciprocal teaching lesson. At first, the teacher plays a major role in the application of reciprocal teaching, modeling the four strategies, making corrections, and providing guidance when necessary. Gradually, the students take more responsibility for leading discussions and applying the strategies.

FYI

- Some students may have difficulty composing questions. Supply these students with model questions. As they begin to catch on to the process, provide prompts or partial questions until they are able to create questions on their own.
- Reciprocal teaching can be used with nonreaders, the major difference being that the teacher reads the selection to the students. The process can also be adapted to a peer-tutoring situation in which a good reader is trained in the strategies and works with a poor reader (Palincsar & Brown, 1986).
- Develop dialogue along with strategies (Benson-Castagna, 2005). The objective of reciprocal teaching is to develop students' self-awareness of their learning and to turn thinking into language. Thus, through discussions, students can become more aware of their thinking and share their thinking with each other. ■

The following is a sample reciprocal teaching lesson based on the reading of a selection about Daisy Low, the founder of the Girl Scouts of America.

(Lead-in question)

Carmen (student discussion leader): My question is, how did Daisy Low help people and animals?

Paula: She fed stray cats and dogs.

Frank: She got clothes for needy children.

(Clarification request)

Charles: I think we should clarify *needy.*

Ann: I think needy children need stuff, like clothes and maybe food.

Teacher: What would be another word for *needy?*

James: *Poor.* I think *poor* means the same thing as *needy.*

Teacher: Good answer. *Poor* and *needy* mean just about the same thing. I have another question. Why did Daisy put a blanket on the cow?

Paula: She was afraid it would get cold.

James: I think that should be clarified. Do cows get cold?

Teacher: Does anybody know? Did any of you ever live on a farm? How can we find out?

Paula: We could look in the encyclopedia.

John: My grandfather raised cows. He's visiting us. I could ask him.

Teacher: That's a great idea. You ask him and report back to us. Maybe your grandfather could come in and talk to the class about life on a farm. By the way, Carmen, do you feel that your question has been answered?

Carmen: I think the story tells about some more things that Daisy Low did to help people. Can anyone tell me what they were?

Ann: Yes, she started a children's group called Helping Hands.

Frank: And the first sentence says that she was the founder of the Girl Scouts in America.

Teacher: Those are good answers. Can you summarize this section of the story, Carmen?

(Summary)

Carmen: The paragraph tells about Daisy Low.

Teacher: That's right, Carmen. The paragraph tells us about Daisy Low. In a summary, you give the main idea and main details. What does the paragraph tell us about Daisy Low?

Carmen: She helped animals and children who were in need.

(Prediction)

Teacher: Very good. What do you predict the article will tell next?

Carmen: I think the article will tell how Daisy Low started the Girl Scouts.

Teacher: Does anyone have a different prediction? Okay. Let's read the next section to see how our prediction works out. Who would like to be the leader for this section?

During the session, the teacher provides guidance through prompts and probes, where needed, and also models the four strategies. For instance, creating questions is difficult for many students. The teacher might show how she or he would go about creating a question, supply question words—*who, what, why, when, where,* and *how,* or use prompts to help students reformulate awkward questions. Ultimately, students should be able to apply the strategy lessons they have learned. Research suggests that this does happen: Students who were trained in the use of the strategies were apparently able to apply them to their social studies and science reading; their rankings in content-area evaluations shot up from the 20th to the 50th percentile (Brown, 1985).

Reciprocal teaching can be used in literature circles and other book discussion groups (see Chapter 10 for information about literature discussion groups). Oczkus (2003) used reciprocal teaching with literature circles to bolster students' comprehension: "Reciprocal teaching adds a 'read and learn to comprehend' dimension to literature circles because it gives students the basics for comprehending well" (p. 134). Some teachers introduce reciprocal teaching in small groups or to the whole class early in the year and by spring have students use reciprocal teaching in their literature discussion groups.

An entire class can use reciprocal teaching if the technique is adapted in the following two ways. First, students use the headings in a selection to make two predictions about the content of the text they are about to read. Second, after reading a segment, they write two questions and a summary, as well as list any items that require clarification. The predictions, summaries, and clarification requests are discussed after the selection has been read. Even with these whole-group adaptations, students' comprehension improved 20 percent after using the approach for just one month (Palincsar & Brown, 1986).

Why is reciprocal teaching so powerful? Reciprocal teaching leads students to a deeper processing of text. It may also change the way students read. It focuses their attention on trying to make sense of what they read, instead of just decoding words (Rosenshine & Meister, 1994).

Questioning the Author (QTA)

Another highly effective technique that emphasizes collaboration and discussion is Questioning the Author (QTA). Based on their research, McKeown, Beck, and Sandora (1996) found that fifth-graders weren't learning very much from content-area texts. The researchers devised QTA to help the students get more out of their reading. In contrast to reciprocal teaching, QTA focuses on content rather than strategies. "A potential drawback of strategy-based instruction . . . is that both teachers' and students' attention may be drawn too easily to the surface features of the strategies themselves rather than to the meaning of what is being read" (Beck & McKeown, 2006, p. 24). A second difference that distinguishes QTA from some other approaches is that students construct meaning and discuss the text during reading rather than after reading. Beck and colleagues set up a program in which students read brief segments of text and then responded to teacher queries, so they were cooperatively constructing meaning as they processed the text instead of reading the entire text and then answering questions. The purpose of discussion was to "ensure that students are indeed comprehending what they read" (Beck & McKeown, 2006, p. 29). The teacher's role was to make sure everyone understood. Consequently, active construction of meaning was emphasized. Students were told that sometimes the author's meaning wasn't clear, so they would have to ask themselves questions like "What is the author trying to say here?"

FYI

The teacher might assign roles to students in implementing reciprocal teaching; for example, one student predicts, one creates questions, and one summarizes. Students might work in pairs or small groups to fulfill their roles and complete their preparation before the larger group meets. ■

Using Technology

The video *Reciprocal Teaching Strategies at Work: Improving Reading Comprehension, Grades 2–6* (Oczkus, 2005), provides examples of reciprocal teaching. Clips for the second edition which is designed for K-12, are available at http://www.reading.org/General/Publications/Books/SupplementalContent/BK507_SUPPLEMENT.aspx ■

FYI

In Questioning the Author, the teacher asks students to tell what an author is saying and builds on the students' responses (Beck & McKeown, 2006). The teacher follows up on responses and uses them to create a focused discussion. Questions should be carefully planned; if not, they may lead students away from the text. Questions focusing on personal connections, for instance, might lead into a discussion of experiences not closely related to key concepts. ■

Having students ask such questions made reading a more active process. Rather than simply extracting information from text, readers had to build a genuine understanding of the text. Beck, McKeown, Hamilton, and Kucan (1997) compared it to the difference between building a model ship and being given one. The student who has assembled a model ship knows a great deal more about its parts than the one who has simply looked at the model.

The teacher used general queries to get the discussion started and to keep it moving. Initiating queries included: "What is the author trying to say here? What is the author's message? What is the author trying to tell us?" Follow-up queries were designed to help the students construct meaning. If a passage didn't seem clear, the teacher might ask, "What did the author mean here? Did the author explain this clearly?" Questions could also be asked that helped students connect ideas that had been encountered previously: "How does this connect to what the author told us before? How do these two ideas fit together?" Other kinds of questions lead students to seek reasons: "Does the author tell us why? Why do you think the author included this information?" Questions might also help students see how what they are learning relates to what they know: "How does this fit in with what you know?"

To structure the discussion so that it helps students construct meaning, the teacher uses six QTA moves: marking, turning back, revoicing, modeling, annotating, and recapping.

Marking.   The teacher highlights a student's comment or idea that is important to the meaning being built. The teacher might remark, "You are saying that immigration was a good thing. It helped the United States grow and develop." Or the teacher might simply say, "Good point!"

Turning back.   The teacher turns students' attention back to the text so that they can get more information, fix a misreading, or clarify their thinking: "Yes, I agree that people should have been pleased to have so many newcomers to build railroads and work in factories. But what does the author tell us about how the newcomers were actually treated?"

Revoicing.   The teacher helps students clearly express what they were attempting to say: "So what you're telling us is that the newcomers put up with hardships and worked long hours so that their children would have a better life."

Modeling.   The teacher shows how he or she might go about creating meaning from text. The teacher may model how to clarify a difficult passage, draw a conclusion, visualize a complex process, or use context to derive the meaning of a difficult word. The teacher might say, "Here's what was going through my mind as I read that passage," or "Here's how I figured out what the author meant," or, "When an author explains how something works, I try to picture the steps in my mind."

Annotating.   The teacher fills in information that is missing from a discussion but that is important for understanding key ideas. It might be information that the author failed to include: "The author tells us that factory goods were so cheap that people stopped making clothes and household items at home and bought them instead. What the author doesn't say is that more and more people became dependent on a job. Up to this time, they had raised their own food and made much of what they needed. Now they needed money to live."

Recapping.   The teacher highlights key points and summarizes. "Now that we understand how immigrant parents sacrificed for their children, let's see whether the children benefited from all those sacrifices." Lesson 7.7 presents the steps in a QTA lesson.

LESSON 7.7

Questioning the Author

Objectives
- Students will construct personal meaning by seeking to understand what the author is trying to say in a text.
- Students will expand and refine their understanding of a text by discussing it with others.

Step 1.
Analyze the text and decide what you want students to know or understand as a result of reading the text. List two or three major understandings.

Step 2.
Note any potential difficulties in the text that might hamper students' comprehension. Problems might include difficult vocabulary or concepts or a lack of background knowledge.

Step 3.
Segment the text into readable blocks. A segment could be a single sentence or paragraph or several paragraphs. A block should generally encompass one major idea.

Step 4.
In light of the understandings you wish students to attain and the possible difficulties in the text, plan your queries. Plan queries for each segment.

Step 5.
Introduce the selection. Clarify difficult vocabulary and other hindrances to comprehension in a particular segment before students read that segment.

Step 6.
Students read the first segment silently.

Step 7.
Students and teacher discuss the first segment.

Step 8.
Students go on to the next segment.

Step 9.
At the conclusion, the class, with the teacher's help, sums up what they have read.

Step 10. Evaluation and Review
Note students' ability to construct a logical meaning and to go beyond a literal level. Note also students' ability to profit from discussions about text. Model strategies and discussion techniques as needed.

FYI

Some theorists see reading as a holistic attempt to construct meaning rather than a problem-solving attempt to apply specific strategies (Kucan & Beck, 1996). This text views reading as a combination of the two: strategies, once learned, are ultimately applied in a holistic, integrated fashion. ■

Using Technology

Cool Sites for Kids presents dozens of sites on a variety of topics. These sites are good for applying comprehension strategies and are recommended by the American Library Association.
http://www.ala.org/alsc/children_links.html ■

Although QTA emphasizes content rather than strategies, the teacher does model strategies as the need arises. For instance, the teacher might model monitoring for meaning, questioning, or inferring if students seem to need to use these strategies. In a sense, students implement strategies as they process text in QTA. Teachers should remind students to use the same processes when reading independently that they use in QTA sessions: " . . .They should pause occasionally during reading, ask themselves what's going on, consider what they have read, reread sections as needed, consider what connects to what and whether it all makes sense" (Beck & McKeown, 2006, p. 120).

Adapting Instruction for Struggling Readers and Writers

In their highly successful Memphis Comprehension Framework, Flynt and Cooter (2005) recommended teaching a single skill for three weeks. They also recommended reading aloud narrative and expository text to students, along with silent reading and discussion to build higher-level comprehension. Guided oral responses, graphic organizers, and guided written responses were used as scaffolds. ■

 Making Strategy Instruction Work

Strategy instruction works best when students evidence a need for a strategy, when the strategy taught is applied to a selection, when the teacher repeatedly models and explains the strategy, when the students have many opportunities to use the strategy, and when assessment is based on comprehension of the text and the use of the strategy (Duffy, 2002). The key element is the teacher's ability to adapt instruction to students' understanding and to provide sufficient instruction. In teaching how to identify the main idea, for instance, the most effective teachers provided extensive modeling and adjusted guided practice to help students overcome shortcomings in their thinking. If students identify a main idea that is too broad, teachers use prompts that help the students narrow their main idea. When students select details that are very interesting but are not really statements of the main idea, teachers use prompts to help students redirect their thinking. Strategy instruction also works best when it is integrated.

Integration of Strategies

For the sake of clarity, the major comprehension strategies presented in this chapter have been discussed in isolation. However, it should be emphasized that reading is a holistic act. Often, several interacting strategies are being applied simultaneously. As Pressley, Borkowski, Forrest-Pressley, Gaskins, and Wiley (1993) explained,

> Strategies are rarely used in isolation. Rather, they are integrated into higher-order sequences that accomplish complex cognitive goals. For example, good reading may begin with previewing, activation of prior knowledge about the topic of a to-be-read text, and self-questioning about what might be presented in the text. These prereading activities are then followed by careful reading, reviewing, and rereading as necessary. General strategies (e.g., self-testing) are used to monitor whether subgoals have been accomplished, prompting the reader to move on when it is appropriate to do so or motivating reprocessing when subgoals have not been met. That is, good strategy users evaluate whether the strategies they are using are producing progress toward goals they have set for themselves. (p. 9)

Learning to use a strategy is a long process. Although researchers may get positive results after twenty lessons on predicting or summarizing, it may actually take students many months to master a particular strategy (Pressley, 1994). In addition, strategies learned at one level may have to be refined when used at higher levels with more complex materials.

Importance of Affective Factors

Being attentive, active, and reflective are key factors in strategy use. Provide students with a rationale for being attentive: The more attentive you are, the more you learn and remember. Attentiveness is enhanced by applying strategies covered here—predicting, inferring, and monitoring—all of which require active student involvement. Students are also more motivated and more involved when they are consulted and given choices and when they have the opportunity to collaborate with classmates. Reflection is also important. Taking time to think about what we have read improves comprehension and retention. Provide students with questions that require careful thinking about what they have read. And provide time for them to reflect (Gaskins, 1998).

Explicit Versus Nonexplicit Instruction of Strategies

Strategy instruction varies in its explicitness. Guided reading, for instance, focuses on having students and the teacher mutually construct a representation of the text. Strategies might not be taught explicitly. The assumption is that after repeated encounters students will infer that they should use these strategies on their own. Explicit teaching grew out of concern for struggling readers who might not pick up strategies without direct instruction. As Duffy (2002) explains,

Explicit teaching is intentional and direct about teaching individual strategies on the assumption that clear and unambivalent information about how strategies work will put struggling readers in a better position to control their own comprehension; other approaches, on the other hand, emphasize quality interaction with text content but avoid explicit teacher talk designed to develop students' metacognitive awareness of when and how to use a particular strategy. . . . Many struggling readers cannot, by simply watching a teacher guide their reading, figure out what they are supposed to do on their own. Consequently, they remain mystified and do not achieve the desired "inner control." (pp. 30–31)

In other approaches, the goal is student comprehension of text. In explicit teaching, the goal is student mastery of strategies. Approaches in which the focus is on comprehension of text rather than mastery of strategies include the guided reading lesson and the directed reading-thinking activity (which are covered in Chapter 8) and KWL.

Summary

Comprehending involves activating a schema, which is a unit of organized knowledge. Comprehension can also be viewed as a process of constructing situation models. While processing text, the reader continually reconstructs or updates the situation model.

Major types of comprehension strategies include preparational, organizational, elaboration, and monitoring (metacognition). Preparational strategies are activities a reader engages in just before reading a selection. Organizational strategies involve selecting the most important details in a piece and constructing relationships among them. Elaboration strategies involve constructing relationships between prior knowledge and knowledge obtained from print. Monitoring strategies include being aware of oneself as a learner and of the learning task, regulating and planning comprehension activities, monitoring one's comprehension, and repairing it when it is faulty.

Reciprocal teaching integrates predicting, question generating, clarifying, and summarizing. Questioning the Author breaks a text into brief segments to allow for intensive, collaborative construction of meaning. Integrating strategies and establishing an environment conducive to learning foster comprehension. Students' motivation, willingness to pay attention, active involvement, and reflection also have an impact on comprehension.

Extending and Applying

1. Plan a direct instruction lesson for teaching one of the comprehension strategies. Select a strategy that is based on your analysis of students' work and students' apparent needs. If possible, teach the lesson and evaluate its effectiveness.

2. Using the think-aloud technique explained on p. 350, obtain information about a student's use of comprehension strategies. Use challenging informational text that is on the student's instructional level. Based on what you learn about the student's strengths and needs, plan a series of lessons for the student.

3. Introduce ReQuest or reciprocal teaching to a group of students or try it out with a group of classmates. What seem to be the advantages and disadvantages of the technique? Reflect on your experience. (If you choose to try out reciprocal teaching, be aware that it will take some time. This is a complex technique with many parts, but its effectiveness makes it worth the effort.)

4. Try out one of the strategies introduced in this chapter in your own reading for at least a week. Note its effectiveness. Did you encounter any difficulties in implementing it?

5. To gain insight into the comprehension process, do a think-aloud with a partner as you read a challenging selection. What processes and strategies did you use? What difficulties, if any, did you experience? How did you cope with these difficulties?

Professional Reflection

Do I ...

___ Have an understanding of the how comprehension is constructed?

___ Have an understanding of how comprehension develops?

___ Have an understanding of the many factors that play a role in comprehension?

___ Have an understanding of the key strategies in comprehension?

___ Have an understanding of the different levels of comprehension?

Am I able to ...

___ Teach the key strategies?

___ Conduct a classroom discussion that fosters comprehension?

___ Use reciprocal techniques for building comprehension?

___ Apply both background knowledge and strategy approaches to teaching comprehension?

___ Assess and monitor students' comprehension and plan and differentiate instruction based on this assessment?

Reflection Question

How well do your students use comprehension strategies? How might you find out how effective their strategy use is? How might you bolster their strategy use?

Which strategies would you emphasize? What steps might you take to see that the strategies are thoroughly learned and applied?

Building Competencies

To build competencies, consult the following sources for more detailed information:

Beck, I. L., & McKeown, M. G. (2006). *Improving comprehension with questioning the author: A fresh and expanded view of a powerful approach.* New York: Scholastic.

Keene, E. O., & Zimmermann, S. (2007). *Mosaic of thought: The power of comprehension strategy instruction.* 2nd ed. Portsmouth, NH: Heinemann.

National Reading Panel. (2000). *National Reading Panel report*, Chapter 4, Part II, "Text comprehension instruction, pp. 4-39–4-95. Washington, DC: U.S. Department of Education. http://www.nationalreadingpanel.org (The report can be read online or downloaded, or a free copy may be ordered.)

Pressley, M. (2001). Comprehension instruction: What makes sense now, what might make sense soon. *Reading Online.* http://www.readingonline.org/articles/art_index.asp?HREF=handbook/pressley/index.htm

Questioning the Author is described in a report from the Florida Center for Reading Research: http://www.fcrr.org/FCRRReports/PDF/QuestioningAuthorFinal.pdf

Reading Comprehension http://www.literacy.uconn.edu/compre.htm has links to a number of excellent sites on comprehension.

Shanahan, T., Callison, K., Carriere, C., Duke, N. K., Pearson, P. D., Schatschneider, C., & Torgesen, J. (2010). *Improving reading comprehension in kindergarten through 3rd grade: A practice guide.* NCEE 2010-4038. Washington, DC: National Center for Education Evaluation and Regional Assistance, Institute of Education Sciences, U.S. Department of Education. http://ies.ed.gov/ncee/wwc/publications/practiceguides

MyEducationLab™

Go to the Topic "Comprehension" in the MyEducation-Lab (www.myeducationlab.com) for your course, where you can:

- Find learning outcomes for "Comprehension" along with the national standards that connect to these outcomes.
- Complete Assignments and Activities that can help you more deeply understand the chapter content.
- Apply and practice your understanding of the core teaching skills identified in the chapter with the Building Teaching Skills and Dispositions learning units.
- Examine challenging situations and cases presented in the IRIS Center Resources.
- Check your comprehension on the content covered in the chapter by going to the Study Plan in the Book

Resources for your text. Here you will be able to take a chapter quiz, receive feedback on your answers, and then access Review, Practice, and Enrichment activities to enhance your understanding of chapter content. (optional)

A+RISE® Standards2Strategy™ is an innovative and interactive online resource that offers new teachers in grades K–12 just-in-time, research-based instructional strategies that meet the linguistic needs of ELLs as they learn content, differentiate instruction for all grades and abilities, and are aligned to Common Core Elementary Language Arts standards (for the literacy strategies) and to English language proficiency standards in WIDA, Texas, California, and Florida.

8 Comprehension

Text Structures and Teaching Procedures

Anticipation Guide

For each of the following statements related to the chapter you are about to read, put a check under "Agree" or "Disagree" to show how you feel. Discuss your responses with classmates before you read the chapter.

	Agree	Disagree
1. The structure of a piece of writing influences its level of difficulty.	_____	_____
2. Talking about the structure of a story ruins the fun of reading it.	_____	_____
3. How you ask a question is more important than what you ask.	_____	_____
4. Struggling learners should be asked a greater proportion of lower-level questions.	_____	_____
5. Students should play the most important role in class discussions.	_____	_____
6. Structured reading lessons usually work better than unstructured ones.	_____	_____
7. Critical (evaluative) reading skills have never been more important or more neglected.	_____	_____

Using What You Know

The emphasis in Chapter 7 was on learners and the strategies they might use to construct meaning. Of course, strategies have to be integrated with text, and that determines the types of strategies that can be applied. This chapter emphasizes the role of text, both narrative and expository, in comprehension. It also explores a number of teaching procedures, such as the use of questions and techniques for asking them, reading lessons, and the cloze procedure, which consists of supplying missing words. The chapter also includes a section on critical (evaluative) reading. Taking into consideration your own learning background, what do you already know about text structure? How might that knowledge improve your comprehension? What kinds of questions might foster comprehension? How should questions be asked? What procedures did your teachers use? What aspects of those procedures worked best?

Nature of the Text

A text has both content and organization. Students are prepared for the content when the teacher activates a schema or builds background; however, they also have to interact with the structure. Therefore, they develop another schema for organizational patterns. Knowledge of structure provides a blueprint for constructing a situation model of a story or informational piece. As students read, they transform text into ideas or details known as **propositions**. Propositions are combined, deleted, and integrated to form a macrostructure. The **macrostructure** is a running summary of the text. The propositions are organized according to their relative importance in a hierarchy. A general statement is toward the top of the hierarchy. Details are lower. A reader who is able to detect the main idea of a text and its supporting details will better understand and retain information in the text than will a reader who fails to use the text's organization. Likewise, a reader who has a good sense of story structure can use the structure of a story as a framework for remembering it (Gordon, 1989).

Narrative Text and Story Schema

Hearing the phrase "Once upon a time . . ." triggers an immediate expectation in both children and adults: They expect to hear a story, most likely a traditional tale that took place many years ago, in some far-off land. It will probably have a hero or heroine and some sort of evil character. A problem or conflict will most likely develop and be resolved, perhaps with the help of magic. The story might end with the phrase ". . . and they all lived happily ever after."

Having heard a variety of stories over a period of years, children as young as 4 develop a schema for them—that is, an internal representation or sense of story. This sense of story continues to grow, and students use it to guide them through a tale, remember the selection, and write stories of their own. They "use a sort of structural outline of the major story categories in their minds to make predictions and hypotheses about forthcoming information" (Fitzgerald, 1989, p. 19). To put it another way, the reader uses structure to construct a situation model of the story.

Various **story grammars**, or schemes, are available for analyzing a story into its parts. Although each may use different terminology, they all tend to concentrate on setting, characters, and plot. Plot is divided into the story problem and/or the main character's goal, the principal episodes, and the resolution of the problem. In most story grammars, characters are included in the setting; however, as *setting* is a literary word that has long been used to indicate only time and place, it is used in that sense in this book. Different types of stories have different types of structures, and, as students progress through the grades, both stories and structures become more complex. Goals and motivations of major characters become more important. Settings may be exotic and include mood as well as time and place.

Narratives progress primarily in terms of the main character's goals. The reader comprehends the story in terms of the main character's attempts to resolve a problem or conflict. For instance, readers comprehend *The Barn* (Avi, 1994) in terms of Ben's goal of building a barn so that his father will be inspired to recover.

Narratives differ in their overall orientation. Some are action-oriented. Mystery novels, such as those in the *Cam Jansen* or *Nate the Great* series, tend to fall in this category. They stress actions. Others emphasize characters' consciousness and explore thoughts, feelings, and motivations. *The Pinballs* (Byars, 1977), a story of children in a foster home, and *Charlotte's Web* (White, 1952) delve into the characters' emotions. In action-oriented narratives, the tale is composed of a series of episodes arranged in the order in which they happened. Little space is devoted to the psychological states of the main characters. The story is usually told from the perspective of a third-person narrator (Westby, 1999). More complex are stories that embody the consciousness of the characters. These are often told from the perspectives of several characters and are more complex because they require an understanding of human motivation. This involves understanding the actions of others in terms of their goals and plans (Bruce, 1980). Most stories combine action and consciousness but emphasize one or the other.

What can be done to build a sense of story? The most effective strategy is to read aloud to students from a variety of materials, from preschool right through high school. Most children gain a sense of story simply from this exposure, but it is also helpful to highlight major structural elements. This can be done by discussing the story's setting, characters, plot, and main problem. Discussions about story structure can be guided through questions, such as the following (Sadow, 1982):

When and where does the story take place?

Who are the characters?

FYI

Bartlett (1932), a British psychologist, asked subjects to read and retell an Indian folk tale, which contained an unfamiliar structure. In the retelling, aspects of the tale were changed so that the reconstructed tale was more like that of a traditional English tale. Bartlett concluded that we tend to reinterpret tales in terms of our own experience. ■

Adapting Instruction for English Language Learners

Some ESL students and even some native-speaking students may come from cultures that have different norms for storytelling. In some cultures, children only listen to stories. They don't tell them until they are teenagers (Westby, 1999). ■

Adapting Instruction for Struggling Readers and Writers

If students have limited experience hearing stories, spend additional time reading to them, and encourage parents and grandparents to also spend time reading and telling stories. Provide specific suggestions for caregivers. ■

■ A **proposition** is a statement of information. "Janice hit the ball" is a proposition; "Janice hit the red ball" is two propositions because it contains two pieces of information: Janice hit the ball. The ball is red.

■ **Macrostructure** is the overall organization of a selection, including the main idea or overall meaning of the selection. *Microstructure* refers to the details of a selection.

■ A **story grammar** is a series of rules designed to show how the parts of a story are interrelated.

What problem does the main character face?

What does the main character do about the problem? Or, what happens to the main character as a result of the problem?

How is the problem resolved?

These questions will help students create an understanding of action-oriented narratives. However, to promote understanding of consciousness-oriented narratives, it is necessary to ask questions about motives and feelings: "Why did Marty lie to his parents? How do you think he felt about it? How would you feel if you lied to your parents?" Consciousness-oriented narratives have a double level: the level of action and the level of thought and emotion. The student must be prepared to grasp both levels.

Asking what, how, and why questions fosters understanding. What questions generally assess literal understanding; why and how questions help the reader integrate aspects of the story and create causal or other relationships. Why questions also foster making inferences (Trabasso & Magliano, 1996).

Discussions should also include an opportunity for students to construct personal responses. The structure is the skeleton of a story. The reader's response is the heart of the piece.

Another technique for reinforcing story structure is having students fill out generic guide sheets. Students reading significantly below grade level found that guide sheets and maps based on story structure helped them better understand the selections they read (Cunningham & Foster, 1978; Idol & Croll, 1985). In their review of the research, Davis and McPherson (1989) concluded that **story maps** are effective because they require students to read actively to complete the maps and also require self-monitoring.

A generic story map based on McGee and Tompkins's (1981) simplified version of Thorndyke's (1977) story grammar is presented in Figure 8.1. As students meet increasingly complex stories, other elements can be added—for example, theme, conflict, and multiple episodes. Maps can be filled in by students working alone or in small groups, with each student having a different part to work on. They can also be used in the prereading portion of the lesson. The teacher might give students a partially completed map and ask them to finish it after reading.

Retelling   One of the best devices for developing both comprehension and awareness of text structure—**retelling**—has been around since the dawn of speech but is seldom used in classrooms. It has proved to be effective in improving comprehension and providing a sense of text structure for average and struggling learners (Koskinen, Gambrell, Kapinus, & Heathington, 1988; Rose, Cundick, & Higbee, 1983); it also develops language skills. According to research by Morrow (1985), children who retell stories use syntactically more complex sentences, gain a greater sense of story structure, and evidence better comprehension than those who simply draw pictures of the stories that are read to them. Combining questions with retelling enhances the effectiveness of the technique. This was especially true in Morrow's study, when the questions prompted students whose retelling was flagging or helped students elaborate. Kindergarten students who retold stories and answered questions did better than those who only retold stories or only answered questions. They also seemed to become more confident and were better at story-sequencing tasks.

Although all of us engage in retelling everyday, it is more complex than it might first seem. Retelling begins with meaning. If children fail to grasp the meaning of a selection, they will not be able to retell it. To be successful at retelling, students must not only comprehend the story, they must also understand the components of a story, be able to analyze the story, have the language required to retell the story, and have the cognitive tools

FYI

Encourage students to retell stories to parents and siblings. This provides additional practice and a home-school connection. ■

FYI

• For more information on developmental retelling, see *The Power of Retelling: Developmental Steps for Building Comprehension* (Benson & Cummins, 2000).
• Props such as puppets or felt board figures are visual reminders of main characters and help shy children, who tend to forget themselves and assume the identities of the puppets.
• A retelling has several advantages over the question-answer discussion format. A retelling is more holistic. It avoids the fragmentation of questions and answers about specific parts of a story. A retelling helps students assimilate the concept of story structure (Morrow, 1985). ■

■ **Story maps** provide an overview of a story: characters, setting, problem, plot, and ending.

■ **Retelling** is telling a story that one has read or heard. Retelling is used to check comprehension or gain insight into a student's reading processes.

FIGURE 8.1   A Generic
Story Map

Setting	Where does the story take place?
	When does the story take place?
	_____
	_____
Characters	Who are the main people in the story?
	_____
	_____
Problem	What problems does the main character face?
	_____
	_____
Goal	What is the main character's goal?
	What is he or she trying to do?
	_____
	_____
Plot	What are the main things that happened in the story?
	_____
	_____
Outcome	How was the story problem resolved?
	_____
	_____

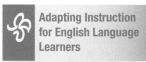

Assessing for Learning

Students who do not retell the main parts of a narrative may lack an understanding of story structure. Those who don't organize a retelling according to the structure of an informational piece may not understand structures used in expository writing or may not be making use of them (Leslie & Caldwell, 2011). ■

Adapting Instruction for English Language Learners

Because they are still learning English, retelling a story will be more difficult for ELLs but could be a valuable tool for developing language. Model the process and provide prompts. Also, start with simple stories and work up to more complex ones. ■

to retell the selection in sequence (Benson & Cummins, 2000). Some children have formed a detailed representation of a story but lack the skill to relate that representation to others. Some students have difficulty with retelling because they have had few opportunities to hear and discuss stories. English language learners may be able to construct representations in their home language but might not have sufficient grasp of English to retell stories. In addition, because retelling requires remembering the whole text, it places greater demands on memory and also communication skills than asking a series of questions would (Caldwell & Leslie, 2011).

Developmental Retelling   Developmental retelling is a way of improving students' comprehension of selections as well as their language and cognitive skills by building prerequisite skills and fostering retelling skills that match students' level of development (Benson & Cummins, 2000). Major developmental levels consist of pretelling, guided retelling, and written retelling.

Pretelling   At the pretelling level, students learn to explain everyday tasks, such as making a sandwich, taking a pet for a walk, playing a game, catching a baseball, covering a book, or using a new computer program. To retell, the child must be able to think backward to reconstruct the steps of a task and then think forward to put the steps in order. The best activities are those that can be conducted within the classroom. Students can take part in the activity and then identify the steps in the activity. As with other strategies, model the process. In demonstrating the steps in making a paper bag puppet, for instance, show each step while explaining what you are doing. Then in reconstructing the steps, hold up the puppet and show and explain what was done first, what was done second, and so forth. Then model putting the steps in order by writing them on the chalkboard, chart paper, overhead, or interactive white board. Emphasize the use of the sequence-signaling words *first*, *second*, *third*, and *last*. After more modeling, invite students to share in pretellings. When ready, students pretell with partners and then alone.

When students are able to retell the key steps in an activity, introduce guided retelling. Since guided retelling requires familiarity with story structure, read aloud and discuss books that have a strong story structure. Books with a clearly delineated plot should be introduced first, followed by books in which the setting is key, followed by books with characters that stand out. Continue to read aloud and discuss books until students have acquired a strong sense of story structure. At that point, introduce guided retelling.

Guided Retelling   In guided retelling, students are aided first by illustrations and then by artifacts. Read selections aloud and show how you use the illustrations to help you retell the story. Select pieces that have illustrations that do a particularly good job of depicting a story. Once students catch on to the idea of using illustrations to retell a story, invite them to join in as you retell with illustrations. Then have them engage in illustration-supported retellings. Encourage students to use only the illustrations when retelling. In fact, it's probably best if you use correction tape or some other means to cover up the words. Once students have caught on to retelling with illustrations, have them use props. Props can be puppets; artifacts such as a ball, a bat, a glove, and a baseball cap for a baseball story; or pictures of objects or people. However, the props do not convey every element in the selection the way pictures do in an illustration-aided retelling. Props might consist of four or five pictures or artifacts that represent highlights of the selection. Felt boards or pocket charts might be used to hold the props.

After mastering retelling with props, students use story maps or graphic organizers to aid their retellings. Graphic organizers help students pick out key elements and note relationships among elements. The graphic organizer might be a story map as in Figure 8.1, a time line as in Figure 8.2 (which could be used for biographies as well as stories), or another type of graphic organizer. The type of graphic organizer will depend on the type of selection being retold and the purpose for retelling. Graphic organizers also provide good preparation for written retelling. At each stage, model the process of retelling but gradually turn the process over to students.

Reenactments   In a reenactment, students act out a scene or story they have read or heard (Martinez, 1993). Since reenactments involve the replaying of a tale, they are excellent devices for building an understanding of the structure of narratives. They also result in improved retellings. To promote reenactments, read lots of stories to students and reread favorites. Include stories that are tightly structured, such as *Are You My Mother?* (Eastman, 1960) and *Caps for Sale* (Slobodkina, 1966). Model reenactments and help students plan and carry them out. In staging reenactments, students might use puppets or fellow students. Props are optional but can be helpful. Include reenactment activities in the dramatic play center. Because reading is not required, reenactments can be initiated by young children. In one study, students acted

> **FYI**
>
> In five-finger retelling, students use their five fingers or a glove as an aid to retelling a story. Each finger represents a key element in the story: Who are the main characters? Where does the story take place? What happened in the beginning? What happened in the middle? What happened at the end? ■

REFLECTION

Which students might have difficulty with a retelling? What techniques might you use to help them?

FIGURE 8.2   Lincoln Time Line

1809 — Born
1834 — Elected to state legislature
1842 — Married Mary Todd
1846 — Elected to U.S. Congress
1860 — Elected President
1861 — Civil War started
1862 — Issued Emancipation Proclamation
1863 — Delivered Gettysburg Address
1865 — Civil War ended; Shot and killed

Expository text provides greater challenges for students.

out favorite stories on their own or in groups after reenactment was modeled for them on a number of occasions. Second-graders were enlisted to create props and reenact stories for kindergartners.

Writing Stories   Story structure can also be used as a framework for composing stories. Laura Pessah, a staff developer at P.S. 148 in New York City, introduced students to the fact that picture books have different patterns of development (Calkins & Harwayne, 1991). Students discovered that some are a series of snapshots; others are circular, as the ending returns to the beginning; still others embody contrasts. Studying these structures gave students ideas about how they might organize picture books they were creating. However, students should be encouraged to follow the dictates of their own imaginations. As Calkins and Harwayne noted, too strict an adherence to structure could limit individual visions. Fitzgerald (1989) cautioned, "Strict adherence to a particular story structure could have a detrimental effect, resulting in formulaic stories" (p. 20).

Comprehension of Narratives   Fostering the comprehension of narratives requires being aware of the students' level of knowledge of narratives. To assess students' understanding of narrative schema, ask them to retell a familiar story or to compose a story based on a wordless picture book. Also note students' understanding of a story that they have read. Ask questions that probe the students' understanding of a story: "How did Yvonne feel at the end of the game? Why do you think she felt that way? What might she do to make up for her error?" Students with poorly developed story schema will compose or retell stories as a string of unrelated episodes or will have difficulty composing or retelling a coherent story. Younger students and struggling learners will also have difficulty inferring goals, motivations, emotions, and characteristics. The ability to grasp what characters think, feel, and believe undergoes a fuller development between the ages of 9 and 11, as does the ability to view situations through the perspective of more than one character (Westby, 1999).

Fostering the comprehension of narratives also requires being aware of the students' culture. In European American culture, the best-known fairy tales follow a story grammar type of organization in which there is a problem and a sequential series of episodes that lead to a resolution of the problem. However, other cultures use different structures. African American children, who use more roundabout methods of telling a story, often include a series of events that might seem unrelated but which lead to the theme of the story. Japanese American children tend to recount their stories in condensed fashion.

Expository Text

Generally speaking, stories are easier to read than science articles, how-to features, and descriptions of historical events (Graesser, Golding, & Long, 1991). Children's schema for **expository text** develops later than that for narration. Expository text has a greater variety of organizational patterns, and, typically, young students have limited experience hearing and reading it. Narrative text is linear; there is generally an initiating event followed by a series of episodes that lead to a climax or high point, a resolution of the story problem, and the ending. Because of its structure and linear quality, narrative text is generally more predictable than expository text.

Narrative and expository text are also based on different ways of thinking. We think in narrative

Using Technology

Using sophisticated computer software, the Coh-Metrix Easability Index provides an analysis of the text structure cues and other cohesive devices used in a text and provides information that can be used to plan instruction (McNamara, Graesser, Cai, & Kulikowich, 2011). A site for the index is being created. ■

■ **Expository text** is writing that is designed to explain or provide information.

fashion. Narrative texts are based on this more straightforward style of thinking, whereas expository text is based on the more complex logical–scientific style (Bruner, 1986). If children are presented with narrative text only, they tend to focus on linear thinking (Trussell-Cullen, 1994). A mix of narrative and expository text is needed to promote a full range of thinking and comprehension skills.

One key to comprehension of expository text is understanding the **text structure**— that is, the way the author has organized her or his ideas. The author may develop an idea by listing a series of reasons, describing a location, supplying causes, or using some other technique. Often, content dictates structure. In science texts, students expect to see both descriptive passages that tell, for example, what a nerve cell is or what an anteater looks like and explanatory paragraphs that tell how a nerve cell passes on impulses or how an anteater obtains food.

Knowledge of structure has a three-fold payoff: It focuses attention on individual ideas, it provides a clearer view of the relationship among ideas, and it is a framework to aid retention of information (Slater & Graves, 1989). The reader can use text structure to organize information from the text and build a situation model.

Types of Expository Text Structure   Following are some of the most important types of expository text structure (Armbruster & Anderson, 1981; Meyer & Rice, 1984). Each description includes examples of words that are used to signal the structure. These signal words are clearly the kind of academic language that should be taught directly to ELLs. ELLs should learn how to read these words and also how to use them in their writing.

1. *Enumeration–description.*   This type of structure lists details about a subject without giving any cause–effect or time relationship among them. Included in this category are structures that describe, give examples, and define concepts. This structure uses no specific signal words except in pieces that provide examples, where *for example* and *for instance* may be used as signals.
2. *Time sequence.*   This type of structure is similar to enumeration; however, time order is specified. Signal words include the following:

after	first	and then
today	next	finally
afterward	second	earlier
tomorrow	then	dates
before	third	later

3. *Explanation–process.*   An explanation tells how something works, such as how coal is formed, how a diesel engine works, or how a bill becomes law. Sequence may be involved, but steps in a process rather than time order are stressed. An explanation structure may include some of the same signal words as those found in a time-sequence structure.
4. *Comparison–contrast.*   This type of structure presents differences and/or similarities. Signal words and phrases include the following:

although	similar	on the one hand
but	different	on the other hand
however	different from	

5. *Problem–solution.*   A statement of a problem is followed by a possible solution or series of solutions. Signal words are *problem* and *solution*.
6. *Cause–effect.*   An effect is presented along with a single cause or a series of causes. Signal words and phrases include the following:

because	therefore	thus
cause	since	for this reason
effect	as a result	consequently

CCSS

Analyze the structure of texts, including how specific sentences, paragraphs, and larger portions of the text (e.g., a section, chapter, scene, or stanza) relate to each other and the whole.

FYI

• To foster awareness of paragraph organization, one teacher divides a bulletin board into six segments, one for each type of paragraph organization. Students are encouraged to bring in examples of different types of paragraphs. Before the teacher places the sample, she reads it aloud, and the class discusses which category to place it in (Devine, 1986).
• Although cause–effect structure aids comprehension, it is one that younger students may be less familiar with (Richgels, McGee, & Slaton, 1989). ■

■ **Text structure** is the way a piece of writing is organized: main idea and details, comparison–contrast, problem–solution, etc.

Some kinds of text structure can facilitate comprehension and retention. Readers understand more and retain information better from text having a cause–effect or comparison–contrast structure than they do when the text has an enumeration–description structure (Pearson & Camperell, 1994):

> These structures apparently provide readers with additional schemata to help them understand and remember the information.... [A comparison–contrast structure] indicates that the information will be about opposing views.... Cause–effect structures indicate that the information will be about problems and solutions.... Enumeration–description structures are more loosely organized, however, and do not provide additional information. (p. 460)

When reading, students need to activate two kinds of schemata: prior knowledge and text structure. The content of a text cannot be separated from the way that content is expressed. Teachers are "well advised to model for students how to figure out what the author's general framework or structure is and allow students to practice finding it on their own" (Pearson & Camperell, 1994, p. 463).

Teaching Expository Text Structure   Being aware of how a text is structured will help readers build a coherent representation of the text (Dymock, 2005). Dymock recommends using the CORE model (Connect, Organize, Reflect, Extend) when teaching expository text. In the Connect step, the teacher helps the students build on the known by connecting what they know to the topic the text will investigate. In the Organize step, the teacher helps the students to see how the information in the text is structured. Each major text structure is explicitly taught. Students learn to diagram the text, or display elements of its organization. In the Reflect step, students think over how the text is organized and how knowing the organization helps them better understand it. Then the teacher might ask, "What was the structure of the text that we read today? What would be a good way to diagram it?" In the Extend step, students extend their learning. If they used a web in the Organize step to diagram information from the expository text, they might gather additional information to add to the web.

Direct instruction in the recognition of text patterns is also helpful. Text patterns should be introduced one at a time. Start off with well-organized, single paragraphs that reflect the structure being taught. Present any signal words used in that structure. To provide practice in the recognition of signal words, use a cut-up paragraph or article and have students recreate the piece by using signal words and the sense of the piece as guides. For instance, students might use dates to help them rearrange a chronologically organized piece. Or they might use the signal words *first*, *second*, *next*, and *last* to arrange sentences or paragraphs explaining a step-by-step process. Gradually, work up to longer selections. Whole articles and chapters often use several text structures, and students should be aware of that. However, in many cases, a particular structure dominates.

English language learners might need extensive instruction in expository structures. ELLs might not be familiar with this type of advanced structure because they are not used often in informal speech; yet a grasp of these structures is essential to understand informational text and to write for a variety of purposes. Instruction might start with single sentences that incorporate a structure word: "*First*, we will talk about a number of possible topics. *Then* we will pick a topic. *Next* we will get information about our topic. *Finally*, we will write about our topic." When teaching text structures to ELLs, encourage the ESL teacher and the content-area teachers to explore the structures with the students.

Using Graphic Organizers   As a postreading activity, students might fill in a time line, as in Figure 8.2, to capitalize on both content and structure. Or they may use a graphic organizer, in which concepts are written in circles, rectangles, or triangles, and interrelationships are shown with lines and arrows. Generally, the more important ideas are shown at the top of the display and subordinate concepts are shown at the bottom. Graphic organizers are helpful to all students but, because of their visual nature, are

FYI

Through hearing stories, reading, and writing, children develop a schema for narrative tales. Expository works are harder to read than narratives, but knowledge of text structures can foster comprehension. Questions and an atmosphere conducive to open discussion play a role in facilitating comprehension. ■

FYI

• One way to teach expository text structure is to have students read a variety of expository materials: periodicals, trade books, content-area textbooks, recipes, sets of directions, and other real-world materials. Teachers should also read expository prose aloud to students, beginning in preschool.

• Before preparing students to read an expository piece, examine it for content and structure. Purpose questions and discussion questions should reflect both features. For example, a brief biography of Abraham Lincoln may highlight the main events of his life and use a time-sequence structure. Instruct students to note these events and their dates to help keep them in order. ■

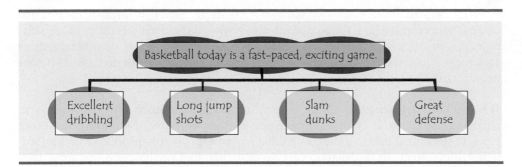

FIGURE 8.3 Graphic Organizer for Enumeration–Description Structure

especially helpful to ELLs. The organizers can be constructed to reflect a variety of patterns (Sinatra, Stahl-Gemeke, & Berg, 1984; Sinatra, Stahl-Gemeke, & Morgan, 1986). After reading a selection, students complete an appropriate graphic organizer and, in so doing, organize the major concepts in a text and discover its underlying structural pattern. Graphic organizers for two major types of text structures, enumeration–description and time sequence, are presented in Figures 8.3 and 8.4.

Students might also use photos or drawings to help them grasp a selection's organizational pattern. For time sequence, they might sequentially arrange photos of a vacation trip they have taken with their family. For explanation–process, they might create a series of drawings showing how to plant tomato seeds. They might use a series of photos to compare or contrast two vehicles, two countries, or two animals. After arranging the graphics, students can add a title, headings, and captions.

Using Questions to Make Connections Identifying the structure of a text is only a first step. The reader must then make two kinds of connections: internal (how ideas in the text are related to each other) and external (how text ideas are related to the reader's background) (Muth, 1987). The right kinds of questions can help students detect relationships among ideas in a text. For instance, if the text has a cause–effect structure, you can ask questions that highlight that relationship among the ideas. Your questions can seek out causes or effects. Questions can also help the students relate ideas in the text to their own backgrounds. Here are some questions (adapted from Muth, 1987) that might be asked to help students make internal connections after reading a piece about the process of rusting:

What causes rusting?

What are some effects of rusting?

Under what conditions does rusting take place fastest? Why?

These questions focus on helping students make external connections:

What kinds of things rust in your house? Why?

In what areas of the house do things rust? Why?

What can be done to prevent rusting? Why would these preventive steps work?

 FYI

To help students incorporate structure in their writing, use frames, in which students fill in blanks with details, or planning sheets, which lead students step by step through the writing of a well-organized piece. Both of these are covered in detail in Chapter 12. ■

FIGURE 8.4 Graphic Organizer for Time-Sequence Structure

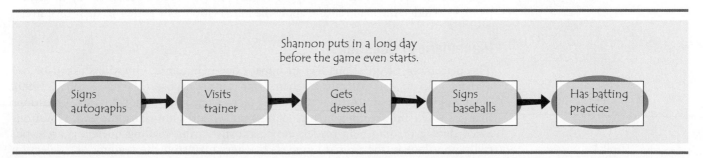

Note that all these questions require students to establish internal or external cause–effect relationships. Questions can also be posed that facilitate establishing relationships in texts having comparison–contrast, problem–solution, or other kinds of structures. Once students have grasped the concept, have them create their own connection questions.

Writing for Organization   Another way to teach expository text structure is to encourage students to compose pieces that employ comparison–contrast and other types of structures. After reading a text that has an explanation–process structure, students might write an explanation of a process they find intriguing. Over time, they should have the opportunity to practice with all the major types of structures.

To help ELLs make use of expository text structures in their writing, provide frame sentences.

- I like _____ because _____. (cause-effect)
- _____ is different from _____. (comparison-contrast)
- To _____, first you _____. Then you _____. Finally, you _____(explanation-process)

Frame paragraphs can be found on page 505.

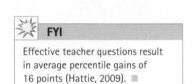

The Role of Questions in Comprehension

Questions play a central role in facilitating comprehension. They can be used to develop concepts, build background, clarify reasoning processes, and even lead students to higher levels of thinking. In one study, second-graders became more adept at making inferences simply by being asked inferential questions (Hansen & Pearson, 1980).

Questions foster understanding and retention. When students are asked questions about information in text, they remember that information longer. Asking higher-level questions is especially helpful. Questioning that demands integrating information in a text "will promote deeper processing, and therefore more learning and better remembering than questions that require recall of specific facts only" (Sundbye, 1987, p. 85). As Wixson (1983) put it, "What you ask about is what children learn" (p. 287). If you ask questions about trivial facts, then those facts are what children will focus on and remember. The questions we ask shape students' comprehension and also their concept of what is important in a text.

Planning Questions

Because of their importance, questions need to be planned carefully. They should be used to establish the main elements in a story or the main concepts in a nonfiction selection (Beck, Omanson, & McKeown, 1982). Poor readers benefit from questions that elicit the basic elements in a selection (Medley, 1977). Once the basic plot of a story or the main facts in an article are established, students can be led to a deeper understanding of the material. It is important to ask questions that help children see relationships among ideas, relate new information to their background of experience, and modify their schema. Students must also have opportunities to respond in a personal way to literary pieces—to judge the material and apply the information they gather to their own lives.

Placement of Questions

The placement of questions has an impact on their effect. Questions asked before reading help readers activate a schema and set a purpose (Harris & Sipay, 1990). They guide readers into the text and tell them what information to seek. Questions that are asked after reading help readers organize and summarize the text. Questions asked during reading help readers process text. During-reading questions are especially prevalent in the primary grades. Teachers may stop the reading of a selection halfway through or even at the end of each page and pose questions. Such questioning can clarify any confusing elements in text just read and prepare students to read the upcoming segment. Questions can also be embedded in text at key points. Embedded questions help readers to maintain an ongoing summary of what they have read, to reflect on their reading, and to monitor their reading.

Types of Questions

One way of looking at questions is to examine the kinds of thinking processes involved in asking and answering them. An arrangement of skills from least demanding to those that require the highest mental powers is known as a **taxonomy**. The following taxonomy of types of questions is based on Weinstein and Mayer's (1986) system, which has also been used to classify the comprehension strategies described in this text. However, the lowest level, comprehending, is drawn from Bloom's (1957) taxonomy.

Comprehending. Students understand prose on a literal level. They can recite five facts stated in a selection, name the main characters, and indicate dates and places. This level also includes having students put information in their own words. Similar to portion of Bloom's Comprehension level.

Organizing. Students select important details from the selection and construct relationships among them. This involves identifying or constructing main ideas, classifying, noting sequence, and summarizing. Similar to portions of Bloom's Comprehension level.

Elaborating. Elaborating entails making connections between information from the text and prior knowledge and includes a wide range of activities: making inferences, creating images and analogies, and evaluating or judging. Except for evaluating, is similar to portion of Bloom's Comprehension level. Evaluating and judging are similar to Bloom's Analysis level.

Monitoring. Monitoring involves being aware of cognitive processes. It entails knowing whether a selection makes sense and knowing what steps might be taken to improve comprehension.

Listed below are examples of each type of question. They are drawn from *Supergiants: The Biggest Dinosaurs* (Lessem, 1997).

Comprehending

Which of the dinosaurs was the biggest? When was the biggest dinosaur discovered? Which of the dinosaurs was the longest?

Organizing

In what ways were the biggest dinosaurs alike? In what ways were they different?

Elaborating

How do you know that Professor Rodolfo is determined and hard-working?

In your mind, picture Argentinosaurus. What does Argentinosaurus look like?

What is the area where Argentinosaurus lives like? What sounds do you hear?

Monitoring

Did you find any confusing parts?

Did you run into any words that you couldn't read or whose meanings you didn't know? If so, what did you do?

Can you summarize each dinosaur's main characteristics? If you forget some important details, what might you do?

FYI

A revision of Bloom's taxonomy can be found in Anderson, L. W., & Krathwohl, D. R. (eds.). (2001). *A taxonomy for learning, teaching, and assessing: A revision of Bloom's taxonomy of educational objectives.* New York: Longman. ■

Adapting Instruction for Struggling Readers and Writers

There is a tendency to ask struggling readers mostly lower-level questions. Be sure to include some higher-level questions, but provide scaffolding and prompts as necessary. ■

■ A **taxonomy** is a classification of objectives, types of questions, or other items, based on difficulty.

■ **Wait time** is a period of silence between asking a question and repeating or rephrasing the question, calling on another student, or making some sort of comment.

FYI

Wait time requires practice and patience; you will have to make a conscious effort to implement it. Try counting to five thousand by thousands after asking a question or after a student has halted an initial response. Ask a colleague to evaluate your beginning attempts. ■

FYI

• Teacher's guides may include an excessive number of questions. If so, ask only the most relevant ones. Note the major concepts or ideas that you want students to take away from their reading and then restrict questions to the ones that lead to those learnings. If questions aren't satisfactory, create your own.
• A question such as "What is the main idea of the selection?" is so general that it fails to provide the kind of structure that helps prompt a response (Searfoss & Readence 1994). It would be better to ask several questions that are more specific and provide better support. ■

Using Wait Time

One way of extending responses is to make use of **wait time**. Teachers often expect an immediate answer and, when none is forthcoming, call on another student. Waiting 5 seconds results in longer, more elaborative responses, higher-level thought processes, and fewer no-responses and I-don't-knows. Teachers who use wait time become more proficient at helping students clarify and expand their responses (Dillon, 1983; Gambrell, 1980). It would be difficult to find a better instructional use of 5 seconds of silence.

Silence after an answer is given also helps. Used to rapid-fire responding, teachers tend to call on another pupil the second the respondent stops talking. Often, however, students have more to say if given a few moments to catch their mental breath. Dillon (1983) suggested waiting from 3 to 5 seconds when a student pauses, seems to be unable to continue, or seems to be finished speaking. Often the student will resume talking and may even supply the most thoughtful part of the response at that point. The postresponse wait time must be a genuine grace period. Maintain eye contact and do not turn away. Failing to maintain eye contact and turning away are cues that your attention is being diverted and will shut down any additional response that the student is about to make (Christenbury & Kelly, 1983).

Classroom Atmosphere

Even more important than using wait time or asking thought-provoking questions is establishing the right classroom atmosphere. The spirit of inquiry and exploration should be obvious. The teacher must be warm and accepting, so students will feel free to speculate, go out on an intellectual limb, or take an unpopular stand without being criticized. Criticism by teachers or classmates actually leads to lowered performance. Less emphasis should be placed on the rightness or wrongness of an answer and more on the reasons supporting the response.

Questions should be democratic, with everyone's contribution valued. That means calling on underachieving students as often as achieving ones and giving introverts as much opportunity to respond as extroverts. Ironically, research suggests that bright students are not only asked more questions than slow students, they are also given more prompts (Brophy & Good, 1970). All too often, the teacher calls on another student as soon as a slower learner begins to falter. Thus, those who would profit the most from prompting receive the least.

The teacher should establish a classroom atmosphere that is receptive to all responses from students.

Techniques for Asking Questions

Discussions should be considered opportunities to expand students' background and enhance their verbal and thinking skills. All too often, however, discussions become oral quizzes with a focus on correct answers; emphasis should instead be on helping the child. If a student is unable to provide an answer, it may be the fault of the question—rephrase it, or ask an easier one (Pearson & Johnson, 1978). Some students, because of shyness or because they come from an environment that does not prepare them for the types of questions asked in school, have difficulty answering higher-level questions (Heath, 1991). They may know the answers but must be prompted to help shape their responses. If students' answers are too brief, use an elaboration probe: "Would you please tell me more?" If a response is unclear, you might use a restating–crystallizing probe. You restate what you believe the student said and then ask whether your restatement is correct: "You seem to be saying that Gopher should have told someone about his problem. Is that right?" The purpose of a restating–crystallizing probe is to help the speaker clarify her or his thoughts. It can also be used to keep the speaker on track if she or he has gotten off the subject (Hyman, 1978). *It is also helpful to affirm students' responses:* " I like the way you described the character's actions to prove your point." This lets them know that they are on the right track.

A classic, research-based technique for using questions to evoke higher-level thinking processes was devised by Taba (1965). Known by the acronym FELS, it consists of asking questions and using prompts and probes that are Focusing, Extending, Lifting, and Substantiating. Focusing questions direct students' attention to a particular topic—for example, the peculiar behavior of Sam, a character in a story. The teacher asks literal questions designed to help students describe that behavior.

Extending questions are designed to elicit clarification and elaboration. By extending students' thoughts on the same level, the teacher can encourage them to seek additional information about a character or event and clear up points of confusion. Extending is important because it prepares students for the next step and provides slower students with an opportunity to become involved.

Lifting is the crucial stage. Through questioning or other means, the teacher lifts the discussion to a higher level. Through focusing and extending, the teacher has established that Sam refused to go into the reptile house on the class trip to the zoo, would not get out of the car when the family stopped for a picnic in the woods, and has not visited his friend Joe since Joe obtained a pet snake. The teacher asks, "What do all these actions tell us about Sam?" Now, instead of just giving factual responses, students are asked to draw the conclusion that Sam is afraid of snakes.

Substantiating questions ask students what evidence they found or what standards or criteria they used to draw a conclusion, make a judgment, or prove a point—for example, the evidence that allowed them to conclude that Sam is afraid of snakes.

The following example shows how FELS might be used to build higher-level comprehension. The questions are based on a selection about Andrea, a knowledgeable backpacker who is trekking through a forest.

Focusing

Teacher: Where was Andrea?

Student: In a forest.

Teacher: What did she watch out for?

Student: Snakes.

Teacher: What was she wearing?

Student: Shirt and jeans.

Extending

Teacher: What else did she watch out for besides snakes?

Student: I don't know.

Teacher: Let's look back over the story.

Student: Oh, I see. She was watching out for poison ivy.

Teacher: What kind of shirt was she wearing?

Student: Old.

Using Technology

An approach known as Accountable Talk also makes use of probes and prompts. information about it can be found at http://www.institute-forlearning.org ■

FYI

Based on their research, Langer and Applebee (2006) concluded that when teachers spend more time building on student responses, ask a larger proportion of higher-level questions, and promote extended discussions, the achievement of urban students increases significantly. ■

Adapting Instruction for Struggling Readers

Often underachieving students can formulate a response if given systematic prompts such as those suggested in FELS. ■

FYI

All too often, teachers' responses to correctly answered questions are a lukewarm "That's right" or "Uh-huh." Try using a stronger response such as "You're absolutely right!" or "That's a very thoughtful observation!" (Hyman, 1978). ■

Teacher: What kind of sleeves did it have?

Student: Long.

Lifting

Teacher: We usually judge people by their actions. Think over Andrea's actions. What do they tell us about her? What kind of person does she seem to be?

Student: Careful.

Substantiating

Teacher: Which actions led you to believe that Andrea is careful?

Student: She watched out for snakes and poison ivy. She wore a shirt with long sleeves so she wouldn't get poison ivy or insect bites.

Frequent shifting from level to level may produce lack of sustained achievement at any level and result in a return to a more basic level. It is also important for teachers to encourage students to reason out and substantiate their answers. If teachers do the students' thinking for them, the strategy is ineffective. Timing and pacing are also important. The teacher has to know, for example, when to proceed to a higher level. Moving to lifting before building a solid understanding of the selection through focusing and extending hinders students' progress. It is also important that the FELS procedure be individualized, as some students require more time on a level than others (Taba, 1965). (For additional discussion techniques see pp. 445–453.)

Responsive Elaboration Despite use of a carefully constructed questioning procedure such as FELS, students' thought processes sometimes go astray. They may have misinterpreted instructions or may be misapplying a strategy. A procedure that works well in these instances is **responsive elaboration** (Duffy & Roehler, 1987). Responsive elaboration is not an introduction to or a new explanation of a strategy or skill but an elaboration. It is responsive because it is based on students' answers, which are used as guides to students' thought processes.

To use responsive elaboration, teachers listen to answers to determine how students arrived at those responses. Instead of asking, "Is this answer right or wrong?" they ask, "What thought processes led the student to this response?" And, if the answer is wrong, "How can those thought processes be redirected?" Instead of calling on another student, telling where the answer might be found, or giving obvious hints, teachers ask questions or make statements that help put students' thinking back on the right track. The key to using responsive elaboration is asking yourself two questions: "What has gone wrong with the student's thinking?" and "What can I ask or state that would guide the student's thinking to the right thought processes and correct answer?"

The following is an example of how a teacher might use responsive elaboration with a student who has inferred a main idea that is too narrow in scope:

Student **(giving incorrect main idea):** Getting new words from Indians.

Teacher: Well, let's test it. Is the first sentence talking about new words from the Indians?

Student: Yes.

Teacher: Is the next?

Student: Yes.

Teacher: How about the next?

Student: No.

Teacher: No. It says that Indians also learned new words from the settlers, right? Can you fit that into your main idea?

■ **Responsive elaboration** is a procedure in which the teacher analyzes a student's thought processes in order to determine how to adjust or elaborate instruction so as to redirect the student's thinking.

Student: The Indians taught the settlers words and the settlers taught the Indians words.

Teacher: Good. You see, you have to think about all the ideas in the paragraph to decide on the main idea. (Duffy & Roehler, 1987, p. 517)

Prompting ELLs   English language learners may not respond to teachers' questions because they don't know the answer or they can't understand the question. Or, they may come from a culture where students are expected to be passive and quiet (Mohr & Mohr, 2007). They might also be unsure of their response skills. Based on their observations, Mohr and Mohr (2007) concluded that teachers need to make an extra effort to develop the responding skills of ELLs. In addition to the prompts discussed in the previous sections, you might use the following:

- Request a response in the student's native language and have someone translate it if you don't speak that language: "Can you explain that in _____ (student's language)?"
- If the student gives an incorrect response that might be due to a misunderstanding of content or language, say: "Help me to understand what you mean. Tell me more so that I can understand your thinking."
- If the student says nothing or "I don't know," but you think the student might be able to answer the question, say: "I think you know something about this, and I would like to hear what you have to say." You might also rephrase the question and/or request a yes/no response. Or you might prompt a nonverbal response: "Can you show me what you know by acting it out or drawing it?"

When ELLs say, "I don't know," they may mean that they don't know how to express their knowledge in English. The keys to fostering participation are to value all responses and provide scaffolding.

> One way to think about classroom interaction is to "beckon, broaden, and build" students' language and conceptual knowledge. Teachers must seek student input by beckoning their participation and the contribution of their ideas. Once offered, students' contributions should be elaborated or broadened to address more of the instructional content and develop more sophisticated language use. Finally, the teacher can build the student's concept knowledge and language competence by exploring the context, emphasizing the key components, and rephrasing structures. (Mohr & Mohr, 2007, p. 447)

Hold informal discussions and conversations. These can prepare students for more formal discussions. Learn some key phrases in the students' native language. Seeing that you are attempting to use a new language might encourage your students to do the same.

Every-pupil responses, in which all students in the room respond by raising their hands, turning thumbs up or down, or answering chorally, can help make ELLs feel part of the group. Having students engage in preliminary discussions in pairs or small groups can prepare them for answering in large groups. You can also teach students how to respond. Model responding and provide starter sentences on a sentence wall (Carrier & Tatum, 2006). Sentence walls display useful expressions that help students take part in classroom discussions and ask questions. They may contain key phrases from the content that students are about to read. To create sentences for the wall, predict the kinds of questions students might be asking or the kinds of statements they might be making. The sentences on the wall might be the language objective for the lesson. Teach students how and when to use the sentences and how to say them.

- What happens when _____?
- What causes _____?
- What is _____ made of?
- How does _____ affect _____?

REFLECTION

Why does questioning play such a critical, multifaceted role in fostering engagement and comprehension? How might questioning be used to improve the performnce of a struggling student?

Exemplary Teaching

A Steppingstone Approach

To build the background knowledge of struggling readers, intervention teachers using the Interactive Strategies Extended Approach had students study thematic units that covered the same content covered by the subject-matter curriculum (Gelzheiser, 2010). To prepare below-level readers to comprehend the challenging texts used to cover key concepts and that are typically used in content-area classes, the teachers first identified the challenging target texts and then analyzed the skills and understandings needed to comprehend them (Gelzheiser, 2010). The teachers next chose easier texts that provided preparation for reading the challenging text. For instance, for an American history unit, a teacher might select key biographical figures, such as Benjamin Franklin and Abigail Adams, and then locate five biographies of gradually increasing difficulty for both of these historical figures. In steppingstone fashion, students read the easier texts first. These prepared them for the more difficult texts. By the time they finished reading as many as five preparatory books, the students had increased their background knowledge and vocabulary and were experts on the subjects they had read about. For struggling readers, this was quite a boost to their self-identity as a student. Having never been experts in school, they began to see that they were capable students.

Along with using a steppingstone approach to reading the texts, the teachers used a conversational approach to building students' comprehension of the text. By talking about the text in a conversational style, the teachers were able to lead students to a deeper level of understanding in a nonthreatening way. The struggling readers' past experience with comprehension discussions had been largely negative, so they generally resisted answering traditional comprehension questions lest their confusion be found out. In a conversational approach, the students were free to ask questions about portions of the text that they didn't understand and also to build on what they did understand. A conversational approach also promotes independent thinking. In a conversational approach, students were encouraged to lead discussions, but they were still asked to justify and explain responses using the text and their background knowledge. Teachers also made it a point to affirm students' growing ability to understand what they had read. Used with fourth- and seventh-graders for a series of 50 to 60 lessons, the students, all of whom were in special education programs, made significant progress.

- How are _____ and _____ similar? How are they different?
- The main causes of _____ are _____.
- _____ and similar because _____.

Think-Pair-Share   Think-Pair-Share is an easy-to-use but powerful technique for fostering discussing and thinking (Lyman, 1981). In the Think step, the teacher poses a question or idea and the students reflect on it. As an option, they can write a brief response. The purpose is to give them some time to gather their thoughts. In the Pair step, students share their thinking with a partner. This helps students develop and organize their thoughts and also allows them to hear another perspective. As an option, two pairs can then share their ideas. This further expands the students' thinking. In the Share step, the pairs or groups share with the whole class via a spokesperson, who shares not only his or her own thoughts but also those of his or her partner or group. The technique can be streamlined by simply having pairs of students share with each other. You might give them specific directions, such as "Share your prediction with your partner and explain what led you to that prediction." Model the sharing technique. Show students what the speaker does and what the listener does, so that they have an understanding of both roles. Whole-class sharing is usually enriched when students have had some time to think and the opportunity to share with a partner. Think-pair-share is especially helpful for struggling students and ELLs.

FYI

Turn and talk is a simplified version of Think-Pair-Share. Students simply turn and talk to a partner. You might give students a specific direction, such as "Tell your partner what your favorite after-school activity is and why that is your favorite" (Calkins & Mermelstein, 2003). ∎

Frameworks for Fostering Comprehension

Asking the right kinds of questions, building background, activating schema, learning to use strategies, and monitoring one's cognitive processes are all essential elements in fostering comprehension. Systematic but unified approaches that incorporate all these elements are required so that building background and vocabulary and prereading and postreading questions are all related to the selection's major concepts and the students' needs. Two such frameworks are guided reading and the directed reading–thinking activity.

Guided Reading

Guided reading, which is also known as the *directed reading activity (DRA)*, is a framework within which the teacher supplies whatever assistance or guidance students need to read a selection successfully (Fountas & Pinnell, 1996, 2001a). Guided reading is used with individuals or with groups of students who are on approximately the same level of reading development. Selections are provided that match the students' level of development. Students should know most but not all of the words (at least 95 percent). Selections should contain some challenge so that students can apply strategies but should not contain so many new words or unfamiliar concepts as to be overwhelming. "The ultimate goal in guided reading is to help children learn how to use independent reading strategies successfully" (Fountas & Pinnell, 1996, p. 2). Independent reading strategies include both word recognition and comprehension strategies. Students read silently and, as they progress in skill, read increasingly more difficult selections or whole books.

Guided reading can be initiated as soon as students have a firm sense of what reading is, know some initial consonant correspondences, and have learned some high-frequency words. Students are able to take part in guided reading when they can read the kinds of books listed at the Caption/Frame level on page 116.

A guided reading lesson consists of five steps: introducing the text (preparation), reading the text, discussing the text, rereading or revisiting the text, and extending the text (follow-up) (Fountas & Pinnell, 1996, 2001c, 2006). Extending the text is optional.

FYI

- See Chapter 11 for suggestions for managing guided reading and providing the rest of the class with useful activities while you are working with groups.
- Even if they have the necessary background knowledge, students don't automatically activate it. Plan questions or activities that will help students recall what they know.
- The guided reading lesson is the model for basal reader lessons and the foundation for the informal reading inventory. ■

Steps in a Guided Reading Lesson

A guided reading lesson proceeds as follows.

Introducing the Text   The introductory phase might use discussion, demonstrations, video clips or other audiovisual aids, and/or simulations to give students guidance in the following areas:

- **Experiential background or concepts.** Experiential gaps that impede understanding of the selection's major concepts are filled in. If students are about to read a piece about solar power but have no experience with the subject, the teacher might demonstrate the workings of a solar toy. Concepts or ideas crucial to understanding the selection are also developed. Batteries would be an important concept in this instance; however, in the discussion, students might indicate that they know that batteries are necessary to make certain devices run, but they do not know why. The battery's use as a device for storing energy would then be discussed. At times, students have the necessary background or schema but need help activating it. Students don't automatically activate their schema.
- **Critical vocabulary.** Vocabulary necessary for understanding the selection is presented. For a factual article about Australia's animals, the words *kangaroos, marsupials,* and *herbivores* are presented. Care is taken to show how these words are related to each other.

■ **Guided reading** is an instructional framework within which the teacher supplies whatever help or guidance students need to read a story successfully. It is an updated version of a framework known as the directed reading activity.

FYI

• To establish the purpose for reading, students might complete a graphic organizer or a reading guide.

• Very beginning readers typically read audibly even when asked to read silently. They move through five kinds of reading: oral, whisper, mumble (reading that is audible but not decipherable), lip movement, and silent (Wright, Sherman, & Jones, 2004). (You might ask students who are reading out loud to read in a whisper instead.) By year's end, most first-graders will be reading silently or in the lip movement phase, but may regress when given difficult material. An increase in audible reading is a sign that the selection is too difficult. ■

Assessing for Learning

As the group reads silently, unobtrusively tap students on the shoulder as a signal to read orally to you (Fountas & Pinnell, 2006). Note needs and supply assistance. For word recognition needs, use the prompts presented on pages 227–228. ■

FYI

To foster comprehension, use checkup questions placed at strategic points. Encourage students to use sticky notes to identify puzzling passages. You might also break into the silent reading to remind students to use a particular strategy or to clarify a passage they are having difficulty with. ■

- **Reading strategies.**   Students have to know how a selection is to be read. Most selections require a mix of preparational, organizational, and elaboration strategies. However, some strategies work better than others with certain kinds of materials. An editorial, for example, requires evaluation. A fictional story might require students to visualize the setting. At times, the format of a selection might be unfamiliar. For example, before tackling a play, students should be given tips on reading stage directions and dialogue. Because teaching a strategy is time-consuming, it is best if the needed strategy is taught beforehand and then briefly reviewed or cued during the introductory discussion.

- **Purpose for reading.**   Whether set by the teacher or by the class, the purpose for reading usually embraces the overall significance of the selection. It may grow out of the introductory discussion. Students discussing hearing-ear dogs might want to find out how they are chosen, and that would become the purpose for reading. On other occasions, the teacher might set the reading purpose. The purpose can be a question or a series of questions to answer or a prediction to evaluate. It can also be completing a strategy guide of thoughtful questions or a graphic organizer.

- **Interest or connection.**   Last but not least, the teacher tries to create interest in the selection. To do this for a piece about an explorer lost in a jungle, the teacher might read the portion of the selection that describes the imminent dangers the explorer faced. The teacher might also help students make connections between what they are about to read and their own lives (Neubert & Wilkins, 2004). If they are reading about solar power, they might talk about relatives or neighbors who have solar water heaters or they might learn that the calculators they use in math run on power from sunlight or artificial light.

For the purpose of clarity, the elements in the introductory step have been described separately, but in actual practice they are merged. For instance, background concepts and the vocabulary used to label them are presented at the same time. The purpose for reading flows from the overall discussion; and, throughout the discussion, the teacher tries to create an interest in the selection. Reading strategies might become a part of the purpose: "Read the story straight through, but read it carefully to find out how the Great Brain solved the mystery" (reading purpose). "Look for clues as you read the story and try to figure out what they mean" (reading strategy).

Reading the Text   The first reading is usually silent. Silent reading is preferred because reading is a meaning-obtaining process rather than a speech activity. What a student understands is more important than how the selection's words are pronounced. During silent reading, a student might reread a difficult portion of text, get help from an illustration, use context, look up a word in the glossary, or take other steps to foster comprehension. Normally, none of these steps would be taken during an oral reading (Hammond, 2001). During the silent reading, the teacher should be alert to any problems students might be having. If the class is listless, the piece may be too difficult or too boring. If it is humorous and no one is chuckling, perhaps the humor is too sophisticated or too childish. Finger pointing and lip movement are signs that individuals are having difficulty with the selection. The teacher should also be available to give assistance as needed, making note of who requested help and what kinds of help were supplied. Those students can then be scheduled for added instruction or practice in those areas. Reading speed should also be noted. Very fast reading with good comprehension might be a sign that materials are too easy. Very slow reading might be a sign that they are too difficult.

During the silent reading, students should monitor their comprehension to check whether they adequately understand what they are reading and, if necessary, take appropriate steps to correct any difficulties. They might take notes, complete a graphic organizer, or use stick-on notes to signal puzzling passages. Students might respond mentally or in writing to inserted questions. The teacher should note students' monitoring and repair strategies. In some classrooms, steps for attacking unfamiliar words or repairing comprehension failure are posted in prominent spots.

The teacher should be actively involved during the silent reading step. In addition to helping those who request assistance or who are obviously struggling, the teacher should unobtrusively interrupt readers to see how they are doing and ask them to tell about any difficulties they have experienced, passages that were puzzling, or words that were difficult. The teacher might also interrupt the silent reading to remind students to use a key strategy that has been the focus of recent lessons (Neubert & Wilkins, 2004). A student could be asked to read a brief passage orally. The student might select a favorite passage or might locate and read a passage that answers a question posed by the teacher. In this way, the teacher can provide individual assistance within a group approach.

The text might be read straight through, or it might be read in sections. Younger readers and struggling readers find text easier to comprehend when it is read in sections. When the text is complex, all readers benefit from reading it in sections. Reading section by section can be more interactive because the teacher can provide more support and guidance. As Cooper and Kiger (2005) comment, "With interactive guided reading, the teacher guides, directs or coaches students through the silent reading of meaningful chunks of text by asking them a question, giving prompts, or helping them formulate questions that they then try to answer as they read the designated section of text" (p. 32). Guided reading lessons in basal anthologies are generally broken up into sections. For instance, a story entitled "The Three Little CyberPigs," from Harcourt's fourth-grade anthology, can be read in nine sections to answer the key questions. However, you might decide to have students read the story straight through and then go back and answer the questions. The Harcourt anthology also offers the option of using the approach known as Questioning the Author, in which brief segments of text are read and followed by open-ended questions and teacher–student interactive processing (see pp. 353–355 for a fuller discussion of QTA).

Struggling readers might read along with a recorded version of the text or a digitized version in which difficult words or whole passages can be highlighted and pronounced. Usually, for guided reading, it's best if the text is at students' level rather than so difficult that they need some sort of aid.

Discussion   The discussion complements the purpose for reading. Students read a selection for a specific purpose; the discussion begins with the purpose question. If the students read about how hearing-ear dogs are trained, the purpose question is "How are hearing-ear dogs trained?" During the discussion, concepts are clarified and expanded, background is built, and relationships between known and unknown, new and old are reinforced.

Difficulties applying comprehension and word-attack strategies are corrected spontaneously, if possible. The teacher also evaluates students' performance, noting whether they are able to consider evidence carefully and draw conclusions and noting weaknesses in concepts, comprehension, word attack, and application. Any difficulties students are having provide direction not only for immediate help for problems that can be resolved on the spot, but also for future lessons for problems that require more work. Although the discussion is partly evaluative, it should not be regarded as an oral quiz. Its main purpose is to build understanding, not test it. Questioning techniques such as probes, prompts, FELS, and wait time should be used. Part of the discussion might also be devoted to asking students to describe their use of strategies, with a focus on the strategy being emphasized.

The discussion can also provide an opportunity to use new vocabulary words. If the word *arrogant* was previously introduced, the teacher might ask: "What evidence do you have that the main character was arrogant? What is your idea of being arrogant?"

 Adapting Instruction for English Language Learners

Discussions can take a number of forms. Students might discuss in pairs or in small groups. These discussions can be ends in themselves or preparation for discussions by the whole class. If ELLs discuss a selection in pairs or small groups, they will be better prepared for a large-group discussion (Neubert & Wilkins, 2004). ∎

Discussion can occur between or among students. Students might meet with a partner or in a small group to discuss the text. Later the group might meet with the teacher.

Revisiting   In most lessons, revisiting takes the form of rereading selected passages and blends in naturally with the discussion. Revisiting may be done to correct misinformation, to obtain additional data, to enhance appreciation or deepen understanding, or to give students opportunities for purposeful oral reading. During the discussion of hearing-ear dogs, students might indicate that they believe the dogs are easy to train (a mistaken notion). Students can then be directed to locate and read aloud passages that describe how long training takes. If students disagree about the main character traits such dogs should possess, they can be asked to locate and read orally passages that support their assertions.

On occasion, revisiting may be an entirely separate step. For instance, students might dramatize a story that has a substantial amount of dialogue or reread a selection to gain a deeper appreciation of the author's style. A separate reading is generally undertaken for a new purpose, although it may be for a purpose that grows out of the discussion. Revisiting is not a necessary step. Some selections are not worth reading a second time, or students might grasp the essence in the first reading.

In the revisiting stage, oral reading should not be overemphasized. Unless a selection is being dramatized, it is generally a poor practice to have students reread an entire selection orally. Oral rereading should be for specific purposes: to clarify a point, to listen to a humorous passage or enjoy an especially vivid description, or to substantiate a conclusion or an answer to a question.

Extending   Extension activities offer opportunities to work on comprehension or word-attack weaknesses evidenced during the discussion phase, to provide additional practice, to extend concepts introduced in the selection, or to apply skills and strategies. These activities may involve any or all of the language arts or creative arts. Students might read a selection on the same topic or by the same author, draw illustrations for the selection, hold a panel discussion on a controversial idea, create an advertisement for the text, or write a letter to the author. The possibilities are virtually limitless, but the follow-up should grow out of the selection and should encompass worthwhile language or creative arts activities. As with revisiting, it is not necessary to have follow-up or extension activities for every reading. In fact, extension activities should be conducted sparingly. "Extending every book (brief books that can be read in a single sitting) through art, writing, or drama is impractical and could interfere with time needed to read widely" (Fountas & Pinnell, 1996, p. 3).

Guided Reading for Beginning Readers   The amount of guidance provided in a guided reading lesson varies, depending on students' abilities and the complexity of the selection to be read. For beginning readers, the guidance might consist of going through the text page by page and discussing the selection and highlighting unfamiliar expressions, unknown concepts, and difficult words. The lesson that follows illustrates what a thorough introduction to a selection might look like. Because the teacher figuratively walks the students through the selection page by page and pictures are used to provide an overview of the selection, this type of heavily guided lesson is sometimes called a text walk or picture walk.

During a guided reading discussion, students may be asked to go back to the text to find support for a statement.

FYI

In the series Junior Great Books, selections are always read at least twice. In the first reading, students get the general gist of the selection. In the second reading, students take directed notes. They mark passages that help them to engage in shared inquiry. Shared inquiry is the exploration and discussion of an open-ended, interpretive question (Great Books Foundation, 2006). ■

As part of an analysis of the book *Up the Ladder, Down the Slide* (Everitt, 1998), a book on a primer level, the teacher noted that readers would need to know what things you might do if you went to the park to have a picnic. The expressions "sun peeks out" and "blow a kiss" might be unfamiliar to some students, including ELLs. Students might also have difficulty decoding words such as *spread*, *peeks*, *shout*, *ladder*, *slide*, and *share*.

FYI

- For more information about the text walk technique, see the article "Introducing a New Storybook to Young Readers" (Clay, 1992).
- As you walk students through the selection, summarize what is happening and highlight elements that might be difficult. "The children are going to the park to play. Now the sun peeks out. What does that mean? Can you find *peeks*?" ■

LESSON 8.1
Text Walk for Beginning Readers

Objectives
- Students will learn the words, concepts, and language structures in a text they are about to read so that students will be prepared to read the selection.
- Students will read to answer a question or fulfill a purpose.

Step 1. Introducing the text

Introduce the title, *Up the Ladder, Down the Slide*, to the students. Point to each word as you read the title. Ask students to tell where the children are. Invite them to predict what might happen in the story. Walk the students through the first twenty-four pages of the story page by page or picture by picture so that they get an overview of the tale. Knowing the gist of the selection and being familiar with the format, the students will be better able to use contextual and other clues to achieve a successful reading. As you walk the students through the story, preview words, concepts, and language structures that you think students might have difficulty understanding. Paraphrase key portions of the text that contain difficult items. Then help the students point out these items. For instance, after paraphrasing the second page, in which the unfamiliar word *spread* is used, ask students to point to the word *spread*. On the next page, discuss the expression "sun peeks out." Then have students point to the word *peeks*. After paraphrasing the following page, have students point to the word *shout*. Go through the rest of the book in this same fashion. Stop three or four pages from the end and have students predict what the rest of the story will tell. Then have students read the book on their own to find out about the rest of the story.

Step 2. Reading the text

Encourage the students to read the story on their own, but provide guidance and support as needed. Generally, stories are read silently first. However, selected portions might be read aloud during the discussion to back up or clarify responses or dramatize a portion of the text.

Step 3. Discussing the text

Discuss the story. Start with the students' purpose for reading, which was to find out the rest of the story. Discuss with students what the children did at the park. You might have them read aloud passages that tell what the children did. As children read selected portions aloud, note whether the selection seems to be on the appropriate level and also analyze the students' performance to see what strategies they are using and which strategies they might need to work on. Also take the opportunity to reinforce students' use of strategies. Begin by affirming students' efforts. Praise the students for their use of strategies: "I like the way you used the meaning of the story to help you read *with*." Call attention to strategies that might need introducing or refining: "You read this word (pointing to *fold*) as *hold*. The word *hold* makes sense in the story. But what letter does *hold* begin with? What letter does this word begin with? What word that begins with *f* and rhymes with *hold* might make sense here?"

Step 4. Rereading

Encourage the students to dramatize the story. Each student might read one or two pages and pantomime the actions described.

Step 5. Extension

Students might draw pictures that show what they like to do at the park or playground and write captions for their pictures.

> **Step 6. Evaluation and review**
> Note students' ability to comprehend the story and to read difficult words, especially words that were pointed out during the text walk.

Guided Reading for ELLs   Because of language and cultural factors, ELLs may need additional help during guided reading with complex syntactical structures, common words that would be known by native speakers of English, figures of speech, homophones, homographs, or words and expressions that don't have a literal translation, such as *never mind* (Avalos, Plasencia, Chavez, & Rascón, 2007). As part of the preparation step, the teacher might point out and discuss sentences or phrases likely to cause difficulty because of their unfamiliarity. ELLs might need background building or explanation of holidays and customs (for example, how celebrating the Fourth of July may involve attending a parade or having a picnic). A text or picture walk might be helpful for ELLs. A guided reading lesson for the story "Three Little CyberPigs," mentioned earlier, suggests that before reading, ELLs become acquainted with the fairy tale characters that play an essential role. Guided reading might be preceded by a shared reading, or the teacher might read the whole text or a portion of the text aloud as students follow along. Vocabulary to highlight might include two to three words for the students' receptive vocabulary and five or more words for their expressive vocabulary. Receptive words are content words that are needed for an understanding of the selection but don't occur very frequently. Expressive words are words that occur in speech and/or reading with a high degree of frequency; these words are worthwhile for ELLs to learn to use. A writing activity can be a productive addition: ELLs may be able to express in writing ideas that they would have a difficult time expressing orally. Writing can also be good preparation for discussion.

Guided Reading with More Advanced Students   More advanced students don't usually need to be walked through a text page by page. However, they do need the kind of thorough preparation detailed in the following section.

Preparing a Guided Reading Lesson   Creating a guided reading lesson starts with an analysis of the selection to be read. After reading the selection, the teacher decides what she or he wants the students to learn from it. Content analysis of fiction may result in statements about plot, theme, character, setting, or author's style. For nonfiction, the statements concern the main principles, ideas, concepts, rules, or whatever the children are expected to learn. After analyzing the selection, the teacher chooses two or three ideas or story elements that she or he feels are most important. The piece may be saturated with important concepts; however, more than two or three cannot be handled in any depth at one time and could diffuse the focus of the activity. Even if an accompanying teacher's guide lists important concepts or provides key story events, the teacher should still complete a content analysis. That way, the teacher, not the textbook author, decides what is important for the class to learn. For example, for a piece entitled "Dream Cars for Tomorrow," the teacher lists the following major learnings. These will provide the focus for prereading and postreading activities and determine key strategies for prereading, during reading, and postreading.

> The T-X will be easier to care for, repair, and guide.
>
> The T-X will be safer and more flexible.
>
> The Express will be faster.

After selecting these major ideas, the teacher lists vocabulary necessary to understand them. As a general rule, no more than five or six vocabulary words should be chosen. If the list contains a dozen terms, the teacher knows that is too many to attempt to cover. An excessive number of difficult words may be a sign that the selection is too difficult.

The teacher selects the words that will be difficult for the students. From the list of difficult words, those most essential to an understanding of the selection are chosen. For example, the following words are chosen as most essential to the three learnings listed for the dream cars selection and as being ones that students are likely to find difficult: *turbine engine*, *protective devices*, *sensors*, *communicate*, and *satellites*. Examining these words gives the teacher a sense of what prior knowledge or schema the passage requires. A mental assessment of the students helps the teacher decide whether additional background has to be built. For example, poor or urban children whose families do not own a car may have very limited experience with cars and so would require more background than middle-class children or children from the suburbs whose families own one or two cars.

Once the major understandings and difficult vocabulary words have been chosen, the teacher looks over the selection to decide what cognitive and reading strategies are necessary to understand it. For the dream cars selection, visualizing and using illustrations would be helpful strategies. Comprehension should be improved if students visualize the futuristic vehicles and their major capabilities and characteristics. In addition, the photos illustrating the cars being described should help students understand the text.

Building background and vocabulary, activating schema, piquing interest, setting purposes, and giving guidance in reading and cognitive strategies are all done in the preparatory segment of the lesson. Generally, this takes the form of a discussion. Key vocabulary words are written on the board, overhead, or interactive white board. When discussing each word, the teacher points to it on the board so that students become familiar with it in print. Lesson 8.2 presents a sample guided reading lesson for "Dream Cars for Tomorrow."

FYI

The guided reading lesson in Lesson 8.2 is just one of many possible lessons. Another teacher might choose to stress different understandings and would tailor discussion and other activities to match her or his teaching style and the abilities, backgrounds, and interests of the students. The teacher might also choose different purposes for revisiting or elect not to have any extension. ■

LESSON 8.2

A Sample Guided Reading Lesson

Objectives
- Students will use visualizing strategy and other strategies, activate background knowledge, and use knowledge of key vocabulary to understand expository text.
- Students will use discussion and rereading to develop a deeper understanding of text.

Step 1. Introducing the text

During the introduction, the teacher presents vocabulary words and concepts that might be difficult for students. (These are italicized below.) As the teacher mentions the words, she or he points to each, which has already been written on the board, overhead, or interactive white board. To start the discussion, the teacher asks, "What is your favorite car? What do you like best about that car? If you were a designer of cars for the future, what kind of a dream car would you build? What kind of an engine would you put in it? A *turbine engine*? Why or why not? (Explain that a turbine engine is used on jets.) How many passengers would your car hold? What kind of *protective devices* would it have? Protective devices are things like air bags and seat belts that help keep passengers safe in case of a crash. Would you have any devices that would help you *communicate*? What do we do when we communicate? Would your car make use of *satellites*? What are satellites, and how might they help car drivers? What kind of *sensors* might the car have? What do sensors do? (Although judged to be difficult for students, the key words *module* and *guidance system* are not introduced because it is felt that they are adequately explained in the selection.) Now that we have talked over some of the parts of a future car, put all your ideas together, close your eyes, and picture your dream car and its main parts. (Students are given a few minutes to picture their dream cars.) What do your dream cars look like? (Students discuss possible dream cars.) Read 'Dream Cars for Tomorrow.' Find out what two of tomorrow's dream cars, the T-X and the Express, are like. As you read, use the imaging strategy that we have been studying. (Teacher briefly goes over the steps of the strategy, which are posted in the front of the room.) Try to picture in your mind what the car or car part looks like or what's happening in the car. Also look at the pictures of the T-X and Express. They will help you to understand the selection."

Step 2. Reading

During silent reading, the teacher looks around to get a sense of the students' reactions to the story. Their silence suggests that they are intrigued. She notes that most of them are glancing at the photos as they read. One student raises his hand and asks for help with the word *ambulance*. The teacher suggests that he look for pronounceable word parts and put them together; when he is unable to do so or to decode the word through an analogy or a contextual strategy, she asks whether the word *ambulance* or *animal* would fit the sense of the selection. Another student has difficulty with *anniversary*, a third with *efficiently*, and a fourth with *kilometers*. The teacher makes a note to work with polysyllabic words in the future.

Step 3. Discussion

The teacher begins the discussion with the purpose question "What are the T-X and Express like?" Additional questions flow from the students' responses; however, the teacher keeps in mind the three major understandings that she wants students to learn and makes sure that they are explored: "Why might a variety of people buy the T-X? What could an owner who needed more passenger room do? How many passengers will the T-X hold?" There is some disagreement, and the teacher asks the class to go back over the story to find a passage that will answer the question. Then she asks, "How will the T-X use a satellite link?" The class seems confused. *Satellite link* is an important concept. The teacher decides that it is worth some in-depth teaching. She directs the class to go back over the part that tells about it. She reminds students to try to picture in their minds how the satellite link operates and suggests that after rereading the section, they make a drawing showing how it works. The drawings are discussed, demonstrating students' improved understanding. The teacher asks further questions: "How will the driver and the car use the satellite link? Why will the T-X be hard to steal? Why do you think there will be fewer accidents with a T-X? In case of an accident, would the passengers be safer than if they were in a regular car? What is the Express like? Which car do you like better? How do these cars compare with your dream car?" The teacher also asks about students' use of strategies: "What strategies did you use to help you read the story? How did the pictures help? How did imaging help? Which parts of the selection did you image? What did your image look like? Did it have sounds? What were the sounds like?"

Step 4. Revisiting the text

During the discussion, the teacher notes that the students had difficulty scanning through the selection to find facts that would justify their responses. The next day, she reviews the skill of scanning. She models the process and explains why it is important and when it is used. She gives the class a series of questions whose answers are numerals, alerting them to this fact so that they know to look for numerals rather than words. The questions are "How fast does the T-X go? How fast does the Express go? When will cars like the Express be seen?"

The teacher also reviews methods for attacking multisyllabic words and stresses the importance of both syllabication and context. Students scan to find the words *information*, *ambulance*, *notified*, *location*, *kilometers*, and *anniversary*, and then examine the words in context. Students use both syllabication and context clues to figure them out. As a review of vocabulary, students create and then discuss semantic maps for words they learned in "Dream Cars for Tomorrow."

Step 5. Extending the text

Some students design their own dream cars and create ads for them. Others read books about transportation in the future or other books about cars. Still others elect to read about satellites. A few write to auto manufacturers to obtain information about the newest experimental cars. One group checks the Internet for information about experimental cars. They look under the heading "Concept Cars." The class also makes plans to visit an auto show.

Step 6. Evaluation and review

Note students' silent reading, especially signs of difficulty, and students' comprehension during discussion. Discuss with students how they used visualizing and other strategies.

FYI

During the discussion, confusions can be clarified. Strategies can be reviewed, reaffirmed, and reinforced. Incorporate into the discussion the vocabulary words that were previewed. ■

Guided Reading for Fiction   Lesson 8.2 was written for an informational text. A lesson for a piece of fiction would incorporate the same features; however, it might use a **story elements map** instead of a list of main concepts as the framework. Created by Beck, Omanson, and McKeown (1982), the story elements map results in better questions and improved comprehension. Basically the teacher asks himself or herself, "What is the core of this story?" and then focuses questions for students on the core. To reach the core, the teacher decides what the starting point of the story is and then lists "the major events and ideas that constitute the plot or gist of the story, being sure to include implied ideas that are part of the story though not part of the text, and the links between events and ideas that unify the story" (Beck, Omanson, & McKeown, 1982, p. 479). A sample story elements map is presented in Figure 8.5.

A story elements map provides a sense of the most important elements in a story, allowing the teacher to gear preparatory and postreading activities to understanding those elements. Preliminary questions lead up to the story; postreading questions enhance understanding of its main elements. Questions about style and questions that lead to appreciation of the author's craft are asked after the reader has a grasp of the essentials. However, some provision should be made for eliciting a personal response.

How do you get started with guided reading? Start off with reading aloud, shared reading, and other group activities. Also, introduce independent reading. As students are reading independently or working in centers, administer an abbreviated informal reading inventory if you don't know the students' reading levels. To save time, use only the oral selections. Based on inventory results and other data that you have, form groups. You may wish to start with just one small group and gradually form additional groups.

Directed Reading–Thinking Activity

The guided reading lesson is primarily a teacher-directed lesson. The **DR–TA (directed reading–thinking activity)** has been designed to help students begin to take responsibility for their own learning. Although based on the guided reading lesson, the DR–TA puts the ball in the students' court. The teacher leads them to establish their own purposes for reading, to decide when these purposes have been fulfilled, and to attack unfamiliar words independently. The DR–TA works best

Using Technology

Guided Reading, Essential Elements, the Skillful Teacher is a video training program created by Fountas and Pinnell (2005) that provides a number of examples of guided reading lessons. ∎

CCSS

Read and comprehend complex literary and informational texts independently and proficiently.

FYI

One problem with using the DR–TA is that a teacher might neglect to develop students' background knowledge and vocabulary prior to reading a selection (Tierney, Readence, & Dishner, 1995). To build background, spend additional time with the predicting phase. While discussing the title and illustrations and other elements needed to make predictions, build essential background and vocabulary. One indicator that students may not have adequate background is difficulty in making reasonable predictions. ∎

■ A **story elements map** lists the key components of a story: theme, problem, plot, setting, and needed concepts. One way of creating a story elements map is to begin by noting the problem or the conflict. Then list the major events leading up to the resolution. At that point, use that information to compose the story's theme or moral. You might also list the key characters and identify and list any vocabulary or concepts needed to understand the key elements of the story. Then create questions that focus on the central elements of the story.

■ **Directed reading–thinking activity (DR–TA)** is an adaptation of the guided reading lesson (or the directed reading activity) in which readers use preview and prediction strategies to set their own purposes for reading.

Title:	*Leo the Late Bloomer*
Author:	Robert Kraus
Theme:	Some people take longer than others to develop.
Problem:	Leo can't do the things that others his age can do.
Plot:	Leo can't do anything right.
	Leo's mom says he is a late bloomer.
	Leo's father watches for signs of blooming, but nothing happens.
	Leo's mother tells the father to stop watching, but nothing happens.
	At last, Leo can do things.
Ending:	Leo says, "I made it."
Needed Concepts or Ideas:	*Bloom* means "to grow and develop." Late bloomers are people who take longer to develop.

FIGURE 8.5   A Story Elements Map

Exemplary Teaching

Guided Reading for Older Students

Adapting guided reading for middle-grade students, Sandra Athans, Denise Ashe Devine, and Robin Parente (2008) worked together to construct a four-part approach, consisting of strategy instruction, applying the strategies, independent activities, and assessment. Based on their reading levels, students are placed in small groups, where they are taught key comprehension strategies. Although a total of nine strategies are taught, the teachers typically start by teaching just three or four. Students apply the strategies by reading high-interest trade books. Read-along guides prepared by the teachers help students apply the strategies that were taught in the small groups. Along with other activities, the guides request written responses in which students demonstrate their grasp of strategies. The guides also provide a way for the teachers to monitor students' progress. Work in the read-along guides is followed by independent activities. Independent activities vary according to students' needs and may include additional reading, added strategy practice, additional writing, work on individual projects, or self-selected reading. Rubrics and observational notes, as well as formal assessment at the end of each unit, are used to assess students' progress.

REFLECTION

Under what circumstances and for which students would DR–TA be an especially effective technique?

Under what circumstances and for which students would guided reading be an especially effective technique?

Adapting Instruction for Struggling Readers and Writers

One adaptation of the DR–TA involves reading the selection to students if it is too difficult for them to read on their own. In a directed listening–thinking activity (DL–TA), the prediction portion is the same. As you read, stop periodically to involve students in discussing predictions and modifying them, summarizing, asking questions about text, and clarifying key terms and confusing passages. ■

when students have background knowledge to bring to the selection and can attack difficult words independently. If students lack background or have weak word analysis skills, then the guided reading lesson is a better choice.

Stauffer (1970), the creator of the DR–TA, based the approach on people's penchant for predicting and hypothesizing. By nature, we have an innate tendency to look ahead. We are also decision-making creatures who need opportunities as well as the freedom to make decisions. Building on these propensities, Stauffer structured a predict–read strategy that has the following facets:

- **Setting purposes.** Students have to know how to ask questions about text they are about to read.
- **Obtaining information.** Students have to know how to sift through reading material to get the information they need to answer a question.
- **Keeping goals in mind.** Students must be able to work within the constraints of their goals, noting information that fits in with these goals and not being led astray by information that does not.
- **Keeping personal feelings in bounds.** Students have to be able to suspend personal judgments when reading a piece that contains ideas with which they might not agree, at least until they have finished the piece and have a good grasp of what the author is trying to say.
- **Considering options.** Students must be able to consider a number of choices as they make their predictions and also be flexible enough to change or refine a prediction in the light of new information.

Like the guided reading lesson, the DR–TA has five steps, as outlined in Lesson 8.3. The major difference is that students are given a more active role in the DR–TA (Stauffer, 1969).

The Cloze Procedure

Another approach used to foster comprehension is cloze; it is illustrated in the following exercise. As you read the paragraph, supply the missing words.

If we see a part of a person or object, we tend to fill in the missing portions. If someone omits the final word of a sentence, we supply it _____ her or him. There is something about the human _____ that can't _____ incompleteness. This tendency to fill in what's _____ is the basis of cloze, a technique by which readers achieve closure by filling in the _____ words in a selection. Based on the concept of gestalt _____, cloze was first proposed as a _____ for measuring the difficulty _____ of reading material. Today it is also used to test reading ability and to build comprehension.

LESSON 8.3
A DR–TA

Students will use background knowledge and textual clues to make and revise predictions. Students will use predictions to construct meaning of text.

Step 1. Introducing the text

Students are led to create their own purposes for reading. The title of the selection, headings and subheads, illustrations, and/or the beginning paragraph are used to stimulate predictions about the content of the selection. For example, in preparation for reading "Live Cargo!" which is the first chapter of *Misty of Chincoteague* (Henry, 1947), the teacher might have the students examine the title of the chapter. After discussing it, the teacher would have the students examine the first illustration—a Spanish galleon—and then ask them what they think the chapter might be about. Responses, which might include slaves, prisoners, horses, and cattle, would be written on the board, overhead, or Interactive White Board. Because the DR–TA is an active process, all students are encouraged to make a prediction or at least to indicate a preference for one of the predictions made by others. The teacher reads the predictions aloud and asks students to raise their hands to show which one they think is most likely.

Step 2. Reading the text

Students read silently until they are able to evaluate their predictions; this might entail reading a single page, several pages, or a whole chapter. Students are encouraged to modify their initial predictions if they find information that runs counter to them.

Step 3. Discussion

This stage is almost identical to Step 3 of the guided reading lesson, except that it begins with the consideration of the class's predictions. After reading a portion of "Live Cargo!" students evaluate their predictions and identify which ones were correct and which required rethinking. Additional questions flowing from the sense of the selection are then asked: "Where were the ponies being taken? Why was the captain headed for trouble? What is a stallion?" During the discussion, students offer proof of the adequacy of their predictions or clarify disputed points by reading passages orally. As in the guided reading lesson, the teacher develops comprehension, background, and concepts as the need arises and opportunities present themselves. The discussion also leads students into making further predictions, as the teacher asks, "Why do you think the captain is angry with the stallion? What do you think will happen next?" If students do not respond to these prediction-making questions, the questions should be rephrased or altered. For instance, after getting no response to the question "What do you think will happen next?" the teacher might ask, "What do you think will happen to the stallion and the ponies?" The teacher might also read a few paragraphs aloud to stimulate predictions. As in Step 1, predictions are written on the board, overhead, or IWB and students select the ones they believe are best or most probable.

Step 4. Revisiting the text

This is the same as Step 4 of the guided reading lesson (see p. 384).

Step 5. Extending the text

This is the same as Step 5 of the guided reading lesson (see p. 384).

Step 6. Evaluation and review

Note students' silent reading, especially signs of difficulty, and students' comprehension during discussion. Discuss with students how their predictions worked out and what they did if a prediction was not working out.

The DR–TA should be used with both fiction and nonfiction. If students apply the strategies of surveying, predicting, sifting, and verifying to fiction only, they may not develop the ability to transfer them to nonfiction. In time, the strategies practiced in the DR–TA should become automatic.

Cloze is an excellent device for building comprehension. Filling in missing words forces a reader to use semantic and syntactic clues together with symbol–sound information and to predict meaning. It also activates the reader's background knowledge. The reader's knowledge of the world must be used to figure out which words should be put in the blanks. Cloze works especially well with students who are concentrating so hard on sounding out words that they fail to read for meaning.

Classic Cloze

In classic cloze, the teacher deletes words at random from a narrative or expository passage. The first and last sentences are left intact, and no proper nouns are removed; otherwise, every fifth, sixth, seventh, eighth, ninth, or tenth word is deleted. (Generally, the interval for word deletion should be no fewer than every fifth and no more than every tenth.)

The teacher explains the purpose of cloze, gives tips such as the following for completing the exercise, and models the process of completing a cloze activity.

• Read the whole exercise first.
• Use all the clues given in a passage.
• Read past the blank to the end of the sentence. Sometimes the best clues come after a blank.
• If necessary, read a sentence or two ahead to get additional clues.
• Spell as best you can. You lose no points for misspelled words.
• Do your best, but do not worry if you cannot correctly complete each blank. Most readers will be able to fill in fewer than half the blanks correctly.
• After you have filled in as many blanks as you can, reread the selection. Make any changes that you think are necessary.

Scoring Cloze

Exact Replacement   There are two ways of scoring a cloze exercise. When it is used as a test, only exact replacements are counted as correct. Otherwise, marking becomes both time-consuming and subjective. Scores are noticeably lower on cloze exercises than they are on multiple-choice activities; a score of 50 percent is adequate. Criteria for scoring a cloze procedure using exact replacement are shown below:

Level	Percentage
Independent	>57
Instructional	44–57
Frustration	<44

Substitution Scoring   When cloze is used for instructional purposes, substitution scoring is generally used. A response is considered correct if it fits both semantically and syntactically. Thus, the following sentence would have a number of correct responses, such as *wagon, toy, ball, bike, coat,* and *dress*:

The child pointed to the red _____ and cried, "I want that!"

Discussion for Comprehension

Discussion enhances the value of cloze as a comprehension building technique (Jongsma, 1980). Discussions can be led by the teacher or by students. During the discussion, participants talk over their responses and give reasons for their choices, thus justifying their responses and

■ **Cloze** is a procedure in which the reader demonstrates comprehension by supplying missing words. Cloze is short for "closure," which is the tendency to fill in missing or incomplete information.

clarifying their thinking processes. They also compare their answers; in the process, they broaden vocabulary, concepts, and experience and learn to consider and value different perspectives.

Constructing Cloze Exercises

The first rule for constructing cloze exercises is to choose selections that are interesting so that students will be motivated to complete them. It is best to start with easier exercises and progress to more difficult ones. In general, the following items affect the difficulty of a cloze exercise (Rye, 1982):

- **Number of deletions.**   The fewer the deletions, the easier the task.
- **Types of words deleted.**   Content words such as nouns, verbs, adverbs, and, to a lesser degree, adjectives are more difficult to replace than structure words such as articles, prepositions, and conjunctions.
- **Location of deletion.**   Deletions in the beginning of a sentence are more difficult to replace than those in the middle or end.

In early exercises, the teacher may want to delete just one word out of ten—mainly structure words that occur in the second half of a sentence. In time, the number of deletions can be increased, more content words can be omitted, and a proportion of words can be taken out of the beginnings of sentences. The kinds of deletions will be dictated by instructional objectives. If the teacher wants students to work on seeing relationships, she may delete structure words such as *if, then, and, but, moreover,* and *however.* Deleting nouns and verbs and, to a lesser extent, adjectives and adverbs will place the focus on content. Deleting adjectives and adverbs could be a device for having students note how modifiers alter a selection.

Variations on Cloze

Traditional cloze exercises are not recommended until students are in fourth grade or have achieved a fourth-grade reading level. However, variations on cloze activities can be introduced earlier.

Word Masking   As children begin to acquire some reading skills, word masking is used. A nursery rhyme, poem, or story is shared with students. Students follow along as the teacher reads the selection in a big book. During the second reading, some of the words are covered over. When the teacher gets to one of them, he or she pauses and the children predict what it might be. After they respond, the teacher uncovers the word and asks students whether they were correct (Hornsby, Sukarna, & Parry, 1986).

Modified Cloze   In modified cloze, which is also known as mazes, each blank is accompanied by answer choices so that students do not have to supply the word; they simply identify the best of three or four possible choices. This is a format employed by a number of commercial workbooks and some tests. Although they provide valuable practice, these exercises shift the focus from predicting a word to considering which alternative is best. The task is changed from constructing meaning to recognizing meaning, a subtle but significant alteration. However, modified cloze can be good preparation for completing classic cloze exercises.

 ## Critical Reading

Today's students are barraged with an overwhelming number of sophisticated, slick television and print ads. Even the youngest readers encounter slanted writing, illogical arguments, and persuasive techniques of all types. In addition, the Internet has become a major source of information. Virtually anyone can put information on the Internet.

Adapting Instruction for English Language Learners

Cloze activities are more difficult for ELLs than they are for native speakers because ELLs are less familiar with the language and find it harder to retrieve or predict words that fit in the blanks. ■

FYI

Modified cloze is used in a number of tests: Degrees of Reading Power (DRP), Star (Renaissance Learning), Scholastic Reading Inventory, and Mazes (aimsweb.com). ■

C.C.S.S

Delineate and evaluate the argument and specific claims in a text, including the validity of the reasoning as well as the relevance and sufficiency of the evidence.

FYI

An affective as well as a cognitive skill, critical reading involves willingness to suspend judgment, consider another point of view, and think carefully about what one reads. Thoughtful reading and discussion promote critical thinking. ■

TABLE 8.1 Critical Reading Skills

Identifying the uses of words (e.g., to describe, to judge)
Recognizing denotations and connotations
Identifying persuasive language
Verifying factual statements
Distinguishing between facts and opinions
Identifying words that signal opinions
Identifying an author's purpose
Drawing logical conclusions
Supporting conclusions
Judging sources of information
Identifying slanted or biased writing
Identifying major propaganda techniques

Unlike book and periodical publishers, Web site sponsors do not necessarily have any editors or reviewers to check the accuracy or fairness of the information. Many of the sites and services provided on the Internet are sponsored by commercial enterprises, so the information may be biased. The ability to evaluate what one hears and reads has never been more important.

Children who read critically judge what they read. This judgment is not a mere opinion but an evaluation based on either internal or external standards. In the process of learning to evaluate what they read, students deal critically with words, statements, and whole selections.

Critical reading is an affective as well as a cognitive skill. To read critically, students must be able to suspend judgment and consider other viewpoints. Generally, people tend to interpret what they read in light of their beliefs. Some readers (and this seems to be especially true of poor readers) reject information that contradicts their beliefs. On the other hand, some readers suffer from a malady that one educator called the "Gutenberg syndrome" (J. Rothermich, personal communication, January 1980): If a statement appears in print, it must be true. Students have to challenge what they read and realize that a printed or online statement might be erroneous or simply be someone else's opinion.

To encourage critical reading, a teacher must create a spirit of inquiry. Students must feel free to challenge statements, support controversial ideas, offer divergent viewpoints, and venture statements that conflict with the majority view. When they see that their own ideas are accepted, they are better able to accept the ideas of others. The program, of course, must be balanced. The idea is not to turn students into mistrustful young cynics but to create judicious thinkers.

There are dozens of critical reading skills. The suggested skills listed in Table 8.1 are based on examination of professional materials and analysis of critical reading tasks. There is no timetable for acquiring these skills.

Uses of Language

A good starting point for a study of critical reading is to examine how language is used. What do words do? What functions do statements fulfill? Words are used in four main ways: to describe, to evaluate, to point out, and to interject (Wilson, 1960). The words *car*, *take*, and *dog* describe bits of reality. The words *evil* and *stupid* evaluate, going beyond mere description to judgment. Some words both describe and evaluate: *jalopy*, *steal*, and *mutt* describe objects and actions, but

Higher-Level Literacy

Critical reading skills should be a part of virtually all reading that students do. They should always be evaluating the reliability and credibility of what they read and hear. ■

■ **Critical reading** refers to a type of reading in which the reader evaluates or judges the accuracy and truthfulness of the content.

they also incorporate unfavorable evaluations. A key strategy in critical reading is to note whether words offer neutral descriptions, evaluations, or both.

To introduce the concept of the uses of words, write a series of sentences similar to the following on the board:

The horse weighs 950 pounds.

The horse is black with white spots.

The horse is lazy.

The horse is wonderful.

Discuss which words just tell about the horse and which judge it. Guide students as they locate words in their texts that describe, judge, or do both. While discussing selections that students have read, note words that are used to judge. To extend the concept of uses of words, introduce the concept of connotations; have students note words that have favorable connotations (*thrifty, slim*) and those that have unfavorable ones (*selfish, skinny*). For younger students, you may want to use phrases like "sounds better" and "sounds worse," instead of "favorable connotations" and "unfavorable connotations."

Introduce the concept of persuasive language by bringing in ads and package labels. Have students locate words that sell or persuade on online ads and in television and print ads—*fresh, delicious, new,* and *improved.* They can even compose their own persuasive advertising.

Understanding Factual Statements and Opinions

Factual statements are those that can be verified through objective evidence or through analyzing language. The statement "It is raining" can be verified by looking outside. Even if the sun is shining, the statement is a factual one rather than an opinion because it can be verified. If the sun is shining, the statement is verified to be inaccurate. The statement "A hurricane is called a *typhoon* when it occurs over the Pacific Ocean" cannot be verified by observing hurricanes or typhoons. It is verified by analyzing the statement to see whether the language is being used accurately. Analytic statements of this type are frequently verified by using a reference. Because the word *fact* suggests something that is true, it is better to use the term *factual statement* rather than *fact*.

To introduce the concepts of factual statements and opinions, place sentences similar to the following on the board, overhead, or interactive white board:

We have twenty-five players on our soccer team.

We have won twelve games in a row.

Our uniforms are red.

Soccer is the best sport.

Show students that the first three sentences can be proved in some way, but the last one cannot. It is simply an opinion, a statement that tells how someone feels. Help students locate statements of fact and opinion in their texts. To reinforce and extend this concept, plan lessons and activities such as the following.

Recognizing the Author's Purpose

The three main purposes for writing are to inform, to entertain, and to persuade. Recognizing which one applies to a particular selection enables students to match their reading strategy to the selection. For example, knowing that a writer is attempting to persuade, they will look at the piece with a critical eye. To introduce the concept of purpose, read aloud an ad or an editorial, an encyclopedia article, and a short story, and discuss each author's purpose. Help students suggest other writings that are designed to inform, entertain, and persuade.

Adapting Instruction for English Language Learners

As with figurative language, ELLs might need expanded explanations and examples to help them understand connotations and denotations. ■

C.C.S.S.

Assess how point of view or purpose shapes the content and style of a text.

REINFORCEMENT ACTIVITIES

Extending the Concepts of Factual Statements and Opinions

- Present words that signal opinions, such as *good*, *bad*, *worse*, *terrible*, *wonderful*, and *awful*. Ask students to use these and other signal words in differentiating between factual statements and opinions.

- Introduce the concept of verifying factual statements. Explain to students that factual statements can be proved in some way—by measuring, weighing, observing, touching, hearing, counting, and so on. Bring in a kiwi or other unusual fruit, and encourage students to make factual statements about it—for example, "The kiwi is brown" and "It has fuzzy skin." Discuss how each statement might be proved. Bring in a scale and a measuring tape so that the kiwi can be weighed and measured. Have students make other factual statements and tell how they might prove them—that is, whether they would mainly count, measure, weigh, touch, listen, or observe to prove the statements.

- Let students examine an object and make at least five factual statements about it based on counting, measuring, weighing, touching, listening, observing, or checking a reference book. Then ask them to write down their personal opinions about that object. This might be an opportunity for them to be especially imaginative and creative.

- Ask students whether a particular statement in a reading selection is factual or an opinion. Take special note of opinions that might be mistaken for facts.

CCSS

Delineate and evaluate the argument and specific claims in a text, including the validity of the reasoning as well as the relevance and sufficiency of the evidence.

To extend the concept, have students predict the author's purpose before reading a selection and then discuss their predictions after reading. For each book report that students complete, have them identify the author's purpose. Students can also decide what their own purpose is before writing a piece. Let them write editorials for the school newspaper or letters to the editor. Bring in persuasive pieces, and discuss them with the class. Help the class see what persuasive techniques are being used.

Drawing Logical Conclusions

A conclusion is a type of inference. Drawing a conclusion usually entails examining several facts or details and coming to some sort of reasoned judgment based on the information. In critical reading, stress is placed on drawing conclusions that are logical, have sufficient support, and consider all the evidence. In many instances, different conclusions can be applied to a set of facts. Students should be shown that they should reach the most likely conclusion while keeping an open mind because other conclusions are possible.

To introduce drawing logical conclusions, model the process and provide guided practice. Have students apply the skill to all content areas, drawing conclusions about the main character in a piece of fiction, about experiments in science, and about historical events and figures in social studies. Stress the need to consider the evidence very carefully.

REFLECTION

In what way is critical (evaluative) reading a matter of attitude as well as reading skill?

Judging Sources

Because students tend to believe everything they read, whether in print or on a computer screen, they should understand that some sources are better than others. Three main criteria are used to judge a source: whether the source has expert knowledge about the subject, whether the information is up to date, and whether the source is unbiased.

Encourage students to examine their textbooks to see whether they are written by experts and are up to date. When students read nonfiction, have them note who wrote the information and then examine the book jacket or another source of information to see whether the author seems to be an expert. For a Web site, students should see whether the author's name is given and whether the author's credentials are provided. Students should also check the date of publication. When examining Web sites, students can note when the site was last updated. Also, discuss the issue of author bias. For instance, talk over why a book or Web site on coal mining written by someone who works for a coal company might be considered to be written by an expert but could be biased in favor of the coal industry.

When using the Internet, students might also determine what the URL tells them about a site. Students can tell whether the site is educational (edu), governmental (gov), organizational (org), or commercial (com) (Caruso, 1997). A tilde (~) in the Internet address indicates that the Web site is the work of an individual. One might have more trust in a site sponsored by a library, university, or government agency than in one sponsored by a commercial entity or an individual.

When using a Web site, students should evaluate the accuracy and fairness of information.

Slanted Writing Slanted, or biased, writing uses emotionally charged words and specially chosen details to create an unfairly favorable or unfavorable impression about a person, place, object, or idea. It is found in political speeches, personal opinion columns in magazines and newspapers and Internet sites, sports articles, biographies and autobiographies, and history texts.

Show students how words and details can be selected so as to shape readers' opinions. Discuss why it is important to recognize slanted writing. Assign selections, some of which are slanted and some of which are neutral, and ask students to decide which are which. They should take note of techniques used to slant writing. Most important, they must be able to detect it as they are reading. To reinforce this skill, keep a file of examples of slanted writing, and, from time to time, share and discuss some of them with the class. Encourage students to bring in examples of slanted writing, and discuss these also. Have students look for examples of slanted writing in what they themselves write.

 Using Technology

Checklists for evaluating Web sources can be found in the following:
Kathy Schrock's *Guide for Educators: Critical Evaluation Information*
http://school.discoveryeducation.com/schrockguide/eval.html ■
Evaluating Internet Resources: A Checklist
http://www.infopeople.org/resources/select.html ■
How to Critically Analyze Information Sources
http://www.library.cornell.edu/okuref/research/skill26.htm ■

 STUDENT STRATEGIES
Judging Sources

 FYI

Visual appeal is the main element most adults use when evaluating the credibility of a Web site (Fogg, Soohoo, Danielson, Marable, Stanford, & Tauber, 2003). ■

Once students seem to grasp the concept of judging sources for fairness, help them develop a set of questions that they might use to assess printed sources and Web sites they consult:

Is the source up to date?
Who is the author?
Is the author unbiased? Is there any reason that the author would be in favor of one side or one position?
Is the writing fair, or does it seem to be slanted?
Does the author give enough proof for all conclusions?
Who is the publisher? Is it a well-known company, an educational institution, a company, or an individual?
Is the Web site an educational, governmental, organizational, or commercial site, or is it the site of an individual?

You might post the questions as a reminder for students to use them when they are reading. The questions might also be adapted and used in evaluating speeches and informational TV programs.

Summary

Through hearing stories, reading, and writing, children develop a schema for narrative tales. Generally, expository works are harder to read than narratives, but knowledge of text structures can foster improved comprehension. Questioning and an atmosphere conducive to open discussion also play a role in facilitating comprehension.

Guided reading is a highly useful framework for conducting reading lessons. The DR–TA (directed reading–thinking activity) gives students more responsibility for their learning. Cloze is valuable for building comprehension because it forces students to read for meaning, use context, and make predictions.

An affective as well as a cognitive skill, critical reading involves willingness to suspend judgment, consider another point of view, and think carefully about what one reads. Thoughtful reading and discussion promote critical thinking.

Extending and Applying

1. Plan a guided reading lesson for a chapter of a children's book, a short story, an informational piece, or an article from a Web site. Teach the lesson and evaluate its effectiveness.
2. Create and teach a cloze or modified cloze lesson. Evaluate its effectiveness.
3. Try out the FELS technique for asking questions in a class. Also use wait time and create an accepting atmosphere. Do this for a week. Have a colleague observe your performance and give you objective feedback.

4. Examine a lesson from a basal series that is no more than three or four years old. Examine the questions for three selections and classify them according to Weinstein and Mayer's taxonomy. What percentage of the questions are on a comprehending level? Organizing level? Elaborating level? Monitoring level?
5. Collect samples of biased writing from children's periodicals and textbooks.

Professional Reflection

Do I …

___ Have an understanding of narrative and expository text structures and the roles they play in comprehension?

___ Have an understanding of the role of questions in comprehension?

___ Have an understanding of frameworks and techniques, such as guided reading, DR-TA, and cloze?

___ Have an understanding of critical (evaluative) reading skills?

Am I able to …

___ Use questioning techniques to foster comprehension?

___ Plan and teach text structure, guided reading, DR-TA, and cloze lessons?

___ Teach a variety of critical reading (evaluative) reading skills?

Reflection Question

Of all the techniques discussed in this chapter, which one would be of most benefit to my students? How might I go about implementing this technique?

Building Competencies

To build competencies, consult the following sources for more detailed information:

Athans, S. K., & Devine, D. A. (2008). *Quality comprehension: A strategic model of reading instruction using read-along guides, grades 3–6*. Newark, DE: International Reading Association.

Guided Reading   wik.ed.uiuc.edu/index.php/Guided_Reading

National Reading Panel. (2000). *National Reading Panel report*, Chapter 4, Part II, "Text comprehension instruction," pp. 4-39–4-95. Washington, DC: U.S. Department of Education. http://www.nationalreadingpanel.org

(The report can be read online or downloaded, or a free copy may be ordered.)

Analyze two or more texts using the Coh-Metrix Easability Index. Note the information provided and how that information might be used to plan instruction.

MyEducationLab™

Go to the Topic "Comprehension" in the MyEducationLab (www.myeducationlab.com) for your course, where you can:

- Find learning outcomes for "Comprehension" along with the national standards that connect to these outcomes.
- Complete Assignments and Activities that can help you more deeply understand the chapter content.
- Apply and practice your understanding of the core teaching skills identified in the chapter with the Building Teaching Skills and Dispositions learning units.
- Examine challenging situations and cases presented in the IRIS Center Resources.
- Check your comprehension on the content covered in the chapter by going to the Study Plan in the Book

Resources for your text. Here you will be able to take a chapter quiz, receive feedback on your answers, and then access Review, Practice, and Enrichment activities to enhance your understanding of chapter content. (optional)

A+RISE A+RISE® Standards2Strategy™ is an innovative and interactive online resource that offers new teachers in grades K–12 just-in-time, research-based instructional strategies that meet the linguistic needs of ELLs as they learn content, differentiate instruction for all grades and abilities, and are aligned to Common Core Elementary Language Arts standards (for the literacy strategies) and to English language proficiency standards in WIDA, Texas, California, and Florida.

9

Reading and Writing in the Content Areas and Study Skills

Anticipation Guide

For each of the following statements related to the chapter you are about to read, put a check under "Agree" or "Disagree" to show how you feel. Discuss your responses with classmates before you read the chapter.

	Agree	Disagree
1. Content-area textbooks should be simplified.	_____	_____
2. The strategies that are most effective in promoting comprehension of content-area material are those that are used after students have read the text.	_____	_____
3. When teaching reading of content-area material, a teacher should stress content rather than strategies.	_____	_____
4. Content-area teachers should be responsible for teaching the reading skills students need to use their subjects' texts.	_____	_____
5. Content-area information should be presented to poor readers through discussions, experiments, and audiovisual aids rather than through texts that might be too difficult for them.	_____	_____
6. Most students learn effective study techniques without any formal instruction.	_____	_____

Using What You Know

Chapters 7 and 8 presented a variety of strategies for improving comprehension of narrative and expository text. This chapter focuses on applying those strategies to improve literacy in the content areas. Additional aids to comprehension are introduced, and some special difficulties inherent in reading in the content areas are explained. The chapter also explores study skills and techniques for remembering content-area information and other material. Before reading this chapter, reflect on your knowledge of reading in science, history, and other content areas. Do you use any special strategies to comprehend what you read in the content areas? If so, what are they? How well do they work for you? Do you have any problems reading in the content areas? Do you have any problems studying? How might you improve your comprehension and retention of the material? How might you help students improve their reading in the content areas? How might you help them improve their studying?

Importance of Content-Area Literacy

Most of the reading required in college and career is informational rather than literary. Moreover, science and social studies build background and vocabulary and provide students with invaluable opportunities to apply their reading skills and learn new ones. In fact, Common Core Stare Standards (2010) call for a greater emphasis on informational reading. The Common Core State Standards call for having students read literacy texts 50 percent of the time and expository text 50 percent of the time. This doesn't mean that students will read fewer stories or poems. It does mean that much of the informational reading must take place in the content areas. As Common Core notes,

"By reading texts in history/social studies, science, and other disciplines, students build a foundation of knowledge in these fields that will also give them the background to be better readers in all content areas" (p. 10).

The Challenge of Content-Area Literacy

Content-area text has a different, more complex structure. Instead of following a narrative, readers must understand complex processes and identify causes and effects as well as problems and solutions. Readers must also cope with greater density of ideas and more technical vocabulary and concepts for which they may have a very limited background. However, what really sets content-area reading apart from other reading is its purpose, which is to allow children to learn about a subject area and, ultimately, to be able to apply what is learned.

Instructional Techniques Building Conceptual Understanding

The first principle of content-area reading instruction is to help students build conceptual understanding. In their study of upper elementary school students reading a U.S. history text, researchers McKeown, Beck, and Sandora (1996) found that students took "one swift pass through the words on a page, and then formed them into a shallow representation of the text" (p. 101). They didn't seek out key ideas or relate what they were reading to what they already knew. Conceptual understanding means going beyond the facts or the events and building a deeper understanding. Simply answering factual end-of-chapter questions will promote only shallow understanding.

In an approach known as Understanding by Design, the focus is on essential questions and teaching for understanding (Wiggins & McTighe, 2006). Planning begins by specifying the essential questions that students will be answering and the big idea that they will be considering. In a study of the presidency, for instance, the essential question might be: "What qualities should a president have?" For a social studies unit, the question might be "What makes a community special?" Students are asked concrete questions such as "How do people in your community help each other?" that enable them to build on personal experiences. In their reading and discussions, they examine the influence of geography, history, and culture in a community. The teacher provides prompts as necessary and uses techniques, such as graphic organizers and opportunities to engage in genuine discussions, to organize and deepen thinking. As students gather information to answer the essential question, they make inferences, synthesize, and summarize. Most important of all, they generalize. Based on their reading, writing, viewing, and discussions, they formulate specific conclusions that can be synthesized into an overall generalization. For the presidential unit, they might go beyond answering the question: "What qualities should a good president have?" to "What qualities should a good leader have?" Students transfer their generalizations to real-life situations. Gaskins (2011) led her students to conclude that geography determines how a civilization develops. In subsequent studies of ancient civilizations, students were able to predict the people's way of life by examining their geography.

It is also important that students make connections. Concepts are stored in networks. Students can understand and retain new information better if they relate it to already existing schemata. For instance, if students have a well-developed schema for World War I, they are better able to understand how economic hardship and the humiliation of the Treaty of Versailles set the stage for Germany's aggression and the beginning of World War II. Instead of being isolated bits of knowledge, information about the two wars becomes a part of a larger web of knowledge about wars. Going beyond dates of battles and names of countries and leaders, looking at the big picture, including the underlying causes and effects of the war, will also foster a deeper understanding. Questions and activities that involve students in making comparisons, connecting bits of information, and drawing conclusions help students construct a conceptual understanding. For instance, students might compare World War II with recent wars and current conflicts and draw conclusions about wars in general.

Because the text is a key source of information in the content areas, being able to use effective reading and learning strategies will help students acquire the information that forms a base for building a conceptual understanding. Specific techniques for helping students get more out of their content-area reading are used before reading, during reading, and after reading.

Realizing that many of their students struggle with texts, some teachers instead use lectures, discussions, and other activities to present content. This deprives students of the opportunity to learn to read in the content areas.

Before Reading

In preparing to read a text, strategic readers survey the text, activate appropriate prior knowledge, predict what the text will be about, set goals, and decide how to read the material. To help the reader learn and apply these strategies independently, the teacher uses DR–TA, ReQuest, reciprocal teaching, or Questioning the Author, techniques that were introduced in Chapters 7 and 8. Another technique that can be used is the anticipation guide.

Anticipation Guides There is nothing like a good old-fashioned debate to perk up a class. Everyone, young and old, enjoys expressing opinions on controversial subjects. One device that capitalizes on this predilection is the **anticipation guide**—a listing of three or more debatable statements about a topic on which students indicate whether they agree with each statement before they read about the topic. (An adapted anticipation guide introduces each chapter in this book.)

Besides building interest, the anticipation guide activates prior knowledge. Readers have to activate information that they possess to decide whether they agree or disagree with each statement. Deeper processing is fostered if students justify a response by jotting down a sentence explaining why they agree or disagree or share their justification orally with a partner. The guide also gives students a purpose for reading: to evaluate their responses. In addition, it opens the students' minds. Some students, especially those who are younger or who are poor readers, tend to reject statements in print that contradict concepts they might have (Lipson, 1984; Maria & MacGinitie, 1987). By comparing their responses with what the author said and by listening to the class discussion of the statements, they can correct and clarify these ideas.

The anticipation guide can be used with any age group and works best when students have some familiarity with the subject. If they do not know anything about it, they do not have much to agree or disagree with. The guide is also most effective when used with subjects about which students have misconceptions—for example, diet, pollution, legal rights, snakes, and insects. Students can complete the guide individually, in pairs, or in small groups. If students are working in pairs or small groups, listening in on their discussions is a good way to get an overview of their background knowledge, including any misconceptions (Wood, Lapp, Flood, & Taylor, 2008).

The recommended steps for constructing and using an anticipation guide are described in Lesson 9.1 (Head & Readence, 1986).

 FYI

• Responding to pressure to do well on state proficiency tests in reading, many schools have abbreviated or eliminated content-area reading, especially in the lower grades. Ironically, in so doing, they are eliminating a potential solution to closing the gap. Content-area reading is an excellent means for building vocabulary, background, advanced comprehension strategies, and critical thinking.
• Realizing that many of their students struggle with texts, some teachers instead use lectures, discussions, and other activities to present content. This deprives students of the opportunity to learn to read in the content areas. ∎

 FYI

The anticipation guide should help students refine erroneous concepts because it involves confronting erroneous beliefs. ∎

∎ An **anticipation guide** is an instructional technique designed to activate and have students reflect on background knowledge.

LESSON 9.1
Using an Anticipation Guide

Step 1. Identification of major concepts and establishing objectives

List two to four major concepts that you wish students to learn and state objectives.

Step 2. Determination of students' background

Consider the experiential and cultural backgrounds of your students. Ask yourself how their backgrounds will affect their knowledge and beliefs about the topic under study. What misconceptions might they have?

Step 3. Creation of statements for the guide

Write three to five statements (or more) that are sufficiently open-ended or general to encourage a discussion. Do not choose simple, factual statements. Instead, think of those that might touch on students' misconceptions or involve areas in which students have partial knowledge. The statements can be arranged in the order in which the concepts they reflect appear in the selection or from simplest to most complex. They may be written on the chalkboard or on paper.

Step 4. Introduction of the guide

Introduce and explain the guide and have students respond to the statements. Emphasize that they should think about their responses because they will be asked to defend them. Students may work individually, in pairs, or in small groups. As an option, ask students to justify each response by jotting down a sentence explaining why they agree or disagree or by sharing their reason orally with a partner.

Step 5. Whole-class discussion of responses

Talk over each statement. You might begin by having students raise their hands if they agree with a statement. Ask volunteers to tell why they agreed or disagreed.

Step 6. Reading of the text

Sum up the main points of the discussion and have students read the text to compare their responses with what the material states. In some instances, the text may contain information that proves or disproves a statement. However, if the statements have been constructed carefully, they will be sufficiently open-ended that students will find information that may support a position but will not prove it one way or another.

Step 7. Discussion of text and statements and evaluation

Talk over each statement in light of the information in the text. Ask students whether they changed their responses because of information in the text. Ask what that information was and why it changed their minds. Responses can be discussed in small or large groups. If small groups are used, bring the whole class together for a summary after the groups have finished their discussions. Evaluate students' grasp of key understandings. You might want to go over at greater length any statements that seem especially controversial or confusing.

The anticipation guide can be extended. In an extended anticipation guide, students note next to each response whether they have found support for their responses. If the text contains information that runs counter to a response, they then write a summary statement of that information next to their response. This helps students to correct misconceptions.

During Reading

During reading, strategic readers construct meaning. They distinguish between important and unimportant details, organize information from the text, summarize sections, and generate questions. They also integrate information from the text with prior knowledge, make inferences, check predictions, seek clarification, and, perhaps, create images of scenes and events portrayed by the text. They use the structure of the text as an aid to comprehension. Strategic readers also regulate their rate of reading and monitor their understanding of the passage. They may reread or seek clarification if their comprehension breaks down. During-reading strategies include using chapter organization and text structure, think-alouds, and strategy guides.

Textual Features That Foster Learning

A number of features promote learning from a textbook. These include chapter overviews, summaries, questions, clear explanations, use of cohesive ties, and use of typographical aids. Figure 9.10 displays a page that uses a number of typographical aids. Although typographical aids are often used to preview a chapter, they should also be used as the reader interacts with the text. Personal observation and experience suggest that they are given only limited attention, however. Perhaps students do not realize their full value. With the help of a textbook that makes especially good use of these elements, explain the purpose and value of each one. Then model how you might use them to aid your understanding of the content.

Think-Alouds

Think-alouds are just what their name suggests. The teacher models a silent reading strategy by thinking aloud as she or he processes a text, thus making explicit skills that normally cannot be observed. Originally a research technique for studying reading processes, think-alouds are used to model comprehension processes, such as making predictions, creating images, linking information in text with prior knowledge, monitoring comprehension, and using a repair strategy when there is a problem with word recognition or comprehension. In addition to being a demonstration technique, think-alouds can be used by students to become more aware of their reading processes and to make needed changes in the way they read.

Lesson 9.2 illustrates how the technique is put into operation to help students understand content-area materials.

LESSON 9.2
Think-Alouds

Step 1. Establishing objectives

Objectives are stated in terms of what students should know and be able to do.

Step 2. Explanation and Modeling

The teacher explains what think-alouds are and how they will help students to become better readers by becoming more aware of the ways in which they read so they can then take steps to read more effectively The teacher reads a brief passage aloud, showing what her or his thoughts are when the text does not make sense and what repair strategies she or he might implement:

> Like a camera, the picture of the outside world which lands on the retina is upside down. The brain turns it the right way up as it interprets the messages from the retina. (Baldwin & Lister, 1984, p. 9)

Then the teacher thinks aloud, "I don't get this. I don't know where the retina is. I'll take a look at the diagram. There it is; it's the lining at the back of the eyeball, and there's the optic nerve. The optic nerve goes from the retina to the brain. Now I understand."

Step 3. Working with partners

Students take turns reading brief passages orally to each other. The selections should be fairly difficult or contain problems. The reader thinks aloud to show what processes he or she is using, what problems he or she is encountering, and how he or she is attempting to solve those problems. The partner is encouraged to ask questions: "Are you trying to picture the main character as you read? Do you see any words you don't know?"

Step 4. Practicing

Students practice thinking through materials as they read them silently. Self-questionnaires or checklists are used to encourage readers to use active processes and to monitor their reading. A sample self-questionnaire, to which students may respond orally or in writing, is shown in Figure 9.1.

As an alternative to a self-questionnaire, you might use a checklist such as the one in Figure 9.2 It assesses use of before-, during-, and after-reading strategies. When using a checklist, include only strategies that have been introduced. Also, model the use of the self-questionnaire or checklist before using it. An even simpler device is to have students place a sticky note next to passages that pose problems. Problem passages can be discussed later.

Step 5. Applying think–alouds

Students apply the strategy to everyday and content-area material. During post-reading discussions, the teacher asks students to tell about their comprehension processes: "What pictures did you create in your mind as you read? Were there any confusing passages? How did you handle them?" Discussing strategies helps the student to clarify his or her use of strategies. It also helps the members of the class learn how others process text.

Step 6: Evaluating and reviewing

Note whether students are able to use the strategy effectively and whether they find it to be a useful strategy. Provide follow-up lessons and demonstrations.

FYI

See Wood, Lapp, Flood, and Taylor (2008) for a variety of strategy guides. ■

FIGURE 9.1   Think-Aloud Self-Questionnaire

A. Before reading
   1. How do I prepare for reading?
B. During reading
   1. What do I do to improve my understanding of what I am reading?
   2. What do I do if I come across a word I don't know?
   3. What do I do if the selection doesn't make sense?
C. After reading
   1. Do I do anything special with the information I just read? If so, what?

Strategy Guides   Strategy guides, which evolved from study guides, are flexible devices that help students comprehend and organize information during as well as after reading, listening, or viewing. Their purpose is to help students become independent, strategic learners (Wood et al., 2008).

The procedure for creating a strategy guide is outlined below:

1. Analyze the selection to be read, listened to, or viewed. Note the major concepts that you think students should learn. Make a note of the sections that students must comprehend to grasp the concepts. Some sections may cover concepts you do not consider important. For printed text, indicate those pages so that students can skip them.
2. Consider elements of the text that might pose problems for students, such as difficult vocabulary, figurative language, confusing explanations, or complex organization. Think about the kinds of difficulties that students are having. The strategy guide should provide assistance with these difficulties.

Put a check next to the things you did before, during, and after you read.

Before Reading	During Reading	After Reading
Surveyed title, headings, illustrations _____	Predicted what might happen next _____	Summarized what I had read _____
Thought about what I know about the topic _____	Inferred ideas not stated _____	Thought about what I had read _____
Predicted what the text might be about or what might happen _____	Got main idea of section _____	Connected what I had read to what I already knew _____
Made up a question to answer _____	Got important details _____	Applied what I had learned in the selection _____
Other (describe) _____ _____	Summarized each section _____	Other (describe) _____ _____
	Created images about parts of the selection _____	
	Thought about what I had read _____	
	Judged whether information was true or the story seemed real _____	
	Made up questions to be answered _____	
	Checked to make sure I was understanding what I read _____	
	Repaired by rereading puzzling parts, getting meaning of hard words, etc. _____	
	Other (describe) _____ _____	

FIGURE 9.2   Think-Aloud Checklist

3. Assess the organizational pattern of the text, such as enumeration–description, time sequence, explanation–process, or other pattern (see Chapter 8 for a description of organizational patterns). Keep in mind that more than one pattern may be used.
4. Note strategies or skills that students might use to get the most out of their reading, listening, or viewing.
5. Construct a strategy guide that leads students to focus on critical content, aids them in overcoming potential hindrances to comprehension, and directs them in the use of appropriate strategies and skills. Strategy guides can take several forms.

Pattern Guides   Detecting the pattern of writing in a piece fosters both understanding and retention (Herber, 1970). For example, if readers realize that the author is using a comparison pattern to discuss U.S. Presidents Harry Truman and Franklin D. Roosevelt, they can mentally sort the information into the proper categories. If readers know that a piece is organized with a main idea and supporting details, they can mentally file the details under the main idea.

A pattern guide can be a partially completed outline in which just the main ideas are included. Or it may ask students to identify causes and effects or to compare and contrast (Estes & Vaughn, 1985). The sample pattern guide in Figure 9.3 not only helps students obtain essential information from the selection, it also assists them in organizing that information so that they can note the main ideas and see how the details relate to them.

Glosses   A gloss is a special type of comprehension aid in which technical items or difficult concepts are explained in marginal notes. An easy way of creating a gloss is to photocopy one or more pages and write explanatory notes in the margins and distribute copies to students. Or line up a sheet of paper next to the text and write your gloss notes next to the target text. Make copies and distribute to students. The gloss may define a hard word, explain a key idea, paraphrase a difficult passage, tap prior knowledge, or emphasize a key point (Gunning, 2002). Glosses can also include various kinds

FYI

Identifying similarities and differences results in an average percentile gain of 20 points (Haystead & Marzano, 2009). ■

Using Technology

With some kinds of digital texts, the teacher can insert explanations, suggestions, and learning aids or even rewrite portions of the text to make it more understandable. ■

FIGURE 9.3   A Pattern
Guide for a Selection on Plants
as Food Makers

All living creatures must have food to stay alive, even plants. Plants make food for
themselves, for animals, and for us. Read "Food Makers," pp. 330–335. Find out
where plants store their food, what kinds of food-producing plants there are, and
what forms of food plants make. After reading the section, complete the outline by
listing supporting details under main ideas.

A. Where food is stored in plants
   1. Roots—carrots
   2.
   3.
B. Types of food producers in a water community
   1. Plants with roots—cattails
   2.
   3.
   4.
C. Types of food producers in a forest community
   1. Ground layer—mosses
   2.
   3.
D. Forms of food made by plants
   1. Starch—beans
   2.

Source: Text drawn from *Merrill Science 5* (pp. 98–99), by J. K. Hackett, R. H. Moyer, and D. K. Adams, 1989, Columbus, OH: Merrill.

of questions: those that help students relate new information to old, those that help
students use a key comprehension strategy, or those that help students set a purpose
for reading (Richgels & Hansen, 1984).

Glosses can be particularly helpful for struggling readers or ELLs. If a text is too
difficult, glosses may summarize key information in simpler language and direct the
students to illustrations, charts, maps, and other graphic aids, which are easier to
read. As you write glosses, think of terms or concepts that may pose problems for
your students. Provide explanations or guidance that will help students cope with
these items.

WIRC (Writing Intensive Reading Comprehension) Thinksheets   Typically,
students write after they read. As an after-reading activity, writing becomes a way of
responding to and extending reading. In the typical reading guide, students read the
text and then respond to the items on the guide. They do not refer to the text as
they fill in the guide. However, writing can also be a during-reading tool for fostering comprehension. WIRC thinksheets guide students through brief segments of text
with specific questions to be answered (Collins & Madigan, 2010). Thinksheets are
designed to be used as students are reading. This leads to "two-handed" reading. The
thinksheets are laid out in such a way that the text and questions are aligned as in
Figure 9.4. Students read with one hand and take notes or answer questions with the
other. Struggling readers who might have difficulty responding to questions that they
attempt to answer after reading a whole piece have improved comprehension when
they use thinksheets and respond to brief segments of text.

Students read and write in segments that last about five to ten minutes. Their
response are then discussed in pairs, small groups, or whole class. The brief writing
reading and writing periods allow students to focus their attention without being
overwhelmed. Although breaking down tasks into more manageable segments

Wind Chill

What is wind chill?

_____

_____

What does wind chill do?

_____

_____

_____

During the winter, you often hear the term "wind chill." Wind chill is a combination of air temperature and wind speed. Wind combined with air temperature makes your body feel even colder than the actual temperature. The wind removes the warm air that surrounds the body and replaces it with cold air. You experience that feeling when you get out of the pool or ocean in the summer.

Why is wind chill dangerous?

_____

_____

When is a wind chill advisory issued?

_____

_____

In winter, wind chill can be dangerous. Exposed skin will freeze faster when there is a wind chill. A wind chill advisory is issued when there is wind speed of 10 miles and the wind chill is –15 or lower. A wind chill warning is issued when the wind speed is 10 miles an hour or faster and the wind chill temperature is –25 or lower.

When is a wind chill warning issued?

_____

_____

_____

What is the 30-30-30 rule?

_____

_____

In the Antarctic, there is a 30-30-30 rule. When the temperature is 30 below, and the wind is 30 miles per hour, a person can live only 30 minutes outside.

Source: Text adapted from NOAA (2011). Owlie Skywarn Brochure. Available online at http://www.nws.noaa.gov/om/brochures/OwlieSkywarnBrochure.pdf.

FIGURE 9.4   Sample Adapted WIRC Thinksheet

helped struggling readers, they then had difficulty integrating the segments. A graphic organizer such as a semantic map or frame was added to the thinksheets to help students integrate their responses. In a final step, students put all the information together and composed an extended response (Collins & Madigan, 2010). As students grow in proficiency, segments of reading and writing can be lengthened and the complexity of questions and text can be increased.

Other Types of Strategy Guides   The questions or activities on strategy guides can take a variety of forms: Students may be asked to match items; to indicate whether statements are true or false; to fill in blanks; to complete a time line, an anticipation guide, a semantic map, a structured overview, or a comparison–contrast chart; to list the steps of a process; or to take part in a reciprocal teaching lesson.

After Reading

After completing reading, strategic readers reflect on what they have read, continue to integrate new information with old information, may evaluate the new information or use it in some way, and may seek additional information on the topic. To help students learn to use after-reading strategies, the teacher can apply several instructional procedures in addition to summarizing, retelling, and other postreading strategies covered in previous chapters. These additional procedures include creating graphic organizers and applying and extending.

R E F L E C T I O N

Which of the during-reading techniques might you use in your teaching? What adaptations might you make so that they fit the demands of your content area and the needs of your students?

 FYI

Trade books and periodicals can expand students' knowledge and their ability to think deeply about key concepts and events. It is important that students see connections and grasp the big picture—and not just learn isolated facts. ■

 Using Technology

Kids News Central
   Provides links to news articles for young people.

http://www.kidsturncentral.com/links/newslinks.htm ■

FYI

Hyerle's key graphic organizers provide a means of teaching higher-level thinking. Each of the eight types of organizers is based on a cognitive skill, such as comparing and contrasting, sequencing, classifying, or cause-effect reasoning. Along with learning how to construct graphic organizers, students should learn when, where, and why to use a particular organizer. ■

FYI

Using graphic organizers results in an average percentile gain of 13 points (Haystead & Marzano, 2009). ■

Using Technology

Designs for Thinking presents more information on Thinking Maps®. http://www.mapthemind.com ■

Creating Graphic Organizers   One of the most effective ways to understand and retain complex content-area information is to use some sort of **graphic organizer** to represent key concepts, main points, or basic steps. In addition to highlighting essential information, graphic organizers show how ideas are interrelated. The content and structure of material and the teaching–learning purpose dictate the type of organizer used: tree diagram, time line, or an organizer that highlights the steps in a process, contrasts elements, or identifies causes. Hyerle (2001) recommends that schools adopt a common set of graphic organizers. He matched each of eight kinds of thinking with a graphic organizer that fosters that specific kind of cognitive processing (see Table 9.1). The key graphic organizers are an adaptation of Hyerle's Thinking Maps®. Whatever form it takes, the visual display should focus on the most essential information and do so vividly. Key concepts should "jump out at the students as soon as their eyes meet the page" (Robinson, 1998, p. 100).

The structured overview (or tree diagram) is one of the most useful graphic organizers because it uses key vocabulary words to show subordinate relationships. Figure 9.5 shows a structured overview for the concept of galaxies. The structured overview can be used for preparing students to read. It can also be created or added to as an after-reading activity. It then enhances understanding and retention of important concepts, especially if students play an active role in creating it. After the selection has been read, the overview's elements are discussed again. Information obtained from reading might be placed on lines beneath each element. For example, a brief definition of the word *galaxy* might be given, together with descriptions of irregular, spiral, and elliptical galaxies. If given their own copies of the overview, students can add information about the elements as they read. They can also use drawings to illustrate concepts, such as irregular, spiral, and elliptical galaxies.

Another kind of graphic organizer that can be used as a postreading aid was presented in Chapter 8—this kind of organizer reflects the actual structure of the text (enumeration–description, time sequence, explanation–process, comparison–contrast, problem–solution,

TABLE 9.1   Key Graphic Organizers

Organizer	Thinking Skill	Example
Descriptive map (web)	Locate and assemble main idea and details.	
Classification map (semantic map)	Categorize and classify.	
Sequence map	Arrange in chronological order.	

(*continued*)

■ **Graphic organizers** are visual devices designed to help the reader note relationships between key concepts, main points, basic steps, or major events in a selection.

TABLE 9.1 Key Graphic Organizers *(Continued)*

Organizer	Thinking Skill	Example
Process map (chain or flow map)	Arrange in step-by-step fashion.	
Cyclical map	Arrange in circular fashion to show a process.	
Structured overview (tree diagram)	Categorize and classify in hierarchical fashion.	
Frame matrix (or Venn diagram)	Compare and contrast.	
Cause-effect map	Locate or infer causes and/or effects.	

or cause–effect). Building as it does on structure, this kind of organizer enhances understanding of the interrelationships of the ideas covered in the text or the process being explained. For instance, an explanation–process organizer can be used to show how an engine operates, how solar cells turn sunlight into energy, how the water cycle operates, or

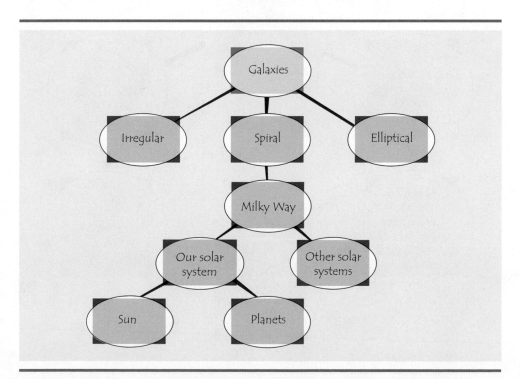

FIGURE 9.5 A Structured Overview (Tree Diagram) on Galaxies

Source: Based on text from *Fearon's United States Geography*, by W. Lefkowitz, 1990, Belmont, CA: Fearon Education.

FYI

Graphic organizers may also lead to dual encoding. They may be encoded and stored in memory verbally and visually. This dual encoding would make the information easier to recall (Robinson, 1998). ■

FYI

In order to construct graphic organizers, "students have to engage in powerful information processing and higher order thinking skills such as using cues to recognize important information, making decisions about what is important or essential, consolidating information and identifying main ideas and supporting details, [and] making decisions about the best way to structure the information" (Ellis, 2004). ■

how numerous other systems work (see Figure 9.6). Boxes or circles containing explanatory text show the steps in the process, with arrows indicating the flow of the process.

For some elements, the best graphic organizer is a diagram. For example, a diagram is the best way to show the parts of the eye (see Figure 9.7). Initially, a diagram can be drawn or traced by the teacher. However, having students create their own diagrams makes reading an active process.

For reading material that has a chronological organization, a time chart is a useful way to highlight major events (see Figure 9.8 for an example). A time line or sequence map serves the same function and may be used instead of a time chart. Often, two or more kinds of graphic organizers can be combined. For instance, a map showing the voyages of the French explorers might be used together with the time chart in Figure 9.8.

Applying and Extending   A particularly effective way of deepening comprehension is to reflect on one's own reading, which often results in a sense of not knowing enough or wanting to know more. Encourage students to use and extend what they know by expanding their knowledge. They can do this by reading books that explore a particular topic in detail or that provide enjoyment while increasing knowledge—for example, a book of math puzzles, one on bird watching, or a piece of historical fiction.

KWL: A Technique for Before, During, and After Reading

A technique designed to give students an active role before, during, and after reading is **KWL**: Know, Want to Know, and Learn (Ogle, 1989). The before-reading stage of KWL consists of four steps: brainstorming, categorizing, anticipating or predicting,

FIGURE 9.6 An Explanation–Process Organizer (Cyclical Map)

Using Technology

Everyday Mysteries: Fun Science Facts from the Library of Congress answers intriguing questions, such as "What is GPS? How does it work? Why is it hot in summer and cold in winter? Why and how do cats purr?" Let students decide which questions they wish to read about.
http://www.loc.gov/rr/scitech/mysteries/archive.html ■

FYI

Funded by the National Science Foundation and having inquiry-based science activities as its core, Seeds • Roots is designed to build literacy and science knowledge and skills for students in grades 2 through 5. It fosters both scientific inquiry and comprehension. ■

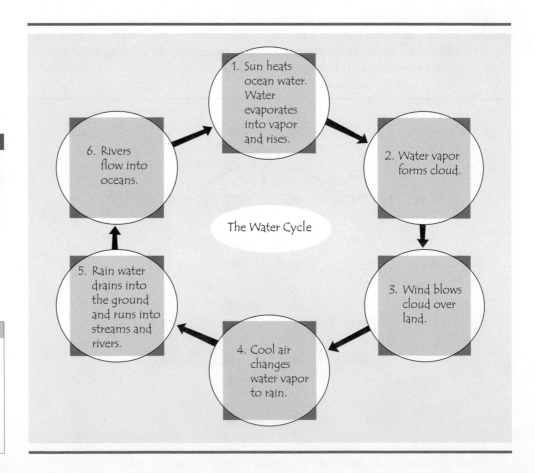

and questioning. Brainstorming begins when the teacher asks the class what they know about a topic. If they are about to read a selection about army ants, for example, the teacher asks what they know about these insects. Responses are written on the board and discussed. If a disagreement occurs or students seem puzzled by a statement, this cognitive conflict can be used to create a what-we-want-to-find-out question. Brainstorming activates prior knowledge so that students become more aware of what they know. The students then write about their personal knowledge of army ants in the first column of a KWL worksheet.

Next, in a step similar to semantic mapping, students categorize their prior knowledge. The process of categorization is modeled. Brainstormed items already written on the board are placed in appropriate categories. Students then label the items in the "What we know" column with letters that indicate category names, as shown in Figure 9.9 H = habitat, C = characteristics, and F = food. Students also anticipate what categories of information the author will provide. This helps them both anticipate the content of the text and organize the information as they read it. The process of anticipating categories is modeled. The teacher might ask, for example, what kinds of information an author might provide about army ants. Students then write these categories at the bottom of the KWL worksheet.

In the third step, questions are created. As a group, the class discusses what they want to know about army ants. Questions are written on the chalkboard. Each student then records in the second column of the worksheet her or his own questions.

With these questions in mind, the class reads the text. After reading, students discuss what they learned and the teacher writes their responses on the chalkboard. Information is organized, misconceptions are clarified, and emerging concepts are developed more fully. After the discussion, students enter what they learned on their own in the third column. In light of this information, they cross out any misconceptions they wrote in the first column. They may find that they still have questions about the topic, so a fourth column—with the heading "What we still want to know"—can be added to the worksheet. The teacher can discuss with the students how they might go about finding the answers to the questions they still have. A completed KWL worksheet is presented in Figure 9.9. Ogle (1989) presents a fuller description of KWL, including a sample lesson.

Using Content-Area Textbooks

Content-area textbooks account for an estimated 75 to 90 percent of the material presented in subject-matter classes. Fortunately, the best of today's content-area texts provide a wealth of support for the reading and writing skills needed to comprehend and remember key concepts and foster many of the strategies discussed in this and previous chapters. They build background and vocabulary and provide previews, overviews, lots of helpful graphics, review questions, and activities. In one social studies program, students are taught a

FIGURE 9.7   Diagram of the Eye

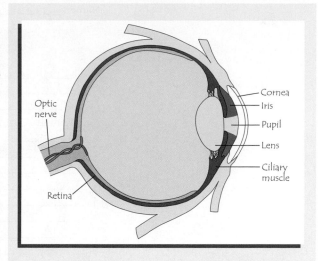

REFLECTION

Which of the after-reading techniques might you use in your teaching? What adaptations might you make so that they fit the demands of your content area and the needs of your students?

FIGURE 9.8   A Time Chart

1524—Verrazano explored the eastern coast of North America.

1535—Jacques Cartier sailed up the Saint Lawrence River and claimed that area for France.

1608—Samuel de Champlain founded Quebec, the first permanent French colony in the Americas.

1673—Father Marquette and Louis Joliet set out on a journey that took them to the Mississippi River.

1682—Robert de La Salle reached the Gulf of Mexico after canoeing down the Mississippi River. He claimed the area for France.

■ **KWL** (Know, Want to Know, and Learn) is a technique designed to help readers build and organize background and seek out and reflect on key elements in a reading selection.

FIGURE 9.9 A KWL
Worksheet

Name: _____ Topic: _Army ants_ Date: _____

What we know	What we want to find out	What we learned	What we still want to know
H Live in the jungle	How large a	Tens of thousands	Do army ants
C Are fierce	group do army	form a group.	harm people?
H Live in the	ants form?	The queen lays	What are larvae
ground	Why are there so	100,000 to	and pupae?
F Eat plants	many army ants	300,000 eggs	
C Work together	in a group?	at a time.	
F Eat insects	Why do the ants	Form armies to	
	form armies?	get food for	
	What do army	larvae and pupae.	
	ants eat?	Kill other insects	
		and small	
		animals and take	
		them back to	
		their home	
		Live in the ground	
		or in trees in the	
		jungles of South	
		America	

Categories of information we expect to see

Habitat
Food
Characteristics
Society
Travel
Appearance

Source: From Scott Foresman Social Studies, *The United States,* by Caol Berkin, et al. © 2011 by Pearson Education, Inc. Used by permission.

FYI

• The categorizing and anticipating steps in KWL are frequently skipped and can be considered optional.
• KWL is excellent preparation for writing a report. Each category of information can be written up as a separate paragraph. ■

FYI

Primary-grade teachers might use KWL strictly as a group technique until students have sufficient writing ability to fill out the worksheet individually. However, teachers have found that just discussing what we know, what we want to find out, and what we have learned is helpful. The ultimate purpose is to lead students to ask these questions automatically as they read. ■

FYI

• Texts should be on the appropriate level of difficulty. There should be a match between students' reading levels and the texts they are required to read.
• The teacher should decide on objectives and topics to be covered and then select the materials. The textbook should be supplemented with informational children's books, periodicals, primary sources, audiovisual aids, computer software, and information from the Internet. ■

target reading strategy that will assist them as they read the chapter (Berkin et al., 2011). In a chapter on the American Revolutionary War, students are taught to recognize cause-and-effect structure and to make use of this structure to comprehend the text (see Figure 9.10).

After being taught the skill, they are provided guided practice by reading an article on causes leading up to the Revolutionary War and answer cause-effect question such as "What caused the British to tax the colonies? What effect did the Americans' reaction to the Stamp Act have?" (Berkin et al., 2011, p. 265). They then apply the skill throughout the chapter. Questions build on the skill and lead students to apply it. For instance, students are asked questions like these: "What effect did the Sons of Liberty have on the Stamp Act? What caused British leaders to pass the Townshend Acts?" Graphic organizers also reinforce skills as students fill in missing causes on a cause–effect organizer.

Writing is used to foster learning. Students are asked to imagine being a member of the Virginia House of Burgesses and write a speech opposing or supporting the Stamp Act. Assessment is also tied to instruction. For instance, if students are

FIGURE 9.10   Reading Aids
in a Content-Area Textbook

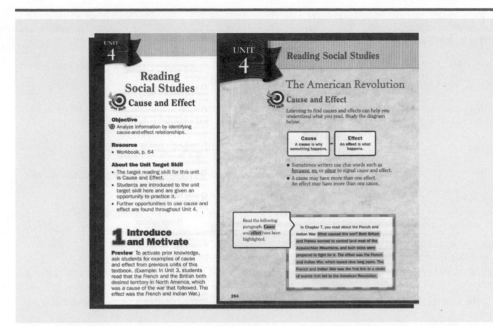

Source: From Scott Foresman Social Studies, *The United States,* by Caol Berkin, et al. © 2011 by Pearson Education, Inc. Used by permission.

unable to tell how the Townshend Acts were similar to but different from the Stamp Act, it is suggested that the teacher guide students as they create a graphic organizer designed to show differences and similarities. The text also contained a glossary, atlas, gazetteer, biographical dictionary, copies of historical documents, and facts about states and presidents. Maps, time lines, photos, and primary sources are also featured.

The best content-area texts are so carefully designed that they are potentially more effective for building literacy skills than many of the literacy programs designed specifically to develop such skills. This doesn't mean that the history teacher has become a teacher of reading and writing. It means that the teacher is helping students acquire skills needed to learn history. Through acquiring effective learning strategies, students learn more content.

Textual Features That Foster Use of Learning Strategies

From a reading standpoint, a number of features promote learning from a textbook. As noted in Chapter 7, the five major types of strategies (excluding rehearsal) are preparing to read; selecting and organizing relevant information; elaborating on the information once it has been selected, which means integrating the new information with existing knowledge structures or schemata; monitoring for meaning; and implementing affective or motivational strategies. Table 9.2 presents textual features that foster these processes.

Differentiating Instruction

In many classrooms, the entire class reads the same textbook, generally one designed for the average student. In the average class, however, such a book will be too difficult for at least one child out of four. On the other hand, advanced readers will be able to use a more challenging book. Some provision has to be made for these varying reading abilities, especially for students reading significantly below the level of the textbook. Possibilities are providing extra help with the text, obtaining an audio or digital

Adapting Instruction for Struggling Readers and Writers

• The typical sequence for reading content-area texts is read-listen-discuss. Students read a chapter, perhaps for homework, which the teacher then explains. After the explanation, the class discusses the text. A more effective sequence might be listen-read-discuss, in which the teacher gives a 5- to 15-minute explanation of the material, directs the students to read it, and then has the class discuss it. Because the explanation precedes the reading of the text, the students are better prepared to read it. ■

Adapting Instruction for Struggling Readers and Writers

For students who have severe reading difficulties, obtain recorded versions of their texts and review ways of studying information from an oral source. Recordings for the Blind and Dyslexic (20 Roszel Road, Princeton, NJ 08540) provides taped versions of school textbooks for students with reading problems. Recorded periodicals and children's books are available from Talking Books, National Library Service for the Blind and Physically Handicapped (includes dyslexia), Library of Congress, Washington, DC. ■

Adapting Instruction for Struggling Readers and Writers

In some content-area programs, the core text is accompanied by below-level, on-level, and advanced readers, all of which cover the same content or topic. These leveled readers are accompanied by a teacher's guide that contains graphic organizers. ■

TABLE 9.2 Textual Features That Foster Use of Learning Strategies

Benefit	Examples
Help students prepare.	Chapter overview that lets students activate schemata Semantic maps or other graphic organizers Headings and illustrations that allow students to make predictions Key terms and explanations Glossary
Help students select relevant information and organize it.	Introduction and summaries to highlight important information Headings and subheadings highlighting main ideas Details that clearly support main ideas Topics developed in sufficient detail but not so much as to overwhelm readers Clear, well-written text with connectives and transitions where needed Graphic aids Questions and activities at the end of each chapter Explanations to relate new knowledge to readers' background
Help students elaborate or integrate important information.	Questions or activities that help readers relate what they have read to their prior knowledge or experience
Help students monitor reading.	Questions at the end of each chapter or interspersed throughout chapters that ask students to check their understanding
Foster students' motivation.	Illustrations and other graphic devices that give the text an appealing look Interesting style that engages the reader; use of anecdotes Relationships drawn between content and students' lives

Source: Adapted from *Textual Features That Aid Learning from Text,* unpublished manuscript by B. Armbruster, 1987. Champaign, IL: Center for the Study of Reading.

text-to-speech version of the text, reading the text to students and then cooperatively composing a summary of key points, using trade books on an easier reading level (content-area teacher's manuals generally contain lists of recommended trade books on various levels), using easier texts, or some combination of these techniques. Among publishers that issue easy-to-read content-area texts are Pearson AGS, Pearson Globe, Pearson Pacemaker, and Steck Vaughn. Whichever approach you choose, make sure that students do some content-area reading. Otherwise, they will never acquire needed skills.

Using Trade Books

In addition to or instead of using content-area textbooks with poor readers, you might use easy-to-read trade books about the topic being studied. For instance, when

Content-area texts have a more complex structure.

studying the Civil War or Abraham Lincoln, students might read *Just a Few Words, Mr. Lincoln* (Fritz, 1993), which is written on a third-grade level but appeals to older students. When studying ancient Egypt, students might read *Tut's Mummy Lost . . . And Found* (Donnelly, 1988), which is also written on a third-grade level but is of high interest. Additional excellent sources of brief, heavily illustrated, easy-to-read trade books are the Harper's Trophy series and Random House's Step into Reading series, which feature a variety of lively, easy-to-read books on dinosaurs, whales, dolphins, sharks, and historical figures. Other easy-to-read informational books include the following:

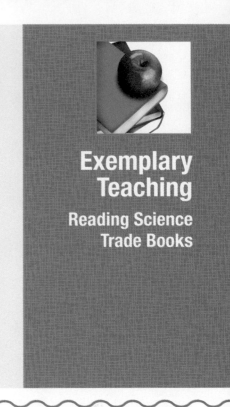

Exemplary Teaching
Reading Science Trade Books

With help from the community, Veronica, a third-grade teacher, was able to obtain more than 600 books for her classroom, 200 of which were science books (Brassell, 2006). At first, few students chose to read the science books, but interest increased dramatically after Veronica started reading the books aloud. As one student observed, "I like it when [Veronica] reads about science stuff. I like to take the books home and show my brother" (p. 339). Veronica read three times a day but chose a book on a different level each time. In that way, she was able to highlight books for underachieving, average, and above-average readers.

She used students' interests to help her decide which books to read. When one student asked how things were invented, she read excerpts from *First to Fly: How Wilbur & Orville Wright Invented the Airplane* (Busby, 2003), *Accidents May Happen* (Foltz Jones, 1998), and *Brainstorm: The Stories of Twenty American Kid Inventors* (Tucker, 1998). Inspired by what they had heard, the students started creating their own inventions. Later in the year, reading about ecology led to a number of save-the-earth projects.

Reading nonfiction fostered the development of vocabulary. Understanding nonfiction tends to require learning more new words (Pellegrini, Perlmutter, Galda, & Brody, 1990). Read-alouds also stimulated more discussion. As Veronica explained, "Luis was a shy kid who didn't speak much English and never showed much interest in class before. Now he constantly raises his hand during read-aloud time to ask questions and share personal experiences. . . . His turnaround has been extraordinary" (Brassell, 2006, p. 341). The read-alouds and focus on science led to a dramatic increase in voluntary reading, so much so that Veronica scheduled a 30-minute period of self-selected reading at the end of each day.

- Scholastic Rookie Biographies. New York: Scholastic. Written on a second-grade level.
- On My Own Biography Biographies. Minneapolis, MN: Carolrhoda. Written on a second- to third-grade level.
- Hameray Biography Series. San Diego, CA: Hameray. Thirty titles featuring a variety of historical and contemporary figures. Written on a third- to fifth-grade level.
- *Rookie Read-About Science.* Chicago: Children's Press. Easy readers that cover a wide range of topics, including seasons, weather, the five senses, mammals, and plants. Written on a second- and third-grade level.
- Seymour Simon See More Books. San Francisco, CA: Chronicle Books. Written on a third- and fourth-grade level.

CCSS

Analyze how two or more texts address similar themes or topics in order to build knowledge or to compare the approaches the authors take.

Trade books aren't just for struggling readers. A multitude of trade books are written for achieving readers, too. Trade books fully develop topics that are barely mentioned in today's overcrowded social studies and science texts. They can make difficult concepts clear and bring to life important discoveries and events. They might also offer a different perspective. Students might compare textbook coverage of a topic with that provided by a trade book. They can also be motivational—they can make students want to learn more about a topic. From a pragmatic point of view, there is probably no better way to build students' background knowledge and vocabulary than by having them read informational trade books. To locate titles of suitable books on a variety of topics and levels, use BookLink software, or visit the Web site of Renaissance Learning, MetaMetrics (Lexile Framework), Scholastic's Book Wizard, or Titlewave. Books can be searched by title, author, subject, maturity level, or readability level. Google Books lists millions of books (go to http://books.google.com/), where they can be purchased and their prices, or where they can be borrowed from libraries. If the book is in the public domain or permission has been granted, a pdf version can be downloaded. Many of the books can be previewed. However, no reviews or readability levels are provided.

Using E-books and Online Texts

Because they are in a digital format, e-books and online texts have a number of advantages. First, most can be read by a screen reader or a talking word-processing program. This makes them accessible to struggling readers. Second, to make them even more accessible, e-books can be linked to a dictionary so that students can readily get help with difficult words. A third advantage is that some texts can be added to or altered. You might add explanatory notes or illustrations or even rewrite difficult portions. E-books are readily available on the Internet from a number of sources, including Project Gutenberg (http://www.promo.net/pg) and the University of Virginia (http://etext.virginia.edu/subjects/Young-Readers.html), which has a Young Readers collection of public domain texts. The Awesome Talking Library has links to a number of e-book sites. CAST UDL Book Builder, which is an easy-to-use program for creating an e-book, offers a variety of e-books. CAST's Book Builder features a number of devices, including tools for creating a glossary and linking the definitions to the text, virtual coaches that provide prompts or explanations as students are reading the text, a library of illustrations, ability to add spoken commentary or even read the selection, and a library of illustrations and clips. Bookshare™ (http://bookshare.org/) is an online library of digital books for people with print disabilities. Bookshare offers free memberships to U.S. schools and qualifying U.S. students. Lerner, Rosen, Pearson, and other publishers also offer extensive listings of e-books.

Using e-Readers

CCSS

Integrate and evaluate content presented graphically, visually, orally, and multimodally as well as in words within and across print and digital sources.

One of the advantages of Kindle, Nook, iPad, and other e-readers is that they offer instant access to hundreds of thousands of books. Generally, e-books are cheaper than their paper versions. In addition, e-readers offer access to thousands of books that are out of copyright and can be downloaded at no charge. E-books also have the advantage of portability. In some schools, students' texts are loaded into e-readers so students don't have to carry four or five heavy textbooks home each night.

Using a Language-Experience Approach to Provide Accessible Text

If textbooks or trade books are simply too difficult for students, you might try a language-experience approach. In a language-experience approach, students, with your help, create their own texts. First, students have an experience. This might be conducting a science experiment, going on a field trip, engaging in a simulation, listening to a lecture, viewing a video, or summarizing a selection that was read to them. The experience is discussed. The students then decide how they are going to organize the experience and, with the help of teacher prompts, dictate an account of it. Acting as a scribe, you record their dictation. Summaries may be dictated by individuals, by small groups, or by the whole class. Dictated summaries become the students' texts. It provides them with text to read and study. After studying machines, for example, the teacher can discuss the main ideas and have the class dictate an experience text that highlights the ideas. Duplicated copies of the text can be distributed and collected into a science booklet; as an option, students can then illustrate their booklets with drawings or clip art.

The sample experience text shown in Figure 9.11 is drawn from a section of a sixth-grade science text, *Discovery Works* (Badders et al., 1999). The text was too difficult for one group of students to read on their own, so the teacher read it out loud instead.

FIGURE 9.11 Density and Rotten Eggs

> Knowing about density can keep you from eating a rotten egg. A fresh egg has a greater density than a rotten egg. Density is the amount of matter in space. Pick up a piece of wood and a piece of iron that are the same size. The piece of iron is heavier. That is because iron has more matter in the same amount of space than a piece of wood.
>
> Density can tell you whether something will sink or float. If an object has a greater density than water, it will sink. If it has a density that is less than that of water, it will float. Water has a density of 1.0 g/mL. That means it has one gram of matter for each milliliter of space. A fresh egg has a density of about 1.2 g/mL. A rotten egg has a density of about 0.9 g/mL. That is why a rotten egg will float. So if you are going to boil an egg for breakfast and it floats, throw it away!

The group then composed an experience story summarizing the segment, which the teacher scribed. The teacher read the summary to the students and discussed ways in which they could improve it. The segment was revised and edited by the group, with the help of teacher prompts. The teacher reread the revised text to them, and the group discussed it. They discussed what density is and why it could be used to predict whether something would sink or float. To make sure that students could read key words in the selection, the teacher asked them to read sentences orally. They were asked to read the sentence that tells what density is and the sentence that tells what the density of water is. They also discussed what a *gram* is and what a *milliliter* is.

Using Periodicals and Web Sites

Keeping up to date in our fast-changing world means reading periodicals as well as books. Periodicals are especially important in social studies because they usually present current events; periodicals also offer the opportunity to look at a topic from a different perspective. Students might compare the coverage of a topic in a periodical versus the coverage in the textbook or trade book. Weekly Reader, Scholastic, National Geographic, Time, and other publishers offer a variety of high-quality periodicals for students.

Web sites are another source of added information. They can be used to supplement and amplify textbook information. For instance, a middle school science text may contain just two pages of information on acid rain, but the Acid Rain Program sponsored by the EPA presents more than a dozen pages of information and describes nine easy-to-conduct experiments (go to http://www.epa.gov/acidrain/what/index.html). Related Web sites are also noted. Reutzel (2011) recommends supplementing information presented in a read-aloud with a carefully chosen clip from YouTube or another source. The clips can reinforce and extend key concepts and build additional background knowledge. After hearing a read-aloud about hummingbirds, students might view a hummingbird clip from http://www.butterflywebsite.com or another source.

Writing to Learn

Writing is a way of learning as well as a method of communication. However, some kinds of writing are better than others for learning. Different kinds of writing lead students to think in different kinds of ways. Writing short answers aids recall over the short term. However, activities in which students manipulate information lead to increased recall over a longer period of time and to deeper understanding. Writing that involves comparing, contrasting, concluding, and evaluating has a greater impact than writing that requires only restating. Writing in which students have a sense of ownership, in which they see value because it fosters their learning, and that they feel

 REFLECTION
How might you differentiate instruction in your class to make key concepts understandable to all students? What steps might you take to make the texts you use in your class accessible to all students?

Using Technology
By using an advanced Google search, users can determine whether the readability of articles is estimated to be basic, intermediate, or advanced. Basic is about a middle school level. The user can also select articles listed by reading level. http://www.google.com/support/websearch/bin/answer.py?hl=en&answer=1095407 ■

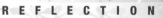 **REFLECTION**
What role might trade books and technology play in your content classroom?

FYI
Students should do the kinds of writing assignments, such as those involving comparing and contrasting, concluding, or judging, that foster the development of higher-level thinking skills. ■

Writing is a way of learning.

competent to undertake seems to work best (Langer & Applebee, 1987). Writing activities such as the following can help clarify complex topics:

• Comparing, contrasting, or evaluating key points in a chapter

• Writing critical reports on famous people or events or taking on the role of a famous person or describing a key event as though one were there

• Interpreting the results of a science experiment conducted in class

• Writing an essay on a social studies or science topic

Students' writing in the content areas often consists of simply retelling information. One solution is to have them conduct firsthand investigations and report the results. They might undertake activities such as the following:

• Writing observations about a natural phenomenon (for example, changes in plants that are being grown from seed)

• Describing birds that visit a bird feeder, changes in a tree from season to season, or changes in a puppy or kitten as it develops over a period of months

• Summarizing and interpreting the results of a classroom poll

• Interviewing older family members about life when they were growing up

A writing activity that can be used in any content-area class is having students explain a process to someone who has no knowledge of it. Processes include finding the area of a rectangle or describing how magnets work, how the president is elected, and how to find a particular state on a map. Students might include graphics to help explain a process.

Other writing-to-learn activities include the following (Noyce & Christie, 1989):

• Writing letters to convey personal reactions or request information on a topic

• Writing scripts to dramatize key events in history

• Writing historical fiction

• Writing a children's book on an interesting social studies or science topic

• Writing an editorial or commentary about a social issue

• Creating captions for photos of a scientific experiment

Learning Logs

One easy device that combines personal reaction with exploration of content is the **learning log**. It consists of a notebook that is

> . . . informal, tentative, first draft, and brief, usually consisting of no more than ten minutes of focused free writing. The teacher poses questions and situations or sets themes that invite students to observe, speculate, list, chart, web, brainstorm, role-play, ask questions, activate prior knowledge, collaborate, correspond, summarize, predict, or shift to a new perspective: in short, to participate in their own learning. (Atwell, 1990, p. xvii)

The class can discuss their learning logs, or the teacher can collect them and respond to them in writing.

The main purpose of logs is to have students examine and express what they are learning, not to air personal matters (Atwell, 1990). Whether students pose a question, jot down a reaction, or create a semantic map, the writing stimulus should help them think as scientists, historians, or mathematicians and think about what they are learning. At times,

■ A **learning log** is a type of journal in which students record and reflect on concepts that they are studying.

they can draft free responses in their learning logs; at other times, the teacher might want to provide a prompt. For a unit on weather, one of the following prompts might be provided for any one log-writing session:

- What do I know about weather forecasting?
- What questions do I have about weather?
- What is the worst kind of storm? Why?
- What kind of weather do I like best? Least? Why?
- How does weather affect my life?
- What kinds of people might be most affected by the weather?
- What causes fog?
- What are some of the ways in which people who are not scientists predict the weather?

Prompts that foster reflection, manipulation of information, evaluation, and relating information to one's personal life also foster higher-level thinking skills.

Students can also write prelearning and postlearning entries in their logs. Before reading a selection on snakes, they might write what they know about snakes and then share their knowledge with a partner. Talking to a partner helps them to elicit more information. Students then read the selection and make log entries indicating what they know now. Prelearning and postlearning entries help students become more metacognitive, more aware of what they know and are learning (Santa, 1994).

Brief Writing-to-Learn Activities

A number of brief writing activities can be used to spark or summarize learning. At the beginning of a class or as part of homework, students can compose admit slips. At the end of class, they compose exit slips. Both activities take no more than 5 minutes. Admit slips can be used to have students reflect on the homework assignment or a topic covered the day before or to set the stage for the day's lessons. Possible prompts include "What was the most important thing you learned from reading the homework assignment? What questions do you have about the causes of the Great Depression? What do you know about alternative energy?" Exit slips might contain a summary or a reaction to the day's lesson: "What did you learn about alternative energy? What questions do you have about alternative energy? What was the most surprising thing that you learned? Which of today's activities did you find most helpful? Explain why." Slips can be written on three-by-five cards, slips of paper, loose-leaf notebook paper, or specially created forms. They can be anonymous or signed. Some teachers assign a grade to each student's overall collection of slips. Discussing some of the slips allows students to hear examples of especially good slips and so improve their own.

In the middle of a lesson, you might use a **quickwrite**, an activity in which students respond to a prompt on what they are learning, what is confusing, or what they know about a topic. In a quickwrite activity known as Question All-Write, the teacher stops and asks a question about the material that has just been presented (Yell, 2002). Sentence Synthesis is a quickwrite activity that helps students summarize their learning. Students are given three or four key words about a topic or concept that has been presented or is about to be presented and are asked to compose a sentence that uses all of those key words to explain the topic or concept. For the topic of the separation of powers among the branches of the federal government, the teacher might supply the following words: *separation*, *Constitution*, and *branch* (Yell, 2002). Quickwrites are discussed by pairs, small groups, and/or the whole class.

These brief writing-to-learn activities activate prior knowledge and foster active learning and reflection. They also

- A **quickwrite** is a brief written response to a text passage, lecture, discussion, lesson, or prompt.

provide insights into what students have learned, helping you make adjustments to clarify misconceptions or provide more practice or more detailed examples. As you do with other kinds of writing, model the process of completing these assignments, and provide instruction in how to complete them. When giving a prompt, also provide a writing tip: "Remember to explain why you believe that this was the most important fact in the lesson."

Sheltered English for English Language Learners

Introduced in the 1980s by Krashen (1991), **sheltered English** is a way of fostering the learning of English through the study of content areas. As students learn science and social studies, they develop English language skills. Sheltered English is generally taught by content-area specialists who have training in teaching English, but some of the techniques employed in sheltered English can be adapted by classroom teachers. The following steps can be taken to make content understandable:

- The presentation should be as understandable as possible. Speak at a slower pace with deliberate enunciation. Use simple, straightforward language. Avoid figurative language, idioms, and cultural references that students might not recognize (Gunning, 2003).
- Use visuals to support the verbal presentation. Use audiovisual aids, gestures, facial expressions, and demonstrations to make the language more meaningful. When introducing a new word, show a picture of what it represents, if possible, and write it on the board. When mentioning a place, write its name on the board and show it on a map. Pantomime actions and demonstrate processes. Use time lines, graphs, videos, and filmclips. Use manipulatives such as globes.
- When giving directions, show students what to do in addition to telling them. If possible, model the process for them. Then ask students to carry out directions or apply a concept under your guidance. Provide additional help as needed.
- Plan lots of hands-on activities, drawings, webs, maps, and other graphic organizers so that students can use techniques that are less language dependent to extend their understanding and express their knowledge.
- Use brainstorming, quickwrites, and similar techniques to activate background knowledge.
- Modify use of text. Conduct text walks, or read and explain portions of the text. Make generous use of the text's illustrations. Also point out cognates. You might use Questioning the Author or reciprocal teaching to help students construct meaning.
- Obtain texts that use simpler language.
- Make use of the students' native language. Provide explanations of complex concepts in the students' native language. If you are unfamiliar with their native language, ask another student who knows the language to provide the explanation. Encourage students to discuss content in their native language as well as in English.
- Scaffold instruction. Provide prompts and other assistance as needed. Use prompts that encourage students to clarify or expand responses: "That's interesting. I'd like to hear more about that. Can you explain that? Can you tell us more? So what happened next?"
- Plan opportunities for students to talk over ideas. This could be in whole-class discussions, pairs, or small groups. This gives ELLs the opportunity to use academic language as they engage in activities and discuss procedures and findings. ELLs are more willing to engage in discussions in small groups than they are in larger groups.

■ **Sheltered English** combines learning English language skills with the study of content areas. As students learn science and social studies, they develop English language skills.

- Use real-world materials such as signs, recycling and nutrition labels, menus, job applications, and bank deposit slips.
- Provide wait time. Instead of requiring students to answer as soon as you pose a question, wait a few seconds. This is helpful to all students (Lake, 1973; Rowe, 1969) but is especially beneficial to ELLs because, being less familiar with the language, they need extra time to formulate their responses.
- When assessing students' work, allow students to demonstrate their knowledge in multiple ways. If possible, include ways that don't rely so heavily on language. Students might conduct an experiment, draw a diagram, or complete a project.

Systematic vocabulary instruction is also essential for ELLs. "In order to provide ELLs with access to content-area curriculum and, in turn, to increase their academic achievement, effective vocabulary instruction must be frequent, intensive, systematic, and complex. It must occur in all classrooms, from kindergarten through 12th grade, and be cohesive and consistent across the grade levels" (Francis, Rivera, Lesaux, Kieffer, & Rivera, 2006, p. 21). In addition to teaching content-area and general vocabulary, it is also important to teach academic language, the language of instruction, so students understand what they are to do when they are asked to *compare, contrast, discuss, illustrate, predict, summarize,* or *give examples.* Here is how one teacher combined instruction in content vocabulary with instruction in academic language while introducing the concept of buoyancy (Echevarria, Vogt, & Short, 2000). Mr. Lew explained that the purpose of the unit was to find out why some objects float and others sink. As he said the word *float*, he pointed to an orange floating in a tank. As he said the word *sink*, he placed a peeled orange in the tank and the class watched as it sank. He also told the students that at the end of the unit, they would be able to calculate and predict whether an object would be buoyant enough to float. The words *float, sink, buoyant, calculate,* and *predict* were written on the board. Mr. Lew used the word *calculate* on purpose. He could have used the word *figure*, but he believed that students would recognize *calculate* more readily because it is a cognate of *calcular* in Spanish, and most of his students were native speakers of Spanish.

Sentence Walls for ELLs and Struggling Learners

Each content area has technical vocabulary as well as certain expressions that are used to talk about the subject. To help students read, write, and talk about a content-area topic, analyze the topic and note the words needed to understand it as well as the kinds of sentences that might be used to explain the topic and the kinds of sentences students might use in order to write and talk about the topic (Carrier & Tatum, 2006). You can devote a portion of a sentence wall to vocabulary words, a portion to statements about the topic, and a portion to questions. For a unit on the water cycle, Carrier and Tatum (2006) included vocabulary words such as *evaporation, condensation, precipitation*, and open-ended questions such as "What happens when_____? What causes _____?" Sentences included "Snow falls when water _____. When water evaporates, it _____." Vocabulary for a unit on the sun and the Earth might include *sun, Earth, revolve, orbit, rotates, axis, seasons, day*, and *year*. Statements might include these: "Earth rotates on _____. Earth revolves _____. The rotation of the Earth causes _____. The orbit of the Earth around the sun causes _____. Summer comes when _____. Winter comes when _____." Inquiry questions for this unit might include: "How long does it take the Earth to rotate on its axis? What causes day? What causes night? What makes days longer? What makes days shorter? How long does it take the Earth to revolve around the sun? What causes a change in the seasons?" Students are taught how to use the sentence wall to pose questions, discuss the topic, and write answers. Sentences and vocabulary on the wall become the language lesson for ELLs and may also be helpful to struggling learners. You might enlist the aid of the ESL teacher in composing such a sentence wall.

REFLECTION

How might you develop both the content knowledge and language skills of ELLs that you teach now or might teach in the future?

Reading to Remember

Some students seem to learn on their own how to study for different types of tests, while others require instruction. Teachers should let students know what types of tests they intend to give and should explain how to study for each one. For example, essay tests require knowing the main ideas of the material; objective tests require more attention to details. Teachers should also discuss the difference between studying for multiple-choice tests, which require only that one recognize correct answers, and studying for fill-in-the-blank exams, which require recalling names, dates, or terms. Recognizing is, of course, far easier than recalling.

Studying also has an affective component. When students are convinced of the value of study skills, they are more likely to use them (Schunk & Rice, 1987). Another crucial element in study strategy instruction is proving to students that these strategies work—they need to see that better studying leads to better grades.

Study habits develop early, and effective study skills take many years to learn. Locating, organizing, and taking steps to retain information should be an integral part of the elementary and middle school curriculum. From the very beginning, students should be taught how to preview a book to get an overview of its content and how to use the table of contents. Students should also be taught in the earliest grades how to preview a section of text, make predictions, create questions, summarize, and then apply what they read. Instruction in these strategies will help build a solid foundation for effective study skills. This instruction will pave the way for the teaching of more formal study strategies such as SQ3R.

Fostering Retention

Knowing how memory works is the key to devising techniques to improve retention. Memory has three stages: encoding, storing, and retrieving. Encoding should be clear and purposeful; text that is vaguely understood will be quickly forgotten. Storage works best when the material is meaningful. Students will remember a piece of information better if they concentrate on its meaning rather than on the exact words used, which is why it is best to respond to questions in one's own words. Retrieval, or remembering, works best when the material is carefully encoded.

Depth of processing also has an impact on memory (Craik & Lockhart, 1972). Repeating information, such as a date we wish to remember, requires only shallow processing. Organizing information, relating new information to old information, evaluating the validity of information, and applying information involve a deeper level of processing. Deeper processing elaborates the representation of the information in memory (Ashcroft, 1994). Material that students read will become more memorable if, as they read, they seek out connections between ideas in the passage or between what they are reading and what they know.

Elaborating information also aids memory. For example, suppose a student reads and wants to remember the following three facts from a selection about anteaters:

1. They have a long, thin snout.
2. They have sharp claws.
3. They have sticky tongues.

The student elaborates on the text by asking herself or himself why anteaters have a long, thin snout, sharp claws, and a sticky tongue and determines that an anteater can use its long snout to poke into underground ant nests, its claws to rip open the nests, and its sticky tongue to pick up the ants. This elaboration aids long-term storage and retrieval.

The more connections that are constructed between items of information in memory, the greater the number of retrieval paths (Atkinson, Atkinson, Smith, & Hilgard, 1987). "Questions about the causes and consequences of an event are particularly effective elaborations because each question sets up a meaningful connection, or retrieval path, to the event" (p. 269).

Principles for Improving Memory

The following principles are based on the way memory is believed to work and should aid retention:

- Get a clear, meaningful encoding of the material to be learned.
- Have a purposeful intention to learn. Activate strategies that will aid retention.
- Organize and elaborate information so that it will have a greater number of meaningful connections and thus will be easier to store and retrieve. Creating outlines, summaries, and maps; taking notes; reflecting; and applying information promote retention.
- Overlearning aids retention. **Overlearning** means that a person continues to study after material has been learned. This extra practice pays off in longer-lasting retention. Novice students often make the mistake of halting their study efforts as soon as they are able to recite the desired material. Added practice sessions should help maintain the level of performance.
- When it is not possible to structure meaningful connections between material to be learned and prior knowledge, use memory devices to create connections. Some popular memory devices are described in the following section.
- Give your mind a rest. After intensive studying, take a break, rest, and get enough sleep. Sleep, it is believed, gives the brain the opportunity to organize information.

Memory Devices

Conceptual Understanding   The best way to remember new material is to achieve conceptual understanding. Bransford (1994) gives an example of a student who is studying arteries and veins for a test: The student knows that one type of blood vessel is thick and elastic, and one is thin and nonelastic, but he is not sure which is which. He can use a number of strategies to help him remember. He could use simple rehearsal and just say, "artery, thick, elastic" over and over. But a far better approach would be to seek conceptual understanding and ask, "Why are arteries thick and elastic?" The student has read that blood is pumped from the heart through the arteries in spurts and reasons, therefore, that the arteries must be elastic so that they can contract and expand as the heart pumps. They have to be thick because they must withstand the pressure of the blood. If the explanation that enables the learner to see the significance of the information is not provided in the reading, the learner must seek it out.

Rehearsal   The simplest memory device of all is **rehearsal**. Rehearsal may be used when conceptual understanding is not feasible or possible. For instance, one has to memorize a list of dates. In its most basic form, rehearsal involves saying the item to be memorized over and over again. It is the way students learn the names of the letters of the alphabet, the names of the vowels, and their home addresses and telephone numbers. Rehearsal works because it focuses the learner's attention on the items to be learned and transfers material into long-term memory (Weinstein & Mayer, 1986).

Young children use rehearsal strategies, but they may not do so spontaneously. They may have to be taught how to use such strategies, and then they may have to be reminded to apply them. Natural development is also a factor. Older children, even when not instructed to do so, tend to use rehearsal more frequently than younger children do. A program of study skills for elementary and middle school students

- **Overlearning** refers to the practice of continuing to study after material has been learned in order to foster increased retention.
- **Rehearsal** refers to the process of memorizing information.

would have to balance students' development with careful instruction. As students grow older, they can learn to use more complex rehearsal strategies, such as rereading text aloud or silently. They also learn how to test themselves.

Mnemonic Method   Rehearsal is an inefficient way to remember material. If at all possible, a more meaningful approach should be used. If conceptual understanding is not possible, learners might use a mnemonic method that constructs connections that are artificially meaningful. **Mnemonics** are artificial memory devices, such as the verse used to remember how many days there are in each month ("thirty days has September, April, June, and November"). Mnemonics are used when it is not possible to create more meaningful connections.

Mnemonic Rhymes   Many traditional rhymes were written specifically to help school children with memory tasks:

> In fourteen hundred and ninety-two
>
> Columbus sailed the ocean blue. . . .
>
> Use *i* before *e* except after *c*
>
> or when sounded like *a* as in *neighbor* and *weigh*.

Acronyms   Words made from the first letters of a series of words are often used to assist memory. Common **acronyms** include *roy g. biv* for the colors of visible light in the order in which they appear in the spectrum (red, orange, yellow, green, blue, indigo, violet); and *homes* for the Great Lakes (Huron, Ontario, Michigan, Erie, and Superior).

Acrostics   In **acrostics**, a simple phrase is used to learn a series of words or letters. For instance, *Every Good Boy Does Fine* has long been used as an aid in memorizing the letters (E, G, B, D, and F) representing the tuning of guitar strings or the notes on the treble clef in written music. Similarly, *My Very Educated Mother Just Served Us Noodles* can help people remember the names of the eight planets (Mercury, Venus, Earth, Mars, Jupiter, Saturn, Uranus, Neptune). Acrostics and acronyms work because they provide a way to organize information that is essentially random.

The best mnemonic devices are those that students create for themselves. Help the class create rhymes or other devices for remembering important dates, names, rules, or other items that have to be memorized.

Importance of Practice

Practice is essential for a number of reasons. First, practice enables students to reach a certain level of competence. With practice, a student learns to write an essay that contains a beginning, a middle, and an end (Willingham, 2009). Practice also makes skills automatic. Periodic practice also aids retention. If reviews are spaced, the skills or information is retained longer. Because it deepens understanding and awareness, practice also fosters transfer to new situations. If students work a number of problems with a similar structure, they are more likely to be able to work a new problem that has a different surface structure but has the underlying structure of the problems they solved previously (Willingham, 2009). For instance, say that a student has just learned that the word *hemisphere* refers to the parts of the brain; when she or he comes to the word *hemisphere* while reading about the brain, the student might need

FYI

Practice results in an average percentile gain of 14 points (Hattie, 2009). ■

■ **Mnemonics** are artificial devices (such as a rhyme) used to aid memory. Mnemonics represent a level of processing deeper than simply saying an item over and over.

■ An **acronym** is a word made up of the first letter of each of a series of words.

■ An **acrostic** is a device in which the first letters in a series of words spell out a word or phrase or correspond to the first letters in another series of words to be memorized.

to pause and think about the meaning of the word *hemisphere* in this context. With repeated reading (practice) about the brain and meeting the word *hemisphere*, the correct meaning of *hemisphere* is immediately retrieved and so takes no mental capacity. In similar fashion, procedures needed to solve problems become automatic with practice (Willingham, 2009).

To be effective, practice has to meet certain requirements (Willingham, 2009). Effective practice requires intentionality and feedback. Intentionality means that you want to improve and are taking steps to do so. Practice also requires feedback from a knowledgeable source. The knowledgeable source can let you know when you need to make adjustments or move on to a higher level.

Providing More Effective Practice   One method of helping students learn to apply a process or strategy is to provide them with model examples. To get the best results with this activity, alternate or interleave studying of model examples that have already been completed with exercises that have to be completed independently (Pashler et al., 2007). Students who alternate back and forth between analyzing completed examples and doing exercises on their own do better than students who completed a series of exercises after having read over a series of similar exercises. By interleaving exercises to be worked out with models or explanations, students get a chance to try out the strategy and see which elements they might not understand. When they get to the next model example, they can seek explanations for elements not understood. For instance, students selecting a main idea statement might realize that they have been choosing statements that are too narrow, but they might then be aided by the interleaved model and explanation. For homework, rather than having to select the main idea for nine paragraphs, it would be more effective if students were given three sets that consist of a worked example and two practice paragraphs. Having the sample example provides students with help for judging the next set of items, so they are motivated to consider the sample carefully because it will help them make better judgments on items they have to classify on their own. As students grow in expertise, they can spend more time judging items and less time studying them.

Distributed Versus Massed Practice   Generally speaking, short practice sessions work better than long ones, especially when students are memorizing. Brief reviews are also important to forestall forgetting. Distributed practice, or studying that is spread over a number of sessions, is often preferable to massed practice. Concentration can be best maintained for short periods, and there is less chance for the student to become bored. This is especially true when the student is engaged in rote tasks, such as studying spelling words or a list of dates. Massed practice or studying for extended periods of time, works best when the material has a wholeness that would be lost if it were split into separate segments. Reading a long story or writing an essay would fall into this category. Lengthier study periods also seem to work better for students who have difficulty settling down and tend to fritter away the first 15 minutes of a study session.

 FYI

Nuthall's (2000) research indicates that it takes three or four presentations "for a new knowledge construct to be created" (p. 93). Sessions devoted to developing new knowledge may be relatively close. Those devoted to review can be spaced more widely, between 5 to 20% of the time the material is to be retained. ■

Providing Judicious Review

Teachers can enhance the impact of students' studying through judicious review. In addition to helping students develop effective study habits and techniques, it also helps students learn and retain more if key concepts are reviewed. Key concepts should be presented at least twice. Presentations designed to develop new concepts should be scheduled so that they are relatively close. Presenting a concept twice or more promotes deeper understanding and retention. In one experiment, middle school students taught mitosis in one lesson were compared with students taught mitosis over several sessions. Three weeks later, when quizzed, students taught under spaced conditions demonstrated that they had learned 50 percent more. Re-presentation requires retrieving information from long-term memory. Doing so requires active engagement and so fosters retention. In addition, each presentation may have a different context. For instance, students taught mitosis in a spaced approach learned about mitosis in terms of animal reproduction and plant reproduction. These spaced presentations allow "'variable encoding'—chances to encode the information in different ways, get different perspectives on it, understand it a little bit differently, relate it to prior knowledge. All of these things are instrumental in learning and good retention" (McDaniels, 2008).

However, if the review or re-presentation is too close in time, it is not very effective. It is also not effective if the re-presentation is delayed for a very long period of time. Pashler and colleagues (2007) recommend that the interval between presentations should not be less than 5 percent of the time that the information has to be retained. if the information has to be retained for 60 days, then it would probably be better to wait two or three days and then two weeks or so. The delayed reexposures can take the form of homework, quizzes, review sessions, applications, or similar exercises.

SQ3R: A Theory-Based Study Strategy

A five-step technique known as SQ3R—Survey, Question, Read, Recite, and Review—implements many of the principles presented in this chapter. Devised in the 1940s, it is the most thoroughly documented and widely used study technique in English-speaking countries. SQ3R, or a method based on it, appears in nearly every text that discusses studying. It is very effective when properly applied (Caverly & Orlando, 1991).

Principles of SQ3R   SQ3R is based on the following principles, derived from F. P. Robinson's (1970) review of research on studying:

- Surveying headings and summaries increases speed of reading, helps students remember the text, and, perhaps most importantly, provides an overview of the text.
- Asking a question before reading each section improves comprehension.
- Reciting from memory immediately after reading slows down forgetting. If asked questions immediately after reading, students are able to answer only about half of them. After just one day, 50 percent of what was learned is forgotten. Students are then able to answer just 25 percent of questions asked about a text. However, those who review the material have a retention rate of more than 80 percent one day later. In another study, students who spent 20 percent of their time reading and 80 percent reciting were able to answer twice as many questions as those who simply read the material (Gates, 1917).
- Understanding major ideas and seeing relationships among ideas help comprehension and retention.
- Having short review sessions, outlining, and relating information to students' personal needs and interests are helpful.

Applying any one of Robinson's (1970) principles should result in more effective studying. However, Robinson based SQ3R on all of them. Applied as described in the following Student Strategies box, SQ3R prepares students to read and helps them organize, elaborate, and rehearse information from text.

In general, special elements should be treated the same way as text. The titles of graphs, tables, and maps are turned into questions and the information in the graph, table, or map is then used to answer the questions (Robinson, 1970). A diagram may be as important as the text and merit special effort. After examining the diagram carefully, students should try to draw it from memory and then compare their drawings with the diagram in the book (Robinson, 1970). Drawing becomes a form of recitation.

 FYI

- SQ3R cannot be mastered in a day or even a month. Each element requires extensive practice and guidance. Students also have to be able to recognize whether they are applying the technique correctly and, if they are not, what they can do about it.
- Although devised over sixty years ago, SQ3R incorporates many strategies recently recommended by cognitive psychologists: predicting or surveying, setting goals, constructing questions, summarizing, monitoring for meaning, and repairing. ■

 FYI

- In addition to needing many opportunities to apply the technique, students using SQ3R require individual feedback so that they can make necessary adjustments in the way the technique is applied.
- SQ3R requires not only the development of component skills but also the replacement of old habits. Instead off simply reading through a chapter, for instance, students must first survey it (Early & Sawyer, 1984, p. 422). ■

Teaching SQ3R   Although originally designed for college students, SQ3R works well with elementary and middle school students. In fact, if SQ3R or some of its elements are not taught in the early grades, college may be too late. By the upper elementary and middle school years, unless students have learned otherwise, they may have acquired inefficient study habits that are resistant to change (Walker, 1995). Very young readers can and should be taught to survey material, make predictions, and read to answer questions they have composed or to check how accurate their predictions were. Answering questions and reacting to predictions is a form of recitation. Once students are reading large amounts of text (in fourth grade or so) and are expected to remember information for tests, they should be introduced to all the principles of SQ3R. If students are to be tested, they must know how to prepare for tests. To use SQ3R fully, students should be able to generate main ideas. It also helps if they have some knowledge of text structures (Walker, 1995).

Test-Enhanced Learning

Although primarily used for evaluation, quizzes can be a device for fostering understanding and retention of material. Self-testing is one of the reasons why SQ3R is effective. Quizzes should contain items, such as filling in the blanks, or constructed responses that require retrieval of information. Tests that require students to produce answers, even if the answers to be produced are brief, are more effective than multiple-choice tests. Taking a test is more effective than spending extra time studying. The act of recalling information to answer a question helps to establish it in memory. The quiz could be in a gamelike format. Corrective feedback should be provided. Otherwise, incorrect information will be retained. Students can also be taught to test themselves.

FYI

Numerous adaptations have been made to SQ3R. A step that several practitioners advocate adding is reflecting (Pauk, 1989; Thomas & Robinson, 1972; Vacca & Vacca, 1986). After reading, students are encouraged to think about the material and how they might use it. Before reading, students reflect on what they already know about the topic. ■

REFLECTION

Which of the suggestions for improving students' learning and study skills would you most likely implement? How might you adapt them for use in your content area?

STUDENT STRATEGIES
Applying SQ3R

1. *Survey.*   Survey the chapter that you are about to read to get an overall picture of what it is about. Glance over the title and headings. Quickly read the overview and summary. Note what main ideas are covered. This quick survey will help you organize the information in the chapter as you read it.

2. *Question.*   Turn each heading into a question. The heading "Causes of the Great Depression" would become "What were the causes of the Great Depression?" Answering the question you created gives you a purpose for reading.

3. *Read.*   Read to answer the question. Having a question to answer focuses your attention and makes you a more active reader.

4. *Recite.*   When you come to the end of the section, stop and test yourself. Try to answer your question. If you cannot, go back over the section and then try once again to answer the question. The answer may be oral or written. Note, however, that a written answer is preferable because writing things down is more active than simply saying them; writing forces you to summarize what you have learned. The answer should also be brief; otherwise, SQ3R takes up too much time.

    Do not take notes until you have read the entire section. Taking notes before completing the section interrupts your reading and could interfere with your understanding of the section. Repeat steps 2, 3, and 4 until you have read the entire selection.

5. *Review.*   When you have finished the assignment, spend a few minutes reviewing what you read. If you took notes, cover them up. Then, asking yourself the questions you created from the headings, try to recall the major points that support the headings. The review helps you put information together and remember it longer.

This is known as test-enhanced learning. In their advice to students, researchers Roediger, McDaniel, and McDermott (n.d.) recommend:

> As you read text material, make up questions (or use the ones supplied at the end of the chapter) and then later test yourself. If you can retrieve the information from memory, great; having retrieved it once, you will remember it even better. If you can't retrieve the answer, study the material again and retest yourself until you're sure you know it. But even if you were able to retrieve the answer once, don't stop. Test yourself repeatedly and keep retrieving answers. Repeated retrieval is the key to long-term retention (Karpicke & Roediger, 2007, pp. 3–4)

Test-Taking Strategies

Students in grades 3 through 8 must be assessed in reading and math each year. Results of the tests are used to judge the proficiency of students and the effectiveness of schools. States and local school districts may also decide to give additional tests. The best way to prepare students for high-stakes tests of this type is to have in place a high-quality literacy program and intervention programs for students who need them. In addition, students also need to know how to take tests. In their study of standardized test-taking among elementary school students, Calkins, Montgomery, and Santman (1998) found that a number of students had poor test-taking skills. They failed to follow directions, did not take guesses when it was to their benefit to do so, did not look back over a passage to find the right answer, did not check answers, and often used background rather than text knowledge to answer questions.

To gain insight into students' test-taking skills, observe them as they take a practice test. Ask students to put a stick-on note on any part of the test that is confusing them. Note those students who seem overly anxious, who rush through the test, who aren't putting forth effort, or who aren't following directions. While students are taking a practice test, do think-alouds with individual students. Have them tell you what's going on in their minds as they read test items or passages and answer questions. For answers that are clearly wrong, ask students to explain their answers. You might also interview students after they have taken a practice test or have a whole-class discussion in which you ask students to tell what they found easy and what was hard or confusing. Invite them to tell how they went about answering questions that were hard or confusing. Analyze your observations, students' stick-on notes, and the think-alouds. Also observe students during discussions and while they complete written responses as part of regular class work. Are they able to locate answers and support their responses? If not, what kinds of prompts and probes help them? Use your analysis of class work and the practice test to plan instruction.

To construct an effective program to prepare students for tests, follow these steps.

Step 1: **Align instructional objectives with test objectives.** For instance, if the test is assessing the ability to make inferences, that should be one of the instructional objectives. However, also note the kinds of test responses that are called for. Students might have good comprehension but have difficulty responding to open-ended questions. For example, an analysis of the constructed responses of 45 third-graders and sample responses to more than 200 open-ended questions on NAEP revealed that students had difficulty supporting their responses (Gunning, 2005). They failed to provide reasons, causes, examples, and explanations. Instruction has to be two-pronged: teaching students how to comprehend and teaching them how to write about what they comprehend.

Step 2: **Model how you would go about taking a test.** Explain your thinking processes as you read and follow directions. For multiple-choice items, explain that you answer the easiest items first and how you go about eliminating answer choices when you are not sure about an answer. Model the process of checking answers and pacing yourself. Provide extra coaching for students whose responding style lowers their scores: those who work too rapidly and fail to check answers as well as those who work too slowly and are overly concerned with making a mistake.

To model a constructed response, read the question and then the selection with the students. Emphasize the steps you would take to obtain the necessary information and construct a response. For example, if the question asks what kind of person the main character is, you think over her actions and decide that she was brave. You note that the question also asks for two examples of actions that show what kind of person the character is, so you go back over the selection and underline, highlight, or use stick-on notes to indicate two examples. You also number the examples. Adding the extra step of numbering the details helped ensure that students included support from the passage.) Emphasize the importance of locating and recalling information as explained on pages 433–434.

Step 3: **Create a rubric for assessing a sample response to an open-ended test question.** Using the rubric, involve the class in assessing the response.

Step 4: **As a group, have the class cooperatively respond to a similar test question.** Using the rubric as a guide, assess the group's response.

Step 5: **Provide guided practice as students respond to similar open-ended test questions.** Initially, give extra assistance or scaffolding as needed. Have students complete partially finished responses. Have students complete items in which the lead sentence and a detail have been supplied and they must add two more supporting details.

Two aids that you can use for guided practice are the answer organizer and the answer frame (Boyles, 2002). In an answer organizer, you lay out step by step what students are to do, as in the example in Figure 9.12, which is in response to this test question: "Did the main character make the right decision? Use details given in the passage to support your answer." Answer frames provide even more assistance than answer organizers do. In an answer frame, you fill in a portion of the answer and have students finish it. As you can see in Figure 9.13, in addition to providing step-by-step directions, the answer frame shows the students what words to use. Answer frames help students who would not be able to complete the task without this higher level of support (Boyles, 2002). As students learn how to formulate responses, answer frames

FIGURE 9.12   An Answer Organizer

Topic sentence: Write a sentence that tells whether you think the main character made the right decision.

_____

_____

Supporting Sentences: Underline and number at least three details in the passage that support your answer. On the lines, write sentences that give the details. Write one sentence for each reason.

Detail 1. _____

Detail 2. _____

Detail 3. _____

Concluding Sentence: Write a concluding sentence that sums up what you have said and repeats the idea that the main character did or did not make the right decision.

_____

_____

FIGURE 9.13 An Answer
Frame

Tell whether you think the main character made the right decision.

The decision that the main character made was _____.
Underline and number at least three details in the passage that support your answer. On the
lines below, give the details by finishing the sentences. Finish one sentence for each detail.

For one thing, _____.
For another thing, _____.
Last of all, _____.

Now finish the concluding sentence that sums up what you have said and repeats the idea
that the main character did or did not make the right decision.

And so you can see from these reasons that _____.

should contain fewer clues or shortened clues and should gradually be eliminated. Boyles (2002) estimates that students should complete five assisted test questions before attempting to create a response on their own.

Step 6: **Have students take a practice test.** Using the rubric, analyze responses and provide additional instruction as needed. Provide individual guidance to students who do not pass the test. If possible, provide sufficient guidance and practice so that they do pass a retest.

Step 7: **Have students apply their skills by taking a real test.** Although the test might be graded, also use it as learning experience. Provide corrective instruction to students so that they improve sufficiently to achieve a passing grade or better. Adopt a mastery approach. Look at tests as a means of providing information on which to base instruction rather than as a device for grading. Reteach those skills that students had difficulty with until they have mastered them to the point where they can pass the test.

On a regular basis, perhaps once a week, provide instruction in responding to open-ended questions and/or multiple-choice items. Tie this instruction in with your overall literacy program. If you are emphasizing summarizing, use a question that involves summarizing. If you are focusing on developing characters, pose a question that asks students to cite examples to show what kind of a person a main character is. Most important, embed instruction in test-taking skills in the curriculum. Don't attempt to cover all types of response strategies in a single year. The most ambitious program could probably cover one a month, but five to eight a year would probably be a more realistic goal (Gunning, 2008).

Provide Practice at Students' Reading Level

Most high-stakes tests are written on grade level. However, students' practice materials should be on their instructional reading level. It isn't possible for students to learn new skills and strategies while coping with material that contains a high percentage of words they don't know in print. Fifth-graders reading on a third-grade level should be provided with materials on a third-grade level. Giving them grade-level material will have a negative impact: It will discourage them and deprive them of the opportunity to advance their skills by engaging in helpful practice. The best thing you can do to help such students is to provide added instruction and opportunities to read on their instructional level so that they can move up to higher levels.

Unfortunately, a large number of students will be required to take tests that are above their instructional level. Prepare the students as best you can. Show them how they might be able to answer some questions by carefully reading the question and then going back over the selection to find the answer. Encourage them to answer as many questions as they can. Try to compensate for this obvious blow to their self-esteem by pointing out the growth in literacy that they have experienced but which the test might not have assessed.

Locate and Recall: An Essential Test-Taking Skill

Locate and recall is a technique for comprehending explicitly stated text, such as supporting details, and basic story elements, such as setting, characters, and plot. Locating and recalling have a natural working relationship. When we fail to recall information, we go back to the text to locate it. For test-taking, it might be one of the most important skills of all. Indeed, the number-one shortcoming of students' responses on high-stakes tests is the failure to support responses (Gunning, 2006). Students need to learn how to go back to a passage to locate details, to verify information, and to find support for a position. On the easiest level, students simply locate directly stated information. On a higher level, they make inferences and draw conclusions from information they have located. QAR can be adapted to test-taking and can be effective in helping students decide whether the answer is "right there" (and so they can go back over the passage and find the information they need) or whether it's "author and me" (so they have to make an inference based on information contained in the passage).

Locating should be explained, modeled, and practiced so that it becomes virtually automatic. To introduce locating, explain to students that we can't remember everything we read, but we can go back to check facts or find details that we can't recall. Do a think-aloud with a sample multiple-choice test. Explain as you come to a challenging question that you are not sure which is the correct answer, so you go over the test passage and locate information that will help you. Show how you quickly skim over the passage to find the pertinent information. Provide students with a lengthy, fact-packed passage and lots of questions. As a class, read the passage and then respond to the questions. Help students as they go back over the passage to locate information. Provide practice with this skill.

Embed instruction in ongoing class activities. During discussions, encourage students to go back over a selection when they can't answer questions. Also, ask them to read from a selection to support a point they are making. Ask questions like these: "Can you read the sentence that tells us at what age the inventor thought up the idea for TV?" "Can you read the part that suggests that the old woman was kind?" When students are completing assignments or taking tests, remind them of the importance of looking back.

As students become accustomed to going back to a passage to verify information or locate a detail, introduce the skill of using information from a passage to construct a response. Along with reinforcing this skill in discussions, provide instruction and practice in applying this skill when writing.

Practice in test-taking skills does improve performance, especially if the format of the upcoming test is unfamiliar. Students taking a test with items having an analogy, cloze, or other unfamiliar format should be provided with exercises that familiarize them with the format. However, instruction should be limited. Excessive time spent on test preparation is time taken away from an activity that might be more valuable.

Test-taking preparation should be ethical. Providing students with items from the actual test is unethical. It is also unethical to raise students' scores without also

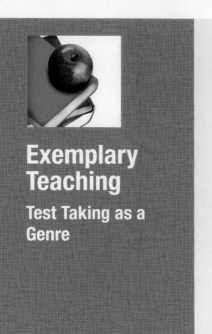

Exemplary Teaching

Test Taking as a Genre

Realizing that students might need special instruction for the high-stakes tests that they would soon be taking, intermediate-level teacher Suzette Serafini-Youngs created a unit on test-taking skills (Serafini, 2006). Before beginning the unit, she attempted to demystify the tests. She explained how they are constructed, how the results are used, and under what conditions they are administered. To initiate the unit, she discussed with students the experiences they had with high-stakes tests. This helped her identify effective and ineffective strategies that students used on past tests and negative attitudes that they acquired. The class then examined sample test passages and questions, which were released items from past tests. A chart of the test questions was created. The class noted any specialized language that was used, including terms such as *define, compare, contrast, list, identify,* and *summarize.* Once the needed skills were identified, instruction and practice in applying the skills was provided. Serafini-Youngs also developed students' attention and stamina, since these are important elements in successful performance. She builds students' confidence so they are not overly anxious.

Although not in agreement with the nature of the high-stakes tests, Serafini-Youngs works hard to ensure that students are as well prepared as possible for the challenges of those tests: "Many of our students have the required reading skills yet have trouble demonstrating these skills in the context of a standardized test" (p. 170). However, test preparation time is limited to a few weeks before the tests are administered. Serafini-Youngs realizes that the best preparation for standardized tests is the well-rounded, high-quality literacy program that she conducts year-round.

REFLECTION

What do you see as your responsibility to prepare students for tests? How might you implement a program in such a way that students receive adequate preparation in test-taking skills without detracting from your instructional program?

increasing their underlying knowledge and skills (Popham, 2000). The goal of test-taking preparation is to instruct students so that they have the test-taking skills to enable them to show what they know and can do. Test-taking preparation should not be so extensive that it displaces other valuable literacy activities, and it should go beyond merely providing practice. Speaking of commercial test-preparation materials, Raphael and Au (2005) comment:

> Test preparation typically takes the form of having students complete workbook exercises with items of a form and content ostensibly similar to those on upcoming tests. In general, students practice by reading short passages and responding to multiple-choice items. Most test preparation packages involve little or no instruction by the teacher. The problem with practice-only activities is that students who have not already acquired reading comprehension strategies gain little or nothing from the large amounts of time spent on these activities. (p. 206)

Wide reading, both in school and out, should be fostered. As Guthrie (2002) notes, the strongest predictor of achievement on standardized tests is the amount of reading students do:

> If a fifth grader is facing a high-stakes test in April, the best thing the student can do is to begin reading widely and frequently in October. If a teacher will encounter a high-stakes test for her classroom in April, her best preparation is to increase motivation of students for extended, learning-focused, independent reading as early as possible in the academic year. (p. 384)

Metacognitive Study Strategies

Metacognitive strategies that apply to virtually all study tasks are listed in Table 9.3 (Nisbet & Shucksmith, 1986). Students involved in writing reports and other long-term projects should learn to go through the six stages: asking questions, planning, monitoring, checking, revising, and self-testing, as shown in the table. These stages, in adapted, abbreviated form, can also be used in studying for tests and completing daily

TABLE 9.3 Metacognitive Study Strategies

Strategy	Description
Asking questions: What do I want to learn?	This includes setting up hypotheses, setting aims, defining boundaries of area to be explored, discovering audience, and relating task to previous work.
Planning: How will I go about the task?	This includes deciding on tactics and subdividing the overall task into subtasks.
Monitoring: Am I answering my questions?	This is a continuing attempt to see whether the results of one's efforts match the questions posed or purposes set.
Checking: How have I done so far?	This is a preliminary check to assess results and tactics.
Revising: What do I have to change?	Tactics, results, or goals may have to be changed.
Self-testing: How did I do? What did I learn?	In this final evaluation, both the results and the method of achieving them are assessed.

homework assignments. Initially, you should walk the students step by step through these stages. Gradually, they should assume responsibility for each stage on their own; ideally, the strategies will become automatic.

Along with applying these metacognitive strategies, students also need to use self-regulatory behaviors to complete academic tasks. They must use self-discipline and perseverance in order to overcome obstacles and forge ahead. Students work best when they understand why they are undertaking a project and what they are to do, feel that the task is doable, and have the necessary materials and strategies. Encourage students to tell you about any obstacles that they encounter. Discuss how they might overcome these obstacles. Provide guidance and encouragement as needed (Gensemer, 1998).

Summary

Content-area textbooks, which account for most of the material covered in subject-matter classes, pose special problems because they are more complex than narrative materials and may contain a high proportion of difficult concepts and technical vocabulary. Trade books, periodicals, Web sites, and other materials enliven content-area instruction and can be used along with or instead of textbooks.

Students can use numerous strategies to foster understanding before, during, and after reading. Teaching content and teaching strategy use should be combined. Increased content knowledge makes strategies easier to apply. Writing is a powerful way to promote learning in the content areas. With sheltered English, students learn both content and English.

Studying requires remembering in addition to understanding material. Retention of important information is improved by understanding, organization, and elaboration. Rehearsal (including the use of mnemonics) is an appropriate strategy for learning materials that lack meaningful connections.

A study strategy that has been effective with a variety of students is SQ3R (Survey, Question, Read, Recite, and Review). Studying should be metacognitive. Help for struggling readers and writers includes making on-level content information accessible to students and providing hands-on experiences.

Extending and Applying

1. Create a lesson showing how you would introduce KWL or another technique to a class. If possible, teach the lesson and evaluate its effectiveness.

2. Try out one of the learning strategies described in this chapter for at least a week. Use a learning log to keep a record of your experience. How well does the strategy work? How hard is it to use? How practical is it?

3. Examine an up-to-date content-area book. Using the Fry readability graph or the Qualitative Assessment of Texts (Chall, Bissex, Conard, & Harris-Sharples, 1996) with at least three separate passages of 100 words or more, obtain an estimate of the readability of the book. Check to see if ATOS (http://www.arbookfind.com) or lexile readabilities (http://www.lexile.com) have been provided for the book. How do they compare with each other and the estimates you obtained? Also note textual features, such as those listed in Table 9.2 How readable is the book? What are its strengths and weaknesses? What special problems might this text pose for ELLs? What might be done to make the text accessible to ELLs and struggling learners?

Professional Reflection

Do I ...

____ Have an understanding of techniques for improving students' understanding of content-area reading?

____ Have an understanding of the basic principles for improving students' study and test-taking skills?

____ Have an understanding of adaptations that might be used to improve ELLs' development of content knowledge and related language skills?

____ Have an understanding of ways to differentiate content-area literacy instruction?

Am I able to ...

____ Use a variety of learning materials, including textbooks, trade books, periodicals, and media to develop students' content knowledge?

____ Use a variety of approaches and techniques to improve students' understanding of content-area reading?

____ Use a variety of approaches and techniques to improve students' study and test-taking skills?

Reflection Question

A number of key techniques and principles for studying and retaining material were discussed in this chapter. Which of these techniques seem most valuable? How might you incorporate these techniques into your teaching? For instance, how might you use tests and quizzes to increase students' retention of material? How might you improve practice activities?

Building Competencies

To build competencies, consult the following sources for more detailed information:

Boyles, N. (2002). *Teaching written response to text.* Gainesville, FL: Maupin House.

IRA podcast. *Writing to learn across the curriculum.* http://www.reading.org Click on Teaching Tools and then Podcasts.

Lenz, B. K., Deshler, D. D., & Kissam, B. R. (2004). *Teaching content to all: Evidence-based inclusive practices in middle and secondary schools.* Boston: Allyn & Bacon.

Serafini, F. (2006). *Around the reading workshop in 180 days: A month-by-month guide to effective instruction.* Portsmouth, NH: Heinemann. Refer to Chapters 5 and 8.

Pashler, H., Bain, P., Bottge, B., Graesser, A., Koedinger, K., McDaniel, M., and Metcalfe, J. (2007). *Organizing instruction and study to improve student learning.* NCER 2007-2004. Washington, DC: National Center for Education Research, Institute of Education Sciences, U.S. Department of Education. http://ncer.ed.gov

MyEducationLab™

Go to the Topic "Reading and Writing in the Content Areas" in the MyEducationLab (www.myeducationlab.com) for your course, where you can:

- Find learning outcomes for "Reading and Writing in the Content Areas" along with the national standards that connect to these outcomes.
- Complete Assignments and Activities that can help you more deeply understand the chapter content.
- Apply and practice your understanding of the core teaching skills identified in the chapter with the Building Teaching Skills and Dispositions learning units.
- Examine challenging situations and cases presented in the IRIS Center Resources.
- Check your comprehension on the content covered in the chapter by going to the Study Plan in the Book

Resources for your text. Here you will be able to take a chapter quiz, receive feedback on your answers, and then access Review, Practice, and Enrichment activities to enhance your understanding of chapter content. (optional)

A+RISE A+RISE® Standards2Strategy™ is an innovative and interactive online resource that offers new teachers in grades K–12 just-in-time, research-based instructional strategies that meet the linguistic needs of ELLs as they learn content, differentiate instruction for all grades and abilities, and are aligned to Common Core Elementary Language Arts standards (for the literacy strategies) and to English language proficiency standards in WIDA, Texas, California, and Florida.

10 Reading Literature

Anticipation Guide

For each of the following statements related to the chapter you are about to read, put a check under "Agree" or "Disagree" to show how you feel. Discuss your responses with classmates before you read the chapter.

	Agree	Disagree
1. A literature program for the elementary and middle schools should emphasize the classics.	_____	_____
2. The main danger of a literature approach to reading is that selections will be overanalyzed.	_____	_____
3. Students need to rely on the teacher for an accurate interpretation of literature.	_____	_____
4. Students should have some say in choosing the literature they read.	_____	_____
5. It does not really matter what children read just as long as they read something.	_____	_____
6. Setting aside a period each day for voluntary reading is an excellent use of time.	_____	_____

Using What You Know

How do you go about reading a piece of literature? Do you read it in the same way that you read a popular novel? If your approach is different, how is it different? When reading literature, students use many of the same processes that they use when reading more mundane materials; word-attack skills and comprehension strategies are necessary. However, reading literature involves going beyond mere comprehension. The focus is on appreciation, enjoyment, and reader response. This chapter explores ideas for building understanding and appreciation of folklore, myths, poems, plays, and novels and ends with suggestions for promoting voluntary reading. What are your favorite kinds of literature? What experiences have you had that created a love of literature? What experiences have you had that may have created negative feelings about literature? How might literature be taught so that students learn to understand and appreciate it without losing the fun of reading it? What might be done to make students lifelong readers of high-quality novels, poetry, plays, and biographies?

> ### FYI
>
> Students interpret literature in terms of their own experience. In their discussions of *Maniac Magee* (Spinnelli, 1990), a tale of a homeless boy and race relations in a small town, students spoke of how characters in the book reminded them of family members (Lehr & Thompson, 2000). They made connections between events in their lives and what was happening to the characters. One student, who had been shuffled between his mother's and grandmother's houses, identified with Maniac Magee's satisfaction at finally having an address. ■

Experiencing Literature

Reading literature involves a dimension beyond reading ordinary material. If read properly, a classic tale draws out a feeling of wholeness or oneness, a carefully drawn character or situation evokes a feeling of recognition, and a poem that speaks to the heart engenders a feeling of tranquility. Louise Rosenblatt (1978) identified this response as characteristic of **aesthetic reading**: "In aesthetic reading, the reader's attention is centered directly on what he is living through during his relationship with that particular text" (p. 25).

In contrast to aesthetic reading is **efferent reading**, in which the reader's attention is directed to "concepts to be refined, ideas to be tested, actions to be performed after the reading" (Rosenblatt, 1978, p. 24). In efferent reading, the reader "carries away"

"The signs of the aesthetic response . . . [may include]: picturing and imagining while reading or viewing; imagining themselves in a character's place . . . ; questioning . . . about a story; making associations with other stories and their own life experiences; and mentioning feelings evoked" (Cox & Many, 1992, pp. 32–33). ■

Readers who make aesthetic responses enjoy a richer experience and produce more elaborated written responses. Efferent responses are more likely to consist of a barebones retelling of the tale and a brief evaluation of literary elements (Many, 1990, 1991). ■

meaning. In aesthetic reading, the reader is carried away by feelings evoked by the text. Text can be read efferently or aesthetically, depending on the reader's stance. For example, we could read an essay efferently for ideas or information, but if we respond to its biting satire or subtle humor, our stance becomes aesthetic. Thus, reading is not an either/or proposition but falls on a continuum, with the reader moving closer to one stance or the other depending on her or his expectations and focus (Dias, 1990). As Rosenblatt (1991) explained, "We read for information, but we are conscious of emotions about it and feel pleasure when the words we call up arouse vivid images and are rhythmic to the inner ear" (p. 445).

Rosenblatt cautioned that it is important to have a clear sense of purpose when asking children to read a particular piece. The purpose should fit in with the nature of the piece and the objective for presenting it. By its nature, for instance, poetry generally demands an aesthetic reading. But if the focus of the reading is on literal comprehension, then the experience will be efferent. The reading is aesthetic if the focus is on experiencing the poem or story and savoring the sounds, sights, and emotions that the words conjure up. Reading aesthetically results in a deeper level of involvement for students (Cox & Many, 1992). They imagine scenes, actions, and characters. They might wonder what happens to the characters after the story is over and imagine possible scenarios or create alternative endings. Students might also identify with a particular character and wonder how they might act if they were that character and experienced the story events.

Reader Response

How does one go about eliciting reader response? Probst (1988) described the following general steps:

1. **Creating a reader response environment.** Establish a setting in which students feel free to respond and each response is valued so that students do not worry about rightness or wrongness.
2. **Preparing to read the literary piece.** Preparation for reading a literary piece is basically the same as that for reading any text: A guided reading framework might be used. In the preparatory stage, a schema is activated, new concepts and vocabulary words are taught, interest in reading the selection is engendered, and a purpose is set. The purpose generally is open-ended, to evoke a response. As an alternative, the teacher might read aloud and discuss the first portion, especially if it is a chapter book or novel.
3. **Reading the literary piece.** Students read the work silently. However, if it is a poem, the teacher may elect to read it aloud, as the sound of poetry is essential to its impact.
4. **Small-group discussion.** The literary piece is discussed by groups of four or five students. In small groups, each student has a better opportunity to express her or his response to the piece and compare it with those of others. Discussion is essential, because it leads to deeper exploration of a piece.

Students need assistance in holding discussions. Set ground rules and have a group role-play the process. ■

The list of response prompts is a menu of questions. Choose those that are most appropriate for your circumstances. ■

To foster a fuller discussion, students might be asked to jot down their responses before they discuss them. Writing facilitates careful consideration. Questions that might be used to evoke a response include the following, some of which were suggested by Probst (1988). Four or five questions should be sufficient to evoke a full discussion.

- Which part of the selection stands out in your mind the most?
- Picture a part of the piece in your mind. Which part did you picture? Why?
- Was there anything in the selection that bothered you?
- Was there anything in it that surprised you?
- What main feeling did it stir up?

■ **Aesthetic reading** refers to emotions experienced or evoked while reading a piece of writing.

■ **Efferent reading** means reading to comprehend the information conveyed by a piece of writing.

- What is the best line or paragraph in the piece?
- Does this selection make you think of anything that has happened in your life?
- As you read, did your feelings change? If so, how?
- Does this piece remind you of anything else that you have read?
- If the author were here, what would you say to her or him?
- What questions would you ask?
- If you were the editor, what changes might you suggest that the author make?
- What do you think the writer was trying to say?
- What special words, expressions, or writing devices did the author use? Which of these did you like best? Least?
- If you were grading the author, what mark would you give her or him? Why? What comments might you write on the author's paper?

5. **Class discussion.** After the small groups have discussed the piece for about 10 minutes, extend the discussion to the whole class. The discussion should center on the responses, beginning with those made in the small groups. Ask each group, "How did your group respond to the piece? How were the responses the same? Is there anything about the work that we can agree on? How were the responses different? Did your response change as your group discussed the piece? If so, how?"

Throughout the discussion, you, as the teacher, must remain neutral and not intervene with your interpretations. Students have to be empowered to construct their own interpretations, and they need opportunities to develop their interpretive skills. Lesson 10.1 shows how a reader response lesson might be presented using the poem "The Land of Counterpane" (Stevenson, 1885).

FYI

Choose literary works that touch students' lives and with which they identify and to which they can respond. "The Land of Counterpane" would probably work best with third-graders. ■

LESSON 10.1
Reader Response

Step 1. Preparing to read the literary piece

Ask students to tell what they do when they aren't feeling well and have to spend the day in bed. Explain that the author of the poem they are about to read, Robert Louis Stevenson, was a sickly child and often spent time in bed. Also explain that *counterpane* is an old-fashioned word for *bedspread*.

Step 2. Reading the literary piece

Have students read "The Land of Counterpane" or listen as you read it. Their purpose should be to see what feelings, thoughts, or pictures the poem brings to mind.

The Land of Counterpane

When I was sick and lay a-bed,
I had two pillows at my head,
And all my toys beside me lay
To keep me happy all the day.
And sometimes for an hour or so
I watched my leaden soldiers go,
With different uniforms and drills,
Among the bed-clothes, through the hills;
And sometimes sent my ships in fleets

FYI

- Rosenblatt (1991) comments: "Textbooks and teachers' questions too often hurry students away from the lived-through experience. After the reading, the experience should be recaptured, reflected on. It can be the subject of further aesthetic activities—drawing, dancing, miming, talking, writing, role-playing, or oral interpretation. It can be discussed and analyzed efferently. Or it can yield information. But first, if it is indeed to be literature for these students, it must be experienced" (p. 447). ■
- Refrain from asking "Why?" after a reader has described his response. "Why?" implies that the youngster must justify his or her response, which tends to make him or her defensive. Instead, request that the student "tell me more about how you're thinking" (McClure & Kristo, 1994, p. xvi) or ask, "What makes you think that?" ■

FYI

Notice how the suggested questions in step 3 are geared to the readers' feelings or affective responses. Unlike typical comprehension questions—such as "What did the boy do?"—the questions ask the students to tell about what they pictured or felt as they read or to explain what impact the poem had on them. ■

FYI

• One problem with using response journals or logs is that students may fall into a rut. Provide creative prompts that invite students to see selections in new ways. Share entries from your journal so that you can model "new ways of thinking about literature" (Temple, Martinez, Yokota, & Naylor, 1998, p. 463). ■

• Although students should be given choices concerning their written responses to literature, assigned writing can sometimes lead students to investigate themes and issues that they might not have considered (Lehr & Thompson, 2000). When students were asked to write a letter from the point of view of the main character, they saw life from the character's perspective and began to problem-solve. ■

FYI

Writing to learn results in an average percentile gain of 8 points (Graham & Perin, 2007). ■

Using Technology

To see Dennis-Shaw's well-planned lesson on using double-entry journals, visit the Read•Write•Think site. http://www.readwritethink.org/lessons/lesson_view.asp?id=228 ■

All up and down among the sheets;
Or brought my trees and houses out,
And planted cities all about.
I am the giant great and still
That sits upon the pillow-hill,
And sees before him, dale and plain,
The pleasant land of counterpane.

Step 3. Responding to the piece

Have students write a brief response to each of the following questions:

• What feelings, thoughts, or pictures come to mind as you read the poem?
• After reading the poem, what stands out most in your mind?
• Was there anything in the poem that bothered you or surprised you?
• Does the poem remind you of anything that has ever happened to you?
• Have you ever had a day like the boy had?

Step 4. Small-group discussion

Students talk over their responses in groups of four or five. Each question should be discussed. Students will have been taught previously to accept everyone's responses, but they can ask for explanations or justifications. Each group should have a discussion leader and a spokesperson. The leader keeps the discussion moving and on track. The spokesperson sums up the group's reactions.

Step 5. Whole-class discussion

Have the whole class discuss the responses. Being careful not to inject your own interpretation, guide the discussion to obtain a full range of responses, thereby making it possible for students to hear them all. You can first take a quick survey of reactions by calling on the spokesperson for each group. Probe and develop those responses by calling on other members of the class. Encourage students to justify their responses by reading phrases or lines from the poem. As the opportunity presents itself, discuss how the language of the poem helps create feelings, images, and thoughts. Also, talk about the mental pictures the poem evokes. Students might want to discuss mental pictures they have formed of the boy.

Step 6. Extension

Have students read other poems by Robert Louis Stevenson. Many of his poems for children can be found in his classic collection, *A Child's Garden of Verses.*

Using Journals to Elicit Responses   **Response journals**, or literary logs, can also be used to encourage responses to literature. After reading a chapter in a novel, students might write their thoughts and reactions in a response journal. These responses could be open-ended or could be the result of prompts. Parsons (1990) suggested that questions similar to the following be used as prompts:

• What surprised you about the section that you read today? How does it affect what might happen next in the story?
• As you read today, what feelings did you experience in response to events or characters; for example, did you feel anger, surprise, irritation, or disappointment? Why do you think you responded that way?
• What startling, unusual, or effective words, phrases, expressions, or images did you come across in your reading that you would like to have explained or clarified?
• What characters and situations in the story reminded you of people and situations in your own life? How are they similar, and how do they differ?

■ A **response journal** is a notebook in which students write down their feelings or reactions to selections they have read. They may also jot down questions that they have about a selection.

Two other response prompts that might be used are "What if . . . " and "If I were in the story . . . ." In response to the

"What if . . . " prompt, readers speculate what might have happened if a character had taken a different course of action or if a key event in the story had been different. In responding to "If I were in the story . . . ," readers tell what they would have done if they had been a part of the story's action (Raphael & Boyd, 1997).

Generally, students would be provided with just one or two prompts but should feel free to respond to other concerns or situations. Gradually, the prompts should be faded so that students can come up with their own concerns. Responses in the journals become the basis for discussion of the next day's selection. In supplying prompts for journals, Meyers (1988) took a different tack. She supplied students with a list of twenty questions, similar to those listed above and earlier in this chapter. They were free to choose two or three questions from the list.

Three other kinds of journals are literary, double-entry, and dialogue journals. In the literary journal, the student assumes the role of one of the characters in a selection and writes as though he or she were that character. A student assuming the role of Carlie in *The Pinballs* (Byars, 1977) might tell how she felt when she saw how sick Harvey had become.

Double-entry journals have two columns. In the left column, the student records information or a quote from the text. In the right column, the student reflects on or questions the material in the left column. In a model lesson on using double-entry journals, Dennis-Shaw (2006) had students note in the left column specific passages that reminded them of something in their lives. In the right column, they described the personal connection that they were able to make.

In dialogue journals, students write to the teacher and the teacher responds, or pairs of students might write to each other. Dialogue journals help the teacher keep close contact with students and also extend their understanding of selections. The journal writing should be a genuine exchange between teacher and student and not simply a means for checking on students' reading. If viewed as a checking device, journals may lose their vitality. In a study by Bagge-Rynerson (1994), students' responses in their dialogue journals were more lively after the teacher modeled the kinds of responses that might be written and also made her own responses more personal and more affirming.

Journal entries can be used to foster the process of reading. For instance, to encourage students to make connections as they read, provide a prompt that includes making connections, such as "How did the events in this story remind you of something that has happened to you?" In your dialogue with the students, discuss the connections that they made. As appropriate, encourage them to make deeper connections or connections they might not have thought of (K. Dayton, personal communication, November 25, 2003).

Other Forms of Response Having students respond in a variety of imaginative ways builds interest and motivation. It also gives students multiple ways of responding and so builds multiple skills. For instance, by responding both visually and verbally, students are building both areas. In addition, some selections lend themselves to one mode of response but not to another. Students might compose an ad for the piece, create a film clip of key scene, interview the main character, imagine text messages sent between two key characters, or create a collage depicting key events in the story.

Using Literature Discussion Groups to Elicit Responses

One effective technique for fostering a genuine response to literature is to form a literature discussion group, an interpretative community that

An aesthetic reading of a literary selection fosters a deeper appreciation and understanding.

shares a text much as a group of adults might do. This sharing can be both formal and informal. It can take place in whole-class discussions, small groups, or between partners. Students can complete their reading for discussion groups in various ways. They can read at home, in class, or in both places. Vicki Yousoofian, a first-grade teacher, sends books home over the weekend to be read with parents. Included with the books is a letter that explains literature circles and suggests ways that parents might discuss the books with their children (Noe, 2002). Stick-on notes are provided so that students can use them to mark favorite passages. Realizing that not all children will receive the suggested help, the teacher schedules time for the children to read over their books on Monday before they gather in their circles.

Students can respond in a variety of ways to their reading (Noe, 2002). They can fill out role sheets, make notes on bookmarks, use stick-on notes to record observations, and respond in logs or journals, with journals being more reflective than logs. They can respond to questions or prompts, or their responses can be more open-ended. You might use some of the reader response prompts listed on pages 436 and 437. Teachers have found it helpful to have students suggest prompts or to report on prompts that have worked especially well. A favorite prompt is "What if . . . ?" which leads students to reflect on what might have happened if the main character had taken a different course of action or if something else in the story had been changed.

Literature discussion groups, which are also known as literature circles, literature study groups, conversational discussion groups, and book clubs, can be organized in a variety of ways. Students may have roles. Or they might simply gather for discussion without having predetermined roles. In some instances, the teacher might appoint a starter who initiates the discussion. The teacher may be an active member, an occasional visitor, or an observer. Literature discussion groups can meet once a week or even every day. The teacher can have one group meet each day or can have all groups meeting simultaneously. Table 10.1 presents the general procedures to be used by literature discussion groups.

An essential part of the literature discussion group is the development of discussion abilities. One highly effective, research-based approach to discussion is quality talk.

Quality Talk Extensively researched, quality talk draws from nine high-quality discussion approaches, including Questioning the Author and Junior Great Books Shared Inquiry (Wilkinson, 2009; Reninger & Wilkinson, 2010). Quality talk is a shared approach in which both teacher and students play essential roles. The teacher typically selects the text and the topic, and provides an authentic question to begin the discus-

TABLE 10.1 Procedures for Literature Discussion Groups

Procedure	Description
Book selection	Students choose from among about five books; each student might list three choices. Or teacher might select book.
Formation of groups	Teacher forms groups based on students' selections. Reading ability can be a factor.
Agreement on procedures	Class formulates basic procedures for completing assignments and discussing books.
Group discussions	Groups meet one or more times a week. Groups can be teacher- or student-led. Students can use role sheets, respond to teacher prompts, or use stick-on notes to highlight passages for discussion.
Debriefing	Group talks about how discussions went and decides on ways to improve discussions.
Whole-class sharing	Groups periodically talk with the rest of the class about the books they are reading.

sion. An authentic question is one for which there is no definite answer or for which there are several possible answers: What other decision might the main character have made? Should sugary foods be banned from school lunches? The teacher emphasizes asking questions that will engage students.

The teacher models higher-level talk and scaffolds students' responses. However, students are encouraged to respond freely and to ask their own questions. Uptake is fostered. Uptake occurs when students build on each other's responses. Teacher modeling and scaffolding are especially important in the earlier stages. Without teacher involvement, talk might remain at an exploratory level (Wilkinson, 2009). Questions should be both analytical and affective. Discussions work best if there is an emotional component, if students feel deeply about their positions or views. Quality talk also requires an atmosphere of trust and curiosity. Quality discussions don't happen automatically. Ground rules need to be established and practiced.

FYI

Giving students some say in creating rules for discussion groups builds community and ownership. One way of eliciting rules is to have students describe a good conversation or discussion and then note what made it so (Adler & Rougle, 2005). It takes time for students to learn how to conduct discussions. Almasi, O'Flahavan, and Arya (2001) found that it takes at least five meetings before students learn to function together. ■

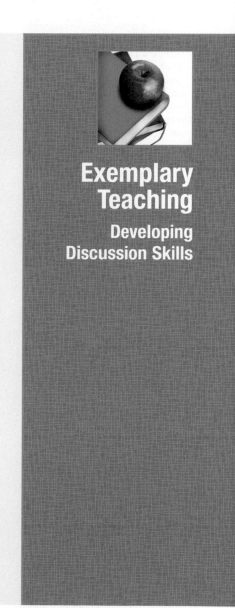

Exemplary Teaching

Developing Discussion Skills

So that her third-graders would get the most out of literature discussion groups, Mrs. P. provided extensive preparation (Maloch, 2004). She stressed the need for a sense of caring and being responsible for each other. The class also participated in self-selected reading and teacher-led whole-class or guided reading discussions. These activities gave them experience selecting and discussing books. As more direct preparation, in whole-class discussions of *Charlotte's Web* (White, 1952), Mrs. P. posed the kinds of questions that she hoped students would ask each other in their discussion groups. After whole-group discussions, she arranged for students to work with partners. They were given a choice of two topics and were to write about one of them in their response journals and then discuss their responses with their partners. The topics stressed making personal connections: "Charlotte consoled Wilbur when he had gotten some bad news. Write about a time that you either helped someone out or a time when you needed help and someone helped you" (Maloch, 2004, p. 8). Gradually, Mrs. P. turned responsibility for the selection of the writing and discussion topics over to the students. Students were asked to select "something that was important to you in that chapter, something that the two of you think will be a good thing to write about" (p. 8). Students shared their written responses in the whole group. During this whole-group sharing, Mrs. P. was able to provide students with suggestions for improving topic selection and discussions.

After students developed some skill working in pairs, they began working in groups of four. As the groups of students discussed, Mrs. P. visited each one and provided assistance and instruction as needed. She addressed issues of behavior, emphasizing the need to respect each other and to learn to solve interpersonal issues. After discussions, students reflected on these questions: "What did I do/say in my group that was helpful? What did I do to make it work?" (p. 13). Mrs. P. also scaffolded students' discussion techniques, such as building on what others have said and providing support for one's positions. And she fostered students' ability to ask higher-level questions and to consider key issues, so that they would move beyond a retelling of the plot or a superficial comparison of characters. By observing and listening carefully to her students' responses, Mrs. P. was able to determine what kinds of guidance the students needed to solidify and expand their comprehension and discussion skills.

The building of interpersonal skills took most of their time, but as students learned how to work together, Mrs. P. could focus more on developing discussion and thinking skills. At the end of the preparatory period and before moving into literature discussion groups, students articulated the elements of an effective discussion group by brainstorming answers to this query: "What makes a good literature group?" (p. 14). Having had guided experience with whole-class, paired, and small-group discussions, the third-graders were ready to work responsibly and profitably in literature discussion groups.

Adapting Instruction for Struggling Readers and Writers

Although similar to book clubs, literature discussion groups provide students with choice and also can be organized according to cooperative learning principles, with each student having a well-defined role. Because students have a choice of materials, struggling readers can select books that are closer to their level. Struggling ELLs and many members of minority groups do better in cooperative learning groups. ■

FYI

Literature discussion groups meet for about 20 minutes. Discussions might be student-led, teacher-led, or a combination of the two (Temple, Martinez, Yokota, & Naylor, 1998). Students feel freer to express themselves when the teacher isn't present, but the teacher can provide expert assistance. Even if the discussion is student-led, in the beginning the teacher can assist the group in getting started and might model the kinds of literary questions that students are learning to ask. The teacher should also monitor each group to make sure it is on task and everyone is participating. From time to time, the teacher might drop in to model higher-level questioning or to perk up a flagging group. ■

R E F L E C T I O N

Which forms of response to literature do you like best? Which forms do you think might work best with your students?

FYI

If there are more roles than students, some students may fulfill more than one role, or roles may be combined. ■

Junior Great Books uses the following guidelines. These guidelines can be adapted to fit your situation.

1. Read the selection before participating in the discussion.
2. Support your ideas with evidence from the text.
3. Discuss the ideas in the selection and try to understand them fully before exploring issues that go beyond the selection.
4. Listen to others and respond to them directly.
5. Expect the leader to ask questions, rather than answer them. (Great Books Foundation, n. d.)

Literature Discussion Groups as Cooperative Learning Groups   Some literature discussion groups incorporate the principles of cooperative learning to provide more structure (Bjorklund, Handler, Mitten, & Stockwell, 1998). The groups are composed of five or six students who have chosen to read the same book. Students choose from six books the three they would most like to read. Books could cover the same theme or topic, be in the same genre, or have the same author. They might all be biographies, or they might all have survival in the wilderness as a theme, for instance. The books should represent a range of interests and difficulty levels so that students have a genuine choice, and the list of choices should include books that are appropriate for average, below-average, and above-average readers.

The books are presented. The teacher provides an overview of each one, and students are invited to examine the books to see whether they are interesting and whether they are on the right level of challenge. Students are urged to read two or three pages at scattered intervals in order to judge the difficulty level of the book. Students then list their top three choices.

Based on the students' choices, the teacher forms four or five groups. The teacher tries to get a mix of students in each group so that a number of perspectives are represented and a number of personalities are included. The teacher also tries to match below-average readers with books that they can handle.

Once the groups have been formed, roles are assigned by the teacher, or the group decides who will fulfill which role. Key roles are the discussion leader, summarizer, literacy reporter, illustrator, word chief, and connector. The discussion leader develops questions for the group and leads the discussion. The summarizer summarizes the selection. The literacy reporter locates passages that stand out because they are funny, sad, contain key incidents, or feature memorable language. The reporter can read the passages out loud, ask the group to read them silently and discuss them, or, with other members of the group, dramatize them. An illustrator illustrates a key part of the selection with a drawing or graphic organizer. The word chief locates difficult words or expressions from the selection, looks them up in the dictionary, and writes down their definitions. At the group meeting, the word chief points out and discusses the words with the other members. The connector finds links between the book and other books the group has read or between the book and real events, problems, or situations. The connector describes the connection and discusses it with the group. Although each student has a certain role to fulfill in the group, any student may bring up a question for discussion, a passage that stands out, a confusing word, a vivid figure of speech, or a possible connection.

The roles reflect the kinds of things that students should be doing as they read a text. They should be creating questions in their minds, making connections, visualizing, summarizing, noting key passages, coping with difficult words and confusing passages, and appreciating expressive language and literary techniques. Students switch roles periodically so that each student has the opportunity to carry out each of the roles.

To help students fulfill their roles, they are given job sheets. A sample job sheet for a discussion leader is shown in Figure 10.1. Each of the roles is also modeled and discussed. The class, as a whole, also practices each of the jobs by applying it to a brief,

FIGURE 10.1 Discussion Leader Job Sheet

The discussion leader's job is to ask a series of questions about the part of the book that your group will be discussing. Ask questions that will make the other students in your group think carefully about what they read and walk in the shoes of the main characters. Here are some possible questions:

How do you feel about this part of the story?

Was there anything that bothered or surprised you?

What would you have done if you had been the main character?

What do you think will happen in the next part of the story?

Write your questions on the lines below.

1. _____

2. _____

3. _____

4. _____

Adapted from Daniels, H. (1994). *Literature Circles, Voice and Choice in the Student-Centered Classroom.* York, ME: Stenhouse.

relatively easy selection. Creation of questions is given special attention. Questions that lead to in-depth sharing of responses are stressed. Discussions are modeled. The teacher might do this by training a group and then having them demonstrate before the class. Job sheets are a way of providing structure and scaffolding students' efforts. Like all scaffolds, they should be gradually reduced or eliminated so that students can take control of the literature circles. Otherwise, the job sheets tend to limit students' performance and engagement (Daniels, 2008). On the other side of the coin, if literature circles are flagging, introducing or reintroducing roles might shore them up.

Students are given two or three weeks to complete a book. After a group has been formed, the group meets and sets up a schedule for how much reading members will do each evening. A written schedule is created and pasted to the inside cover of the response journal. If students are doing most or all of their work in school, they meet every other day. Days they don't meet are used to complete their reading and related tasks.

The teacher visits each group and, in the early stages, might model asking questions or responding to a selection. As students become more adept, the teacher takes on the role of participant. Students also rely less on their job sheets. Job sheets are a temporary scaffold designed to show students how to analyze and respond to text and discuss it (Daniels, 2002). As students learn basic skills involved in reading, responding, and discussing, the job sheets can be phased out or used only to prepare for the discussion. If students hold onto the job sheets too long, they may limit their discussions to what's written on the sheets rather than having a fuller, more spontaneous discussion of the text. However, job sheets might also be used to shore up flagging discussions if students haven't used them previously.

Whole-class sessions are held each day so that groups can share with each other. This is also a good time to present minilessons or perhaps read aloud a selection that pertains to the theme or topic of the books being read.

After the books have been completely read and discussed, students meet in groups according to the roles they fulfilled. All the discussion leaders meet, as do all the summarizers, connectors, illustrators, word chiefs, and literary reporters. In these groups, students give an overview of the book they read and their opinion of the book. They also discuss the books they read from the point of view of their roles. In this way, all of the students become acquainted with the books read in other groups.

FYI

• Encourage parents to discuss books with their children. Book discussions foster both reading and language development. It is important, however, that you give parents sufficient guidance and encouragement.

• Students in schools in Chicago that used literature circles as part of a reading-writing workshop showed significant gains on citywide reading tests (Daniels, 2002). In one school, the number of students reading at the national average tripled. ■

Using Technology

The video *Looking into Literature Circles* (Stenhouse) portrays three real literature circles.

LiteratureCircles.com features book recommendations, management ideas, and tips from veteran teachers. http://www. literaturecircles.com

Literature Circles Resource Center provides information and resources on literature circles. http://www. litcircles.org ■

Students can eventually conduct literature discussion groups on their own, without much teacher involvement.

R E F L E C T I O N

What are the benefits of teacher-led discussion groups versus student-led discussion groups? Which do you prefer? Why might it be a good idea to have both teacher-led and student led groups?

FYI

Literature circles can embrace nonfiction. Stien and Beed (2004) made the transition from fiction to nonfiction circles by using biographies. Roles were altered slightly. The Fantastic Fact Finder collected important facts; the Timeline Traveler kept track of key dates; and the Vital Statistics Collector assembled basic information about the subject. After growing in proficiency, instead of using role sheets, students used sticky notes to mark passages they wanted to discuss. ■

FYI

Rearranging the furniture can cause a change in response patterns. Students are more likely to respond to each other when they are facing each other. ■

Each group also makes a brief presentation of its book to the whole class. This might be in the form of an ad, a skit based on the book, a panel discussion, an interview of the main character, or a dramatization of a key passage.

Literature discussion groups can be less structured so that students don't have specific roles. However, teachers who have used a structured approach find that in time, students automatically carry out the various roles as they read.

Strategic Literature Discussions   While observing students involved in a literature discussion group, researchers Clark and Berne (2005; Berne & Clark, 2006) noticed that students were using comprehension strategies to construct meaning, but they were not using a full range of strategies and were not using the strategies very effectively. As Berne and Clark (2006) comment, "Students need to be taught how to employ comprehension strategies to assist themselves and group members as they collaboratively puzzle through ideas in the text." To deepen comprehension, teach key strategies explicitly and prompt the use of the strategies during discussions. For instance, the following prompts, some of which are taken directly from Clark and Berne (2005, 2006) and some of which have been adapted from Clark and Berne (2005, 2006), might be used for the strategies noted:

Summarizing

- There were so many details here. What were the main things that happened?
- If you had to tell me what this was about very briefly, what would you say?

Analyzing the author's craft

- What did the author do to help us understand the text?
- What special techniques did the author use?

Questioning

- Are there parts that were hard to understand?
- As you read, what did you wonder?
- As you read, what questions came to mind?

Making connections

- This makes me think of another story that we read that had a mystery in it. How was the mystery in that story like the mystery in this one?
- How did the main character feel? Have you ever felt the way the main character did?

At the Sandy Hook School in Connecticut, the fourth- and fifth-grade teachers fostered appreciation through the use of literature circles. Students were given a choice of six books to read. The books explored a common question or topic (survival, for instance), or they constituted an author study (all being written by the same author). Students listed three books they would most like to read, and based on their choices, groups were formed. The groups were heterogeneous, so all the poorest readers or all the best readers didn't end up in the same group. However, the teacher matched up books and students so that all students, including below-level readers, had books they could handle.

After the groups were formed and jobs were assigned (jobs included discussion leader, summarizer, literacy reporter, illustrator, word chief, and connector), students were given a calendar and asked to make up a schedule for reading their book and completing their jobs. Students were required to complete the book in two weeks, but they decided how many pages they would read each night. They could choose to do the most reading on days when they had few afternoon activities. After the schedule was created, students were given two copies of it, one for home and one to be kept at school.

Students seldom missed their assignments. Having been able to choose their reading and set up their schedules, they were committed to completing their assignments. Besides, there was considerable peer pressure. If they didn't complete an assignment, they were letting the group down. If students did not complete their assignments, they were not allowed to take part in the circle. Instead, they worked by themselves to complete the missed work.

Each day, just two of the four groups met for discussion. The other two groups worked on their assignments. By having just two groups meet each day, each teacher was better able to oversee their discussions and provide any needed help. But mostly, the teacher took on the role of participant. To be a realistic participant, the teacher responded to the story in her journal and then brought her journal to the circle. Thus, she was a genuine participant and not just someone who came to direct or assess.

Students were enthusiastic about their circles, and they also improved their ability to appreciate and respond to literature. By year's end, they incorporated the six roles into their reading; as they read, they were asking themselves questions, summarizing, visualizing, appreciating the author's craft, making connections, and noting difficult words and confusing passages.

What was the secret of the teachers' success? Through careful planning and implementation, they let the students know what was expected and set them up for success. The teachers also were caring and enthusiastic (Bjorklund, Handler, Mitten, & Stockwell, 1998).

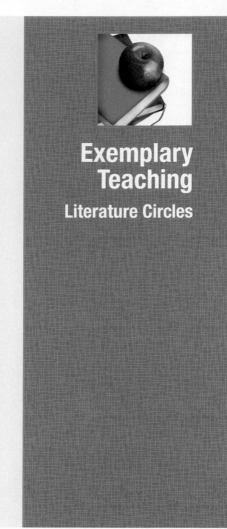

Exemplary Teaching

Literature Circles

Looking back

- What in the story makes you say that?
- What makes you think the girl was clever?
- Can you read the line that explains why the boy wasn't prepared for the test?

A key strategy in discussions is going back to the text for clarification or to locate support for a position.

With proper preparation and supervision, literature discussion groups have the potential to develop students' comprehension strategies as well as their understanding of a selection.

Envisionments

To foster a deeper engagement and understanding, help students build envisionments (Langer, 2011). An envisionment is "the understanding that a particular person has at a given point in time." (p. 10). The students progress from forming an initial understanding to developing interpretations, to reflecting on personal experience and proceed to evaluating the reading and, in some instances, apply what they have built in one envisionment to the creation of a new envisionment. Careful questioning can help students develop their envisionments. Initially, you might pose the kinds of questions that lead to deeper understanding, but, over time, with your guidance, students should take more responsibility for asking these kinds of questions in their literature discussion groups. Langer (1990) suggests that teachers pose four levels of questions.

 Using Technology

Making Meaning in Literature: A Video Library, Grades 6–8
  Series of high-quality videos demonstrate the implementation of the envisionment process:
www.learner.org/libraries/makingmeaning/makingmeaning/ ■

 FYI

A natural way to begin discussions is to pose questions about aspects of a selection that are puzzling (Adler & Rougle, 2005). After listening to or reading a selection, students compose "wonder questions" on slips of paper. The wonder questions are placed in a hat. Students then take turns drawing a wonder question, which is read aloud and discussed. ■

CCSS

Read closely to determine what the text says explicitly and to make logical inferences from it; cite specific textual evidence when writing or speaking to support conclusions drawn from the text.

FYI

Envisionment questions can be a guide for discussing literature. You can use general questions from each of the four levels. Or use the levels to compose your own more specific questions. Some teachers create a list of envisionment questions for students to use as a guide as they read (Adler & Rougle, 2005). When using envisionment questions, it isn't necessary to begin at the lowest level and work your way up. You might start a discussion with an evaluative question but use a lower-level question to provide support. ■

CCSS

• Analyze the structure of texts, including how specific sentences, paragraphs, and larger portions of the text (e.g., a section, chapter, scene, or stanza) relate to each other and the whole.

• Assess how point of view or purpose shapes the content and style of a text.

1. **Initial understandings.**   Ask typical reader response questions, which enable students to share their reactions to the piece: "Which part of the work stands out in your mind? Was there anything in the work that bothered you? Was there anything in it that surprised you? Do you have any questions about the work?"

2. **Developing interpretations.**   Ask questions that encourage students to think more deeply about the story. These questions can help students think about motivations, character development, theme, or setting: "Do you think the main character acted responsibly? What do you think made the main character confess, even though he was innocent? What is the author trying to say here?" Helping students develop interpretations of character is especially important. As Westby (1999) notes, "Understanding of characters' emotions, thoughts, and beliefs [is] the glue that ties the action of stories together" (p. 172). Students may experience difficulty drawing inferences about characters because they focus on action rather than on inner states; they misinterpret the character's emotions and motivations because they mistakenly believe the character is just like them, because they fail to consider the whole story, or because they focus on the perspective of just one of the characters (Westby, 1999). One way of helping children think about character traits as well as expand their vocabularies is to develop labels for traits. The teacher discusses a character and his or her traits, lists the traits on a chart, and then introduces new words for the traits (Manyak, 2007a). For example, *courageous* is offered as a synonym for *brave*. Other characters are introduced, and their traits are listed and discussed, with synonyms supplied. A chart is constructed with character trait words appropriate for the grade level. Lists of character trait words for all grade levels could be collected by the school. In that way, character trait words could be built on and reinforced in subsequent grades.

3. **Reflecting on personal experience.**   Ask questions that help students relate what they have read to personal knowledge or experience. These questions can help them reconsider current or previous understandings or feelings. Some of the reader response questions will work well here: "Does the main character remind you of anyone you know? Have you ever been in a situation similar to the one he was in? How would you have handled it? Does this story make you think of anything that has happened in your life?"

There seems to be a difference between the "associations" that students frequently offer when they discuss a text and the critical "connections" that undergird deeper comprehension. . . . Miller (2002) contended that classroom conversations often stop with associations rather than probing for their roots. It's the kind of familiar (to teachers) talk that begins: "I have a puppy (uncle, grandmother, toy castle), too!" without following that association to its significance in the story world. (Roser, Martinez, Fuhrken, & McDonnold, 2007, p. 555)

Connections need to go beyond surface associations to the underlying emotion or other element that connects the story and real life: "I had a dog and I had to give it away, too, just like Jason, the boy in the story. I felt sad for a long time just like Jason."

4. **Evaluating.**   Once students have responded to the work, refined their interpretations, and looked at the work in terms of their own background knowledge and experiences, help them step back and take a critical look at the piece as a work of art. They might compare it with other pieces they have read and evaluate it in terms of character development, originality and plausibility of the plot, development of the theme, suitability of setting, style, and overall impact. Students should consider the author's craft so they might come to a better understanding of the creative process and perhaps apply some of the techniques they experienced to their own writing. The following questions might be asked: "Does this piece remind you of anything else that you read? What was the best line or paragraph in the piece? Did the characters seem real? What made them seem real? Was the plot believable? What special words, expressions, or writing devices did the author use? Which of these did you like best? Least? If you were the author's editor, what would you say to the author? What changes might you ask the author to make? What point of view did the author use? How might the story have been different if the author had told the story from a third-person point of view rather than the first?"

Discussion Moves

Approaches that attempt to foster students' discussion of literature vary in their effectiveness. All increase the amount of talk. However, their impact on comprehension varies from minimal to quite significant (Murphy & Edwards, 2004). Overall, two of the most effective approaches are Junior Great Books and Questioning the Author. Both approaches provide extensive training and have a well-planned, systematic implementation plan. A key feature of both is that discussion moves are spelled out. Discussion moves are statements that students can make to maintain a discussion or that the teacher may make to foster effective discussion. For example, instead of saying, "You're wrong," a student would say something like this: "I understand what you are saying about the father, but I think the father was wrong to get rid of the dog."

Table 10.2 lists discussion moves from a number of approaches, including Junior Great Books and Questioning the Author. The moves marked with an asterisk are typically used by the teacher but might sometimes be used by students. Conversely, the teacher might use some of the moves that students typically use.

 Assessing for Learning

To keep track of students' responses, create a seating chart and record students' responses (Great Books Foundation, 1999). This will help you to see who is responding, who needs encouraging, and who is having difficulty, as well as to gauge the overall quality of the discussion. ■

 Adapting Instruction for Struggling Readers and Writers

On occasions when you wish to involve all students in the discussion, including those who cannot read the book on their own, read aloud to the class and have students follow along. However, make sure that struggling readers have ample opportunities at other times to read texts on their level.

TABLE 10.2   Major Discussion Moves

Discussion Move	Description	Example(s)
Stating	Stating an idea or opinion	This is what I think happened that day.
Explaining	Explaining a statement	Here is what I meant when I said that Alex made a mistake.
Supporting/ substantiating	Providing details or examples to prove or back up an assertion	This is why I believe the main character was a genius.
Agreeing	Expressing agreement with a position and often explaining why	I agree with you, Anna, because. . . .
Disagreeing	Expressing disagreement with a position and often explaining why	I understand what you are saying about the father, but I think the father was wrong to get rid of the dog.
Building	Building on what others say	I'd like to add to what Monique said about Amelia Earhart's courage.
Extending/ following/expanding	Seeking elaboration	Tell me more about that.
Clarifying	Asking to have a confusing point clarified	I'm not sure what you mean here. (If a response is not clear, the student or teacher might restate what he or she believes the student said and then ask if the restatement is correct: "You seem to be saying that having a pet gave Tyrique a sense of responsibility, which carried over to his school work.")
Initiating/opening*	Opening discussion	What is the author trying to say here?
Inviting*	Inviting others to respond	Josh, what do you have to say about Franklin? Do you think he acted responsibly?
Connecting*	Inviting others to make connections with another part of the text, another text, or the world	What is the connection between getting a pet in the first part of the story and Manuel's attitude at the end of the story? What story that we read does this one remind you of? Has anything like this ever happened to you?
Monitoring*	Facilitating discussion	Let's hold our responses until we hear what Milano has to say.
Summarizing*	Highlighting main points	From what we have discussed, what seem to be the main causes of the problem?
Including*	Inviting students who have not responded to participate	We haven't heard from James yet. James, what is your opinion of the main character?

 Using Technology

Great Books Foundation offers extensive information about Junior Great Books and features film clips of discussion techniques.
http://www.greatbooks.org ■

(continued)

TABLE 10.2   Major Discussion Moves (*Continued*)

Discussion Move	Description	Example(s)
Modeling*	Demonstrating a discussion technique, reasoning, or reading strategy	Sometimes I find myself thinking about what I want to say rather than listening to the person speaking. Here is what I do. . . .
Prompting strategy use*	Prompting the use of questioning, comparing, connecting, imaging, appreciating, evaluating, or another strategy	What questions came to mind as you read? How would you compare Chuck and Lisa? Does this remind you of another story that we have read? Something that has happened to you? Did you make any pictures in your mind as you read about the fierceness of the dog? What did the author do to build suspense? Did the characters seem true to life?
Debriefing/ reflecting*	Assessing quality and impact of a discussion	Did the discussion change your views? We seemed to be getting off topic. What might we do to stay on topic?

* These moves are typically used by the teacher but can be used by students.

Responding in Writing

In addition to responding to literary works during discussions, students need to learn to respond in writing. Writing affords the opportunity to think more deeply about a selection and to take the time to organize one's thoughts. As a practical matter, many high-stakes tests assess students' ability to construct a written response to a passage.

Types of Literature

Folklore

A good place to start the study of literature is with folklore, which includes folktales, myths, rituals, superstitions, songs, and jokes. **Folklore** follows an oral tradition. As Taylor (1990) put it, "The tales of the tongue are a good introduction to the tales of the pen." Having stood the test of time, folklore has universal appeal.

Every culture has produced its own **folktales**. Students can investigate those drawn from the culture of their ancestors. African American students might look into one of Verna Aardema's works, such as *Why Mosquitoes Buzz in People's Ears: A West African Folk Tale* (1975), or one of Harold Courlander's collections of African folktales. Closer to home is Virginia Hamilton's (1985) *The People Could Fly: American Black Folktales*. Latino students might enjoy one of Alma Flor Ada's tales from *Tales Our Abuelitas Told: A Hispanic Folktale Collection* (Ada & Campoy, 2006) or another source. Other outstanding sources of materials about diverse cultures are *Kaleidoscope: A Multicultural Booklist for Grades K–8*, 4th ed. (Hansen-Krening, Aoki, & Mizokawa, 2003), and *Multicultural Teaching: A Handbook of Activities, Information, and Resources*, 8th ed. (Tiedt & Tiedt, 2010). To provide follow-up after students have read and discussed a piece of folklore, have them dramatize the tale or compare it to other tales.

Poetry

Students like poetry that has humor and a narrative element and that rhymes. Include both light verse and more thoughtful pieces. Before reading a poem to the class, practice it so that your reading is strong and dramatic. Briefly discuss vocabulary words or concepts that might interfere with students' understanding or enjoyment. Give students a

■ **Folklore** refers to the tales, rituals, superstitions, nursery rhymes, and other oral works created by people.

■ **Folktales** are stories handed down orally from generation to generation. Folktales include fairy tales, myths, legends, and tall tales.

purpose for listening, such as creating images in their minds, awaiting a surprise ending, or hearing unusual words.

You might emphasize questions that evoke a personal response: "What about the poem stands out most in your mind? What pictures came to mind as you listened? Which line do you like best? How does the poem make you feel? Is there anything in the poem that you do not like? Is there anything in it that surprises you?" Better yet, invite students to ask questions about anything in the poem that may have confused them. Gear discussions toward personal responses and interpretations. The emphasis should be "upon delight rather than dissection" (Sloan, 1984, p. 86).

Model how to read a poem, especially one that is complex. Explain how the images create a certain mood or meaning. Much of the magic of poetry arises from its language. Read alliterative verse such as Eleanor Farejon's "Mrs. Peck Pigeon" and Rachel Field's "Something Told the Wild Geese," as well as poems that contain excellent examples of onomatopoeia, such as Rhoda Bracemesseter's "Galoshes" and David McCord's "Song of the Train." Also, help students discover how poets use sensory words, as in Mary O'Neil's "Sound of Water" and Polly Chase Boyden's "Mud." Through becoming aware of language, students develop an ear for poetry.

The following Student Reading List presents a sampling of some of the many fine poetry anthologies available for young people. As the Exemplary Teaching feature shows, students enjoy selecting and sharing favorite poems.

STUDENT READING LIST
Poetry

Bagert, B. (2007). *Shout! Little poems that roar*. New York: Penguin. Exuberant poems for younger students. Designed to be shouted. Has written similar collections.

Brooks, G. (1956, 1984, 2007). *Bronzeville boys and girls*. New York: HarperCollins. Reissue of Gwendolyn Brooks' classic collection. For 8- to 10-year-olds.

Brown, C. (2006). *Flamingos on the roof: Poems and paintings*. Boston: Houghton Mifflin. A collection of easy-to-read humorous poems.

Ciardi, J. (1962). *You read to me, I'll read to you*. New York: HarperCollins. Features thirty-five lighthearted poems.

Dyer, G. L., Jr. (2001). *40 Poems for "T": The fun of writing poetry*. Catskill, NY: Tige. Letters to a young boy explain what poetry is, how to collect ideas for poems, and how to write them.

Foxworth, J. (2008) *Dirt on my shirt*. New York: HarperCollins. Humorous easy-to-read poems.

Hopkins, L. B. (ed.). (1986). *Surprises*. New York: Harper. Thirty-eight easy-to-read poems on a variety of subjects ranging from pets to flying.

Hopkins, L. B. (2000). *My America: A poetry atlas of the United States*. New York: Simon & Schuster. Fifty-one poems celebrate different sections of the United States.

Hudson, W. (1993). *Pass it on: African-American poetry for children*. New York: Scholastic. An illustrated collection of poetry by such African American poets as Langston Hughes, Nikki Giovanni, Eloise Greenfield, and Lucille Clifton.

Hughes, L. (1993). *The dream keeper and other poems*. New York: Knopf. A collection of sixty-six poems selected by the author for young readers, including lyrical poems and songs, many of which explore the African American tradition.

Kennedy, C. (2005). *A family of poems, My favorite poetry for children*. New York: Hyperion. Collection of a variety of poems organized around the themes of self, humor, animals, seasons, seashore, adventure, and bedtime.

CCSS

Determine the meaning of words and phrases as they are used in a text, including figurative and connotative meanings; analyze the impact of a specific word choice on meaning and tone.

REFLECTION

What has been your experience with poetry as a teacher and a student? Why do you think many students have a negative attitude toward poetry? How might you go about developing students interest in and appreciation of poetry?.

Using Technology

Children's poetry is published on KitLit Poetry Gallery.
http://mgfx.com/kidlit/kids/artlit/poetry/index.htm
Poetry workshops for student poets are presented by Jack Prelutsky (grades 1–4), Karla Kuskin (grades 4–8), and Jean Marzollo (grades 2–5). Writing tips are so specific that every student should be able to write a poem.
http://teacher.scholastic.com/writewit/poetry/index.htm
Poet Bruce Lasky has more than a dozen suggestions for writing poems at Giggle Poetry: Poetry Class.
http://www.gigglepoetry.com/poetryclass.aspx
Yahoo! Kids School Bell: Language Arts: Poetry links to a wide variety of sites.
http://kids.yahoo.com/directory/School-Bell/Language-Arts/Poetry ∎

See Appendix B of the Common Core State Standards for a listing of possible novels and stories to read. http://www.corestandards.org/ assets/Appendix_B.pdf

Kuskin, K. (1992). *Soap soup and other verses.* New York: HarperCollins. Features a variety of easy-to-read poems.

Kuskin, K. (2003). *Moon, have you met my mother?* New York: HarperCollins. Comprehensive collection of poems on animals, insects, food, the seasons, and many other topics.

Lawson, J. (2006). *Black stars in a white night sky.* Honesdale, PA: Boyds Mill. A collection of thought- and emotion-provoking poems for middle grade and middle school readers.

Martin, B. & Sampson, M. (eds.). (2008) *The Bill Martin, Jr. big book of poetry.* New York: Simon & Schuster. Features nearly 200 classic and contemporary poems.

Prelutsky, J. (2008). *Pizza, pigs, and poetry: How to write a poem.* New York: Greenwillow. Tips on writing poetry, including poetry starters from the children's poet laureate.

Yolen, J. (2007). *Here's a little poem: A very first book of poetry.* Cambridge, MA: Candlewick. A variety of poems for children in grades 1 to 3.

FYI

Through prompts, teachers can lead students to practice a variety of literacy and comprehension strategies. Prompts might ask students to predict what will happen next or make inferences about a character based on the character's actions, for instance. Or prompts might ask students to create character webs or note examples of figurative language. ■

Chapter Books and Novels

In a literature-based program, chapter books or novels are often set aside as a separate unit of study. Before embarking on a chapter book or novel, students should receive some guidance to build the background essential for understanding the text. Their interest in the book should also be piqued. Place particular emphasis on understanding the first chapter. If students, especially poorer readers, have a thorough understanding of the first chapter, they will have a solid foundation for comprehending the rest of the text. It will also build their confidence in their ability to read the rest of the book (Ford, 1994).

Generally, students are asked to read a chapter or more each day. The teacher may provide questions to be considered during reading, or students might make predictions and read to evaluate them. Students might also keep a response journal for their reading. Responses might be open-ended, with students jotting down their general reactions to the segment being read, or students might respond to questions posed by the teacher.

After a segment has been read, it is discussed. Students might also do some rereading to clarify confusing points or might dramatize exciting parts. A cumulative plot outline or story map could be constructed to keep track of the main events. If the story involves a long journey, the characters' progress might be charted on a map. Extension activities can be undertaken once the book has been completed. The novel might be presented within the framework of an extended guided reading lesson or directed reading–thinking activity, or it might be discussed as a grand conversation in a literature discussion group. Emphasis is on building appreciation and evoking a response; skills are secondary.

Both content and form should be discussed. Design questions to help students understand what is happening in the story and to see how the setting, plot, characters, theme, point of view, and author's style work together. However, take care that you do not overanalyze a piece or ask too many questions at any one time. Balance analysis with eliciting personal responses. Response should precede analysis and general discussion. Once the reader has responded, she or he is in a better position to analyze the piece. Part of the analysis might involve discovering what elements in the piece caused the student to respond (see the earlier section on reader response for some questions). Some general questions for novels are outlined in Table 10.3. Do not attempt to ask all the questions listed; choose only those that seem most appropriate for your students.

The following Student Reading List identifies some outstanding chapter books and novels (in the list, C indicates challenging books, and E indicates easy ones).

Story Element Activities   Several activities help students gain a deeper understanding and appreciation of story elements.

STUDENT READING LIST
Chapter Books and Novels

Grade 1
Bridwell, N. (1972). *Clifford the small red puppy.* New York: Scholastic.
Keats, E. J. (1964). *Whistle for Willie.* New York: Puffin.
Minarik, E. H. (1968). *A Kiss for little bear.* New York: HarperCollins.
Rylant, C. (1990). *Henry and Mudge, the first book.* New York: Simon & Schuster.
Seeger, L. V. (2007). *Dog and Bear: Two friends • three stories.* New Milford, CT: Roaring Brook.

Grade 2
Byars, B. (1996). *My brother, Ant.* New York: Viking.
Diakite, P. (2006). *I lost my tooth in Africa.* New York: Scholastic.
Hoban, R. (1964). *Bread and jam for Frances.* New York: HarperCollins.
Keats, E. J. (1962). *The snowy day.* New York: Viking.
Krensky, S. (1996). *Lionel and his friends.* New York: Dial.
Lobel, A. (1979). *Days with Frog and Toad.* New York: HarperCollins.
Look, L. (2004). *Ruby Lu, brave and true.* New York: Atheneum.
Marshall, J. (1992). *Fox be nimble.* New York: Penguin.
Zion, G. (1956). *Harry the dirty dog.* New York: HarperCollins.

Grade 3
Ada, A. F. (1993). *My name is Maria Isabel.* New York: Simon & Schuster.
Cleary, B. (1981). *Ramona Quimby, age 8.* New York: Dell. C
Cohen, B. Z. (1983). *Molly's pilgrim.* New York: Bantam Doubleday Dell.
Dahl, R. (1961). *James and the giant peach.* New York: Puffin.
Dalgliesh, A. (1954). *Courage of Sarah Noble.* New York: Scribner's.
Surat, M. M. (1983). *Angel child, dragon child.* New York: Scholastic.

Grade 4
Bulla, C. R. (1975). *Shoeshine girl.* New York: Crowell. E
Gardiner, J. R. (1980). *Stone Fox.* New York: HarperCollins. E
Krumgold, J. (1953). *And now Miguel.* New York: Crowell.
MacLachlan, P. (1985). *Sarah, plain and tall.* New York: HarperCollins.
Taylor, M. (1976). *Roll of thunder, hear my cry.* New York: Puffin.
White, E. B. (1952). *Charlotte's web.* New York: HarperCollins.
Wilder, L. I. (1932). *Little house in the big woods.* New York: HarperCollins.

Grade 5
Burnett, F. H. (1912). *The secret garden.* New York: HarperCollins.
Byars, B. (1977). *The pinballs.* New York: HarperCollins.
Cleary, B. (1983). *Dear Mr. Henshaw.* New York: Morrow.
Clements, A. (2006). *A mystery or two.* New York: Simon & Schuster.
Codell, E. R. (2003). *Sarah special.* New York: Hyperion.
Dahl, R. (1964). *Charlie and the chocolate factory.* New York: Penguin.
Giff, P. R. (1997). *Lily's crossing.* New York: Delacorte.
Kadohata, C. (2004). *Kira-kira.* New York: Aladdin.
Konigsburg, E. L. (1967). *From the mixed-up files of Mrs. Basil E. Frankweiler.*
    New York: Atheneum.
Lewis, C. S. (1950). *The lion, the witch, and the wardrobe.* New York: HarperCollins.
Lin, G. (2009). *Where the mountain meets the moon.* Boston: Little, Brown.
Lowry, L. (1989). *Number the stars.* Boston: Houghton Mifflin.
Naylor, P. R. (1991). *Shiloh.* New York: Dell. E
O'Dell, S. (1960). *Island of the blue dolphins.* Boston: Houghton Mifflin. E

Grade 6
Blos, J. W. (1979). *A gathering of days.* New York: Aladdin. C
Byars, B. (1970). *Summer of the swans.* New York: Viking. E
DiCamillo, K. (2000). *Because of Winn-Dixie.* Cambridge, MA: Candlewick Press.

FYI

Chapter books and novels sometimes deal with mature or controversial issues. Before recommending a book to students, make sure that its content is suitable for them. ■

Fox, P. (1984). *One-eyed cat*. New York: Bantam Doubleday Dell.
Gutman, D. (2006). *Satch and me*. New York: HarperCollins. E.
Juster, N. (1961). *The phantom toll booth*. New York: Knopf.
Konigsburg, E. L. (1996). *The view from Saturday*. New York: Atheneum. C
L'Engle, M. (1962). *A wrinkle in time*. New York: Bantam Doubleday Dell.
Lowry, L. (1993). *The giver*. New York: Bantam Doubleday Dell. C
O'Brien, R. C. (1971). *Mrs. Frisby and the rats of NIMH*. New York: Aladdin.
Paterson, K. (1977). *Bridge to Terabithia*. New York: HarperCollins.
Paulsen, G. (1987). *Hatchet*. New York: Simon & Schuster. E
Sachar, L. (1998). *Holes*. New York: Farrar, Straus & Giroux.
Sperry, A. (1940). *Call it courage*. New York: Macmillan.
Spinelli, J. (1996). *Crash*. New York: Knopf. E
Taylor, T. (1969). *The cay*. New York: Avon. E

Grades 7 and 8
Collier, J. L. (1974). *My brother Sam is dead*. New York: Scholastic. E
Craighead, J. G. (1959). *My side of the mountain*. New York: Puffin.
Curtis, C. P. (1999). *Bud, not Buddy*. New York: Delacorte Press.
Forbes, E. (1943). *Johnny Tremain*. New York: Dell.
Hunt, I. (1986). *Across five Aprils*. New York: Berkeley.
London, J. (1903/1996). *The call of the wild*. New York: Viking. C
Perkins, L. R. (2005). *Criss Cross*. New York: Greenwillow.
Stevenson, R. L. (1883/2006). *Treasure Island*. New York: Scribner's.
Twain, M. (1876/2002). *Adventures of Tom Sawyer*. New York: Penguin.
Yep, L. (1990). *Child of the owl*. New York: HarperCollins. E

TABLE 10.3   Possible Questions for Novels

Setting	Where does the story take place?
	When does the story take place?
	Could the story have happened in a different place at a different time?
	Why or why not?
	When you close your eyes and imagine the setting, what do you see?
Characters	Who are the main characters?
	What kinds of people are they?
	Do they seem like real people? Why or why not?
	How does the author let you know what the main characters are like?
	Did the characters change? If so, how?
	Can you picture the characters in your mind? What do they look like? What do they do? What do they say?
	Do you know anyone like them?
	Would you like to meet them? Why or why not?
Plot	What event started the story?
	What is the main problem?
	What is making the problem better?
	What is making the problem worse?
	What has been the most exciting part of the story so far?
	How is the problem resolved?
Point of view	How is the story told?
	Is it told by a narrator who is a part of the story and who calls himself "I"?
	Is it told in the second person, using the pronoun "you"?
	Is the story told by someone outside, a person who can see all and tell all?
	How does the author seem to feel about the characters?
Theme	What seems to be the main or most important idea in the story?
	What main idea do you take away from the story?

Style	What are some especially well-written passages? What are some examples of colorful words that the author uses? Does the author use figures of speech or images? If so, give some examples. What special writing techniques does the author use? Give some examples. Would you like to read another book by this same author or about this same subject? Why or why not? Would you recommend this book to a friend? Why or why not? If you could, would you make changes in this book? Why or why not? Give some changes you would make.

Character Analysis   A number of devices can be used to analyze characters in a story. One such device is the character chart (see Figure 10.2). Students list the facts that an author uses to create a character and note what these facts reveal about the character. The facts are listed in the chart under "What the story says." The facts are interpreted in the adjoining column, headed "What the reader can infer." When introducing the character chart, think aloud as you fill it in.

Another device for character analysis is an opinion–proof, in which readers write an opinion about a character and cite proof to back it up. The proof could be the character's actions or comments made about the character by other characters or the author (Santa, 1988). Figure 10.3 presents an opinion–proof for Chibi from *Crow Boy* (Yashima, 1955).

Plot Analysis   Understanding the structure of a story aids comprehension and gives students a framework for composing their own stories. A plot chart shows the story

FIGURE 10.2   Character Chart

Name of character _____

	What the story says	**What the reader can infer**
Character's actions		
Character's thoughts		
Character's conversations		
What others say about the character		
What the author says about the character		

FIGURE 10.3   Opinion–Proof for Chibi from *Crow Boy*

Opinion	**Proof**
Chibi knew the ways of nature.	He could hold insects in his hand. He knew where wild grapes and wild potatoes grew. He knew about flowers. He could imitate the voices of crows.

FYI

• Children aged 10 and younger have a more difficult time comprehending the internal states of characters than they do the more concrete elements in a story, such as characters' specific actions (van den Broek, Lynch, Naslund, Ievers-Landis, & Verduin, 2003).
• A character continuum can be used to show how characters change (Barton & Sawyer, 2003). For example, a continuum for the prince in *The Whipping Boy* (Fleschman, 1986) might show how the prince started out being selfish and self-centered but gradually became self-reliant and caring. ■

CCSS

Describe how a particular story's or drama's plot unfolds in a series of episodes as well as how the characters respond or change as the plot moves toward a resolution. Explain how an author develops the point of view of the narrator or speaker in a text.

FIGURE 10.4   Illustrated Plot Chart for *Crow Boy*

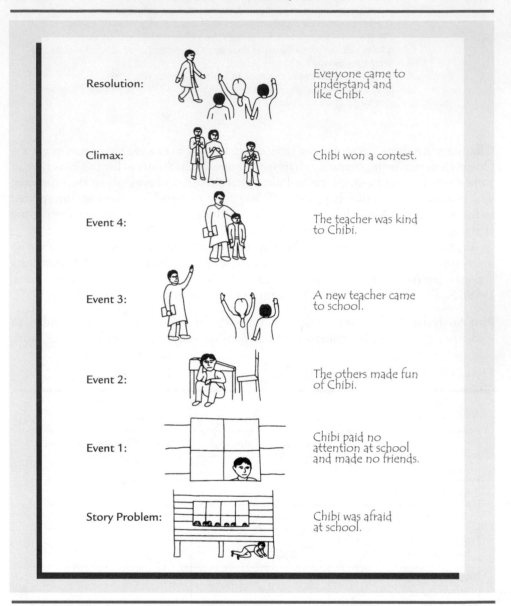

REFLECTION

What were your favorite novels or
chapter books when you were your
students' ages? How might you
promote choice in your program
but still provide students with the
common experience of reading
and discussing **some of the** same
works?

problem, the main actions or events leading up to the climax, the climax, the resolution of the problem, and the ending. It could be a series of rectangles, a diagram, or a picture. Figure 10.4 provides an example of a plot chart.

Students might also draw pictures of major events of a story or put the events on a time line. Acting out key scenes or putting on a puppet show could highlight the action. To help them choose the most exciting parts, have students pretend that they are making a movie of the story and must decide which scenes to depict in a preview of coming attractions and which scene to show on a poster advertising the movie.

Theme Analysis   Theme is the underlying meaning of a story; it can be a universal truth or a significant statement about society, human nature, or the human condition (Stauffer, 1999). The theme is not the same as a lesson or moral. In children's books, the theme often "reflects those developmental values inherent in the process of growing up. The theme may be concerned with overcoming jealousy or fear, adjusting to a physical handicap, or accepting a stepparent" (Sutherland, 1997, p. 31). Thus, analysis of changes that major characters undergo can provide insight into a particular theme.

To illustrate the importance of helping students understand big ideas, or themes, Walmsley (2006) cites the example of *Chrysanthemum* (Henkes, 1991), a book about a mouse named after the flower, who is teased at school. After a class reads this book, discussion invariably revolves around students' names. However, a class discussion about not judging on the basis of outward appearances or not being swayed by the opinions of others would elicit the theme of the book. Similarly, a presentation of "Itsy Bitsy Spider" to preschool or kindergarten children should include a discussion of the importance of trying again if at first you don't succeed.

Developing the concept of theme is a two-part process. In the first part, students draw generalizations or themes from the text; in the second part, they seek support for these generalizations or themes (Norton, 1989). Readers are seeking the answers to two questions: "What is the author trying to tell us that would make a difference in our lives? How do we know the author is telling us _____?" (Norton, 1989, p. 431).

Identifying themes can be a difficult task. When asked to identify the theme, students might retell the story. Remind them to think about what the author is trying to say in the story. To help them understand the concept of theme, read a short story or picture book to students. Read a selection that is brief but has a well-developed theme. Before reading the selection, set a purpose. Have students listen to discover what important thing the author is trying to tell readers about life. Discuss possible themes with students. List the possible themes on the chalkboard or overhead projector. Read the selection again. This time have students listen to the story in order to find support for the themes. List the evidence under each theme.

Most chapter books and novels lend themselves to a variety of follow-up activities. Plan activities such as the following to deepen students' understanding and appreciation of a book and to promote the development of language arts skills.

REINFORCEMENT ACTIVITIES
Chapter Books and Novels

- Read a sequel or another book by the same author or a book that develops the same theme or can be contrasted with the book just completed.
- Dramatize portions of the book.
- Create a print, TV, or Internet ad for the book.
- Create a dust cover for the book, complete with blurbs that highlight the story and that tell about the author.
- View a movie based on the book, then compare the two.
- Create a montage, diorama, or other piece of art related to the book.
- Write a review of the book for the school newspaper.
- Have a Characters' Day, during which students dress up and act the parts of characters in the book.
- Arrange for a panel discussion of the book. The panel might be composed of the book's characters.
- Describe books on the school's or class's homepage. Include links to the author's site, if there is one.

Drama

Plays are a welcome change of pace but require some special reading skills. Although designed to be acted out or at least read orally, plays should first be read silently so that students get the gist of the work. Students need to be taught to read stage directions

CCSS
For a listing of possible plays to be read and performed, see Appendix B of the Common Core State Standards.
http://www.corestandards.org/assets/Appendix_B.pdf.

 FYI
Drama and arts result in an average percentile gains of 12 points in language and related skills (Hattie, 2009).

Using Technology

The site Cre8tive Drama features many teaching resources.

http://www.cre8tivedrama.com

At Kids' Vid, students can use Storyboard to plan and create a film clip, going step by step through an outline, a script, a treatment, and a storyboard. The storyboard notes setting, actors, lighting, transitions, camera, and sound.

http://kidsvid.altec.org ■

FYI

• Students might also like to try role-playing, improvisation, and use of puppets. Role-playing works well with all ages, but seems to work best with younger children; improvisation seems to suit older children better. Using improvisation, students spontaneously dramatize a story or situation. Improvisation might be used to portray a character in a tale or extend a story. It might also be used to dramatize a concept in science or social studies.

• Introduce students to a variety of types of reading: short stories, novels, biographies, poems, plays, and informational pieces. Students may have a favored genre or may exclude informational texts. They need to experience a full range of literary genres. ■

so that they can picture the setting. They also require practice in reading dialogue, which does not contain the familiar transitions and descriptive passages of their usual reading. If possible, students should see plays put on by local professional or amateur groups to give them first-hand experience with theater.

Plays are found in many basal readers. Scripts from TV shows and movies are often included in children's magazines. The magazine *Plays* is, of course, an excellent source. The following Student Reading List identifies a number of anthologies of children's plays.

STUDENT READING LIST
Drama

Barchers, S. I. (1993). *Reader's theatre for beginning readers.* Englewood, CO: Teachers Ideas Press.

Barchers, S. I. (2001). *From Atlanta to Zeus: Reader's theatre from Greek mythology.* Littleton, CO: Libraries Unlimited.

Barchers, S., & Ruscoe, M. (2008). *Against all odds: Readers theater for grades 3–8.* Westport, CT: Libraries Unlimited/Teachers Ideas Press.

Blau, T. (2000). *The best of reader's theatre.* Bellevue, WA: One from the Heart Publications.

Braun, W., & Braun, C. (2000). *A reader's theatre treasury of stories.* Winnipeg, Manitoba, CAN: Portage & Main Press.

Chanda, J. (2008). *Acting out.* New York: Atheneum.

Friedman, L. (2001). *Break a leg! The kid's guide to acting and stagecraft.* New York: Workman.

Kamerman, S. E. (ed.). (2001). *Plays of great achievers: One-act plays about inventors, scientists, statesmen, humanitarians, and explorers.* Boston: Plays.

McBride-Smith, B. (2001). *Tell it together: Foolproof scripts for story theatre.* Little Rock, AR: August House.

Dramatizations To dramatize a story, actors must understand the action and must think carefully about the characters they are portraying. Instead of settling for passive comprehension, readers as actors must put themselves into the piece. They must make the characters come alive by giving them voice, expression, and motivation. This requires that readers think carefully and creatively about what they have read.

Story Theater In **story theater**, students pantomime a selection—a folktale, a realistic story, or a poem—while a narrator reads it aloud. Actions need not be limited to those performed by human characters. For example, the sun, the wind, trees swaying in the breeze, and a babbling brook can all be pantomimed. The teacher will probably have to help students organize the production, at least in the beginning. As students become familiar with the technique, they should be able to work out production details for themselves. Working out the details encourages cooperative learning and also involves all the language arts.

Reader's Theater. In **reader's theater**, participants dramatize a selection by reading it aloud. A whole selection or just one portion of it can be dramatized. Selections that contain a generous amount of dialogue work best. A narrator reads the portions not spoken by characters. Parts are not memorized but are read from the text. Even though they do not have to memorize their parts, readers should spend time developing their interpretation of the dialogue and rehearsing. A reader's theater production might be implemented in the following way (Pike, Compain, & Mumper, 1994):

1. **Select or write the script.** When starting out, it might be helpful to use scripts that have already been prepared for reader's theater. Any script used

■ **Story theater** is a form of dramatization in which participants pantomime a selection while a narrator reads it aloud.

■ **Reader's theater** is a form of dramatization in which the participants read aloud a selection as though it were a play.

should include extensive dialogue, be interesting to your students, and be on the appropriate level of difficulty. A script should have from three to eight parts for students to read. Scripts can also be written by the students, but this takes more time and effort. Composing a script could be a fruitful cooperative learning project. However, students will need some guidance.

2. **Assign parts.** The parts can be either assigned by the teacher or decided on by students.

3. **Rehearse the script.** Although the scripts are read aloud, they should be rehearsed. Before students rehearse a script, they should have read and discussed the selection. As a group, students should decide how each part is to be read. Focus should be on interpreting the character's mood and feelings. Should a character sound angry, sad, or frightened? How are these emotions to be portrayed? Students then rehearse individually and as a group.

4. **Plan a performance.** Students decide where they want to stage their performance. Although no props are needed, they may want to place their scripts in colorful folders. They may use stools if they are available, or they may stand.

Literary Nonfiction

Common Core State Standards recommends the reading of literary nonfiction. This includes famous speeches, essays, historical documents, and biographies.

Biographies Although biographies generally rank poorly when students are asked to tell what types of books they like best, the lives of interesting and relevant subjects are often runaway favorites. Biographies of sports heroes and pop music stars are among some of the most heavily circulated books in the children's departments of libraries.

When properly motivated, students show an intense, long-lasting interest in historical figures. In one elementary school, students were involved in reading and writing biographies for as long as three months. (Zarnowski, 1990). The key to motivating children to become interested in biography is to choose the right subject. Above all, the subject should have led an interesting life and should be someone that the students can relate to and care about. Zarnowski (1990) chose such people as Benjamin Franklin, Martin Luther King, Jr., and Eleanor Roosevelt. The following Student Reading List presents some high-quality biographies.

Using Technology

Aaron Shepard's RT Page gives an overview of reader's theater and provides a number of scripts for students in grades 3 and up.
http://www.aaronshep.com/rt ■

CCSS

By the end of the year, read and comprehend literature, including stories, dramas, and poems, in their grade band text complexity proficiently, with scaffolding as needed at the high end of the range.

Adapting Instruction for English Language Learners

The graphics in nonfiction books can assist struggling readers and ELLs (Duthie, 1996). ■

Adapting Instruction for Struggling Readers and Writers

• One advantage of nonfiction reading is that students need not read the entire book. They can simply read the part that interests them or that answers the questions they have.

• Several publishers have created easy-to-read biography series: Troll's First-Start Biographies are written on a second-grade level. Holiday House's Picture Biographies are written on a third-grade level. Simon & Schuster's Childhoods of Famous Americans includes a large number of easy biographies. ■

Reading aloud to students is a valuable activity at all grade levels.

FYI

Effective read-alouds require selecting books that are interesting and matched to students' developmental level, previewing selections so that the oral reading is smooth and expressive, establishing a purpose for reading, modeling fluent reading during the read-aloud, stopping periodically to pose questions and involve students, and making connections to students' other reading and writing activities (Fisher, Flood, Lapp, & Frey, 2004). ■

FYI

Teachers should set a purpose or provide an overview for reading aloud. The read-aloud should fit in with other things that are happening in the class, such as helping to develop the theme the class is exploring. There might be a follow-up to the read-aloud, or the read-aloud might provide an introduction to the next activity. New words in the read-aloud might be highlighted on a word wall (Fisher et al., 2004). ■

Using Technology

At Young Reviewers, children from all over the country read and evaluate many of the books considered by the Children's Book Committee. Check the Web site for more information: http://www.bankstreet.edu/bookcom/reviewers.html ■

FYI

To foster active listening or reading, have students mark the text as you read it or as they read it. They might circle unknown words, put a question mark next to a puzzling passage, an exclamation mark next to a surprising passage, a *C* next to a connection, and a star next to a passage that is memorable (Adler & Rougle, 2005). ■

Adapting Instruction for English Language Learners

Dynamic Read-Aloud Strategies for English Learners (Hickman & Pollard-Durodola, 2009) has excellent suggestions for conducting read-alouds with English learners. ■

STUDENT READING LIST

Biographies

Adler, D. A. (1991). *A picture book of Eleanor Roosevelt.* New York: Holiday House.
Alcott, S. (1992). *Young Amelia Earhart: A dream to fly.* Mahwah, NJ: Troll.
Anderson, W. (1992). *Laura Ingalls Wilder: A biography.* New York: HarperCollins.
Deans, K. (2007). *Playing to win: The story of Althea Gibson.* New York: Holiday House.
Freedman, R. (1987). *Lincoln: A photobiography.* New York: Clarion.
Fritz, J. (1993). *Just a few words, Mr. Lincoln.* New York: Grosset & Dunlap.
Gutman, D. (2006). *Jackie Robinson and the big game* (Ready to Read). New York: Aladdin.
Haskins, J. (1977). *The life and death of Martin Luther King, Jr.* New York: Lothrop.
Jemison, M. (2001). *Find where the wind goes: Moments from my life.* New York: Scholastic.
Kehret, P. (1996). *Small steps: The year I got polio.* Morton Grove, IL: Whitman.
Kramer, S. A. (1997). *Basketball's greatest players.* New York: Random House.
Lakin, P. (2002). *Helen Keller and the big storm.* New York: Aladdin.
Meltzer, M. (1987). *Mary McLeod Bethune: Voice of black hope.* New York: Viking.
Peare, C. O. (1959). *The Helen Keller story.* New York: Crowell.
Schaefer, L. M. (1999). *César Chávez.* Mankato, MN: Pebble Books.
Taylor-Butler, C. (2008). *Explorers of North America.* New York: Scholastic.
Walker, A. (1974). *Langston Hughes: American poet.* New York: Crowell.
Walker, P. R. (1988). *Pride of Puerto Rico: The life of Roberto Clemente.* New York: Harcourt.

Reading Aloud to Students

Although often associated with the primary grades, reading aloud is a valuable activity throughout all the grades—both at school and at home. Five middle school teachers who were concerned about students' negative attitudes toward reading decided to read to students every day (Trelease, 2001). The percentage of students who read at home for pleasure increased from 40 to 75 percent. The teachers had the following suggestions for structuring a read-aloud program:

- Select books that you enjoy. Your enjoyment of the book will shine through. Also ask students to suggest titles that they would like to hear read aloud.
- If your students change classes, read aloud at the beginning of the period so the bell doesn't interrupt the reading.
- Decide ahead of time how much time you will spend reading aloud. It could be 10 to 15 minutes, or longer.
- Shorter books work better than longer ones.
- Follow up with talks about books that students might enjoy reading.
- Be imaginative and creative in book selections. You might read picture or joke books on occasion.
- Read slightly above students' reading levels, but not too far.
- Prepare your reading in advance. Note difficult vocabulary that might have to be discussed. Also note stopping points.

It's important to set routines for reading aloud, so that you do it at a certain time and for a designated period of time. That way read-alouds aren't relegated to an activity that is undertaken when everything else is done. Read-alouds are valuable enough that they should be regularly scheduled.

Read-alouds should be previewed. You want to prepare your read-aloud. You also want to make sure that there is nothing in the text that would embarrass students or that is not appropriate for them.

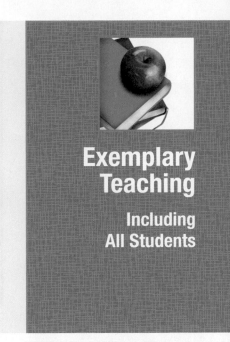

Believing that their expertise is limited, classroom teachers sometimes cede responsibility for ELLs to the specialists who work with them. As a result, these students may feel isolated and unaccepted and may be ignored by classmates who, following the teacher's lead, don't see them as full members of the classroom community. Understandably, ELLs are more anxious in their mainstream classes than in their ESL classes (Yoon, 2007) and so need more support.

Noting the silence of ELLs in her class, Mrs. Young, after reading aloud *The Leaving Morning* (Johnson, 1996), invited them to share their experiences of moving. When talking about Thanksgiving, Mrs. Young asked her ELLs if they had a similar holiday. Dae, a recent arrival from Korea, explained how the people in Korea have a similar holiday and eat a rice cake called *songpyun*. Before reading aloud from the first chapter of the book *My Name Is Brain* (Betancourt, 1995), Mrs. Young asked Dae to tell about some ways in which schools in Korea were different. By carefully involving Dae and other ELLs in book discussions, Mrs. Young made them true members of the class community. She was also fostering their language growth and broadening the experiences of all the students. As she commented, "I want non-ESL kids to know that their beliefs and their cultures are different. I want them to understand and to enjoy and appreciate those things. . . . I really enjoy having all the ESL kids on our team. It adds a dimension that we would not have otherwise" (Yoon, 2007, pp. 222–223).

Exemplary Teaching

Including All Students

Voluntary (Self-Selected) Reading

The key to improved reading achievement is very simple: Encourage students to read on their own for 10 minutes a day. According to carefully conducted research, these extra 10 minutes result in significant improvements in reading (Fielding, Wilson, & Anderson, 1986). What can be done to motivate students to read on their own? First, demonstrate that reading is both personally fulfilling and fun and put children in contact with books that they will enjoy. Attractive classroom libraries attract readers. In a large-scale study of children's reading, the classroom library was the major source of books for most of the children. Students also like to choose their books, and they like to talk about them with other students and the teacher. Students frequently select a book to read because a friend or a teacher recommended it (Gambrell, Codling, & Palmer, 1996).

Step 1. Determining Interests and Attitudes

A good starting point for creating a voluntary (or self-selected) reading program is to determine students' reading interests and their attitudes toward reading. Close observation of your students yields useful information about these factors. In addition, you probably have a good sense of who likes to read and who does not. Through observation, classroom discussions, and conversations with individual children, you probably also know who likes sports, who prefers mysteries, and who is interested in animals. An easy way to obtain an overview of the kinds of books your students might enjoy reading voluntarily is to duplicate several pages listing books at their grade level from the catalog of a distributor of children's books. Ask students to circle the titles that interest them. One experienced librarian recommended indirect questioning when exploring children's interests:

> The best way to learn what any child likes to read is to ask, but a direct question may not elicit clear information. A bit of probing may be necessary. What does he do with leisure time? What are his favorite television programs? The last good book he read? (Halstead, 1988, p. 35)

IRA POSITION STATEMENT ON KEY ISSUE
Providing Books and Other Print Materials for Classroom and School Libraries

"Children who are allowed to self-select and who have access to varied sources of print materials in their classrooms, school libraries, town libraries, and at home, read more and read more widely, both for pleasure and for information" (International Reading Association, 1999b, p. 2). Frequent reading develops language and improves comprehension, word analysis skills, and fluency. It also builds background and vocabulary. "Given that there are approximately 180 days in the school year, a child should be able to select within the classroom a new book to read each day. This averages to about seven books per student in each classroom library. . . . " (International Reading Association, 1999b, p. 3). School libraries should have a minimum of twenty books per child. In addition, it is recommended that each year one new book per student should be added to every classroom library and two new books per child should be added to the school library collection.

FYI

- Many libraries make special provision for teachers and will loan them a hundred or more books.
- See *Guiding Readers and Writers, Grades 3–6* (Fountas & Pinnell, 2001a) for a thorough step-by-step explanation of setting up a program of voluntary reading. ∎

FYI

Voluntary reading is a key means for extending reading skills. If you can't get parents to take their children to the library, maybe you can get children to take their parents. In one school in San José, California, the children enjoyed the books that they were reading in school so much that they persuaded their parents to take them to the library so that they could read more books by the same authors (Maldonado-Colon, 2003). ∎

Using Technology

For information on the latest and best-selling children's books, consult the Web sites of online book stores, such as these:

Amazon.com
http://www.amazon.com

Barnes and Noble
http://www.bn.com

IPL2 For Kids offers a wealth of reading activities, including a story hour.
http://www.ipl.org/IPLBrowse/GetSubject?vid=12&cid=3&tid=4248&parent=0

Accelerated Reading (AR) (Renaissance Learning), Reading Counts (Scholastic), and Book Adventure use computerized quizzes and a point system to motivate reading. AR and Reading Counts are fee-based, but Book Adventure is free:
http://bookadventure.org ∎

Step 2. Building the Classroom Library

Once you have a sense of what your class might like to read, start building a classroom library and involve students in the process. When books are close by and easy to check out, students will read more. If students feel they have a stake in the classroom library, they will be more highly motivated to read. Invite students, their parents, and the community at large to contribute books to your classroom library. You might also be able to obtain some volumes from the school librarian and other local librarians.

Obtaining Books on a Variety of Levels   Students need reading material they can handle. They are most likely to read on their own when they have books (or periodicals) that are interesting and when they feel competent enough to read the materials (Gambrell, Codling, & Palmer, 1996). Although students will read books that are beyond their level if they have a special interest in the subject, a steady diet of such books can be discouraging. A study of sixth-graders found that both good and poor readers chose books on the same level; however, a higher percentage of good readers finished their books (Anderson, Higgins, & Wurster, 1985). If the less-able readers had selected books closer to their ability, perhaps they would have completed them. Young children may require special provisions during self-selected reading. Kaissen (1987) observed that voluntary reading works well with first-graders if several books are available to them, including those that have been read to them previously.

The reading levels of books in classroom and school libraries should be determined and marked on the books. This is especially important at the lower levels. However, don't overemphasize levels. Focus on choosing books that students can read smoothly or that will help them grow as readers (Calkins, 2001). Instead of saying, "You need to read books that have a blue dot," say, "You might be able to read a blue dot book faster and more smoothly" or "Why don't you try a blue dot book for now and try the green dot books after you read some blue dot ones?" Or you might ask, "Is this a stop-and-go book—are you stopping a lot to try to figure out hard words? Try a blue dot book. You won't have so many stops" (Calkins, 2001). At the upper levels, instead of marking books with dots, you might have a section of "fast reads" intended for below-level readers. However, encourage all students to select from these fast reads; otherwise, the books become stigmatized. Also select materials that represent a wide range of cultures and interests. Consider choosing digital materials including e-books.

Setting up the Classroom Library   Make the classroom library as appealing as possible. Display books with their covers showing. You might also have special displays of books on high-interest topics. Update the collection periodically—at least once a month, add new titles to keep children interested.

Managing the Classroom Library   Wilson (1992) suggested that the teacher involve the poorest readers in helping with the management of the classroom collection. By helping display, advertise, and keep track of the collection, poor readers become familiar with its contents. Involve students in setting up check-out procedures and rules. Keep the rules simple; if they are complicated and punitive, they will discourage borrowing (Wilson, 1986). Inevitably, some books will be lost or damaged. Consider this part of the cost of "doing business." Do not charge late fines or fees for lost or damaged books; these could be a genuine hardship for poor children. Instead, have a talk with students about being more responsible. If it is not a hardship, students could contribute replacement books, which do not necessarily have to have the same titles as the lost books.

Step 3.   Setting Up a Management System
Discuss with the class the purpose of self-selected reading and explain how the books are organized. Set aside a time each day for self-selected reading. A typical session might last 20 to 30 minutes. However, it might be necessary to start with shorter sessions, in order to build stamina, especially for younger children. It is generally a good idea to have students select and check out their books before the session begins so that they are ready to read as soon as it starts. Also, have books available to read during transitional times or during spare moments of the day. Encourage students to check out more than one book. If they don't like their first selection, they have a backup. You might have students check out several books at the beginning of the week; these become the basis for the week's voluntary reading.

Step 4.   Teaching Students How to Select Books
Model book selection techniques. Show how you judge a book by examining the cover, seeing who the author is, reading the blurb on the jacket, glancing through the book, and reading brief parts. Discuss with students how they choose books. Post book selection suggestions such as those in Figure 10.5. Guide students, especially those who are reading below grade level, as they select books. Have them read a passage or two. If the passage seems too hard, suggest an easier book. Set aside time for students to recommend books they think others in the class might enjoy.

In one study, students cited word difficulty, length, and lack of interest as the main reasons they didn't finish reading books (Wutz & Wedwick, 2005). After discussions with students, Wutz created a list of criteria for selecting books and posted it. She also modeled each of the criteria—for example, how to select a book that doesn't have too many hard words or that isn't too long. After students had a chance to try out a criterion, they discussed how they were able to use it to choose books.

FIGURE 10.5   Checklist for Choosing Books

- Does the book look interesting?
- Is the book about as hard as other books I have read?
- Can I read most of the words?
- Can I understand what the book is saying?

FYI

Encourage students to talk about books they enjoyed. Students are more likely to read a book when it is recommended by a friend than when it is suggested by a parent, teacher, or librarian (Gallo, 1985). ■

FYI

Gear activities to the level of the students' reading development. Students whose reading is very limited will not benefit from self-selected reading or reading with a partner. Have them read along with a recorded selection or CD, or try echo reading. Novice and struggling readers need lots of experience with contextual reading (Carbo, 1997). Read Jodi Crum Marshall's (2002) account of how she set up a voluntary reading program for middle school students. ■

Assessing for Learning

- Book selection is an essential skill. By observing students as they select books and discussing with them how they go about selecting a book, you can decide whether they need help choosing books and what form that help might take.
- When students are selecting books, Hoonan (2006) asks, "What are you doing to help you choose a book?" Responses enable him to help them implement selection strategies. ■

FYI

Having students read on their own during free time and at home is a highly effective way to help below-level readers catch up, as long as they are reading books on their level. ■

Students should have time during the day when they can read books of their own choosing.

Step 5.   Teaching Students How to Talk about Books

Students read more and get more out of their reading if they have a chance to talk about books. You might have students gather in groups of three or four to discuss their books—to engage in *buddy buzz* (Fountas & Pinnell, 2001a). So that buddy buzz may be profitable, students are given a prompt beforehand. They might be asked, for instance, to attach sticky notes to two passages that they would like to share. During the buzz, they read the passages they marked and explain why they chose them. They also ask each other questions. Before engaging in buddy buzz, students are taught to be respectful of each other, listen attentively, ask questions after each presentation, and take turns. They also learn how to provide support for their statements and how to politely voice opposing opinions.

Possible prompts for buddy buzz sessions are as follows:

- Mark two passages that you would like to share.
- Mark two passages that are funny, exciting, or sad.
- Mark two passages that tell you things you didn't know.
- Mark two passages that you think the others in the group would like to hear.
- Mark two passages that contain interesting language.
- Mark two passages that give you information you can use.

Step 6.   Teaching Students How to Work Together

Elicit from students guidelines for working together: reading silently, holding questions or concerns until the teacher is available (unless it's an emergency), and so forth.

Case Study
Creating a Better Self-Selected Reading Program

Realizing the importance of extensive reading, Jodi Crum Marshall (2002) initiated a self-selected reading program. At first, she thought the program was working well. The room was quiet. There were no complaints. But then she noticed that the room was too quiet. There was no expression of excitement or enjoyment. And while there were no complaints, there were no positive comments either. After discussing the self-selected reading program with her students, Marshall concluded that she had made a series of blunders. She had failed to set expectations or goals for the program with students. They saw the session as a free period. If they didn't raise a fuss, they could quietly do whatever they wanted. She had not included them in setting up the program or acquiring books. Although her classes were made up of sixth-, seventh-, and eighth-grade struggling readers, she had failed to acquire books on the appropriate levels. Most were too difficult. And she hadn't really done anything to spark an interest in reading. Because the books were difficult and lacking in appeal, many of the students weren't really reading. Some would begin to read a book but quit when they found that it was too difficult. As one student put it, none of the books "make sense."

Marshall reformed the program. First, she had conversations with students about the program. The students wanted more books and more time to read. They also wanted to discuss their books, but they didn't want the discussions to seem like quizzes. Responding to the issues that students raised, Marshall changed discussions so that they were more like conversations than oral quizzes. She also held individual conversations with students. And she encouraged students to keep logs of their reading. This served a practical purpose, because often they forgot where they had left off reading the day before. She also began reading aloud to the class. This motivated students to read the books that she was reading to them. She also passed out book catalogs to students and had them mark the books they would like to read. These and other titles were added to the class library. But perhaps the most important thing she did was to get to know her students, their reading strengths and weaknesses, and their interests. Using this knowledge, she was able to match them up with books that they could read and wanted to read. Not surprisingly, students' attitudes changed. And their gains on tests of reading comprehension and language were better than expected.

Step 7. Teaching Students to Recommend Books
Display books that students have recommended on a special shelf or rack. Discuss with students how they might decide whether to recommend a book and how they might compose a recommendation.

Activities for Motivating Voluntary Reading

To motivate voluntary reading, be enthusiastic, accepting, and flexible. Present reading as an interesting, vital activity. Include a wide range of material from comics to classics. Share reading with students in the same way that you might share with friends. By doing so, you are accepting students as serious readers. Above all, be a reader yourself. Some activities for motivating voluntary reading follow:

- **Match books with interests.** Make personal recommendations. For a Gary Paulsen fan, you might say, "Joe, I know you enjoy Gary Paulsen's books. The school library has a new book by him. I read it, and it's very interesting."
- **Use the indirect approach.** Choose a book that would be appropriate for your students and that you would enjoy reading. Carry the book to class with you. Mention that the book is interesting and tell students that they can borrow it when you're finished.

 FYI
- Sometimes known as sustained silent reading, self-selected reading (SSR) is a time when all the students in a class, or even in a school, read materials of their own choosing.
- We want children to read the best that has been written. However, students must be allowed to choose what they wish to read. Once students experience the joy of reading, then, through skillful guidance, they might be led to experience high-quality literature. ■

R E F L E C T I O N

How much do your students read voluntarily? What might you do to increase both the quantity and quality of what they read but at the same time instill a love of reading in them? What special provision might you make for **struggling readers?**

FYI

A reinforcer for voluntary reading is to have students keep a record of their reading. This might be a list or a graph showing the number of books or pages read, or number of minutes spent reading. Since students differ in reading speed, and the number of words on a page varies, the fairest measurement is number of minutes spent reading. ■

FYI

Richgels and Wold (1998) involved parents of first-graders in their children's reading by sending home "Three for the Road" backpacks. Each backpack contained three books; three sock puppets, which students could use to talk about their reading; a response notebook; markers and pencils; a letter to parents; and suggestions for using the backpack. ■

Adapting Instruction for Struggling Readers and Writers

Some struggling readers select books that are beyond their capability because they want to read the same books that their friends are reading. Have available books that are interesting but easy. From time to time, highlight these books and allow everyone to read them so that they don't become stigmatized as "baby books." ■

- **Pique students' interest.** Read a portion of a book and stop at a cliff-hanging moment, then tell students that they can read the rest themselves if they want to find out what happened.
- **Use clips to preview books.** Show a portion of a movie based on a book, then encourage students to find out what happened by reading the book.
- **Substitute voluntary reading for workbook or other seatwork assignments.** The Center for the Study of Reading (1990) made the following statement: "Independent, silent reading can fulfill many of the same functions as workbook activities—it permits students to practice what they are learning, and it keeps the rest of the class occupied while you meet with a small group of students" (p. 5).
- **Have students visit author sites on the Web to learn of the latest books by their favorite authors.**
- **Have students keep records of books they read voluntarily.** Recording books read gives students a sense of accountability and accomplishment.
- **Encourage partner reading.** Young and less able readers might be willing to attempt a challenging book if they get some help and support from a partner. Such readers might also be more willing to read on their own if given a "running start" that gets them solidly into the book (Castle, 1994).
- **Recommend books by a popular series author.** Students who have enjoyed one of Beverly Cleary's books about Ramona Quimby or Henry Huggins might not be aware that other equally funny books feature these same characters.
- **Introduce students to book clubs that cater to school-age populations.** Book clubs offer a variety of interesting books at bargain prices. When students choose and pay money for a book, it is highly likely that they will read it. Make alternative provisions for economically disadvantaged children.
- **Do not overlook community resources.** Invite the public librarian and a representative from a local bookstore to visit the class and tell students what is "hot" in children's books. Inform speakers beforehand about the reading levels and interests of students so that they can suggest suitable titles.
- **Encourage students to build personal libraries with a few inexpensive paperbacks.** They can add to their collection by requesting books as gifts.
- **Once a month, give students the opportunity to trade books they have read.** Before the trading session, students might want to post a list or announce titles that they will swap. You might also have a trading shelf in the classroom from which students may take any book they wish, as long as they put one in its place.
- **Suggest and have on hand books that relate to people or subjects being taught in the content areas.** Reading a brief biography of John F. Kennedy, for instance, could help shed light on his presidency and the early 1960s.
- **Use the Web.** On the class or school homepage, list books that parents might obtain for their children at either the local library or a bookstore.
- **Set up book clubs based on students' interests.** In Queens, New York, adolescents interested in graphic novels spend many hours at branch libraries reading and discussing the books (Barnard, 2010). One library held weekly meetings of graphic novel readers that drew up to 40 young people. Similar reading clubs might be set up to read and discuss books about sports, hobbies, digital devices, or other topics of interest to young people.

Incentives seem to work best when the nature of the reward fits with the nature of the activity and when the incentive is tied to meeting a specific goal rather than simply engaging in the activity. In Running Start, a reading incentive program, the goal was reading twenty brief books within ten weeks. As an incentive, students could select a book to keep (Gambrell, Codling, & Palmer, 1996).

On the first day of school, third-grade teacher Cathy Clarkson (2000) gathers her students in a circle on the rug. Piled in front of Clarkson are her favorite books from childhood. During that first session and in subsequent sessions, she shares some of her favorites with her students. She also invites students to bring in their favorite books. If students don't have favorite books to bring in, they can select books from a collection of favorite books. Included in that collection are books that previous teachers read to Clarkson's students. Throughout the year, students share past and current favorites.

Exemplary Teaching
Motivating Reading

Summary

Until recently, reading was looked upon as being primarily a skills subject. Today, the emphasis is on reading quality materials. Reading literature involves fostering appreciation and enjoyment as well as understanding. The focus is on eliciting personal responses and valuing students' interpretations. Students should read a variety of types of literature. Voluntary reading should also be fostered. Key elements of a successful voluntary reading program include providing lots of materials on a variety of topics and levels, setting aside time for reading, teaching students how to select books, talking about books, and using a variety of intrinsic, and, if necessary, extrinsic motivators.

Extending and Applying

1. Plan a lesson in which you introduce a poem, play, or other literary piece. In your lesson, stress appreciation, enjoyment, and personal response. Teach the lesson and evaluate it.
2. Create a literature unit. Include standards (objectives), activities, materials, and assessment. Also explain how you would introduce the unit.
3. With a group of classmates, start a literature discussion group in which you discuss children's books. Reflect on the group's discussions. What are their strengths? What are some ways in which they might be improved? What has being in a discussion group taught you about having discussion groups in a class that you teach or plan to teach?
4. Read at least three current anthologies of children's poetry. Which poems did you like best? Which do you think would appeal to your students?
5. Try out one of the suggestions listed in this chapter or an idea of your own for increasing voluntary reading. Implement the idea and evaluate its effectiveness.

Professional Reflection

Do I ...

___ Have an understanding of response to literature?

___ Have an understanding of the distinguishing characteristics of major literary genres?

___ Have an understanding of ways in which students might be led to respond to, understand, and appreciate major literary genres?

Am I able to ...

___ Select literary and general reading materials that represent a range of levels and that are appropriate for students and that appeal to them?

___ Conduct activities that elicit an aesthetic response?

___ Conduct a literature discussion group that leads to a higher level of understanding and deeper appreciation?

___ Lead students to conduct and participate productively in a literature discussion group?

___ Set up and manage a voluntary reading program that leads to increased free reading and a greater enjoyment of reading for all students?

 ## Reflection Question

How might you discover what your students like to read? How might you use that knowledge to plan intriguing lessons and to motivate students, especially those who struggle, to read on their own?

 ## Building Competencies

To build competencies, consult the following sources for more detailed information:

Literature Circles Resource Center presents information and resources on literature circles for elementary and middle school teachers.

http://www.litcircles.org

Making Meaning in Literature

http://www.learner.org/libraries/makingmeaning/makingmeaning/introducing/

High-quality videos show the envisionment process. Although designed for students in grades 6–8, the techniques could be adapted for students in grades 3–5.

MyEducationLab™

Go to the Topic "Comprehension" in the MyEducation-Lab (www.myeducationlab.com) for your course, where you can:

- Find learning outcomes for "Comprehension" along with the national standards that connect to these outcomes.
- Complete Assignments and Activities that can help you more deeply understand the chapter content.
- Apply and practice your understanding of the core teaching skills identified in the chapter with the Building Teaching Skills and Dispositions learning units.
- Examine challenging situations and cases presented in the IRIS Center Resources.
- Check your comprehension on the content covered in the chapter by going to the Study Plan in the Book Resources for your text. Here you will be able to take

a chapter quiz, receive feedback on your answers, and then access Review, Practice, and Enrichment activities to enhance your understanding of chapter content. (optional)

A+RISE A+RISE® Standards2Strategy™ is an innovative and interactive online resource that offers new teachers in grades K–12 just-in-time, research-based instructional strategies that meet the linguistic needs of ELLs as they learn content, differentiate instruction for all grades and abilities, and are aligned to Common Core Elementary Language Arts standards (for the literacy strategies) and to English language proficiency standards in WIDA, Texas, California, and Florida.

11 Approaches to Teaching Reading

Anticipation Guide

For each of the following statements related to the chapter you are about to read, put a check under "Agree" or "Disagree" to show how you feel. Discuss your responses with classmates before you read the chapter.

	Agree	Disagree
1. A structured approach to reading is most effective.	_____	_____
2. Extensive reading of children's books should be a part of every elementary and middle school reading program.	_____	_____
3. Teacher and method are equally important.	_____	_____
4. A writing approach to reading works best with young children.	_____	_____
5. An individualized reading program is hard to manage.	_____	_____
6. A commercial reading program, such as a basal series or literature anthology, is best for new teachers because it shows them step by step how to teach reading.	_____	_____
7. Teachers should combine the best parts of each reading approach.	_____	_____
8. Teachers should be free to choose the approach to reading that they feel works best.	_____	_____

Using What You Know

There are really just two main ways of learning to read: by reading and by writing, or some combination of the two. The approach that uses writing is known as language experience. Reading approaches use textbooks (including basal anthologies and linguistic reading series) and children's books. Children's books are used in the individualized and literature-based approaches. Of course, these approaches can also be combined in various ways. Teachers who use basals or literature anthologies often supplement their programs with language-experience stories and children's books. Which of these approaches are you familiar with? What are the characteristics of the approaches? What are their advantages? Their disadvantages?

Changing Approaches to Teaching Reading

Reading instruction is now undergoing a major change. With the goal of having every student college and career ready and the advent of the widely accepted Common Core State Standards, reading instruction is set to become more challenging. Because of an apparent gap between the demands made by college and career reading and the capabilities of high school seniors, students will be expected to read at higher levels beginning in grade two and extending up into high school so that the gap is eliminated. The Standards also call for increased reading of informational text. However, informational reading is more demanding than narrative fictional reading, so this also will make the literacy program more challenging. Because informational text requires its own specific set of skills and strategies or adaptations of general skills and strategies, it means that literacy instruction will need to be expanded. The Common Core Standards call for approaches to literacy instruction that are more rigorous and more effective but that consider the needs of all students.

Effective approaches incorporate the basic principles of teaching literacy that have been emphasized throughout this book:
Students become readers and writers by reading and writing.

- Literacy programs should include a rich variety of interesting, appropriate material and should stress a great deal of reading and writing.
- Strategies that promote independence in word recognition and comprehension should be taught.
- Literacy programs should be language-based. Provision should be made for developing speaking and listening as well as reading and writing skills.
- Because reading fosters writing development and writing fosters reading development, literacy programs should develop both.
- Provision should be made for individual differences. Because students differ in terms of interests, abilities, learning rate, experiential background, and culture, the approach used should take into consideration the needs of all students. Provision needs to be made for struggling readers and English language learners.
- Students' progress should be monitored, and provision should be made for helping students fully develop their potential.

This chapter examines the major approaches to teaching reading and writing. Each approach has its strengths and weaknesses. Suggestions are made for adapting each approach to take advantage of its strengths and compensate for its weaknesses. For instance, ways to make the basal approach more holistic are suggested. Thus, if it has been mandated that you use a basal series but you prefer a holistic approach, you can adapt your instruction to make the program more holistic and still keep within the guidelines of the school or school district that employs you.

Basal/Anthology Approach

How were you taught to read? Chances are you were taught through **a basal/anthology reading program**. Basal readers are the main approach to teaching reading in the United States. A complex package based on a relatively simple concept, the basal program includes a series of readers or anthologies and supplementary materials that gradually increase in difficulty, thus serving as stepping stones along a path that begins with emergent literacy and extends through sixth-grade reading. Accompanying teacher's manuals provide guidance so that the classroom teacher can lead students upward.

Designed to be integrated language arts programs, today's basals have comprehension, spelling, grammar, oral language, listening, and vocabulary components and, at the lower levels, systematic instruction in phonics. Created to meet the needs of most students, basals have materials for average, above average, and below-level readers and ELLs. They also have accompanying intervention programs. In addition to anthology selections, they include supplementary books and read-aloud anthologies. In some series, materials are written on the three difficulty levels but have the same topic, vocabulary, and strategies so that they can be used, at least in part, for whole-class instruction. In addition, basals have related workbooks, detailed teacher's manuals packed with teaching suggestions, big books, supplementary libraries of excellent children's books, read-aloud books, e-books, a wide array of games and manipulatives, audio recordings, digital versions of some text, computer software, video discs, inservice programs, home-school programs, posters, charts, unit, benchmark, and end-of-book tests, placement and diagnostic tests, observation guides, portfolio systems, Web sites, and more.

Some of the basal series have become partially digitized. Using a Web-based management system, teachers can plan lessons by consulting the online teacher's manual and noting which of the many resources they would like to use. Most of the basals have portions of the students' materials in

■ A **basal/anthology reading program** is a comprehensive program for teaching reading that includes readers or anthologies that gradually increase in difficulty, teacher's manuals, workbooks, and assessment measures. In grades 7 and 8 and sometimes in grade 6, teachers use literature texts instead of basals.

digital format. Using the digital versions, students can highlight text and take notes as they read, and answer checkup questions by writing responses. They can also have words pronounced, and meanings provided. They can even have selections read aloud. One program has a dual speed for read-alouds: one for slower intensive reading and one at natural speed so as to model fluency. Another program allows ELL students to move back and forth between English and Spanish.

At one time, there were more than a dozen basal reading programs. Today, there are just four: Houghton Mifflin Harcourt, Macmillan/McGraw-Hill, Scott Foresman, and Open Court (SRA/McGraw-Hill). The programs from Houghton Mifflin Harcourt, Macmillan/McGraw-Hill, and Scott Foresman are more alike than different. However, each one has an area of relative strength. Houghton Mifflin Harcourt's basal reading program has a strong vocabulary component. Macmillan/McGraw-Hill's has a strong word study component that features sorting. Scott Foresman's has a focus on New Literacies. Open Court's basal reading program is somewhat different from the other three in that it is a scripted program. A scripted program is one in which the teacher is expected to closely follow the teacher's manual and even use the words indicated. Open Court also offers the most extensive word analysis component.

Today's basals are bigger and better than ever. But the real question is "Are today's basals good enough?" The answer is yes and no. Basals have many advantages, but they also have some shortcomings.

Using Technology

Programs, such as Reading Mastery (SRA), have been written specifically to reinforce phonic elements. Reading Mastery is a highly scripted program with a strict behaviorist approach. However, it has been used successfully with at risk learners. The National Institute for Direct Instruction provides more information on the theory behind Reading Mastery. http://nifdi.org ∎

Advantages of Basals

Basals offer teachers a convenient package of materials, techniques, and assessment devices, as well as a plan for orchestrating the various components of a total literacy program. In their anthologies, which, for the most part, gradually increase in difficulty, basals offer students a steady progression from emergent literacy through a sixth-grade reading level. They also offer varied reading selections, an abundance of practice material, carefully planned units and lessons, and a wealth of follow-up and enrichment activities.

Disadvantages of Basals

Despite a major overhaul, basals are still driven by the same engine. The core of the basal reading program is the trio of anthology, workbook, and teacher's manual. Although the contents of the anthology are much improved, its function remains the same—to provide a base of materials for all students to move through. However, students have diverse interests and abilities and progress at different rates. Although basal selections are meant to be of high quality, they will not all be of interest to all students. The sports biography that delights one child is a total bore to another.

A second shortcoming has to do with the way basal readers are assembled: They are anthologies and often contain excerpts from whole books. For example, the fourth-grade reader from a typical series contains "The Diary of Leigh Botts," a delightful tale of a budding young writer that is excerpted from Beverly Cleary's 1983 Newbury Award winner, *Dear Mr. Henshaw*. If reading the excerpt is worthwhile, reading the whole book should be even better.

There is also the question of pacing and time spent with a selection. Students often move through basals in lockstep fashion. Part of the problem is the nature of the teacher's manuals; they offer too much of a good thing. Stories and even poems are overtaught. There are too many questions asked before a selection is read, too many asked after the piece has been read, and too many follow-up activities. A class might spend three days on a thousand-word story. To be fair, the manuals do present activities as choices. Teachers can choose those they wish to undertake and omit the others. Teachers may even be provided a choice of ways of presenting a story: interactively, with the teacher modeling strategies; independently, with the teacher providing a minimum of assistance; or with support, which means that students follow along as the

Teachers sometimes use minibooks in their guided reading lessons.

 FYI

In her comparison of students who were read *to* and students who read *with* her, Kuhn (2004) found that students showed more growth when they read rather than being read to. ■

teacher reads the story. All in all, the typical basal lesson has many fine suggestions, but the ideas are "canned," that is, created by someone in an editorial office far from the classroom. Designed to be all things to all teachers, the activities are not designed for a specific class of students with specific needs and interests.

Perhaps the biggest disadvantage of basals is the organizational pattern they suggest. Basal reading series have core selections in anthologies and also supplementary reading in libraries of leveled readers. The core basal selections are presented to the whole class. The selections are generally appropriate for average students but may not be challenging enough for the best readers and are too hard for as many as the one student out of four in the typical classroom who is reading below grade level. Suggestions are made for adapting instruction for all learners. This may mean reading selections to the poorest readers or providing them with an audio or digital version of the selection so that they can read along. Or, the teacher might simply read the selection to the whole class. Whatever your approach, you need to provide access for all students. If you do read the selection to students, have them follow along in their text. This provides them with exposure to print. To keep them involved, from time to time, call on the whole group to read a portion with you in choral reading style.

In addition to reading or listening to the core selection, students also read in guided reading groups. All basal series have sets of books on three levels—easy, average, and challenging—giving all students the opportunity to read books on their level. However, a key question remains: Which students do the least reading? Since the average and above-average students read the core selection and the least advanced group listens to the selection or reads along with it, those students most in need of reading practice do the least amount of reading. If you are using a basal, you need to make adjustments so that struggling readers are reading more, not less, than the other students. Some basals offer an alternative selection for struggling readers, which is related to the theme in the core selection but is easier to read. If available, you might use this option.

Unfortunately, even the use of both interactive read-alouds and guided reading groups does not quite solve the problem of meeting the needs of below-level readers. All of a theme's (or unit's) activities revolve around the core selection, including phonics or other decoding lessons and workbook exercises. However, these activities are on the same level as the core selection and so are too difficult and/or inappropriate for below-level readers. For instance, consider a basal core selection that is on a mid–first-grade level. The phonics lesson introduces the final-*e* long-*i* pattern, but the below-level readers haven't yet mastered short-vowel patterns. Long-vowel patterns are beyond their grasp. Workbook exercises reinforce the pattern. The core selection, *The Kite* by Alma Flor Ada, also provides practice with the pattern. Listening to the core selection would be useful for below-level readers, but taking part in the phonics lesson or attempting the workbook exercises would not be appropriate and, in fact, could undermine the confidence of the below-level readers, as noted in Chapter 5. What's the solution?

Above all, struggling readers need materials and instruction on their level. The "trickle-down" approach does not meet the needs of these readers. Instead of using the core on-level selection with struggling readers, obtain materials on their instructional level so that they are actually reading rather than simply listening to or reading along with selections too difficult for them to read on their own. They need decoding instruction and selections that reinforce the decoding skills they have been taught. The teacher might use texts and activities from the program that are on these students' level. For example, first-grade struggling readers might be placed in theme 2 (out of ten themes covered in a year's time) rather than theme 5, which is where the achieving readers are working. Second-graders who are below level might work in first-grade readers, perhaps starting with theme 6 or 7, depending on their reading level and the skills they have mastered. Using lower-level materials that match struggling readers' reading levels is generally the best solution, since it allows them to develop the skills needed to make progress in the program and provides coordination between the skills taught, the practice activities, and the key selections being read.

Another solution is to use the resources provided in the basal reading program. All basals include below-level books and phonics readers created for the series, as well as a listing of below-level trade books. These materials can be used with struggling readers, as long as they match those students' reading levels. Although these materials can provide much needed practice and application, they are not accompanied by essential decoding instruction. You will need to supply this.

A third solution is to use an intervention program. Most basal programs include an intervention program, or you can obtain a stand-alone program. Of course, you can combine these solutions. A good combination is to use the lower-level reader or anthology of the basal program that matches struggling readers' needs and an intervention program that provides added instruction and practice so that the struggling readers can catch up.

Adapting Basals

Despite the criticisms voiced here and elsewhere, there is nothing intrinsically wrong with basals. Over the years, thousands of teachers have successfully used basals to teach millions of children. However, in keeping with today's research and promising practices, basals should be adapted in the following ways.

Although basal manuals have been criticized as being too didactic (Goodman, 1994a), the fault may be with the professionals who use them. Manuals and, in fact, the entire basal program should be viewed as a resource. The manual is a treasure chest of ideas, and the anthologies are good, representative collections of children's literature. As professionals, we should feel free to use those selections that seem appropriate and to use the manual as a resource rather than a guide. Select only those suggestions and activities that seem appropriate and effective.

As a new teacher in a large urban school system, I had the good fortune to work for administrators who encouraged the integration of language arts and the use of themed units but frowned on the use of teacher's manuals and workbooks. In fact, a manual was not available for the basal that I used. Not having a teacher's manual, I planned my own units and my own lessons. In retrospect, I realize that some of my lessons fell flat. However, others worked extremely well. I still recall with pride being asked to present a model lesson for other new teachers at one of our monthly meetings. Good, bad, or indifferent, the lessons were my own, and so I had made a commitment to them. When I planned my lessons, I kept in mind the needs and interests of my students. I especially enjoyed building interest in a story so that they really wanted to read it. And I did not present any stories I disliked or thought the students would not like.

Other adaptations that might be made to make basals more effective include the following:

- *Use workbooks and other practice materials judiciously.* Workbooks and other practice materials have both management and instructional roles. Students can work in them independently while the teacher meets with a small group or individual children. Some workbook exercises provide valuable reinforcement. However, as Pincus (2005) comments, "Many workbook tasks are not interesting, do not provide rich instructional possibilities, lack clear objectives, allow false-positive feedback, consume teachers' time in scoring them, and, most importantly, occupy time that can be otherwise spent teaching students what they do not already know" (p. 79).

Adapting Instruction for Struggling Readers

To provide added reinforcement with phonics patterns, use the books listed on pp. 212–214. ∎

FYI

Three of the four major basal series offer teachers a variety of instructional choices. However, the Open Court series is scripted. It tells teachers what to say and offers a tightly structured sequence of teaching activities. Although novice teachers might welcome the guidance, veteran teachers may desire more flexibility, despite the good results that this series often obtains. ∎

R E F L E C T I O N

What has been your experience with a basal/anthology program? Did you learn to read with a basal approach? Are you using one now? What do you see as the advantages and disadvantages of the basal/anthology approach? How might you deal with the issue of making sure that struggling readers were given more time reading on their level rather than less?

FYI

Reading programs vary in the rate at which they introduce skills, the number of words they introduce, and the amount of practice they provide (Hiebert, Martin, & Menon, 2005; Dewitz, Jones, & Leahy, 2009). If your program does not offer enough practice or introduces skills too rapidly, use supplementary materials or children's books for added reinforcement or to bridge gaps. ∎

Before using a workbook exercise, ask yourself these questions: Is the exercise worth doing? Does it reinforce a skill in which students need added practice? How should the exercise be completed? Should it be done independently, or does it require instruction? Also make sure that the exercise is on the appropriate level for your students. Especially valuable are workbook exercises that provide additional reading of paragraphs or other text, added experience with vocabulary words, or practice with graphic organizers. If a workbook exercise fails to measure up, it should be skipped. The teacher should provide alternative activities, such as having students read children's books or work in learning centers. Reading builds background and gives students an opportunity to integrate and apply skills. Instead of just practicing for the main event, they are taking part in it. In fact, students get far better practice reading children's books than they do completing workbook exercises. Writing, drawing, discussing, and preparing a presentation also provide superior alternatives to workbook exercises.

• *Emphasize wide reading of a variety of materials.*   No matter how well the basal program has been put together, students need to read a broader range of fiction and nonfiction materials, including books, magazines, newspapers, sets of directions, brochures, ads, menus, schedules, and other real-world materials. Make use of the extensive libraries of children's books offered by basal publishers to supplement the basal materials; excellent suggestions for additional reading are also provided in basal manuals.

• *Focus on a few key skills or strategies.*   Teach and use key skills and strategies in context. Today's basal series offer instruction in a wide variety of skills or strategies. In trying to cover so many areas, they typically spread themselves too thin and so fail to present crucial skills in sufficient depth. It may take twenty lessons or more before students are able to draw inferences or identify main ideas, but a basal program might present just two or three lessons on such skills. For instance, in one program the target strategy for the first week is summarizing; the next week, monitoring; the third week, visualizing. Although a summarizing question is in the selection read the second week, there is no review or extension of the strategy. Summarizing is not addressed in the third week. Make necessary adaptations so that skills and strategies are given the instruction and practice they require. In this instance, adapt instruction so that some summarizing activities are included, such as asking questions that require summarizing or provide practice in summarizing content-area reading in which students engage.

• *Provide opportunities for struggling readers to read appropriate-level material every day.*   Make use of the supplementary programs or leveled libraries designed for struggling readers. In this era of college and career readiness and RTI, struggling readers should be given added instruction and do more reading so that they can catch up.

• *Gradually take control of your literacy program.*   Decide what your philosophy of teaching literacy is. List the objectives you see as most important, aligning them, of course, with the standards set by your school and school district. If possible, work with other professionals to create a literacy program that makes sense for your situation. Consider basals as only one source of materials and teaching ideas. Basals are neither a method nor an approach to teaching reading. They are simply carefully crafted sets of materials. The core of any reading program is the teacher. It is the teacher who should decide how and when to use basals and whether to choose alternative materials. As Tyner (2004) recommends, "A basal reading program was never meant to provide a complete program, only a starting point. Basal readers are most effective when they are used flexibly and as part of a comprehensive, balanced program of instruction" (p. 2). Also use your professional expertise. For instance, if the basal your school district is using doesn't provide enough practice using strategies, arrange

■ **Linguistic patterns** are regularities in the spelling of English words. A linguistic patterns approach presents patterns by comparing and contrasting words that have minimal differences (*pat–pan*) so that students can see how they differ. Although such an approach isn't used by many classroom teachers, it is frequently employed by remedial specialists.

for more practice. If the series fails to take advantage of regularities when teaching high-frequency words, adapt instructions so as to point out the regularities *wh* = /w/ and *t* =/t/ in a word such as *what* (Scott Foresman's Reading Street and Sidewalks follow this practice).

Basal readers extend only to grade 6. In grade 7 and beyond, students use literature anthologies or sets of texts that have literary value instead of basal readers. The main difference between basal readers and literature anthologies is the focus on literature. Literature anthologies also place emphasis on appreciation. However, the anthologies often provide some coverage of reading skills. Today's literature anthologies are very comprehensive. They typically feature a mix of contemporary works and classics. A full-length novel may accompany the anthology. The best of these anthologies provide a host of materials that teachers can use to prepare students to read the selections and to extend their appreciation and understanding. Well-designed literature anthologies also feature a program of skill development for struggling readers. In general, literature anthologies have the same advantages and disadvantages as basal series.

Minibook Series

A number of beginning-reading programs consist of series of minibooks of increasing difficulty. The series ease children into reading and move them from emergent to fluent reading. Books at the emergent stage are designed so that students can enjoy them before they can actually read them. Illustrations help children predict what the text might say. The text itself is brief, often consisting of a single sentence that contains a repetitive phrase. Each page of the book might contain the same repeated phrase. The books are read through shared reading, and eventually students can, with the help of illustrations, read the books on their own. At this point, students are primarily "reading" pictures rather than text. The intent is to emphasize reading for enjoyment and meaning. Of course, students are also picking up concepts about print.

After students have enjoyed a number of books and shown an interest in reading print, text-reading strategies are introduced. Difficulty and length of text are carefully controlled so that students gradually grow into reading. As students gain in skill, they move into more challenging stages. Some of the best-known kits include Story Box® (The Wright Group), Sunshine™ Series (The Wright Group), and Literacy by Design (Houghton Mifflin Harcourt). Literacy by Design provides instruction in phonemic-awareness, phonics, vocabulary, comprehension, fluency, and writing. One drawback of these series is that the texts at the early levels do not adequately reinforce decoding patterns. The series are not decodable. A minibook series that provides reinforcement for phonics patterns without resorting to tongue-twisting tales is Ready Readers (Modern Curriculum Press). Minibook series enjoy widespread use, especially in grade 1, and are often used as supplements to a basal or other approach. In fact, all of today's basal series have supplementary kits of easy-to-read booklets, which feature decodable texts at the early levels.

Closing the Gap: Providing Better Reinforcement

With the right kind of intervention, it is possible for struggling readers to catch up. In one study of first-graders, struggling readers caught up to average readers in just 15 weeks (Menon & Hiebert, 2003). The control group had a typical basal. The intervention group was given a series of 150 minibooks that were designed to reinforce the phonics patterns they had been taught but were not written in the sing-song fashion characteristic of some decodable texts. The minibooks were carefully sequenced so that in all instances easier books were presented before more difficult books. The books gradually became more challenging. In addition to reading books that were more carefully sequenced and did a better job of reinforcing patterns that had been

FYI

Programs such as Breakthrough to Literacy and Lightspan make heavy use of technology. In addition to computerized lessons, Breakthrough to Literacy includes big books, pupil books, and take-home books. Lightspan uses the Internet as well as traditional methods to provide ongoing assessment, professional development, and additional learning activities. ■

Using Technology

Titlewave offers lists of books to be used in conjunction with popular textbook programs (including basal anthologies), books for guided and leveled reading, and award-winning books.

Can search its database of 50,000 books by level, grade, genre, or general interest.

http://www.flr.follett.com/

See also Book Wizard

http://bookwizard.scholastic.com/tbw/homePage.do ■

taught, the intervention group read a greater variety of words. They read between 500 and 1,000 words a week. The basal group read an average of 250 words. The basal group, which devoted a full week to a selection, reread the same story several times, so they may have read as many words as the intervention group, but they did this by reading the same words over and over again. Reading several books seems to be more effective than reading the same book over and over again.

Literature-Based Approach

More and more teachers are using literature as the core of their programs. Today's basal anthologies feature high-quality selections drawn from children's literature. Increasingly, basals are including children's books in their entirety as an integral part of the program or as a recommended component. Although there is some overlap between a basal program and a literature-based approach, the term **literature-based approach** is used here to describe a program that uses sets of children's books as a basis for providing instruction in literacy. A major advantage of this approach is that teachers, independently or in committees, choose the books they wish to use with their students; thus, the reading material is tailored to students' interests and needs.

A literature-based program may be organized in a variety of ways. Three popular models are core literature, text sets, and thematic units or transactional units. Transactional units are theme-based units that begin with an overall plan just as traditional thematic units do, but the plan is subject to modification depending on students' needs and interests. The unit becomes a "blend of preplanned lessons and response-centered teaching" (Serafini, 2006, p. 23).

Core Literature

Core literature is literature that has been selected for a careful, intensive reading. Core selections are often read by the whole class, but may be read by selected groups. Core literature pieces might include such children's classics as *The Little House* (Burton, 1942) and *Aesop's Fables* or more recent works such as *Shiloh* (Naylor, 1991), *Number the Stars* (Lowry, 1989), *Lunch Money* (Selznick, 2007), *Where the Mountain Meets the Moon* (Linn, 2009), or *Winn–Dixie* (DiCamillo, 2000).

Serafini (2006) uses what he calls *cornerstone texts* in his reading units. The cornerstone text introduces the unit and provides a foundation for discussing subsequent texts. For instance, for a unit on reading informational texts, the cornerstone text was *Volcano* (Magloff, 2003). *Volcano* has a rich array of access features: photos, charts, graphs, diagrams, headings, sidebars, glossary, and index. After being introduced to the use of these elements in *Volcano*, students were prepared to make use of them as they read other informational texts. *Volcano* was also used to demonstrate previewing and other key strategies for reading informational texts. After discussing *Volcano*, students selected topics of inquiry and read related high-quality informational texts.

In addition to providing students with a rich foundation in the best of children's literature, the use of core selections also builds community (Ford, 1994). It gives students a shared experience, thereby providing the class with common ground for conversations about selections and also a point of reference for comparing and contrasting a number of selections. The use of core literature should help boost the self-esteem of the poorer readers, who are often given less mature or less significant reading material. As Cox and Zarillo (1993) noted, in the core literature model, "no child is denied access to the best of children's literature" (p. 109).

However, there are some obvious problems with the core literature approach. Children have diverse interests and abilities. What is exciting to one child may be boring to another. An easy read for one child may be

CCSS

See Appendix B of Common Core State Standards.
for a listing of possible core literature texts.
http://www.corestandardsorg/assets/Appendix_B.pdf

FYI

Provide students with choices in their reading. They might choose from a selection of three to five novels, for instance. ■

■ The **literature-based approach** is a way of teaching reading by using literary selections as the primary instructional materials.

■ **Core literature** is literature selected to be read and analyzed by a group or an entire class. In a core literature approach, students read the same book.

an overwhelming task for another. Careful selection of core books with universal appeal should take care of the interest factor. It is difficult, for instance, to imagine any child not being intrigued by Wilder's *Little House in the Big Woods* (1932). Selections can also be presented in such a way as to be accessible to all. Suggestions for presenting texts to students of varying abilities can be found in Chapter 2.

Core selections might also be overanalyzed. Move at a lively pace when working with a core book. Do not move so slowly that the book becomes boring—but do not rush through the book so that slower readers cannot keep up. Do allow students to read ahead if they want to. If they finish the text early, they might read related books or books of their own choosing. Also, avoid assigning too many activities. Activities should build reading and writing skills or background knowledge and should deepen or extend students' understanding of the text. In addition, if you do use core books, make sure that students are provided with some opportunities to select books, so that teacher-selected texts are balanced by student-selected ones. Also provide for individual differences in reading ability. If core books are too difficult for some students, provide additional assistance, or, if necessary, read the books to them or obtain audiotapes of the texts. If audiotapes are available for all to use, there will be no stigma attached to using them. However, make sure that low-achieving readers have ample opportunity to read books on their level. This may entail scheduling sessions in which books on their level are introduced and discussed.

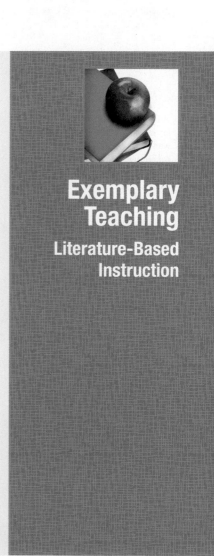

Exemplary Teaching
Literature-Based Instruction

Coming to a second-grade classroom composed primarily of poor children, many of whom were reading on a beginning reading level, researcher James Baumann set up a balanced literature-based program that reflected three principles: reading of high-quality children's books, explicit instruction in skills and strategies, and engaging in a significant amount of reading and writing each day.

The program was implemented through a series of routines that included reading aloud to students; intensive instruction in skills and strategies; providing students opportunities to read and discuss high-quality literature selections; providing time for self-selected, independent reading; and conducting writer's workshops. In addition, Baumann related reading and writing, used a variety of grouping patterns so that individual needs were met, and conducted a study buddies program with the fifth-grade class next door. In the study buddies program, half of Baumann's class went next door to meet their study buddies. The other half stayed where they were, and the study buddies came to them. During the 30-minute sessions, the second-graders worked on reading and writing with the help of their study buddies.

Baumann made use of a wide variety of techniques, including reading aloud, shared reading, choral reading, direct instruction, functional phonics lessons, and guided reading. Although explicit instruction was stressed, it was conducted within the context of real reading or writing. Baumann used an 80–20 rule, which meant that 80 percent of the time was spent reading and 20 percent was spent in skills/strategy instruction.

Working closely with parents, Baumann kept them informed about their children's progress and the work the class was doing. In notes sent home and in formal and informal conferences, parents were given suggestions for supporting their children's work. To foster reading at home, Baumann invited the children to take turns taking home Leo, the Read-With-Me Lion, or Molly, the Read-With-Me Monkey. Both stuffed animals had a pocket to hold a book and a parent card describing techniques that the parents might use to share the book with the child.

Assessment was conducted through observation, interviews, and examination of samples of the children's work. An abbreviated informal reading inventory was also administered. Inventory results showed that the children gained an average of two years. More importantly, they became avid readers. As Baumann commented, "They read up a storm" (Baumann & Duffy, 1997; Baumann & Ivey, 1997).

Text Sets

Text sets are groups of related books. Reading text sets fosters the making of connections. When students can make connections, their reading of all related texts is enriched (Harste, Short, & Burke, 1988). In addition to deepening readers' background, text sets broaden readers' framework for thinking about literature. Having read two or more related books, they can compare and contrast them. Discussions are also enlivened because students have more to talk about. If students read books on the same topic, understanding can be developed in greater depth.

Thematic Units

Another model of literature-based instruction is the **unit**, which has a theme or other unifying element. Its unifying element may be the study of a particular author, a genre—mystery or picture books, for example—or a theme. Possible themes include such diverse topics as heroes, distant places, sports and hobbies, animals, teddy bears, friendship, plants, or the Westward Movement. A unit's theme may involve only the language arts, or it may cut across the curriculum and include social studies, science, math, and the visual and performing arts.

Thematic organization has a number of advantages, the principal one being that it helps students make connections among reading, writing, listening, speaking, and viewing activities and among different pieces of literature. If the language arts are integrated with other subjects, even broader and more numerous connections can be constructed. However, Routman (1991) cautioned that before the language arts are integrated with content area subjects, they should first be integrated with each other.

Routman (1991) also warned that some thematic units lack depth and "are nothing more than suggested activities clustered around a central focus or topic" (p. 277). In her judgment, this is correlation rather than integration. In order for true integration to occur, the unit must develop some overall concepts or understandings, and activities must be designed to support those concepts or understandings. For instance, a unit may revolve around famous people, with students reading and writing about such people, but the unit is not truly integrated unless the reading and related activities developed a genuine theme or core idea. "Famous people" is a topic rather than a theme because it does not express a unifying idea. A unifying idea for a unit might be expressed as "Successful people have had to overcome obstacles on their way to success" or "Successful people have many characteristics in common." An excellent way to integrate such a unit is to create broad questions to be answered by students: "What are the secrets of success?" or "What are successful people like?" Ideally, these are questions that students have had a hand in creating. As part of the unit's activities, students read about successful people, then interview and write about them in order to integrate information from the unit and answer broad questions. They might look at successful people in science, social studies, and the arts.

A suggested procedure for creating and implementing a thematic unit follows:

1. *Select a topic or theme that you wish to explore.* When deciding upon a theme, select one that encompasses concepts that are an important part of the curriculum and that will facilitate the development of essential language arts goals. The theme should be significant and interesting to students.
2. *Involve students in the planning.* Determine through a modified KWL or similar technique what they know about the topic and what they would like to learn.

3. *State the overall ideas that you wish the unit to emphasize.* Include questions that your students might have about the topic (Routman, 1991). Key reasons for a unit on the West-

■ A **text set** is a group of related books. Because the books are related, reading and comparing them deepen readers' understanding of the unifying theme or topic.

■ A **unit** is a way of organizing instruction around a central idea, topic, or focus.

ward Movement might include: reasons for moving west, problems encountered during the move, transportation in the west, and life in a frontier settlement (DiLuglio, Eaton, & de Tarnowsky, 1988). Also, compose a list of language arts objectives. What literary appreciations and comprehension, study, writing, or other skills and strategies will the unit develop? These objectives should tie in with the unit's overall ideas. They should help students understand the nature of the Westward Movement. Included in the list of skill/strategy objectives are reading skills, such as summarizing, and writing skills, such as report writing, that students need in order to investigate the Westward Movement. Because the unit is interdisciplinary, objectives are listed for each content area.

4. ***Decide on the reading materials and activities that will be included in the unit.***   You may wish to focus on a core book that will become the center of the unit. Using a semantic map or web, show how you might integrate each of the language arts. Show, too, how you might integrate science, social studies, and other areas. Each activity should advance the theme of the unit. Activities should also promote skill/strategy development in the language arts and other areas. For instance, in the Westward Movement unit, students might simulate a journey west. As part of the simulation, they could write journal entries and track their progress on a map.

5. ***List and gather resources, including materials to be read, centers to be set up, audiovisual aids, Web sites, and guest speakers or resource personnel.***   Be sure to work closely with school and town librarians if students will be doing outside reading or research. The "Westward Movement" unit might list *Sarah, Plain and Tall* (MacLachlan, 1985), *Caddie Woodlawn* (Brink, 1935), *A Gathering of Days* (Blos, 1979), and other high-quality selections (Di-Luglio, Eaton, & de Tarnowsky, 1988). These texts vary in difficulty level from grade 3 to grade 7, so all the students might have materials on an appropriate level of difficulty.

6. ***Plan a unit opener that will set the stage for the unit.***   A unit opener might involve showing a film or video, reading a poem or the first chapter of the core book, or staging a simulation. The opener might involve brainstorming with students to decide which aspect of the topic they would like to explore. For the "Westward Movement" unit, students might imagine how it might feel if they were making a long, dangerous trip across the country.

7. ***Evaluate.***   Evaluation should be broad-based and keyed to the objectives that you have set for your students or that they have set for themselves in collaboration with you. It should include the unit's major concepts or ideas as well as skills and strategies that were emphasized. For example, if the ability to visualize was emphasized, it needs to be assessed. If you emphasized the ability to take notes or to write journals, that might be assessed through holistic evaluation of students' written pieces. As part of the evaluation, you must decide whether students learned the concepts and skills or strategies listed in the objectives. If not, reteaching is in order. In addition, you should evaluate the unit itself and determine what might be done to improve it. You might eliminate activities or materials that proved boring or ineffective and revise other elements as necessary.

Self-Selection

Reading a chapter book, novel, or full-length biography is a major commitment of time. Students will be more willing to put forth the necessary effort if they enjoy the book and have some say in its selection. Even when working with groups, it is possible to allow some self-selection. Obtain several copies of a number of appropriate books. Give a brief overview of each, and have students list them in order of preference. Group students by their preferences into literature discussion groups or similar groups (see the discussion of literature discussion groups in Chapter 10). You can even allow some self-selection when using a core literature approach with the entire class. Give

FYI

Units may encompass a single area, such as language arts or social studies, or they may be integrated and cut across subject matter areas. Integrated units apply the language arts to one or more content areas. The focus is on a theme topic, such as the essential role immigrants played in the development of the United States. Curriculum lines are dropped, and all activities are devoted to that topic. ■

FYI

Self-selection of reading fosters engagement, as does taking part in a conference with a teacher. ■

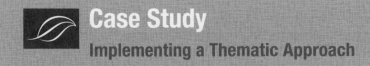

Case Study

Implementing a Thematic Approach

In a multiyear project with struggling readers and writers in grades 6 through 8, teachers in Memphis, Tennessee, implemented a thematic approach that involved cooperating across subject-matter boundaries. The idea behind the project was to "move curriculum from an unlinked catalog of texts, collection of superficially related works, or sequential or chronological structure to a more integrated whole of episodes echoing one another in support of ongoing curricular conversations" (Athanases, 2003, p. 110). In other words, teachers structured activities so as to make connections among key ideas to give students a broader perspective on major concepts and a deeper understanding of them. Ideas introduced in language arts class were reinforced and expanded in history and science classes. While the theme of community was being developed through reading literary works, the science teacher further developed the theme by exploring one of the theme's big ideas: interdependence. Family history was linked to science themes of nature versus nurture. Subthemes of discovery, motivation, and curiosity were developed through historical biographies of exploration and scientific experimentation.

As students were studying community, a tornado ripped through Memphis, causing enormous damage but also providing numerous opportunities for people of all economic, racial, and ethnic groups to come together and help each other out. Having studied interdependence in their community unit, students were able to arrive at a deeper understanding of what was happening in their city and do a better job writing about it.

At the outset, students' concepts of community were simplistic and tended to be limited to concepts of neighborhood. By year's end, students' concepts of community had grown considerably in breadth and depth. They were able to use analogies and metaphors in their discussions of community. They were also able to draw from the literature they had read. As their teacher commented:

> That was exciting to me to see that all of a sudden literature wasn't just born in books that sit on the shelf. It was "literature and my life." There is some connection there and I think the themes do that.... (Athanases, 2003, p. 116)

the students a choice of two or three core books from which to select. If it is necessary for the entire class to read a particular book, plan some activities in which students can select their own reading materials. You might also alternate teacher selection with self-selection: After teaching a unit that revolves around a teacher-selected book, plan a unit in which students select books.

Choosing Materials

One of the most important tasks in structuring a literature-based program is choosing the books. If the program is to be schoolwide or districtwide, teachers at each grade level should meet and decide which books might be offered at that level. Quality and appeal of the materials must be considered. Teachers also have to think about students' reading abilities, with easy, average, and challenging books provided for each grade. All genres should be included: novels, short stories, poems, plays, myths, and well-written informational books. And, of course, as noted above, students should have a voice in the selection of books to be read.

Advantages and Disadvantages of a Literature-Based Approach

The primary advantage of a literature-based approach is that books can be chosen to meet students' needs and interests. The major disadvantage of a literature-based program is that fine literature may be misused, by being made simply a means for developing reading skills rather than a basis for fostering personal response and an aesthetic sense. A second major disadvantage is that the books chosen may not be equally appealing to all students and may in some cases be too difficult for struggling readers.

Using Technology

Many authors and publishers of children's books maintain Internet sites. Some of the sites offer free teaching guides and other instructional resources. ∎

Adapting a Literature-Based Approach

In a literature-based approach, selections can be read in one of three ways: whole-class, small-group, or individually. Whole-class reading creates a sense of community and builds a common background of knowledge but neglects individual differences in reading ability and interest. Working in small groups does not build a sense of larger community but can better provide for individual differences. Individualized reading, which is described in the next section, provides for individual differences and fosters self-selection but may be inefficient. If you do use whole-class reading, use it on a limited basis and complement it with small groups or an individualized approach and self-selection.

In an individualized approach, students might pursue a favorite author.

Individualized Reading/Reading Workshop

The **individualized reading** approach is designed to create readers who can and do read. As Serafini (2006) explains, "Reading workshop is a place for engaged reading." Each student chooses her or his own reading material and has periodic conferences with the teacher to discuss it. The most popular form of individualized reading is known as **reading workshop**. Reading workshop is similar to writing workshop, but the focus is on reading. Reading workshop has three major components: preparation time, self-selected reading and responding, and student sharing (Atwell, 1987; Cooper, 1997; Reutzel and Cooter, 1991).

Preparation Time

Reading workshop begins with preparation time, which includes a state-of-the-class conference and a minilesson. The state-of-the-class conference is a housekeeping procedure and can be as brief as a minute or two. During this time, the schedule for the workshop is set, and students note what they will be doing. In the minilesson, the teacher presents a skill or strategy lesson based on a need evidenced by the whole class. It could be a lesson on making inferences, predicting, using context clues, deciphering multisyllabic words, or interpreting metaphors. Or it could be a lesson on selecting a book, finding more time to read, or how to share a book with a partner (Calkins, 2001). The minilesson might be drawn from the basal series or a literature guide or might be created by the teacher (Cooper, 1997). It should be presented within the framework of a story or article that students have read or listened to, and it should be applicable to the reading that they will do that day. The minilesson should last approximately 10 minutes, but could be longer.

Although brief, minilessons should be memorable and effective. Calkins (2001) has found a five-part format to be effective. The parts are connection, teaching, active involvement, link, and follow-up. The connection explains why a particular strategy or topic was chosen. For instance, the teacher might say, "When I'm reading a book about a new topic, I use the pictures to help me. Yesterday, I was reading about robots. I don't know much about robots, but the illustrations really helped." The teaching is the actual instruction. The teacher shows specifically how the illustrations and diagrams added to his or her understanding of robots and clarified some ideas that weren't

FYI

• Reading workshop can be time-consuming to plan and implement. Bookshop (Mondo) is a commercial program designed for grades K through 5 that includes a wide variety of children's books and other materials and extensive lesson plans. In several research studies, Bookshop has been shown to be an effective intervention program (Crévola & Vineis, 2004). ■

■ **Individualized reading** is a system of teaching reading in which students select their own reading material, read at their own pace, and are instructed in individual conferences and whole-class or small-group lessons.

■ **Reading workshop** is a form of individualized reading in which students choose their own books and have individual or group conferences but may meet in groups to discuss books or work on projects. There may also be whole-class or small-group lessons.

- Pinnell and Fountas (2002) recommend that guided reading be a part of a reading workshop for students in grade 3 and beyond.
- Minilessons may not allow sufficient time for instruction in complex skills. When introducing a skill, especially a complex one, you may need to extend the lesson. A shorter lesson might suffice when you are reviewing a skill.
- Literature discussion groups can be a part of a reading workshop. ∎

FYI

Independent reading, as described by Fountas and Pinnell (2001a), is a modified version of individualized or personalized reading and functions as a structured version of voluntary reading. ∎

clear. In the active involvement part of the minilesson, students try out the strategy or a portion of it for at least a few minutes. For example, the teacher gives students a handout that describes several unusual animals but contains no illustrations. The teacher then gives students the same handout with illustrations. The students briefly discuss how the second handout helped them better understand the selection. The link part connects the strategy with a story that the students are about to read. If students are reading informational books of their own choosing, the teacher could suggest that they use the illustrations to help them better understand the topics they are reading about. In the follow-up, students are asked to tell or demonstrate how they applied the strategy. The teacher asks students to tell how illustrations helped them better understand what they read.

Serafini (2006) uses read-alouds of literary selections to prepare his students for reading. Read-alouds are used to demonstrate fluent reading, key strategies, ways to respond to others in discussions, and ways to listen to and talk about literary selections. Read-alouds are also a way to introduce new authors, books, themes, and genres and to build a community of readers. After a book has been read aloud, a copy of its cover is posted so that the book may easily be referred to in subsequent sessions.

Self-Selected Reading and Responding

At the heart of the reading workshop is the time when students read self-selected books, respond to their reading, or engage in group or individual conferences. Self-selected reading may last approximately 30 minutes; if time is available, this period can be extended. If children have difficulty reading alone for that period of time, a portion of the period might be set aside for reading with a partner or in a small group. Because students will be reading their self-selected books independently, they should be encouraged to use appropriate strategies. Before reading, they should survey, predict, and set a purpose for reading. As they read, they should use summarizing, inferencing, questioning, and imaging strategies—if appropriate—and should monitor for meaning. As they read, students can use sticky notes to indicate a difficult word or puzzling passage. Or, as suggested by Atwell (1987), they can record difficult words and the page numbers of puzzling passages on a bookmark. A full bookmark could be a sign that a book is too difficult. After reading, students should evaluate their original prediction and judge whether they can retell the selection and relate it to their own experiences.

Response time may last from 15 to 30 minutes or longer. During response time, students may meet in a literature discussion group to discuss their reading, write in their journals, work on an extension activity, plan a reader's theater or other type of presentation, work at one of the classroom's centers, continue to read, or attend a conference. During response time, hold individual and/or group conferences. If time allows, circulate around the room, giving help and guidance as needed. Visiting literature discussion groups should be a priority.

Conferences Just as for writing workshop, conferences are a key part of reading workshop. Both individual and group conferences are recommended, each having distinct advantages.

FYI

- In the original version of individualized reading, teachers held individual conferences with students. In reading workshop, teachers hold group as well as individual conferences.
- Instead of filling out a response sheet (or in addition to doing so), students might use sticky notes to mark interesting or puzzling passages, difficult words, or other items they would like to talk about in a conference. ∎

Individual Conferences Although time-consuming, the individual conference allows each student to have the teacher's full attention and direct guidance and instruction for at least a brief period. It builds a warm relationship between teacher and student and provides the teacher with valuable insights into the needs of each child. While individual conferences are being held, other students are engaged in silent reading. No interruption of the conference is allowed, and those involved in silent reading are not to be disturbed.

An individual conference begins with some questions designed to put the student at ease and to get a general sense of the student's understanding of the book. Through questioning, the teacher also attempts to elicit the child's personal response to the text and encourages the child to relate the text to her or his own life. The teacher poses questions to clear up difficulties and to build comprehension—and concepts, if necessary—and reviews difficult vocabulary. If the teacher has taught a particular skill or strategy, such as analyzing characters, using context clues, or making personal connections, that might be the focus of a conference. In addition, the teacher assesses how well the student understood the book, whether she or he enjoyed it, and whether she or he is able to apply the strategies and skills that have been taught. The teacher notes any needs the student has and may provide spontaneous instruction or give help later.

As part of the conference, the teacher might conduct a brief running record that lasts just a minute or two (Reutzel, Jones, & Newman, 2010). The running record might be conducted at the beginning of the conference. Students' performance on the running record can be used to plan on-the-spot instruction as well as future lessons.

To prepare for individual conferences, students choose a favorite part of the book to read to the teacher and also give a personal assessment of the book, telling why they did or did not like it or what they learned from it. Students also bring words, ideas, or items they want clarified or questions that they have about the text. In addition, students may be asked to complete a generic response sheet or a specific response sheet geared to the book they have read. Figure 11.1 presents a generic response form designed to elicit a personal response from students. To avoid having students do an excessive amount of writing, you might focus on just a few of the personal response questions, or have students respond to the questions orally rather than in writing.

Another way that students can prepare for an individual conference is to keep track of their reading in journals. Students note the date, the title and author of the book, and their personal response to the piece, answering questions such as these: How does the selection make me feel? What will I most remember about it? Was there anything in it that bothered me (Gage, 1990)? Did it remind me of a person or event in my life? Do I have any questions about the piece (Parsons, 1990)? For an informational book, students answer such questions as these: What did I learn? Which details did I find most interesting? How might I use the information? What questions do I still have about the topic? Questions should not be so time-consuming or arduous to answer that children avoid reading so that they will not have to answer them. As an alternative, you might have students keep a dialogue journal, as described later in this chapter. Younger children may respond to a book by drawing a picture. Whatever form the response takes, it should be geared to the maturity level of the child and the nature of the text.

Students should keep a record of all books that they read. While helping the teacher keep track of students' reading, such records are also motivational. Students get a sense of accomplishment from seeing their list grow.

Individual conferences can last anywhere from 5 to 10 minutes. At least one individual or group conference should be held for each student each week. However, not every book needs a conference. A student who is reading two or three books a week should decide on one book to talk about. On the other hand, if the student is a slow reader, a conference may be held when she or he is halfway through the book. Conferences should be scheduled. A simple way to do this is to have students who are ready for conferences list their names on the chalkboard. The teacher can then fill in the times for the conferences.

After the conference is over, the teacher should make brief notes in the student's folder, including date, title of book read, assessment of student's understanding and satisfaction with the book, strategies or skills introduced or reinforced, student's present and future needs, and student's future plans. A sample conference report form is presented in Figure 11.2.

Group Conferences   Group conferences are an efficient use of time and can be used along with or instead of individual conferences. The teacher has the opportunity to work with five or six students rather than just one. Conferences can be held to discuss books by the same author, those with a common theme, or those in the same genre.

Assessing for Learning

After holding a conference, be sure to summarize it. Include date, selection read, and student's reaction to the text: Did the student enjoy it? Is she or he able to respond to it? Is the book too difficult or too easy? Does the student select books wisely? Did you note any needs? If so, how will these be provided for? Will she or he engage in an extension or enrichment activity? Will she or he read another book? ■

FYI

Teachers might hold conferences during silent reading and during response time. A main reason that teachers found individualized reading unmanageable in the past was the demand that conferences made on their time. However, with group conferences, this should no longer be a major hindrance. ■

FIGURE 11.1 Response
Sheet for Fiction

Name: _____   Date: _____

Title of book: _____   Publisher: _____

Author: _____   Date of publication: _____

Plot

　　　　Problem: _____
　　　　　　　　　_____

Main happenings: _____
　　　　　　　　　_____
　　　　　　　　　_____
　　　　　　　　　_____

　　　　Climax: _____
　　　　　　　　_____

　　　Outcome: _____

Answer any three of the following questions:

1. What did you like best about the book?

　　_____
　　_____
　　_____

2. Is there anything in the book that you would like to change? If so, what? Also
　 tell why you would like to make changes.

　　_____
　　_____
　　_____
　　_____

3. Is there anything in the book that puzzled you or bothered you?

　　_____
　　_____
　　_____

4. Would you like to be friends with any of the characters in the book? Why or
　 why not?

　　_____
　　_____
　　_____

5. If other students your age asked whether you thought they might like to read
　 this book, what would you tell them?

　　_____
　　_____
　　_____

Group conferences work best when students have read the same book. If several copies of a book are available, they can be given to interested students, who then confer.

A group conference includes three types of questions: an opening question to get the discussion started, following questions to keep the discussion moving, and process questions to "help the children focus on particular elements of the text" (Hornsby, Sukarna, & Parry, 1986, p. 62). Process questions focus on comprehending and appreciating a piece and are similar to those asked in the discussion and rereading portions of a guided reading lesson. They are often related to reading strategies and might ask students to summarize a passage, compare characters, predict events, clarify difficult terms, or locate proof for an inference. Students should also have the

Name: *Althea S.*　　　　　　　Date: *10/19*

Title: *Owl at Home*　　　　　Author: *Arnold Lobel*

Understanding of text
and personal response:　　*Discussion of Ch. 1 of text: Saw humor in story.
Remembered time when furnace broke and apartment
was cold but became cozy again.*

Oral reading:　　*Fairly smooth. Good interpretation. Some difficulty reading
dialogue. 97% accuracy.*

Needs:　　*Read behav for behave. Needs to integrate context and
phonics.*

Future plans:　　*Plans to finish book by end of week. Will join Arnold Lobel
Literature Circle and compare Owl books with Frog and
Toad books. Will share funniest incident with whole class.*

FIGURE 11.2　A Sample
Conference Report Form

opportunity to respond personally to the text. Process and response questions might be interwoven. The teacher should lead the discussion, although students eventually may take on that role. Just as in individual conferences, the teacher evaluates students' performance, notes needs, and plans future activities based on those needs. Along with or instead of a group conference, students might take part in a literature discussion group.

Using Dialogue Journals　If you are working with older students, you might try **dialogue journals** as an alternative or supplement to conferences. In a dialogue journal a student responds freely to a piece of writing or to a prompt about the writing provided by the teacher. The teacher then responds to the student's response. Having the opportunity to write about their reading gives students time to reflect and leads to deeper insights (Atwell, 1987). The give and take of dialogue journals leads students to develop their thoughts and reconsider interpretations. In addition to providing students with an opportunity to respond, dialogue journals yield insight into students' growth as readers. Thus, they offer the teacher a rich source of ideas for teaching lessons. Because responding to each student's journal on a daily basis could be overwhelming, you might want to have one fifth of the class turn in their journals each day. That way you respond each day to just a few students, but you see each student's journal once a week.

Student Sharing

During the student-sharing portion of reading workshop, which should last from 10 to 20 minutes, students share their reading with the entire class. They might give the highlights of a book they especially enjoyed, read an exciting passage, share a poem, make a recommendation, enact a reader's theater performance, or share in some other way. "Sharing time advertises and promotes the excitement of literacy learning and helps to promote the class as a community of readers" (Cooper, 1997, p. 491). As an alternative to whole-class sharing, the teacher might arrange for small-group sharing with about four students in each group. The teacher can then visit with the groups as a participant or observer (Cooper, 1997).

 Building Language

To develop students' use of language, you can ask them to expand on responses. If a student said that he liked *Heads or Tails* (Gantos, 1994) because it was funny, ask him to tell what made it funny or to tell what the funniest part was. ■

 FYI

Through the use of dialogue journals, you can prompt students to look more deeply at characters and theme and to think more critically about their reading. ■

 FYI

Dialogue journals allow teachers to model and scaffold more mature expression (Atwell, 1987). Through comments and questions, they can elicit more elaborated responses and can direct students to look at essential aspects of the texts being discussed. Closed questions such as "Which character did you like best?" tend to elicit a limited response. Open questions such as "The story sounds interesting—tell me about it" tend to bring forth a fuller response. ■

■ A **dialogue journal** is a journal in which the student reacts to or makes observations about reading selections and the teacher responds by writing in the journal.

Organizing the Program

The classroom must be organized carefully. Just as in a library, it should have an inviting browsing area where students can choose books and settle down comfortably to read. Routines should be established for selecting books, keeping track of books circulated, taking part in conferences, and completing independent activities. The nature of the activity should determine the types of rules and routines. Because they are expected to follow these procedures, students should have a role in formulating them. The teacher might describe the situation and have students suggest ways to make it work.

The following basic conditions must be met: (1) the teacher must be able to hold individual or group conferences with students without interruptions; (2) students must be able to work on their own without disturbing others; and (3) students must be responsible for choosing books on their own and reading them. Rules and routines might include the following:

- *Book selection.* The number of students choosing books at one time is limited to five; students may select two books at one time; students may make one exchange. Some students, especially those who are struggling with their reading, may waste a great deal of time choosing books. Instead of having students select books during reading workshop, you might have students gather books from the school or classroom library prior to reading. Younger students might gather four or five books that they intend to read. Older students might gather two or three. These can be kept in book boxes or accordion folders or oversized envelopes along with students' reading logs and conference sheets and any other reading aids, such as a model words chart (Calkins, 2001).
- *Circulation.* Students are responsible for the books they check out; a card, sign-out sheet, or computerized system is used to keep track of books; students are in charge of the circulation system; books may be taken home.
- *Conference time.* No one may interrupt the teacher during conferences; students must come prepared to conferences; students (or the teacher) must arrange for periodic conferences.

Advantages and Disadvantages of Reading Workshop

Self-selection, moving at one's own pace, using group processes, and relating reading and writing are the major advantages of reading workshop. Disadvantages include potential neglect of skills and the possibility that the teacher might spread himself or herself too thin in an attempt to meet with a variety of groups and individuals and respond to students' journal entries. Also, reading workshop might be unsuitable for students who have a difficult time working independently or whose skills are so limited that there are few books they can read on their own.

Adapting Reading Workshop

Reading workshop can be used instead of a basal series or along with one. For instance, you might use a basal three days and reading workshop two days. Or you might use a basal for a part of the day and reading workshop for a portion. Use whole-class instruction as appropriate. For instance, teach book selection and strategies needed by all students to the whole class. Use small-group instruction for those children who evidence a specific need for additional help. Obtain multiple copies of selected titles, just as you might do for a literature-based approach, and periodically invite students to choose one of the titles and read it as part of a small-group guided reading lesson. Use efficient management techniques, and do not overextend yourself. If you use reading workshop with younger students whose writing skills are still rather limited, gradually lead them into the use of dialogue journals. They might begin by drawing pictures in response to selections they read.

It is essential that students be taught basic skills and strategies and be provided with adequate opportunities to apply them. Instructing students in the selection of books and regularly holding conferences are also essential elements (Hiebert & Reutzel, 2010).

Language-Experience Approach

The **language-experience approach**, introduced in Chapter 4, is very personal. Children's experiences, expressed in their own language and written down by the teacher or an aide, become their reading material. Because both the language and the experience are familiar, this method presents fewer difficulties for children who are learning to read. It also integrates thinking, listening, speaking, reading, and writing. Through discussion, the teacher can lead students to organize and reflect on their experiences. If time order is garbled, the teacher can ask, "What happened first? What happened next?" If details are scant, the teacher can request that the children tell more or can ask open-ended questions, such as "How do you think the dinosaur tracks got there? What do the tracks tell us about dinosaurs?" Through comments that show an interest in the children and the topic, the teacher affirms them and encourages them to elaborate.

Whereas the teacher should affirm, support, encourage, and scaffold, she or he needs to be careful not to take over. When recording students' stories, it is important to write their exact words. Rephrasing what they have dictated shows a lack of acceptance for the language used. In addition, if the story is expressed in words that the child does not normally use, the child may have difficulty reading it. However, when a group story is being written, the situation is somewhat different. The story and the way it is written reflect the language structures that the group typically uses. To record a nonstandard structure might confuse some members of the group and result in criticism of the child who volunteered the structure. Displaying group stories containing nonstandard structures might

■ The **language–experience approach** to teaching reading involves students dictating a story based on an experience they have had. The dictated story is written down by a teacher or aide and used to instruct the students in reading. Shared writing and interactive writing are language-experience activities.

LESSON 11.1
Group Language-Experience Chart

Day 1

Step 1. Building experiential background for the story

The students have an experience that they share as a group and that they can write about. It might be a field trip, the acquisition of a pet for the classroom, the baking of bread, or another experience.

Step 2. Discussing the experience

Students reflect on their experience and talk about it. During the discussion, the teacher helps them organize the experience. In discussing a visit to the circus, the teacher might ask them to tell what they liked best so that they do not get lost in details. If they baked bread, the teacher would pose questions in such a way that the children would list in order the steps involved.

Step 3. Dictating the story

The children dictate the story. The teacher or aide writes it on large lined paper, an overhead transparency, or on the chalkboard or might type it on a computer that has an attachment to magnify the input and project it on a screen. The teacher reads aloud what she or he is writing so that children can see the spoken words being written. The teacher reads each sentence to make sure it is what the child who volunteered the sentence wanted to say. The teacher sweeps her or his hand under the print being read so that students can see where each word begins and ends and that reading is done from left to right. For students just learning to read, each sentence is written on a separate line, when possible.

Step 4. Reviewing the story

After the whole story has been written, the teacher reads it aloud once more. Children listen to see that the story says what they want it to say. They are invited to make changes.

Step 5. Reading of story by teacher and students

The teacher reads the story, running her or his hand under each word as it is read. The children read along with the teacher.

Step 6. Reading of familiar parts by students

Volunteers are asked to read sentences or words that they know. The teacher notes those children who are learning words and phrases and those who are just getting a sense of what reading is all about.

Day 2

Step 1. Rereading of story

The story is reread by the teacher, who points to each word as it is read. The children read along. The story might then be read in unison by the teacher and students. The teacher continues to point to each word. Volunteers might be able to read some familiar words or phrases.

Step 2. Matching of story parts

The teacher has duplicated the story and cut it into strips. The teacher points to a line in the master story, and students find the duplicated strip that matches it. Individual words might also be matched. A volunteer reads the strip, with the teacher helping out as necessary. For students who can go beyond matching, the teacher plans activities that involve reading, asking questions such as the following: "Which strip tells where we went? Which strip tells what we saw?" Students identify and read the strips. On a still more advanced level, students assemble the strips in correct order. This works best with stories that have no more than four or five sentences. Individual sentences can also be cut up into words that students assemble into sentences. This can be done as a pocket chart activity. The scrambled words are displayed, and volunteers read each one. Then a volunteer reads the word that should come first, puts it in its place, and reads it once more. A second volunteer reads the word that should come next and places it after the first word. The teacher reads the two words that have been correctly placed or calls on a volunteer to do so. This continues until the sentence has been assembled correctly. Once the entire strip has been assembled, the teacher or a volunteer reads it. The class listens to see whether the sentence has been put together correctly. Once students agree that it has, they read it in unison. This technique works best with short sentences.

FYI

Working with individual words helps both the least able and the most able readers. It helps poor readers see where words begin and end and more advanced readers learn to read words automatically. When words are looked at individually, students note their characteristics, such as which letter comes first. ■

also result in protests from parents and administrators (Cunningham & Allington, 1999).

The language-experience approach can be used with individuals or groups. Lesson 11.1 describes the steps for a group language-experience story.

Personalizing Group Stories

One way to personalize group language-experience stories is to identify the name of each contributor. After a volunteer has supplied a sentence, the teacher writes the student's name and the sentence, as shown in Figure 11.3. When the story is reread, each student can read the sentence that she or he contributed originally. Seeing their names in print gives students a sense of ownership of the story. It also helps them remember the sentences that they supplied.

FYI

If your students are creating individual language-experience stories, it's helpful to have an aide or volunteers assist with dictation. First, explain the process to your helpers, and let them observe you until they feel they can undertake it on their own. ■

> ## OUR PETS
>
> *Billy said, "I have a dog.*
>
> *My dog's name is Ralph."*
>
> *Amy said, "I have a cat.*
>
> *My cat's name is Sam."*
>
> *Julio said, "My pets are goldfish.*
>
> *They don't have names.*
>
> *They just swim and swim."*

FIGURE 11.3 Personalized Group Language-Experience Story

An Individual Approach

Individual language-experience stories are similar to group stories, except that they are more personalized. (Figure 4.2 on p. 140 is an individual language-experience story about a trip to an apple orchard.) Just as in the group approach, the child dictates a story and the teacher, an aide, or a volunteer writes it down and uses it as the basis for teaching reading. Often, an individual language-experience story starts out as a drawing. The child then dictates a story that tells about the drawing. A photo can also be used to illustrate a story or as a stimulus for dictating one.

When dictating a language-experience story, a child may bring up experiences that are highly personal or that reveal private family matters. Affirm the child's feelings, but suggest a more appropriate way for the child to relate the experience: "I'm pleased that you trusted me enough to share that with me, but I think maybe you should tell your mom or dad about it." If the child uses language that is unsuitable for the classroom, have her or him use more appropriate language: "Can you think of another way to say it?" (Tierney, Readence, & Dishner, 1995). Maintaining the child's dignity and self-concept is of primary importance. Handle delicate situations with sensitivity and careful professional judgment.

Other Uses for the Language-Experience Approach

The language-experience approach can be used to compose booklets on science and social studies topics, thank-you notes to a visiting author, a letter to a classmate who is hospitalized, an invitation to a guest speaker, recipes, a set of directions for the computer, class rules, charts, lists, captions, diaries, booklets, plays, and similar items that are suitable for the language-experience approach. When possible, the pieces should be written for real purposes.

Shared writing is another way in which the language-experience approach might be used. Shared writing is a cooperative venture involving teacher and students. In a regular language-experience story, the teacher records students' exact words. In shared writing, the teacher draws from the children the substance of what they want to say but may rephrase it (Cunningham & Allington, 1999). For instance, at the end of the day, the teacher may ask the students what they learned that day. Summarizing the contributions of many children, the teacher records the day's highlights. In doing so, the teacher is modeling how spoken language is transformed into written language.

FYI

- Because the language-experience approach is based on students' individual backgrounds, it allows each student to share her or his culture, experience, and mode of self-expression. The approach has the power to promote understanding and community among students whose backgrounds may differ.
- How to handle dialect is a controversial issue. Shuy (1973) made the point that it is developmentally inappropriate to introduce another dialect to a young child. The child will be confused and will not pick up the second dialect. As students grow older, they may choose to use other dialects to be able to communicate more effectively with diverse groups. This does not mean that they will surrender their home dialect. ■

Using Technology

Language experience stories can be composed on interactive white boards, computer words processing programs, PowerPoint or other electronic format and can be enlivened by importing photos, music, or filmclips. ■

FYI

• Group language-experience stories can be used beyond the beginning or early reading level to demonstrate writing techniques. One way of showing students how to write a letter to the editor or a persuasive essay is to have the class compose the item as a group.
• See the discussion of language-experience stories in Chapter 4. ■

REFLECTION

What are some highly effective uses for the language experience approach? How might you adapt the language experience approach for use with your students?

Advantages and Disadvantages of the Language-Experience Approach

The language-experience approach is most frequently used as a supplement to other programs and is especially useful with children who are in the beginning stages of learning to read. The major advantage of the approach is that it builds on children's language and experience. A major disadvantage of using it as the sole approach to teaching reading is that the child's reading will be limited to his or her own experiences. However, in a sense this disadvantage is an advantage. By sharing experiences, students have the opportunity to learn about each other. As Landis, Umolu, and Mancha (2010) comment, "Teachers and students who participate in LEA reading and writing activities are introduced to the power of language to create opportunities for learning that bridge different language, cultural expectations, and values about diverse events and life experiences" (p. 588).

Adapting the Language-Experience Approach

Because it neglects published reading materials and limits children's reading experiences, language experience should not be the sole approach to reading instruction. However, it makes an excellent supplement to any of the other approaches presented in this chapter, especially at the emergent and early stages of reading.

FYI

• Not all teachers favor learning centers. Having students read independently or meet with a literature discussion group or a cooperative learning group can be more productive than working at learning centers, especially with students in grades 2 and above.
• Centers should contain puzzles, magnets, word games, magazines, and manipulatives that are appealing to children and allow them to make discoveries on their own. The best centers are those that children would want to work at even if they weren't assigned to do so (Cunningham & Allington, 2003). ■

Adapting Instruction for Struggling Readers and Writers

Specialists in one elementary school helped teachers plan their learning centers and incorporate activities that would assist struggling learners (Guastello & Lenz, 2005). To check on the effectiveness of the centers, teachers had students take turns reporting what they learned. ■

Guided Reading

Guided reading is a way of organizing reading instruction that uses grouping (see pp. 377–385 for a discussion of guided reading). In guided reading, students are grouped and instructed according to their level of development (Fountas & Pinnell, 1996, 2001c, 2006). The groups meet daily for 10 to 30 minutes or more. The teacher may organize as many groups as she believes are necessary, but the more groups assembled, the less time there is for each one. As a practical matter, three or four groups are the most that can be handled efficiently. Grouping, however, is flexible. When appropriate, students are moved into other groups.

What does the rest of the class do while the teacher is working with guided reading groups? Students can engage in a number of independent activities. These activities should provide students with the opportunity to apply and extend their skills. One of the best activities for developing reading skills is, of course, to read. Students can

• read independently in the reading corner,
• read with a buddy,
• read along with an audiotape or CD,
• read charts and stories posted around the room,
• meet with a literature discussion group,
• meet with a cooperative learning group,
• work on a piece of writing,
• research a project in the library or on the Internet,
• work on a carefully chosen Web site that fosters literacy, or
• work at one of the classroom learning centers.

Learning Centers

Learning centers can provide practice for skills, provide enrichment, or allow students to explore interests. Many of the reinforcement activities suggested throughout this text can be made into learning centers. For instance, word-analysis centers can be set up that include sorting activities. The nature of the centers should be dictated by learning outcomes.

■ A **dialect** is a variant of a language that may differ somewhat in pronunciation, grammar, and vocabulary.

Case Study
Guided Reading

After whole-group shared reading and writing, students in Pat Loden's first-grade class assemble for guided reading. Loden has four groups of four or five students. Students are grouped according to their levels and needs. While Loden is meeting with a group, other students read independently for 20 minutes. They reread books that were read during guided reading or select new books. A record is kept of books read, and each student responds to at least one book each week. After 20 minutes of silent reading, students engage in journal writing. After completing journal writing, they work in learning centers that focus on Internet penpals, science, literacy, poetry, writing, letter and word work, and read-the-room exercises. Reading-the-room consists of using a pointer while reading signs, charts, and other materials posted around the room. Each center contains directions for completing the activity. Students also make a note of the work that they complete at a center.

Meanwhile, Loden conducts her guided reading lessons. Each lesson begins with a minilesson designed to teach a skill related to the reading of the day's text. Children read the text silently. While the group reads silently, Loden has each of the children in the group read a passage orally to her. After students finish reading the selection, they discuss it. Loden then signals another group to come to the guided reading table (Morrow & Asbury, 2001).

What do you want students to know or be able to do as a result of using the centers? Centers offer an almost infinite number of possibilities. However, most classrooms feature a reading center or book corner in which students choose and read books or periodicals; a listening center in which students listen to or view recorded stories; an Internet center in which students engage in Web-related activities; a writing center in which students compose messages, poems, or stories; a word-work center that might feature riddles, word games, or sorting activities; and a drama center that might feature books or scripts and puppets that can be used to dramatize selections or compose scripts. There might also be math, science, art, and social studies centers. For younger students, there might be a pretend play or role-playing center.

Connect the centers to the curriculum. The centers should extend skills and themes students are currently working on. Each center should have an objective. If your curriculum is standards-based, you might want to note the standard that a center addresses. This prevents having centers that are fun and interesting but don't really further any educational objective. Also, have a means for tracking students' performance at the centers. After working at a center, students might record the title of a book and the number of pages they read, or they might produce a piece of writing or note a story that they dramatized. Also, have students discuss with the class the kinds of things they are doing at the centers. This helps keep the work at the centers related to the overall objectives of the classroom. Components of a learning center include title, activities, directions, materials, and assessment. See Table 11.1 for a description of the activities in two typical centers.

Involve students in the creation of learning centers. Change the content of the centers frequently to keep them interesting. Although the nature of a center might stay the same, change the activities and materials periodically. Assess the centers. Which ones seem most popular? Which ones seem to result in the most learning?

Where possible, provide choices. Students might practice a phonics skill by reading a selection along with an ebook version, or they might complete a crossword puzzle or a sorting activity. The objective is the same in each case, but the means for getting there vary.

The Internet is an excellent resource for centers. The LiteracyCenter.net, for instance, offers a range of interactive alphabet-recognition, letter-formation, and word-creation activities for students in pre-K and kindergarten. The teacher needs to provide directions for logging on, select activities, and assess students' performance.

Adapting Instruction for English Language Learners

Center activities should reinforce themes so that concepts are extended and vocabulary is reinforced. This added reinforcement is especially helpful to ELLs. ∎

Using Technology

A to Z Teacher Stuff offers links to a number of sites for creating literacy centers:

http://www.atozteacherstuff.com/Lesson_Plans/Learning_Centers/Literacy_Centers/index.shtml ∎

Using Technology

Examples of centers and resources.

Classroom Centers
http://www.mrsmcdowell.com/centers.htm

ABC Teach
http://www.abcteach.com/directory/learning_centers/ ∎

TABLE 11.1 Two Sample Learning Centers

Type	Objective	Sequence of Activities
Listening/viewing post	Building fluency	1. Students listen to or view a brief recorded play. 2. Students read along with the recorded play. Each student reads a part. 3. Students listen to the recorded play again. 4. Students dramatize the play (Ford, 2004).
Word study	Building word recognition	1. Working in pairs, students sort words. 2. One student sorts as the other observes and makes corrections when necessary. The student sorting explains why each word is sorted: has the same sound as the headword or picture or follows the same pattern. 3. The second student sorts and explains. 4. Students sort several more times in order to obtain speed and accuracy. 5. Students fill out a response form, supplying their names, the title of their sort, and the number of sorts.

R E F L E C T I O N

How might guided reading be used with virtually any approach? What are some of the challenges of implementing guided reading? How might you meet these challenges in your teaching situation?

Managing Learning Centers To manage the use of learning centers, a magnetic schedule board or pocket chart can be helpful. On the board or chart, list the possible activities, as in Figure 11.4.

Depending on the length of time students will be working independently, they may complete two or three activities. In Figure 11.4, students have each been assigned three activities. Students may be required to complete certain activities, or they might be given choices. Some teachers post a schedule so that students know exactly what they are to do. This allows visits to centers to be staggered so that the centers don't become too crowded.

Advantages and Disadvantages of Guided Reading

A key advantage of guided reading is that students are instructed on their level and are given the support and instruction they need. The approach works especially well if the grouping is flexible and if students not meeting in groups are provided with worthwhile activities. However, unless carefully planned, learning centers can deteriorate into busy-work. Tyner (2004, 2006) recommends integrating word study and writing into a guided reading approach. Word study prepares students for the text they will be

FIGURE 11.4 Pocket Chart Schedule of Learning Centers

Wednesday, November 15			
Edna, Ashley, Kayla, Michael, Dylan	ABC	🎧	✏️
Luis, Juan, Alyssa, William	💻	✏️	📖
Jacob, Aaron, Maria, Marisol	🎧	📖	ABC
Rachel, Edith, Latasha, Carlos	📖	💻	🎧
Raymond, Nicole, Michael, Angel	✏️	ABC	💻

reading, and writing reinforces and extends the reading and the word study. As she points out, this integration is especially important for struggling readers.

At a computer center, students can follow a story in print as it is read to them.

An Integrated Approach

A large-scale comparison of approaches to teaching reading in the 1960s came up with no clear winner (Bond & Dykstra, 1967, 1997). All of the approaches evaluated were effective in some cases but ineffective in others. The study suggested that the teacher is more important than the method and that a method successful in one situation may not be successful in all. Combinations of approaches were recommended. Adding language experience to a basal program seemed to strengthen the program. A word-attack element also seemed to be an important component, a conclusion that was reached repeatedly in a number of studies and research reviews (Adams, 1990; Anderson, Hiebert, Scott, & Wilkinson, 1985; Chall, 1967, 1983a; Dykstra, 1974; Snow, Burns, & Griffin, 1998).

Another interpretation of the research strongly suggests that what is really most effective is using the best features of all approaches. Draw from holistic literature-based approaches the emphasis on functional–contextual instruction, the use of children's literature, and integration of language arts. From basal programs, adopt some of the structure built into the skills and strategies components. From individualized approaches, take the emphasis on self-selection of students' reading material. From the language-experience approach, adopt the practice of using writing to build and extend literacy skills.

Above all else, use your professional judgment. This book presents a core of essential skills and strategies in word recognition, comprehension, reading in the content areas, and study skills. Use this core of skills as a foundation when implementing your literacy program, regardless of which approach or approaches you use. If a skill or strategy is omitted or neglected in one approach, then add it or strengthen it. For instance, not all basals recommend the use of pronounceable word parts or analogy strategies. If you are using a basal and these elements are missing, add them.

IRA POSITION STATEMENT ON KEY ISSUE
Using Multiple Methods of Beginning Reading Instruction

Several large-scale studies of reading methods have shown that no one method is better than any other method in all settings and situations (International Reading Association, 1999a). For every method studied, some children learned to read very well while others had great difficulty. Perhaps the most important reason for a search for the best method is that there are a significant number of children who do not read as well as they must to function in a society that has increasing demands for literacy. Reading is not being taught as well as it should be. "Because there is no clearly documented best way to teach beginning reading, professionals who are closest to the children must be the ones to make the decisions about what reading methods to use, and they must have the flexibility to modify those methods when they determine that particular children are not learning" (International Reading Association, 1999a, p. 5).

Summary

A number of approaches are used to teach reading. The basal approach uses anthologies, which may be complemented by children's books. The literature-based approach and reading workshop use children's books. The language-experience approach uses writing to teach reading. Each approach has advantages and disadvantages and may be combined with other approaches and/or adapted to individual teaching goals.

Guided reading can be used along with most approaches to teaching reading. Guided reading is a way of grouping and instructing students according to their needs.

According to research, no single approach to teaching reading yields consistently superior results. A combination is probably best. Teachers should use their professional judgment and know-how to adapt programs to fit the needs of their students. Struggling readers need materials on their level and will benefit from additional instruction.

Extending and Applying

1. Plan a series of language-experience lessons, either for an individual or for a group of students, in which an experience story is written and used to present or reinforce appropriate literacy understandings or skills and strategies. Evaluate the effectiveness of your lessons.
2. Adapt a lesson in a basal/anthology reading program to fit the needs of a group of students you are teaching. Teach the lesson and assess its effectiveness. In what ways was the program's teacher's manual a helpful resource? What adaptations did you have to make?
3. Examine a current basal series. Look at a particular level and assess the interest of the selections, the kinds of strategies and teaching suggestions presented in the teacher's manual, and the usefulness of the workbook exercises. Summarize your findings. (You may be able to examine a series online. Some of the current series have their manuals and many of the reading and support materials available online.)
4. Examine your philosophy of teaching reading. Make a list of your beliefs and your teaching practices. Also note the approach that best fits in with your philosophy. Do your practices fit your beliefs? If not, what might you do to align the two?

Professional Reflection

Do I ...

___ Have an understanding of the major components of an effective reading program?
___ Have an understanding of the major approaches to teaching reading and the advantages and disadvantages of each?

Am I able to ...

___ Select the reading approach or combination that is most appropriate for my students?
___ Teach reading using a variety of approaches?
___ Adapt reading approaches to meet the needs of my students?

Reflection Question

Which of the approaches or combinations discussed in this chapter best suit your philosophy and style of teaching? How would you go about implementing your preferred approach? In many school, an approach or materials are chosen by the administration.

What adaptations might you make if you are working in a system that has chosen a basal? What adaptations might you make if you are working in a system that has chosen a workshop approach?

Building Competencies

To build competencies, consult the following source for more detailed information:

Serafini, F. (2006). *Around the reading workshop in 180 days: A month-by-month guide to effective instruction.* Portsmouth, NH: Heinemann.

Landis, D., Umolu, J., & Mancha, S. (2010). The power of language experience for cross-cultural reading and writing. *The Reading Teacher, 63,* 580–589.

MyEducationLab™

Go to the Topic "Organization and Management" MyEducationLab (www.myeducationlab.com) for your course, where you can:

- Find learning outcomes for "Organization and Management" along with the national standards that connect to these outcomes.
- Complete Assignments and Activities that can help you more deeply understand the chapter content.
- Apply and practice your understanding of the core teaching skills identified in the chapter with the Building Teaching Skills and Dispositions learning units.
- Examine challenging situations and cases presented in the IRIS Center Resources.
- Check your comprehension on the content covered in the chapter by going to the Study Plan in the Book

Resources for your text. Here you will be able to take a chapter quiz, receive feedback on your answers, and then access Review, Practice, and Enrichment activities to enhance your understanding of chapter content. (optional)

A+RISE A+RISE® Standards2Strategy™ is an innovative and interactive online resource that offers new teachers in grades K–12 just-in-time, research-based instructional strategies that meet the linguistic needs of ELLs as they learn content, differentiate instruction for all grades and abilities, and are aligned to Common Core Elementary Language Arts standards (for the literacy strategies) and to English language proficiency standards in WIDA, Texas, California, and Florida.

12 Writing and Reading

Anticipation Guide

For each of the following statements related to the chapter you are about to read, put a check under "Agree" or "Disagree" to show how you feel. Discuss your responses with classmates before you read the chapter.

	Agree	Disagree
1. Reading and writing are two sides of the same coin.	_____	_____
2. New writers should write short pieces to keep their mistakes to a minimum.	_____	_____
3. Students should be allowed to choose their own topics.	_____	_____
4. Completing endings for unfinished stories written by others is good practice for budding fiction writers.	_____	_____
5. The most time-consuming part of the writing process is revising.	_____	_____
6. Teachers should mark all uncorrected errors after a student has edited a piece.	_____	_____
7. Emphasis in a writing program for elementary and middle school students should be on content rather than form.	_____	_____

Using What You Know

Writing and reading are related processes that are mutually supportive. Reading improves writing, and vice versa. Innovations in technology have had a major impact on writing. Much of our oral communication has given way to written exchanges. Increasingly, phone conversations and face-to-face meetings have been replaced by e-mails and text messages. In addition, testing has increased dramatically, and most of the tests require written responses. What is your writing process? What steps do you take before you begin writing? What elements do you consider when you choose a topic? How do you plan your writing? How do you go about revising and editing your writing? How are your reading and writing related? What impact does your reading have on your writing? What impact does writing have on your reading?

The Roots of Writing

The roots of writing go deep and begin their growth early. Writing evolves from the prespeech gestures children make and from the language they hear and later use, as well as from the developing realization that the spoken word is not the only way to represent reality. Children discover pictures and words in storybooks that are read aloud to them. They draw pictures of mommy and daddy and their house. They scribble for the fun of it. In time, these scribbles become invested with meaning. Ultimately, children discover that not only can they draw pictures of people and objects, but they can also represent people and objects with words.

Writing processes develop and change with age and experience. Novice writers use a knowledge-telling process, in which writing is similar to telling a story orally or providing an oral explanation. It requires "no greater amount of planning or goal setting than ordinary conversation" (Bereiter & Scardamalia, 1982, p. 9). Novice

> **FYI**
>
> • *Units of Study for Primary Writing: A Yearlong Curriculum (K–2)* (Calkins et al., 2003) and *Units of Study for Teaching Writing, Grades 3–5* (Calkins et al., 2006) provide step-by-step suggestions for teaching writing to young writers. Both contain numerous real-life examples.
> • Students in any one class can range from those who are having difficulty composing a basic message to those who are well on their way to becoming proficient writers. ■

Building Language

In preparation for having students write, build the language they will need. For example, for a set of directions, students need words that signify sequence: *first, next, last.* Encourage students to use these words as they orally give sets of directions. Also read sets of directions to students so they can see how they are written. ■

CCSS

With some guidance and support from peers and adults, develop and strengthen writing as needed by planning, revising, editing, rewriting, or trying a new approach.

FYI

• Writing is not a linear process. We don't plan and then write and then revise. As we write, we plan and revise.

• The process approach to writing needs to be applied flexibly. Writing a friendly letter requires a bare minimum of planning and doesn't usually involve revising and editing. A letter to the editor, however, might require very careful planning, revising, and editing. ■

FYI

Prewriting results in average percentile gains of 11 points (Graham & Perin, 2007). ■

writers also use a what-next strategy, in which they write from one sentence to the next without having an overall plan for the whole piece (Dahl & Farnan, 1998). The sentence currently being written provides a springboard for the next sentence.

Gradually, writers acquire a knowledge-transforming ability that allows them to alter their thoughts as they write. As they compose, their writing affects their thinking, and their thinking affects their writing. Instead of merely summarizing thoughts, writers are reconsidering and drawing conclusions, which are reflected in their writing. Thus, as students progress, some of the writing activities provided should go beyond having them merely list or summarize and should ask them to compare, contrast, conclude, and evaluate. Research suggest that the process approach is a highly effective way to develop students' writing. In a compilation of writing research studies, implementing key elements of the process approach resulted in average percentile gains of 28 points (Graham & Perin, 2007).

The Process Approach to Writing

In the **process approach**, writing instruction is based on writing processes that professional writers and students actually use. The research of Graves (1983), Emig (1971), and others describes a series of steps that reflect how writers write. The steps are prewriting, composing, revising, editing, and publishing. However, these steps are not linear; they are recursive. Writers may engage in prewriting activities after composing and may be revising while composing

Part of teaching the writing process is helping students see the power and importance of writing in their lives. We need to show students the part that writing plays in our lives and encourage them to share the role that writing plays in their lives. We might share how, through writing, we keep in touch with friends, explore topics of interest, record the everyday events of our lives, or entertain or enlighten others, and invite our students to do the same (Calkins, 1994).

Prewriting

Easily the most important step, prewriting encompasses all necessary preparation for writing, including topic selection, planning, and rehearsing.

Topic Selection   Topic selection is the hallmark of the process approach. Letting students choose their own topics is one of the keys to good writing, because there is a greater chance that students will invest more of themselves in a piece that means something to them. When 7-year-olds were allowed to choose their topics, they wrote four times as much as a group of peers who were assigned subjects (Graves, 1975). However, Graves (2004) cautions that students might "latch on to stale TV plots, violent action scenarios, or insipid sentiments involving Care Bears—the kinds of stories they encounter on television and in computer games" (p. 89). To counter this tendency, Graves recommends that teachers "read the world," which means that they help students discover the important things that are happening in their lives and all around them. As Graves explains, "Students need to choose most of their own topics. But we need to show them all the places writing comes from, that it is often triggered by simple everyday events" (p. 91). Graves also stresses the importance of going beyond the personal narrative.

Murray (1989) suggested that teaching writing is mainly a matter of helping students discover what they have to say and how to say it. The teacher should model the process of selecting a topic and begin by discussing what he or she has done, seen, or learned that would be interesting to others. The teacher then jots down three or four topics on the chalkboard. They might be similar to the following:

■ The **process approach** is an approach to teaching writing that is based on the way professionals and students actually write.

I saw a real whale close up.

I saw the tallest building in the world.

I saw the longest baseball game ever played.

As the class listens, the teacher goes through the process of choosing a topic. The teacher rejects the first two because many people have seen whales and the tallest building, but only a handful of fans watched the longest game ever played. Most important, that is the topic that holds the greatest interest for the teacher.

Once the teacher has demonstrated the process, he or she asks the class to **brainstorm** topics and then lists them on the board. This helps others discover subjects of interest. After a discussion, each student lists three or four tentative topics and, later, chooses one to develop. In group discussions and one-on-one conversations or conferences with the teacher, students discover additional topics. With the teacher's questioning as a stimulus, they find subjects in which they have expertise, that they would like to explore, and that they would like to share.

Knowing that they will be writing nearly every day and so must have many subjects to write about, students search for topics continuously. They find them on television, in their reading, in their other classes, in their homes, in writing notebooks, on the Internet, and in outside activities. They can keep lists of topics in their folders or in special notebooks or journals (Calkins, 1994; Calkins & Harwayne, 1991). Students might also keep a list of questions. Questions to be answered are an excellent source of topics. The list could include personal questions, questions about sports or hobbies, or questions about a topic they are studying or an interesting fact that they heard (Spandel, 2001).

Journals are a favorite repository for writers' observations and ideas. In their writing journals, students can list topic ideas, outline observations they have made, or explore ideas. They can also record passages from their reading that were especially memorable or that contained distinctive language. Students might also use their journals to test out writing techniques or experiment with story ideas. Journals keep ideas germinating until they are ready to flower. When students keep writing journals or notebooks, prewriting might consist primarily of selecting an anecdote or question from the notebook to explore or elaborate.

With students, establish guidelines for journals. If you plan to read the journals, make that known to students so that the journals do not become private diaries. Reading students' writing journals has several advantages. It makes the journals part of the writing program and encourages students to make entries. It also provides you with the opportunity to gain insight into students' thoughts about writing and to respond. Students could highlight any items that they would like you to focus on, and they can mark as private or fold over a page containing any item that they do not want you to see. Journals are not graded, and corrections are not made, because doing so will shut off the flow of ideas. However, you should write a response.

One of the shortcomings of journals is that they can, over time, become diaries of mundane events. Encourage students to take a broader look at the world and also to dig beneath the surface. The student's journal entry "I struck out three times in the Little League game" might draw the following responses from the teacher: "What happened because you struck out? How did you feel? Why do you think you struck out? What might you do about it? Could this be the start of a story?" You might also encourage students to write for several days on a topic they care about (Routman, 2000). From time to time, model the process of composing journal entries. Show students how you develop topics or try out new techniques in your journal.

Planning   Research and preparation are also essential parts of prewriting. For older students, preparation might take the form of discussing, brainstorming, creating semantic maps or webs, reading, consulting Web sites and basic references, devising a plot outline or general outline. For younger

FYI

• Pressured to prepare students for competency tests, teachers require students to write to test-type prompts. While it is important to prepare students for tests, practice should not be excessive. Students' abilities are best developed through a balanced program.
• Teachers in the Columbia Writing Project suggest that students record their topic ideas in a small spiral notepad (Calkins et al., 2003). To model the practice, the teacher jots down possible topics in full view of the students as ideas strike him or her. ■

FYI

It isn't necessary for students to have a piece blocked out in their minds before they begin writing. In a way, writing is an exploration. Writers may not be sure what they want to say until they've said it. ■

FYI

An excellent repository of topics is the idea folder. Idea folders hold newspaper clippings, notes from the Internet or other sources, and magazine articles that could become stories. For example, intriguing articles about flying snakes or the return of monarch butterflies can be stored for future reference. With the current emphasis on expository writing, idea folders can be especially useful for gathering background information. ■

■ **Brainstorming** is a process in which members of a group generate ideas by spontaneously vocalizing or writing thoughts without evaluating them.

students, it could be discussing topics or drawing a picture. Drawing is especially useful, as it provides a frame of reference. Drawing also helps older students who have difficulty expressing themselves verbally.

A particularly effective prewriting strategy is to have students brainstorm words that they think they might use to develop their topics. Brainstorming is a free-flowing, spontaneous activity. All ideas should be accepted and recorded but not critiqued. Everyone should contribute. After brainstorming, ideas generated can be discussed, elaborated on, and clarified. Related ideas can also be introduced.

Brainstorming helps students note details to include in their pieces (Bereiter & Scardamalia, 1982). D'Arcy (1989) recommended several different kinds of brainstorming. The simplest form involves writing down names—of birds, famous people, or mystery places, for example. Students jot down the results of their brainstorming rather than simply thinking aloud. This gives them a written record of their associations as well as concrete proof of the power of brainstorming to draw out items. Students then share their lists with partners, which may result in additional items. At this point, students might circle the name of a bird, famous person, or place that they know the most about and brainstorm that item. Later, they brainstorm questions about the item they have chosen: "Where do bald eagles live? What kinds of nests do they have? Are they still in danger of becoming extinct? What do they eat? How fast do they fly?" The questions can be the basis for exploring and writing pieces about the topic.

Memories, feelings, images, and scenes can also be brainstormed. For instance, students might go down their lists of items and note the one that aroused the strongest feelings or created the sharpest image. Words to describe the feelings or details that describe the image could be brainstormed and listed.

Clustering and freewriting are versions of brainstorming. **Clustering** is a kind of mapping in which students jot down the associations evoked by a word. Lines and circles are used to show relationships. In **freewriting**, students write freely for approximately 10 minutes on an assigned or self-selected topic, about a real event or an imagined one. The idea is to have students catch the flow of their thoughts and feelings by writing nonstop. Ideas or themes generated can then become the basis for more focused work. In some instances, freewriting might be an end in itself—an exercise that promotes spontaneity in writing.

To help students flesh out their writing and determine what kinds of details they might include, model how you might brainstorm possible questions that the readers of your article might have. For instance, if students plan to write about flying snakes, they might brainstorm questions such as these: "How do the snakes fly? Where do they live? Are they poisonous? How big are they? What do they eat? Why do they fly out of trees?"

Orally sharing ideas is another form of preparing for writing. Discussing helps students "order their thoughts and generate many more ideas and angles for writing" (Muschla, 1993, p. 37). This technique is especially effective when students work in pairs. After students have generated ideas through brainstorming, clustering, or some other method, have them talk over their ideas with their partners. The listener should summarize what the speaker has said, ask the speaker to clarify any parts that are not clear, and answer questions that the speaker might have, thereby helping the speaker shape and clarify his or her ideas.

Role playing can be an effective way to draw out ideas (Muschla, 1993). Students can role-play fictional or actual events, including historical events or events that they have personally experienced. Role playing can also help students elaborate on and clarify what they want to say. For instance, if students are about to write a letter to a classmate who has moved away, they might work in pairs and role-play the writer of the letter and the intended receiver. Students might role-play situations that they intend

---

■ **Clustering** is a form of brainstorming that involves creating a map of words and associations linked by lines and circles.

■ **Freewriting** is a form of writing in which participants write for a brief period of time on an assigned or self-selected topic without prior planning and without stopping. Freewriting can be used as a warm-up activity or a way of freeing up the participant's writing ability. One danger of freewriting is that students might get the mistaken idea that writing is an unplanned, spontaneous activity.

In preparation for having her middle school students write a feature article, Ms. Hernandez had her students read a number of feature articles in *Time for Kids*. Students chose a favorite article and discussed why they liked it. They discussed the importance of writing about interesting topics. Under Ms. Hernandez' direction, the students also analyzed favorite articles to see how they were written. They noted that the articles had leads: These were beginnings designed to draw the reader in. They also noted different kinds of leads, such as a startling fact, a challenging question, and a surprising incident. Then they noted that the articles were fleshed out with interesting details or examples and that the articles often ended with a thought-provoking idea. To lend authenticity to the instruction, Ms. Hernandez arranged for an interview with a feature writer. Students prepared questions ahead of time. The interview was held via the Internet through the free service known as Skype. In the interview, the feature writer reinforced the key concept that Ms. Hernandez had introduced. The writer also provided some practical tips for writing feature articles.

Exemplary Teaching

Interviewing a Writer

to write about: persuading the town to fix up the park or requesting that the local health department get rid of rats in the neighborhood. Students might also role-play Washington's crossing of the Delaware, the landing of astronauts on the moon, or other historical occasions. Or they could role-play a Little League coach giving her team a pep talk, the principal confronting two students who have been arguing, or a zookeeper answering questions about the newly acquired giraffe.

Actually beginning to write is another way of getting started. "Writing is generative. The hardest line to write is the first one" (Spandel, 2001, p. 135). Often, after writers get that first sentence down, the ideas begin to flow.

Rehearsing Experienced writers do a substantial amount of **rehearsing**, or writing in their heads, composing articles, stories, and even parts of books at odd moments during the day or before going to sleep. In a way, rehearsing is a way of looking at life. Throughout the day, the writer is aware of episodes or objects that might become a topic for writing or an element in a story. An item in a newspaper or an overheard conversation might trigger a story. A puzzling question might set off an exploration and result in an essay or informational book. Throughout the day, students should be alert to possible sources of writing topics and record these in their journal notebooks.

Composing

Composing is the act of writing a piece. The idea is for the writer to put her or his thoughts down on paper without concern for neatness, spelling, or mechanics. A writer who is concerned about spelling is taking valuable time away from the more important job of creating. Reassure students that they will have time later to revise and edit. Model how you go about composing a piece. As you compose your piece, explain what is going on in your mind so that students can gain insight into the process.

Experienced writers generally have far more information than they can use, and discard much of it either before or after it is put on the page. However, students often do not seem to have enough to say. Finding enough to say may be essentially a problem of access (Scardamalia & Bereiter, 1986). Younger students are used to oral conversations in which the responses of the listener act as cues for retrieving knowledge. When the speaker fails to supply enough information, the listener's blank look or questions ferret out more talk:

Written speech is more abstract than oral speech. . . . It is speech without an interlocutor. This creates a situation completely foreign to the conversation

---

FYI

• Composing is difficult because writing is decontextualized. The writer must compose the whole message without the prompts supplied in conversation, must create a context so the message is understandable, and must compose for an unseen audience. Prewriting activities and conferences help supply some of the support that is provided in conversation but not composition.

• For younger writers, planning and composing are very similar operations. Young writers' composing duplicates their planning notes. ■

■ **Rehearsing** is that part of the writing process in which the writer thinks over or mentally composes a piece of writing.

■ **Composing** is that part of the writing process in which the writer creates a piece.

FYI

• Because much of the writing students will be asked to do in life and in content-area subjects will be expository, the program should include a balance of narrative and expository writing. One way of achieving this balance is to include writing in all areas of the curriculum.

• Composing is an uneven process. We sometimes can't get our ideas down fast enough. At other times, we labor to get a few words down so the paper won't look so blank. ■

Building Language

Before students can write stories, they must be acquainted with the language of stories. Reading to them and discussing stories will help, as will providing story books as models for their writing. After reading *A Dinosaur Named after Me* (Most, 1991), children might imitate the author's style as they write about their favorite dinosaur. ■

the child is accustomed to. In written speech, those to whom the speech is directed are either absent or out of contact with the writer. Written speech is speech with a white sheet of paper, with an imaginary or conceptualized interlocutor. Still, like oral speech, it is a conversational situation. Written speech requires a dual abstraction from the child. (Vygotsky, 1987, pp. 202–203)

This need to supply the missing listener when writing explains, perhaps, why prewriting activities are so important and why postdrafting conferences are so helpful in evoking a full written response from younger students. Scardamalia, Bereiter, and Goelman (1982) found that just encouraging young writers, who claimed to have written everything they knew, doubled their output. What the students had apparently done was extract their top-level memories, which are the main ideas, the generalities. They had not mined the lower-level memories, the examples, details, and explanations, that give body to the general ideas. With encouragement, they proceeded to do so.

Instruction for novice writers might begin with narrative writing. Narrative writing is easier and more natural for young writers than is expository writing. They are used to hearing and reading stories. A number of techniques foster the development of narrative writing. Shared reading can be used to present models of narrative writing. One easy type of writing is to use the structure of a familiar piece but substitute one's own ideas or words. For instance, using the structure of *Brown Bear, Brown Bear, What Do You See?* (Martin, 1983), students might write a story entitled "Gray Owl, Gray Owl, What Do You Spy?"

After students have acquired some experience writing narratives, wordless picture books, such as the Carl series (Farrar, Straus, & Giroux), might be used to encourage young students to create a story that goes along with the illustrations. Also, have students use toys, puppets, a felt board, or other props to create a story (Education Department of Western Australia, 1994). This helps them structure their stories.

For older students, cut out a series of pictures and have students sequence the pictures and create a story to accompany the pictures. This could be a whole-class or small-group activity. Students might also create a storyboard. A storyboard is a series of drawings used by creators of ads, TV shows, movies, and film clips to show the plot of their work. The storyboard might show the main scenes, actions, or events.

For novice writers, the mechanical production of letters and words may take an extraordinary amount of effort. Place less emphasis on handwriting and mechanics so that students can focus on content and style.

Composing is not a smooth process. If a writer is primed and the ideas flow, he or she may produce page after page of text, in seemingly effortless, almost automatic fashion. Another writer may simply stare at the page for endless moments before finally producing a tortured paragraph. A third writer may write in fits and starts, with an initial burst of writing followed by intense reflection, which is then followed by another burst of writing.

Preparation can help the composing process, but perseverance is required. A writer must be prepared to overcome various obstacles and blocks. By using strategies that experienced writers employ, the writer can avoid certain pitfalls. A key pitfall for elementary school students is believing that the **first draft** is the last draft, which blocks their writing through an overconcern with correctness and neatness. Students need to know that their first writing is just a draft and that the focus should be on getting thoughts down. There is plenty of time for revising and correcting later.

Beginnings are often the most difficult part of a piece to create. If students are blocked by an inability to create an interesting beginning, advise them to write down the best beginning they can think of and then return to it after they have completed their first draft. This same principle applies to other aspects of composing. If students cannot remember a fact, a name, or how to spell a word, they can leave a blank or insert a question mark and come back later. Nothing should interrupt the forward flow of the composing process.

■ A **first draft** is the writer's initial effort and is not intended to be a finished product.

■ **Revising** is that part of the writing process in which the author reconsiders and alters what she or he has written.

Some students freeze at the sight of a blank piece of paper. Discuss some possible opening sentences. If nothing else works, suggest to the students that they just start writing. Their first sentence might simply be a statement that they are having difficulty getting started. As they continue to write, it is very likely that other thoughts will come to them. If this doesn't work, you might supply them with some easy-to-develop sentence starters: Did you ever wonder why _____? You are not going to believe this, but _____ . If I had three wishes, I would _____. _____ is a truly amazing animal. Some of the best things in life are free. _____ overcame incredible odds to become _____. It was hard work, but _____ was worth the effort.

Focusing on Audience   Although we make lists or diary entries strictly for ourselves, most of our writing is geared toward an audience. A sense of audience helps shape our writing. As we write, we consider the backgrounds and interests of our readers. We try to think of ways of making our writing appealing as well as informative. Young writers typically lack a sense of audience and may assume that the readers already know whatever the writers know. A first step in writing is to define whom one is writing for. To help young students write for a particular audience, help them ponder the following questions (Learning Media, 1991):

What is my topic?

Why am I writing this piece?

Who will read my piece?

What might they already know about the topic?

What do they need to know?

The answers to these questions should help sharpen students' focus and provide them with a plan for gathering information. As they look over what they need to know and what they want to tell their audience, students can begin collecting information from books, family members, Web sites, computer databases, or experts. They might then use semantic webs or other diagrams to organize their information. Again, audience comes into play as students ask themselves, "How can I present this information so that my audience will understand it?" Teacher modeling, minilessons, and conferences with teacher and peers might be used to help students organize their material.

To help students gain a sense of audience, have them share what they have written. Students should focus on communicating with others rather than writing to meet a certain standard of performance or earn a certain grade. As they get feedback, they can clarify confusing details or add examples if that is what their audience seemed to need. The teacher can model sharing by reading pieces she has written and inviting students to respond.

Revising

For many students, revising means making mechanical corrections—putting in missing periods and capital letters and checking suspicious spellings. Actually, **revising** goes to the heart of the piece and could involve adding or deleting material, changing the sequence, getting a better lead, adding details, or substituting more vivid words for overused expressions. Revising means rethinking a work and can, in fact, lead to a total reworking of the piece. Revision may be aided by a peer conference or a conference with the teacher. However, before they can revise, students need to be able to reread their writing with a critical eye. As Graves (2004) warns, "Until children are able to read their work critically, revision is anathema" (p. 90).

Modeling the Revision Process   One way of conveying the concept of rereading one's work critically is for the teacher to model the process. The teacher puts an original draft that she or he has written on the chalkboard or overhead and poses pertinent questions: "Does this piece say what I want it to say? Have I fully explained what I want to say? Is it clear? Is it interesting? Is it well organized?" The teacher can then

 FYI

- Composing requires focus, discipline, and time. Make the writing period as long as possible, and if your schedule permits, allow students whose writing is flowing to continue for a longer stretch of time.
- Once students gain a sense of audience, their writing becomes more restricted. They begin to worry whether their peers will approve of their writing. ■

 FYI

Show students how you read and reread a draft and decide what changes need to be made. With the class, devise a revision checklist. A key question to ask is "Does it sound right?" Students should develop an ear for good writing. ■

 FYI

If students are using word-processing programs, show them the mechanics of making revisions: how to check spelling, how to replace and delete items, how to use the thesaurus. Demonstrate how they might make major changes by adding ideas or shifting around sentences or whole paragraphs. ■

show how to add details, clarify a confusing passage, or switch sentences around. The teacher might also model some highly productive revising routines. Essential routines include rewriting for clarity, rewriting beginnings and endings to give them more impact, substituting more vivid or more appropriate words, rearranging sentences or paragraphs, and adding additional examples or details.

Another helpful approach is to use samples of published pieces and students' writing to demonstrate effective writing. When working on improving leads, for instance, show students a variety of pieces in which writers have composed especially effective openings. Also, encourage students to note particularly creative leads in their reading. Do the same with endings and middles. Summarize by looking at pieces that do all three well.

To dramatize the power of good leads, share a piece that has an especially good opening, but omit the opening. Instead, have students select from three leads the one they think the author wrote. Do the same with conclusions.

Over a series of lessons, the teacher shows students how to make revisions, focusing on the kinds of writing challenges that students are facing. One group might be grappling with lead sentences, whereas another group might not be fully developing ideas. In time, students can demonstrate to their peers how they successfully revised a piece. Having professional writers such as children's authors and newspaper reporters visit the class to demonstrate how they revise will emphasize the importance of revision and the fact that virtually everyone who writes must do it.

Have students practice by revising someone else's paper. The paper could be one that you have composed for this purpose, one from a published source, or one done by a student in a former class. The author, of course, should be anonymous. Start with papers that obviously need revising but aren't so hopelessly bad that they would overwhelm students. Revise some of the papers as a group exercise. Allow students to add or delete details or examples so that they aren't just rewording the piece. After students have caught on to the idea of revising, have them work in pairs and then individually. When working in pairs, they should discuss the reasons for any changes they made. As they work individually, they revise their own writing. However, after revising a paper, they might then confer with a partner.

FYI

- Revising takes objectivity. To distance themselves from their writing, professional writers usually let a piece sit for at least 24 hours and then take a hard look at it.
- Revising should not be neglected, but there is some danger in overemphasizing it. Although all pieces should be reread carefully, they may not have to be revised or may require only minor changes. This is especially true if the writer is experienced and has prepared carefully before writing. Knowing when to revise and when not to revise is an important skill. ■

Instruction should also include the mechanical techniques of revision. Students can cross out, cut and paste, and use carets to insert to their hearts' content. Long insertions may be indicated with an asterisk and placed on a separate sheet of paper. Students should be encouraged to revise as much as they feel they have to. To remind students of the kinds of things they should be doing when they revise, you might develop a revision checklist. Figure 12.1 presents a sample checklist. From an early concern with spelling and handwriting, students can be led to add information to their pieces and, later, to make more complex revisions, such as reordering sentences or clarifying confusing points. One of the last revision skills to develop is the ability—and willingness—to delete material that should be left out.

Conferences help students move beyond mechanical revisions. "Revisions that children make as a result of the conference can be at a much higher level than those made when the child is working and reading alone" (Graves, 1983, p. 153). As with other cognitive activities, younger students are less likely to monitor their writing. For example, they may fail to consider the background or interests of their intended audience (Maimon & Nodine, 1979). Through skillful questioning in conferences, the teacher can help students see their writing from the point of view of the audience. This helps them figure out what they want to say and how to say it so others will understand. The teacher provides an executive structure to help students revise effectively (Scardamalia & Bereiter, 1986). In time, students internalize such a structure, which allows them to monitor their writing, just as they learn with experience and instruction to monitor their reading.

FIGURE 12.1 A Sample Revision Checklist

____ Does the piece say what I want it to say?
____ Will the audience understand it?
____ Is it interesting?
____ What might I do to make it more interesting?
____ Did I give enough details or examples?
____ Does it sound right?

During the revision process, focus on one element. Revision is more effective when the focus is on just one element at a time—the lead, details, word choices, or concluding sentence (Spandel, 2001).

Editing

In the **editing** stage, students check carefully for mechanical errors, adding commas and question marks and correcting misspelled words. Ideally, all mechanical errors should be corrected. Realistically, the teacher should stress certain major elements. For some students, correcting all errors could be a very discouraging process. The degree of editing depends on students' maturity and proficiency.

Editing can begin as early as kindergarten, with students checking to make sure they put names, dates, and page numbers on their pieces (Calkins, 1986). As new skills are acquired, the items to be checked increase to include spelling, punctuation, capitalization, and so on.

Just as with revision, editing should be modeled. Students should also have access to editing tools: pencils, a dictionary, easy style guides, and editing checklists. Such checklists help support students' evolving executive function and encourage them to focus on the conventions of writing, which requires looking at writing objectively and abstractly. Such a checklist should be geared to the students' expertise and experience; a sample is presented in Figure 12.2. Peer editing can also be employed. However, this is just an additional check. Student writers need to realize that, ultimately, it is their own responsibility to correct errors.

As part of learning the editing process, students should be introduced to the use of a writer's indispensable tool—the dictionary. Although students may understand that the dictionary is used to look up the meanings and spellings of unfamiliar words, they may not realize that dictionaries can be used to check capitalization and usage and that most dictionaries contain sections on grammar, punctuation, forming endings, ways to address dignitaries, and correct forms for business and friendly letters and thank-you notes. Model the various ways in which the dictionary can be used in editing and, as the need arises, encourage and guide students in their use of the dictionary. If possible, each student should have a copy of a dictionary on the appropriate level. Also, model and encourage the use of style guides and thesauruses. If these tools along with a spelling and grammar check are available on word-processing programs used by the class, model and help students implement their use. A useful device, especially for struggling readers and writers, is a talking word-processing program.

When deciding which editing skills to introduce, examine students' current writing and see what is most needed. Sometimes, the nature of the writing will dictate the skill.

In the editing stage, students check carefully for mechanical errors.

■ **Editing** is that part of the writing process in which the author searches for spelling, typographical, and other mechanical errors.

 Using Technology

With talking word-processing programs, students can listen as the program recites their pieces. Hearing their pieces read, they are better able to note dropped -*ing*s and -*ed*s, omitted words, and awkward expressions. ■

FIGURE 12.2   A Sample Editing Checklist

____ Is my story clear? Will readers be able to understand it?

____ Did I write in complete sentences?

____ Did I capitalize the first word of every sentence?

____ Did I capitalize the names of people, cities, towns, and other places?

____ Did I end each sentence with a period, question mark, or exclamation point?

____ Did I spell all the words correctly?

FIGURE 12.3 Editing Reminder

> *Underline the titles of books, magazines, newspapers, and movies:*
> <u>*Charlotte's Web*</u>, <u>*Weekly Reader*</u>, <u>*Sports Illustrated for Kids*</u>, <u>*Jurassic Park*</u>.
> *(If you are using a word processor, italicize instead of underlining. Underlining is used to tell whoever is printing the piece to use italics.)*

Source: Adapted from *Writing Workshop Survival Kit* by G. R. Muschla, 1993, West Nyack, NY: Center for Applied Research in Education.

REFLECTION

What has been your experience using the writing process? What has helped you to improve as a writer? With what aspects do you struggle? What tips might you have for novice writers?

FYI

Collect children's books and periodicals that provide good models for writing. For instance, when introducing a question-and-answer format, use *What Food Is This?* (Hausherr, 1994), *Ask Me Anything about Dinosaurs* (Phillips, 1997), or similar question-and-answer texts as models. ■

If students are writing pieces in which they will be referring to titles of books, introduce italicizing and underlining. After you have taught a skill, have students add it to their editing checklists. Also, display a brief explanation or example of the skill's use on the bulletin board, as shown in Figure 12.3, so that students have a reminder of it (Muschla, 1993).

As a final editing check, the teacher should examine the piece before approving it to be copied on clean paper or typed. The teacher might decide to note all errors with an advanced student and to focus on only one or two with a less advanced student. If the piece is to be published, however, all errors should be corrected. Noting the corrections should be done gently; you want the student to continue to feel pride in her or his product. Making such corrections must be recognized for the lower-level, mechanical skill that it is.

The writing process has been described here step by step to make it more understandable; however, in reality, many steps may be operating at the same time, and the steps are not necessarily executed in order. For example, writers mentally plan and revise and edit as they compose (Scardamalia & Bereiter, 1986). Books designed to assist young writers are listed in the following Student Reading List.

STUDENT READING LIST
Books for Young Writers

Bauer, M. D. (1992). *What's your story? A young person's guide to writing fiction.* New York: Clarion Books. Practical tips for writing fiction from a highly regarded writer.

Christopher, D. (2004). *Behind the desk with . . . Matt Christopher: The #1 sports writer for kids.* Boston: Little, Brown. Describes how Matt Christopher goes about his writing.

Fletcher, R. J. (2000). *How writers work: Finding a process that works for you.* New York: Harper. Has many practical suggestions for student writers.

Jacobs, P. D. (2005). *Putting on a play: Drama activities for kids.* Layton, UT: Gibbs Smith. Includes suggestions for writing a script as well as putting on a play.

Kehret, P. (2002). *Five pages a day: A writer's journey.* Morton Grove, IL: Whitman. Discusses how Kehret became a writer and why she writes.

Leedy, L. (2004). *Look at my book: How kids can write and illustrate terrific books.* New York: Holiday House. Explains to students how they can create a picture book.

Loewen, N. (2010). *Make me giggle, writing your own silly story.* Minneapolis, MN: Picture Window Books. Explains the key elements of a silly story and illustrates the parts by creating a silly story.

Otfinoski, S. (2005). *Extraordinary short story writing.* New York: Franklin Watts. Gives step-by-step advice for writing stories.

Strauss, L. L. (2011). *Drop everything and write!* Sausalito, CA: E&E Publishing. Provides practice suggestions in an easy-to-read style for choosing characters, creating a plot, and establishing a setting.

Terban, M. (2007). *Ready! Set! Research! Your fast and fun guide to writing research papers that rock.* New York: Scholastic. Provides tips for writing an interesting research paper.

Publishing

According to Elbow (2002), writing should be treated as a way of communicating, just as oral language is. All too often it is treated as an academic exercise in which the students write and the teacher corrects. Elbow isn't calling for a casual, careless kind of writing replete with errors. He is suggesting that pieces be written to real people for real purposes. He sees publishing as the antidote for lifeless prose. As he put it, "I believe publication is the single strongest way to help encourage students to revise and copyedit" (2002, p. 5). Knowing that others will be reading their words, students work hard to produce the best writing possible.

Students' work can be published in varied ways. Poems are collected in anthologies. Stories are bound in books, which are placed in the library. Essays and reports are shared and placed on classroom and school bulletin boards or on the class or school Web site. Scripts are dramatized. Essays and stories are entered in contests and printed in class and school publications or submitted to Web sites and children's magazines that print young people's works. Other ways of **publishing** include creating charts, posters, ads, brochures, announcements, sets of directions, book reviews, video- or audiotapes, supervised blogs, and Wikis.

To emphasize the importance of the writer, the teacher might arrange to have a student share his or her writing orally through use of the **author's chair**. Seated in this special chair, the author reads her or his piece to the class and invites comments. Special assemblies can also honor authors. Professional writers are invited to share with the other writers in the class. With publication and celebration, students put their hearts into their writing.

Conferences

In a typical conference, three types of questions are asked: opening, following, and process. They are nonjudgmental and are intended to evoke an open and honest response. Opening questions might take one of the following forms: "How is it going? How is your piece coming? What are you working on today?" The student's response provides clues for following questions, which are asked to find out more about how the student's writing is progressing. Process questions such as "What will you do next?" prompt students to make plans or take action. However, do not be so concerned about asking questions that you forget to listen. Calkins (1986) cautioned, "Our first job in a conference, then, is to be a person, not just a teacher. It is to enjoy, to care, and to respond" (p. 119).

Sometimes, a human response is all that is necessary. At other times, the teacher reflects the student's line of thinking but gently nudges the student forward. The student might say, for example, "I'm not sure how to describe my dog. My dog isn't a purebred." The teacher reflects that concern by saying, "You're not sure how to describe your dog because he is just an ordinary dog?" The repetition is an expression of interest that encourages the student to elaborate and continue the flow. If that does not work, more directed responses might include such questions as "You say your dog isn't a purebred, but is there anything special about him? What does your dog look like? Can you think of anything about the way your dog acts or looks that might set him apart from other dogs?" The teacher must take care not to make questions too directed, however, to avoid taking over the writing. The purpose of the questioning is to have writers explore ways in which they might develop their work.

If a piece is confusing, the teacher might say, "I liked the way you talked about the funny things your dog did, but I don't understand how you taught him to roll over." The

Using Technology

One way of publishing students' work is to post it on the class's homepage. Go to the following Web page for a list of sites that publish children's writing. Click on "Writing by Children."

http://www.ala.org/greatsites ■

FYI

• In helping young writers, teachers tend to stress content, which is as it should be. However, some attention has to be paid to form, especially when children are exploring new modes, such as their first informational piece or mystery.

• When conferencing with a student, if a portion of the piece isn't fully developed or clear, you might read the piece to the student so that he or she can be helped to notice a part that might not be clear to the reader or a part where the reader might want more information (Calkins, 2003). ■

■ **Publishing** is that part of the writing process in which an author makes a piece of writing public.

■ **Author's chair** is the practice of having a student author share his or her work with the rest of the class.

■ **A conference** is a conversation between teacher and student(s) or between students designed to foster the development of one or more aspects of the writing process.

Through sharing their writing, students develop a sense of audience.

student will then tell how she or he taught the dog to roll over and most likely realize that this is an element to be included in the piece.

If a student has not developed a piece adequately, the teacher might say, "You said your dog was always getting into trouble. Can you tell me what kind of trouble he gets into?" Often, the response will be an oral rehearsal of what to write in the next draft. "They tell me what they are going to write in the next draft, and they hear their own voices telling me. I listen and they learn" (Murray, 1979, p. 16).

Through questioning, the teacher comes to an understanding of the writer. Using this understanding, the teacher is better able to supply the guidance that will best help the writer develop. A teacher should wonder, "Of all that I could say to this student, what will help her most?" (Calkins, 1994). Questions are geared to the nature and needs of the student and the student's level of writing development.

In their extensive studies, Donovan and Smolkin (2011) and Smolkin (2011) analyzed the expository writing of students in grade K to 5 and noted a series of stages or phases. The earliest writing consists of composing labels. Labels describe what the student has written and are generally written in the present tense: "This is my dog." However, the label could consist of a single word or phrase: "dog, my dog." Or, it could consist of several sentences: "This is my dog. This is my dog's house." Fact statements go beyond labels by adding information: "My dog is a golden retriever." As they progress, they add more facts and details: "My dog is a golden retriever. My dog is ten years old. My dog likes to swim." A student may have as many as a dozen details. However, the details are provided in listlike fashion. The details tell about the topic but are not related to each other. The details are not elaborated upon or explained. The student doesn't explain what a golden retriever looks like or describe what a ten-year-old dog is like or why his dog likes to swim or how he knows his dog likes to swim. As their writing develops, students elaborate on it. They explain and answer the questions how and why, organize their writing, and show relationships: "Golden retrievers were bred to retrieve ducks and other birds that were shot by hunters and fell into the water. They like water and are good swimmers." As their writing develops, students group ideas. They use main idea or topic sentences, and use cohesive devices, such as repeating key words and connecting words:

> Golden retrievers were bred to retrieve ducks and other birds that were shot by hunters and fell into the water. They like water and are good swimmers. Their coat is thick and keeps the water out.

> Golden retrievers make good pets. They are friendly and gentle. I know because my dog is a golden retriever.

Using instruction and prompts, the teacher gradually leads students to elaborate on labels and facts and organize the information being presented. Instead of using the traditional prompt of telling me more about plants or dogs or lions, which may well result in more labels or more unrelated facts, the teacher uses prompts that lead students to a higher level of elaboration and organization. Information prompts ask for more details. The students might not have supplied enough. Elaboration prompts lead to development of detail. Organizational prompts may lead to greater use of cohesive devices such as repeating key words (*elephants*, for instance), using pronouns-antecedents (*elephants-they*), or using words that signal relationships (*because, and, also*). For instance, if a student has produced the label "This is an elephant," the teacher can use the prompt "Yes, that is an elephant. Can you tell me something about the elephant?" or "Make up a sentence that begins with the word *elephant* and tell me something about the elephant," so that the student produces a fact statement such as the following: "The elephant has a trunk." To prompt more information, ask the students what else they can tell you about elephants: "What else do you know about elephants' trunks?" If the student has difficulty providing information, have her or him take a closer look at the illustration or book being used or seek out a suitable reference. If students are having difficulty getting their thoughts down on paper, Smolkin and Donovan (2011) recommend eliciting more information. Otherwise, you might use prompts that help students elaborate on information. How and why prompts are especially effective: "How do elephants use their trunks? Why are Asian elephants easier to train? Why does the elephant use its trunk to spray itself with water?"

If students have a long list of unconnected facts, the teacher might have them cut the individual facts into strips and then group them. Which ones describe the elephant? Which ones tell how the elephant gets its food? Which one tells how it protects its young? In future activities, students might also be encouraged to compose a topic sentence and, in a later activity, use signal words. Creating a graphic organizer also helps students organize their information (Donovan & Smolkin, 2011). Mentor texts can be used as models of organization. Mentor books exist on a variety of levels of organization, from labels and lists of facts to carefully organized paragraphs. For instance, the text *Stegosaurus Up Close* (Dodson, 2011) has a very clear organizational pattern that uses both headings and topic sentences to group major categories of information. The key to effective instruction is to determine the processes students are currently controlling and what kinds of scaffolding will enable them to use more advanced processing. Table 12.1 presents some common writing situations or difficulties that students encounter and teacher prompts that might be used to scaffold students' efforts.

TABLE 12.1 Teacher Prompts in Response to Common Writing Situations

Writing Situation	Teacher Prompts
Has written a label sentence.	Yes, that is an elephant. Can you tell me something about the elephant? Make up a sentence that begins with the word *elephant* and tell me something about the elephant.
Has not supplied enough information.	What else can you tell me about elephants? What else do you know about elephants' trunks?
Has supplied a list of unconnected or unordered details, but details are not explained.	You said that Asian elephants are trained to do work. Why are Asian but not African elephants trained? How are they trained?
Lack of focus or order.	What are you trying to say here? What might be a good topic or opening sentence? What kind of graphic organizer might we use to show this information?
Lack of coherence or unity.	What is your main purpose here? Do all your ideas fit? Are your ideas in the best order? Let's cut your paragraph apart and group the sentences that go together. Which sentences describe _____? Which sentences tell how _____ gets food? Let's look at how (mentor author) organizes information? How might we use her organization? How might we use the signal words like *first*, *next*, and *last* to organize our explanation?
Topic is too broad.	What is your purpose in writing this? What's the most important or most interesting idea here? How might you develop that?
Piece lacks details or examples.	I like your piece about _____. But I don't know very much about _____. Can you tell more about it?
Needs an interesting beginning sentence.	How might you start this off? What might you say to pull your reader into this story?
Inadequate conclusion or lack of ending.	How might you sum up what you've said? What thought or idea do you want your reader to take away from this?

Adapted from Donovan, C. A., & Smolkin, L. B. (2011). Supporting informational writing in the elementary grades. *The Reading Teacher, 64*, 406–416. And Muschla, G. R. (1993). *Writing workshop survival kit*. West Nyack, NY: Center for Applied Research in Education.

R E F L E C T I O N

What experience have you had with conferences? Can you think of some conferences that were especially helpful to you as a writer? Based on your experiences and the suggestions that you have read so far, what might you do to improve the effectiveness of writing conferences?

FYI

Peer assistance results in average percentile gains of 26 points (Graham & Perin, 2007). ■

In every conference, include something positive about the student's work. However, also make a teaching point (Calkins, 2003). You might ask a student to reread her piece to see if it has all the details that the readers need. If the student doesn't notice that essential details are missing, read the piece to her and have her listen to see if there is something missing. If necessary, use a prompts such as the ones in Table 12.1 or, if that doesn't work, point out the difficulty and help the student revise her piece. After the revision, review what has been done so that the student can apply this to future writing: "Good work, Sabrina. You have added a detail that tells why your dog had to be taken to the vet. A good piece of writing tells why things happened. Look over your story and see if there are any other things that need to be explained." After each conference, note the student's writing strengths, needs, plans, and other pertinent information. A sample writing conference summary sheet is shown in Figure 12.4.

Peer Conferences   What all writers need is feedback from an audience. Student partners might perform this function for each other. With instruction and practice, they can bounce ideas off each other and get feedback that will help them to make audience-friendly revisions. As appropriate, have pairs or small groups of students talk over topic ideas and read each other's drafts. Partners can affirm each other by telling what they like about a piece. They can promote improvement by raising questions about puzzling passages, asking for more information, or pointing out passages that might be made more interesting.

Effective peer conferencing is a learned behavior. Discuss the ingredients of a successful conference and then model and supervise the process. In addition to being effective and producing improved writing, conferences should build a sense of community and respect. Some general principles of conferencing include the following:

- Students should learn to listen carefully.
- Students should lead off with a positive comment about the piece.

FIGURE 12.4 Writing Conference Summary

Name	Date	Topic	Strengths	Needs	Plans
Angel	11/15	Football game	Exciting opening.	Key part not clear.	Tell how he caught pass.
Amy	11/15	Pet rabbit	Interesting subject.	Not developed enough.	Give examples of pet's tricks.
James		Little sister			
Keisha		Making friends			
Maria		Dream vacation			
Marsha		Recycling trash			
Robert		Letter to sports star			
Stephanie		New bicycle			

Key
P: Planning   PE: Peer editing   PC: Peer conference
D: Drafting   PUB: Publishing   TC: Teacher conference
R: Revising   M: Making final copy   AC: Author's circle
E: Editing   RE: Researching   S: Sharing

Source: Adapted from *Writing Workshop Survival Kit* by G. R. Muschla, 1993, West Nyack, NY: Center for Applied Research in Education.

- Students should make concrete suggestions.
- Suggestions should be put in positive terms.

Highly effective teachers carefully instruct students in the art of conducting successful writing and reading conferences. They might even have a group of students from a previous year model a conference. Teachers also continue to monitor conferences to make sure that they are as productive as they can be (Wharton-McDonald, 2001). Working with a student, model a peer conference and show how suggestions can be used to make revisions.

FYI

In addition to modeling skills, use students' writing to show how a skill was used. For instance, if you are teaching students how to use vivid verbs, show how a student used vivid verbs in her piece. ■

Authors' Circle   One form of peer conference is the **authors' circle**. When students have pieces they wish to share, they gather at an authors' table and read their works to each other. The teacher may also join the circle. The only requirement is that everyone in the circle have a work he or she wishes to read (Harste, Short, & Burke, 1988). The authors' circle is designed for rough drafts rather than edited pieces. By seeking and listening to the reactions of others, students can determine whether their works need clarification and which parts might have to be revised. Both authors and listeners benefit from the circle.

The ultimate purpose of conferences is to help writers internalize the process so that they ask themselves questions like these: "How is my writing going? What will I do next? Do I like what I have written? Is there anything I would like to change?"

Writing Workshop

Just as students learn to read by reading, they learn to write by writing. The **writing workshop** is a way of providing students with the opportunity to try out newly introduced strategies under the teacher's guidance (Collins, 1998). Through individual or small-group conferences, the teacher can help students adapt and implement strategies that were taught in whole-class or guided writing sessions. Writing workshop consists of the following elements: minilessons, guided writing, writing time, conferences, and sharing. If possible, the workshop should be held every day.

Minilesson

Minilessons are generally presented to the whole group. The purpose of a minilesson is to present a needed writing skill. The minilesson lasts for only about 10 minutes, so the skill should be one that is fairly easy to understand. The skill could be capitalizing titles, selecting topics, using correct letter form, or any one of a dozen fairly easy-to-teach skills. Minilessons can also be used to explain workshop procedures.

Guided Writing (or Strategic Writing)

During guided writing, students are taught writing strategies in small groups in which all members are at the same stage of writing development or have similar needs. To teach a writing strategy, provide examples of the target strategy as it appears in selections that students are reading and also in pieces written by their peers and you. Just as in other sample lessons, discuss the strategy and how it will help their writing. Model the use of the strategy, showing, for instance, how you might write an interesting lead. Provide guided practice, and have students apply the skill by using it in their own writing. Revision and evaluation should focus on the element introduced. The skill should be reviewed and reintroduced in conferences and follow-up lessons until it becomes virtually automatic. Here is a sample writing strategy lesson. Notice that this lesson is more extensive than a minilesson and may take 10 to 20 minutes to teach.

■ An **authors' circle** is a form of peer conference in which several students meet to discuss their drafts and obtain suggestions for possible revision.

■ **Writing workshop** is a way of organizing writing instruction that includes a minilesson, time for students to write, individual and group conferences, and whole-class sharing.

■ The **minilesson** is a brief lesson on a needed writing skill. The skill is usually applied in the writing workshop.

LESSON 12.1
Writing Strategy: Adding Specific Details

Objective

- Students will add elaborative details to a piece of writing.

Step 1.

Show a paragraph, such as the following, that calls out for elaboration. Do not use a student's paragraph, as this will embarrass the writer.

The Strange Day

I turned on the radio. The announcer said to stay inside. She said that the streets were very dangerous. My father said that the announcement was a joke. But it wasn't.

Invite students to read the paragraph. Ask students whether they have questions that they might like to have answered. Write students' questions on the board. Discuss the author's failure to include needed details.

Step 2.

Show the students how the writer could make the piece come alive by adding details. Add needed details and compare the revised paragraph with the original.

The Strange Day

On my way to my place at the breakfast table, I switched on the radio. My favorite song was being played. Suddenly, the music stopped. "We have an important news flash for our listeners," the announcer said. "A monkey stole keys from the zoo keeper and opened all the cages. The streets are now full of dangerous, wild animals. The elephants have already smashed five cars. Stay in your homes. If you spot any wild animals, call the police immediately. But do not let the animals into your home."

"Hey, Mom and Dad," I shouted. "Come quick. There's trouble in the streets." When I told them what I had heard, they started laughing. Dad pointed to the calendar. "Don't you remember what day this is? It's April first. It's April Fool's Day. Somebody is playing a trick on the town."

Dad was still laughing when he headed out the door for work. But he wasn't laughing seconds later when he rushed back inside and slammed the door shut. "Call 911!" he shouted. "There's a tiger sitting on the roof of my car."

Step 3. Guided practice

Provide one or two practice paragraphs that lack details. Working with students, add needed details.

Step 4. Application

Encourage students to flesh out their stories by adding details. During the ensuing workshop session, provide any needed assistance.

Step 5. Extension

As a follow-up, have volunteers show how they added details to their stories. In subsequent lessons, discuss the many ways in which writing can be elaborated.

Step 6. Assessment and review

In conferences and while looking over various drafts of students' writing, evaluate whether they are fully developing their pieces. Provide additional instruction as needed.

FYI

Provide parents with an overview of your writing program and ways in which they might help. If students are writing about interesting moments in their lives, encourage parents to talk with their children about such moments. This helps children develop the topic. ∎

There are a number of ways of introducing strategies. In addition to showing how a piece might be improved, as in the sample lesson, you might have students compare two pieces, one of which is more effective because it uses the target strategy. You might examine the works of published writers to see how they used strategies that you wish to present, give a demonstration of how you use a particular strategy, or introduce a strategy through individual coaching and prompting. Regardless of how a writing strategy is taught, be sure to name it and tell why it is used so that students will adopt it: "Writers use details to make their stories seem real to their readers." Post a chart of strategies with brief examples of their use (Calkins, 2006).

Writing Strategies   There are dozens of writing strategies. Listed below are those that seem most essential for students. The strategies are listed in approximate order of difficulty. However, some strategies are taught at every level. For instance, writing an interesting lead is important for writers throughout the elementary and middle school grades but is a more complex undertaking in the upper grades than in the lower ones.

Expository Writing

- Writing clear, complete sentences.
- Writing a lead or beginning sentence. The lead or beginning sentence often gives the main idea of a piece and should grab the reader's interest and entice her or him to read the piece.
- Developing informational pieces. Informational pieces can be developed with details, including facts, opinions, examples, and descriptions. Failure to develop a topic is a major flaw in students' writing.
- Writing an effective ending. An effective ending should provide a summary of the piece and/or restate the main point of the piece in such a way that it has an impact on the reader.
- Using precise, varied, and vivid words—finding substitutes for *said* or *good*, for instance.
- Using a thesaurus to help achieve a varied vocabulary.
- Gathering appropriate and sufficient information for a piece. Writers do their best work when they are overflowing with information and can't wait to put it down on paper.
- Using figurative language, including similes and metaphors.
- Using advanced writing devices such as alliteration and rhetorical questions.
- Using varied sentence patterns.
- Combining short sentences into longer ones.
- Writing in a variety of forms: poems, stories, plays, letters, advertisements, announcements, expository pieces, newspaper articles, essays.
- Writing for a variety of purposes and audiences.
- Providing transitions so that one thought leads into another and the writing flows.
- Creating headings and subheadings for longer pieces.
- Eliminating details that detract from a piece.

Narrative or Fiction Writing

- Writing a story that has a well-developed beginning, middle, and end.
- Developing believable characters by using description, action, and dialogue.
- Creating a setting.
- Developing an interesting plot.
- Creating an interesting ending or even a surprise ending.
- Writing dialogue that sounds natural.
- Creating a title that makes the reader want to read the piece.
- Building suspense.
- Using advanced fiction techniques, such as the flashback or starting in the middle of the story (*in media res*).

 FYI

- One way of making the transition from narrative writing to expository writing is to have students write a how-to piece (Calkins, 2003). How-to pieces have a format that differs from that of a narrative, but they range in difficulty and thus can be created by kindergartners as well as eighth-graders.
- For suggestions on helping primary-grade children write how-to pieces, see Calkins et al. (2003).

 Using Technology

The Biography Maker provides step-by-step directions for composing biographies.
http://bellinghamschools.org/department-owner/curriculum/biography-maker ∎

Writing Time

Writing time, which is the core of the writing workshop, lasts for 30 minutes or longer. During that time, students work on their individual pieces, have peer or teacher conferences, meet in small groups to discuss their writing, or meet in their guided writing groups. Before beginning this portion of the lesson, you may want to check with students to see what their plans are for this period.

As students write, hold one or two guided writing sessions. As time allows, circulate in the classroom and supply help or encouragement as needed. You might show one student how to use the spell checker, applaud another who has just finished a piece, encourage a third who is searching for just the right ending, and discuss topic possibilities with a student who cannot seem to decide what to write about. You might also have scheduled conferences with several students or sit in on a peer conference that students have convened.

You should also plan for a mid-workshop teaching point (Calkins & Martinelli, 2006). About midway through the workshop or when students' efforts seem to be lagging, take about 2 minutes to remind students of the target skill from the minilesson or to provide a teaching tip based on your observations during the workshop. However, if students are doing well, you might skip the mid-workshop teaching point.

Group Sharing

At appropriate times, such as at the end of the workshop or day, students gather for group sharing. Volunteers read their pieces. The atmosphere is positive, and other students listen attentively and tell the author what they like about the piece. They also ask questions and make suggestions and might inquire about the author's future plans for writing. Group sharing builds a sense of community. Student writers are shown appreciation by their audience. They also have the opportunity to hear what their peers are writing about, what techniques their peers are using, and what struggles they are having.

Management of Writing Workshop

Active and multifaceted, writing workshop requires careful management. The room should be well organized. The classroom should be set up as a writer's workshop. Younger students need an assortment of soft lead pencils, crayons, magic markers, and sheets of unlined paper. Older students can get by with pencil and paper but should have some choices, too. At times, they might feel the need to write on a yellow legal pad or with a pink magic marker. You should have a round table or two for group meetings, a word-processing or editing corner, and a reference corner that contains a dictionary, style guide, almanac, and other references. Staplers, paper, and writing instruments of various kinds should be placed in the supply corner. Writing folders or portfolios should be arranged alphabetically in cartons. Involve students in helping with housekeeping chores. They can take turns seeing that materials are put away and that writing folders are in order.

Before starting the workshop, explain the setup of the room and show where supplies and materials are located. With the class, develop a series of rules and routines. Before students engage in peer conferences or small sharing groups, discuss and model these activities.

Be aware of students' productivity. Students should have specific plans for each day's workshop: revise a piece, confer with the teacher, obtain additional information about a topic, start a new piece. Make sure that peer conferences are devoted to writing and not last night's TV programs.

Writing workshop with a minilesson.

FIGURE 12.5 Daily Log: Students' Plans for Writing Workshop

Name	Topic	M	T	W	Th	F
Angel	Football game	D–1, TC	RE			
Amy	Pet rabbit	E, TC	PE			
James	Little sister	AC	R, TC			
Keisha	Making friends	AC	M			
Maria	Dream vacation	TC, D–2	E			
Marsha	Recycling trash	M	P, S			

Key
P:	Planning	PE:	Peer editing	PC:	Peer conference
D:	Drafting	PUB:	Publishing	TC:	Teacher conference
R:	Revising	M:	Making final copy	AC:	Author's circle
E:	Editing	RE:	Researching	S:	Sharing

It is important to note the social dynamics of peer conferences. Lensmire (1994) found teasing in the peer groups in his third-grade classroom. And he found that students who were not socially accepted in general were mistreated in the peer conferences. Lensmire suggested that students work toward a common goal, such as investigating a particular genre. With a common goal to guide them, he hoped that the focus would be on working toward the goal rather than on peer relationships. He also recommended more teacher guidance in the workshop setting. Getting feedback from students on the impact of peer and teacher conferences and other aspects of the workshop on their development as writers is also helpful (Dahl & Farnan, 1998).

Note students who do more conferencing than writing, those who never seem to confer, and those who have been working on the same piece for weeks. You might keep a record of students' activities in a daily log. A sample daily log, adapted from Muschla (1993), is presented in Figure 12.5.

As you circulate in the room, note students' strengths and weaknesses. During the guided writing or sharing period, call attention to the positive things that you saw: Mary Lou's colorful use of language, Fred's title, Jamie's interesting topic. Needs that you note might be the basis for a future minilesson or guided writing lesson, a brief one-on-one lesson, or—if several students display a common need—a small-group lesson.

Most of all, serious writing demands time. Even professionals need a warm-up period to get into their writing. Once the thoughts begin to flow on paper, however, writers have to keep on writing. If possible, at least 30 minutes to 1 hour a day, three to five days a week, should be set aside for writing.

Written Conversations and Quickwrites

In a **written conversation**, two students or a student and a teacher converse by writing to each other. Either party may initiate the conversation, which may be conducted at a table or other convenient spot. The teacher might start with a question such as "How is your

R E F L E C T I O N

What might you do to improve the effectiveness of a writing workshop? If you have not set up a writing workshop, how might you go about setting up one that would work particularly well in your teaching situation? What adaptations might you need to make?

■ **Written conversation** is a type of writing in which teacher and student or two students carry on a conversation by writing a series of notes to each other.

new puppy?" The student responds, and then the teacher replies. As one student is responding, the teacher can initiate a written conversation with a second student, and then a third.

Written conversations provide practice in both reading and writing. The teacher's writing is geared to the student's reading level. If the student's reading level is very limited, the teacher can read her letter to the student. If a student's writing ability is so rudimentary that the teacher cannot understand it, the student is asked to read it.

Quickwrites are brief first drafts written in response to reading a short piece of literature, a line from a poem or essay, or a prompt. Quickwrites can also be used to react to concepts learned in a content area, to summarize a lesson, or to react to an idea. The purpose of quickwrites is to get ideas down on paper and to write frequently. Because the task is brief and limited, the quickwrite can be especially effective with struggling writers. As a bonus, quickwrites provide practice in writing on demand in a timed situation.

Students who have difficulty responding with words can use stick figures to represent their response. They might also use stick figures to describe an event or tell a story. After telling a story in stick figure format, students can then add words. For some struggling readers, drawing stick figures is a highly effective aid.

If writers wish, they can expand their quickwrites into more extended pieces. Rief (2003), a middle school teacher, has her students collect their quickwrites in a section of their response journals. From time to time, students reexamine their quickwrites and may decide to expand some of them. Rief checks the quickwrites regularly, and if she sees one that cries out for elaboration, she might suggest that to the writer.

Writing in Major Genres

Just as students read a variety of genres—realistic fiction, folk tales, essays, poems, informational pieces—they should also be able to write in a variety of genres.. Major types or genres include narrative; explanatory, informational, and persuasive writing; and reports.

Composing Narratives

Narrative writing includes nonfiction as well as fiction. Often, narratives are used to introduce or enliven argumentative or explanatory writing. A narrative paints a picture of what happened. It introduces the character(s) and describes the setting or scene and events in vivid detail so that the reader can see and hear what happened. Following the "show, don't tell" principle, the narrative uses a variety of devices to portray the event: dialogue, actions, comments by others or the narrator. It might include motivation (Writing Across the Curriculum, 2010). Why did the participants do what they did? It might also include suspense and humor. However, the narrative is selective. It does not include every possible detail. Since a narrative typically includes a series of events, writers use transitional phrases to maintain the flow and coherence of the piece. Also to be considered is point of view. Who will tell what happened? Will the narrator be speaking in the first person? In the third person? Will the narrator be the person who experienced the event? Students should try out both first- and third-person narratives. Most of all, the narrative should express an event that has significance to the person telling it and the person reading it.

Composing Explanatory/Informational Texts

Having background knowledge on a topic doesn't guarantee that students will be able to express that knowledge in writing. When asked to explain how a fire extinguisher worked, students provided a series of steps for operating the extinguisher but failed to explain why the extinguisher was able to put out the fire, even though in their science class the students had discussed how carbon dioxide smothered fire (Klein & Rose, 2010). Students described key steps but failed to explain why the steps occurred. To rectify this failure, the teachers directed students to do the following:

- Obtain the necessary information.
- Describe each step.
- Tell why each step works.

Students also need to be taught the language needed to express relationships found in explanations. Many of the explanations were awkwardly phrased. One way of familiarizing students with the rhetoric of explanations is to provide them with step-by-step hands-on experiences and then have students explain them. For instance, they might observe a dancing raisins experiment in which raisins are dropped into cups of diet soda and then explain what happened and why. The key is to stop at each step and get a clear description of what happened and then a reasoned explanation (Klein & Rose, 2010).

Composing Argumentation Texts

Composing arguments is a key writing task. Students are asked to take positions on issues and support them, respond to literacy pieces and justify their responses, write persuasive essays and letters to the editors, and respond to prompts that call for taking a position and justifying it. Argumentation isn't new to students. Chances are they started arguing almost as soon as they learned to talk. However, composing written argumentation is a complex task that develops gradually over a number of years. Oral arguments don't make heavy cognitive demands. In an oral argument, one person responds to what the other person said. However, in a written argument, the writer is on her or his own. There is no one there to supply cues. The writer must supply and organize the argument both for and against a claim (Piolat, Roussey, & Gombert, 1999). The ability to compose arguments goes through the following phases:

- Students at ages 7 to 8 produce nonargumentative text. They state, for instance, that we should cut down on the use of plastic bags but don't provide any supporting reasons for doing so.
- Students at 9 to 10 produce arguments that are supported by a simple listing of reasons or data.
- Students at 11 to 14 produce arguments that include reasons for and against the claim. Students are gaining the ability to consider opposing points of view. Organization also improves.

Composing an effective argument involves clearly stating a claim and supporting it, while at the same time refuting counterclaims. The evidence should be relevant, credible, and compelling. The piece should be well organized, with a clear introduction and a strong conclusion. Students do best in writing about claims that they agree with: being able to choose their own books, for instance. Students should also be taught to focus on their audience so they can anticipate what kinds of arguments would be convincing and what kinds of opposition might be presented. Students are typically better at supporting their claims than they are at answering possible objections.

Students have difficulty learning content and a rhetorical structure at the same time. Begin with topics or issues that are familiar so that they grasp the rhetorical structure before applying it to complex content (Klein & Rose, 2010). Activities that might be used to build the skills needed to compose an argument include:

- Holding debates in which students are taught how to formulate arguments. Debating an issue helps students bring to the fore their arguments and support.
- Encouraging students to support their positions in class and small-group discussions and modeling how to do so.

FYI

- How-to books provide models for children to follow. How-to pieces are particularly good assignments because they provide a one-step-at-a-time structure that aids children in composing and revising (Duthie, 1996).
- To foster expository writing, read informational pieces aloud so that students get a feel for the language of expository prose. ■

CCSS

Write arguments to support claims with clear reasons and relevant evidence.

 Using Technology

Docs Teach Contains more than 3,000 primary sources. Includes photos, diaries, journals, and film clips. Has ready-made lessons and tools for creating lessons that help students weigh support for an issue or note the sequence of events or causes and effects.

http://docsteach.org ■

 Using Technology

Persuade Star helps students in grade 5 and above plan and write persuasive pieces. The site includes a feature that allows students to read and analyze essays.

http://persuadestar.4teachers.org ■

- Having students read and analyze opinion pieces in newspapers and magazines and note how the authors state and support their claims and refute the claims of others. Older students might also read historical documents that discuss issues of the day.
- Having students read and discuss two sample arguments and decide which one is better and why. List on the board the rhetorical features that are especially effective.
  Students should try out the rhetorical devices that they found to be effective.
- Having students read several pieces and rank them, and explain their ranking.

Guiding the Writing of Reports

For young students, writing a report poses problems. The earliest reports are lists of details about a topic (New Standards Primary Literacy Committee, 1999). They tell what the writer knows about the topic, but lack organization. By about third grade, students' reports have a clearly defined beginning, middle, and end.

In writing reports, students differ greatly in the degree of elaboration and in the organization. Writing an organized report involves analyzing the information and classifying it by category. Analyzing and classifying information are easier if students are writing about a familiar topic. If students are writing about an unfamiliar topic, they will have difficulty highlighting important information. Because the information is new to them, they won't be able to distinguish important ideas from trivial details. Organization will also be a problem. They will lack the understanding needed to create categories of information and will probably simply use the headings contained in their source material.

To help students improve their report writing, try the following:

- Make sure that students understand the nature and purpose of the assignment. With as much student input as possible, compose a rubric so that students have a clear idea of what is expected.
- If possible, students should be given a choice of topics so that they have a sense of ownership. They will then be willing to invest the time and energy needed to create a thoughtfully composed report. Before students make a final choice of a topic, encourage them to do some preliminary exploration so that they are better able to determine whether this is a topic that interests them and that there is enough information available for them to develop the topic. The information should not be so difficult or complex that students would not be able to understand it.
- With your help, students select sources of information. Make sure that you have materials on a variety of levels so that below-level readers have accessible sources. Finding relevant information is surprisingly complex (Gans, 1940). Model the process and provide guided practice. Pose questions or topics and have students search through indices and tables of contents or lists of Web sites to locate what seems to be relevant information. Then have the class read the information and decide whether the information is relevant.
- Students complete a planning guide that includes a brief description of the audience, the topic, key supporting subtopics, and a list of sources of information.
- Students compile relevant information. Because younger students and less-expert writers have a tendency to copy, they need instruction in taking notes. Students might be taught a paraphrasing strategy in which they read a relevant passage, recall what they have read, and summarize what they have read in their own words on physical or electronic note cards.
- Students organize their information by grouping physical or electronic cards that contain information on the same subtopic. Groups of cards are then placed in sequential or some other kind of logical order.

CCSS

Conduct short research projects to answer a question, drawing on several sources and refocusing the inquiry when appropriate.

FYI

- Composing nonfiction pieces may result in "dump truck" writing, in which the author simply dumps in facts and neglects style (Duthie, 1996). The resulting piece lacks voice and interest. Encourage students to put their unique stamp on nonfiction writing.
- Encourage students to explore the use of visuals in their nonfiction writing. ■

CCSS

Gather relevant information from multiple print and digital sources; assess the credibility of each source; and quote or paraphrase the data and conclusions of others while avoiding plagiarism and providing basic bibliographic information for sources. Draw evidence from literary or informational texts to support analysis, reflection, and research.

 Using Technology

The ePals site provides opportunities for classroom-to-classroom communication. It has more than 10,000 participating classrooms in nearly 100 countries.

http://www.epals.com ■

- Using information they have compiled, students compose their reports. When using multiple sources, students use a cut-and-paste synthesis or a discourse synthesis. In a cut-and-paste synthesis, students simply jot down information from one source and then information from a second source. In discourse synthesis, students integrate the information from two or more sources. To help students use a discourse synthesis, model the process and provide guided practice.
- Students review their reports to make sure they are accurate and contain sufficient information (Many, Fyfe, Lewis, & Mitchell, 1996). Students also examine their reports to make sure they are interesting and that the mechanics are correct.

Because report writing is complex, you might do a shared report involving the whole class or a guided writing group. The next step would be to have cooperative groups compose reports. If available, provide students with sample reports written by former students. To make the task of writing a report more manageable, you might also break it down into segments: The first segment might be topic selection, preliminary exploration, and completion of a planning guide. The second segment might be the first draft. The third segment could be revising and editing. The final segment might be the finished report.

Sharpening the Focus of Report Writing

Traditionally, students report on animals, states, countries, presidents, inventors, and other famous people, and their reports are sometimes simply recitations of facts. These are worthwhile topics, but more thoughtful, more interesting reports could result if the report-writing assignment were made more focused as well as more intriguing (Thibault & Walbert, 2008). As you create report assignments, ask yourself, "What are my content objectives? What do I want students to know and understand as a result of composing this report?" A report on an inventor that focuses on the chronology of the invention process will differ from one that focuses on the impact of the invention or the characteristics of the inventor. To add interest, you might ask students to focus on young inventors, such as Philo Farnsworth, or inventors who failed to benefit from their work. Or you might have them investigate a controversy: "Who really invented TV?" Also consider what it is that you want students to be able to do as a result of working on the report. At the most basic level, you might simply want students to be able to summarize the life of an inventor and use such basic tools as an encyclopedia and a children's book on the subject. On a more advanced level, you might want students to use multiple sources and compose a cause–effect piece that looks at the impact of an invention or a comparison–contrast piece that assigns credit for a disputed invention.

Helping ELLs with Their Writing

There is no need to wait for ELLs to have a basic command of English before they begin to write in English. In fact, these students should be encouraged to write from the beginning of their endeavor to learn English. Writing fosters the learning of language. And, in some ways, writing is easier than speaking because writers have time to formulate what they want to say. As Crawford (2003) notes, "Writing begins when children can draw, and there is no need to wait for reading. We can certainly extend these ideas to English language learners, especially if they have writing skills in their primary language. The errors they make should be viewed in the same way that we view errors in oral production, as part of the natural process of acquisition" (p. 177). However, as Coppola, Dawson, McPhillips, George, and MacLean (2005) advise, ELLs need opportunities to learn vocabulary and need to be taught sentence patterns, ways of organizing writing, and words that link ideas, such as *however* and *but*.

FYI

- Part of students' difficulty in writing about an unfamiliar topic may be rooted in their reading. Because the material is new, their understanding may be so limited that they are forced to use the author's words. Chances are they will not understand the material well enough to put it into their own words. Writing in which students use a few phrases of their own to string together material taken directly from their source material is known as "patch" writing.
- Building a deeper understanding of background material can foster more effective report writing. Students do best when they have a deep understanding of their material and when they are provided with the type of guidance that helps them select relevant information and organize it (New Standards Primary Literacy Committee, 1999). ■

Adapting Instruction for English Language Learners

For more examples of frames, see p. 370. ■

Academic Language in Writing

In addition to having specific vocabulary of its own, academic writing requires mastering a complex style of expression that differs in many respects from the informal personal narratives that students might be used to. Having less experience with the written forms of English, ELLs need to do more reading so that they become better acquainted with the forms of academic writting. They need to read as writers and note the ways in which authors express themselves. Before writing a persuasive essay, students should read a variety of essays and take a careful look at the ways in which the essays are constructed. They need to develop a writer's ear for what sounds right.

In developing ELLs' expository writing abilities, you need to teach them overall organization (for instance, topic or lead sentence, development of topic, and conclusion), basic sentence structures, key vocabulary, and academic language. Here are steps you might take to introduce students to expository writing. Have them start by composing a simple enumeration/description paragraph whose structure uses a main idea and supporting details, since this is one of the easiest structures to create.

Step 1. Build a general language background by reading and discussing informational texts that are similar to what students will be writing. Encourage written responses to questions about the informational text: "List the three most important facts you learned about recycling." Writing responses in the form of sentences should be modeled, and models should be posted. Remember that you are teaching students how to write sentences as well as developing comprehension.

Step 2. Analyze simple but well-written paragraphs of the type that you wish students to compose. An easy-to-read series such as the First Facts series (Capstone Press) can be used to show students how an author puts the main idea in the first sentence and then follows with details that support the main idea.

Step 3. Model the writing of simple enumeration/description paragraphs.

Step 4. Under your guidance, have the students compose an enumeration/description paragraph as a group.

Step 5. Have students complete frames of enumeration/description paragraphs like this one:

The platypus looks like a mixture of several animals. It has the bill and webbed feet of a _____. It has the fur of a _____. And it has the tail of a _____. The scientist who discovered the platypus had a hard time _____

_____.

As students' ability to compose improves, reduce the stem sections of the frame sentences.

Step 6. Have students compose enumeration/description paragraphs based on a writing guide. In a writing guide, you lay out step by step what students are to do, as in the example in Figure 12.6 (Boyles, 2002).

Step 7. Have students compose other enumeration/description paragraphs with a partner and then on their own.

Extension: Move into more complex types of descriptions and other genres. When discussing selections that students have read, help them recognize the author's craft. Read aloud well-written informational text so that students develop an ear for it.

ELLs might also have to learn new approaches to writing. Writing in English is typically linear and direct. Speakers of Arabic might compose texts that have parallel rather than linear structures and that emphasize moral teaching. Chinese students might use circular rather than linear patterns; they might not use a beginning-to-end structure (Diaz-Rico & Weed, 2002).

Assessing and Improving Writing: The Key Traits Approach

Improving writing requires having a concept of what good writing is, being able to explain to and show students the traits of good writing, and having an assessment system that enables students and teachers to judge whether a piece of writing contains those characteristics. The final requirement is devising a plan for teaching students how to revise their writing so as to strengthen key characteristics (Spandel, 2001). In a sense, it's creating a rubric that students can use to plan their writing, assess their writing, and revise their writing. The teacher can use this same rubric to plan instruction and assess students' writing. Such a system enables a teacher to base instruction on assessment.

The main element in effective writing as determined by Six Traits Plus, a popular writing assessment system, is content. These are the ideas or information that the piece conveys or, for a narrative, the story that it tells. The remainder of the characteristics have to do with form, the way the content is presented. Form can be subdivided into organization, word choice, sentence construction, and mechanics. A final element is voice, which reflects the individual personality of the author.

To help students become aware of the components of good writing, invite them to tell what they think these components are. Write their responses on the board and create a web of the elements. Their responses will tell you what they think the important elements are and, by implication, where they put their efforts when they are writing. Share samples of good writing with students. Discuss with students what it is about these pieces that makes them effective. This will help students broaden their concept of what good writing is (Spandel, 2001). Provide an overview of the characteristics, but then focus on them one by one. You can start with any trait you want, but because content is key, most teachers start with that.

To help students become familiar with the traits and to provide practice for assessing writing, have students assess the writing of unknown writers. You might start with published writers who have written works on the students' level. One good source would be periodicals designed for young people. For third-graders, for instance, look at samples from *Weekly Reader*, *Scholastic Magazine*, and *Time for Kids* (*News Scoop*). If you don't subscribe to these and they are not available in your school library, sample articles are usually available on the publishers' Web sites. Collect pieces of writing that

FYI

• Describing key characteristics of good writing is somewhat subjective. First of all, you as a teacher need to have a sense of the characteristics of good writing at your grade level. One way of doing this is to examine the best pieces of writing in your class to determine what traits make these pieces of writing especially effective. Such a review is even more effective when done on a schoolwide or districtwide basis.

• The Six Traits Plus analytical model for assessing and teaching writing focuses on these elements: Ideas, the heart of the message; Organization, the internal structure of the piece; Voice, the personal tone and flavor of the author's message; Word Choice, the vocabulary a writer chooses to convey meaning; Sentence Fluency, the rhythm and flow of the language; Conventions, the mechanical correctness; and Presentation, how the writing actually looks on the page.

• Voice is the distinctive style or personality that writers put into their work. To foster voice, Simmons (1996) suggests that teachers read and respond as readers. The initial reading should be directed to what the student is saying and how he or she is saying it. Students also need to see models of pieces that have a distinctive voice and they need time to develop voice. ■

FIGURE 12.6 A Writing Guide

Writing Guide

1. Write a topic sentence that states the main idea of your paragraph.

_____

2. Write three details that support the main idea. Use words such as *also*, *and*, and *too* to glue your details together.

Detail 1: _____

Detail 2: _____

Detail 3: _____

Conclusion: Write a closing sentence that sums up the main idea of the paragraph.

_____

_____

Exemplary Teaching

Teaching English Language Learners to Write

Working in an urban elementary school with a large number of ELLs, first-, second-, and third-grade teachers Susan McPhillips, Joanne George, and Diane MacLean used models and scaffolding to foster those students' writing (Coppola, Dawson, McPhillips, George, & MacLean, 2005). Realizing that ELLs needed to learn sentence patterns as well as vocabulary in order to write in English, the teachers analyzed children's trade books to find ones that provided models of basic sentence patterns. They used texts such as *The Snowy Day* (Keats, 1962/1996), *Brave Irene* (Steig, 1987), and *Owl Moon* (Yolen, 1987) to illustrate narrative patterns and descriptions, and texts such as *From Tadpole to Frog* (Pfeiffer, 1994) to illustrate nonfiction patterns. Instruction was scaffolded through the use of graphic organizers and frames. The graphic organizers included words that the students might need to use. For a sequence paragraph, the graphic organizer included *first, second, next, then,* and *finally*. The frames included ones for topic and concluding sentences. Although the teachers' classrooms already featured lists of words that students might need in their writing, many of the ELLs needed additional support. The teachers created supplementary word lists and special word notebooks for them. The literacy specialist helped out during writing workshop so that additional support could be provided. The classroom teachers also coordinated with the ESL teacher, who reread to ELLs the books featured in regular class read-aloud sessions or read them texts with similar patterns. For instance, after rereading *Rosie's Walk* (Hutchins, 1986) with ELLs, the ESL teacher helped them compose their own walk stories.

FYI

Setting goals, purpose, and characteristics of the piece to be written-results in average percentile gains of 24 points (Graham & Perin, 2007). ■

FYI

• A writing program should do more than just prepare students for writing assessments. Speaking of high-stakes writing tests, Thomas (2004) warns, "When assessment rubrics and sample essays become templates for students to follow, we lose any chance of achieving authentic or valuable writing instruction. When a test wields power like this, teachers abdicate their expertise as writing instructors."

• To help students understand rubrics, distribute examples of good, middling, and poor responses to a writing assignment—preferably ones written by students in the previous year's class (with names removed). Using a rubric, students rank the responses and then articulate what features of each response led to its ranking (Saddler & Andrade, 2004). ■

illustrate key elements in writing. Collect examples of both good and bad writing so that you can show how the two differ. After students have had some practice assessing the writing of others, have them assess their own writing (Spandel, 2001). The key characteristics should be translated into a rubric (see Table 3.13 on p. 88). Although a generic rubric is helpful, rubrics geared to each major kind of writing would be more effective because they would offer more specific guidance. In addition, different types of writing have different demands. Focusing on key elements, the most effective rubrics are concise and contain only three to seven evaluative criteria. Each evaluative criterion must encompass a teachable skill. For instance, evaluative criteria for a how-to piece might include a clear description of steps; list of needed materials; effective, sequential organization; and correct use of mechanics. All of these criteria are teachable. A sample rubric for an explanatory piece is presented in Table 12.2. Rubrics for major genres at grade levels K–5 can be found in *Using Rubrics to Improve Student Writing, Revised Edition* (Hampton, Murphy, & Lowry, 2009).

Develop rubrics with your students for the writing they do. You might ask them to use markers or highlighters to color-code evidence in their compositions that shows that their writing meets each criterion in the rubric (Saddler & Andrade, 2004). For instance, the rubric might ask for at least two examples that support the main idea. Students mark their examples, and if they can't find them, they make a note to add them.

So that they can more readily assess their progress over time, students should have a place to store and keep track of their completed works, works in progress, and future writing plans. File folders make convenient, inexpensive portfolios. Two for each student are recommended—one for completed works and one for works in progress. The works-in-progress folder should also contain a listing of the key characteristics of good writing, an editing checklist, a list of skills mastered, a list of topics attempted, and a list of possible future topics.

The works-completed folder, or portfolio, provides a means of examining the student's development. If all drafts of a piece are saved, the teacher can see how the student progressed through the writing steps. A comparison of current works with beginning pieces will show how the writer has developed over the course of the year. Careful examination of the portfolio's contents should reveal strengths and weaknesses

TABLE 12.2 Rubric for Assessing Writing to Explain

	Skillful	Sufficient	Developing	Needs Support
Introduction	States topic clearly and invokes reader's interest.	States topic fully.	States topic but does not fully explain it.	Does not state topic or states topic but does not explain it.
Development of ideas	Clear explanation of whole and full discussion of main parts.	Explanation of most parts of the subject.	Some explanation of the subject.	Little or no explanation of the subject.
Details and examples	Clear general and specific details and examples to support understanding.	Details and examples adequately support explanation, but development may be uneven.	Some relevant details and examples, but they are not developed enough.	Details or examples are brief, general, undeveloped, or not relevant to the explanation.
Organization	Ideas are logically grouped. Relationships among ideas are mostly clear. Transitions clearly convey relationships among ideas.	Ideas are logically grouped. Relationships among ideas are mostly clear. Few or no transitions.	Ideas are mostly logically grouped. Relationships among ideas are sometimes unclear. Few or no transitions.	Groupings of ideas are mostly illogical or nonexistent. Relationships among ideas are mostly unclear.
Word choice	Uses precise language and domain-specific vocabulary to inform about or explain the topic.	Language is usually precise, with some use of domain-specific language.	Language sometimes lacking in specificity. Limited use of domain-specific language.	Often unclear and inappropriate.
Conclusion	Provides a strong concluding statement or section related to the information or explanation presented.	Provides a concluding statement or section related to the information or explanation presented.	Concluding statement is weak or vague.	Lacks a concluding statement or concluding statement is not related to the topic.
Conventions	Grammar, usage, and mechanics are usually correct with a few distracting errors, but meaning is clear.	Grammar, usage, and mechanics are mostly correct with some distracting errors, but meaning is clear.	Grammar, usage, and mechanics are mostly correct but with some distracting errors that may occasionally impede understanding.	Grammar, usage, and mechanics are sometimes correct but with frequent distracting errors that often impede understanding.

Adapted from National Assessment Governing Board. (2010). *Writing framework for the 2011 National Assessment of Educational Progress.* Washington, DC: Author and Writing Standards K–5, Common Core State Standards for English Language Arts & Literacy in History, Social Studies, Science, and Technical Subjects.

and provide insights into interests and abilities. While reading through the portfolio, the teacher might try to ascertain whether a student is finding his or her own voice, has a pattern of interests, is showing a bent for certain kinds of writing, is applying certain techniques, and is being challenged to grow and develop. The teacher then decides what will best help the student progress further.

Students should also examine their portfolios with a critical eye. What have they learned? What topics have they explored? What pieces do they like best? What kinds of writing do they enjoy most? What are some signs of growth? What questions do they have about their writing? What would help them become better writers? Are there some kinds of writing that they have not yet attempted but would like to try? Of course, teacher and student should confer about the portfolio, reviewing past accomplishments, discussing current concerns, and setting up future goals and projects. (For more information on portfolio assessment, see Chapter 3.)

Technology and Writing

Word-processing programs have made revising and editing easier, but students need to be taught how to use these features. Word-processing and desktop publishing programs have also made publishing feasible for students. The last step in the writing process, publishing is often ignored. However, it is the step that gives purpose to writing. **Desktop publishing**, as its name suggests, facilitates numerous publishing opportunities. With it, students can produce high-quality posters, banners, signs, forms, brochures, résumés, classroom

 FYI

The Writing Observation Framework (Henk, Marinak, Moore, & Mallette, 2003) is a guide used to assess writing instruction. You might fill it out yourself or invite a colleague to observe your class and fill it out. ■

Using Technology

Kidspiration (Inspiration) uses questions and illustrations to prompt students' writing. It also has a speech component that reads students' writing.
www.inspiration.com ■

■ **Desktop publishing** is the combining of word processing with layout and other graphic design features that allow the user to place print and graphic elements on a page.

CCSS

Use technology, including the Internet, to produce and publish writing, and link to and cite sources, as well as to interact and collaborate with others.

REFLECTION

How might you assess your students' writing so it is almost sure to lead to improvements in their writing? What special provision might you make for assessing and instructing ELLs?

FYI

Using word processing results in average percentile gains of 19 points (Graham & Perin, 2007). ■

FYI

• Text-to-speech word processing programs such as *Write: Outloud* (Don Johnston) say the words that students type in and are especially helpful for students with impaired vision and for very young students. They can also be used by students who have difficulty detecting errors. Students who reread a written piece without detecting a dropped *-ed* or *-ing*, missing words, or awkward phrases often notice these errors when they hear the computer read the piece. ■

FYI

"Writers read differently than other people do. Writers notice and think about how texts are written, in addition to what texts are about. . . . Talk with students about what they notice writers doing in books (the craft of the writing) and help them imagine how they could write like that in their own books" (Ray, 2004, p. 15). ■

or school newspapers, reports, and club newsletters. They can also illustrate stories or write stories based on illustrations. With some programs, students can add background music, sound effects, animation, and speech to their text. Using Web 2.0 capabilities, students can also contribute to classroom Wikis and use blogs or instant messaging to communicate with the teacher and each other. See Chapter 13 for more information on the use of technology in writing.

Reading and Writing

Hampton and colleagues (2009) note that learning about genres helps both reading and writing. "Readers develop expectations that enable them to anticipate where a text is going so that they can make sense of it as they read. Writers know how to order and present thoughts in language patterns readers can recognize and follow" (p. 1).

Students can also learn stylistic features from their reading. After a trip to the zoo, one first-grade teacher read *The Day Jimmy's Boa Ate the Wash* (Noble, 1980) to the class. The book begins with the query "How was your trip to the zoo?" and goes on to recount a series of amazing and amusing incidents. A student also began his piece with "How was your trip to the zoo?" However, the rest of his work told how one class member became lost and was found watching the tigers. The boy used *The Day Jimmy's Boa Ate the Wash* to shape his piece but not to determine its content (Franklin, 1988). The stylistic device of using an opening question was borrowed, but the content was original.

Students have a better chance of learning about writing through reading if they "read like a writer," which means that as they read, they notice the techniques the author uses to create a story. This process is enhanced if students respond to their reading in journals. As they begin to look at characters' motives and other story elements, they might then begin to incorporate them in their own writing (Hiebert, Pearson, Taylor, Richardson, & Paris, 1998). It also helps if students take note of authors' techniques during discussions of books read. Teachers might make specific recommendations of pieces that students could use as models or sources of techniques. For example, one of Beverly Cleary's or Betsy Byars's works might help a student who is attempting to write conversational prose.

A Full Menu

Students should engage in a full range of writing activities. With guidance, everyone can and should write poetry, plays, stories, explanatory, and persuasive pieces. How can we tell what our limits are unless we try? Exploring a new genre helps students understand that particular form and provides them with a different kind of writing experience (Read, 2010). Another advantage is that the skills learned in one mode often transfer to other modes. Writing poetry improves word choice and figurative language. Writing plays helps improve dialogue when writing fiction. Fictional techniques enliven expository writing.

Budding writers need a full menu of writing experiences. They should write everything from thank-you notes to poetry, the most demanding kind of writing. Table 12.3 lists some of the kinds of writing activities that might be introduced in an elementary or middle school. It is not a definitive list and offers only suggestions. It should be adapted to fit the needs of your students and your school district's curriculum.

TABLE 12.3 Suggested Writing Activities

Strategy	When Used	Prompt
Academic	*Social*	*Creative*
Book review/book report	E-mail	Story
Essay test	Text message	Poem/verse
State competency test	Friendly letter	Essay (humorous or serious)
Computer-assisted presentation	Postcard	Play/script
Web site	Thank-you note	Story board for video clip
Business/Economic	Get-well card and note	Digital stories
Business letter	Special occasion card and note	
Consumer complaint	Invitation	*Personal*
Correcting a mistake	Fan letter	Diary
Seeking information		Journal
Ordering a product	*General Communication*	
Civic/Personal Development Letters	Announcement	*Writing to Learn*
Letter to the editor	Newsletter	Descriptions of characters, persons, places, events, experiments
Making a suggestion	*Newspaper*	Comparisons of characters, places, events, issues, processes
Protesting a government decision Requesting help	Ad	Explanation of processes, events, movements, causes, and effects
	Editorial	
Seeking information	Feature	Diary of events
	Letter to editor	Journal of observation
Everyday/Practical	News story	Summary of information
Directions	Photo essay/caption	Synthesis of several sources of information
List		
Message (computer, telephone)		Critique of a story, play, movie, Web site, or TV program
Notice		

FYI

Prepare a handout suggesting some specific things parents might do to foster their children's writing development. They can provide the tools of writing and a place to write; explain the kinds of writing they do; share in a writing task, such as writing a note to a relative or sending an e-mail; act as a helpful resource and answer questions about style and format; provide research resources by taking their children to the library; and explain how the Web might be used as a resource. Most important of all, parents can affirm their children's efforts. ■

FYI

In *Dear Mr. Henshaw* (Cleary, 1983), Leigh Botts keeps a diary in which he pretends to write to his favorite author. This diary could be a model for keeping a diary and letter writing. ■

Using Technology

The National Writing Project provides information about writing research and instruction. www.nwp.org ■

Assessing for Learning

Conduct think-alouds to gain insights into students' reasoning processes and the strategies they use to respond to higher-level questions. Use these insights to get ideas for helping students. ■

Summary

Writing evolves from the prespeech gestures children make and from the language they hear and later use. Writing develops in stages. Instruction should be geared to students' stage of writing development. Needed writing strategies should be identified, presented, practiced, and applied.

Once viewed primarily as a product, writing today is viewed as both process and product. Major processes involved in writing include prewriting (topic selection, planning, and rehearsing), composing, revising, editing, and publishing.

Essential techniques for teaching writing include modeling, conferencing, sharing, and direct teaching of skills and strategies and using mentor texts. Instruction is most effective when it is geared to the students' level of development. Improving writing also requires knowing what the characteristics of good writing are. These can be translated into rubrics or checklists that help students better understand the requirements of a piece of writing and that provide guidance for assessment and revision. Portfolios in the form of file folders are recommended for storing and keeping track of students' writing.

Although the emphasis in writing instruction is on content, form is also important. Good form improves content. A balanced writing program includes instruction and exploration of a variety of narrative and expository forms.

Instruction in composing and mechanical skills should be geared to students' current needs and should be continuing and systematic, including daily instruction as well as on-the-spot aid when problems arise.

Good readers tend to be good writers, and vice versa. Also, students who read more tend to be better at writing. Their writing reflects structures and stylistic elements learned through reading. Through reading, they also pick up ideas for topics.

Extending and Applying

1. Plan a writing lesson. Using the process approach, focus on topic selection and planning. If possible, teach the lesson. Compose a written overview and a reflection on the results.
2. Examine a student's permanent writing folder. Track the student's progress. Note gains and needs as well as the types of topics the student has explored and the kinds of writing the student has done. With the student, make plans for future activities.
3. Observe a group of students as they write. Note how they go about prewriting, composing, revising, and editing. What strategies do they use? How effectively do they employ them? What other strategies might they use?
4. Try writing for a short period of time 3 to 5 days a week to gain insight into the process. If possible, have conferences with a colleague. Note your strengths and areas that need work.

Professional Reflection

Do I ...
___ Have an understanding of the writing process?
___ Have an understanding of guided writing and writing workshop?
___ Have an understanding of ways of assessing writing?
___ Have an understanding of how technology might be implemented in a writing program?

Am I able to ...
___ Implement writing process with all students?
___ Hold effective writing conferences?
___ Conduct guided writing lessons?
___ Use technology in the writing program?
___ Use a range of approaches to assesses writing?
___ Set up and manage writing workshop?

Reflection Question

How might you translate the information contained in this chapter into specific action steps designed to improve the writing of all of your students? For instance, how might you make use of models of good writing or mentor texts to improve students' writing? How might you make writing goals more specific? How might you make use of rubrics?

 Building Competencies

To build competencies, consult the following sources for more detailed information:

6+1 Trait® Writing (MCREL)

http//:www.nwrel.org/assessment

presents a wealth of information on writing instruction and assessment.

Donovan, C. A., & Smolkin, L. B. (2011). Supporting informational writing in the elementary grades. *The Reading Teacher, 64,* 406–416. A landmark article on using prompts and other techniques to develop students' writing.

Rog, L. J. (2011). *Marvelous minilessons for teaching intermediate writing, grades 4–6.* Newark, DE: International Reading Association. Features many practical ideas.

MyEducationLab™

Go to the Topic "Writing" in the MyEducationLab (www.myeducationlab.com) for your course, where you can:

- Find learning outcomes for "Writing" along with the national standards that connect to these outcomes.
- Complete Assignments and Activities that can help you more deeply understand the chapter content.
- Apply and practice your understanding of the core teaching skills identified in the chapter with the Building Teaching Skills and Dispositions learning units.
- Examine challenging situations and cases presented in the IRIS Center Resources.
- Check your comprehension on the content covered in the chapter by going to the Study Plan in the Book Resources for your text. Here you will be able to take a chapter quiz, receive feedback on your answers, and then access Review, Practice, and Enrichment activities to enhance your understanding of chapter content. (optional)

A+RISE A+RISE® Standards2Strategy™ is an innovative and interactive online resource that offers new teachers in grades K–12 just-in-time, research-based instructional strategies that meet the linguistic needs of ELLs as they learn content, differentiate instruction for all grades and abilities, and are aligned to Common Core Elementary Language Arts standards (for the literacy strategies) and to English language proficiency standards in WIDA, Texas, California, and Florida.

13 Creating and Managing a Literacy Program

Anticipation Guide

For each of the following statements related to the chapter you are about to read, put a check under "Agree" or "Disagree" to show how you feel. Discuss your responses with classmates before you read the chapter.

	Agree	Disagree
1. Students should be grouped heterogeneously rather than homogeneously for reading instruction.	_____	_____
2. Teaching small groups of students with common needs is just about the best way to provide for individual differences.	_____	_____
3. Ultimate responsibility for the progress of struggling readers rests with the classroom teacher.	_____	_____
4. Without parental support, literacy programs have a greatly diminished chance for success.	_____	_____
5. Instruction in the use of the Internet should be a part of the literacy program.	_____	_____
6. Educators have been oversold on the educational value of technology.	_____	_____

Using What You Know

The best teachers are caring individuals who have solid knowledge of their field, broad knowledge of children and how they learn, and a firm grasp of effective teaching strategies. In addition, they must be skilled managers. They must have goals and objectives and the means to meet them. They must make wise and efficient use of their resources: time, materials, and professional assistance. They must also have positive interactions with students, administrative and supervising staff, resource personnel, parents, and the community at large. Clearly, a tall order. Think of some teachers you have had who were excellent managers. What management strategies did they use? What routines did they devise to keep the class running smoothly? As you read this chapter, try to visualize how you might implement those strategies and routines. Also think about the components of a successful literacy program. What elements does such a program have?

Constructing a Literacy Program

Previous chapters provided the building blocks for a literacy program. Constructing a program means assembling the blocks in some logical way and then reassembling them when necessary. Effective programs have some common features, such as a philosophy that all students can learn to read, high expectations for students, objectives that are specific and clearly stated, varied and appropriate materials, effective teaching strategies, motivation, building a sense of community, efficient use of time and increased time on task, continuous monitoring of progress, involvement of parents, cooperation among staff, a consistent program that builds on past learnings, prevention and intervention as necessary, and a process for evaluating the program (Hiebert, Pearson, Taylor, Richardson, & Paris, 1998; Hoffman, 1991; Samuels, 1988a).

FYI

Building higher-level literacy requires that students change their views of themselves as learners. They must see their role as one of generating understanding by making connections between new information and what they already know by evaluating. Up to this point, they may have thought that their role was to memorize and record (Wittrock, 1991). ■

 FYI

"A clear understanding of a school's shared goals is the cornerstone to successful reading programs" (Hiebert et al., 1998, p. 3). ■

 FYI

Setting goals results in an average percentile gain of 25 points (Haystead & Marzano, 2009). ■

R E F L E C T I O N

Do I have a comprehensive set of goals and objectives for my program? What provision have I made to see if goals and objectives are being met? Do I share goals and objectives with students?

 FYI

Additional information on the use of computers and today's technology in a literacy program is offered later in this chapter. ■

 Adapting Instruction for Struggling Readers and Writers

When selecting materials, make sure that the readability of the materials is appropriate for your students. It is especially important to have plentiful material for below-level readers. See Chapter 3 for suggestions for assessing the difficulty of materials. ■

Construction of a literacy program starts with the students. To build an effective program, you need to ask, "What are the students' needs? What are their interests? What aspirations do their parents have for them? What literacy skills do they need in order to survive and prosper now and in the future?"

Setting Goals

Once you have acquired some basic information about students , you can start setting goals. In setting goals, you might consider the school and school district's curriculum framework, state and national standards. Most states have adopted and are implementing Common Core State Standards. Setting goals should be a collaborative activity among the staff in a school. Teachers need to create a shared vision of what they want their literacy program to do and what shape it will take. Once they agree on common objectives, they can begin planning activities that help them meet those objectives and select the kinds of assessment devices that will keep them aware of how they are doing and flag problem areas. Ultimately, goals and objectives will be determined by the needs of the students. As a practical matter, you must consider the high-stakes tests that students will be required to take. However, providing clear goals and tracking students' progress are two of the most essential elements in an effective program (Marzano, 2011a).

Choosing Materials

Goals and philosophy lead naturally into a choice of materials and activities. Materials should be varied and should include children's books, both fiction and informational. Because children's interests and abilities are diverse, the selection should cover a wide variety of topics and include easy as well as challenging books. There should also be reference books, children's magazines and newspapers, pamphlets, menus, and directions for activities as diverse as planting seeds and operating the classroom computer, telephone books and online references materials, such as weather forecasts, phone books, maps, and encyclopedias.

Supplementary materials, such as a DVD player, audio recorders, interactive white board, document camera, tablet and regular computers and software and apps, and digital devices including e-readers, should also be available. There should be safe access to the Internet. Basals and other commercial materials should be on hand if the teacher chooses to use them.

Selecting Techniques and Strategies

The heart of the instructional program is the quality of the teaching. Effective teachers will have mastered a variety of techniques that they can adapt to fit the needs of their students. Some basic techniques for teaching literacy are listed in Table 13.1.

Teachers must also decide when it is time to substitute one technique or approach for another. For instance, if discussion techniques such as KWL or Questioning the Author aren't working, the teacher might try direct, explicit teaching of strategies. The important point is that the teacher chooses the techniques to be used and makes adjustments when necessary.

Some key student strategies are listed in Table 13.2. It is important to teach students a variety of strategies: Research suggests that, because of the novelty factor, changing strategies enhances achievement.

Building Motivation

Instruction should also take into account affective factors so that students become engaged learners. In a series of studies on effective instruction, Pressley (2001) discovered that motivation had a significant impact on students' learning. Motivation, the

Technique	Appropriate Grade Level
Reading to students	All grades
Shared or assisted reading	Primary grades/remedial
Language experience	Primary grades/remedial
Inductive phonics lesson	Primary grades/remedial
Word building	Primary grades/remedial
Pattern approach to syllabication	Grade 2 and up
Morphemic analysis	Grade 3 and up
Direct instructional lesson for skills and strategies	All grades
Modeling	All grades
Think-aloud lesson	All grades
Guided reading (DRA)	All grades
DR–TA	All grades
Text walk	All grades
Cooperative learning	All grades
Literature discussion groups	All grades
ReQuest	Grade 3 and up
Reciprocal teaching	All grades
KWL	All grades
Questioning the Author (QTA)	Grade 3 and up
Quality Talk	Grade 3 and up
Responsive elaboration	All grades
Process approach to writing	All grades

TABLE 13.1   Essential Techniques for Teaching Literacy

FYI

Teaching strategies to students results in an average percentile gain of 20 points (Hattie, 2009). ■

REFLECTION

Which of the techniques listed in Table 13.1 would be most valuable for you in your teaching situation? How might you go about becoming proficient in the implementation of these techniques? Which technique would you start learning first?

Using Technology

The What Works Clearinghouse provides information about research on instructional practices. http://ies.ed.gov/ncee/wwc ■

researcher discovered, is mainly a matter of creating a positive and encouraging but challenging environment. Students get the feeling that they're valued and competent and that they are engaged in interesting, worthwhile learning activities. The following characteristics of the learning context are also important in fostering motivation (Boothroyd, 2001; Marzano, 2011b):

- Variety of techniques are used. Techniques are matched to students' needs.
- Routines and procedures are well established. The classroom is orderly.
- Effort is emphasized. Praise and reinforcement are used as appropriate.
- The teacher builds a sense of excitement and enthusiasm.
- Cooperation rather than competition is emphasized.
- Manipulatives and hands-on activities are prominent. However, the activities engage students' minds and have legitimate learning goals.
- The teacher notes when students are not engaged and adjusts instruction.
- The teacher maintains a lively pace.

Building a Sense of Community

In an effective literacy program, the teacher focuses on building a community of learners. Traditionally, the focus in schools has been on the individual. As the importance of learning from others through scaffolding, discussion, cooperative learning, and consideration of multiple perspectives has become apparent, it is clear that the focus must be on group learning. In an ideal community of learners, all students' contributions are valued. Activities and discussions are genuine because students feel that they are a valuable part of the learning community. For the teacher, building relationships with students is an essential element of an effective program (Marzano, 2011b). This means getting to know students, their interests and backgrounds, and showing all students that they are valued and respected.

FYI

Teachers' knowledge of techniques should be metacognitive. Not only should they know how to teach the techniques, they should also know where and when to use them. For example, a group of students who need a maximum of structure and assistance should be taught within a guided reading (DRA) framework. As their work habits improve, the DR–TA can be introduced to foster independence. Later, reciprocal teaching might be employed. ■

FYI

Student engagement results in average percentile gains of 21 points (Hattie, 2009). ■

FYI

Based on observations of 827 first-grade classrooms, researchers in a federal study concluded that both behavior and engagement in academic activities were improved in classrooms that provided both emotional and academic support (NICHD Early Child Care Research Network, 2002). Observations of 780 third-grade classrooms resulted in similar findings (NICHD Early Child Care Research Network, 2005). ■

 FYI

Classroom cohesion results in an average percentile gain of 18 points (Hattie, 2009). ■

 FYI

• One source of help for struggling readers, and the rest of the class, too, is tutors. Tutors should be screened, trained, supervised, and appreciated. See Wasik (1999) for excellent suggestions for using volunteers.

• To make better use of time, avoid teaching students what they already know and stop having them practice skills they have mastered. When introducing new words for a selection, do not spend time on those that are already familiar. One study found that students already knew 80 percent of the words recommended for instruction in the basal materials (Stallman et al., 1990). If the unknown words are words that students recognize when they hear them but do not know in print, do not waste time teaching the meanings. Emphasize the phonic form of the words, which is the unknown element. ■

TABLE 13.2   Learning Strategies and Related Instructional Techniques

	Student's Learning Strategies	Teacher's Instructional Techniques
Preparational	Activating prior knowledge Previewing Predicting Setting purpose SQ3R	Brainstorming Discussion KWL DR–TA Guided reading Text walk Discussing misconceptions Modeling Direct instruction Questioning the Author (QTA) Quality Talk Reciprocal teaching, ReQuest Think-alouds Responsive elaboration
Selecting/ organizing	Selecting important or relevant details Identifying main idea Summarizing Questioning Using graphic organizers SQ3R	Think-alouds DR–TA Guided reading Modeling Direct instruction Reciprocal teaching KWL Discussing Questioning the Author Quality Talk Strategy guide Responsive elaboration
Elaborational	Inferring Evaluating Applying Imaging SQ3R	Direct instruction DR–TA Guided reading Modeling Think-alouds Reciprocal teaching Questioning the Author Discussing Quality Talk KWL Responsive elaboration
Monitoring/ metacognitive	Monitoring for meaning SQ3R Using fix-up strategies	Think-alouds Modeling Reciprocal teaching Direct instruction Questioning the Author
Affective	Attending/concentrating Staying on task Using self-talk	Think-alouds Modeling Discussing Encouraging
Rehearsal/study	Using understanding Using mnemonic devices Rehearsing SQ3R Self-testing	Modeling Think-alouds Direct instruction Judicious practice Interleaving

(continued)

TABLE 13.2 Learning Strategies and Related Instructional Techniques (*Continued*)

	Student's Learning Strategies	Teacher's Instructional Techniques
Word recognition	Using pronounceable word parts Using analogies Sounding out words Using context Using morphemic analysis Using syllabic analysis Using the dictionary Integrating word-attack skills	Modeling Word building Direct instruction Think-alouds Responsive elaboration

Adapted from Jones, Palincsar, Ogle, & Carr, 1986.

 ## Managing a Literacy Program

A teacher of literacy must be an efficient manager, determining how to handle physical setup, materials, time, paid classroom assistants, and volunteers. With the current emphasis on inclusion and collaboration, the teacher must also coordinate his or her efforts with a number of specialists: the special education teacher, Title 1 personnel, the reading consultant, and the bilingual and ESL teachers. The teacher must consult with the school social worker, nurse, vice principal, principal, and supervisory personnel and must enlist the support of parents. Promoting collegiality and seeking mentorship in areas of need and interest are essential characteristics of an effective teacher (Marzano & Toth, 2011).

Using Time Efficiently

Although time on task is a major ingredient in learning, the nature of the task plays a key role. If the task is too easy, too difficult, or not educationally valid, the time is wasted. A better measure of time use is academic learning time. Academic learning time (ALT) is the amount of time a student spends attending to relevant academic tasks while performing those tasks with a high rate of success (Berliner, 1984; Caldwell, Huitt, and Graeber, 1982). For primary grades, aim for a minimum of 90 minutes for literacy instruction, but 120 is more desirable. For the upper grades, aim for a minimum of 60 minutes, but 90 is more desirable.

Pacing Teachers must eliminate those activities that have limited or no value. They should critically examine every activity, asking whether it results in effective learning or practice. Also, eliminate unnecessary seatwork. Use cooperative learning, have students read self-selected books, meet in literature discussion groups, and work at learning centers. Well-planned centers can provide excellent opportunities for exploration and skills application. To be effective, each center should have a specific objective. The key is to arrange a sequence of valuable activities that students can perform without teacher direction. If some of the planned activities involve partners or small groups, students can obtain feedback and elaboration from each other. Table 13.3 describes two sample learning centers.

 FYI

Classroom management results in an average percentile gain of 18 points (Hattie, 2009). ▪

 FYI

Middle-class students gain 0.13 over the summer. Economically disadvantaged lose about 0.14. Summer school results in a gain of 0.23 (Hattie, 2009). These gains and losses may seem small, but over a period of years can be quite substantial. In one study, students who engaged in a summer reading program gained as much as 5 months (White & Kim, 2010). A program of summer reading can also result in encouraging gains (Allington et al., 2010). ▪

An effective literacy program is well managed and fosters group learning and a sense of community.

Exemplary Teaching

Organizing for Self-Regulated Learning

In an intensive study of ten fourth- and fifth-grade literacy classes, Ms. Kurtz's students stood out. Although the atmosphere in her class was friendly, it was also purposeful. Students were actively engaged in their learning, were seldom seen to be wasting time, were highly motivated, and had excellent work habits.

What was the secret of Ms. Kurtz's success? Involvement and instruction. Whenever possible, she gave students choices, and she also actively involved them in planning activities. Ms. Kurtz's instruction was organized around thematic units, with theme topics including survival, mysteries, the Revolutionary War, and others. After a unit was planned, she provided students with a list of unit activities and let them decide when to complete the activities. Instead of leaving them to their own devices, she actively promoted self-regulated learning. She assisted students with decision making and helped them plan their assignments. Students were also encouraged to reflect on and evaluate their work.

She expected students to be independent, but she taught them how to work on their own. Having been given the tools to become independent and the motivation to use them, the students lived up to expectations (Pressley, Wharton-McDonald, Mistretta-Hampston, & Echevarria, 1998).

TABLE 13.3   Two Sample Learning Centers

Type	Objective	Sequence of Activities
Word study center	Building decoding skills	1. Students follow directions to make new words by substituting clusters for single consonants. 2. Students read the new words. 3. Students assemble the words and read the message they created (see Secret Messages, p. 216). 4. Students write the message in their learning center logs.
Making and doing center	Following directions	1. Students select an activity that requires following directions. 2. Students read the directions to get an overview. 3. Students check to see that they have needed materials. 4. Students follow the directions. 5. Students describe the finished activity in their logs.

Source: Adapted from Ford, 1994.

FYI

With inclusion, today's classrooms are more diverse than ever. In first grade, the range of achievement in a class can be expected to be two or more years; in fourth grade, four years or more; by sixth grade, six years or more (Kulik, 1992). ■

Providing for Individual Differences

One way of providing for individual differences is to use reading and writing workshops, which were explained in Chapters 11 and 12. A second technique is to give extra help to low-achieving students through Response to Intervention (RTI) and other approaches. Those students might be given one-on-one or small-group instruction during school hours, before or after school, on Saturdays, or in special summer programs. A third technique is to adapt or modify the program to meet individual needs. Adaptations have been discussed throughout the text and include providing added instruction, easier materials, or specialized aids to learning and changing the learning environment or using assistive technology. A fourth technique is to use varied, **flexible grouping**. Possible groups include whole-class groups, guided reading groups, temporary skills groups, cooperative learning groups, and interest groups.

Whole-Class Grouping   **Whole-class instruction** can be efficient and build a sense of community. Reading aloud to students, shared reading, and introducing new concepts and strategies lend themselves to whole-class instruction. Reading and writing workshops begin and end with whole-class activities. Preparation for reading a selection is provided to the whole class. Anticipating difficulties that students might have with the text, the teacher develops background knowledge, activates schema, builds vocabulary, sets a purpose, and creates interest in the selection.

Although the initial preparatory instruction may be the same for all students, students might read the text in different ways. Adapting instruction to students' varied reading approaches is known as **tiered instruction**. When using tiered instruction, teachers teach the same concept or skill but adjust the level of difficulty of materials, how the materials are to be presented, how much help is provided, or the difficulty level of the assignment. Higher-achieving students read independently. Others can receive varying degrees of assistance. The teacher might spend additional time reviewing vocabulary, reading a portion of the selection to get the students started, or guiding students through the selection section by section. For children who have more serious reading problems, the teacher might use shared or assisted reading or allow them to listen to a recorded version or allow them to listen to or view an electronic version of the selection.

After the selection has been read, the whole class discusses it. Having read and discussed a story together builds community among students. However, it should be emphasized that although the selection might have been easy or just slightly challenging for some students, it was probably very difficult for others. For this reason, whole-group reading of selections should be used sparingly, and some teachers might choose not to use it at all. If used, whole-group reading should be balanced by providing lower-achieving students with opportunities to read on their instructional or independent levels.

Guided Reading   In guided reading, students are grouped by reading proficiency (Fountas & Pinnell, 1996, 2001c). The groups meet daily for 10 to 30 minutes or more. The teacher may organize as many groups as she or he believes are necessary, but the more groups assembled, the less time there is for each one. As a practical matter, three or four groups are the most that can be handled efficiently. Grouping, however, is flexible. When appropriate, students are moved into other groups.

Temporary Skills Groups   In **skills groups**, students are grouped based on the need for a particular skill. Once the skill has been mastered, the group is disbanded. For example, if a number of students are having difficulty monitoring their comprehension, you might group them for lessons and practice sessions on how to use strategies in this area. Make sure that skills groups provide for the special needs of high-achieving students so that the groups are not stigmatized as being remedial (Radencich, 1995).

Study Buddies   Pairs of students can work together in a variety of ways—for example, as reading partners who take turns reading to each other, as study buddies who work on an assignment together, or as peer editors who read and comment on each other's written pieces.

Interest Groups   Students who are interested in a particular topic, author, or genre can join together in **interest groups**. The group creates questions to be answered and uses trade books and other sources to gather information. The students work together in cooperative-learning style. One advantage of this type of grouping is that it includes students with diverse abilities and acts as a counterbalance to ability or achievement grouping. It also provides students with choices.

■ Because **flexible grouping** allows students to be in a variety of groups, some based on need, some on interest, some on personal choices, students are not tracked into low, average, or above-average groups. Flexible grouping makes it easier for specialists to work with small groups. While the specialist is working with one group, the classroom teacher can be working with another (Ogle & Fogelberg, 2001).
■ **Whole-class instruction** is the practice of teaching the entire class at the same time. Although whole-class grouping is efficient and builds a sense of community, it does have disadvantages. Teaching tends to be teacher-centered, there is less opportunity to provide for individual differences, and students have less opportunity to contribute (Radencich, 1995).
■ **Tiered instruction** consists of differentiating instruction so that the same concept or skill is presented in appropriate ways to students of varying abilities.

Regrouping   Regrouping is the practice of assigning students from several classes who are reading on the same grade level to instructional groups. If the reading, special education, and other specialists agree to take groups, groups can be relatively small. A variation of regrouping is the Joplin plan, in which students from different grade levels are regrouped according to reading level. Regrouping on an informal basis can also be effective. Two fifth-grade teachers might agree that one will take the lowest-level and the other will take the highest-level students. This cuts down on the range of pupils and number of groups. Disadvantages of regrouping include time lost going from class to class and lack of flexibility in the schedule: Students must move into their groups at a certain time.

Balanced Grouping   Grouping patterns should be balanced and flexible. At times, it is best for the class to work as a whole; at other times, small groups or pairs work best, and students should also have some experience working individually. By employing several patterns, the teacher gives students the opportunity to mix with a greater variety of their peers, and there is less of a chance that lower-achieving students will brand themselves as "slow" learners. The foundation of balanced grouping lies in the building of a sense of community. Realizing that they are valued and have a common purpose, students are better able to work with each other.

Grouping can result in gains of an extra two or three months on reading achievement tests. However, grouping is only effective when instruction is tailored to the group (Kulik, 1992). There is no gain when students are placed in groups but all are taught essentially the same material in the same way. It is also critical that students be assessed frequently and that group placement be changed when called for. Limiting the number of groups so that each group gets as much teacher attention as possible is also helpful (Slavin, 1987a).

Advantages and Disadvantages of Grouping   Grouping reduces variability in achievement and so makes it easier for the teacher to target instruction to the students' needs. The teacher is able to move at a faster pace for achieving students and provide more review and practice for struggling readers. However, grouping can be harmful to the self-concepts of struggling readers, who may begin to see themselves as slow learners. Students in the lowest groups are also deprived of the opportunity to learn from the example and ideas of achieving readers. There is also a danger that low expectations will be set for struggling readers and that they will be given activities that are geared to lower-level skills, thus depriving them of opportunities to develop high-level thinking skills (Barr & Dreeben, 1991).

If students are grouped heterogeneously, it should be done in such a way that all students benefit. Based on her observations of mixed-level groups, Poole (2008) found that struggling readers were stigmatized because they stumbled over a large number of words. In addition, the only help they were given was directed toward getting them through the passages they were reading orally rather than fostering the use of needed decoding strategies. Indeed, overall, instruction neglected decoding because some of the students in the heterogeneous groups were reading on grade level. Either heterogeneous groups should be given text that even struggling readers can handle or the struggling readers should be provided with advance preparation so that the text is accessible. Poole's research also indicated that oral reading is a problematic activity when some students in a group are dysfluent.

Intervention Programs

Intervention programs are another means of differentiating instruction. Intervention programs are designed to help students who are at risk of not making adequate progress as well as students who have fallen behind. The best known intervention program is Reading Recovery. The idea behind Reading Recovery is to intervene early, before students are discouraged by failure and before they pick up unproductive reading strategies. The program is designed for the lowest-achieving 20 percent of a class. In 30-minute, one-on-one daily sessions, students read whole books, write, and are taught how to use a variety of decoding and monitoring strategies. A key element in Reading Recovery's success is the teacher's guidance, which is based on close observation of each student. Instructors are highly trained and have a thorough knowledge of the reading process.

Other Intervention Programs   Today's basal/anthology reading programs also make provisions for struggling readers. One advantage of these intervention programs is that they are closely tied to the core program. The core program and the intervention program are mutually reinforcing, giving struggling readers maximum assistance. For a listing of other commercial intervention programs, see Table 13.4.

TABLE 13.4   Commercial Intervention Programs

Title	Publisher	Interest Level	Grade Level	Main Characteristics
AMP	Pearson	6–12	3–6	Develops vocabulary and key comprehension strategies.
Bookshop	Mondo	K–3	K–3	Workshop approach; PA, decoding, comprehension, writing, language.
Corrective Reading	SRA	4–12	1–5+	Scripted direct instruction; decoding, comprehension.
Edmark	Great Source	P–12	1–2	Whole-word approach, simplified text; designed for students with cognitive deficits.
Fast Track	Macmillan/McGraw-Hill	4–8	1–5+	Decoding, comprehension.
High Noon	High Noon	3–12	1–4+	Decoding, comprehension.
High Point	Hampton Brown	4–12	1–6	Decoding, comprehension, writing, oral language; emphasis on ELL.
Intervention by Design	Rigby	K–5	K–5	Phonemic awareness, decoding, fluency, vocabulary, comprehension.
Language	Sopris West	4–12	1–9	Comprehensive literacy intervention curriculum designed for students reading two or more years below grade level or at the 30th percentile or below. Features 540 lessons in 18 strands that include reading, writing, spelling, vocabulary, and grammar. Has a special component for ELLs.
Leveled Literacy Intervention	Heinemann	K–3	K–3	Separate phonics/word study, oral language, writing; emphasis on reading predictable texts.
Lightspan Early Reading	Lightspan	K–3	K–3	Computer-based program; PA, decoding, comprehension, vocabulary, background knowledge.
Ramp Up Literacy	America's Choice	6	3–6+	Develops phonics, comprehension, vocabulary, fluency, and writing. Includes cross-age tutoring and self-selected reading.
Read 180	Scholastic	4–8+	1.5–8.9	Includes software, student books, audiobooks, and paperbacks for independent reading. A high-tech program.
Read Naturally	Read Naturally	1–8	1–8	Emphasis on fluency; also has materials for reinforcing phonics.
Reading Mastery	SRA	K–6	K–6	Scripted direct instruction; decoding and comprehension.
Reading Rescue	Literacy Trust	1–2	1–2	PA, decoding, fluency, vocabulary, comprehension; uses Ready Readers.
Ready Readers	Modern Curriculum Press	K–3	K–3	PA, decoding; stresses sorting; texts are decodable but readable.
REWARDS	Sopris West	4–6 6–12	2–4+ 2–4+	Syllabic analysis, fluency, vocabulary, comprehension.
Road to the Code	Brookes	K–2	K–1	Phonemic awareness and beginning consonants.
Road to Reading	Brookes	1–2+	1–2+	Decoding single-syllable and multisyllabic words, fluency.
Sidewalks	Scott Foresman	1–5	1–5	PA, decoding, fluency, vocabulary, comprehension.
SIPPS	Developmental Studies Center	K–3 4–12	K–3 1–4+	PA, single-syllable phonics, syllabic analysis.

(continued)

TABLE 13.4 Commercial Intervention Programs (*Continued*)

Title	Publisher	Interest Level	Grade Level	Main Characteristics
Soar to Success	Houghton Mifflin	K–8	K–8	Phonemic awareness (at K–2), phonics, fluency, comprehension; uses high-interest trade books.
System 44	Scholastic	3–12	1–2	Adaptive software delivers systematic phonics instruction. Also builds vocabulary.
S.P.I.R.E	EPS	1–8	1–5+	Develops decoding, spelling, fluency, vocabulary, and comprehension. Designed for severely disabled readers.
Success for All	Success for All Foundation	K–8	K–8	Whole-school program; PA, decoding, comprehension, writing.
Voyager Reading Intervention	Voyager	K–8	K–8	PA, decoding, comprehension, writing.
Wilson	Wilson	3–12	1–4+	Provides extensive instruction in phonics, spelling, and fluency. Designed for severely disabled readers.
Word Building	Phoenix	K–4	K–3	PA, decoding, modified cloze comprehension.
Word Detectives	Benchmark School	1–5+	1–5	PA, decoding.
Wright Group Early Reading Intervention	Wright Group	K–3	K–3	PA, decoding, spelling, fluency, comprehension.

Note: PA = Phonological awareness. Separate phonics programs are those in which the phonics skills taught in a particular lesson are not reinforced by the selection read during that lesson.

A Framework Based on an Overview of Intervention Programs Although the intervention programs differ in specifics, all stress the importance of providing ample opportunity for students to read materials on the appropriate level, teaching students to be strategic readers, monitoring their progress, evaluating the program, providing inservice training, and having strong leadership. Programs at the early levels also have a strong decoding component. Successful programs are additive. They provide instruction that is in addition to the regular classroom program. Most of the techniques presented in this chapter are the same as those discussed in previous chapters. In general, the techniques that work with achieving readers also work with students who are at risk. The chief difference in working with at-risk students is the need to make appropriate adaptations and modifications.

The following framework for planning a classroom intervention program is based on the major principles covered in this chapter and the exemplary intervention programs discussed in this section. The framework is flexible and can be used with students who are experiencing difficulty with any or all of the following: word recognition, comprehension, vocabulary, study skills, and writing.

Building Literacy: A Classroom Intervention Program

Goals and Objectives: Objectives should be those that are most likely to result in maximum improvement in literacy and should be clearly communicated to learners.

Direct, Systematic Instruction: Struggling readers and writers need direct, systematic instruction geared to their strengths. High-quality instructional techniques need to focus on building phonemic awareness, word building and sorting words, guided reading (including text walk), shared reading, language experience (including shared writing and interactive writing), and use of graphic organizers, ReQuest, reciprocal teaching, and Questioning the Author (QTA).

Selecting Students: Select students with the greatest needs in reading and writing. Depending on students' levels, use an informal reading inventory (IRI) and/or assessment devices from the appendix of this book. Also use observations, samples of students' work, and portfolios, if available.

Size of Group: A group of six or seven is the maximum size that can be taught effectively. However, the more serious the difficulties, the smaller the group should be.

Scheduling Instruction: Intervention is most beneficial when it's given in addition to the instruction already provided to the whole class. Students who are behind need more instructional time if they are expected to catch up. Before school, after school, Saturday, and/or summer sessions are recommended. However, if this is not practical, arrange intervention sessions when they will best fit into the daily schedule. You might hold intervention sessions when the rest of the class is engaged in sustained reading, working at learning centers, or working on individual or group projects. Intervention sessions should be scheduled every day, if possible, but not less than three times a week. Sessions can last from 20 to 45 minutes, with 40 minutes being the recommended duration.

Materials: Use high-interest materials. Select materials that are attractive and well illustrated and that don't have a lot of print on a page. Make sure that materials are on the appropriate level of difficulty. Also, students should use technology, such as talking software, to help them overcome learning difficulties.

Evaluation: Continuously monitor students' progress. Keep records of books read, and conduct a running record or modified informal reading inventory monthly or weekly, if possible. If decoding is a problem area, use the Phonics Inventory or a similar instrument (see the appendix). Observe and make note of students' daily progress. Maintain a portfolio of work samples. At least once a month, review each student's progress and make any necessary adjustments to the program.

Parental Involvement: Let parents know about the program. Keep them informed about their children's progress. Also, enlist their support. Students in the program should read 20 minutes a night at least four times a week. Discuss with parents how they might help their children fulfill this requirement. Parents might also help out as volunteers, perhaps working with the rest of the class while you are teaching the intervention group. Or they might work with individuals on language-experience stories or listen to them read.

Professional Support: Discuss your program with the principal and enlist her or his support. Also, talk it over with other professionals. They may have suggestions for improvement or be able to provide assistance if problems arise.

Parts of a Building Literacy Lesson: A building literacy lesson for an intervention session should include certain key elements: At a minimum, there should be a review of past material, an introduction to or extension of a new skill or strategy, and an opportunity to apply that skill or strategy by reading a selection. If time allows, there should be a writing activity. Conclude the session with a brief activity chosen by the students: a game, computer time, or reading of a riddle or verse, for instance. Students should also have a take-home activity, such as a book or periodical to read or reread.

Continuous Monitoring of Progress

A near universal finding of research on effective teaching is that it is essential to know where students are (Hoffman, 1991). **Monitoring** should be continuous. Continuous monitoring assumes that if something is lacking in the students' learning, the program will be modified. In a Response to Intervention (RTI) approach, all students are monitored at least three times a year. Students who are not making adequate progress are provided with increasingly intensive help.

Involving Parents

Parents have a right to be kept informed about their child's literacy program. As a practical matter, keeping them up to date, especially if the program is a new one, will forestall complaints due to misunderstanding and will build support.

REFLECTION

What provision might you make for struggling students? What help would you provide in the classroom? What help would you seek for students who need assistance beyond the classroom? How might you work with reading and learning disabilities specialists to maximize struggling students' progress?

FYI

When parents are involved with their children's schools, their children do better and so does the school. Teachers feel more appreciated and are reaffirmed by the improved performance of their students. See the IRA position statement on family and school partnerships:
http://www.reading.org/General/AboutIRA/PositionStatements/FamilySchoolPosition.aspx ∎

■ **Monitoring** refers to the assessment of students' progress to see whether they are performing adequately.

IRA POSITION STATEMENT ON KEY ISSUE
Family-School Partnerships

"Educators need to view partnerships with families as an integral part of good teaching and student success. . . . School programs and educator practices to organize family-school connections are equalizers to help families who would not become involved on their own" (Epstein & Dauber, 1991). "The benefits of developing collaborative relationships with all families are many, and they accrue to educators, families, and students. . . . Children from low-income and culturally and racially diverse families experience greater success when schools involve families, enlist them as allies, and build on their strengths. Family involvement in a child's education is a more important factor in student success than family income or education" (International Reading Association, 2002a, para. 3).

Adapting Instruction for English Language Learners

Parents of ELLs can help their children more fully develop their first language by encouraging its use. They can discuss current events and topics that are being studied in school. If their children are literate in their first language, parents can encourage them to read in that language. ∎

FYI

Involving parents results in an average percentile gain of 17 points (Hattie, 2009). ∎

Using Technology

To increase communication with parents and to provide help with homework, supply students and parents with an e-mail address where they can get in touch with you, or explain the homework assignment on the school's voicemail. You might also create a Web page that contains information valuable to parents. ∎

FYI

Parents tend to have a bottom-up view of reading (Evans, Fox, Cremaso, & McKinnon, 2004)—that is, they favor systematic instruction in reading with lots of practice and accurate oral reading. If your approach is more holistic, you will need to clearly explain its benefits. ∎

Prior to changes made to improve the effectiveness of the program in an impoverished elementary school in Southern California, teachers incorrectly assumed that parents lacked the time, ability, or motivation to help their children (Goldenberg, 1994). Although the parents were not well educated, they had high aspirations for their children. The school sent home reading materials and suggestions for ways in which the materials might be used. Even though parents were interested and supportive, merely making suggestions at the beginning of the year wasn't enough. The teachers found that it was important to use follow-up notes, phone calls, and regular homework assignments. With follow-through and monitoring, parents began providing assistance and students' achievement increased. The lesson is clear: The school must establish and maintain contact with parents. Quarterly report cards and PTA notices are a start, but more is necessary. Encourage students to take their papers home to show their parents and to read to their parents from their basals and/or trade books. This is especially important for novice readers. After students have finished a level in their basals or completed a trade book, help them prepare a passage to read to their parents.

Working with Other Professionals

Working with Resource Personnel   With the emphasis on inclusion and the implementation of RTI, classroom teachers are taking more responsibility for all students, including those who struggle, and are working more closely with the special education teacher, the reading–language arts coach, and other specialists. Through collaboration, classroom teachers can obtain services and materials for struggling learners and special needs students and can also learn teaching and management techniques that will help them more effectively instruct these students. Often, the techniques and strategies recommended by resource personnel work well with all students and might be used in the regular classroom.

Collaboration works best when the professionals involved meet regularly, establish common goals, and are flexible but work diligently to meet their common goals and make adjustments as necessary. Carefully planned and implemented collaboration can result in improved learning for all students.

Using Reading to Close the Gap

To catch up, students who are behind must read more. Adding reading time to a crowded day can be a problem. However, one solution is to make better use of the time available. Having efficient management routines can save time. If the guided reading group gets started promptly, they might have 5 more minutes of reading time. If students have carefully chosen their books for voluntary or self-selected reading and are engaged in their reading, instead of leafing through the book or looking at pictures, that, too, can add valuable minutes to reading time. Any reading in content areas, of course, adds to reading time. And having books on the appropriate level makes it possible for below-level readers to get maximum benefit from added reading time (Guthrie, 2004).

Making significant progress in reading takes extended effort. A fourth-grader who is two years behind might need an extra hour of reading each school day for a period of two years to catch up. The key is not how many minutes the students have books in their hands. The key is how many minutes they are engrossed in reading text that is on the appropriate level of challenge.

Literacy and Technology: The New Literacies

Although sometimes known as New Literacies, digital literacy relies heavily on the old literacies of activating prior knowledge, previewing, inferring, summarizing, and evaluating. Students need to be taught how reading strategies and skills learned in the classroom can be applied to online reading. Coiro (2009) suggests comparing online and offline reading. Specifically, compare the text features. Note features such as hyperlinks, digitized speech, embedded glossaries, and interactive questions that are present in online reading but not in offline reading. Also stress the increased importance of setting a purpose for reading and reading to fulfill that purpose. It's easy to lose sight of one's purpose for reading when confronted with an excess of information. Skimming and scanning also take on a new importance. Think-alouds, in which the teacher demonstrates and explains how she or he reads online, are especially effective. Students might also share techniques and strategies that they already use and feel are effective.

An approach known as Internet reciprocal teaching uses a series of lessons to develop needed skills. For instance, students used the following reciprocal teaching strategies to investigate the reliability of Web sites (Internet Reciprocal Teaching, 2009):

Predict: Do you think your site is a reliable source of information?

Question: How do you know that a Web site has accurate information?

Clarify: How do you go about checking the validity of Web sites?

Summarize: Which strategies were most useful? Which were not?

Part of learning the new literacies is developing skills needed for collaborating. Just as in literature circles, students need to learn to treat each other with respect and to adopt a cooperative, collaborative approach so that everyone contributes. In addition to learning traditional face-to-face collaborative skills, students need to learn how to use online communication tools in a respectful, cooperative manner. They may be using online communication tools to collaborate with classmates and students in other schools and in other lands. Last but not least, students need to learn how to use digital technologies ethically. They need to learn about property rights, copying, citing sources, and using information and online tools in an ethical manner.

Creating WebQuests

A WebQuest (http://webquest.org) is an inquiry-based learning task that makes use of Internet resources (Dodge, 2001). Typical WebQuests might involve giving a PowerPoint presentation on the deserts of the world and offering solutions to the problem of desertification based on material found at several Web sites, comparing the biographies of two authors after visiting their sites, deciding what most likely happened to the Mayan civilization, creating a newspaper report of an historical event after reviewing sites containing primary sources, designing an energy-efficient home using information from pertinent sites, and persuading others of your viewpoint after visiting sites that contain information about controversial issues.

Because the sites for a WebQuest are chosen for students, students make efficient use of their time. They don't spend a lot of time surfing the Net. Because the sites

FYI

In one elementary school in Connecticut, the writing strategies taught by the learning disabilities specialist were so effective that they were adopted by the whole school. Through collaboration, classroom teachers learned about effective strategies and learning disabilities teachers increased their knowledge of the curriculum. ■

FYI

Use of computers results in average percentile gains of 13 points (Hattie, 2009). ■

Using Technology

"Using the Internet requires . . . that you identify a question that you want to answer. You then have to plan a search. You have to determine the best source of information and also when you have sufficient information. You must evaluate the information. You must also integrate and synthesize information" (Leu, 2006). The following contains an extensive listing of teaching and learning resources for teachers:
http://www.free.ed.gov ■

are selected by the teacher, they are high quality and safe and geared to the teacher's instructional objectives. Listed below are suggested steps for creating a WebQuest.

Steps in Creating a WebQuest

Step 1. *Stating objectives.* What is it that you want students to know or be able to do as a result of the WebQuest? You might want them to be able to write a poem, compare contrasting opinions on a timely topic, or create a Web site by following directions.

Step 2. *Finding appropriate sites.* Find sites that enable students to achieve their learning objective. For instance, if the goal is to have them write a poem, you might select sites that contain a variety of poems, explain how poems are created, and provide templates for the creation of easy-to-compose poems.

Step 3. *Organize the WebQuest.* Create a guide that explains the purpose of the WebQuest and how to implement it. For each site they visit, students might be provided a brief overview as well as questions to be answered or a task to be completed. The questions or tasks should foster higher-level thinking as well as basic understanding. The WebQuest should go beyond merely having students retell information.

Step 4. *Establish outcome activities.* Decide how you want students to use this knowledge or skill that they have gained through engaging in the WebQuest. Will they write a letter of protest? Will they create a modern-day fable? Will they share information with younger students?

Step 5. *Assessing the WebQuest.* Using a rubric or other assessment device, evaluate the students' learning and also the effectiveness of the WebQuest. Did they attain the learning objectives? Did the WebQuest spark interest and higher-level thinking? How might it be improved?

Selecting and Using Internet Sites

There are thousands of sites designed for elementary and middle school students. Here is a list of recommended sites:

- Awesome Library provides links to 22,000 carefully reviewed resources for students of all ages. The browser is available in a dozen languages and has a translation feature: http://www.awesomelibrary.org
- Enchanted Learning features a wealth of information about animals and other topics, and a variety of activities and illustrations that can be printed out. Materials are in English and Spanish, including a Little Explorer's Picture Dictionary: http://www.enchantedlearning.com
- IPL2 features a wide range of resources. Chosen by librarians, only high-quality, informative, reliable sites are listed. Also has special sections with resources for kids and for teens, and links to hundreds of newspapers and magazines: http://www.ipl2.org
- Billed as the best homework and reference resource, Kid Info/School Subjects is arranged by subject area and linked to many of the best educational sites online. http://www.kidinfo.com
- Great Sites for Kids is compiled by members of the American Library Association for students, teachers, librarians, and parents: http://www.ala.org/greatsites

Using Technology

VuSafe:

Teachers can search for and preview video clips from YouTube and other sources through the Web site, and can add clips to their school's VuSafe video library. This protects students from inappropriate clips. http://www.m86vusafe.com/i ■

Using Web 2.0 Tools

Search tools help students locate information and are known as Web 1.0 tools. Web 2.0 tools enable students to share and produce information on the Web. Many elementary and middle school students create literary content on their own. For instance, one fifth-grader who struggled somewhat with reading and writing in school produced several well-planned videos explaining and demonstrating how to care for a pet gecko and posted them on YouTube. The videos were highly informative. Had his language arts teacher known of the student's out-of-school literacy creations, he or she could have built on them and had the student share with the class his knowledge of taking care of geckos and producing videos. Some other Web 2.0 tools are listed below.

Blogging   A blog (a combination of the words *web* and *log*) is a Web site on which the creator periodically adds content, with the latest content being placed first. A key advantage of blogs is that readers can, in many instances, respond by posting comments. Blogs have been set up to replace or complement traditional discussion groups, such as literature circles and other literary discussion groups. Blogs have also been used as a forum for sharing writing or discussing ideas. Teachers who have used blogs note that that they are motivational (Boling, Castek, Zawilinski, Barton, & Nierlich, 2008). Students often put in extra time on their blogs. They also encourage students who are normally reticent to contribute, and they provide students with a genuine audience and feedback. Blogs can be private, accessible only to a select group, or they can be public, open to anyone using the Internet. As with discussion groups, rules for blogging must be established. Students need to be respectful of each other. If the blogs are open to the public, procedures for online safety need to be established. Some teachers monitor blogs by checking them before posting.

Wikis   Wikis can be used to create a database of information about a topic that includes a listing of recommended books, examples of misleading advertising, a glossary of important terms, results of a science experiment, lists of recommended Web sites, and ways in which students have used what they learned in class, or a class cooperative report in which individuals or groups contribute sections. Wikis can be open or private. Using a closed wiki, a group of special education second-graders posted stories, which they shared with each other and with their e-pals, teacher candidates at a local university (Andes & Claggett, 2011).

Podcasts   Podcasts are auditory or video digital files. A number of educational and commercial organizations, such as PBS, the Discovery Channel, and the International Reading Association, offer podcasts. Podcasts can be used to provide multimedia content. Students can also create podcasts. A group of second- and third-graders created reader's theater productions using a podcast (Vasinda & McLeod, 2011). The podcast enriched the experience. The podcasts made the production seem "real" to students. It also broadened their audience and made the students feel important.

Issues of Safety

For all its potential value, the Internet can be a source of harm to young people. The Internet is essentially unregulated, so objectionable material is available. Filtering software can be used to restrict access to some objectionable sites. Software that keeps track of sites that have been visited is also available. There is also the issue of security. Unfortunately, some adults have used the Internet to prey on children. The best defense is to educate students and their parents about the dangers of the Internet and precautions that might be taken. In many schools, parents and students sign an agreement to use the Internet ethically and responsibly. Students also need to be supervised when using the Internet. As a practical matter, monitors should be set up so that teachers can readily see what students are viewing.

Other Uses of Computers

Computers are most powerful in literacy learning when they are used as a tool. They can help locate data, retrieve information, organize data, compose information, and present information.

Word Processing   Computers are most frequently used as aids to composition. The major advantage of word-processing software is that students can revise without rewriting or retyping the whole piece. See Chapter 12 for additional information about word processing and desktop publishing.

Using the Computer as a Source of Information   The increased power of computers allows students to have access to dictionaries, encyclopedias, thesauruses, picture libraries, atlases, and other databases of information They often come with features that help students locate and organize information.

Selecting Programs

The key to making effective use of the computerized devices is to obtain high-quality programs. Before selecting software or other electronic program, decide what you want it to do and how you might use it. Decide what educational objective you wish to fulfill. In addition to being appealing and motivational, the program should fulfill an educational purpose.

It is important that technology, no matter how promising or exciting or complex, be seen as a tool and not the focus of instruction. A long-term study of the effect of technology on students found that "students worked best when technology was not the topic itself but was integrated into the entire curriculum" (Bitter, 1999, p. 109).

Teacher Tools

Technology has also created a variety of valuable tools for the teacher. For instance, using *Wynn Reader* (Freedom Scientific), the teacher can make adaptations in electronic text. Text can be added, deleted, or simplified. Study aids, such as voice notes, and a built-in dictionary are available. *Worksheet Magic Plus* (Gamco Educational Software) makes it possible to create fifteen different kinds of practice activities, including crossword puzzles and word searches. Crossword puzzles can also be created at the Read•Write•Think site (http://www.readwritethink.org/materials/crossword). EdHelper.com (http://www.edhelper.com), which charges a yearly subscription fee, also offers a variety of tools for creating puzzles, along with lesson plans and other teaching resources. *Inspiration* (Inspiration Software) can be used by both students and teachers to make graphic organizers.

TeacherTube (http://www.teachertube.com) is an online community for sharing instructional videos. Videos display teaching methods and techniques or introduce concepts, skills, and practice activities to students. Topics range from methods for teaching phonics to demonstrations of the use of the Smart Board in a literacy class.

IRA POSITION STATEMENT ON KEY ISSUE

Integrating Literacy and Technology in the Curriculum

"The Internet and other forms of information and communication technology (ICT) such as word processors, Web editors, presentation software, and e-mail are regularly redefining the nature of literacy. To become fully literate in today's world, students must become proficient in the new literacies of ICT. Therefore, literacy educators have a responsibility to effectively integrate these technologies into the literacy curriculum in order to prepare students for the literacy future they deserve" (International Reading Association, 2001a, para. 1).

On its Ning site, the National Council of Teachers of English (www.ncte.org) hosts a number of discussion groups for middle school teachers. Other useful sites include:

- PBS Teachersource lists sites selected for curriculum content, arranged by subject areas; http://www.pbs.org/teachersource.
- Library of Congress has a special page for teachers that includes a listing of primary source materials and suggestions: http://www.loc.gov/teachers.

Universal Design For Learning and Adaptive Technology

Universal design for learning (UDL) fits in with the concept of universal access. UDL calls for flexibility in methods of presentation, flexibility in response options, and flexible options for engagement (CAST, 2009). UDL also uses technology to help meet the needs of all learners. For students who have serious reading problems, text-to-speech systems such as the *Kurzweil 3000* (http://kurzweiledu.com), *Read and Write Gold* (http://readwritegold.com), and *Wynn Wizard* (http://www.freedomscientific.com) are available. The text that the student wishes to read is scanned into the program. Once scanned in, it is read aloud by the computer's voice synthesizer at the same time that it is highlighted on the screen so that the student can follow along. In addition, the systems have a number of useful study tools, including an audible spellchecker, note-taking feature, and access to a dictionary and other reference materials.

The National Library Service (NLS) for the Blind and Physically Handicapped offers a variety of books and periodicals in Braille and recorded form for persons who are blind or who have an organically based reading disability. Also available are playback devices that play at variable speeds so the listener can pick a reading rate that is comfortable.

e-Readers

E-book readers have the potential to change the way students read. When given e-readers, students adjusted the font size, listened to parts of the story by activating the text-to-speech feature, highlighted key passages or vocabulary, used the built-in dictionary, searched for keywords, and added notes (Larson, 2010). The students were more active and more highly engaged when using e-readers.

Literacy in Today's and Tomorrow's Worlds

Increasingly, literacy includes the ability to use computers and other technology. Students need to know how to use resources such as the Internet and how to construct multimedia reports. They also need to understand how to get the most out of interactive encyclopedias and other sophisticated sources of information. Computer literacy still requires traditional skills: the ability to read with understanding, to write coherently, and to think clearly. However, today's technology also requires more sophisticated literacy skills. Internet searches allow students to obtain a greater amount of information on a particular topic, but only some of that information might be relevant and important. Thus, a key reading skill for the era of the information superhighway is the ability to decide quickly and efficiently whether an online document merits reading. With so much more information available, it is essential that students not waste time reading texts that are not pertinent or worthwhile. Having more information to work with also means that students must be better at organizing it, evaluating it, drawing conclusions, and conveying its essence to others. They also need cognitive flexibility to make use of the growing amounts of information in solving the increasingly complex problems sure to arise in the coming years.

 FYI

The December/January 2005 issue of *The Reading Teacher* (pp. 388–393) contains rubrics for assessing your performance on running records, guided reading, and graphic organizers. ∎

Assessing and Improving the Program

Current concern with preparing all students for college and career and RTI have turned the spotlight on the literacy gap that exists in many schools and highlighted the need to improve the effectiveness of instruction for struggling readers and writers. In today's data-driven schools, a broad range of sources of information can be used to assess and improve instruction. Reading data might include scores on state tests and criterion-referenced tests, informal classroom assessments, progress monitoring and benchmark assessments, student-work samples, and portfolios (Mokhtari, Rosemary, & Edwards, 2007). Instructional data might include video of lessons, lesson plans, observational notes, sample assignments, results from observation protocols such as the Early Language and Literacy Classroom Observation toolkit (ELLCO) (Smith & Dickinson, 2004) or the Classroom Literacy Environmental Profile (CLEP) (Wolfersberger, Reutzel, Sudweeks, & Fawson, 2004), and observations conducted by administrators and literacy coaches.

In addition to looking at the results of instruction, schools can look at the key activities and materials being used and the use of time. A careful analysis can identify activities and materials that are effective, those that need improving, and those that are ineffective. As an informed neutral observer, a perceptive coach or experienced teacher can find ways to improve instruction in even the best of classrooms. Suggestions are most palatable when they are made in terms of improving students' learning rather than in terms of improving or changing the teacher.

Professional Development

In a recent study of what makes a difference in literacy growth, the researchers concluded that "what matters for student achievement are approaches that fundamentally change what teachers and students do every day" (Slavin, Cheung, Groff, & Lake, 2008, p. 309). In other words, approaches that reflect effective professional development work best. To keep up with the latest developments in the fields of reading and writing instruction, it is necessary to be professionally active—to join professional organizations, attend meetings, take part in staff-development activities, and read in the field. The International Reading Association (100 Barksdale Road, Newark, DE 19714) and the National Council of Teachers of English (1111 Kenyon Road, Urbana, IL 61801) are devoted to professional improvement in reading and the language arts. The IRA publishes the widely read periodicals *The Reading Teacher* and *Journal of Adolescent and Adult Literacy*. The NCTE publishes *Language Arts*. Both organizations have local and state chapters and sponsor regional and national conferences.

Study Groups and Grade-Level Meetings

In many schools, teachers meet in study groups or grade-level or department meetings to discuss the latest children's books, techniques for teaching comprehension, or ways to help struggling learners. A study group provides a forum in which teachers can share ideas and work together on a common problem (Gunning, 2006). Participants can develop collaborative units, share lesson plans, develop materials, adapt programs, view videos, read and discuss a professional text, or investigate areas of concern (Murphy, 1992). As a result of their study, the group members may decide to make some changes in the literacy program. As members implement any change, they can advise and support each other.

As a follow-up to a grade-level or department meeting, teachers might observe each other trying out a new technique. Or a teacher might want some feedback from a colleague on a procedure or technique that isn't working well. Peer observations are less threatening than official evaluation and can be very helpful. Also, if the school has a literacy coach, he or she can model new techniques or procedures. The coach can also observe lessons in the classroom and provide expert advice or work with a teacher on an area of concern. Literacy coaches are a valuable resource that is too often underused.

FIGURE 13.1   Checklist for an Effective Literacy Program

Directions: To read each question, insert the phrase "Do I" before it (e.g., "Do I read aloud regularly?"). Then circle the appropriate response. If you are not in the teaching situation described, respond as though you were. When finished, analyze your answers. What are your strengths? What are some areas in which you might need improvement?

Teaching Practices: General	Never	Seldom	Often	Usually
Read aloud regularly	1	2	3	4
Directly teach key strategies and skills	1	2	3	4
Model reading and writing processes	1	2	3	4
Use think-alouds to make reading and writing processes explicit	1	2	3	4
Provide adequate guided practice	1	2	3	4
Provide opportunities for application	1	2	3	4
Integrate reading, writing, listening, and speaking	1	2	3	4

Teaching Practices: Comprehension/Study Skills				
Build background and activate prior knowledge	1	2	3	4
Set or encourage the setting of purposes	1	2	3	4
Present a variety of comprehension strategies	1	2	3	4
Teach monitoring/strategic reading	1	2	3	4
Provide adequate practice/application	1	2	3	4

Teaching Practices: Word Recognition				
Provide systematic instruction in major skill areas: phonics, context clues, syllabication, morphemic analysis, dictionary skills	1	2	3	4
Provide systematic instruction in use of major cueing systems: phonological, syntactic, semantic	1	2	3	4
Encourage the use of a variety of decoding strategies	1	2	3	4
Provide opportunities for students to read widely so skills become automatic	1	2	3	4

Teaching Practices: Content Area				
Use high-quality content-area texts	1	2	3	4
Supplement content-area texts with informational books and nonprint materials	1	2	3	4
Provide texts on appropriate levels of difficulty or make adjustments	1	2	3	4
Present skills and strategies necessary to learn from informational texts	1	2	3	4

Teaching Practices: Writing				
Encourage self-selection of topics	1	2	3	4
Use a process approach	1	2	3	4
Provide guided instruction in writing strategies	1	2	3	4
Provide frequent opportunities for writing	1	2	3	4
Provide opportunities to compose in a variety of forms	1	2	3	4

(continued)

FIGURE 13.1 Checklist for an Effective Literacy Program *(Continued)*

Materials	Never	Seldom	Often	Usually
Use a variety of print materials	1	2	3	4
Children's books, fiction and nonfiction	1	2	3	4
Supplementary materials	1	2	3	4
Literature anthology	1	2	3	4
Periodicals	1	2	3	4
Real-world materials	1	2	3	4
Pamphlets, brochures	1	2	3	4
Pupil-written works	1	2	3	4
Use a variety of nonprint materials	1	2	3	4
e-reader	1	2	3	4
VCR	1	2	3	4
Videodiscs/DVDs	1	2	3	4
Applications for digital devices	1	2	3	4
Computer software	1	2	3	4
Web sites	1	2	3	4
Web 2.0 applications	1	2	3	4
Adapt materials to students' needs	1	2	3	4
Provide materials for slow as well as bright students	1	2	3	4
Evaluate materials before using them	1	2	3	4
Evaluation				
Set goals and objectives (standards) for the program	1	2	3	4
Align standards (objectives) and assessment	1	2	3	4
Screen students and monitor progress	1	2	3	4
Collect formal and informal data to use as a basis for evaluating the program	1	2	3	4
Encourage self-assessment	1	2	3	4
Assess data-collection instruments in terms of validity and reliability	1	2	3	4
Assemble a portfolio for each student	1	2	3	4
Share assessment data with students and parents	1	2	3	4
Use assessment data to improve instruction for each student and to improve the program	1	2	3	4
Organization/Management				
Provide for individual differences	1	2	3	4
Use a variety of grouping strategies	1	2	3	4
Use time and materials efficiently	1	2	3	4

Other Sources of Professional Development

As was mentioned earlier, the Web site Read•Write•Think offers a wide range of high-quality lesson plans. These can provide models for new techniques to try out in your classroom. Video clips accompany some of the lesson plans. In addition, a variety of video clips showing highly effective lessons are cited throughout this text. When it isn't possible to observe excellent teachers in real time, viewing video clips of such instructors is an appropriate alternative.

Another alternative is to engage in self-study. Sometimes it isn't possible to be part of a professional development group. An organization known as iObservation offers a program known as *iGrow* (http://www.igrow.net). For a relatively nominal fee, *iGrow* offers access to a professional library and provides self-assessment tools, guidelines for reflective instruction in a variety of key areas, and videos with expert commentary that demonstrate key concepts and teaching techniques. Teachers can subscribe individually or in pairs or as a group.

Reflection and Setting Professional Goals

Marzano and Toth (2011) recommend evaluative reflections in which teachers identify specific areas of strength and weaknesses, analyzing the effectiveness of units and lessons, and their effectiveness with groups of students. Perhaps, the average students are doing well, but the gifted aren't being challenged and the underachieving students aren't making adequate progress.

As with any other vital endeavor, teachers should set both long-term goals and short-term professional objectives, asking such questions as the following:

- Where do I want to be professionally five years from now?
- What steps do I have to take to get there?
- What are my strengths and weaknesses as a teacher of reading and writing?
- How can I build on my strengths and remediate my weaknesses?
- What new professional techniques, skills, or areas of knowledge would I most like to learn?

The answers should result in a plan of professional development. Just as when working with students, you should monitor your progress and make adjustments as necessary.

Filling out the checklist in Figure 13.1 will help you create a profile of your strengths and weaknesses as a reading and writing teacher. The checklist covers the entire literacy program and incorporates the major principles covered in this text. As such, it provides a review of the book as well as a means of self-assessment.

Summary

The construction of a literacy program starts with consideration of the needs and characteristics of students, the parents' wishes, and the nature of the community. General goals and specific objectives are based on these factors. Other elements in the construction of a literacy program include high-quality teaching, use of varied materials, continuous monitoring of students' progress, involvement of parents, efficient management of time and resources, provision for individual differences, and collaboration with other professionals.

Literacy includes the ability to use technology. Technology should be integrated into the literacy program. Effective use of the Internet requires instruction in efficient searching techniques and the ability to judge the relevance and reliability of information. Word-processing and Web 2.0 programs can be used to enable students to become producers of information.

Extending and Applying

1. Respond to the questions about professional goals and objectives on page 549. Complete the checklist in Figure 13.1. If you are not teaching now, base your responses on how you believe you will conduct yourself when you are a teacher. What strengths and weaknesses do your responses reveal? Based on your responses, set up a plan for professional development. Pick one or two areas on which to focus. Make a specific plan for each area. Explain how you will acquire and apply the desired knowledge and skills. If you are teaching, proceed to apply the knowledge and/or skills and reflect on your performance. Monitor your progress toward achieving your objectives. Obtain feedback from other professionals if possible and your students, and implement their suggestions. As you make changes, use observation and informal assessment, such as running records or comprehension quizzes, to note changes in students' performance. Reflect on your overall experience.

2. Set up goals and objectives for a reading/language arts program that you are now teaching or plan to teach. Discuss your goals and objectives with a colleague or classmate.

3. For a week, keep a record of the activities in your reading or language arts class. Which seem to be especially valuable? Which, if any, seem to have limited value or take up excessive time? Based on your observations, construct a plan for making better use of instructional time. If you are not teaching now, arrange to observe a teacher who has a reputation for having a well-managed classroom. Note the strategies that teacher uses to keep the class running smoothly and to make efficient use of time.

4. Assess parental involvement in your literacy program. Based on your assessment and the suggestions made in this chapter, make any needed changes.

 ## Professional Reflection

Do I ...

___ Have an understanding of the key elements of a literacy program?

___ Have an understanding of ways in which I might develop professionally?

Am I able to ...

___ Use a variety of learning materials and techniques?

___ Manage my literacy program so that all students are learning to the fullest?

___ Differentiate instruction so that all students' needs are being met?

___ Make effective use of technology?

___ Create a home-school connection?

___ Plan, implement, and monitor a program of professional development?

 ## Reflection Question

Based on the information presented in this chapter, how would you rate your literacy program? What are its strengths? What are some areas needing improvement?

What are some immediate steps that you might take to improve your program? What are some long-term steps you will consider?

Building Competencies

To build competencies, consult the following sources for more detailed information:

The site of the New Literacies Research Team at the University of Connecticut has a wealth of information about the New Literacies.

http://www.newliteracies.uconn.edu

Marzano, R. J. (2007). *The art and science of teaching*. Alexandria, VA: ASCD. Describes research-based principles for improving instruction.

MyEducationLab™

Go to the Topic "Organization and Management" in the MyEducationLab (www.myeducationlab.com) for your course, where you can:

- Find learning outcomes for "Organization and Management" along with the national standards that connect to these outcomes.
- Complete Assignments and Activities that can help you more deeply understand the chapter content.
- Apply and practice your understanding of the core teaching skills identified in the chapter with the Building Teaching Skills and Dispositions learning units.
- Examine challenging situations and cases presented in the IRIS Center Resources.
- Check your comprehension on the content covered in the chapter by going to the Study Plan in the Book

Resources for your text. Here you will be able to take a chapter quiz, receive feedback on your answers, and then access Review, Practice, and Enrichment activities to enhance your understanding of chapter content. (optional)

A+RISE A+RISE® Standards2Strategy™ is an innovative and interactive online resource that offers new teachers in grades K–12 just-in-time, research-based instructional strategies that meet the linguistic needs of ELLs as they learn content, differentiate instruction for all grades and abilities, and are aligned to Common Core Elementary Language Arts standards (for the literacy strategies) and to English language proficiency standards in WIDA, Texas, California, and Florida.

Appendix

Name _____   Total number correct _____

Date _____   Estimated level _____

PHONICS INVENTORY

1. hat	_____	18. truck	_____	35. store	_____
2. man	_____	19. must	_____	36. first	_____
3. sit	_____	20. black	_____	37. shirt	_____
4. big	_____	21. make	_____	38. smart	_____
5. can	_____	22. ride	_____	39. clear	_____
6. top	_____	23. place	_____	40. morning	_____
7. hen	_____	24. hope	_____	41. brook	_____
8. bug	_____	25. sheep	_____	42. blue	_____
9. hot	_____	26. use	_____	43. broom	_____
10. wet	_____	27. sail	_____	44. ground	_____
11. sand	_____	28. play	_____	45. yawn	_____
12. back	_____	29. coat	_____	46. growl	_____
13. pick	_____	30. night	_____	47. toy	_____
14. drip	_____	31. turn	_____	48. fault	_____
15. fill	_____	32. girl	_____	49. noise	_____
16. sock	_____	33. fair	_____	50. could	_____
17. step	_____	34. card	_____		

Directions: Explain to the student that he or she will be asked to read a series of words. Say that some of the words might be difficult but that the student is expected to try her or his hardest. Put the words on cards or have them read from the list. Mark each response with a check (✓) for correct or with a check with a tail for incorrect, and write incorrect responses in the blanks as time allows. If the student doesn't respond within 5 seconds, supply the word. Stop when the student gets five words in a row wrong. The student's level is the highest one at which she or he gets 8 out of 10 words correct. Students should be instructed at a level if they get more than 2 out of 10 wrong. Each level has ten items: 1–10, short-vowel patterns; 11–20, short vowels with clusters; 21–30, long vowels; 31–40, *r*-vowels; 41–50, other vowels.

Source: From T. Gunning (2008). *Teacher's Guide for Word Building* (2nd ed.). Honesdale, PA: Phoenix Learning Resources. Reprinted by permission of Galvin Publications.

Name _____   Total number correct _____

Date _____   Estimated level _____

GRADUATED SYLLABLE SURVEY

1. admit _____	18. charter _____	35. subdivided _____
2. minus _____	19. approach _____	36. vulture _____
3. dentist _____	20. lumber _____	37. invention _____
4. vacant _____	21. voyage _____	38. discussion _____
5. discuss _____	22. awkward _____	39. special _____
6. human _____	23. loosen _____	40. treasure _____
7. problem _____	24. avoid _____	41. famous _____
8. frozen _____	25. powder _____	42. enclosure _____
9. plastic _____	26. wooden _____	43. conclusion _____
10. music _____	27. pronounce _____	44. partial _____
11. remain _____	28. destroy _____	45. courageously _____
12. barber _____	29. continue _____	46. observation _____
13. indeed _____	30. applause _____	47. disadvantage _____
14. former _____	31. complicated _____	48. astonishment _____
15. increase _____	32. disadvantage _____	49. communicate _____
16. further _____	33. responsibility _____	50. circumstances _____
17. frighten _____	34. advisable _____	

Directions: Give one copy of the Graduated Syllable Survey to the student and keep one copy for marking. Mark each response with a check (✓) for correct or with a check with a tail for incorrect. (When you use a check with a tail rather than a minus sign, x, or zero, the student can't tell whether their answers are being marked correct or incorrect, so a source of stress is reduced.) If possible, write down each incorrect response for later analysis. Start with the first item and continue testing until the student gets five in a row wrong. A score of 5 or below indicates that the student probably needs instruction in basic decoding skills. Administer the Phonics Inventory. A score of 6 to 44 indicates a need for instruction in syllabic analysis. A score of 45 or higher indicates mastery of basic syllabic analysis. The test words assess key syllabic patterns. Words 1–10: odd numbers, short vowels; even numbers, long vowels and short vowels. 11–20: odd numbers, long-vowel digraphs and short vowels; even numbers, *r* vowels and short vowels. Words 21–30: other vowels: /aw/, /oy/, /ow/, short and long *oo*; 31–35: prefixes and suffixes. Words 36–45: *ture, tion, ion, cial, ous*. Words 46–50: words that have four or more syllables. Note areas where students had difficulty and plan instruction accordingly.

Source: Adapted from: Gunning, T. (2011). *Teacher's Guide for Word Building Book D* (2nd ed.). Unionville, CT: Galvin Publishing; Honesdale, PA: Phoenix Learning Resources.

References

Professional

Abedi, (2009). Validity of assessments for English language learning students in a national/ international context. *Estudios sobre Educación*, 16, 167–183.

Abedi, J., Leon, S., Kao, J., Bayley, R., Ewers, N., Herman, J., & Mundhenk, K. (2010). *Accessible reading assessments for students with disabilities: The role of cognitive, grammatical, lexical, and textual/ visual features* (CRESST Report 785). Los Angeles, CA: University of California, National Center for Research on Evaluation, Standards, and Student Testing (CRESST).

Achievement First (n. d.) *The essentials of effective teaching*. Available online at http://www.achievementfirst.org/resources/login/

ACT. (2006). *Reading between the lines: What the ACT reveals about college readiness in reading*. Iowa City, IA: Author. Available online at http://www.act.org/research/policymakers/pdf/reading_report.pdf.

Adams, M. J. (1990). *Beginning to read: Thinking and learning about print: A summary*. Cambridge, MA: MIT Press.

Adams, M. J. (1994). Modeling the connections between word recognition and reading. In R. B. Ruddell, M. R. Ruddell, & H. Singer (Eds.), *Theoretical models and processes of reading* (4th ed.) (pp. 838–863). Newark, DE: International Reading Association.

Adams, M. J., & Higgins, A. W. F. (1985). The growth of children's sight vocabulary: A quick test with educational and theoretical implications. *Reading Research Quarterly, 20*, 262–281.

Afflerbach, P. (1990). The influence of prior knowledge on expert readers' main idea construction strategies. *Reading Research Quarterly, 25*, 31–46.

Afflerbach, P., & Johnston, P. H. (1986). What do expert readers do when the main idea is not explicit? In J. F. Baumann (Ed.), *Teaching main idea comprehension* (pp. 49–72). Newark, DE: International Reading Association.

Afflerbach, P., Pearson, P., & Paris, S. G. (2008). Clarifying differences between reading skills and reading strategies. *The Reading Teacher, 61*, 364–373.

Ahlmann, M. E. (1992). Children as evaluators. In K. S. Goodman, L. B. Bird, & Y. M. Goodman (Eds.), *The whole language catalog: Supplement on authentic assessment* (p. 95). Santa Rosa, CA: American School Publishers.

Akroyd, S. (1995). Forming a parent reading-writing class: Connecting cultures, one pen at a time. *The Reading Teacher, 48*, 580–584.

Alber, S. R., & Foil, Carolyn R. (2003). Drama activities that promote and extend your students' vocabulary proficiency. *Intervention in School & Clinic, 39*(1), 22–29.

Allen, V. (1991). Teaching bilingual and ESL children. In J. Flood, J. M. Jensen, D. Lapp, & J. R. Squire (Eds.), *Handbook of research on teaching the English language arts* (pp. 356–364). New York: Macmillan.

Allen, V. (1994). Selecting materials for the reading instruction of ESL children. In K. Spangenberg-Urbschat & R. Pritchard (Eds.), *Kids come in all languages: Reading instruction for all ESL students* (pp. 108–131). Newark, DE: International Reading Association.

Allington, R. L. (2006). Fluency: Still waiting after all these years. In S. J. Samuels & A. E. Farstrup (Eds.), *What research has to say about fluency instruction* (pp. 94–105). Newark, DE: International Reading Association.

Allington, R. L., McGill-Franzen, A., Camilli, G., Williams, L., Graff, J., Zeig, J., Zmach, C., & Nowak, R. (2010). Addressing summer reading setback among economically disadvantaged elementary students. *Reading Psychology, 31*, 411–427.

Alvermann, D. E., & Phelps, S. F. (1994). *Content area reading and literacy: Succeeding in today's diverse classrooms*. Boston: Allyn & Bacon.

Alvermann, D. E., Young, J. P., Weaver, D., Hinchman, K. A., Moore, D. W., Phelps, S. F., Thrash, E. C., & Zaleewski, P. (1996). Middle and high school students' perceptions of how they experience text-based discussions: A multicase study. *Reading Research Quarterly, 31*, 244–267.

Anderson, G., Higgins, D., & Wurster, S. R. (1985). Differences in the free-reading books selected by high, average, and low achievers. *The Reading Teacher, 39*, 326–330.

Anderson, R. C. (1984). Role of the reader's schema in comprehension, learning, and memory. In R. C. Anderson, J. Osborn, & R. J. Tierney (Eds.), *Learning to read in American schools: Basal readers and content texts* (pp. 469–482). Hillsdale, NJ: Erlbaum.

Anderson, R. C. (2006, May). *Collaborative reasoning: An approach to literature discussion that promotes children's social and intellectual development*. Paper presented at the Reading Research Conference, Chicago.

Anderson, R. C., Hiebert, E. H., Scott, J. A., & Wilkinson, I. A. G. (1985). *Becoming a nation of readers: The report of the commission on reading*. Washington, DC: National Institute of Education.

Andes, L., & Claggett, E. (2011). Wiki writers: Students and teachers making connections across communities. *The Reading Teacher, 64*, 345–350.

Andre, M. E. D. A., & Anderson, T. H. (1978–1979). The development and evaluation of a self-questioning study technique. *Reading Research Quarterly, 14*, 605–623.

Anthony, A. (2008). Output strategies for English-language learners: Theory to practice. *The Reading Teacher, 61*, 472–482.

Anthony, H. M., Pearson, P. D., & Raphael, T. E. (1989). *Reading comprehension research: A selected review* (Technical Report No. 448).

Champaign: University of Illinois, Center for the Study of Reading.

Anthony, J. L., & Lonigan, C. J. (2004). The nature of phonological awareness: Converging evidence from four studies. *Journal of Educational Psychology, 96,* 43–55.

Appel, R., & Vermeer, A. (1996). Speeding up the acquisition of Dutch vocabulary by migrant children. Uitbreiding van de Nederlandse woordenschat van allochtone leerlingen in het basisonderwijs, *Pedagogische Studieen, 73,* 82–92.

Applegate, M. D., Quinn, K. B., & Applegate, A. J. (2002). Levels of thinking required by comprehension questions in informal reading inventories. *The Reading Teacher, 56,* 174–180.

Applegate, M. D., Quinn, K. B., & Applegate, A. J. (2006). Profiles in comprehension. *The Reading Teacher, 60,* 48–57.

Arciero, J. (1998, October). *Strategies for shared text reading responses.* Paper presented at Connecticut Reading Association meeting, Waterbury.

Armbruster, B. B., & Anderson, T. H. (1981). *Content area textbooks* (Technical Report No. 23). Champaign: University of Illinois, Center for the Study of Reading.

Asch, S., & Nerlove, H. (1967). The development of double function terms in children: An exploratory investigation. In J. P. Cecco (Ed.), *The psychology of thought, language, and instruction* (pp. 283–291). New York: Holt.

Ash, K. (2011). Classroom-tested tech tools used to boost literacy. *Education Week, 4*(2), 22–44. Available online at http://www.edweek.org/dd/articles/2011/02/09/02literacy.h04.html.

Ashcroft, M. H. (1994). *Human memory and cognition.* New York: HarperCollins.

Ashton-Warner, S. (1963). *Teacher.* New York: Simon & Schuster.

Athanases, S. Z. (2003). Thematic study of literature: Middle school teachers, professional development, and educational reform. *English Education, 35,* 107–121.

Athans, S. K., & Devine, D. A. (2008). *Quality comprehension: A strategic model of reading instruction using read-along guides, grades 3–6.* Newark, DE: International Reading Association.

Athans, S. K., Devine, D. A., & Parente, R. (2008). *Beyond guided reading: A practical model of instruction to enhance comprehension through the intermediate levels.* Paper presented at the International Reading Association Convention, Atlanta.

Atkinson, R. L., Atkinson, R. C., Smith, E. E., & Hilgard, E. R. (1987). *Introduction to psychology* (9th ed.). New York: Harcourt.

Atwell, N. (1987). *In the middle.* Portsmouth, NH: Boynton/Cook.

Atwell, N. (1990). *Coming to know: Writing to learn in the intermediate grades.* Portsmouth, NH: Heinemann.

Au, K. H. (1994). Portfolio assessment: Experiences at the Kamehameha elementary education program. In S. W. Valencia, E. H. Hiebert, & P. P. Afflerbach (Eds.), *Authentic reading assessment: Practices and possibilities* (pp. 103–126). Newark, DE: International Reading Association.

Aud, S., Hussar, W., Planty, M., Snyder, T., Bianco, K., Fox, M., Frohlich, L., Kemp, J., & Drake, L. (2010). *The condition of education 2010* (NCES 2010–028). Washington, DC: National Center for Education Statistics, Institute of Education Sciences, U.S. Department of Education.

August, D., Calderón, M., & Carlo, M. (2001). *Transfer of skills from Spanish to English: A study of young learners, report for practitioners, parents, and policy makers.* Office of English Language Acquisition, Language Enhancement, and Academic Achievement for Limited English Proficient Students (OELA), U.S. Department of Education. Available online at http://www.cal.org/pubs/articles/skillstransfer-nabe.html.

Australian Ministry of Education. (1990). *Literacy profiles handbook.* Victoria, Australia: Author.

Avalos, M. A., Plasencia, A., Chavez, C., & Rascón, J. (2007). Modified guided reading: Gateway to English as a second language and literacy learning. *The Reading Teacher, 61,* 318–329.

Bader, L. A., & Pearce, D. L. (2009). *Reading and language inventory* (6th ed.). Upper Saddle River, NJ: Prentice Hall.

Bagge-Rynerson, B. (1994). Learning good lessons: Young readers respond to books. In T. Newkirk (Ed.), *Workshop 5: The writing process revisited* (pp. 90–100). Portsmouth, NH: Heinemann.

Baker, B. (2010, September). *Examining the validity of oral reading fluency assessments with Dr. Sheila Valencia* [podcast]. Available online at http://www.voiceofliteracy.org/posts/40043.

Baker, L., & Brown, A. L. (1984). Metacognitive skills and reading. In P. D. Pearson, R. Barr, M. L. Kamil, & P. Mosenthal (Eds.), *Handbook of reading research* (pp. 353–394). New York: Longman.

Bandeira de Mello, V. (2011). Mapping state proficiency standards onto the NAEP scales: variation and change in state standards for reading and mathematics, 2005–2009 (NCES 2011–458). National Center for Education Statistics, Institute of Education Sciences, U.S. Department of Education, Washington, DC: Government Printing Office

Banks, J. A. (1994). *Introduction to multicultural education.* Boston: Allyn & Bacon.

Banks, J. A., & Banks, C. A. M. (1997). *Multicultural education* (2nd ed.). Boston: Allyn & Bacon.

Barnard, A. (2010, May 17). At Queens libraries, a passion for Japanese comics endures. *The New York Times,* A21.

Barr, C, & Gillespie, J. T. (2010). *Best books for children preschool through grade 6* (9th ed.). Libraries Unlimited.

Barr, R. (1974). Instructional pace differences and their effect on reading acquisition. *Reading Research Quarterly, 9,* 526–554.

Barr, R., & Dreeben, R. (1991). Grouping students for reading instruction. In R. Barr, M. L. Kamil, P. Mosenthal, & P. D. Pearson (Eds.), *Handbook of reading research* (Vol. II, pp. 885–910). New York: Longman.

Barton, J., & Sawyer, D. M. (2003). Our students are ready for this: Comprehension instruction in the elementary school. *The Reading Teacher, 57,* 322–333.

Barton, P. E., & Cooley, R. J. (2008). *Windows on achievement and inequality.* Princeton, NJ: Educational Testing Service.

Bauer, G. F. (1995). *The poetry break.* New York: H.W. Wilson.

Bauman, G. A. (1990, March). *Writing tool selection and young children's writing.* Paper presented at the spring meeting of the National Conference of Teachers of English, Colorado Springs, CO.

Baumann, J. F. (1986). The direct instruction of main idea comprehension ability. In J. F. Baumann (Ed.), *Teaching main idea comprehension* (pp. 133–178). Newark, DE: International Reading Association.

Baumann, J. F., & Duffy, A. M. (1997). *Engaged reading for pleasure and learning: A report from the National Reading Research Center.* Athens, GA: National Reading Research Center.

Baumann, J. F., & Ivey, G. (1997). Delicate balances: Striving for curricular and instructional equilibrium in a second-grade, literature/strategy-based classroom. *Reading Research Quarterly, 32,* 244–275.

Baumann, J. F., Kame'enui, E. J., & Ash, G. (2003). Research on vocabulary instruction: Voltaire redux. In J. Flood, D. Lapp, J. Jensen, & J. R. Squire (Eds.), *Handbook of research on teaching the English language arts* (2nd ed.) (pp. 752–785). New York: Macmillan.

Baumann, J. F., & Serra, J. K. (1984). The frequency and placement of main ideas in children's social studies textbooks: A modified replication of Braddock's research on topic sentences. *Journal of Reading Behavior, 16,* 27–40.

Bear, D. R. (1995). *Word study: A developmental perspective based on spelling stages.* Paper presented at the annual meeting of the International Reading Association, Anaheim, CA.

Bear, D. R., Invernizzi, M., Templeton, S., & Johnston, F. (2008). *Words their way: Word study for phonics, vocabulary, and spelling instruction* (4th ed.). Upper Saddle River, NJ: Prentice Hall.

Bear, D. R., & Templeton, S. (1998). Explorations in developmental spelling: Foundations for learning and teaching phonics, spelling, and vocabulary. *The Reading Teacher, 52,* 222–242.

Beck, I. L., et al. (2008). *Storytown series.* Orlando, FL: Harcourt.

Beck, I. L., & Juel, C. (1995). The role of decoding in learning to read. *American Educator, 9*(2), 8, 21–25, 39–42.

Beck, I. L., & McKeown, M. G. (1983). Learning words well—a program to enhance vocabulary and comprehension. *The Reading Teacher, 36,* 622–625.

Beck, I. L., & McKeown, M. G. (2001). Text talk: Capturing the benefits of read-aloud experiences for young children. *The Reading Teacher, 55,* 10–20.

Beck, I. L., & McKeown, M. G. (2006). *The three Cs of comprehension instruction.* Comprehension Forum. Pacific Resources for Education and Learning.

Beck, I. L., McKeown, M. G., Hamilton, R. L., & Kucan, L. (1997). *Questioning the author: An approach for enhancing student engagement with text.* Newark, DE: International Reading Association.

Beck, I. L., McKeown, M. G., & Kucan, L. (2002). *Bringing words to life: Robust vocabulary instruction.* New York: Guilford.

Beck, I. L., McKeown, M. G., & Kucan, L. (2008). *Creating robust vocabulary: Frequently asked questions and extended examples.* New York: Guilford.

Beck, I. L., McKeown, M. G., & Omanson, R. C. (1987). The effects and uses of diverse vocabulary instructional techniques. In M. G. McKeown & M. E. Curtis (Eds.), *The nature of vocabulary acquisition* (pp. 147–163). Hillsdale, NJ: Erlbaum.

Beck, I. L., Omanson, R. C., & McKeown, M. G. (1982). An instructional redesign of reading lessons: Effects on comprehension. *Reading Research Quarterly, 17,* 462–481.

Beers, K. (2003). *When kids can't read, what teachers can do: A guide for teachers 6–12.* Portsmouth, NH: Heinemann.

Behavioral Research and Teaching. (2005). *Oral reading fluency: 90 years of assessment* (Technical Report No. 33). Eugene: University of Oregon.

Benson, V., & Cummins, C. (2000). *The power of retelling: Developmental steps for building comprehension.* Bothell, WA: Wright Group/McGraw-Hill.

Benson-Castagna, V. (2005). *Reciprocal teaching, a workshop.* Houston, TX: Author.

Bereiter, C., & Scardamalia, M. (1982). From conversation to composition: The role of instruction in a developmental process. In R. Glass (Ed.), *Advances in instructional psychology* (Vol. 2, pp. 1–64). Hillsdale, NJ: Erlbaum.

Berkin, C. (2011). *Scott, Foresman social studies: The United States.* Glenview, IL: Scott Foresman.

Berliner, D. C. (1984). The half-full glass: A review of research on teaching. In P. Hosford (Ed.), *Using what we know about teaching.* Alexandria, VA: Association for Supervision and Curriculum Development.

Berne, J. I., & Clark, K. F. (2006, May). *Strategic literary discussion: Teachers and students test new ground for comprehension strategy use.* Paper presented at the International Reading Association convention, Chicago.

Bertrand, J. E. (2000). "I hate words": Bridging the gap with learning disabled fourth graders. In C. F. Stice & J. E. Bertrand (Eds.), *Teaching at-risk students in the K–4 classroom: Language, literacy, learning* (pp. 79–94). Norwood, MA: Christopher-Gordon.

Beyer, B. (2001). What research says about teaching thinking skills. In A. L. Costa (Ed.), *Developing minds: A resource book for teaching thinking* (3rd ed.) (pp. 275–282). Alexandria, VA: Association for Supervision and Curriculum Development.

Bielenberg, B., & Fillmore, L. W. (2004). The English they need for the test. *Educational Leadership, 62*(4), 45–49.

Biemiller, A. (1994). Some observations on acquiring and using reading skill in elementary schools. In C. K. Kinzer & D. J. Leu (Eds.), *Multidimensional aspects of literacy research, theory, and practice* (43rd yearbook of the National Reading Conference) (pp. 209–216). Chicago: National Reading Conference.

Biemiller, A. (2005). Size and sequence in vocabulary development: Implications for choosing words for primary vocabulary instruction. In E. Hiebert & M. Kamil (Eds.), *Teaching and learning vocabulary: Bringing research to practice* (pp. 223–242). Mahwah, NJ: Erlbaum.

Birnbaum, R. K. (1999). *NewPhonics.* Pittsford, NY: NewPhonics Literacy System.

Bissex, G. L. (1980). *GNYS AT WRK.* Cambridge, MA: Harvard University Press.

Bitter, G. G. (1999). *Using technology in the classroom* (4th ed.). Boston: Allyn & Bacon.

Bjorklund, B., Handler, N., Mitten, J., & Stockwell, G. (1998, October). *Literature circles: A tool for developing students as critical readers, writers, and thinkers.* Paper presented at the 47th annual conference of the Connecticut Reading Association, Waterbury.

Blachman, B. A., Ball, E. W., Black, R., & Tangel, D. M. (2000). *Road to the code.* Baltimore: Brookes.

Blachman, B. A., Tangel, D. M., Ball, E., Black, R., & McGraw, C. K. (1994). Kindergarten teachers develop phonological awareness and word recognition skills: A two-year intervention with lowincome, innercity children. *Reading and Writing: An Interdisciplinary Journal, 11,* 239–273.

Blachowicz, C. L. Z. (1977). Cloze activities for primary readers. *The Reading Teacher, 31,* 300–302.

Blachowicz, C. L. Z., & Fisher, P. (2000). Vocabulary instruction. In M. L. Kamil, P. B. Mosenthal, P. D. Pearson, & R. Barr (Eds.), *Handbook of reading research* (Vol. III, pp. 503–523). Mahwah, NJ: Erlbaum.

Blachowicz, C. L. Z., & Obrochta, C. (2005). Vocabulary visits: Virtual field trips for content vocabulary development. *The Reading Teacher, 59,* 262–268.

Black, P., & Wiliam, D. (1998). Inside the black box: Raising standards through classroom assessment. *Phi Delta Kappan, 80*(2), 139–148. Available online at http://www.pdkintl.org/kappan/kbla9810.htm.

Blamey, K. L., & Beauchat, K. A. (2011). Word walk: Vocabulary instruction for young children. *The Reading Teacher, 65,* 71–75.

Block, C. C., & Israel, S. E. (2004). The ABCs of performing highly effective think-alouds. *The Reading Teacher, 58,* 154–167.

Bloom, B. (Ed.). (1957). *Taxonomy of educational objectives.* New York: McKay.

Bloom, B. (1976). *Human characteristics and school learning.* New York: McGraw-Hill.

Blum, I. H., Koskinen, P. S., Tennant, S., Parker, E. M., Straub, M., & Curry, C. (1995). Using audiotaped books to extend classroom literacy instruction into the homes of second-language learners. *Journal of Reading Behavior, 27,* 535–564.

Bodrova, E., & Leong, D. J. (2007). *Tools of the mind, The Vygotskian approach to early childhood education* (2nd ed.). Upper Saddle River, NJ: Merrill.

Boehm, A. E. (1971). *Boehm test of basic concepts manual.* New York: Psychological Corporation.

Boling, E., Castek, J., Zawilinski, L., Barton, K., & Nierlich, T. (2008). Collaborative literacy: Blogs and internet projects. *The Reading Teacher, 61,* 504–506.

Bond, G. L., & Dykstra, R. (1967). The cooperative research program in first-grade reading instruction. *Reading Research Quarterly, 2,* 1–142.

Bond, G. L., & Dykstra, R. (1997). The cooperative research program in first-grade reading instruction. *Reading Research Quarterly, 32,* 348–427.

Boote, C. (2006, May). *Reading comprehension requires word meaning knowledge: A classroom model for teaching word meanings in primary grades.* Paper presented at the Reading Research Conference, Chicago.

Boothroyd, K. (2001, December). *Being literate in urban third-grade classrooms.* Paper presented at the annual meeting of the National Reading Conference, San Antonio, TX.

Borders, S., & Naylor, A. P. (1993). *Children talking about books*. Phoenix, AZ: Oryx.

Boulware-Gooden, R., Carreker, S., Thornhill, A., & Joshi, R. (2007). Instruction of metacognitive strategies enhances reading comprehension and vocabulary achievement of third-grade students. *The Reading Teacher, 61*, 70–77.

Boyd-Batstone, P. (2004). Focused anecdotal records assessment: A tool for standards-based, authentic assessment. *The Reading Teacher, 58*, 230–239.

Boyle, C. (1996). *Efficacy of peer evaluation and effects of peer evaluation on persuasive writing*. Unpublished master's thesis, San Diego State University, San Diego, CA.

Boyles, N. (2002). *Teaching written response to text*. Gainesville, FL: Maupin House.

Boyles, N. (2004). *Constructing meaning*. Gainesville, FL: Maupin House.

Bradley, B. A., & Jones, J. (2007). Sharing alphabet books in early childhood classrooms . *The Reading Teacher, 60*, 452–463.

Bradshaw, A. C., Bishop, J. L., Gens, L. S., Miller, S. L., & Rogers, M. A. (2002). The relationship of the World Wide Web to thinking skills. *Educational Media International, 39* (3 & 4), 275–284.

Bransford, J. D. (1994). Schema activation and schema acquisition: Comments on Richard C. Anderson's remarks. In R. B. Ruddell, M. R. Ruddell, & H. Singer (Eds.), *Theoretical models and processes of reading* (4th ed.) (pp. 483–495). Newark, DE: International Reading Association.

Bransford, J. D., Stein, B. S., Shelton, T. S., & Owings, R. A. (1981). Cognition and adaptation: The importance of learning to learn. In J. Harvey (Ed.), *Cognition, social behavior, and the environment*. Hillsdale, NJ: Erlbaum.

Brassell, D. (2006). Inspiring young scientists with great books. *The Reading Teacher, 60*, 336–342.

Brewster, P. G. (Ed.). (1952). *Children's games and rhymes*. Durham, NC: Duke University Press.

Bridge, C. A., Winograd, P. N., & Haley, D. (1983). Using predictable materials vs. preprimers to teach beginning sight words. *The Reading Teacher, 36*, 884–891.

Bromley, K. D. (1998). *Language arts: Exploring connections* (3rd ed.). Boston: Allyn & Bacon.

Brophy, J. E., & Good, T. L. (1970). Teachers' communication of differential expectations for children's classroom performance: Some behavioral data. *Journal of Educational Psychology, 61*, 365–375.

Brown, A. L. (1985). *Reciprocal teaching of comprehension strategies: A natural history of one program for enhancing learning* (Technical Report No. 334). Champaign: University of Illinois, Center for the Study of Reading.

Brown, A. L., & Day, J. D. (1983). Macrorules for summarizing text: The development of expertise. *Journal of Verbal Learning and Verbal Behavior, 22*(1), 1–14.

Brown, C. S., & Lytle, S. L. (1988). Merging assessment and instruction: Protocols in the classroom. In S. M. Glazer, L. W. Searfoss, & L. M. Gentile (Eds.), *Reexamining reading diagnosis: New trends and procedures* (pp. 94–102). Newark, DE: International Reading Association.

Brown, J. J. (1988). *High impact teaching: Strategies for educating minority youth*. Lanham, MD: University Press of America.

Brown, K. J. (2003). What do I say when they get stuck on a word? Aligning teachers' prompts with students' development. *The Reading Teacher, 56*, 720–733.

Bruce, B. (1980). Plans and social actions. In R. J. Spiro, B. C. Bruce, & W. F. Brewer (Eds.), *Theoretical issues in reading comprehension* (pp. 367–384). Hillsdale, NJ: Erlbaum.

Bruck, M. (1992). Persistence of dyslexics' phonological awareness deficits. *Developmental Psychology, 28*, 874–886.

Bruner, J. (1975). The ontogenesis of speech acts. *Journal of Child Languages, 2*, 1–40.

Bruner, J. (1986). *Actual minds, possible worlds*. Cambridge, MA: Harvard University Press.

Buettner, E.G. (2002). Sentence by sentence self-monitoring. *The Reading Teacher, 56*, 34–44.

Bunce, B. H. (1995). *Building a language-focused curriculum for the preschool classroom. Volume II: A planning guide*. Baltimore: Brookes.

Burns, J. M., & Richgels, D. S. (1989). An investigation of task requirements associated with the invented spelling of 4-year-olds with above average intelligence. *Journal of Reading Behavior, 21*, 1–14.

Buros Institute. (2007). *The seventeenth mental measurements handbook*. R. A. Spies, B. S. Plake, & K. F. Geisinger (Eds.). Lincoln: University of Nebraska.

Bus, A. G., & van IJzendoorn, M. H. (1999). Phonological awareness and early reading: A meta-analysis of experiential training studies. *Journal of Educational Psychology, 91*, 403–414.

Bush, C., & Huebner, M. (1979). *Strategies for reading in the elementary school* (2nd ed.). New York: Macmillan.

Button, K., Johnson, M. J., & Ferguson, P. (1996). Interactive writing in a primary classroom. *The Reading Teacher, 49*, 446–454.

Byrne, B. (1992). Studies in the acquisition procedure for reading: Rationale, hypotheses, and data. In P. B. Gough, L. C. Ehri, & R. Treiman (Eds.), *Reading acquisition* (pp. 1–35). Hillsdale, NJ: Erlbaum.

Calder, L., & Carlson, S. (2002). *Using "think alouds" to evaluate deep understanding*. Policy Center on the First Year of College. Available online at http://www.brevard.edu/fyc/listserv/remarks/calderandcarlson.htm.

Caldwell, J. H., Huitt, W. G., & Graeber, A. O. (1982). Time spent in learning: Implications from research. *Elementary School Journal, 82*, 471–480.

Caldwell, J., & Lauren, L. (2010) . Thinking aloud in expository text: Processes and outcomes. *Journal of Literacy Research, 42*, 308–340.

California Department of Education. (2007). *Reading/language arts framework for California public schools*. Sacramento: Author. Available online at http://www.cde.ca.gov/ci/cr/cf/documents/rlafw.pdf.

Calkins, L. (1986). *The art of teaching writing*. Portsmouth, NH: Heinemann.

Calkins, L. (1994). *The art of teaching writing* (new ed.). Portsmouth, NH: Heinemann.

Calkins, L. (2001). *The art of teaching reading*. Portsmouth, NH: Heinemann.

Calkins, L. (2003). *Nuts and bolts of teaching writing*. Portsmouth, NH: Heinemann.

Calkins, L. (2006). *A guide to the writing workshop*. Portsmouth, NH: Heinemann.

Calkins, L., Hartman, A., & White, Z. (2003). *Units of study for primary writing: A yearlong curriculum (K–2)*. Portsmouth, NH: Heinemann.

Calkins, L., & Harwayne, S. (1991). *Living between the lines*. Portsmouth, NH: Heinemann.

Calkins, L., Martinelli, M., Kesler, T., Gillette, C., McEvoy, M., Chiarella, M., & Cruz, C. (2006). *Units of study for teaching writing, grades 3–5*. Portsmouth, NH: Heinemann.

Calkins, L., & Mermelstein, L. (2003). *Nonfiction writing: Procedures and reports. Units of study for primary writing: A yearlong program*. Portsmouth, NH: Heinemann.

Calkins, L., Montgomery, K., & Santman, D. (1998). *A teacher's guide to standardized reading tests*. Portsmouth, NH: Heinemann.

Campbell, R. (1998). Looking at literacy learning in preschool settings. In R. Campbell (Ed.), *Facilitating preschool literacy* (pp. 70–83). Newark, DE: International Reading Association.

Campbell, R. (2001). *Read-alouds with young children*. Newark, DE: International Reading Association.

Carbo, M. (1997). *What every principal should know about teaching reading: How to raise test scores and nurture a love of reading*. Syosset, NY: National Reading Styles Institute.

Carbo, M., Dunn, R., & Dunn, K. (1986). *Teaching students to read through their individual learning styles.* Boston: Allyn & Bacon.

Carlisle, J. F., & Stone, C. (2005). Exploring the role of morphemes in word reading. *Reading Research Quarterly, 40,* 428–449.

Carlson, N. R., & Buskist, W. (1997). *Psychology: The science of behavior* (5th ed.). Boston: Allyn & Bacon.

Carnine, D., Kame'enui, E. J., & Coyle, G. (1984). Utilization of contextual information in determining the meaning of unfamiliar words. *Reading Research Quarterly, 19,* 188–204.

Carnine, D., Silbert, J., & Kame'enui, E. J. (1990). *Direct instruction in reading.* Columbus, OH: Merrill.

Carr, E., Dewitz, P., & Patberg, J. P. (1989). Using cloze for inference training with expository text. *The Reading Teacher, 42,* 380–385.

Carr, K. S. (1983). The importance of inference skills in the primary grades. *The Reading Teacher, 36,* 518–522.

Carrier, K. A., & Tatum, A. W. (2006). Creating sentence walls to help English-language learners develop content literacy. *The Reading Teacher, 60,* 285–288.

Cartwright, C. P., Cartwright, C. A., & Ward, M. E. (1989). *Educating special learners.* Belmont, CA: Wadsworth.

Caruso, C. (1997). Before you cite a site. *Educational Leadership, 55*(3), 24–25.

Carver, R. (1990). *Reading rate: A review of research and theory.* San Diego, CA: Academic.

Cassidy, J., Valadez, J. M., Garrett, S. D., & Barrera IV, E. S. (2010). Commentary: Adolescent and adult literacy: What's hot, what's not. *Journal of Adolescent & Adult Literacy, 53,* 448–456.

CAST. (2009). *Research & development in universal design for learning.* Wakefield, MA: Author. Available online at http://cast.org/research/index.html.

Castle, M. (1994). Helping children choose books. In E. H. Cramer & M. Castle (Eds.), *Fostering the love of reading: The affective domain in reading education* (pp. 145–168). Newark, DE: International Reading Association.

Cattagni, A., & Westnat, E. F. (2001). *Internet access in U.S. public schools and classrooms: 1994–2000.* Washington, DC: U.S. Department of Education, National Center for Educational Statistics. Available online at http://nces.ed.gov/pubs2001/2001071.pdf.

Center for the Study of Reading. (1990). *Suggestions for the classroom: Teachers and independent reading.* Urbana: University of Illinois Press.

Center on Education Policy. (2006). *From the capital to the classroom: Year 4 of the No Child Left Behind Act.* Available online at http://www.cepdc.org/nclb/Year4/Press.

Centers for Disease Control and Prevention. (2011). *Intellectual disability.* Available online at http://www.cdc.gov/ncbddd/dd/ddmr.htm.

Chadwell, G. B. (2002). *Developing an effective writing program for the elementary grades.* West Newbury, MA: Collins Education Associates.

Chadwell, G. B. (2009). *Twelve assignments every middle school student should write.* Newbury, MA: Collins Education Associates.

Chall, J. S. (1967). *Learning to read: The great debate.* New York: McGraw-Hill.

Chall, J. S. (1983a). *Learning to read: The great debate* (rev. ed.). New York: McGraw-Hill.

Chall, J. S. (1983b). *Stages of reading development.* New York: McGraw-Hill.

Chall, J. S. (1996). *Stages of reading development* (2nd ed.). Fort Worth, TX: Harcourt.

Chall, J. S., Bissex, G. L., Conard, S. S., & Harris-Sharples, S. H. (1996). *Qualitative assessment of text difficulty: A practical guide for teachers and writers.* Cambridge, MA: Brookline.

Chall, J. S., & Dale, E. (1995). *The new Dale-Chall readability formula.* Cambridge, MA: Brookline.

Chall, J. S., Jacobs, V. A., & Baldwin, L. E. (1990). *The reading crisis: Why poor children fall behind.* Cambridge, MA: Harvard University Press.

Chamot, A. U., & O'Malley, J. M. (1994). Instructional approaches and teaching procedures. In K. Spangenberg-Urbschat & R. Pritchard (Eds.), *Kids come in all languages: Reading instruction for ESL students* (pp. 82–107). Newark, DE: International Reading Association.

Chapman, J. W., Tunmer, W. E., & Prochnow, J. E. (2001). Does success in the Reading Recovery program depend on developing proficiency in phonological-processing skills? A longitudinal study in a whole language instructional context. *Scientific Studies of Reading, 5,* 141–176.

Chappuis, S., Chappuis, J., & Stiggins, R. (2009). The quest for quality. *Educational Leadership, 67*(3), 14–19.

Chard, N. (1990). How learning logs change teaching. In N. Atwell (Ed.), *Coming to know: Writing to learn in the intermediate grades* (pp. 61–68). Portsmouth, NH: Heinemann.

Charney, R. S. (2002). *Teaching children to care: Classroom management for ethical and academic growth, K–8.* Turners Falls, MA: Northeast Foundation for Children.

Chicago Public Schools. (2000). *Rubrics.* Available online at http://intranet.cps.k12.il.us/Assessments/Ideas_and_Rubrics.html.

Children and Adults with Attention-Deficit/Hyperactivity Disorder (CHADD). (2006). *About AD/HD: Statistical prevalence.* Available online at http://www.help4adhd.org/en/about/statistics.

Chomsky, N. (1968). *Language and mind.* New York: Harcourt, Brace, & World.

Chomsky, N. (1976). *Reflections on language.* London: Temple Smith.

Christenbury, L., & Kelly, P. (1983). *Questioning: A path to critical thinking.* Urbana, IL: National Council of Teachers of English.

Christie, J. F. (1990). Dramatic play: A context for meaningful engagements. *The Reading Teacher, 43,* 542–545.

Clark, K. F., & Berne, J. (2005, December). *A microanalysis of intermediate grade students' comprehension strategy use during peerled discussions of text: An initial inquiry.* Paper presented at the National Reading Conference, Miami.

Clark, K. F., & Berne, J. (2006, May). *Sentence starters.* Paper presented at the International Reading Association convention, Chicago.

Clarke, L. K. (1988). Invented vs. traditional spelling in first graders' writings: Effects on learning to spell and read. *Research in the Teaching of English, 22,* 281–309.

Clarke, L. W., & Holwadel, J. (2007). "Help! What is wrong with these literature circles and how can we fix them?" *The Reading Teacher, 61,* 20–29.

Clarkson, C. (2000). Discovering children and creating curriculum in one small-town third grade. In C. F. Stice & J. E. Bertrand (Eds.), *Teaching at-risk students in the K–4 classroom: Language, literacy, learning.* Norwood, MA: Christopher-Gordon.

Clay, M. M. (1972). *Reading: The patterning of complex behavior.* Auckland, New Zealand: Heinemann.

Clay, M. M. (1975). *What did I write?* Auckland, New Zealand: Heinemann.

Clay, M. M. (1982). *Observing young readers.* Portsmouth, NH: Heinemann.

Clay, M. M. (1991). *Becoming literate: The construction of inner control.* Portsmouth, NH: Heinemann.

Clay, M. M. (1992). Introducing a new storybook to young readers. *The Reading Teacher, 45,* 264–272.

Clay, M. M. (1993a). *An observation survey of early literacy achievement.* Portsmouth, NH: Heinemann.

Clay, M. M. (1993b). *Reading Recovery: A guidebook for teachers in training.* Portsmouth, NH: Heinemann.

Clay, M. M. (2000a). *Concepts about print: What have children learned about the way we print language?* Portsmouth, NH: Heinemann.

Clay, M. M. (2000b). *Running records for classroom teachers.* Portsmouth, NH: Heinemann.

Clay, M. M. (2006). *An observation survey of early literacy achievement* (rev. 2nd ed.). Portsmouth, NH: Heinemann.

Clowes, G. A. (1999, November). Helping teachers raise student achievement: An interview with William L. Sanders. *School Reform News*, The Heartland Institute. http://www.heartland.org/ policybot/results/11119/Helping_Teachers_Raise_Student_ Achievement_an_interview_with_William_L_Sanders.html.

Cohen, J. (1992). A power primer. *Psychological Bulletin, 112*, 155–159.

Cohn, M., & D'Alessandro, C. (1978). When is a decoding error not a decoding error? *The Reading Teacher, 32*, 341–344.

Coiro, J. (2009). Promising practices for supporting adolescents' online literacy development. In K. D. Wood & W. E. Blanton (Eds.), *Literacy instruction for adolescents* (pp. 442–471). New York: Guilford.

Coiro, J. (2010, April). *Measuring online reading comprehension to inform instruction: Challenges, considerations, and practical ideas.* Paper presented at the International Reading Association Convention, Chicago.

Coiro, J., & Dobler, E. (2007). Exploring the online reading comprehension strategies used by sixth-grade skilled readers to search for and locate information on the Internet. *Reading Research Quarterly, 42*, 214–257.

Cole, A. D. (1998). Beginner-oriented texts in literature-based classrooms: The segue for a few struggling readers. *The Reading Teacher, 51*, 488–501.

Cole, A. D. (2006). Scaffolding beginning readers: Micro and macro cues teachers use during student oral reading. *The Reading Teacher, 59*, 450–459.

Collins, J., & Madigan, T. P. (2010). Using writing to develop struggling learners' higher level reading comprehension. In J. Collins & T. Gunning (Eds.), *Building struggling students higher level literacy* (pp. 125–161). Newark, DE: International Reading Association.

Collins, A., & Smith, E. (1980). *Teaching the process of reading comprehension* (Technical Report No. 182). Urbana: University of Illinois, Center for the Study of Reading.

Collins, J. L. (1998). *Strategies for struggling writers.* New York: Guilford.

Collins, M. F. (2005). ESL preschoolers' English vocabulary acquisition from storybook reading. *Reading Research Quarterly, 40*, 406–408.

Colorín Colorado (2008). *A bilingual site for families and educators of English language learners.* Available online at http://www.colorincolor.

Combs, M. (1987). Modeling the reading process with enlarged texts. *The Reading Teacher, 40*, 422–426.

Constantino, M. (1999, May). *Reading and second language learners: Research report.* Olympia, WA: Evergreen State College. Available online at http://www.evergreen.edu/user/K-12/ readingSecondLangLearners.htm.

Cook, M. (2006). *A journal for Corduroy: Responding to literature.* Read•Write•Think. Available online at http://www.readwritethink. org/lessons/lesson_view.asp?id=30.

Cook, V. (2001). *Second language learning and language teaching* (3rd ed.). New York: Oxford University Press.

Cooper, C. R., & Odell, L. (1977). *Evaluating writing: Describing, measuring, judging.* Urbana, IL: National Council of Teachers of English.

Cooper, D. J., & Kiger, N. D. (2005). *Literacy: Helping children construct meaning* (6th ed.). Boston: Houghton Mifflin.

Cooper, P. D. (1997). *Literacy: Helping children construct meaning* (3rd ed.). Boston: Houghton Mifflin.

Cooper, P. D., & Pikulski, J. J. (2005). *Houghton Mifflin reading.* Boston: Houghton Mifflin.

Cooter, K. S., & Cooter, R. B., Jr. (2004). One size doesn't fit all: Slow learners in the reading classroom. *The Reading Teacher, 57*, 680–684.

Coppola, J., Dawson, C. J., McPhillips, S., George, J., & MacLean, D. (2005). "In my country, we don't write stories, we tell our stories": Writing with English-language learners in the primary grades. In R. Indrisano & J. R. Paratore (Eds.), *Learning to write,* *writing to learn: Theory and research in practice* (pp. 40–56). Newark, DE: International Reading Association.

Corson, D. J. (1985). *The lexical bar.* Oxford, UK: Pergamon Press.

Corson, D. J. (1995). *Using English words.* Dordrecht, The Netherlands: Kluwer Academic.

Cote, N., Goldman, S. R., & Saul, E. U. (1998). Students making sense of informational text: Relations between processing and representation. *Discourse Processes, 25*, 1–53.

Cox, C., & Many, J. E. (1992). Towards an understanding of the aesthetic stance towards literature. *Language Arts, 66*, 287–294.

Cox, C., & Zarillo, J. (1993). *Teaching reading with children's literature.* New York: Merrill.

Crafton, L. K. (1991). *Whole language: Getting started . . . moving forward.* Katonah, NY: Richard C. Owen.

Craik, F. I. M., & Lockhart, R. S. (1972). Levels of processing. *Journal of Verbal Learning and Verbal Behavior, 11*, 671–684.

Crawford, A. (2003). Communicative approaches to second-language acquisition: The bridge to second-language literacy. In G. C. Garcia (Ed.), *English learners: Reaching the highest level of English literacy* (pp. 152–181). Newark, DE: International Reading Association.

Crévola, C., & Vineis, M. (2004). *Building essential literacy with bookshop, a research-based reading program.* New York: Mondo.

Culham, R. L., & Coutu, R. (2008). *Using picture books to teach writing.* New York: Scholastic.

Cummins, J. (1994). The acquisition of English as a second language. In K. Spangenberg-Urbschat & R. Pritchard (Eds.), *Kids come in all languages: Reading instruction for all ESL students* (pp. 36–62). Newark, DE: International Reading Association.

Cummins, J. (2001). Assessment and intervention with culturally and linguistically diverse learners. In S. R. Hollins & J. V. Tinajero (Eds.), *Literacy assessment of second language learners* (pp. 115–129). Boston: Allyn & Bacon.

Cunningham, A. E., & Stanovich, K. E. (1998). What reading does for the mind. *American Educator* (Spring/Summer), 1–8.

Cunningham, J. W., Erickson, K., Spadorcia, S. A., Koppenhaver, D. A., Cunningham, P. M., Yoder, D. E., & McKenna, M. C. (1999). Assessing decoding from an onset-rime perspective. *Journal of Literacy Research, 31*, 391–414.

Cunningham, J. W., & Foster, E. O. (1978). The ivory tower connection: A case study. *The Reading Teacher, 31*, 365–369.

Cunningham, J. W., & Moore, D. W. (1986). The confused world of main idea. In J. F. Baumann (Ed.), *Teaching main idea comprehension* (pp. 1–17). Newark, DE: International Reading Association.

Cunningham, J. W., Spadorcia, S. A., Erickson, K. A., Koppenhaver, D. A., Sturm, J. M., & Yoder, D. E. (2005). Investigating the instructional supportiveness of leveled texts. *Reading Research Quarterly, 40*, 410–427.

Cunningham, P. M. (1978). Decoding polysyllabic words: An alternative strategy. *Journal of Reading, 21*, 608–614.

Cunningham, P. M. (1998). The multisyllabic word dilemma: Helping students build meaning, spell, and read "big" words. *Reading and Writing Quarterly: Overcoming Learning Disabilities, 14*, 189–218.

Cunningham, P. M., & Allington, R. L. (1999). *Classrooms that work: They can all read and write* (2nd ed.). New York: Longwood.

Cunningham, P. M., & Allington, R. L. (2003). *Classrooms that work: They can all read and write* (3rd ed.). Boston: Allyn & Bacon.

Cunningham, P. M., & Cunningham, J. W. (1992). Making words: Enhancing the invented spelling-decoding connection. *The Reading Teacher, 46*, 106–115.

Cunningham, P. M., & Hall, D. P. (1997). *Month-by-month phonics for first grade.* Greensboro, NC: Carson-Dellosa.

Cunningham, P. M., Yoder, D. E., & McKenna, M. C. (1999). Assessing decoding from an onset-rime perspective. *Journal of Literacy Research, 31*, 391–414.

Curtis, M. E. (1987). Vocabulary testing and vocabulary instruction. In M. G. McKeown & M. E. Curtis (Eds.), *The nature of vocabulary acquisition* (pp. 37–51). Hillsdale, NJ: Erlbaum.

Dahl, K. (1992). Kidwatching revisited. In K. S. Goodman, L. B. Bird, & Y. M. Goodman (Eds.), *The whole language catalog: Supplement on authentic instruction* (p. 50). Santa Rosa, CA: American School Publishers.

Dahl, K., & Farnan, N. (1998). *Children's writing: Perspectives from research*. Newark, DE: International Reading Association & National Reading Conference.

Dahl, K., & Freppon, P. (1995). A comparison of inner city children's interpretations of reading and writing instruction in the early grades in skills-based and whole language classrooms. *Reading Research Quarterly, 31*, 50–75.

Dale, E., & O'Rourke, J. (1971). *Techniques of teaching vocabulary.* Chicago: Field.

Dalton, B., & Grisham, D. L. (2011). eVoc strategies: 10 Ways to use technology to build vocabulary. *The Reading Teacher, 64*, 306–317.

Daane, M. C., Campbell, J. R., Grigg, W. S., Goodman, M. J., and Oranje, A. (2005). *Fourth-grade students reading aloud: NAEP 2002 Special Study of Oral Reading* (NCES 2006–469). U.S. Department of Education. Institute of Education Sciences, National Center for Education Statistics. Washington, DC: Government Printing Office.

Daniels, H. (2002). *Literature circles: Voice and choice in book clubs and reading groups.* York, ME: Stenhouse.

Daniels, H. (2008, November). *What's new with literature circles?* Paper presented at the Annual Conference of the Connecticut Reading Association, Cromwell, CT.

Danielson, C. (2010). *Implementing the framework for teaching and enhancing professional practice.* Alexandria, VA: ASCD.

D'Arcy, P. (1989). *Making sense, shaping meaning: Writing in the context of a capacity-based approach to learning.* Portsmouth, NH: Boynton/Cook.

Darling-Hammond, L., & Pecheone, R. (2009). Reframing accountability: Using performance assessments to focus learning on higher-order skills. In L. M. Pinkus (Ed.), *Meaningful measurement: The role of assessments in improving high school education in the twenty-first century* (pp. 25–53). Washington, DC: Alliance for Excellent Education.

Davis, F. B. (1968). Research on comprehension in reading. *Reading Research Quarterly, 3*, 449–545.

Davis, G., Jackson, J., & Johnson, S. (2000, May). *Guided writing: Leveling the balance.* Paper presented at the annual meeting of the International Reading Association, Indianapolis, IN.

Davis, Z. T., & McPherson, M. D. (1989). Story map instruction: A road map for reading comprehension. *The Reading Teacher, 43*, 232–240.

DeFord, D. E. (1985). Validating the construct of theoretical orientation in reading instruction. *Reading Research Quarterly, 20*, 351–367.

Deighton, L. C. (1959). *Vocabulary development in the classroom.* New York: Columbia University Press.

Delpit, L. D. (1990). *A socio-cultural view of diversity and instruction.* Paper presented at the Annual Conference on Reading Research, Atlanta.

DeNavas-Walt, C., Proctor, B. D., &. Smith, J. C. (2010). *U.S. Census Bureau, Current population reports, P60–238, Income, poverty, and health insurance coverage in the United States: 2009.* Washington, DC: U.S. Government Printing Office.

Dennis-Shaw, S. (2006). *Guided comprehension: Making connections using a double-entry journal.* Read•Write•Think. Available online at http://www.readwritethink.org/lessons/lesson_view.asp?id=228.

Deno, S. L., Fuchs, L. S., Marston, D., & Shin, J. (2001). Using curriculum-based measurement to establish growth standards for students with learning disabilities. *School Psychology Review, 30*, 507–524.

Denton, C. A., Ciancio, D. J., & Fletcher, J. M. (2006). Validity, reliability, and utility of the Observation Survey of Early Literacy Achievement. *Reading Research Quarterly, 41*, 8–34.

Denton, K., & West, J. (2002). *Children's reading and mathematics achievement in kindergarten and first grade.* Washington, DC: National Center for Educational Statistics. Available online at http://nces.ed.gov/pubs2002/kindergarten.

Denton, K., West, J., & Walston, J. (2003). *Reading—young children's achievement and classroom experiences.* Washington, DC: National Center for Education Statistics. Available online at http://nces.ed.gov/programs/coe/2003/analysis/sa05.asp.

DeRuvo, S., & Barcus, B. (2008). *RTI process steps: A small elementary school's approach to implementation.* Schools Moving Up. Available online at http://www.schoolsmovingup.net/cs/wested/view/e/2840.

Devine, T. G. (1986). *Teaching reading comprehension: From theory to practice.* Boston: Allyn & Bacon.

Dewitz, P., Carr, E. M., & Patberg, J. P. (1987). Effects of inference training on comprehension and comprehension monitoring. *Reading Research Quarterly, 22*, 99–121.

Dewitz, P., & Dewitz, P. K. (2003). They can read the words, but they can't understand: Refining comprehension assessment. *The Reading Teacher, 56*, 422–435.

Dewitz, P., Jones, J., & Leahy, S. (2009). Comprehension strategy instruction in core reading programs. *Reading Research Quarterly, 44*, 102–126.

Dias, P. (1990). A literary-response perspective on teaching reading comprehension. In D. Bogdan & S. B. Straw (Eds.), *Beyond communication: Reading comprehension and criticism* (pp. 283–299). Portsmouth, NH: Boynton/Cook.

Diaz-Rico, L. T. (2004). *Teaching English learners: Strategies and methods* (2nd ed.). Boston: Allyn & Bacon.

Diaz-Rico, L. T., & Weed, K. W. (2002). *The cross-cultural, language, and academic development handbook: A complete K–12 reference guide.* Boston: Allyn & Bacon.

Dickinson, D. K., & Smith, M. W. (1994). Long-term effects of preschool teachers' book reading on low-income children's vocabulary and story comprehension. *Reading Research Quarterly, 29*, 104–122.

Dierking, C. (2006). *Growing up literate: Orchestrating speaking, writing, and reading.* Paper presented at the International Reading Association's Reading Research Conference, Chicago.

Dillon, J. T. (1983). *Teaching and the art of questioning.* Bloomington, IN: Phi Delta Kappa.

DiLuglio, P., Eaton, D., & de Tarnowsky, J. (1988). *Westward wagons.* North Scituate, RI: Scituate School Department.

District of Columbia Public Schools. (2010). *IMPACT: The DCPS effectiveness assessment system for school-based personnel.* Washington, DC: Author.

Dodge, B. (2001). *FOCUS: Five rules for writing a great WebQuest.* Available online at http://www.iste.org/L&L/archive/vol28/no8/featuredarticle/dodge/index.html.

Dodson, P. (2011). *Stegosaurus up close.* Berkeley Heights. NJ: Enslow.

Doing What Works (2007). *Preschool language and literacy.* U.S. Department of Education, What Works Clearinghouse. Available online at ttp://dww.ed.gov/Preschool-Language-and-Literacy/topic/index.cfm?T_ID=15.

Dole, J. S., Duffy, G. G., Roehler, L. R., & Pearson, P. D. (1991). Moving from the old to the new: Research on reading comprehension. *Review of Educational Research, 61*, 239–264.

Donovan, C. A., &. Smolkin, L. B. (2001). Genre and other factors influencing teachers' book selection for science instruction. *Reading Research Quarterly, 36*, 421–440.

Donovan, C. A., & Smolkin, L. B. (2011). Supporting informational writing in the elementary grades. *The Reading Teacher, 64*, 406–416.

Dorn, L. (2010, April). *Response to intervention: A comprehensive and systemic design.* Paper presented at the International Reading Association Convention, Chicago.

Dowhower, S. L. (1987). Effects of repeated reading on second-grade transitional readers' fluency and comprehension. *Reading Research Quarterly, 22*, 389–406.

Doyle, B., & Bramwell, W. (2006). Promoting emergent literacy and social-emotional learning through dialogic reading. *The Reading Teacher, 59*, 554–564.

Duncan, G. J., & Magnson, K. A. (2005). Can family socioeconomic resources account for racial and ethnic test score gaps? *The Future of Children 15* (1), 35–54.

Duffelmeyer, F. A. (1985). Main ideas in paragraphs. *The Reading Teacher, 38,* 484–486.

Duffy, G. G. (2002). The case for direct explanation of strategies. In C. C. Block & M. Pressley (Eds.), *Comprehension instruction: Research based best practices* (pp. 28–41). New York: Guilford.

Duffy, G. G., & Roehler, L. R. (1987). Improving reading instruction through the use of responsive elaboration. *The Reading Teacher, 40,* 514–520.

Duffy, R. (1994). It's just like talking to each other: Written conversation with five-year-old children. In N. Hall & A. Robinson (Eds.), *Keeping in touch: Using interactive writing with young children* (pp. 31–42). Portsmouth, NH: Heinemann.

Duke, N. K. (2003, July). *Comprehension difficulties.* Presentation at the CIERA Summer Institute, Ann Arbor, MI.

DuPaul, G. J., & Eckert, T. L. (1996). Academic interventions for students with attention-deficit/hyperactivity dis-order: A review of the literature. *Reading and Writing Quarterly: Overcoming Learning Difficulties, 14,* 58–82.

Durgunoglu, A. Y., & Oney, B. (2000). *Literacy development in two languages: Cognitive and sociocultural dimensions of cross-language transfer.* (A research symposium on high standards in reading for students from diverse language groups: Research, practice & policy.) Washington, DC: U.S. Department of Education, Office of Bilingual Education and Minority Languages Affairs. Available online at http://www.ncbe.gwu.edu/ncbepubs/symposia/reading/reading3.html.

Duthie, C. (1996). *True stories: Nonfiction literacy in the primary classroom.* York, ME: Stenhouse.

Dykstra, R. (1974). Phonics and beginning reading instruction. In C. C. Walcutt, J. Lamport, & G. McCracken (Eds.), *Teaching reading: A phonic/linguistic approach to developmental reading* (pp. 373–397). New York: Macmillan.

Dymock, S. (2005). Teaching expository text structure awareness. *The Reading Teacher, 59,* 177–181.

Dzaldov, B., & Peterson, S. (2005). Book leveling and readers. *The Reading Teacher, 59,* 222–229.

Echevarria, J., Vogt, M. E., & Short, D. (2000). *Making content comprehensible for English language learners: The SIOP model.* Boston: Allyn & Bacon.

Education Department of Western Australia. (1994). *Writing resource book.* Melbourne, Australia: Longman.

Education Week. (2006). *Quality counts at 10: A decade of standards-based education.* Available online at http://www.edweek.org/ew/articles/2006/01/05/17execsum.h25.html.

Edwards, L. (2000). "We teached ourselves." In C. F. Stice & J. E. Bertrand (Eds.), *Teaching at-risk students in the K–4 classroom: Language, literacy, learning* (pp. 1–18). Norwood, MA: Christopher-Gordon.

Ehren, B. (2009). Looking through an adolescent literacy lens at the narrow view of reading. *Language, Speech, and Hearing Services in Schools, 40,* 192–195.

Ehri, L. C. (1991). Development of the ability to read words. In R. Barr, M. L. Kamil, P. Mosenthal, & P. D. Pearson (Eds.), *Handbook of reading research* (Vol. II, pp. 383–417). New York: Longman.

Ehri, L. C. (1994). Development of the ability to read words: Update. In R. B. Ruddell, M. R. Ruddell, & H. Singer (Eds.), *Theoretical models and processes of reading* (4th ed.) (pp. 323–358). Newark, DE: International Reading Association.

Ehri, L. C. (1998). Research on learning to read and spell: A personal-historical perspective. *Scientific Studies of Reading, 2,* 97–114.

Ehri, L. C., & McCormick, S. (1998). Phases of word learning: Implications for instruction with delayed and disabled readers. *Reading and Writing Quarterly: Overcoming Learning Disabilities, 14,* 135–163.

Ehri, L. C., Satlow, E., & Gaskins, I. (2009). Grapho-phonemic enrichment strengthens keyword analogy instruction for struggling young readers. *Reading & Writing Quarterly, 25,* 162–191.

Elbow, P. (2002). The role of publication in the democratization of writing. In C. Weber (Ed.), *Publishing with students: A comprehensive guide* (pp. 1–8). Portsmouth, NH: Heinemann.

Elbow, P. (2004). Writing first! *Educational Leadership, 62* (2), 9–13.

Elkonin, D. B. (1973). Reading in the USSR. In J. Downing (Ed.), *Comparative reading* (pp. 551–579). New York: Macmillan.

Elley, W. B. (1989). Vocabulary acquisition from listening to stories. *Reading Research Quarterly, 24,* 174–187.

Elley, W. B. (1992). *How in the world do students read?* The Netherlands: IEA.

Elliott, S. N. (1999). *A multi-year evaluation of the Responsive Classroom® approach: Its effectiveness and acceptability in promoting social and academic competence* (Final report, 1996–1998). Madison: University of Wisconsin–Madison.

Ellis, E. (2004). *Workshop resources. Think sheet presentations: Comparison frames.* Masterminds Publishing. Available online at http://graphicorganizers.com/resources.html.

Emig, J. (1971). *The composing processes of twelfth-graders.* Urbana, IL: National Council of Teachers of English.

Engelmann, S. (1999). *Student-program alignment and teaching to mastery.* Paper presented at the 25th National Direct Instruction Conference, Eugene, OR.

Enz, B, (1989, May). *The 90 percent success solution.* Paper presented at the International Reading Association annual convention, New Orleans, LA.

Epstein, J. L., & Dauber, S. L. (1991). School programs and teacher practices of parent involvement in innercity elementary and middle schools. *The Elementary School Journal, 91,* 290–305.

Ericson, L., & Juliebo, M. F. (1998). *The phonological awareness handbook for kindergarten and primary teachers.* Newark, DE: International Reading Association.

Estes, T., & Vaughn, J. (1985). *Reading and learning in the content classroom* (2nd ed.). Boston: Allyn & Bacon.

Evans, A. M., Fox, M., Cremaso, L., & McKinnon, L. (2004). Beginning reading: The views of parents and teachers of young children. *Journal of Educational Psychology, 96,* 130–141.

Farr, R. (1991). Current issues in alternative assessment. In C. P. Smith (Ed.), *Alternative assessment of performance in the language arts: Proceedings* (pp. 3–17). Bloomington, IN: ERIC Clearinghouse on Reading and Communication Skills & Phi Delta Kappa.

Farr, R. (2003). Appendix A: Purposeful reading. In W. J. Popham (Ed.), *Crafting curricular aims for instructionally supportive assessment* (pp. 19–29). Available online at http://www.education.unm.edu/NCEO/Presentations/CraftingCurricular.pdf.

Farr, R., & Carey, R. F. (1986). *Reading: What can be measured?* Newark, DE: International Reading Association.

Farr, R., & Farr, B. (1990). *Integrated assessment system.* San Antonio, TX: Psychological Corporation.

Feitelson, D., Kita, B., & Goldstein, Z. (1986). Effects of reading series stories to first-graders on their comprehension and use of language. *Research in the Teaching of English, 20,* 339–356.

Ferdig, R. E., & Trammell, K. D. (2004, February). Content delivery in the "Blogosphere." *The Journal.* Available online at http//:www.thejournal.com/articles/16626.

Ferreiro, E. (1986). The interplay between information and assimilation in beginning literacy. In W. H. Teale & E. Sulzby (Eds.), *Emergent literacy* (pp. 15–49). Norwood, NJ: Ablex.

Ferreiro, E., & Teberosky, A. (1982). *Literacy before schooling.* Portsmouth, NH: Heinemann.

Fielding, L. G., Wilson, P. T., & Anderson, R. C. (1986). A new focus on free reading: The role of trade books in reading instruction. In T. E. Raphael (Ed.), *The contexts of school-based literacy* (pp. 149–160). New York: Random House.

Fielding-Barnsley, R. (1997). Explicit instruction of decoding benefits children high in phonemic awareness and alphabet knowledge. *Scientific Studies of Reading, 1* (1), 85–98.

Fields, M. W., Spangler, K., & Lee, D. M. (1991). *Let's begin reading right: Developmentally appropriate beginning literacy* (2nd ed.). New York: Macmillan.

Fiene, J., & McMahon, S. (2007). Assessing comprehension: A classroom-based process. *The Reading Teacher, 60,* 406–417.

Fillmore, L. W. (1976). *The second time around: Cognitive and social strategies in second language acquisition.* Dissertation Abstracts International, 37, 10A, P.6443 (University Abstracts International No. AAG7707085).

Fillmore, L. W., & Valdez, C. (1986). Teaching bilingual learners. In M. E. Wittrock (Ed.), *Handbook of research on teaching* (pp. 648–685). New York: Macmillan.

Fischbaugh, R. (2004). Using book talks to promote high-level questioning skills. *The Reading Teacher, 58,* 296–298.

Fisher, D., Flood, J., Lapp, D., & Frey, N. (2004). Interactive read-alouds: Is there a common set of implementation practices? *The Reading Teacher, 58,* 8–17.

Fisher, D., & Frey, N. (2007a). *Checking for understanding: Formative assessment techniques for your classroom.* Alexandria, VA: ASCD.

Fisher, D., & Frey, N. (2007b). Implementing a schoolwide literacy framework: Improving achievement in an urban elementary school. *The Reading Teacher, 61,* 32–43.

Fitzgerald, J. (1989). Research on stories: Implications for teachers. In K. P. Muth (Ed.), *Children's comprehension of text: Research into practice* (pp. 2–36). Newark, DE: International Reading Association.

Fitzgerald, J., Amendum, S. J., & Guthrie, K. M. (2008). Young Latinos growth in all-English classrooms. *Journal of Literacy Research, 40,* 6–58.

Fletcher, J. M., Lyon, G. R., Fuchs, L. S., & Barnes, A. (2007). *Learning disabilities, from identification to intervention.* New York: Guilford.

Flexner, S. B., & Hauck, L. C. (Eds.). (1994). *The Random House dictionary of the English language* (2nd ed., rev.). New York: Random House.

Flood, J., Medcaris, A., Hasbrouk, J. E., Paris, S., Hoffman, J., Stahl, S., Lapp, D., Tinejero, J. V., & Wood, K. (Eds.). (2001). *McGraw-Hill reading.* New York: McGraw-Hill.

Florida Center for Reading Research (2009). *Use of ongoing progress monitoring to improve reading instruction.* Tallahassee, FL: Author.

Florida Department of Education (2008). *2008 Florida Cella communiqué #3.* Available online at http://www.fldoe.org/aala/pdf/CELLACommunique3.pdf.

Flynt, E., & Cooter, R. B., Jr. (2005). Improving middle-grade reading in urban schools: The Memphis comprehension framework. *The Reading Teacher, 58,* 774–780.

Foorman, B. R., Fletcher, J. M., Francis, D. J., Schatschneider, C., & Mehta, P. (1998). The role of instruction in learning to read: Preventing reading failure in at-risk children. *Journal of Educational Psychology, 90,* 37–55.

Ford, M. P. (1994, November). *Keys to successful whole group instruction.* Paper presented at the annual conference of the Connecticut Reading Association, Waterbury.

Fountas, I. C. (1999). *Little readers for guided reading teacher's manual.* Boston: Houghton Mifflin.

Fountas, I. C., & Pinnell, G. S. (1996). *Guided reading: Good first teaching for all children.* Portsmouth, NH: Heinemann.

Fountas, I. C., & Pinnell, G. S. (2001a). *Guiding readers and writers, grades 3–6.* Portsmouth, NH: Heinemann.

Fountas, I. C., & Pinnell, G. S. (2001b). *The primary literacy video collection: Guided reading.* Portsmouth, NH: Heinemann.

Fountas, I. C., & Pinnell, G. S. (2001c). *Using guided reading to strengthen students' reading skills at the developing level grades 1–3.* Portsmouth, NH: Heinemann.

Fountas, I. C., & Pinnell, G. S. (2006). *Teaching for comprehending and fluency.* Portsmouth, NH: Heinemann.

Fountas, I. C., & Pinnell, G. S. (2009). Leveled book list, K-8+. 2010–2012. Portsmouth, NH: Heinemann.

Fox, E. (2009). The role of reader characteristics in processing and learning from informational text. *Review of Educational Research, 79,* 197–261.

Francis, D., Rivera, M., Lesaux, N., Kieffer, M., & Rivera, H. (2006). *Practical guidelines for the education of English language learners: Research-based recommendations for instruction and academic interventions* (Under cooperative agreement grant S283B050034 for U.S. Department of Education). Portsmouth, NH: RMC Research Corporation, Center on Instruction. Available online at http://www.centeroninstruction.org/files/ELL1-Interventions.pdf.

Franklin, E. A. (1988). Reading and writing stories: Children creating meaning. *The Reading Teacher, 42,* 184–190.

Fredericks, A. D. (1986). Mental imagery activities to improve comprehension . *The Reading Teacher, 40,* 78–81.

Freeman, Y. S., & Freeman, D. E. (1998). Effective literacy practices for English learners. In C. Weaver (Ed.), *Practicing what we know: Informed reading instruction* (pp. 409–438). Urbana, IL: National Council of Teachers of English.

Fry, E. (1977a). *Elementary reading instruction.* New York: McGraw-Hill.

Fry, E. (1977b). Fry's readability graph: Clarifications, validity, and extension to level 17. *Journal of Reading, 21,* 242–252.

Fuchs, D., & Fuchs, L. (n.d.). *Letter sound fluency test.* Nashville, TN: Vanderbilt University.

Fuchs, L. S., Fuchs, D., & Compton, D. L. (2004). Monitoring early reading development in first grade: Word identification fluency versus nonsense word fluency. *Exceptional Children, 71* (1), 7–21.

Gage, F. C. (1990, November). *An introduction to reader-response issues: How to make students into more active readers.* Paper presented at the annual meeting of the Connecticut Reading Conference, Waterbury.

Gallo, D. R. (1985). Teachers as reading researchers. In C. N. Hedley & A. N. Baratta (Eds.), *Contexts of reading* (pp. 185–199). Norwood, NJ: Ablex.

Gambrell, L. B. (1980). Think time: Implications for reading instruction . *The Reading Teacher, 34,* 143–146.

Gambrell, L. B., & Bales, R. J. (1986). Mental imagery and the comprehension monitoring performance of fourth- and fifth-grade poor readers. *Reading Research Quarterly, 21,* 454–464.

Gambrell, L. B., Wilson, R. M., & Gantt, W. N. (1981). Classroom observations of good and poor readers. *Journal of Educational Research, 24,* 400–404.

Gans, R. (1940). *Study of critical reading comprehension in intermediate grades* (Teachers College Contributions to Education, No. 811). New York: Bureau of Publications, Teachers College, Columbia University.

García, G. E. (1990). *Response to "A socio-cultural view of diversity and instruction."* Paper presented at the annual Conference on Reading Research, Atlanta.

García, G. E., Pearson, P. D., & Jiménez, R. T. (1994). *The atrisk situation: A synthesis of reading research.* Champaign, IL: University of Illinois, Center for the Study of Reading.

Garner, R., Hare, V. C., Alexander, P., Haynes, J., & Winograd, P. (1984). Inducing use of a text lookback strategy among unsuccessful readers. *American Educational Research Journal, 21,* 789–798.

Garner, R., MacCready, G. B., & Wagoner, S. (1984). Readers' acquisition of the components of the text look-back strategy. *Journal of Educational Psychology, 76,* 300–309.

Gaskins, I. W. (1998). *What research suggests are ingredients of a grades 1–6 literacy program for struggling readers.* Paper presented at International Reading Association Convention, Orlando, FL.

Gaskins, I. W. (2005). *Success with struggling readers: The Benchmark School approach.* New York: Guilford.

Gaskins, I. W. (2011, April). *The evidence base for successful interventions with struggling readers.* Paper presented at the International Reading Association convention, Orlando, FL.

Gates, A. I. (1917). Recitation as a factor in memorizing. *Archives of Psychology, 40,* 65–104.

Geisinger, K. F., Spies, R. A., Plake, B. S., & Carlson, A. (Eds.). (2007) *The seventeenth mental measurements handbook.* Lincoln: University of Nebraska, Buros Institute.

Gelzheiser, L. M. (2010, April). *Interactive strategies approach: Part 2, older struggling readers.* Paper presented at the International Reading Association Convention, Chicago.

Gensemer, E. (1998, May). *Teaching strategies for taking charge of task, text, situation, and personal characteristics.* Paper presented at International Reading Association Convention, Orlando, FL.

Germeroth, C., Barker, J., Aren, A., & Wang, X (2009). *Our kids, A McREL report prepared for Foundation's Learning System.* Denver, CO: McREL.

Gersten, R., Baker, S. K., Shanahan, T., Linan-Thompson, S., Collins, P., & Scarcella, R. (2007). *Effective literacy and English language instruction for English learners in the elementary grades: A practice guide* (NCEE 2007–4011). Washington, DC: National Center for Education Evaluation and Regional Assistance, Institute of Education Sciences, U.S. Department of Education. Available online at http://ies.ed.gov/ncee.

Gibson, E. J., Gibson, J. J., Pick, A. D., & Osser, H. (1962). A developmental study of the discrimination of letter-like forms. *Journal of Comparative and Physiological Psychology, 55,* 897–906.

Gibson, E. J., & Levin, H. (1975). *The psychology of reading.* Cambridge, MA: MIT Press.

Gibson, E. J., Osser, H., & Pick, A. (1963). A study in the development of grapheme-phoneme correspondences. *Journal of Verbal Learning and Verbal Behavior, 2,* 142–146.

Gipe, J. P. (1980). Use of a relevant context helps kids learn. *The Reading Teacher, 33,* 398–402.

Glass, G. G. (1976). *Glass analysis for decoding only: Teacher's guide.* Garden City, NY: Easier to Learn.

Glenberg, A. M., Gutierrez, T., Levin, J. R., Japuntich, S., & Kaschak, M. P. (2004). Activity and imagined activity can enhance young children's reading comprehension. *Journal of Educational Psychology, 96,* 424–436.

Glenberg, A. M., Jaworski, B., Rischal, M., & Levin, J. (2007). What brains are for: Action, meaning, and reading comprehension. In D. S. McNamara (Ed.), *Reading comprehension strategies, theories, interventions, and technologies* (pp. 221–240). New York: Lawrence Erlbaum.

Gold, J., & Fleisher, L. S. (1986). Comprehension breakdown with inductively organized text: Differences between average and disabled readers. *Remedial and Special Education, 7,* 26–32.

Goldenberg, C. (1994). Promoting early literacy development among Spanish-speaking children: Lessons from two studies. In E. H. Hiebert & B. M. Taylor (Eds.), *Getting reading right from the start* (pp. 171–200). Boston: Allyn & Bacon.

Good, R. H., & Kaminski, R. A. (Ed.). (2003). *Dynamic indictors of basic early literacy skills* (6th ed.). Longmont, CO: Sopris West.

Good, R. H., Kaminski, R. A., Smith, S. B., Simmons, D. C., Kame'enui, E., & Wallin, J. (2003). Reviewing outcomes: Using DIBELS to evaluate a school's core curriculum and system of additional intervention in kindergarten. In S. R. Vaughn & K. L. Briggs (Eds.), *Reading in the classroom: Systems for the observation of teaching and learning.* Baltimore: Brookes.

Goodman, K. S. (1974). Miscue analysis: Theory and reality in reading. In J. E. Merritt (Ed.), *New horizons in reading* (pp. 15–26). Newark, DE: International Reading Association.

Goodman, K. S. (1986). *What's whole in whole language?* Portsmouth, NH: Heinemann.

Goodman, K. S. (1994a). Foreword: Lots of changes, but little gained. In P. Shannon & K. Goodman (Eds.), *Basal readers: A second look* (pp. xiii–xxvii). Katonah, NY: Richard C. Owen.

Goodman, K. S. (1994b). Reading, writing, and written texts: A transactional sociopsycholinguistic view. In R. B. Ruddell, M. R. Ruddell, & H. Singer (Eds.), *Theoretical models and processes of reading* (4th ed.) (pp. 1093–1130). Newark, DE: International Reading Association.

Goodman, K. S., & Goodman, Y. M. (1978). *Reading of American children whose language is a stable rural dialect of English or a language other than English.* Detroit: Wayne State University Press. (ERIC Document Reproduction Service No. ED 182 465)

Goodman, Y. M. (1985). Kidwatching: Observing children in the classroom. In A. Jagger & M. T. Smith-Burke (Eds.), *Observing the language learner* (pp. 9–18). Newark, DE: International Reading Association.

Gordon, C. J. (1985). Modeling inference awareness across the curriculum. *Journal of Reading, 28,* 444–447.

Gordon, C. J. (1989). Teaching narrative text structure: A process approach to reading and writing. In K. P. Muth (Ed.), *Children's comprehension of text: Research into practice* (pp. 79–102). Newark, DE: International Reading Association.

Gormley, W. T., Gayer, T., Phillips, D., & Dawson, B. (2005). The effects of universal pre-K cognitive development. *Developmental Psychology, 41,* 872–884.

Goswami, U. (2001). Early phonological development and acquisition of literacy. In S. B. Neuman & D. K. Dickinson (Eds.), *Handbook of early literacy research* (pp. 111–125). New York: Guilford.

Gough, P. B., & Hillinger, M. L. (1980). Learning to read: An unnatural act. *Bulletin of the Orton Society, 30,* 179–196.

Gough, P. B., Juel, C., & Griffith, P. L. (1992). Reading, spelling, and the orthographic cipher. In P. B. Gough, L. C. Ehri, & R. Treiman (Eds.), *Reading acquisition* (pp. 35–48). Hillsdale, NJ: Erlbaum.

Gough, P. B., Larson, K. C., & Yopp, H. (2001). *The structure of phonemic awareness.* Unpublished paper. Austin: University of Texas.

Graesser, A. C. (2007). An introduction to strategic reading comprehension. In D. S. McNamara (Ed.), *Reading comprehension strategies, theories, interventions, and technologies* (pp. 3–26). New York: Lawrence Erlbaum

Graesser, A. C., Golding, J. M., & Long, D. L. (1991). Narrative representation and comprehension. In R. Barr, M. L. Kamil, P. Mosenthal, & P. D. Pearson (Eds.), *Handbook of reading research* (Vol. II, pp. 171–205). New York: Longman.

Graham, S., & Perin, D. (2007). *Writing next: Effective strategies to improve writing of adolescents in middle and high schools—A report to Carnegie Corporation of New York.* Washington, DC: Alliance for Excellent Education.

Graves, D. H. (1975). Examination of the writing processes of seven-year-old children. *Research in the Teaching of English, 9,* 221–241.

Graves, D. H. (1983). *Writing: Teachers and children at work.* Exeter, NH: Heinemann.

Graves, D. H. (2004). What I've learned from teachers of writing. *Language Arts, 82,* 88–94.

Graves, M. F. (1987). Roles of instruction in fostering vocabulary development. In M. G. McKeown & M. E. Curtis (Eds.), *The nature of vocabulary acquisition* (pp. 165–184). Hillsdale, NJ: Erlbaum.

Graves, M. F., & Dykstra, R. (1997). Contextualizing the first-grade studies: What is the best way to teach children to read? *Reading Research Quarterly, 32,* 342–344.

Graves, M. F., & Hammond, H. K. (1980). A validated procedure for teaching prefixes and its effect on students' ability to assign meaning to novel words. In M. Kamil & A. Moe (Eds.), *Perspectives of reading research and instruction* (pp. 184–188). Washington, DC: National Reading Conference.

Graves, M. F., Juel, C., & Graves, B. B. (2001). *Teaching reading in the 21st century* (2nd ed.). Boston: Allyn & Bacon.

Gray, W. S., & Holmes, E. (1938). *The development of meaning vocabulary in reading.* Chicago: University of Chicago.

Great Books Foundation. (1999). *An introduction to shared inquiry: A handbook for Junior Great Books leaders* (4th ed.). Chicago: Author.

Great Books Foundation. (2006). *Junior Great Books.* Chicago: Author.

Greenwood, S. C., & Flanigan, K. (2007). Overlapping vocabulary and comprehension: Context clues complement semantic gradients . *The Reading Teacher, 61,* 249–254.

Griffith, P. L., & Olson, M. W. (1992). Phonemic awareness helps beginning readers break the code. *The Reading Teacher, 45,* 516–523.

Guastello, E., & Lenz, C. (2005). Student accountability: Guided reading kidstations. *The Reading Teacher, 59,* 144–156.

Gunning, T. (1975). *A comparison of word attack skills derived from a phonological analysis of frequently used words drawn from a juvenile corpus and an adult corpus.* Unpublished doctoral dissertation, Temple University, Philadelphia.

Gunning, T. (1982). Wrong level test: Wrong information. *The Reading Teacher, 35,* 902–905.

Gunning, T. (1994). *Word building book D.* New York: Phoenix Learning Systems.

Gunning, T. (1995). Word building: A strategic approach to the teaching of phonics. *The Reading Teacher, 48,* 484–488.

Gunning, T. (1996, November). *Choosing and using books for beginning readers.* Paper presented at the annual meeting of the Connecticut Reading Conference, Waterbury.

Gunning, T. (1998). *Assessing and correcting reading and writing difficulties.* Boston: Allyn & Bacon.

Gunning, T. (2000a). *Assessing the difficulty level of material in the primary grades: A study in progress.* Paper presented at the annual meeting of the National Reading Conference, Scottsdale, AZ.

Gunning, T. (2000b). *Best books for building literacy for elementary school children.* Boston: Allyn & Bacon.

Gunning, T. (2000c). *Phonological awareness and primary phonics.* Boston: Allyn & Bacon.

Gunning, T. (2001, December). *An analysis of second graders' attempts to read multisyllabic words.* Paper presented at the annual meeting of the National Reading Conference, San Antonio, TX.

Gunning, T. (2002). *Assessing and correcting reading and writing difficulties* (2nd ed.). Boston: Allyn & Bacon.

Gunning, T. (2003). *Building literacy in the content areas.* Boston: Allyn & Bacon.

Gunning, T. (2005, November). *Assessing the comprehension processes of good decoding but poor comprehending students.* Paper presented at the National Reading Conference, Miami, FL.

Gunning, T. (2006). *Closing the literacy gap.* Boston: Allyn & Bacon.

Gunning, T. (2007). *Reading, reasoning, responding, and reflecting: Developing higher-level literacy.* Boston: Allyn & Bacon.

Gunning, T. (2008). *Teacher's guide for word building book B* (2nd ed.). Honesdale, PA: Phoenix Learning Resources.

Gunning, T. (2010). *Reading comprehension boosters: 100 lessons for building higher-level literacy.* San Francisco, CA: Jossey-Bass.

Guthrie, J. T. (1980). Research views: Time in reading programs. *The Reading Teacher, 33,* 500–502.

Guthrie, J. T. (2002). Preparing students for high-stakes test taking in reading. In A. E. Farstrup & S. J. Samuels (Eds.), *What research has to say about reading instruction* (pp. 370–391). Newark, DE: International Reading Association.

Guthrie, J. T. (2004). Teaching for literacy engagement. *Journal of Literacy Research, 36,* 1–28.

Gutnick, A. L., Robb, M., Takeuchi, L., & Kotler, J. (2011). *Always connected: The new digital media habits of young children.* New York: The Joan Ganz Cooney Center at Sesame Workshop.

Guzman-Johannessen, G. (2006, May). *Stages of second-language acquisition.* Paper presented at the International Reading Association conference, Chicago.

Hackett, J. K., Moyer, R. H., & Adams, D. K. (1989). *Merrill science 5.* Columbus, OH: Merrill.

Hagerty, P., Hiebert, E., & Owens, M. (1989). Students' comprehension, writing, and perceptions in two approaches to literacy instruction. In S. McCormick & J. Zutell (Eds.), *38th yearbook of the National Reading Conference* (pp. 453–459). Chicago: National Reading Conference.

Halstead, J. W. (1988). *Guiding gifted readers.* Columbus, OH: Ohio Psychology.

Hamilton, L., Halverson, R., Jackson, S., Mandinach, E., Supovitz, J., & Wayman, J. (2009). *Using student achievement data to support instructional decision making* (NCEE 2009–4067). Washington, DC: National Center for Education Evaluation and Regional Assistance,

Institute of Education Sciences, U.S. Department of Education. Available online at http://ies.ed.gov/ncee/wwc/publications/practiceguides/.

Hammond, D. W. (2001, May). *The essential nature of teacher talk and its effect on students' engagement with expository text.* Paper presented at the annual meeting of the International Reading Association, New Orleans, LA.

Hampton, S., Murphy, S., & Lowry, M. (2009). *Using rubrics to improve student writing, grade 1* (rev.). Pittsburgh, PA: New Standards and National Center on Education and the Economy.

Hampton, S., & Resnick, L. B. (2009). *Reading and writing with understanding: Comprehension in fourth and fifth grades.* Washington, DC: National Center on Education and the Economy; Newark, DE: International Reading Association.

Hansen, J. (1981). The effects of inference training and practice on young children's reading comprehension. *Reading Research Quarterly, 16,* 391–417.

Hansen, J., & Pearson, P. D. (1980). *The effects of inference training and practice on young children's comprehension* (Technical Report No. 166). Urbana: University of Illinois, Center for the Study of Reading.

Hansen, J., & Pearson, P. D. (1982). *Improving the inferential comprehension of good and poor fourth-grade readers* (Report No. CSRTR-235). Urbana: University of Illinois, Center for the Study of Reading. (ERIC Document Reproduction No. ED 215–312)

Hansen-Krening, N., Aoki, E. M., & Mizokawa, D. T. (Eds.). (2003). *Kaleidoscope: A multicultural booklist for grades K–8* (4th ed.). Urbana, IL: National Council of Teachers of English.

Harcourt Educational Measurement. (2000). *Some things parents should know about testing: A series of questions and answers.* Available online at http://www.hbem.com/library/parents.htm.

Hardman, M. L., Drew, C. J., Egan, M. W., & Wolf, B. (1993). *Human exceptionality* (4th ed.). Boston: Allyn & Bacon.

Hare, V. C., & Borchardt, K. M. (1984). Direct instruction of summarization skills. *Reading Research Quarterly, 20,* 62–78.

Harlem Children's Zone. (2002, Summer/Fall). The baby college. *Quarterly Report from the Zone 1* (1). Available online at http://www.hcz.org/images/stories/pdf.

Harlem Children's Zone. (2011). *The baby college* [film clip]. New York: Author.

Harlem Children's Zone. (n. d.). *Whatever it takes: A white paper on the Harlem Children's Zone.* Available online at http://www.hcz.org/images/stories/HCZ%20White%20Paper.pdf.

Harmon, J. M. (1998). Constructing word meanings: Strategies and perceptions of four middle school learners. *Journal of Literacy Research, 30,* 561–599.

Harper, L. (1997). The writer's toolbox: Five tools for active revision instruction. *Language Arts, 74,* 193–200.

Harris, A. J., & Jacobson, M. D. (1982). *Basic reading vocabularies.* New York: Macmillan.

Harris, A. J., & Sipay, E. R. (1990). *How to increase reading ability* (9th ed.). New York: Longman.

Harris, T. L., & Hodges, R. E. (1995). *The literacy dictionary: The vocabulary of reading and writing.* Newark, DE: International Reading Association.

Harrison Group (2010). *Kids and family reading report.* New York: Scholastic. Available online at mediaroom. scholastic.com/KFRR.

Harste, J. C., Short, K. G., & Burke, C. (1988). *Creating classrooms for authors: The reading-writing connection.* Portsmouth, NH: Heinemann.

Harste, J. C., Woodward, V. A., & Burke, C. L. (1984). *Language stories and literacy lessons.* Ports-mouth, NH: Heinemann.

Hart, B., & Risley, T. (1995). *Meaningful differences in the everyday experience of young American children.* Baltimore: Brookes.

Hartman, D. K. (1994). The intertextual links of readers using multiple passages: A postmodern semiotic/cognitive view of meaning making. In R. B. Ruddell, M. R. Ruddell, & H. Singer (Eds.), *Theoretical models and processes of reading* (4th ed.) (pp. 616–636). Newark, DE: International Reading Association.

Hasbrouck, J., & Tindal, G. A. (2006). Oral reading fluency norms: A valuable assessment tool for reading teachers. *The Reading Teacher, 59,* 636–644.

Hattie, J. (2009). *Visible learning: A synthesis of over 800 meta-analyses relating to achievement.* London: Routledge.

Haystead, M. W., & Marzano, R. J. (2009). *Meta-analytic synthesis of studies conducted at Marzano Research Laboratory on instructional strategies.* Englewood, CO: Marzano Research Laboratory.

Head, M. H., & Readence, J. E. (1986). Anticipation guides: Meaning through prediction. In E. K. Dishner, T. W. Bean, J. E. Readence, & D. W. Moore (Eds.), *Reading in the content areas* (2nd ed.) (pp. 229–234). Dubuque, IA: Kendall/Hunt.

Heath, S. B. (1991). The sense of being literate: Historical and cross-cultural features. In R. Barr, M. L. Kamil, P. Mosenthal, & P. D. Pearson (Eds.), *Handbook of reading research* (Vol. II, pp. 3–25). New York: Longman.

Heimlich, J. E., & Pittelman, S. D. (1986). *Semantic mapping: Classroom applications.* Newark, DE: International Reading Association.

Helman, L. (2004). Building on the sound system of Spanish: Insights from the alphabetic spellings of English-language learners. *The Reading Teacher, 57,* 452–460.

Helper, S. (1989). A literature program: Getting it together, keeping it going. In J. Hickman & B. Culliman (Eds.), *Children's literature in the classroom: Weaving Charlotte's Web* (pp. 209–220). Needham Heights, MA: Christopher-Gordon.

Henderson, E. H. (1990). *Teaching spelling.* Boston: Houghton Mifflin.

Henk, W. A., Marinak, B. A., Moore, J. C., & Mallette, M. H. (2003). The writing observation framework: A guide for refining and validating writing instruction. *The Reading Teacher, 57,* 322–333.

Henry, M. K. (1990). Reading instruction based on word structure and origin. In P. G. Aaron & R. M. Joshi (Eds.), *Reading and writing disorders in different orthographic systems* (pp. 25–49). Dordrecht, The Netherlands: Kluwer Academic.

Herber, H. L. (1970). *Teaching reading in content areas.* Englewood Cliffs, NJ: Prentice Hall.

Herber, H. L., & Herber, J. N. (1993). *Teaching in content areas with reading, writing, and reasoning.* Boston: Allyn & Bacon.

Herman, P. A., Anderson, R. C., Pearson, P. D., & Nagy, W. E. (1987). Incidental acquisition of word meanings from expositions with varied text features. *Reading Research Quarterly, 22,* 263–284.

Hidi, S., & Anderson, V. (1986). Producing written summaries: Task demands, cognitive operations, and implications for instruction. *Review of Educational Research, 56,* 473–493.

Hiebert, E. H., Martin, L. A., & Menon, S. (2005). Are there alternatives in reading textbooks? An examination of three beginning reading programs. *Reading and Writing Quarterly, 21,* 7–32.

Hiebert, E. H., & Reutzel, D. R. (2010). Revisiting silent reading in 2020 and beyond. In E. H. Hiebert & D. R. Reutzel (Eds.), *Revisiting silent reading, New directions for teachers and researchers* (pp. 290–299). Newark, DE: International Reading Association.

Hiebert, E. H., & Taylor, B. M. (2000). Beginning reading instruction: Research on early interventions. In M. L. Kamil, P. B. Mosenthal, P. D. Pearson, & R. Barr (Eds.), *Handbook of reading research* (Vol. III, pp. 455–482). Mahwah, NJ: Erlbaum.

Hiebert, E. H., Valencia, S. W., & Afflerbach, P. P. (1994). Definitions and perspectives. In S. W. Valencia, E. H. Hiebert, & P. P. Afflerbach (Eds.), *Authentic reading assessment: Practices and possibilities* (pp. 6–25). Newark, DE: International Reading Association.

Hildreth, G. (1950). *Readiness for school beginners.* New York: World.

Hirsch, E. D. (1987). *Cultural literacy: What every American needs to know.* Boston: Houghton Mifflin.

Hodgkinson, H. (2003). *Leaving too many children behind.* Washington, DC: Institute of Educational Leadership.

Hoffman, J. V. (1991). Teacher and school effects in learning to read. In R. Barr, M. L. Kamil, P. Mosenthal, & P. D. Pearson (Eds.), *Handbook of reading research* (Vol. II, pp. 911–950). New York: Longman.

Hoffman, J. V., Sailors, M., & Patterson, E.U. (2003). *Decodable texts for beginning reading instruction: The year 2000 basals* (CIERA Report #1–016). Available online at http://www.ciera.org/library/reports/inquiry-1/1–016/1–016fm.html.

Holdaway, D. (1979). *The foundations of literacy.* New York: Ashton Scholastic.

Hoonan, B. (2006). *Using literature and providing access to books.* Paper presented at the International Reading Association Conference, Chicago.

Hornsby, P., Sukarna, P., & Parry, J. (1986). *Read on: A conference approach to reading.* Portsmouth, NH: Heinemann.

Hosp, M. L., Hosp, J. L., & Howell, K. W. (2007). *The ABCs of CBM: A practical guide to curriculum-based measurement.* New York: Guilford.

Hulit, L. M., & Howard, M. R. (2002). *Born to talk.* Boston: Allyn & Bacon.

Hyerle, D. (2001). Visual tools for mapping minds. In A. L. Costa (Ed.), *Developing minds: A resource book for teaching thinking* (3rd ed.) (pp. 401–407). Alexandria, VA: Association for Supervision and Curriculum Development.

Hyman, R. T. (1978). *Strategic questioning.* Englewood Cliffs, NJ: Prentice-Hall.

Hyson, M., Marion, C., & Hyson, M. C. (2003). *Emotional development of young children. Building an emotion-centered curriculum.* New York: Teachers College Press.

Idol, L., & Croll, V. (1985). Story mapping training as a means of improving reading comprehension. *Learning Disability Quarterly, 10,* 214–229.

Individuals with Disabilities Act Amendments of 1997. 20 U.S.C. 1400 et seq.

International Reading Association. (1988). *New directions in reading instruction.* Newark, DE: Author.

International Reading Association. (1998a). *Multiple methods of beginning reading instruction.* Newark, DE: Author. Available online at http://www.reading.org/positions/begin_reading.html.

International Reading Association. (1998b). *Social promotion and grade retention.* Newark, DE: Author. Available online at http://www.reading.org/positions/social_promotion.html.

International Reading Association. (1999a). *High stakes assessments in reading: A position statement of the International Reading Association.* Newark, DE: Author.

International Reading Association. (1999b). *Providing books and other print materials for classroom and school libraries.* Newark, DE: Author. Available online at http://www.reading.org/positions/media_center.html.

International Reading Association. (1999c). *The role of phonics in reading instruction: A position statement of the International Reading Association.* Newark, DE: Author.

International Reading Association. (2001a). *Integrating literacy and technology in the curriculum.* Newark, DE: Author. Available online at http://www.reading.org/positions/technology.html.

International Reading Association. (2001b). *Second-language literacy instruction.* Newark: DE: Author. Available online at http://www.reading.org/positions/second_language.html.

International Reading Association. (2002a). *Family-school partnerships: Essential elements of reading instruction in the United States.* Newark, DE: Author. Available online at http://www.reading.org/positions/family-school.html.

International Reading Association. (2002b). *What is evidence-based reading? A position statement of the International Reading Association.* Newark, DE: Author. Available online at http://www.reading.org/resources/issues/positions_evidence_based.html.

International Reading Association (2010). *Standards for reading professionals—Revised 2010.* Available online at http://reading.org/General/CurrentResearch/Standards/ProfessionalStandards2010.aspx.

International Reading Association & National Association for the Education of Young Children. (1998). Learning to read and write: Developmentally appropriate practices for young children. *The Reading Teacher, 52,* 193–216.

Invernizzi, M., & Hayes, L. (2004). Developmental-spelling research: A systematic imperative. *Reading Research Quarterly, 39*, 216–228.

Invernizzi, M., Meier, J. D., Swank, L., & Juel, C. (2001). *PALS-K, Phonological awareness literacy screening, 2000–2001.* Charlottesville: University of Virginia.

iObservation (2010). *Supervising and supporting effective teachers in every classroom.* Available online at http://www.iobservation.com/iobservation/

Irwin, P. A., & Mitchell, J. N. (1983). A procedure for assessing the richness of retellings. *Journal of Reading, 26*, 391–396.

Jenkins, J. R., Matlock, B., & Slocum, T. A. (1989). Approaches to vocabulary instruction. *Reading Research Quarterly, 24*, 215–235.

Jett-Simpson, M. (Ed.) (1990). *Toward an ecological assessment of reading progress.* Schofield: Wisconsin State Reading Association.

Jiganti, M. A., & Tindall, M. A. (1986). An interactive approach to teaching vocabulary. *The Reading Teacher, 39*, 444–448.

Jiménez, R. T. (1997). The strategic reading abilities and potential of five low-literacy Latina/o readers in middle school. *Reading Research Quarterly, 32*, 224–243.

Jiménez, R. T. (2004). More equitable literacy assessment for Latino students. *The Reading Teacher, 57*, 576–578.

Johns, J. (2008). *Basic reading inventory* (10th ed.). Dubuque, IA: Kendall/Hunt.

Johnson, D. D., Moe, A. J., & Baumann, J. F. (1983). *The Ginn word book for teachers: A basic lexicon.* Lexington, MA: Ginn.

Johnson, D. D., & Pearson, P. D. (1984). *Teaching reading vocabulary* (2nd ed.). New York: Holt.

Johnson, E., Mellard, D. F., Fuchs, D., & McKnight, M. A. (2006). *Response to intervention (RTI): How to do it.* Lawrence, KS: National Research Center on Learning Disabilities. Available online at http://www.nrcld.org/rti_manual/.

Johnson, M. S., & Kress, R. A. (1965). *Developing basic thinking abilities.* Unpublished manuscript, Temple University, Philadelphia.

Johnson, M. S., Kress, R. A., & Pikulski, J. J. (1987). *Informal reading inventories* (2nd ed.). Newark, DE: International Reading Association.

Johnston, F. R. (1999). The timing and teaching of word families. *The Reading Teacher, 53*, 64–75.

Johnston, F. R. (2001). The utility of phonic generalizations: Let's take another look at Clymer's conclusions. *The Reading Teacher, 55*, 132–150.

Johnston, P. H. (2000). *Running records: A self-tutoring guide.* Portland, ME: Stenhouse.

Johnston, P. H., & Rogers, R. (2001). Early literacy development: The case for "informed assessment." In S. B. Neuman & D. K. Dickinson (Eds.), *Handbook of early literacy research* (pp. 377–389). New York: Guilford.

Joint Task Force on Assessment. (1994). *Standards for the assessment of reading and writing.* Newark, DE & Urbana, IL: International Reading Association & National Council of Teachers of English.

Jones, B. F., Palincsar, A. S., Ogle, D. S., &. Carr, E. G. (Eds.). (1986). *Strategic teaching and learning: Cognitive instruction in the content areas* (pp. 73–91). Alexandria, VA: Association for Supervision and Curriculum Development.

Jongsma, E. (1980). *Cloze instruction research: A second look.* Newark, DE: International Reading Association.

Juel, C. (1994). *Learning to read and write in one elementary school.* New York: Springer-Verlag.

Juel, C., & Minden-Cupp, C. (2000). Learning to read words: Linguistic units and instructional strategies. *Reading Research Quarterly, 35*, 458–492.

Juel, C., & Roper-Schneider, D. (1985). The influence of basal readers on first-grade reading. *Reading Research Quarterly, 20*, 134–152.

Jurek, D. J. (1995). *Teaching young children.* Torrance, CA: Good Apple.

Kahlenberg, R. D. (2009). *Turnaround schools that work: Moving beyond separate but equal.* New York: Century Foundation. Available online at http://tcf.org/events/pdfs/ev264/turnaround.pdf.

Kaissen, J. (1987). SSR/Booktime: Kindergarten and first grade sustained silent reading. *The Reading Teacher, 40*, 532–536.

Kallick, B., & Troxell, B. (2011, April 14) *New common core standards, uncommon shifts in practice* [Webinar]. Sungard. K –12 Education.

Kame'enui, E. J., Dixon, R. C., & Carnine, D. W. (1987). Issues in the design of vocabulary instruction. In M. E. McKeown & M. E. Curtis (Eds.), *The nature of vocabulary instruction* (pp. 129–145). Hillsdale, NJ: Erlbaum.

Kamhi, A. G., & Catts, H. W. (1999). Language and reading: Convergences and divergences. In H. W. Catts & A. G. Kamhi (Eds.), *Language and reading disabilities* (pp. 1–24). Boston: Allyn & Bacon.

Karpicke, J. D., & Blunt, J. R. (2011). Retrieval practice produces more learning than elaborative studying with concept mapping. *Science, 331*, 772–775.

Karpicke, J. D., & Roediger, H. L. (2007). The critical importance of retrieval for learning. *Science, 319*, 966–968.

Keene, E. O., & Zimmermann, S. (1997). *Mosaic of thought: Teaching comprehension in a reader's workshop.* Portsmouth, NH: Heinemann.

Keene, E. O., & Zimmermann, S. (2007). *Mosaic of thought: The power of comprehension strategy instruction* (2nd ed.). Portsmouth, NH: Heinemann.

Kelley, M. J., & Clausen-Grace, N. (2009). Facilitating engagement by differentiating independent reading. *The Reading Teacher, 63*, 313–318.

Kemple, J., Corrin, W., Nelson, E., Salinger, T., Herrmann, S., & Drummond, K. (2008). *The enhanced reading opportunities study: Early impact and implementation findings* (NCEE 2008–4015). Washington, DC: National Center for Education Evaluation and Regional Assistance, Institute of Education Sciences, U.S. Department of Education. Available online at http://ies.ed.gov/ncee/pdf/20084017.pdf.

Kibby, M. W. (1989). Teaching sight vocabulary with and without context before silent reading: A field test of the "focus of attention" hypothesis . *Journal of Reading Behavior, 21*, 261–278.

Kibby, M. W., Rapaport, W. J., & Wieland, K. M. (2004). *Contextual vocabulary acquisition: From algorithm to curriculum.* Paper presented at the International Reading Association Convention, Reno, NV. Available online at http://www.cse.buffalo.edu/?rapaport/CVA/cvaslides.html.

Kibby, M. W., Rapaport, W. J., Wieland, K. M., & Dechert, D. A. (2006). *CSI: Contextual semantic investigation for word meaning.* Available online at http://www.cse.buffalo.edu/?rapaport/CVA/CSI.

Kids Count. (2008). *Children in poverty.* Kids Count Data Center. Available online at http://www.kidscount.org/datacenter.

Kieffer, M. J., & Lesaux, N. K. (2007). Breaking down words to build meaning: Morphology, vocabulary, and reading comprehension in the urban classroom. *The Reading Teacher, 61*, 134–144.

Kimmel, S., & MacGinitie, W. H. (1984). Identifying children who use a perseverative text processing strategy. *Reading Research Quarterly, 19*, 162–172.

Kintsch, W. (1994). Test comprehension, memory, and learning. *American Psychologist, 49*, 294–303.

Kintsch, W., & Kintsch, E. (2005). Comprehension. In S. G. Paris & S. A. Stahl (Eds.), *Children's reading comprehension and assessment* (pp. 71–92). Mahwah, NJ: Erlbaum.

Klein, P. D., & Rose, M. A. (2010). Teaching argument and explanation to prepare junior students for writing to learn. *Reading Research Quarterly, 45*, 433–461.

Klesius, J. P., & Griffith, P. L. (1996). Interactive storybook reading for at-risk learners. *The Reading Teacher, 49*, 552–560.

Kletzien, S. B. (1991). Strategy use by good and poor comprehenders reading expository text of differing levels. *Reading Research Quarterly, 26*, 67–86.

Kobayashi, W. (2005, May). An investigation of method effects on reading comprehension test performance. In *Lifelong Learning: Proceedings of the 4th Annual JALT Pan-SIG Conference.* Tokyo, Japan: Tokyo Keizai University. Available online at http://jalt.org/pansig/2005/HTML/Kobayashi.htm.

Kober, N., Chudowsky, N., & Chudowski, V. (2008). *Has student achievement increased since 2002? State test score trends through 2006–07*. Washington, DC: Center on Education Policy.

Koskinen, P. S., Gambrell, L. B., Kapinus, B. A., & Heathington, B. S. (1988). Retelling: A strategy for enhancing students' reading comprehension. *The Reading Teacher, 41*, 892–896.

Krashen, S. D. (1991). Sheltered subject matter teaching. *Cross Currents, 18*, 183–189.

Krashen, S. D. (1997–1998). Bridging inequity with books. *Educational Leadership, 55* (4), 18–21.

Krashen, S. D. (2003) *Explorations in language acquisition and use.* Portsmouth, NH: Heinemann.

Kucan, L., & Beck, I. L. (1996). Thinking aloud and reading comprehension research: Inquiry, instruction, and social interaction. *Review of Educational Research, 67*, 271–299.

Kuhn, M. (2004). Helping students become accurate, expressive readers: Fluency instruction for small groups. *The Reading Teacher, 58*, 338–344.

Kuhn, M. R., & Stahl, S. A. (2003). Fluency: A review of developmental and remedial practices. *Journal of Educational Psychology, 95*, 3–21.

Kulik, J. A. (1992). *An analysis of the research on ability grouping: Historical and contemporary perspectives*. Storrs: The National Research Center on the Gifted and Talented, University of Connecticut. (ERIC Document Reproduction Service No. ED350 777.)

Labbo, L. D., Eakle, A. J., & Montero, M. K. (2002). Digital language experience approach: Using digital photographs and software as a language experience approach innovation. *Reading Online, 5* (8). Available online at http://www.readingonline.org/electronic/elec_index.asp?HREF=labbo2/index.html.

Laberge, D., & Samuels, S. J. (1974). Toward a theory of automatic information processing in reading. *Cognitive Psychology, 6*, 293–323.

Lake, J. H. (1973). *The influence of wait time on the verbal dimensions of student inquiry behavior*. Dissertations Abstracts International, 34, 6476A. (University Microfilms No. 74–08866.)

Lalas, J., Solomon, M., & Johannessen, G. (2006). *Making adaptations in content area reading and writing: A gateway to academic language development for English language learners*. Paper presented at the International Reading Association convention, Chicago.

Landis, D., Umolu, J., & Mancha, S. (2010). The power of language experience for cross-cultural reading and writing. *The Reading Teacher, 63*, 580–589.

Lane, B. (1993). *After the end: Teaching and learning creative revision.* Portsmouth, NH: Heinemann.

Lane, B. (1998). *The reviser's toolbox*. Shoreham, VT: Discover Writing Press.

Langer, J. A. (1986). Reading, writing, and understanding: An analysis of the construction of meaning. *Written Communication, 3*, 219–266.

Langer, J. A. (1990). Understanding literature. *Language Arts, 67* (8), 817–823.

Langer, J. (2011). *Envisioning literature: Literary understanding and literature instruction.* New York: Teachers College Press.

Langer, J. A., & Applebee, A. N. (1987). *How writing shapes thinking.* Urbana, IL: National Council of Teachers of English.

Langer, J. A., & Applebee, A. N. (2006, April). *The partnership for literacy: A study of professional development, instructional change and student growth.* Paper presented at the Reading Research Conference, Chicago.

Language Enrichment Activities Program. (2004). *Teacher training overview*. Available online at http://www.leapsandbounds.org/trainingoverview.htm.

Larson, L. C. (2010). Digital readers: The next chapter in e-book reading and response. *The Reading Teacher, 64*, 15–22.

Law, B., & Eckes, M. (2002). *The more than just surviving handbook: ESL for every classroom teacher*. Winnipeg, Canada: Portage & Main.

Learning Media. (1991). *Dancing with the pen: The learner as writer*. Wellington, New Zealand: Ministry of Education.

Lee, J. (2006). *Tracking achievement gaps and assessing the impact of NCLB on the gaps: An indepth look into national and state reading and math outcome trends*. Cambridge, MA: Civil Rights Project at Harvard University, Harvard Education Publishing Group. Available online at http://www.civilrightsproject.harvard.edu.

Lee, J., Grigg, W., & Donahue, P. (2007). *The nation's report card: Reading 2007* (NCES 2007–496). Washington, DC: National Center for Education Statistics, Institute of Education Sciences, U.S. Department of Education.

Lehr, S., & Thompson, D. L. (2000). The dynamic nature of response: Children reading and responding to *Maniac Magee* and "The Friendship." *The Reading Teacher, 53*, 480–493.

Lembke, E. (2008, April 28). *Webinar: Data utilization within a CBM screening and progress monitoring system*. National Center on Student Progress Monitoring. Available online at http://www.student-progress.org/library/Webinars.asp.

Lensmire, T. (1994). *When children write: Critical revisions of the writing workshop*. New York: Teachers College Press.

Lesaux, N. K., Kieffer, M. J., Faller, S., & Kelley, J. G. (2010). The effectiveness and ease of implementation of an academic vocabulary intervention for linguistically diverse students in urban middle schools. *Reading Research Quarterly, 45*, 196–228.

Leseman, P. P. M., & deJong, P. F. (1998). Home literacy: Opportunity, instruction, cooperation and social-emotional quality predicting early reading achievement. *Reading Research Quarterly, 33*, 294–318.

Leslie, L., & Caldwell, J. (2006). *Qualitative reading inventory–4*. Boston: Allyn & Bacon/Longman.

Leslie, L., & Caldwell, J. (2011). *Qualitative reading inventory–5*. Boston: Pearson Education.

Lessow-Hurley, J. (2003). *Meeting the needs of second-language learners: An educator's guide*. Alexandria, VA: Association for Supervision & Curriculum Development.

Leu, D. J., Jr. (2006, May). *The new literacies*. Paper presented at the International Reading Association's Reading Research Conference, Chicago.

Leung, C. B. (1992). Effects of word-related variables on vocabulary growth through repeated read-aloud events. In C. K. Kinzer & D. J. Leu (Eds.), *Literacy research, theory, and practice: Views from many perspectives* (pp. 491–498). Chicago: National Reading Conference.

Levin, M. (2002). Putting students in charge. In C. Weber (Ed.), *Publishing with students: A comprehensive guide* (pp. 31–37). Portsmouth, NH: Heinemann.

Lewis, M., & S. J. Samuels. *Read more—read better? A meta-analysis of the literature on the relationship between exposure to reading and reading achievement*. Minneapolis, MN: University of Minnesota, 2003. Available online at http://www.tc.umn.edu/~samue001/publications.htm.

Li, G. (2011). The role of culture in literacy, learning, and teaching. In M. Kamil, P. D. Pearson, E. B. Moje, & P. Afflerbach (Eds.), *Handbook of reading research* (Vol. 4, pp. 515–538). New York: Routledge.

Liberman, I. Y., & Shankweiler, D. (1991). Phonology and beginning reading: A tutorial. In L. Rieben & C. A. Perfetti (Eds.), *Learning to read: Basic research and its implications* (pp. 3–18). Hillsdale, NJ: Erlbaum.

Lima, C. W., & Thomas, R. L. (2010). *A to zoo: Subject access to children's picture books* (8th ed.). Westport, CT: Libraries Unlimited.

Lindamood, P., & Lindamood, P. (1998). *The Lindamood phoneme sequencing program for reading, spelling, and speech: LIPS*. Austin, TX: Pro-Ed.

Linden, M., & Wittrock, M. C. (1981). The teaching of reading comprehension according to the model of generative learning. *Reading Research Quarterly, 17*, 44–57.

Linn, R. L., Baker, E. L., & Betebenner, D. W. (2002). *Accountability systems: Implications of requirements of the No Child Left Behind Act of 2001* (CSE Technical Report 567). Los Angeles: UCLA, National Center for Research on Evaluation. Available online at http://www.cse.ucla.edu/CRESST/pages/reports.htm.

Lipson, M. Y. (1984). Some unexpected issues in prior knowledge and comprehension. *The Reading Teacher, 37,* 760–764.

Lipson, M. Y., Valencia, S. W., Wixson, K. K., & Peters, C. W. (1993). Integration and thematic teaching and learning. *Language Arts, 70,* 252–263.

Lipson, M. Y., & Wixson, K. K. (1997). *Assessment and instruction of reading disability: An interactive approach* (2nd ed.). Boston: Allyn & Bacon.

Lipson, M. Y., & Wixson, K. K. (2008). *Assessment and instruction of reading and writing difficulties* (4th ed.). Boston: Allyn & Bacon.

Long, T. W., & Gove, M. K. (2003–2004). How engagement strategies and literature circles promote critical response in a fourth-grade, urban classroom. *The Reading Teacher, 57,* 350–361.

Lonigan, C. J., Schatschneider, C., & Westberg, L. (2007). Identification of children's skills and abilities linked to later outcomes in reading, writing, and spelling. In *Report of the National Early Literacy Panel.* Washington, DC: National Institute for Literacy.

Lovett, M. W., Lacerenza, L., & Borden, S. L. (2000). Putting struggling readers on the phast track: A program to integrate phonological and strategy-based remedial reading instruction and maximize outcomes. *Journal of Learning Disabilities, 33,* 458–477.

Lubliner, S., & Smetana, L. (2005). The effects of comprehensive vocabulary instruction on Title 1 students' metacognitive word-learning skills and reading comprehension. *Journal of Literacy Research, 37,* 163–199.

Luria, A. R. (1983). The development of writing in the child. In M. Martlew (Ed.), *The psychology of written language* (pp. 237–277). New York: Wiley.

Lyman, F. (1981). The responsive classroom discussion. In A. S. Anderson (Ed.), *Mainstreaming digest* (pp. 109–113). College Park: University of Maryland, College of Education.

Lyon, G. R. (2003). *The critical need for evidence-based comprehensive and effective early childhood programs.* Available online at http://olpa.od.nih.gov/hearings/108/session1/testimonies/headstart.asp.

MacDonald, M. R. (1982). *The storyteller's sourcebook: A subject, title, and motif index to folklore for children.* Farmington Hills, MI: Gale.

MacDonald, M. R., & Sturm, B. W. (2001). *The storyteller's sourcebook: A subject, title, and motif index to folklore collections for children 1983–1999.* Farmington Hills, MI: Gale.

Maimon, E. P., & Nodine, B. F. (1979). Measuring syntactic growth: Errors and expectations in sentence-combining practice with college freshmen. *Research in the Teaching of English, 12,* 233–244.

Maloch, B. (2004). On the road to literature discussion groups: Teacher scaffolding during preparatory experiences. *Reading Research and Instruction, 44,* 1–20.

Mansell, J., Evans, M. A., & Hamilton-Hulak, L. (2005). Developmental changes in parents' use of miscue feed-back during shared book reading. *Reading Research Quarterly, 40,* 294–317.

Many, J. (1990). The effect of reader stance on students' personal understanding of literature. In J. Zutell & S. McCormick (Eds.), *Literacy theory and research: Analyses from multiple paradigms* (39th yearbook of the National Reading Conference) (pp. 51–63). Chicago: National Reading Conference.

Many, J. (1991). The effects of stance and age level on children's literary responses. *Journal of Reading Behavior, 21,* 61–85.

Many, J., Fyfe, R., Lewis, G., & Mitchell, E. (1996). Traversing the topical landscape: Exploring students' self-directed reading-writing-research processes. *Reading Research Quarterly, 31,* 122–135.

Manyak, P. C. (2007a). Character trait vocabulary: A schoolwide approach. *The Reading Teacher, 60,* 574–577.

Manyak, P. C. (2007b). A framework for robust literacy instruction for English learners. *The Reading Teacher, 61,* 197–199.

Manyak, P. C. (2008). What's your news? Portraits of a rich language and literacy activity for English-language learners. *The Reading Teacher, 61,* 197–199.

Manzo, A. V. (1969). The ReQuest procedure. *Journal of Reading, 13,* 123–126.

Manzo, A. V., & Manzo, U. C. (1993). *Literacy disorders.* Fort Worth, TX: Harcourt.

Manzo, A. V., Manzo, U. C., & Albee, J. J. (2004). *Reading assessment for diagnostic-prescriptive teaching* (2nd ed.). Belmont, CA: Thomson Learning.

Marcell, B. (2007). Traffic light reading: Fostering the independent usage of comprehension strategies with informational text. *The Reading Teacher, 60* (8), 778–781.

Maria, K. (1990). *Reading comprehension instruction: Issues and strategies.* Parkton, MD: York Press.

Maria, K., & MacGinitie, W. (1987). Learning from texts that refute the reader's prior knowledge. *Reading Research and Instruction, 26,* 222–238.

Marshall, J. C. (2002). *Are they really reading? Expanding SSR in the middle grades.* Portland, ME: Stenhouse.

Martin, M. (1995). *Spelling in the kindergarten.* Paper presented at the annual meeting of the International Reading Association, Anaheim, CA.

Martinez, M. (1993). Motivating dramatic story reenactments. *The Reading Teacher, 46,* 682–688.

Martinez, M., & Teale, W. H. (1987). The ins and outs of a kindergarten writing program. *The Reading Teacher, 40,* 444–451.

Marzano, R. J. (2007). *The art and science of teaching.* Alexandria, VA: ASCD.

Marzano, R. J. (2010a). *Marzano collection.* iObservation. Available online at http://www.iObservation.com/Marzano.

Marzano, R. J. (2010b). *On excellence in teaching.* Bloomington, IN: Solution Tree Press.

Marzano, R. J. (2011a). Designing and teaching learning goals and objectives [Webinar]. Available online at http://www.marzanoresearch.com/Free_Resources/event_presentations_webinars.aspx.

Marzano, R. J. (2011b). The highly engaged classroom [Webinar]. Available online at http://www.marzanoresearch.com/Free_Resources/event_presentations_webinars.aspx.

Marzano, R. J., Gaddy, B. B., & Dean, C. (2000). *What works in classroom instruction.* Aurora, CO: Mid-continent Research for Education and Learning.

Marzano, R. J., & Marzano, J. S. (1988). *A cluster approach to elementary vocabulary instruction.* Newark, DE: International Reading Association.

Marzano, R., & Toth, M. (2011). *Art and science of teaching causal teacher evaluation model—raising student achievement.* Learning Sciences International.

Maslin, P. (2003). *Comparing basal pro-grams.* Charlottesville: University of Virginia. Available online at http://readingfirst.virginia.edu/pdfs/Maslin_whitepaper.

Mason, J. M., Peterman, C. L., & Kerr, B. M. (1988). *Fostering comprehension by reading books to kin-dergarten children* (Technical Report No. 426). Champaign: University of Illinois, Center for the Study of Reading.

Mathes, P. G., Denton, C. A., Fletcher, J. M., Anthony, J. L., Francis, D. J., & Schatschneider, C. (2005). The effects of theoretically different instruction and student characteristics on the skills of struggling readers. *Reading Research Quarterly, 40,* 148–182.

Mathes, P. G., & Fuchs, L. S. (1993). Peer-mediated reading instruction in special education resource rooms. *Learning Disabilities Research and Practice, 8,* 233–243.

McArthur, T. (Ed.). (1992). *The Oxford companion to the English language.* New York: Oxford University Press.

McCabe, D. (2010). *Sequential spelling.* Available online at http://www.avko.org/sequentialspelling.html.

McClure, A. A., & Kristo, J. V. (Eds.). (1994). *Inviting children's responses to literature.* Urbana, IL: National Council of Teachers of English.

McCormick, S. (1992). Disabled readers' erroneous responses to inferential comprehension questions: Description and analysis. *Reading Research Quarterly, 27,* 55–77.

McCracken, R. A. (1991). *Spelling through phonics.* Grand Forks, ND: Pegasus.

McDaniels, M. (2008, March). Key concepts in spacing learning over time [transcript]. In U.S. Department of Education, What Works Clearinghouse, *Doing what works: How to organize your teaching.* Available online at http://dww.ed.gov/launcher.cfm?media/CL/OIS/SL/Learn/528_sl_video.

McGee, L. M., & Schickedanz, J. A. (2007). Re-peated interactive read-alouds in preschool and kindergarten. *The Reading Teacher, 60,* 742–751.

McGee, L. M., & Tompkins, G. E. (1981). The videotape answer to independent reading comprehension activities. *The Reading Teacher, 34,* 427–433.

McGinley, W. J., & Denner, P. R. (1987). Story impressions: A prereading/writing activity. *Journal of Reading, 31,* 248–253.

McKenna, M. C., & Kerr, D. J. (1990). Measuring attitude toward reading: A new tool for teachers. *The Reading Teacher, 43,* 626–639.

McKenna, M. C., & Picard, M. (2006). Revisiting the role of miscue analysis in effective teaching. *The Reading Teacher, 60,* 378–380.

McKenna, M. C., & Walpole, S. (2005). How well does assessment inform our reading instruction? *The Reading Teacher, 59,* 84–86.

McKeown, M. G. (1993). Creating effective definitions for young word learners. *Reading Research Quarterly, 28,* 16–32.

McKeown, M. G. (2006). *Understanding text: What does it mean, why is it hard, and how can we support students to do it?* Paper presented at the Reading Research conference, Chicago.

McKeown, M. G., Beck, I. L., & Blake, R. K. (2009). Rethinking reading comprehension instruction: A comparison of instruction for strategies and content approaches. *Reading Research Quarterly, 44,* 218–253.

McKeown, M. G., Beck, I. L., & Sandora, C. A. (1996). Questioning the author: An approach to developing meaningful classroom discourse. In M. F. Graves, P. van den Broek, & B. M. Taylor (Eds.), *The first R, every child's right to read* (pp. 97–119). New York: Teachers College Press.

McLane, J. B., & McNamee, G. D. (1990). *Early literacy.* Cambridge, MA: Harvard University Press.

McLaughlin, B., August, D., Snow, C., Carlo, M., Dressier, C., White, C., Lively, T., & Lippman, D. (2000). *Vocabulary knowledge and reading comprehension in English language learners* (Final performance report). Washington, DC: Office of Educational Research and Improvement. Available online at http://www.ncela.gwu.edu/ncbepubs/symposia/reading/6august.

McMackin, M. C., & Witherell, N. L. (2005). Different routes to the same destination: Drawing conclusions with tiered graphic organizers. *The Reading Teacher, 59,* 242–252.

McMaster, J. C. (1998). "Doing" literature: Using drama to build literacy. *The Reading Teacher, 51,* 574–584.

McNamara, D. S., Graesser, A. C., Cai, Z., & Kulikowich, J. M. (2011, April). *Coh-Metrix Easability components: Aligning text difficulty with theories of text comprehension.* Paper presented at the AERA conference, New Orleans, LA.

McNamara, T. P., Miller, D. L., & Bransford, J. D. (1991). Mental models and reading comprehension. In R. Barr, M. L. Kamil, P. Mosenthal, & P. D. Pearson (Eds.), *Handbook of reading research* (Vol. II, pp. 490–511). New York: Longman.

McNeil, J. D. (1987). *Reading comprehension: New directions for classroom practice* (2nd ed.). Glenview, IL: Scott, Foresman.

Medley, D. M. (1977). *Teacher competence and teacher effectiveness: A review of process-product research.* Washington, DC: American Association of Colleges for Teacher Education.

Mehigan, K. (2005). The strategy toolbox: A ladder to strategic teaching. *The Reading Teacher, 58,* 552–566.

Meichenbaum, D., & Biemiller, A. (1998). *Nurturing independent learners: Helping students take charge of their learning.* Cambridge, MA: Brookline Books.

Menke, P. J., & Pressley, M. (1994). Elaborative interrogation: Using "why" questions to enhance the learning from text. *Journal of Reading, 37,* 642–645.

Menon, S., & Hiebert, E. H. (2003, April). *A comparison of first graders' reading acquisition with little books and literature anthologies.* Paper presented at the annual meeting of the American Educational Research Association, Chicago.

Mesmer, H. A. (1999). Scaffolding a crucial transition using text with some decodability. *The Reading Teacher, 53,* 130–142.

Mesmer, H. A., & Griffith, P. L. (2005). Every-body's selling it—but just what is explicit, systematic phonics instruction? *The Reading Teacher, 59,* 366–376.

Metsala, J. L. (1999). The development of phonemic awareness in reading-disabled children. *Applied Psycholinguistics, 20,* 149–158.

Meyer, B. J. F., & Rice, G. E. (1984). The structure of text. In P. D. Pearson, R. Barr, M. L. Kamil, & P. Mosenthal (Eds.), *Handbook of reading research* (pp. 319–351). New York: Longman.

Meyer, K. (2010). A collaborative approach to reading workshop in the middle years. *The Reading Teacher, 63,* 501–507.

Meyers, K. L. (1988). Twenty (better) questions. *English Journal, 77* (1), 64–65.

Miller, D. (2002). *Reading with meaning: Teaching comprehension in the primary grades.* Portland, ME: Stenhouse.

Miller, K. (2000). Hoa means "flower": language, learners, and culture in an ESL multi-age classroom. In C. F. Stice, & J. E. Bertrand (Eds.), *Teaching at-risk students in the K-4 classroom: Language, literacy, learning* (pp. 95–112). Norwood, MA; Christopher-Gordon.

Miranda, A., Villaescusa, M. I., & Vidal-Abarca, E. (1997). Is attribution retraining necessary? Use of self-regulation procedures for enhancing the reading comprehension strategies of children with learning disabilities. *Journal of Learning Disabilities, 30,* 503–512.

Moats, L. C. (2000). *Speech to print: language essentials for teachers.* Baltimore: Brookes.

Moats, L. C. (2004). *Language essentials for teachers of reading and spelling. Module 2: Phonetics, phonology, and phoneme awareness.* Longmont, CO: Sopris West.

Modiano, N. (1968). National or mother language in beginning reading: A comparative study. *Research in the Teaching of English, 2,* 32–43.

Mohr, K. J., & Mohr, E. S. (2007). Extending English-language learners' classroom interactions using the response protocol. *The Reading Teacher, 60,* 440–450.

Mokhtari, K., & Reichard, C. A. (2002). Assessing students' metacognitive awareness of reading strategies. *Journal of Educational Psychology, 94,* 249–259.

Mokhtari, K., Rosemary, C. A., & Edwards, P. A. (2007). Making instructional decisions based on data: What, how, and why . *The Reading Teacher, 61,* 354–359.

Moldofsky, P. B. (1983). Teaching students to determine the central story problem: A practical application of schema theory. *The Reading Teacher, 38,* 377–382.

Moore, D. W., & Moore, S. A. (1986). Possible sentences. In E. K. Dishner, T. W. Bean, J. E. Readence, & D. W. Moore (Eds.), *Reading in the content areas: Improving classroom instruction* (2nd ed.) (pp. 174–179). Dubuque, IA: Kendall/Hunt.

Moore, D. W., Moore, S. A., Cunningham, P. M., & Cunningham, J. W. (1986). *Developing readers and writers in the content areas.* New York: Longman.

Morris, D. (2008). *Diagnosis and correction of reading problems.* New York: Guilford.

Morris, D., Bloodgood, J. R., Lomax, R. G., & Perney, J. (2003). Developmental steps in learning to read: A longitudinal study in kindergarten and first grade. *Reading Research Quarterly, 38,* 302–328.

Morris, D., & Gaffney, M. (2011). Building reading fluency in a learning-disabled middle school reader. *Journal of Adolescent & Adult Literacy, 54,* 331–341.

Morrow, L. M. (1985). Reading and retelling stories: Strategies for emergent readers. *The Reading Teacher, 38,* 871–875.

Morrow, L. M. (1988). Young children's responses to one-to-one story readings in school settings. *Reading Research Quarterly, 23,* 89–107.

Morrow, L. M. (1997). *Literacy development in the early years: Helping children read and write* (3rd ed.). Boston: Allyn & Bacon.

Morrow, L. M. (2002). *The literacy center: Contexts for reading and writing.* Portland, ME: Sten-house.

Morrow, L. M., & Asbury, E. B. (2001). Patricia Loden. In M. Pressley, R. L. Allington, R. Wharton-McDonald, C. C. Block, & L. M. Morrow (Eds.), *Learning to read: Lessons from exemplary first-grade classrooms* (pp. 184–202). New York: Guilford.

Mosenthal, J. H. (1990). Developing low-performing, fourth-grade, inner-city students' ability to comprehend narrative. In J. Zutell & S. McCormick (Eds.), *Literacy theory and research: Analyses from multiple paradigms* (39th yearbook of the National Reading Conference) (pp. 275–286). Chicago: National Reading Conference.

Moustafa, M. (1995). Children's productive phonological recoding. *Reading Research Quarterly, 30,* 464–476.

Moustafa, M., & Maldonado-Colon, E. (1999). Whole-to-part phonics instruction: Building on what children know to help them know more. *The Reading Teacher, 52,* 448–458.

Mullis, I. V. S., Martin, M. O., Gonzalez, E. J., & Kennedy, A. M. (2003). *PIRLS 2001 international report: IEA's study of reading literacy achievement in primary schools in 35 countries.* Chestnut Hill, MA: Boston College.

Murphy, C. (1992). Study groups foster school-wide learning. *Educational Leadership, 50* (3), 71–74.

Murphy, L. L., Spies, R. A., & Plake, B. S. (Eds.). (2006). *Tests in print VII.* Lincoln: University of Nebraska.

Murphy, P. K., & Edwards, M. E. (2004, April). *What the studies tell us: A meta-analysis of discussion approaches.* Paper presented at the meeting of American Educational Research Association, Montreal.

Murray, B. (2006a). How to help beginners with oral reading. *The Reading Genie.* Available online at http://www.auburn.edu/academic/education/reading_genie/oralrdg.html.

Murray, B. (2006b). Making friends with phonemes. *The Reading Genie.* Available online at http://www.auburn.edu/academic/education/reading_genie/phon.html.

Murray, B. (2006c). Overview: How children learn to read words. *The Reading Genie.* Available online at http://www.auburn.edu/academic/education/reading_genie/overview.html.

Murray, B. (2006d). Adopting a reading series? *The Reading Genie.* Available online at http://auburn.edu/academic/education/reading_genie.

Murray, D. (1979). The listening eye: Reflections on the writing conference. *College English, 41,* 13–18.

Muschla, G. R. (1993). *Writing workshop survival kit.* West Nyack, NY: Center for Applied Research in Education.

Muter, V., & Snowling, M. (1998). Concurrent and longitudinal predictors of reading: The role of metalinguistic and short-term memory skills. *Reading Research Quarterly, 33,* 320–337.

Muth, K. D. (1987). Teachers' connection questions: Prompting students to organize text ideas. *Journal of Reading, 31,* 254–259.

NAEYC. (2009). *Where we stand on learning to read and write.* Available online at http://www.naeyc.org/positionstatements/learning_read-write.

Nagy, W. E. (1988). *Teaching vocabulary to improve reading comprehension.* Newark, DE: International Reading Association.

Nagy, W. E., & Anderson, R. C. (1984). How many words are there in printed English? *Reading Research Quarterly, 19,* 304–330.

Nagy, W. E., Anderson, R. C., & Herman, P. A. (1987). Learning word meanings from context during normal reading. *American Educational Research Journal, 24,* 237–270.

Nagy, W. E., & Herman, P. A. (1987). Breadth and depth of vocabulary knowledge: Implications for acquisition and instruction. In M. G.

McKeown & M. E. Curtis (Eds.), *The nature of vocabulary acquisition* (pp. 19–35). Hills-dale, NJ: Erlbaum.

Nagy, W. E., & Scott, J. A. (2000). Vocabulary processes. In M. L. Kamil, P. B. Mosenthal, P. D. Pearson, & R. Barr (Eds.), *Handbook of reading research* (Vol. III, pp. 269–284). Mahwah, NJ: Erlbaum.

Nation, P. (2001). *Learning vocabulary in another language.* Cambridge, UK: Cambridge University Press.

National Center on Education and the Economy & University of Pittsburgh. (1997). *Performance standards: Vol. 1, Elementary school.* Washington, DC: New Standards.

National Center for Education Statistics. (2009). *The nation's report card: Reading 2009* (NCES 2010–458). Washington, DC: Institute of Education Sciences, U.S. Department of Education. National Center on Quality Teaching and Learning. (2011). *Curriculum, assessment and the head start framework: An alignment review tool.* Available online at http://eclkc.ohs.acf.hhs.gov/.../docs/Alignment-Guide-1.pdf.

National Center on Response to Intervention (2011). Ask the expert — Lou Danielson. Why does The National Center on RTI use the term "levels of prevention" instead of "tiers" when describing the RTI framework? [Video script]. Author. Available online at www.rti4success.org

National Clearinghouse for English Acquisition and Language Instruction Education Programs. (2008). *NCELA FAQ. Q: How has the English language learner (ELL) population changed in recent years?* Available online at http://www.ncela.gwu.edu/expert/faq/08leps.html.

National Governors Association Center for Best Practices and Council of Chief State School Officers. (2010a). *The standards: English language arts stan-dards.* Available online at http://www.corestandards.org/the-standards/englishlanguage-arts-standards.

National Governors Association Center for Best Practices and Council of Chief State School Officers. (2010b). *Common Core State Standards for English language arts and literacy in history/social studies & science. Appendix A: Research supporting key elements of the standards.* Available online at http://www.corestandards.org/Files/K12ELAAppendixA.pdf.

National Governors Association Center for Best Practices and Council of Chief State School Officers. (2010c). *Common Core State Standards for English language arts & literacy in history/social studies, science, and technical subjects. Appendix B: Text exemplars and sample performance, tasks.* Available online at http://www.corestandards.org/assets/Appendix_B.pdf.

National Reading Panel. (2000). *National Reading Panel report.* Washington, DC: U.S. Department of Education.

Nessel, D. (1987). The new face of comprehension instruction: A closer look at questions. *The Reading Teacher, 40,* 604–606.

Neubert, G. A., & Wilkins, E. A. (2004). *Putting it all together: The directed reading lesson in the secondary content classroom.* Boston: Pearson.

Neuman, S. B. (1997). *Getting books in children's hands: A study of access to literacy.* Paper presented at National Reading Conference, Scottsdale, AZ.

Neuman, S.B. How we neglect knowledge— and why. (2006, spring). *American Educator,* 24–27.

Neuman, S. B., & Roskos, K. (2005). Whatever happened to developmentally appropriate practice in early literacy? *Journal of the National Association for the Education of Young Children (Beyond the Journal).* Available online at http://www.journal.naeyc.org/btj/200507/02Neuman.asp.

New Literacies Research Team. (2006). *Results summary reports 1–6 from the survey of Internet us-age and online reading.* Storrs: University of Connecticut, Neag School of Education. Available online at http://www.newliteracies.uconn.edu/pubs.html.

New Standards Primary Literacy Committee. (1999). *Reading and writing grade by grade: Primary literacy standards through third grade.* Washington, DC: National Center on Education and the Economy & University of Pittsburgh.

New Standards Speaking and Listening Committee. (2001a). *Reading and writing grade by grade: Primary literacy standards through third grade*. Washington, DC: National Center on Education and the Economy & University of Pittsburgh.

New Standards Speaking and Listening Committee. (2001b). *Speaking and listening for preschool through third grade*. Washington, DC: National Center on Education and the Economy & University of Pittsburgh.

NICHD Early Child Care Research Network. (2002). The relation of global first grade classroom environment to structural classroom features and teacher and student behaviors. *The Elementary School Journal, 102*, 367–387.

NICHD Early Child Care Research Network. (2005). Pathways to reading: The role of oral language in the transition to reading. *Developmental Psychology, 41*, 428–442.

Nichols, C. N. (2007). *The effect of three methods of introducing vocabulary words to elementary students: Traditional, friendly definitions, and parsing*. Unpublished doctoral dissertation, University of Pittsburgh, Pittsburgh.

Nicholson, T., & Whyte, B. (1992). Matthew effects in learning new words while listening to stories. In C. K. Kinzer & D. J. Leu (Eds.), *Literacy research, theory, and practice: Views from many perspectives* (pp. 499–501). Chicago: National Reading Conference.

Nilsson, N. L. (2008). A critical analysis of eight informal reading inventories. *The Reading Teacher, 61*, 526–536.

Nisbet, J., & Shucksmith, J. (1986). *Learning strategies*. London: Routledge & Kegan Paul.

No Child Left Behind Act of 2001, Public Law PL 107–110, Sec. 1001.

Noe, K. L. S. (2002, May). *Literature circles: Fostering thinking and response*. Paper presented at the annual convention of the International Reading Association, San Francisco.

Noll, E., & Watkins, R. (2003–2004). The impact of homelessness on children's literacy experiences. *The Reading Teacher, 57*, 362–371.

Northwest Regional Educational Laboratory. (2003). *Overview of second language acquisition theory*. Available online at http://www.nwrel.org/request/2003may/overview.html.

Northwest Regional Educational Laboratory. (2008). *The beginning writing continuum*. Available online at http://www.nwrel.org/assessment/pdfGeneral/BWC.pdf.

Norton, D. E. (1989). *Through the eyes of a child*. Columbus, OH: Merrill.

Oakhill, J., & Yuill, N. (1996). Higher-order factors in comprehension disability: Processes and remediation. In C. Cornoldi & J. Oakhill (Eds.), *Reading comprehension difficulties: Processes and intervention* (pp. 69–92). Mahwah, NJ: Erlbaum.

Oczkus, L. (2005). *Reciprocal teaching strategies at work: Improving reading comprehension, grades 2–6* [video recording]. Newark, DE: International Reading Association.

Office of Special Education and Rehabilitation. (2005). *IDEA-reauthorized statute Individualized Education Program (IEP)*. Available online at http://www.ed.gov/about/offices/list/osers/index.html.

Ogle, D., & Fogelberg, E. (2001). Expanding collaborative roles of reading specialists: Developing an intermediate reading support program. In V. J. Risko & K. Bromley (Eds.), *Collaboration for diverse learners: Viewpoints and practices*. Newark, DE: International Reading Association.

Ogle, D. M. (1989). The know, want to know, learn strategy. In K. D. Muth (Ed.), *Children's comprehension of text* (pp. 205–223). Newark, DE: International Reading Association.

Ogle, L., Sen, A., Pahlke, E., Jocelyn, L., Kastberg, D., Roey, S., & Williams, T. (2003). *International comparisons in fourth-grade reading literacy: Findings from the Progress in International Reading Literacy Study (PIRLS) of 2001* (NCES 2003–073). Washington, DC: U.S. Department of Education, NCES. Available online at http://nces.ed.gov/pubs2004/pirlspub.

Oken-Wright, P. (1998). Transition to writing: Drawing as a scaffold for emergent writers. *Young Children, 53* (2), 76–81.

Olson, J. L. (1987). Drawing to write. *School Arts, 87* (1), 25–27.

Onofrey, K. A., & Theurer, J. (2007). What's a teacher to do: Suggestions for comprehension strategy instruction. *The Reading Teacher, 60*, 681–684.

Opitz, M. F., & Harding-DeKam, J. L. (2007). Understanding and teaching English-language learners. *The Reading Teacher, 60*, 590–593.

Oregon Department of Education (2008). *Test administration manual 2008–2009 school year*. Salem, OR: Author.

O'Rourke, J. P. (1974). *Toward a science of vocabulary development*. The Hague: Mouton.

Owens, R. E. (1992). *Language development: An introduction*. Boston: Allyn & Bacon.

Palincsar, A. S., & Brown, A. L. (1986). Interactive teaching to promote independent learning from text. *The Reading Teacher, 39*, 771–777.

Palincsar, A. S., Winn, J., David, Y., Snyder, B., & Stevens, D. (1993). Approaches to strategic reading instruction reflecting different assumptions regarding teaching and learning. In L. J. Meltzer (Ed.), *Strategy assessment and instruction for students with learning disabilities: From theory to prac-tice* (pp. 247–292). Austin, TX: Pro-Ed.

Paratore, J. R. (1995). Implementing an intergenerational literacy project: Lessons learned. In L. M. Morrow (Ed.), *Family literacy: Connections in schools and communities* (pp. 37–53). Newark, DE: International Reading Association.

Paratore J. R., Cassano C. M., & Schickedanz J. A. (2011). Supporting early (and later) literacy development at home and at school: The long view. In M. Kamil, P. D. Pearson, E. B. Moje, & P. Afflerbach (Eds.), *Handbook of reading research* (Vol. 4, pp. 107–135). New York: Routledge.

PARCC (2011). *Draft Model content frameworks for English language arts/literacy*. Available online at http://parcconline.org/

Paris, S. G., Wasik, B. A., & Turner, J. C. (1991). The development of strategic readers. In R. Barr, M. L. Kamil, P. Mosenthal, & P. D. Pearson (Eds.), *Handbook of reading research* (Vol. II, pp. 609–640). New York: Longman.

Parker, D. (2002). *Accelerated literacy for English language learners (ELLs): A field-tested, research-based model of training and learning*. Paper presented at the annual convention of the International Reading Association, San Francisco.

Parsons, L. (1990). *Response journals*. Portsmouth, NH: Heinemann.

Pashler, H., Bain, P., Bottge, B., Graesser, A., Koedinger, K., McDaniel, M., & Metcalfe, J. (2007). *Organizing instruction and study to improve student learning* (NCER 2007–2004). Washington, DC: National Center for Education Research, Institute of Education Sciences, U.S. Department of Education. Available online at http://ies.ed.gov/ncee/wwc/pdf/practiceguides/20072004.pdf.

Paterson, W. A., Henry, J. J., O'Quin, K., Ceprano, M. A., & Blue, E. V. (2003). Investigating the effectiveness of an integrated learning system on early emergent readers. *Reading Research Quarterly, 38*, 172–207.

Pauk, W. (1989). The new SQ3R. *Reading World, 23*, 386–387.

Paul, R., & Elder, L. (2001). *Critical thinking: Tools for taking charge of your learning and your life*. New York: Prentice Hall.

Pearman, C. J. (2008). Independent reading of CD-ROM storybooks: Measuring comprehension with oral retellings. *The Reading Teacher, 61*, 594–602.

Pearson, P. D. (1985). Changing the face of reading comprehension instruction. *The Reading Teacher, 38*, 724–738.

Pearson, P. D. (2003, May). *Maintaining momentum: Getting inside the problem*. Paper presented at the annual convention of the International Reading Association, Orlando, FL.

Pearson, P. D., & Camperell, K. (1994). Comprehension of text structures. In R. B. Ruddell, M. R. Ruddell, & H. Singer (Eds.), *Theoretical models and processes of reading* (4th ed.) (pp. 448–568). Newark, DE: International Reading Association.

Pearson, P. D., & Gallagher, M. C. (1983). The instruction of reading comprehension. *Contemporary Educational Psychology, 8,* 317–345.

Pearson, P. D., & Johnson, D. D. (1978). *Teaching reading comprehension.* New York: Holt.

Pearson Education (2008). *The Longman dictionary of American English* (4th ed.). Essex, ENG: Author.

Pellegrini, A. D., Perlmutter, J. C., Galda, L., & Brody, G. H. (1990). Joint reading between Head Start children and their mothers. *Child Development, 61,* 443–453.

Pellegrino, J. W., Jones, L. R., and Mitchell, K. J. (Eds.). (1999). *Grading the nation's report card: Evaluating NAEP and transforming the Assessment of Educational Progress.* Washington, DC: National Academy Press.

Peregoy, S. F., & Boyle, O. F. (2001). *Reading, writing, & learning in ESL: A resource book for K–12 teachers.* New York: Longman.

Perfetti, C. A. (1985). *Reading ability.* New York: Oxford University Press.

Petty, W., Herold, C., & Stoll, E. (1968). *The state of the knowledge of the teaching of vocabulary* (Cooperative Research Project No. 3128). Champaign, IL: National Council of Teachers of English.

Pianta, R. C., & La Paro, K. (2003). Improving early school success. *Educational Leadership, 60* (7), 24–29.

Pike, K., Compain, R., & Mumper, J. (1994). *New connections: An integrated approach to literacy.* New York: HarperCollins.

Pikulski, J. J. (2006). Fluency: A developmental and language perspective. In S. J. Samuels & A. E. Farstrup (Eds.), *What research has to say about fluency instruction* (pp. 70–93). Newark, DE: International Reading Association.

Pincus, A. (2005). Teaching tips: What's a teacher to do? Navigating the worksheet curriculum. *The Reading Teacher, 59,* 75–79.

Ping-Yun, S. (2003). Using drama and theatre to promote literacy development: Some basic classroom applications . *The Clearinghouse on Reading, English, and Communication Digest 187.* Available online at http://reading.indiana.edu/ieo/digests/d187.html.

Pinkus, L. M. (2009). *Meaningful measurement: The role of assessments in improving high school education in the twenty-first century.* Washington, DC: Alliance for Excellent Education.

Pinnell, G. S. (2006). Every child a reader: What one teacher can do. *The Reading Teacher, 60,* 78–83.

Pinnell, G. S., & Fountas, I. C. (1998). *Word matters.* Portsmouth, NH: Heinemann.

Pinnell, G. S., & Fountas, I. C. (2002). *Leveled books for readers grades 3–6.* Portsmouth, NH: Heinemann.

Pinnell, G. S., Pikulski, J. J., Wixson, K. K., Campbell, J. R., Gough, P. B., & Beatty, A. S. (1995). *Listening to children read aloud.* Washington, DC: U.S. Department of Education, National Center for Education Statistics.

Piolat, A., Roussey, J., & Gombert, A. (1999). The development of argumentative schema in writing. In J. Andriessen & P. Coirier (Eds.), *Foundations of argumentative text processing* (pp. 117–136). Amsterdam: Amsterdam University Press.

Pitcher, S. M., Albright, L. K., DeLaney, C. J., Walker, N. T., Seunarinesingh, K., Mogge, S., Headley, K. N., Ridgeway, V., Peck, S., Hunt, R., & Dunston, P. J. (2007). Assessing adolescents' motivation to read. *Journal of Adolescent & Adult Literacy, 50,* 378–396.

Platt, P. (1978). Grapho-linguistics: Children's drawings in relation to reading and writing skills. *The Reading Teacher, 31,* 262–268.

Poole, D. (2008). Interactional differentiation in the mixed-ability group: A situated view of two struggling readers. *Reading Research Quarterly, 43,* 228–250.

Popham, W. J. (2000). *Modern educational measurement: Practical guidelines for educational leaders.* Boston: Allyn & Bacon.

Popham, W. J. (2004). "Teaching to the test": An expression to eliminate. *Educational Leadership, 62* (3), 82–83.

Prawat, R. S. (1989). Promoting access to knowledge, strategy, and disposition in students: A research synthesis. *Review of Educational Research, 59,* 1–41.

Pressley, M. (1994, November). *What makes sense in reading instruction according to research.* Paper presented at the annual meeting of the Connecticut Reading Association, Waterbury.

Pressley, M. (2001, December). *Teachers who motivate, students who learn to read and write.* Paper presented at the annual meeting of the National Reading Conference, San Antonio, TX.

Pressley, M. (2006, April). *What the future of reading research could be.* Paper presented at the Reading Research Conference, Chicago.

Pressley, M., & Afflerbach, P. (1995). *Verbal protocols of reading: The nature of constructively responsive reading.* Hillsdale, NJ: Erlbaum.

Pressley, M., Allington, R. L., Wharton-McDonald, R., Block, C. C., & Morrow, L. M. (2001). The nature of first-grade instruction that promotes literacy achievement. In M. Pressley, R. L. Allington, R. Wharton-McDonald, C. C. Block, & L. M. Morrow (Eds.), *Learning to read: Lessons from exemplary first-grade classrooms* (pp. 48–69). New York: Guilford.

Pressley, M., Borkowski, J. G., Forrest-Pressley, D., Gaskins, I. W., & Wiley, D. (1993). Closing thoughts on strategy instruction for individuals with learning disabilities: The good information-processing perspective. In L. Meltzer (Ed.), *Strategy assessment and instruction for students with learning disabilities: From theory to practice* (pp. 355–377). Austin, TX: Pro-Ed.

Pressley, M., Gaskins, I. W., & Fingeret, L. (2006). Instruction and development of reading fluency in struggling readers. In S. J. Samuels & A. E. Farstrup (Eds.), *What research has to say about fluency instruction* (pp. 47–69). Newark, DE: International Reading Association.

Pressley, M., Johnson, C. J., Symons, S., McGoldrick, J. A., & Kurita, J. A. (1989). Strategies that improve children's memory and comprehension of what is read. *Elementary School Journal, 89,* 3–32.

Pressley, M., Wharton-McDonald, R., Mistretta-Hampston, J., & Echevarria, M. (1998). Literacy instruction in 10 fourth- and fifth-grade classrooms in upstate New York. *Scientific Studies of Reading, 2,* 159–194.

Probst, R. (1988). Dialogue with a text. *English Journal, 77* (1), 32–38.

Purcell-Gates, V. (1997). Stories, coupons, and the TV guide: Relationships between home literacy experiences and emergent literacy knowledge, *Reading Research Quarterly, 31,* 406–428.

QuanSing, J. (1995, May). *Developmental teaching and learning using developmental continua as maps of language and literacy development which link assessment to teaching.* Paper presented at the annual meeting of the International Reading Association, Anaheim, CA.

Radencich, M. C. (1995). *Administration and supervision of the reading/ writing program.* Boston: Allyn & Bacon.

Raines, S., & Isbell, R. (1994). *Stories: Children's literature in early education.* Albany, NY: Delmar.

Rapaport, W. J. (2004). *What is "context" in contextual vocabulary acquisition? Lessons learned from artificial intelligence and verbal protocol of good readers when they encounter unknown words in context.* Paper presented at the International Reading Association convention, Reno, NV.

Raphael, T. E. (1984). Teaching learners about sources of information for answering questions. *The Reading Teacher, 28,* 303–311.

Raphael, T. E. (1986). Teaching question/answer relationships, revisited. *The Reading Teacher, 39,* 516–522.

Raphael, T. E., & Au, K. H. (2005). QAR: Enhancing comprehension and test taking across grades and content areas. *The Reading Teacher, 59,* 206–221.

Raphael, T. E., & Boyd, F. B. (1997). When readers write: The book club writing component. In S. I. McMachon & T. E. Raphael (Eds.), *The book club connection: Literacy learning and classroom talk* (pp. 69–88). New York: Teachers College Press.

Raphael, T. E., & Englert, C. S. (1990). Writing and reading: Partners in constructing meaning. *The Reading Teacher, 43,* 388–400.

Raphael, T. E., Englert, C. S., & Kirschner, B. W. (1989). Acquisition of expository writing skills. In J. M. Mason (Ed.), *Reading and writing connections* (pp. 261–290). Boston: Allyn & Bacon.

Rashotte, C. A., & Torgesen, J. K. (1985). Repeated reading and reading fluency in learning disabled children. *Reading Research Quarterly, 20,* 180–188.

Rasinski, T., & Hamman, P. (2010). Fluency: Why it is not hot. *Reading Today, 28* (1), 26.

Ray, K. W. (2004). When kids make books. *Educational Leadership, 62* (2), 14–19.

Rayner, K., & Pollatsek, A. (1989). *The psychology of reading.* Englewood Cliffs, NJ: Prentice Hall.

Read, C. (1971). Preschool children's knowledge of English phonology. *Harvard Educational Review, 41,* 1–34.

Read, S. (2010). A model for scaffolding writing instruction: *The Reading Teacher, 64,* 47–52.

Readence, J. E., Bean, T. W., & Baldwin, R. S. (1992). *Content area literacy: An integrated approach* (4th ed.). Dubuque, IA: Kendall/Hunt.

Reading Recovery Council of North America. (2006). *Reading Recovery facts and figures (1984–2005).* Available online at http://readingrecovery.org/sections/reading/facts.asp.

Renaissance Learning (2006). *Using readability levels to guide students to books.* Wisconsin Rapids, WI: Author.

Renaissance Learning (2009). *Atos vs. lexile. Which formula is better?* Wisconsin Rapids, WI: Author.

Reninger, K. B., & Wilkinson, I. A. G. (2010). Using discussions to promote striving readers' higher level comprehension of literary texts. In J. L. Collins & T. G. Gunning (Eds.), *Building struggling students' higher level literacy: Practical ideas, powerful solutions* (pp. 57–83). Newark, DE: International Reading Association.

Resnick, L. B. (1999). Making America smarter. *Education Week on the Web, 18* (June 16). Available online at http://www.edweek.org/ew/vol18/40resnick.h18

Resnick, L. B., & Hall, M. W. (2001). *The principles of learning: Study tools for educators* [CD-ROM, version 2.0]. Pittsburgh, PA: University of Pittsburgh, Learning Research and Development Center, Institute for Learning.

Reutzel, D. R. (2008). *Effective letter recognition in kindergarten and first grade: Lessons learned from research and from working with early readers in high poverty settings.* Paper presented at the International Reading Association Convention, Atlanta.

Reutzel, D. R. (2011). *Teaching early literacy and beginning readers.* Paper presented at the International Reading Association Convention, Orlando.

Reutzel, D. R., & Cooter, R. B. (1991). Organizing for effective instruction: The reading workshop. *The Reading Teacher, 44,* 548–555.

Reutzel, D. R., Jones, C. D., & Newman, T. H. (2010). Scaffolded silent reading: Improving the conditions of silent reading practice in classrooms. In E. H. Hiebert & D. R. Reutzel (Eds.), *Revisiting silent reading: New directions for teachers and researchers* (pp. 129–150). Newark, DE: International Reading Association.

Rhodes, J. A., & Milby, T. M. (2007). Teacher-created electronic books: Integrating technology to support readers with disabilities. *The Reading Teacher, 61,* 255–259.

Rhodes, L. K. (1990, March). *Anecdotal records: A powerful tool for ongoing literacy assessment.* Paper presented at the National Council of Teachers of English Conference, Colorado Springs, CO.

Rhodes, L. K., & Dudley-Marling, C. (1988). *Readers and writers with a difference: A holistic approach to teaching learning-disabled and remedial students.* Portsmouth, NH: Heinemann.

Richek, M. (2005). Words are wonderful: Interactive, time-efficient strategies to teach meaning vocabulary. *The Reading Teacher, 58,* 414–423.

Richgels, D. J., & Hansen, R. (1984). Gloss: Helping students apply both skills and strategies in reading content texts. *Journal of Reading, 27,* 312–317.

Richgels, D. S., McGee, L. M., & Slaton, E. A. (1989). Teaching expository text structure in reading and writing. In K. D. Muth (Ed.), *Children's comprehension of text* (pp. 167–184). Newark, DE: International Reading Association.

Richgels, D. S., & Wold, L. S. (1998). Literacy on the road: Backpacking partnerships between school and home. *The Reading Teacher, 52,* 18–29.

Riddle Buly, M., & Valencia, S. W. (2002). Below the bar: Profiles of students who fail state reading assessment. *Educational Evaluation and Policy Analysis, 24,* 219–239.

Rideout, V. J., Foehr, U. G., & Roberts, D. F. (2010). *Generation M2: Media in the lives of 8- to18-year-olds. A Kaiser Family Foundation study.* Available online at http://www.kff.org/entmedia/upload/8010.pdf.

Riedel, B. W. (2007). The relation between DIBELS, reading comprehension, and vocabulary in urban first-grade students. *Reading Research Quarterly, 42,* 546–567.

Rief, L. (2003). *100 quickwrites.* New York: Scholastic.

Riley, J. (1996). *The teaching of reading.* London: Paul Chapman.

Rimm-Kaufman, S. E., Fan, X., Chiu, Y. I., & You, W. (2006, April). *The contribution of the Responsive Classroom® approach on children's academic achievement: Results from a three-year longitudinal study.* Paper presented at the American Education Research Association Conference, San Francisco.

Risley, T. (2003, May). *Meaningful differences in the everyday experiences of young American children.* Paper presented at the annual convention of the International Reading Association, Orlando, FL.

Ritchey, K. D. (2004). From letter names to word reading: The development of reading in kindergarten (IRA Outstanding Dissertation Award for 2004). *Reading Research Quarterly, 39,* 374–376.

Rittle-Johnson, B., & Siegler, R. S. (1999). Learning to spell: Variability, choice, and change in children's strategy use. *Child Development, 70,* 332–348.

Robinson, D. H. (1998). Graphic organizers as aids to text learning. *Reading Research and Instruction, 37,* 85–105.

Robinson, F. P. (1970). *Effective study* (4th ed.). New York: Harper.

Rodriguez-Brown, F. V. (2011). Family literacy: A current view of research on children and parents learning together. In M. Kamil, P. D. Pearson, E. B. Moje, & P. Afflerbach (Eds.), *Handbook of reading research* (Vol. 4, pp. 726–753). New York: Routledge.

Roediger, H. L., McDaniel, K. B, & McDermott, M. A. (n.d.). *Using testing to improve learning and memory.* St Louis, MO: St. Louis University .

Romance, N. R., & Vitale, M. R. (2001). Implementing an indepth expanded science model in elementary schools: Multi-year findings, research issues, and policy implications. *International Journal of Science Education, 23* (4), 272–304.

Rose, M. C., Cundick, B. P., & Higbee, K. L. (1983). Verbal rehearsal and visual imagery: Mnemonic aids for learning disabled children. *Journal of Learning Disabilities, 16,* 352–354.

Rosenblatt, L. (1978). *The reader, the text, the poem.* Carbondale: Southern Illinois University Press.

Rosenblatt, L. (1991). Literature—S. O. S.! *Language Arts, 68,* 444–448.

Rosenblatt, L. (1994). The traditional theory of reading and writing. In R. B. Ruddell, M. R. Ruddell, & H. Singer (Eds.), *Theoretical models and processes of reading* (4th ed.) (pp. 1057–1092). Newark, DE: International Reading Association.

Rosenshine, B., & Meister, C. (1994). Reciprocal teaching: A review of the research. *Review of Educational Research, 64,* 479–530.

Rosenshine, B., Meister, C., & Chapman, S. (1996). Teaching students to generate questions: A review of the intervention studies. *Review of Educational Research, 66,* 181–221.

Roser, N. (2011, May). *Teaching early learners: Remixing literacy, technology, and motivation.* Paper presented at the International Reading Association convention, Orlando, FL.

Roser, N., Martinez, M., Fuhrken, C., & McDonnold, K. (2007). Characters as guides to meaning.*The Reading Teacher, 60,* 548–559.

Rosier, P. (1977). *A comparative study of two approaches introducing initial reading to Navajo children: The direct method and the native language method.* Unpublished doctoral dissertation, Northern Arizona University, Flagstaff.

Routman, R. (1991). *Invitations: Changing as teachers and learners K–12.* Portsmouth, NH: Heinemann.

Routman, R. (2000). *Conversations.* Portsmouth NH: Heinemann.

Rowe, D. (2005). Writing as an instructional factor in early literacy development. In C. M. Connor (Ed.), *International Reading Association–National Institute for Child Health and Human Development conference on early childhood literacy research: A summary of presentations and discussions.* Available online at http://reading.org/resources/issues/reports/iranichd_conference.html.

Rowe, M. B. (1969). Science, silence, and sanctions. *Science for Children, 6* (6), 11–13.

Ruddell, M. R. (1992). *Integrated content and long-term vocabulary learning with the vocabulary self-collection strategy.* In E. K. Dishner, T. W. Bean, J. E. Readence, & D. W. Moore (Eds.), *Reading in the content areas: Improving classroom instruction* (3rd ed.) (pp. 190–196). Dubuque, IA: Kendall/Hunt.

Ruddell, R. B. (1995). Those influential literacy teachers: Meaning negotiators and motivators. *The Reading Teacher, 48,* 454–463.

Ruddell, R. B., & Boyle, O. F. (1989). A study of cognitive mapping as a means to improve summarization and comprehension of expository text. *Reading Research and Instruction, 29* (1), 12–22.

Ruddell, R. B., & Ruddell, M. R. (1995). *Teaching children to read and write: Becoming an influential teacher.* Boston: Allyn & Bacon.

Rumelhart, D. (1980). Schemata: The building blocks of cognition. In R. J. Spiro, B. C. Bruce, & W. F. Bruner (Eds.), *Theoretical issues in reading comprehension* (pp. 33–58). Hillsdale, NJ: Erlbaum.

Rumelhart, D. (1984). Understanding understanding. In J. Flood (Ed.), *Understanding reading comprehension* (pp. 1–20). Newark, DE: International Reading Association.

Rye, J. (1982). *Cloze procedure and the teaching of reading.* London: Heinemann.

Saddler, B., & Andrade, H. (2004). The writing rubric. *Educational Leadership, 62* (2), 48–52.

Sadow, M. K. (1982). The use of story grammar in the design of questions. *The Reading Teacher, 35,* 518–522.

Sadowski, M., & Paivio, A. (1994). A dual coding view of imagery and verbal processes in reading comprehension. In R. B. Ruddell, M. R. Ruddell, & H. Singer (Eds.), *Theoretical models and processes of reading* (4th ed.) (pp. 582–601). Newark, DE: International Reading Association.

Salahu-Din, D., Persky, H., & Miller, J. (2008). *The nation's report card: Writing 2007* (NCES2008–468). Washington, DC: National Center for Education Statistics, Institute of Education Sciences, U.S. Department of Education.

Salinger, T. (2001). Assessing the literacy of young children: The case for multiple forms of evidence. In S. B. Neuman & D. K. Dickinson (Eds.), *Handbook of early literacy research* (pp. 390–418). New York: Guilford.

Samuels, S. J. (1979). The method of repeated reading. *The Reading Teacher, 32,* 403–408.

Samuels, S. J. (1988a). Characteristics of exemplary reading programs. In S. J. Samuels & P. D. Pearson (Eds.), *Changing school reading programs: Principles and case studies* (pp. 3–9). Newark, DE: International Reading Association.

Samuels, S. J. (1988b). Decoding and automaticity: Helping poor readers become automatic at word recognition. *The Reading Teacher, 41,* 756–760.

Samuels, S. J. (1994). Toward a theory of automatic information processing in reading revisited. In R. B. Ruddell, M. R. Ruddell, & H. Singer (Eds.), *Theoretical models and processes of reading* (4th ed.) (pp. 816–837). Newark, DE: International Reading Association.

Samuels, S. J. (2006). Fluency: Toward a model of reading fluency. In S. J. Samuels & A. E. Farstrup (Eds.), *What research has to say about fluency instruction* (pp. 24–46). Newark, DE: International Reading Association.

Samuelstuen, M. S., & Bråten, I. (2005). Decoding, knowledge, and strategies in comprehension of expository text. *Scandinavian Journal of Psychology, 46,* 107–117.

Sanders, W. L., & Rivers, J. C. (1996). *Cumulative and residual effects of teachers on future student academic achievement.* Knoxville, TN: University of Tennessee Value-Added Research and Assessment Center.

Santa, C. M. (1989). *Comprehension strategies across content areas.* Paper presented at the annual conference of the New England Reading Association, Newport, RI.

Santa, C. M. (1994, October). *Teaching reading in the content areas.* Paper presented at the International Reading Association's Southwest Regional Conference, Little Rock, AR.

Santa, C. M., Havens, L. T., & Maycumber, E. M. (1996). *Creating independence through student-owned strategies* (2nd ed.). Dubuque, IA: Kendall.

Scanlon, D. M., (2010, April). *The interactive strategies approach: Early literacy.* Paper presented at the International Reading Association Convention, Chicago.

Scanlon, D. M., & Anderson, K. I. (2010). Using the interactive strategies approach to prevent reading difficulties in an RTI context. In M. Y. Lipson & K. K. Wixson (Eds.), *Successful approaches to RTI: Collaborative practices for improving K–12 literacy* (pp. 20–65). Newark, DE: International Reading Association.

Scardamalia, M., & Bereiter, C. (1986). Research on written composition. In M. C. Wittrock (Ed.), *Handbook of research on teaching* (pp. 778–863). New York: Macmillan.

Scardamalia, M., Bereiter, C., & Goelman, H. (1982). The role of production factors in writing ability. In M. Nystrand (Ed.), *What writers know: The language, process, and structure of written discourse* (pp. 173–210). New York: Academic.

Schatz, E. K., & Baldwin, R. S. (1986). Context clues are unreliable predictors of word meanings. *Reading Research Quarterly, 21,* 439–453.

Schickedanz, J. A. (1999). *Much more than the ABCs: The early stages of reading and writing.* Washington, DC: National Association for the Education of Young Children.

Schneider, J. J., & Jackson, S. A. W. (2000). Process drama: A special space and place for writing. *The Reading Teacher, 54,* 38–51.

Schnorr, J. A., & Atkinson, R. C. (1969). Repetition versus imagery instructions in the short- and long-term retention of paired associates. *Psychonomic Science, 15,* 183–184.

Scholastic. (n.d.). *Accuracy matters: Reducing measurement error by targeted SRI testing.* New York: Author.

Scholastic. (2010). *Turning the page in the digital age.* New York: Author. Available online at http://mediaroom.scholastic.com/themes/bare_bones/2010_KFRR.pdf.

Schunk, D. H., & Rice, J. H. (1987). Enhancing comprehension skill and self-efficacy with strategy value information. *Journal of Reading Behavior, 19,* 285–302.

Schunk, D. H., & Zimmerman, B. J. (1997). Developing self-efficacious readers and writers: The role of social and self-regulatory processes. In J. T. Guthrie & A. Wigfield (Eds.), *Reading engagement: Motivating readers through integrated instruction* (pp. 34–50). Newark, DE: International Reading Association.

Schwanenflugel, P. J., Hamilton, A. M., Kuhn, M. R., Wisenbaker, J. M., & Stahl, S. A. (2004). Becoming a fluent reader: Reading skill and prosodic features in the oral reading of young readers. *Journal of Educational Psychology, 96,* 119–129.

Schwartz, R. M. (2005). Decisions, decisions: Responding to primary students during guided reading. *The Reading Teacher, 58,* 436–443.

Scott, T. (1998, May). *Using content area text to teach decoding and comprehension strategies.* Paper presented at the annual meeting of the International Reading Association, Orlando, FL.

Serafini, F. (2006). *Around the reading workshop in 180 days: A month-by-month guide to effective instruction.* Portsmouth, NH: Heinemann.

Shanahan, T. (2007). Early literacy development: Sequence of acquisition. In *Encyclopedia of language and literacy development* (pp. 1–6). London, ON: Canadian language and Literacy Research Network. Available online at http://www.literacyencyclopedia.ca/pdfs/topic.php?topId=225.

Shanahan, T., Callison, K., Carriere, C., Duke, N. K., Pearson, P. D., Schatschneider, C., & Torgesen, J. (2010). *Improving reading comprehension in kindergarten through 3rd grade: A practice guide* (NCEE 2010–4038). Washington, DC: National Center for Education Evaluation and Regional Assistance, Institute of Education Sciences, U.S. Department of Education. Retrieved from http://ies.ed.gov/ncee/wwc/publications/practiceguides

Shany, M. T., & Biemiller, A. (1995). Assisted reading practice: Effects on performance for poor readers in grades 3 and 4. *Reading Research Quarterly, 30*, 382–395.

Sharp, A. C., Sinatra, G. M., & Reynolds, R. E. (2008). The development of children's orthographic knowledge: A microgenetic perspective. *Reading Research Quarterly, 43*, 206–226.

Shearer, B. (1999, December). *The vocabulary self-collection strategy (VSS) in a middle school.* Paper presented at the 49th annual meeting of the National Reading Conference, Orlando, FL.

Shefelbine, J. (1990). A syllabic-unit approach to teaching decoding of polysyllabic words to fourth- and sixth-grade disabled readers. In J. Zutell & S. McCormick (Eds.), *Literacy theory and research: Analyses from multiple paradigms* (39th yearbook of the National Reading Conference) (pp. 223–229). Chicago: National Reading Conference.

Shefelbine, J. (1997). *Beginning Phonics Skills Test (BPST).* Sacramento, CA: Author.

Shefelbine, J., & Newman, K. K. (2000). *SIPPS (systematic instruction in phoneme awareness, phonics, and sight words): Challenge level.* Concord, CA: Developmental Studies Center.

Shuy, R. (1973). Nonstandard dialect problems: An overview. In J. L. Laffey & R. Shuy (Eds.), *Language differences: Do they interfere?* (pp. 3–16). Newark, DE: International Reading Association.

Silvaroli, N. J., & Wheelock, A. (2001). *Classroom reading inventory* (9th ed.). New York: McGraw-Hill.

Simmons, J. (1996). What writers know with time. *Language Arts, 73*, 602–605.

Sinatra, G. M., Brown, K. J., & Reynolds, R. E. (2002). Implications of cognitive resource allocation for comprehension strategies instruction. In C. C. Block & M. Pressley (Eds.), *Comprehension instruction: Research-based best practices* (pp. 62–76). New York: Guilford.

Sinatra, R. C., Stahl-Gemeke, J., & Berg, D. N. (1984). Improving reading comprehension of disabled readers through semantic mapping. *The Reading Teacher, 38*, 22–29.

Sinatra, R. C., Stahl-Gemeke, J., & Morgan, N. W. (1986). Using semantic mapping after reading to organize and write original discourse. *Journal of Reading, 30*, 4–13.

Singer, H., & Donlan, D. (1989). *Reading and learning from text* (2nd ed.). Hillsdale, NJ: Erlbaum.

Skillings, M. J., & Ferrell, R. (2000). Student-generated rubrics: Bringing students into the assessment process. *The Reading Teacher, 53*, 452–455.

Skjelfjord, V. J. (1976). Teaching children to segment words as an aid to learning to read. *Journal of Learning Disabilities, 9*, 39–48.

Slater, W. H., & Graves, M. F. (1989). Research on expository text. Implications for teachers. In K. D. Muth (Ed.), *Children's comprehension of text* (pp. 140–166). Newark, DE: International Reading Association.

Slavin, R. E. (1987a). Ability grouping and student achievement in elementary schools: A best-evidence synthesis. *Review of Education Research, 57*, 293–336.

Slavin, R. E. (1987b). Cooperative learning and the cooperative school. *Educational Leadership, 45* (3), 7–13.

Slavin, R. E. (1997–1998). Can education reduce societal inequity? *Educational Leadership, 55* (4), 6–10.

Slavin, R. E., & Cheung, A. (2005). A synthesis of research on language of reading instruction for English language learners. *Review of Educational Research, 75* (2), 247–284.

Slavin, R. E., Cheung, A., Groff, C., & Lake, C. (2008). Effective reading programs for middle and high schools: A best-evidence synthesis. *Reading Research Quarterly, 43*, 290–322.

Sloan, G. D. (1984). *The child as critic* (2nd ed.). New York: Teachers College Press.

Smith, L. (2006). Think-aloud mysteries: Using structured, sentence-by-sentence text passages to teach comprehension strategies. *The Reading Teacher, 59*, 764–773.

Smith, M. W., & Dickinson, D. K. (2002). *User's guide to the early language & literacy classroom observation kit.* Baltimore: Brookes.

Smith, T. E., Polloway, E. A., Patton, J. R., & Dowdy, C. A. (1998). *Teaching students with special needs in inclusive settings* (2nd ed.). Needham Heights, MA: Allyn & Bacon.

Smolkin, L. B. (2011, May). *Introduction to a developmental framework to support children's informational writing.* Paper presented at the International Reading Association Convention, Orlando.

Smolkin, L. B., & Donovan, C. A. (2011, May). *A developmental framework to support children's informational writing.* Paper presented at the International Reading Association Convention, Orlando.

Snider, M. A., Lima, S. S., & DeVito, P. J. (1994). Rhode Island's literacy portfolio assessment project. In S. Valencia, E. H. Hiebert, & P. P. Afflerbach (Eds.), *Authentic reading assessment: Practices and possibilities* (pp. 71–88). Newark, DE: International Reading Association.

Snow, C. (2010). Academic language and the challenge of reading for learning about science. *Science, 328*, 450–452.

Snow, C. E., Burns, M. S., & Griffin, P. (1998). *Preventing reading difficulties in young children.* Washington, DC: National Academy Press.

Spandel, V. (2001). *Creating writers through 6-trait writing assessment and instruction.* New York: Longman.

Spandel, V., & Stiggins, R. J. (1997). *Creating writers: Linking writing assessment and instruction* (2nd ed.). New York: Longman.

Spires, H. A., & Donley, J. (1998). Prior knowledge activation: Inducing engagement with informational texts. *Journal of Educational Psychology, 90*, 249–260.

Stahl, S. A. (1990, May). *Responding to children's needs, styles, and interests.* Paper presented at the 35th annual convention of the International Reading Association, Atlanta.

Stahl, S. A. (1998). Teaching children with reading problems to decode: Phonics and "not-phonics" instruction. *Reading and Writing Quarterly: Overcoming Learning Disabilities, 14*, 165–188.

Stahl, S. A., & Fairbanks, M. M. (1986). The effects of vocabulary instruction: A model-based meta-analysis. *Review of Educational Research, 56*, 72–110.

Stahl, S. A., Heubach, K., & Crammond, P. (1997). *Fluency-oriented reading instruction* (Reading Research Report No. 79). Athens, GA: National Reading Research Center. (ERIC Document Reproduction Service No. ED 405–554)

Stahl, S. A., & McKenna, M. M. (2002). *The concurrent development of phonological awareness, word recognition, and spelling.* Atlanta: University of Georgia, Center for the Improvement of Early Reading Achievement. Available online at http://www.ciera.org/library/archive/2001–07/200107.htm.

Stahl, S. A., Osborne, J., & Lehr, F. (1990). *Beginning to read: Thinking and learning about print: A summary.* Urbana-Champaign: University of Illinois, Center for the Study of Reading.

Stauffer, M. H. (1999). *Outline on literary elements.* Tampa: University of South Florida. Available online at http://www.cas.usf.edu/lis/lis6585/class/litelem.html.

Stauffer, R. G. (1969). *Directing reading maturity as a cognitive process.* New York: Harper.

Stauffer, R. G. (1970). *Reading-thinking skills.* Paper presented at the annual reading conference at Temple University, Philadelphia.

Stecher, B. M., Barron, S., Kaganoff, T., & Goodwin, J. (1998). *The effects of standards-based assessment on classroom practices: Results of the 1996–97 RAND survey of Kentucky teachers of mathematics and writing*

(CSE Technical Report 482). Los Angeles: University of California, Graduate School of Education & Information Studies, Center for the Study of Evaluation, National Center for Research on Evaluation, Standards and Student Testing (CRESST) & RAND Education.

Sternberg, R. J. (1987). Most vocabulary is learned from context. In M. G. McKeown & M. E. Curtis (Eds.), *The nature of vocabulary acquisition* (pp. 89–105). Hillsdale, NJ: Erlbaum.

Sticht, T. G., & James, J. H. (1984). Listening and reading. In P. D. Pearson, R. Barr, M. L. Kamil, & P. Mosenthal (Eds.), *Handbook of reading research* (pp. 293–317). New York: Longman.

Stien, D., & Beed, P. L. (2004). Bridging the gap between fiction and nonfiction in the literature circle setting. *The Reading Teacher, 57,* 510–518.

Stiggins, R. (2004). New assessment beliefs for a new school mission. *Phi Delta Kappan, 86* (1), 22–27.

Stiggins, R. (2006). Assessment for learning: A key to motivation and achievement. *Edge, 2* (2), 3–19.

Stiggins, R., & Chappuis, J. (2005). Using student-involved classroom assessment to close achievement gaps. *Theory Into Practice 44* (1), 11–18.

Strategic Education Research Partnership (2009). *Word generation.* Available online at http://wordgeneration.org/

Strickland, D. (1998). Educating African American learners at risk: Finding a better way. In C. Weaver (Ed.), *Practicing what we know: Informed reading instruction* (pp. 394–408). Urbana, IL: National Council of Teachers of English.

Strickland, D. (2008, May). *When DAP meets GAP: Strategies for promoting peaceful coexistence between developmentally-appropriate practice and the need to address the achievement gap.* Paper presented at the International Reading Association Convention, Atlanta.

Strickland, D., & Shanahan, T. (2004). What research says about reading: Laying the groundwork for literacy. *Educational Leadership, 61* (6), 74–77.

Strickland, D., & Taylor, D. (1989). Family storybook reading: Implications for children, curriculum, and families. In D. S. Strickland & L. M. Morrow (Eds.), *Emerging literacy: Young children learn to read and write* (pp. 27–33). Newark, DE: International Reading Association.

Sulzby, E. (1985). Children's emergent reading of favorite storybooks. *Reading Research Quarterly, 20,* 458–481.

Sulzby, E. (1989a). Appendix 2.1: Forms of writing and rereading from writing, example list. In J. M. Mason (Ed.), *Reading and writing connections* (pp. 51–63). Boston: Allyn & Bacon.

Sulzby, E. (1989b). Assessment of writing and of children's language while writing. In L. Morrow & J. Smith (Eds.), *The role of assessment and measurement in early literacy instruction* (pp. 83–109). Englewood Cliffs, NJ: Prentice-Hall.

Sulzby, E., & Barnhart, J. (1992). The development of academic competence: All our children emerge as writers and readers. In J. W. Irwin & M. A. Doyle (Eds.), *Reading/writing connections, learning from research* (pp. 120–144). Newark, DE: International Reading Association.

Sulzby, E., Barnhart, J., & Hieshima, J.A. (1989). Forms of writing and rereading from writing: A preliminary report. In J. M. Mason (Ed.), *Reading and writing connections* (pp. 31–50). Boston: Allyn & Bacon.

Sulzby, E., Teale, W., & Kamberelis, G. (1989). Emergent writing in the classroom: Home and school connections. In D. S. Strickland & L. M. Morrow (Eds.), *Emerging literacy: Young children learn to read and write* (pp. 63–79). Newark, DE: International Reading Association.

Sundbye, N. (1987). Text explicitness and inferential questioning: Effects on story understanding and recall. *Reading Research Quarterly, 22,* 82–98.

Sutherland, Z. (1997). *Children and books* (9th ed.). Glenview, IL: Scott, Foresman.

Sutton, C. (1989). Helping the nonnative English speaker with reading. *The Reading Teacher, 42,* 684–688.

Swain, M. (2005). The output hypothesis: Theory and research. In E. Hinkel (Ed.), *Handbook on research in second language teaching and learning* (pp. 471–484). Mahwah, NJ: Lawrence Erlbaum.

Sweet, A. P. (1997). Teacher perceptions of student motivation and their relation to literacy learning. In K. Guthrie & A. Wigfield (Eds.), *Reading engagement: Motivating readers through integrated instruction* (pp. 86–101). Newark, DE: International Reading Association.

Sylvester, R., & Greenidge, W. (2009). Digital storytelling: Extending the potential for struggling writers. *The Reading Teacher, 63,* 284–295.

Taba, H. (1965). The teaching of thinking. *Elementary English, 42,* 534–542.

Tabors, P. O. (1997). *One child, two languages: A guide for preschool educators of children learning English as a second language.* Baltimore: Brookes.

Tanner, T. M. (2010). Los Angeles teacher ratings. *The Los Angels Times.* Available online at http://projects.latimes.com/value-added/teacher/tracey-michelle-tanner/

Taylor, B. M. (2001). *The Early Intervention in Reading Program (EIR®). Research and development spanning twelve years.* Edina, MN: Web Education Company. Available online at http://www.earlyinterventioninreading.com/pdfs/taylor_research3.pdf.

Taylor, D., & Dorsey-Gaines, C. (1988). *Growing up literate: Learning from innercity families.* Portsmouth, NH: Heinemann.

Taylor, K. K. (1986). Summary writing by young children. *Reading Research Quarterly, 21,* 193–208.

Teale, W. H. (2008). *What it takes for readalouds to make a difference with children in early literacy.* Paper presented at the International Reading Association Convention, Atlanta.

Teale, W. H., & Sulzby, E. (1986). *Emergent literacy: Writing and reading.* Norwood, NJ: Ablex.

Temple, C., Martinez, M., Yokota, J., & Naylor, A. (1998). *Children's books in children's hands: An introduction to their literature.* Boston: Allyn & Bacon.

Temple, C., Nathan, R., Temple, F., & Burris, N. A. (1993). *The beginnings of writing* (3rd ed.). Boston: Allyn & Bacon.

Terman, L. M. (1954). The discovery and encouragement of exceptional talent. *American Psychologist, 9,* 221–230.

Terry, A. (1974). *Children's poetry preferences.* Urbana, IL: National Council of Teachers of English.

Texas Instrument Foundation, Head Start of Greater Dallas, & Southern Methodist University. (1996). *LEAP into a brighter future.* Paper presented at Head Start's 3rd National Research Conference, Dallas. Available online at http://www.ti.com/corp/docs/company/citizen/foundation/leapsbounds/leap.pdf.

Thames, D. G., & York, K. C. (2003). Disciplinary border crossing: Adopting broader, richer view of literacy. *The Reading Teacher, 56,* 602–610.

Thibault, M., & Walbert, D. (2008). *Rethinking reports.* Learn NC Editions. Chapel Hill: Chapel Hill School of Education, University of North Carolina. Available online at http://learnnc.org/lp/editions/rethinking-reports/719.

Thomas, E. L., & Robinson, H. A. (1972). *Improving reading in every class: A sourcebook for teachers.* Boston: Allyn & Bacon.

Thomas, P. (2004) The negative impact of testing writing skills. *Educational Leadership, 62* (2), 76–79.

Thomas, W. P., & Collier, V. P. (1997). *School effectiveness for language minority students.* Washington, DC: National Center for Bilingual Education. Available online at http://www.ncela.gwu.edu/pubs/resource/effectiveness.

Thomas, W. P., & Collier, V. P. (2002). *A national study of school effectiveness for language minority students' long-term academic achievement final report: Project 1.1.* University of California–Berkeley: Center for Research on Education, Diversity and Excellence. Available online at http://crede.ucsc.edu/research/llaa/1.1_final.html#top.

Thonis, E. (1983). *The English-Spanish connection: Excellence in English for Hispanic children through Spanish language and literacy development.* Compton, CA: Santillana.

Thorndike, R. L. (1973). Reading as reasoning. *Reading Research Quarterly, 9,* 135–147.

Thorndyke, P. (1977). Cognitive structures in comprehension and memory of narrative discourse. *Cognitive Psychology, 9,* 77–110.

Thornley, C., Selbie, J., & McDonald, T. (2011). Focused feedback for inference in expository text. *The Reading Teacher, 64,* 358–362.

Thurlow, M. L., Laitusis, C. C., Dillon, D. R., Cook, L. L., Moen, R. E., Abedi, J., & O'Brien, D. G. (2009). *Accessibility principles for reading assessments.* Minneapolis, MN: National Accessible Reading Assessment Projects.

Tiedt, P. M., & Tiedt, I. M. (2010). *Multicultural teaching: A handbook of activities, information, and resources* (8th ed.). Boston: Allyn & Bacon.

Tierney, R. J., Carter, M. A., & Desai, L. E. (1991). *Portfolio assessment in the reading-writing classroom.* Norwood, MA: Christopher-Gordon.

Tierney, R. J., & Readence, J. E. (2000). *Reading strategies and practices: A compendium* (5th ed.). Boston: Allyn & Bacon.

Tierney, R. J., Readence, J. E., & Dishner, E. K. (1995*). Reading strategies and practices: A compendium* (4th ed.). Boston: Allyn & Bacon.

Tindal, G., Hasbrouck, J., & Jones, C. (2005). *Oral reading fluency: 90 years of measurement* (Technical Report No. 33). Eugene, OR: Behavioral Research and Teaching, College of Education.

Tompkins, G. E., & Yaden, D. B. (1986). *Answering questions about words.* Urbana, IL: National Council of Teachers of English.

Topping, K. (1987). Paired reading: A powerful technique for parent use. *The Reading Teacher, 40,* 608–609.

Topping, K. (1989). Peer tutoring and paired reading: Combining two powerful techniques. *The Reading Teacher, 42,* 488–494.

Topping, K. (1998). Effective tutoring in America Reads: A reply to Wasik. *The Reading Teacher, 52,* 42–50.

Topping, K. (2006). Building reading fluency: Cognitive, behavioral, and socioemotional factors and the role of peer-mediated learning. In S. J. Samuels & A. E. Farstrup (Eds.), *What research has to say about fluency instruction* (pp. 106–129). Newark, DE: International Reading Association.

Torgesen, J. K., Wagner, R. K., Rashotte, C. A., Burgess, S. R., & Hecht, S. A. (1997). The contributions of phonological awareness and rapid automatic naming ability to the growth of word reading skills in second to fifth grade children. *Scientific Studies of Reading, 1,* 161–185.

Touchstone Applied Science Associates. (1994). *DRP handbook.* Brewster, NY: Author.

Touchstone Applied Science Associates. (1997). *Text sense, summary writing: Teacher's resource manual.* Brewster, NY: Author.

Touchstone Applied Science Associates. (2006). The DRP model of reading. *TASA Talk.* Available online at http://www.tasaliteracy.com/tasatalk/tasatalk-main.html.

Trabasso, T., & Magliano, J. P. (1996). How do children understand what they read and what can we do to help them? In M. F. Graves, P. van den Broek, & B. M. Taylor (Eds.), *The first R, every child's right to read* (pp. 160–188). New York: Teachers College Press & International Reading Association.

Trelease, J. (2001). *The new read-aloud handbook* (5th ed.). New York: Penguin.

Trelease, J. (2006). *The new read-aloud handbook* (6th ed.). New York: Penguin.

Trussell-Cullen, A. (1994, November). *Celebrating the real strategies for developing nonfiction reading and writing.* Paper presented at the annual meeting of the Connecticut Reading Association, Waterbury.

Tunmer, W. E., & Chapman, J. W. (1999). Teaching strategies for word identification. In G. B. Thompson & T. Nicholson (Eds.), *Learning to read: Beyond phonics and whole language* (pp. 74–102). Newark, DE: International Reading Association.

Tyner, B. (2004). *Small-group reading instruction: A differentiated teaching model for beginning and struggling readers.* Newark, DE: International Reading Association.

Tyner, B. (2006). *Small-group reading instruction: A differentiated teaching model for intermediate readers, grades 3–8.* Newark, DE: International Reading Association.

Tyson, E. S., & Mountain, L. (1982). A riddle or pun makes learning words fun. *The Reading Teacher, 36,* 170–173.

U.S. Department of Education. (1991, September 16). *Memorandum: Clarification of policy to address the needs of children with attention deficit disorders with general and/or special education.* Washington, DC: Author.

U.S. Department of Education. (2010). A blueprint for reform: The reauthorization of the Elementary and Secondary Education Act. Available online at www2.ed.gov/policy/elsec/leg/blueprint.

Vacca, R. T., & Vacca, J. L. (1986). *Content area reading* (2nd ed.). Boston: Little, Brown.

Valdes, G. (1996). *Con respeto—bridging the distances between culturally diverse families and schools: An ethnographic portrait.* New York: Teachers College Press.

Valencia, S. W. (1990). Assessment: A portfolio approach to classroom reading assessment: The whys, whats, and hows. *The Reading Teacher, 43,* 338–340.

Valencia, S. W., Smith, A. T., Reece, A. M., Li, M., Wixson, K. K., & Newman, H., (2010). Oral reading fluency assessment: Issues of construct, criterion, and consequential validity. *Reading Research Quarterly, 45*(3), 270–291.

Valencia, S. W. (2001). *Integrated theme tests, Levels 2.1–2.2.* Houghton Mifflin Reading. Boston: Houghton Mifflin.

Valencia, S. W., & Place, N. A. (1994). Literacy portfolios for teaching, learning, and accountability: The Bellevue literacy assessment project. In S. W. Valencia, E. H. Hiebert, & P. P. Afflerbach (Eds.), *Authentic reading assessment: Practices and possibilities* (pp. 134–156). Newark, DE: International Reading Association.

Van Bon, W. H. J., Bokesbeld, L. M., Font Freide, T. A., & Van den Hurk, A. J. (1991). A comparison of three methods of reading-while-listening. *Journal of Learning Disabilities, 24,* 471–477.

van den Broek, P., & Kremer, K. E. (2000). The mind in action: What it means to comprehend during reading. In B. Taylor, M. F. Graves, & P. van den Broek (Eds.), *Reading for meaning: Fostering comprehension in the middle grades* (pp. 1–31). New York: Teachers College Press.

van den Broek, P., Lynch, J. S., Naslund, J., Ievers-Landis, C. E., & Verduin, K. (2003). The development of comprehension of main ideas in narratives: Evidence from the selection of titles. *Journal of Educational Psychology, 95,* 707–718.

Vandervelden, M. C., & Siegel, L. S. (1997). Phonological recoding and phoneme awareness in early literacy: A developmental approach. *Reading Research Quarterly, 30,* 854–876.

Vasinda, S., & McLeod, J. (2011). Extending Readers Theatre: A powerful and purposeful match with podcasting. *The Reading Teacher, 64,* 486–497.

Vaughn, S., Klinger, J., & Schumm, J. (n.d.). *Collaborative strategy instruction: A manual to assist with staff development.* Miami, FL: University of Miami.

Vaughn, S., Linan-Thompson, S., Mathes, P. G., Cirino, P. T., Carlson, C. D., Pollard-Durodola, S. D., Cardenas-Hagan, E., & Francis, D. J. (2006). Effectiveness of Spanish intervention for first-grade English language learners at risk for reading difficulties. *Journal of Learning Disabilities, 39,* 56–73.

Vellutino, F. R., Scanlon, D. M., Sipay, E. R., Small, S. G., Pratt, R., Chen, R., & Denckla, M. B. (1996). Cognitive profiles of difficult-to-remediate and readily remediated poor readers: Early intervention as a vehicle for distinguishing between cognitive and experiential deficits as basic causes of specific reading disability. *Journal of Educational Psychology, 88,* 601–638.

Venezky, R. L. (1965). *A study of English spelling-to-sound correspondences on historical principles*. Unpublished doctoral dissertation, Stanford University, Stanford, CA.

Venn, E. C., & Jahn, M. D. (2004). *Teaching and learning in the preschool*. Newark, DE: International Reading Association.

Verhallen, M., & Schoonen, R. (1993). Vocabulary knowledge of monolingual and bilingual children. *Applied Linguistics, 14*, 344–363.

Vogt, M., & Nagano, P. (2003). Turn it on with light bulb reading! Sound-switching strategies for struggling readers. *The Reading Teacher, 57*, 214–221.

Vukelich, C., Christie, J. F., & Enz, B. J. (2012). *Helping young children learn language and literacy: Birth through kindergarten* (3rd ed.). Boston: Allyn & Bacon.

Vygotsky, L. S. (1962). *Mind and society: The development of higher psychological processes*. Cambridge, MA: MIT Press.

Vygotsky, L. S. (1978). *Thought and language*. Cambridge, MA: MIT Press.

Vygotsky, L. S. (1987). The development of scientific concepts in childhood. In R. F. Rieber & A. S. Carton (Eds.), *The collected works of L. S. Vygotsky* (N. Mnick, Trans.) (Vol. 1, pp. 167–241). New York: Plenum.

Wade, S. E. (1990). Using think-alouds to assess comprehension. *Reading Teacher, 43*, 442–451.

Walczyk, J. J., & Griffith-Ross, D. A. (2007). How important is reading skill fluency for comprehension? *The Reading Teacher, 60*, 560–569.

Walker, M. L. (1995). Help for the "fourth-grade slump"—SRQ2R plus instruction in text structure or main idea. *Reading Horizons, 36*, 38–58.

Walmsley, S. A. (1978–1979). The criterion referenced measurement of an early reading behavior. *Reading Research Quarterly, 14*, 574–604.

Walmsley, S. A. (2006). Getting the big idea: A neglected goal for reading comprehension. *The Reading Teacher, 60* (3), 281–285.

Wasik, B. A. (1999). Reading coaches: An alternative to reading tutors. *The Reading Teacher, 52*, 653–656.

Wasik, B. A., Bond, M. A., & Hindman, A. (2006). The effects of a language and literacy intervention on Head Start children and teachers. *Journal of Educational Psychology, 98*, 63–74.

Watkins, C. (1985). *The American Heritage dictionary of Indo-European roots*. Boston: Houghton Mifflin.

Watson, A. J. (1984). Cognitive development and units of print in early reading. In J. Downing & R. Valten (Eds.), *Language awareness and learning to read* (pp. 93–118). New York: Springer-Verlag.

Weaver, C. (1994). Understanding and educating students with attention deficit hyperactivity disorders: Toward a system-theory and whole language perspective. In C. Weaver (Ed.), *Success at last: Helping students with AD(H)D achieve their potential*. Portsmouth, NH: Heinemann.

Webb, N. L. (1999). *Alignment of science and mathematics standards and assessments in four states* (Research Monograph No. 18). Madison: University of Wisconsin–Madison, National Institute for Science Education.

Weber, R. M., & Longhi-Chirlin, T. (2001). Beginning in English: The growth of linguistic and literate abilities in Spanish-speaking first graders. *Reading Research and Instruction, 41*, 19–50.

Weinstein, C., & Mayer, R. (1986). The teaching of learning strategies. In M. C. Wittrock (Ed.), *Handbook of research on teaching* (pp. 315–327). New York: Macmillan.

Wells, G. (1986). *The meaning makers: Children learning language and using language to learn*. Portsmouth, NH: Heinemann.

West, J., Denton, K., & Germino-Hausken, E. (2000). *Early childhood longitudinal study: Kindergarten class of 1998–99*. Washington, DC: National Center for Educational Statistics. Available online at http://nces.ed.gov/pubsearch/pubsinfo.asp?pubid=2000070.

Westby, C. E. (1999). Assessing and facilitating text comprehension problems. In H. W. Catts & A. G. Kamhi (Eds.), *Language and reading disabilities* (pp. 154–223). Boston: Allyn & Bacon.

Westmont Psychology Department. (2008). *Theories of personality*. Westmont College, Santa Barbara, CA. Available online at http://westmont.edu/_academics/.../15personality/cognitivebehavioral.html.

Wharton-McDonald, R. (2001). Teaching writing in first grade: Instruction, scaffolds and expectations. In M. Pressley, R. L. Allington, R. Wharton-McDonald, C. C. Block, & L. M. Morrow (Eds.), *Learning to read: Lessons from exemplary first-grade classrooms* (pp. 70–91). New York: Guilford.

What Works Clearing House. (2007). *Intervention: Reading Recovery*. Institute of Education Sciences, U.S. Department of Education. Washington, DC. Available online at http://ies.ed.gov/ncee/wwc/reports/beginning_reading/reading_recovery/.

White, T. G. (2005). Effects of systematic and strategic analogy-based phonics on grade 2 students' word reading and reading comprehension. *Reading Research Quarterly, 40*, 234–255.

White, T. G., & Kim, J. S. (2010). Can silent reading in the summer reduce socioeconomic differences in reading achievement? In E. H. Hiebert & D. R. Reutzel (Eds.), *Revisiting silent reading: new directions for teachers and researchers* (pp. 67–91). Newark, DE. International Reading Association.

White, T. G., Power, M. A., & White, S. (1989). Morphological analysis: Implications for teaching and under-standing vocabulary growth. *Reading Research Quarterly, 24*, 283–304.

White, T. G., Sowell, J., & Yanagihara, A. (1989). Teaching elementary students to use word-part clues. *The Reading Teacher, 42*, 302–308.

Wigfield, A. (1997). Children's motivations for reading and writing engagement. In J. Guthrie & A. Wigfield (Eds.), *Motivating readers through integrated instruction* (pp. 14–33). Newark, DE: International Reading Association.

Wiggins, G., & McTighe, J. (2006). *Understanding by design* (expanded 2nd ed.). Alexandria, VA: ASCD.

Wilde, S. (1995). *Twenty-five years of inventive spelling: Where are we now?* Paper presented at the annual meeting of the International Reading Association, Anaheim, CA.

Wilkinson, I. A. G. (2009, February). *Quality Talk about text to promote high-level reading comprehension*. Invited paper presented at the Research Conference of the International Reading Association, Phoenix, AZ.

Williams, J. P. (1986a). Identifying main ideas: A basic aspect of reading comprehension. *Topics in Language Disorders, 8*, 1–13.

Williams, J. P. (1986b). Research and instructional development on main idea skills. In J. F. Baumann (Ed.), *Teaching main idea comprehension* (pp. 73–95). Newark, DE: International Reading Association.

Willingham, D. T. (2009). *Why don't students like school?* San Francisco: Jossey-Bass.

Wilson, B. (1999). *Wilson reading system overview presentation* (3rd ed.) [video recording]. Millbury, MA: Wilson Language Training Corporation.

Wilson, J. (1960). *Language and the pursuit of truth*. London: Cambridge University Press.

Wilson, P. (1986). *Voluntary reading*. Paper presented at the annual convention of the International Reading Association, Philadelphia.

Wilson, P. (1992). Among nonreaders: Voluntary reading, reading achievement, and the development of reading habits. In C. Temple & P. Collins (Eds.), *Stories and readers: New perspectives on literature in the elementary class-room* (pp. 157–169). Norwood, MA: Christopher-Gordon.

Winne, R. H., Graham L., & Prock, L. (1993). A model of poor readers' text-based inferencing: Effects of explanatory feedback. *Reading Research Quarterly, 28*, 536–566.

Winstead, L. (2004). Increasing academic motivation and cognition in reading, writing, and mathematics: Meaning-making strategies. *Educational Research Quarterly, 28*, 29–49.

Wittrock, M. C. (1991). Generative teaching of comprehension. *Elementary School Journal, 92*, 169–180.

Wixson, K. K. (1983). Questions about a text: What you ask about is what children learn. *The Reading Teacher, 37*, 287–293.

Wolf, M., & Katzir-Cohen, T. (2001). Reading fluency and its intervention. *Scientific Studies of Reading, 5*, 211–238.

Wolf, M. K., Herman, J. L.,& Dietel, R. (2010). *Improving the validity of English language learner assessment systems*. Los Angeles: National Center for Research, on Evaluation, Standards, & Student Testing.

Wolfersberger, M. E., Reutzel, D. E., Sudweeks, R., & Fawson, P. C. (2004). Developing and validating the Classroom Literacy Environmental Profile (CLEP): A tool for examining the "print richness" of early childhood and elementary classrooms. *Journal of Literacy Research, 36,* 83–144.

Wood, K. D., Lapp, D., Flood, J., & Taylor, D. B. (2008). *Guiding readers through text, Strategy guides for new times* (2nd ed.). Newark, DE: International Reading Association.

Woolfolk, A. (2001). *Educational psychology* (8th ed.). Boston: Allyn & Bacon.

Word Generation. (2010). *Teacher's extended word form chart: Week 5 focus words*. Available online at wordgeneration.org/observe/images/.../Y03.05Twordchart.pdf.

Wright, G., Sherman, R., & Jones, T. B. (2004). Are silent reading behaviors of first graders really silent? *The Reading Teacher, 57,* 546–553.

Writing across the Curriculum. (2010). *How to write a narrative.* Northern Illinois University. Available online at http://www.engl.niu.edu/wac/personass.html#narr.

Wutrz, J., & Wedwick, L. (2005). Bookmatch: Scaffolding book selection for independent reading. *The Reading Teacher, 59,* 16–32.

Yaden, D. B., Tam, A., Madrigal, P., Brassell, D., Massa, J., Altamirano, S., & Armendariz, J. (2001). *Early literacy for innercity children: The effects of reading and writing interventions in English and Spanish during the preschool years* (CIERA Article #00–04). Available online at http://www.ciera.org/ciera/publications/report-series/.

Yell, M. (2002). Putting gel pen to paper. *Educational Leadership, 60* (3), 60–66.

Yoon, B. (2007). Offering or limiting opportunities: Teachers' roles and approaches to English-language learners' participation in literacy activities. *The Reading Teacher, 61,* 216–225.

Yopp, H., & Stapleton, L. (2008). Conciencia fonémica en Español (Phonemic awareness in Spanish).*The Reading Teacher, 61,* 374–382.

Yuill, N., & Oakhill, J. (1991). *Children's problems in text comprehension: An experimental investigation* (Cambridge Monographs & Texts in Applied Psycholinguistics). New York: Cambridge University Press.

Zarnowski, M. (1990). *Learning about biographies: A reading-and-writing approach for children*. Urbana, IL: National Council of Teachers of English.

Zeno, S. M., Ivens, S. H., Millard, R. T., & Duvvuri, R. (1995). *The educator's word frequency guide*. Brewster, NY: Touchstone Applied Science Associates.

Zevenbergen, A. A., & Whitehurst, G. J. (2003). Dialogic reading: A shared picture book reading intervention for preschoolers. In A. van Kleeck, S. A. Stahl, & E. B. Bauer (Eds.), *On reading books to children: Parents and teachers* (pp. 177–200). Mahwah, NJ: Erlbaum.

Zieky, M., & Perie, M. (2006). *A primer on setting cut scores on tests of educational achievement*. http://www.ets.org/.

Zimmermann, S., & Hutchins, C. (2003). *7 Keys to Comprehension: How to help your kids read it and get it!* New York: Prima Lifestyles.

Zinsser, W. (1988). *Writing to learn*. New York: Harper.

Zorfass, J., Corley, P., & Remy, A. (1994). Helping students with disabilities become writers. *Educational Leadership, 51* (7), 62–66.

Zutell, J. (1998). Word sorting: A developmental spelling approach to word study for delayed readers. *Reading and Writing Quarterly: Overcoming Learning Difficulties, 14,* 219–238.

Zwiers, J. (2008). *Building academic language: Essential practices for content classrooms*. San Francisco, CA: Jossey-Bass.

Children's

Aardema, V. (1975). *Why mosquitoes buzz in people's ears: A West African folk tale*. New York: Dial.

Ada, A. F. (1999). *The kite*. Miami, FL: Santillana.

Ada, A. F., & Campoy, F. I. (2006). *Tales our abuelitas told: A Hispanic folktale collection*. New York: Atheneum.

Aiken, J. (1962). *Wolves of Willoughby Chase*. New York: Dell.

Albee, S. (1997). *I can do it*. New York: Random House.

Alexander, A. (1961). *Boats and ships from A to Z*. New York: Rand McNally.

Arnold, C. (2001). *Did you hear that?* Watertown, MA: Charlesbridge.

Atwater, R., & Atwater, F. (1938). *Mr. Popper's penguins*. Boston: Little, Brown.

Avi. (1994). *The barn*. New York: Orchard.

Baldwin, D., & Lister, C. (1984). *Your five senses*. Chicago: Children's Press.

Banks, K. (2006). *Max's words*. New York: Farrar, Straus & Giroux.

Barracca, S. (1990). *The adventures of taxi dog*. New York: Dial.

Barton, B. (1982). *Airport*. New York: Crowell.

Bauer, C. (1984). *Too many books*. New York: Viking.

Berger, M., & Berger, G. (1995). *What do animals do in winter?* Nashville, TN: Ideals Children's Books.

Betancourt, J. (1995). *My name is Brain Brian*. New York: Apple Paperbacks/Scholastic.

Blos, J. W. (1979). *A gathering of days: A New England girl's journal*. New York: Scribner's.

Bonsall, C. (1974). *And I mean it, Stanley*. New York: Harper.

Bridwell, N. (1972). *Clifford the small red puppy*. New York: Scholastic.

Brink, C. (1935). *Caddie Woodlawn*. New York: Macmillan.

Brown, A. (2001). *Hoot and holler*. New York: Knopf.

Brown, C. M. (1991). *My barn*. New York: Greenwillow.

Brown, J. G. (1976). *Alphabet dreams*. Englewood Cliffs, NJ: Prentice-Hall.

Burnford, S. (1961). *Incredible journey*. New York: Bantam.

Burningham, J. (1986). *Colors*. New York: Crown.

Burton, L. L. (1942). *The little house*. Boston: Houghton Mifflin.

Busby, P. (2003). *First to fly: How Wilbur & Orville Wright invented the airplane*. New York: Crown.

Byars, B. (1970). *Summer of the swans*. New York: Viking.

Byars, B. (1977). *The pinballs*. New York: Harper.

Cameron, A. (1994). *The cat sat on the mat*. Boston: Houghton Mifflin.

Carle, E. (1969). *The very hungry caterpillar*. New York: Philomel.

Carle, E. (1973). *Have you seen my cat?* New York: Watts.

Carle, E. (1987). *Papa, please get the moon for me*. New York: Simon & Schuster.

Carlson, N. (1996). *Sit still*. New York: Viking Penguin.

Carroll, L. (2000). *Alice's adventures in Wonderland*. New York: Signet Classics.

Choi, Y. (2001). *The name jar*. New York: Knopf.

Cleary, B. (1975). *Ramona the brave*. New York: Morrow.

Cleary, B. (1981). *Ramona Quimby, age 8*. New York: Morrow.

Cleary, B. (1983). *Dear Mr. Henshaw*. New York: Morrow.

Cleland, J. (2009). *Boats! Boats! Boats!* Vero Beach, FL: Rourke.

Clements, A. (2007). *Lunch money*. New York: Atheneum.

Clifford, E. (1979). *Flatfoot Fox and the case of the bashful beaver*. Boston: Houghton Mifflin.

Clifford, E. (1997). *Help! I'm a prisoner in the library!* New York: Scholastic.

Cohen, B. (2005). *Molly's pilgrim*. New York: Harper.

Cole, H. (1995). *Jack's garden*. New York: Greenwillow.

Cole, J. (1992). *The magic school bus on the ocean floor*. New York: Scholastic.

Cole, J. (1997). *The magic school bus and the electric field trip*. New York: Scholastic.

Cole, J., & Calmenson, S. (1993). *Six sick sheep: 101 tongue twisters*. New York: Morrow.

Coxe, M. (1996). *Cat traps*. New York: Random House.

Crews, D. (1984). *Schoolbus*. New York: Greenwillow.

Curtis, F. (1977). *The little book of big tongue twisters*. New York: Harvey House.

Dalgliesh, S. (1954). *Courage of Sarah Noble.* New York: Scribner's.

Degen, B. (1983). *Jamberry.* New York: Harper.

dePaola, T. (1973). *Andy: That's my name.* Englewood Cliffs, NJ: Prentice-Hall.

dePaola, T. (1998). *Big Anthony, his story.* New York: Putnam & Grosset.

DiCamillo, K. (2000). *Because of Winn-Dixie.* Cambridge, MA: Candlewick Press.

Douglas, B. (1982). *Good as new.* New York: Lothrop.

Eastman, P. D. (1960). *Are you my mother?* New York: Random House.

Eastman, P. D. (1962). *Go, dog, go!* New York: Random House.

Ehlert, L. (2001). *Waiting for wings.* San Diego, CA: Harcourt.

Ellwand, D. (1996). *Emma's elephant & other favorite animal friends.* New York: Dutton.

Emberley, E. (1987). *Cars, boats, planes.* New York: Little, Brown.

Everitt, B. (1998). *Up the ladder, down the slide.* New York: Harcourt.

Fitzgerald, J. D. (2000). *The great brain.* New York: Dial.

Fleschman, S. (1986). *The whipping boy.* New York: Greenwillow.

Folsom, M., & Folsom, M. (1986). *Easy as pie.* New York: Clarion.

Foltz Jones, C. (1998). *Accidents may happen.* New York: Delacorte.

Freeman, D. (1978). *A pocket for Corduroy.* New York: Viking.

Gág, W. (1928). *Millions of cats.* New York: Coward.

Galdone, P. (1975). *The gingerbread boy.* New York: Clarion.

Gantos, J. (1994). *Heads or tails: Stories from the sixth grade.* New York: Harper.

Garten, J. (1964). *The alphabet tale.* New York: Random House.

Geisel, T. S. (Dr. Seuss). (1957). *The cat in the hat.* New York: Random House.

Geisel, T. S. (Dr. Seuss). (1961). *The cat in the hat comes back.* New York: Random House.

Geisel, T. S. (Dr. Seuss). (1974). *There's a wocket in my pocket.* New York: Beginner.

Geisel, T. S. (Dr. Seuss). (1996). *The foot book.* New York: Random House.

George, J. C. (2000). *My side of the mountain.* New York: Puffin.

Gershator, D., & Gershator, P. (1997). *Palampam Day.* New York: Marshall Cavendish.

Gibbons, G. (1992). *Recycle! A handbook for kids.* Boston: Little, Brown.

Grahame, K. (1966). *The reluctant dragon.* New York: Holiday House.

Greydanus, R. (1988). *Let's get a pet.* New York: Troll.

Gwynne, F. (1987). *The king who rained.* Englewood Cliffs, NJ: Prentice-Hall.

Gwynne, F. (1988a). *A chocolate moose for dinner.* New York: Aladdin.

Gwynne, F. (1988b). *A little pigeon toad.* New York: Simon & Schuster.

Hall, K. (1995). *A bad, bad day.* New York: Scholastic.

Hamilton, V. (1971). *The planet of Junior Brown.* New York: Simon & Schuster.

Hamilton, V. (1985). *The people could fly: American black folktales.* New York: Knopf.

Henkes, K. (1991). *Chrysanthemum.* New York: Greenwillow.

Hausherr, R. (1994). *What food is this?* New York: Scholastic.

Heling, K., & Hembrook, D. (2003). *Mouse's hide-and-seek words.* New York: Random House.

Henry, M. (1947). *Misty of Chincoteague.* New York: Rand McNally.

Hill, E. (1980). *Where's Spot?* New York: Putnam.

Hoban, L. (1981). *Arthur's funny money.* New York: Harper.

Hoban, R. (1964). *Bread and jam for Frances.* New York: Harper.

Hutchins, P. (1976). *Don't forget the bacon!* New York: Mulberry.

Hutchins, P. (1987). *Rosie's walk.* New York: Simon & Schuster.

Johnson, A. (1996). *The leaving morning.* London: Orchard/Hatchett.

Juster, N. (1961). *The phantom tollbooth.* New York: Knopf.

Juster, N., & Raschka, C. (2005). *The hello, goodbye window.* New York: Hyperion.

Keats, E. J. (1962). *The snowy day.* New York: Viking.

Keats, E. J. (1964). *Whistle for Willie.* New York: Viking.

Kipling, R. (1992). *The jungle book.* New York: Tor Books.

Komori, A. (1983). *Animal mothers.* New York: Philomel.

Krauss, R. (1945). *The carrot seed.* New York: Harper.

Kremetz, J. (1986). *Jamie goes on an airplane.* New York: Random House.

L'Engle, M. (1962). *A wrinkle in time.* New York: Farrar.

Lessem, D. (1997). *Supergiants: The biggest dinosaurs.* Boston: Little, Brown.

Lewis, C. S. (1950). *The lion, the witch, and the wardrobe.* New York: Macmillan.

Lewison, W. C. (1992). *Buzz said the bee.* New York: Scholastic.

Linn, G. (2009). *Where the mountain meets the moon.* Boston: Little, Brown.

Lionni, L. (1963). *Swimmy.* New York: Knopf.

Lobel, A. (1972). *Frog and Toad together.* New York: Harper.

Lowry, L. (1989). *Number the stars.* Boston: Houghton Mifflin.

MacLachan, P. (1985). *Sarah, plain and tall.* New York: Harper.

Magloff, L. (2003). *Volcano.* New York: Dorling Kindersley.

Maitland, B. (2000). *Moo in the morning.* New York: Farrar.

Malam, J. (1998). *Leonardo da Vinci.* Minneapolis, MN: Carolrhoda.

Martin, B., Jr. (1983). *Brown bear, brown bear, what do you see?* New York: Holt.

Martin, B., Jr., & Archambault, J. (1989). *Chicka chicka boom boom.* New York: Simon & Schuster.

Mazer, H. (2001). *A boy at war: A novel of Pearl Harbor.* New York: Simon & Schuster.

McCloskey, R. (1941). *Make way for ducklings.* New York: Viking.

McGovern, A. (1968). *Stone soup.* New York: Scholastic.

McKissack, P., & McKissack, F. (1988). *Bugs.* Chicago: Children's Press.

Minarik, E. H. (1961). *Little Bear's visit.* New York: HarperCollins.

Minor, W. (2011). *My farm friends.* New York: Putnam.

Modesitt, J. (1990). *The story of z.* Saxonville, MA: Picture Book Studio.

Most, B. (1991). *A dinosaur named after me.* Orlando, FL: Harcourt.

Naylor, P. (1991). *Shiloh.* New York: Atheneum.

Naylor, P. (1996). *Fear place.* New York: Aladdin.

Naylor, P. (1997). *Ducks disappearing.* New York: Atheneum.

Nedobeck, D. (1981). *Nedobeck's alphabet book.* Chicago: Children's Press.

Nixon, J. (2011). *Trucks.* New York: Franklin Watts.

Nobisso, J. (2002). *In English, of course.* Westhampton Beach, NY: Gingerbread House.

Noble, T. H. (1980). *The day Jimmy's boa ate the wash.* New York: Dial.

Nodset, J. L. (1963). *Who took the farmer's hat?* New York: Harper.

Oelschlager, V. (2008). *What pet will I get?* Akron, OH: VanitaBooks.

Parish, P. (1964). *Thank you, Amelia Bedelia.* New York: Harper.

Paterson, K. (1978). *The great Gilly Hopkins.* New York: HarperCollins.

Petrie, C. (1983). *Joshua James likes trucks.* Chicago: Children's Press.

Pinkwater, D. (2010). *I am the dog.* New York: HarperCollins.

Pfeiffer, W. (1994). *From tadpole to frog.* New York: HarperCollins.

Phillips, L. (1997). *Ask me anything about dinosaurs.* New York: Avon.

Pomerantz, C. (1984). *Where's the bear?* New York: Greenwillow.

Potter, B. (1908). *The tale of Peter Rabbit.* London: Warne.

Rau, D. M. (2009). *Guess who swims.* Book-worms. Guess Who series. New York: Marshall Cavendish Benchmark.

Richards, J. (2002). *Howling hurricanes.* Broomall, PA: Chelsea House.

Rockwell, A. (1984). *Cars.* New York: Dutton.

Rolfer, G. (1990). Game day. *Sports Illustrated for Kids, 2* (8), 25.

Rosa-Mendoza, G. (2011). *Cars, trucks and planes.* New York: Windmill Books.

Ryan, P. (2010). *Freight trains.* New York: PowerKids Press.

Rylant, C. (1985). *The relatives came.* New York: Bradbury.

Rylant, C. (1987). *Henry and Mudge, the first book.* New York: Scholastic.

Schotter, R. (2006). *The boy who loved words.* New York: Schwartz & Wade.

Segal, L. (1973). *All the way home.* New York: Farrar.

Sendak, M. (1963). *Where the wild things are.* New York: Harper.

Shaw, N. (1986). *Sheep in a jeep.* Boston: Houghton Mifflin.

Shaw, N. (1992). *Sheep on a ship.* Boston: Houghton Mifflin.

Shaw, N. (1996). *Sheep in a shop.* Boston: Houghton Mifflin.

Shuter, J. (1997). *The ancient Greeks.* Des Plaines, IL: Heinemann.

Slepian, J., & Seidler, A. (1992). *The hungry thing goes to a restaurant.* New York: Scholastic.

Slobodkina, E. (1966). *Caps for sale.* New York: HarperCollins.

Smalley, G. (1989). *Numbers.* New York: Bantam.

Snow, P. (1984). *A pet for Pat.* Chicago: Children's Press.

Sobol, D. (1961). *The Wright brothers at Kitty Hawk.* New York: Dutton.

Soto, G. (1998). *Big, bushy mustache.* New York: Knopf.

Soto, G. (2003). *Cesar Chavez: A hero for everyone.* New York: Alladin.

Souza, D. M. (1998). *Fish that play tricks.* Minneapolis, MN: Carolrhoda.

Speare, E. (1958). *The witch of Blackbird Pond.* Boston: Houghton Mifflin.

Spinelli, J. (1990). *Maniac Magee.* New York: Scholastic.

Steig, W. (1987). *Brave Irene.* New York: Gollancz.

Stevenson, R. L. (1885). *A child's garden of verses.* London: Longman.

Stevenson, R. L. (1967). *Treasure island.* Feltham, UK: Hamlyn.

Stone, L. M. (1985). *Antarctica.* Chicago: Children's Press.

Stone, L. M. (1998). *Brown bears.* Minneapolis, MN: Lerner.

Strauss, L. L. (2011). *Drop everything and write!* Sausalito, CA: E&E Publishing.

Sullivan, L. H. (2011). *Trains on the move.* Minneapolis, MN: Lerner.

Thompson, S. E. (1998). *Built for speed: The extraordinary, enigmatic cheetah.* Minneapolis, MN: Lerner.

Tolkien, J. R. R. (2002). *The hobbit.* New York: Houghton Mifflin.

Tucker, T. (1998). *Brainstorm: The stories of twenty American kid inventors.* Geneva, IL: Sunburst.

White, E. B. (1952). *Charlotte's web.* New York: Harper.

Whitebird, M. (2001). *Ta-Na-E-Ka.* In J. Flood et al. (Eds.), McGraw-Hill Reading. New York: McGraw-Hill.

Wilder, L. I. (1932). *Little house in the big woods.* New York: Harper.

Wilder. L. I. (1941). *Little house on the prairie.* New York: Harper.

Wildsmith, B. (1982). *Cat on the mat.* New York: Oxford University Press.

Williams, M. (1926). *The velveteen rabbit.* New York: Doubleday.

Winrich, R. (2005). *The sun.* Mankato, MN: Capstone.

Winthrop, E. (2006). *Counting on Grace.* New York: Random House.

Withers, C. (Ed.). (1948). *A rocket in my pocket: The rhymes and chants of young Americans.* New York: Holt.

Yashima, T. (1955). *Crow boy.* New York: Viking.

Yep, L. (1975). *Dragonwings.* New York: Harper.

Yep, L. (1991). *The star fisher.* New York: Morrow.

Yolen, J, (1987). *Owl moon.* New York: Putnam.

Ziefert, H. (1984). *Sleepy dog.* New York: Random House.

Ziefert, H. (1993). *Jason's bus ride.* New York: Puffin.

Ziefert, H. (1998). *I swapped my dog.* Boston: Houghton Mifflin.

Zion, G. (1956). *Harry the dirty dog.* New York: Harper.

Photo Credits

Page	Source
434, 435, 439	©Myrleen Pearson/Alamy
444	©Dennis MacDonald/Alamy
457	©Alamy
462	©Tetra Images/Alamy
468, 469, 472	©First Light/Alamy
481	©Monshee Frantz/Alamy
493	©Michael Newman/PhotoEdit
496, 497, 505	©Myrleen Ferguson Cate/PhotoEdit
508	©Robin Nelson/PhotoEdit
514	©Image 100 RF
528, 529	©Michael Newman/PhotoEdit
533	©David Buffington/Photodisc/Getty Images

Index